Table of Contents

Published by Home Planners, LLC, wholly owned by Hanley-Wood, Inc.

Editorial and Corporate Offices:
3275 West Ina Road, Suite 110
Tucson, Arizona 85741

Distribution Center:
29333 Lorie Lane
Wixom, Michigan 48393

Rickard D. Bailey, CEO and Publisher
Cindy Coatsworth Lewis, Director of Publishing
Jan Prideaux, Senior Editor
Lorie Anderson, Project Editor
Paul Fitzgerald, Senior Graphic Designer
Jay Walsh, Graphic Designer
Matthew Kauffman, Graphic Designer

D0470620

Photo Credits

Front Cover: Design 9705, Jon Riley
Design 9871, Dave Dawson Photography
Design 9410, Bob Greenspan

Back Cover: Design 6636, Oscar Thompson
Design 8013, Peter Loppacher

First Printing, September, 1997

10 9 8 7 6 5 4 3 2

Library of Congress: 97-071442

ISBN Softcover: 1-881955-36-2

On the front cover: Design 9705 from Donald A. Gardner Architects, Inc., page 88; Design 9871 from Design Traditions, page 15; Design 9410 from Alan Mascord Design Associates, Inc., page 332.

On the back cover:
Design 6636 from The Sater Design Collection, page 281; Design 8013, from Larry E. Belk Designs, page 201.

Photo by Dave Rowland Photography

Design 9453

Square Footage: 3,524

■ Just about any "extra" you might ever conceive of has been thoughtfully incorporated into this striking one-story home. Tray vaulted ceilings are found in the breakfast nook, sitting room, master bedroom, dining room and living room. The den and the foyer have raised ceilings also. Notice the entertainment center in the sunken family room and the area set aside for exercise, with built-in wet bar. The master suite has a mitered corner window, an unbelievably large walk-in closet and a spa-style bath. The rear terrace could be a fine precursor to a swimming pool.

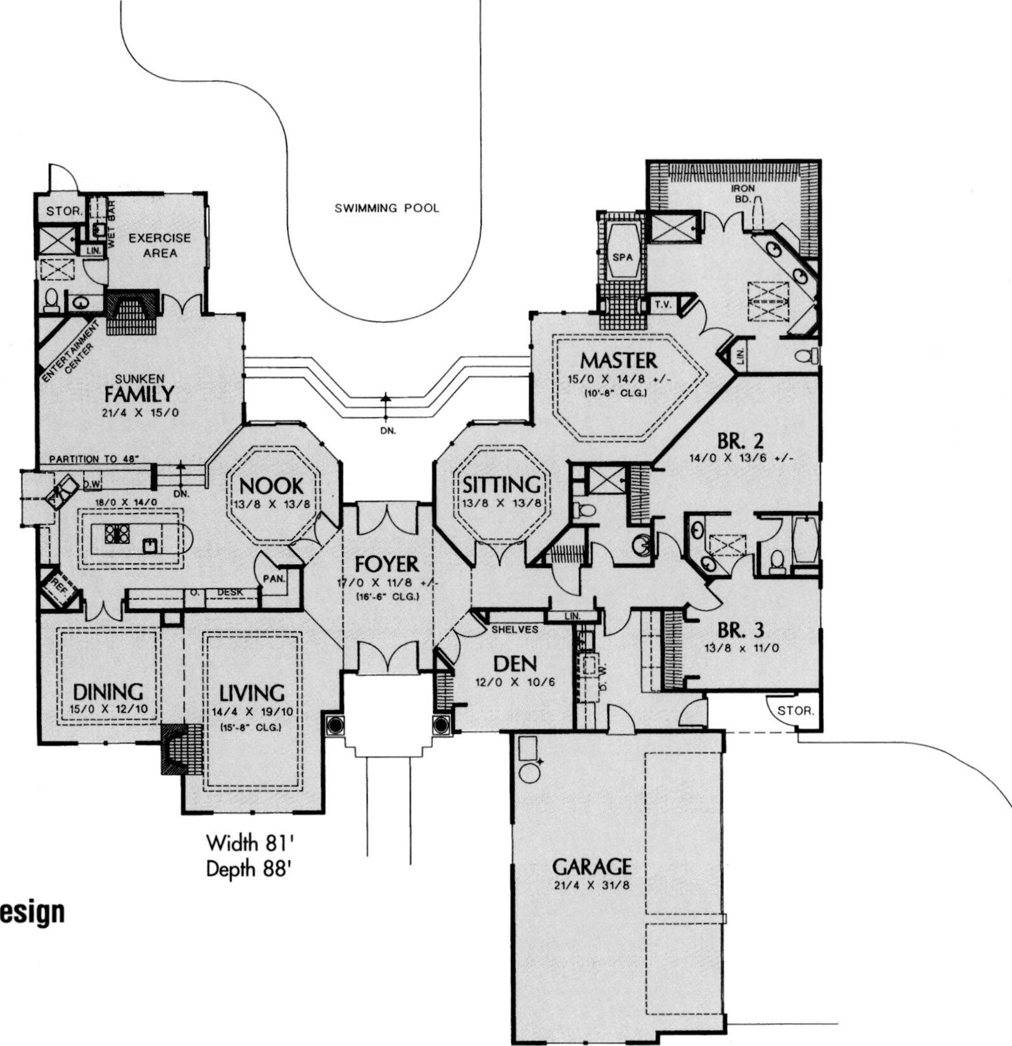

SWIMMING POOL
STOR.
WET BAR
LIN.
EXERCISE AREA
ENTERTAINMENT CENTER
SUNKEN FAMILY
21/4 X 15/0
PARTITION TO 48"
D.W.
18/0 X 14/0
DN.
REF.
DESK
PAN.
NOOK
13/8 X 13/8
DN.
FOYER
17/0 X 11/8 +/-
(16'-6" CLG.)
SITTING
13/8 X 13/8
IRON BD.
SPA
T.V.
LIN.
MASTER
15/0 X 14/8 +/-
(10'-8" CLG.)
BR. 2
14/0 X 13/6 +/-
BR. 3
13/8 x 11/0
LIN.
SHELVES
DEN
12/0 X 10/6
STOR.
DINING
15/0 X 12/10
LIVING
14/4 X 19/10
(15'-8" CLG.)
GARAGE
21/4 X 31/8
Width 81'
Depth 88'

Design by
Alan Mascord Design Associates, Inc.

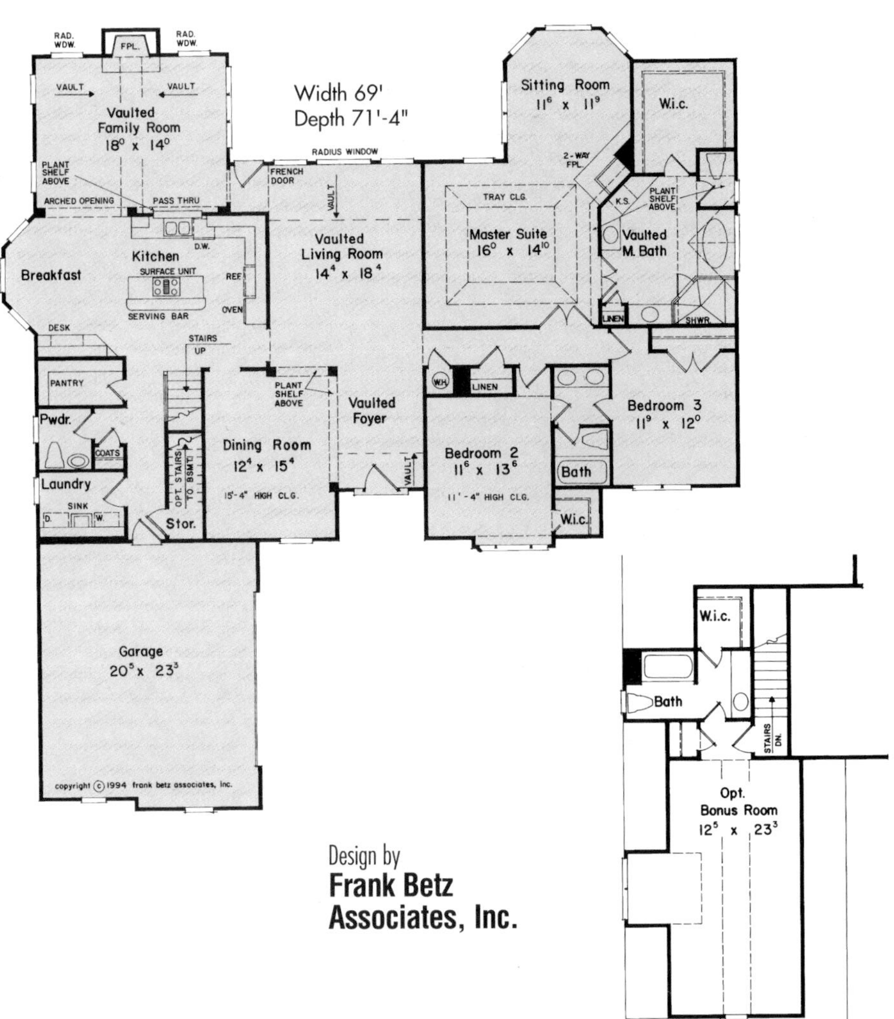

RAD. WDW.
FPL.
RAD. WDW.
VAULT
VAULT
Vaulted Family Room 18⁰ x 14⁰
Width 69'
Depth 71'-4"
Sitting Room 11⁶ x 11⁹
W.i.c.
RADIUS WINDOW
PLANT SHELF ABOVE
ARCHED OPENING
PASS THRU
FRENCH DOOR
VAULT
2-WAY FPL.
TRAY CLG.
K.S.
PLANT SHELF ABOVE
Master Suite 16⁰ x 14¹⁰
Vaulted M. Bath
Breakfast
Kitchen
D.W.
SURFACE UNIT
REF
OVEN
SERVING BAR
Vaulted Living Room 14⁴ x 18⁴
LINEN
SHWR
DESK
STAIRS UP
PANTRY
PLANT SHELF ABOVE
Vaulted Foyer
W.H.
LINEN
Bedroom 3 11⁹ x 12⁰
Pwdr.
COATS
Dining Room 12⁴ x 15⁴
OPT. STAIRS TO BSMT.
Bedroom 2 11⁶ x 13⁶
Laundry
SINK
15'-4" HIGH CLG.
VAULT
11'-4" HIGH CLG.
Bath
W.i.c.
Stor.
Garage 20⁵ x 23³
copyright © 1994 frank betz associates, inc.
W.i.c.
Bath
STAIRS DN.
Opt. Bonus Room 12⁵ x 23³

Design by
Frank Betz Associates, Inc.

Design P234

Square Footage: 2,622
Bonus Room: 478 square feet

■ Striking design and an open floor plan contribute to the gracious atmosphere of this one-story home. The front-facing dining room is set off from the foyer and formal living room with columns and a plant shelf, creating an open, yet elegant area for entertaining. The gourmet-inspired kitchen features a cooktop island with a serving bar, a bayed breakfast nook and a pass-through to the cozy family room. A vaulted ceiling and fireplace accent the family room. Sleeping quarters are headlined with a luxurious master suite that's designed for relaxing with a sunny sitting room, three-sided fireplace and a spa bath. Two family bedrooms have private access to a compartmented bath. The optional bonus room would make a comfortable guest suite. Please specify basement or crawlspace foundation when ordering.

Photo by Design Basics, Inc.

Design 9206

First Floor: 1,421 square feet
Second Floor: 578 square feet
Total: 1,999 square feet

■ Growing families will love this unique plan. Start with the living areas — a spacious great room with high ceilings, windows overlooking the back yard, a through-fireplace to the kitchen and access to the rear deck. A dining room with hutch space accommodates formal occasions. The hearth kitchen features a well-planned work area and a bay-windowed breakfast area. The master suite with a whirlpool and a walk-in closet is found downstairs while three family bedrooms are upstairs. Notice the abundant attic storage.

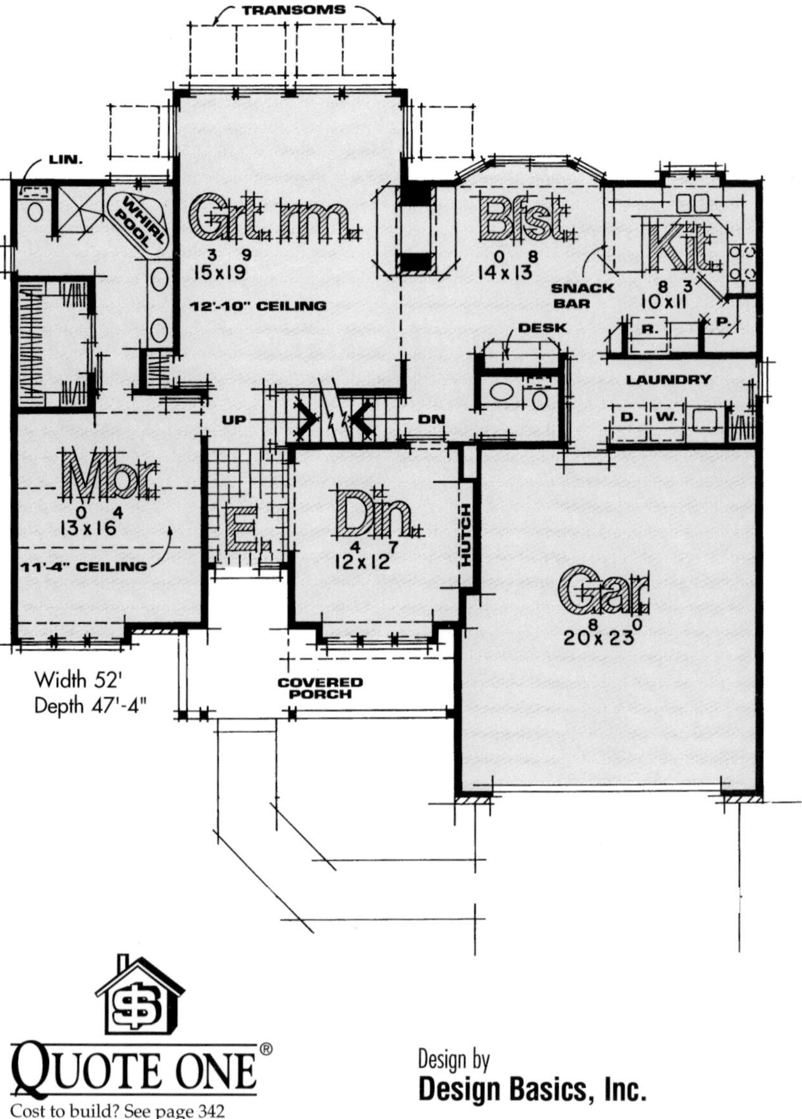
TRANSOMS
LIN.
WHIRLPOOL
Grt. rm.
15³x19⁹
12'-10" CEILING
Bfst.
14⁰x13⁸
SNACK BAR
Kit.
10⁸x11³
DESK
R.
P.
LAUNDRY
D.
W.
UP
DN
Mbr.
13⁰x16⁴
11'-4" CEILING
E.
Din.
12⁴x12⁷
HUTCH
Gar.
20⁸x23⁰
COVERED PORCH

Width 52'
Depth 47'-4"

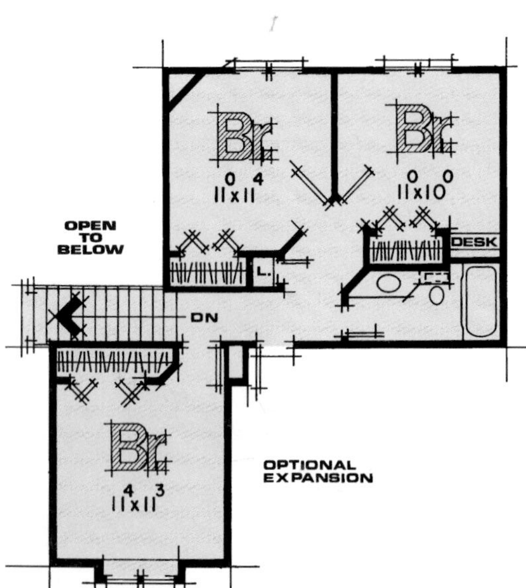
Br.
11⁰x11⁴
Br.
11⁰x10⁰
OPEN TO BELOW
DESK
L.
DN
Br.
11⁴x11³
OPTIONAL EXPANSION

QUOTE ONE®

Cost to build? See page 342 to order complete cost estimate to build this house in your area!

Design by
Design Basics, Inc.

Photo by John Dillon

Design 9242

First Floor: 1,322 square feet
Second Floor: 1,272 square feet
Total: 2,594 square feet

■ Here's the luxury you've been looking for—from the wraparound covered front porch to the bright sun room at the rear off the breakfast room. A sunken family room with fireplace serves everyday casual gatherings, while the more formal living and dining rooms are reserved for special entertaining situations. The kitchen has a central island with snack bar and is located most conveniently for serving and cleaning up. Upstairs are four bedrooms, one a lovely master suite with French doors into the master bath and a whirlpool tub in a dramatic bay window. A double vanity in the shared bath easily serves the three family bedrooms.

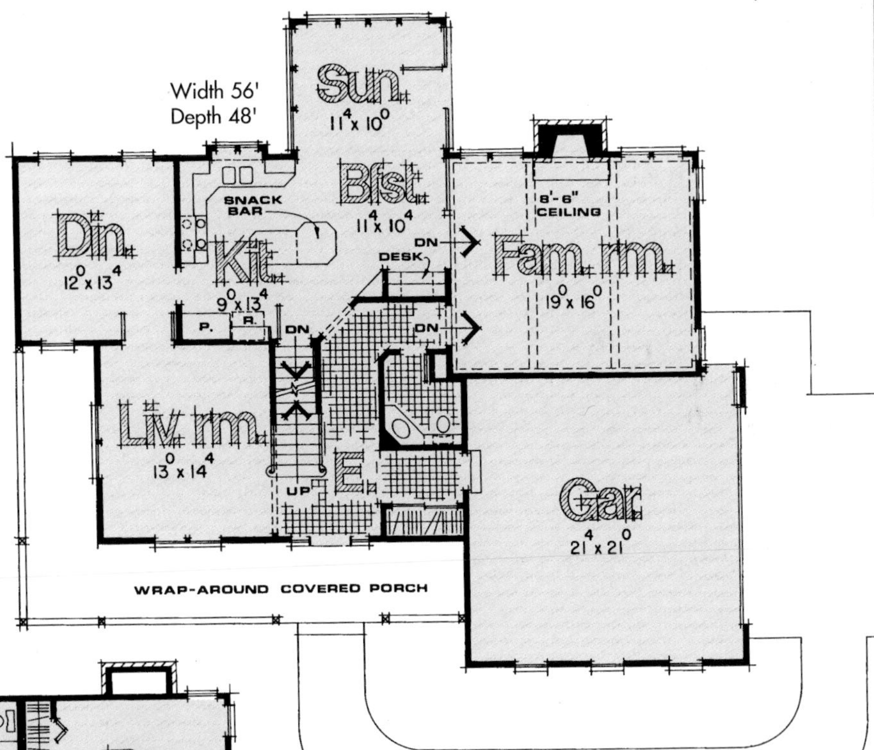
Width 56'
Depth 48'
Sun 11⁴ x 10⁰
Bfst 11⁴ x 10⁴
SNACK BAR
Din. 12⁰ x 13⁴
Kit. 9⁰ x 13⁴
DESK
DN
8'-6" CEILING
Fam. rm. 19⁰ x 16⁰
P.
R.
Liv. rm. 13⁰ x 14⁴
UP
E.
Gar. 21⁴ x 21⁰
WRAP-AROUND COVERED PORCH

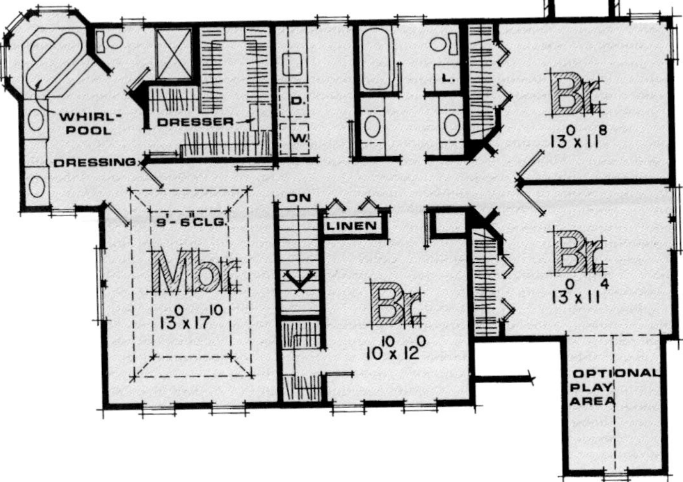
WHIRLPOOL
DRESSER
D.
W.
L.
DRESSING
Br. 13⁰ x 11⁸
DN
9'-6" CLG.
LINEN
Mbr. 13⁰ x 17¹⁰
Br. 10¹⁰ x 12⁰
Br. 13⁰ x 11⁴
OPTIONAL PLAY AREA

Design by
Design Basics, Inc.

QUOTE ONE®

Cost to build? See page 342 to order complete cost estimate to build this house in your area!

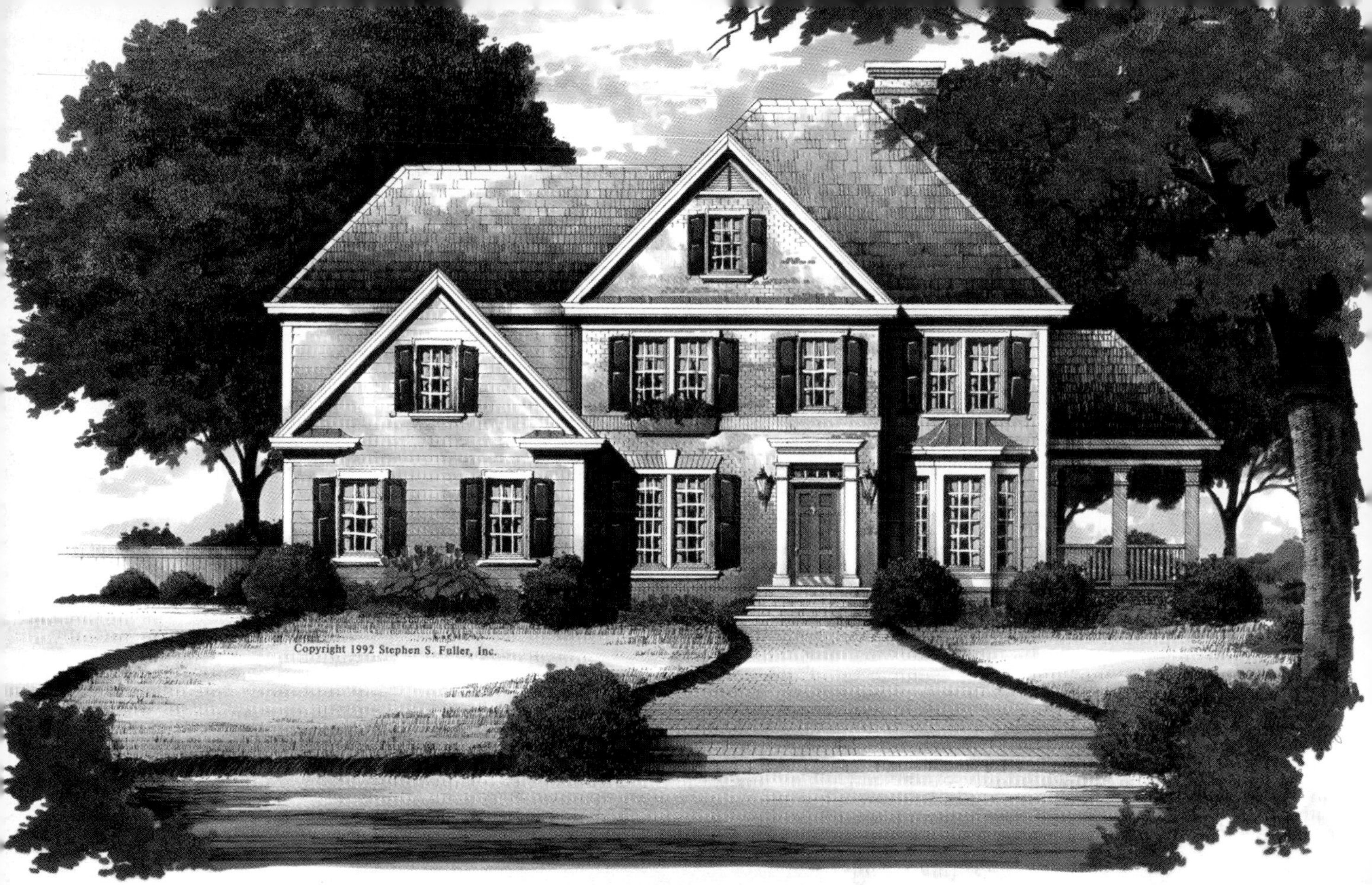

Width 52'-6"
Depth 43'-6"

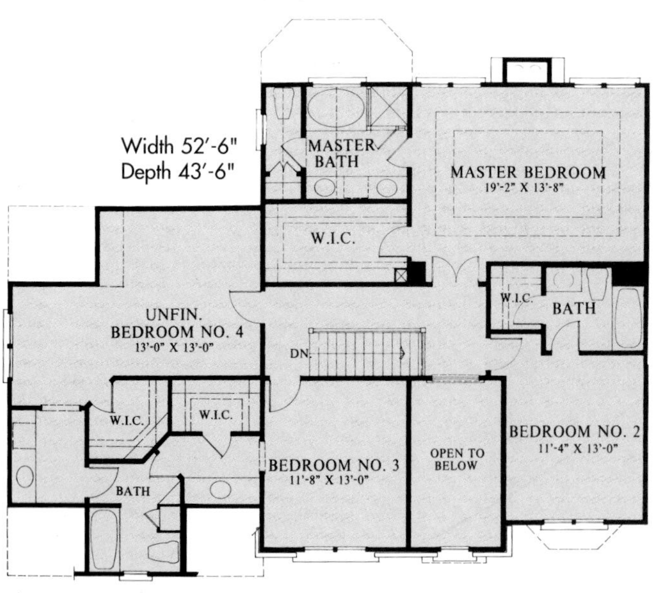
MASTER BATH
MASTER BEDROOM
19'-2" X 13'-8"
W.I.C.
W.I.C.
BATH
UNFIN. BEDROOM NO. 4
13'-0" X 13'-0"
DN.
W.I.C.
W.I.C.
BATH
BEDROOM NO. 3
11'-8" X 13'-0"
OPEN TO BELOW
BEDROOM NO. 2
11'-4" X 13'-0"

Design by
Design Traditions

Design 9892

First Floor: 1,205 square feet
Second Floor: 1,160 square feet
Total: 2,365 square feet

QUOTE ONE®

Cost to build? See page 342 to order complete cost estimate to build this house in your area!

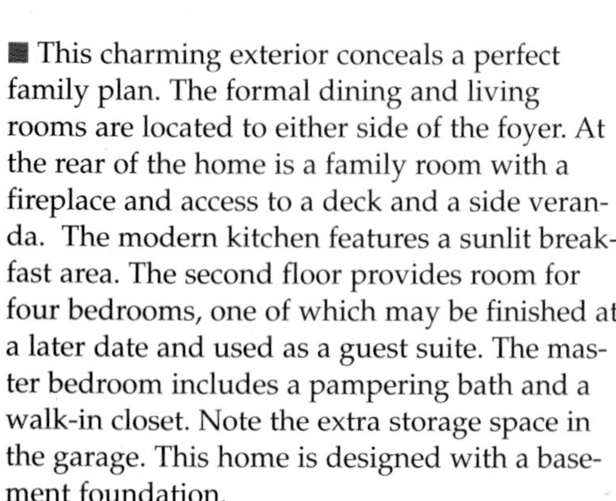

■ This charming exterior conceals a perfect family plan. The formal dining and living rooms are located to either side of the foyer. At the rear of the home is a family room with a fireplace and access to a deck and a side veranda. The modern kitchen features a sunlit breakfast area. The second floor provides room for four bedrooms, one of which may be finished at a later date and used as a guest suite. The master bedroom includes a pampering bath and a walk-in closet. Note the extra storage space in the garage. This home is designed with a basement foundation.

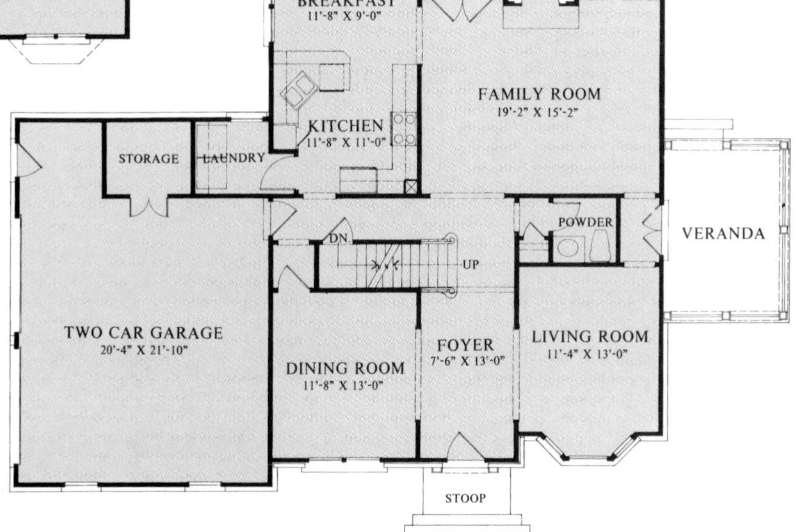
DECK
BREAKFAST
11'-8" X 9'-0"
FAMILY ROOM
19'-2" X 15'-2"
KITCHEN
11'-8" X 11'-0"
STORAGE
LAUNDRY
POWDER
VERANDA
DN.
UP
TWO CAR GARAGE
20'-4" X 21'-10"
DINING ROOM
11'-8" X 13'-0"
FOYER
7'-6" X 13'-0"
LIVING ROOM
11'-4" X 13'-0"
STOOP

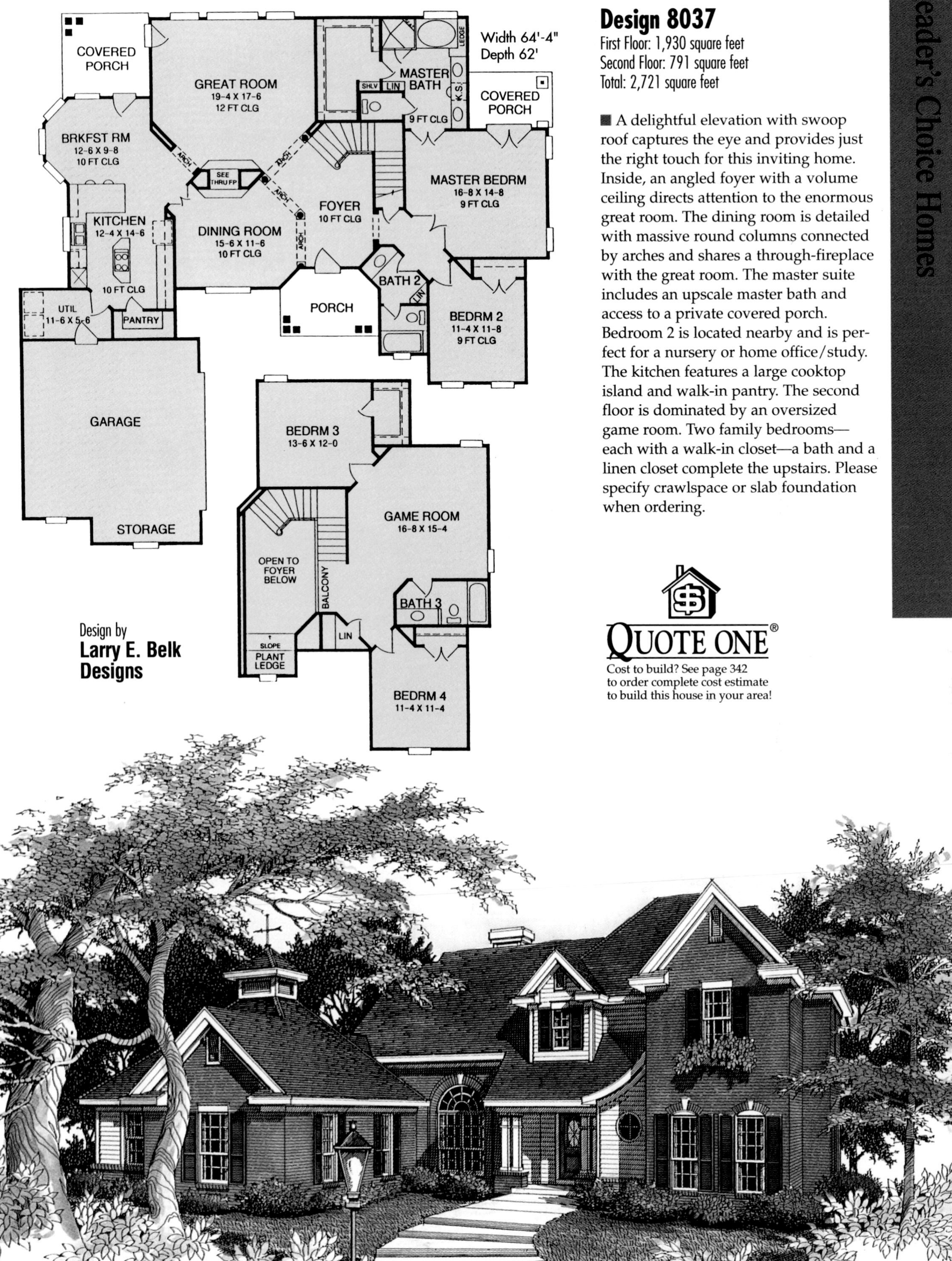
COVERED PORCH
GREAT ROOM
19-4 X 17-6
12 FT CLG
MASTER BATH
SHLV
LIN
K.S.
LEDGE
9 FT CLG
COVERED PORCH
BRKFST RM
12-6 X 9-8
10 FT CLG
ARCH
SEE THRU FP
MASTER BEDRM
16-8 X 14-8
9 FT CLG
FOYER
10 FT CLG
KITCHEN
12-4 X 14-6
DINING ROOM
15-6 X 11-6
10 FT CLG
10 FT CLG
BATH 2
LIN
UTIL
11-6 X 5-6
PANTRY
PORCH
BEDRM 2
11-4 X 11-8
9 FT CLG
GARAGE
STORAGE
BEDRM 3
13-6 X 12-0
GAME ROOM
16-8 X 15-4
OPEN TO FOYER BELOW
BALCONY
BATH 3
LIN
SLOPE
PLANT LEDGE
BEDRM 4
11-4 X 11-4
Width 64'-4"
Depth 62'

Design 8037

First Floor: 1,930 square feet
Second Floor: 791 square feet
Total: 2,721 square feet

■ A delightful elevation with swoop roof captures the eye and provides just the right touch for this inviting home. Inside, an angled foyer with a volume ceiling directs attention to the enormous great room. The dining room is detailed with massive round columns connected by arches and shares a through-fireplace with the great room. The master suite includes an upscale master bath and access to a private covered porch. Bedroom 2 is located nearby and is perfect for a nursery or home office/study. The kitchen features a large cooktop island and walk-in pantry. The second floor is dominated by an oversized game room. Two family bedrooms—each with a walk-in closet—a bath and a linen closet complete the upstairs. Please specify crawlspace or slab foundation when ordering.

Design by
Larry E. Belk Designs

QUOTE ONE®
Cost to build? See page 342 to order complete cost estimate to build this house in your area!

Design 9089

Square Footage: 1,849

■ A wonderful floor plan is found on the interior of this one-story plan. The large living room and conveniently placed dining room both open from the raised foyer. In between is the galley kitchen with huge pantry and attached breakfast area. French doors flanking the fireplace in the living room open to the rear yard. To the right of the plan is the master bedroom with a walk-in closet and double lavatories. To the left of the plan are two family bedrooms sharing a full bath in between.

QUOTE ONE®

Cost to build? See page 342 to order complete cost estimate to build this house in your area!

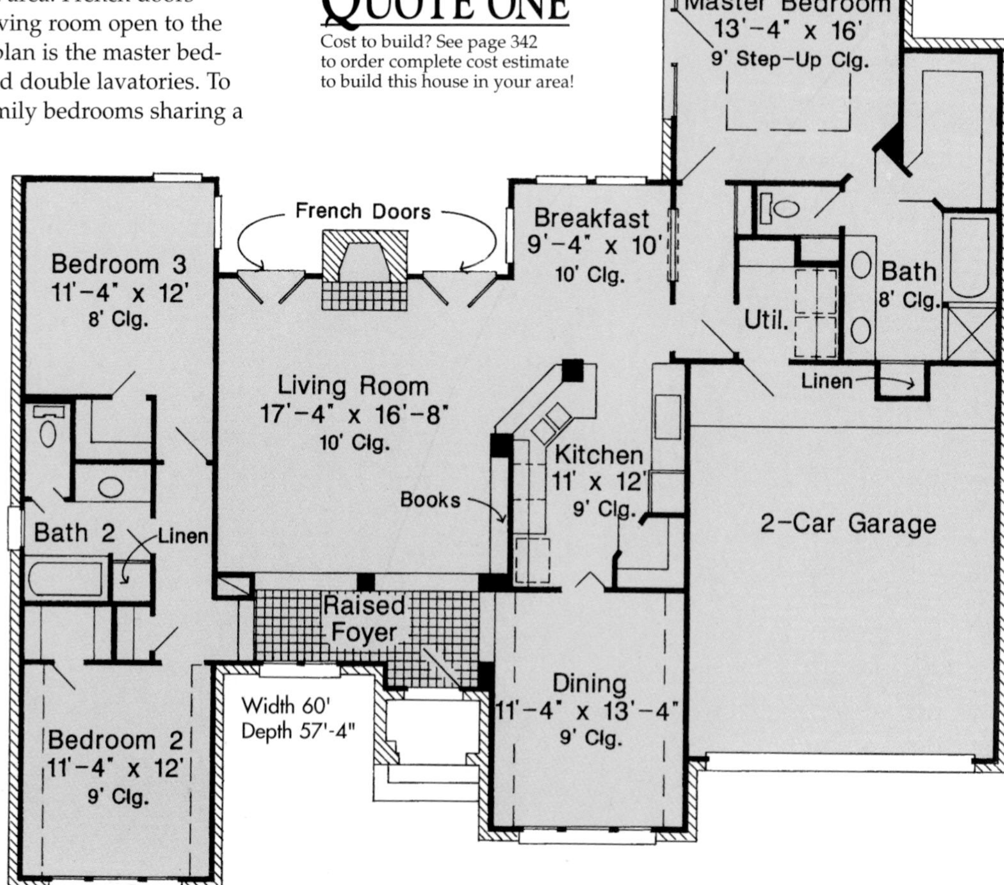

Master Bedroom
13'-4" x 16'
9' Step-Up Clg.
French Doors
Breakfast
9'-4" x 10'
10' Clg.
Bath
8' Clg.
Util.
Linen
Bedroom 3
11'-4" x 12'
8' Clg.
Living Room
17'-4" x 16'-8"
10' Clg.
Kitchen
11' x 12'
9' Clg.
Books
2-Car Garage
Bath 2
Linen
Raised Foyer
Dining
11'-4" x 13'-4"
9' Clg.
Bedroom 2
11'-4" x 12'
9' Clg.
Width 60'
Depth 57'-4"

Design by
Larry W. Garnett & Associates, Inc.

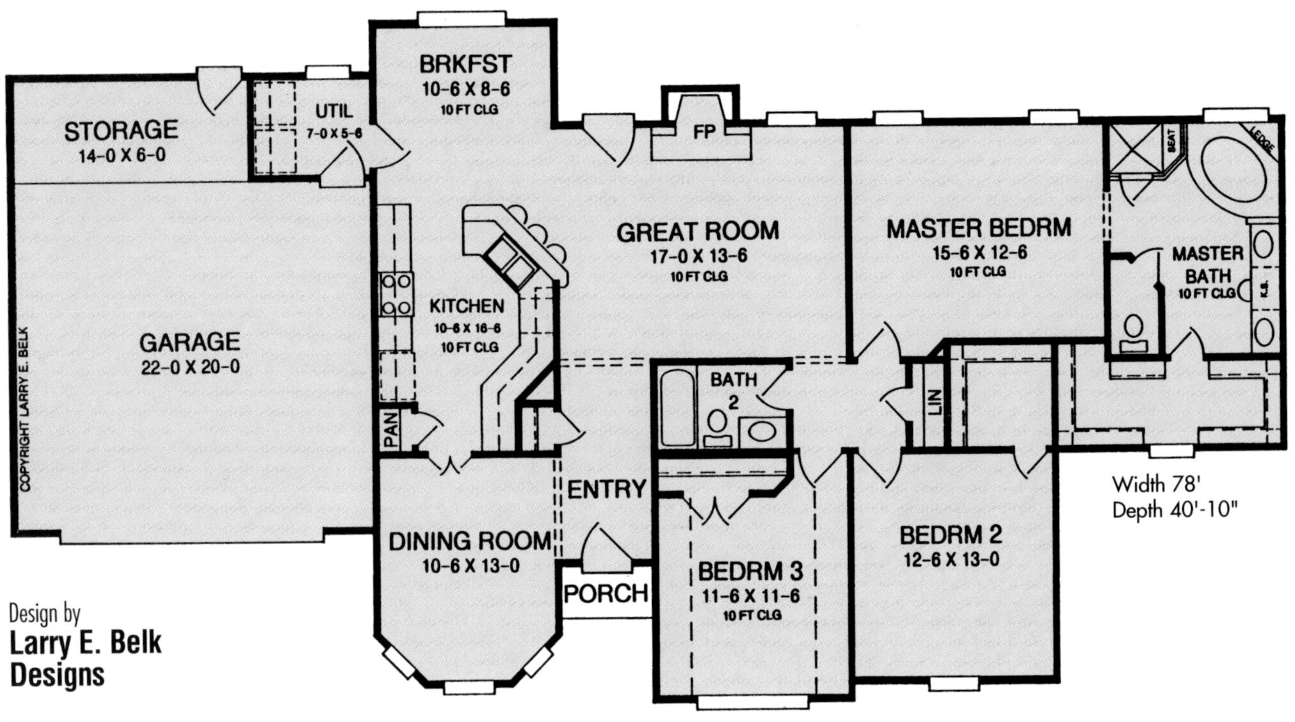
STORAGE
14-0 X 6-0
UTIL
7-0 X 5-6
BRKFST
10-6 X 8-6
10 FT CLG
FP
GREAT ROOM
17-0 X 13-6
10 FT CLG
MASTER BEDRM
15-6 X 12-6
10 FT CLG
MASTER BATH
10 FT CLG
SEAT
LEDGE
GARAGE
22-0 X 20-0
COPYRIGHT LARRY E. BELK
KITCHEN
10-6 X 16-6
10 FT CLG
PAN
BATH 2
LIN
ENTRY
DINING ROOM
10-6 X 13-0
PORCH
BEDRM 3
11-6 X 11-6
10 FT CLG
BEDRM 2
12-6 X 13-0
Width 78'
Depth 40'-10"

Design by
Larry E. Belk Designs

Design 8064

Square Footage: 1,742

■ This traditional elevation fronts a compact layout with all the frills normally found in a larger home. Ten-foot ceilings in all major living areas give the home an open, spacious feel. The kitchen features an angled eating bar, a pantry and lots of cabinet and counter space. The master suite is highlighted by a luxury bath. Standard features include His and Hers vanities with knee space, a corner whirlpool tub and a separate shower with a seat. An enormous walk-in closet with a window for natural light completes this owner's retreat. Bedrooms 2 and 3 and a large linen closet are nearby. Bedroom 2 is notable for its oversized walk-in closet. Please specify basement or crawlspace foundation when ordering.

© The Sater Group, Inc.

Design 6602

Square Footage: 2,794

■ Classic columns, circle-head windows and a graceful bow window give this stucco home a wonderful street presence. The foyer leads into the formal living and dining rooms. An arched buffet server separates these rooms and gives an open feeling. The kitchen, nook and leisure room join for a casual and sunny living area. A desk/message center in the island kitchen, art niches in the nook and a fireplace with an entertainment center and shelves add custom touches. Two secondary suites have private-access baths and offer full privacy from the master wing. The master suite hosts a private garden area that's visible through a mitered glass window. The master bath features a walk-in shower that overlooks the garden, a compartmented toilet and garden tub. Large His and Hers walk-in closets complete these private quarters.

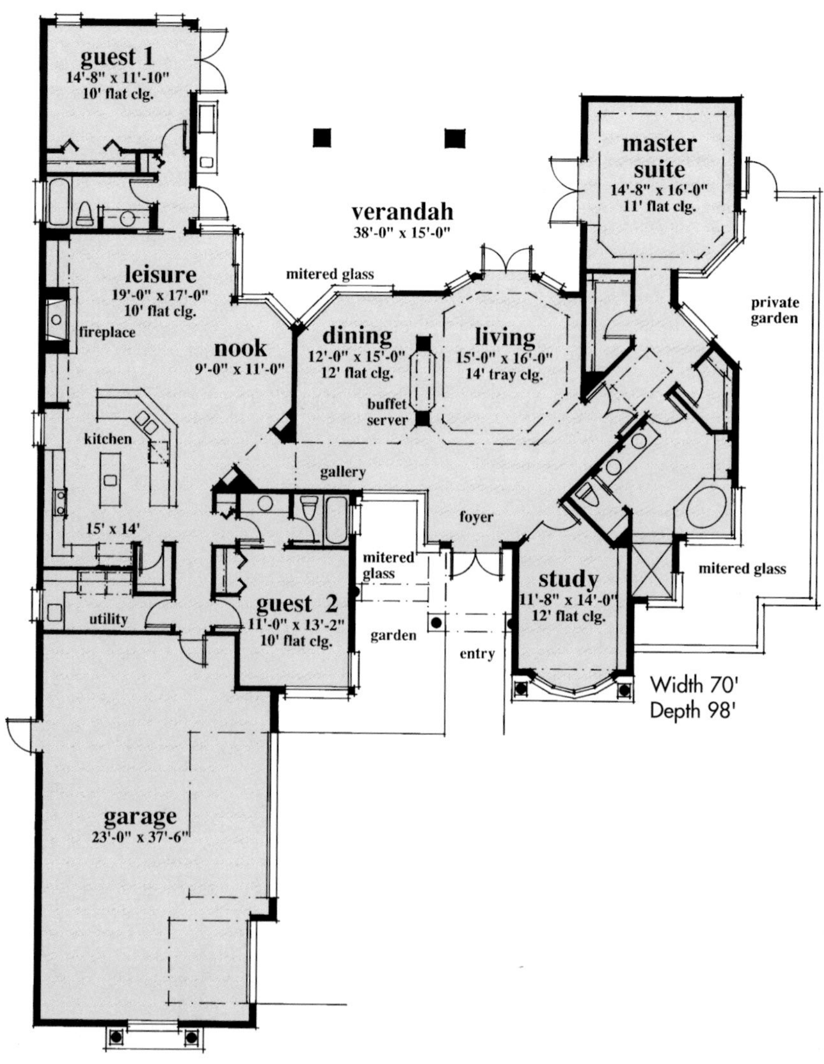
guest 1
14'-8" x 11'-10"
10' flat clg.
verandah
38'-0" x 15'-0"
master suite
14'-8" x 16'-0"
11' flat clg.
leisure
19'-0" x 17'-0"
10' flat clg.
mitered glass
private garden
fireplace
nook
9'-0" x 11'-0"
dining
12'-0" x 15'-0"
12' flat clg.
living
15'-0" x 16'-0"
14' tray clg.
buffet server
kitchen
gallery
15' x 14'
foyer
mitered glass
study
11'-8" x 14'-0"
12' flat clg.
mitered glass
utility
guest 2
11'-0" x 13'-2"
10' flat clg.
garden
entry
Width 70'
Depth 98'
garage
23'-0" x 37'-6"

Design by
The Sater Design Collection

Design by
Alan Mascord Design Associates, Inc.

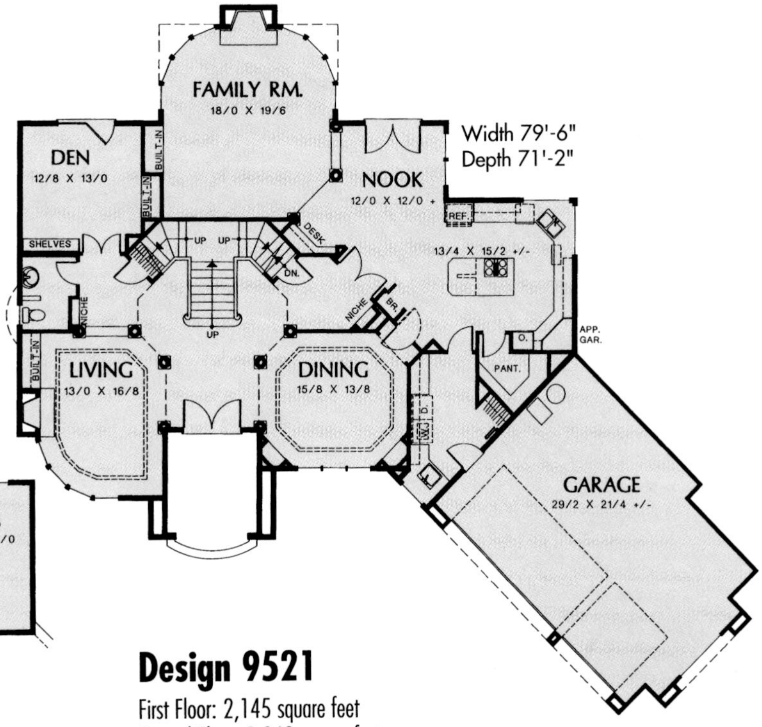

Width 79'-6"
Depth 71'-2"

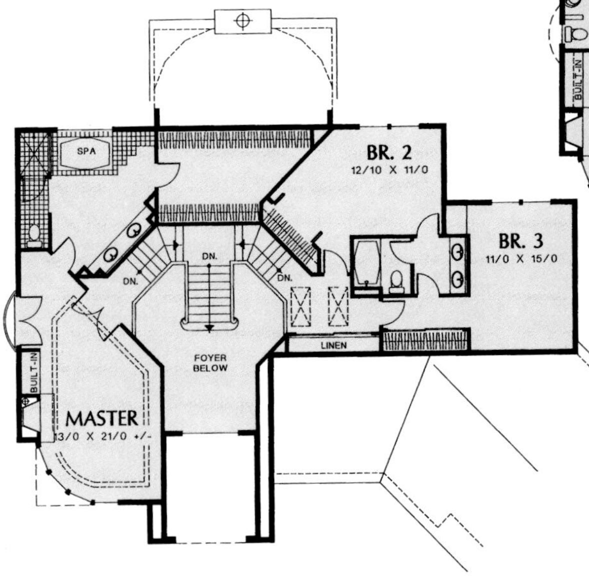

Design 9521

First Floor: 2,145 square feet
Second Floor: 1,342 square feet
Total: 3,487 square feet

■ The best of contemporary design to suit the best of contemporary times. A dynamic floor plan is housed in this elegant exterior. Enter the foyer and find the living room to the left and the dining room to the right—both accented with an expanse of windows. Straight ahead, the spacious family room sports a fireplace with high, curved windows flanking each side. Columned arches lead into the dining nook with double doors opening to the rear grounds. A wrap-around kitchen features a double-windowed corner sink, a large walk-in pantry and a convenient cooktop prep island. A den with built-ins and shelves, a powder room and a sizable laundry room complete the first floor. Upstairs, double doors open to a master suite finished with a cozy fireplace and a pampering bath with relaxing spa tub and giant walk-in closet. Two family bedrooms and a full bath complete the second floor.

Photo by Andrew D. Lautman

Design 9055

First Floor: 997 square feet
Second Floor: 1,069 square feet
Total: 2,066 square feet

Design by
Larry W. Garnett & Associates, Inc.

■ With its exceptional detail and proportions, this home is reminiscent of the Queen Anne Style. The foyer opens to a living area with a bay-windowed alcove and a fireplace with flanking bookshelves. Natural light fills the breakfast area with a full-length bay window and a French door. Upstairs, the master bedroom offers unsurpassed elegance and convenience. The sitting area has an eleven-foot ceiling with arch-top windows. The bath area features a large walk-in closet, His and Hers lavatories and plenty of linen storage. Plans for a two-car detached garage are included.

QUOTE ONE®
Cost to build? See page 342 to order complete cost estimate to build this house in your area!

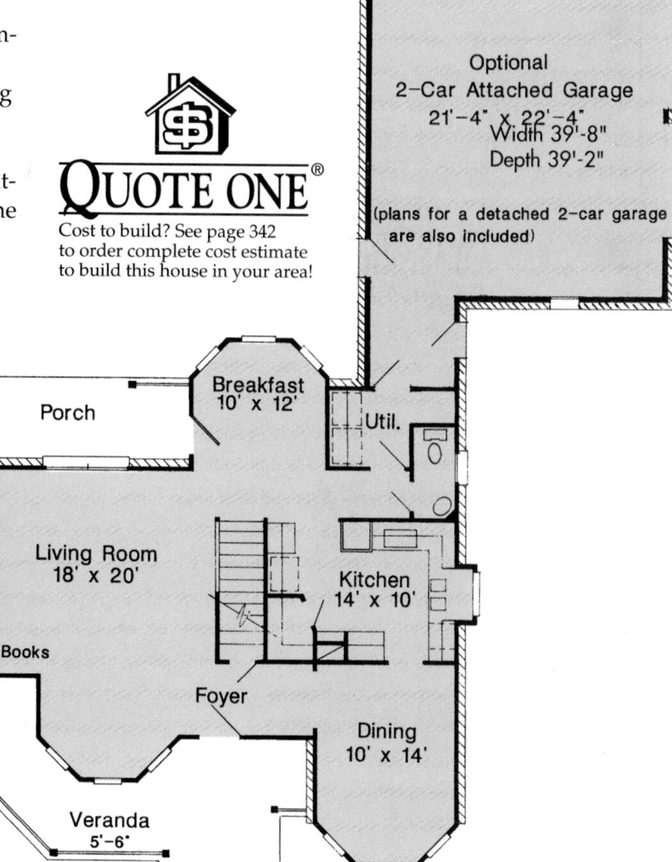
Optional
2-Car Attached Garage
21'-4" x 22'-4"
Width 39'-8"
Depth 39'-2"
(plans for a detached 2-car garage are also included)
Breakfast
10' x 12'
Porch
Util.
Living Room
18' x 20'
Kitchen
14' x 10'
Books
Foyer
Dining
10' x 14'
Veranda
5'-6"

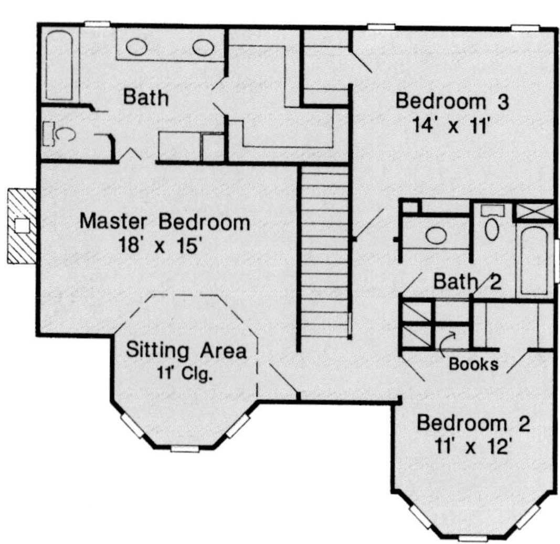
Bath
Bedroom 3
14' x 11'
Master Bedroom
18' x 15'
Bath 2
Sitting Area
11' Clg.
Books
Bedroom 2
11' x 12'

■ Quaint, yet as majestic as a country manor on the Rhine, this European-styled stucco home enjoys the enchantment of arched windows to underscore its charm. The two-story foyer leads through French doors to the study with its own hearth and coffered ceiling. Coupled with this cozy sanctuary is the master suite with tray ceiling and large accommodating bath. The large, sunken great room is highlighted by a fireplace, built-in bookcases, lots of glass and easy access to a back stair and large gourmet kitchen. Upstairs are three secondary bedrooms. One spacious upstairs bedroom gives guests the ultimate in convenience with a private bath and walk-in closet. This home is designed with a basement foundation.

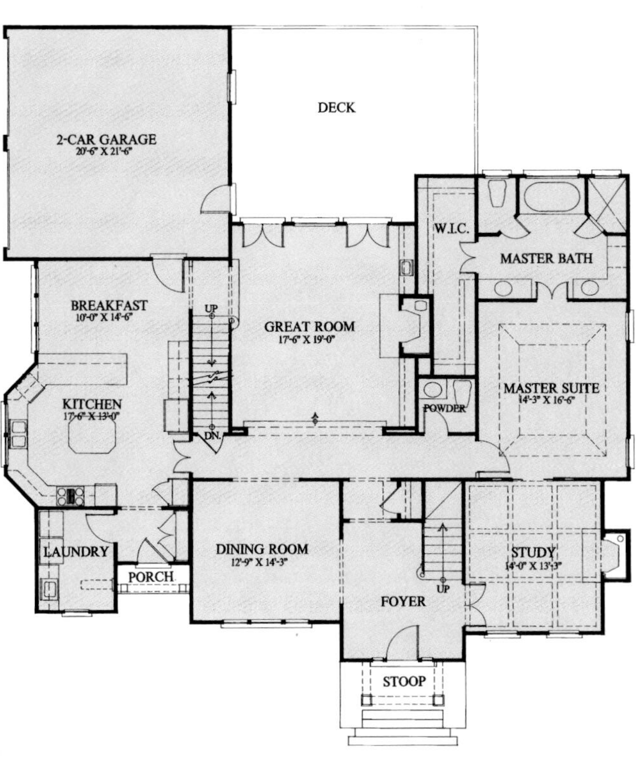
DECK
2-CAR GARAGE
20'-6" X 21'-6"
W.I.C.
MASTER BATH
BREAKFAST
10'-0" X 14'-6"
UP
GREAT ROOM
17'-6" X 19'-0"
KITCHEN
17'-6" X 13'-0"
POWDER
MASTER SUITE
14'-3" X 16'-6"
DN.
LAUNDRY
DINING ROOM
12'-9" X 14'-3"
STUDY
14'-0" X 13'-3"
PORCH
FOYER
UP
STOOP

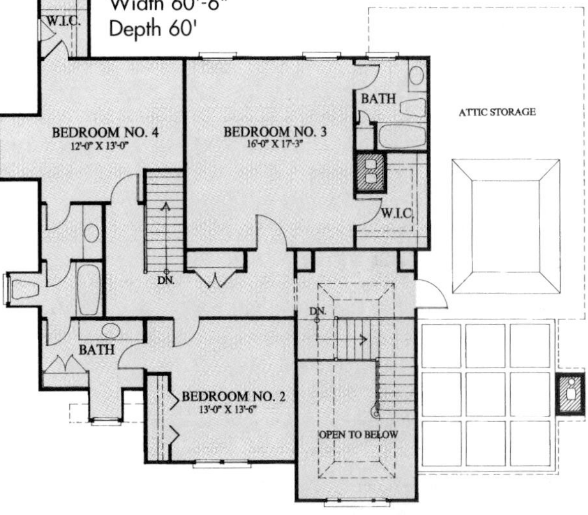
Width 60'-6"
Depth 60'
W.I.C.
BATH
ATTIC STORAGE
BEDROOM NO. 4
12'-0" X 13'-0"
BEDROOM NO. 3
16'-0" X 17'-3"
W.I.C.
DN.
DN.
BATH
BEDROOM NO. 2
13'-0" X 13'-6"
OPEN TO BELOW

QUOTE ONE®

Cost to build? See page 342
o order complete cost estimate
o build this house in your area!

Design by
Design Traditions

Design 9871

First Floor: 2,208 square feet
Second Floor: 1,250 square feet
Total: 3,458 square feet

Photo by Dave Dawson, courtesy of Design Traditions

Design by
Frank Betz
Associates, Inc.

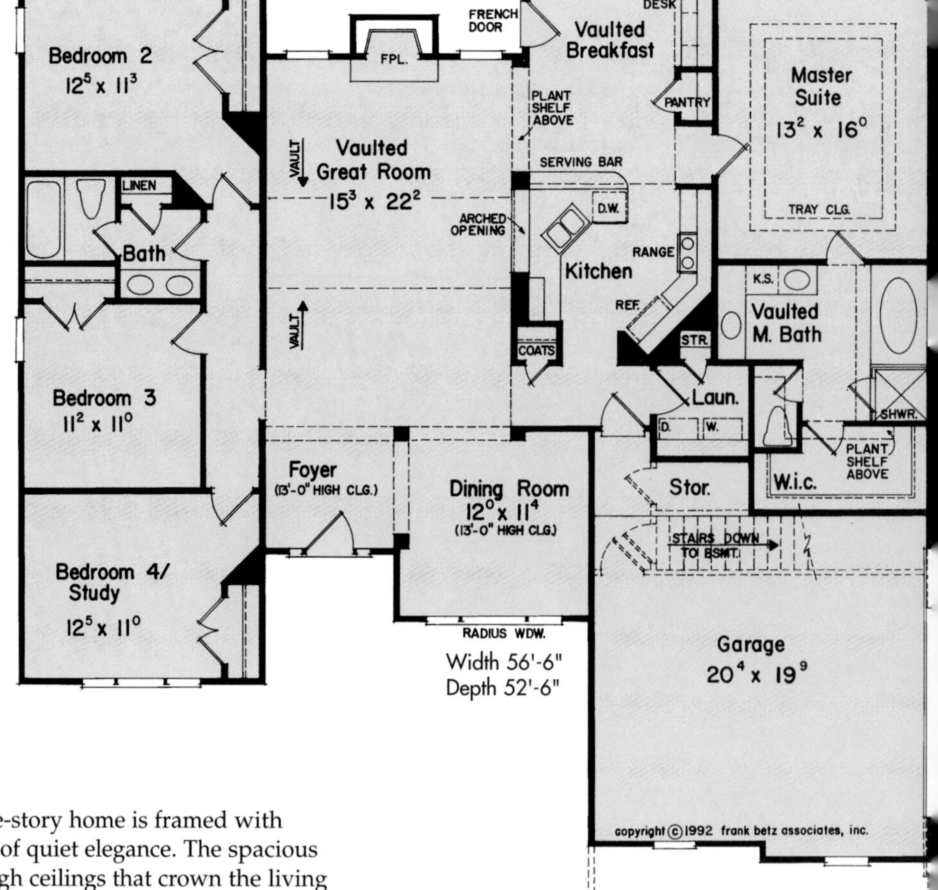
Bedroom 2
12⁵ x 11³
FRENCH DOOR
FPL.
Vaulted Breakfast
DESK
Master Suite
13² x 16⁰
PANTRY
PLANT SHELF ABOVE
VAULT
Vaulted Great Room
15³ x 22²
SERVING BAR
TRAY CLG.
LINEN
ARCHED OPENING
D.W.
Bath
RANGE
K.S.
Kitchen
Vaulted M. Bath
REF.
VAULT
COATS
STR.
Bedroom 3
11² x 11⁰
Laun.
SHWR.
D.
W.
Foyer
(13'-0" HIGH CLG.)
Dining Room
12⁰ x 11⁴
(13'-0" HIGH CLG.)
Stor.
W.i.c.
PLANT SHELF ABOVE
STAIRS DOWN TO BSMT.
Bedroom 4/ Study
12⁵ x 11⁰
RADIUS WDW.
Width 56'-6"
Depth 52'-6"
Garage
20⁴ x 19⁹
copyright © 1992 frank betz associates, inc.

Design P100

Square Footage: 1,945

■ The stately brick facade of this one-story home is framed with stucco quoins and accents for a look of quiet elegance. The spacious feeling is enhanced with the extra-high ceilings that crown the living areas starting with the foyer, columned dining room and oversized great room. An angular kitchen located between the formal dining room and breakfast nook maintains an open feel, with the serving bar and arched pass-through to the great room. The master suite has a stylish tray ceiling and a pampering bath with a dual vanity, compartmented toilet and garden tub. Three family bedrooms and a compartmented hall bath are situated off a private hall. Please specify basement or crawlspace foundation when ordering.

Design 8229

Square Footage: 1,955

■ A finely detailed covered porch and arch-topped windows announce a scrupulously designed interior, replete with amenities. A grand foyer with 10-foot ceiling and columned archways sets the pace for the entire floor plan. Clustered sleeping quarters to the left feature a luxurious master suite with a sloped ceiling, corner whirlpool bath and walk-in closet, and two family bedrooms which share a bath. Picture windows flanking a centered fireplace lend plenty of natural light to the great room, which is open through grand, columned archways to the formal dining area and bay windowed breakfast room. The roomy kitcher is conveniently positioned between the dining and breakfa rooms and shares an informal eating counter with the gr room. A utility room and walk-in pantry are tucked ne to the side of the plan. Please specify crawlspace or sl foundation when ordering.

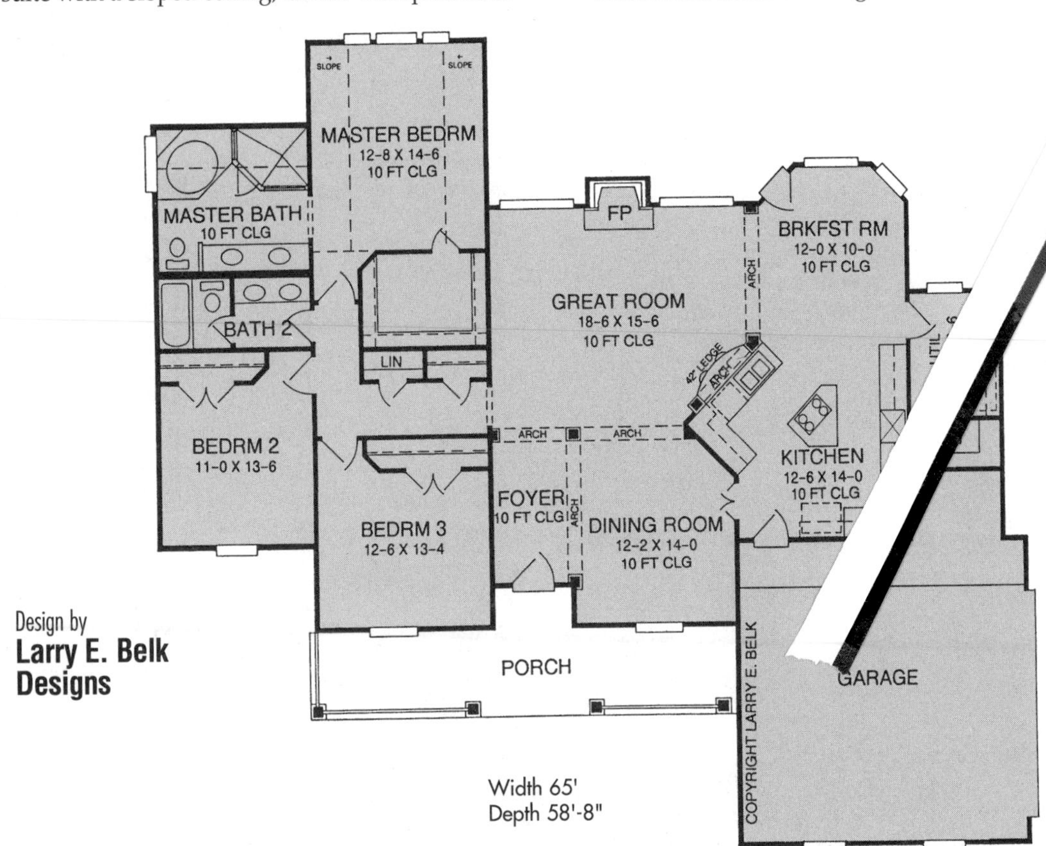
SLOPE
SLOPE
MASTER BEDRM
12-8 X 14-6
10 FT CLG
MASTER BATH
10 FT CLG
FP
BRKFST RM
12-0 X 10-0
10 FT CLG
ARCH
GREAT ROOM
18-6 X 15-6
10 FT CLG
BATH 2
LIN
42" LEDGE
ARCH
ARCH
ARCH
BEDRM 2
11-0 X 13-6
KITCHEN
12-6 X 14-0
10 FT CLG
FOYER
10 FT CLG
ARCH
DINING ROOM
12-2 X 14-0
10 FT CLG
BEDRM 3
12-6 X 13-4
PORCH
GARAGE
COPYRIGHT LARRY E. BELK
Width 65'
Depth 58'-8"

Design by
Larry E. Belk Designs

Design P235

Square Footage: 1,070

■ This modest home takes a creative look at space to design an efficient floor plan that's comfortable yet compact. The vaulted family room has a lovely corner fireplace and sliding glass doors to the rear yard. A galley kitchen is designed for efficiency and includes a hidden laundry center and a window over the sink. The breakfast room offers an optional bay window. The master suite has a tray ceiling and a large walk-in closet. Two family bedrooms and a hall bath round out the plan.

Design by
Frank Betz Associates, Inc.

OPT. BAY WINDOW
D.
D.W.
W.
Kitchen
REF.
Breakfast
Vaulted Family Room 13³x20¹⁰
FPL.
TUB
Vaulted M. Bath
W.i.c.
PLANT SHELF
TRAY CLG.
Master Suite 14⁶x12⁰
VAULT
Stor.
OPT. STAIRS TO BSMT.
Garage
W.H.
COATS
LIN.
copyright © 1990 frank betz associates, inc.
Covered Porch
Bedroom 2 10⁰x10⁰
Bedroom 3 11¹x10⁰

Width 48'
Depth 36'

Design P107

Square Footage: 1,373

■ A steep gable roofline punctuated with dormer windows and a columned front porch give a traditional welcome to this family home. A vaulted ceiling tops the family and dining rooms, which are nicely accented with a fireplace and bright windows. An amenity-filled kitchen opens to the breakfast room. The master suite has a refined tray ceiling and a vaulted master bath. Two family bedrooms, a laundry center and a full bath—with private access from Bedroom 3—complete this stylish plan. Please specify basement or crawlspace foundation when ordering.

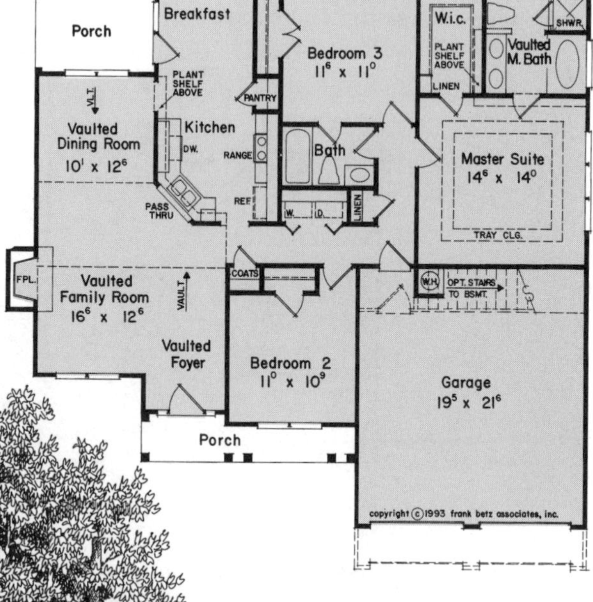

Porch
Breakfast
Bedroom 3 11⁶ x 11⁰
W.i.c.
PLANT SHELF ABOVE
SHWR.
Vaulted M. Bath
LINEN
PLANT SHELF ABOVE
PANTRY
Vaulted Dining Room 10' x 12⁶
Kitchen
DW.
RANGE
Bath
Master Suite 14⁶ x 14⁰
PASS THRU
REF.
W.
D.
LINEN
TRAY CLG.
FPL.
Vaulted Family Room 16⁶ x 12⁶
COATS
W.H.
OPT. STAIRS TO BSMT.
Vaulted Foyer
Bedroom 2 11⁰ x 10⁹
Garage 19⁵ x 21⁶
Porch
copyright © 1993 frank betz associates, inc.

Width 50'-4"
Depth 45'

Design by
Frank Betz Associates, Inc.

Design 9760

Square Footage: 1,475

■ The front porch of this timeless design leads to the columned foyer. A cathedral ceiling in the great room lends height and a feeling of openness. A fireplace here is framed by doors leading to a rear deck. The kitchen easily serves the dining room while remaining open to the great room. The quiet master bedroom is accented with a tiered ceiling, a private bath and a walk-in closet. Two secondary bedrooms share a full hall bath. The two-car garage is located, out of sight, at the rear of the plan.

Design by
Donald A. Gardner, Architects, Inc.

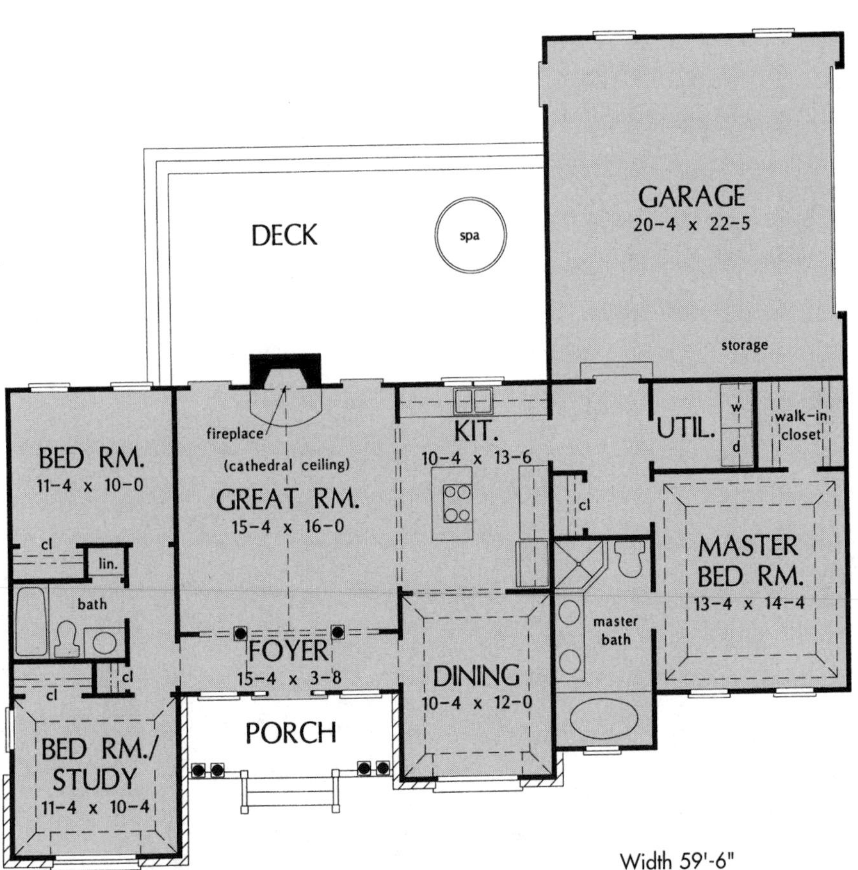
GARAGE
20-4 x 22-5
DECK
spa
storage
fireplace
(cathedral ceiling)
GREAT RM.
15-4 x 16-0
KIT.
10-4 x 13-6
UTIL.
w
d
walk-in closet
BED RM.
11-4 x 10-0
cl
lin.
bath
cl
MASTER BED RM.
13-4 x 14-4
master bath
FOYER
15-4 x 3-8
DINING
10-4 x 12-0
cl
cl
PORCH
BED RM./ STUDY
11-4 x 10-4

Width 59'-6"
Depth 54'-7"

Design P189

Square Footage: 1,502

■ This ambitious plan masterfully combines stylish architectural elements in a smaller square footage. Elegant ceiling details, decorative columns and fancy window treatment prevail throughout this split-bedroom design. The great room is fashioned with a fireplace and has an open view into the breakfast room and serving bar. The modified galley kitchen has a convenient rear entry to the formal dining room and a service entrance through the two-car garage. Two family bedrooms and a full bath are neatly tucked behind the breakfast nook. The master suite is truly an owner's retreat with a cozy sitting room that's accented with a vaulted ceiling and sunny windows. The compartmented bath has a twin vanity and a walk-in closet. Please specify slab or basement foundation when ordering.

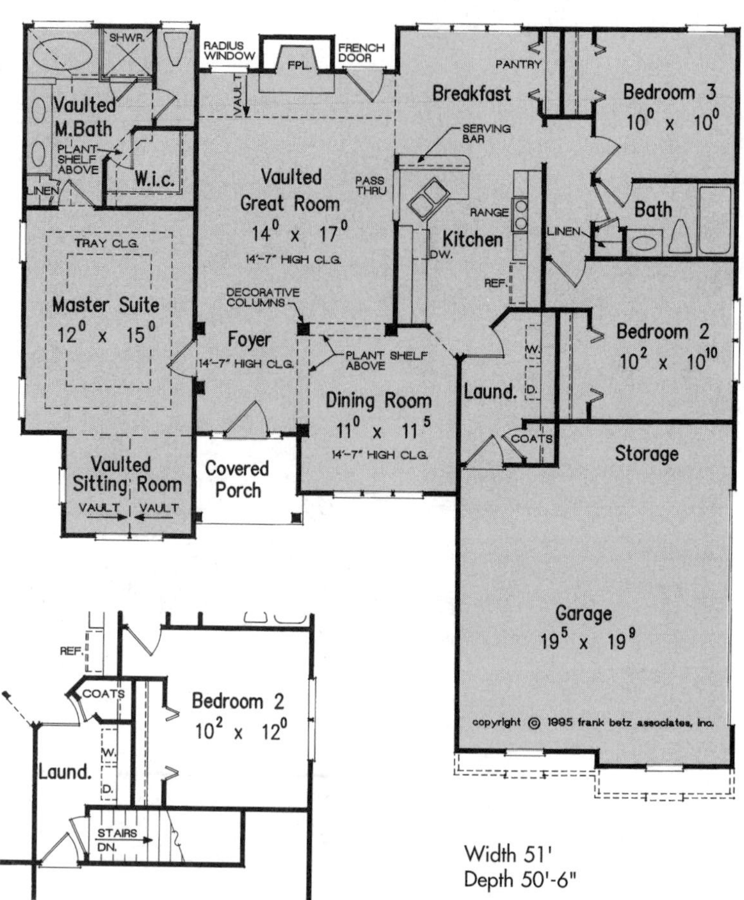
SHWR.
Vaulted M.Bath
PLANT SHELF ABOVE
LINEN
W.i.c.
RADIUS WINDOW
FPL.
FRENCH DOOR
VAULT
PANTRY
Breakfast
Bedroom 3
10⁰ x 10⁰
SERVING BAR
Vaulted Great Room
14⁰ x 17⁰
14'-7" HIGH CLG.
PASS THRU
RANGE
Kitchen
DW.
REF.
LINEN
Bath
TRAY CLG.
Master Suite
12⁰ x 15⁰
DECORATIVE COLUMNS
Foyer
14'-7" HIGH CLG.
PLANT SHELF ABOVE
Dining Room
11⁰ x 11⁵
14'-7" HIGH CLG.
Laund.
W.
D.
Bedroom 2
10² x 10¹⁰
COATS
Storage
Vaulted Sitting Room
VAULT
VAULT
Covered Porch
Garage
19⁵ x 19⁹
copyright © 1995 frank betz associates, inc.
REF.
COATS
Bedroom 2
10² x 12⁰
W.
Laund.
D.
STAIRS DN.
Width 51'
Depth 50'-6"

Design by
Frank Betz Associates, Inc.

Design by
Larry E. Belk
Designs

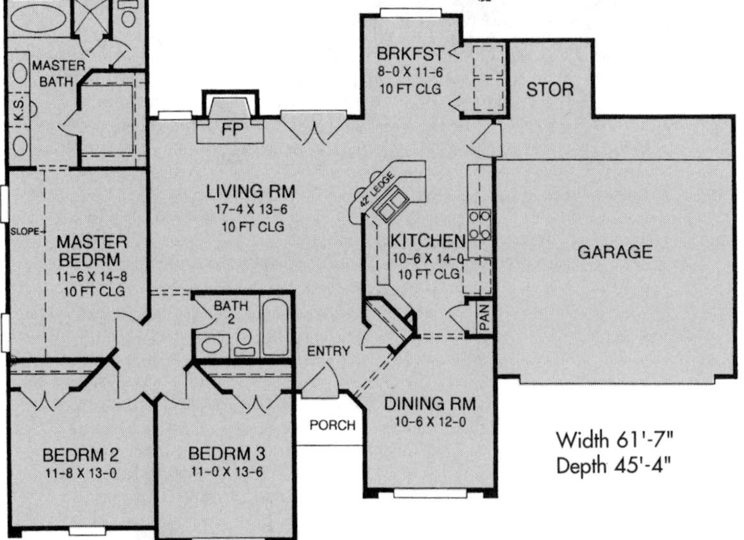
MASTER BATH
K.S.
SLOPE
MASTER BEDRM
11-6 X 14-8
10 FT CLG
FP
LIVING RM
17-4 X 13-6
10 FT CLG
42" LEDGE
BRKFST
8-0 X 11-6
10 FT CLG
STOR
KITCHEN
10-6 X 14-0
10 FT CLG
PAN
GARAGE
BATH 2
ENTRY
PORCH
DINING RM
10-6 X 12-0
BEDRM 2
11-8 X 13-0
BEDRM 3
11-0 X 13-6

Width 61'-7"
Depth 45'-4"

Design 8061

Square Footage: 1,553

■ Two striking brick gables give a balanced look to this lovely starter home. The living room features a ten-foot ceiling and cozy fireplace. A formal dining room is located to the right of the foyer and has easy access to the kitchen. Ten-foot ceilings throughout the kitchen and breakfast nook give the home a spacious feel. Minimal corridor space in the sleeping zone allows for larger family bedrooms. The master suite features a bath appointed with double vanities, a whirlpool tub and a separate shower. Please specify crawlspace or slab foundation when ordering.

Design 9328

Square Footage: 1,496

■ Sleek rooflines, lap siding and brick accents highlight the exterior of this three-bedroom home. A tiled entry views the spacious great room featuring a sloping cathedral ceiling and window-framed fireplace. Natural light adds comfort to the bayed breakfast area with its pantry, handy planning desk and the peninsula kitchen. Both secondary bedrooms share a full bath and linen closet. Bedroom 3 is easily converted to a den or home office. With the nine-foot-high boxed ceiling, walk-in closet, sunlit whirlpool tub and double vanities, the master suite is soothing and luxurious.

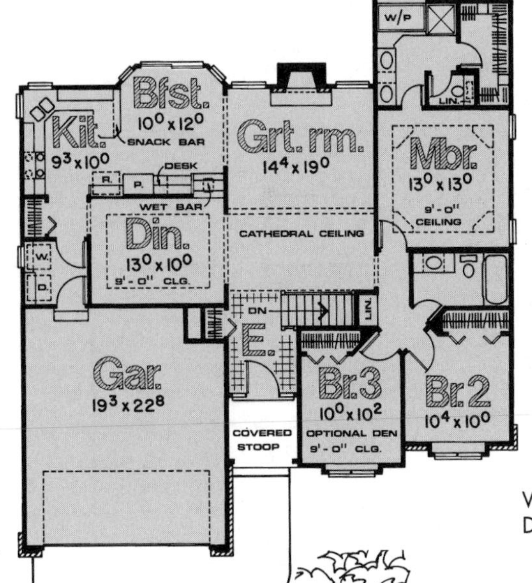
W/P
LIN.
Bfst.
10⁰ x 12⁰
SNACK BAR
Kit.
9³ x 10⁰
DESK
R.
P.
WET BAR
Grt. rm.
14⁴ x 19⁰
Mbr.
13⁰ x 13⁰
9'-0" CEILING
CATHEDRAL CEILING
Din.
13⁰ x 10⁰
9'-0" CLG.
W.
D.
DN
LIN
E.
Gar.
19³ x 22⁸
Br.3
10⁰ x 10²
OPTIONAL DEN
9'-0" CLG.
Br.2
10⁴ x 10⁰
COVERED STOOP

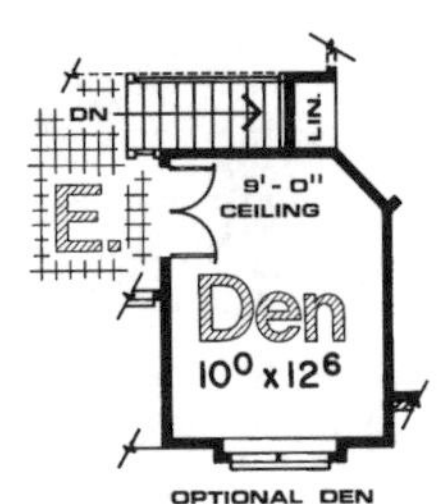
DN
LIN
E.
9'-0" CEILING
Den
10⁰ x 12⁶
OPTIONAL DEN

Width 48'
Depth 52'

Design by
Design Basics, Inc.

Design P233

Square Footage: 1,671

■ A play on symmetry in the elevation of this one-story home will surely encourage a second glance. Inside, custom amenities accent every room. The vaulted family room features a centerpiece fireplace flanked by windows and a French door, a multi-angled serving bar and, for that decorator's touch, a stylish plant shelf. The kitchen is designed for efficiency, placed between the formal dining room and the breakfast nook and service entrance. The expansive master suite is comprised of a sitting room with a vaulted ceiling, a large bedroom with tray ceiling detail and a French door to the rear yard, and a compartmented bath. Two family bedrooms and a hall bath round out the sleeping quarters.

Dining Room
11⁰x11⁰
FRENCH DOOR
FPL.
FRENCH DOOR
TRAY CLG.
Master Suite
13⁰x16⁰
SHWR
Vaulted M.Bath
W.i.c.
OPT. FPL.
SERVING BAR
REF
Kitchen
RANGE
D.W.
PANTRY
Vaulted Family Room
15⁵x17⁵
15'-4" HIGH CLG.
VAULT
Bath
Vaulted Sitting
14⁰x10⁰
RADIUS WINDOW
PLANT SHELF ABOVE
Breakfast
Laund.
WH
Foyer
15'-4" HIGH CLG.
LINEN
COATS
OPT. STAIRS TO BSMT.
Bedroom 2
11⁵x11⁰
Bedroom 3
10⁹x13⁶
Covered Porch
Garage
19⁵ x 19⁷
copyright © 1992 frank betz associates, inc.

Width 50'
Depth 51'

Design by
Frank Betz Associates, Inc.

Design by
Larry E. Belk Designs

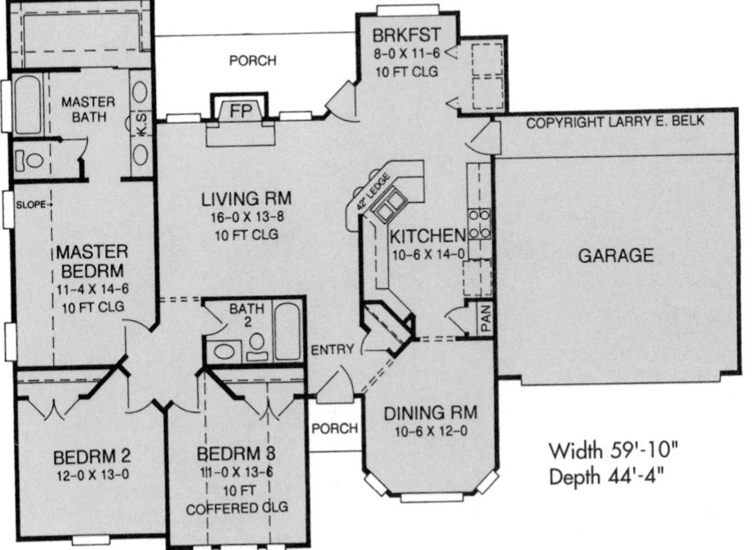
PORCH
BRKFST
8-0 X 11-6
10 FT CLG
MASTER BATH
K.S.
FP
COPYRIGHT LARRY E. BELK
SLOPE
LIVING RM
16-0 X 13-8
10 FT CLG
42" LEDGE
KITCHEN
10-6 X 14-0
GARAGE
MASTER BEDRM
11-4 X 14-6
10 FT CLG
BATH 2
PAN
ENTRY
PORCH
DINING RM
10-6 X 12-0
BEDRM 2
12-0 X 13-0
BEDRM 3
11-0 X 13-6
10 FT
COFFERED CLG

Width 59'-10"
Depth 44'-4"

Design 8181

Square Footage: 1,500

■ A spacious interior is implied from the curb with the lofty, hipped rooflines of this economical family home. From the entry, the large living room is fully visible, as is the rear yard, through windows flanking the fireplace. The kitchen is partially open to the living room via a snack bar and has full access to the breakfast room. A formal dining room just off the kitchen will serve entertaining needs with style. The master bedroom features a compartment bath with a sit-down vanity. Two family bedrooms share a full hall bath. Please specify crawlspace or slab foundation when ordering.

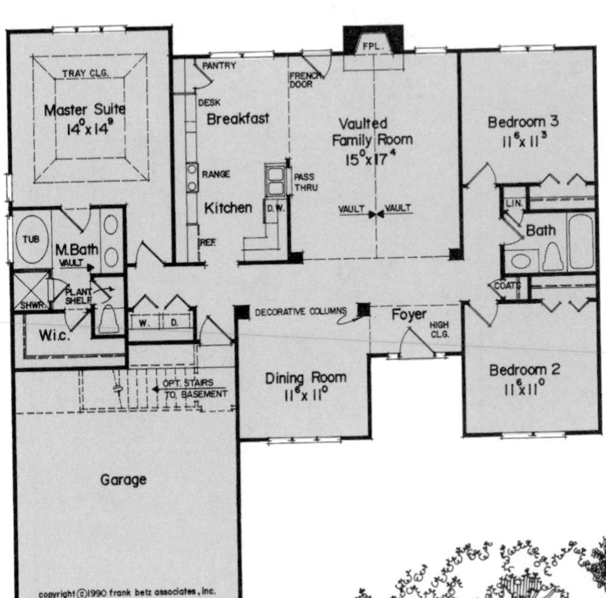
TRAY CLG.
Master Suite
14^{0}x14^{9}
PANTRY
FRENCH DOOR
FPL.
DESK
Breakfast
Vaulted Family Room
15^{0}x17^{4}
Bedroom 3
11^{6}x11^{3}
RANGE
PASS THRU
Kitchen
D.W.
VAULT
VAULT
LIN.
Bath
TUB
M.Bath
VAULT
REF
PLANT SHELF
SHWR.
COATS
DECORATIVE COLUMNS
Foyer
HIGH CLG.
W.
D.
Wi.c.
Dining Room
11^{6}x11^{0}
Bedroom 2
11^{6}x11^{0}
OPT. STAIRS TO BASEMENT
Garage
copyright © 1990 frank betz associates, inc.

Design P111

Square Footage: 1,553

■ This traditional, split floor plan is quite manageable in size while featuring amenities found in much larger homes. Decorative columns frame the entrances to the dining room and the expansive family room that's fashioned with a vaulted ceiling and a French door to the rear yard. The step-saving kitchen has a planning desk, breakfast area and pass-through to the family room. A dramatic tray ceiling crowns the bedroom of the master suite that's rounded out with a compartmented bath and walk-in closet. Two family bedrooms, just off the family room, share a hall bath.

Width 52'
Depth 49'-6"

Design by
Frank Betz Associates, Inc.

Design 8168

Square Footage: 1,628

■ A lovely traditional facade complements this up-to-date floor plan. Inside, the open angled breakfast bar connects the kitchen and breakfast room to the main living area beyond. Ten-foot ceilings give the home a spacious feel. The master suite features a roomy walk-in closet, double vanities and a separate shower and whirlpool tub. Two family bedrooms have stylish angled entries and share a hall bath. Please specify crawlspace or slab foundation when ordering.

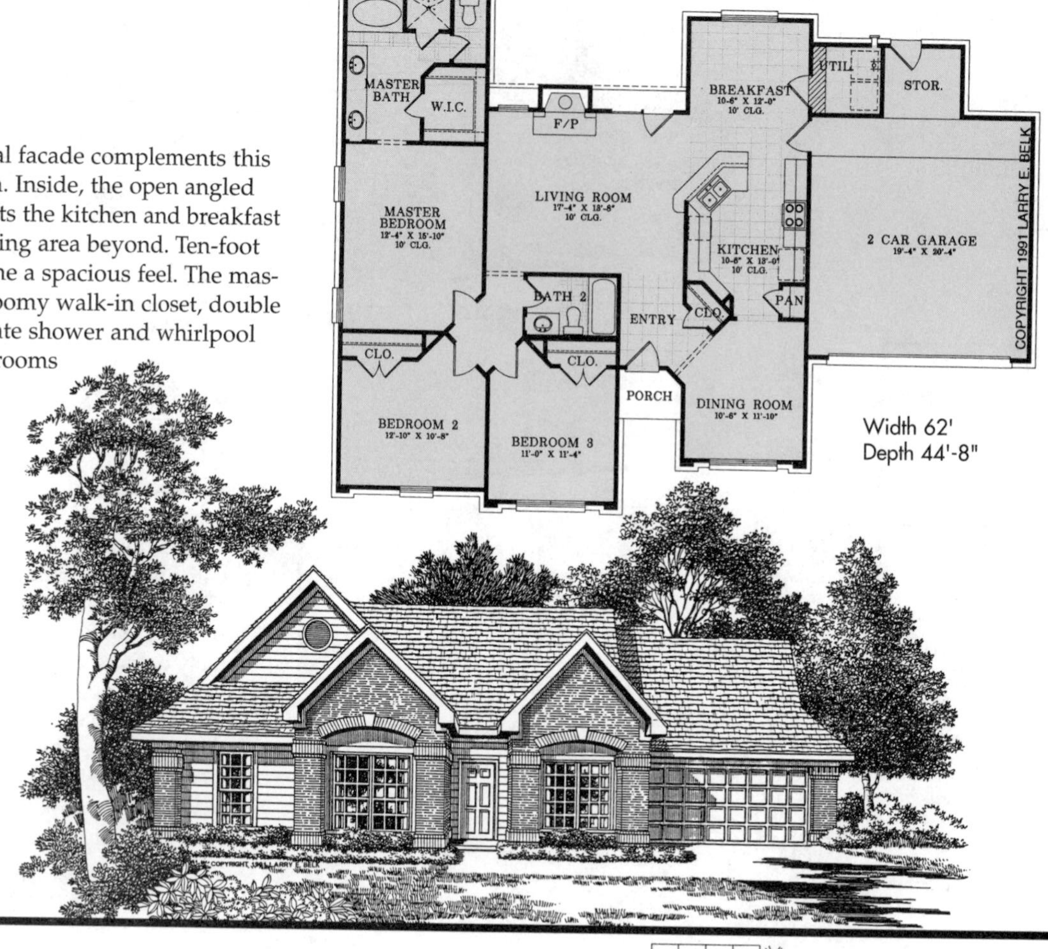

MASTER BATH
W.I.C.
F/P
BREAKFAST
10'-6" X 12'-0"
10' CLG.
UTIL.
STOR.
MASTER BEDROOM
12'-4" X 15'-10"
10' CLG.
LIVING ROOM
17'-4" X 18'-8"
10' CLG.
KITCHEN
10'-8" X 13'-0"
10' CLG.
2 CAR GARAGE
19'-4" X 20'-4"
COPYRIGHT 1991 LARRY E. BELK
BATH 2
ENTRY
CLO.
PAN
CLO.
CLO.
PORCH
BEDROOM 2
12'-10" X 10'-8"
BEDROOM 3
11'-0" X 11'-4"
DINING ROOM
10'-8" X 11'-10"
Width 62'
Depth 44'-8"

Design by
Larry E. Belk Designs

Design 9427

Square Footage: 1,687

■ Intriguing rooflines create a dynamic exterior for this home. The interior floor plan is equally attractive. Toward the rear a wide archway forms the entrance to the spacious family living area with its centrally placed fireplace and bay-windowed nook area. An island, mitered corner window and a walk-in pantry complete the efficient kitchen. This home also boasts a terrific master suite complete with walk-in wardrobe, spa tub with corner windows and a compartmented shower and toilet area. Two family bedrooms share a hall bath.

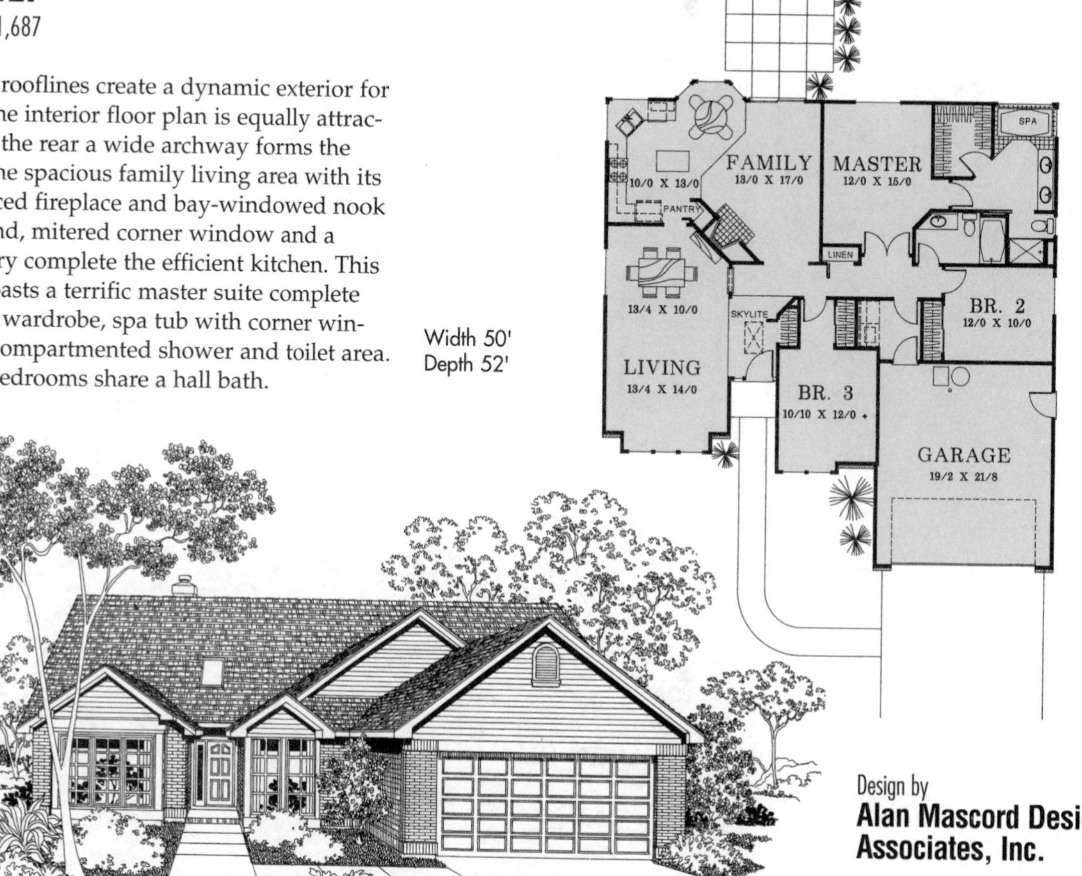

Width 50'
Depth 52'
SPA
FAMILY
13/0 X 17/0
MASTER
12/0 X 15/0
10/0 X 13/0
PANTRY
LINEN
13/4 X 10/0
SKYLITE
BR. 2
12/0 X 10/0
LIVING
13/4 X 14/0
BR. 3
10/10 X 12/0 +
GARAGE
19/2 X 21/8

Design by
Alan Mascord Design Associates, Inc.

Design 9894

Square Footage: 1,733

■ Delightfully different, this brick one-story home has everything for the active family. The entry foyer opens to a formal dining room on the right, accented with four columns, and a great room with fireplace and French doors to the rear deck. The efficient kitchen has an attached, light-filled breakfast nook. Bedrooms are split with the master suite on the right and family bedrooms to the left. The master bath features His and Hers walk-in closets, a double vanity and huge garden tub. The other full bath is compartmented to serve both secondary bedrooms. This home is designed with a basement foundation.

DECK
BREAKFAST 11'-4" X 8'-6"
BEDROOM NO. 3 11'-6" X 11'-0"
GREAT ROOM 14'-0" X 17'-6"
KITCHEN 11'-4" X 10'-0"
MASTER BEDROOM 12'-4" X 15'-6"
BATH
DN.
HIS
FOYER 6'-6" X 6'-6"
MASTER BATH
PWDR.
BEDROOM NO. 2 11'-0" X 14'-8"
DINING ROOM 11'-4" X 10'-6"
LAUNDRY
HERS
TWO-CAR GARAGE 20'-4" X 19'-4"
Width 55'-6"
Depth 57'-6"

QUOTE ONE®

Cost to build? See page 342 to order complete cost estimate to build this house in your area!

Design by
Design Traditions

Design 9619

Square Footage: 2,021

■ Simplicity embraces elegance in this three bedroom home. A special feature of this plan is the sunroom with hot tub accessed from the master bath and the great room. Details in the great room include a fireplace, cathedral ceiling and sliding glass door with arched window above. The spacious master bedroom has a walk-in closet and master bath with double-bowl vanity, shower and garden tub. Two family bedrooms are located at the other end of the house for privacy. Please specify basement or crawlspace foundation when ordering.

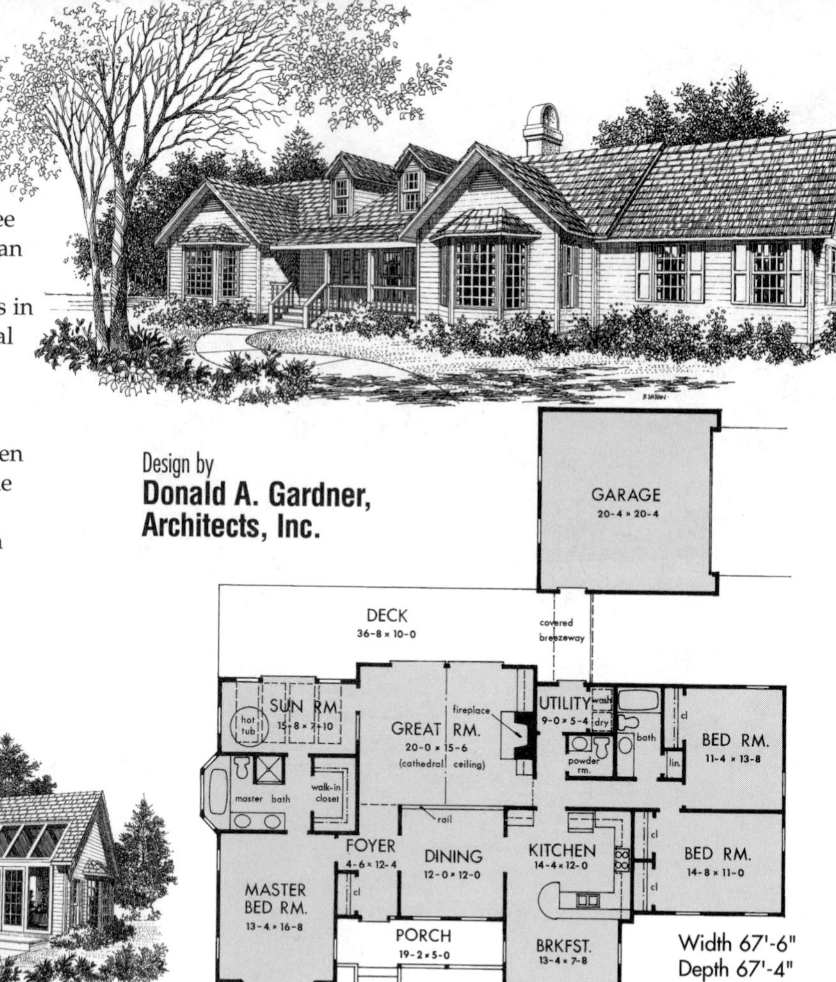
GARAGE
20-4 × 20-4
DECK
36-8 × 10-0
covered breezeway
SUN RM.
15-8 × 7-10
hot tub
GREAT RM.
20-0 × 15-6
(cathedral ceiling)
fireplace
UTILITY
9-0 × 5-4
wash
dry
powder rm.
bath
lin.
cl
BED RM.
11-4 × 13-8
master bath
walk-in closet
rail
FOYER
4-6 × 12-4
DINING
12-0 × 12-0
KITCHEN
14-4 × 12-0
BED RM.
14-8 × 11-0
MASTER BED RM.
13-4 × 16-8
PORCH
19-2 × 5-0
BRKFST.
13-4 × 7-8

Design by
Donald A. Gardner, Architects, Inc.

Width 67'-6"
Depth 67'-4"

Design 9622

Square Footage: 1,842

■ The angular nature of the plan allows for flexibility in design—lengthen the great room or family room, or both, to suit individual space needs. Special amenities include cathedral ceilings in both the great and family rooms and a fireplace in the great room. The master bedroom features cathedral ceiling, private deck and master bath with whirlpool tub. Two secondary bedrooms share a full bath. An expansive deck area with hot tub wraps around for enhanced outdoor living. Please specify basement or crawlspace foundation when ordering.

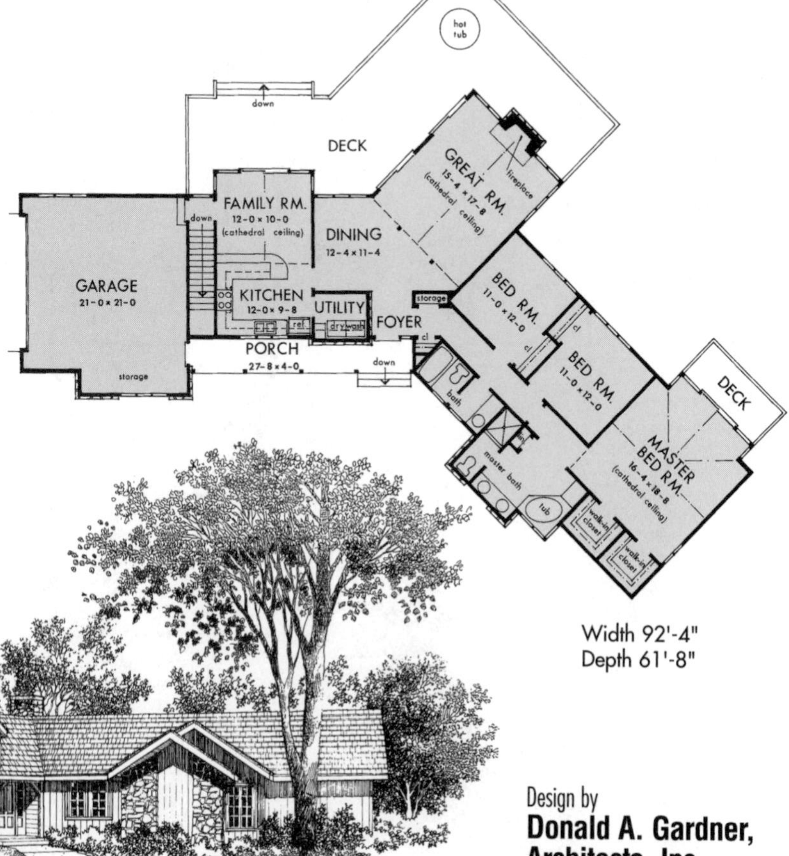
hot tub
down
DECK
GREAT RM.
15-4 × 17-8
(cathedral ceiling)
fireplace
FAMILY RM.
12-0 × 10-0
(cathedral ceiling)
DINING
12-4 × 11-4
GARAGE
21-0 × 21-0
KITCHEN
12-0 × 9-8
UTILITY
storage
FOYER
BED RM.
11-0 × 12-0
BED RM.
11-0 × 12-0
PORCH
27-8 × 4-0
storage
bath
DECK
MASTER BED RM.
16-4 × 18-8
(cathedral ceiling)
master bath
tub
walk-in closet

Width 92'-4"
Depth 61'-8"

Design by
Donald A. Gardner, Architects, Inc.

Design by
Donald A. Gardner, Architects, Inc.

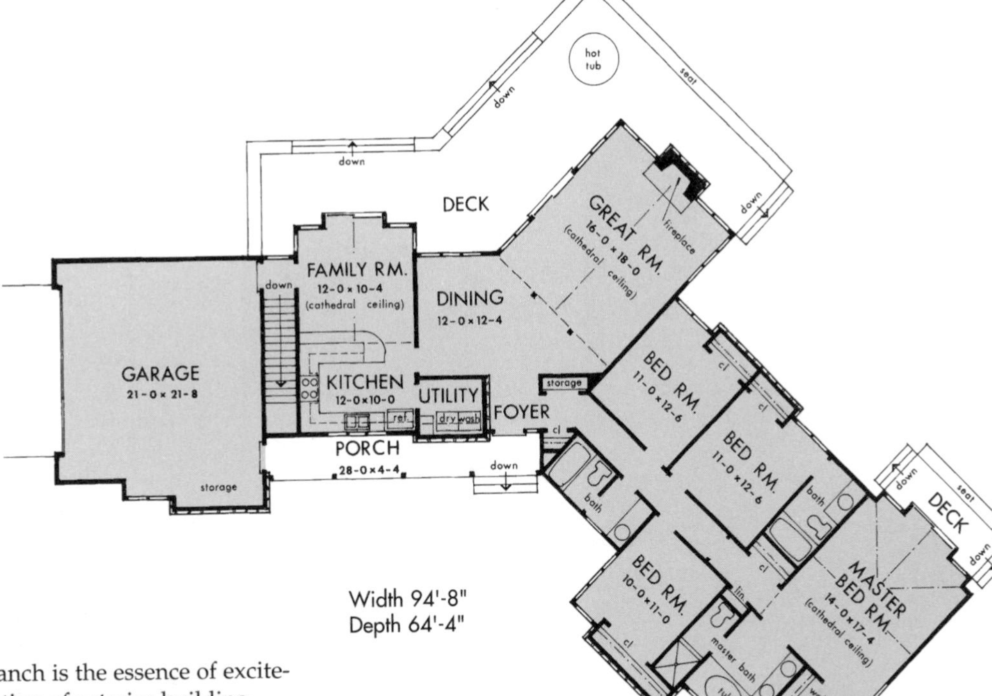
hot tub
seat
down
down
DECK
down
GREAT RM.
16-0 x 18-0
(cathedral ceiling)
fireplace
down
FAMILY RM.
12-0 x 10-4
(cathedral ceiling)
DINING
12-0 x 12-4
GARAGE
21-0 x 21-8
KITCHEN
12-0 x 10-0
UTILITY
ref.
dry wash
FOYER
storage
cl
PORCH
28-0 x 4-4
down
storage
BED RM.
11-0 x 12-6
BED RM.
11-0 x 12-6
bath
bath
DECK
seat
down
down
MASTER BED RM.
14-0 x 17-4
(cathedral ceiling)
BED RM.
10-0 x 11-0
lin
cl
master bath
tub
walk-in closet
Width 94'-8"
Depth 64'-4"

Design 9601

Square Footage: 1,988

■ This country-style ranch is the essence of excitement with its combination of exterior building materials and interesting shapes. Because it is angled, it allows for flexibility in design—the great room and/or the family room can be lengthened to meet family space requirements. Both family room and great room have cathedral ceilings. The great room is framed with a dramatic wall of windows and has a cozy fireplace. The master bedroom has a cathedral ceiling, a walk-in closet, private deck and a spacious master bath with whirlpool tub. There are three family bedrooms—two that share a full bath and one that has a private bath. Expansive deck area with space for a hot tub wraps around interior family gathering areas. Please specify basement or crawlspace foundation when ordering.

NATHAN INC

Design 9748

Square Footage: 1,737

■ Inviting porches are just the beginning of amenities found in this lovely country home. Casual lifestyles will love the massive great room with a cathedral ceiling, built-in bookshelves and a fireplace. An octagonal dining room with a tray ceiling makes every meal a special occasion. The breakfast area is a perfect extension to the efficient kitchen that includes an island cooktop and built-in pantry. The master bedroom, set to the rear of the plan, offers privacy and comfort.

Width 65'-10"
Depth 59'-8"

Design by
Donald A. Gardner, Architects, Inc.

Design 9873

Square Footage: 2,078

■ A porch with column detailing covers the entry to this single-story American classic. Once inside, the foyer opens to the living room with a wall of windows and French doors that lead outside. The spacious kitchen with work island opens to a sunlit breakfast area and great room featuring a warming hearth and doors to the rear deck. The master suite is framed with a large window section and door to the rear yard. The bath has twin vanities, garden tub and walk-in closet. Two family bedrooms have spacious closets and a shared private bath. This home is designed with a basement foundation.

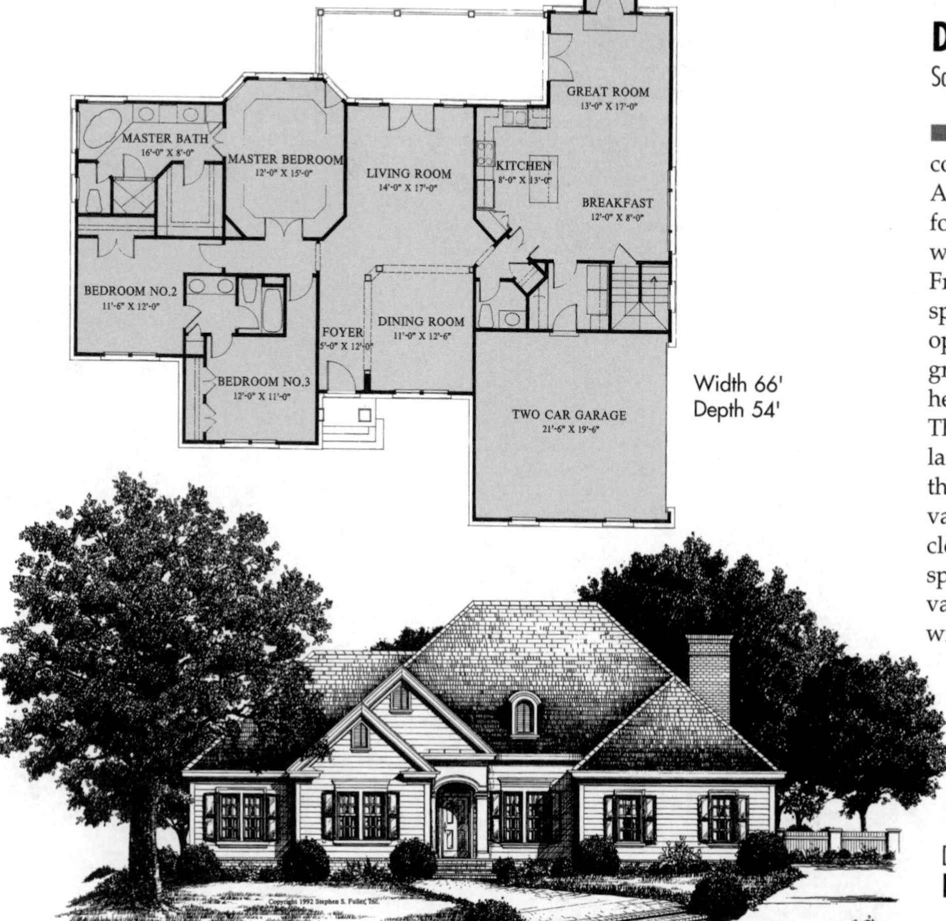

GREAT ROOM
13'-0" X 17'-0"
MASTER BATH
16'-0" X 8'-0"
MASTER BEDROOM
12'-0" X 15'-0"
LIVING ROOM
14'-0" X 17'-0"
KITCHEN
8'-0" X 13'-0"
BREAKFAST
12'-0" X 8'-0"
BEDROOM NO.2
11'-6" X 12'-0"
FOYER
5'-0" X 12'-0"
DINING ROOM
11'-0" X 12'-6"
BEDROOM NO.3
12'-0" X 11'-0"
TWO CAR GARAGE
21'-6" X 19'-6"
Width 66'
Depth 54'

Design by
Design Traditions

Design 9734

Square Footage: 1,977
Basement Foundation: 2,025 square feet
Bonus Room: 430 square feet

■ A two-story foyer with a Palladian window above sets the tone for this sunlit home. Columns mark the passage from the foyer to the great room, where a centered fireplace and built-in cabinets are found. A screened porch with four skylights above and a wet bar provides a pleasant place to start the day or wind down after work. The kitchen is flanked by the formal dining room and the breakfast room with sliding glass doors to the large, rear deck. Hidden quietly in the rear, the master suite includes a bath with dual vanities and skylights. Two family bedrooms (one an optional study) share a bath with twin sinks. Please specify basement or crawlspace foundation when ordering.

seat
spa
DECK
skylights
SCREEN PORCH
16-0 x 11-0
wet bar
MASTER BED RM.
13-4 x 18-8
master bath
walk-in closet
BED RM.
12-4 x 11-8
GREAT RM.
16-0 x 17-4
BRKFST.
12-0 x 8-6
UTIL.
lin.
storage
up
fireplace
cabinets
KITCHEN
12-0 x 12-8
GARAGE
22-0 x 20-4
cl
lin.
bath
FOYER
12-4 x 5-6
DINING
12-0 x 13-8
storage
PORCH
BED RM./ STUDY
12-0 x 12-0

Width 69'-8"
Depth 67'-6"

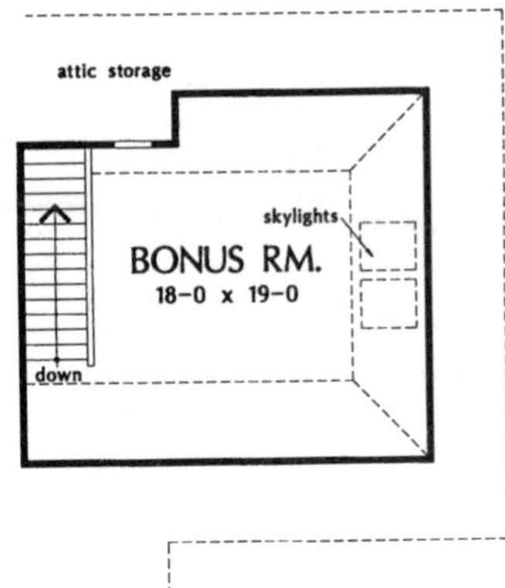
attic storage
skylights
BONUS RM.
18-0 x 19-0
down

QUOTE ONE®

Cost to build? See page 342 to order complete cost estimate to build this house in your area!

Design by
Donald A. Gardner, Architects, Inc.

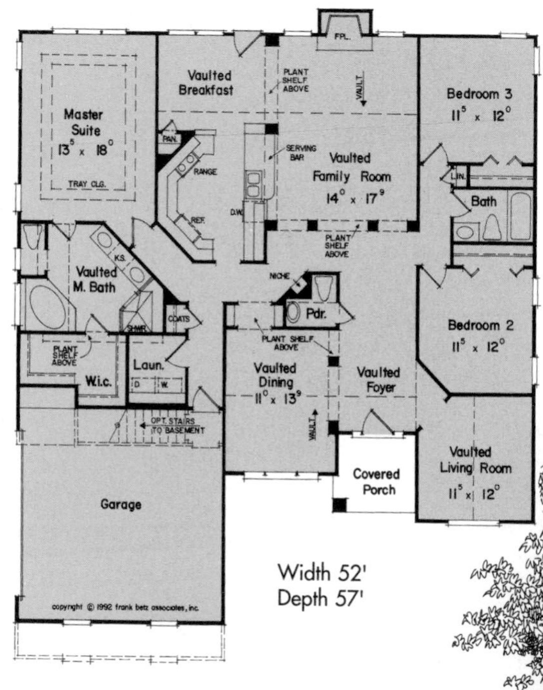

Vaulted Breakfast
PLANT SHELF ABOVE
FPL.
VAULT
Bedroom 3
$11^5 \times 12^0$
Master Suite
$13^5 \times 18^0$
TRAY CLG.
PAN.
RANGE
SERVING BAR
Vaulted Family Room
$14^0 \times 17^9$
LIN.
Bath
REF.
D.W.
PLANT SHELF ABOVE
K.S.
Vaulted M. Bath
NICHE
Pdr.
Bedroom 2
$11^5 \times 12^0$
COATS
SHWR.
PLANT SHELF ABOVE
PLANT SHELF ABOVE
Laun.
Vaulted Dining
$11^0 \times 13^9$
Vaulted Foyer
W.i.c.
OPT. STAIRS TO BASEMENT
Vaulted Living Room
$11^5 \times 12^0$
Covered Porch
Garage
Width 52'
Depth 57'
copyright © 1992 frank betz associates, inc.

Design P148

Square Footage: 2,094

■ An elegant brick exterior is brightened with stylish stucco accents and lovely window treatments. Entertaining will be a pleasure with the well-designed formal dining and living rooms; set to the front apart from casual areas, they both have vaulted ceilings. Vaulted ceilings top off the family and breakfast rooms as well. The master suite has a lush bath and large walk-in closet. The two family bedrooms share a hall bath. Please specify basement, slab or crawlspace foundation when ordering.

Design by
Frank Betz Associates, Inc.

Design by
Donald A. Gardner, Architects, Inc.

Design 9660

Square Footage: 2,108

■ Multi-paned windows, dormers, copper-covered bay windows, a covered porch with round columns and brick veneer siding give a sophisticated appearance to this three-bedroom home. A special feature is the sunroom with hot tub adjacent to and accessible from both the master bath and great room. The great room has a fireplace, cathedral ceiling and sliding glass door with arched window above to allow plenty of natural light. The spacious master bedroom contains a walk-in closet and a bath with double-bowl vanity, shower and garden tub. Two family bedrooms are located at the opposite end of the house for privacy.

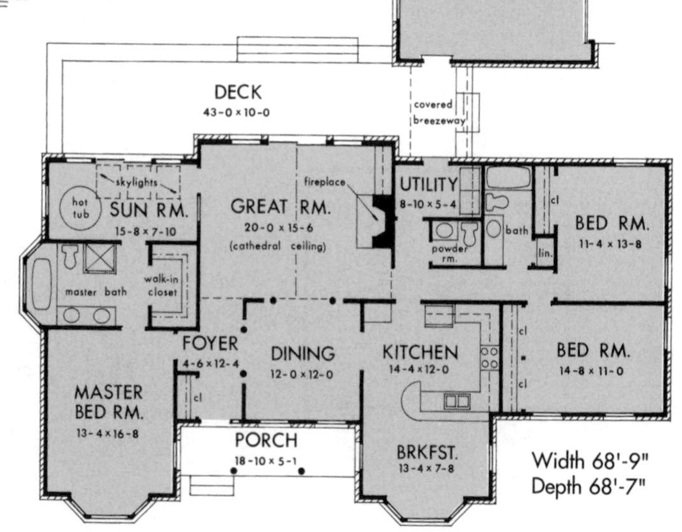

GARAGE
20-4 x 20-4
DECK
43-0 x 10-0
covered breezeway
skylights
hot tub
SUN RM.
15-8 x 7-10
fireplace
GREAT RM.
20-0 x 15-6
(cathedral ceiling)
UTILITY
8-10 x 5-4
powder rm.
bath
cl
lin.
BED RM.
11-4 x 13-8
master bath
walk-in closet
FOYER
4-6 x 12-4
DINING
12-0 x 12-0
KITCHEN
14-4 x 12-0
BED RM.
14-8 x 11-0
MASTER BED RM.
13-4 x 16-8
PORCH
18-10 x 5-1
BRKFST.
13-4 x 7-8
Width 68'-9"
Depth 68'-7"

Design 8126

Square Footage: 2,127
Bonus Room: 338 square feet

■ Three arched windows provide just the right touch of elegance to give this home a picturesque appeal. The large great room with a corner fireplace is located comfortably near the roomy breakfast area and kitchen. Ten-foot ceilings in all major living areas give the plan an open, spacious feel. The master suite includes a luxury bath with a coffered ceiling, large His and Hers closet, a whirlpool tub, a shower with a seat and dual vanities with a seating area. This split-bedroom plan locates Bedrooms 2 and 3 on the opposite side of the home. A stair leads to a bonus room on the second floor—perfect for a game room or home office. Please specify crawlspace or slab foundation when ordering.

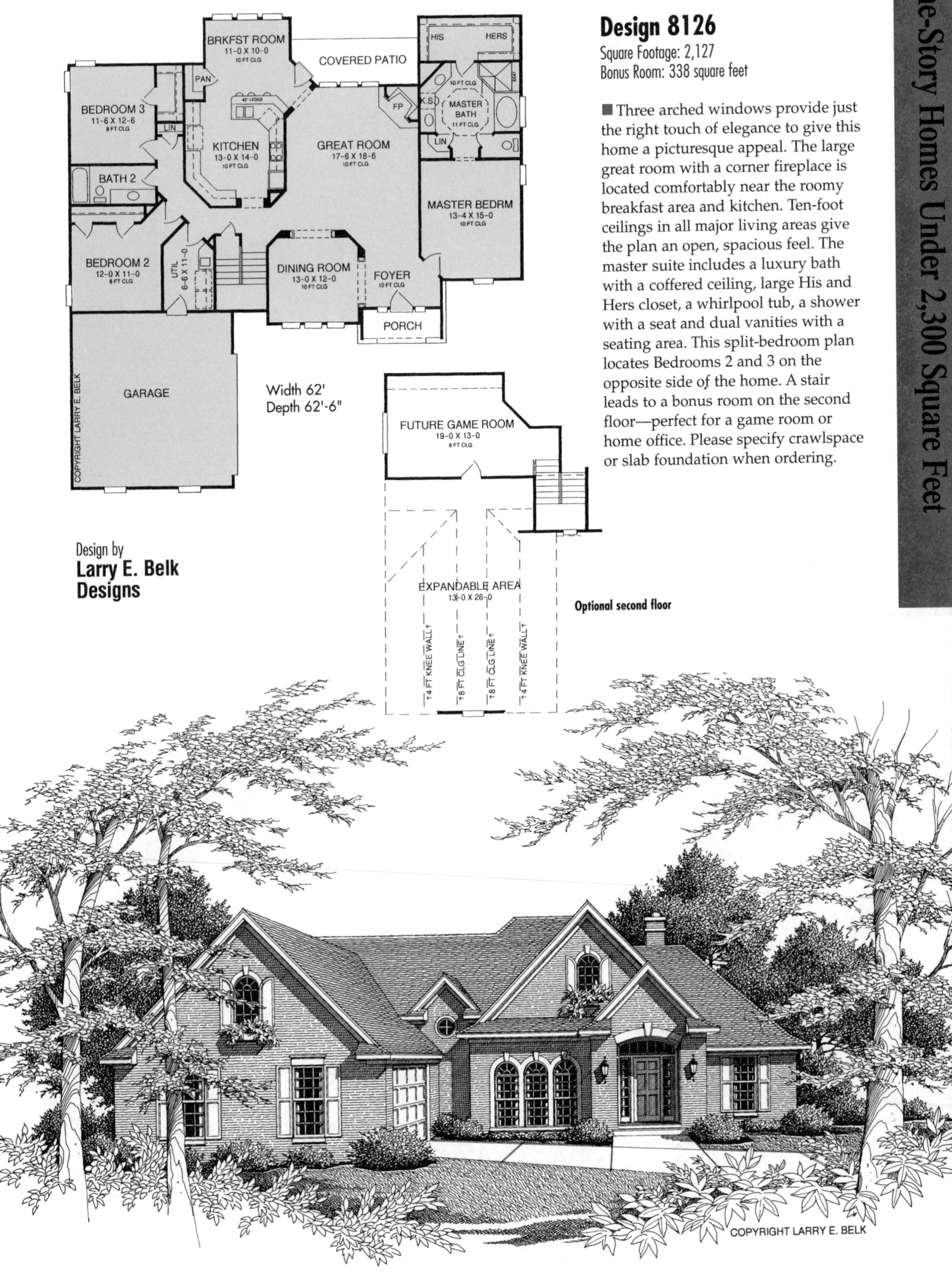
BRKFST ROOM
11-0 X 10-0
10 FT CLG
COVERED PATIO
HIS
HERS
PAN
BEDROOM 3
11-6 X 12-6
8 FT CLG
LIN
KITCHEN
13-0 X 14-0
10 FT CLG
GREAT ROOM
17-6 X 18-6
10 FT CLG
FP
K.S.
MASTER BATH
11 FT CLG
10 FT CLG
LIN
BATH 2
MASTER BEDRM
13-4 X 15-0
10 FT CLG
BEDROOM 2
12-0 X 11-0
8 FT CLG
UTIL
6-6 X 11-0
DINING ROOM
13-0 X 12-0
10 FT CLG
FOYER
10 FT CLG
PORCH
GARAGE
COPYRIGHT LARRY E. BELK
Width 62'
Depth 62'-6"
FUTURE GAME ROOM
19-0 X 13-0
8 FT CLG
EXPANDABLE AREA
13-0 X 26-0
4 FT KNEE WALL
8 FT CLG LINE
8 FT CLG LINE
4 FT KNEE WALL
COPYRIGHT LARRY E. BELK

Optional second floor

Design by
Larry E. Belk Designs

COPYRIGHT LARRY E. BELK

Design by
Larry E. Belk Designs

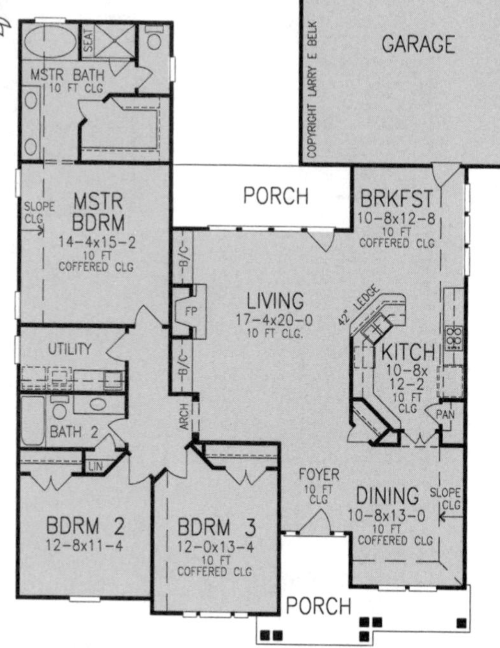
MSTR BATH
10 FT CLG
SEAT
GARAGE
COPYRIGHT LARRY E. BELK
PORCH
BRKFST
10-8x12-8
10 FT
COFFERED CLG
SLOPE CLG
MSTR BDRM
14-4x15-2
10 FT
COFFERED CLG
B/C
FP
LIVING
17-4x20-0
10 FT CLG.
42" LEDGE
KITCH
10-8x
12-2
10 FT
CLG
PAN
UTILITY
BATH 2
LIN
ARCH
FOYER
10 FT
CLG
DINING
10-8x13-0
10 FT
COFFERED CLG
SLOPE
CLG
BDRM 2
12-8x11-4
BDRM 3
12-0x13-4
10 FT
COFFERED CLG
PORCH

Design 8244

Square Footage: 1,948

■ A striking window display and a lofty entrance porch set the tone of this casually elegant home. Open spaces prevail throughout the dining and living rooms. A fireplace flanked by built-in cabinets accents the living room. The kitchen is thoughtfully placed between the formal dining room and the breakfast nook. The sleeping zone is designed for maximum quiet from living areas in a separate hall. The master bedroom has a large compartmented bath and a walk-in closet. Two family bedrooms share a hall bath. Please specify crawlspace or slab foundation when ordering.

Width 50'
Depth 68'

COPYRIGHT LARRY E. BELK

Design by
Larry E. Belk Designs

Design 8155

Square Footage: 1,973

■ An angled foyer is defined by arches and columns to give this traditional home an elegant flavor. Designed as a split-bedroom plan, the master suite is privately located off the entry. Bedrooms 2 and 3 are grouped off the kitchen area. The kitchen includes a large walk-in pantry and lots of counter and cabinet space. An oversized great room provides a roomy area for family gatherings and entertaining. Please specify crawlspace or slab foundation when ordering.

Width 74'-2"
Depth 44'-10"

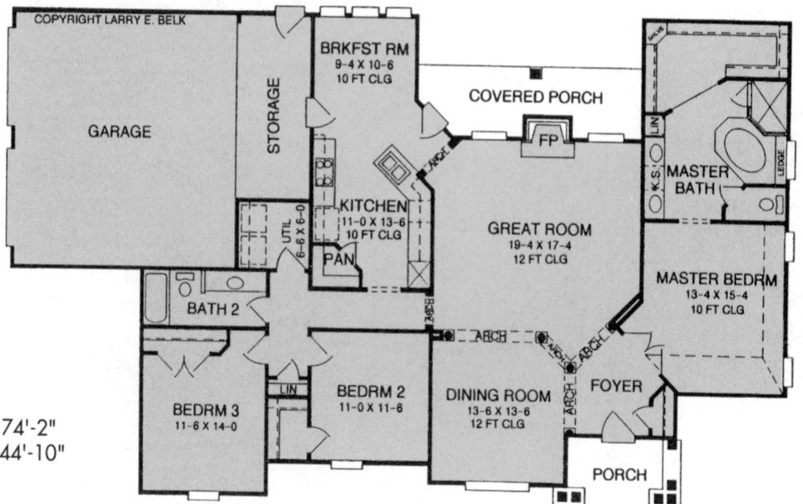
COPYRIGHT LARRY E. BELK
GARAGE
STORAGE
BRKFST RM
9-4 X 10-6
10 FT CLG
COVERED PORCH
FP
KITCHEN
11-0 X 13-6
10 FT CLG
PAN
UTIL
6-6 X 6-0
ARCH
GREAT ROOM
19-4 X 17-4
12 FT CLG
LIN
K.S.
MASTER
BATH
LEDGE
MASTER BEDRM
13-4 X 15-4
10 FT CLG
BATH 2
BEDRM 3
11-6 X 14-0
LIN
BEDRM 2
11-0 X 11-6
DINING ROOM
13-6 X 13-6
12 FT CLG
FOYER
PORCH

Design 8166

Square Footage: 1,955
Bonus Room: 240 square feet

■ A low hipped roof with a projecting gable crowning the entry porch has a strong visual impact and great curb appeal. Open living areas flow into one another through columns that define the great room and dining room. The modified galley kitchen is designed for efficient cooking and easily serves both the formal dining room and the window-framed breakfast gazebo. The master suite is set behind double doors off the foyer and is highlighted with a compartmented bath and large walk-in closet. Two large family bedrooms are split down the angular hall by a comfortable bath. Please specify crawlspace or slab foundation when ordering.

Design by
Larry E. Belk Designs

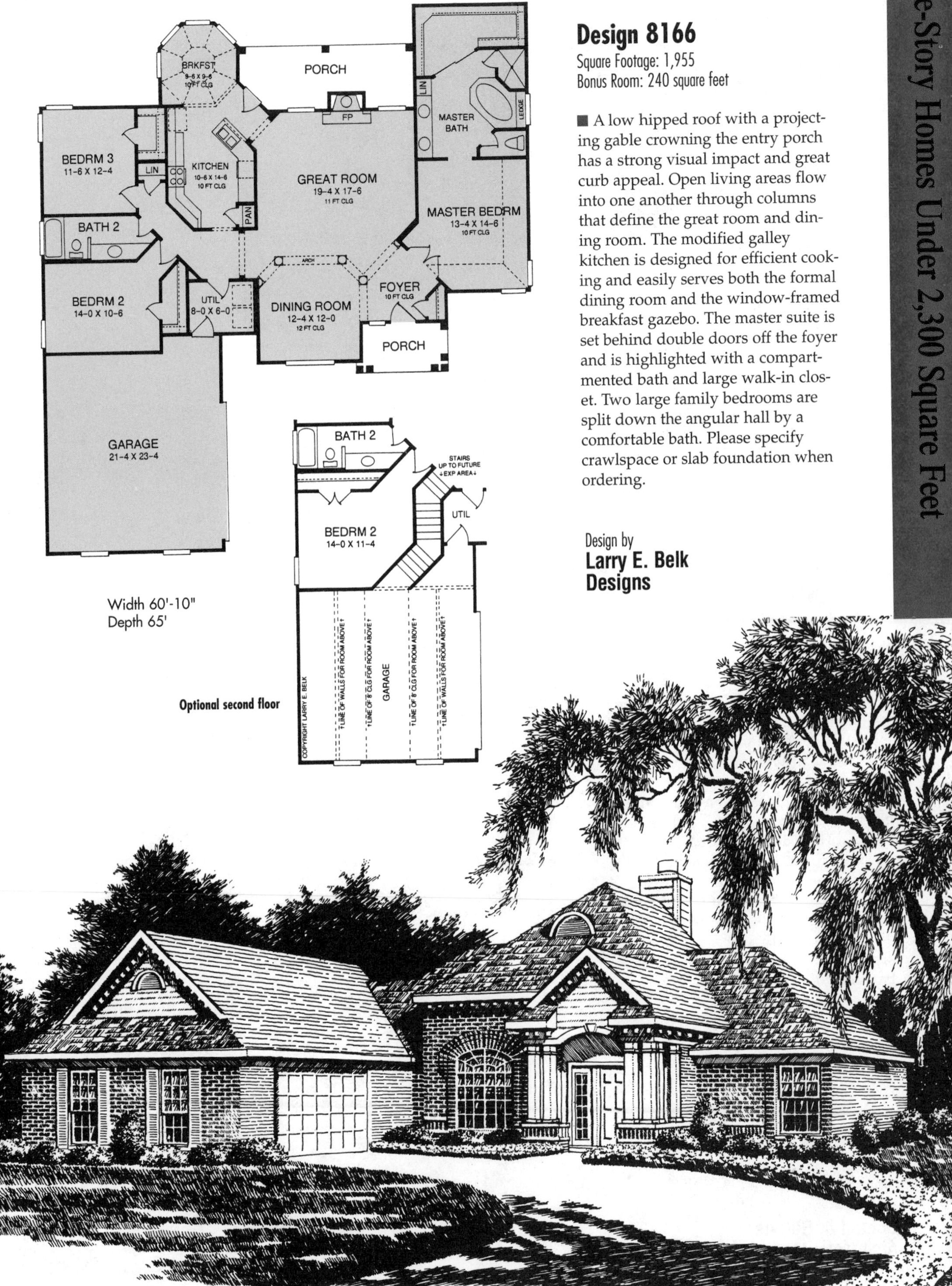
PORCH
BRKFST
KITCHEN
10-6 X 14-6
10 FT CLG
FP
GREAT ROOM
19-4 X 17-6
11 FT CLG
MASTER BATH
LIN
LEDGE
BEDRM 3
11-6 X 12-4
LIN
PAN
MASTER BEDRM
13-4 X 14-6
10 FT CLG
BATH 2
BEDRM 2
14-0 X 10-6
UTIL
8-0 X 6-0
DINING ROOM
12-4 X 12-0
12 FT CLG
FOYER
10 FT CLG
PORCH
GARAGE
21-4 X 23-4
BATH 2
STAIRS UP TO FUTURE EXP AREA
UTIL
BEDRM 2
14-0 X 11-4
GARAGE
COPYRIGHT LARRY E. BELK

Width 60'-10"
Depth 65'

Optional second floor

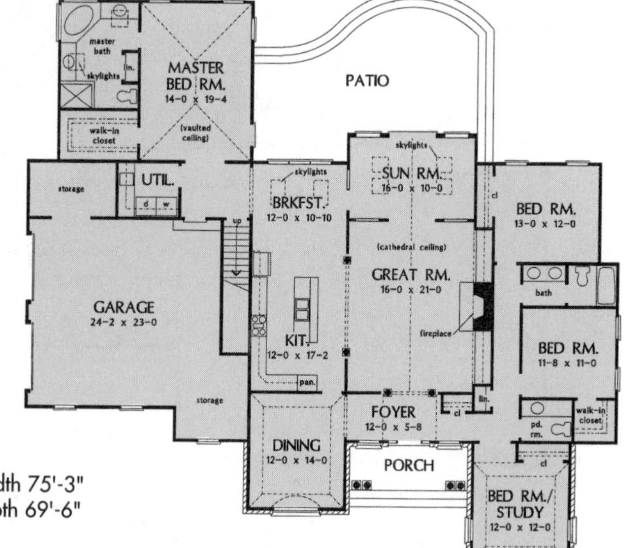

attic storage
BONUS RM.
19-1 x 16-4
skylights
down
attic storage
master bath
skylights
lin.
walk-in closet
MASTER BED RM.
14-0 x 19-4
(vaulted ceiling)
PATIO
skylights
SUN RM.
16-0 x 10-0
storage
UTIL.
d w
skylights
BRKFST.
12-0 x 10-10
up
cl
BED RM.
13-0 x 12-0
(cathedral ceiling)
GREAT RM.
16-0 x 21-0
bath
GARAGE
24-2 x 23-0
KIT.
12-0 x 17-2
fireplace
BED RM.
11-8 x 11-0
pan.
lin.
storage
FOYER
12-0 x 5-8
cl
walk-in closet
pd. rm.
DINING
12-0 x 14-0
PORCH
cl
BED RM./ STUDY
12-0 x 12-0

Design 7623

Square Footage: 2,602

■ A recessed entry porch framed by stately columns is a welcome introduction to this split-bedroom family plan. A traditional foyer directs the flow to either the formal dining room, the family bedrooms or the expansive great room. A vaulted ceiling crowns the great room, which is highlighted with a fireplace and the adjoining sunroom. The presentation kitchen has a full island and is designed to easily serve the formal dining room and breakfast nook. Set back for privacy, the master suite is sure to pamper.

Design by
Donald A. Gardner, Architects, Inc.

Width 75'-3"
Depth 69'-6"

Design 9634

Square Footage: 2,099

■ This enchanting design incorporates the best in floor planning all on one level. The central great room is highlighted with a fireplace and cathedral ceiling. Nearby is a skylit sunroom with sliding glass doors to the rear deck and a built-in wet bar. The galley-style kitchen adjoins a breakfast room. The master suite is split from the family bedrooms and has access to the rear deck. The bathroom amenities include a large walk-in closet and double vanity. Family bedrooms share a full bath, also with double vanity. Please specify basement or crawlspace foundation when ordering.

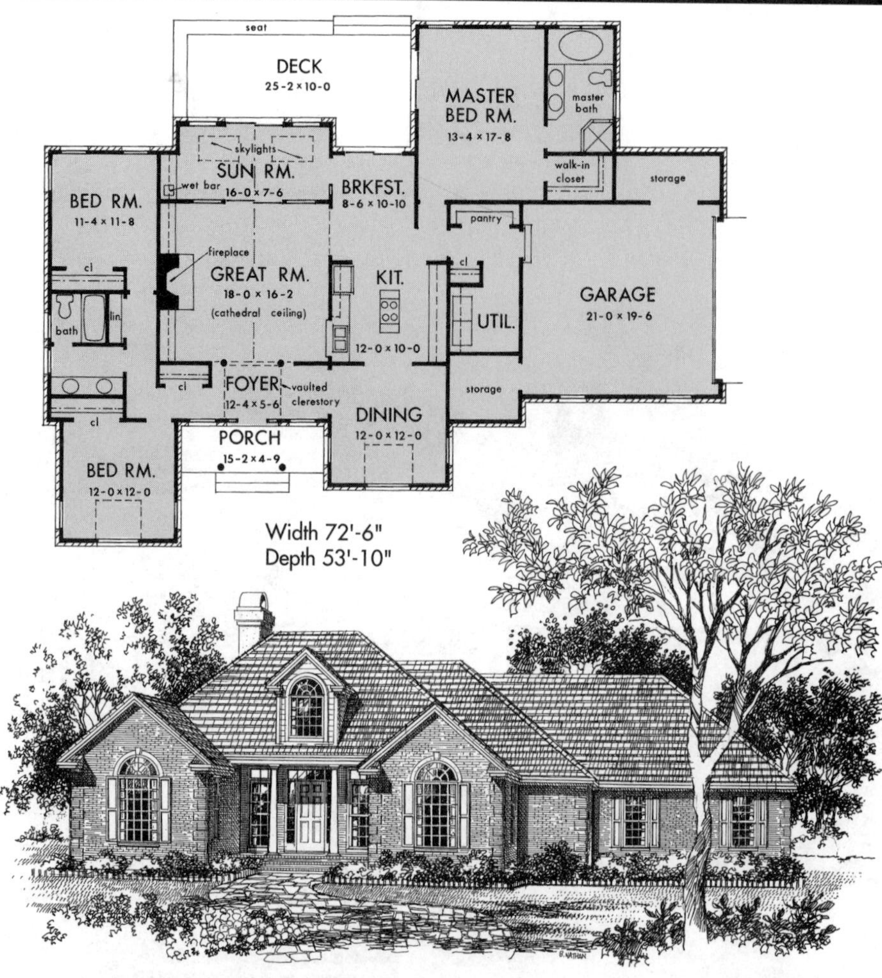

seat
DECK
25-2 x 10-0
MASTER BED RM.
13-4 x 17-8
master bath
skylights
SUN RM.
16-0 x 7-6
wet bar
BRKFST.
8-6 x 10-10
walk-in closet
storage
BED RM.
11-4 x 11-8
pantry
fireplace
GREAT RM.
18-0 x 16-2
(cathedral ceiling)
KIT.
cl
cl
lin.
bath
UTIL.
GARAGE
21-0 x 19-6
12-0 x 10-0
cl
FOYER
12-4 x 5-6
vaulted clerestory
storage
cl
PORCH
15-2 x 4-9
DINING
12-0 x 12-0
BED RM.
12-0 x 12-0

Width 72'-6"
Depth 53'-10"

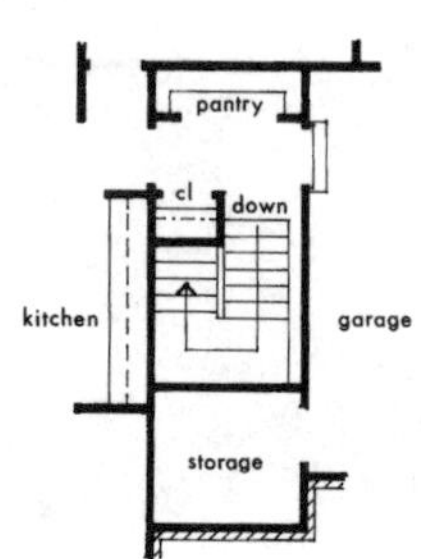

pantry
cl
down
kitchen
garage
storage

Design by
Donald A. Gardner, Architects, Inc.

Design 9728

Square Footage: 1,576

■ This stately, three-bedroom, one-story home exhibits sheer elegance with its large, arched windows, round columns, covered porch, and brick veneer. In the foyer, natural light enters through arched windows in clerestory dormers. In the great room, a dramatic cathedral ceiling and a fireplace set the mood. Through gracious, round columns, the kitchen and breakfast room open up. For sleeping, turn to the master bedroom. Here, a large, walk-in closet and a well-planned master bath with a double-bowl vanity, a garden tub, and a shower will pamper. Two additional bedrooms are located at the opposite end of the house for privacy.

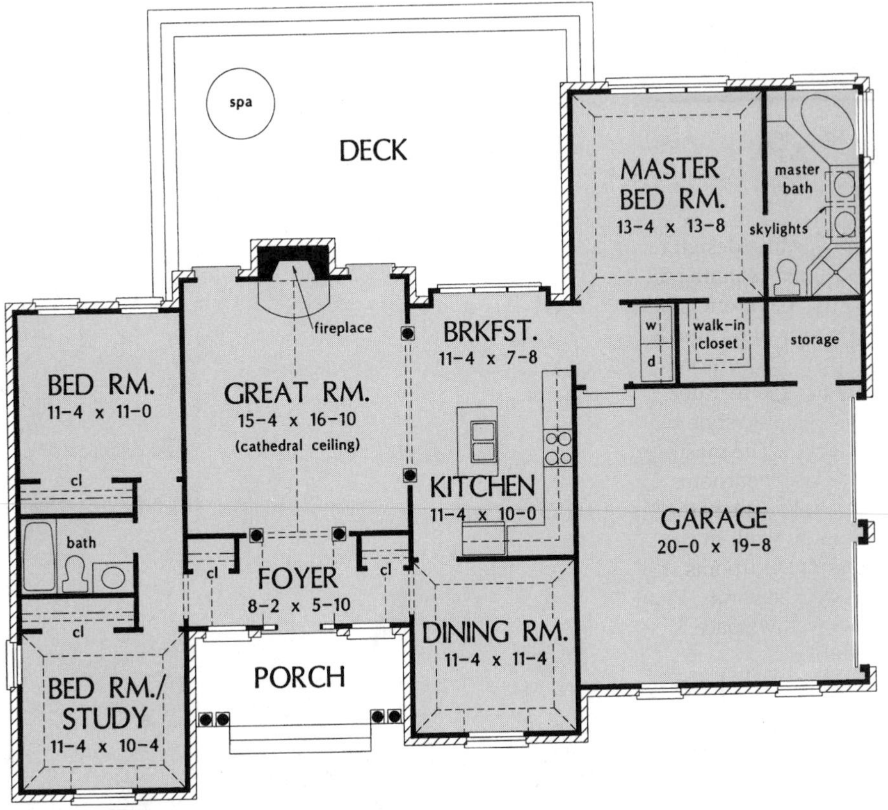
spa
DECK
MASTER BED RM.
13-4 x 13-8
master bath
skylights
w
d
walk-in closet
storage
fireplace
BRKFST.
11-4 x 7-8
BED RM.
11-4 x 11-0
GREAT RM.
15-4 x 16-10
(cathedral ceiling)
KITCHEN
11-4 x 10-0
GARAGE
20-0 x 19-8
cl
bath
cl
FOYER
8-2 x 5-10
cl
cl
DINING RM.
11-4 x 11-4
PORCH
BED RM./ STUDY
11-4 x 10-4

Width 60'-6"
Depth 50'-9"

Design by
Donald A. Gardner, Architects, Inc.

QUOTE ONE®

Cost to build? See page 342 to order complete cost estimate to build this house in your area!

Design by
Design Basics, Inc.

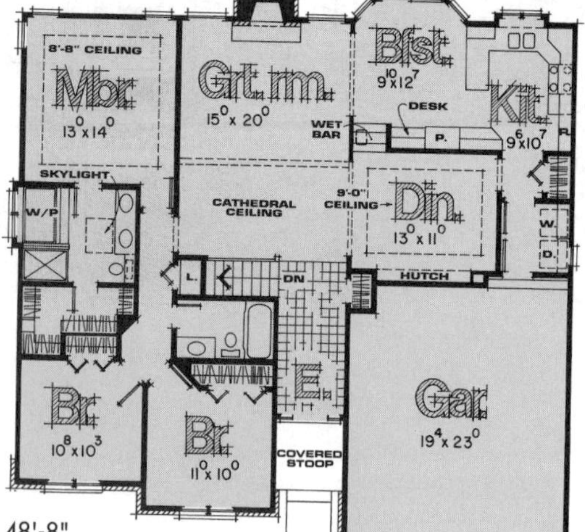
8'-8" CEILING
Mbr.
13⁰x14⁰
Grt.rm.
15⁰x 20⁰
Bfst.
9¹⁰x12⁷
DESK
Kit.
9⁶x10⁷
WET BAR
P.
SKYLIGHT
W/P
CATHEDRAL CEILING
9'-0" CEILING
Din.
13⁰x11⁰
W.
D.
L.
DN
HUTCH
Br.
10⁸x10³
Br.
11⁰x10⁰
E.
Gar.
19⁴x23⁰
COVERED STOOP

Width 48'-8"
Depth 48'

Design 9200

Square Footage: 1,604

■ Thoughtful arrangement makes this uncomplicated three-bedroom plan comfortable. The living and working areas are grouped together for convenience—a great room with cathedral ceiling, dining room with wet bar pass-through and kitchen with breakfast room. The sleeping area features a spacious master suite with skylight bath and whirlpool, and large walk-in closet. Two smaller bedrooms accommodate the rest of the family. Don't miss the deck off the breakfast room—a great spot for outdoor dining. An alternate elevation is available at no extra cost.

Design 9237

Square Footage: 1,697

Design by
Design Basics, Inc.

■ This volume-look home gives the impression of size and scope in just under 1,700 square feet. The large great room with fireplace is perfect for entertaining. Its proximity to the kitchen, with breakfast room, and to the formal dining room ensures easy serving and clean-up. Besides a large walk-in closet, other features in the master bedroom include a whirlpool tub, double vanity, skylit dressing area, and convenient linen storage. Two family bedrooms share a full bath with skylight and offer ample closet space.

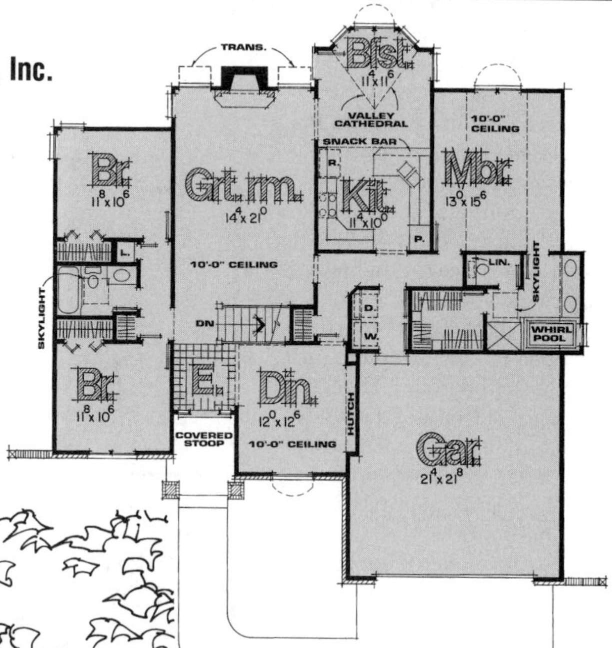

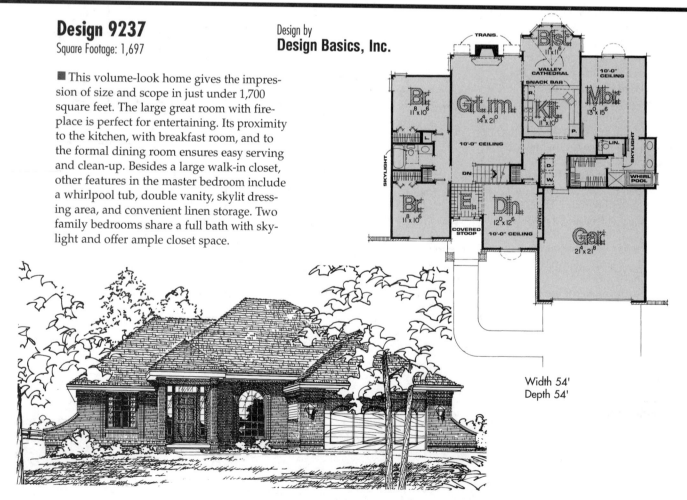

Width 54'
Depth 54'

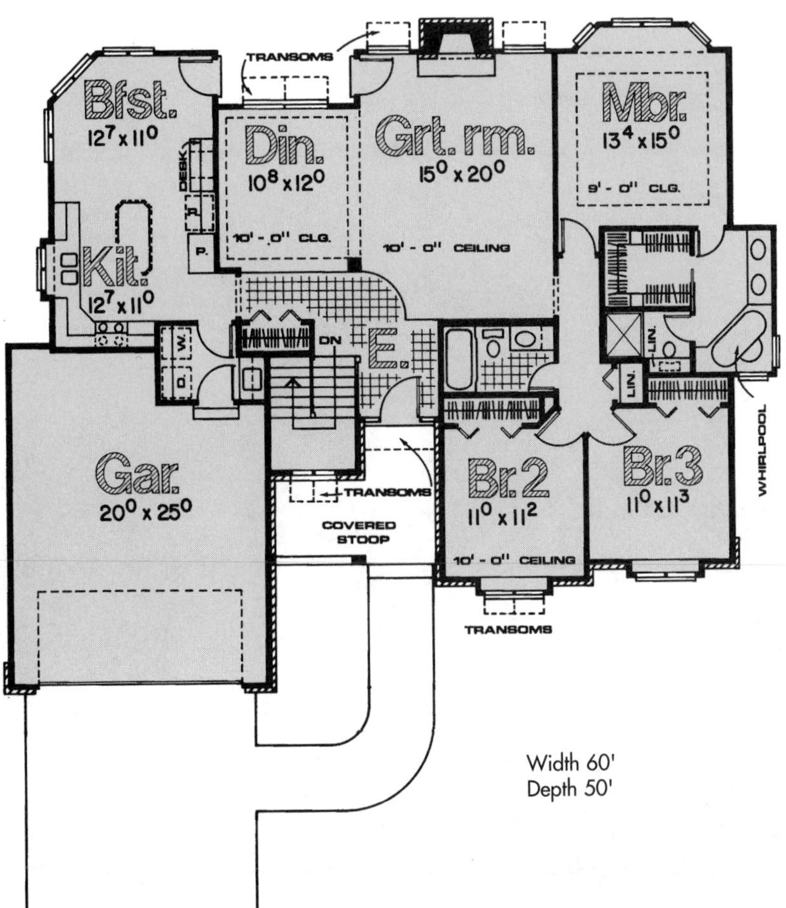
TRANSOMS
Bfst.
12^7 x 11^0
Din.
10^8 x 12^0
10'-0" CLG.
Grt. rm.
15^0 x 20^0
10'-0" CEILING
Mbr.
13^4 x 15^0
9'-0" CLG.
DESK
R
P.
Kit.
12^7 x 11^0
W.
D.
DN
E.
LIN.
LIN.
Gar.
20^0 x 25^0
TRANSOMS
COVERED STOOP
Br. 2
11^0 x 11^2
10'-0" CEILING
Br. 3
11^0 x 11^3
WHIRLPOOL
TRANSOMS

Width 60'
Depth 50'

Design 9257

Square Footage: 1,735

■ A covered porch at the entry to this home welcomes family and guests alike. Ten-foot ceilings at the entry foyer, great room and dining room give a feeling of spaciousness to living areas. The formal dining room sits between the kitchen area and great room—a perfect spot for entertaining. Note the service entrance with laundry just off the kitchen in route to the garage. Three bedrooms include two secondary bedrooms with shared bath and a master suite with an elegant bayed window and a bath with angled whirlpool, double vanity and walk-in closet. An open staircase in the entry allows for the possibility of a finished basement area in the future.

Design by
Design Basics, Inc.

Design 9895

Square Footage: 1,850

■ A side-loaded garage helps maintain a beautiful facade for this brick one-story. The recessed entry opens to a central foyer that leads to the dining room on the left and the great room to the rear. A lovely deck is found beyond the great room and is also accessed from the master suite. The large kitchen has an attached breakfast room with bay window and is just across the hall from the service entrance with laundry. Two secondary bedrooms have plenty of closet space and share a compartmented full bath. This home is designed with a basement foundation.

Design by
Design Traditions

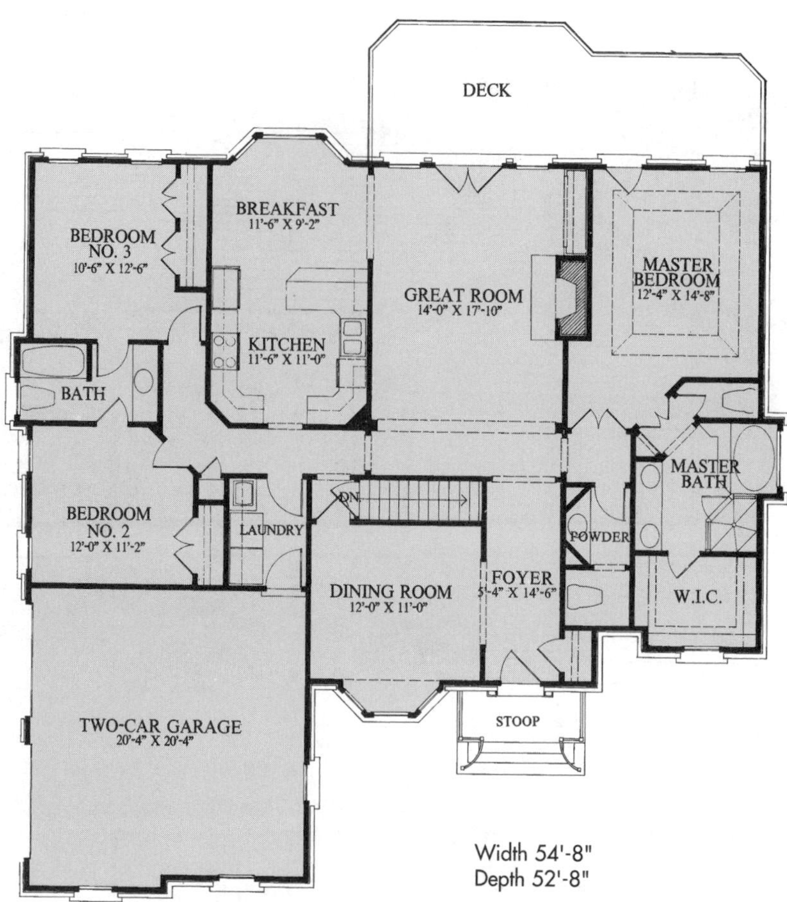

DECK
BREAKFAST
11'-6" X 9'-2"
BEDROOM NO. 3
10'-6" X 12'-6"
GREAT ROOM
14'-0" X 17'-10"
MASTER BEDROOM
12'-4" X 14'-8"
KITCHEN
11'-6" X 11'-0"
BATH
MASTER BATH
BEDROOM NO. 2
12'-0" X 11'-2"
LAUNDRY
DN.
POWDER
DINING ROOM
12'-0" X 11'-0"
FOYER
5'-4" X 14'-6"
W.I.C.
STOOP
TWO-CAR GARAGE
20'-4" X 20'-4"
Width 54'-8"
Depth 52'-8"

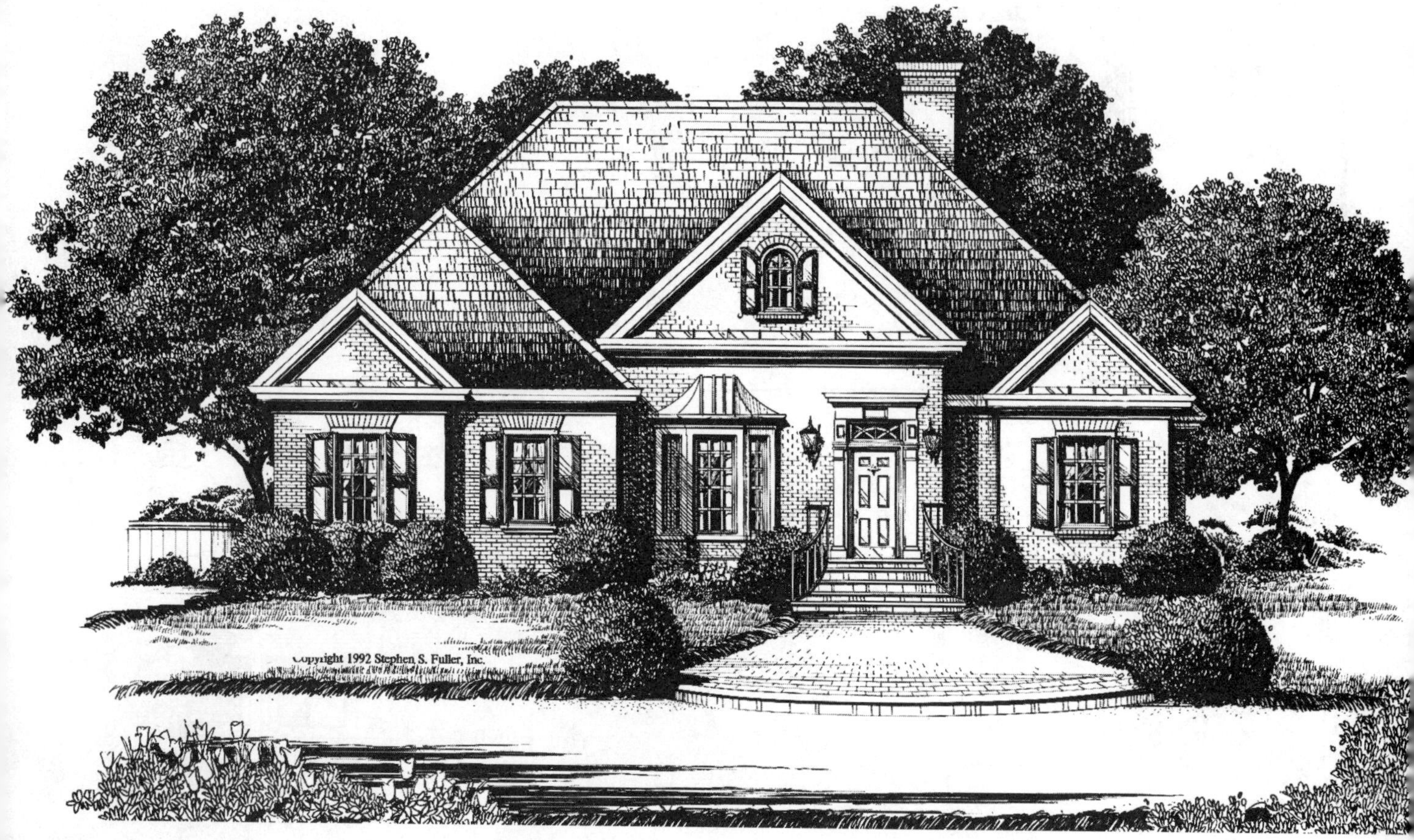

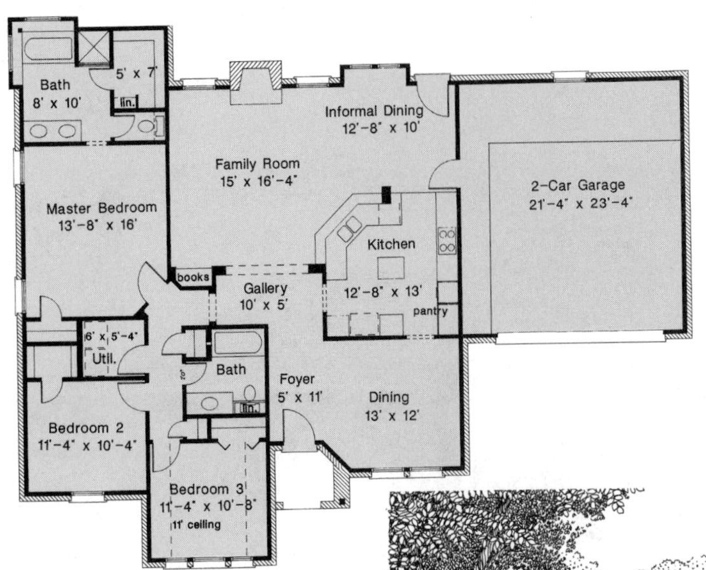
Bath
8' x 10'
5' x 7'
lin.
Informal Dining
12'-8" x 10'
Family Room
15' x 16'-4"
2-Car Garage
21'-4" x 23'-4"
Master Bedroom
13'-8" x 16'
Kitchen
books
Gallery
10' x 5'
12'-8" x 13'
pantry
6' x 5'-4"
Util.
Bath
Foyer
5' x 11'
Dining
13' x 12'
Bedroom 2
11'-4" x 10'-4"
Bedroom 3
11'-4" x 10'-8"
11' ceiling

Width 65'
Depth 50'-6"

Design 8985

Square Footage: 1,800

■ From its hipped rooflines to the corner quoins, this design has plenty of curb appeal. Inside, with large living spaces, this one-story also has plenty of room for great family living. The formal dining room is complemented by an informal eating area, both of which are easily served by the efficient island kitchen. Both connect to the spacious family room, which is complete with a warming fireplace. The large master suite has a compartmented bath and walk-in closet. Two family bedrooms share a hall bath.

Design by
Larry W. Garnett & Associates, Inc.

Design 9202

Square Footage: 1,808

■ Discriminating buyers will love the refined yet inviting look of this three-bedroom plan. A tiled entry with ten-foot ceiling leads into the spacious great room with a large bay window. An open-hearth fireplace warms both the great room and the kitchen. The sleeping area features a large master suite with a dramatic arched window and a bath with a whirlpool, twin vanities and a walk-in closet. Two secondary bedrooms each have private access to the shared bath. Don't miss the storage space in the oversized garage.

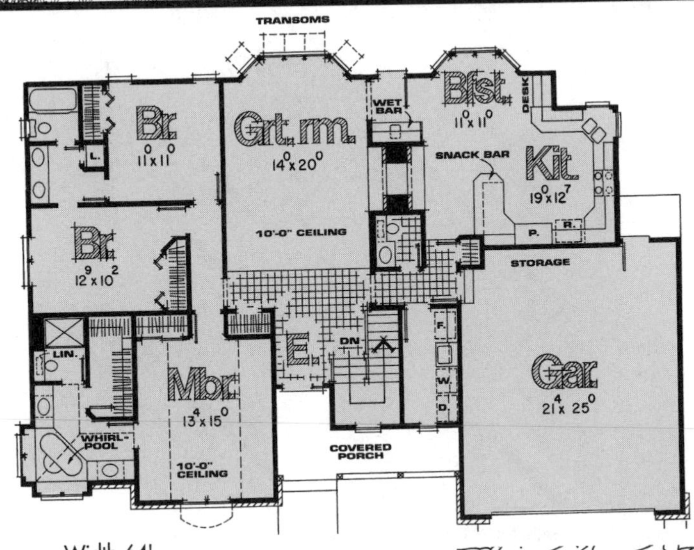
TRANSOMS
Br.
Grt. rm.
$14^{0} x 20^{0}$
WET BAR
Bfst.
$11^{0} x 11^{0}$
DESK
SNACK BAR
Kit.
$19^{0} x 12^{7}$
Br.
$12^{9} x 10^{2}$
10'-0" CEILING
STORAGE
P.
R.
LIN.
E.
DN
F.
W.
D.
Mbr.
$13^{4} x 15^{0}$
Gar.
$21^{4} x 25^{0}$
WHIRL-POOL
10'-0" CEILING
COVERED PORCH

Width 64'
Depth 44'

Design by
Design Basics, Inc.

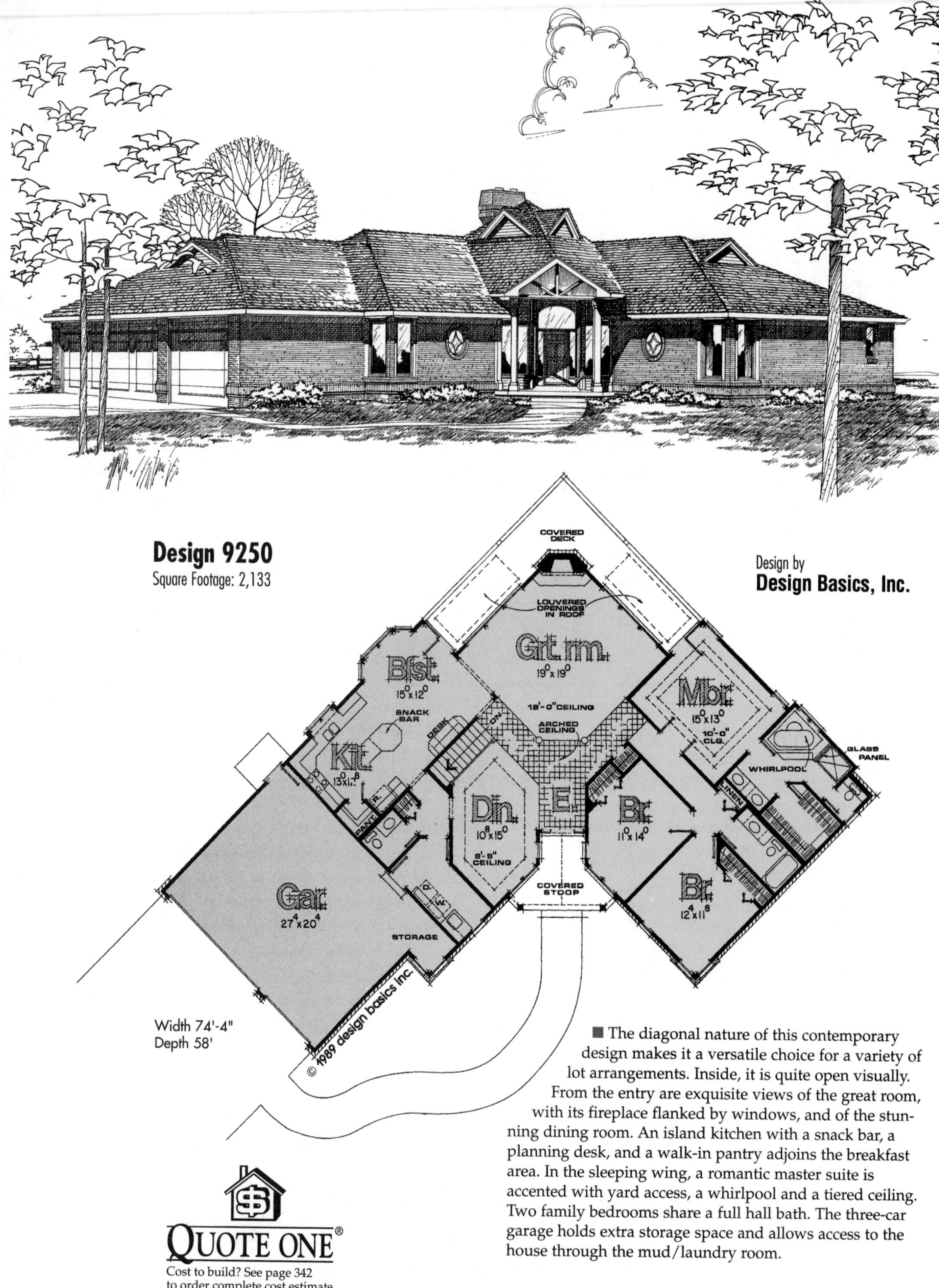
COVERED DECK
LOUVERED OPENINGS IN ROOF
Grt. rm.
19⁰x 19⁰
12'-0" CEILING
ARCHED CEILING
Bfst.
15⁰x 12⁰
SNACK BAR
DESK
Kit.
Mbr.
15⁰x 13⁰
10'-0" CLG.
GLASS PANEL
WHIRLPOOL
LINEN
Din.
10⁸x 15⁰
8'-8" CEILING
E.
Br.
11⁰x 14⁰
Br.
12⁴x 11⁸
COVERED STOOP
Gar.
27⁴x 20⁴
STORAGE
© 1989 design basics inc.

Design 9250

Square Footage: 2,133

Design by
Design Basics, Inc.

Width 74'-4"
Depth 58'

■ The diagonal nature of this contemporary design makes it a versatile choice for a variety of lot arrangements. Inside, it is quite open visually. From the entry are exquisite views of the great room, with its fireplace flanked by windows, and of the stunning dining room. An island kitchen with a snack bar, a planning desk, and a walk-in pantry adjoins the breakfast area. In the sleeping wing, a romantic master suite is accented with yard access, a whirlpool and a tiered ceiling. Two family bedrooms share a full hall bath. The three-car garage holds extra storage space and allows access to the house through the mud/laundry room.

QUOTE ONE®

Cost to build? See page 342 to order complete cost estimate to build this house in your area!

Design by
Design Basics, Inc.

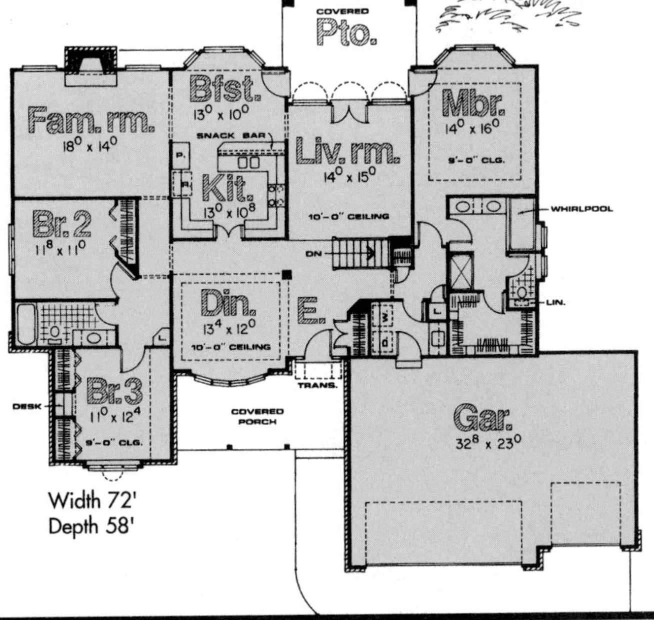

COVERED
Pto.
Bfst.
$13^{0} \times 10^{0}$
SNACK BAR
Fam. rm.
$18^{0} \times 14^{0}$
Liv. rm.
$14^{0} \times 15^{0}$
10'-0" CEILING
Kit.
$13^{0} \times 10^{8}$
Mbr.
$14^{0} \times 16^{0}$
9'-0" CLG.
WHIRLPOOL
Br. 2
$11^{8} \times 11^{0}$
DN
LIN.
Din.
$13^{4} \times 12^{0}$
10'-0" CEILING
E.
TRANS.
Br. 3
$11^{0} \times 12^{4}$
9'-0" CLG.
DESK
COVERED PORCH
Gar.
$32^{8} \times 23^{0}$
Width 72'
Depth 58'

Design 7275

Square Footage: 2,132

■ Upon entering this ranch-style home, the foyer opens onto a formal dining room enhanced by a wall of bowed windows. To the rear is a living room filled with light, compliments of a glass wall. Casual times will be enjoyed in the family room with its warming fireplace. The kitchen is designed to easily serve the bayed breakfast nook and the formal dining room. Split for privacy, the master suite enjoys a bay window and a lush bath. Two family bedrooms share a hall bath.

Design 9739

Square Footage: 2,211
Bonus Room: 408 square feet

■ This home is built for entertaining. The large great room is perfect for parties and the kitchen, with sunny skylights and an adjoining dining room, creates a cozy breakfast buffet. Access from both rooms to the expansive deck completes the picture perfectly. The location of the master bedroom and the other bedrooms allows for quiet comfort. You'll love the bonus room which can be made into a game room or a study.

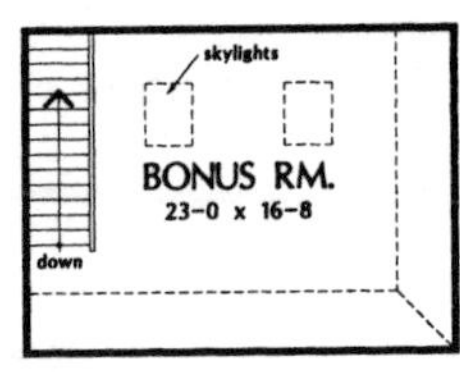

skylights
BONUS RM.
23-0 x 16-8
down

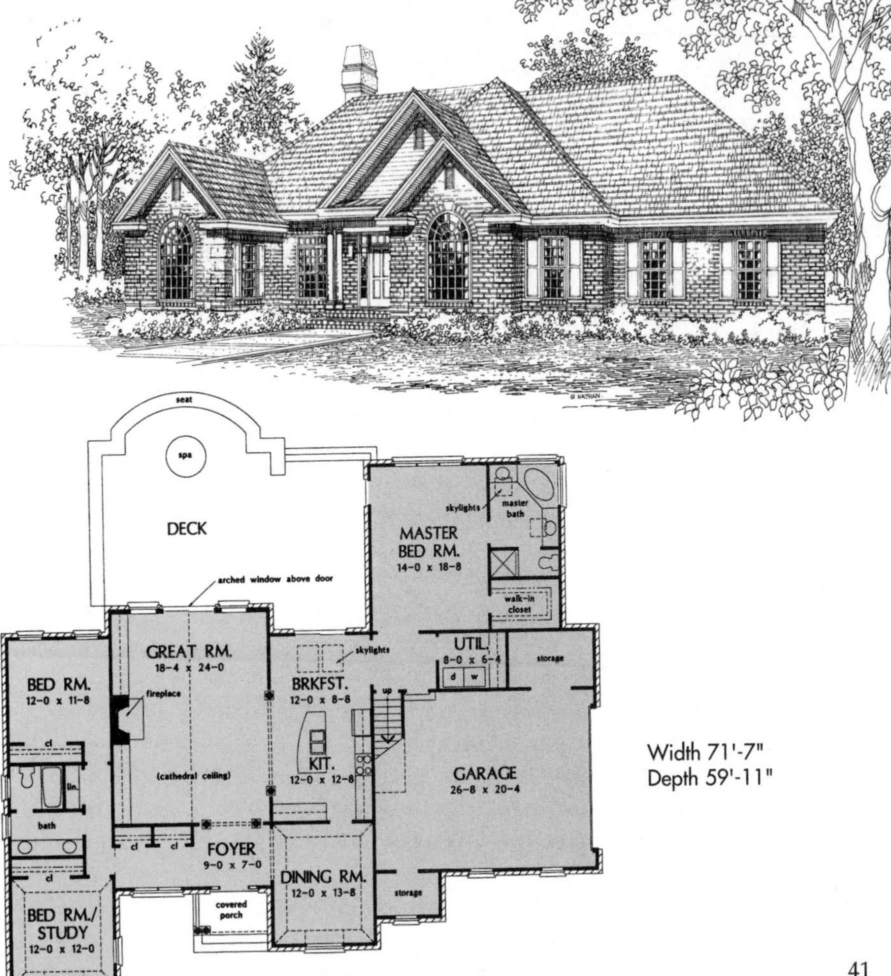

seat
spa
DECK
arched window above door
MASTER BED RM.
14-0 x 18-8
skylights
master bath
walk-in closet
UTIL.
8-0 x 6-4
storage
GREAT RM.
18-4 x 24-0
fireplace
(cathedral ceiling)
BED RM.
12-0 x 11-8
bath
lin.
BRKFST.
12-0 x 8-8
skylights
up
KIT.
12-0 x 12-8
GARAGE
26-8 x 20-4
FOYER
9-0 x 7-0
DINING RM.
12-0 x 13-8
storage
covered porch
BED RM./ STUDY
12-0 x 12-0
Width 71'-7"
Depth 59'-11"

Design by
Donald A. Gardner, Architects, Inc.

Design 9204

Square Footage: 1,911

■ This sophisticated three-bedroom ranch is a welcome addition to any neighborhood. Off the entry are the dining room with twelve-foot detailed ceiling and arched window, and the enormous great room which shares a through-fireplace with the hearth room. The well-planned kitchen features a spacious work area, with snack-bar pass through to the breakfast area. The private master suite features a detailed ceiling, corner windows, whirlpool bath and giant walk-in closet. Two family bedrooms are placed on the other side of the plan to ensure peace and quiet. An alternate elevation is available at no extra cost.

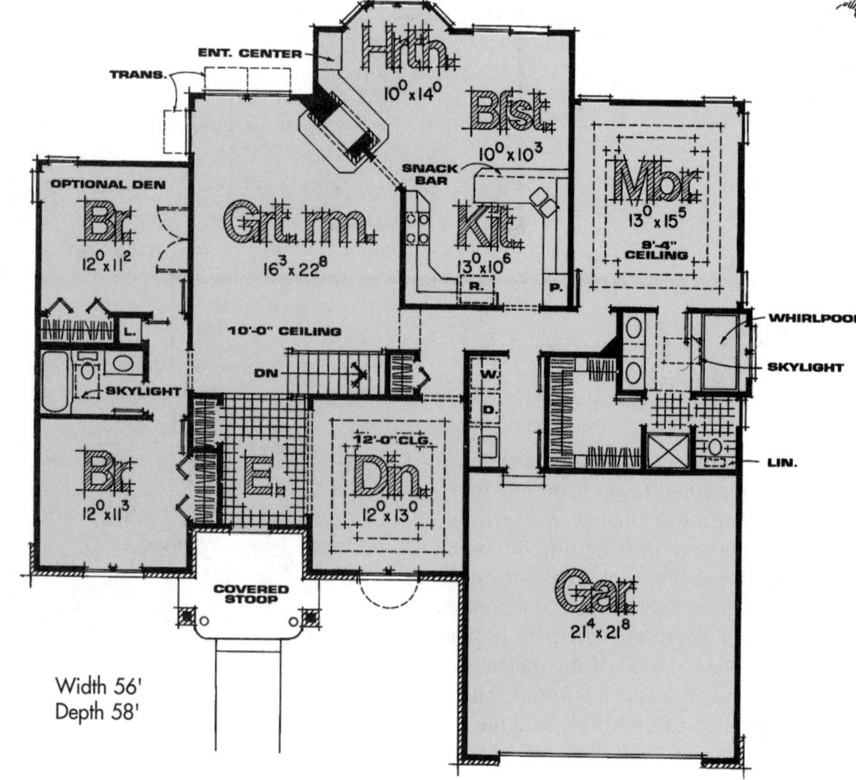

ENT. CENTER
TRANS.
Hrth.
$10^{0} \times 14^{0}$
Bfst.
$10^{0} \times 10^{3}$
SNACK BAR
OPTIONAL DEN
Br.
$12^{0} \times 11^{2}$
Grt. rm.
$16^{3} \times 22^{8}$
Kit.
$13^{0} \times 10^{6}$
R.
P.
Mbr.
$13^{0} \times 15^{5}$
9'-4" CEILING
L.
10'-0" CEILING
WHIRLPOOL
DN
W.
D.
SKYLIGHT
SKYLIGHT
12'-0" CLG.
Br.
$12^{0} \times 11^{3}$
E.
Din.
$12^{0} \times 13^{0}$
LIN.
COVERED STOOP
Gar.
$21^{4} \times 21^{8}$

Width 56'
Depth 58'

Design by
Design Basics, Inc.

QUOTE ONE®

Cost to build? See page 342 to order complete cost estimate to build this house in your area!

QUOTE ONE®

Cost to build? See page 342 to order complete cost estimate to build this house in your area!

Design by
Design Basics, Inc.

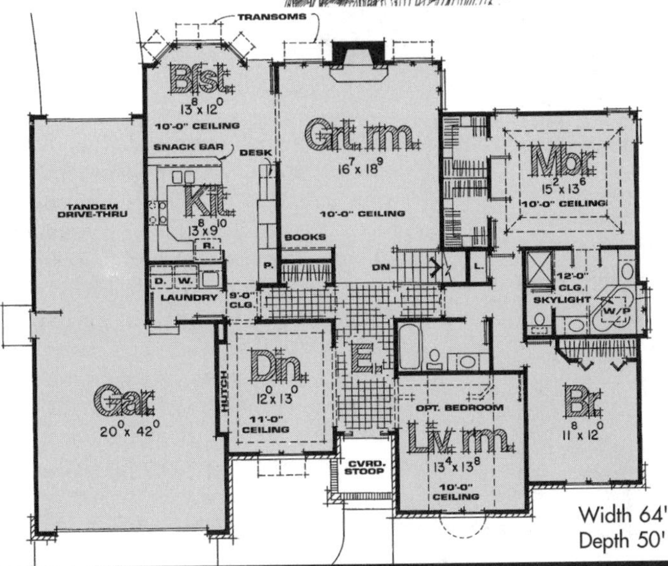
TRANSOMS
Bfst.
13⁸x12⁰
10'-0" CEILING
SNACK BAR
DESK
Grt.rm.
16⁷x18⁹
10'-0" CEILING
Mbr.
15²x13⁶
10'-0" CEILING
TANDEM DRIVE-THRU
Kit.
13⁸x9¹⁰
BOOKS
LAUNDRY
9'-0" CLG.
DN
12'-0" CLG.
SKYLIGHT
Din.
12⁰x13⁰
11'-0" CEILING
HUTCH
Gar.
20⁰x42⁰
E.
OPT. BEDROOM
Liv.rm.
13⁴x13⁸
10'-0" CEILING
Br.
11⁸x12⁰
CVRD. STOOP

Width 64'
Depth 50'

Design 9201

Square Footage: 1,996

■ Practical, yet equipped with a variety of popular amenities, this pleasant ranch home is an excellent choice for empty nesters or small families. The front living room can become a third bedroom if you choose. The great room with dramatic fireplace serves as the main living area. A luxurious master suite features a ten-foot tray ceiling and a large bath with whirlpool, skylight, plant ledge and twin vanities. The kitchen with breakfast room serves both the dining and great rooms. A tandem drive-through garage holds space for a third car or extra storage.

Design 9362

Square Footage: 2,172

■ This one-story with grand rooflines holds a most convenient floor plan. The great room to the rear complements a front-facing living room. The formal dining room sits just across the hall from the living room and is also easily accessible to the kitchen. A bedroom with full bath at this end of the house works as an office or guest bedroom. Two additional bedrooms are to the right of the plan: a master suite with grand bath and one additional bedroom.

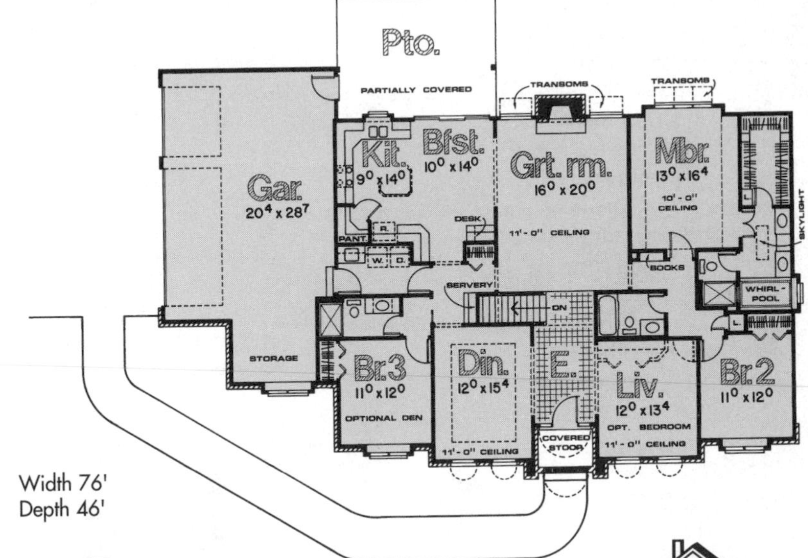
Pto.
PARTIALLY COVERED
TRANSOMS
TRANSOMS
Kit.
9⁰x14⁰
Bfst.
10⁰x14⁰
Grt. rm.
16⁰x20⁰
11'-0" CEILING
Mbr.
13⁰x16⁴
10'-0" CEILING
Gar.
20⁴x28⁷
DESK
PANT
SERVERY
BOOKS
WHIRLPOOL
SKYLIGHT
DN
STORAGE
Br.3
11⁰x12⁰
OPTIONAL DEN
Din.
12⁰x15⁴
11'-0" CEILING
E.
COVERED STOOP
Liv.
12⁰x13⁴
OPT. BEDROOM
11'-0" CEILING
Br.2
11⁰x12⁰

Width 76'
Depth 46'

QUOTE ONE®

Cost to build? See page 342 to order complete cost estimate to build this house in your area!

Design by
Design Basics, Inc.

Design by
Design Basics, Inc.

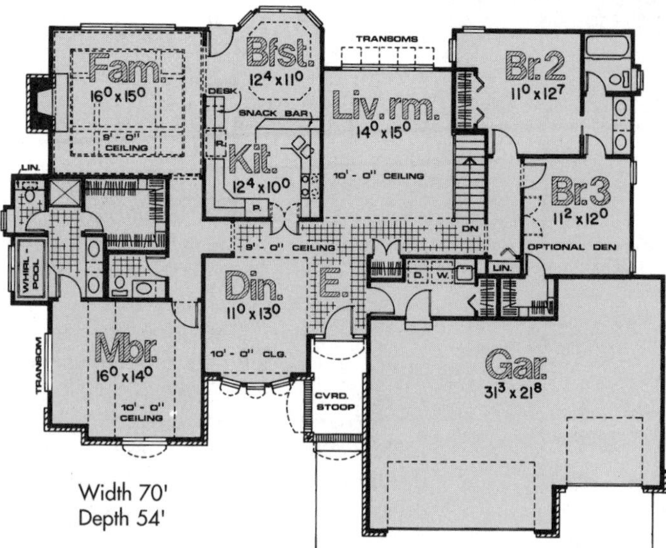

Fam.
16^{0} x 15^{0}
9' - 0" CEILING
Bfst.
12^{4} x 11^{0}
DESK
SNACK BAR
Kit.
12^{4} x 10^{0}
P.
TRANSOMS
Liv. rm.
14^{0} x 15^{0}
10' - 0" CEILING
Br. 2
11^{0} x 12^{7}
Br. 3
11^{2} x 12^{0}
OPTIONAL DEN
DN
LIN.
WHIRL-POOL
9' - 0" CEILING
Din.
11^{0} x 13^{0}
10' - 0" CLG.
E.
D.
W.
LIN.
Mbr.
16^{0} x 14^{0}
10' - 0" CEILING
TRANSOM
CVRD. STOOP
Gar.
31^{3} x 21^{8}

Width 70'
Depth 54'

Design 9347

Square Footage: 2,149

■ Beautiful and accommodating, this ranch home features open entry views into formal rooms plus volume ceilings in major living spaces. The family room has a beamed ceiling and cozy fireplace. The kitchen is equipped with a snack bar open to the breakfast area, a built-in desk and pantry. Sleeping areas are comprised of three bedrooms, including a master suite with walk-in closet, double vanity and whirlpool. Two additional family bedrooms share a private bath. Bedroom 3 may be used as a den with French doors to the hall.

Design by
Design Basics, Inc.

Design 9323

Square Footage: 2,276

■ Drama and harmony are expressed by utilizing a variety of elegant exterior materials. An expansive entry views the private den with French doors and an open dining room. The great room with a window-framed fireplace is joined by the kitchen and bayed breakfast area. Two secluded secondary bedrooms enjoy easy access to a compartmented bath with two sinks. His and Hers closets, a spa-style bath and a built-in entertainment center grace the master bedroom.

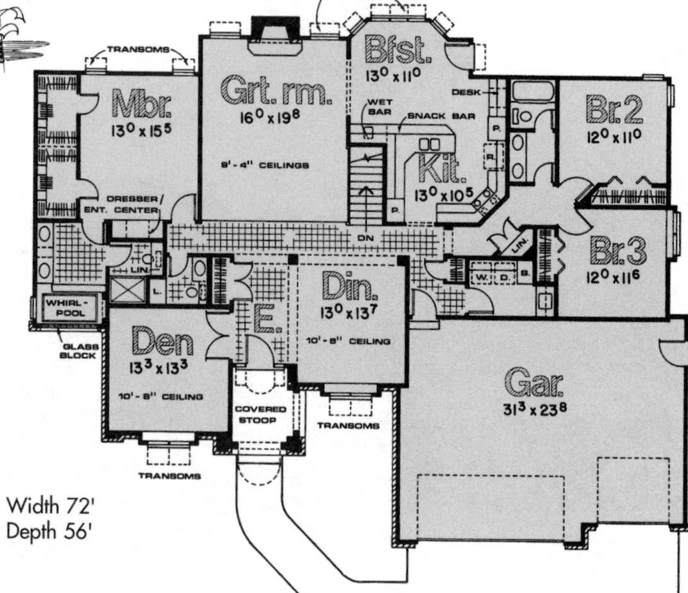

TRANSOMS
Mbr.
13^{0} x 15^{5}
DRESSER/ ENT. CENTER
Grt. rm.
16^{0} x 19^{8}
9' - 4" CEILINGS
WET BAR
Bfst.
13^{0} x 11^{0}
DESK
SNACK BAR
Kit.
13^{0} x 10^{5}
P.
Br. 2
12^{0} x 11^{0}
Br. 3
12^{0} x 11^{6}
DN
LIN.
W. D.
WHIRL-POOL
GLASS BLOCK
Den
13^{3} x 13^{3}
10' - 8" CEILING
E.
Din.
13^{0} x 13^{7}
10' - 8" CEILING
COVERED STOOP
TRANSOMS
Gar.
31^{3} x 23^{8}

Width 72'
Depth 56'

Design 8113

Square Footage: 2,279

■ Spacious rooms and a gracious division of formal and casual living areas makes this three-bedroom home perfect for the active family. Entertaining will be a pleasure in the elegant dining room that's open to the living room through a series of columns. The cozy family room and kitchen are designed for easy living thanks to an oversized fireplace, snack bar and breakfast nook. Two family bedrooms and a large hall bath are split from the master bedroom for privacy. A spa-style bath and a walk-in closet make the master suite a true owner's retreat. Please specify crawlspace or slab foundation when ordering.

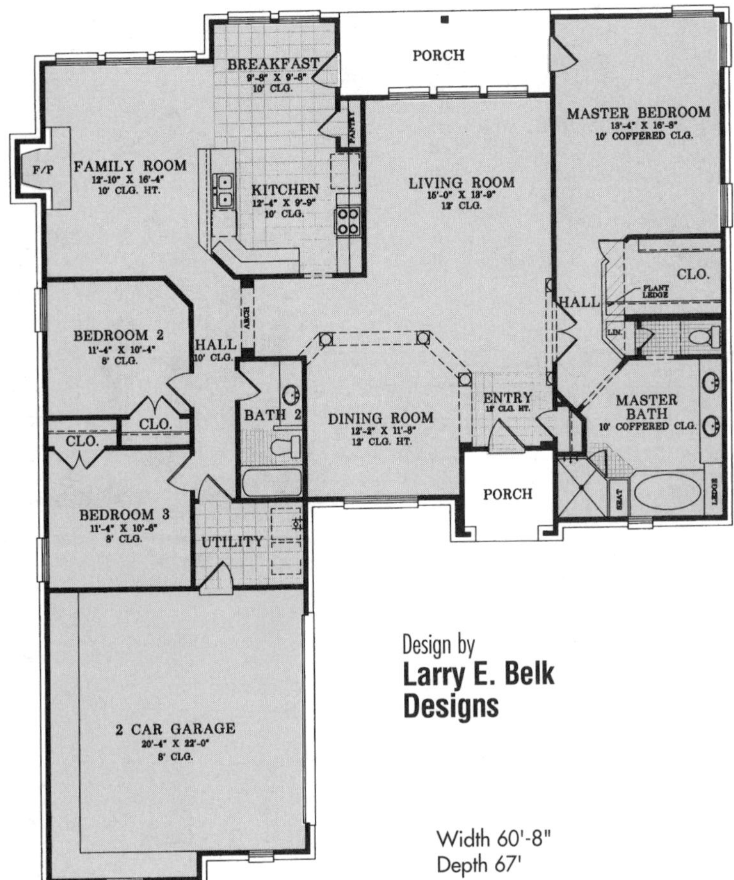
BREAKFAST
9'-8" X 9'-8"
10' CLG.
PORCH
PANTRY
F/P
FAMILY ROOM
12'-10" X 16'-4"
10' CLG. HT.
KITCHEN
12'-4" X 9'-9"
10' CLG.
LIVING ROOM
15'-0" X 13'-9"
12' CLG.
MASTER BEDROOM
13'-4" X 16'-8"
10' COFFERED CLG.
CLO.
PLANT LEDGE
HALL
LIN.
ARCH
BEDROOM 2
11'-4" X 10'-4"
8' CLG.
HALL
10' CLG.
BATH 2
DINING ROOM
12'-2" X 11'-8"
12' CLG. HT.
ENTRY
12' CLG. HT.
MASTER BATH
10' COFFERED CLG.
CLO.
CLO.
PORCH
SEAT
LEDGE
BEDROOM 3
11'-4" X 10'-6"
8' CLG.
UTILITY
2 CAR GARAGE
20'-4" X 22'-0"
8' CLG.

Design by
Larry E. Belk Designs

Width 60'-8"
Depth 67'

Design by
Frank Betz Associates, Inc.

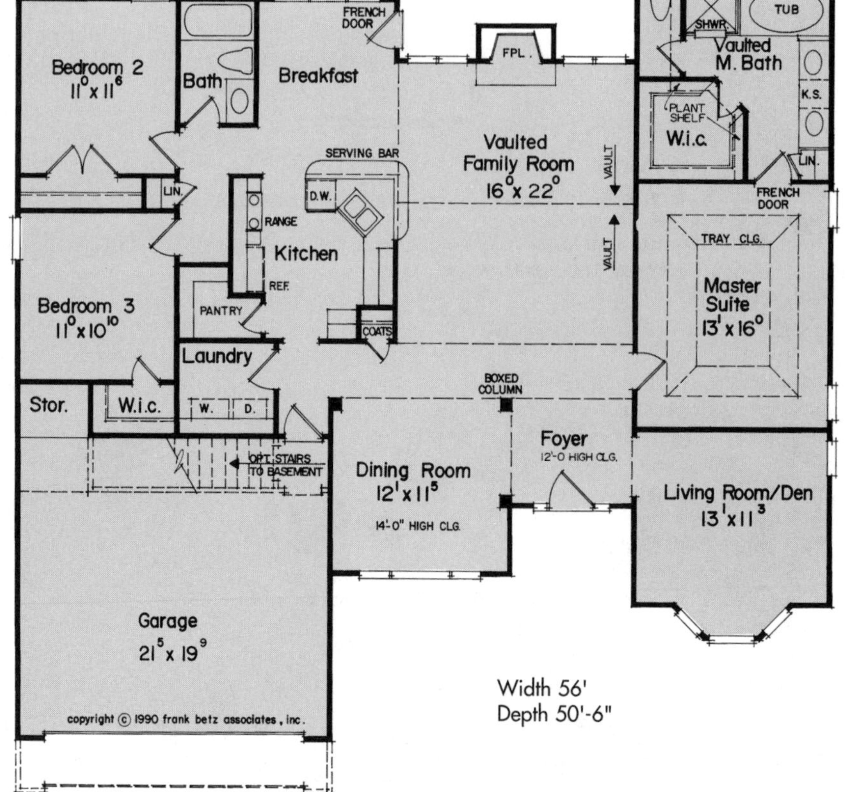

RAD. WDW.
TUB
SHWR.
Vaulted M. Bath
K.S.
PLANT SHELF
W.i.c.
LIN.
FRENCH DOOR
FPL.
Bedroom 2
11⁰x 11⁶
Bath
Breakfast
SERVING BAR
D.W.
RANGE
Kitchen
REF.
Vaulted Family Room
16⁰x 22⁰
VAULT
LIN.
TRAY CLG.
Master Suite
13¹x 16⁰
Bedroom 3
11⁰x 10¹⁰
PANTRY
COATS
Laundry
BOXED COLUMN
Stor.
W.i.c.
W.
D.
Foyer
12'-0 HIGH CLG.
OPT. STAIRS TO BASEMENT
Dining Room
12¹x 11⁵
14'-0" HIGH CLG.
Living Room/Den
13¹x 11³
Garage
21⁵x 19⁹
copyright © 1990 frank betz associates, inc.
Width 56'
Depth 50'-6"

Design P125

Square Footage: 1,875

An oversized picture window gives a cheerful first impression to this well-appointed family home. Boxed columns frame the formal dining room to one side of the foyer. A living room or den is to the other side. A vaulted ceiling soars over the family room. A lovely fireplace flanked by windows and a wraparound serving bar make this room the heart of family gatherings. The kitchen has all the amenities, including a sunny breakfast nook. The master suite is split from the two family bedrooms and features a lush compartmented bath and walk-in closet. Two family bedrooms, a hall bath and laundry room complete this favorite plan. Please specify basement, crawlspace or slab foundation when ordering.

■ Gentle arched lintels harmonize with the high hipped roof to create an elevation that is both welcoming and elegant. This efficient plan minimizes hallway space in order to maximize useable living areas. A favorite feature of this home is the "elbow-bend" galley kitchen that has easy access to the dining room, service entrance, laundry room and breakfast—plus a full length serving bar open to the great room. The master suite has a cozy sitting room and a compartmented bath. Two family bedrooms share a full hall bath. Please specify basement or crawlspace foundation when ordering.

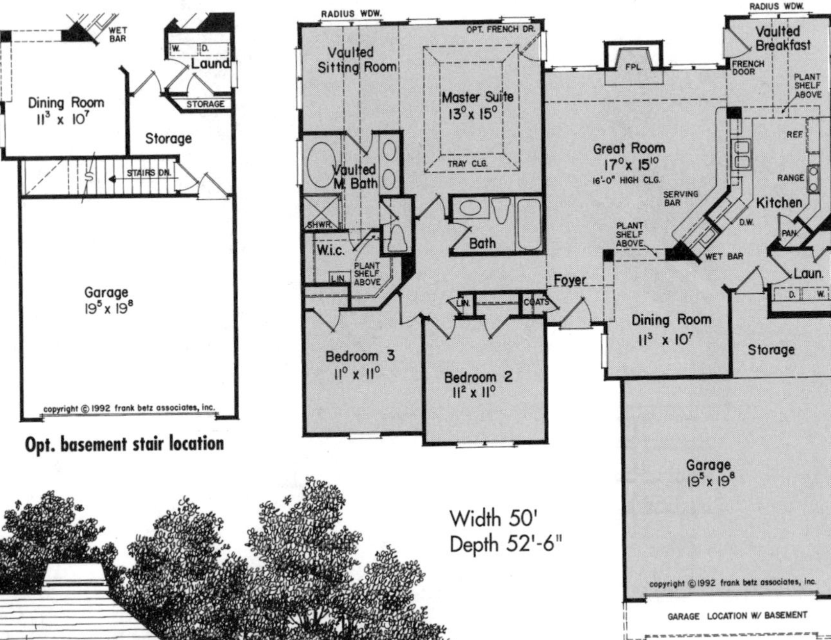

WET BAR
Laund
STORAGE
Dining Room 11³ x 10⁷
Storage
STAIRS DN.
Garage 19⁵ x 19⁸
copyright © 1992 frank betz associates, inc.
RADIUS WDW.
OPT. FRENCH DR.
Vaulted Sitting Room
Master Suite 13⁰ x 15⁰
TRAY CLG.
Vaulted M. Bath
SHWR.
W.i.c.
LIN.
PLANT SHELF ABOVE
Bath
FPL.
Great Room 17⁰ x 15¹⁰
16'-0" HIGH CLG.
SERVING BAR
Vaulted Breakfast
FRENCH DOOR
REF.
RANGE
Kitchen
D.W.
PAN.
WET BAR
Laun.
Foyer
COATS
Dining Room 11³ x 10⁷
Storage
Bedroom 3 11⁰ x 11⁰
Bedroom 2 11² x 11⁰
Garage 19⁵ x 19⁸
copyright © 1992 frank betz associates, inc.
GARAGE LOCATION W/ BASEMENT

Opt. basement stair location

Width 50'
Depth 52'-6"

Design P128

Square Footage: 1,575

Design by
Frank Betz Associates, Inc.

Design P123

Square Footage: 1,715

■ A grand double bank of windows looking in on the formal dining room mirrors the lofty elegance of the extra-tall vaulted ceiling inside. From the foyer, an arched entrance to the great room visually frames the fireplace on the back wall. The wraparound kitchen has plenty of counter and cabinet space, along with a handy serving bar. The luxurious master suite features a front sitting room for quiet times and a large spa-style bath. Two family bedrooms are split from the master for privacy and share a hall bath. Please specify basement or crawlspace foundation when ordering.

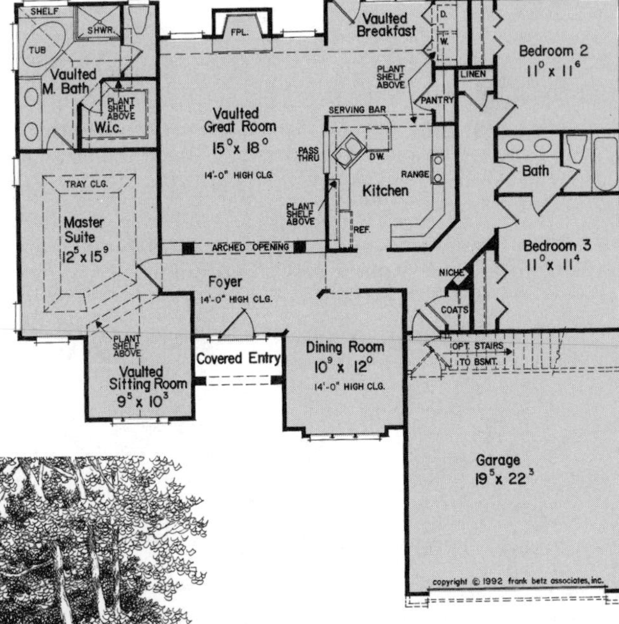

FRENCH DOOR
SHELF
SHWR.
TUB
Vaulted M. Bath
PLANT SHELF ABOVE
W.i.c.
FPL.
Vaulted Breakfast
Vaulted Great Room 15⁰ x 18⁰
14'-0" HIGH CLG.
SERVING BAR
PASS THRU
D.W.
RANGE
Kitchen
REF.
PANTRY
LINEN
Bedroom 2 11⁰ x 11⁶
Bath
TRAY CLG.
Master Suite 12⁵ x 15⁹
ARCHED OPENING
Foyer
14'-0" HIGH CLG.
NICHE
COATS
Bedroom 3 11⁰ x 11⁴
Covered Entry
Vaulted Sitting Room 9⁵ x 10³
Dining Room 10⁹ x 12⁰
14'-0" HIGH CLG.
OPT. STAIRS TO BSMT.
Garage 19⁵ x 22³
copyright © 1992 frank betz associates, inc.

Width 55'
Depth 51'-6"

Design by
Frank Betz Associates, Inc.

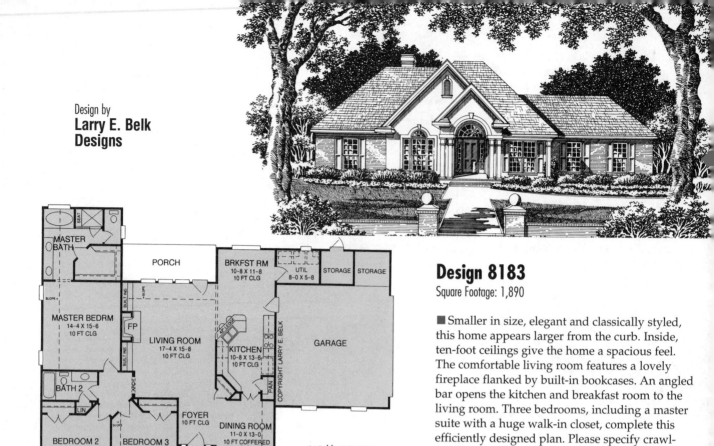

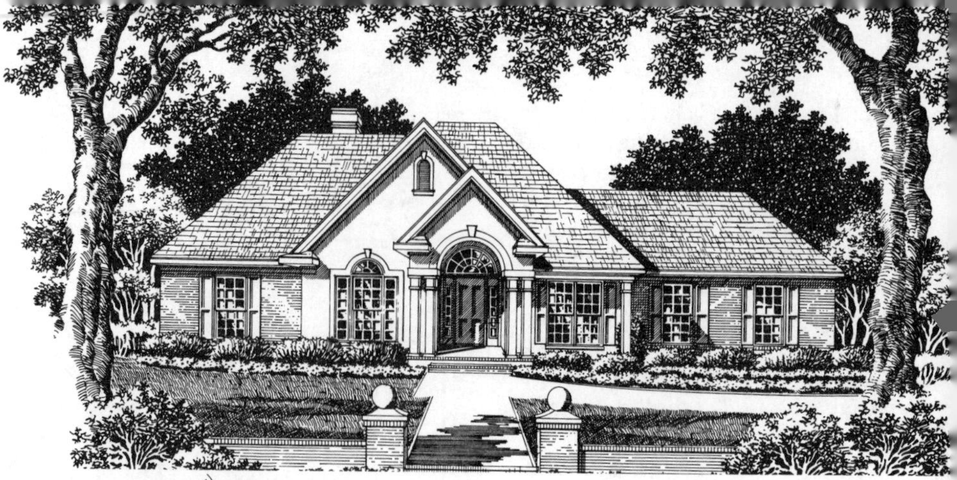

Design by
Larry E. Belk Designs

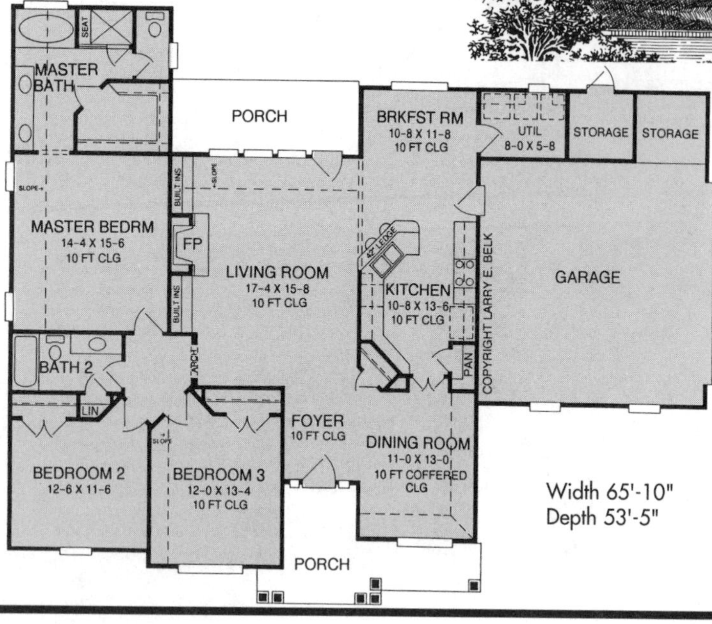

MASTER BATH
SEAT
PORCH
BRKFST RM 10-8 X 11-8 10 FT CLG
UTIL 8-0 X 5-8
STORAGE
STORAGE
MASTER BEDRM 14-4 X 15-6 10 FT CLG
FP
LIVING ROOM 17-4 X 15-8 10 FT CLG
KITCHEN 10-8 X 13-6 10 FT CLG
GARAGE
BATH 2
LIN
FOYER 10 FT CLG
DINING ROOM 11-0 X 13-0 10 FT COFFERED CLG
BEDROOM 2 12-6 X 11-6
BEDROOM 3 12-0 X 13-4 10 FT CLG
PORCH
COPYRIGHT LARRY E. BELK

Width 65'-10"
Depth 53'-5"

Design 8183

Square Footage: 1,890

■ Smaller in size, elegant and classically styled, this home appears larger from the curb. Inside, ten-foot ceilings give the home a spacious feel. The comfortable living room features a lovely fireplace flanked by built-in bookcases. An angled bar opens the kitchen and breakfast room to the living room. Three bedrooms, including a master suite with a huge walk-in closet, complete this efficiently designed plan. Please specify crawlspace or slab foundation when ordering.

Design P122

Square Footage: 1,884

■ Designer lintels and stately corner quoins are just a hint of the attention to detail this well-crafted plan offers. Arched openings, decorative columns and elegant ceiling detail throughout highlight the very livable floor plan. The extra-large country kitchen has a spacious work area, prep island and breakfast nook. The dining room is set to the rear for gracious entertaining and opens to the great room. The master suite is beautifully appointed with a compartmented bath and walk-in closet. Two family bedrooms share a private compartmented bath. Please specify basement or crawlspace foundation when ordering.

Design by
Frank Betz Associates, Inc.

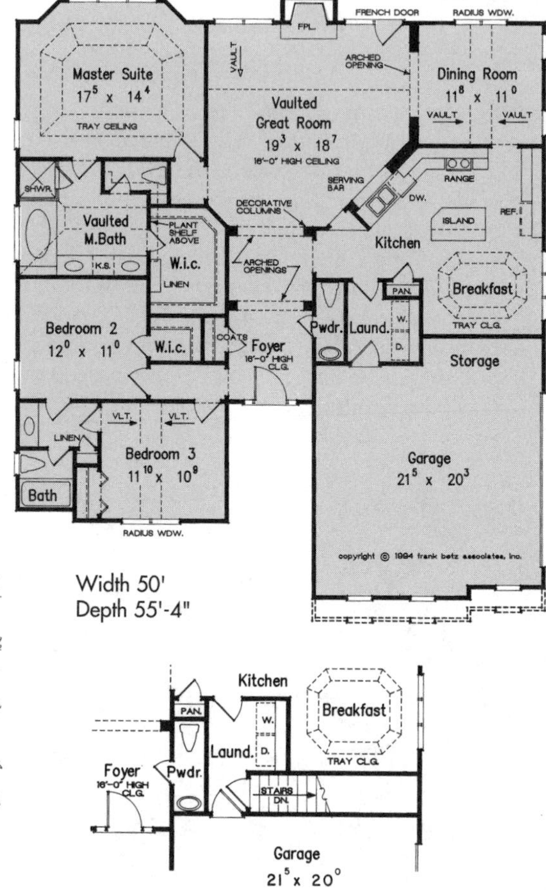

FRENCH DOOR
RADIUS WDW.
FPL.
Master Suite 17^5 x 14^4
TRAY CEILING
Vaulted Great Room 19^3 x 18^7
Dining Room 11^8 x 11^0
VAULT
Vaulted M.Bath
W.i.c.
Kitchen
Breakfast
TRAY CLG.
Bedroom 2 12^0 x 11^0
W.i.c.
Foyer
Pwdr.
Laund.
Storage
Bedroom 3 11^{10} x 10^9
Bath
Garage 21^5 x 20^3
RADIUS WDW.
Width 50'
Depth 55'-4"
Kitchen
Breakfast
Laund.
Foyer
Pwdr.
STAIRS DN.
Garage 21^5 x 20^0
Optional basement stair location

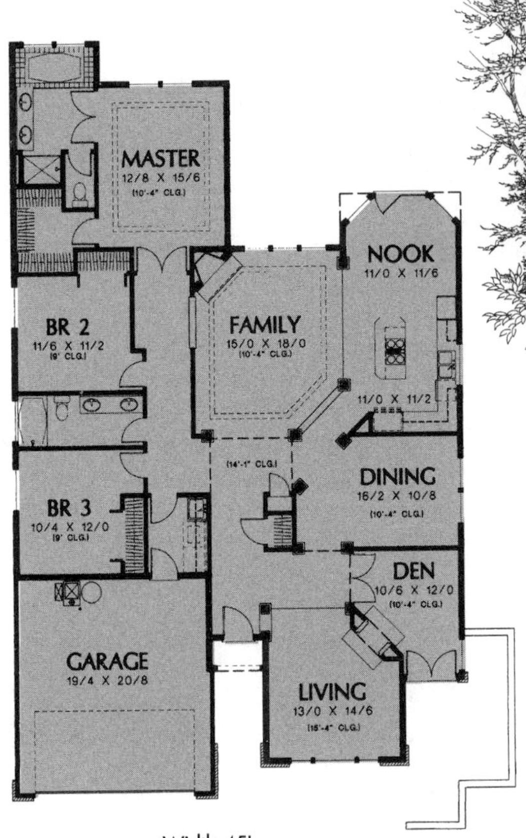
MASTER
12/8 X 15/6
(10'-4" CLG.)
NOOK
11/0 X 11/6
BR 2
11/6 X 11/2
(9' CLG.)
FAMILY
15/0 X 18/0
(10'-4" CLG.)
11/0 X 11/2
(14'-1" CLG.)
DINING
16/2 X 10/8
(10'-4" CLG.)
BR 3
10/4 X 12/0
(9' CLG.)
DEN
10/6 X 12/0
(10'-4" CLG.)
GARAGE
19/4 X 20/8
LIVING
13/0 X 14/6
(16'-4" CLG.)

Width 45'
Depth 73'

Design 9578

Square Footage: 2,225

■ This home exemplifies clever floor patterning. Casual living takes off in the kitchen, nook and family room. A fireplace here will warm gatherings. A dining room is nearby, as are a den and a living room. A see-through fireplace graces these areas. In the master bedroom suite, a garden tub and dual lavatories accommodate the owners. Two secondary bedrooms share a hall bath, also with dual lavatories. A laundry room connects the two-car garage.

Design by
Alan Mascord Design Associates, Inc.

QUOTE ONE®

Cost to build? See page 342 to order complete cost estimate to build this house in your area!

Design P129

Square Footage: 1,845
Bonus: 409 square feet

Design by
Frank Betz Associates, Inc.

■ This thoughtful split floor plan separates the family bedrooms from the master suite for maximum privacy and allows the family living areas to flow together from the entry foyer. The living room is accented with such amenities as a fireplace, French door to the rear yard, a vaulted ceiling and an open view to the dining room. The wraparound kitchen has a handy serving bar and a sunny breakfast nook. The master suite has a compartmented bath and a walk-in closet. Two family bedrooms share a private bath. An optional bonus room over the garage may be completed as needed. Please specify basement or crawlspace foundation when ordering.

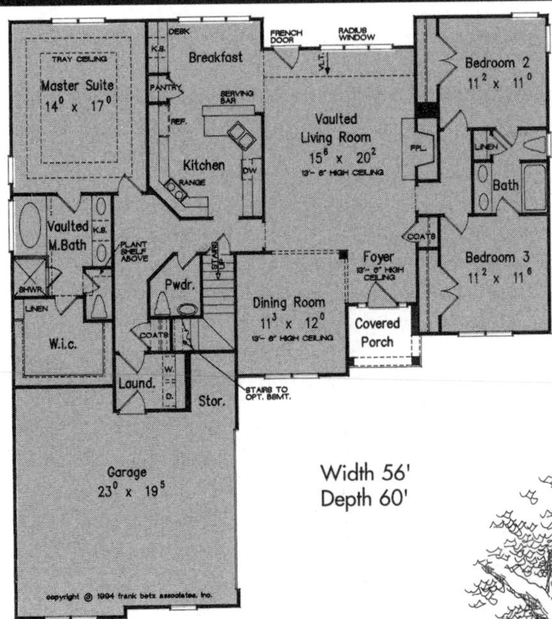
Tray Ceiling
Master Suite
14^{0} x 17^{0}
Breakfast
French Door
Radius Window
Vaulted Living Room
15^{6} x 20^{2}
13'-6" High Ceiling
Bedroom 2
11^{2} x 11^{0}
Kitchen
Serving Bar
Bath
Vaulted M.Bath
Foyer
Bedroom 3
11^{2} x 11^{6}
Pwdr.
Dining Room
11^{3} x 12^{0}
Covered Porch
W.i.c.
Laund.
Stor.
Stairs to Opt. Bsmt.
Garage
23^{0} x 19^{5}
copyright © 1994 frank betz associates, inc.

Width 56'
Depth 60'

Bath
W.i.c.
Stairs DN
Optional Bonus Room
11^{8} x 19^{2}

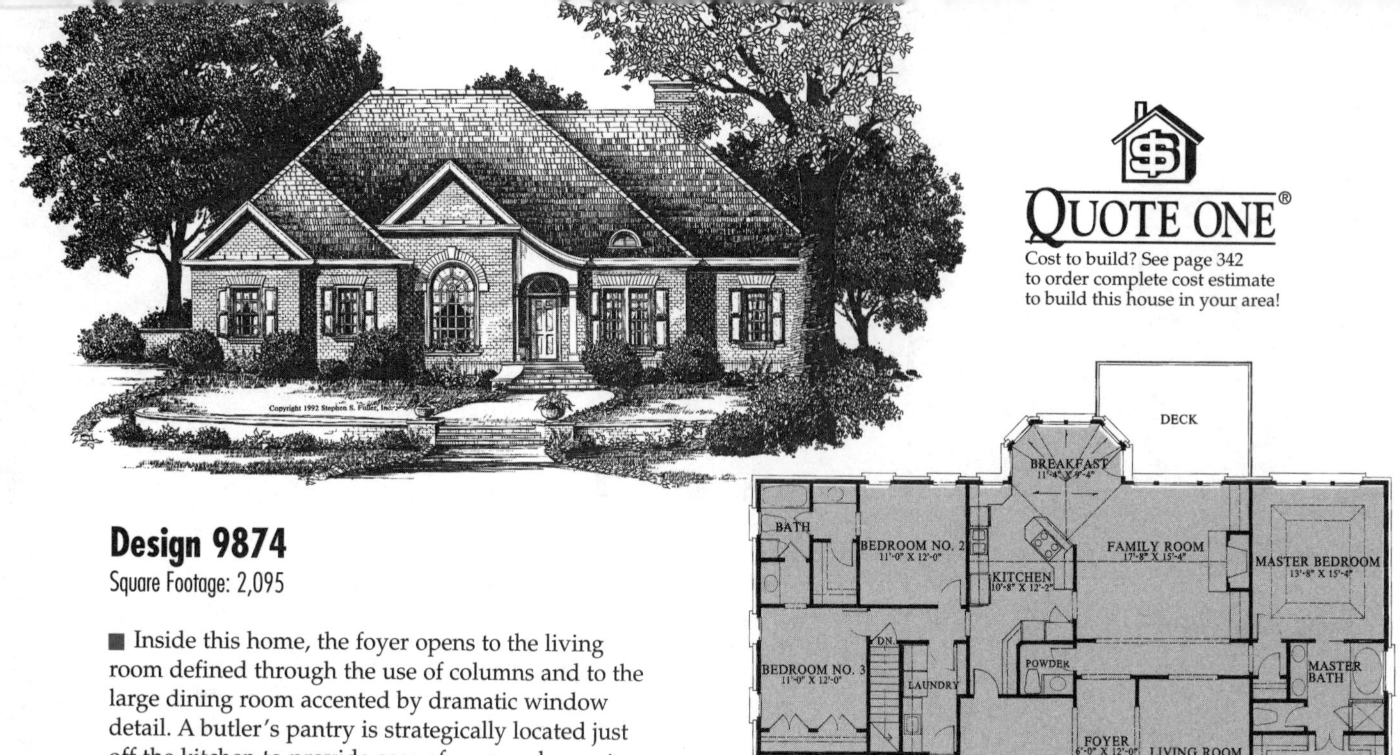
QUOTE ONE®
Cost to build? See page 342 to order complete cost estimate to build this house in your area!
DECK
BREAKFAST
11'-4" X 9'-4"
BATH
BEDROOM NO. 2
11'-0" X 12'-0"
FAMILY ROOM
17'-8" X 15'-4"
MASTER BEDROOM
13'-8" X 15'-4"
KITCHEN
10'-8" X 12'-2"

Design 9874

Square Footage: 2,095

■ Inside this home, the foyer opens to the living room defined through the use of columns and to the large dining room accented by dramatic window detail. A butler's pantry is strategically located just off the kitchen to provide ease of access when entertaining. The open family room displays a fireplace and built-in cabinetry for added storage. In the master suite, a large bath with dual vanities, jacuzzi tub and shower is complete with a spacious walk-in closet. On the opposite side of the home are two additional bedrooms. This home is designed with a basement foundation.

DN.
BEDROOM NO. 3
11'-0" X 12'-0"
LAUNDRY
POWDER
MASTER BATH
FOYER
6'-0" X 12'-0"
LIVING ROOM
11'-4" X 14'-0"
W.I.C.
DINING ROOM
11'-8" X 15'-0"
STOOP
TWO CAR GARAGE
20'-4" X 19'-10"

Width 65'
Depth 55'-11"

Design by
Design Traditions

Design 8136

Square Footage: 2,247

■ The combination of stucco and brick materials gives this one-story home a European feel. The dining room and great room are showcased by the dramatic entry formed by classic columns. A see-through fireplace serves both rooms. All bedrooms are conveniently grouped on one side of the house. A large island kitchen and a breakfast room with a snack bar and porch access complete this efficiently designed plan. Please specify crawlspace or slab foundation when ordering.

Design by
Larry E. Belk Designs

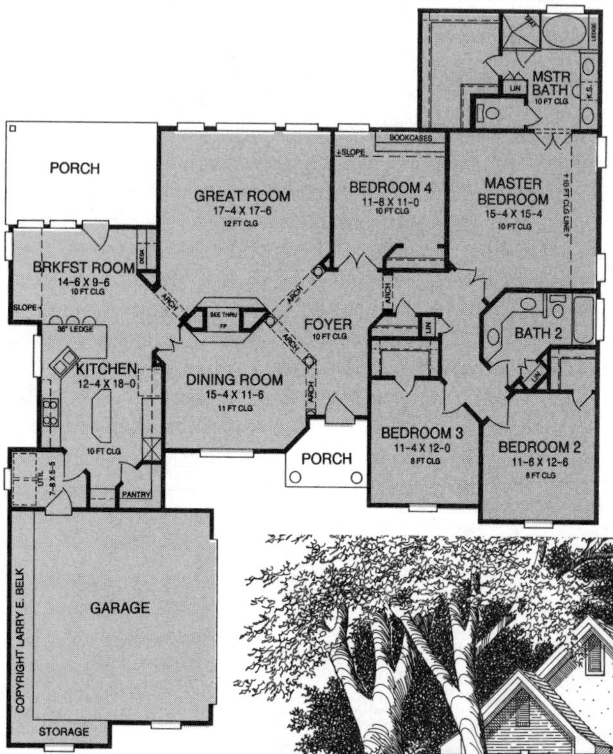

PORCH
GREAT ROOM
17-4 X 17-6
12 FT CLG
BEDROOM 4
11-8 X 11-0
10 FT CLG
MASTER BEDROOM
15-4 X 15-4
10 FT CLG
MSTR BATH
10 FT CLG
BRKFST ROOM
14-6 X 9-6
10 FT CLG
FOYER
10 FT CLG
BATH 2
KITCHEN
12-4 X 18-0
DINING ROOM
15-4 X 11-6
11 FT CLG
BEDROOM 3
11-4 X 12-0
8 FT CLG
BEDROOM 2
11-8 X 12-6
8 FT CLG
PORCH
PANTRY
GARAGE
STORAGE
COPYRIGHT LARRY E. BELK

Width 61'-6"
Depth 73'

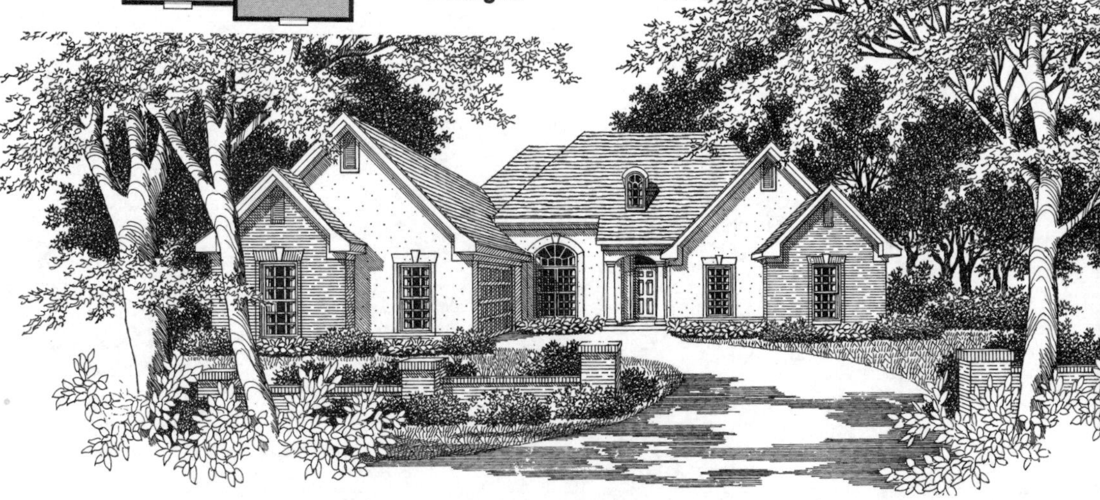

QUOTE ONE®
Cost to build? See page 342 to order complete cost estimate to build this house in your area!
MASTER BATH
MASTER BEDRDOOM
16'-4" X 13'-6"
PORCH
BREAKFAST
13'-4" X 9'-0"
BEDROOM/ OFFICE
10'-4" X 11'-0"
GREAT ROOM
17'-0" X 17'-8"
BEDROOM NO. 2
10'-4" X 12'-0"
KITCHEN
13'-4" X 10'-6"
DN.
BATH
LAUNDRY
BATH
DINING ROOM
11'-4" X 12'-10"
FOYER
5'-4" X 12'-10"
BEDROOM/ STUDY
11'-2" X 12'-0"
TWO CAR GARAGE
20'-6" X 19'-6"
PORCH
Width 61'
Depth 70'-6"

Design 9853

Square Footage: 2,090

■ This traditional home features board-and-batten siding and cedar shingles in an attractively proportioned exterior. Finishing touches include a covered entrance and porch with column detailing and an arched transom, flower boxes and shuttered windows. The foyer opens to both the dining room and great room beyond with French doors opening onto the porch. Through the double doors to the right of the foyer is the combination bedroom/study. A short hallway leads to a full bath and a secondary bedroom with ample closet space. The master bedroom is spacious, with walk-in closets on both sides of the entrance to the master bath. With separate vanities, a shower and a toilet, the master bath forms a private retreat at the rear of the home. Convenient to both the great room and dining room, the kitchen opens to an attractive breakfast area featuring a bay window. An additional room is remotely located off the kitchen, providing a retreat for today's at-home office or guests. This home is designed with a basement foundation.

Design by
Design Traditions

Design 9885

Square Footage: 2,295

■ One-story living takes a lovely traditional turn in this brick one-story home. The entry foyer opens directly to the dining room and great room, with columned accents to separate the areas. A large island kitchen adjoins a combination breakfast room/keeping room with fireplace. The bedrooms are found to the left of the plan. A master suite is cloistered to the rear and has a large master bath and bayed sitting area. Two additional bedrooms share a full bath. This home is designed with a basement foundation.

Design by
Design Traditions

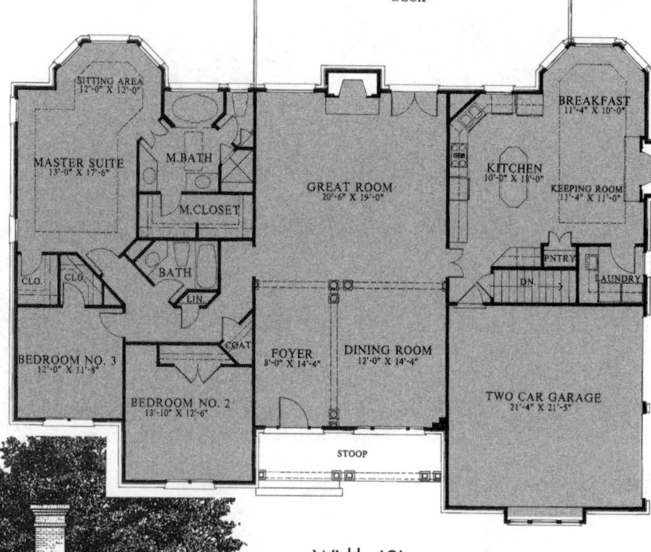
DECK
SITTING AREA
MASTER SUITE
M.BATH
M.CLOSET
GREAT ROOM
BREAKFAST
KITCHEN
KEEPING ROOM
PNTRY
LAUNDRY
DN.
CLO.
CLO.
BATH
LIN.
COAT
BEDROOM NO. 3
BEDROOM NO. 2
FOYER
DINING ROOM
TWO CAR GARAGE
STOOP

Width 69'
Depth 49'-6"

QUOTE ONE®

Cost to build? See page 342 to order complete cost estimate to build this house in your area!

Design 9884

Square Footage: 2,120

■ Arched lintels and fanlight windows act as graceful accents for this wonderful design. A central family room serves as the heart of family activity. It has a fireplace and connects to a lovely sunroom with rear porch access. The formal dining room is to the front of the plan and is open to the entry foyer. A private den also opens off the foyer with double doors. The kitchen area opens to the sunroom and has an island work counter. Bedrooms are split, with the master suite to the right side of the design and family bedrooms to the left. This home is designed with a basement foundation.

Design by
Design Traditions

BATH
BEDROOM NO. 3
BEDROOM NO. 2
SUN ROOM
PORCH
MASTER BATH
W.I.C.
MASTER BEDROOM
BREAKFAST
FAMILY ROOM
LAUNDRY
KITCHEN
BATH
DN.
DINING ROOM
FOYER
DEN
STOOP
TWO CAR GARAGE

Width 62'
Depth 62'-6"

QUOTE ONE®

Cost to build? See page 342 to order complete cost estimate to build this house in your area!

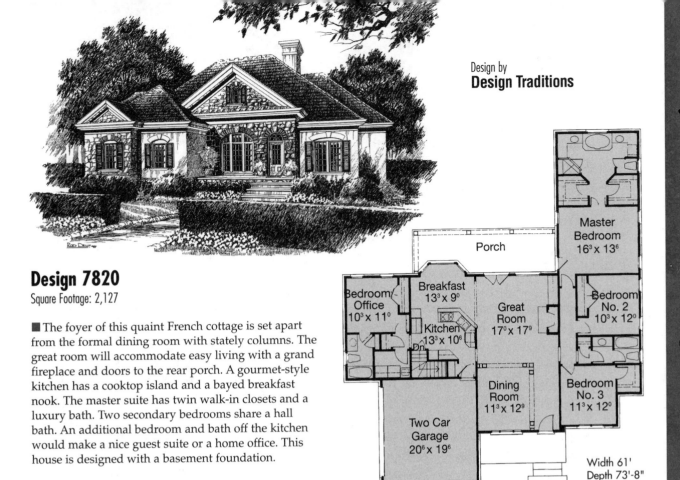

Design by
Design Traditions

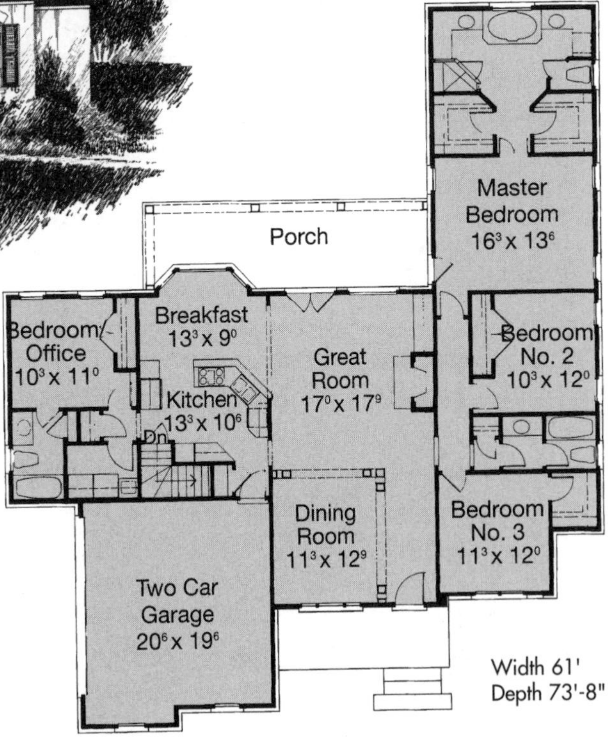

Design 7820

Square Footage: 2,127

■ The foyer of this quaint French cottage is set apart from the formal dining room with stately columns. The great room will accommodate easy living with a grand fireplace and doors to the rear porch. A gourmet-style kitchen has a cooktop island and a bayed breakfast nook. The master suite has twin walk-in closets and a luxury bath. Two secondary bedrooms share a hall bath. An additional bedroom and bath off the kitchen would make a nice guest suite or a home office. This house is designed with a basement foundation.

Porch
Master Bedroom 16^3 x 13^6
Bedroom/Office 10^3 x 11^0
Breakfast 13^3 x 9^0
Kitchen 13^3 x 10^6
Great Room 17^0 x 17^9
Bedroom No. 2 10^3 x 12^0
Dining Room 11^3 x 12^9
Bedroom No. 3 11^3 x 12^0
Two Car Garage 20^6 x 19^6

Width 61'
Depth 73'-8"

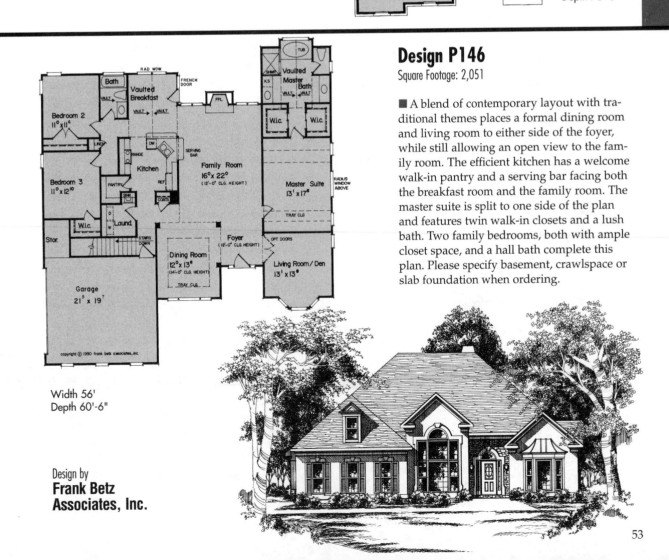

Design P146

Square Footage: 2,051

■ A blend of contemporary layout with traditional themes places a formal dining room and living room to either side of the foyer, while still allowing an open view to the family room. The efficient kitchen has a welcome walk-in pantry and a serving bar facing both the breakfast room and the family room. The master suite is split to one side of the plan and features twin walk-in closets and a lush bath. Two family bedrooms, both with ample closet space, and a hall bath complete this plan. Please specify basement, crawlspace or slab foundation when ordering.

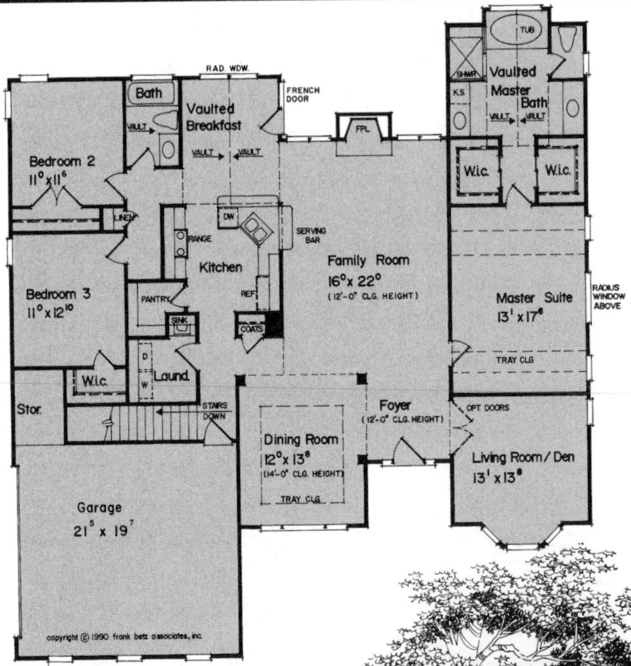

Vaulted Breakfast
Bath
Bedroom 2 11^0 x 11^6
Bedroom 3 11^0 x 12^{10}
Kitchen
Family Room 16^0 x 22^0 (12'-0" CLG. HEIGHT)
Vaulted Master Bath
W.i.c.
Master Suite 13^1 x 17^6
Foyer (12'-0" CLG. HEIGHT)
Dining Room 12^0 x 13^8 (14'-0" CLG. HEIGHT)
Living Room/Den 13^1 x 13^8
Garage 21^5 x 19^7
Stor.
Laund.

copyright © 1990 frank betz associates, inc.

Width 56'
Depth 60'-6"

Design by
Frank Betz Associates, Inc.

Design 9797

Square Footage: 1,417

■ A wide-open floor plan puts the emphasis on family living in this modest, single-story home. A cathedral ceiling stretches the length of the plan, stylishly topping the dining room, great room and master bedroom. Cooks will enjoy working in the presentation kitchen that's open to the dining room and great room. The master suite has a walk-in closet and a compartmented bath with a garden tub and twin vanities. One of the two family bedrooms has a cathedral ceiling as well, making it an optional study. A full hall bath and a convenient hallway laundry center complete this plan.

Design by
Donald A. Gardner, Architects, Inc.

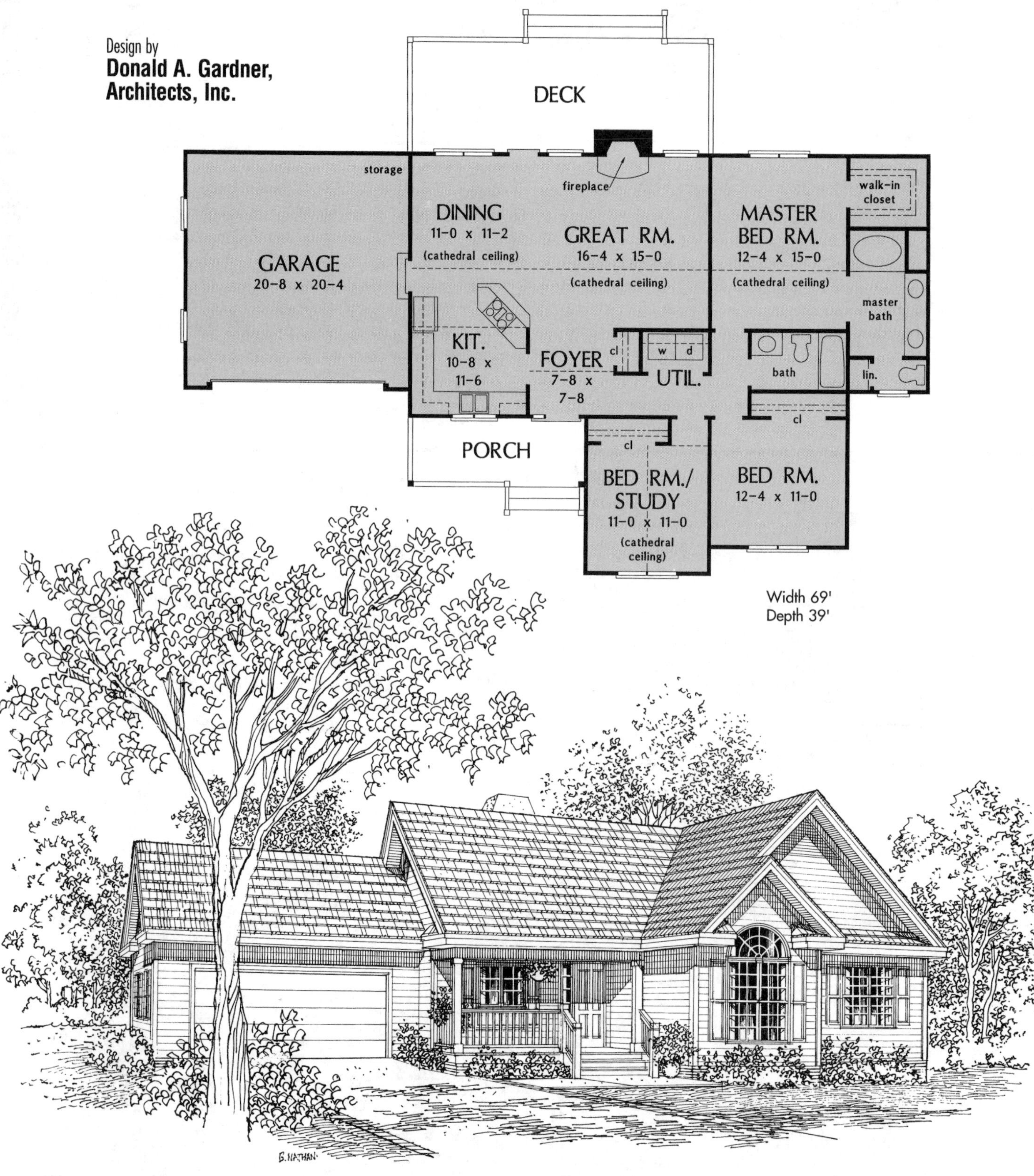
DECK
storage
fireplace
walk-in closet
DINING
11-0 x 11-2
(cathedral ceiling)
GREAT RM.
16-4 x 15-0
(cathedral ceiling)
MASTER BED RM.
12-4 x 15-0
(cathedral ceiling)
GARAGE
20-8 x 20-4
master bath
KIT.
10-8 x 11-6
FOYER
7-8 x 7-8
cl
w d
UTIL.
bath
lin.
cl
PORCH
cl
BED RM./ STUDY
11-0 x 11-0
(cathedral ceiling)
BED RM.
12-4 x 11-0
Width 69'
Depth 39'
B. NATHAN

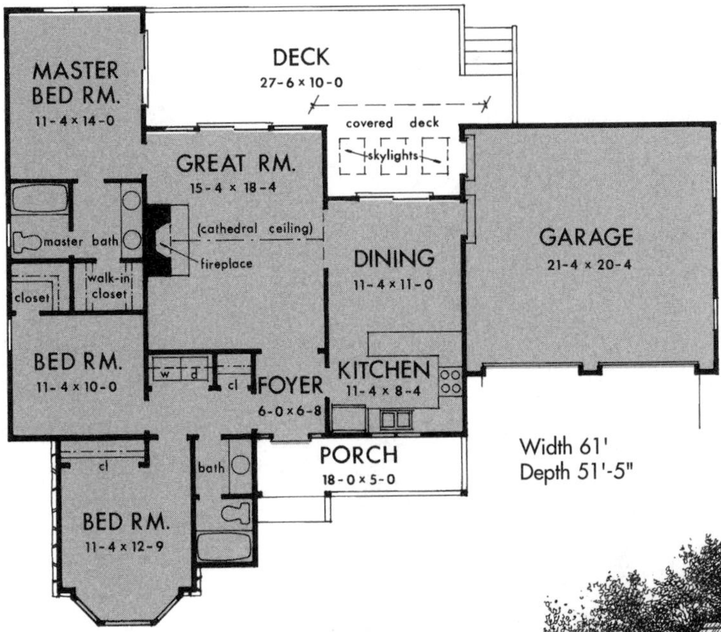

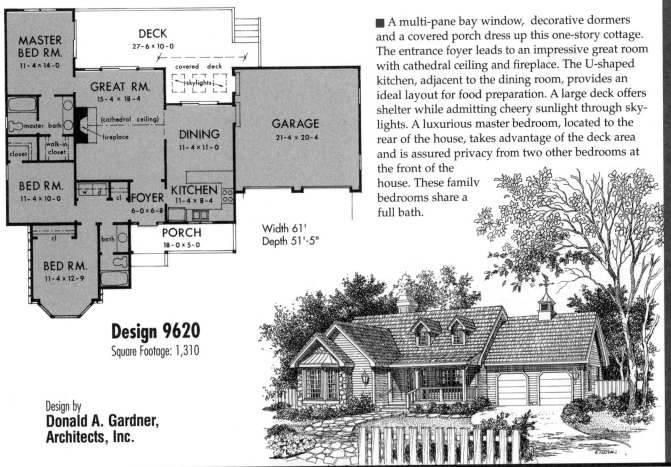

■ A multi-pane bay window, decorative dormers and a covered porch dress up this one-story cottage. The entrance foyer leads to an impressive great room with cathedral ceiling and fireplace. The U-shaped kitchen, adjacent to the dining room, provides an ideal layout for food preparation. A large deck offers shelter while admitting cheery sunlight through skylights. A luxurious master bedroom, located to the rear of the house, takes advantage of the deck area and is assured privacy from two other bedrooms at the front of the house. These familv bedrooms share a full bath.

MASTER BED RM. 11-4 × 14-0
DECK 27-6 × 10-0
covered deck
skylights
GREAT RM. 15-4 × 18-4
(cathedral ceiling)
fireplace
master bath
walk-in closet
closet
DINING 11-4 × 11-0
GARAGE 21-4 × 20-4
BED RM. 11-4 × 10-0
w d
cl
FOYER 6-0 × 6-8
KITCHEN 11-4 × 8-4
cl
bath
PORCH 18-0 × 5-0
BED RM. 11-4 × 12-9

Width 61'
Depth 51'-5"

Design 9620

Square Footage: 1,310

Design by
Donald A. Gardner, Architects, Inc.

Design by
Donald A. Gardner, Architects, Inc.

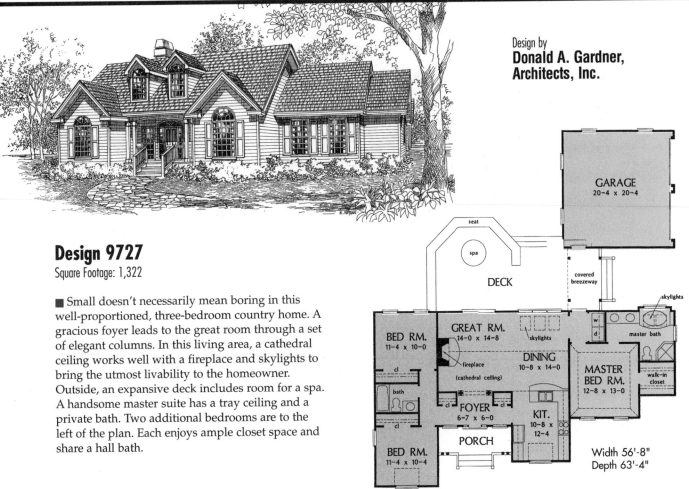

Design 9727

Square Footage: 1,322

■ Small doesn't necessarily mean boring in this well-proportioned, three-bedroom country home. A gracious foyer leads to the great room through a set of elegant columns. In this living area, a cathedral ceiling works well with a fireplace and skylights to bring the utmost livability to the homeowner. Outside, an expansive deck includes room for a spa. A handsome master suite has a tray ceiling and a private bath. Two additional bedrooms are to the left of the plan. Each enjoys ample closet space and share a hall bath.

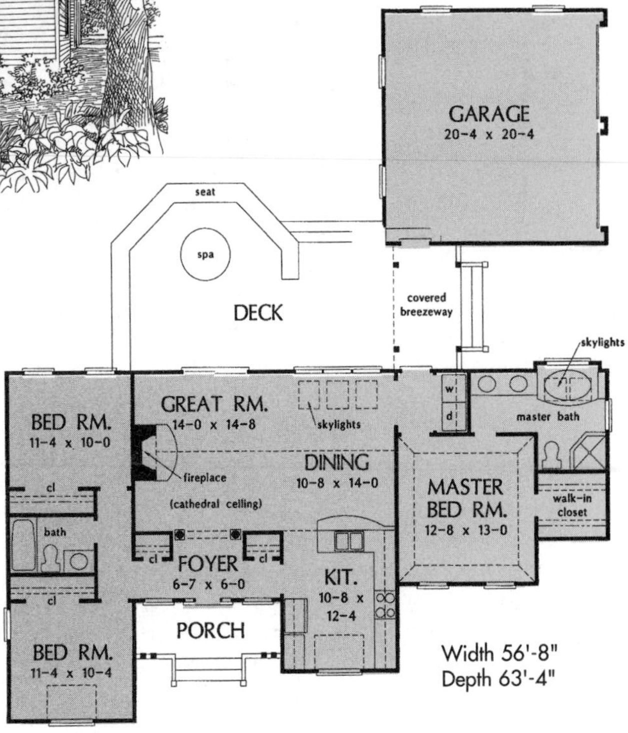

GARAGE 20-4 × 20-4
seat
spa
DECK
covered breezeway
skylights
BED RM. 11-4 × 10-0
GREAT RM. 14-0 × 14-8
skylights
fireplace
(cathedral ceiling)
DINING 10-8 × 14-0
w d
master bath
MASTER BED RM. 12-8 × 13-0
walk-in closet
cl
bath
cl
FOYER 6-7 × 6-0
cl
KIT. 10-8 × 12-4
cl
PORCH
BED RM. 11-4 × 10-4

Width 56'-8"
Depth 63'-4"

B.NATHAN
seat
spa
DECK
arched window above door
GARAGE
19-0 x 22-0
GREAT RM.
15-0 x 17-2
fireplace
(cathedral ceiling)
bath
UTIL.
d
w
BRKFST.
walk-in closet
master bath
lin.
BED RM.
10-0 x 10-0
cl
MASTER BED RM.
13-0 x 14-0
lin.
cl
FOYER
4-8 x 12-4
cl
DINING
10-0 x 12-0
KIT.
10-0 x 17-8
BED RM.
13-0 x 11-8
PORCH
17-8 x 6-0

Design by
Donald A. Gardner, Architects, Inc.

Width 71'
Depth 59'

Design 9639

Square Footage: 1,541

■ This traditional three-bedroom home with front and side porches, arched windows and dormers projects the appearance of a much larger home. The great room features a cathedral ceiling, a fireplace and an arched window above the sliding glass door to the expansive rear deck. A spa here creates the perfect atmosphere for entertaining. Elegant round columns define the dining room. The master suite contains a pampering master bath with a whirlpool tub, a separate shower, a double-bowl vanity and a walk-in closet. Two other bedrooms share a full bath with a double-bowl vanity. Please specify basement or crawlspace foundation when ordering.

Design by
Donald A. Gardner, Architects, Inc.

Design 9753

Square Footage: 1,346

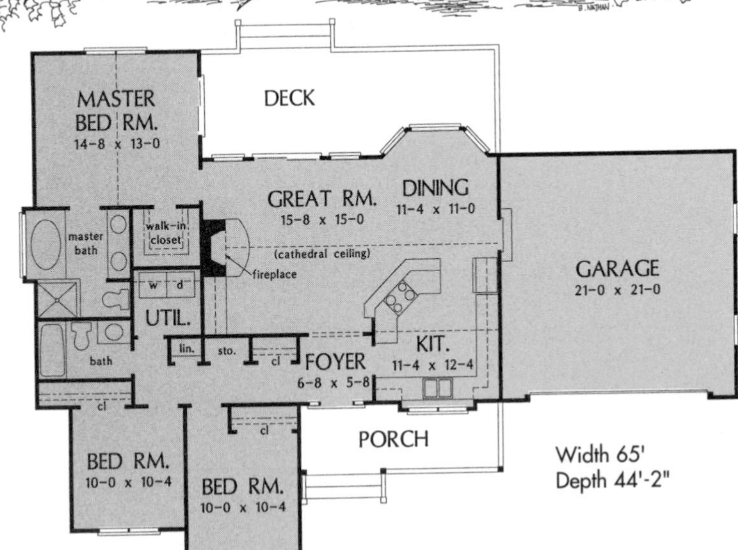
MASTER BED RM.
14-8 x 13-0
DECK
GREAT RM.
15-8 x 15-0
DINING
11-4 x 11-0
master bath
walk-in closet
(cathedral ceiling)
fireplace
GARAGE
21-0 x 21-0
w d
UTIL.
lin.
sto.
cl
FOYER
6-8 x 5-8
KIT.
11-4 x 12-4
bath
cl
cl
PORCH
BED RM.
10-0 x 10-4
BED RM.
10-0 x 10-4
Width 65'
Depth 44'-2"

■ A great room that stretches into the dining room makes this design perfect for entertaining. A cozy fireplace and stylish built-ins, as well as a cathedral ceiling, further this casual yet elegant atmosphere. A rear deck extends living possibilities. The ample kitchen features an abundance of counter and cabinet space, and an angled cooktop and serving bar that overlooks the great room. Two bedrooms, a hall bath and a handy laundry room make up the family sleeping wing while the master suite is privately located at the rear of the plan.

Design 9726

Square Footage: 1,498

■ This country home has quite a welcoming front exterior. Inside, the great room with a dramatic cathedral ceiling commands attention; the kitchen and breakfast room are just beyond a set of columns. The tiered-ceilinged dining room presents a delightfully formal atmosphere for dinner parties or family gatherings. A tray ceiling accents the master bedroom, as do a large walk-in closet and a gracious master bath with dual sinks, garden tub, and separate shower. Two secondary bedrooms and a hall bath are located at the opposite end of the house for privacy. Please specify basement or crawlspace foundation when ordering.

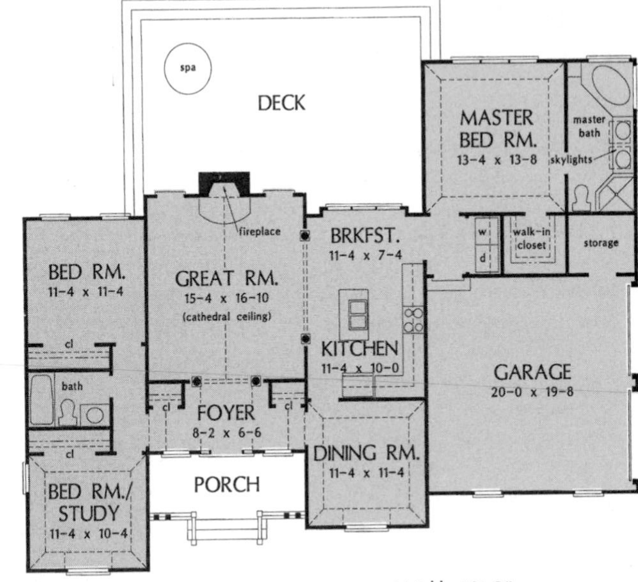
spa
DECK
MASTER BED RM.
13-4 x 13-8
master bath
skylights
fireplace
BRKFST.
11-4 x 7-4
w d
walk-in closet
storage
BED RM.
11-4 x 11-4
GREAT RM.
15-4 x 16-10
(cathedral ceiling)
cl
bath
KITCHEN
11-4 x 10-0
GARAGE
20-0 x 19-8
cl
FOYER
8-2 x 6-6
cl
cl
DINING RM.
11-4 x 11-4
BED RM./ STUDY
11-4 x 10-4
PORCH

Width 59'-8"
Depth 50'-8"

Design by
Donald A. Gardner, Architects, Inc.

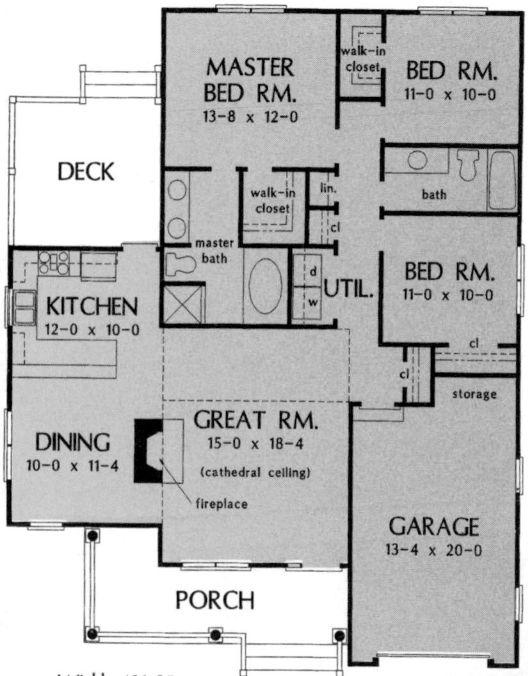

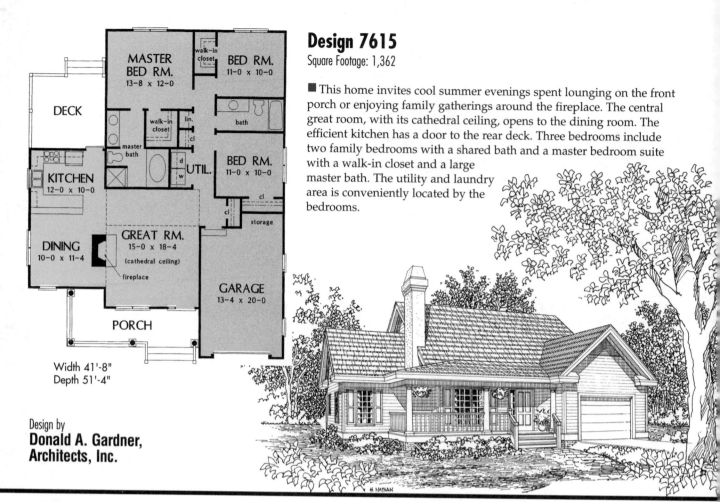

Design 7615

Square Footage: 1,362

■ This home invites cool summer evenings spent lounging on the front porch or enjoying family gatherings around the fireplace. The central great room, with its cathedral ceiling, opens to the dining room. The efficient kitchen has a door to the rear deck. Three bedrooms include two family bedrooms with a shared bath and a master bedroom suite with a walk-in closet and a large master bath. The utility and laundry area is conveniently located by the bedrooms.

Width 41'-8"
Depth 51'-4"

Design by
Donald A. Gardner, Architects, Inc.

Design 7614

Square Footage: 1,306

■ A central kitchen is the focal point for this country ranch home. It gives the opportunity for the cook to be a part of the activities and increases serving ease. The large kitchen offers a snack bar and easy access to both the living and sleeping areas. The great room and dining area are combined, offering access to the front porch, a fireplace and a cathedral ceiling—the perfect area for entertaining. The washer and dryer are conveniently located near the family bedrooms and the shared full bath. The master bedroom and bath include a cathedral ceiling, a walk-in closet and a skylit whirlpool tub.

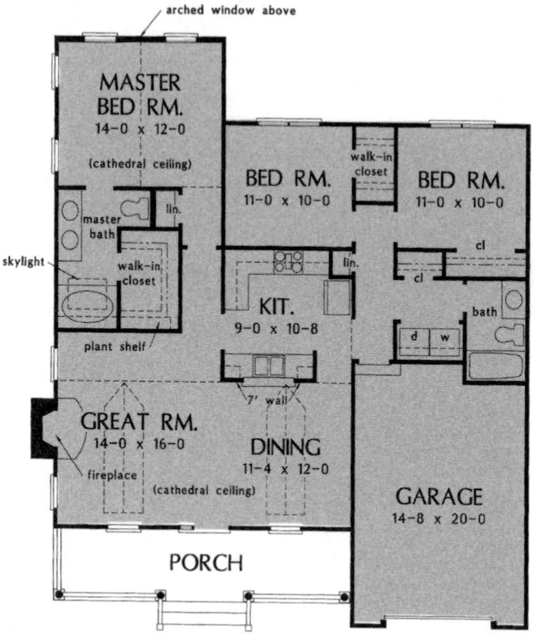

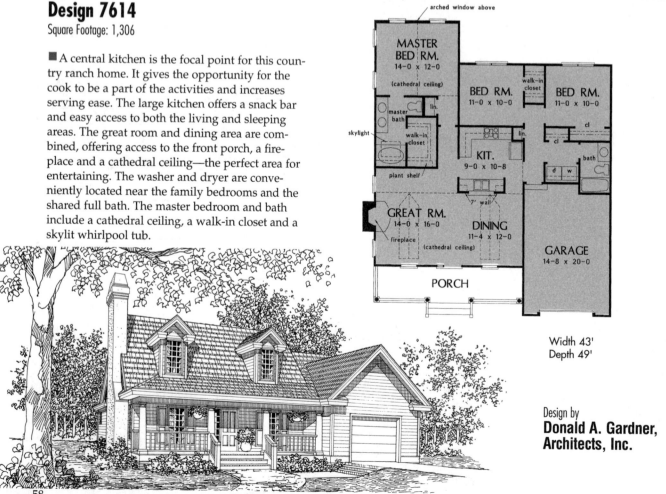

Width 43'
Depth 49'

Design by
Donald A. Gardner, Architects, Inc.

B. NATHAN

Design by
Donald A. Gardner, Architects, Inc.

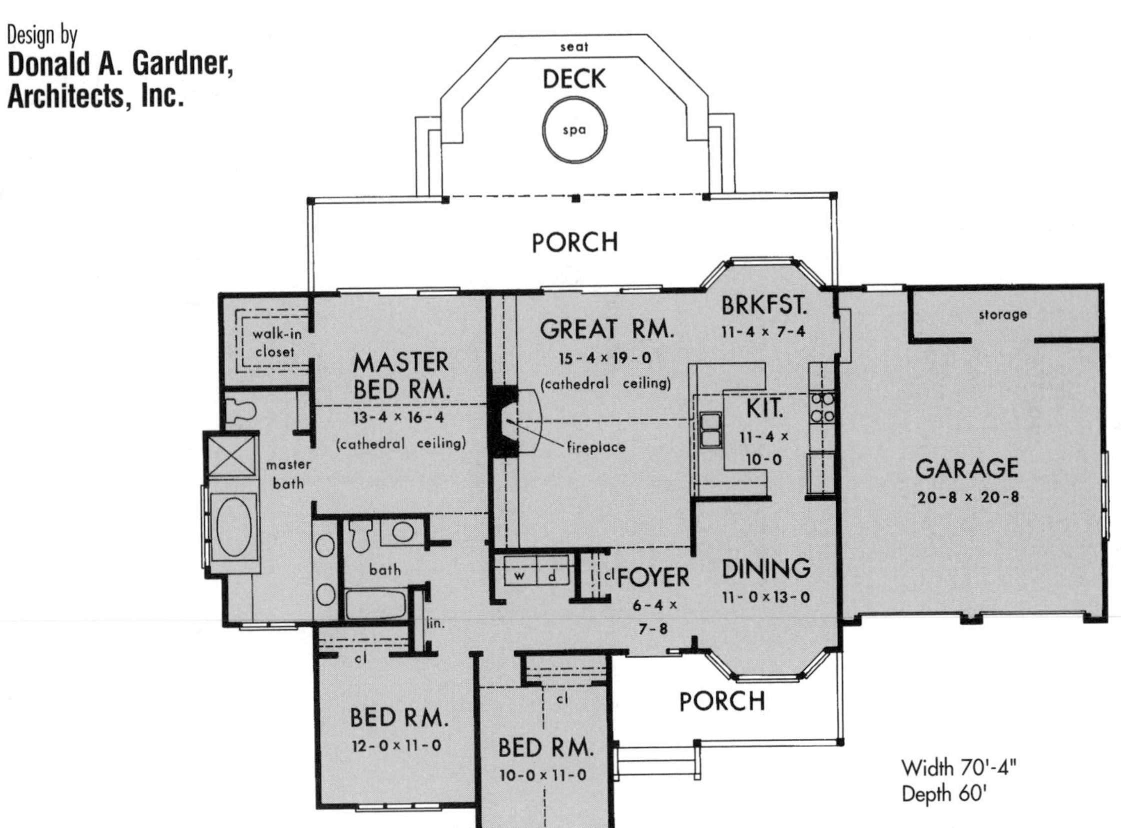
seat
DECK
spa
PORCH
walk-in closet
MASTER BED RM.
13-4 x 16-4
(cathedral ceiling)
master bath
GREAT RM.
15-4 x 19-0
(cathedral ceiling)
fireplace
BRKFST.
11-4 x 7-4
KIT.
11-4 x 10-0
storage
GARAGE
20-8 x 20-8
bath
w d
lin.
cl
FOYER
6-4 x 7-8
DINING
11-0 x 13-0
cl
PORCH
BED RM.
12-0 x 11-0
BED RM.
10-0 x 11-0
Width 70'-4"
Depth 60'

Design 9696

Square Footage: 1,625

■ This family-pleasing design is thoughtful, indeed. Living areas include a kitchen with efficient work triangle, an adjoining breakfast room, a dining room with bay window, and of course, the great room with fireplace and access to a rear porch. The master bedroom also has porch access, along with a walk-in closet and a lavish bath. Two family bedrooms include one featuring a half-round transom window, adding appeal to the exterior and interior. The laundry room is convenient to all three bedrooms.

Design 9780

Square Footage: 1,561

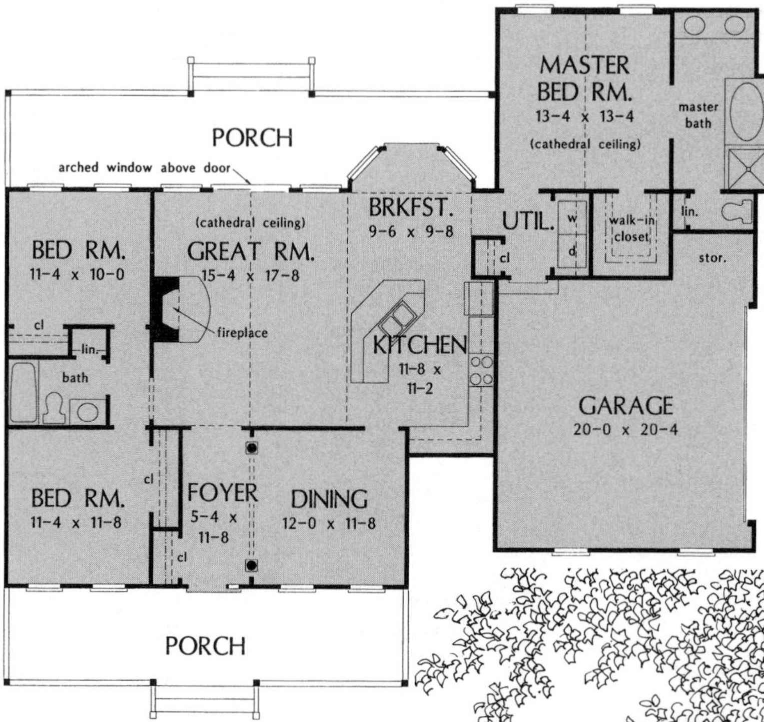

■ Special touches such as interior columns, a bay window and dormers add their own special brand of charm to this wonderful country home. Inside, the centrally located great room features a cathedral ceiling, a welcoming fireplace and a clerestory window that fills the room with natural light. Whether entertaining guests or gathering with the family, you'll find that the adjoining kitchen and sun-filled breakfast area combine with the great room to create an open, comfortable space. Split for privacy, the master bedroom provides a quiet getaway. For ultimate relaxation, indulge yourself in a pampering master bath that has a double-bowl vanity, a separate shower and a whirlpool tub. Two additional bedrooms share a full bath.

Width 60'-10"
Depth 51'-6"

Design by
Donald A. Gardner, Architects, Inc.

PORCH
arched window above door
MASTER BED RM.
13-4 x 13-4
(cathedral ceiling)
master bath
BRKFST.
9-6 x 9-8
UTIL.
w
d
walk-in closet
lin.
cl
stor.
(cathedral ceiling)
BED RM.
11-4 x 10-0
GREAT RM.
15-4 x 17-8
fireplace
KITCHEN
11-8 x 11-2
cl
lin.
bath
GARAGE
20-0 x 20-4
cl
BED RM.
11-4 x 11-8
FOYER
5-4 x 11-8
DINING
12-0 x 11-8
cl
PORCH

skylights
BONUS RM.
24-8 X 11-8
down

Design by
Donald A. Gardner, Architects, Inc.

Design 9750

Square Footage: 1,575
Bonus Room: 276 square feet

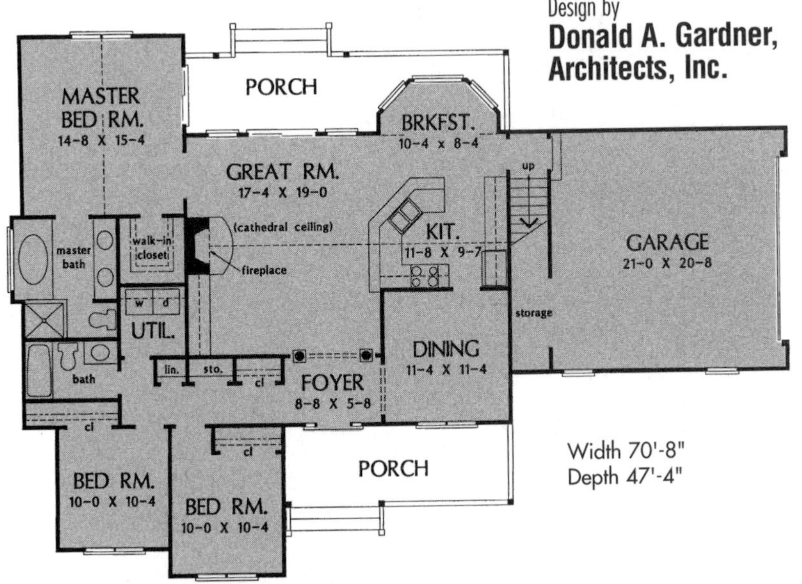

MASTER BED RM.
14-8 X 15-4
PORCH
BRKFST.
10-4 x 8-4
GREAT RM.
17-4 X 19-0
(cathedral ceiling)
fireplace
KIT.
11-8 X 9-7
up
GARAGE
21-0 X 20-8
master bath
walk-in closet
UTIL.
storage
DINING
11-4 X 11-4
bath
lin.
sto.
cl
FOYER
8-8 X 5-8
BED RM.
10-0 X 10-4
BED RM.
10-0 X 10-4
PORCH

Width 70'-8"
Depth 47'-4"

■ A covered porch and dormers combine to create the inviting exterior on this three-bedroom country home. The foyer leads through columns to an expansive great room with a cozy fireplace, built-in bookshelves and access to the rear covered porch. To the right, an open kitchen is conveniently situated to easily serve the bay-windowed breakfast area and the formal dining room. The master suite enjoys access to the covered porch, a walk-in closet and a relaxing master bath. A utility room, two secondary bedrooms and a full bath complete the plan. A bonus room over the garage provides room for future growth.

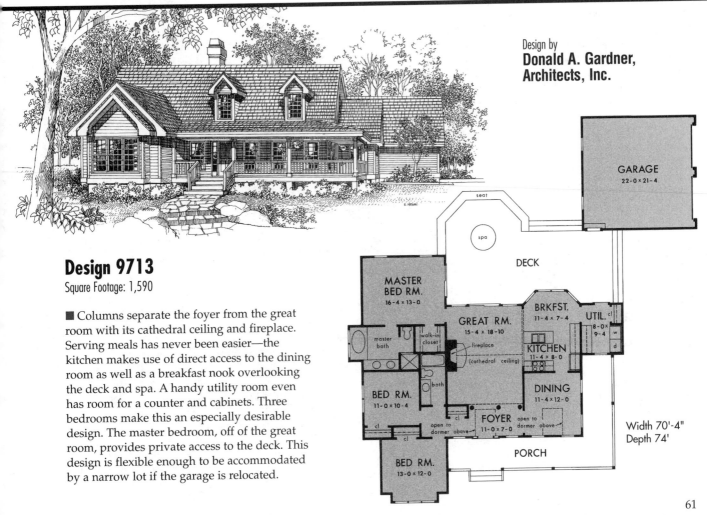

Design by
Donald A. Gardner, Architects, Inc.

Design 9713

Square Footage: 1,590

■ Columns separate the foyer from the great room with its cathedral ceiling and fireplace. Serving meals has never been easier—the kitchen makes use of direct access to the dining room as well as a breakfast nook overlooking the deck and spa. A handy utility room even has room for a counter and cabinets. Three bedrooms make this an especially desirable design. The master bedroom, off of the great room, provides private access to the deck. This design is flexible enough to be accommodated by a narrow lot if the garage is relocated.

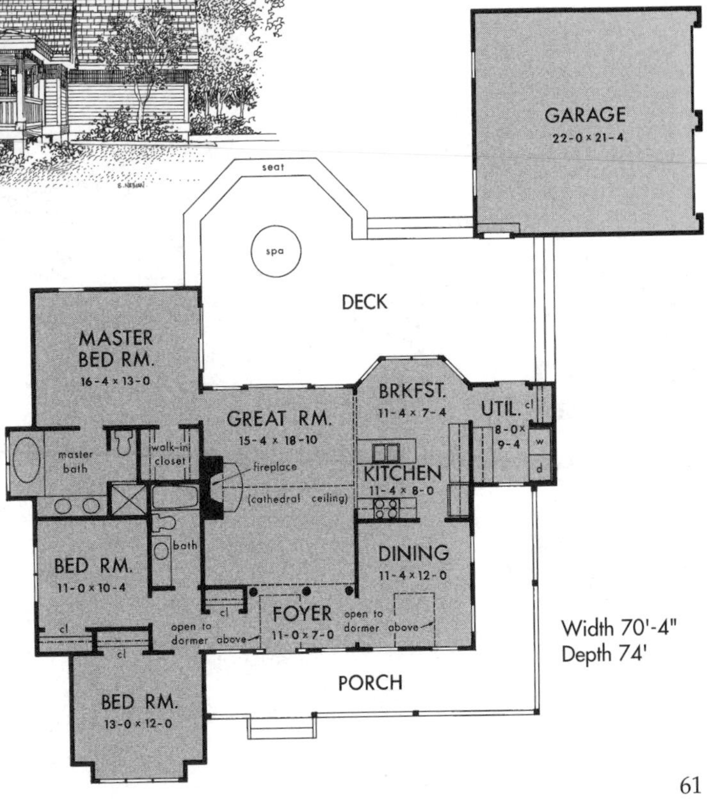

Width 70'-4"
Depth 74'

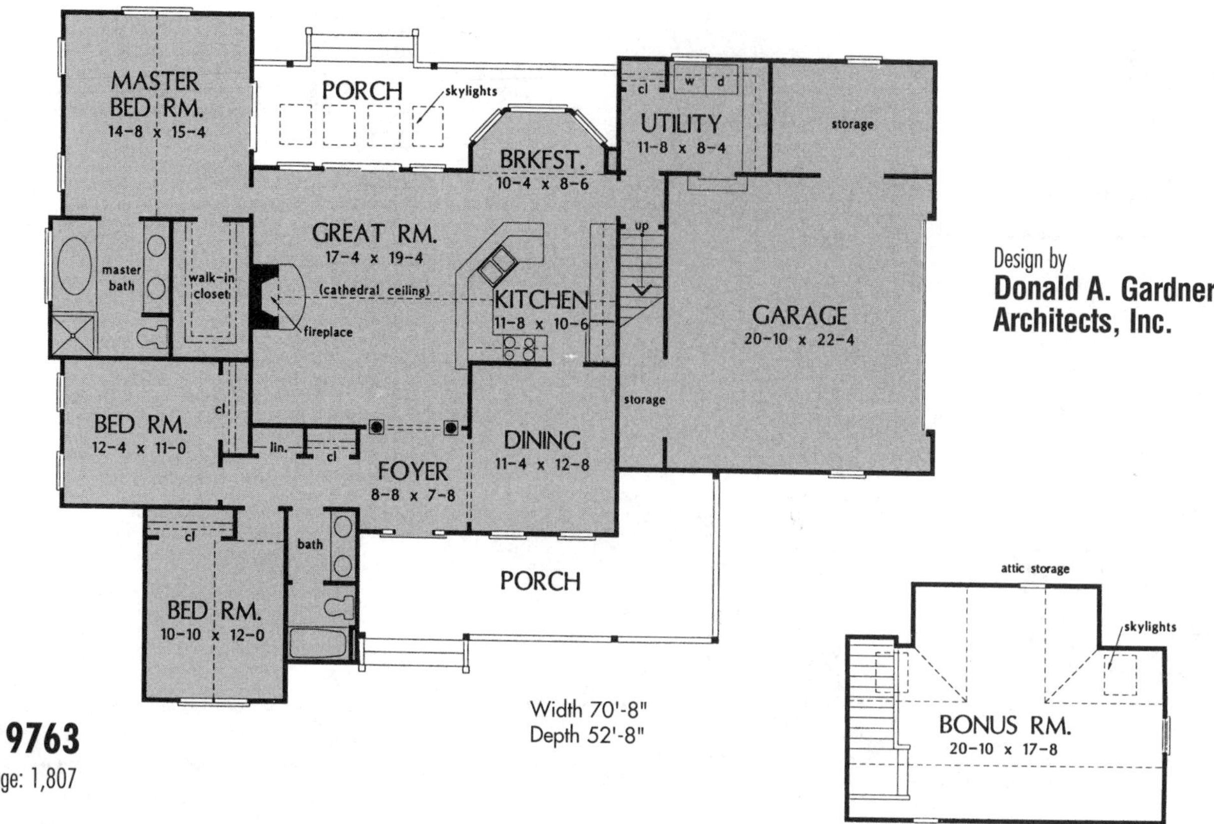
MASTER BED RM.
14-8 x 15-4
PORCH
skylights
BRKFST.
10-4 x 8-6
UTILITY
11-8 x 8-4
cl
w
d
storage
GREAT RM.
17-4 x 19-4
(cathedral ceiling)
fireplace
master bath
walk-in closet
KITCHEN
11-8 x 10-6
up
GARAGE
20-10 x 22-4
storage
BED RM.
12-4 x 11-0
cl
lin.
cl
FOYER
8-8 x 7-8
DINING
11-4 x 12-8
bath
cl
BED RM.
10-10 x 12-0
PORCH
Width 70'-8"
Depth 52'-8"
attic storage
skylights
BONUS RM.
20-10 x 17-8
attic storage

Design by
Donald A. Gardner, Architects, Inc.

Design 9763

Square Footage: 1,807

■ Dormers and arched windows provide this country home with lots of charm. An open kitchen easily serves the great room, the bayed breakfast area and the dining room. Outdoor living is enhanced with a skylit porch located on the rear of the plan. The master bedroom contains a huge walk-in closet and a private bath featuring a whirlpool tub, a separate shower and a double-bowl vanity. Two family bedrooms share a full bath. A bonus room over the garage can be developed as additional space is needed.

Design 9778

Square Footage: 1,655
Basement Option: 1,704 square feet

Design by
Donald A. Gardner, Architects, Inc.

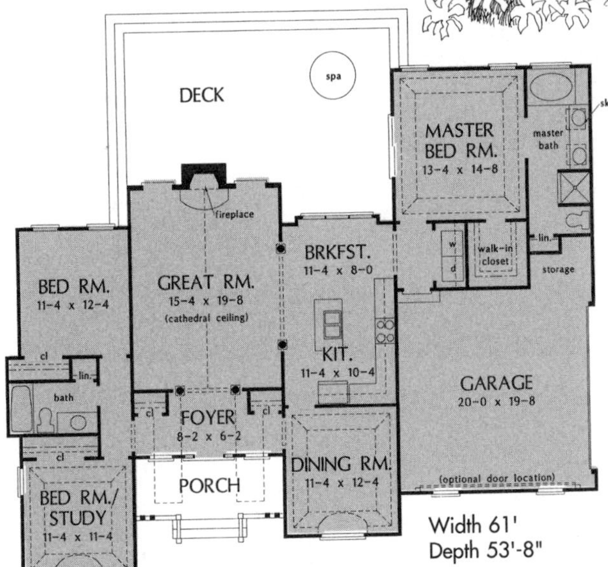
DECK
spa
MASTER BED RM. 13-4 x 14-8
master bath
skylights
fireplace
GREAT RM. 15-4 x 19-8 (cathedral ceiling)
BRKFST. 11-4 x 8-0
walk-in closet
lin.
storage
BED RM. 11-4 x 12-4
KIT. 11-4 x 10-4
GARAGE 20-0 x 19-8
bath
FOYER 8-2 x 6-2
DINING RM. 11-4 x 12-4
PORCH
BED RM./ STUDY 11-4 x 11-4
(optional door location)

Width 61'
Depth 53'-8"

■ Covered front porch dormers and arched windows welcome you to this popular country house. Interior columns open the foyer and the kitchen to the spacious great room. The kitchen, with its food preparation island, easily serves the breakfast area and the formal dining room. The master suite has a tray ceiling and access to the rear deck. Added luxuries include a walk-in closet and a skylit master bath with a double vanity, a garden tub and a shower. Two generous family bedrooms share the second bath. Please specify basement or crawlspace foundation when ordering.

Design 9794

Square Footage: 1,633
Bonus Rooms: 595 square feet

■ This charming country home is ready to grow and change as the family's space needs evolve. For example, one of the two family bedrooms would make a fine study and the bonus room upstairs can be finished off to make a great game room or loft. A soaring cathedral ceiling and a cozy fireplace highlight the great room. The kitchen is thoughtfully set between the dining and breakfast rooms. The master bedroom is also crowned with a cathedral ceiling and has a walk-in closet.

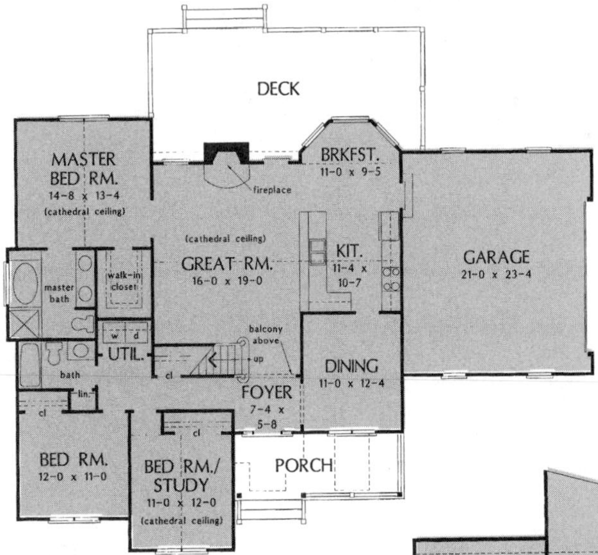

Width 65'-4"
Depth 55'-4"

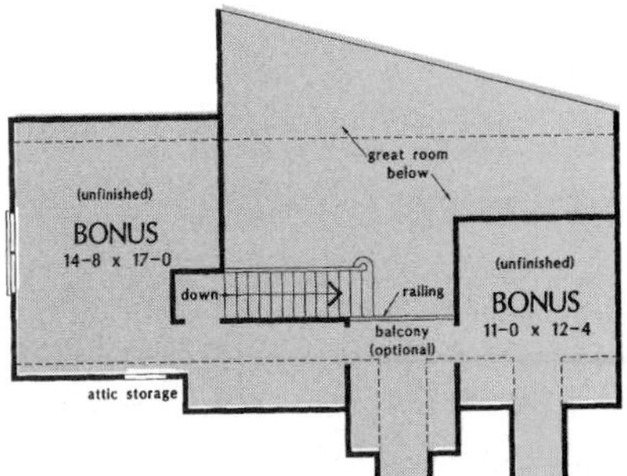

Design by
Donald A. Gardner, Architects, Inc.

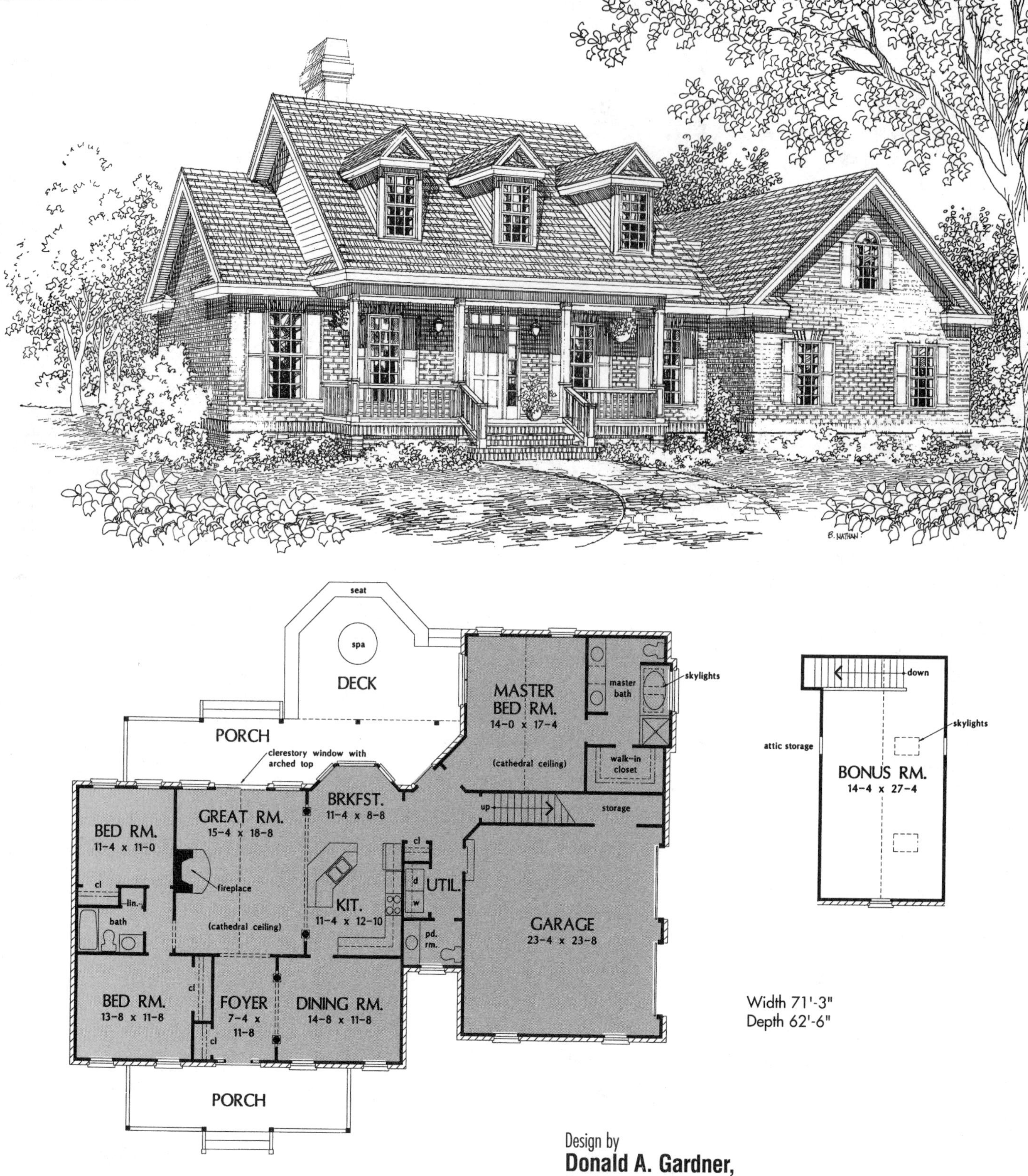

B. NATHAN
seat
spa
DECK
PORCH
clerestory window with arched top
MASTER BED RM.
14-0 x 17-4
(cathedral ceiling)
master bath
skylights
walk-in closet
storage
up
BRKFST.
11-4 x 8-8
GREAT RM.
15-4 x 18-8
fireplace
(cathedral ceiling)
BED RM.
11-4 x 11-0
cl
lin.
bath
KIT.
11-4 x 12-10
cl
d
w
UTIL.
pd. rm.
GARAGE
23-4 x 23-8
BED RM.
13-8 x 11-8
cl
cl
FOYER
7-4 x 11-8
DINING RM.
14-8 x 11-8
PORCH
down
skylights
attic storage
BONUS RM.
14-4 x 27-4
Width 71'-3"
Depth 62'-6"

Design by
Donald A. Gardner, Architects, Inc.

Design 9742

Square Footage: 1,954
Bonus Room: 436 square feet

■ This beautiful brick country home has all the amenities needed for today's active family. Covered front and back porches along with a rear deck provide plenty of room for outdoor enjoyment. Inside, the focus is on the large great room with its cathedral ceiling and welcoming fireplace. To the right, columns separate the kitchen and breakfast room while keeping this area open. Resident gourmets will certainly appreciate the convenience of the kitchen with its center island and breakfast nook. The master bedroom provides a splendid private retreat, featuring a cathedral ceiling and a large walk-in closet. A double-bowl vanity, a separate shower and a relaxing skylit whirlpool tub enhance the luxurious master bath. At the opposite end of the plan, two additional bedrooms share a full bath. A skylit bonus room above the garage allows for additional living space.

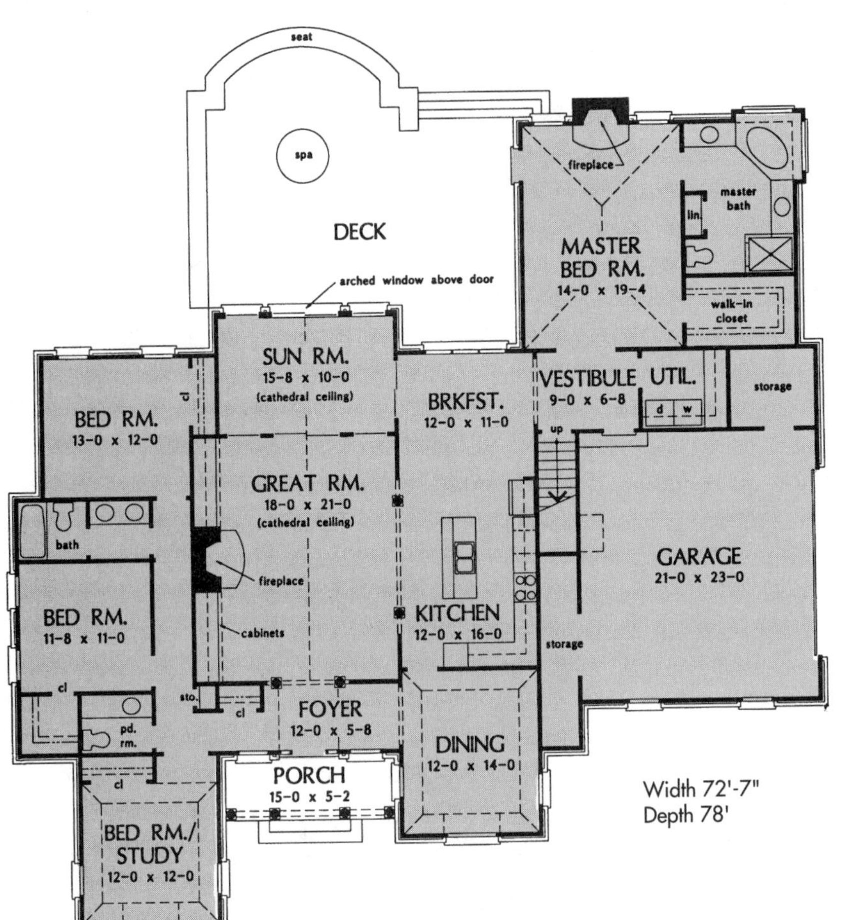
seat
spa
DECK
arched window above door
fireplace
master bath
lin.
MASTER BED RM. 14-0 x 19-4
walk-in closet
SUN RM. 15-8 x 10-0 (cathedral ceiling)
BED RM. 13-0 x 12-0
cl
BRKFST. 12-0 x 11-0
VESTIBULE 9-0 x 6-8
UTIL.
d w
storage
up
GREAT RM. 18-0 x 21-0 (cathedral ceiling)
bath
fireplace
GARAGE 21-0 x 23-0
BED RM. 11-8 x 11-0
cabinets
KITCHEN 12-0 x 16-0
storage
cl
sto.
cl
FOYER 12-0 x 5-8
pd. rm.
DINING 12-0 x 14-0
cl
PORCH 15-0 x 5-2
BED RM./ STUDY 12-0 x 12-0

skylights
BONUS RM. 33-3 x 17-10
attic storage
down
down

Width 72'-7"
Depth 78'

Design 9709

Square Footage: 2,663
Bonus Room: 653 square feet

■ This home features large arched windows, round columns, a covered porch, and brick veneer siding. The arched window in the clerestory above the entrance provides natural light to the interior. The great room boasts a cathedral ceiling, a fireplace, built-in cabinets and bookshelves. Sliding glass doors lead to the sun room. The L-shaped kitchen services the dining room, the breakfast area, and the great room. The master bedroom suite, with a fireplace, uses private passage to the deck and its spa. Three additional bedrooms—one could serve as a study—are at the other end of the house for privacy

Design by
Donald A. Gardner, Architects, Inc.

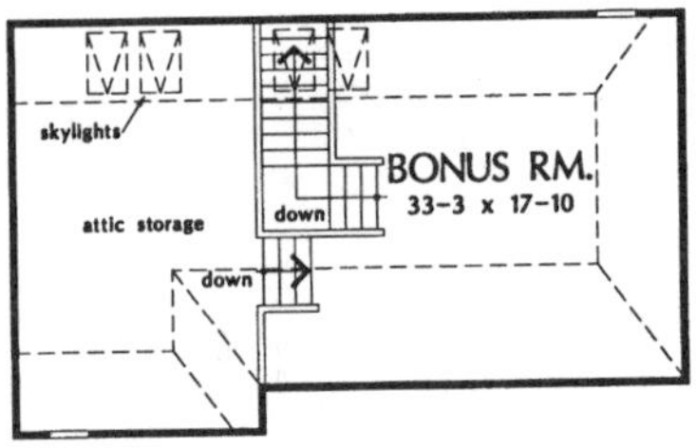

B. NATHAN

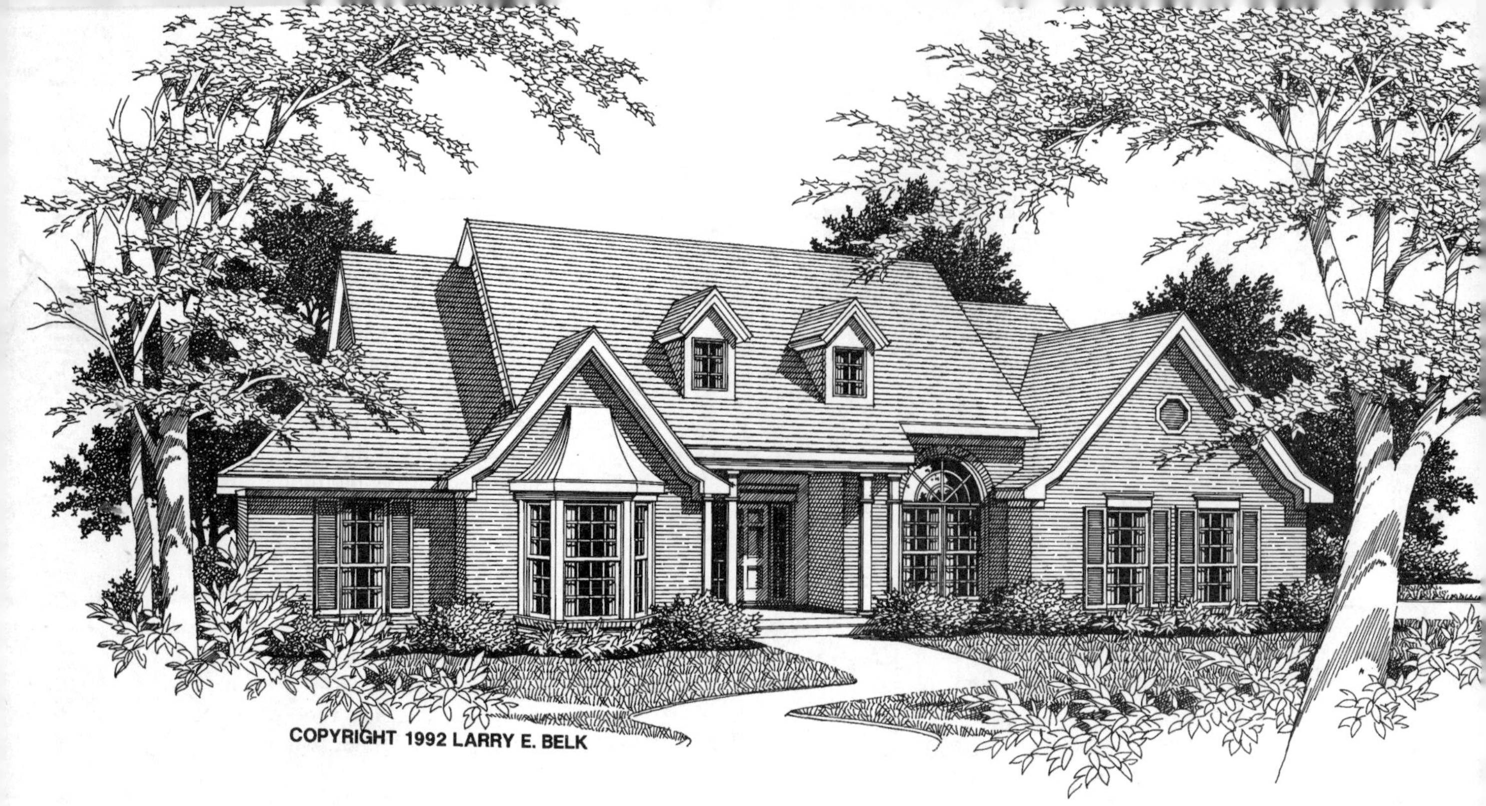

PLANT LEDGE
MASTER BATH
ARCH
F/P
BREAKFAST
10' CLG.
FAMILY ROOM
10' CLG.
13'4" X 14'8"
MASTER BEDROOM
CATHEDRAL CLG.
14'4" X 17'4"
PATIO
BEDROOM 2
PLANT LEDGE
8' CLG.
W.I.C.
LIVING ROOM
10' CLG.
17' X 18'8"
KITCHEN
10' CLG.
13'8" X 12'6"
PDR.
REAR ENTRY
UTIL.
BATH 2
10' CLG.
W.I.C.
PAN.
FOYER
DINING ROOM
10' CLG.
11'8" X 13'4"
2 CAR GARAGE
BEDROOM 3
11' X 11'6"
CLO.
BEDROOM 4 /STUDY
COFFERED CLG.
11'6" X 18'
W.I.C.
RAISED PORCH
PORCH

Width 70'
Depth 65'-6"

Design 8070

Square Footage: 2,561

■ This split-bedroom plan makes a strong impact as the angled foyer steps down into the living room, where built-in display shelving on either side gives plenty of room for collectibles or books. The family room and kitchen are conveniently grouped with the gazebo breakfast room to provide a large area for family gatherings and informal entertaining. The master suite is entered through angled double doors. The luxury bath awaits with a whirlpool tub as the centerpiece. His and Hers vanities, a shower and two large walk-in closets are standard. Three family bedrooms with large walk-in closets and a roomy bath complete this best-selling plan. Please specify crawlspace or slab foundation when ordering.

Design by
Larry E. Belk Designs

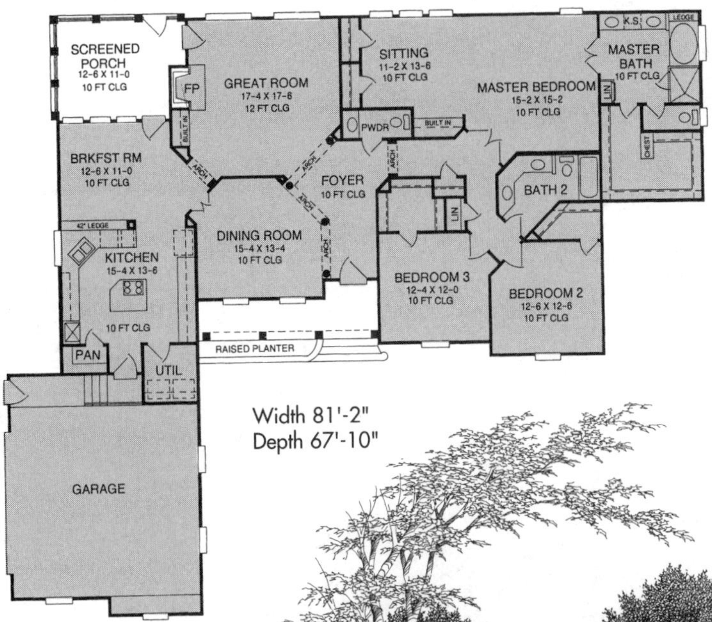

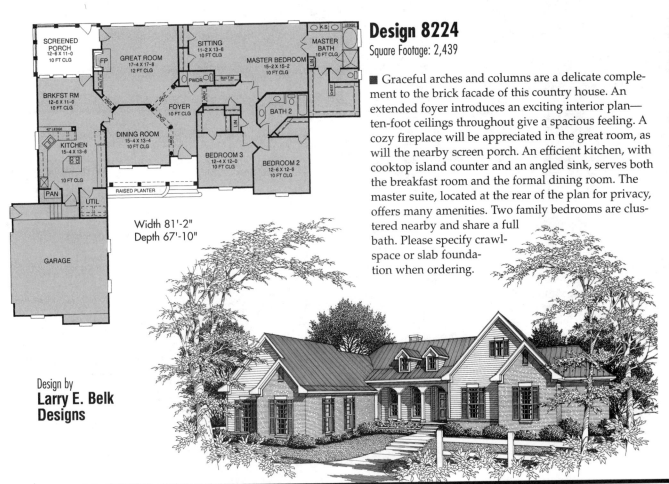

Design 8224

Square Footage: 2,439

■ Graceful arches and columns are a delicate complement to the brick facade of this country house. An extended foyer introduces an exciting interior plan—ten-foot ceilings throughout give a spacious feeling. A cozy fireplace will be appreciated in the great room, as will the nearby screen porch. An efficient kitchen, with cooktop island counter and an angled sink, serves both the breakfast room and the formal dining room. The master suite, located at the rear of the plan for privacy, offers many amenities. Two family bedrooms are clustered nearby and share a full bath. Please specify crawlspace or slab foundation when ordering.

Width 81'-2"
Depth 67'-10"

Design by
Larry E. Belk Designs

Design 9695

Square Footage: 2,526

■ A covered front porch, an arched-window dormer and brick detailing all combine to give this home plenty of curb appeal. A cozy fireplace and built-in cabinets accent the great room. The island kitchen is partially open to the great room, maintaining a spacious feeling. The sunroom and breakfast area will surely brighten each day. The lovely master suite has a romantic fireplace and a pampering bath. Three bedrooms—or two with a study—one full bath and a powder room complete the plan. Please specify basement or crawlspace foundation when ordering.

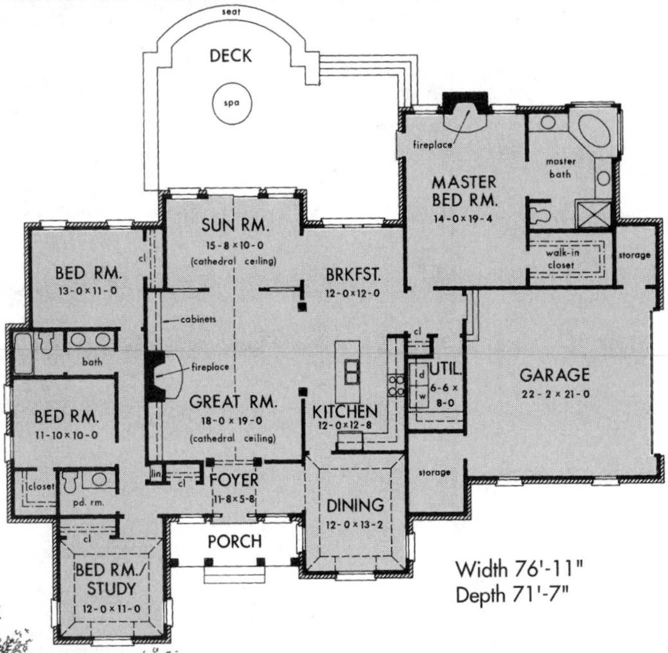

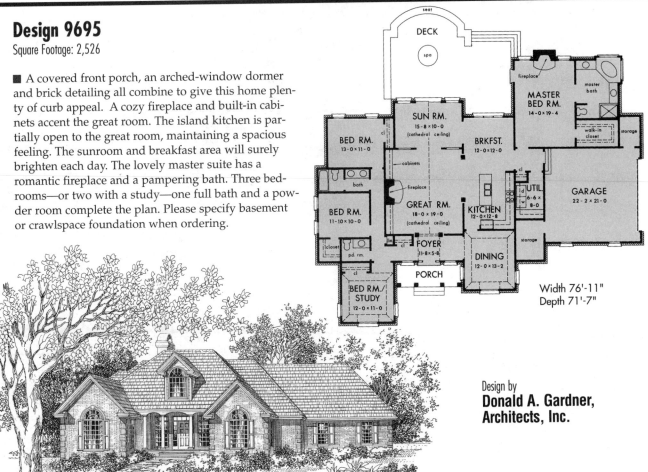

Width 76'-11"
Depth 71'-7"

Design by
Donald A. Gardner, Architects, Inc.

Design 8029

Square Footage: 3,461

■ This home has a commanding entry with an octagonal porch supported by large columns. Through the foyer is a large living room which opens to a covered porch. Flanking the foyer are the dining room and study. The gourmet kitchen has a small bay window over the sink and an adjacent breakfast area with a wet bar. The master bedroom and bath are spacious and provide ample closet space. Two family bedrooms share a hall bath while a fourth bedroom and a full bath are privately located off the kitchen area.

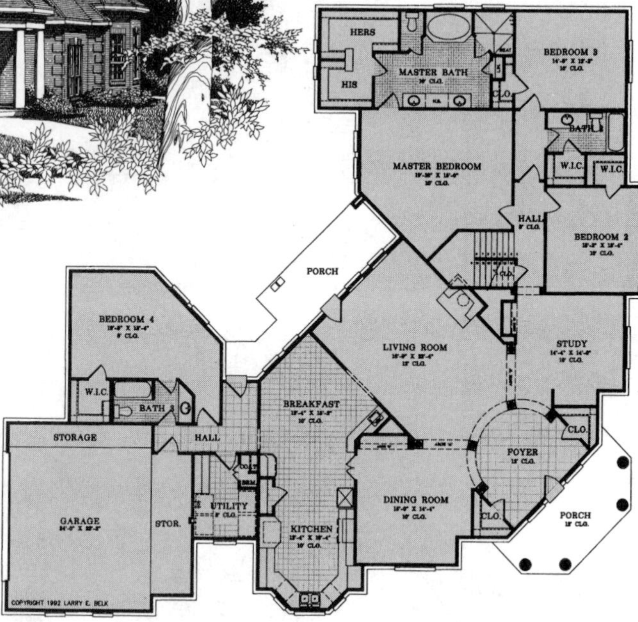

Design by
Larry E. Belk Designs

Width 87'
Depth 77'-4"

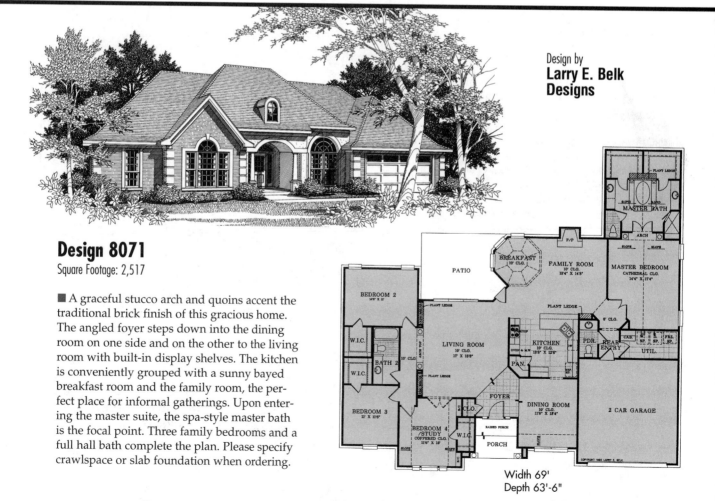

Design 8071

Square Footage: 2,517

■ A graceful stucco arch and quoins accent the traditional brick finish of this gracious home. The angled foyer steps down into the dining room on one side and on the other to the living room with built-in display shelves. The kitchen is conveniently grouped with a sunny bayed breakfast room and the family room, the perfect place for informal gatherings. Upon entering the master suite, the spa-style master bath is the focal point. Three family bedrooms and a full hall bath complete the plan. Please specify crawlspace or slab foundation when ordering.

Design by
Larry E. Belk Designs

Width 69'
Depth 63'-6"

Design 8000

Square Footage: 2,540

■ A gabled stucco entry with oversized columns emphasizes the arched glass entry of this winsome one-story brick home. Arched windows on either side of the front door add symmetry and style to this pleasing exterior. An arched passage, which leads to the three family bedrooms, flanked by twin bookcases and a plant ledge provides focal interest to the living room. Bedroom 4 may also be a study, and can be entered from double French doors off the living room. A large, efficient kitchen shares space with an octagonal breakfast area and a family room with a fireplace. The master bedroom is entered through angled double doors and features a cathedral ceiling. Attention centers immediately on the arched entry to the relaxing master bath and its central whirlpool tub. Please specify crawlspace or slab foundation when ordering.

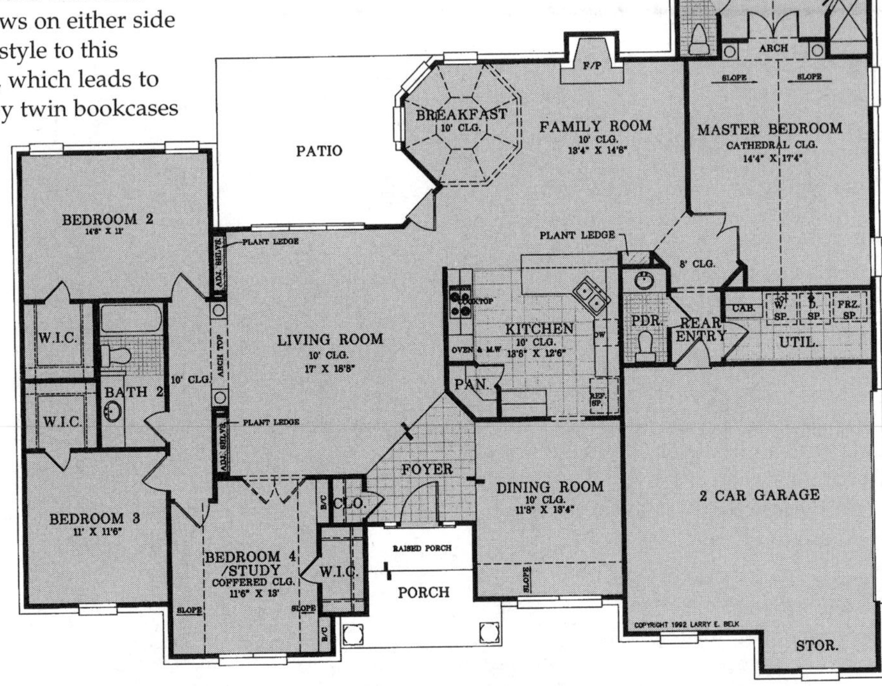
MASTER BATH
ARCH
F/P
BREAKFAST
10' CLG.
FAMILY ROOM
10' CLG.
13'4" X 14'8"
MASTER BEDROOM
CATHEDRAL CLG.
14'4" X 17'4"
PATIO
BEDROOM 2
PLANT LEDGE
8' CLG.
W.I.C.
BATH 2
10' CLG.
LIVING ROOM
10' CLG.
17' X 18'8"
KITCHEN
10' CLG.
13'6" X 12'6"
PDR.
REAR ENTRY
CAB.
UTIL.
PAN.
FOYER
DINING ROOM
10' CLG.
11'8" X 13'4"
2 CAR GARAGE
BEDROOM 3
11' X 11'6"
BEDROOM 4
/STUDY
COFFERED CLG.
11'6" X 13'
W.I.C.
CLO.
RAISED PORCH
PORCH
STOR.

Width 70'
Depth 65'

Design by
Larry E. Belk Designs

Design 9258

Square Footage: 2,498

■ Elegant arches at the covered entry of this home give way to beautiful views of the formal dining room and living room inside. Ceilings in the main living areas and the master bedroom are vaulted. The gazebo dinette is open to the family room and to the gourmet kitchen, which includes an island cooktop and snack bar. Two bedrooms and a den share a compartmented hall bath. Bedroom 3 could become a sitting area for the master suite, if desired. A luxurious master bath provides twin vanities, a large walk-in closet and an oval whirlpool tub.

Design by
Design Basics, Inc.

WHIRLPOOL
TRANSOMS
Bfst.
11³x11³
Kit.
13⁰x14⁰
SNACK BAR
Liv. rm.
15⁰x16⁹
11' - 0" CEILING
Mbr.
15⁰x16⁰
11' - 0" CEILING
Fam. rm.
18⁸x15³
DESK
BOOKS
Br. 3
11'x12⁰
OPT. SITTING
LINEN
DN
Din.
12⁰x14⁰
11' - 0" CLG.
HUTCH
E.
Den
12⁰x13²
OPT. BEDROOM
12' - 0" CLG.
Br. 2
12⁷x11²
Gar.
30⁰x21⁸
COVERED PORCH

Width 76'
Depth 55'-4"

Design 8124

Square Footage: 2,350
Bonus Room: 286 square feet

■ This gracious plan is designed to grow with the family, thanks to the optional nursery/sitting room off the master suite and the expandable area upstairs. A corner fireplace and bright windows to the porch highlight the great room. The wraparound kitchen has plenty of cabinet and counter space, a snack bar and breakfast nook. The master suite has a large bath with a walk-in closet. Two family bedrooms share a full hall bath. Please specify crawlspace or slab foundation when ordering.

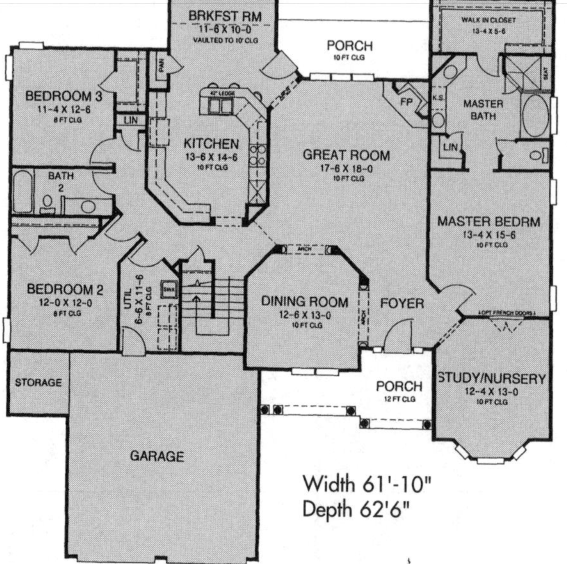
BRKFST RM
11-6 X 10-0
PORCH
10 FT CLG
WALK IN CLOSET
13-4 X 5-6
BEDROOM 3
11-4 X 12-6
8 FT CLG
LIN
KITCHEN
13-6 X 14-6
10 FT CLG
GREAT ROOM
17-6 X 18-0
10 FT CLG
FP
MASTER BATH
LIN
BATH 2
MASTER BEDRM
13-4 X 15-6
10 FT CLG
BEDROOM 2
12-0 X 12-0
8 FT CLG
UTIL
6-6 X 11-6
DINING ROOM
12-6 X 13-0
10 FT CLG
FOYER
STORAGE
PORCH
12 FT CLG
STUDY/NURSERY
12-4 X 13-0
10 FT CLG
GARAGE

Width 61'-10"
Depth 62'6"

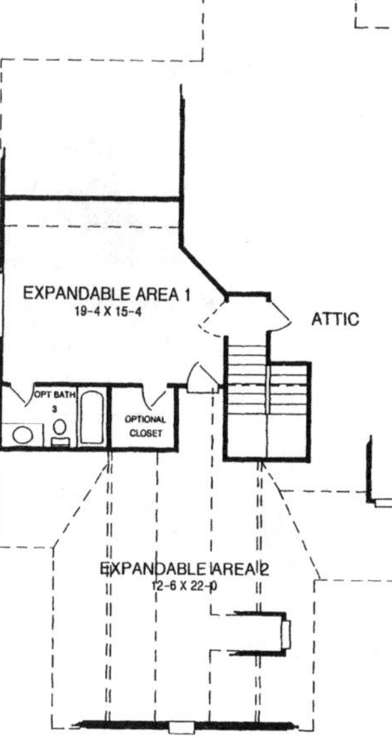
EXPANDABLE AREA 1
19-4 X 15-4
ATTIC
OPT BATH 3
OPTIONAL CLOSET
EXPANDABLE AREA 2
12-6 X 22-0

Design by
Larry E. Belk Designs

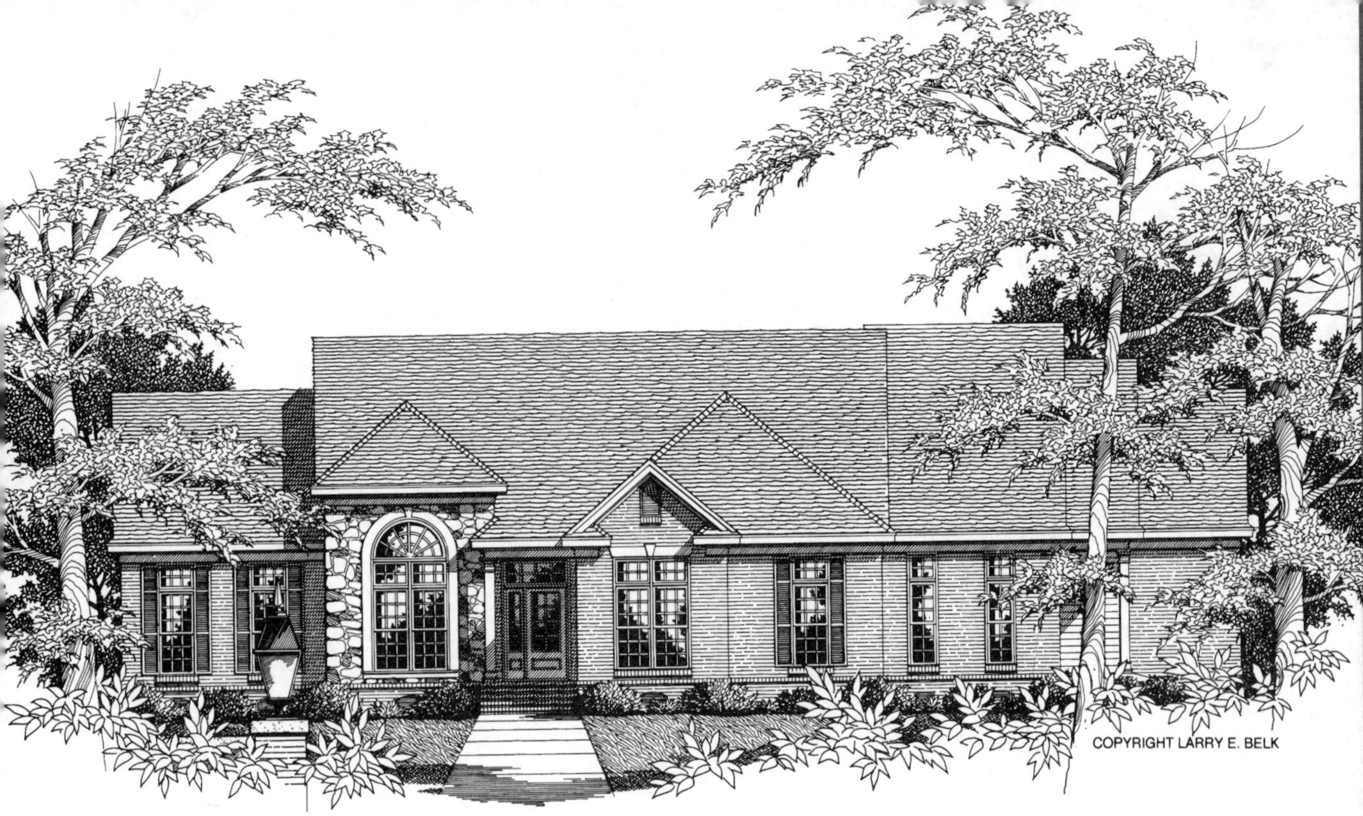

Design 8243

Square Footage: 2,445

■ An arch-top muntin window sets off a refined blend of natural materials on this traditional exterior, while staggered gables give it an eclectic splash. A dazzling arched foyer leads to the formal living room and to the expansive great room, complete with a focal-point fireplace. French doors framed by dramatic archways open to the rear property and set an elegant tone for the interior. A split bedroom plan places the master suite in the left wing. A corner whirlpool tub, a knee-space vanity and two walk-in closets highlight the master bath. Three family bedrooms share a private hall and a full bath.

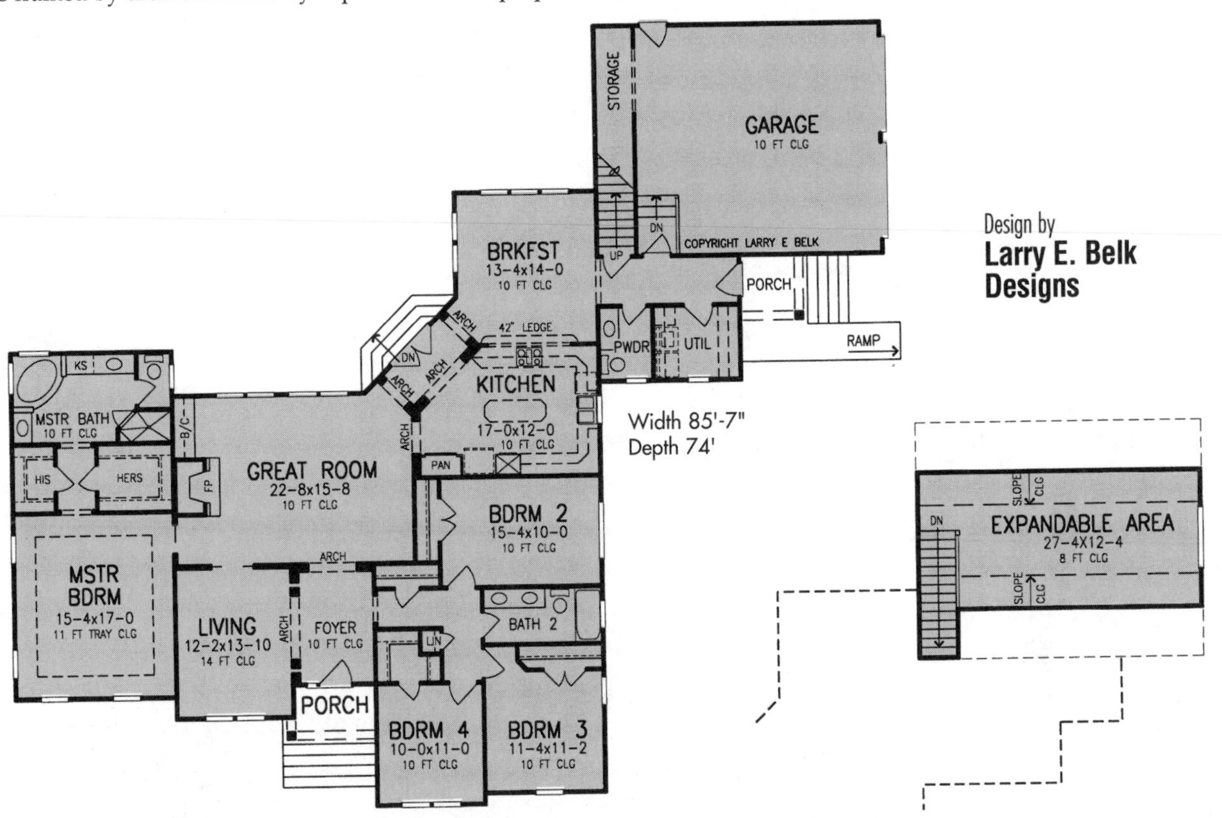
STORAGE
GARAGE
10 FT CLG
COPYRIGHT LARRY E BELK
DN
UP
PORCH
RAMP
BRKFST
13-4x14-0
10 FT CLG
42" LEDGE
ARCH
DN
KITCHEN
17-0x12-0
10 FT CLG
PAN
PWDR
UTIL
KS
MSTR BATH
10 FT CLG
HIS
HERS
B/C
FP
GREAT ROOM
22-8x15-8
10 FT CLG
BDRM 2
15-4x10-0
10 FT CLG
MSTR
BDRM
15-4x17-0
11 FT TRAY CLG
LIVING
12-2x13-10
14 FT CLG
FOYER
10 FT CLG
BATH 2
LIN
PORCH
BDRM 4
10-0x11-0
10 FT CLG
BDRM 3
11-4x11-2
10 FT CLG
Width 85'-7"
Depth 74'
Design by
Larry E. Belk
Designs
EXPANDABLE AREA
27-4x12-4
8 FT CLG
SLOPE
CLG

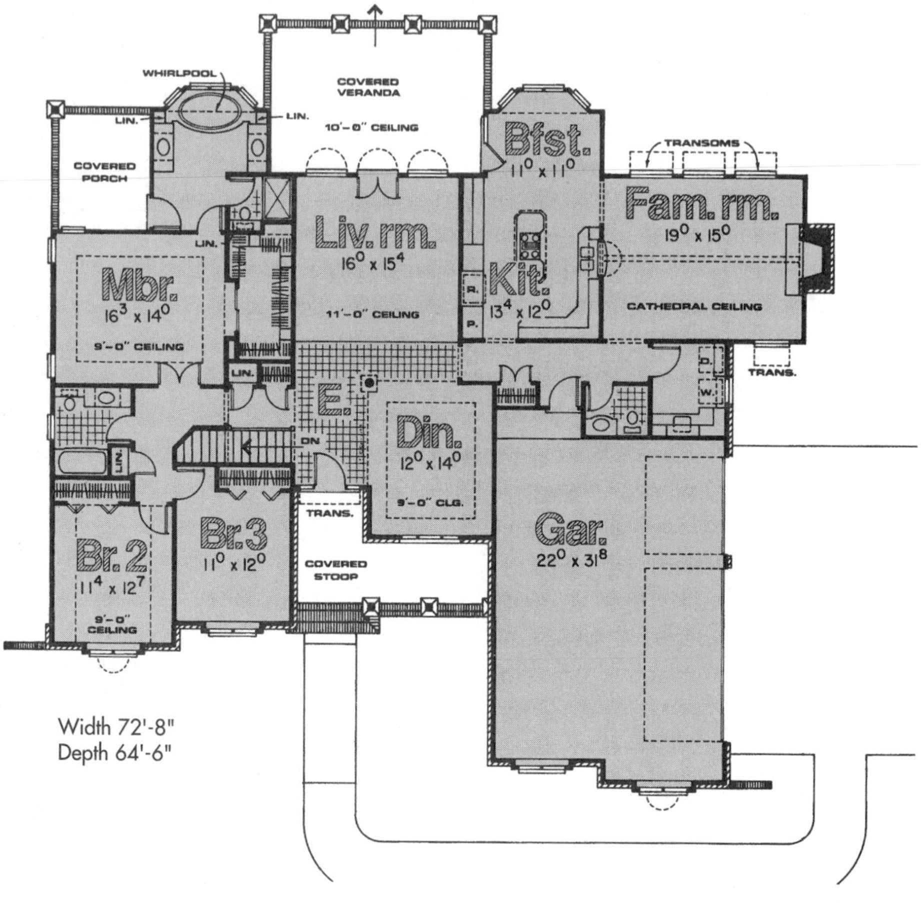

Design 7274

Square Footage: 2,399

■ Interesting window treatments and a charming porch extend the attention-getting nature of this brick ranch home. Beyond the covered porch, the entry showcases the formal dining room to the right and the multi-windowed living room straight ahead. The L-shaped kitchen features an island cooktop and blends with the bay-windowed breakfast room and welcoming family room to create a comfortable area for family gatherings. Located for privacy, the master suite includes a huge walk-in closet. A covered porch accessed from the master bath offers a wonderful outdoor retreat. The amenity-filled master bath contains twin vanities and an oval whirlpool tub. Two secondary bedrooms share a full bath.

Width 72'-8"
Depth 64'-6"

Design by
Design Basics, Inc.

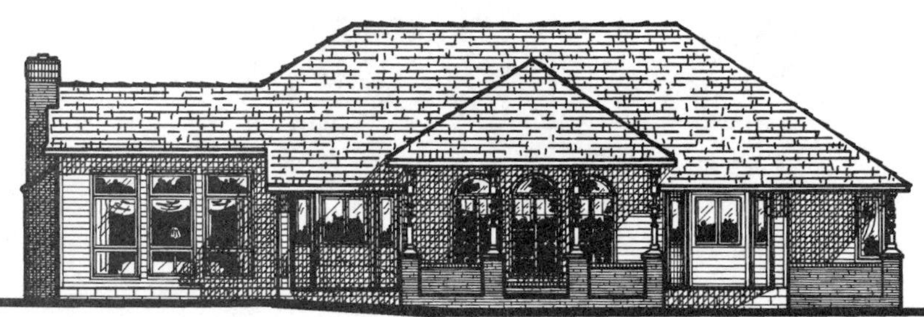

Design 9375

Square Footage: 2,456

Design by
Design Basics, Inc.

■ Tapered columns at the entry create a majestic front elevation. Inside, an open great room features a wet bar, a fireplace, tall windows and access to the covered porch with skylights. An oversized kitchen features a prep island, two pantries and easy laundry access. Double doors open to the master suite where French doors lead to the master bath and the covered porch. The master bath provides beauty and convenience with a whirlpool, dual sinks and a large walk-in closet. Two secondary bedrooms share a compartmented bath.

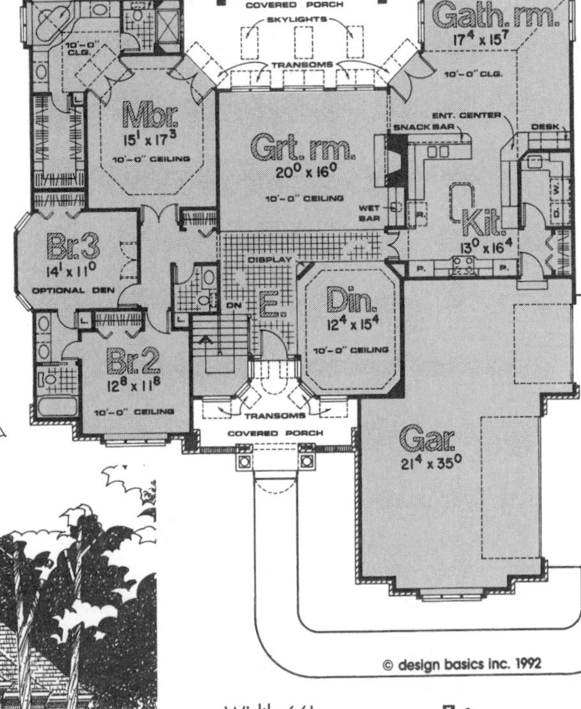
WHIRLPOOL
LIN.
COVERED PORCH
SKYLIGHTS
TRANSOMS
Gath. rm.
17⁴ x 15⁷
10'-0" CLG.
Mbr.
15¹ x 17³
10'-0" CEILING
10'-0" CLG.
Grt. rm.
20⁰ x 16⁰
10'-0" CEILING
ENT. CENTER
SNACK BAR
DESK
WET BAR
Kit.
13⁰ x 16⁴
Br. 3
14¹ x 11⁰
OPTIONAL DEN
DISPLAY
DN
E.
Din.
12⁴ x 15⁴
10'-0" CEILING
Br. 2
12⁶ x 11⁶
10'-0" CEILING
TRANSOMS
COVERED PORCH
Gar.
21⁴ x 35⁰
© design basics inc. 1992

Width 66'
Depth 68'

QUOTE ONE®

Cost to build? See page 342 to order complete cost estimate to build this house in your area!

Design 7276

Square Footage: 2,598

Design by
Design Basics, Inc.

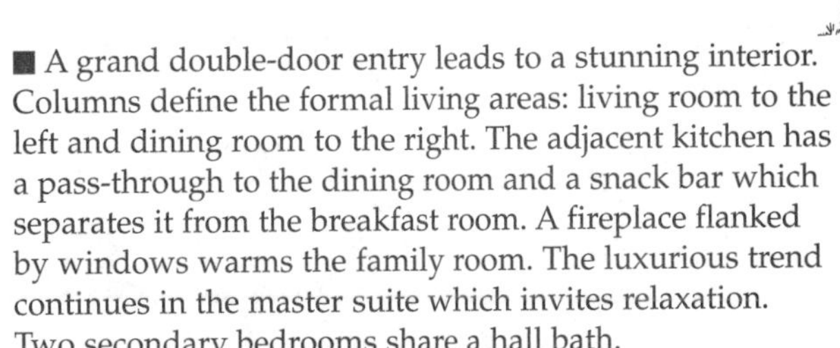

■ A grand double-door entry leads to a stunning interior. Columns define the formal living areas: living room to the left and dining room to the right. The adjacent kitchen has a pass-through to the dining room and a snack bar which separates it from the breakfast room. A fireplace flanked by windows warms the family room. The luxurious trend continues in the master suite which invites relaxation. Two secondary bedrooms share a hall bath.

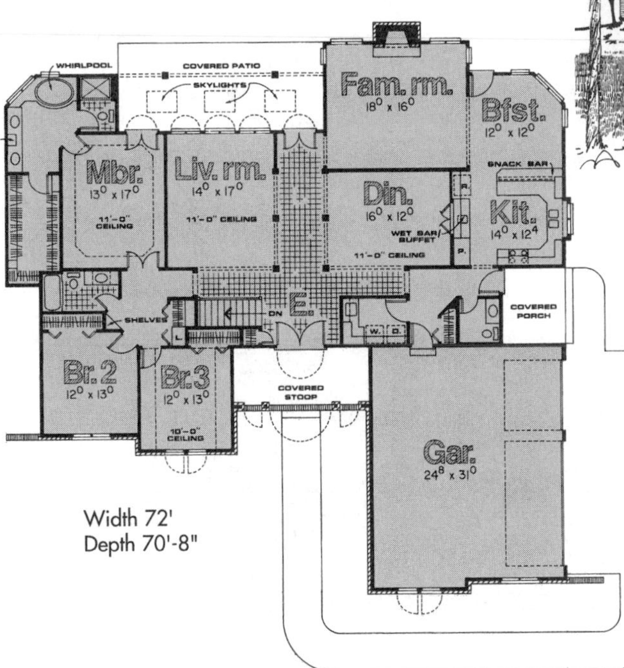
WHIRLPOOL
COVERED PATIO
SKYLIGHTS
Fam. rm.
18⁰ x 16⁰
Bfst.
12⁰ x 12⁰
LIN.
Mbr.
13⁰ x 17⁰
11'-0" CEILING
Liv. rm.
14⁰ x 17⁰
11'-0" CEILING
Din.
16⁰ x 12⁰
WET BAR/BUFFET
11'-0" CEILING
SNACK BAR
Kit.
14⁰ x 12⁴
SHELVES
DN
E.
COVERED PORCH
Br. 2
12⁰ x 13⁰
Br. 3
12⁰ x 13⁰
10'-0" CEILING
COVERED STOOP
Gar.
24⁸ x 31⁰

Width 72'
Depth 70'-8"

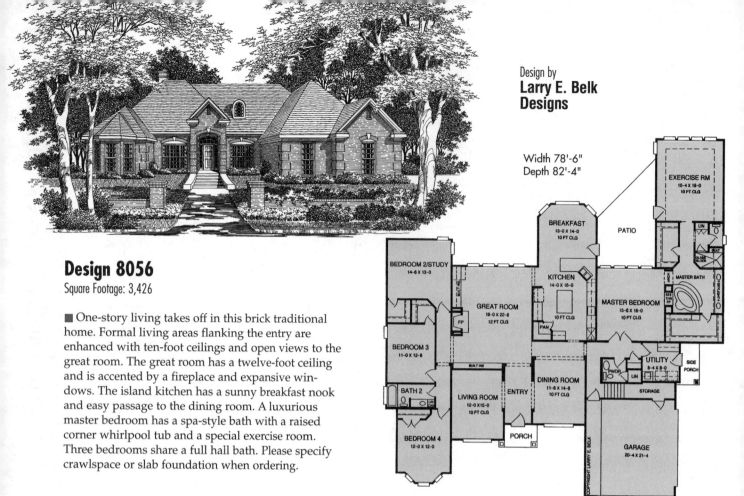

Design by
Larry E. Belk Designs

Width 78'-6"
Depth 82'-4"

Design 8056

Square Footage: 3,426

■ One-story living takes off in this brick traditional home. Formal living areas flanking the entry are enhanced with ten-foot ceilings and open views to the great room. The great room has a twelve-foot ceiling and is accented by a fireplace and expansive windows. The island kitchen has a sunny breakfast nook and easy passage to the dining room. A luxurious master bedroom has a spa-style bath with a raised corner whirlpool tub and a special exercise room. Three bedrooms share a full hall bath. Please specify crawlspace or slab foundation when ordering.

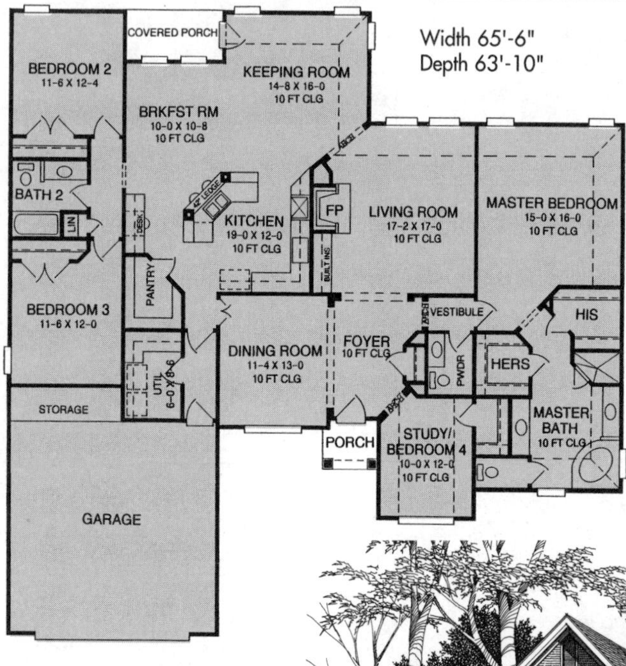

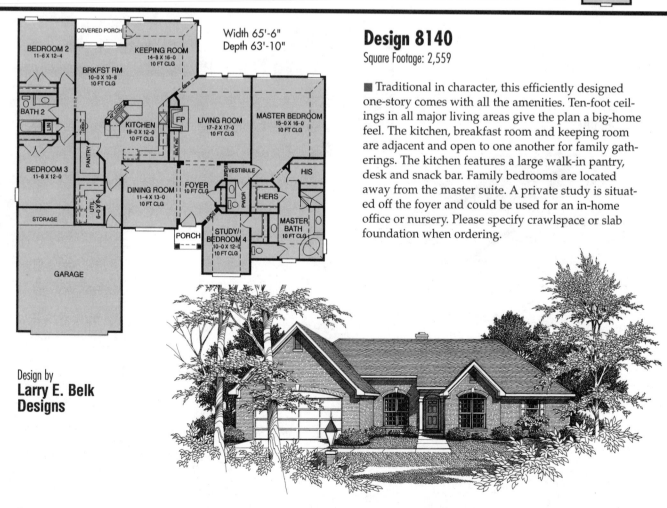

Width 65'-6"
Depth 63'-10"

Design 8140

Square Footage: 2,559

■ Traditional in character, this efficiently designed one-story comes with all the amenities. Ten-foot ceilings in all major living areas give the plan a big-home feel. The kitchen, breakfast room and keeping room are adjacent and open to one another for family gatherings. The kitchen features a large walk-in pantry, desk and snack bar. Family bedrooms are located away from the master suite. A private study is situated off the foyer and could be used for an in-home office or nursery. Please specify crawlspace or slab foundation when ordering.

Design by
Larry E. Belk Designs

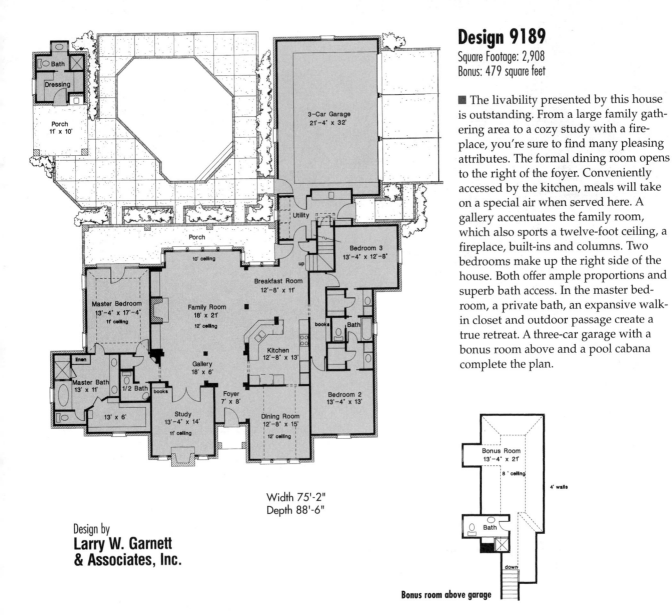

Design 9189

Square Footage: 2,908
Bonus: 479 square feet

■ The livability presented by this house is outstanding. From a large family gathering area to a cozy study with a fireplace, you're sure to find many pleasing attributes. The formal dining room opens to the right of the foyer. Conveniently accessed by the kitchen, meals will take on a special air when served here. A gallery accentuates the family room, which also sports a twelve-foot ceiling, a fireplace, built-ins and columns. Two bedrooms make up the right side of the house. Both offer ample proportions and superb bath access. In the master bedroom, a private bath, an expansive walk-in closet and outdoor passage create a true retreat. A three-car garage with a bonus room above and a pool cabana complete the plan.

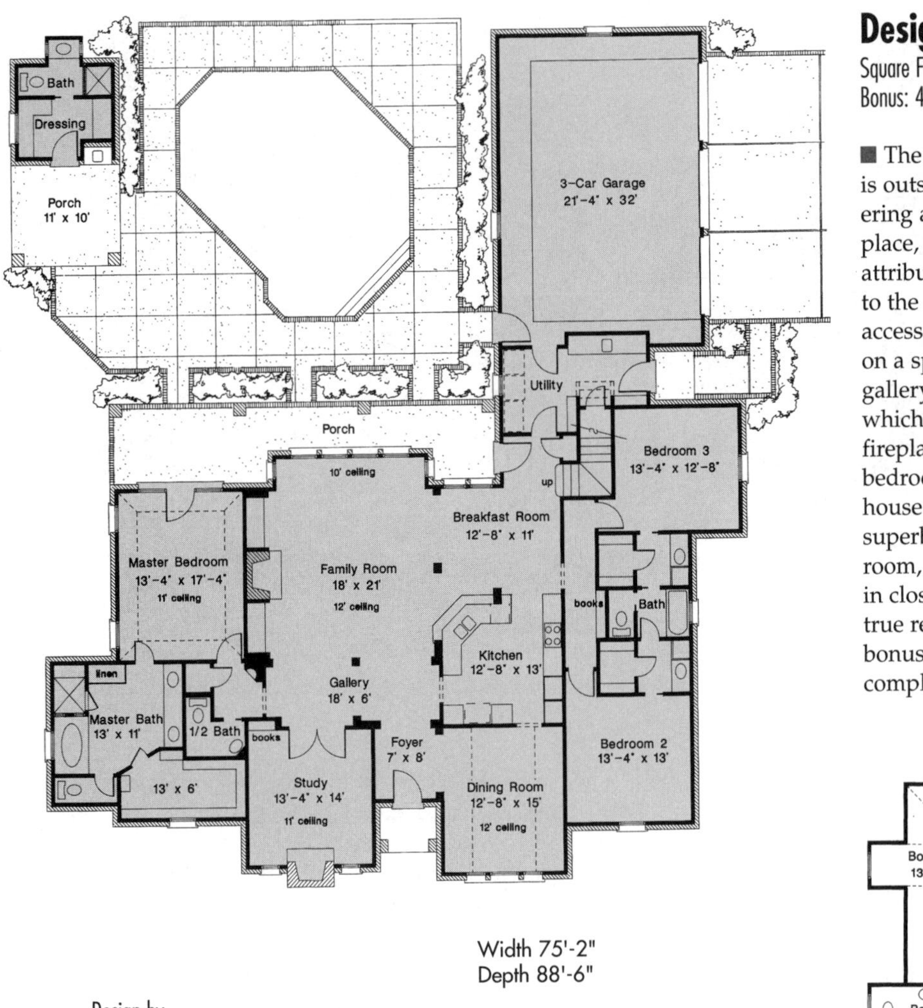
Bath
Dressing
Porch
11' x 10'
3-Car Garage
21'-4" x 32'
Utility
Porch
Bedroom 3
13'-4" x 12'-8"
10' ceiling
up
Breakfast Room
12'-8" x 11'
Master Bedroom
13'-4" x 17'-4"
11' ceiling
Family Room
18' x 21'
12' ceiling
books
Bath
Kitchen
12'-8" x 13'
linen
Gallery
18' x 6'
Master Bath
13' x 11'
1/2 Bath
books
Foyer
7' x 8'
Bedroom 2
13'-4" x 13'
13' x 6'
Study
13'-4" x 14'
11' ceiling
Dining Room
12'-8" x 15'
12' ceiling

Width 75'-2"
Depth 88'-6"

Design by
Larry W. Garnett & Associates, Inc.

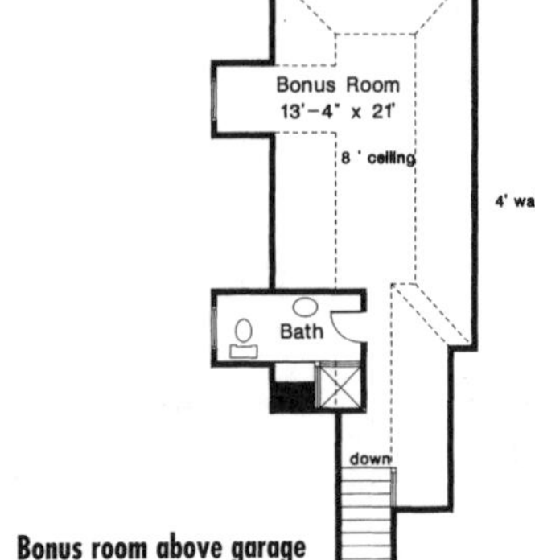
Bonus Room
13'-4" x 21'
8' ceiling
4' walls
Bath
down

Bonus room above garage

Design 8053

Square Footage: 2,506

■ A traditional exterior accented by triple gables introduces this well-appointed one-story. Columns with connecting arched openings define the formal dining room and create a dramatic entrance. An efficiently planned kitchen faces the spacious family room and breakfast room. The corner fireplace with a raised hearth bids a warm welcome, making this a splendid area for informal entertaining. The romantic master suite is designed with a fireplace and an exercise room that includes space for a tanning bed. The master bath has large His and Hers walk-in closets as well as His and Hers baths with separate entrances to a shared shower. Two additional bedrooms featuring walk-in closets and separate dressing areas are located on the opposite side of the home. Please specify crawlspace or slab foundation when ordering.

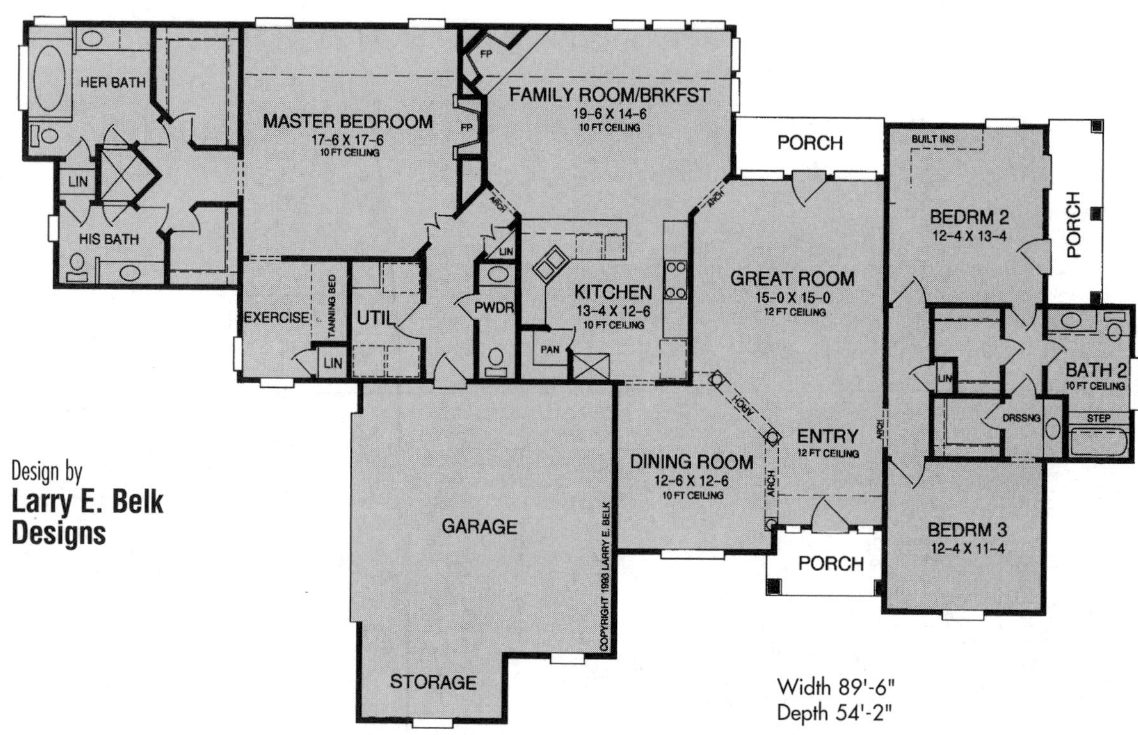

HER BATH
LIN
HIS BATH
MASTER BEDROOM
17-6 X 17-6
10 FT CEILING
FP
FAMILY ROOM/BRKFST
19-6 X 14-6
10 FT CEILING
PORCH
BUILT INS
BEDRM 2
12-4 X 13-4
PORCH
EXERCISE
TANNING BED
UTIL
LIN
PWDR
KITCHEN
13-4 X 12-6
10 FT CEILING
PAN
GREAT ROOM
15-0 X 15-0
12 FT CEILING
BATH 2
10 FT CEILING
DRSSNG
STEP
ARCH
ENTRY
12 FT CEILING
DINING ROOM
12-6 X 12-6
10 FT CEILING
GARAGE
COPYRIGHT 1993 LARRY E. BELK
PORCH
BEDRM 3
12-4 X 11-4
STORAGE

Design by
Larry E. Belk Designs

Width 89'-6"
Depth 54'-2"

QUOTE ONE®

Cost to build? See page 342 to order complete cost estimate to build this house in your area!

Design by
Larry W. Garnett & Associates, Inc.

Design 8923

Square Footage: 2,361

■ The combination of finely detailed brick and shingle siding recalls some of the distinctive architecture of the East Coast. The foyer and gallery provide for a functional traffic pattern. The formal dining room to the front of the home is outlined by columns and features a thirteen-foot ceiling. The extensive living area offers a corner fireplace. A screened porch surrounding the breakfast room is an ideal entertainment area. The master suite features two spacious closets and a bath with a garden tub and an oversized shower. Bedroom 4 can serve as a study, nursery, guest room, or home office.

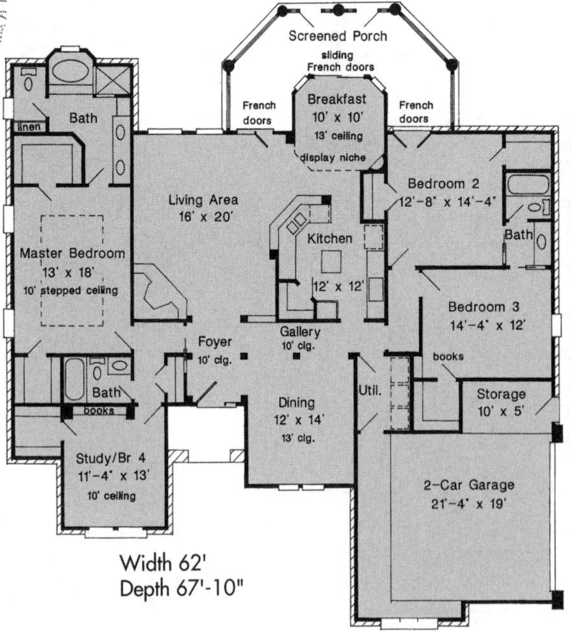
Screened Porch
sliding French doors
French doors
Breakfast 10' x 10' 13' ceiling
display niche
French doors
Bath
linen
Living Area 16' x 20'
Bedroom 2 12'-8" x 14'-4"
Kitchen 12' x 12'
Bath
Master Bedroom 13' x 18' 10' stepped ceiling
Bedroom 3 14'-4" x 12'
Gallery 10' clg.
Foyer 10' clg.
books
Bath
books
Util.
Dining 12' x 14' 13' clg.
Storage 10' x 5'
Study/Br 4 11'-4" x 13' 10' ceiling
2-Car Garage 21'-4" x 19'
Width 62'
Depth 67'-10"

Design by
Larry W. Garnett & Associates, Inc.

3-Car Garage
French Door
French Door
Breakfast 10' x 10'
French Door
Courtyard
Bath
Linen
Mirrored Doors
Desk
Master Bedroom 13'-4" x 22'-4" 10' Clg.
Family Room 14'-8" x 19'-4" 14' Clg.
Kitchen 14' x 11'
French Door
Pantry
Dining 11' x 14' 11' Clg.
Desk
Util.
Bath 2
Living Room 15' x 19'-4" 11' Clg.
Foyer
Bedroom 3 11'-4" x 13'
Bedroom 2 12' x 11' 11' Clg.
Width 75'-4"
Depth 80'-8"

QUOTE ONE®

Cost to build? See page 342 to order complete cost estimate to build this house in your area!

Design 9025

Square Footage: 2,481

■ Multiple gables, bay windows and corner windows with transoms above provide an exterior reminiscent of English countryside homes. The formal dining room features an eleven-foot ceiling, bay window, and French doors that open onto a private dining terrace. A spacious kitchen overlooks the breakfast area and the family room, which boasts a corner fireplace and dramatic fourteen-foot ceiling. Another corner fireplace is located in the master bedroom, which also contains a built-in desk and triple French doors. The luxurious master bath has a large walk-in closet and a whirlpool tub inset in a bay window. Two family bedrooms share a hall bath.

QUOTE ONE®

Cost to build? See page 342 to order complete cost estimate to build this house in your area!

Design by
Design Traditions

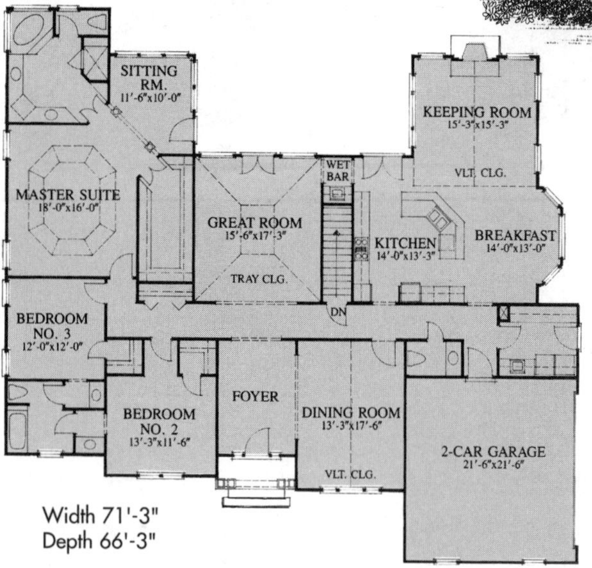
SITTING RM.
11'-6"x10'-0"
KEEPING ROOM
15'-3"x15'-3"
VLT. CLG.
WET BAR
MASTER SUITE
18'-0"x16'-0"
GREAT ROOM
15'-6"x17'-3"
TRAY CLG.
KITCHEN
14'-0"x13'-3"
BREAKFAST
14'-0"x13'-0"
DN
BEDROOM NO. 3
12'-0"x12'-0"
FOYER
BEDROOM NO. 2
13'-3"x11'-6"
DINING ROOM
13'-3"x17'-6"
VLT. CLG.
2-CAR GARAGE
21'-6"x21'-6"

Width 71'-3"
Depth 66'-3"

Design 9808

Square Footage: 2,902

■ To highlight the exterior of this brick home, window jack arches have been artfully combined with arched transoms, gables and a sweeping roofline. Open to the foyer is the great room with its dramatic tray ceiling. The accommodating kitchen, with a generous work island/breakfast bar, adjoins the breakfast area with its bright bay window and the keeping room with a fireplace and abundant windows. Two front bedrooms have a connecting bath offering private vanities. The master suite, with its garden bath and sunny sitting room, provides a quiet and peaceful retreat from the noise and pace of the day. This home is designed with a basement foundation.

Design 9810

Square Footage: 2,770

■ The European savoir-faire of this stucco home can be seen in its artful use of windows. Inside, the spacious foyer leads directly to a large great room with a massive fireplace. The spacious kitchen offers popular amenities such as a walk-in pantry, planning desk, breakfast bar and generous storage space. The master suite features a separate sitting area with a cathedral ceiling and access to the patio. The two additional bedrooms each have their own vanity within a shared bath. This home is designed with a basement foundation.

SITTING
HIS
MASTER BATH
BREAKFAST
DN.
GREAT ROOM
MASTER SUITE
HERS
POWDER
BEDROOM NO. 3
KITCHEN
FOYER
LAUNDRY
DINING ROOM
STOOP
BATH
BEDROOM NO. 2
STORAGE
2-CAR GARAGE

Width 74'
Depth 79'

Design by
Design Traditions

HOLZHAUER
INC. 96

Design by
The Sater Design Collection

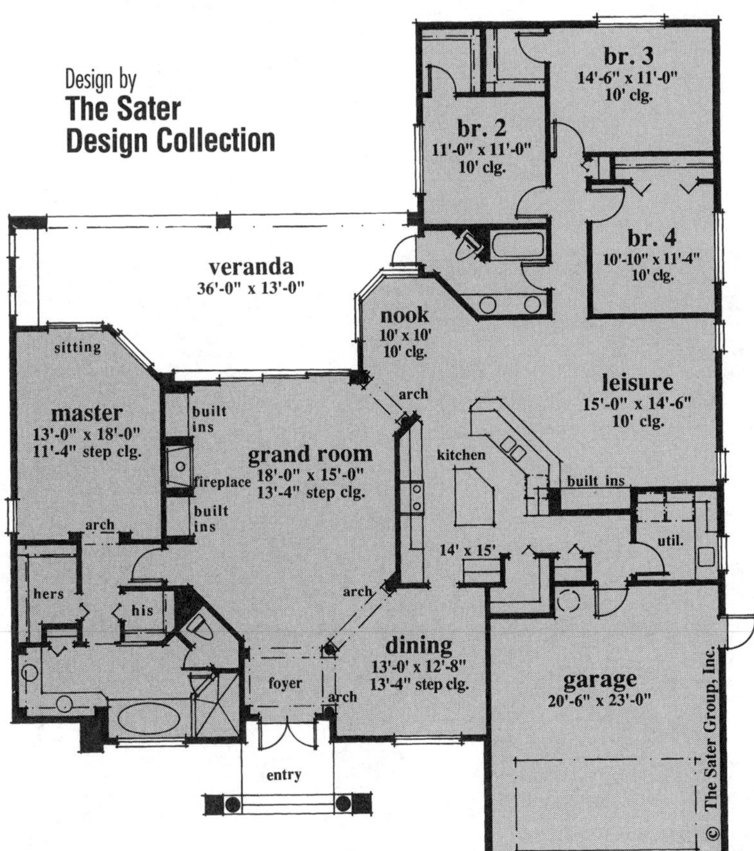
veranda
36'-0" x 13'-0"
sitting
master
13'-0" x 18'-0"
11'-4" step clg.
built ins
fireplace
grand room
18'-0" x 15'-0"
13'-4" step clg.
built ins
arch
hers
his
foyer
arch
entry
nook
10' x 10'
10' clg.
arch
kitchen
14' x 15'
arch
dining
13'-0' x 12'-8"
13'-4" step clg.
br. 2
11'-0" x 11'-0"
10' clg.
br. 3
14'-6" x 11'-0"
10' clg.
br. 4
10'-10" x 11'-4"
10' clg.
leisure
15'-0" x 14'-6"
10' clg.
built ins
util.
garage
20'-6" x 23'-0"
© The Sater Group, Inc.

Width 63'-8"
Depth 72'-8"

Design 6659

Square Footage: 2,659

■ Classic columns are a handsome accent to the multi-plane hipped roof and expansive window treatment in this elegant family home. Formal spaces flow together off the foyer with the dining room to the right and the grand room stretching back with sliding glass doors to the veranda. Family living takes charge in the leisure room that is joined with the kitchen and breakfast nook. Built-ins, a serving bar and sunny windows add to the livability. The grand master suite has a sitting area, doors to the veranda and an oversized, spa-style bath. Three family bedrooms are thoughtfully split off of the leisure area and share a full cabana bath.

Design 9999

Square Footage: 2,721

■ In this design, equally at home in the country or at the coast, classic elements play against a rustic shingle-and-stone exterior. Doric porch columns provide the elegance, while banks of cottage-style windows let in lots of natural light. The symmetrical layout of the foyer and formal dining room blend easily with the cozy great room. Here, a fireplace creates a welcome atmosphere that invites you to select a novel from one of the built-in bookcases and curl up in your favorite easy chair. The adjacent U-shaped kitchen combines with a sunny breakfast room that opens onto a rear porch, making casual meals a pleasure. Split away from family bedrooms for privacy, the master suite occupies the right side of the house and enjoys a dramatic master bath. The left wing contains two secondary bedrooms that share a bath with compartmentalized vanity/dressing areas. This home is designed with a basement foundation.

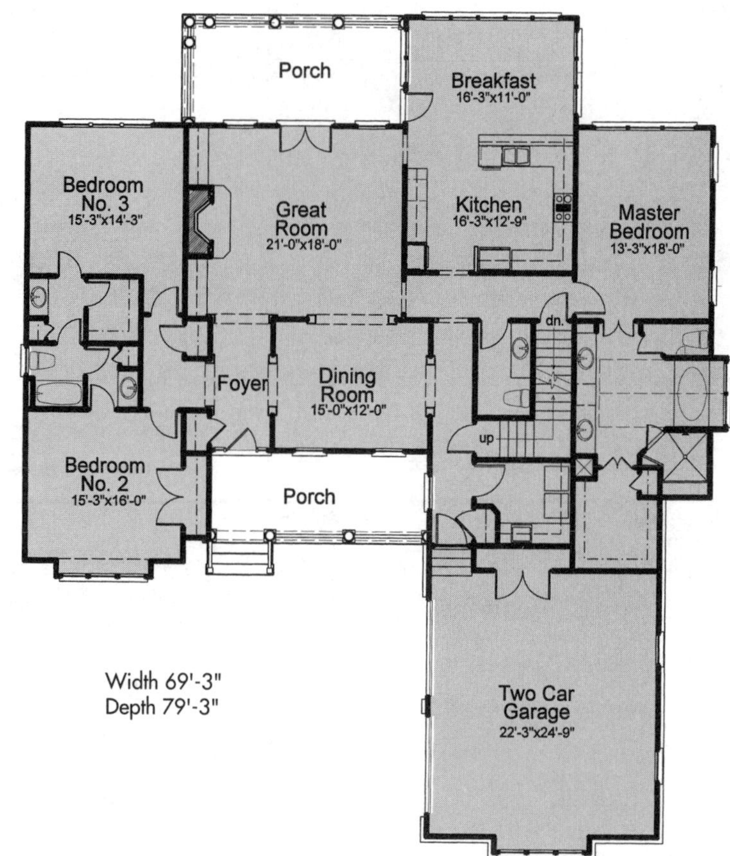
Porch
Breakfast
16'-3"x11'-0"
Bedroom
No. 3
15'-3"x14'-3"
Great
Room
21'-0"x18'-0"
Kitchen
16'-3"x12'-9"
Master
Bedroom
13'-3"x18'-0"
dn.
Foyer
Dining
Room
15'-0"x12'-0"
up
Bedroom
No. 2
15'-3"x16'-0"
Porch
Width 69'-3"
Depth 79'-3"
Two Car
Garage
22'-3"x24'-9"

Design by
Design Traditions

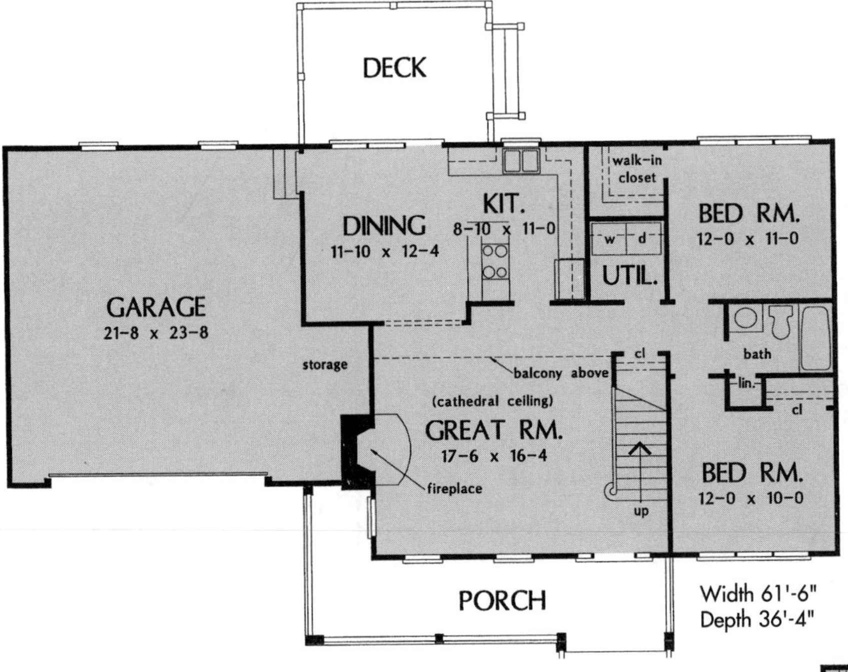
DECK
walk-in closet
KIT.
8-10 x 11-0
DINING
11-10 x 12-4
w d
BED RM.
12-0 x 11-0
UTIL.
GARAGE
21-8 x 23-8
storage
balcony above
cl
bath
lin.
cl
(cathedral ceiling)
GREAT RM.
17-6 x 16-4
fireplace
up
BED RM.
12-0 x 10-0
PORCH
Width 61'-6"
Depth 36'-4"

Design 7605

First Floor: 1,099 square feet
Second Floor: 647 square feet
Total: 1,746 square feet
Bonus: 377 square feet

■ The front gable of this farmhouse design features a clerestory window that illuminates the oversized great room. The efficient kitchen opens to the dining room, which accesses the deck and provides a service entrance from the garage. Family bedrooms on the first floor feature triple windows and a shared full bath. The master retreat, located upstairs, includes a bath with a garden tub and separate vanities, as well as a loft/study that can be converted into an additional bedroom or nursery. A versatile bonus room completes the plan.

Design by
Donald A. Gardner, Architects, Inc.

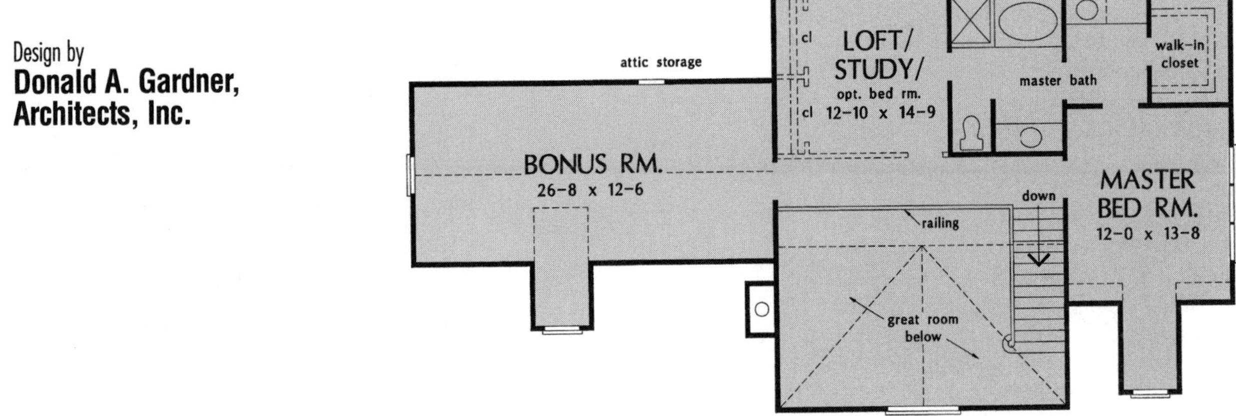
attic storage
cl
LOFT/
STUDY/
opt. bed rm.
cl 12-10 x 14-9
master bath
walk-in closet
BONUS RM.
26-8 x 12-6
down
railing
MASTER
BED RM.
12-0 x 13-8
great room
below

Design by
Donald A. Gardner, Architects, Inc.

Design 9775

First Floor: 1,234 square feet
Second Floor: 609 square feet
Total: 1,843 square feet

■ Interesting room arrangements make this home unique and inviting. From the wide front porch, enter the foyer to find the family bedrooms and a shared full bath on the left and a small hallway on the right that leads to the sunny kitchen. Ahead of the foyer and the kitchen is a combination great room and dining area that features a fireplace, access to the large back porch and plenty of windows and skylights. A large utility area with access to the garage and an abundance of storage space completes the first floor. The second floor is reserved for a grand master suite that features plenty of closet space, a separate loft or study area and a wonderful master bath with a bumped-out whirlpool tub.

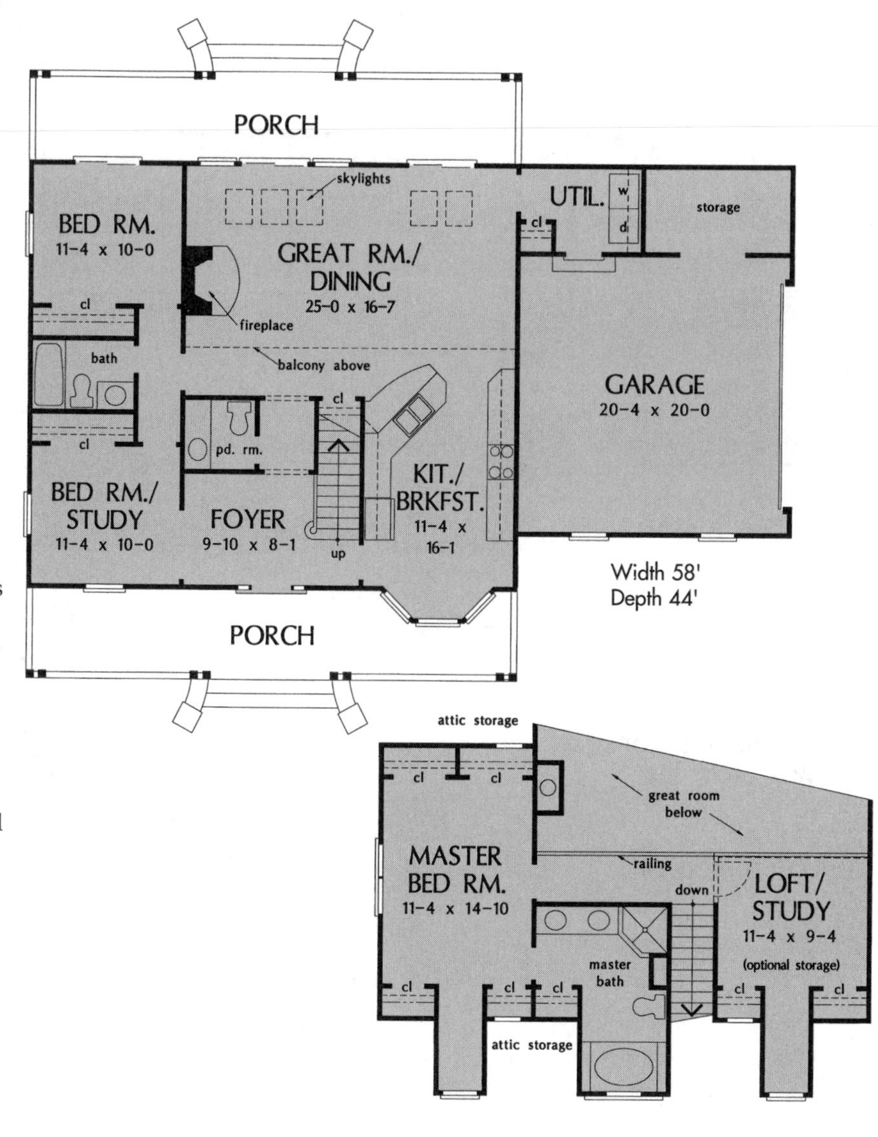
PORCH
skylights
BED RM.
11-4 x 10-0
GREAT RM./
DINING
25-0 x 16-7
fireplace
UTIL.
w
d
cl
storage
cl
bath
balcony above
cl
GARAGE
20-4 x 20-0
cl
pd. rm.
KIT./
BRKFST.
11-4 x
16-1
BED RM./
STUDY
11-4 x 10-0
FOYER
9-10 x 8-1
up
Width 58'
Depth 44'
PORCH
attic storage
cl
cl
great room
below
MASTER
BED RM.
11-4 x 14-10
railing
down
LOFT/
STUDY
11-4 x 9-4
(optional storage)
master
bath
cl
cl
cl
cl
cl
attic storage

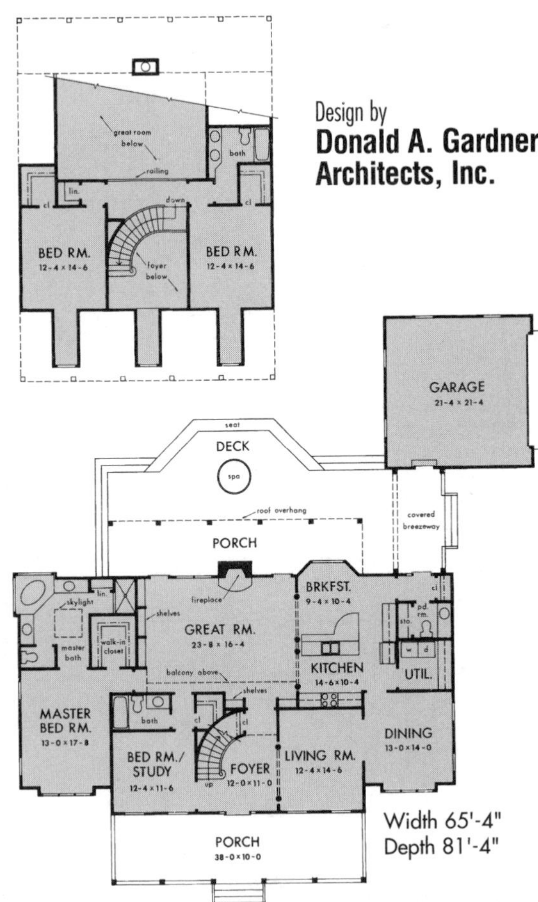
great room below
railing
lin.
bath
cl
down
BED RM. 12-4 x 14-6
foyer below
BED RM. 12-4 x 14-6
GARAGE 21-4 x 21-4
seat
DECK
spa
roof overhang
covered breezeway
PORCH
skylight
lin.
fireplace
shelves
BRKFST. 9-4 x 10-4
pd rm.
GREAT RM. 23-8 x 16-4
master bath
walk-in closet
KITCHEN 14-6 x 10-4
UTIL.
balcony above
shelves
MASTER BED RM. 13-0 x 17-8
bath
cl
DINING 13-0 x 14-0
BED RM./ STUDY 12-4 x 11-6
FOYER 12-0 x 11-0
LIVING RM. 12-4 x 14-6
up
PORCH 38-0 x 10-0

Width 65'-4"
Depth 81'-4"

Design by
Donald A. Gardner, Architects, Inc.

Design 9671

First Floor: 2,156 square feet
Second Floor: 707 square feet
Total: 2,863 square feet

■ This striking country home is enhanced by large front and rear porches and an expansive rear deck for great outdoor living. The foyer with a curved stair adds a touch of elegance along with the round columns between the foyer and living room and between the great room and kitchen/breakfast area. The great room boasts a cathedral ceiling, allowing a second-level balcony overlook. The master bedroom is located on the first level for convenience. The luxurious master bath has a dual vanity, whirlpool and shower. A second bedroom with full bath on the first floor can double as a study. Two large bedrooms with walk-in closets on the second level share a full bath with double-bowl vanity.

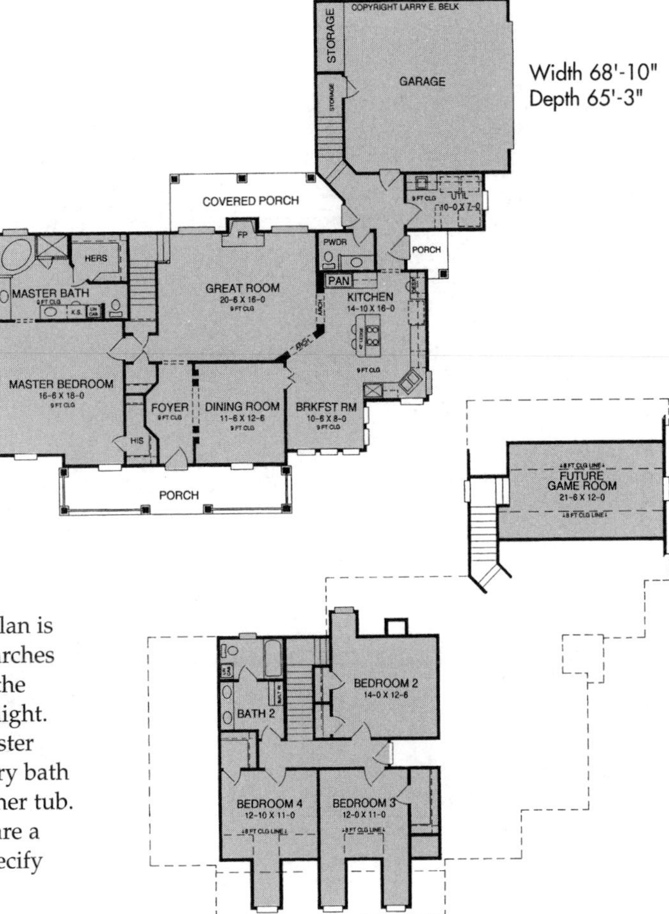
COPYRIGHT LARRY E. BELK
STORAGE
GARAGE
STORAGE
COVERED PORCH
FP
UTIL
PWDR
PAN
PORCH
HERS
MASTER BATH
GREAT ROOM 20-6 X 16-0
KITCHEN 14-10 X 16-0
MASTER BEDROOM 16-6 X 18-0
FOYER
DINING ROOM 11-6 X 12-6
BRKFST RM 10-6 X 8-0
HIS
PORCH
FUTURE GAME ROOM 21-6 X 12-0
BEDROOM 2 14-0 X 12-6
BATH 2
BEDROOM 4 12-10 X 11-0
BEDROOM 3 12-0 X 11-0

Width 68'-10"
Depth 65'-3"

Design 8114

First Floor: 1,785 square feet
Second Floor: 830 square feet
Total: 2,615 square feet
Bonus Room: 280 square feet

Design by
Larry E. Belk Designs

■ Looking to the past for style, the character of this winning plan is vintage Americana. A huge great room opens through classic arches to the island kitchen and the breakfast room. A corner sink in the kitchen gives the cook a view to the outside and brings in sunlight. Nearby, a small side porch provides a charming entry. The master suite is found on the first floor for privacy and features a luxury bath with separate vanities, His and Hers walk-in closets and a corner tub. The three bedrooms upstairs feature dormer windows and share a full bath. A bonus room is located above the garage. Please specify crawlspace or slab foundation when ordering.

Design 9626

First Floor: 1,057 square feet
Second Floor: 500 square feet
Total: 1,557 square feet
Basement Foundation: 1,610 square feet
Bonus Room: 342 square feet

Design by
Donald A. Gardner, Architects, Inc.

■ This cozy country cottage is perfect for the economically conscious family. Its entrance foyer is highlighted by a clerestory dormer above for natural light. The master suite is conveniently located on the first level for privacy and accessibility. The master bath boasts a skylight and lush amenities. Second-level bedrooms share a full bath. Bonus room may be finished above the garage. Please specify basement or crawlspace foundation when ordering.

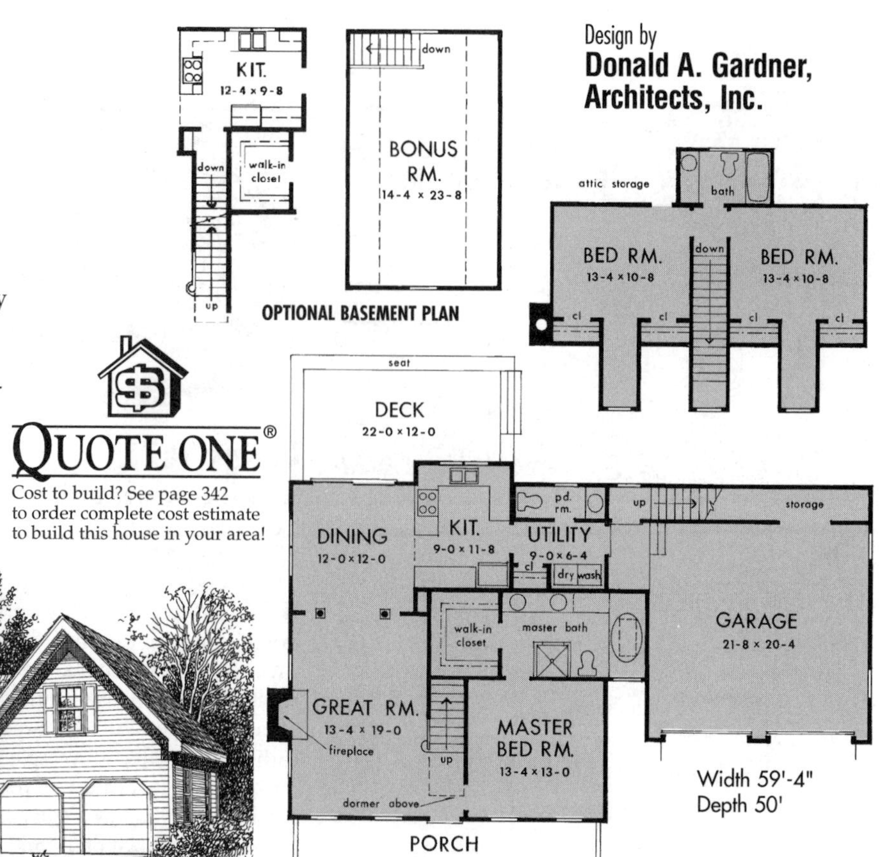
KIT.
12-4 x 9-8
down
walk-in closet
up
BONUS RM.
14-4 x 23-8
OPTIONAL BASEMENT PLAN
attic storage
bath
BED RM.
13-4 x 10-8
BED RM.
13-4 x 10-8
cl
QUOTE ONE®
seat
DECK
22-0 x 12-0
DINING
12-0 x 12-0
KIT.
9-0 x 11-8
pd. rm.
UTILITY
9-0 x 6-4
dry wash
storage
walk-in closet
master bath
GARAGE
21-8 x 20-4
GREAT RM.
13-4 x 19-0
fireplace
MASTER BED RM.
13-4 x 13-0
dormer above
PORCH
30-0 x 6-0
Width 59'-4"
Depth 50'

Cost to build? See page 342 to order complete cost estimate to build this house in your area!

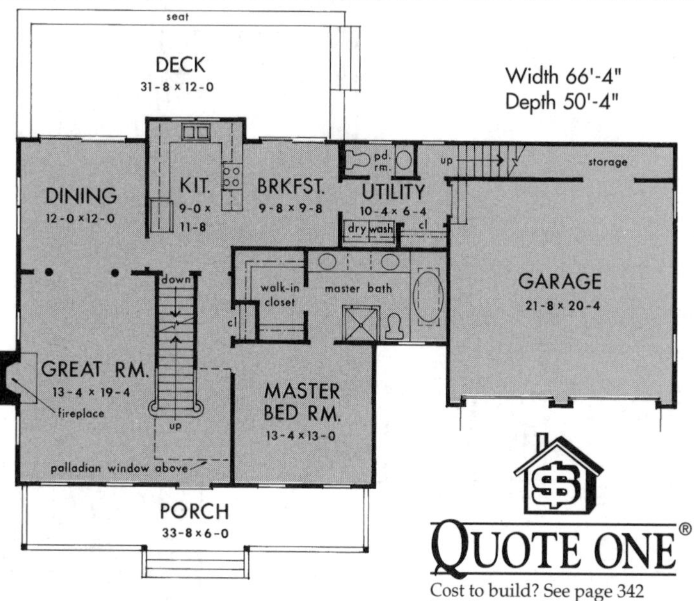
seat
DECK
31-8 x 12-0
Width 66'-4"
Depth 50'-4"
DINING
12-0 x 12-0
KIT.
9-0 x 11-8
BRKFST.
9-8 x 9-8
pd. rm.
UTILITY
10-4 x 6-4
dry wash
storage
walk-in closet
master bath
GARAGE
21-8 x 20-4
GREAT RM.
13-4 x 19-4
fireplace
MASTER BED RM.
13-4 x 13-0
palladian window above
PORCH
33-8 x 6-0
QUOTE ONE®

Design 9606

First Floor: 1,289 square feet
Second Floor: 542 square feet
Total: 1,831 square feet
Bonus Room: 393 square feet

Design by
Donald A. Gardner, Architects, Inc.

■ This cozy country cottage is perfect for the growing family—offering both an unfinished basement option and a bonus room. Enter through the two-story foyer with a Palladian window in a clerestory dormer above. The master suite is on the first floor for privacy and accessibility. Its accompanying bath boasts a whirlpool tub with a skylight above and a double-bowl vanity. The second floor contains two bedrooms, a full bath and plenty of storage. Please specify basement or crawlspace foundation when ordering.

Cost to build? See page 342 to order complete cost estimate to build this house in your area!

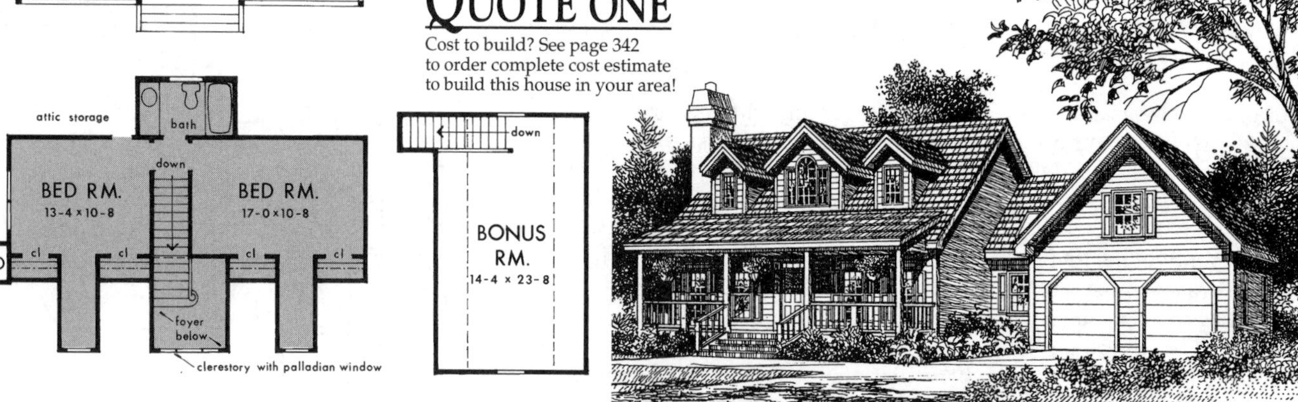
attic storage
bath
down
BED RM.
13-4 x 10-8
BED RM.
17-0 x 10-8
cl
foyer below
clerestory with palladian window
down
BONUS RM.
14-4 x 23-8

COPYRIGHT LARRY E. BELK

Design 8161

First Floor: 2,028 square feet
Second Floor: 558 square feet
Total: 2,586 square feet
Bonus Room: 272 square feet

■ From the curb, this inviting entrance beckons family and friends to enter. The two-story foyer features a ledge perfect for displaying a special picture or tapestry. Arched openings form the entrance to the formal dining room and great room. An angled, see-through fireplace serves the great room, breakfast room and kitchen areas. The kitchen features an abundance of cabinet and counter space, a walk-in pantry and a built-in desk. A sitting area and a luxurious master bath enhance the private master suite. An adjacent secondary bedroom serves well as a guest room, a nursery or a study. Upstairs, two family bedrooms, a full bath and an expandable area complete the layout. Please specify slab or crawlspace foundation when ordering.

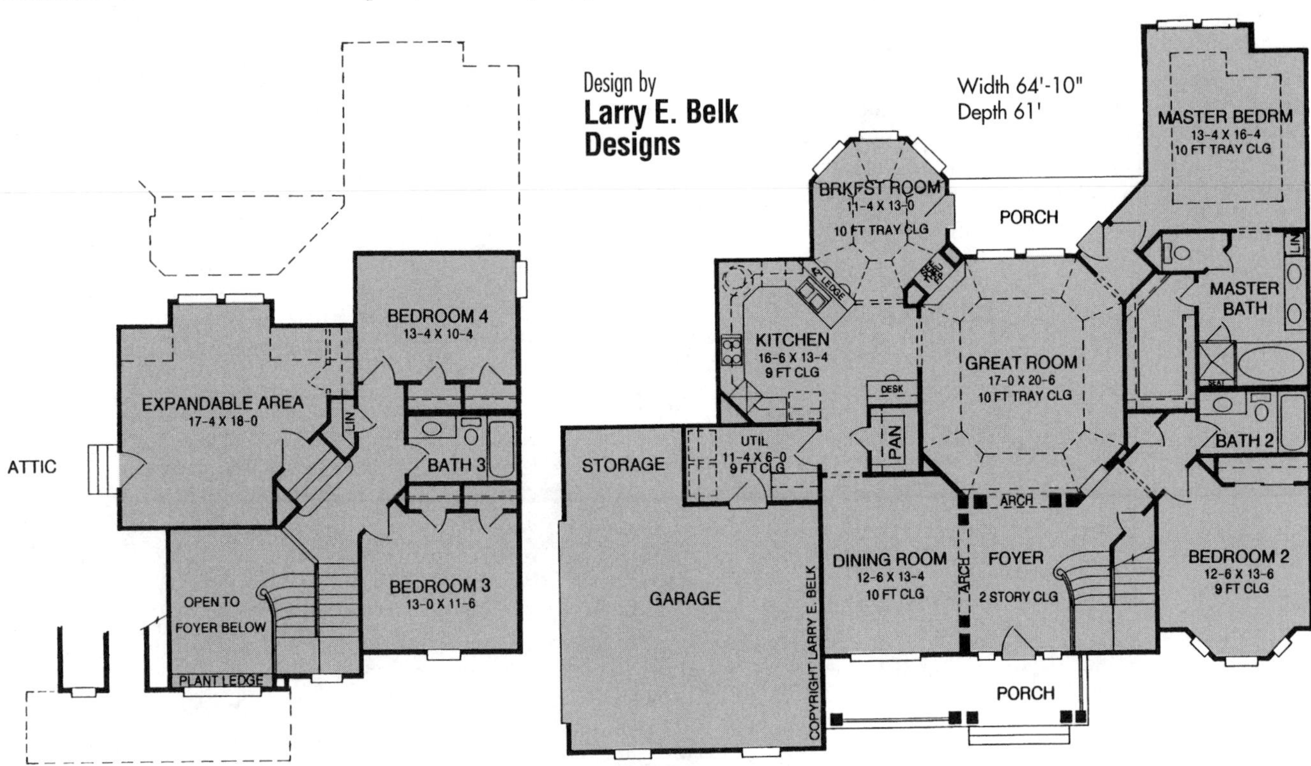
Design by
Larry E. Belk Designs
Width 64'-10"
Depth 61'
BEDROOM 4
13-4 X 10-4
EXPANDABLE AREA
17-4 X 18-0
ATTIC
BATH 3
LIN
BEDROOM 3
13-0 X 11-6
OPEN TO
FOYER BELOW
PLANT LEDGE
MASTER BEDRM
13-4 X 16-4
10 FT TRAY CLG
BRKFST ROOM
11-4 X 13-0
10 FT TRAY CLG
PORCH
LEDGE
KITCHEN
16-6 X 13-4
9 FT CLG
MASTER BATH
GREAT ROOM
17-0 X 20-6
10 FT TRAY CLG
DESK
PAN
SEAT
BATH 2
STORAGE
UTIL
11-4 X 6-0
9 FT CLG
ARCH
GARAGE
DINING ROOM
12-6 X 13-4
10 FT CLG
FOYER
2 STORY CLG
BEDROOM 2
12-6 X 13-6
9 FT CLG
PORCH
COPYRIGHT LARRY E. BELK

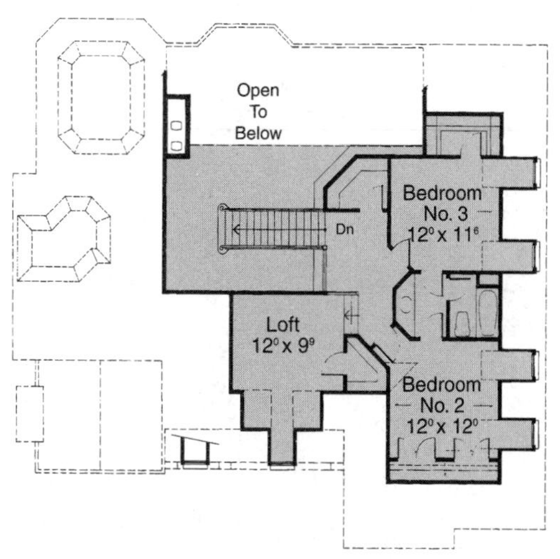
Open
To
Below
Bedroom
No. 3
12^{0} x 11^{6}
Dn
Loft
12^{0} x 9^{9}
Bedroom
No. 2
12^{0} x 12^{0}

Design by
Design Traditions

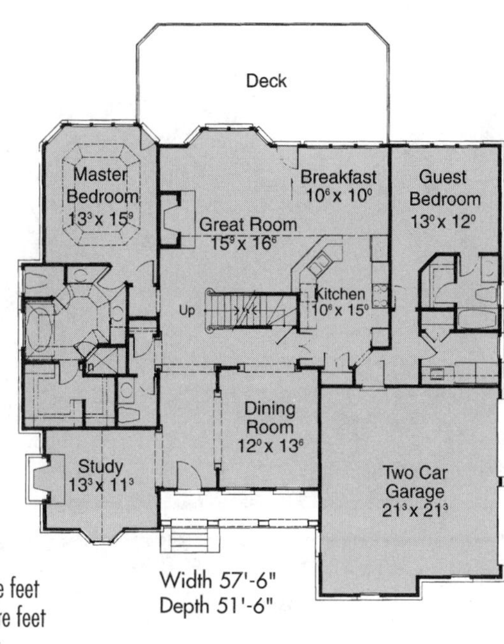
Deck
Master
Bedroom
13^{3} x 15^{9}
Breakfast
10^{6} x 10^{0}
Guest
Bedroom
13^{0} x 12^{0}
Great Room
15^{9} x 16^{8}
Kitchen
10^{6} x 15^{0}
Up
Dining
Room
12^{0} x 13^{6}
Study
13^{3} x 11^{3}
Two Car
Garage
21^{3} x 21^{3}
Width 57'-6"
Depth 51'-6"

Design 7817

First Floor: 2,919 square feet
Second Floor: 543 square feet
Total: 3,462 square feet

■ This lovely home's foyer opens to the formal dining room, defined by decorative columns, and leads to a two-story great room. The kitchen and breakfast room join the great room to create a casual family area. The master suite is finished with a coffered ceiling and a sumptuous bath. A guest suite with a private bath is located just off the kitchen. Upstairs two family bedrooms share a private compartmented bath and a raised loft. This home is designed with a basement foundation.

Design 6662

First Floor: 1,671 square feet
Second Floor: 851 square feet
Total: 2,522 square feet

■ Arches in the foyer of this traditional home echo the porch theme and lead to an open great room with sliding doors to the rear yard. The kitchen, which overlooks the great room, has a walk-in pantry and breakfast nook. Just off the kitchen is a private study or guest suite with a hall bath and door to the veranda. The master suite enjoys a spacious bath and two walk-in closets. Three family bedrooms on the second floor share a hall bath, and two of the three have access to the rear balcony. A computer loft has built-ins for books and software. Please specify basement or slab foundation when ordering.

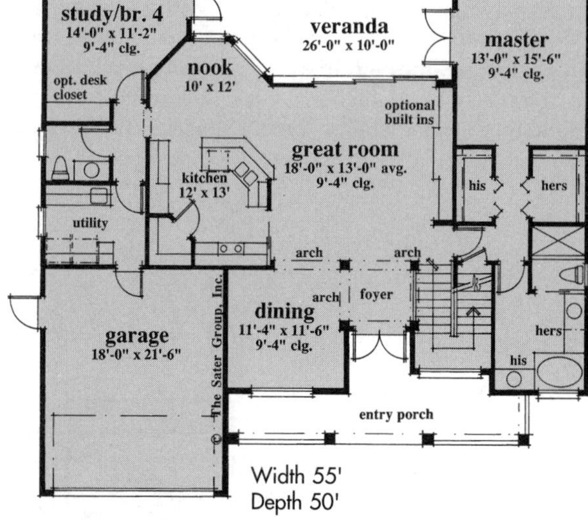
study/br. 4
14'-0" x 11'-2"
9'-4" clg.
opt. desk
closet
nook
10' x 12'
veranda
26'-0" x 10'-0"
master
13'-0" x 15'-6"
9'-4" clg.
optional
built ins
great room
18'-0" x 13'-0" avg.
9'-4" clg.
kitchen
12' x 13'
utility
his
hers
arch
arch
arch
foyer
dining
11'-4" x 11'-6"
9'-4" clg.
garage
18'-0" x 21'-6"
hers
his
entry porch
© The Sater Group, Inc.
Width 55'
Depth 50'

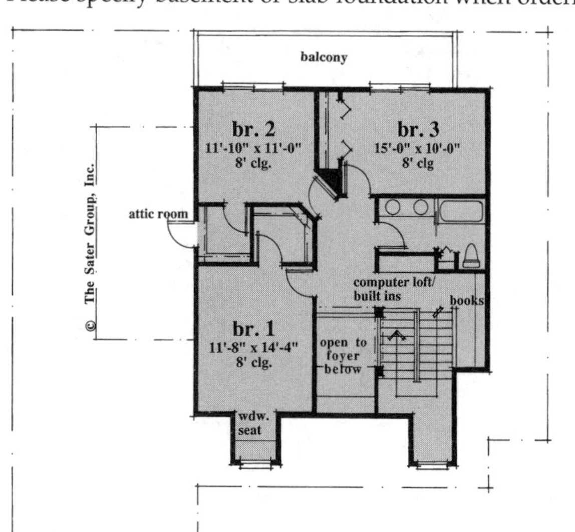
balcony
br. 2
11'-10" x 11'-0"
8' clg.
br. 3
15'-0" x 10'-0"
8' clg
attic room
computer loft/
built ins
books
br. 1
11'-8" x 14'-4"
8' clg.
open to
foyer
below
wdw.
seat
© The Sater Group, Inc.

Design by
The Sater Design Collection

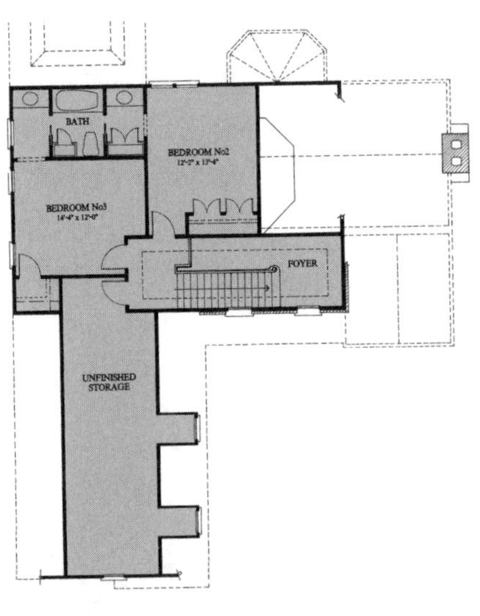
BATH
BEDROOM No2
BEDROOM No3
FOYER
UNFINISHED STORAGE

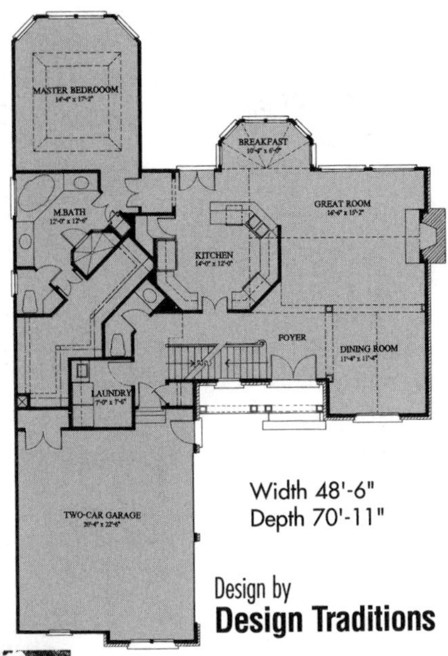
MASTER BEDROOM
BREAKFAST
GREAT ROOM
M.BATH
KITCHEN
FOYER
DINING ROOM
LAUNDRY
TWO-CAR GARAGE

Width 48'-6"
Depth 70'-11"

Design by
Design Traditions

Design 9812

First Floor: 1,580 square feet
Second Floor: 595 square feet
Total: 2,175 square feet
Bonus Room: 290 square feet

■ This home features a front porch which warmly welcomes family and visitors, as well as protecting them from the weather—a true Southern original. Inside, the spacious foyer leads directly to a large vaulted great room with a massive fireplace. A grand kitchen offers both storage and large work areas opening up to the breakfast area. In the privacy and quiet of the rear of the home is the master suite with its garden bath, His and Hers vanities, and oversized closet. The second floor provides two additional bedrooms with a shared bath along with a balcony overlook to the foyer below. Ample amounts of storage space or an additional bedroom can be created in space over the garage. This home is designed with a basement foundation.

QUOTE ONE®

Cost to build? See page 342 to order complete cost estimate to build this house in your area!

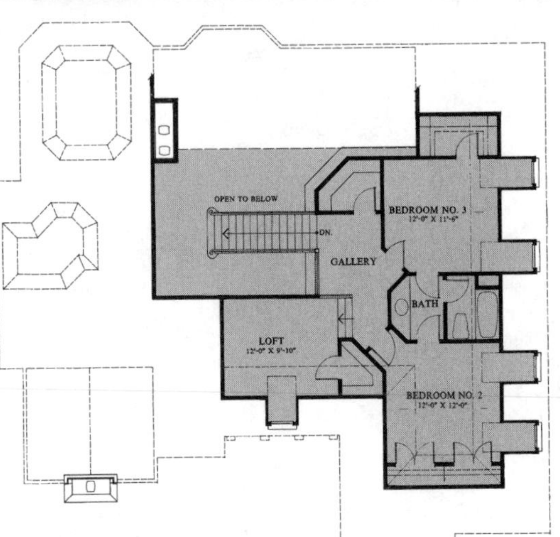
OPEN TO BELOW
DN.
GALLERY
BEDROOM NO. 3
BATH
LOFT
BEDROOM NO. 2

Design 9821

First Floor: 2,070 square feet
Second Floor: 790 square feet
Total: 2,860 square feet

QUOTE ONE®

Cost to build? See page 342 to order complete cost estimate to build this house in your area!

Design by
Design Traditions

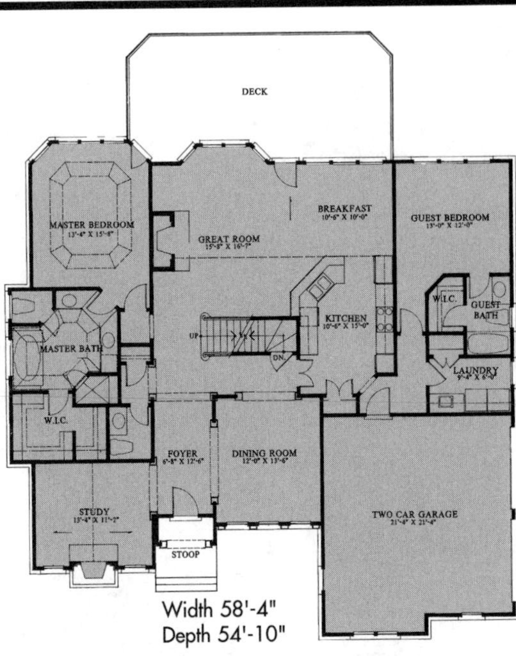
DECK
MASTER BEDROOM
GREAT ROOM
BREAKFAST
GUEST BEDROOM
W.I.C.
GUEST BATH
MASTER BATH
KITCHEN
LAUNDRY
W.I.C.
FOYER
DINING ROOM
STUDY
STOOP
TWO CAR GARAGE

Width 58'-4"
Depth 54'-10"

■ The striking combination of wood frame, shingles and glass create the exterior of this classic cottage. The foyer opens to the main level layout. To the left of the foyer is a study with a warming hearth and a vaulted ceiling. To the right is the formal dining room. A great room with an attached breakfast area is near the kitchen. A guest room is nestled in the rear of the plan for privacy. The master suite provides an expansive tray ceiling, a glass sitting area and easy passage to the outside deck. Upstairs, two bedrooms are accompanied by a sunken loft for a quiet getaway. This home is designed with a basement foundation.

Design 9705

First Floor: 1,675 square feet
Second Floor: 448 square feet
Total: 2,123 square feet
Basement Foundation: 2,203 square feet

Design by
Donald A. Gardner, Architects, Inc.

■ This attractive three-bedroom house projects a refined image with its hip roof, brick veneer and arched windows while offering a touch of country with its covered front porch. The entrance foyer, flanked by dining room and bedroom/study, leads to the spacious great room. The dining room and breakfast room have cathedral ceilings with the kitchen nestled cleverly between. The master bedroom boasts a cathedral ceiling and bath with whirlpool, shower and double-bowl vanity. The second floor has two family bedrooms along with a bonus room. Please specify basement or crawlspace foundation when ordering.

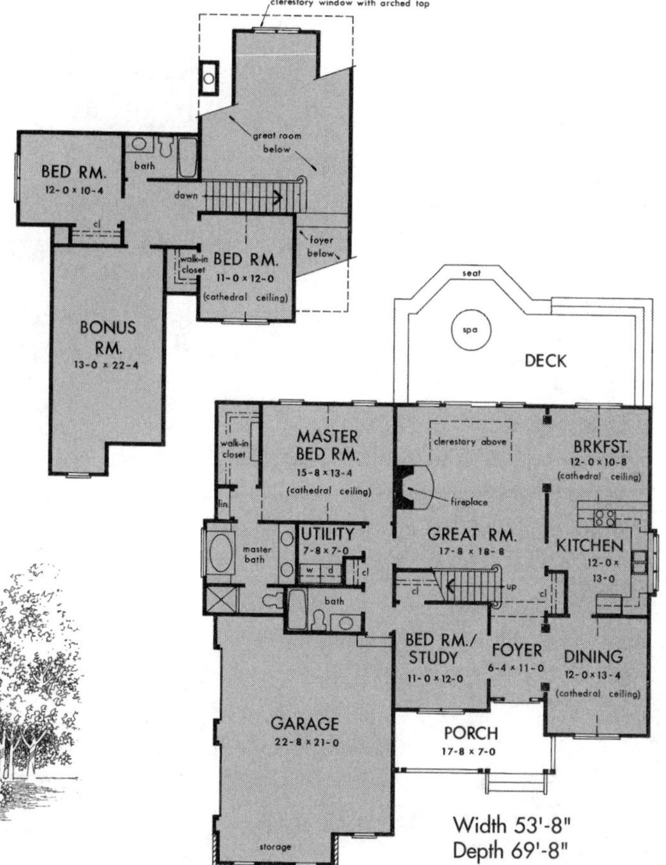
clerestory window with arched top
great room below
BED RM.
12-0 x 10-4
bath
down
foyer below
walk-in closet
BED RM.
11-0 x 12-0
(cathedral ceiling)
BONUS RM.
13-0 x 22-4
seat
spa
DECK
walk-in closet
MASTER BED RM.
15-8 x 13-4
(cathedral ceiling)
clerestory above
BRKFST.
12-0 x 10-8
(cathedral ceiling)
fireplace
master bath
UTILITY
7-8 x 7-0
GREAT RM.
17-8 x 18-8
KITCHEN
12-0 x 13-0
up
bath
BED RM./ STUDY
11-0 x 12-0
FOYER
6-4 x 11-0
DINING
12-0 x 13-4
(cathedral ceiling)
GARAGE
22-8 x 21-0
PORCH
17-8 x 7-0
storage
Width 53'-8"
Depth 69'-8"

Design 7223

First Floor: 1,651 square feet
Second Floor: 634 square feet
Total: 2,285 square feet

Design by
Design Basics, Inc.

■ Soft curves under repeating gables form an inviting elevation. The bayed living room and the formal dining room surround a beautiful two-story entry. The peninsula kitchen opens to a bayed breakfast area with a snack bar between. The family room has a high sloped ceiling. The master suite is finished with a whirlpool tub, twin vanities and a walk-in closet. The upstairs bedrooms share a hall bath with a dual vanity. Unfinished storage space and an optional loft overlooking the family room allow room to grow.

Mbr. 16⁰ x 13⁰
9'-0" CEILING
WHIRLPOOL
10'-0" CLG.
Kit. 10⁰ x 12⁴
Bfst. 11⁰ x 12⁰
SNACK BAR
PANTRY
Fam. rm. 14⁰ x 18⁰
SLOPED CEILING
DN
UP
D. W.
STORAGE 10⁸ x 4⁸
Liv. 12⁰ x 14⁸
10'-0" CEILING
E.
Din. 11⁰ x 14⁰
Gar. 20⁸ x 22⁴
TRANS.
COVERED STOOP

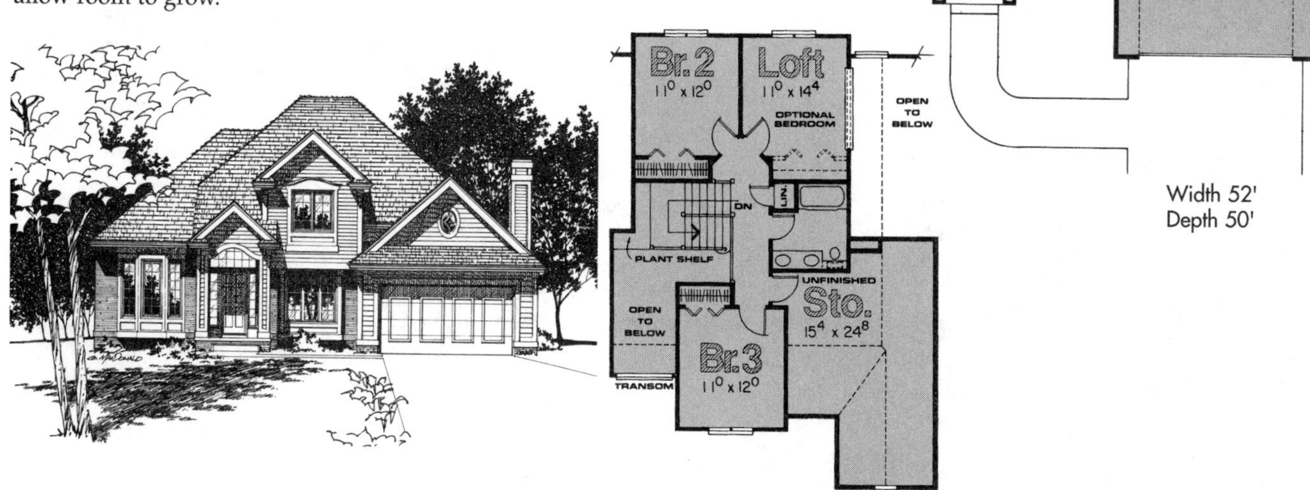
Br. 2
11⁰ x 12⁰
Loft
11⁰ x 14⁴
OPTIONAL BEDROOM
OPEN TO BELOW
DN
PLANT SHELF
OPEN TO BELOW
UNFINISHED
Sto.
15⁴ x 24⁸
Br. 3
11⁰ x 12⁰
TRANSOM

Width 52'
Depth 50'

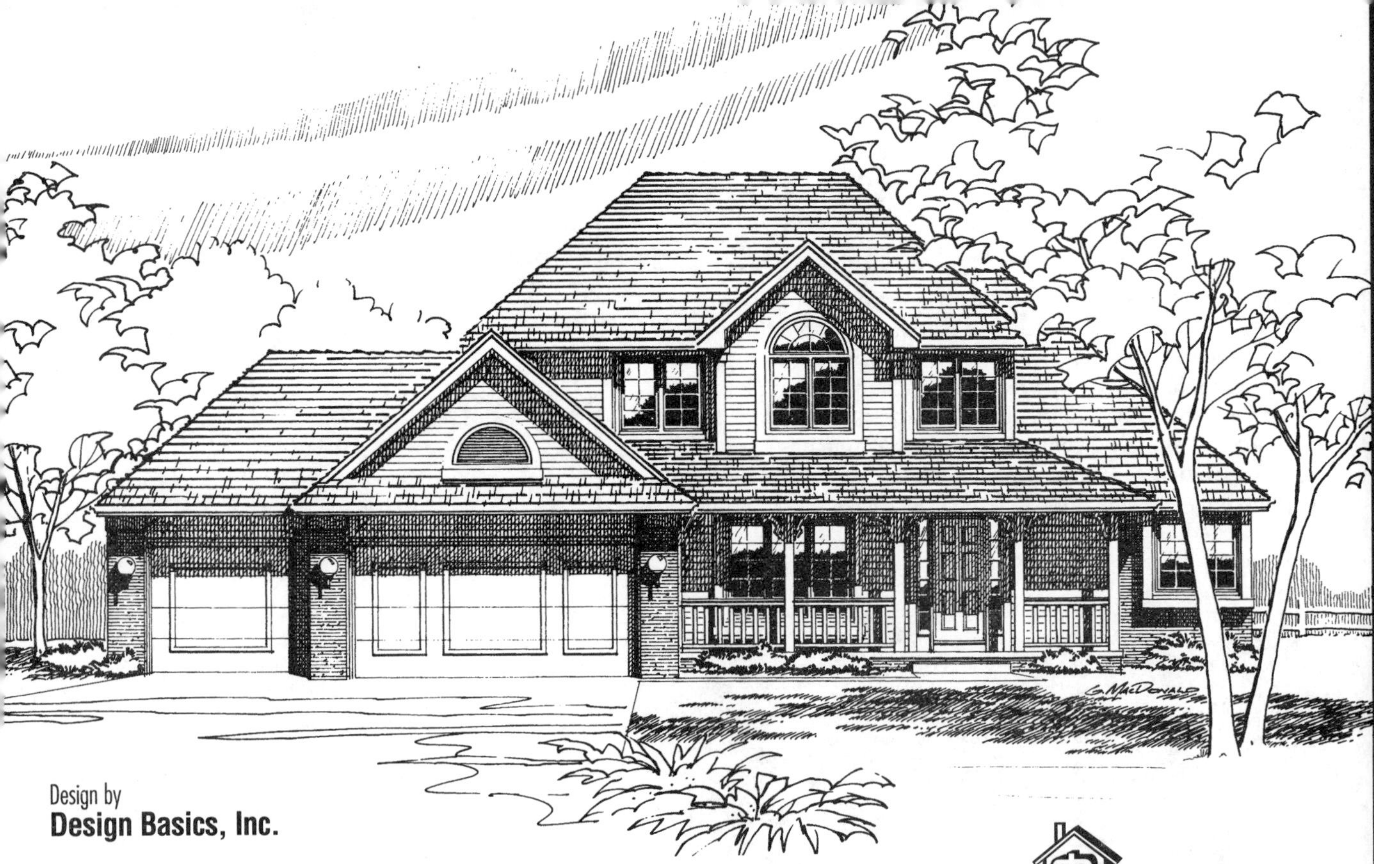

Design by
Design Basics, Inc.

Design 9310

First Floor: 1,505 square feet
Second Floor: 610 square feet
Total: 2,115 square feet

■ Sunny windows, lap siding and a covered porch give this elevation a welcoming country flair. The formal dining room with hutch space is conveniently located near the island kitchen. A main floor laundry room with a sink is discreetly located next to the bright breakfast area with desk and pantry. Highlighting the spacious great room are a raised-hearth fireplace, a cathedral ceiling and trapezoid windows. Special features in the master suite include a large dressing area with a double vanity, a skylight, a step-up corner whirlpool and a generous walk-in closet. Upstairs, the three secondary bedrooms are well separated from the master bedroom and share a hall bath.

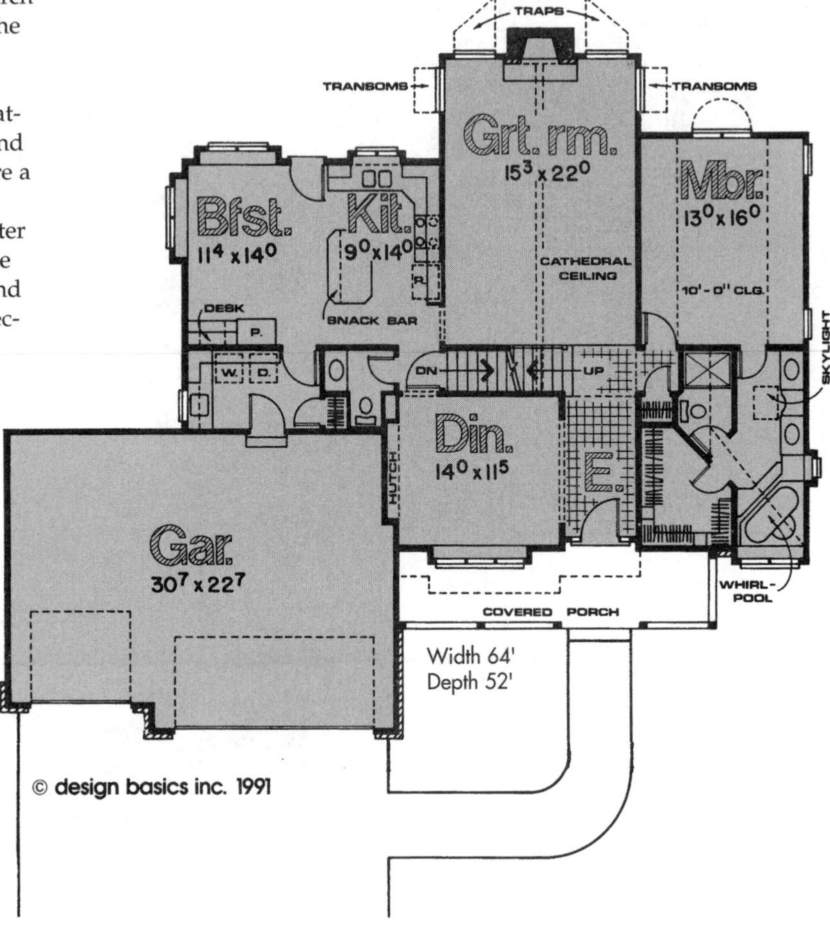
TRAPS
TRANSOMS
TRANSOMS
Grt. rm.
$15^{3} \times 22^{0}$
CATHEDRAL CEILING
Mbr.
$13^{0} \times 16^{0}$
10'-0" CLG.
SKYLIGHT
Bfst.
$11^{4} \times 14^{0}$
Kit.
$9^{0} \times 14^{0}$
R.
DESK
P.
SNACK BAR
W.
D.
DN
UP
Din.
$14^{0} \times 11^{5}$
HUTCH
E.
Gar.
$30^{7} \times 22^{7}$
WHIRL-POOL
COVERED PORCH
Width 64'
Depth 52'
© design basics inc. 1991

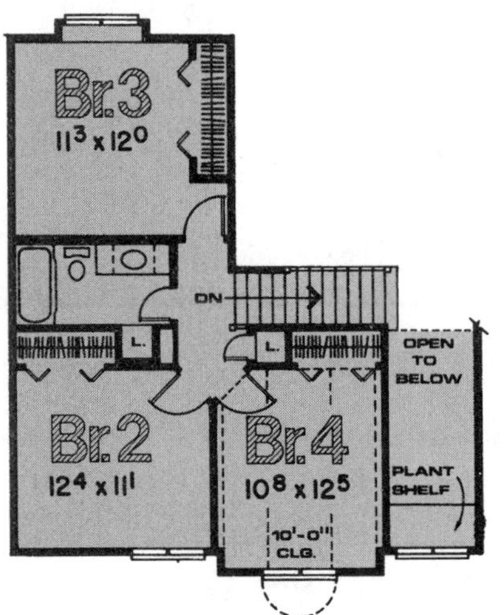
Br.3
$11^{3} \times 12^{0}$
DN
L.
L.
OPEN TO BELOW
Br.2
$12^{4} \times 11^{1}$
Br.4
$10^{8} \times 12^{5}$
10'-0" CLG.
PLANT SHELF

Design P104

First Floor: 1,320 square feet
Second Floor: 554 square feet
Total: 1,874 square feet
Bonus Room: 155 square feet

Design by
Frank Betz Associates, Inc.

■ This plan combines a traditional, stately exterior with an updated floor plan to create a house that will please the entire family. The heart of the plan is surely the wide-open living space consisting of the vaulted family room, breakfast area and gourmet kitchen. Highlights here are a full-length fireplace, a French door to the rear yard and an island cooktop. The master suite has a tray ceiling and a vaulted master bath with a garden tub and walk-in closet. The family sleeping area is on the upper level and gives the option of two bedrooms and a loft overlooking the family room or three bedrooms. Please specify basement or crawlspace foundation when ordering.

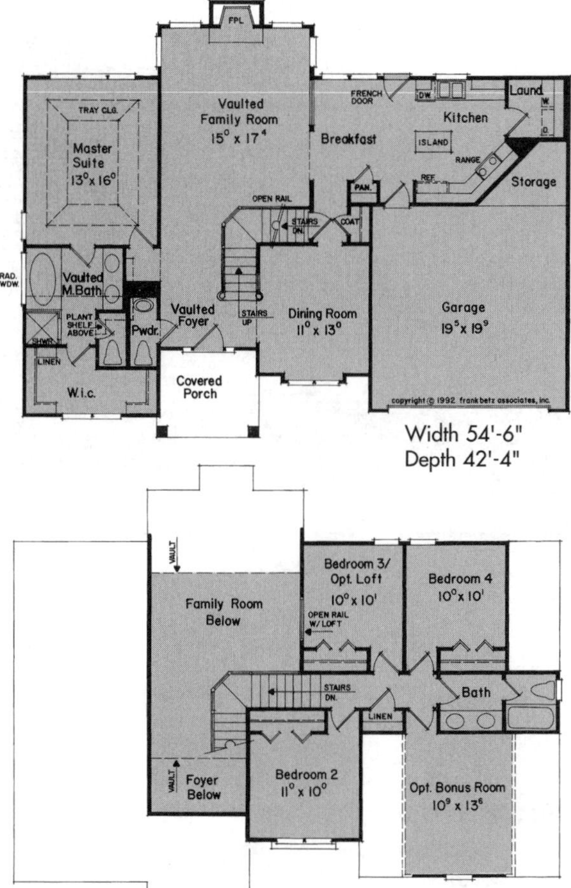
FPL
Vaulted Family Room 15^{0} x 17^{4}
Tray Clg.
Master Suite 13^{0}x 16^{0}
French Door
Kitchen
Laund.
Breakfast
Island
Range
Ref.
Pan.
Storage
Open Rail
Stairs Dn.
Coat
Rad. Wdw
Vaulted M.Bath
Plant Shelf Above
Pwdr.
Vaulted Foyer
Stairs Up
Dining Room 11^{0} x 13^{0}
Garage 19^{5}x 19^{9}
Linen
W.i.c.
Covered Porch
copyright © 1992 frank betz associates, inc.
Width 54'-6"
Depth 42'-4"
Vault
Family Room Below
Bedroom 3/ Opt. Loft 10^{0}x 10'
Open Rail w/Loft
Bedroom 4 10^{0}x 10'
Stairs Dn.
Bath
Linen
Vault
Foyer Below
Bedroom 2 11^{0} x 10^{0}
Opt. Bonus Room 10^{9} x 13^{6}

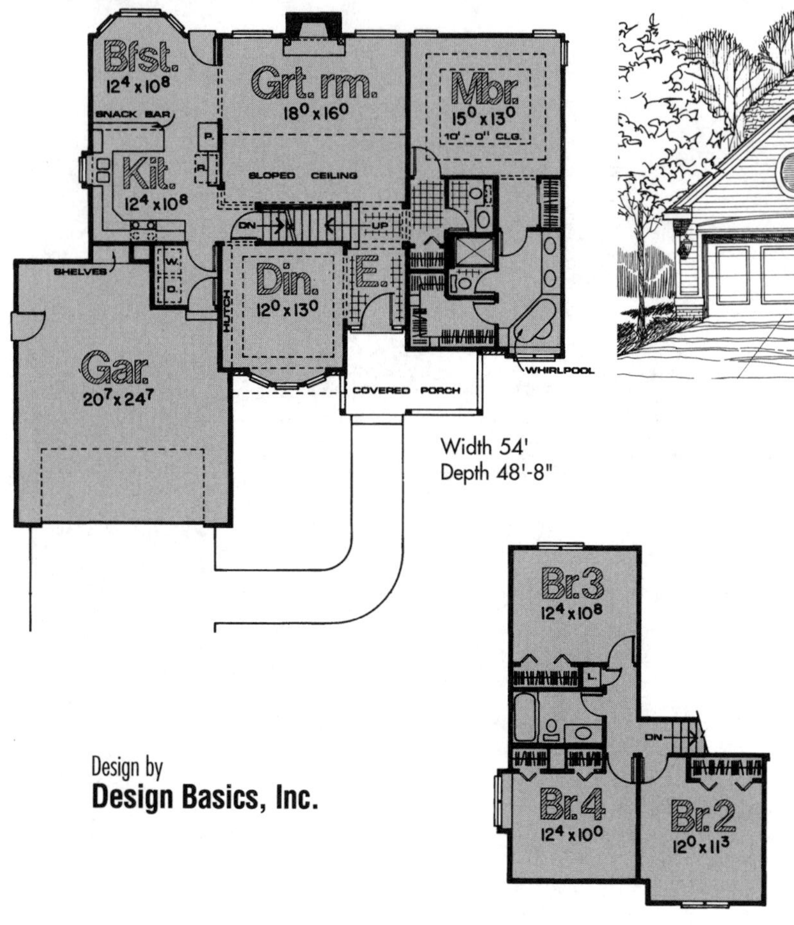
Bfst. 12^{4} x 10^{8}
Snack Bar
Grt. rm. 18^{0} x 16^{0}
Mbr. 15^{0} x 13^{0}
10' - 0" Clg.
Kit. 12^{4} x 10^{8}
Sloped Ceiling
DN
UP
Shelves
Din. 12^{0} x 13^{0}
Hutch
E.
Gar. 20^{7} x 24^{7}
Whirlpool
Covered Porch
Width 54'
Depth 48'-8"
Br. 3 12^{4} x 10^{8}
DN
Br. 4 12^{4} x 10^{0}
Br. 2 12^{0} x 11^{3}

Design by
Design Basics, Inc.

Design 9280

First Floor: 1,348 square feet
Second Floor: 603 square feet
Total: 1,951 square feet

■ Highlighting the elevation of this four-bedroom family home is a covered porch. Upon entering, a spacious great room gains attention. Cooks will enjoy the thoughtfully designed kitchen with a snack bar, a pantry and a window above the sink. A sunny breakfast room is open to this area. In the master suite, a tiered ceiling, double vanities, a corner whirlpool and a large walk-in closet are sure to please. Upstairs, three secondary bedrooms share a hall bath.

Design 9247

First Floor: 1,297 square feet
Second Floor: 558 square feet
Total: 1,855 square feet

■ The covered front porch of this home opens to a great floor plan. From the entry, go left to reach the formal dining room with boxed window. Straight back is the great room with handsome fireplace and tall windows. A snack bar, pantry, and planning desk in the kitchen make it convenient and appealing. The breakfast room has sliding glass doors to the rear yard. The master bedroom is on the first floor and has a luxurious bath with skylit whirlpool. Upstairs are three more bedrooms and a full bath.

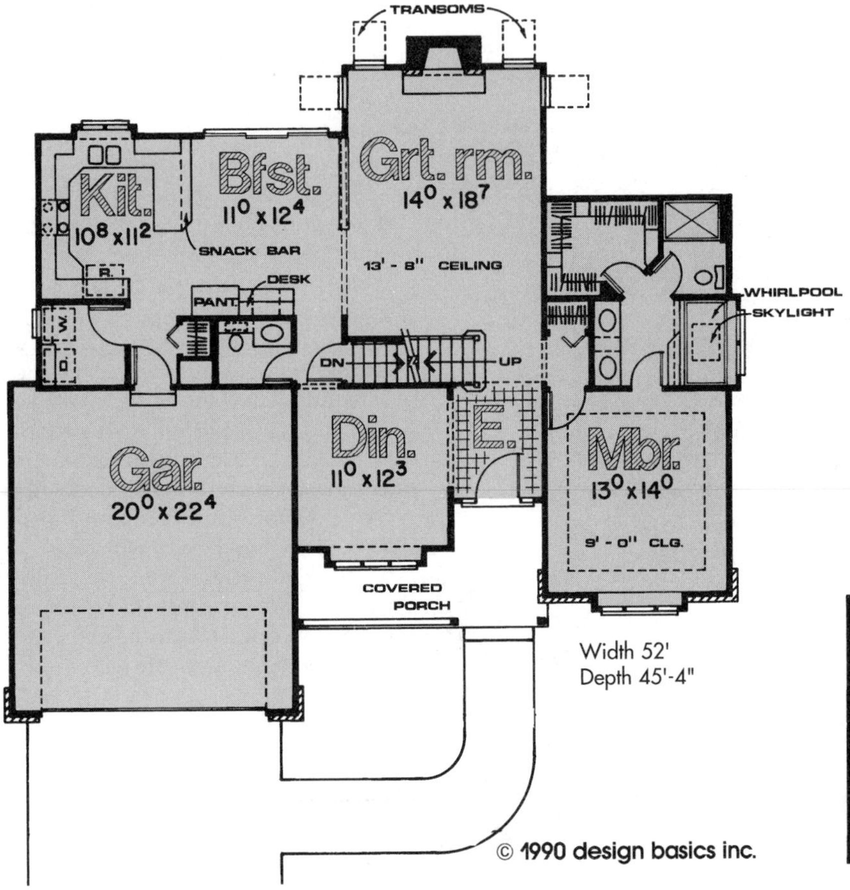

Width 52'
Depth 45'-4"

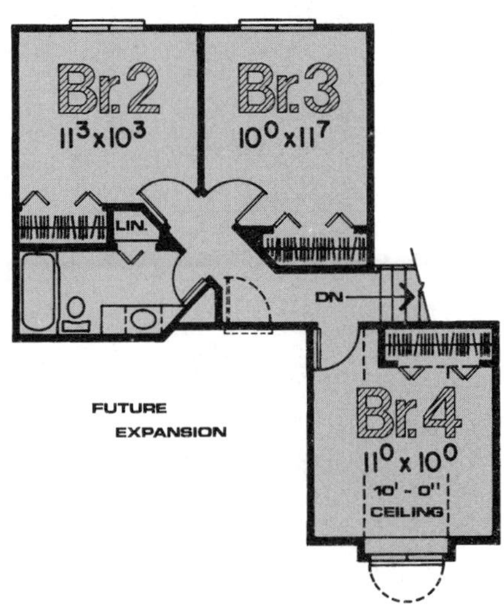
Br. 2
11³x10³
Br. 3
10⁰x11⁷
LIN.
DN
FUTURE EXPANSION
Br. 4
11⁰x10⁰
10' - 0" CEILING

Design by
Design Basics, Inc.

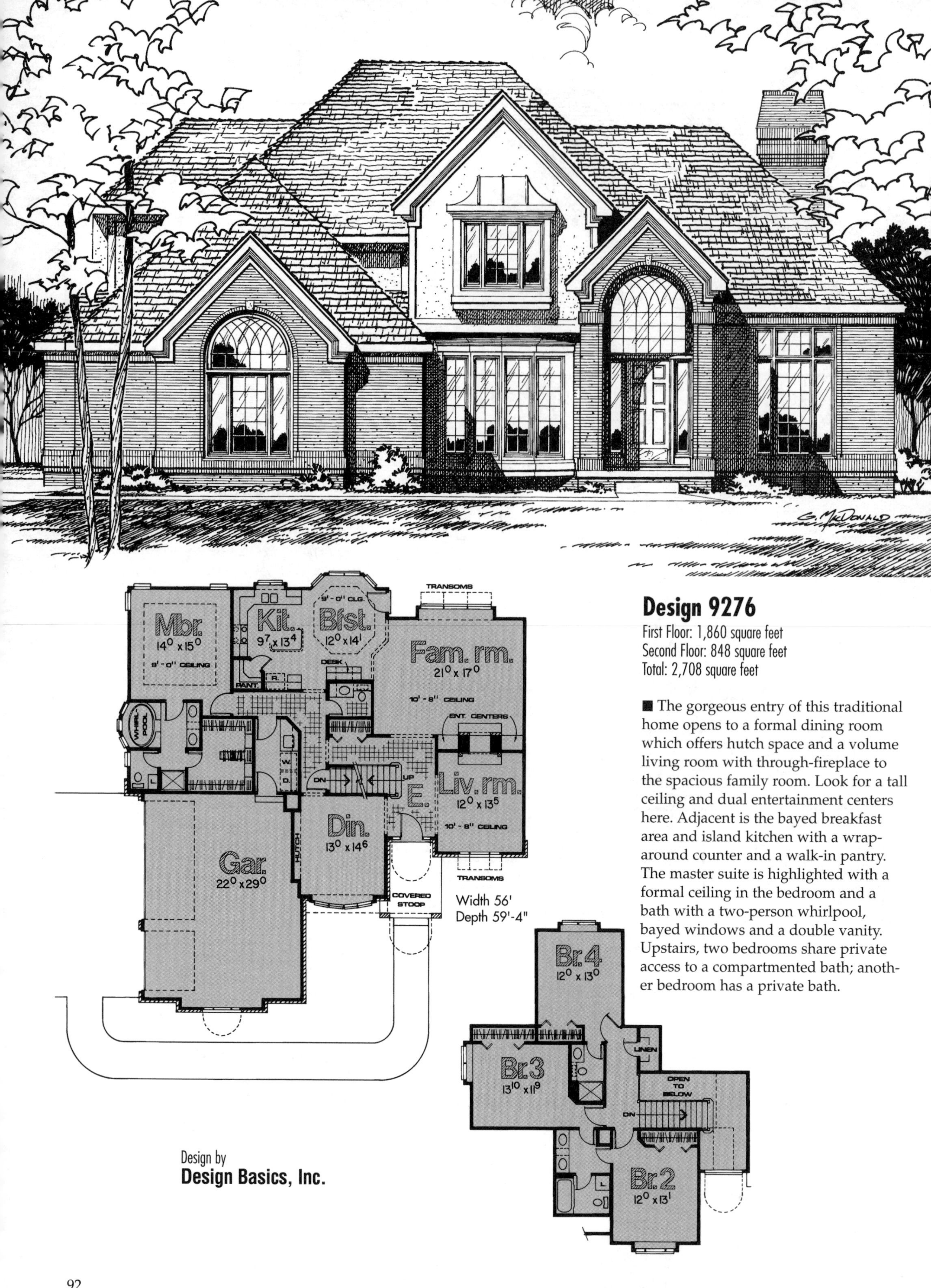
G. McDONALD
TRANSOMS
Mbr.
14⁰ x 15⁰
9'-0" CEILING
Kit.
9⁷ x 13⁴
9'-0" CLG.
Bfst.
12⁰ x 14¹
Fam. rm.
21⁰ x 17⁰
10'-8" CEILING
ENT. CENTERS
DESK
PANT.
R.
WHIRL-POOL
W.
D.
DN
UP
E.
Liv. rm.
12⁰ x 13⁵
10'-8" CEILING
HUTCH
Din.
13⁰ x 14⁶
Gar.
22⁰ x 29⁰
COVERED STOOP
TRANSOMS
Width 56'
Depth 59'-4"
Br. 4
12⁰ x 13⁰
LINEN
Br. 3
13¹⁰ x 11⁹
OPEN TO BELOW
DN
Br. 2
12⁰ x 13¹

Design 9276

First Floor: 1,860 square feet
Second Floor: 848 square feet
Total: 2,708 square feet

■ The gorgeous entry of this traditional home opens to a formal dining room which offers hutch space and a volume living room with through-fireplace to the spacious family room. Look for a tall ceiling and dual entertainment centers here. Adjacent is the bayed breakfast area and island kitchen with a wrap-around counter and a walk-in pantry. The master suite is highlighted with a formal ceiling in the bedroom and a bath with a two-person whirlpool, bayed windows and a double vanity. Upstairs, two bedrooms share private access to a compartmented bath; another bedroom has a private bath.

Design by
Design Basics, Inc.

TRANSOMS
Bfst.
12⁰ x 11⁰
SNACK BAR
Grt. rm.
18⁰ x 15⁵
18'-0" CEILING
Mbr.
14⁰ x 16⁶
11'-8" CEILING
BOOKS
WHIRLPOOL
Kit.
11⁴ x 12⁰
DESK
DN
UP
LIN
HUTCH
Din.
12⁰ x 13⁰
E.
Den
11⁰ x 12⁰
11'-0" CEILING
COVERED STOOP
Gar.
20⁸ x 31⁰
Width 58'
Depth 59'-4"
Br. 2
12³ x 12⁰
OPEN TO BELOW
Br. 3
11³ x 12¹¹
Br. 4
11⁰ x 12⁰
LINEN
10'-0" CEILING

Design 7301

First Floor: 1,777 square feet
Second Floor: 719 square feet
Total: 2,496 square feet

■ Dramatic rooflines, brick detailing and a columned entry highlight this traditional home. The entry overlooks the formal dining room and the den with French doors. The sunken great room features a two-story ceiling and a fireplace flanked by windows and is down a step from the main hall and kitchen. An arched transom window and sloped ceiling accentuate the breakfast area. A peninsula kitchen provides a snack bar, a desk and a pantry. The master bedroom has a volume ceiling and a bay window. The master bath is luxurious and convenient. Three family bedrooms on the second floor share a full bath.

Design by
Design Basics, Inc.

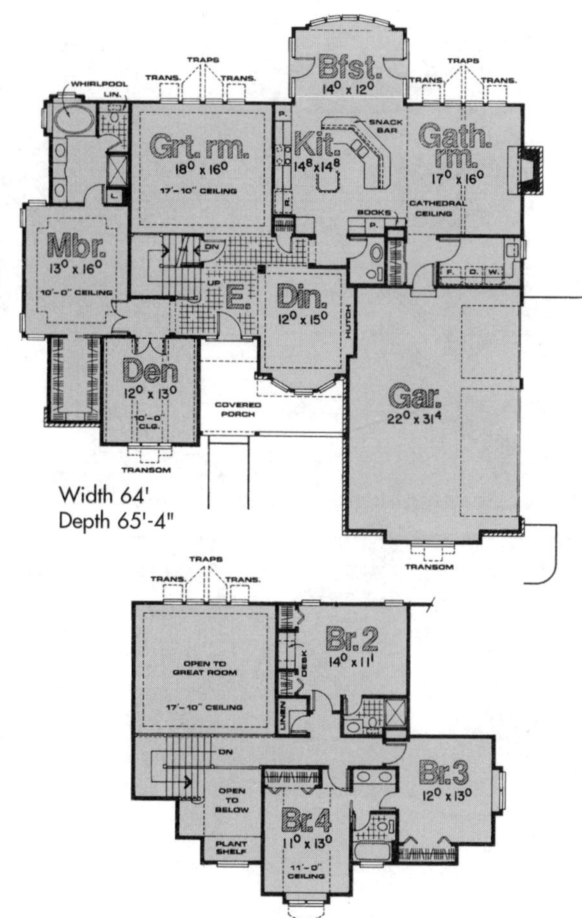

Bfst.
14^0 x 12^0
Grt. rm.
18^0 x 16^0
17'-10" CEILING
Kit.
14^8x14^8
SNACK BAR
Gath. rm.
17^0 x 16^0
CATHEDRAL CEILING
Mbr.
13^0 x 16^0
10'-0" CEILING
WHIRLPOOL
LIN.
TRAPS
TRANS.
BOOKS
E.
Din.
12^0 x 15^0
HUTCH
Den
12^0 x 13^0
10'-0" CLG.
COVERED PORCH
TRANSOM
Gar.
22^0 x 31^4
Width 64'
Depth 65'-4"
OPEN TO GREAT ROOM
17'-10" CEILING
Br. 2
14^0 x 11^1
DESK
LINEN
DN
OPEN TO BELOW
PLANT SHELF
Br. 4
11^0 x 13^0
11'-0" CEILING
Br. 3
12^0 x 13^0

Design 9395

First Floor: 2,158 square feet
Second Floor: 821 square feet
Total: 2,979 square feet

Design by
Design Basics, Inc.

■ The livability present in this design will delight even the most discerning homeowner. Upon entry, an elegant dining room with built-in hutch space commands attention. A two-story great room provides the perfect setting for entertaining. For quieter pursuits, a den is located at the front of the house. Family time is easily spent in the open kitchen, breakfast room, and gathering room. Four bedrooms include a first-floor master suite with a private bath and a large, walk-in closet. Upstairs, two of the secondary bedrooms share a compartmented bath; Bedroom 2 has its own bath.

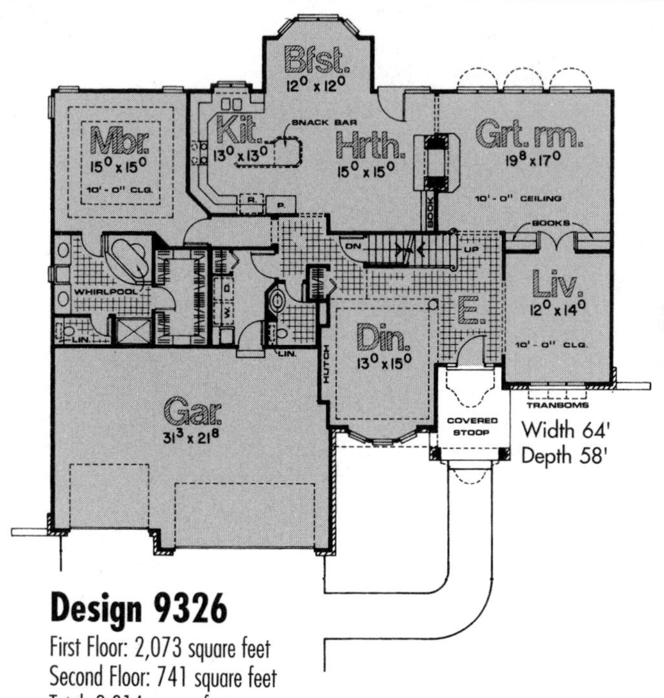

Bfst.
12^0 x 12^0
Mbr.
15^0 x 15^0
10'-0" CLG.
Kit.
13^0 x 13^0
SNACK BAR
Hrth.
15^0 x 15^0
Grt. rm.
19^8 x 17^0
10'-0" CEILING
BOOKS
WHIRLPOOL
LIN.
DN
UP
Liv.
12^0 x 14^0
10'-0" CLG.
E.
Din.
13^0 x 15^0
HUTCH
Gar.
31^3 x 21^8
COVERED STOOP
TRANSOMS
Width 64'
Depth 58'

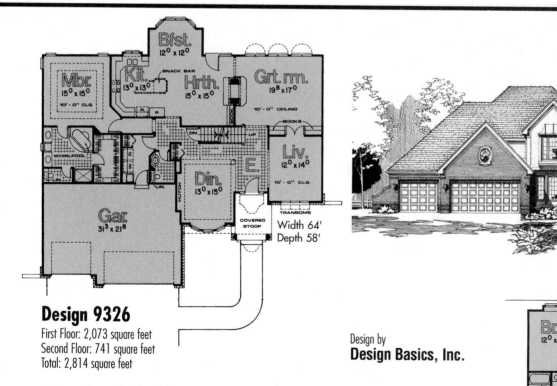

Design 9326

First Floor: 2,073 square feet
Second Floor: 741 square feet
Total: 2,814 square feet

Design by
Design Basics, Inc.

■ From the curbside of this 1½-story home, brick and stucco accents command attention. Ten-foot ceilings enhance the living room and comfortable great room, which are separated by French doors. Family oriented features in the great room include a through-fireplace and bookcases. Special features in the gourmet kitchen and hearth room include a breakfast nook, snack bar and generous counter space. The main-floor master suite offers a tiered ceiling, huge walk-in closet, corner whirlpool, plus His and Hers vanities. Upstairs, three generous secondary bedrooms share a compartmented bath.

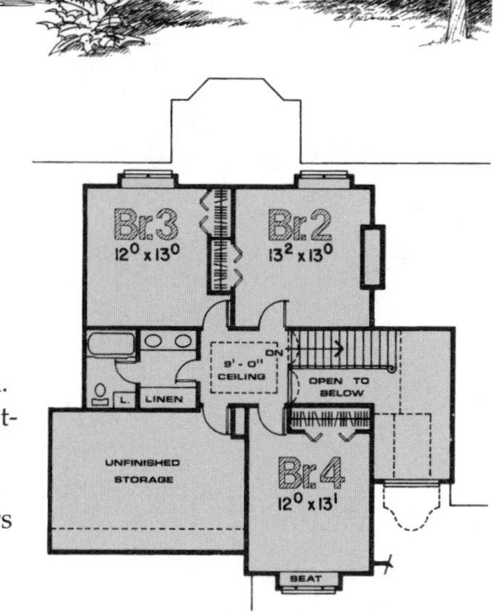

Br. 3
12^0 x 13^0
Br. 2
13^2 x 13^0
9'-0" CEILING
DN
OPEN TO BELOW
LINEN
UNFINISHED STORAGE
Br. 4
12^0 x 13^1
SEAT

G. MacDonald
BOOKS
LIN.
Br. 4
12⁰ x 13⁰
DN
Br. 2
12⁰ x 14⁰
10'-0" CEILING
Br. 3
12⁰ x 14⁰
COVERED VERANDA
WHIRLPOOL
Grt. rm.
18⁰ x 18⁰
11'-8" CEILING
SKYLIGHTS
Hrth.
12⁷ x 15³
Bfst.
11³ x 11³
ENT. CENTER
SNACK BAR
Mbr.
16³ x 14⁰
10'-0" CEILING
UP
DN
Kit.
12⁹ x 12⁸
E.
Den
13³ x 14⁴
10'-4" CLG.
TRANSOMS
Din.
12⁰ x 15⁰
COVERED STOOP
Gar.
21³ x 31³

Design by
Design Basics, Inc.

Width 68'-8"
Depth 60'

Design 9370

First Floor: 2,084 square feet
Second Floor: 848 square feet
Total: 2,932 square feet

■ The combination of brick, stucco, and elegant detail provides this home with instant curb appeal. The entry is flanked by the formal dining room and the den with a fireplace and an intriguing ceiling. The great room offers a through-fireplace to the hearth room and French doors to a covered veranda. A sunny breakfast room and kitchen feature an island with snack bar, wrapping counters and a pantry. The first-floor master suite affords luxury accommodations with two closets, a whirlpool tub, His and Hers vanities and access to the covered veranda. Three secondary bedrooms on the second floor offer walk-in closets and access to bathroom space.

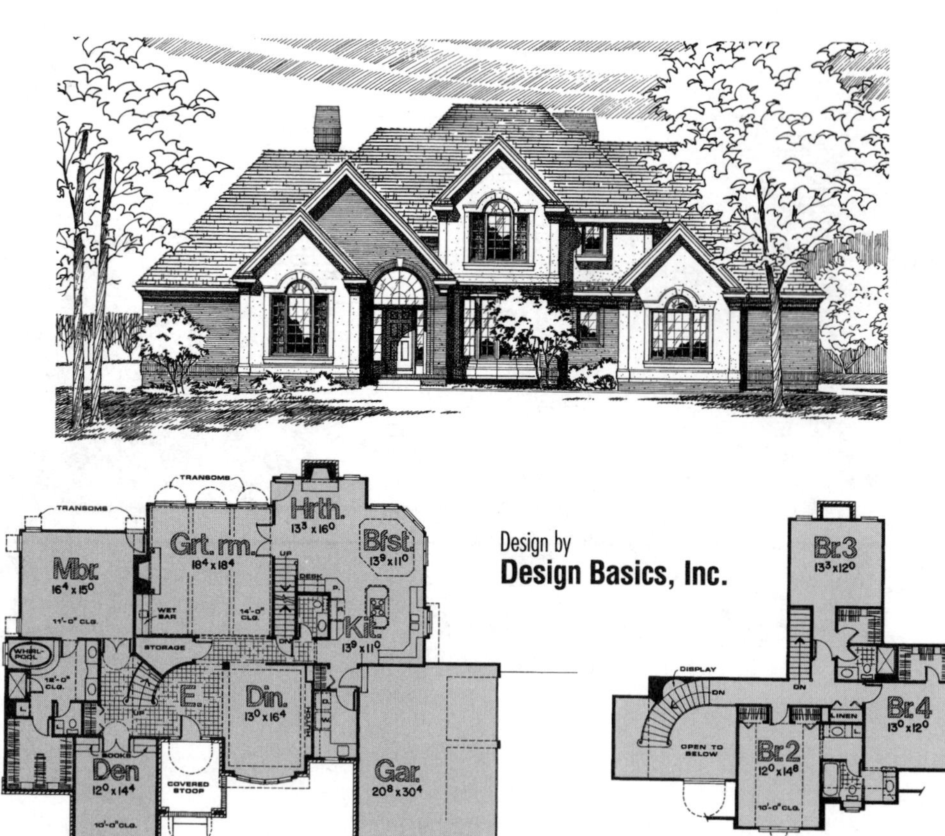
TRANSOMS
TRANSOMS
Hrth.
13³ x 16⁰
Bfst.
13⁹ x 11⁰
Grt. rm.
18⁴ x 18⁴
Mbr.
16⁴ x 15⁰
11'-0" CLG.
WET BAR
14'-0" CLG.
DESK
Kit.
13⁹ x 11⁰
STORAGE
WHIRLPOOL
12'-0" CLG.
E.
Din.
13⁰ x 16⁴
HUTCH
BOOKS
Den
12⁰ x 14⁴
10'-0" CLG.
COVERED STOOP
Gar.
20⁸ x 30⁴
Width 73'-4"
Depth 57'-4"
Design by
Design Basics, Inc.
Br. 3
13³ x 12⁰
DISPLAY
DN
OPEN TO BELOW
LINEN
Br. 4
13⁰ x 12⁰
Br. 2
12⁰ x 14⁸
10'-0" CLG.

Design 9255

First Floor: 2,252 square feet
Second Floor: 920 square feet
Total: 3,172 square feet

■ A curving staircase graces the entry to this beautiful home and hints at the wealth of amenities found in the floor plan. Besides an oversized great room with fireplace and arched windows, there's a cozy hearth room with its own fireplace. The gourmet kitchen has a work island and breakfast area. A secluded den contains bookcases and an arched transom above double doors. The master bedroom is on the first floor, thoughtfully separated from three family bedrooms upstairs. Bedrooms 2 and 4 share a full bath while bedroom 3 has its own private bath. Note the informal stair to the second floor originating in the hearth room.

Design 7204

First Floor: 2,789 square feet
Second Floor: 1,038 square feet
Total: 3,827 square feet

■ The sophisticated lines and elegant brick details of this house are stunning enhancements. The entry surveys a dramatic, curved staircase and French doors to the den. In the dining room, large-sized gatherings are easily accomplished. The living room enjoys an eleven-foot ceiling and a fireplace flanked by transom windows. For more casual living, a family room includes a raised-hearth fireplace and a built-in desk. The gourmet kitchen has two pantries, an island cooktop, a snack bar, and private stairs to the second level. Four bedrooms include a pampering master suite.

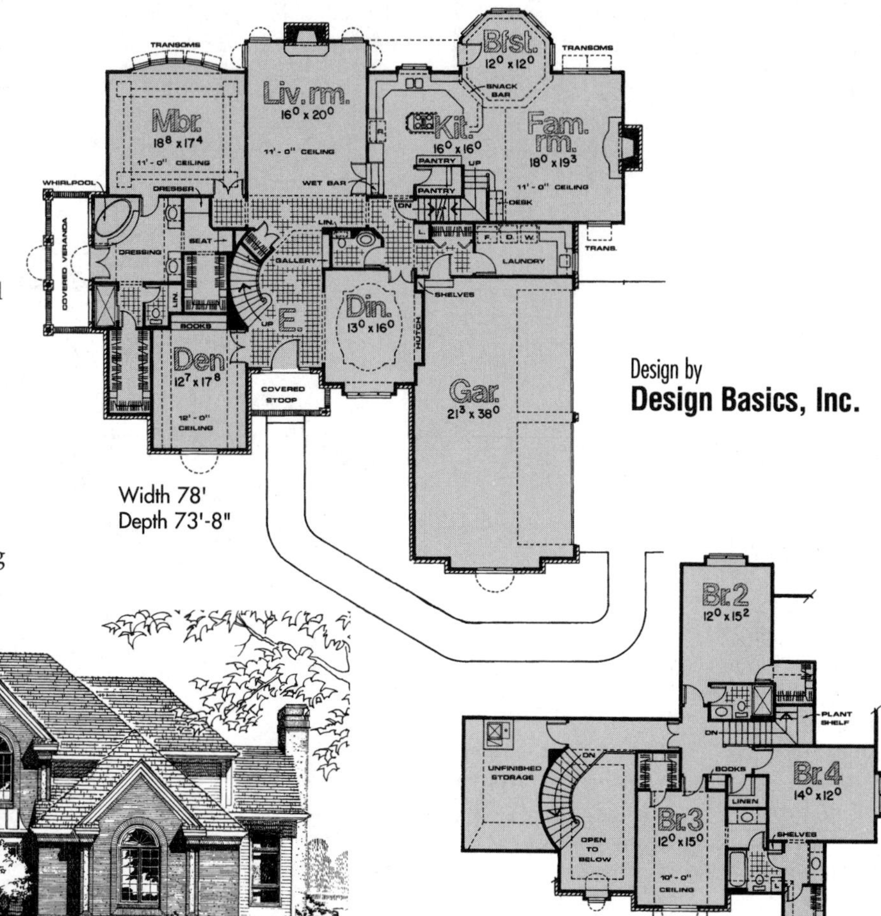
TRANSOMS
Bfst.
12⁰ x 12⁰
TRANSOMS
SNACK BAR
Mbr.
18⁸ x 17⁴
11'-0" CEILING
Liv. rm.
16⁰ x 20⁰
11'-0" CEILING
Kit.
16⁰ x 16⁰
PANTRY
Fam. rm.
18⁰ x 19³
11'-0" CEILING
WHIRLPOOL
DRESSER
WET BAR
PANTRY
DESK
DRESSING
SEAT
LIN.
GALLERY
LAUNDRY
TRANS.
COVERED VERANDA
SHELVES
BOOKS
Din.
13⁰ x 16⁰
HUTCH
E.
Den
12⁷ x 17⁸
12'-0" CEILING
COVERED STOOP
Gar.
21³ x 38⁰
Design by
Design Basics, Inc.
Width 78'
Depth 73'-8"
Br. 2
12⁰ x 15²
PLANT SHELF
UNFINISHED STORAGE
BOOKS
Br. 4
14⁰ x 12⁰
LINEN
Br. 3
12⁰ x 15⁰
10'-0" CEILING
OPEN TO BELOW
SHELVES

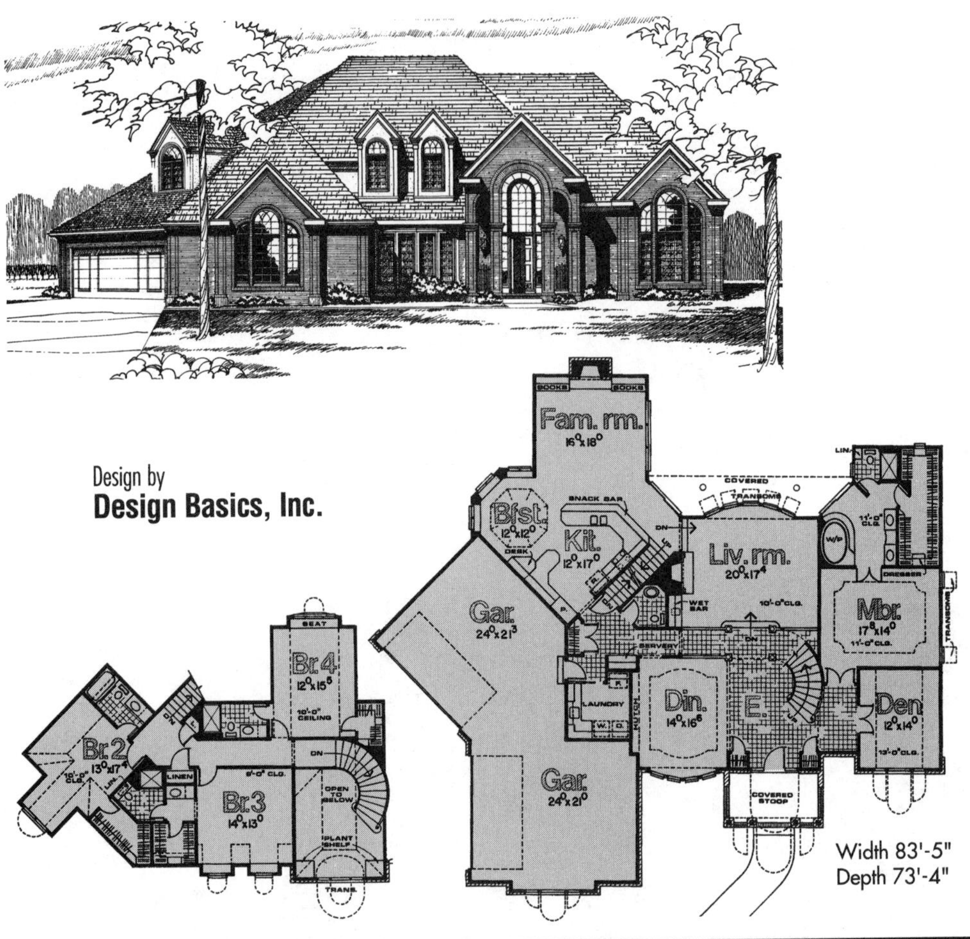
Fam. rm.
16⁰x18⁰
BOOKS
SNACK BAR
Bfst.
12⁰x12⁰
DESK
Kit.
12⁰x17⁰
COVERED
TRANSOMS
Liv. rm.
20⁰x17⁴
10'-0" CLG.
WET BAR
Mbr.
17⁸x14⁰
11'-0" CLG.
Gar.
24⁰x21³
SERVERY
LAUNDRY
HUTCH
Din.
14⁰x16⁶
E.
Den
12⁰x14⁰
12'-0" CLG.
COVERED STOOP
Gar.
24⁰x21⁰
Br. 4
12⁰x15⁶
SEAT
10'-0" CEILING
Br. 2
13⁰x17⁴
LINEN
Br. 3
14⁰x13⁰
9'-0" CLG.
OPEN TO BELOW
PLANT SHELF
TRANS.

Design by
Design Basics, Inc.

Width 83'-5"
Depth 73'-4"

Design 9346

First Floor: 2,617 square feet
Second Floor: 1,072 square feet
Total: 3,689 square feet

■ A spectacular volume entry with curving staircase features columns to the formal areas of this home. The living room contains a fireplace, bowed window and wet bar. The formal dining room contains hutch space and nearby servery. All main-level rooms have nine-foot ceilings. To the rear of the plan is the family room. It has bookcases surrounding a fireplace. French doors lead into the den with a stunning window. The master suite is located on the first floor and has a most elegant bath and huge walk-in closet. Second-floor bedrooms also have walk-in closets and private baths.

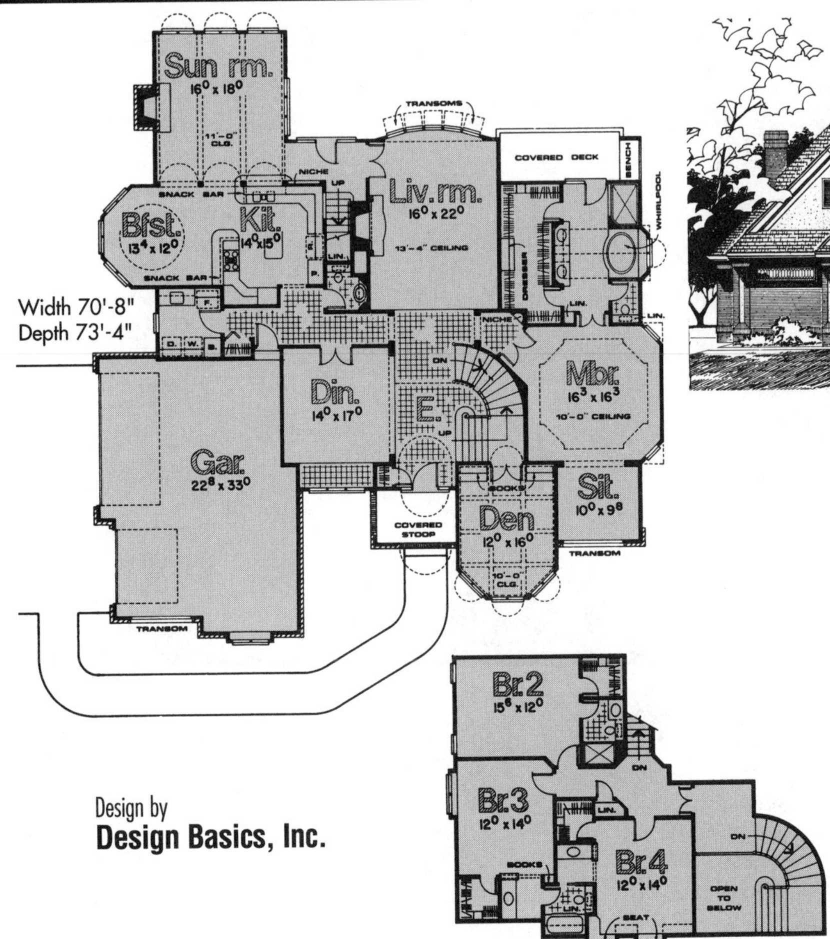
Sun rm.
16⁰ x 18⁰
11'-0" CLG.
TRANSOMS
COVERED DECK
BENCH
WHIRLPOOL
NICHE
SNACK BAR
Bfst.
13⁴ x 12⁰
Kit.
14⁰x15⁰
Liv. rm.
16⁰ x 22⁰
13'-4" CEILING
DRESSER
SNACK BAR
Mbr.
16³ x 16³
10'-0" CEILING
Din.
14⁰ x 17⁰
E.
Gar.
22⁸ x 33⁰
COVERED STOOP
Den
12⁰ x 16⁰
10'-0" CLG.
Sit.
10⁰ x 9⁸
TRANSOM
TRANSOM
Br. 2
15⁶ x 12⁰
Br. 3
12⁰ x 14⁰
Br. 4
12⁰ x 14⁰
BOOKS
SEAT
OPEN TO BELOW

Width 70'-8"
Depth 73'-4"

Design by
Design Basics, Inc.

Design 7245

First Floor: 2,804 square feet
Second Floor: 961 square feet
Total: 3,765 square feet

■ This captivating exterior is accentuated by handsome stone columns and a dramatic cantilevered bay. Inside, formal elegance is captured in the living room that has a volume ceiling, bowed windows and fireplace. The kitchen is enhanced with a prep island, snack bar and pantry. Informal gatherings will be enjoyed in the breakfast nook or the sun room. The master suite has an adjoining sitting room and a luxury bath. Upstairs, at landing level is a den complete with a spider beam ceiling. The second floor houses three bedrooms—two share a bath and one has a private bath.

Design by
Donald A. Gardner, Architects, Inc.

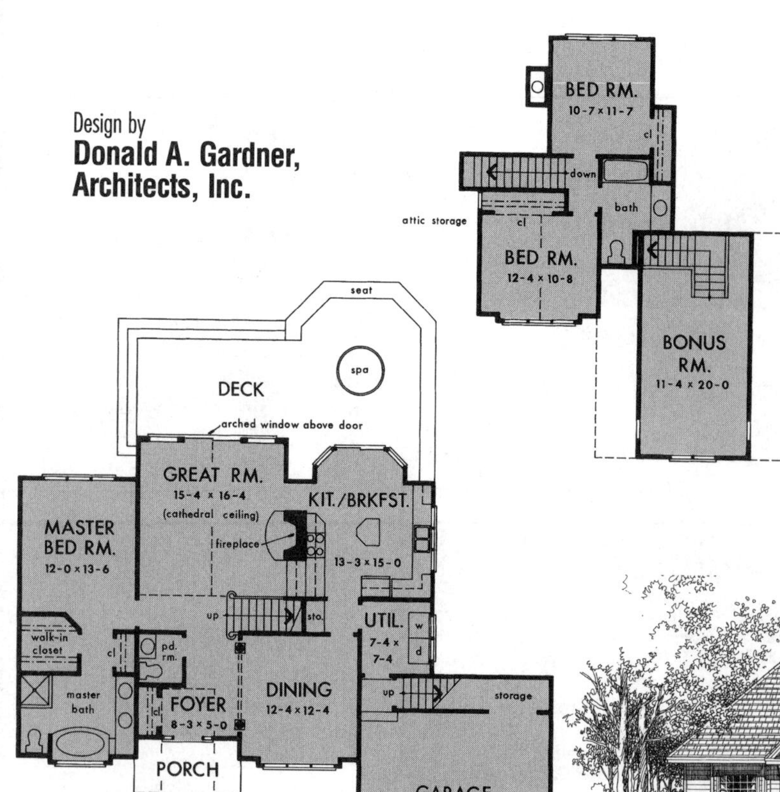

BED RM.
10-7 x 11-7
cl
down
bath
attic storage
cl
BED RM.
12-4 x 10-8
BONUS RM.
11-4 x 20-0
seat
spa
DECK
arched window above door
GREAT RM.
15-4 x 16-4
(cathedral ceiling)
fireplace
KIT./BRKFST.
13-3 x 15-0
MASTER BED RM.
12-0 x 13-6
up
sto.
UTIL.
7-4 x 7-4
w
d
walk-in closet
cl
pd. rm.
master bath
cl
FOYER
8-3 x 5-0
DINING
12-4 x 12-4
up
storage
PORCH
GARAGE
20-0 x 20-0
Width 56'-7"
Depth 64'

Design 9692

First Floor: 1,288 square feet
Second Floor: 410 square feet
Total: 1,698 square feet
Bonus Room: 289 square feet

■ An arched entrance and windows combine with the round columns of this home for an eye-catching exterior. The dining room features round columns at the entrance, while the great room boasts a cathedral ceiling, fireplace and doors to the deck. A large open kitchen has an island and separate entrance to the deck. A master bedroom with plenty of walk-in closet space includes a bath with a double-bowl vanity, shower and whirlpool tub. On the second level are two bedrooms sharing a full bath.

Design 9661

First Floor: 1,416 square feet
Second Floor: 445 square feet
Total: 1,861 square feet
Bonus Room: 284 square feet

■ This charming country home gives a warm welcome inside and out. Designed for maximum livability, the foyer leads to all areas of the house to minimize corridor space. The dining room has round columns at the entrance while the great room boasts a cathedral ceiling, fireplace and arched passage to the large country kitchen that's completed with an angled cooktop island and breakfast nook. In the master suite are two walk-in closets and a lavish bath. On the second level are two bedrooms and a full bath. Bonus space over the garage can be developed later. Please specify basement or crawlspace foundation when ordering.

QUOTE ONE®

Cost to build? See page 342 to order complete cost estimate to build this house in your area!

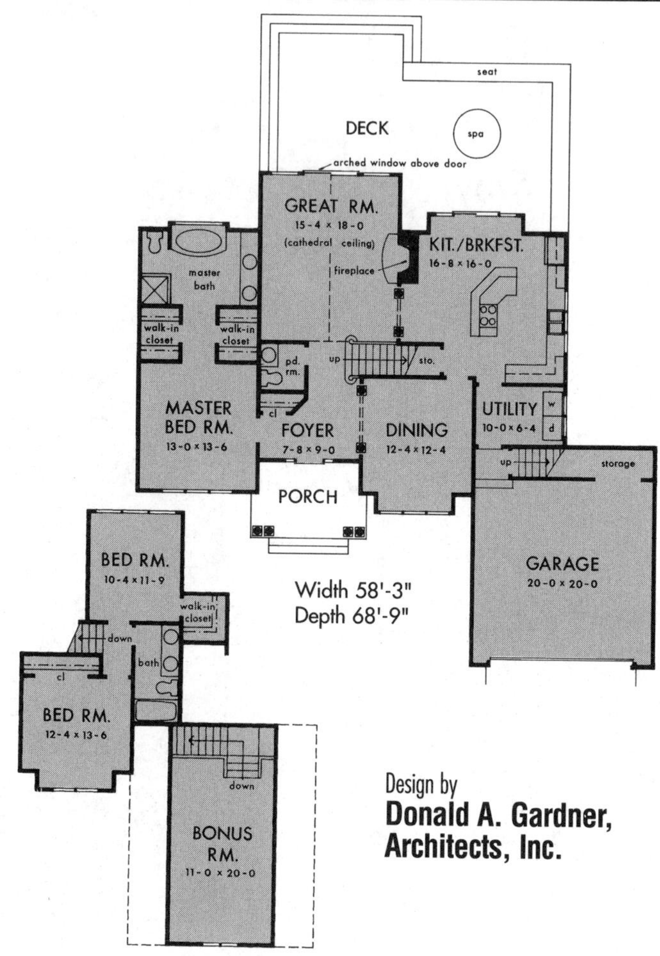

seat
DECK
spa
arched window above door
GREAT RM.
15-4 x 18-0
(cathedral ceiling)
fireplace
KIT./BRKFST.
16-8 x 16-0
master bath
walk-in closet
walk-in closet
pd. rm.
up
sto.
MASTER BED RM.
13-0 x 13-6
cl
FOYER
7-8 x 9-0
DINING
12-4 x 12-4
UTILITY
10-0 x 6-4
w
d
up
storage
PORCH
GARAGE
20-0 x 20-0
Width 58'-3"
Depth 68'-9"
BED RM.
10-4 x 11-9
walk-in closet
down
bath
cl
BED RM.
12-4 x 13-6
down
BONUS RM.
11-0 x 20-0

Design by
Donald A. Gardner, Architects, Inc.

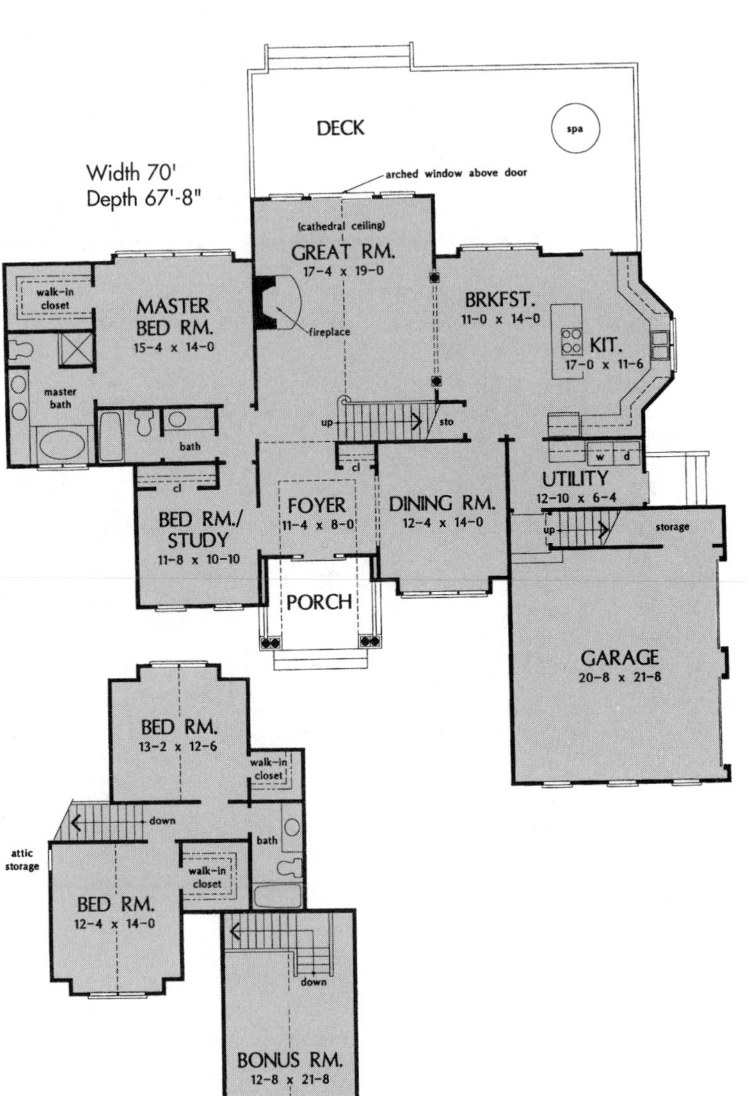
DECK
spa
arched window above door
Width 70'
Depth 67'-8"
(cathedral ceiling)
GREAT RM.
17-4 x 19-0
fireplace
walk-in closet
MASTER BED RM.
15-4 x 14-0
master bath
bath
BRKFST.
11-0 x 14-0
KIT.
17-0 x 11-6
up
sto
cl
BED RM./ STUDY
11-8 x 10-10
FOYER
11-4 x 8-0
DINING RM.
12-4 x 14-0
UTILITY
12-10 x 6-4
storage
PORCH
GARAGE
20-8 x 21-8
BED RM.
13-2 x 12-6
walk-in closet
down
bath
attic storage
walk-in closet
BED RM.
12-4 x 14-0
down
BONUS RM.
12-8 x 21-8
attic storage
attic storage

Design by
Donald A. Gardner, Architects, Inc.

Design 9736

First Floor: 1,839 square feet
Second Floor: 527 square feet
Total: 2,366 square feet
Bonus Room: 344 square feet

■ An arched entrance and windows combine with round columns to give a touch of class on the exterior of this four-bedroom plan. The plan layout allows no wasted space. The foyer leads to all areas of the house, minimizing corridor space. The large, open kitchen with an island cooktop is convenient to the breakfast and dining rooms. The master bedroom suite has plenty of walk-in closet space and a well-planned master bath. A nearby bedroom would make an excellent guest room or study, with an adjacent full bath. An expansive rear deck boasts a location for a spa and generous space for outdoor living. The second level offers two bedrooms, with sloped ceilings and walk-in closets, and a full bath. A bonus room is available over the garage.

Br.2
11⁰x10⁰
DN
Br.3
11⁰x10⁰
TRANSOMS
Kit.
10⁸x11²
SNACK BAR
Bfst.
11⁰x12⁴
Grt. rm.
14⁰x18⁷
12'-4" CEILING
DESK
SKYLIGHT
11'-0" CLG.
W/P
DN
UP
Din.
11⁰x12⁰
E.
Mbr.
13⁰x14⁰
9'-0" CLG.
SEAT
Gar.
20⁰x22⁴
COVERED PORCH
Width 52'
Depth 45'-4"

QUOTE ONE®

Cost to build? See page 342 to order complete cost estimate to build this house in your area!

Design 9265

First Floor: 1,297 square feet
Second Floor: 388 square feet
Total: 1,685 square feet

■ A lovely covered porch welcomes family and guests to this delightful one-story home. From the entry, the formal dining room with boxed windows and the great room with fireplace are visible. A powder room for guests is located just beyond the dining room. An open kitchen/dinette features a pantry, planning desk and a snack-bar counter. The elegant master suite is appointed with formal ceiling detail and a window seat. The skylight above the whirlpool, the decorator plant shelf, and the double lavatories all dress up the master bath. Family bedrooms on the second floor share a centrally located bath.

Design by
Design Basics, Inc.

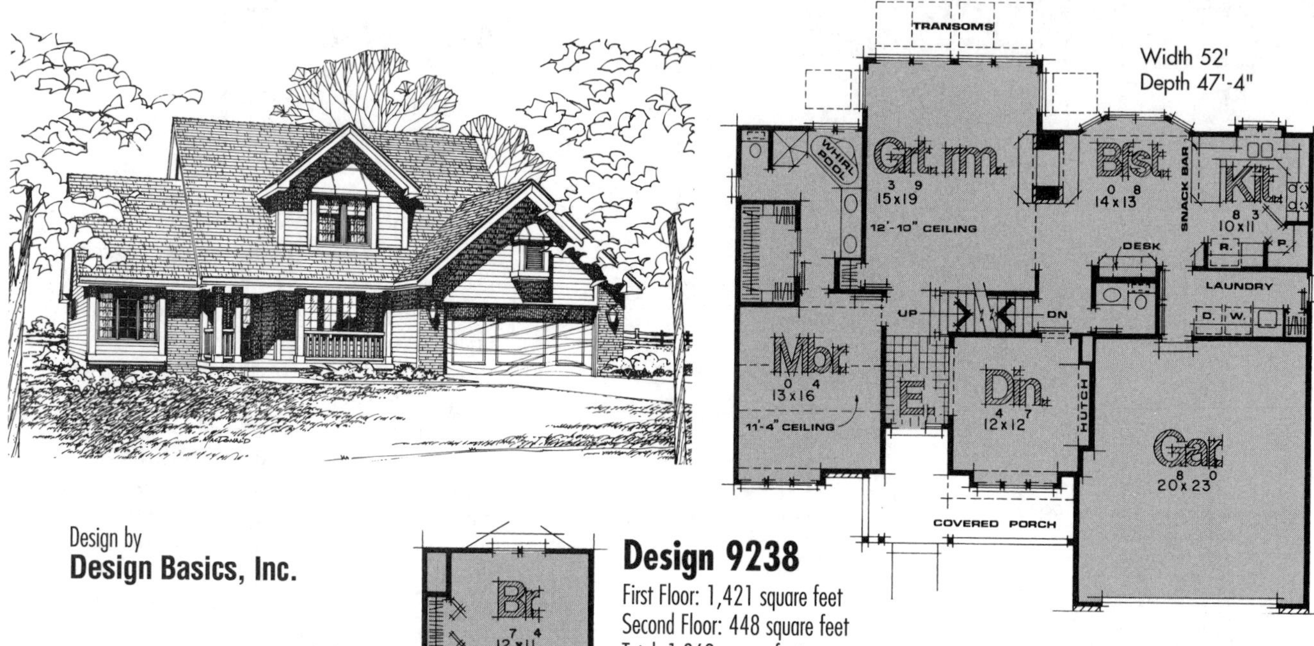

TRANSOMS
Width 52'
Depth 47'-4"
WHIRLPOOL
Grt. rm.
15³x19⁹
12'-10" CEILING
Bfst.
14⁰x13⁸
SNACK BAR
Kit.
10⁸x11³
DESK
LAUNDRY
UP
DN
Mbr.
13⁰x16⁴
11'-4" CEILING
E.
Din.
12⁴x12⁷
HUTCH
Gar.
20⁶x23⁰
COVERED PORCH

Design by
Design Basics, Inc.

Design 9238

First Floor: 1,421 square feet
Second Floor: 448 square feet
Total: 1,869 square feet

■ Always a welcome site, the covered front porch of this home invites investigation of its delightful floor plan. Living areas to the back of the house include the great room, containing a see-through fireplace to the hearth kitchen with bayed dinette, planning desk, and large corner walk-in pantry. The formal dining room is conveniently placed. A split-bedroom sleeping plan puts the master suite with whirlpool tub, walk-in closet, and double vanity on the first floor away from two second-floor bedrooms and a shared full bath.

Br.
12⁷x11⁴
OPEN TO GREAT ROOM
DN
Br.
11⁴x11³

QUOTE ONE®

Cost to build? See page 342 to order complete cost estimate to build this house in your area!

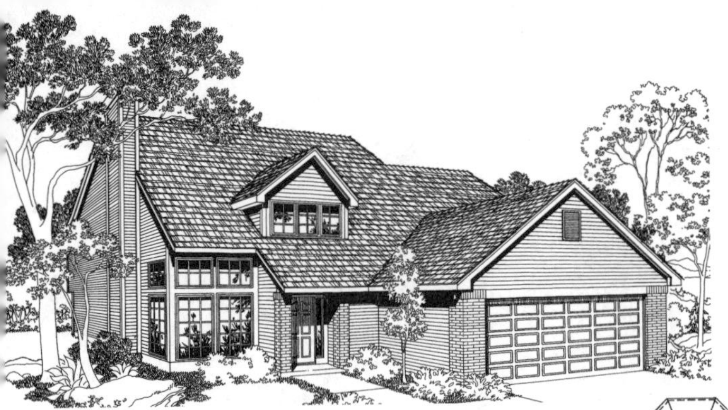

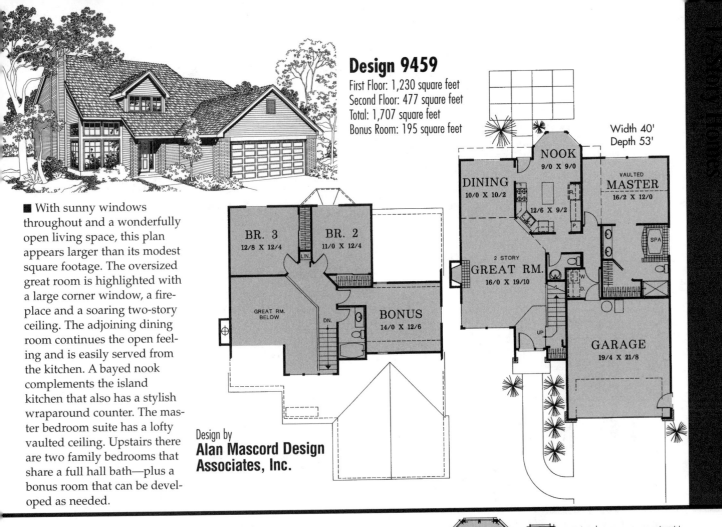

Design 9459

First Floor: 1,230 square feet
Second Floor: 477 square feet
Total: 1,707 square feet
Bonus Room: 195 square feet

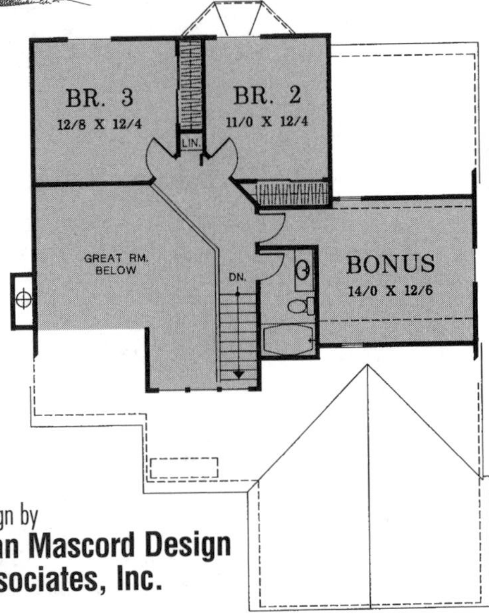

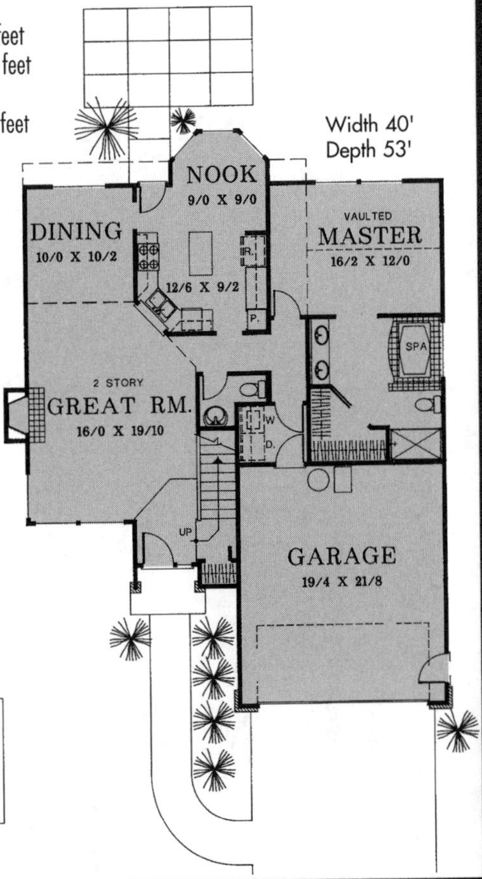

Width 40'
Depth 53'

■ With sunny windows throughout and a wonderfully open living space, this plan appears larger than its modest square footage. The oversized great room is highlighted with a large corner window, a fireplace and a soaring two-story ceiling. The adjoining dining room continues the open feeling and is easily served from the kitchen. A bayed nook complements the island kitchen that also has a stylish wraparound counter. The master bedroom suite has a lofty vaulted ceiling. Upstairs there are two family bedrooms that share a full hall bath—plus a bonus room that can be developed as needed.

Design by
Alan Mascord Design Associates, Inc.

Design by
Design Basics, Inc.

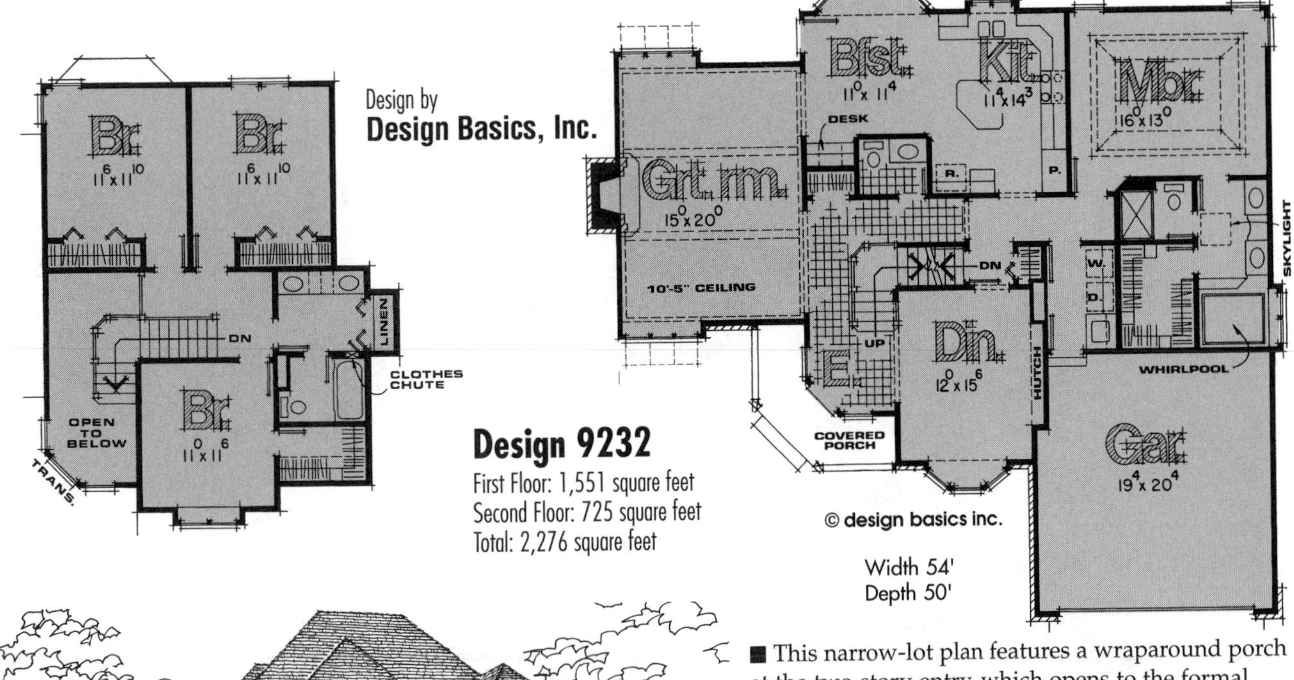

Br. 11⁶x11¹⁰
Br. 11⁶x11¹⁰
Br. 11⁰x11⁶
DN
LINEN
CLOTHES CHUTE
OPEN TO BELOW
TRANS.
Bfst. 11⁰x11⁴
Kit. 11⁴x14³
Mbr. 16⁰x13⁰
DESK
Grt.rm. 15⁰x20⁰
10'-5" CEILING
R.
P.
W.
D.
SKYLIGHT
WHIRLPOOL
UP
E
Din. 12⁰x15⁶
HUTCH
COVERED PORCH
Gar. 19⁴x20⁴

Design 9232

First Floor: 1,551 square feet
Second Floor: 725 square feet
Total: 2,276 square feet

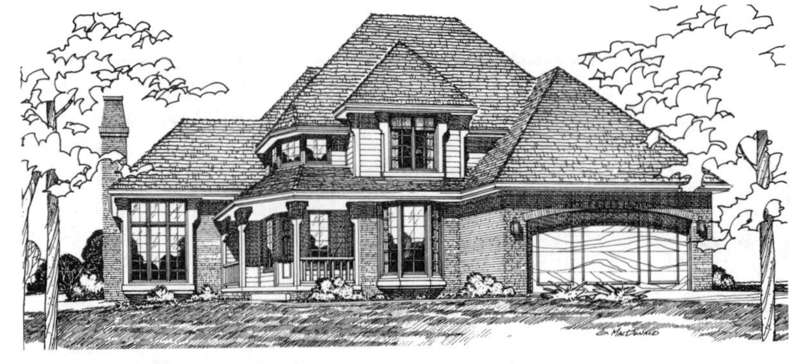

© design basics inc.

Width 54'
Depth 50'

■ This narrow-lot plan features a wraparound porch at the two-story entry, which opens to the formal dining room with beautiful bay windows. The great room features a handsome fireplace and a ten-and-a-half foot ceiling. A well-equipped island kitchen with pantry and built-in desk is designed for the serious cook. The large master bedroom has a vaulted ceiling and a luxury master bath. Upstairs, three secondary bedrooms with ample closet space share a compartmented bath.

Design by
Larry E. Belk Designs

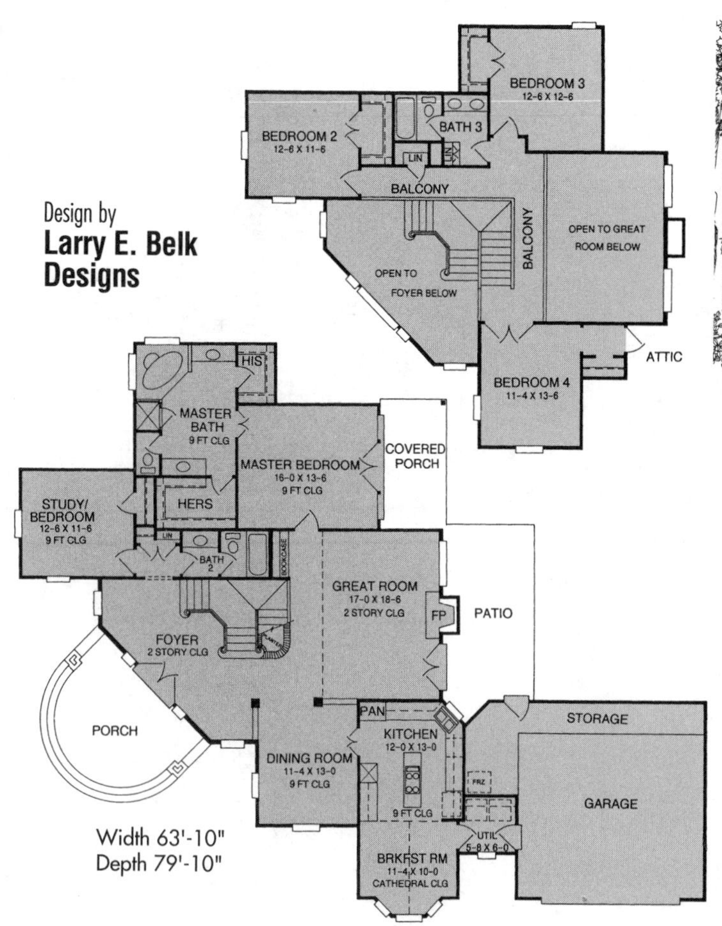

BEDROOM 3
12-6 X 12-6
BEDROOM 2
12-6 X 11-6
BATH 3
LIN
BALCONY
OPEN TO GREAT ROOM BELOW
OPEN TO FOYER BELOW
BALCONY
BEDROOM 4
11-4 X 13-6
ATTIC
HIS
MASTER BATH
9 FT CLG
MASTER BEDROOM
16-0 X 13-6
9 FT CLG
COVERED PORCH
STUDY/ BEDROOM
12-6 X 11-6
9 FT CLG
HERS
BATH 2
GREAT ROOM
17-0 X 18-6
2 STORY CLG
FP
PATIO
FOYER
2 STORY CLG
PORCH
PAN
KITCHEN
12-0 X 13-0
9 FT CLG
STORAGE
DINING ROOM
11-4 X 13-0
9 FT CLG
GARAGE
UTIL
5-8 X 6-0
BRKFST RM
11-4 X 10-0
CATHEDRAL CLG
Width 63'-10"
Depth 79'-10"

Design 8179

First Floor: 1,966 square feet
Second Floor: 872 square feet
Total: 2,838 square feet

■ The grand, two-story foyer of this European-style home leads you into the formal dining room defined by pillars. A deluxe master bedroom suite is full of amenities including His and Hers walk-in closets, a corner garden tub, twin vanities and access to a private covered porch. A study/bedroom and a full bath complete this floor. Upstairs, three bedrooms, each with walk-in closets, share a full hall bath. Please specify crawlspace or slab foundation when ordering.

Design 9244

First Floor: 1,972 square feet
Second Floor: 893 square feet
Total: 2,865 square feet

Design by
Design Basics, Inc.

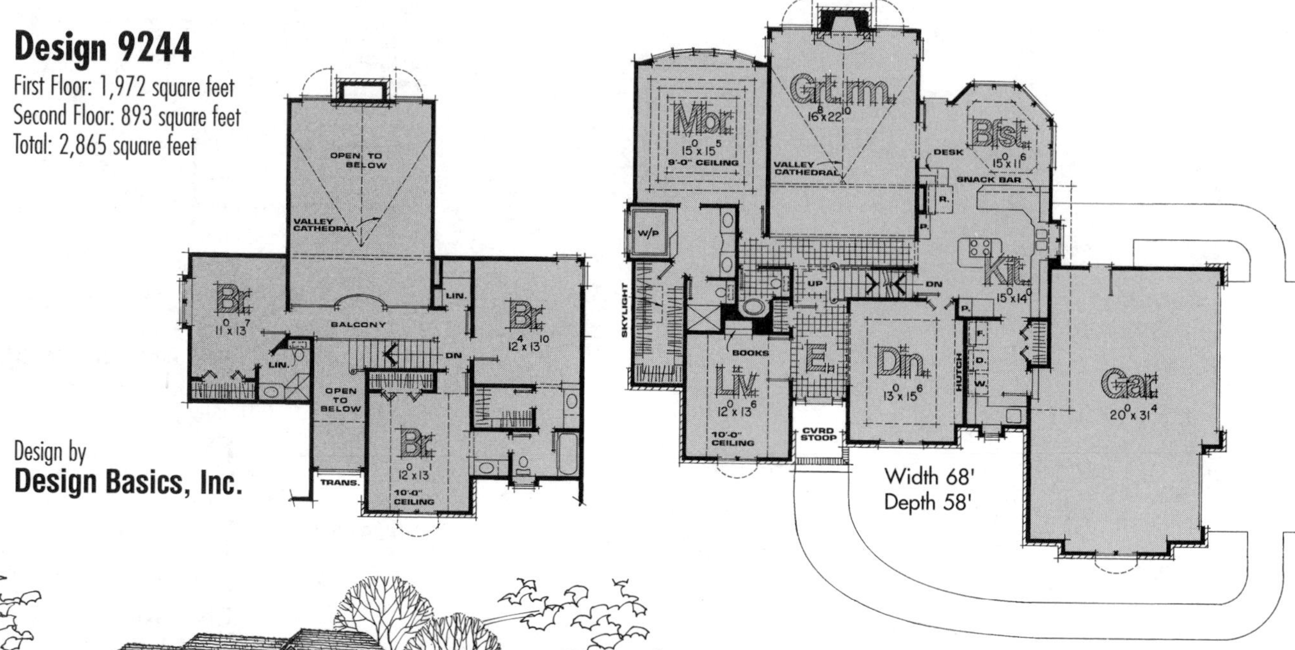

OPEN TO BELOW
VALLEY CATHEDRAL
Br
BALCONY
LIN.
Br
DN
OPEN TO BELOW
Br
10'-0" CEILING
TRANS.
Mbr
9'-0" CEILING
Grt.rm.
VALLEY CATHEDRAL
Bfst.
DESK
SNACK BAR
W/P
SKYLIGHT
UP
DN
Kit.
BOOKS
Liv.
10'-0" CEILING
E.
Din.
HUTCH
Gar.
CVRD STOOP
Width 68'
Depth 58'

■ Natural light from transom windows floods the entry of this home, traditionally flanked by the formal living room and dining room. The large great room to the rear of the plan has a cathedral ceiling and fireplace framed by windows. An island kitchen has two pantries and a gazebo dinette. The sumptuous master suite has a bow window and tiered ceiling, plus a lush bath. Upstairs bedrooms include two with a Hollywood bath and one with its own three-quarter bath.

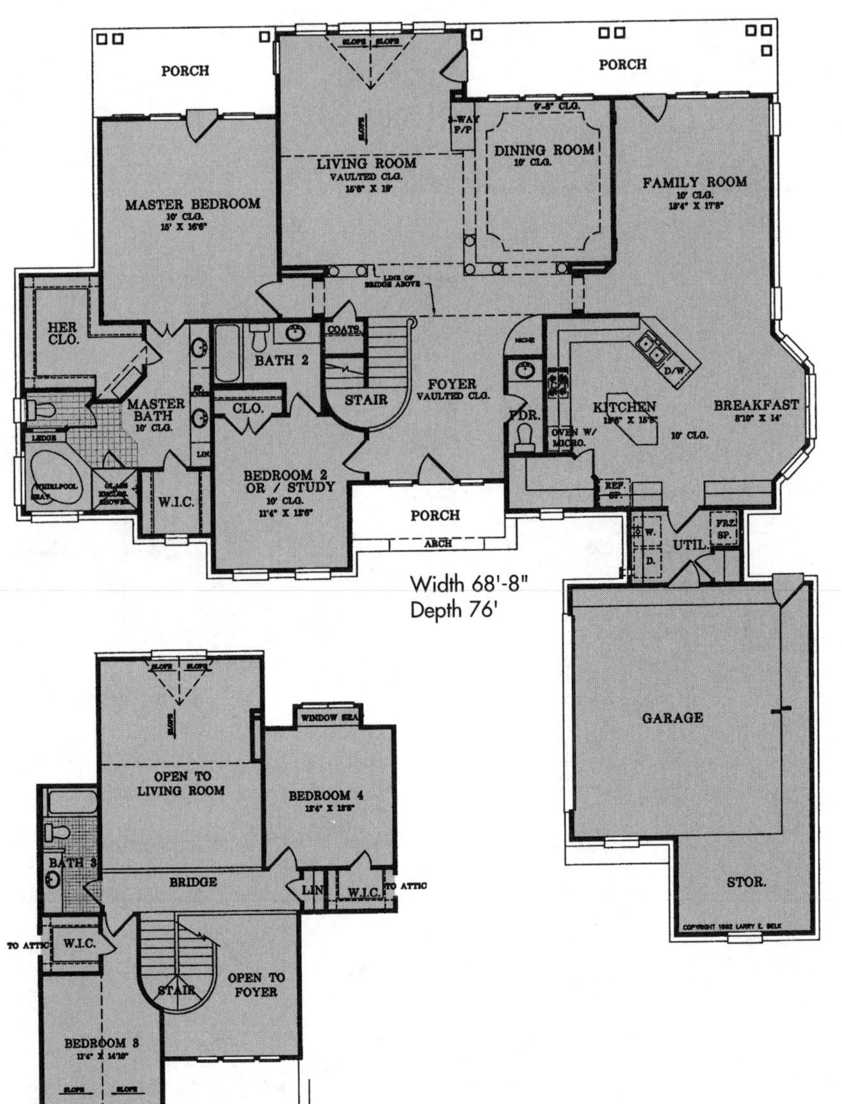
PORCH
PORCH
LIVING ROOM
VAULTED CLG.
DINING ROOM
MASTER BEDROOM
FAMILY ROOM
HER CLO.
BATH 2
COATS
STAIR
FOYER
VAULTED CLG.
MASTER BATH
CLO.
KITCHEN
BREAKFAST
PDR.
W.I.C.
BEDROOM 2
OR / STUDY
PORCH
ARCH
UTIL.
GARAGE
STOR.
Width 68'-8"
Depth 76'
OPEN TO
LIVING ROOM
BEDROOM 4
BATH 3
BRIDGE
LIN
W.I.C.
W.I.C.
OPEN TO
FOYER
STAIR
BEDROOM 3

Design 8022

First Floor: 2,385 square feet
Second Floor: 619 square feet
Total: 3,004 square feet

■ A two-story glass entry banded in stucco provides a striking focal point on this lovely brick home. Inside, the vaulted foyer leads to the formal living room and dining room, which share a three-way fireplace. The family room, breakfast area and kitchen are conveniently grouped for informal family gatherings. The efficient kitchen features a large work island and walk-in pantry, making meal preparation a breeze. An amenity-filled master suite is situated on the first floor with a luxurious bath and access to a rear porch. On the first floor, Bedroom 2 enjoys a full bath while Bedrooms 3 and 4, located upstairs, share a spacious bath.

Design by
Larry E. Belk Designs

Design 9896

First Floor: 1,225 square feet
Second Floor: 563 square feet
Total: 1,788 square feet

■ A 1½-story home with mixed exterior materials is hard to beat. Both casual and formal occasions are accommodated from the great room with fireplace to the formal dining room. An informal breakfast room complements the gourmet kitchen; its bay window makes family dining a treat. The master suite is found on the first floor. It features a huge walk-in closet, corner tub, separate shower and compartmented toilet. There are two family bedrooms on the second floor. Unfinished space on the second floor can function as storage or be developed into a fourth bedroom if needed. This home is designed with a basement foundation.

DECK
BREAKFAST 10'-4" X 9'-0"
MASTER BEDROOM 14'-6" X 12'-6"
GREAT ROOM 12'-0" X 16'-8"
KITCHEN 10'-4" X 10'-4"
MASTER BATH
W.I.C.
DN
UP
FOYER 5'-8" X 6'-8"
DINING ROOM 10'-0" X 12'-4"
POWDER
LAUNDRY
TWO-CAR GARAGE 19'-4" X 20'-0"
Width 42'
Depth 50'
OPEN TO BELOW
BEDROOM NO. 2 12'-8" X 11'-4"
DN
GALLERY
BEDROOM NO. 3 10'-0" X 10'-8"
BATH
UNFIN. BONUS 9'-4" X 21'-10"

Design by
Design Traditions

QUOTE ONE®
Cost to build? See page 342 to order complete cost estimate to build this house in your area!

Design by
Frank Betz Associates, Inc.

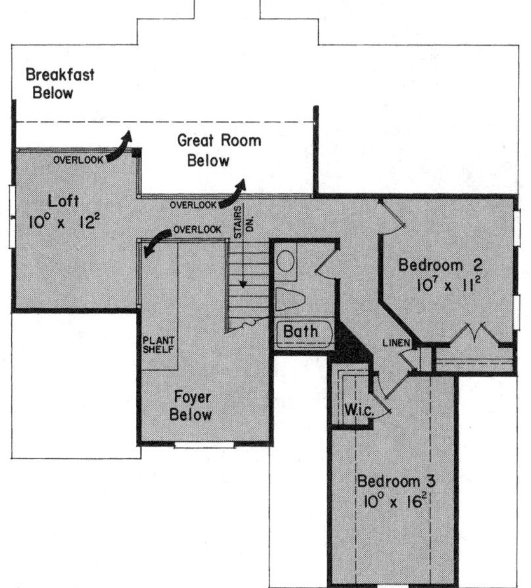
Breakfast Below
OVERLOOK
Great Room Below
Loft 10⁰ x 12²
OVERLOOK
OVERLOOK
STAIRS DN.
Bedroom 2 10⁷ x 11²
PLANT SHELF
Bath
LINEN
Foyer Below
W.i.c.
Bedroom 3 10⁰ x 16²

Design P113

First Floor: 1,133 square feet
Second Floor: 486 square feet
Total: 1,619 square feet
Optional Loft: 135 square feet

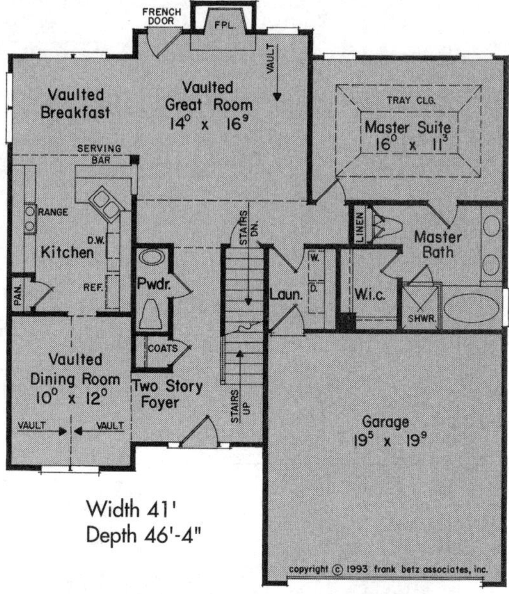
FRENCH DOOR
FPL.
VAULT
Vaulted Breakfast
Vaulted Great Room 14⁰ x 16⁹
TRAY CLG.
Master Suite 16⁰ x 11³
SERVING BAR
RANGE
Kitchen
D.W.
REF.
PAN.
STAIRS DN.
LINEN
W. D.
Master Bath
Pwdr.
Laun.
W.i.c.
SHWR.
COATS
Vaulted Dining Room 10⁰ x 12⁰
Two Story Foyer
VAULT
VAULT
STAIRS UP
Garage 19⁵ x 19⁹
Width 41'
Depth 46'-4"
copyright © 1993 frank betz associates, inc.

■ Stucco and stone provide a pleasing contrast to the large-pane windows on the exterior of this two-story family home. Open planning joins the great room and the breakfast room under a dramatic vaulted ceiling. The modified galley kitchen features a serving bar to the breakfast room and has easy access to the formal dining room. The master suite has a tray ceiling, a compartmented bath and a walk-in closet. Stairs lead up to a balcony overlooking the great room and to two family bedrooms. An optional loft can be converted to a fourth bedroom, if desired.

DECK
BREAKFAST
12'-0" X 10'-0"
MASTER BATH
MASTER BEROOM
13'-0" X 15'-4"
TWO STORY
FAMILY ROOM
14'-6" X 15'-0"
KITCHEN
12'-0" X 14'-8"
POWDER
W.I.C.
DN
LAUNDRY
STORAGE
DINING ROOM
13'-4" X 11'-8"
UP
TWO STORY
FOYER
9'-0" X 15'-0"
TWO CAR GARAGE
22'-4" X 20'-8"
LIVING ROOM
13'-4" X 11'-4"
STOOP

Width 50'
Depth 53'-6"

Design 9876

First Floor: 1,720 square feet
Second Floor: 545 square feet
Total: 2,265 square feet

■ The foyer opens to the living and dining areas, providing a spectacular entrance to this English country cottage. Just beyond the dining room is a gourmet kitchen with work island and food bar opening onto the breakfast room. Accented by a fireplace and built-in bookcase, the family room with a ribbon of windows is an excellent setting for family gatherings. Located off the central hallway, the master suite includes a rectangular ceiling detail and access to the rear deck, while the master bath features His and Hers vanities, garden tub, and spacious walk-in closet. The central staircase leads to the balcony overlook and three bedrooms with spacious closets and baths. This home is designed with a basement foundation.

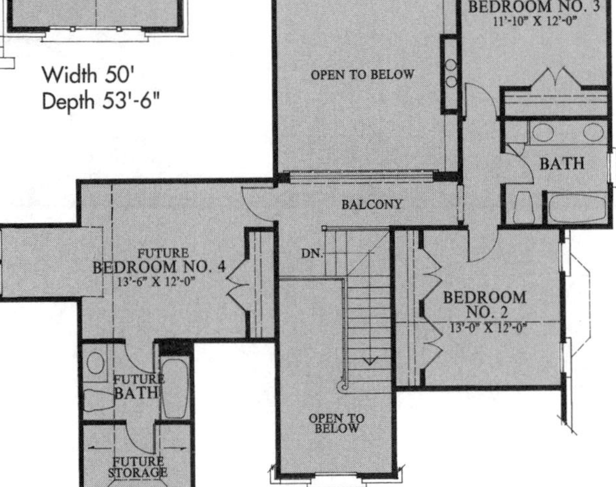

BEDROOM NO. 3
11'-10" X 12'-0"
OPEN TO BELOW
BATH
BALCONY
FUTURE
BEDROOM NO. 4
13'-6" X 12'-0"
DN.
BEDROOM
NO. 2
13'-0" X 12'-0"
FUTURE
BATH
OPEN TO
BELOW
FUTURE
STORAGE

Design by
Design Traditions

Design P112

First Floor: 1,637 square feet
Second Floor: 671 square feet
Total: 2,308 square feet

■ Custom features abound in this traditional home with the inclusion of plant shelves, built-in shelves and niches, a romantic second-floor balcony and a vaulted ceiling in the foyer, formal living, family and breakfast rooms. The kitchen has an abundance of counter and cabinet space. The master suite has an elegant tray ceiling and an oversized bath with a whirlpool and walk-in closet. Upstairs, two family bedrooms and a bonus room share a compartmented hall bath.

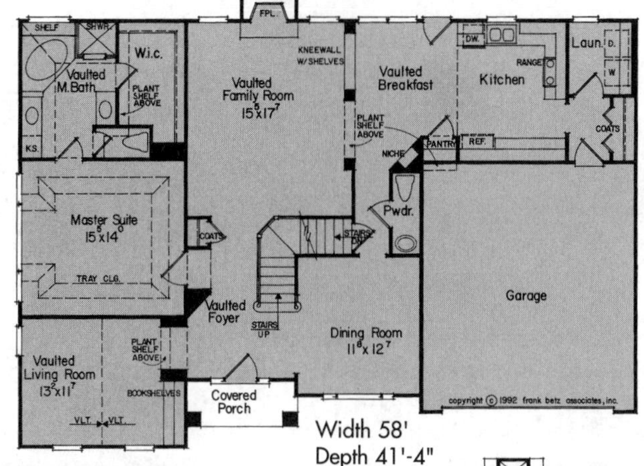

SHELF
SHWR.
W.i.c.
Vaulted M.Bath
PLANT SHELF ABOVE
KS.
FPL.
KNEEWALL W/SHELVES
Vaulted Family Room
15^{5}x17^{7}
Vaulted Breakfast
Kitchen
DW.
RANGE
Laun.
D.
W
PLANT SHELF ABOVE
NICHE
PANTRY
REF.
COATS
Master Suite
15^{5}x14^{0}
TRAY CLG.
COATS
STAIRS DN
Pwdr.
Garage
Vaulted Foyer
STAIRS UP
Dining Room
11^{6}x 12^{7}
Vaulted Living Room
13^{2}x11^{7}
PLANT SHELF ABOVE
BOOKSHELVES
Covered Porch
VLT. VLT.
copyright © 1992 frank betz associates, inc.
Width 58'
Depth 41'-4"

Design by
Frank Betz Associates, Inc.

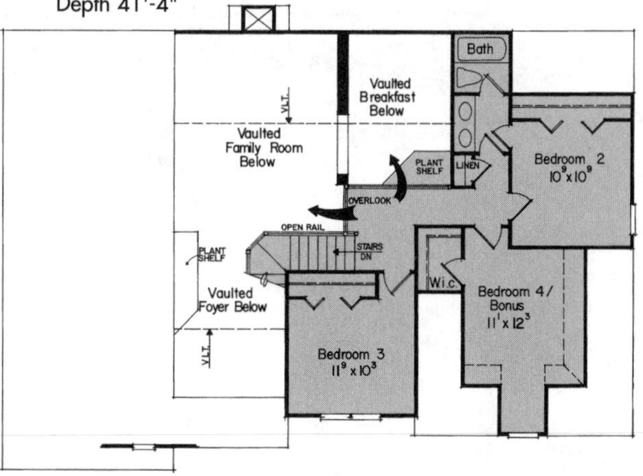

Bath
Vaulted Breakfast Below
VLT.
Vaulted Family Room Below
PLANT SHELF
LINEN
Bedroom 2
10^{9}x10^{9}
OVERLOOK
OPEN RAIL
STAIRS DN
PLANT SHELF
W.i.c.
Bedroom 4/ Bonus
11'x12^{3}
Vaulted Foyer Below
VLT.
Bedroom 3
11^{9}x10^{3}

Design 9757

First Floor: 1,715 square feet
Second Floor: 620 square feet
Total: 2,335 square feet

■ With a decided European flavor, this handsome plan features family living at its best. The foyer opens to a study or living room on the left. The dining room on the right offers large proportions and full windows. The family room remains open to the kitchen and breakfast room. Here, sunny meals are guaranteed with a bay window overlooking the rear yard. In the master suite, a bayed sitting area, a walk-in closet and a pampering bath are sure to please. Upstairs, two bedrooms flank a loft or study area.

Design by
Donald A. Gardner, Architects, Inc.

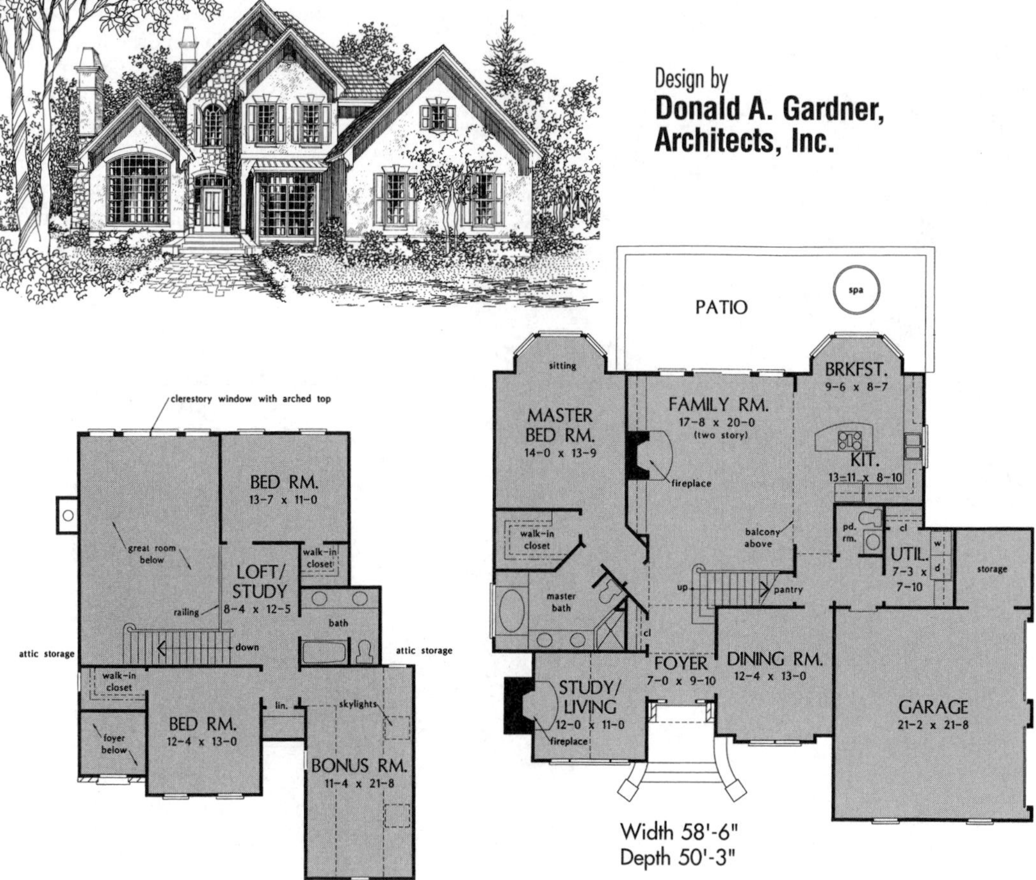

PATIO
spa
sitting
MASTER BED RM.
14-0 x 13-9
FAMILY RM.
17-8 x 20-0
(two story)
fireplace
BRKFST.
9-6 x 8-7
KIT.
13-11 x 8-10
walk-in closet
balcony above
pd. rm.
cl
UTIL.
7-3 x 7-10
storage
master bath
up
pantry
cl
FOYER
7-0 x 9-10
DINING RM.
12-4 x 13-0
STUDY/ LIVING
12-0 x 11-0
fireplace
GARAGE
21-2 x 21-8
Width 58'-6"
Depth 50'-3"
clerestory window with arched top
great room below
BED RM.
13-7 x 11-0
walk-in closet
LOFT/ STUDY
8-4 x 12-5
railing
bath
attic storage
down
attic storage
walk-in closet
foyer below
BED RM.
12-4 x 13-0
lin.
skylights
BONUS RM.
11-4 x 21-8

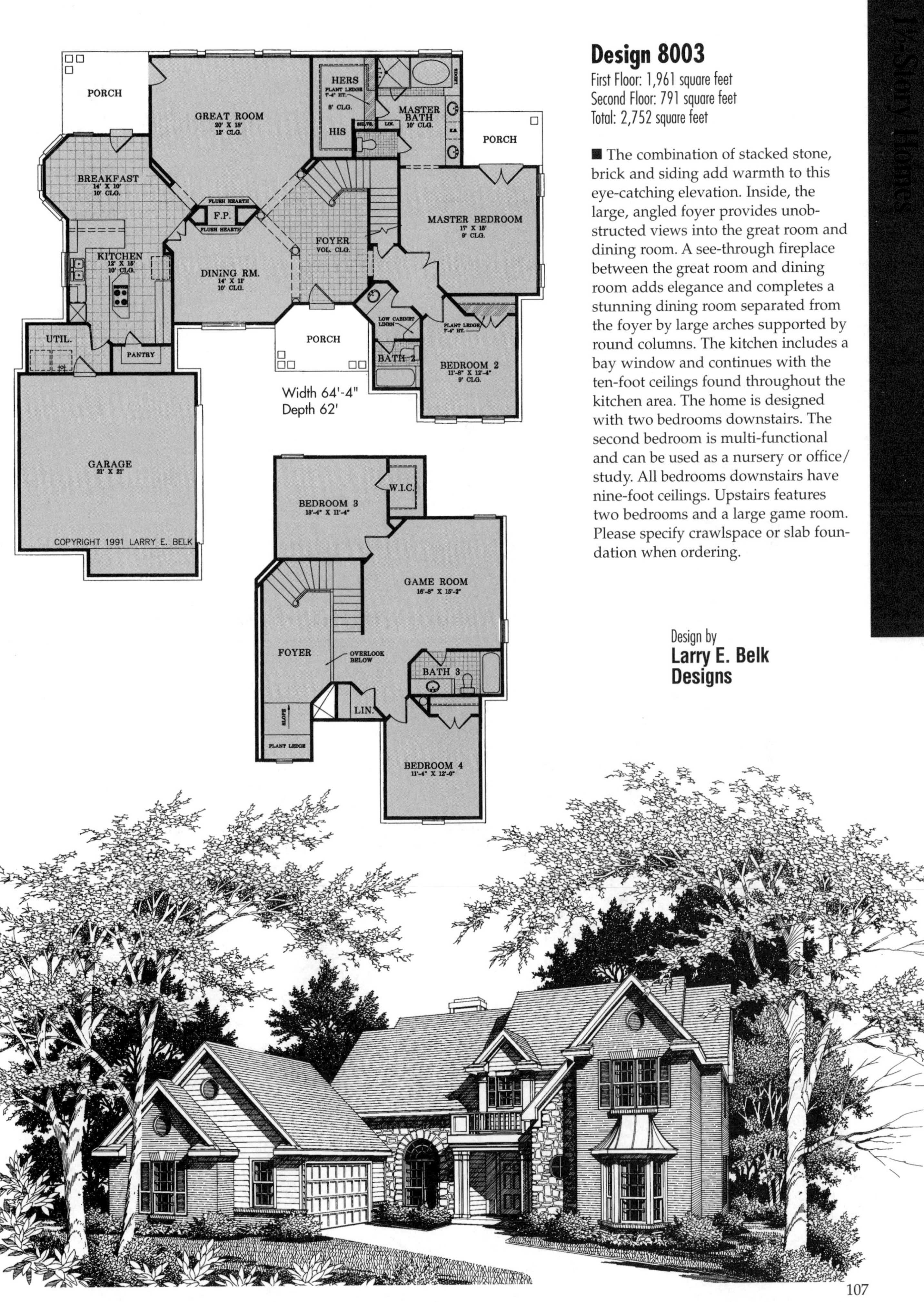
PORCH
GREAT ROOM
20' X 18'
12' CLG.
HERS
PLANT LEDGE
8' CLG.
HIS
MASTER BATH
10' CLG.
PORCH
BREAKFAST
14' X 10'
10' CLG.
F.P.
FLUSH HEARTH
MASTER BEDROOM
17' X 15'
9' CLG.
FOYER
VOL. CLG.
KITCHEN
12' X 15'
10' CLG.
DINING RM.
14' X 11'
10' CLG.
LOW CABINET LINEN
PLANT LEDGE
UTIL.
PANTRY
PORCH
BATH 2
BEDROOM 2
11'-8" X 12'-4"
9' CLG.
Width 64'-4"
Depth 62'
GARAGE
21' X 21'
COPYRIGHT 1991 LARRY E. BELK
BEDROOM 3
13'-4" X 11'-4"
W.I.C.
GAME ROOM
16'-8" X 15'-2"
FOYER
OVERLOOK BELOW
BATH 3
LIN.
SLOPE
PLANT LEDGE
BEDROOM 4
11'-4" X 12'-0"

Design 8003

First Floor: 1,961 square feet
Second Floor: 791 square feet
Total: 2,752 square feet

■ The combination of stacked stone, brick and siding add warmth to this eye-catching elevation. Inside, the large, angled foyer provides unobstructed views into the great room and dining room. A see-through fireplace between the great room and dining room adds elegance and completes a stunning dining room separated from the foyer by large arches supported by round columns. The kitchen includes a bay window and continues with the ten-foot ceilings found throughout the kitchen area. The home is designed with two bedrooms downstairs. The second bedroom is multi-functional and can be used as a nursery or office/study. All bedrooms downstairs have nine-foot ceilings. Upstairs features two bedrooms and a large game room. Please specify crawlspace or slab foundation when ordering.

Design by
Larry E. Belk Designs

Design by
Larry E. Belk Designs

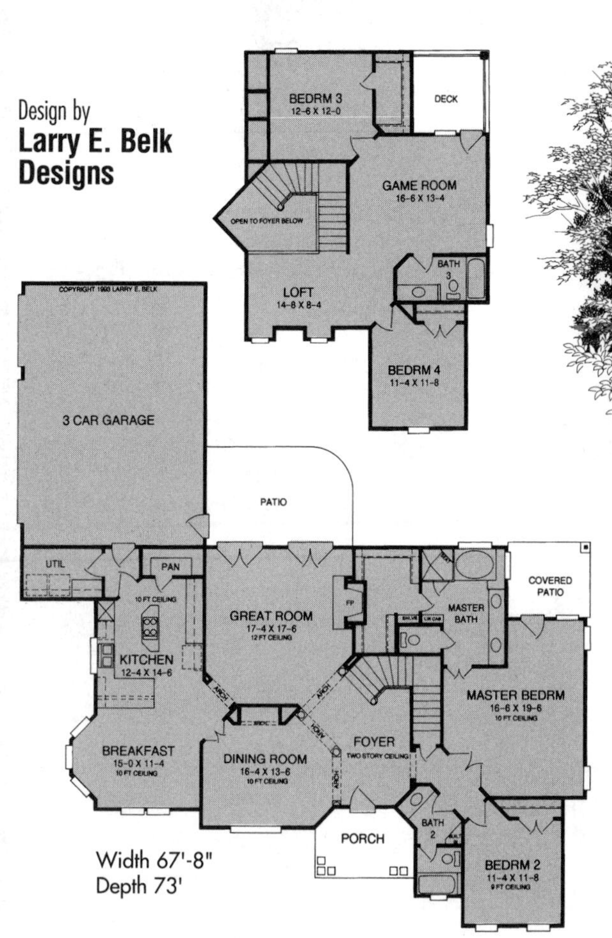
BEDRM 3
12-6 X 12-0
DECK
GAME ROOM
16-6 X 13-4
OPEN TO FOYER BELOW
LOFT
14-8 X 8-4
BATH
3
BEDRM 4
11-4 X 11-8
3 CAR GARAGE
PATIO
UTIL
PAN
GREAT ROOM
17-4 X 17-6
12 FT CEILING
FP
MASTER BATH
COVERED PATIO
KITCHEN
12-4 X 14-6
10 FT CEILING
MASTER BEDRM
16-6 X 19-6
10 FT CEILING
FOYER
TWO STORY CEILING
BREAKFAST
15-0 X 11-4
10 FT CEILING
DINING ROOM
16-4 X 13-6
10 FT CEILING
BATH
2
PORCH
BEDRM 2
11-4 X 11-8
9 FT CEILING

Width 67'-8"
Depth 73'

COPYRIGHT 1993 LARRY E. BELK

Design 8054

First Floor: 2,012 square feet
Second Floor: 832 square feet
Total: 2,844 square feet

■ A large arched window, twin dormers and an entry accented by a swoop roof add charm to this inviting two-story home. A grand entry opens to the formal dining room and great room with a fireplace. The roomy kitchen has a large pantry, cooktop island and snack bar area. Natural sunlight streams in from the bay window in the breakfast area. The master bedroom provides access to a covered patio offering a quiet outdoor retreat. The master bath enjoys a private bath with a large walk-in closet. An adjacent secondary bedroom and full bath is easily a nursery or study. The second floor contains two family bedrooms, a full bath, game room, loft and deck. Please specify crawlspace or slab foundation when ordering.

Design P120

First Floor: 2,130 square feet
Second Floor: 897 square feet
Total: 3,027 square feet

Design by
Frank Betz Associates, Inc.

■ Family living takes on a casually elegant look in this classic 1½-story home. The large foyer opens to the formal dining room, stylishly open to the great room through arches. The two-story great room has French doors to the rear, with a fireplace and wet bar dividing it from casual family living areas. The kitchen has a cooktop island, wrapping counters, a breakfast nook and a cozy keeping room. The luxurious master suite joins a study/sitting room. Upstairs, three bedrooms are fashioned with private bath access and plenty of closet space.

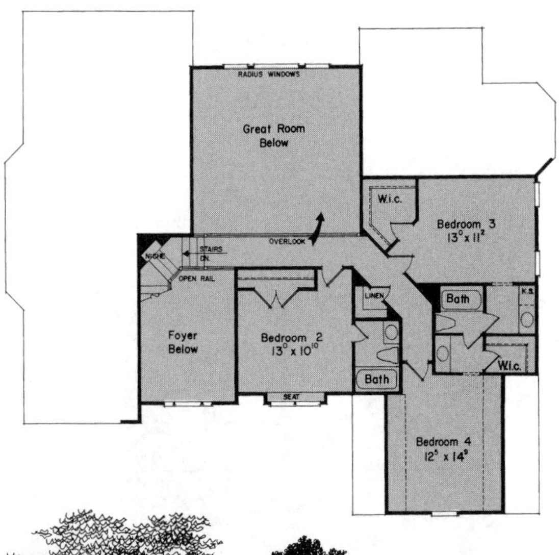
RADIUS WINDOWS
Great Room
Below
W.i.c.
Bedroom 3
OVERLOOK
OPEN RAIL
Foyer
Below
Bedroom 2
Bath
Bath
W.i.c.
SEAT
Bedroom 4

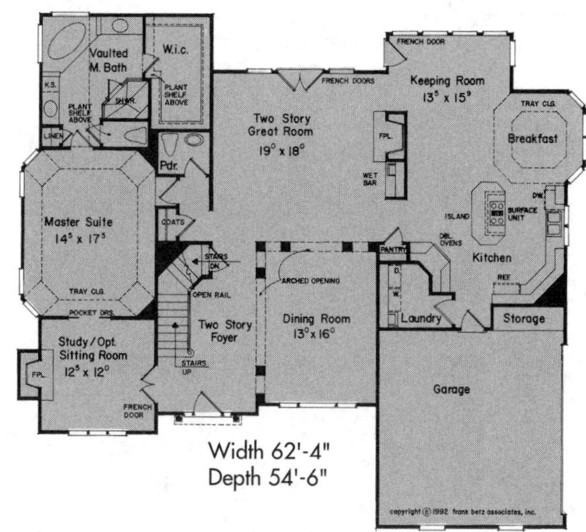
Vaulted
M. Bath
W.i.c.
FRENCH DOOR
FRENCH DOORS
Keeping Room
Two Story
Great Room
Breakfast
Pdr.
WET BAR
Master Suite
COATS
ISLAND
Kitchen
TRAY CLG
POCKET DRS
OPEN RAIL
ARCHED OPENING
PANTRY
Laundry
Storage
Study/Opt.
Sitting Room
Two Story
Foyer
Dining Room
FRENCH DOOR
Garage

Width 62'-4"
Depth 54'-6"

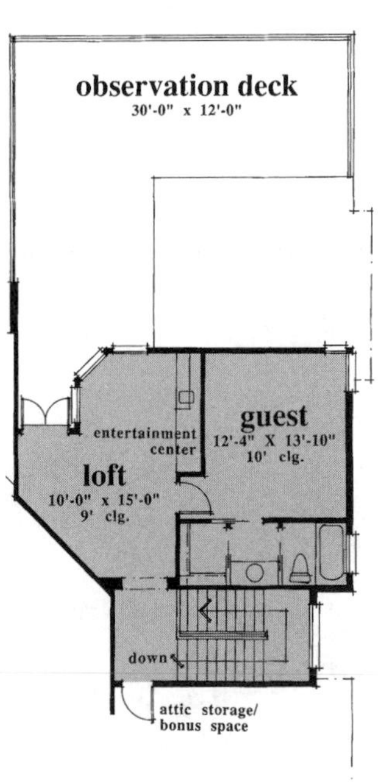

observation deck
30'-0" x 12'-0"
guest
12'-4" X 13'-10"
10' clg.
entertainment center
loft
10'-0" x 15'-0"
9' clg.
down
attic storage/
bonus space

Design by
The Sater Design Collection

Width 67'
Depth 102'

lanai
30'-0" x 10'-0"
outdoor kitchen
leisure
15'-10" x 18'-0"
stepped clg.
fireplace
dry bar
lanai
31'-0" x 10'-0"
nook
8' x 10'
10' clg.
kitchen
12' x 14'
master
17'-0" x 14'-9"
13'-4" tray clg.
living
15'-0" x 15'-0"
14'-4" clg.
arch
up
stor.
w.i.c.
mir.
hooks
study
10' x 11'
13'-4" clg.
foyer
dining
11'-0" x 14'-0"
15'-0" tray clg.
guest
12'-0" x 11'-0"
10' clg.
his
hers
glass shwr.
master garden
planter
entry
util.
storage
garage
21'-0" x 28'-6"
© The Sater Group, Inc.

Design 6653

First Floor: 2894 square feet
Second Floor: 568 square feet
Total: 3,462 square feet

■ The traditional front elevation of this home belies the incredible expanse of windows that stretches the entire rear. Formal and casual living zones are thoughtfully divided, with the elegant living and dining rooms greeting you right off the foyer. Large sliding glass doors open the living room to the lanai. To the rear of the plan lies the open, demonstration-style kitchen with a cooktop island, wrapping counters and a walk-in pantry. A breakfast nook and leisure room with a fireplace are made for family living. The leisure room also has large sliding glass doors that open to the lanai, where a summer kitchen awaits outdoor entertaining. The sumptuous master suite is comprised of an elegant bedroom, a large walk-in closet and an amazing bath that's fashioned with twin vanities, a glass octagonal shower, a compartmented European toilet, corner tub and a private garden. Two guest suites complete the plan—one is on the first floor and the other is joined by a loft and observation deck upstairs.

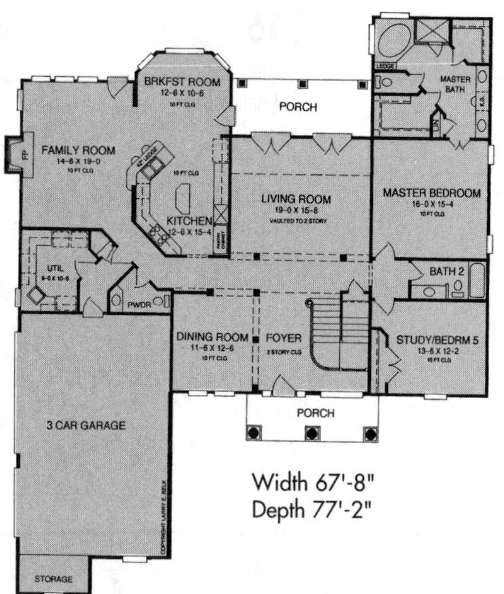

BRKFST ROOM
12-6 X 10-6
10 FT CLG
PORCH
MASTER BATH
FAMILY ROOM
14-6 X 19-0
10 FT CLG
FP
KITCHEN
12-6 X 15-4
LIVING ROOM
19-0 X 15-8
VAULTED TO 2 STORY
MASTER BEDROOM
16-0 X 15-4
10 FT CLG
UTIL
BATH 2
PWDR
DINING ROOM
11-6 X 12-6
10 FT CLG
FOYER
2 STORY CLG
STUDY/BEDRM 5
13-6 X 12-2
10 FT CLG
PORCH
3 CAR GARAGE
STORAGE

Width 67'-8"
Depth 77'-2"

■ A bold entrance leads to a two-story foyer and living room, giving the home an elegant, open feel. The kitchen and breakfast room are open to the large family room—a perfect backdrop for everyday living. The master suite has a compartmented bath and a nearby study or nursery. Upstairs, three comfortable bedrooms each have walk-in closets. Two of the bedrooms share a private bath, another full bath is located in the hall. Please specify crawlspace or slab foundation when ordering.

Design 8103

First Floor: 2,547 square feet
Second Floor: 1,128 square feet
Total: 3,675 square feet
Bonus Room: 357 square feet

Design by
Larry E. Belk Designs

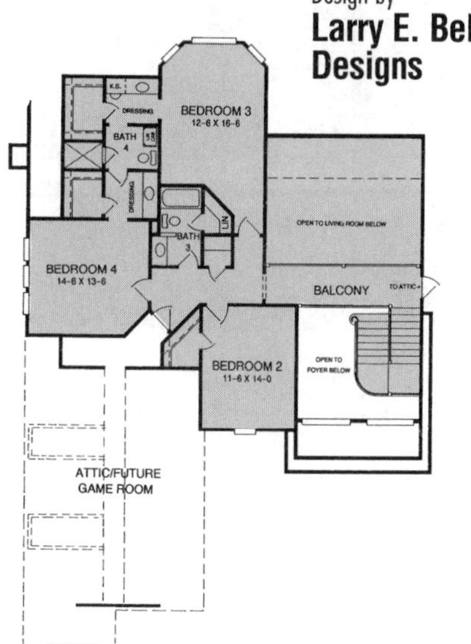

BEDROOM 3
12-6 X 16-6
BATH 4
BEDROOM 4
14-6 X 13-6
BATH 3
OPEN TO LIVING ROOM BELOW
BALCONY
TO ATTIC
BEDROOM 2
11-6 X 14-0
OPEN TO FOYER BELOW
ATTIC/FUTURE GAME ROOM

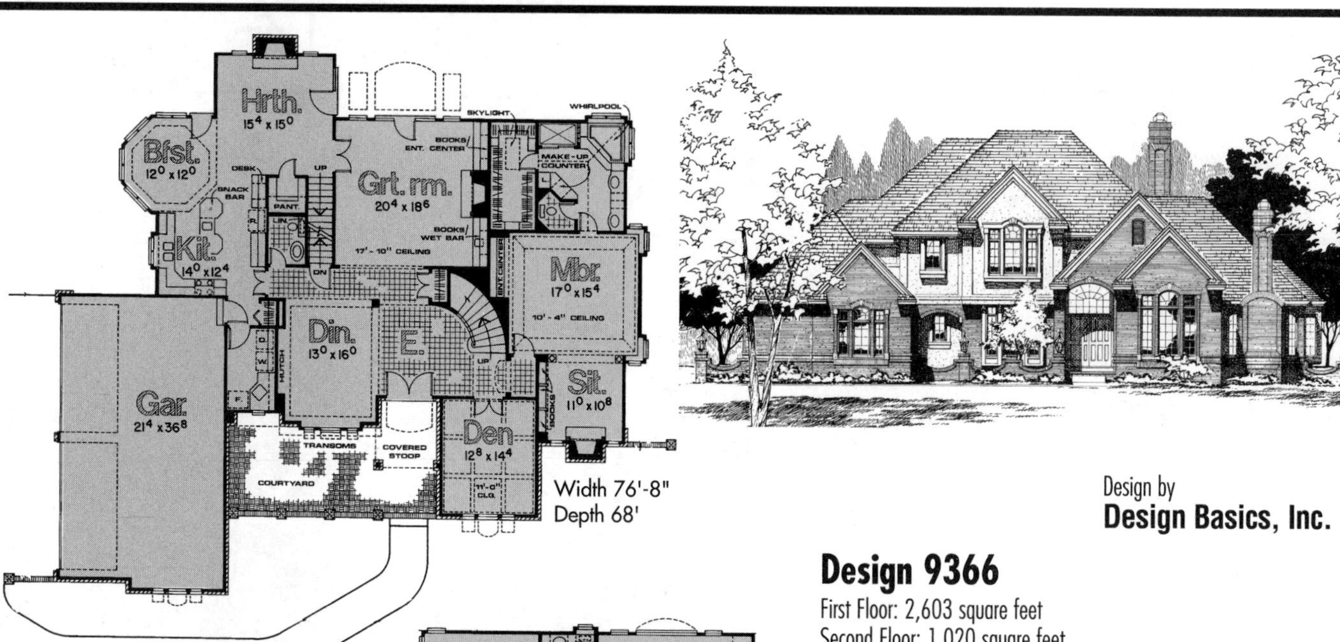

Hrth.
15⁴ x 15⁰
Bfst.
12⁰ x 12⁰
Grt. rm.
20⁴ x 18⁶
17' - 10" CEILING
Kit.
14⁰ x 12⁴
Mbr.
17⁰ x 15⁴
10' - 4" CEILING
Din.
13⁰ x 16⁰
E.
Sit.
11⁰ x 10⁸
Gar.
21⁴ x 36⁸
Den
12⁸ x 14⁴
COVERED STOOP
COURTYARD
TRANSOMS
SKYLIGHT
WHIRLPOOL

Width 76'-8"
Depth 68'

Design by
Design Basics, Inc.

Design 9366

First Floor: 2,603 square feet
Second Floor: 1,020 square feet
Total: 3,623 square feet

Br.2
15³ x 12⁰
9'-0" CEILING
OPEN TO GREAT ROOM
Br.4
12⁰ x 14⁰
9'-0" CEILING
Br.3
12⁰ x 14⁶
9'-0" CEILING
OPEN TO BELOW

■ Perhaps the most notable characteristic of this traditional house is its masterful use of space. The glorious great room, open dining room and handsome den serve as the heart of the house. A cozy hearth room with fireplace rounds out the kitchen and breakfast areas. The master bedroom (which is situated on the first floor) opens up into a private sitting room with fireplace. Three family bedrooms occupy the second floor; each one has its own private bath.

QUOTE ONE®
Cost to build? See page 342 to order complete cost estimate to build this house in your area!

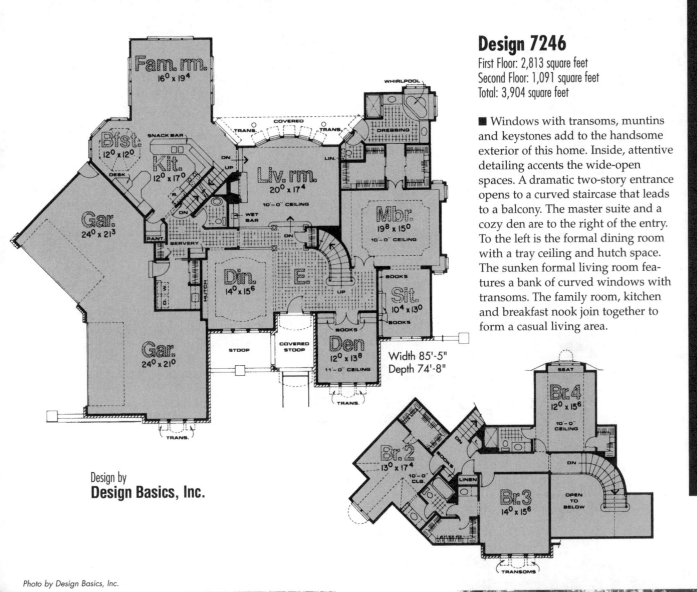

Design 7246

First Floor: 2,813 square feet
Second Floor: 1,091 square feet
Total: 3,904 square feet

■ Windows with transoms, muntins and keystones add to the handsome exterior of this home. Inside, attentive detailing accents the wide-open spaces. A dramatic two-story entrance opens to a curved staircase that leads to a balcony. The master suite and a cozy den are to the right of the entry. To the left is the formal dining room with a tray ceiling and hutch space. The sunken formal living room features a bank of curved windows with transoms. The family room, kitchen and breakfast nook join together to form a casual living area.

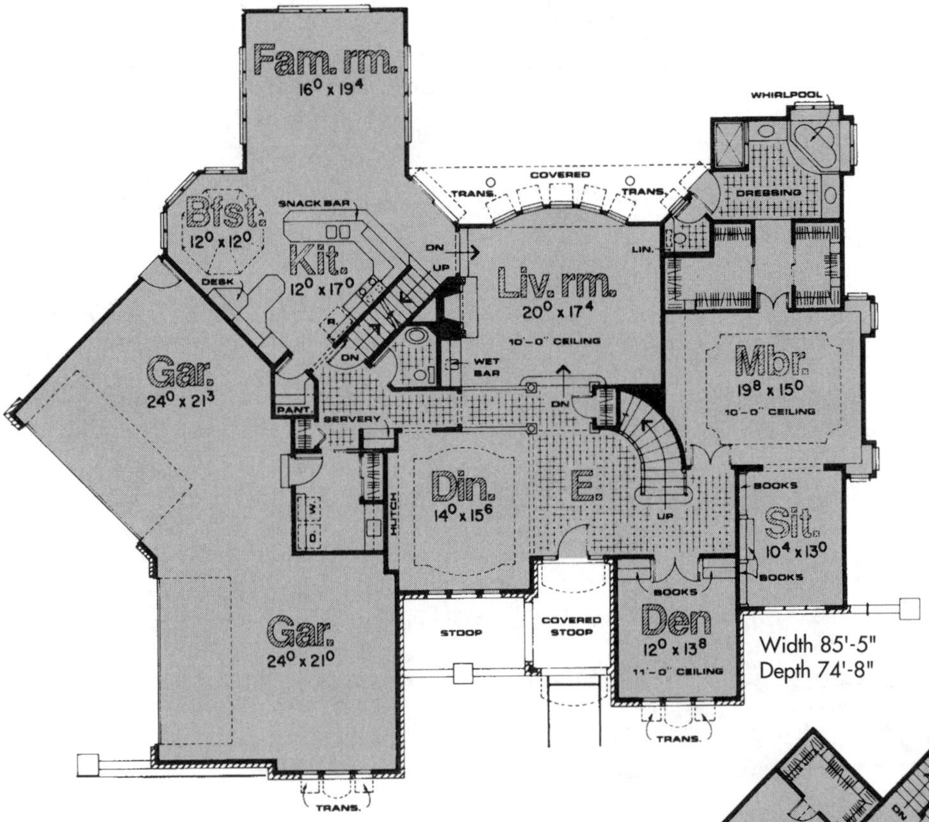

Width 85'-5"
Depth 74'-8"

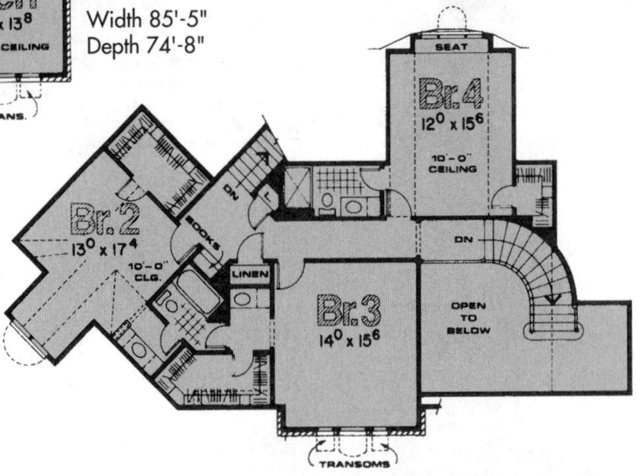

Design by
Design Basics, Inc.

Photo by Design Basics, Inc.

© The Sater Group, Inc.

Design 6646

Design by
The Sater Design Collection

First Floor: 2,551 square feet
Second Floor: 1,037 square feet
Total: 3,588 square feet

■ This beautiful home has many attributes including a bowed dining room and a living room with a fireplace and outdoor access. For family gatherings, the kitchen remains open to the living areas. A study off the foyer will be much appreciated. A full bath leads to the outdoors—perfect for poolside. The master suite enjoys its own personal luxury bath with a whirlpool tub, dual lavatories, a compartmented toilet and bidet and a separate shower. Dual walk-in closets provide ample storage space. Upstairs, two bedrooms share a full bath. A loft with a wet bar accommodates playtime. A wraparound deck is an added feature.

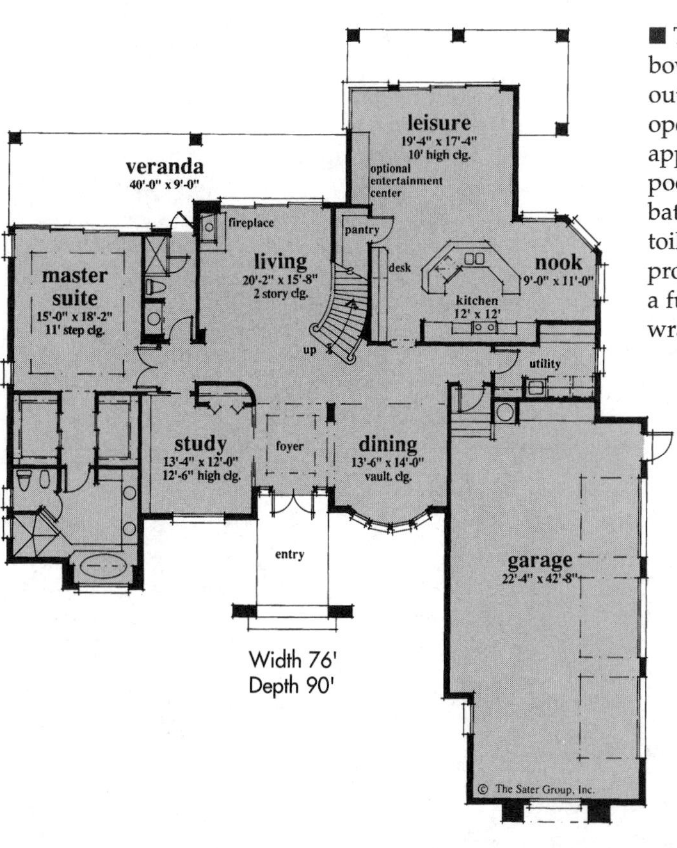
leisure
19'-4" x 17'-4"
10' high clg.
veranda
40'-0" x 9'-0"
optional entertainment center
fireplace
pantry
master suite
15'-0" x 18'-2"
11' step clg.
living
20'-2" x 15'-8"
2 story clg.
desk
nook
9'-0" x 11'-0"
kitchen
12' x 12'
up
utility
study
13'-4" x 12'-0"
12'-6" high clg.
foyer
dining
13'-6" x 14'-0"
vault. clg.
entry
garage
22'-4" x 42'-8"
© The Sater Group, Inc.

Width 76'
Depth 90'

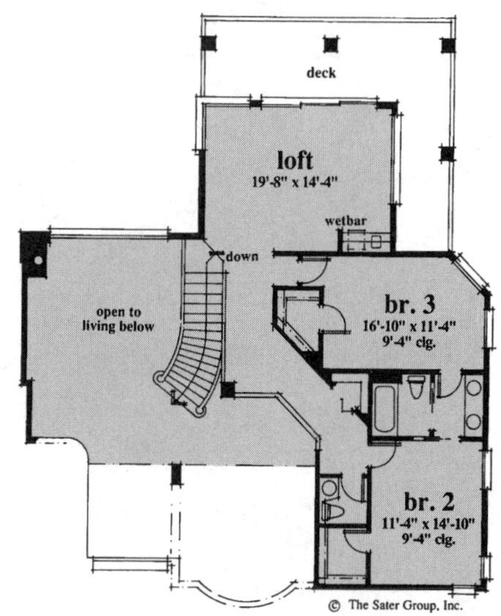
deck
loft
19'-8" x 14'-4"
wetbar
down
open to living below
br. 3
16'-10" x 11'-4"
9'-4" clg.
br. 2
11'-4" x 14'-10"
9'-4" clg.
© The Sater Group, Inc.

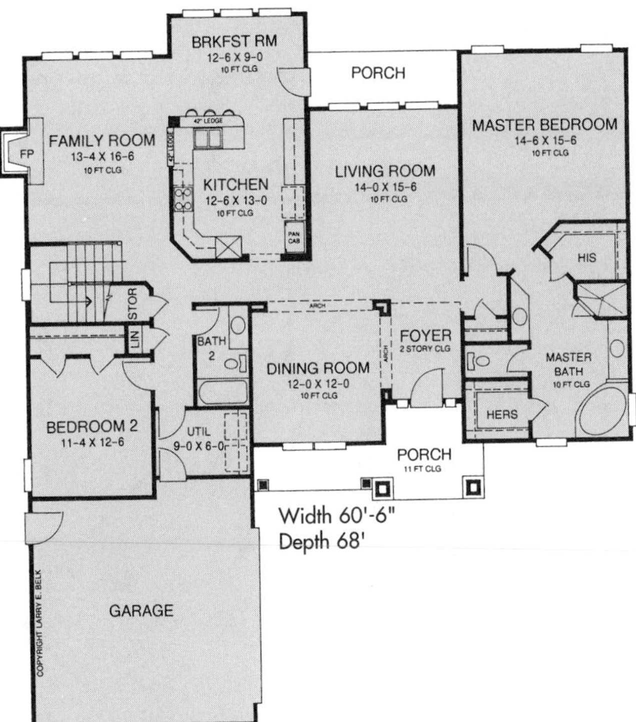
BRKFST RM
12-6 X 9-0
10 FT CLG
PORCH
FAMILY ROOM
13-4 X 16-6
10 FT CLG
FP
KITCHEN
12-6 X 13-0
10 FT CLG
LIVING ROOM
14-0 X 15-6
10 FT CLG
MASTER BEDROOM
14-6 X 15-6
10 FT CLG
HIS
STOR
LIN
BATH
2
DINING ROOM
12-0 X 12-0
10 FT CLG
FOYER
2 STORY CLG
MASTER
BATH
10 FT CLG
HERS
BEDROOM 2
11-4 X 12-6
UTIL
9-0 X 6-0
PORCH
11 FT CLG
Width 60'-6"
Depth 68'
GARAGE
STORAGE
COPYRIGHT LARRY E. BELK

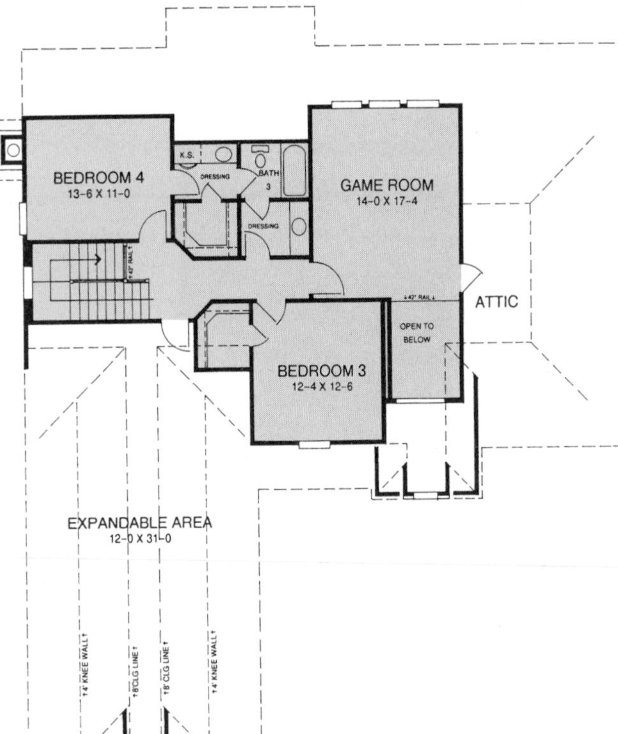
BEDROOM 4
13-6 X 11-0
K.S.
DRESSING
BATH
3
GAME ROOM
14-0 X 17-4
ATTIC
OPEN TO
BELOW
BEDROOM 3
12-4 X 12-6
EXPANDABLE AREA
12-0 X 31-0

Design 8125

First Floor: 2,134 square feet
Second Floor: 863 square feet
Total: 2,997 square feet
Bonus Room: 372 square feet

Design by
Larry E. Belk Designs

■ A country French flair distinguishes this home. The two-story foyer opens to both the formal dining room and the formal living room. The kitchen, the breakfast room and the family room are grouped for great casual living. A nearby bedroom and bath would make a nice guest suite. The master suite is designed for privacy and relaxation. An amenity-filled bath features His and Hers walk-in closets and vanities, a corner whirlpool tub and separate shower. Two bedrooms and a bath with two private vanity areas are located upstairs. A large game room has a loft overlooking the foyer. An expandable area can be finished as needed. Please specify crawlspace or slab foundation when ordering.

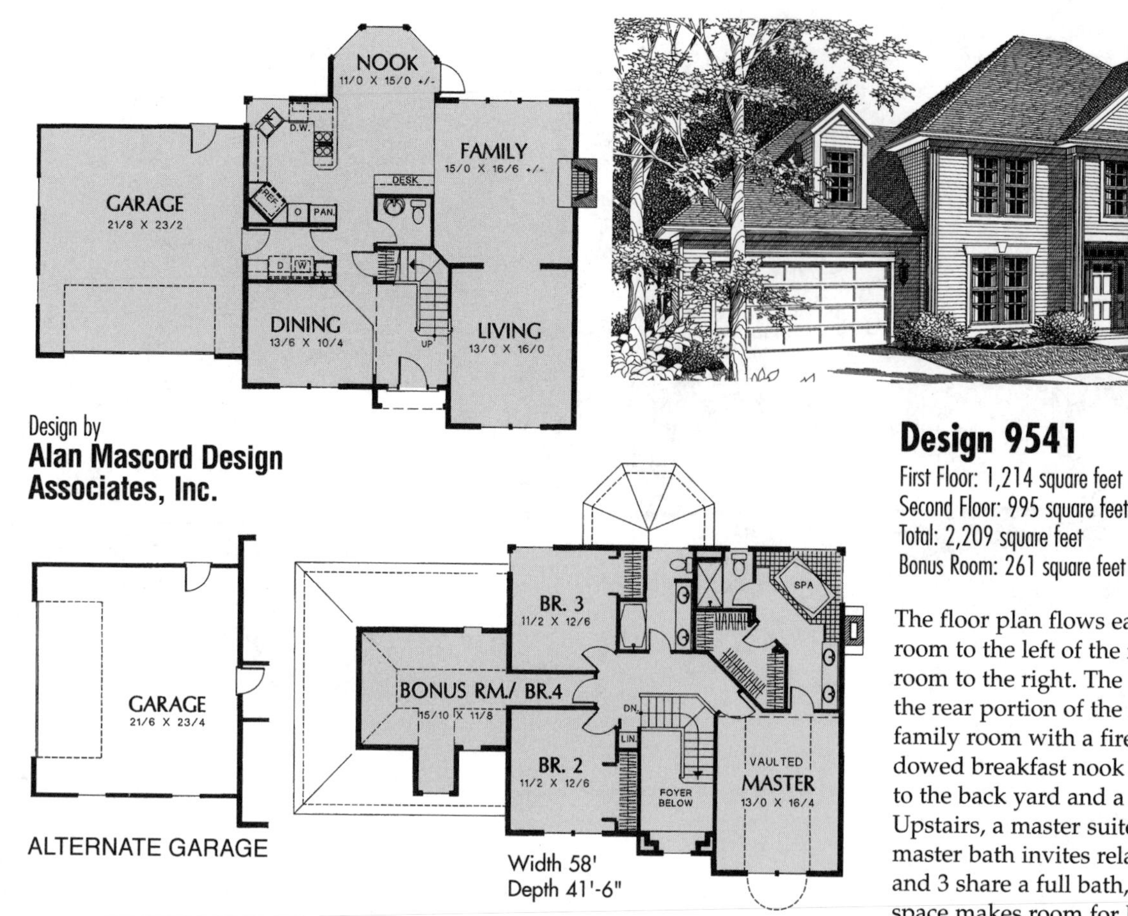
NOOK
11/0 X 15/0 +/-
D.W.
FAMILY
15/0 X 16/6 +/-
DESK
GARAGE
21/8 X 23/2
REF.
O
PAN.
D
W
DINING
13/6 X 10/4
UP
LIVING
13/0 X 16/0
GARAGE
21/6 X 23/4
ALTERNATE GARAGE
BR. 3
11/2 X 12/6
SPA
BONUS RM./ BR.4
15/10 X 11/8
DN.
LIN.
BR. 2
11/2 X 12/6
FOYER
BELOW
VAULTED
MASTER
13/0 X 16/4

Design by
Alan Mascord Design Associates, Inc.

Width 58'
Depth 41'-6"

Design 9541

First Floor: 1,214 square feet
Second Floor: 995 square feet
Total: 2,209 square feet
Bonus Room: 261 square feet

■ A combined hip and gable roof, keystones and horizontal wood siding lend this lovely traditional home an air of distinction. The floor plan flows easily, with the dining room to the left of the foyer and the living room to the right. The combined space at the rear portion of the house contains a family room with a fireplace, a bay-windowed breakfast nook with a door leading to the back yard and a step-saving kitchen. Upstairs, a master suite with a pampering master bath invites relaxation. Bedrooms 2 and 3 share a full bath, while the bonus space makes room for Bedroom 4.

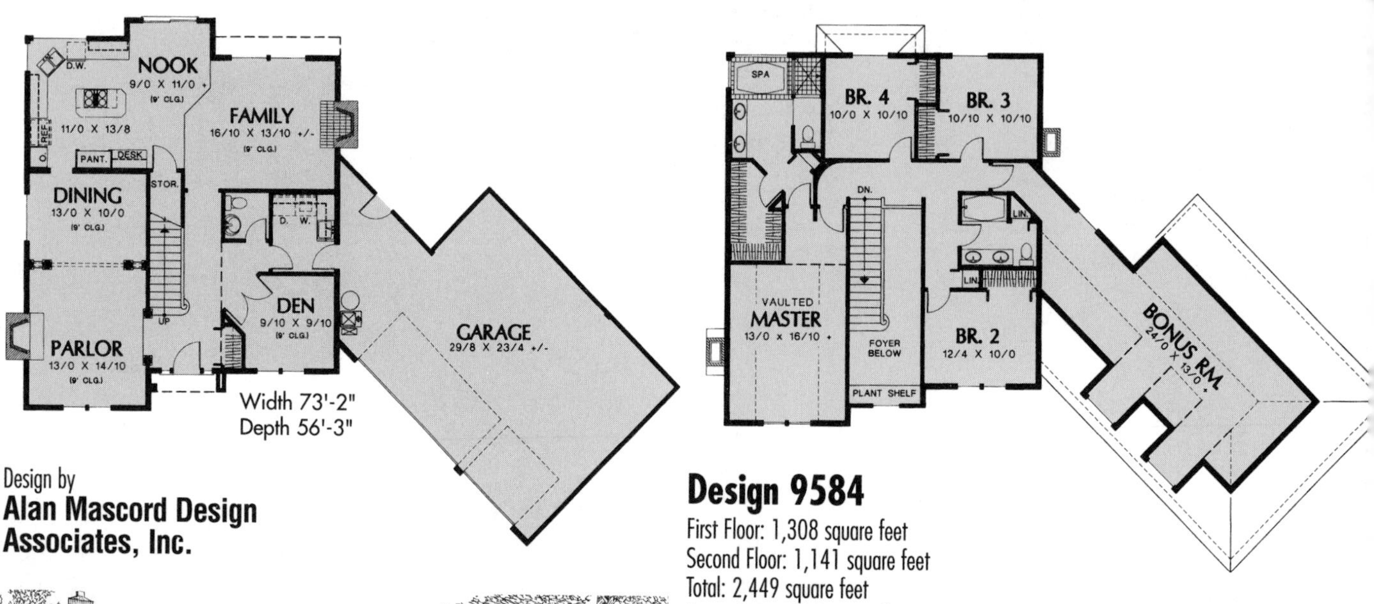
D.W.
NOOK
9/0 X 11/0
(9' CLG.)
11/0 X 13/8
REF.
FAMILY
16/10 X 13/10 +/-
(9' CLG.)
PANT.
DESK
STOR.
DINING
13/0 X 10/0
(9' CLG.)
D.
W.
DEN
9/10 X 9/10
(9' CLG.)
PARLOR
13/0 X 14/10
(9' CLG.)
UP
GARAGE
29/8 X 23/4 +/-
SPA
BR. 4
10/0 X 10/10
BR. 3
10/10 X 10/10
DN.
LIN.
VAULTED
MASTER
13/0 x 16/10
FOYER
BELOW
BR. 2
12/4 X 10/0
PLANT SHELF
BONUS RM.
24/0 X 13/0

Width 73'-2"
Depth 56'-3"

Design by
Alan Mascord Design Associates, Inc.

Design 9584

First Floor: 1,308 square feet
Second Floor: 1,141 square feet
Total: 2,449 square feet
Bonus Room: 266 square feet

■ Set at an angle, this home starts off with distinction. Just off the foyer and down a step, the formal parlor gives a welcoming atmosphere with its large window and warming fireplace. The island kitchen has convenient access to both the formal dining room and the breakfast nook and looks out into the large family room. A den with double French doors completes this level. Upstairs, three secondary bedrooms share a hall bath with a double-bowl vanity while the vaulted master suite is replete with luxuries.

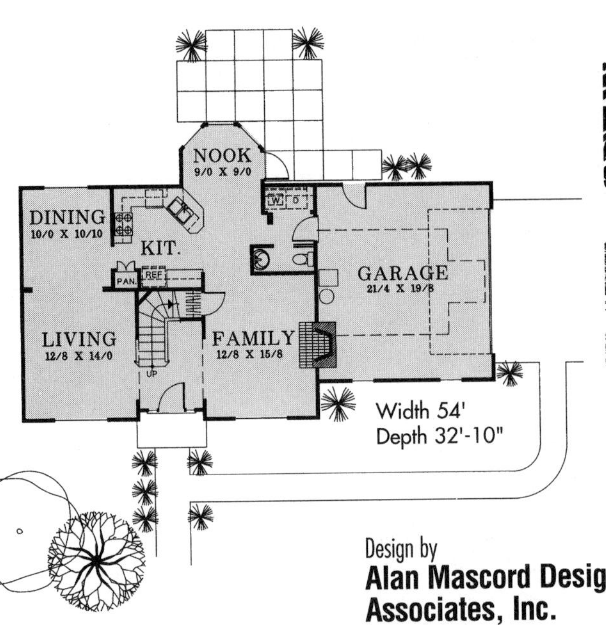
NOOK
9/0 X 9/0
DINING
10/0 X 10/10
KIT.
PAN.
REF.
GARAGE
21/4 X 19/8
LIVING
12/8 X 14/0
FAMILY
12/8 X 15/8
UP
Width 54'
Depth 32'-10"

Design 9462

First Floor: 935 square feet
Second Floor: 772 square feet
Total: 1,707 square feet
Bonus Room: 177 square feet

Design by
Alan Mascord Design Associates, Inc.

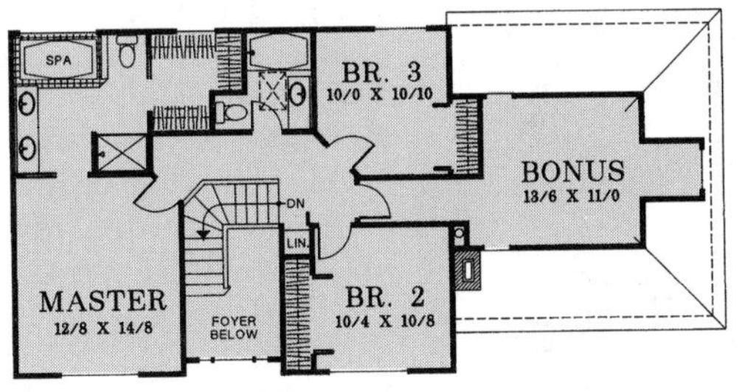
SPA
BR. 3
10/0 X 10/10
BONUS
13/6 X 11/0
ON
LIN.
MASTER
12/8 X 14/8
FOYER
BELOW
BR. 2
10/4 X 10/8

■ Colonial styling gives an efficient form to this popular two-story design. The dramatic two-story foyer with its angled stairway forms the circulation hub for this efficient home. Upstairs is a master bedroom with spa tub, large shower, double vanity and walk-in closet. Two additional bedrooms are provided, along with a bonus room over the garage, which could be the fourth bedroom. A flexible rear-, front- or side-entry garage works well for corner lots or lots served by a lane.

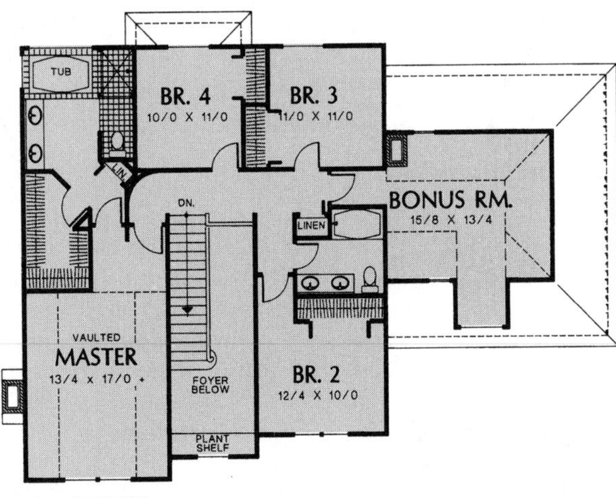
TUB
BR. 4
10/0 X 11/0
BR. 3
11/0 X 11/0
LIN.
DN.
LINEN
BONUS RM.
15/8 X 13/4
VAULTED
MASTER
13/4 x 17/0 +
FOYER
BELOW
BR. 2
12/4 X 10/0
PLANT
SHELF

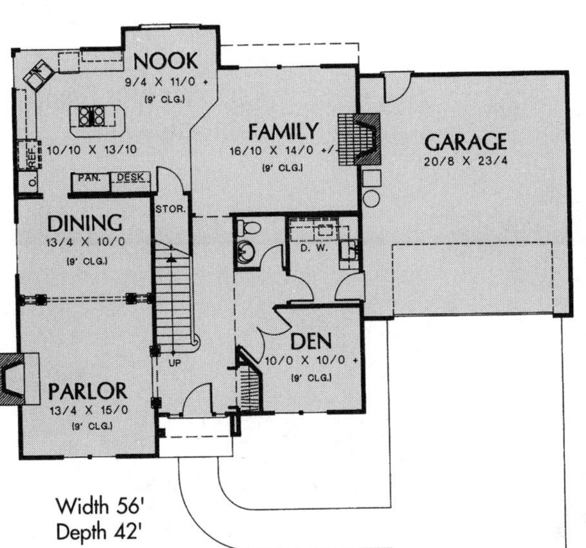
NOOK
9/4 X 11/0 +
(9' CLG.)
10/10 X 13/10
REF.
PAN.
DESK
FAMILY
16/10 X 14/0 +/
(9' CLG.)
GARAGE
20/8 X 23/4
DINING
13/4 X 10/0
(9' CLG.)
STOR.
D. W.
DEN
10/0 X 10/0 +
(9' CLG.)
UP
PARLOR
13/4 X 15/0
(9' CLG.)
Width 56'
Depth 42'

Design 9477

First Floor: 1,308 square feet
Second Floor: 1,141 square feet
Total: 2,449 square feet
Bonus Room: 266 square feet

Design by
Alan Mascord Design Associates, Inc.

■ Quietly stated elegance is the key to this home's attraction. Its floor plan allows plenty of space for formal and informal occasions. The rear of the first floor is devoted to an open area serving as family room, breakfast nook and island kitchen. This area is complemented by a formal parlor and dining room. A private den could function as a guest room with the handy powder room nearby. There are four bedrooms on the second floor. Bonus room over the garage could become an additional bedroom or study.

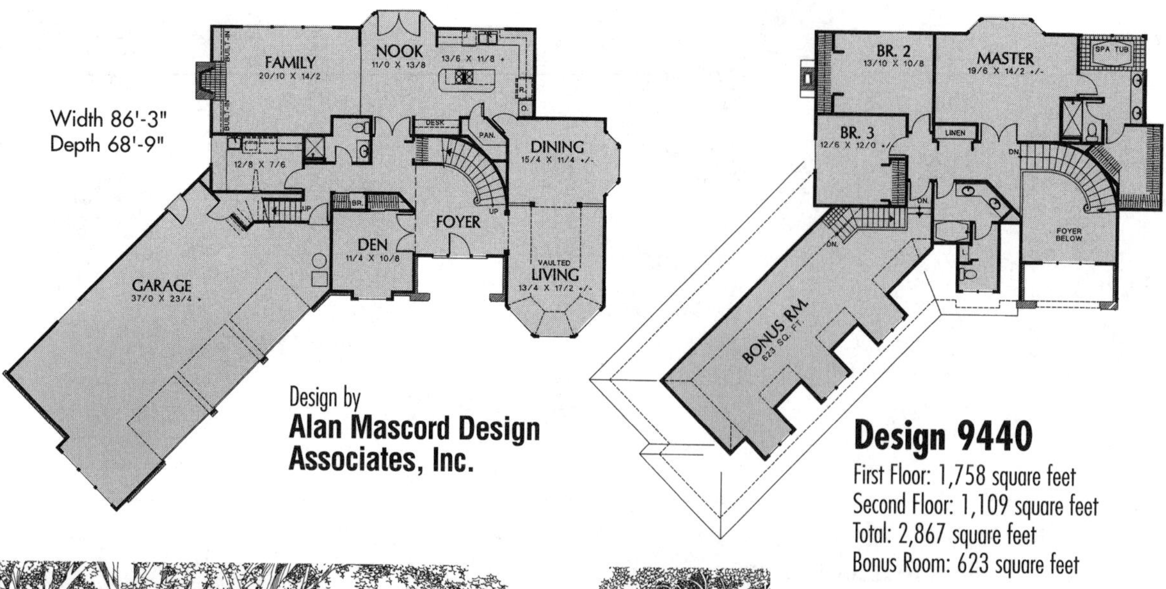
Width 86'-3"
Depth 68'-9"
FAMILY
20/10 X 14/2
NOOK
11/0 X 13/8
13/6 X 11/8 +
DINING
15/4 X 11/4 +/-
12/8 X 7/6
FOYER
DEN
11/4 X 10/8
VAULTED
LIVING
13/4 X 17/2 +/-
GARAGE
37/0 X 23/4 +
BR. 2
13/10 X 10/8
MASTER
19/6 X 14/2 +/-
SPA TUB
BR. 3
12/6 X 12/0 +/-
LINEN
FOYER
BELOW
BONUS RM.
623 SQ. FT.

Design by
Alan Mascord Design Associates, Inc.

Design 9440

First Floor: 1,758 square feet
Second Floor: 1,109 square feet
Total: 2,867 square feet
Bonus Room: 623 square feet

■ Representing elegance in a timeless design, this home offers as its focal point a graciously curved staircase in its two-story foyer. Besides spacious living areas on the first floor, there is a convenient full bath, which allows the den to serve as a guest room when needed. To the rear of the plan is the master suite that contains a bay window overlooking the rear yard. An oversized three-car garage provides enough room for a workshop or additional storage space.

Design 9486

First Floor: 1,368 square feet
Second Floor: 972 square feet
Total: 2,340 square feet
Bonus Room: 344 square feet

■ Special details such as the two dormer windows and double-columned front entry add to the appeal of this well-designed home. Inside, it features formal living and dining rooms, a tucked-away den and large family room with a vaulted ceiling and fireplace. The island kitchen is adjacent to a breakfast nook and has a wonderful walk-in pantry. Upstairs, there are three bedrooms, including a lovely master suite with whirlpool spa. Bonus room over the garage can be developed later into a fourth bedroom, office space or a playroom for children.

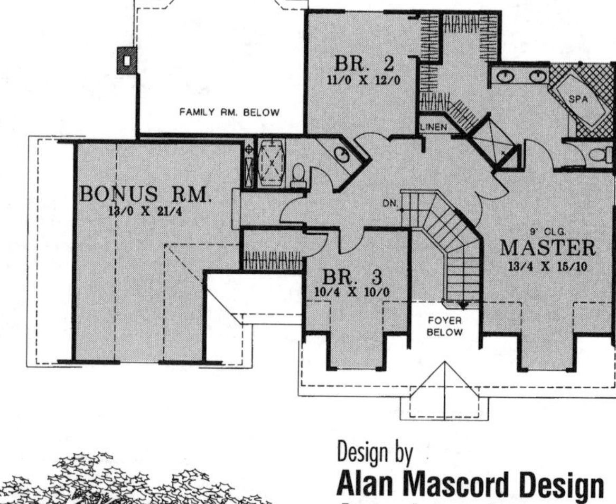
FAMILY RM. BELOW
BR. 2
11/0 X 12/0
SPA
LINEN
BONUS RM.
13/0 X 21/4
BR. 3
10/4 X 10/0
9' CLG.
MASTER
13/4 X 15/10
FOYER
BELOW

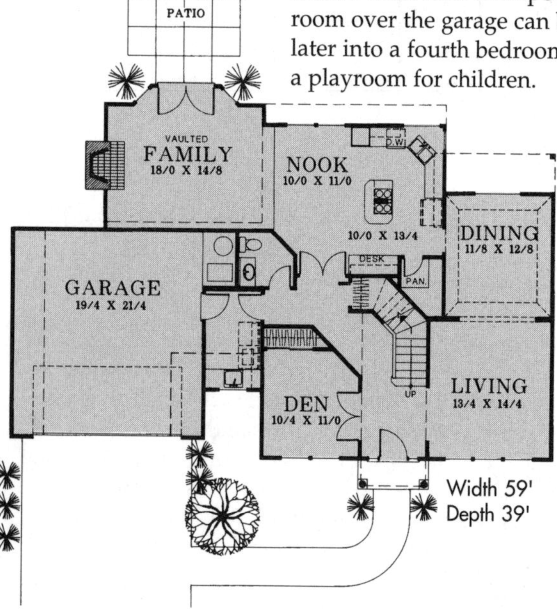
PATIO
VAULTED
FAMILY
18/0 X 14/8
NOOK
10/0 X 11/0
10/0 X 13/4
DINING
11/8 X 12/8
GARAGE
19/4 X 21/4
DEN
10/4 X 11/0
LIVING
13/4 X 14/4
Width 59'
Depth 39'

Design by
Alan Mascord Design Associates, Inc.

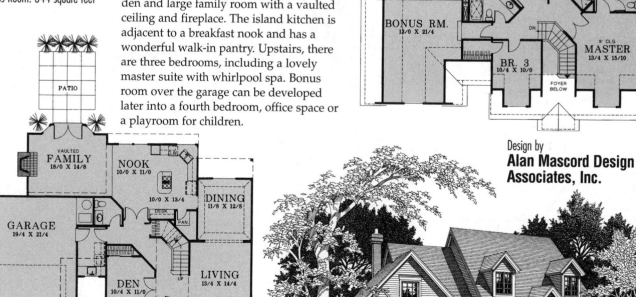

Design 9487

First Floor: 1,175 square feet
Second Floor: 891 square feet
Total: 2,066 square feet

■ This charming two-story home is enhanced by horizontal siding on its exterior and a Palladian window at the den. Inside are formal dining and living rooms, both with transom windows, and a family room with fireplace. The island kitchen has an attached nook with outdoor access. A private den with angled double doors opens off the foyer. Upstairs is a master bedroom with a nine-foot tray ceiling and two secondary bedrooms sharing a full bath.

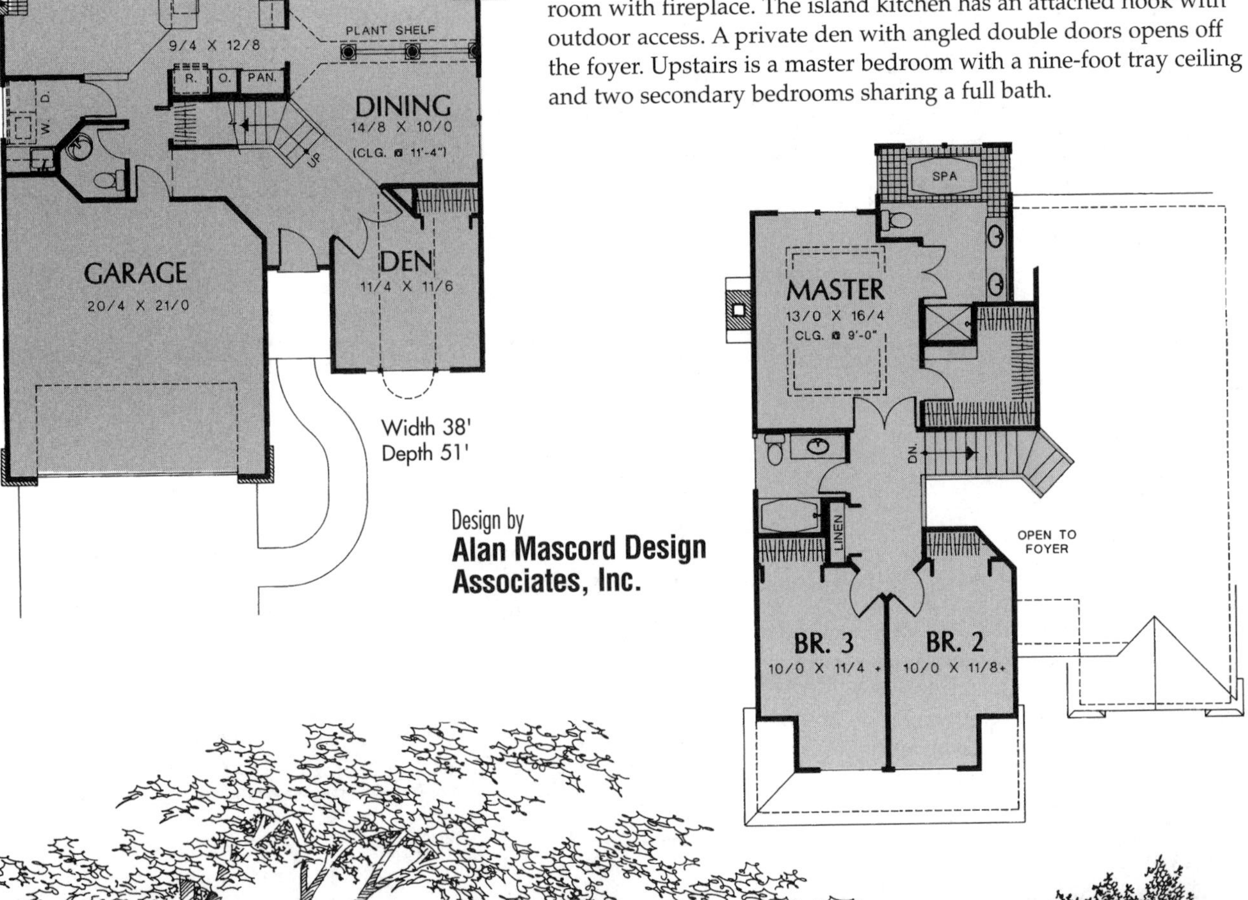
NOOK
10/4 X 18/6
FAMILY
13/0 X 14/6
LIVING
14/8 X 12/10
(CLG. @ 11'-4")
PLANT SHELF
9/4 X 12/8
R.
O.
PAN.
W.
D.
DINING
14/8 X 10/0
(CLG. @ 11'-4")
UP
GARAGE
20/4 X 21/0
DEN
11/4 X 11/6
Width 38'
Depth 51'
SPA
MASTER
13/0 X 16/4
CLG. @ 9'-0"
DN.
LINEN
OPEN TO
FOYER
BR. 3
10/0 X 11/4 +
BR. 2
10/0 X 11/8+

Design by
Alan Mascord Design Associates, Inc.

Design 9260

First Floor: 891 square feet
Second Floor: 759 square feet
Total: 1,650 square feet

■ This modest-size home provides a quaint covered front porch that opens to a two-story foyer. The formal dining room features a boxed window that can be seen from the entry. A fireplace in the great room adds warmth and coziness to the attached breakfast room and the well-planned kitchen. Sliding glass doors lead from the breakfast room to the rear yard. In a nearby utility room a washer and dryer reside and a closet provides ample storage. A powder room is provided nearby for guests. Three bedrooms are on the second floor; one of these includes an arched window under a vaulted ceiling. The deluxe master suite provides a large walk-in closet and a dressing area with a double vanity and a whirlpool.

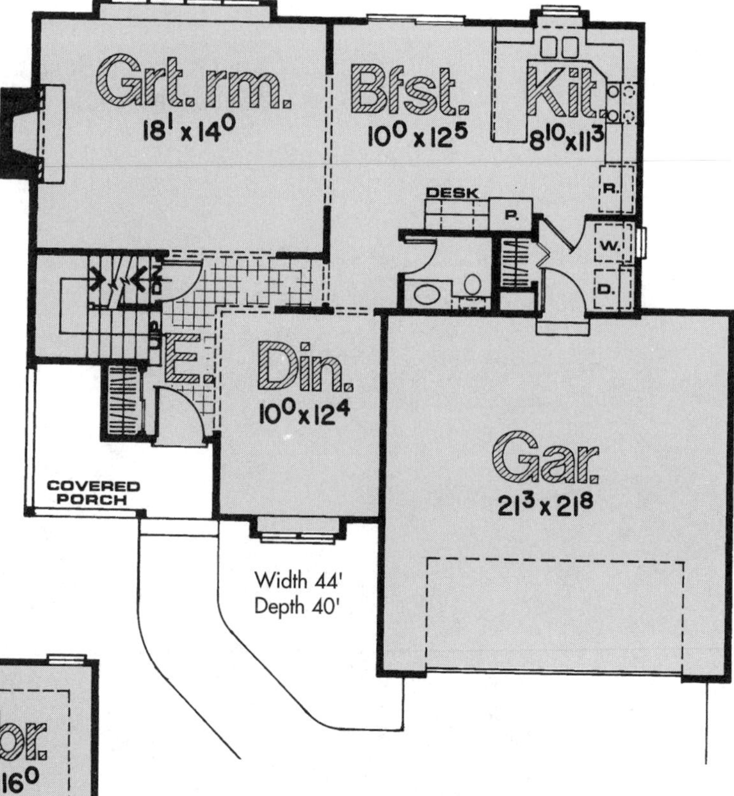
Grt. rm.
$18^{1} \times 14^{0}$
Bfst.
$10^{0} \times 12^{5}$
Kit.
$8^{10} \times 11^{3}$
DESK
P.
R.
W.
D.
E.
Din.
$10^{0} \times 12^{4}$
Gar.
$21^{3} \times 21^{8}$
COVERED PORCH
Width 44'
Depth 40'

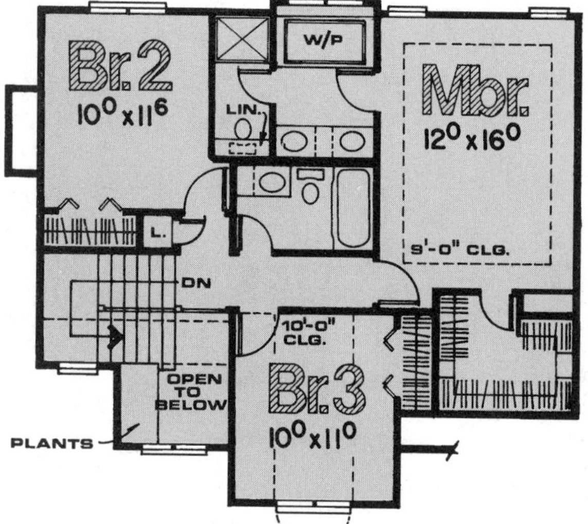
Br. 2
$10^{0} \times 11^{6}$
W/P
LIN.
Mbr.
$12^{0} \times 16^{0}$
9'-0" CLG.
L.
DN
10'-0" CLG.
OPEN TO BELOW
Br. 3
$10^{0} \times 11^{0}$
PLANTS

Design by
Design Basics, Inc.

Design 9235

First Floor: 919 square feet
Second Floor: 927 square feet
Total: 1,846 square feet

■ Wonderful country design begins with the wraparound porch of this plan. The island kitchen with a boxed window over the sink is adjacent to a large bay-windowed dinette. The great room includes many windows and a fireplace. Upstairs, the large master suite contains His and Hers walk-in closets, corner windows and a bath area featuring a double vanity and whirlpool tub. Two secondary bedrooms have interesting angles and a third bedroom in the front features a volume ceiling and arched window.

QUOTE ONE®
Cost to build? See page 342 to order complete cost estimate to build this house in your area!

Design by
Design Basics, Inc.

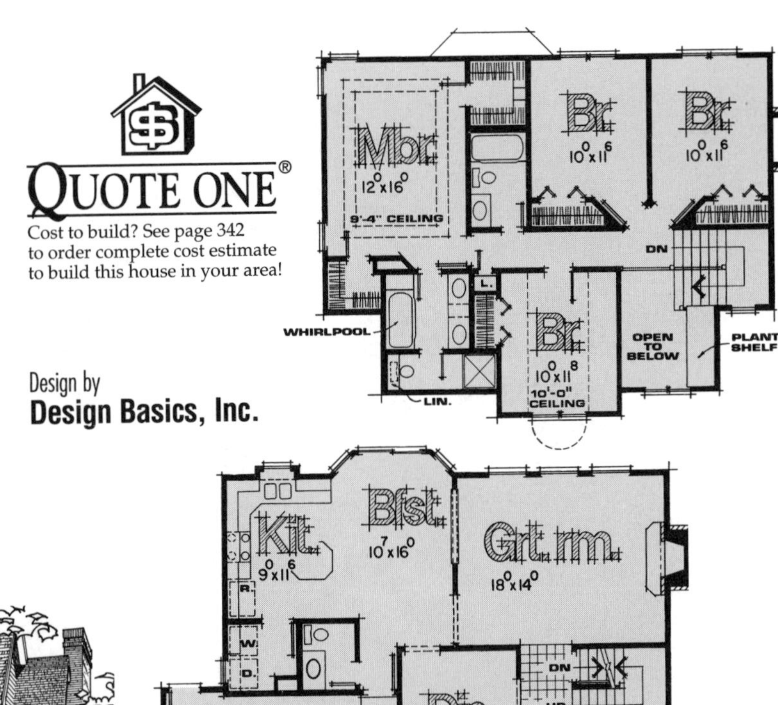

Mbr.
12⁰x16⁰
9'-4" CEILING
Br.
10⁰x11⁶
Br.
10⁰x11⁶
DN
WHIRLPOOL
L.
Br.
10⁰x11⁸
10'-0" CEILING
LIN.
OPEN TO BELOW
PLANT SHELF

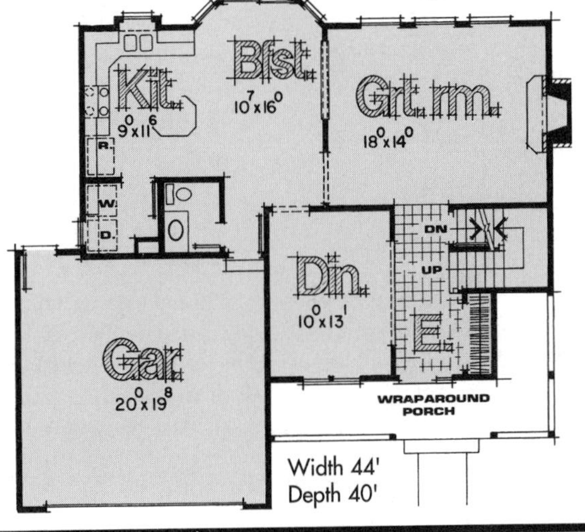

Kit.
9⁰x11⁶
R.
W.
D.
Bfst.
10⁷x16⁰
Grt. rm.
18⁰x14⁰
DN
UP
Din.
10⁰x13¹
E.
Gar.
20⁰x19⁸
WRAPAROUND PORCH
Width 44'
Depth 40'

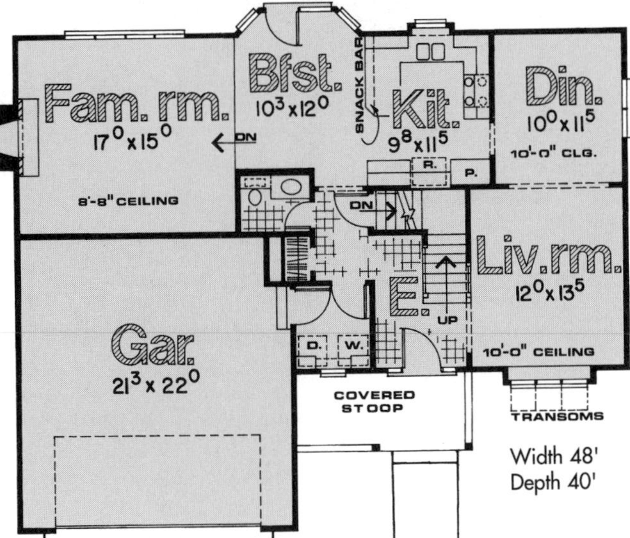

Fam. rm.
17⁰x15⁰
DN
8'-8" CEILING
Bfst.
10³x12⁰
SNACK BAR
Kit.
9⁸x11⁵
R.
P.
Din.
10⁰x11⁵
10'-0" CLG.
DN
Liv. rm.
12⁰x13⁵
E.
UP
10'-0" CEILING
Gar.
21³ x 22⁰
D.
W.
COVERED STOOP
TRANSOMS
Width 48'
Depth 40'

Design 9282

First Floor: 1,042 square feet
Second Floor: 803 square feet
Total: 1,845 square feet

Design by
Design Basics, Inc.

■ Upon entry from the covered front porch, the thoughtful floor plan is immediately evident. To the right of the entry is a formal living room accented with a ten-foot ceiling. The kitchen is set between the formal dining room and the breakfast room for easy service. Off the breakfast area, step down into the family room where a handsome fireplace and wall of windows welcome you. Upstairs, two secondary bedrooms share a hall bath. The private master bedroom has a boxed ceiling, walk-in closet and a pampering dressing area with double vanity and whirlpool.

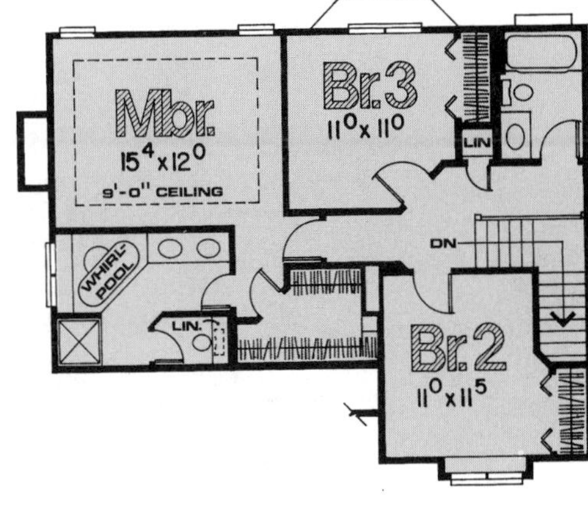

Mbr.
15⁴x12⁰
9'-0" CEILING
Br. 3
11⁰x11⁰
LIN
DN
WHIRLPOOL
LIN.
Br. 2
11⁰x11⁵

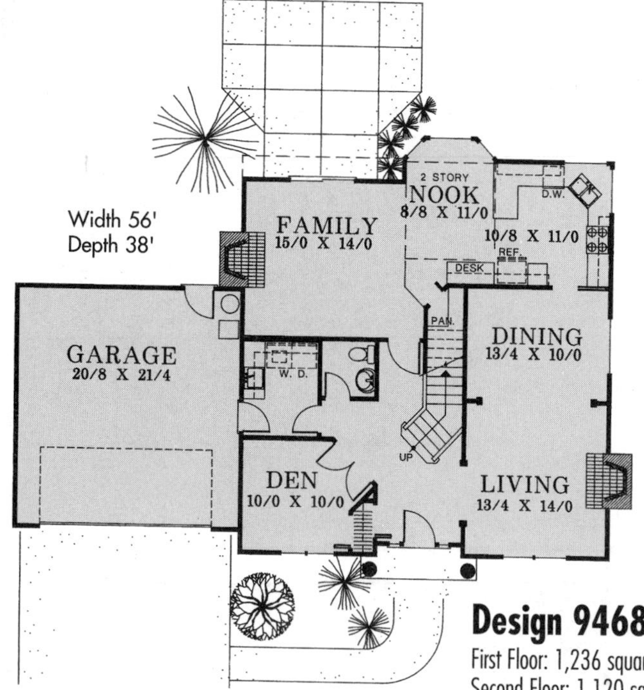

Width 56'
Depth 38'
2 STORY
NOOK
8/8 X 11/0
D.W.
FAMILY
15/0 X 14/0
10/8 X 11/0
REF.
DESK
GARAGE
20/8 X 21/4
PAN.
DINING
13/4 X 10/0
W. D.
UP
DEN
10/0 X 10/0
LIVING
13/4 X 14/0

Design 9468

First Floor: 1,236 square feet
Second Floor: 1,120 square feet
Total: 2,356 square feet
Bonus Room: 270 square feet

Design by
Alan Mascord Design Associates, Inc.

■ This gracious home integrates timeless traditional styling with a functional, cost-effective plan. An interesting feature is the two-story nook area with a bay window set between the gourmet kitchen and the large family room. A conveniently located door in the upper hallway opens to the large bonus room over the two-car garage. Rounding out the upper floor are a sumptuous master suite, with its own private retreat out over the entry, and two family bedrooms.

Design 7261

First Floor: 1,093 square feet
Second Floor: 1,038 square feet
Total: 2,131 square feet

Design by
Design Basics, Inc.

■ The beautifully proportioned design is complemented by a large covered porch framed with a wood railing. The living room is enhanced by a bay window and French doors leading to the family room. The dining room is accented by a built-in curio cabinet and is convenient to the spacious kitchen with a cooktop island and bayed breakfast nook. Upstairs, the master bedroom contains a distinctive vaulted ceiling plus a luxurious bath with a corner whirlpool tub and a large walk-in closet. Three family bedrooms share a compartmented hall bath.

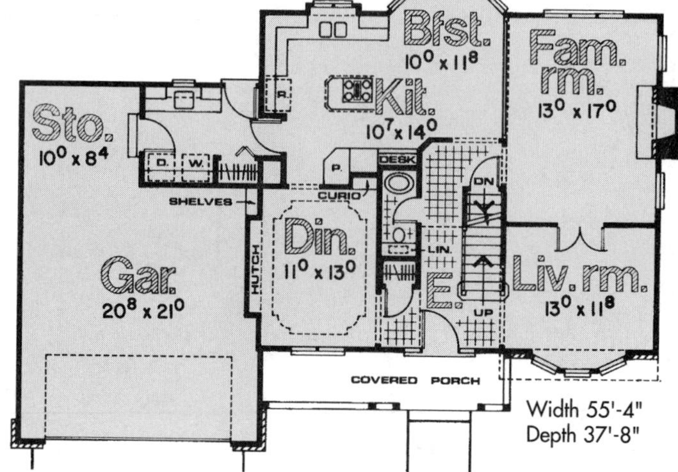

Bfst.
10⁰ x 11⁸
Fam. rm.
13⁰ x 17⁰
Sto.
10⁰ x 8⁴
Kit.
10⁷ x 14⁰
DESK
SHELVES
CURIO
Din.
11⁰ x 13⁰
HUTCH
Gar.
20⁸ x 21⁰
LIN.
Liv. rm.
13⁰ x 11⁸
COVERED PORCH
Width 55'-4"
Depth 37'-8"

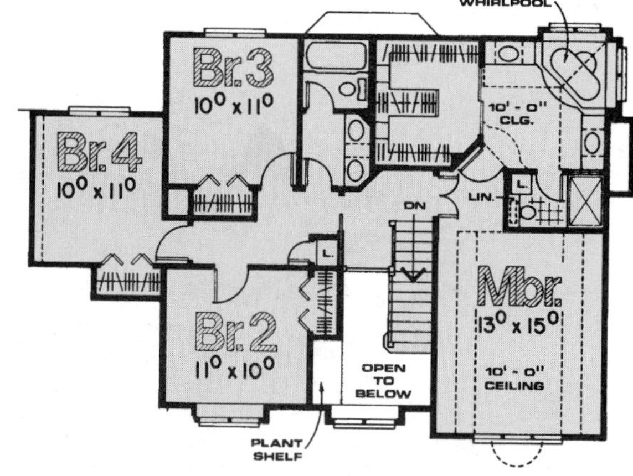

WHIRLPOOL
Br. 3
10⁰ x 11⁰
10' - 0" CLG.
Br. 4
10⁰ x 11⁰
LIN.
DN
Mbr.
13⁰ x 15⁰
Br. 2
11⁰ x 10⁰
OPEN TO BELOW
10' - 0" CEILING
PLANT SHELF

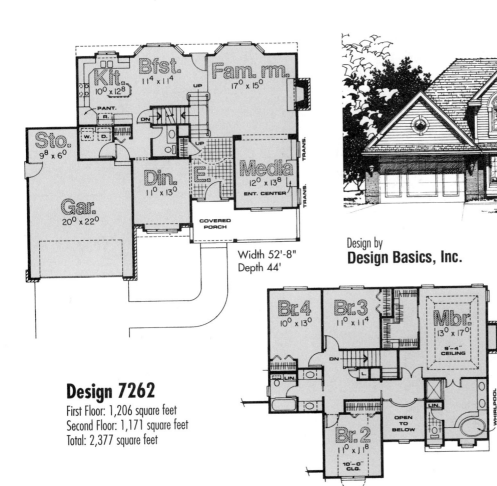

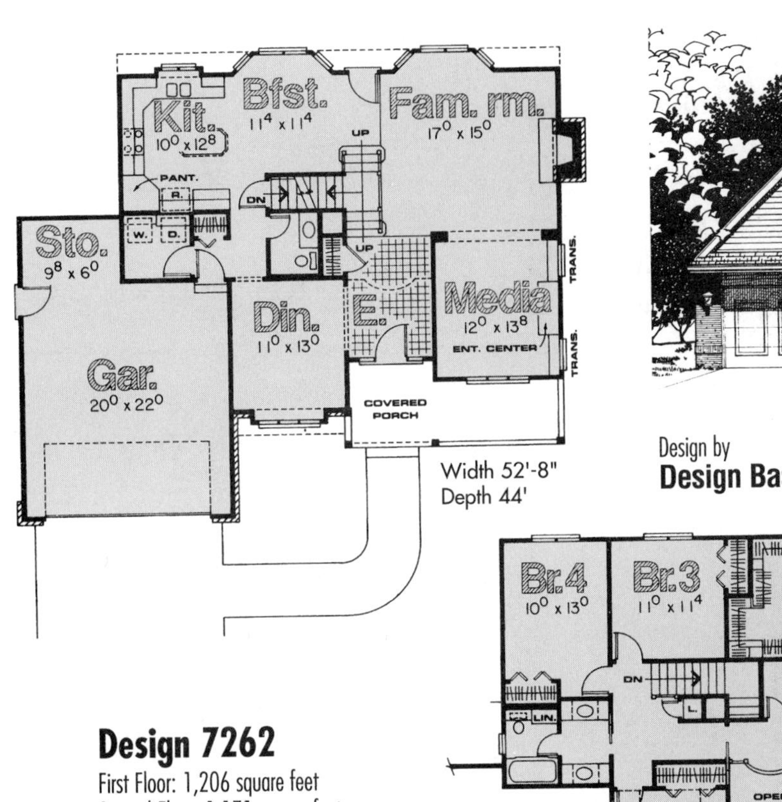
Kit.
$10^0 \times 12^8$
Bfst.
$11^4 \times 11^4$
Fam. rm.
$17^0 \times 15^0$
PANT.
Sto.
$9^8 \times 6^0$
Din.
$11^0 \times 13^0$
E.
Media
$12^0 \times 13^8$
ENT. CENTER
Gar.
$20^0 \times 22^0$
COVERED PORCH
Width 52'-8"
Depth 44'

Design by
Design Basics, Inc.

■ Country charm is found in this home's cozy front porch and bright windows. A media room with a built-in entertainment center is just off the bay-windowed family room. The oversized kitchen has a prep island and spacious breakfast nook. Upstairs, three family bedrooms share a compartmented bath with twin vanities. Elegant French doors lead into the luxurious master suite that is finished with a corner whirlpool, compartmented toilet and walk-in closet.

Design 7262

First Floor: 1,206 square feet
Second Floor: 1,171 square feet
Total: 2,377 square feet

Design 9245

First Floor: 1,132 square feet
Second Floor: 1,087 square feet
Total: 2,219 square feet

Design by
Design Basics, Inc.

■ A front porch graces the entry to this charming transitional design and hints of the great floor plan inside. Note the central core staircase, around which open the formal dining room with tiered ceiling, huge great room with fireplace, and island kitchen with breakfast room. A convenient powder room is found in the hallway to serve guests. Upstairs are four bedrooms, including a master suite with a double vanity and a whirlpool, which is buffered from the family bedrooms. Three secondary bedrooms share a full bath with double vanity.

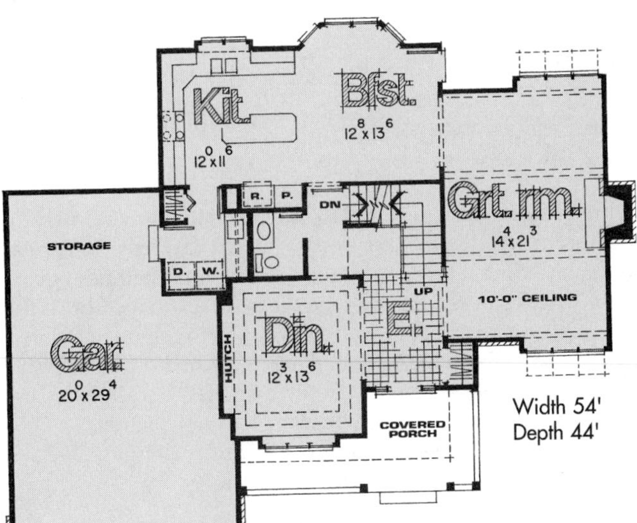
Kit.
$12^0 \times 11^6$
Bfst.
$12^8 \times 13^6$
Grt. rm.
$14^4 \times 21^3$
10'-0" CEILING
STORAGE
Gar.
$20^0 \times 29^4$
HUTCH
Din.
$12^3 \times 13^6$
E.
COVERED PORCH
Width 54'
Depth 44'

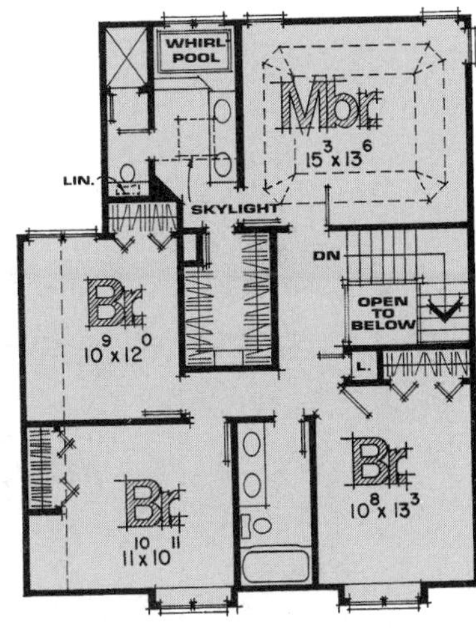
WHIRL POOL
Mbr.
$15^3 \times 13^6$
LIN.
SKYLIGHT
Br.
$10^9 \times 12^0$
OPEN TO BELOW
Br.
$11^{10} \times 10^{11}$
Br.
$10^8 \times 13^3$

■ Exterior detailing is the first attraction to this home: a gabled roof, an arched window and a rustic covered porch. The floor plan inside offers its own delights, such as a formal parlor with a ten-foot ceiling, a breakfast area leading to a covered deck and an island kitchen with a wrapping pantry. The family room is spacious and contains a warming hearth. Upstairs, the secondary bedrooms each feature a built-in desk. A bonus room allows space for a playroom. The master bedroom features an oversized closet and a bath fit for a king.

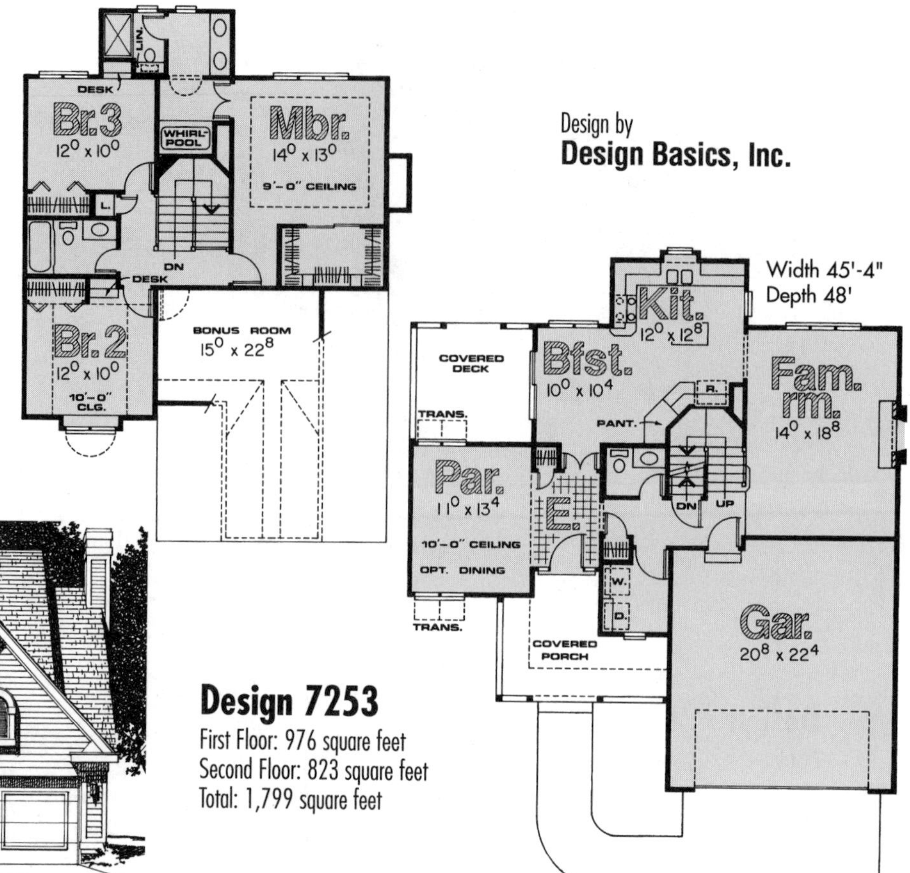

DESK
Br.3
12⁰ x 10⁰
LIN.
WHIRL-POOL
Mbr.
14⁰ x 13⁰
9'-0" CEILING
L.
DN
DESK
Br.2
12⁰ x 10⁰
10'-0" CLG.
BONUS ROOM
15⁰ x 22⁸
Width 45'-4"
Depth 48'
Kit.
12⁰ x 12⁸
COVERED DECK
Bfst.
10⁰ x 10⁴
R.
PANT.
Fam. rm.
14⁰ x 18⁸
TRANS.
Par.
11⁰ x 13⁴
10'-0" CEILING
OPT. DINING
E.
DN
UP
W.
D.
TRANS.
COVERED PORCH
Gar.
20⁸ x 22⁴

Design by
Design Basics, Inc.

Design 7253

First Floor: 976 square feet
Second Floor: 823 square feet
Total: 1,799 square feet

Design 7302

First Floor: 1,273 square feet
Second Floor: 1,035 square feet
Total: 2,308 square feet

Design by
Design Basics, Inc.

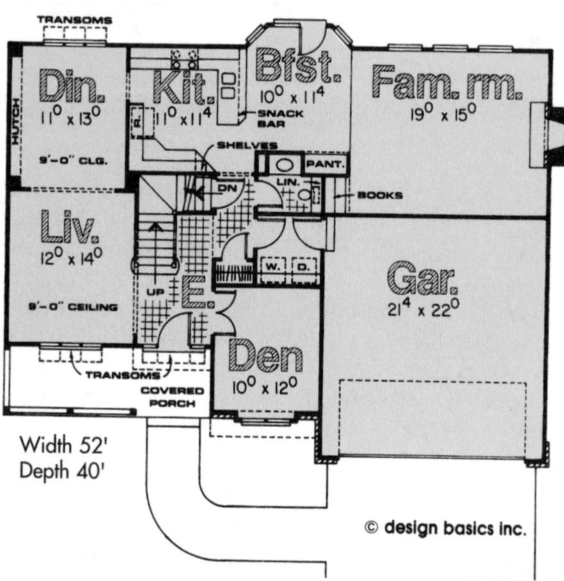

TRANSOMS
Din.
11⁰ x 13⁰
HUTCH
9'-0" CLG.
Kit.
11⁰ x 11⁴
R.
Bfst.
10⁰ x 11⁴
SNACK BAR
Fam. rm.
19⁰ x 15⁰
SHELVES
PANT.
DN
LIN.
BOOKS
Liv.
12⁰ x 14⁰
9'-0" CEILING
UP
E.
W.
D.
Gar.
21⁴ x 22⁰
TRANSOMS
COVERED PORCH
Den
10⁰ x 12⁰

Width 52'
Depth 40'

© design basics inc.

■ From the cozy front porch to the multitude of windows, the enhancements that this home contains are impressive. Formal living and dining areas combine to allow entertainment flexibility. The well-organized kitchen is open to a bayed breakfast area with back yard access and also leads to the huge family room with a fireplace. A private den is located off the entry. The master suite has a high ceiling and a large walk-in closet. The pampering master bath boasts a luxurious sunlit whirlpool tub with separate shower. Three secondary bedrooms share a large, compartmented bath.

Br.3
11⁰ x 11⁴
Br.4
11⁰ x 11⁴
Mbr.
14⁰ x 15⁰
9'-0" CLG.
DN
LINEN
L.
OPEN TO BELOW
LIN.
WHIRL-POOL
Br.2
10⁰ x 12⁰
10'-0" CEILING
PLANT SHELF
UNFINISHED
Sto.
15⁶ x 11⁸

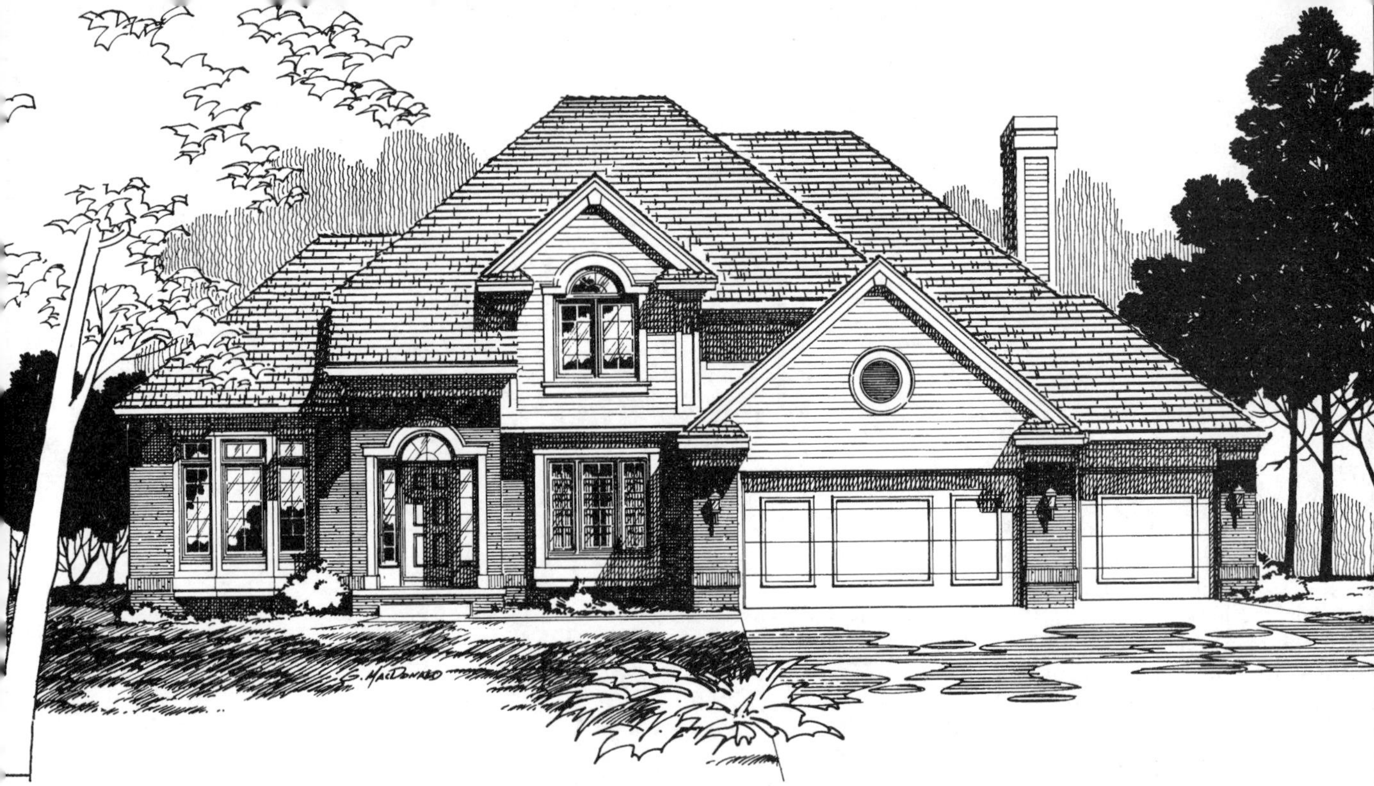

Design by
Design Basics, Inc.

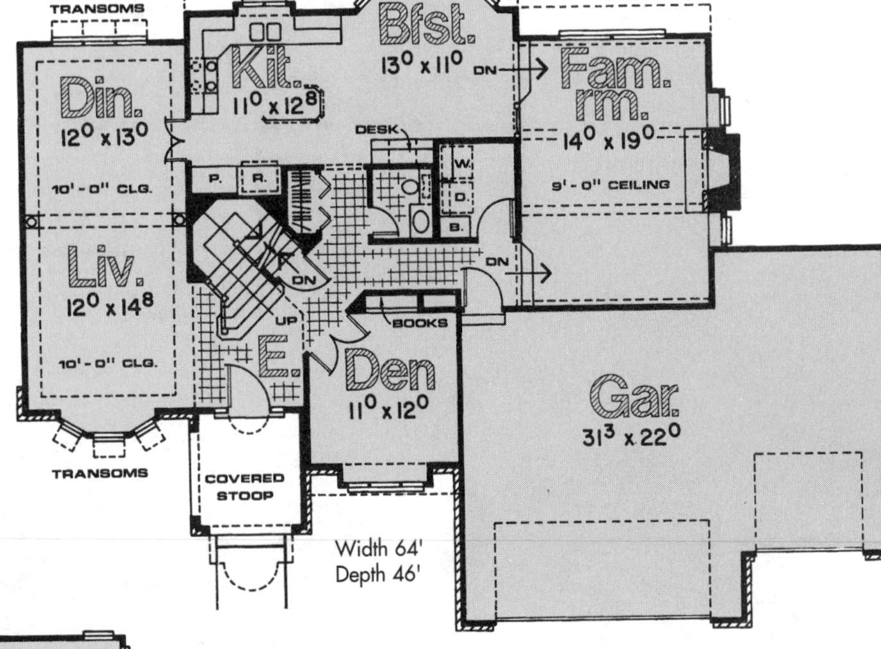
TRANSOMS
Bfst.
13⁰ x 11⁰
Kit.
11⁰ x 12⁸
Din.
12⁰ x 13⁰
10'-0" CLG.
Fam. rm.
14⁰ x 19⁰
9'-0" CEILING
DN
DESK
P.
R.
W.
D.
B.
Liv.
12⁰ x 14⁸
10'-0" CLG.
DN
UP
E.
BOOKS
Den
11⁰ x 12⁰
Gar.
31³ x 22⁰
TRANSOMS
COVERED STOOP
Width 64'
Depth 46'

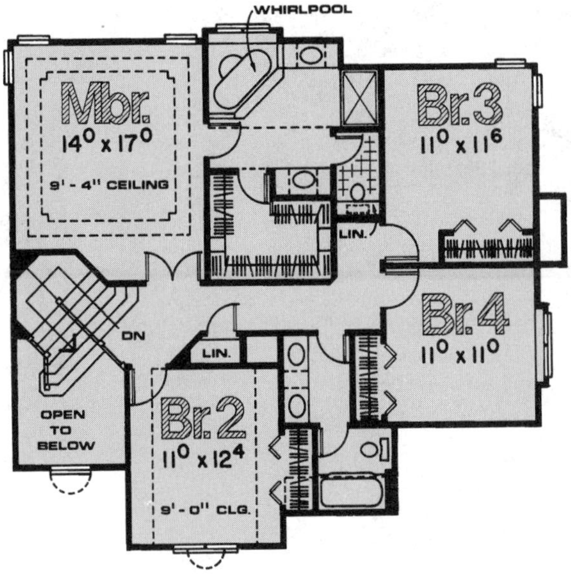

Design 9369

First Floor: 1,369 square feet
Second Floor: 1,111 square feet
Total: 2,480 square feet

■ This delightful plan offers the best in transitional design. Combined dining and living areas provide abundant space for formal entertaining or holiday gatherings. Or if preferred, escape to the den for quiet time with a book—built-in bookshelves fill out one wall of this room. The kitchen makes use of island counter space and breakfast nook. Take a step down into the large family room and enjoy the ambience of a cozy fireplace and beam ceiling. A laundry room and powder room round out the first floor. The master bedroom—with tiered ceiling and bath with whirlpool—highlights the second floor. Three additional bedrooms and another full bath complete the design.

Design 9542

First Floor: 1,465 square feet
Second Floor: 1,103 square feet
Total: 2,568 square feet
Bonus Room: 303 square feet

■ Here's traditional style at its best! The bay-windowed den with built-in bookshelves is conveniently located to the front of the plan, making it ideal for use as an office or home-based business. To the left, the formal area contains a living and dining room, both with a tray ceiling. Cooks will find the kitchen a delight, with its sunlit corner sink, cooktop island, large pantry and built-in planning desk. A bumped-out eating nook opens to the rear yard through double doors. Completing the first floor is a spacious family room with a fireplace. The second floor contains the sleeping zone. A master suite with a relaxing spa tub, a separate shower and a huge walk-in closet is sure to please. Bedrooms 2 and 3 share a full bath. The three-car garage provides ample space for a workshop.

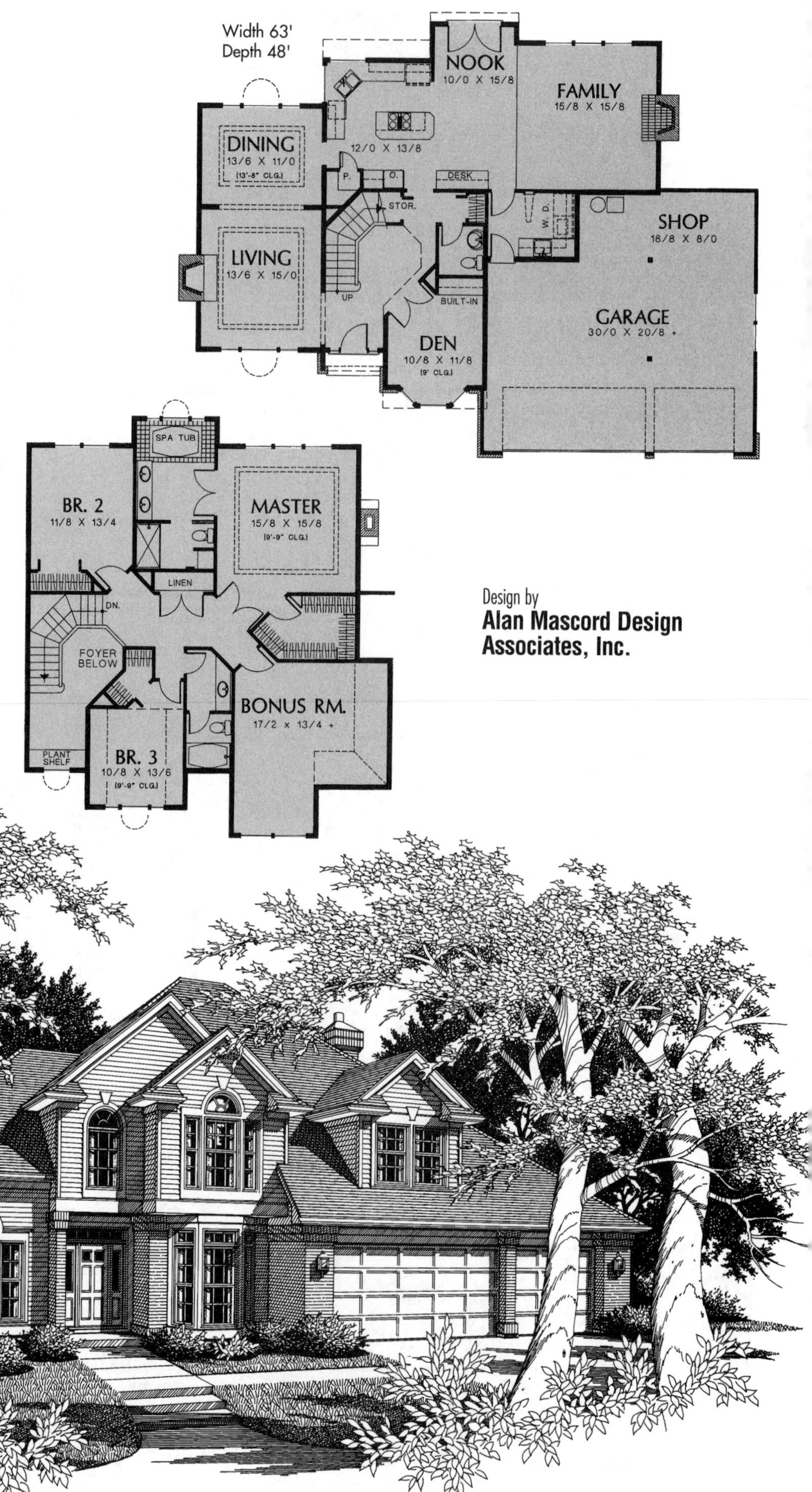

Width 63'
Depth 48'
NOOK
10/0 X 15/8
FAMILY
15/8 X 15/8
DINING
13/6 X 11/0
(13'-8" CLG.)
12/0 X 13/8
P.
O.
DESK
STOR.
W. D.
SHOP
18/8 X 8/0
LIVING
13/6 X 15/0
UP
BUILT-IN
GARAGE
30/0 X 20/8 +
DEN
10/8 X 11/8
(9' CLG.)
SPA TUB
BR. 2
11/8 X 13/4
MASTER
15/8 X 15/8
(9'-9" CLG.)
LINEN
DN.
FOYER
BELOW
BONUS RM.
17/2 x 13/4 +
PLANT
SHELF
BR. 3
10/8 X 13/6
(9'-9" CLG.)

Design by
Alan Mascord Design Associates, Inc.

Design 9272

First Floor: 1,520 square feet
Second Floor: 1,334 square feet
Total: 2,854 square feet

■ This stunning two-story home features an enormous great room with spider-beamed ceiling, built-in bookcases and fireplace; it connects directly to the sunroom with attached wet bar. This skylit area leads to the breakfast room and island kitchen. Complementing these informal gathering areas are the formal living room and dining room. A luxurious master suite features His and Hers walk-in closets and a dressing area with angled, oval whirlpool. Generous bath arrangements are made for the three secondary bedrooms.

Design by
Design Basics, Inc.

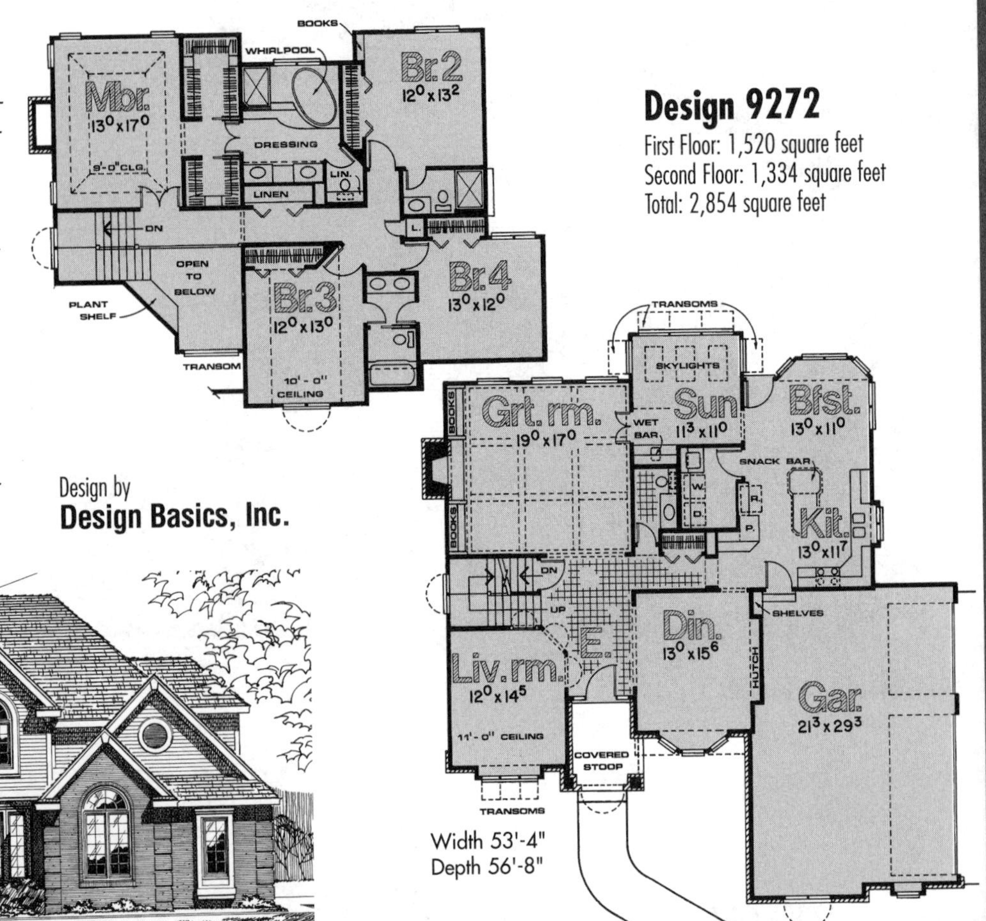

BOOKS
WHIRLPOOL
Mbr.
13⁰x17⁰
9'-0" CLG.
Br.2
12⁰x13²
DRESSING
LINEN
LIN.
DN
OPEN TO BELOW
PLANT SHELF
TRANSOM
Br.3
12⁰x13⁰
10'-0" CEILING
Br.4
13⁰x12⁰
TRANSOMS
SKYLIGHTS
Grt. rm.
19⁰x17⁰
WET BAR
Sun
11³x11⁰
Bfst.
13⁰x11⁰
SNACK BAR
Kit.
13⁰x11⁷
SHELVES
Din.
13⁰x15⁶
HUTCH
Gar.
21³x29³
Liv. rm.
12⁰x14⁵
11'-0" CEILING
COVERED STOOP
TRANSOMS
Width 53'-4"
Depth 56'-8"

Design P119

First Floor: 1,424 square feet
Second Floor: 1,256 square feet
Total: 2,680 square feet

■ A grand two-story foyer takes its charm from a bright clerestory window. Just off the foyer lies the formal living area, where the living room joins the dining room with twin boxed columns that are personalized with shelves. The kitchen is placed to easily serve the dining room while remaining open to the breakfast area and vaulted family room. Upstairs, the master suite and bath are nicely balanced with three family bedrooms, a full hall bath and convenient laundry room. Please specify basement or crawlspace foundation when ordering.

Design by
Frank Betz Associates, Inc.

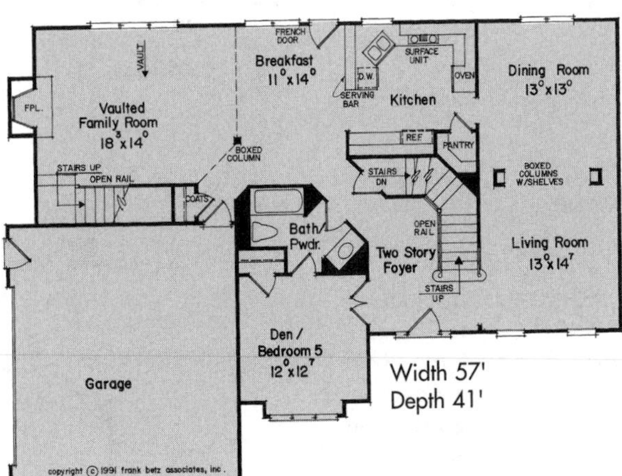

FRENCH DOOR
Breakfast
11⁰x14⁰
Kitchen
Dining Room
13⁰x13⁰
Vaulted Family Room
18⁵x14⁰
FPL.
BOXED COLUMN
PANTRY
BOXED COLUMNS W/SHELVES
Bath/Pwdr.
Two Story Foyer
Living Room
13⁰x14⁷
Den / Bedroom 5
12⁰x12⁷
Garage
copyright © 1991 frank betz associates, inc.

Width 57'
Depth 41'

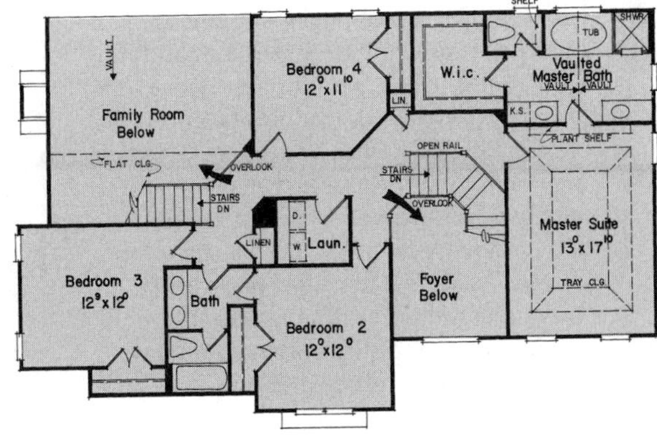

PLANT SHELF
Family Room Below
Bedroom 4
12⁰x11¹⁰
W.i.c.
Vaulted Master Bath
PLANT SHELF
OVERLOOK
STAIRS DN
Laun.
Master Suite
13⁰x17¹⁰
TRAY CLG.
Bedroom 3
12⁹x12⁰
Bath
Foyer Below
Bedroom 2
12⁰x12⁰

Design by
Frank Betz Associates, Inc.

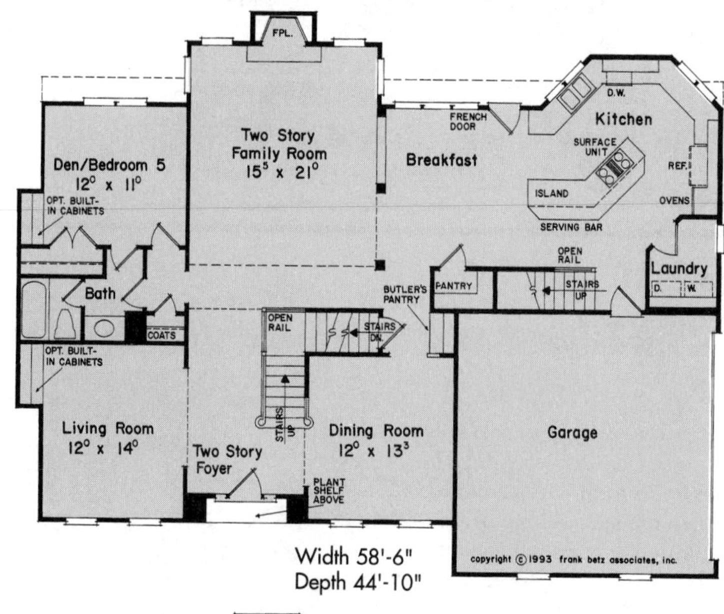

FPL.
Two Story Family Room 15^5 x 21^0
Den/Bedroom 5 12^0 x 11^0
OPT. BUILT-IN CABINETS
Bath
COATS
OPT. BUILT-IN CABINETS
Living Room 12^0 x 14^0
Two Story Foyer
OPEN RAIL
STAIRS DN.
STAIRS UP
Dining Room 12^0 x 13^3
PLANT SHELF ABOVE
FRENCH DOOR
Breakfast
Kitchen
D.W.
SURFACE UNIT
REF.
OVENS
ISLAND
SERVING BAR
OPEN RAIL
STAIRS UP
BUTLER'S PANTRY
PANTRY
Laundry
D. W.
Garage
copyright © 1993 frank betz associates, inc.

Width 58'-6"
Depth 44'-10"

Design P117

First Floor: 1,665 square feet
Second Floor: 1,554 square feet
Total: 3,219 square feet

■ Family living is the focus of this stately transitional home. With the formal living area traditionally placed to flank the two-story foyer, the rear of the plan is devoted to casual living. The two-story family room has a lovely fireplace and windows to the rear yard. The remarkable kitchen has wraparound counters, a breakfast nook and a unique cooktop island that is angled to create a serving bar. A bedroom and full bath would make a comfortable guest suite or a quiet den. Stairs lead to a balcony hall overlooking the family room and foyer, then on to two bedrooms that share a private bath; a third bedroom has its own bath and walk-in closet. The master suite is designed with a tray ceiling and sitting room with a through-fireplace to the vaulted bath. Please specify basement or crawl-space foundation when ordering.

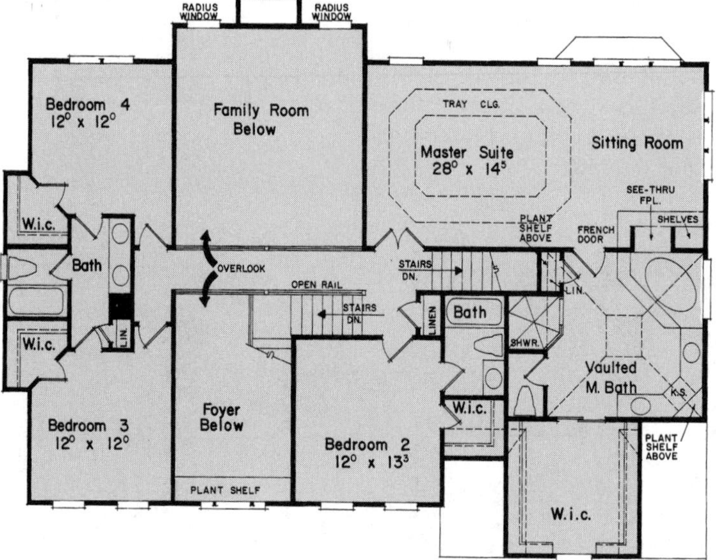

RADIUS WINDOW
RADIUS WINDOW
Bedroom 4 12^0 x 12^0
Family Room Below
TRAY CLG.
Master Suite 28^0 x 14^5
Sitting Room
SEE-THRU FPL.
SHELVES
PLANT SHELF ABOVE
FRENCH DOOR
W.i.c.
Bath
OVERLOOK
OPEN RAIL
STAIRS DN.
STAIRS DN.
LINEN
LIN.
Bath
SHWR.
W.i.c.
Vaulted M. Bath
K.S.
Bedroom 3 12^0 x 12^0
Foyer Below
PLANT SHELF
Bedroom 2 12^0 x 13^3
W.i.c.
PLANT SHELF ABOVE
W.i.c.

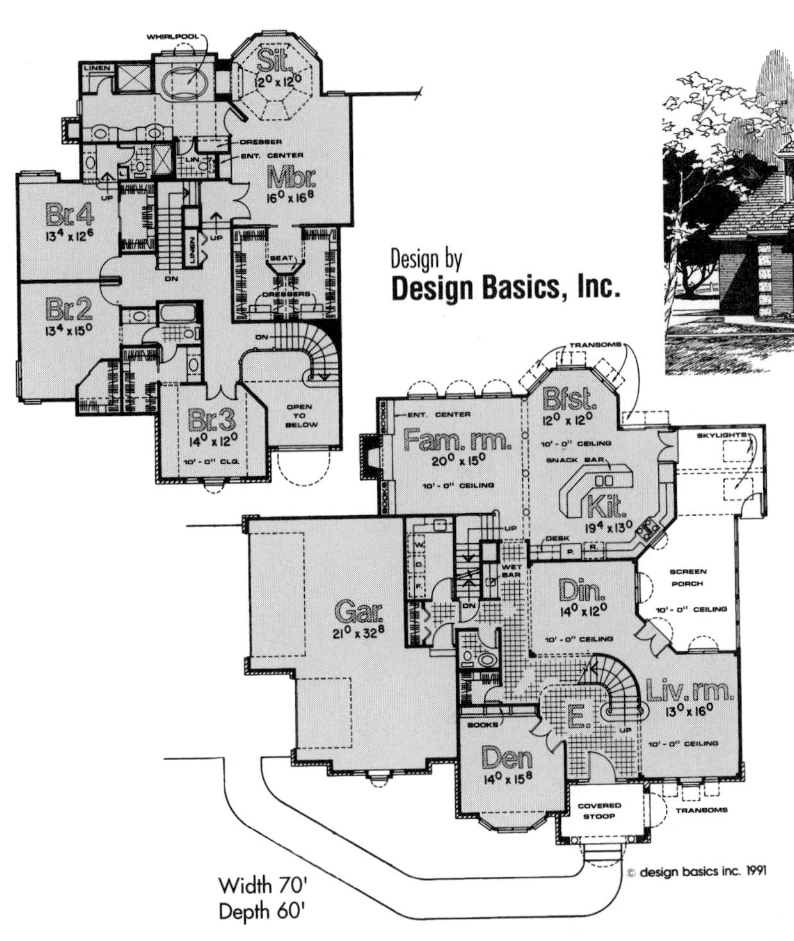
WHIRLPOOL
LINEN
Sit.
12⁰ x 12⁰
DRESSER
ENT. CENTER
Mbr.
16⁰ x 16⁸
Br.4
13⁴ x 12⁶
Br.2
13⁴ x 15⁰
SEAT
DRESSERS
Br.3
14⁰ x 12⁰
10'-0" CLG.
OPEN TO BELOW
TRANSOMS
Bfst.
12⁰ x 12⁰
Fam. rm.
20⁰ x 15⁰
10'-0" CEILING
SNACK BAR
SKYLIGHTS
Kit.
19⁴ x 13⁰
DESK
WET BAR
SCREEN PORCH
Gar.
21⁰ x 32⁸
Din.
14⁰ x 12⁰
10'-0" CEILING
Liv. rm.
13⁰ x 16⁰
BOOKS
Den
14⁰ x 15⁸
COVERED STOOP
TRANSOMS
© design basics inc. 1991
Width 70'
Depth 60'

Design by
Design Basics, Inc.

Design 9337

First Floor: 1,923 square feet
Second Floor: 1,852 square feet
Total: 3,775 square feet

■ Breathtaking details and bright windows highlight this luxurious two-story home. Just off the spectacular entry is an impressive private den. The curved hall between the living and dining rooms offers many formal entertaining options. The family room has three arched windows, a built-in entertainment center and a fireplace. Upstairs, three secondary bedrooms have walk-in closets and private access to a bath. The master suite has a built-in entertainment center and twin walk-in closets. Separated from the whirlpool bath by a through-fireplace, the sitting area adds an elegant touch.

Design 7266

First Floor: 1,631 square feet
Second Floor: 1,426 square feet
Total: 3,057 square feet

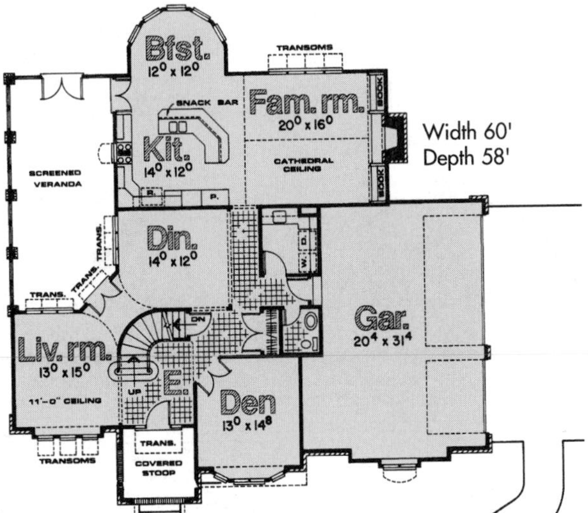

■ A clear division between formal and casual living areas makes this home a joy for the busy family. The living room is delightfully joined to the dining room through a curved hall that opens to the veranda. Casual living will center in the open kitchen with an angular snack bar island and open views to the breakfast nook and family room. Upstairs, three family bedrooms have access to a private bath. The master suite has a sunny sitting nook, two walk-in closets and a luxurious bath.

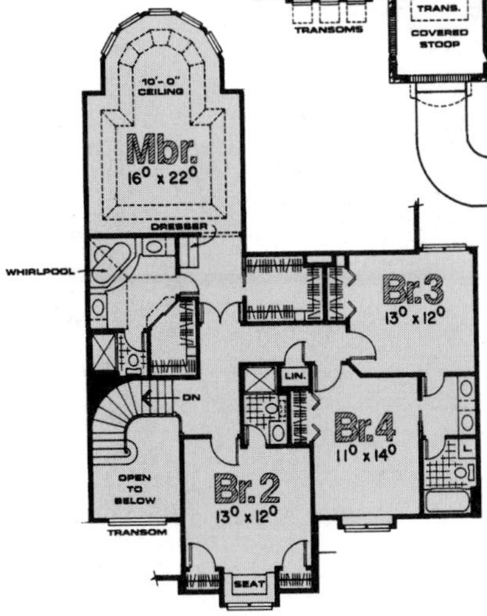

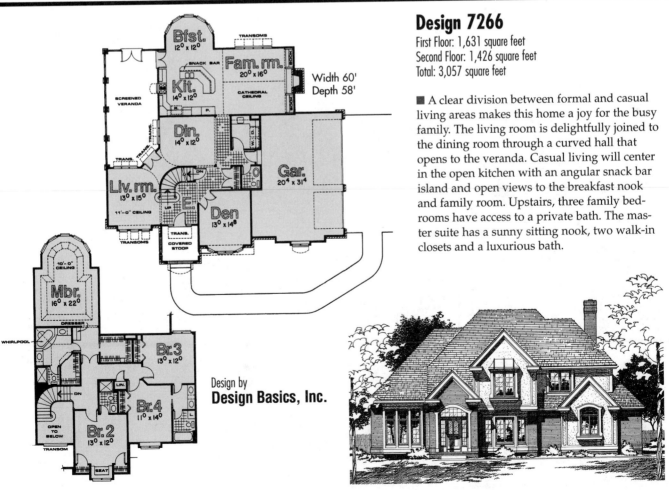

Width 60'
Depth 58'

Design by
Design Basics, Inc.

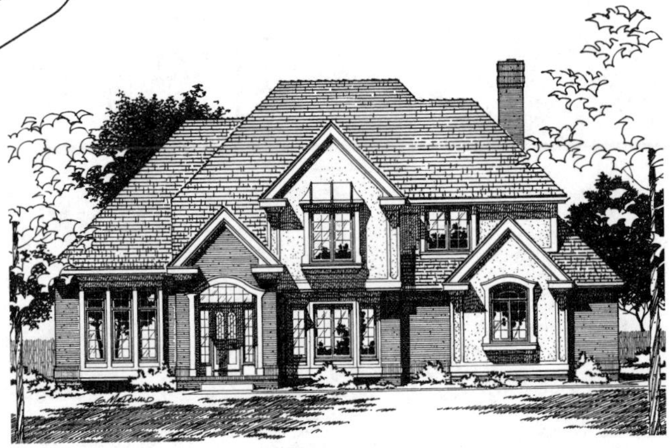

Design by
Frank Betz Associates, Inc.

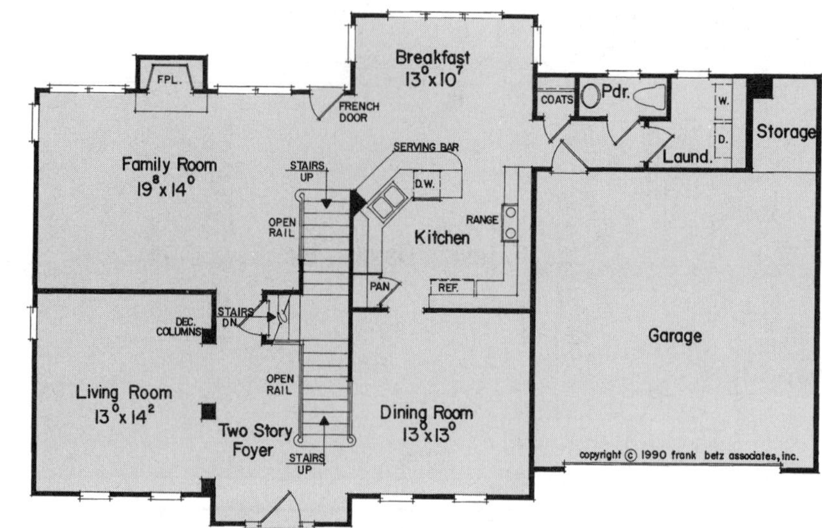

Breakfast
13^{0}x10^{7}
FPL.
FRENCH DOOR
COATS
Pdr.
W.
D.
Storage
Laund.
SERVING BAR
Family Room
19^{8}x14^{0}
STAIRS UP
D.W.
OPEN RAIL
RANGE
Kitchen
PAN
REF.
DEC. COLUMNS
STAIRS DN
Garage
OPEN RAIL
Living Room
13^{0}x14^{2}
Two Story Foyer
Dining Room
13^{0}x13^{0}
STAIRS UP
copyright © 1990 frank betz associates, inc.

Design P231

First Floor: 1,252 square feet
Second Floor: 1,348 square feet
Total: 2,600 square feet

■ Stately corner quoins and an exterior that's symmetrical in design reflect this home's functional yet elegant floor plan. The two-story foyer is framed by the formal living and dining rooms. The large family room has a fireplace flanked by windows and a French door to the rear yard. The efficient kitchen has a serving bar and an abundance of counter and cabinet space. A stylish twin-entry staircase leads to the second level and three family bedrooms and a compartmented bath. The master suite has an oversized bedroom, a sitting room that could double as an exercise area and a spa-style bath with a walk-in closet. Please specify basement or crawlspace foundation when ordering.

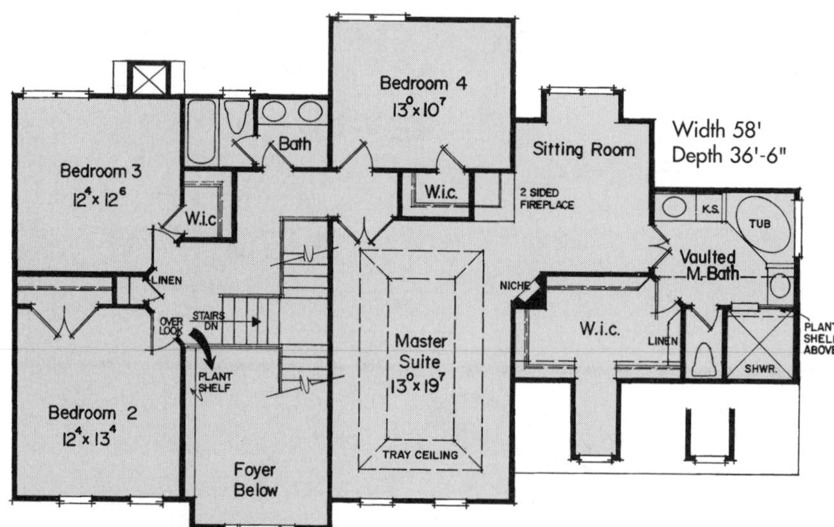

Bedroom 4
13^{0}x10^{7}
Bath
Sitting Room
Width 58'
Depth 36'-6"
Bedroom 3
12^{4}x 12^{6}
W.i.c.
W.i.c.
2 SIDED FIREPLACE
K.S.
TUB
Vaulted M. Bath
LINEN
NICHE
OVER LOOK
STAIRS DN
W.i.c.
LINEN
PLANT SHELF ABOVE
Master Suite
13^{0}x 19^{7}
PLANT SHELF
SHWR.
Bedroom 2
12^{4}x 13^{4}
TRAY CEILING
Foyer Below

Design 9918

First Floor: 1,710 square feet
Second Floor: 1,470 square feet
Total: 3,180 square feet

Design by
Design Traditions

DECK
BREAKFAST
11'-0" X 13'-3"
SCREEN PORCH
13'-6" X 13'-6"
FAMILY ROOM
17'-3" X 20'-0"
KITCHEN
13'-3" X 15'-0"
LAUNDRY
STOR.
BATH
DN.
OPTION ROOM
LIVING RM.
STUDY
GUEST RM.
12'-0" X 14'-6"
DINING ROOM
15'-0" X 19'-6"
2-CAR GARAGE
21'-6" X 21'-6"
UP
FOYER
STOOP

Width 61'-6"
Depth 50'-6"

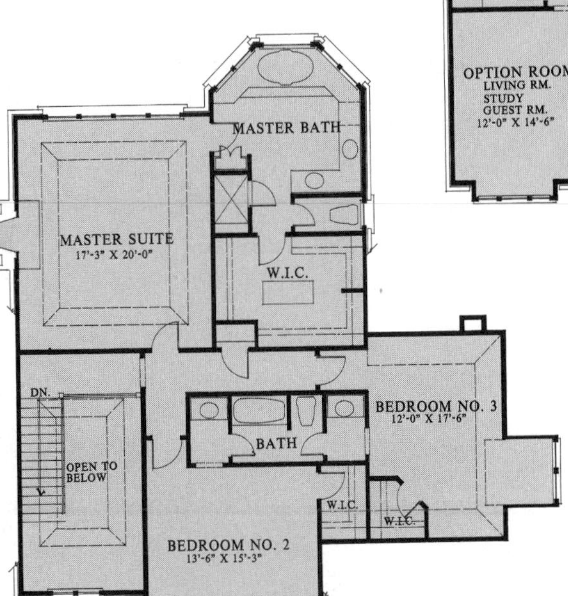
MASTER BATH
MASTER SUITE
17'-3" X 20'-0"
W.I.C.
DN.
OPEN TO BELOW
BATH
BEDROOM NO. 3
12'-0" X 17'-6"
W.I.C.
W.I.C.
BEDROOM NO. 2
13'-6" X 15'-3"

■ Many generously sized, shuttered windows flood this stunning home with the clear, warming light of outdoors—captivating with its classic styling. The two-story foyer with its tray ceiling makes a dramatic entrance. To the right, a banquet-sized dining room offers space for a buffet, while the large kitchen allows easy access to the bay-windowed breakfast room. To the left is a versatile room which can serve as a living room, study or guest room. Beyond the foyer is the great room, which sports a cheerful fireplace flanked by bookcases. An open-railed stairway leads to three bedrooms on the second floor. The exquisite master suite is truly a room to live in, with its stylish tray ceiling and warming fireplace. Its elegance is intensified right down to the bay window and huge walk-in closet with a built-in dressing table. This home is designed with a basement foundation.

Design 9805

First Floor: 2,355 square feet
Second Floor: 987 square feet
Total: 3,342 square feet

■ The front of this transitional home is characterized by the arch pattern evident in the windows, doorway and above the columned front porch. Left of the foyer is the formal dining area and a great room with a fireplace and vaulted ceiling. The large kitchen is constructed with a cooking island, adjoining breakfast room and a keeping room with a corner fireplace. The master suite has a study with a vaulted ceiling just off the foyer, with a dual-opening fireplace that also warms the bedroom. Upstairs are three family bedrooms and two baths. This home is designed with a basement foundation.

Design by
Design Traditions

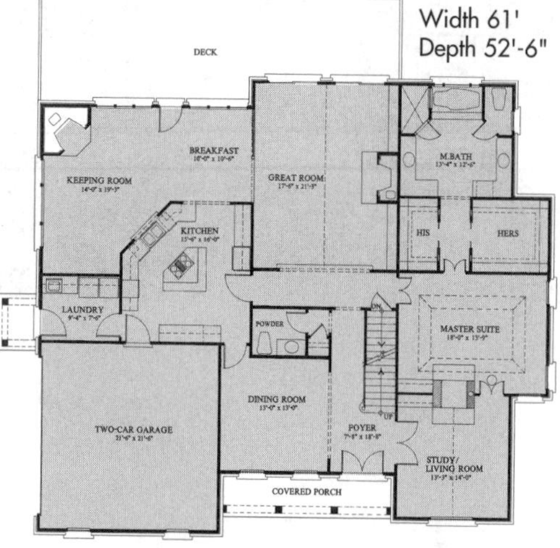
DECK
KEEPING ROOM
BREAKFAST
GREAT ROOM
M.BATH
KITCHEN
HIS
HERS
LAUNDRY
POWDER
MASTER SUITE
DINING ROOM
TWO-CAR GARAGE
FOYER
STUDY/ LIVING ROOM
COVERED PORCH
Width 61'
Depth 52'-6"

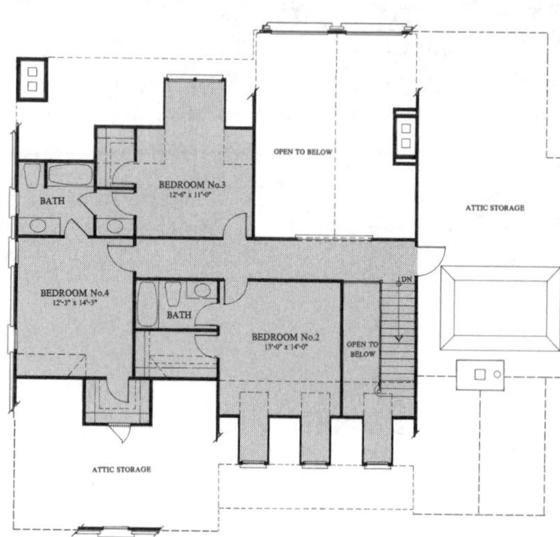
OPEN TO BELOW
BEDROOM No.3
BATH
ATTIC STORAGE
BEDROOM No.4
BATH
BEDROOM No.2
OPEN TO BELOW
ATTIC STORAGE

Design by
Frank Betz Associates, Inc.

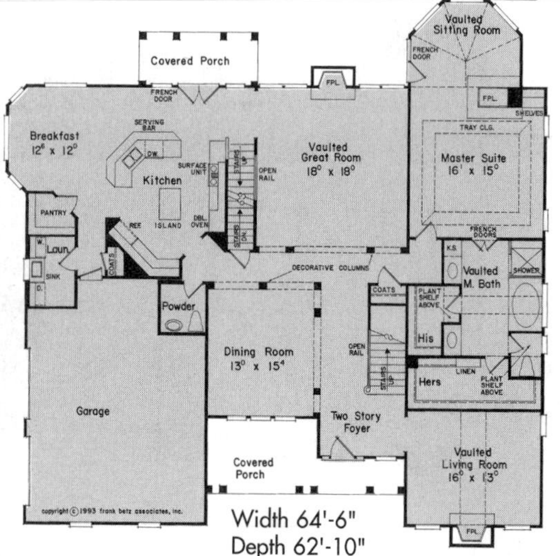
Vaulted Sitting Room
Covered Porch
Breakfast 12⁶ x 12⁰
Kitchen
Vaulted Great Room 18⁰ x 18⁰
Master Suite 16' x 15⁰
Pantry
Laun.
Powder
Vaulted M. Bath
His
Hers
Dining Room 13⁰ x 15⁴
Garage
Two Story Foyer
Covered Porch
Vaulted Living Room 16⁶ x 13⁰
Width 64'-6"
Depth 62'-10"

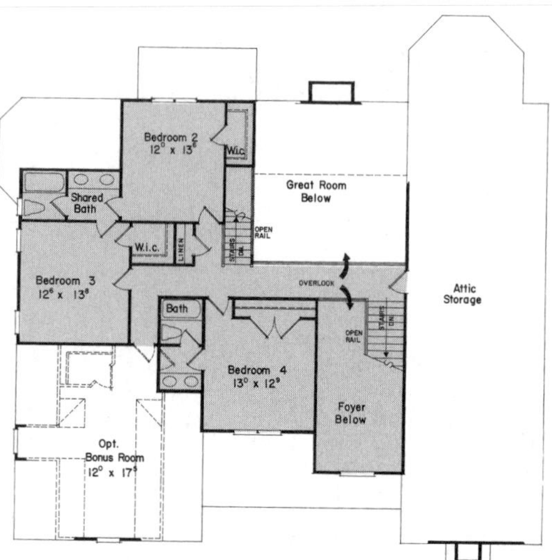
Bedroom 2
Shared Bath
W.i.c.
Great Room Below
Bedroom 3
Bath
Bedroom 4
Attic Storage
Foyer Below
Opt. Bonus Room

Design P152

First Floor: 2,467 square feet
Second Floor: 928 square feet
Total: 3,395 square feet
Bonus Room: 296 square feet

■ A chic combination of European style and farmhouse charm gives this two-story home an eclectic appeal. Apart from the private living room, living areas are open and divided by decorative columns at the dining room and the vaulted great room. The spacious kitchen has wraparound counters, serving bar and a sunny breakfast room. The master suite has a lovely, vaulted sitting room with a three-sided fireplace and a spa-style bath. Upstairs, two bedrooms share a bath, with another having a private bath. Please specify basement, crawlspace or slab foundation when ordering.

Design P230

First Floor: 2,764 square feet
Second Floor: 1,598 square feet
Total: 4,362 square feet

■ This truly elegant home offers the best in gracious living and casual ease in a home designed for the active family. The stunning foyer rises two stories with a grand staircase and leads to the formal dining room and the two-story living room. Amenities abound with plant shelves, decorative columns, French doors and fireplaces throughout the living areas. The vaulted family room and kitchen will be the heart of family gatherings. The gourmet kitchen features a cooktop island, walk-in pantry, a handy back staircase, a butler's pantry and two serving bars. The first-floor master suite is highlighted by the vaulted sitting room and the extravagant master bath. A gallery overlooking the living room and foyer is at the top of the main stair. A balcony hall leads past a loft that overlooks the family room to three family bedrooms, each featuring a walk-in closet and private bath.

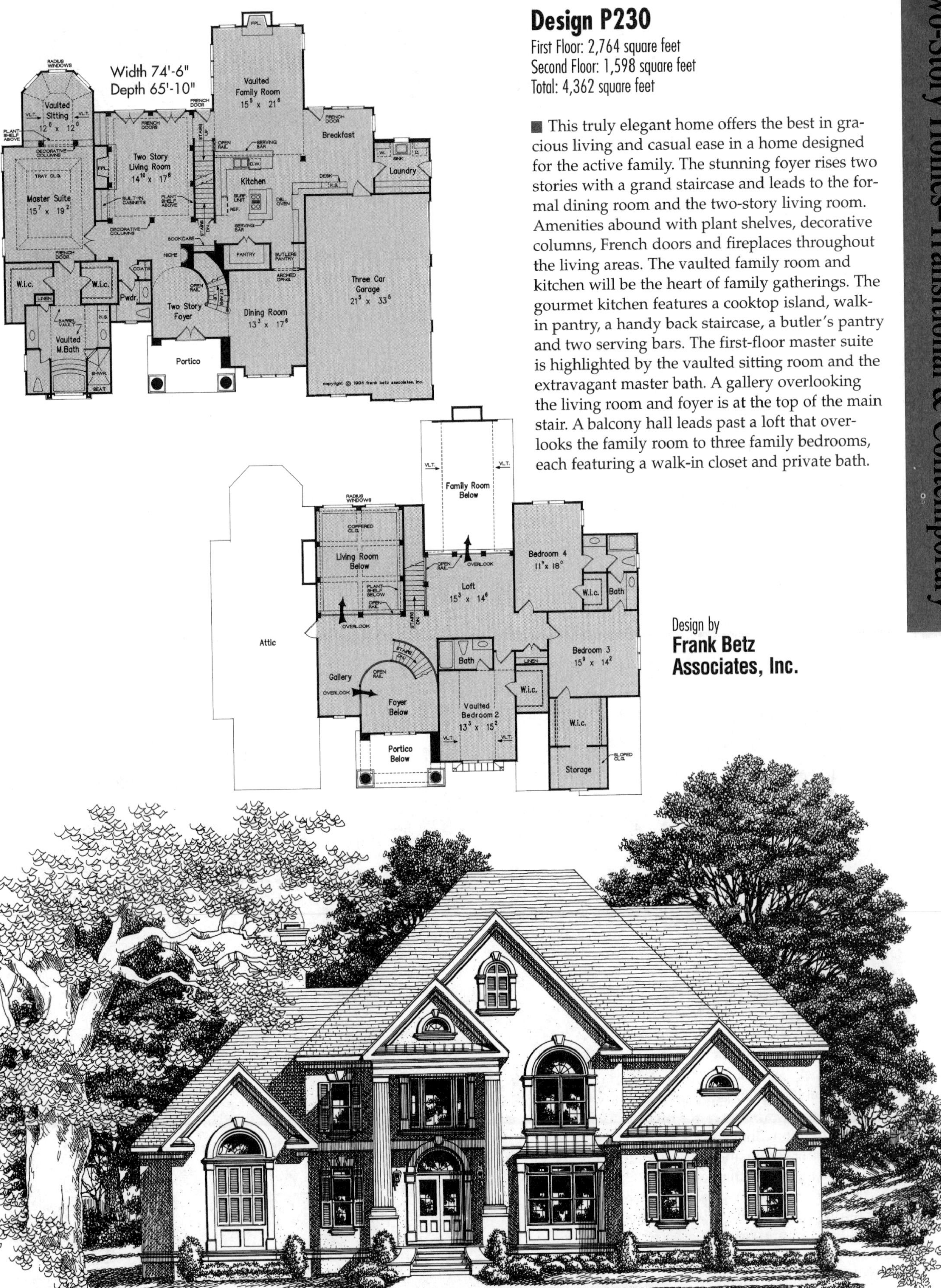
Width 74'-6"
Depth 65'-10"
Vaulted Sitting 12⁰ x 12⁰
Master Suite 15⁷ x 19²
Two Story Living Room 14¹⁰ x 17⁸
Vaulted Family Room 15⁵ x 21⁶
Breakfast
Laundry
Kitchen
W.i.c.
W.i.c.
Pwdr.
Vaulted M.Bath
Two Story Foyer
Dining Room 13³ x 17⁶
Three Car Garage 21⁵ x 33⁵
Portico
Family Room Below
Living Room Below
Loft 15³ x 14⁶
Bedroom 4 11⁵ x 18⁰
Bath
Bedroom 3 15⁹ x 14²
Attic
Gallery
Foyer Below
Vaulted Bedroom 2 13³ x 15²
Storage
Portico Below

Design by
Frank Betz Associates, Inc.

Design 8078

First Floor: 2,648 square feet
Second Floor: 1,102 square feet
Total: 3,750 square feet

Design by
Larry E. Belk Designs

©1993 LARRY E. BELK

■ Put a little luxury into your life with this fine brick home. A great room with a fireplace and expansive windows provides the perfect spot for gatherings of all sorts. A large study nearby creates a quiet environment for working at home. The kitchen has a large cooktop island and a convenient walk-in pantry. In the dining room, bumped-out windows shed light on entertaining. The first-floor master suite has its own fireplace and a pampering bath. A second bedroom with a private bath is nearby. Upstairs, two more bedrooms, a full bath and an expansive game room complete the plan.

Width 91'-6"
Depth 46'-10"

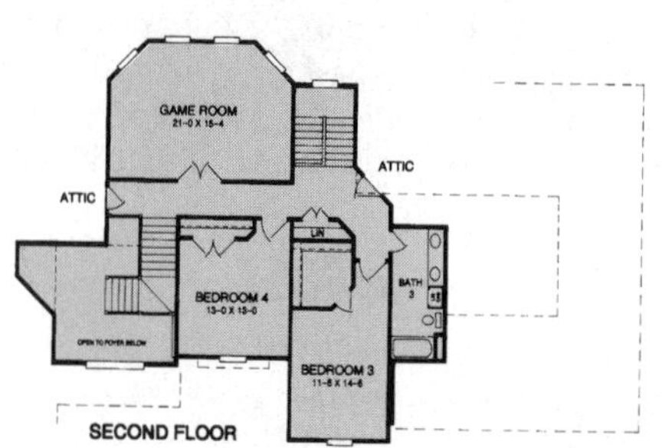
GAME ROOM
ATTIC
ATTIC
BEDROOM 4
BEDROOM 3
SECOND FLOOR

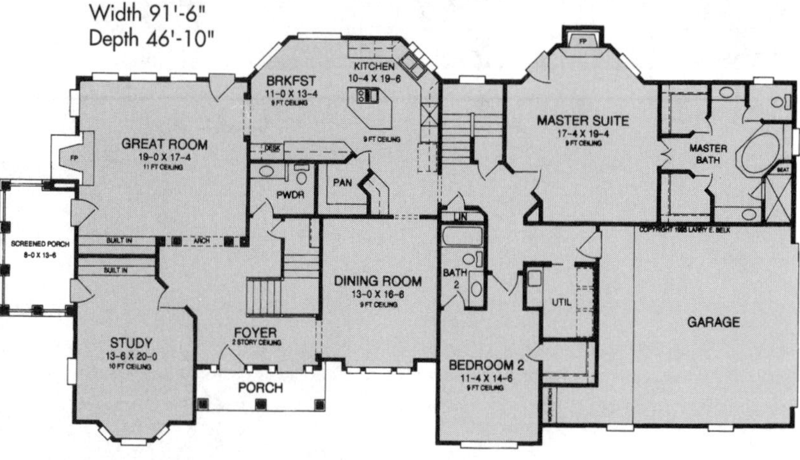
BRKFST
11-0 X 13-4
KITCHEN
10-4 X 19-6
GREAT ROOM
19-0 X 17-4
MASTER SUITE
17-4 X 19-4
MASTER BATH
PWDR
PAN
SCREENED PORCH
DINING ROOM
13-0 X 16-8
BATH 2
UTIL
GARAGE
STUDY
13-6 X 20-0
FOYER
PORCH
BEDROOM 2
11-4 X 14-6

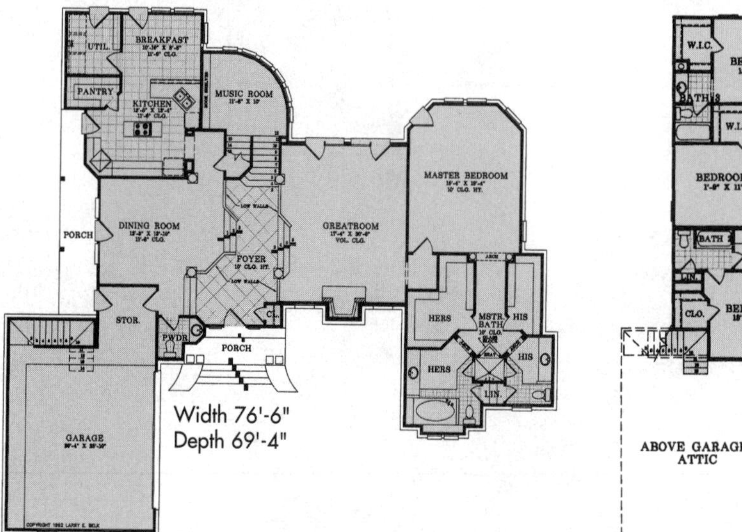
UTIL.
BREAKFAST
PANTRY
KITCHEN
MUSIC ROOM
MASTER BEDROOM
DINING ROOM
PORCH
GREATROOM
FOYER
STOR.
PWDR
PORCH
HERS
MSTR. BATH
HIS
HERS
HIS
LIN.
GARAGE

Design by
Larry E. Belk Designs

Width 76'-6"
Depth 69'-4"

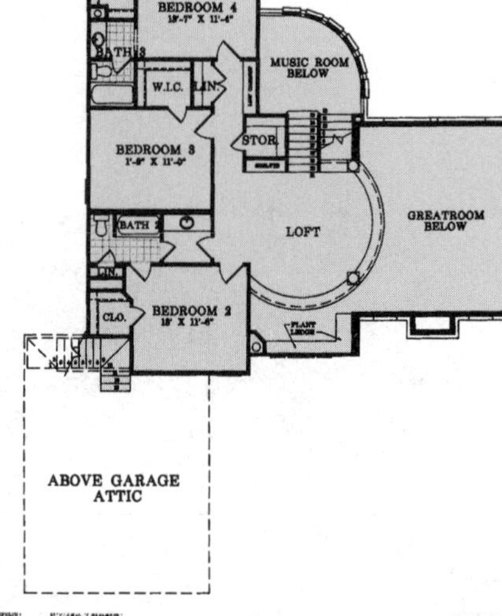
W.I.C.
BEDROOM 4
MUSIC ROOM BELOW
W.I.C.
BEDROOM 3
STOR.
GREATROOM BELOW
LOFT
BEDROOM 2
ABOVE GARAGE ATTIC

Design 8028

First Floor: 2,270 square feet
Second Floor: 1,100 square feet
Total: 3,370 square feet

■ A combination of stacked stone, brick and wood siding makes this home a real beauty from the curb. The foyer steps up into a large great room with a view to the rear grounds. On the other side, steps lead down into the dining room with access to a side porch. The master suite includes a fabulous master bath—really two baths in one—with a His and Hers dressing area and a shared shower between. At the half landing, curved windows frame a traditional music room. Continuing up the stairs, a large circular loft overlooks the great room and leads to three bedrooms and two baths.

Design by
Design Traditions

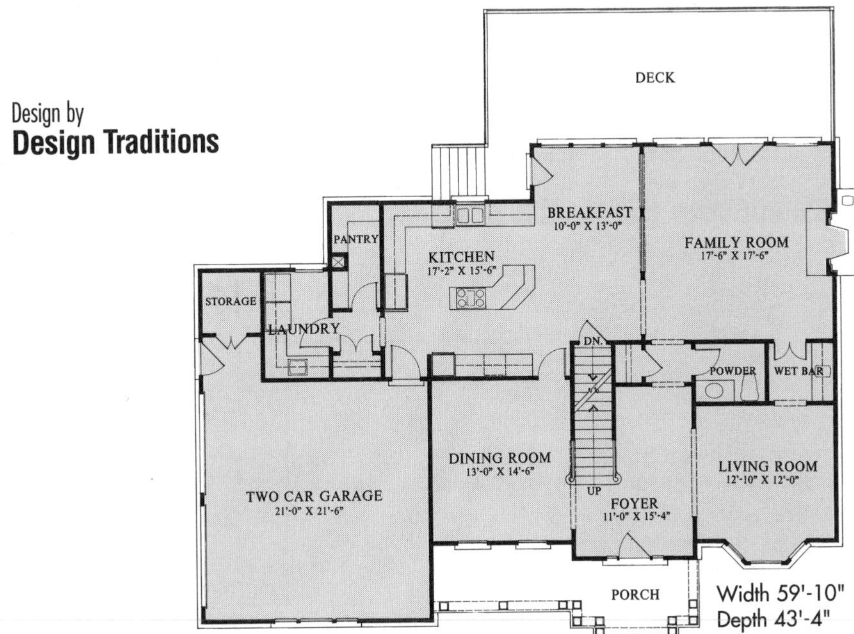
DECK
BREAKFAST
10'-0" X 13'-0"
PANTRY
KITCHEN
17'-2" X 15'-6"
FAMILY ROOM
17'-6" X 17'-6"
STORAGE
LAUNDRY
DN.
POWDER
WET BAR
DINING ROOM
13'-0" X 14'-6"
LIVING ROOM
12'-10" X 12'-0"
TWO CAR GARAGE
21'-0" X 21'-6"
UP
FOYER
11'-0" X 15'-4"
PORCH
Width 59'-10"
Depth 43'-4"

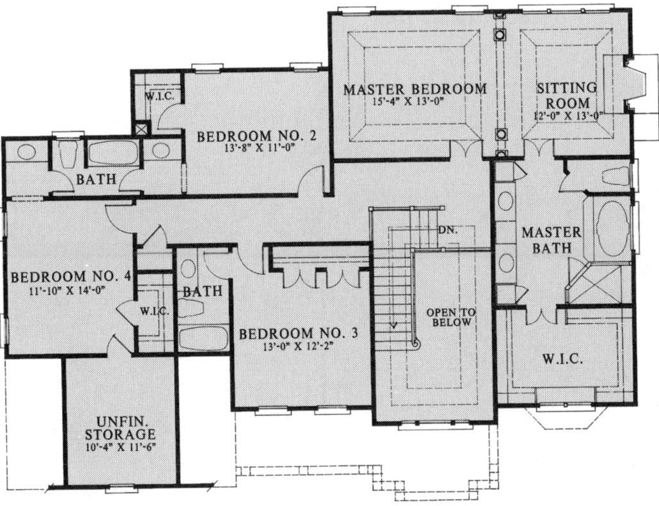
W.I.C.
MASTER BEDROOM
15'-4" X 13'-0"
SITTING ROOM
12'-0" X 13'-0"
BEDROOM NO. 2
13'-8" X 11'-0"
BATH
DN.
MASTER BATH
BEDROOM NO. 4
11'-10" X 14'-0"
BATH
W.I.C.
OPEN TO BELOW
BEDROOM NO. 3
13'-0" X 12'-2"
W.I.C.
UNFIN. STORAGE
10'-4" X 11'-6"

Design 9858

First Floor: 1,570 square feet
Second Floor: 1,630 square feet
Total: 3,200 square feet

■ This classic Americana design employs wood siding, a variety of window styles and a detailed front porch. Upon entry, the large two-story foyer flows into the formal dining room, with arched window accents, and the combination study/living room with a large bay window. A short passage with a wet bar accesses the family room with a wall of windows, French doors and a fireplace. The large breakfast area and open kitchen with cooking island are spacious and airy as well as efficient. The walk-in pantry, laundry and entry to the two-car garage complete this level. Upstairs, the master suite's sleeping and sitting rooms feature architectural details including columns, tray ceilings and a fireplace. The elegant master bath contains a raised oval tub, dual vanities and separate shower. Generous His and Hers closets are located beyond the bath. Additional bedrooms are complete with closets and a variety of bath combinations. This home is designed with a basement foundation.

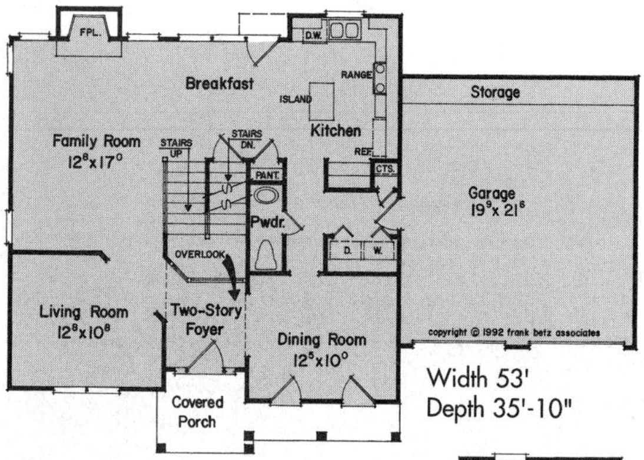

Design by
Frank Betz Associates, Inc.

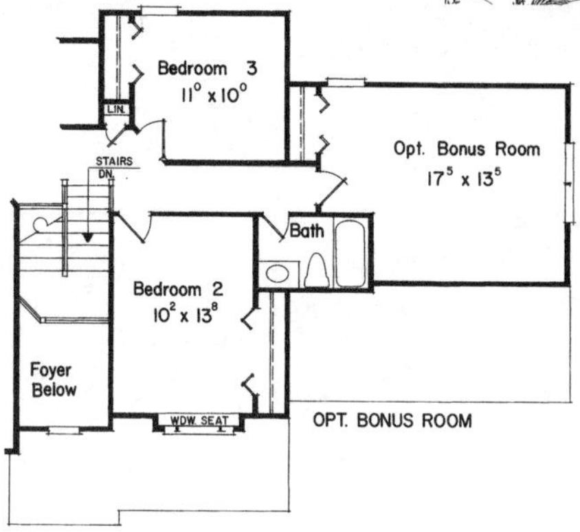

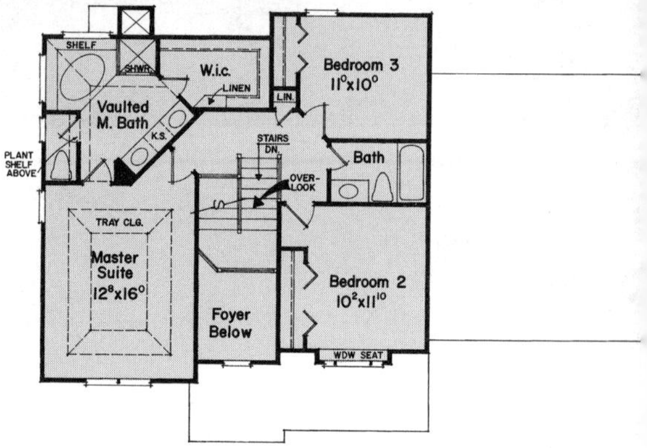

Design P114

First Floor: 926 square feet
Second Floor: 824 square feet
Total: 1,786 square feet
Bonus Room: 282 square feet

■ This charming home goes to great lengths to please the homeowner with a busy family. With formal dining and living rooms traditionally located to the front of the plan, the large family room and kitchen are the focus of casual living. Highlights here include a grand fireplace, breakfast nook and a prep island in the kitchen. Upstairs, a lovely master suite with a vaulted bath and large walk-in closet is balanced by two family bedrooms and a full hall bath.

Design P106

First Floor: 767 square feet
Second Floor: 738 square feet
Total: 1,505 square feet
Bonus Room: 240 square feet

■ A clear focus on family living is the hallmark of this traditional two-story plan. A columned porch leads to an open foyer and family room complete with a fireplace. A dining room with a sliding glass door is thoughtfully placed between the family room and kitchen. A bayed breakfast nook works well with the roomy kitchen. On the second level a large master suite features a tray ceiling, detailed bath and a space-efficient, walk-in closet. Two family bedrooms, a hall bath and convenient laundry center round out the plan. Please specify basement or crawlspace foundation when ordering.

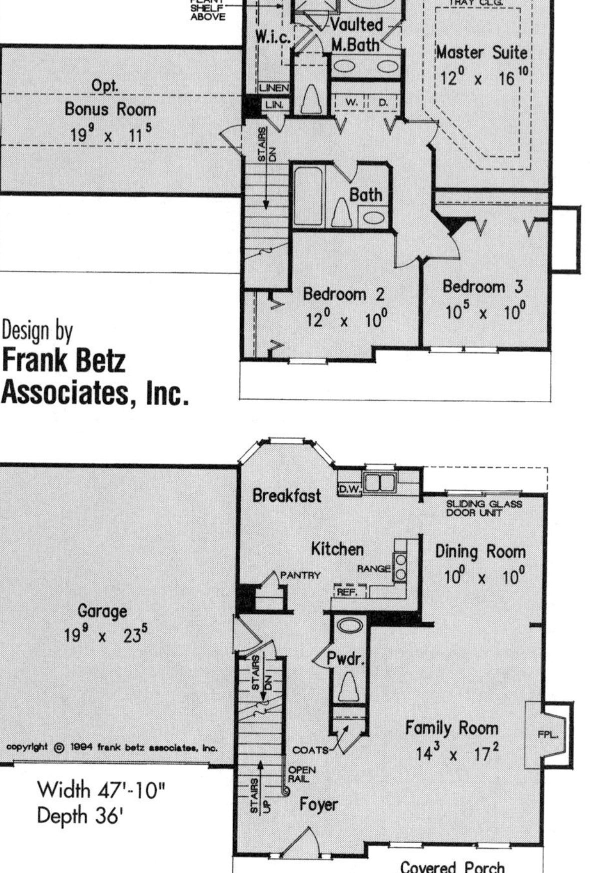
PLANT SHELF ABOVE
W.i.c.
SHWR.
Vaulted M.Bath
TRAY CLG.
Master Suite
12^0 x 16^{10}
Opt. Bonus Room
19^9 x 11^5
LINEN
LIN.
W.
D.
STAIRS DN
Bath
Bedroom 2
12^0 x 10^0
Bedroom 3
10^5 x 10^0
Breakfast
D.W.
SLIDING GLASS DOOR UNIT
Kitchen
RANGE
PANTRY
REF.
Dining Room
10^0 x 10^0
Garage
19^9 x 23^5
STAIRS DN
Pwdr.
Family Room
14^3 x 17^2
FPL.
copyright © 1994 frank betz associates, inc.
COATS
OPEN RAIL
STAIRS UP
Foyer
Width 47'-10"
Depth 36'
Covered Porch

Design by
Frank Betz Associates, Inc.

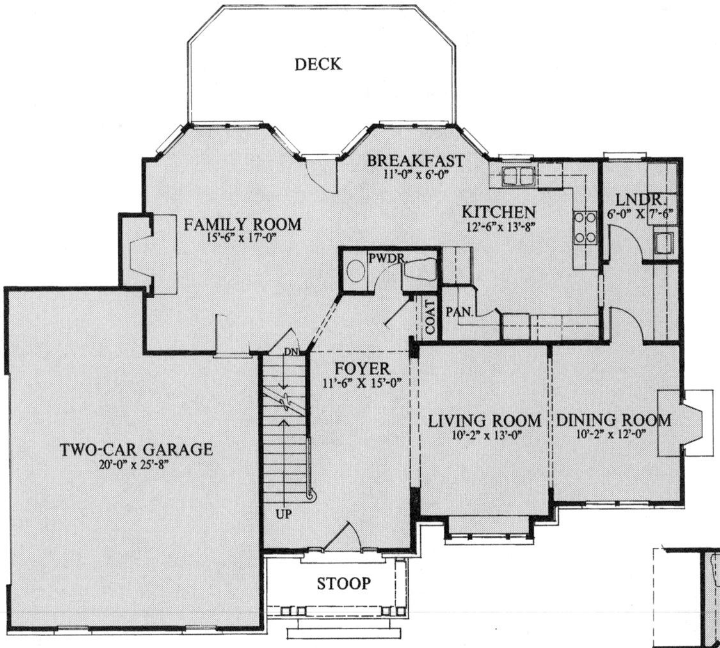

Design by
Design Traditions

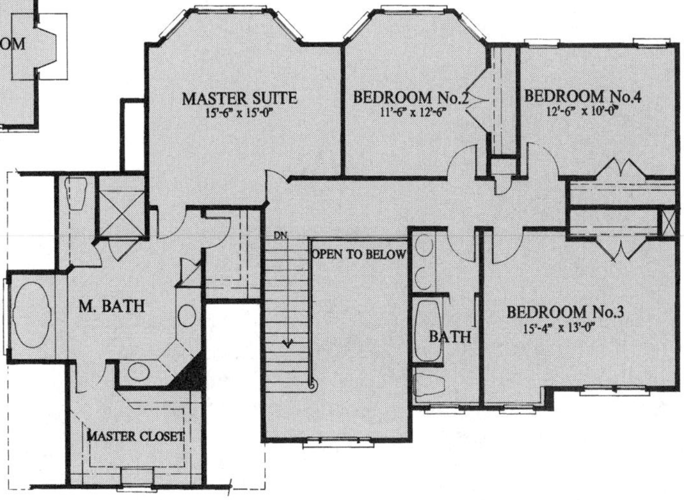

Width 54'
Depth 39'-5"

Design 9857

First Floor: 1,156 square feet
Second Floor: 1,239 square feet
Total: 2,395 square feet

■ This two-story home combines an attractive, classic exterior with an open and sophisticated interior design. The two-story foyer has a staircase to the left and a coat closet and powder room straight ahead. Opening off of the foyer, the living and dining rooms give a lovely backdrop for entertaining. The open design flowing to the breakfast area and family room features two large bay windows. The open foyer staircase leads to the upper level, beginning with the master suite. The master bath contains a luxurious tub, separate shower and dual vanities, as well as a large linen closet. A large, walk-in master closet completes the suite. All three secondary bedrooms share a hall bath with separate vanity and bathing areas. This home is designed with a basement foundation.

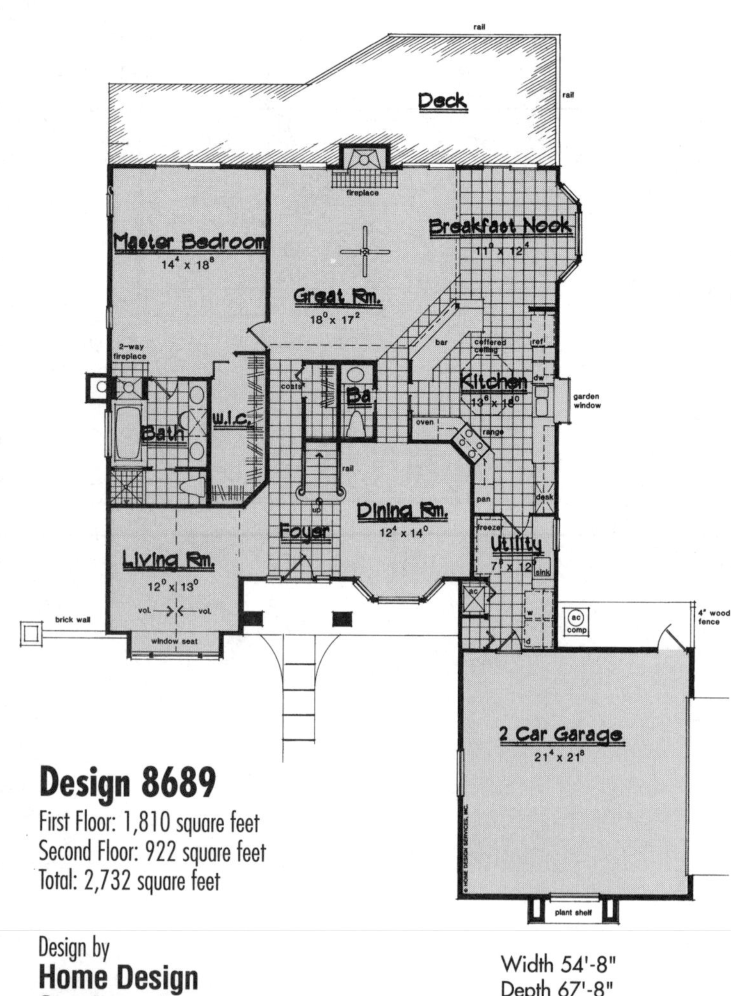

Deck
rail
fireplace
Breakfast Nook
11^{0} x 12^{4}
Master Bedroom
14^{4} x 18^{8}
Great Rm.
18^{0} x 17^{2}
2-way fireplace
Bath
w.i.c.
Ba
bar
coffered ceiling
Kitchen
13^{6} x 18^{0}
ref
dw
garden window
oven
range
pan
desk
Dining Rm.
12^{4} x 14^{0}
Foyer
Living Rm.
12^{0} x 13^{0}
vol.
Utility
7^{4} x 12^{8}
brick wall
window seat
ac comp
4" wood fence
2 Car Garage
21^{4} x 21^{8}
plant shelf

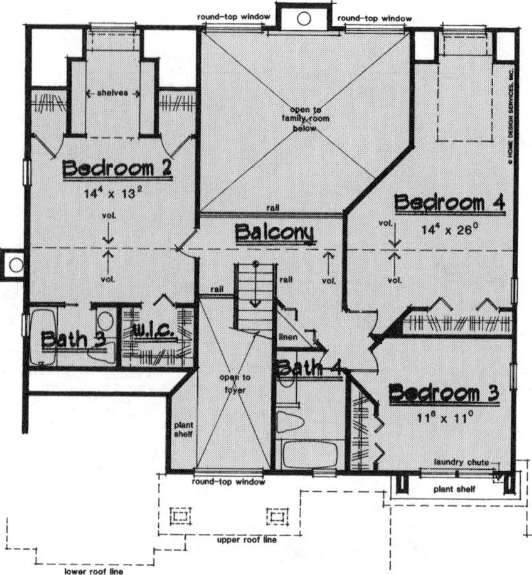

round-top window
shelves
open to family room below
Bedroom 2
14^{4} x 13^{2}
Bedroom 4
14^{4} x 26^{0}
Balcony
rail
vol.
Bath 3
w.i.c.
linen
Bath 4
open to foyer
plant shelf
Bedroom 3
11^{6} x 11^{0}
laundry chute
upper roof line
lower roof line

Design 8689

First Floor: 1,810 square feet
Second Floor: 922 square feet
Total: 2,732 square feet

Design by
Home Design Services, Inc

Width 54'-8"
Depth 67'-8"

■ A lovely radius window crowns this impressive entry and brings you into the foyer which separates the formal living and dining rooms. Efficient planning keeps the casual living area to the rear where the breakfast nook, the great room and the huge kitchen share views of the deck and backyard beyond. A fireplace flanked by sliding glass doors is the focal point of the great room, as is the bay window in the breakfast nook. The master suite features a large bedroom and a deluxe bath containing a spacious walk-in closet and a soaking tub with a through-fireplace. Upstairs, Bedroom 2 has a private bath and a walk-in closet, while two other bedrooms share a full bath.

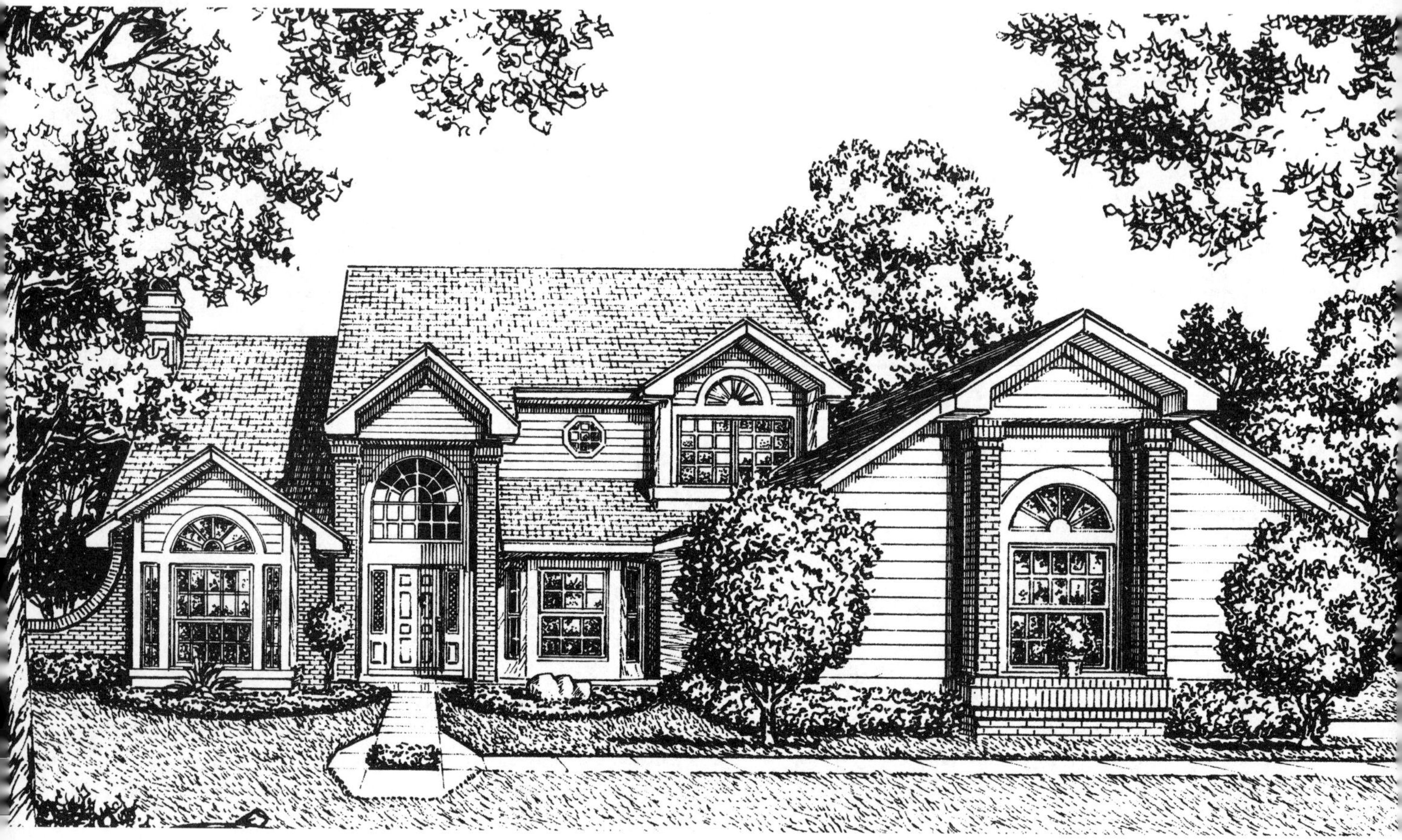

COPYRIGHT 1991 LARRY E. BELK

Design 8011

First Floor: 1,934 square feet
Second Floor: 528 square feet
Total: 2,462 square feet

Design by
Larry E. Belk Designs

■ This charming cottage-style home features sweeping rooflines and an undeniably exquisite exterior. Inside, a two-story foyer opens through a large arch to the living room with another arch defining the dining room. A see-through fireplace is located between the living room and the breakfast area. A large kitchen, utility room, and walk-in pantry complete the area. The master bedroom, with a sitting area and luxury bath, is located on the opposite side of the house. Bedroom 2 and a full bath are located nearby. Two family bedrooms are situated upstairs along with an expandable game room.

BREAKFAST
PORCH
MASTER BEDROOM
MASTER BATH
KITCHEN
LIVING ROOM
W.I.C.
BATH 2
STORAGE
UTILITY ROOM
DINING ROOM
FOYER
BEDROOM 2
GARAGE
PORCH
COPYRIGHT 1991 LARRY E. BELK

Width 64'-10"
Depth 59'-8"

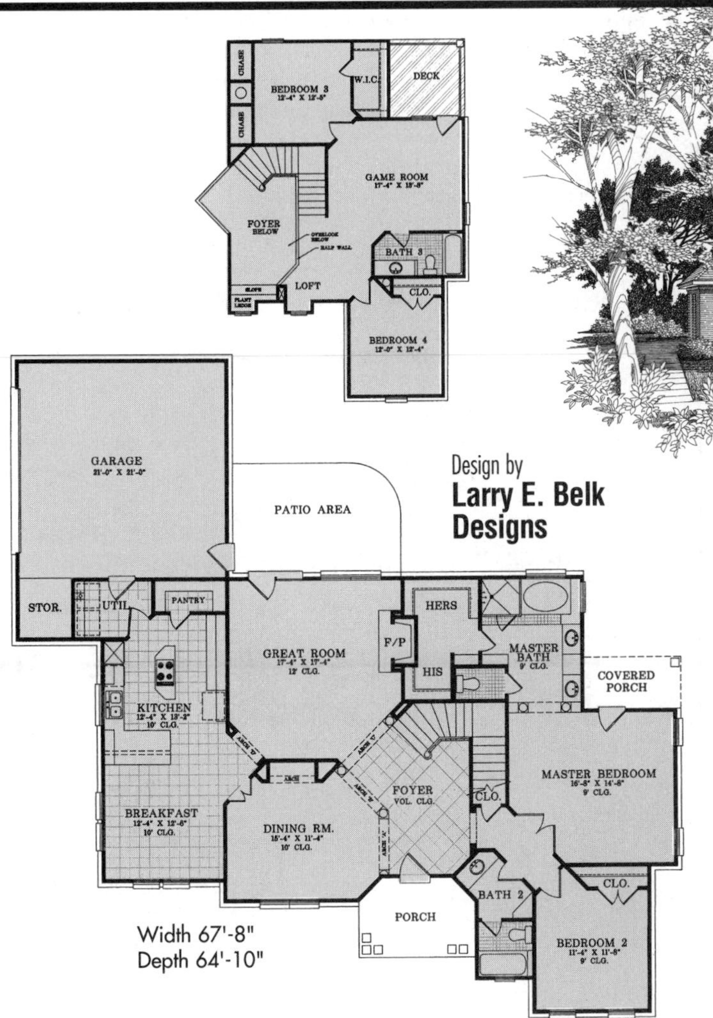
BEDROOM 3
W.I.C.
DECK
GAME ROOM
FOYER BELOW
BATH 3
LOFT
CLO.
BEDROOM 4
GARAGE
PATIO AREA
STOR.
UTIL.
PANTRY
HERS
F/P
MASTER BATH
GREAT ROOM
HIS
COVERED PORCH
KITCHEN
FOYER
MASTER BEDROOM
BREAKFAST
DINING RM.
BATH 2
PORCH
BEDROOM 2

Width 67'-8"
Depth 64'-10"

Design by
Larry E. Belk Designs

Design 8088

First Floor: 1,904 square feet
Second Floor: 792 square feet
Total: 2,696 square feet

■ This charming cottage has all the accouterments of an English manor. Inside, the angled foyer directs the eye to the arched entrances of the formal dining room and the great room with its fireplace and patio access. The master bedroom and a guest bedroom (or possible study) are located at the opposite end of the house for privacy. Two additional bedrooms, a full bath, a game room and an upper deck are located on the second floor. Please specify basement, crawlspace or slab foundation when ordering.

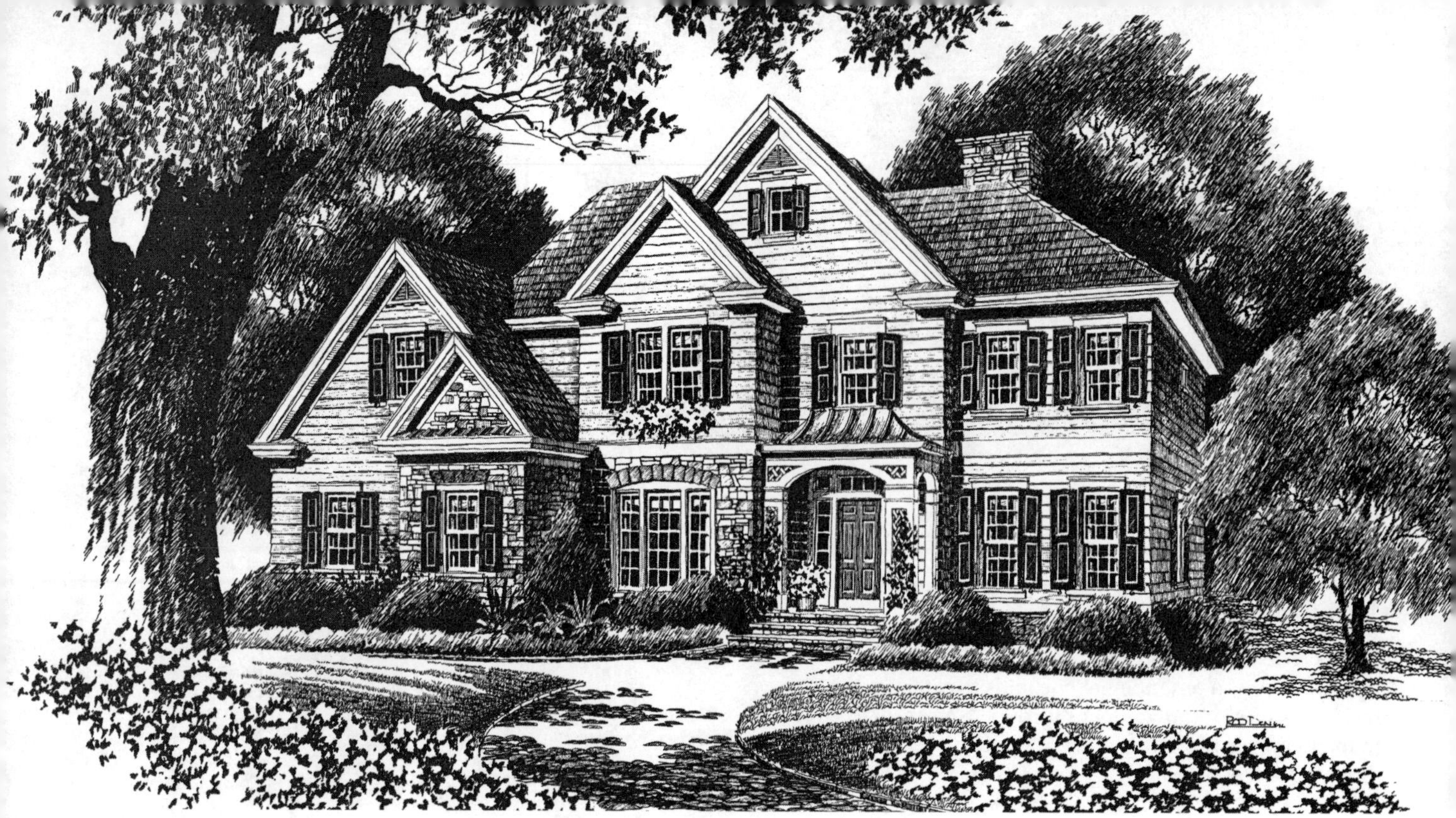

Design 9869

First Floor: 1,475 square feet
Second Floor: 1,460 square feet
Total: 2,935 square feet

■ Through this home's columned entry, the two-story foyer opens to the living room with wet bar. The media room features a fireplace and is accessed from both the main hall and great room. The two-story great room with fireplace is open to the breakfast area, kitchen and rear staircase, making entertaining a pleasure. The kitchen design is ideal with breakfast bar and preparation island and is conveniently located near the laundry room. The dining room is ideal for formal entertaining. The upper level begins with the balcony landing overlooking the great room. The master bedroom features a bay-windowed sitting area and a tray ceiling. The master bath has dual vanities, a corner garden tub, a separate shower, a large walk-in closet and an optional secret room. Across the balcony, two family bedrooms and 3 share a bath, while one bedroom has its own private bath. This home is designed with a basement foundation.

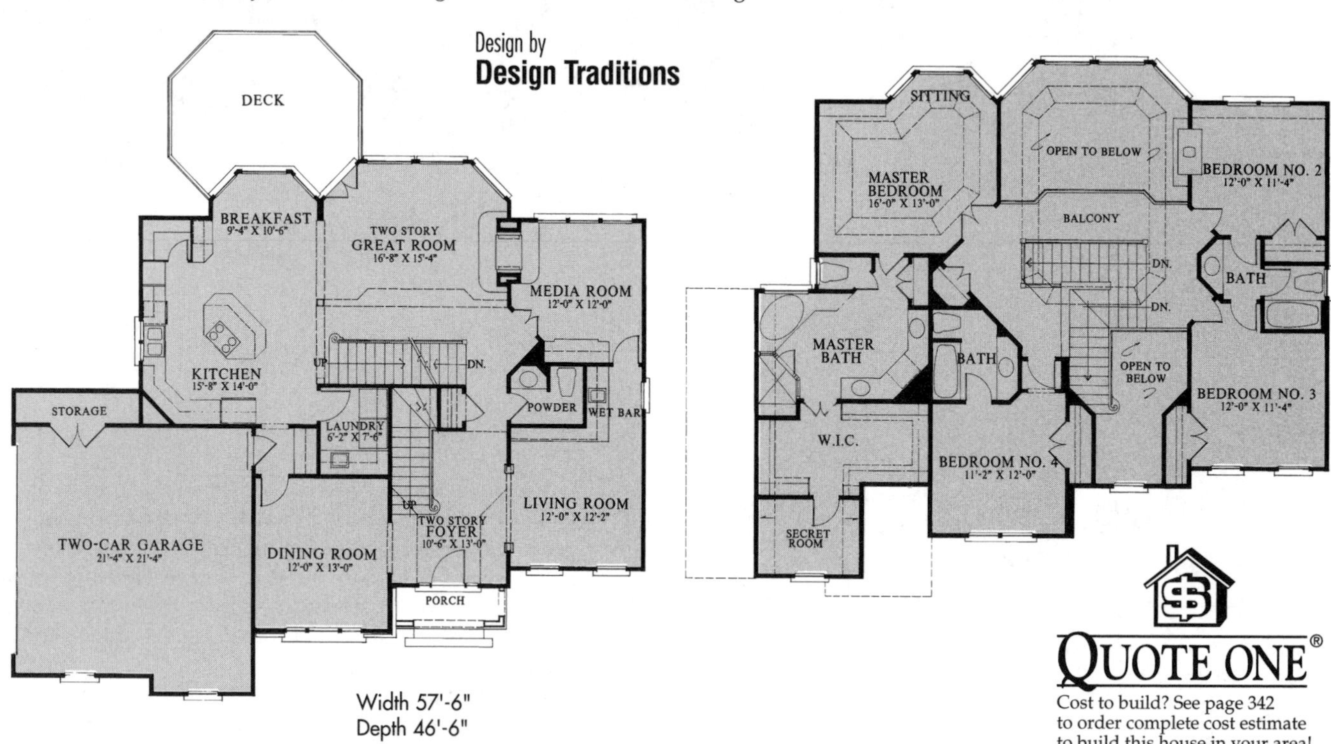
DECK
BREAKFAST 9'-4" X 10'-6"
TWO STORY GREAT ROOM 16'-8" X 15'-4"
MEDIA ROOM 12'-0" X 12'-0"
KITCHEN 15'-8" X 14'-0"
UP
DN.
POWDER
WET BAR
STORAGE
LAUNDRY 6'-2" X 7'-6"
LIVING ROOM 12'-0" X 12'-2"
TWO-CAR GARAGE 21'-4" X 21'-4"
DINING ROOM 12'-0" X 13'-0"
TWO STORY FOYER 10'-6" X 13'-0"
PORCH
SITTING
MASTER BEDROOM 16'-0" X 13'-0"
OPEN TO BELOW
BEDROOM NO. 2 12'-0" X 11'-4"
BALCONY
BATH
MASTER BATH
BATH
OPEN TO BELOW
BEDROOM NO. 3 12'-0" X 11'-4"
W.I.C.
BEDROOM NO. 4 11'-2" X 12'-0"
SECRET ROOM
Width 57'-6"
Depth 46'-6"

Design by
Design Traditions

Design 9829

First Floor: 1,581 square feet
Second Floor: 1,415 square feet
Total: 2,996 square feet

■ Classical details and a stately brick exterior accentuate the grace and timeless elegance of this home. Inside, the foyer opens up to a large banquet-sized dining room with an adjacent formal living room. A central staircase, positioned for common access from all areas of the home, accents the foyer. Just beyond, the two-story great room awaits, featuring a wet bar and warming fireplace. To the left is the sunlit breakfast room and gourmet kitchen with breakfast bar. A large covered porch off the kitchen completes the family center. Upstairs, the master suite features a sitting bay and a private sun deck. The accompanying bath features His and Hers closets. Two bedrooms with a connecting bath complete the second floor. This home is designed with a basement foundation.

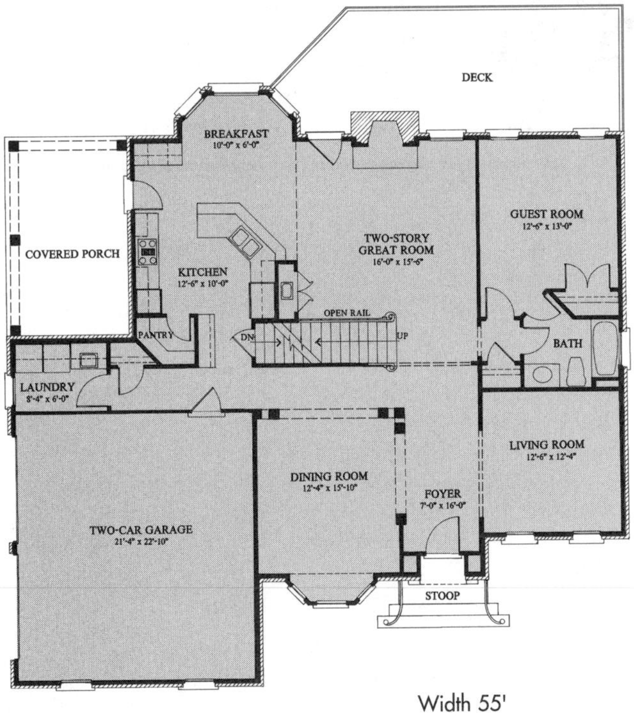

DECK
BREAKFAST 10'-0" x 6'-0"
COVERED PORCH
KITCHEN 12'-6" x 10'-0"
TWO-STORY GREAT ROOM 16'-0" x 15'-6"
GUEST ROOM 12'-6" x 13'-0"
PANTRY
OPEN RAIL
DN
UP
BATH
LAUNDRY 8'-4" x 6'-0"
LIVING ROOM 12'-6" x 12'-4"
DINING ROOM 12'-4" x 15'-10"
FOYER 7'-0" x 16'-0"
TWO-CAR GARAGE 21'-4" x 22'-10"
STOOP

Width 55'
Depth 52'

Design by
Design Traditions

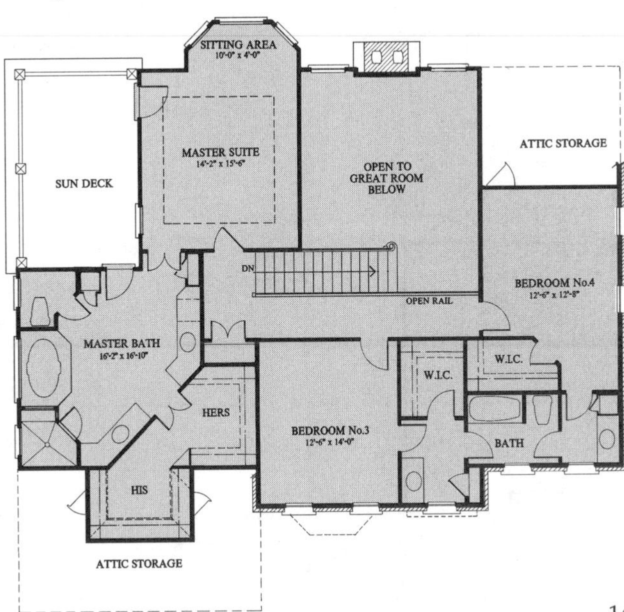
SITTING AREA
10'-0" x 4'-0"
MASTER SUITE
14'-2" x 15'-6"
OPEN TO
GREAT ROOM
BELOW
ATTIC STORAGE
SUN DECK
DN
OPEN RAIL
BEDROOM No.4
12'-6" x 12'-8"
MASTER BATH
16'-2" x 16'-10"
W.I.C.
W.I.C.
HERS
BEDROOM No.3
12'-6" x 14'-0"
BATH
HIS
ATTIC STORAGE

PORCH
STORAGE
GARAGE
GARAGE
HERS
HIS
UTIL 5-4 X 6-6
LINEN
MASTER BATH
BATH 2
LIN
BEDROOM 2 12-6 X 13-0 9 FT CLG
ENTRY
MASTER BEDROOM 16-6 X 17-6 9 FT CLG
PORCH
PLANTING AREA
BALCONY
BRKFST RM 12-4 X 10-6 10 FT CLG
DINING ROOM 12-4 X 16-6 10 FT BARREL CLG
BEDROOM 3 12-8 X 13-0 10 FT CLG
KITCHEN 12-4 X 17-6
ARCH
BATH 3
BUILT INS
FP
FAMILY ROOM 17-0 X 17-6 10 FT CLG
LIVING ROOM 16-6 X 17-0 12 FT CLG
TRACK LIGHTING
SITTING 12-6 X 6-0 10 FT CLG
PORCH
BALCONY
COPYRIGHT LARRY E. BELK

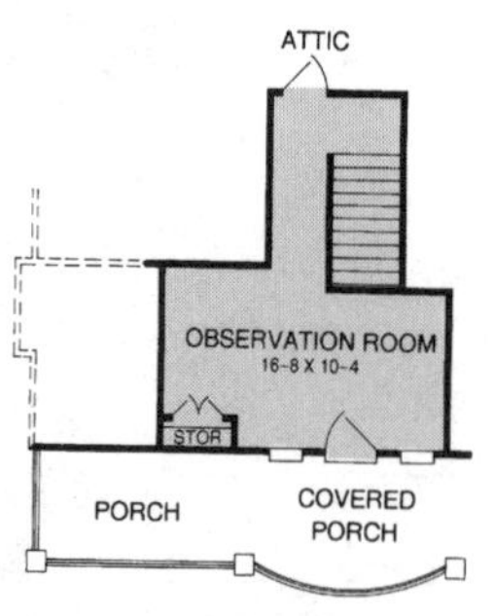
ATTIC
OBSERVATION ROOM 16-8 X 10-4
STOR
PORCH
COVERED PORCH

Design by
Larry E. Belk Designs

Design 8119

First Floor: 1,158 square feet
Second Floor: 1,773 square feet
Third Floor: 173 square feet
Total: 3,104 square feet

Width 39'-10"
Depth 58'-11"

■ The facade of this home is a super prelude to an equally impressive interior. The front porch provides entry to a sleeping level, with the master suite on the right and a secondary bedroom on the left. Upstairs, living areas include a family room with a sitting alcove and a living room with special ceiling treatment. The kitchen serves a breakfast room as well as a barrel-vaulted dining room. A third bedroom and two balconies further the custom nature of this home. On the third floor, an observation room with outdoor access is an extra-special touch. Please specify crawlspace or slab foundation when ordering.

Design 8129

First Floor: 1,755 square feet
Second Floor: 2,275 square feet
Total: 4,030 square feet

■ A perfect combination of traditional elements and contemporary design makes this home a stand-out showpiece. A long courtyard and porch lead to the foyer, where traffic is directed either to the living room or down a sunny hall to the dining room and study. The large kitchen features an oversized island and a bay breakfast nook. Fully accessible balconies frame the second floor, reached by a formal and rear stair. The master suite has a fireplace and luxurious bath. Three family bedrooms each have walk-in closets and private access to a shared bath. Please specify crawlspace or slab foundation when ordering.

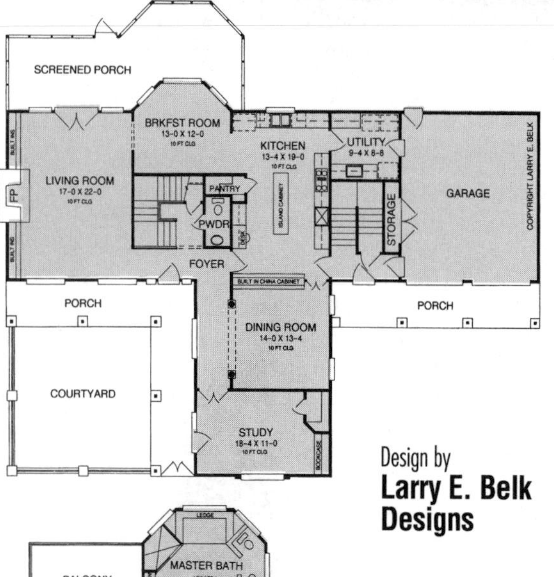
SCREENED PORCH
BRKFST ROOM 13-0 X 12-0
KITCHEN 13-4 X 19-0
UTILITY 9-4 X 6-6
LIVING ROOM 17-0 X 22-0
FP
PANTRY
PWDR
GARAGE
STORAGE
FOYER
BUILT IN CHINA CABINET
PORCH
PORCH
DINING ROOM 14-0 X 13-4
COURTYARD
STUDY 18-4 X 11-0
BOOKCASE
COPYRIGHT LARRY E. BELK

Design by
Larry E. Belk Designs

LEDGE
MASTER BATH
BALCONY
MASTER BEDROOM 17-0 X 22-0 CATHEDRAL CLG
HIS
HERS
BEDROOM 4 13-4 X 13-4
BATH 3
GAME ROOM 19-0 X 22-0 CATHEDRAL CLG
FP
OPEN TO FOYER BELOW
BOOKCASE
BALCONY
BEDROOM 3 13-4 X 10-4
BALCONY
LINEN
BATH 2
BEDROOM 2 13-0 X 11-4

Width 74'
Depth 63'-4"

COPYRIGHT LARRY E. BELK

Design 8131

First Floor: 2,772 square feet
Second Floor: 933 square feet
Total: 3,705 square feet
Bonus Room: 310 square feet

■ A truly grand entry—absolutely stunning on a corner lot—sets the eclectic, yet elegant tone of this contemporary home. The foyer opens to a dramatic circular stair then on to the two-story great room that's framed by a second-story balcony. An elegant dining room is set to the side, distinguished by a span of arches. The gourmet kitchen features wrapping counters, a cooktop island and a breakfast nook. A front study and secondary bedroom are nice accompaniments to the expansive master suite. A through-fireplace, spa-style bath and huge walk-in closet highlight this area. Upstairs, a loft opens to two balconies overlooking the porch and leads to two family bedrooms and a game room. Please specify crawlspace or slab foundation when ordering.

Design by
Larry E. Belk Designs

Width 74'-8"
Depth 61'-10"

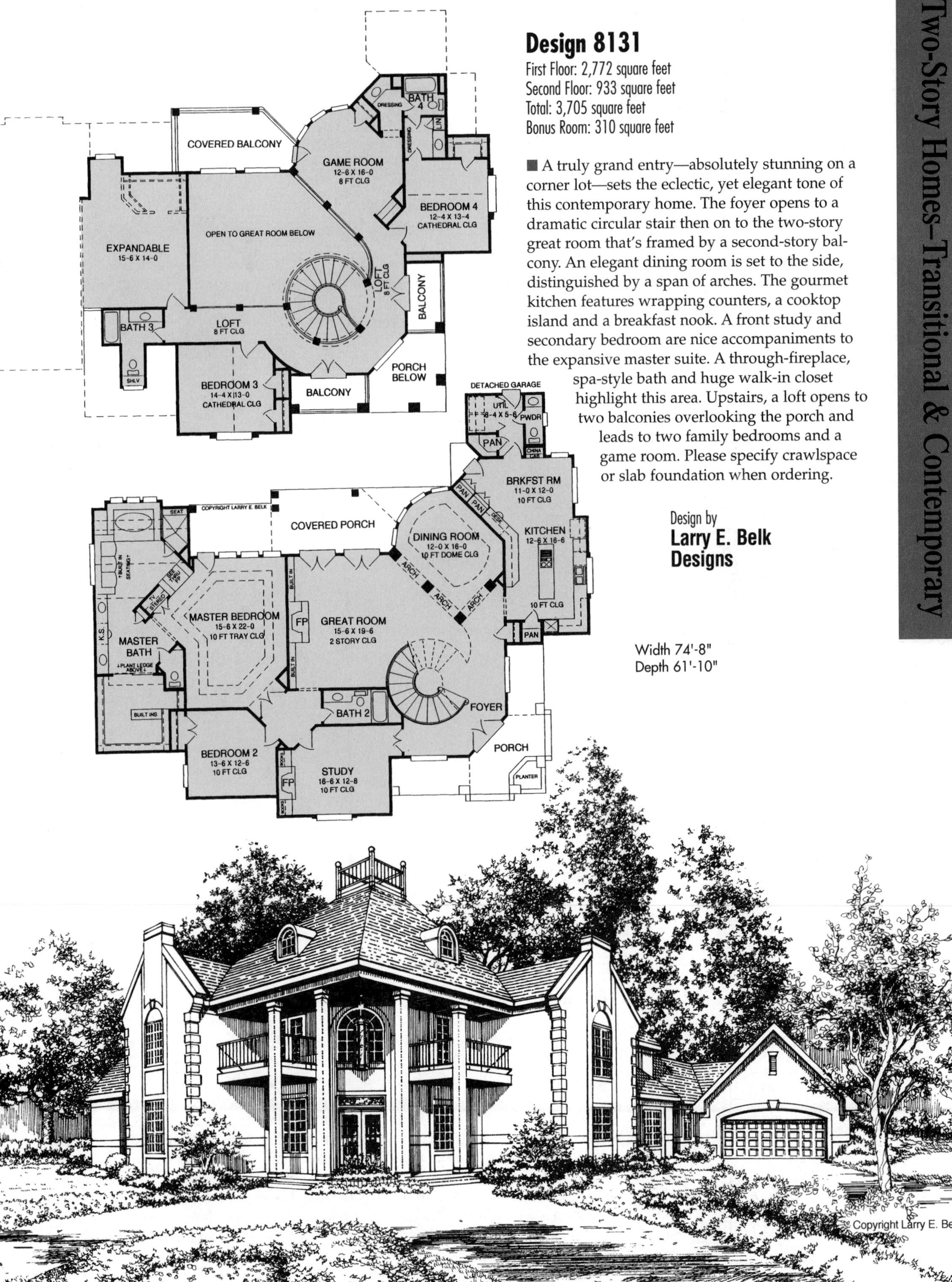
COVERED BALCONY
GAME ROOM
12-6 X 16-0
8 FT CLG
BATH 4
BEDROOM 4
12-4 X 13-4
CATHEDRAL CLG
EXPANDABLE
15-6 X 14-0
OPEN TO GREAT ROOM BELOW
LOFT
8 FT CLG
BALCONY
BATH 3
LOFT
8 FT CLG
PORCH BELOW
BEDROOM 3
14-4 X 13-0
CATHEDRAL CLG
BALCONY
DETACHED GARAGE
UTIL
8-4 X 5-6
PWDR
PAN
BRKFST RM
11-0 X 12-0
10 FT CLG
COPYRIGHT LARRY E. BELK
COVERED PORCH
DINING ROOM
12-0 X 16-0
10 FT DOME CLG
KITCHEN
12-6 X 16-6
10 FT CLG
ARCH
MASTER BEDROOM
15-6 X 22-0
10 FT TRAY CLG
FP
GREAT ROOM
15-6 X 19-6
2 STORY CLG
MASTER BATH
PLANT LEDGE ABOVE
BUILT INS
BATH 2
FOYER
PORCH
PLANTER
BEDROOM 2
13-6 X 12-6
10 FT CLG
STUDY
16-6 X 12-8
10 FT CLG
© Copyright Larry E. Belk

NATHAN INC.

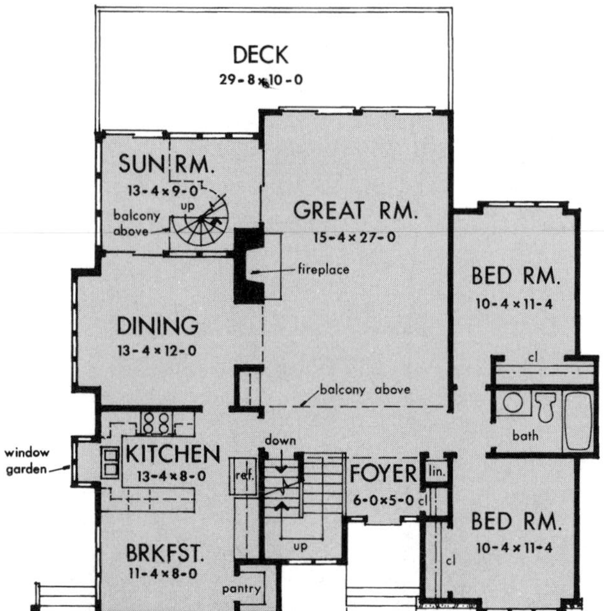

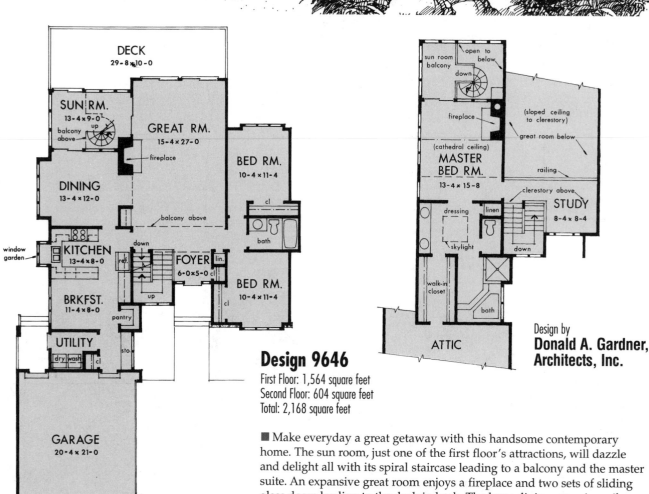

DECK
29-8 x 10-0

SUN RM.
13-4 x 9-0
balcony above
up

GREAT RM.
15-4 x 27-0
fireplace

DINING
13-4 x 12-0

balcony above

BED RM.
10-4 x 11-4

cl

bath

window garden

KITCHEN
13-4 x 8-0

ref.

down

FOYER
6-0 x 5-0

lin.

cl

up

BED RM.
10-4 x 11-4

cl

BRKFST.
11-4 x 8-0

pantry

UTILITY

dry wash

cl

sto.

GARAGE
20-4 x 21-0

Width 47'-4"
Depth 69'

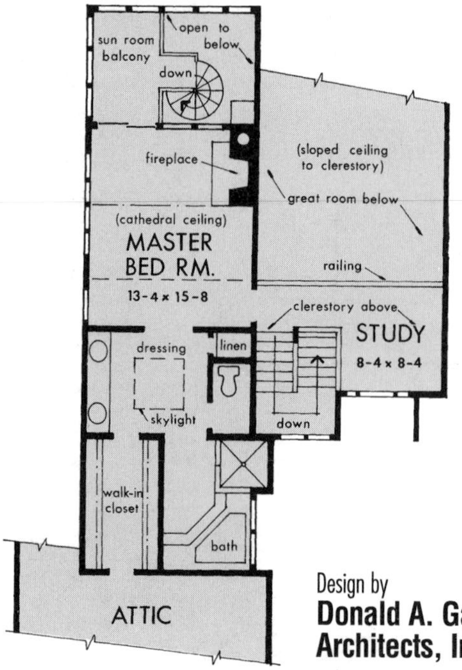

sun room balcony

open to below

down

fireplace

(sloped ceiling to clerestory)

great room below

(cathedral ceiling)

MASTER BED RM.
13-4 x 15-8

railing

clerestory above

STUDY
8-4 x 8-4

dressing

linen

skylight

down

walk-in closet

bath

ATTIC

Design by
Donald A. Gardner, Architects, Inc.

Design 9646

First Floor: 1,564 square feet
Second Floor: 604 square feet
Total: 2,168 square feet

■ Make everyday a great getaway with this handsome contemporary home. The sun room, just one of the first floor's attractions, will dazzle and delight all with its spiral staircase leading to a balcony and the master suite. An expansive great room enjoys a fireplace and two sets of sliding glass doors leading to the deck in back. The large dining room is easily serviced by the kitchen. The U-shaped kitchen lends itself to outstanding convenience with a breakfast room and a nearby utility area to add further to the livability at this end of the house. Three bedrooms include two family bedrooms and a glorious master suite. Located on the second floor, the master bedroom extends a cathedral ceiling, a fireplace, abundant closet space, a generous dressing area with a skylight and a lavish bath and shower area with a whirlpool garden tub. Please specify basement or crawlspace foundation when ordering.

Design 9299

First Floor: 2,063 square feet
Second Floor: 894 square feet
Total: 2,957 square feet

■ An elegant brick elevation and rows of shuttered windows lend timeless beauty to this 1½-story Colonial design. The volume entry surveys formal dining and living rooms and the magnificent great room. Sparkling floor-to-ceiling windows flank the fireplace in the great room with a cathedral ceiling. French doors, bayed windows and a decorative ceiling, plus a wet bar highlight the private den. Special lifestyle amenities in the kitchen and bayed breakfast area include a built-in desk, wrapping counters and island. A boxed ceiling adds elegance to the master suite. In the master bath, note the large walk-in closet, built-in dresser, His and Hers vanities, oval whirlpool and plant shelves. Each secondary bedroom upstairs has a roomy closet and private bath.

Design by
Design Basics, Inc.

QUOTE ONE®

Cost to build? See page 342 to order complete cost estimate to build this house in your area!

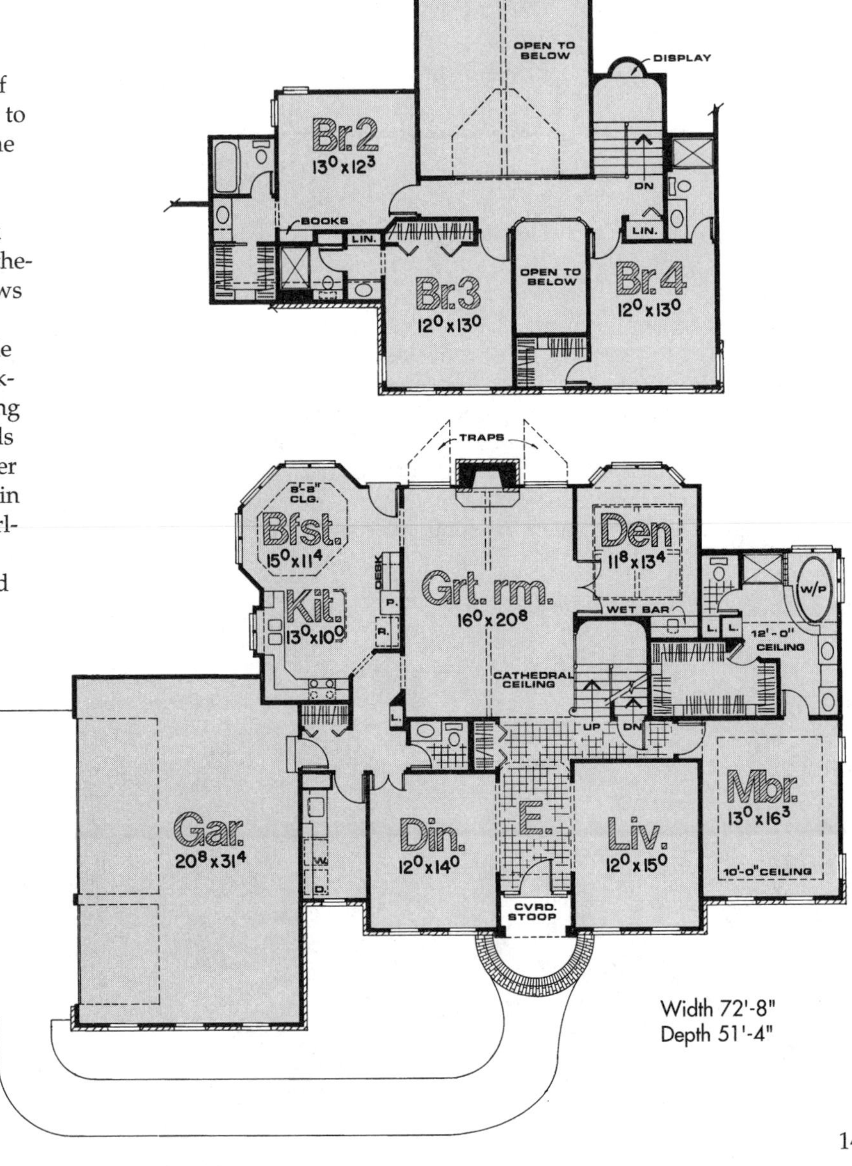
TRAPS
OPEN TO BELOW
DISPLAY
Br.2
$13^0 x 12^3$
BOOKS
LIN.
DN
Br.3
$12^0 x 13^0$
OPEN TO BELOW
Br.4
$12^0 x 13^0$
TRAPS
8'-8" CLG.
Bfst.
$15^0 x 11^4$
DESK
Kit.
$13^0 x 10^0$
Grt. rm.
$16^0 x 20^8$
CATHEDRAL CEILING
Den
$11^8 x 13^4$
WET BAR
W/P
12'-0" CEILING
UP
DN
Gar.
$20^8 x 31^4$
Din.
$12^0 x 14^0$
E.
Liv.
$12^0 x 15^0$
Mbr.
$13^0 x 16^3$
10'-0" CEILING
CVRD. STOOP

Width 72'-8"
Depth 51'-4"

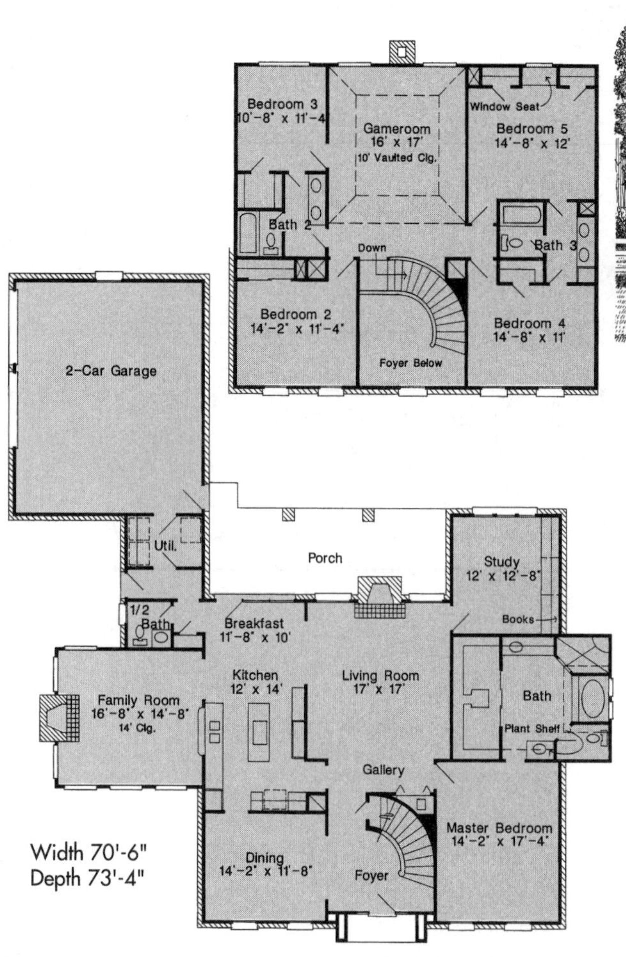

Bedroom 3
10'-8" x 11'-4"
Gameroom
16' x 17'
10' Vaulted Clg.
Window Seat
Bedroom 5
14'-8" x 12'
Bath 2
Bath 3
Down
Bedroom 2
14'-2" x 11'-4"
Bedroom 4
14'-8" x 11'
Foyer Below
2-Car Garage
Util.
Porch
Study
12' x 12'-8"
Books
1/2 Bath
Breakfast
11'-8" x 10'
Kitchen
12' x 14'
Living Room
17' x 17'
Bath
Plant Shelf
Family Room
16'-8" x 14'-8"
14' Clg.
Gallery
Master Bedroom
14'-2" x 17'-4"
Dining
14'-2" x 11'-8"
Foyer

Width 70'-6"
Depth 73'-4"

Design 9126

First floor: 2,157 square feet
Second floor: 1,346 square feet
Total: 3,503 square feet

■ Traditional styling at its best—this plan is a true work of art. The entry foyer contains a curved staircase to the second floor and is open to the formal dining room. The living room has a fireplace as does the family room. A quiet study features built-in shelves and is tucked away to the rear of the plan. Note the master bedroom on the first floor. It boasts a double walk-in closet, corner shower and large tub. Four bedrooms upstairs branch off of game room with vaulted ceiling.

Design by
Larry W. Garnett & Associates, Inc.

QUOTE ONE®
Cost to build? See page 342 to order complete cost estimate to build this house in your area!

Design 9899

First Floor: 1,554 square feet
Second Floor: 1,648 square feet
Total: 3,202 square feet

Design by
Design Traditions

■ The classic styling of this brick American traditional will be respected for years to come. The foyer is flanked by the spacious dining room and the formal study or parlor. A large family room with a full wall of glass conveniently opens to the breakfast room and kitchen. The master suite features a spacious sitting area with its own fireplace and tray ceiling. Two additional bedrooms share a bath, while a fourth bedroom has its own private bath. This home is designed with a basement foundation.

QUOTE ONE®
Cost to build? See page 342 to order complete cost estimate to build this house in your area!

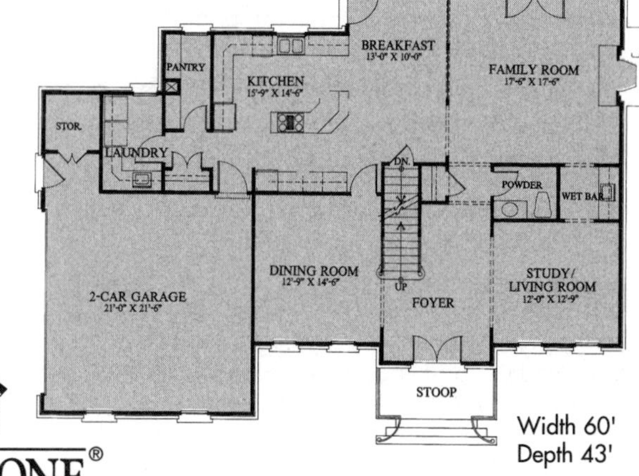

BREAKFAST
PANTRY
KITCHEN
FAMILY ROOM
STOR.
LAUNDRY
DN.
POWDER
WET BAR
DINING ROOM
2-CAR GARAGE
UP
STUDY/
LIVING ROOM
FOYER
STOOP

Width 60'
Depth 43'

W.I.C.
MASTER SUITE
SITTING
BEDROOM NO. 2
BATH
DN.
MASTER BATH
BEDROOM NO. 3
BATH
W.I.C.
OPEN TO BELOW
BEDROOM NO. 4
HIS
HERS
UNFIN.
STORAGE

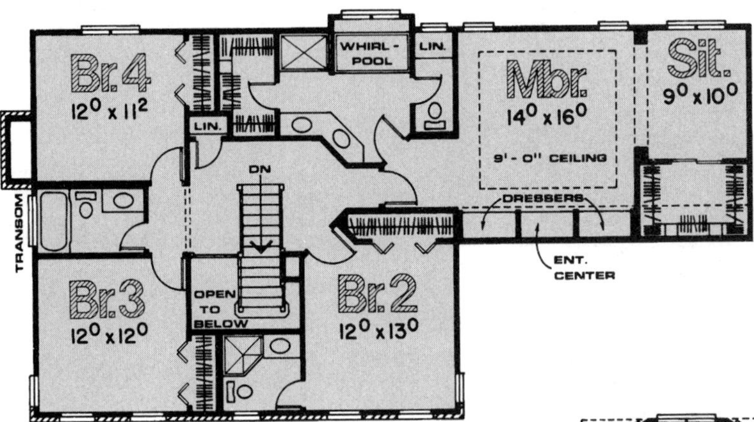

Br.4
12^{0} x 11^{2}
LIN.
WHIRL-POOL
LIN.
Mbr.
14^{0} x 16^{0}
9'-0" CEILING
Sit.
9^{0} x 10^{0}
DN
TRANSOM
DRESSERS
ENT. CENTER
Br.3
12^{0} x 12^{0}
OPEN TO BELOW
Br.2
12^{0} x 13^{0}

Design by
Design Basics, Inc.

Design 9344

First Floor: 1,000 square feet
Second Floor: 1,345 square feet
Total: 2,345 square feet

■ Balanced window detailing, an arched entry and a brick facade highlight the exterior of this modern, two-story Colonial home. Formal rooms at the front provide entertaining ease. The dining room is served by a convenient passageway for quick kitchen service while bright windows and French doors add appeal to the living room. A relaxing family room has a bayed conversation area plus a clear view through the sunny dinette into the effecient kitchen. Features include wrapping counters, a snack bar, two lazy Susans and a generous pantry. Upstairs, a U-shaped hall with a view to below offers separation to all four bedrooms. Bedroom 2 has its own bath. Homeowners will love the expansive master retreat. This oasis features a private sitting room, two walk-in closets, compartmented bath, separate vanities and a whirlpool tub.

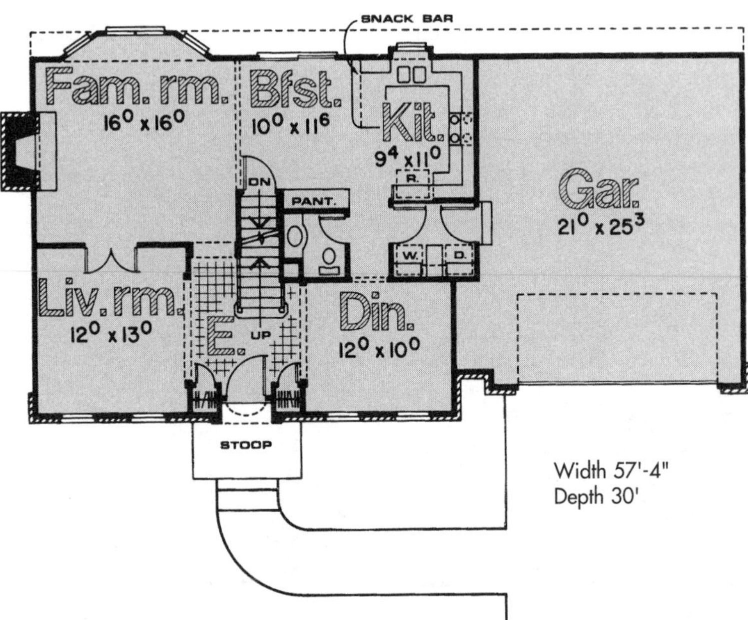

SNACK BAR
Fam. rm.
16^{0} x 16^{0}
Bfst.
10^{0} x 11^{6}
Kit.
9^{4} x 11^{0}
R.
DN
PANT.
Gar.
21^{0} x 25^{3}
W.
D.
Liv. rm.
12^{0} x 13^{0}
E.
UP
Din.
12^{0} x 10^{0}
STOOP

Width 57'-4"
Depth 30'

Design 9389

First Floor: 1,362 square feet
Second Floor: 1,223 square feet
Total: 2,585 square feet

■ Gracing the elevation of this captivating Colonial are decorative windows and brick detailing. Inside, the dining room is complemented by French doors, a distinctive ceiling treatment and space to accommodate a buffet or hutch. A formal parlor provides a place for quiet relaxation. The family room, with a fireplace, is brightened by an airy bowed window. The spacious kitchen provides a large pantry, a snack bar and an abundant counter space. Half baths are placed conveniently near the family room and laundry. On the second floor, a resplendent master suite filled with the most desirable amenities is joined by three family bedrooms. The side-load garage accommodates three cars.

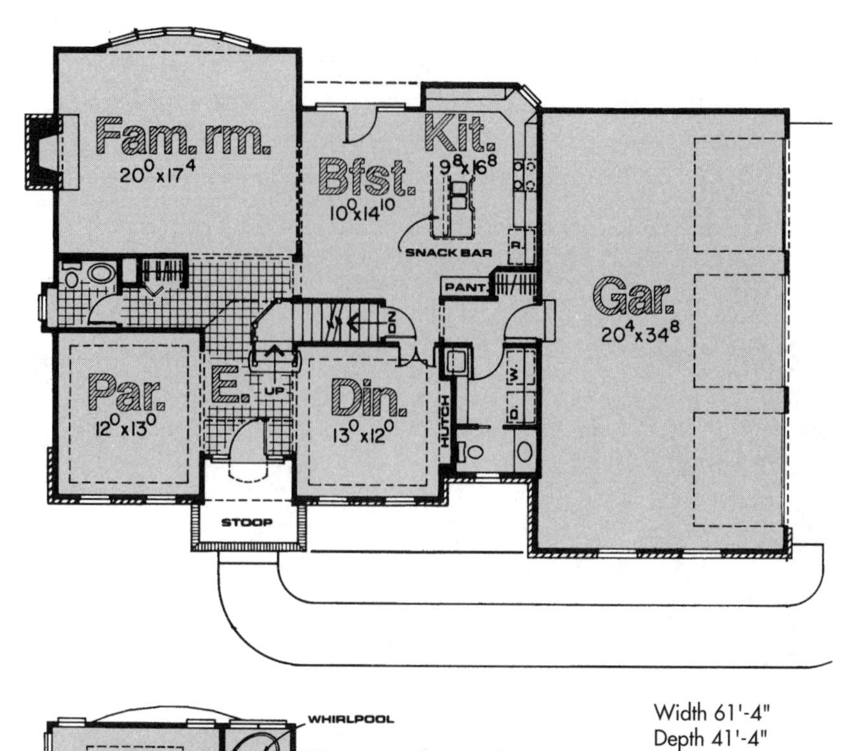

Fam. rm.
$20^0 x 17^4$
Bfst.
$10^0 x 14^{10}$
Kit.
$9^8 x 16^8$
SNACK BAR
PANT.
Gar.
$20^4 x 34^8$
Par.
$12^0 x 13^0$
E.
UP
DN
Din.
$13^0 x 12^0$
HUTCH
W.
D.
R.
STOOP

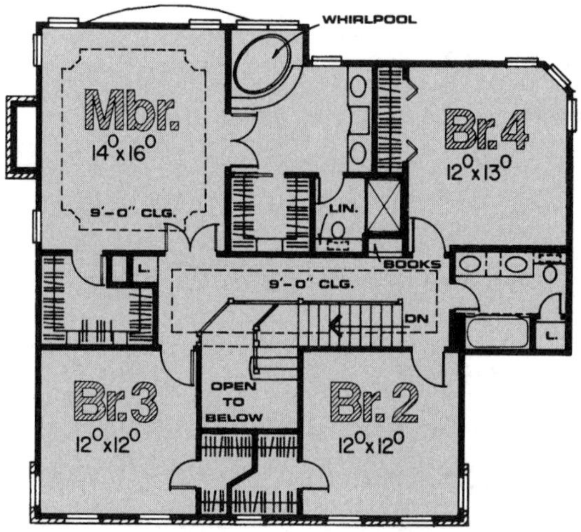

Width 61'-4"
Depth 41'-4"

Design by
Design Basics, Inc.

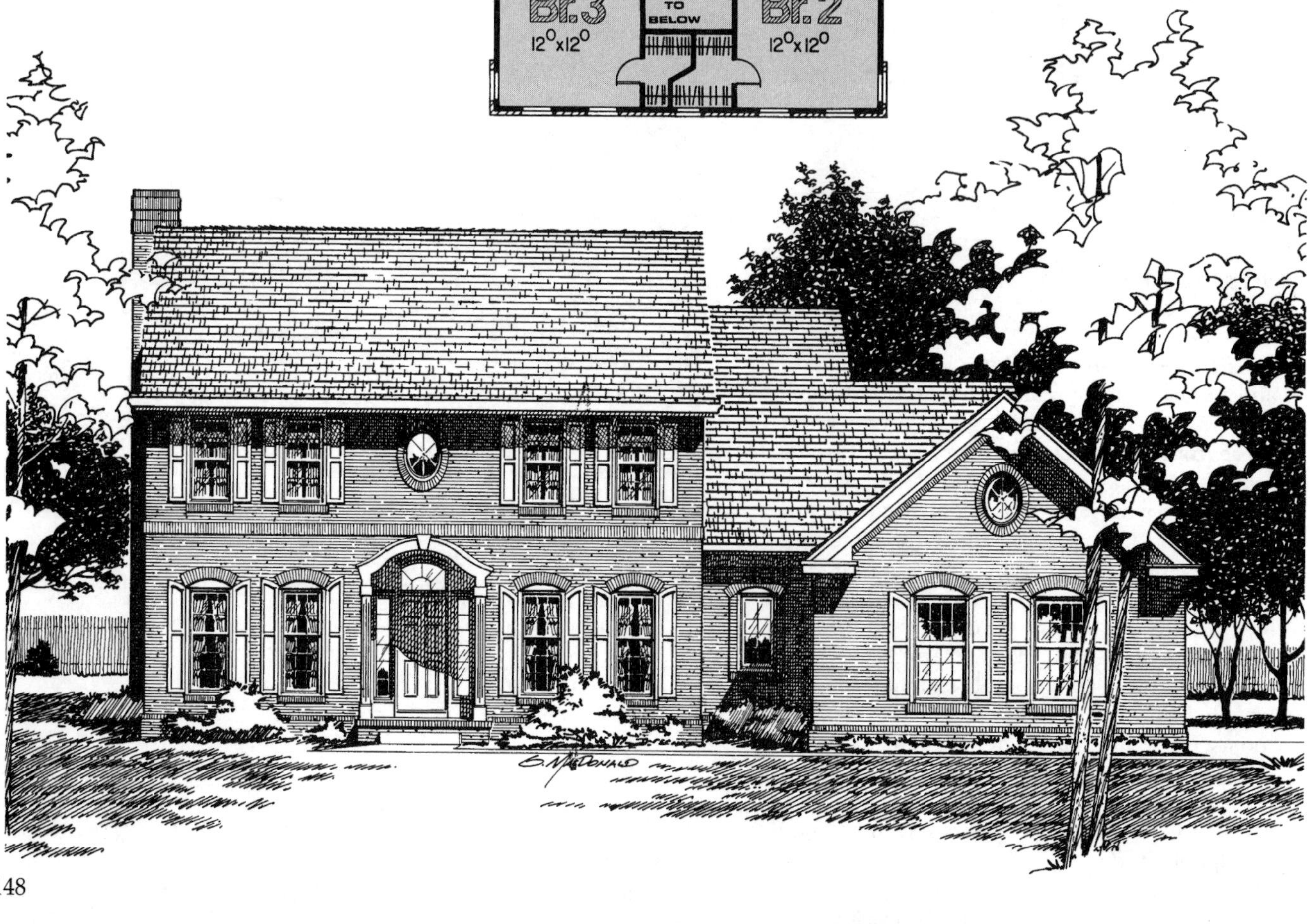

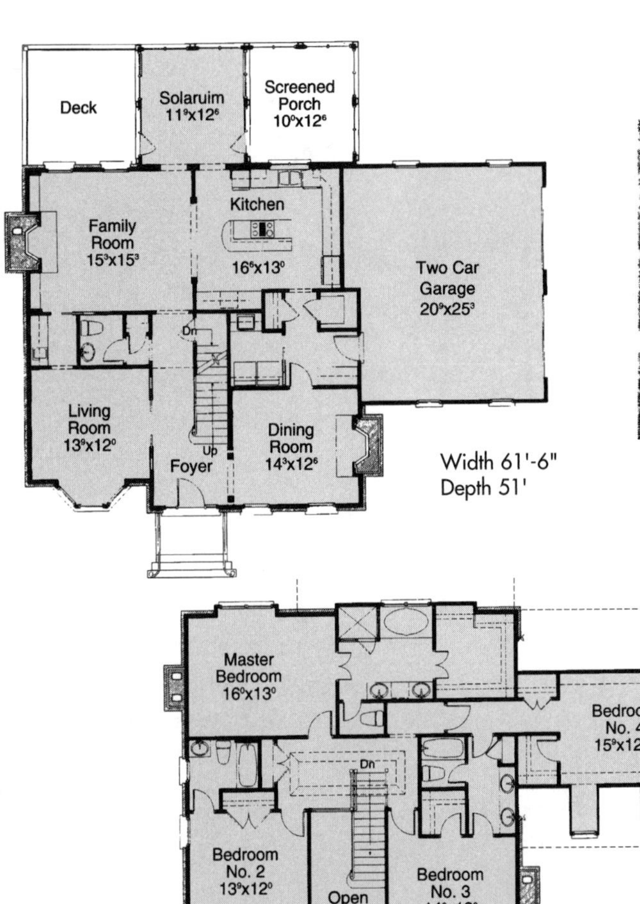
Deck
Solaruim $11^{9}x12^{6}$
Screened Porch $10^{0}x12^{6}$
Kitchen $16^{6}x13^{0}$
Family Room $15^{3}x15^{3}$
Two Car Garage $20^{9}x25^{3}$
Dn
Living Room $13^{9}x12^{0}$
Up
Foyer
Dining Room $14^{3}x12^{6}$
Width 61'-6"
Depth 51'
Master Bedroom $16^{0}x13^{0}$
Bedroom No. 4 $15^{6}x120^{3}$
Dn
Bedroom No. 2 $13^{9}x12^{0}$
Open To Below
Bedroom No. 3 $14^{6}x12^{0}$

Design 9979

First Floor: 1,698 square feet
Second Floor: 1,542 square feet
Total: 3,240 square feet

Design by
Design Traditions

■ Make your mark with this brick traditional. With a walk-out basement, there's lots of room to grow. On the first floor, such attributes as informal/formal zones, a gourmet kitchen and a solarium, deck and screened porch are immediate attention getters. In the kitchen, meal preparation is a breeze with an island work station and plenty of counter space. Four bedrooms make up the second floor of this plan. One of the family bedrooms has a private bath. The master bedroom has its own bath and a giant walk-in closet. This home is designed with a basement foundation.

Bedroom No. 2 $13^{3}x12^{0}$
Bedroom No. 3 $11^{9}x12^{6}$
Width 54'-3"
Depth 70'-3"
Dn
Master Bedroom $15^{9}x17^{0}$
Open To Below
Bedroom No. 4 $15^{9}x12^{0}$
Two Car Garage $21^{3}x22^{6}$
Porch
Breakfast $13^{3}x14^{6}$
Great Room $15^{3}x21^{0}$
Kitchen $15^{0}x13^{3}$
Up
Dn
Living Room $15^{3}x13^{0}$
Foyer
Dining Room $15^{3}x13^{0}$

Design 9981

First Floor: 1,828 square feet
Second Floor: 1,552 square feet
Total: 3,380 square feet

■ A stately appearance and lots of living space give this home appeal. The foyer introduces formal living and dining rooms. For more casual occasions, a great room opens to the back. The breakfast room has convenient proximity to these informal areas. The kitchen has plenty of work space. Four bedrooms on the second floor enjoy complete privacy. In the master bedroom suite, a short hallway flanked by closets leads to a lovely bath with a spa tub, a compartmented toilet, a separate shower and dual lavatories. This home is designed with a basement foundation.

Design by
Design Traditions

Design 9239

First Floor: 998 square feet
Second Floor: 1,206 square feet
Total: 2,204 square feet

Design by
Design Basics, Inc.

■ The bright entry of this two-story home opens to the formal living and dining space. To the back is the casual family room with a fireplace and built-in bookshelves. An island kitchen features a corner sink, pantry, and convenient planning desk. Upstairs, the master bedroom has a vaulted ceiling and a sumptuous master bath with a skylit dressing area, a whirlpool tub, and a walk-in closet. Three family bedrooms and a full bath round out sleeping accommodations. A laundry room is located conveniently on the second floor as well.

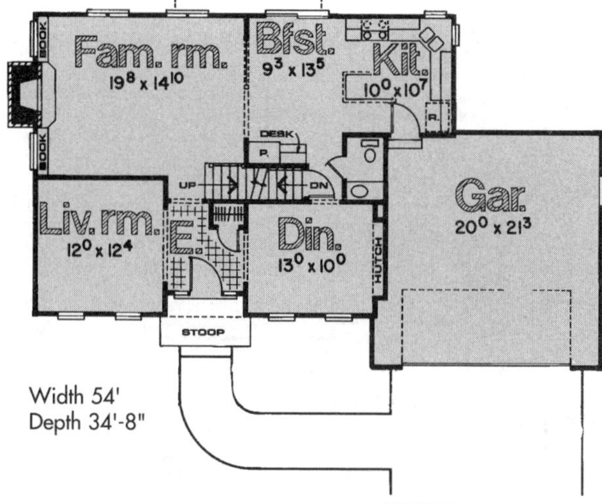

Fam. rm.
19⁸ x 14¹⁰
Bfst.
9³ x 13⁵
Kit.
10⁰ x 10⁷
DESK
UP
DN
Liv. rm.
12⁰ x 12⁴
E.
Din.
13⁰ x 10⁰
HUTCH
Gar.
20⁰ x 21³
STOOP

Width 54'
Depth 34'-8"

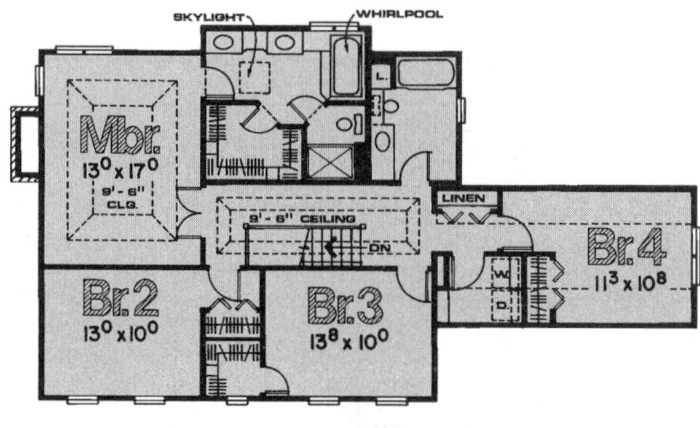

SKYLIGHT
WHIRLPOOL
Mbr.
13⁰ x 17⁰
9'-6" CLG.
9'-6" CEILING
DN
LINEN
Br. 4
11³ x 10⁸
Br. 2
13⁰ x 10⁰
Br. 3
13⁸ x 10⁰

Design P108

First Floor: 719 square feet
Second Floor: 717 square feet
Total: 1436 square feet
Bonus: 290 square feet

■ Traditional wood siding gives a look of down-home comfort to this charming two-story home. A brief foyer opens to the family room that is highlighted with a fireplace and pass through to the kitchen. The efficient kitchen has wrapping counters, a breakfast nook, laundry center and easy service to the dining room. Upstairs, the master suite has elegant ceiling detail, a vaulted bath and roomy walk-in closet. Two family bedrooms share a hall bath. Please specify basement or crawlspace foundation when ordering.

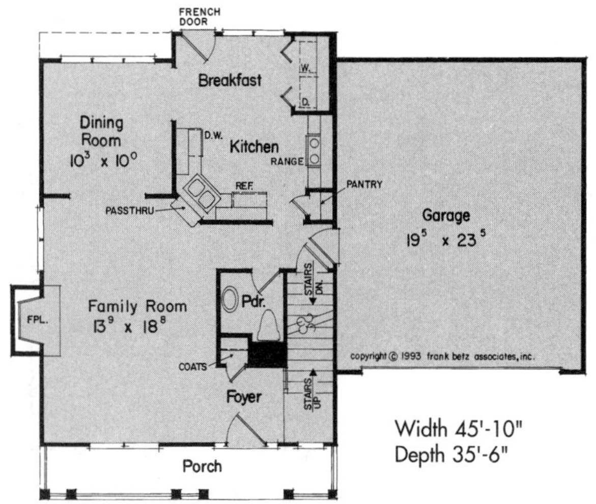

FRENCH DOOR
Breakfast
Dining Room
10³ x 10⁰
D.W.
Kitchen
RANGE
REF.
PANTRY
PASSTHRU
Garage
19⁵ x 23⁵
FPL.
Family Room
13⁹ x 18⁸
Pdr.
STAIRS DN.
COATS
Foyer
STAIRS UP
copyright © 1993 frank betz associates, inc.
Porch

Width 45'-10"
Depth 35'-6"

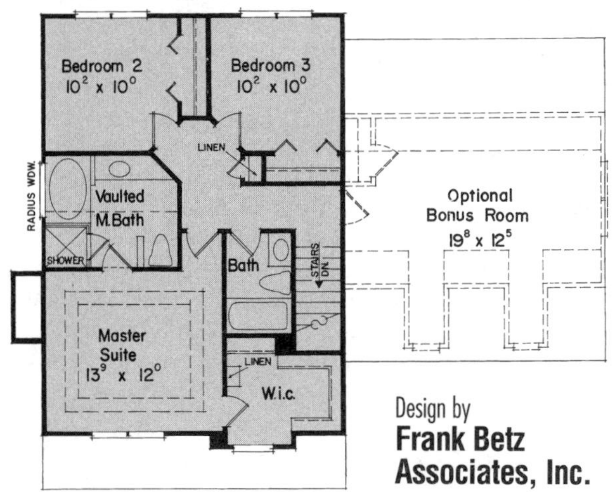

Bedroom 2
10² x 10⁰
Bedroom 3
10² x 10⁰
LINEN
RADIUS WDW.
Vaulted M.Bath
SHOWER
Bath
STAIRS DN.
Optional Bonus Room
19⁸ x 12⁵
Master Suite
13⁹ x 12⁰
LINEN
W.i.c.

Design by
Frank Betz Associates, Inc.

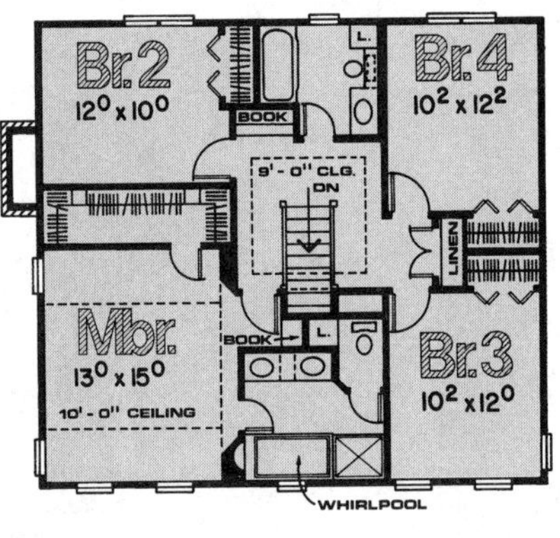
Br. 2
12^0 x 10^0
BOOK
L.
Br. 4
10^2 x 12^2
9' - 0" CLG.
DN
LINEN
Mbr.
13^0 x 15^0
10' - 0" CEILING
BOOK
L.
Br. 3
10^2 x 12^0
WHIRLPOOL

Design 9343

First Floor: 1,000 square feet
Second Floor: 993 square feet
Total: 1,993 square feet

QUOTE ONE®
Cost to build? See page 342 to order complete cost estimate to build this house in your area!

■ This plan captures the heritage and romance of an authentic Colonial home. A central hall leads to the formal rooms at the front where showpiece furnishings can be displayed. For daily living, the informal rooms can't be beat. A bookcase and large linen cabinet are thoughtful touches upstairs. Further evidence of tasteful design is shown in the master suite. A volume ceiling, large walk-in closet and whirlpool tub await the fortunate homeowner. Each secondary bedroom has bright windows to add natural lighting and comfort.

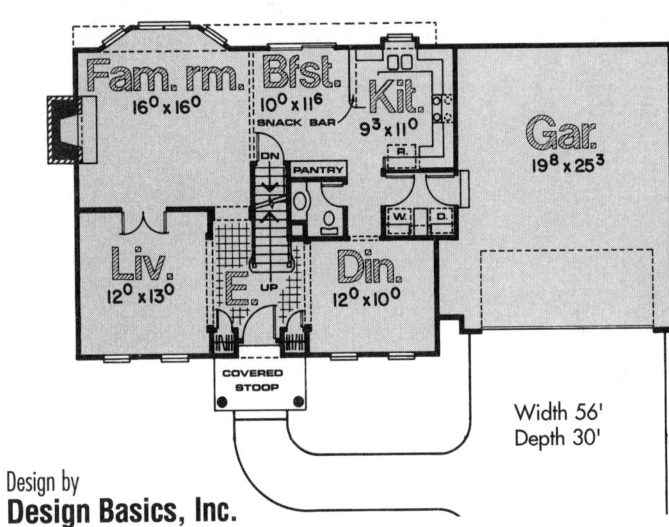
Fam. rm.
16^0 x 16^0
Bfst.
10^0 x 11^6
SNACK BAR
Kit.
9^3 x 11^0
R.
Gar.
19^8 x 25^3
DN
PANTRY
W.
D.
Liv.
12^0 x 13^0
E.
UP
Din.
12^0 x 10^0
COVERED STOOP
Width 56'
Depth 30'

Design by
Design Basics, Inc.

Design 7255

First Floor: 941 square feet
Second Floor: 920 square feet
Total: 1,861 square feet

■ Colonial charm is abundantly displayed in this gracious two-story home. The great room offers views to the covered porch and multi-windowed breakfast area. To the left, a formal dining room provides a special place for dinner parties. An island kitchen with a pantry and plenty of storage has convenient access to all areas. The second floor contains two family bedrooms, a full bath and a master suite. A cathedral ceiling graces the master bedroom. The master bath features a whirlpool bath, an open shower and a generous walk-in closet.

Design by
Design Basics, Inc.

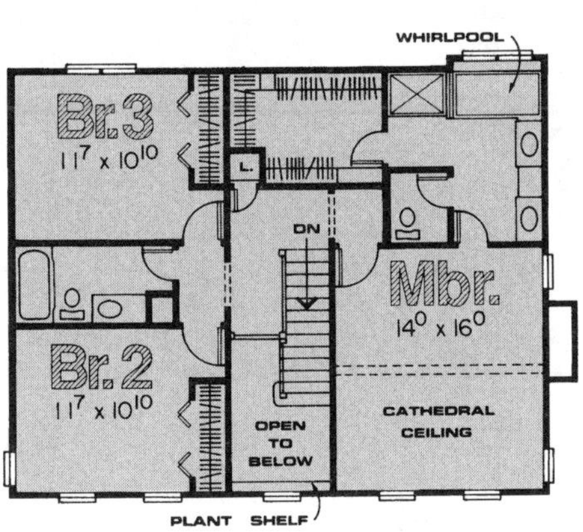
WHIRLPOOL
Br. 3
11^7 x 10^{10}
L.
DN
Mbr.
14^0 x 16^0
Br. 2
11^7 x 10^{10}
OPEN TO BELOW
CATHEDRAL CEILING
PLANT SHELF

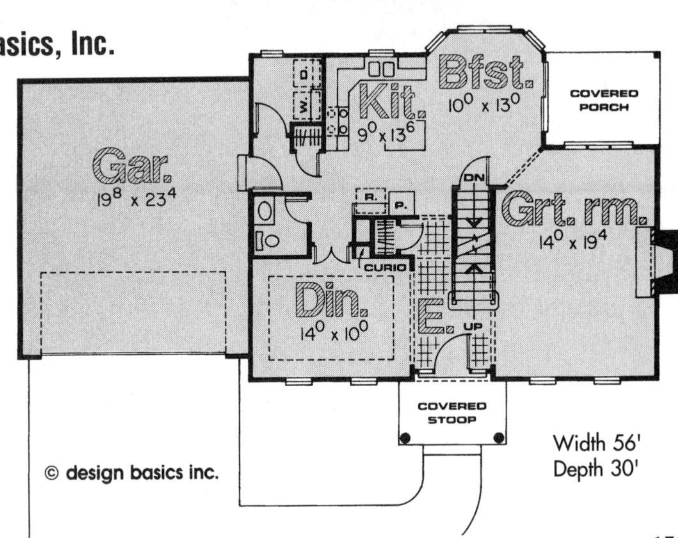
W.
D.
Kit.
9^0 x 13^6
Bfst.
10^0 x 13^0
COVERED PORCH
Gar.
19^8 x 23^4
R.
P.
DN
Grt. rm.
14^0 x 19^4
CURIO
Din.
14^0 x 10^0
E.
UP
COVERED STOOP
Width 56'
Depth 30'

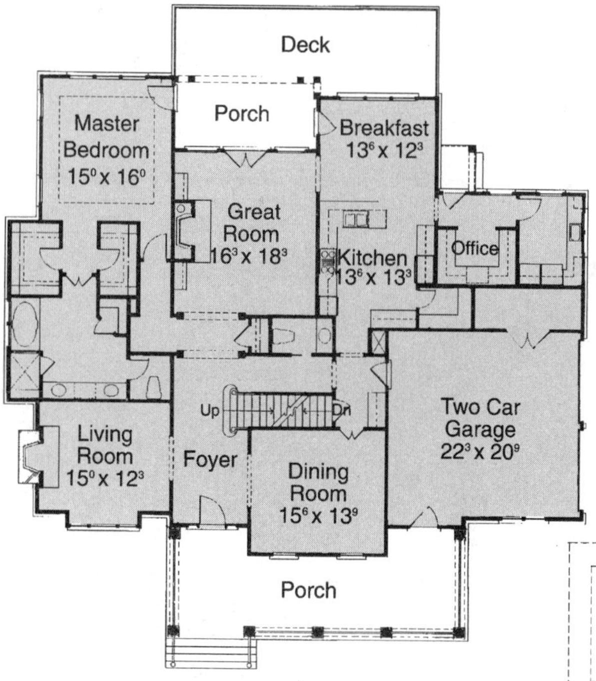

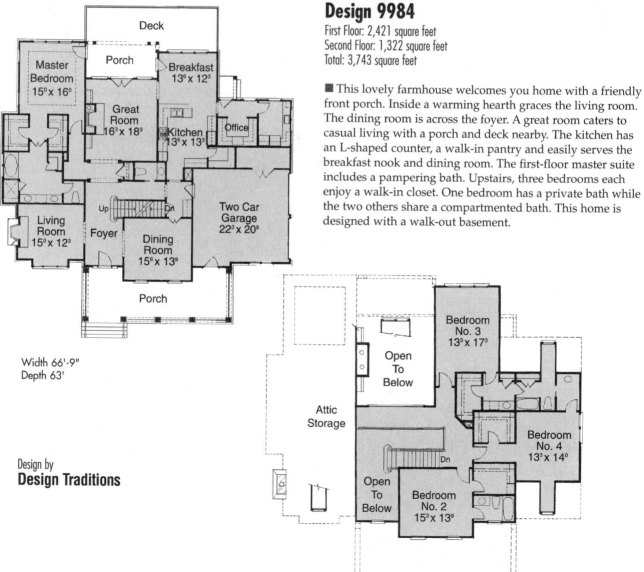

Design 9984

First Floor: 2,421 square feet
Second Floor: 1,322 square feet
Total: 3,743 square feet

■ This lovely farmhouse welcomes you home with a friendly front porch. Inside a warming hearth graces the living room. The dining room is across the foyer. A great room caters to casual living with a porch and deck nearby. The kitchen has an L-shaped counter, a walk-in pantry and easily serves the breakfast nook and dining room. The first-floor master suite includes a pampering bath. Upstairs, three bedrooms each enjoy a walk-in closet. One bedroom has a private bath while the two others share a compartmented bath. This home is designed with a walk-out basement.

Width 66'-9"
Depth 63'

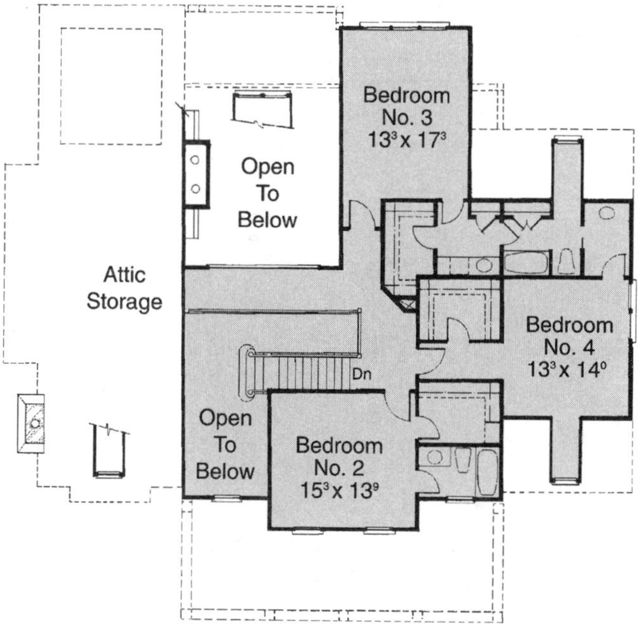

Design by
Design Traditions

Design by
Design Traditions

MASTER SUITE
14'-10" x 15'-8"
M. BATH
W.I.C.
LAUN.
6'-0" x 5'-8"
BEDROOM No.3
10'-0" x 12'-10"
BEDROOM NO. 2
12'-0" X 14'-0"
BATH
DECK
BREAKFAST
10'-0" x 7'-0"
GREAT ROOM
18'-6" x 15'-6"
KITCHEN
12'-0" x 10'-10"
UP
DN
FOYER
DINING
9'-6" x 12'-10"
POWDER
TWO-CAR GARAGE
20'-0" x 21'-0"
PORCH
Width 41'
Depth 40'-6"

Design 9902

First Floor: 830 square feet
Second Floor: 1,060 square feet
Total: 1,890 square feet

■ The pleasing character of this house does not stop behind its facade. The foyer opens up into an encompassing great room with fireplace and the eat-in kitchen. Stairs lead from the great room to the second floor—and here's where you'll find the laundry! The master suite spares none of the amenities: full bath with double vanity, shower, tub and walk-in closet. Bedrooms 2 and 3 share a full bath. This home is designed with a basement foundation.

Design P101

First Floor: 882 square feet
Second Floor: 793 square feet
Total: 1,675 square feet
Bonus Room: 416 square feet

Design by
Frank Betz Associates, Inc.

■ Traditional wood siding is spruced up with a bright window display and quaint flower boxes. Inside, the formal living and dining rooms are distinguished just off the foyer, with casual living at the rear. The comfortable family room is highlighted with a fireplace and its easy flow with the kitchen and breakfast areas. Upstairs, two family bedrooms and a hall bath are a nice complement to the large master suite that's accented with a vaulted bath and walk-in closet. Please specify basement or crawlspace foundation when ordering.

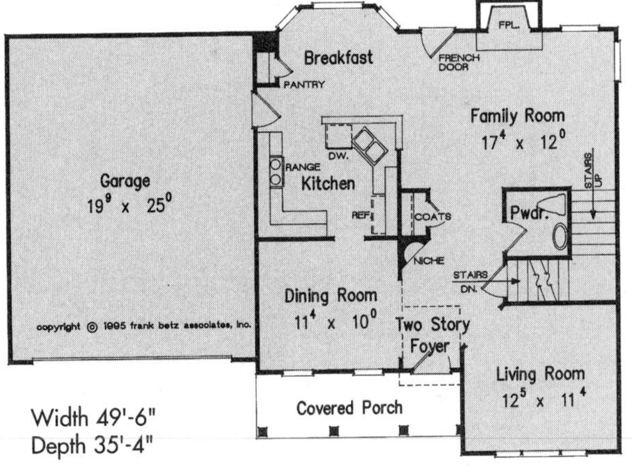
Breakfast
FPL
FRENCH DOOR
PANTRY
Family Room
17^4 x 12^0
Garage
19^9 x 25^0
DW.
RANGE
Kitchen
REF.
COATS
Pwdr.
STAIRS UP
NICHE
STAIRS DN.
Dining Room
11^4 x 10^0
Two Story Foyer
Living Room
12^5 x 11^4
Covered Porch
copyright © 1995 frank betz associates, inc.
Width 49'-6"
Depth 35'-4"

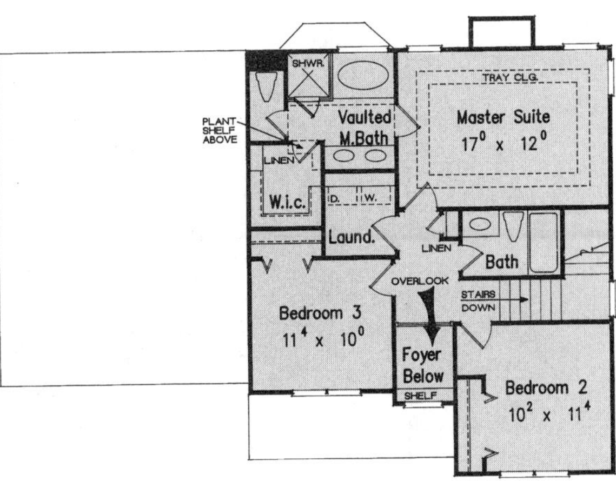
SHWR.
PLANT SHELF ABOVE
Vaulted M.Bath
TRAY CLG.
Master Suite
17^0 x 12^0
LINEN
W.i.c.
D. W.
Laund.
LINEN
Bath
OVERLOOK
STAIRS DOWN
Bedroom 3
11^4 x 10^0
Foyer Below
SHELF
Bedroom 2
10^2 x 11^4

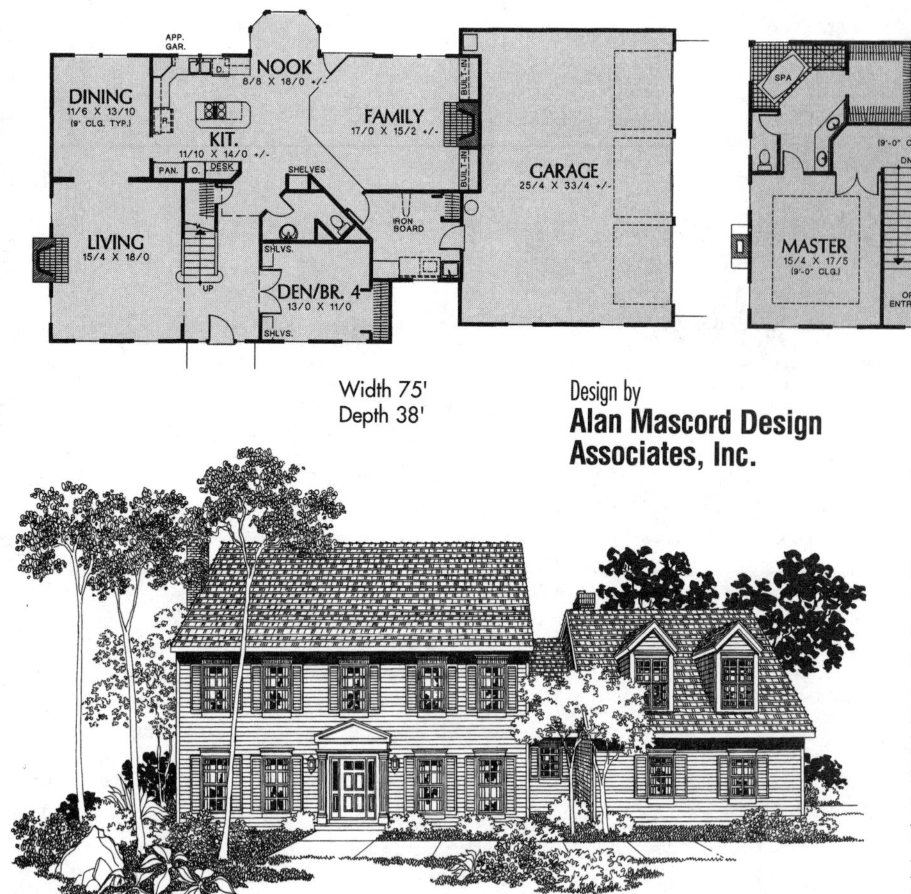
APP. GAR.
NOOK
8/8 X 18/0 +/-
DINING
11/6 X 13/10
(9' CLG. TYP.)
KIT.
11/10 X 14/0 +/-
PAN.
DESK
FAMILY
17/0 X 15/2 +/-
BUILT-IN
GARAGE
25/4 X 33/4 +/-
SHELVES
IRON BOARD
LIVING
15/4 X 18/0
SHLVS.
DEN/BR. 4
13/0 X 11/0
UP

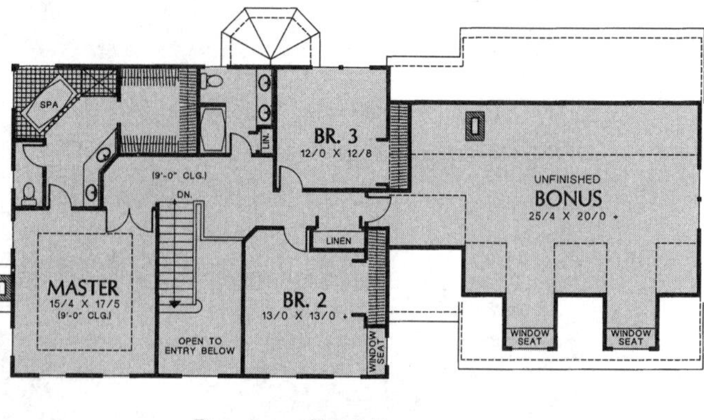
SPA
(9'-0" CLG.)
DN.
LIN.
BR. 3
12/0 X 12/8
UNFINISHED
BONUS
25/4 X 20/0 +
LINEN
MASTER
15/4 X 17/5
(9'-0" CLG.)
BR. 2
13/0 X 13/0 +
OPEN TO ENTRY BELOW
WINDOW SEAT
WINDOW SEAT
WINDOW SEAT

Width 75'
Depth 38'

Design by
Alan Mascord Design Associates, Inc.

Design 9465

First Floor: 1,627 square feet
Second Floor: 1,219 square feet
Total: 2,846 square feet
Bonus: 717 square feet

■ This elegant Colonial is designed to work well on a corner lot thanks to its side-loaded three-car garage. The main floor contains a den that serves nicely as an office and is accessed through a pair of French doors right off the entry. All the bedrooms are generously sized, especially the master which features all the amenities plus a huge walk-in closet. A giant bonus room is provided over the garage, perfect for use as a fourth bedroom or a game room.

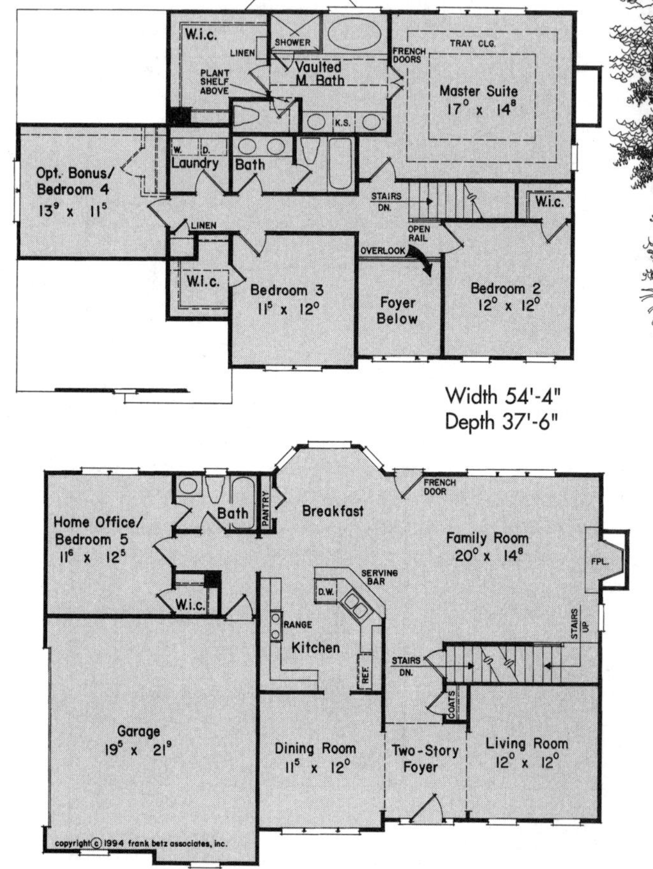
W.i.c.
LINEN
SHOWER
TRAY CLG.
FRENCH DOORS
PLANT SHELF ABOVE
Vaulted M. Bath
Master Suite
17° x 14⁸
K.S.
Opt. Bonus/ Bedroom 4
13⁹ x 11⁵
Laundry
Bath
STAIRS DN.
W.i.c.
LINEN
OPEN RAIL
OVERLOOK
W.i.c.
Bedroom 3
11⁵ x 12°
Foyer Below
Bedroom 2
12° x 12°
Home Office/ Bedroom 5
11⁶ x 12⁵
Bath
PANTRY
Breakfast
FRENCH DOOR
Family Room
20° x 14⁸
FPL.
SERVING BAR
D.W.
W.i.c.
RANGE
Kitchen
REF.
STAIRS DN.
STAIRS UP
COATS
Garage
19⁵ x 21⁹
Dining Room
11⁵ x 12°
Two-Story Foyer
Living Room
12° x 12°
copyright © 1994 frank betz associates, inc.

Width 54'-4"
Depth 37'-6"

Design P105

First Floor: 1,294 square feet
Second Floor: 1,067 square feet
Total: 2,361 square feet
Bonus: 168 square feet

Design by
Frank Betz Associates, Inc.

■ A high, hipped roof makes the stately facade of this traditional home all the more impressive. The striking two-story entry is flanked by the formal dining and living rooms before leading to the expansive family room. A lovely fireplace and understated stair to the second level highlight this room. The efficient kitchen has a great serving bar that angles to the breakfast room. A secluded bedroom off the kitchen would make a super guest room or home office. Upstairs, two family bedrooms and a compartmented bath are joined by an optional bedroom and the grand master suite. Please specify basement or crawlspace foundation when ordering.

Design 9390

First Floor: 1,865 square feet
Second Floor: 774 square feet
Total: 2,639 square feet

■ A magnificent brick facade with a three-car, side-load garage conceals a well-organized floor plan. A tiled foyer leads to the formal dining room, with wet bar and hutch space, on the left and a parlor on the right. Straight ahead is a spacious great room with arched windows flanking a fireplace. The kitchen offers a snack bar peninsula and adjoins a bayed breakfast area. The first-floor master bedroom includes a large, walk-in closet and French doors leading to a master bath with angled whirlpool and a shower with glass block. The second floor provides three bedrooms and two full baths. A reading seat flanked by two cabinets overlooks the volume entry.

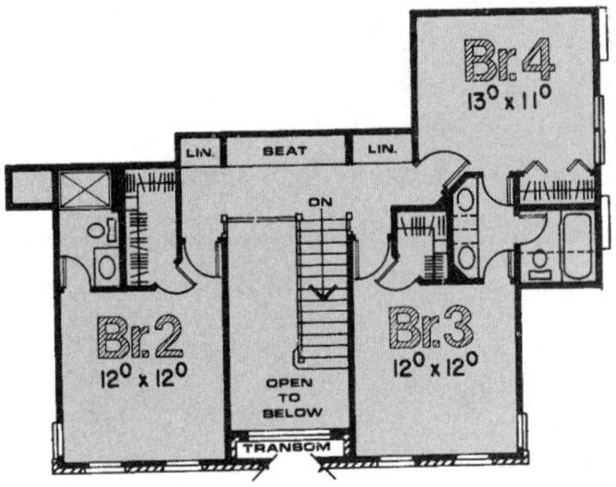

Design by
Design Basics, Inc.

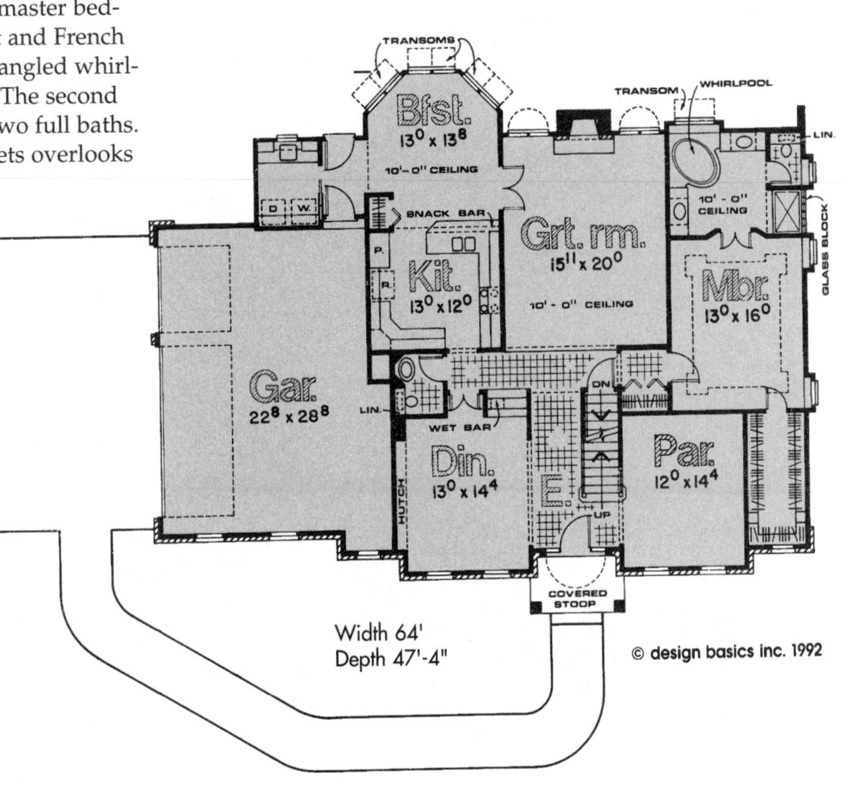
Br. 4
13^0 x 11^0
LIN.
SEAT
LIN.
ON
Br. 2
12^0 x 12^0
Br. 3
12^0 x 12^0
OPEN TO BELOW
TRANSOM
TRANSOMS
Bfst.
13^0 x 13^8
10'-0" CEILING
TRANSOM
WHIRLPOOL
LIN.
10'-0" CEILING
GLASS BLOCK
SNACK BAR
Grt. rm.
15^{11} x 20^0
10'-0" CEILING
Kit.
13^0 x 12^0
Mbr.
13^0 x 16^0
Gar.
22^8 x 28^8
LIN.
WET BAR
DN
Din.
13^0 x 14^4
HUTCH
E.
UP
Par.
12^0 x 14^4
COVERED STOOP

Width 64'
Depth 47'-4"

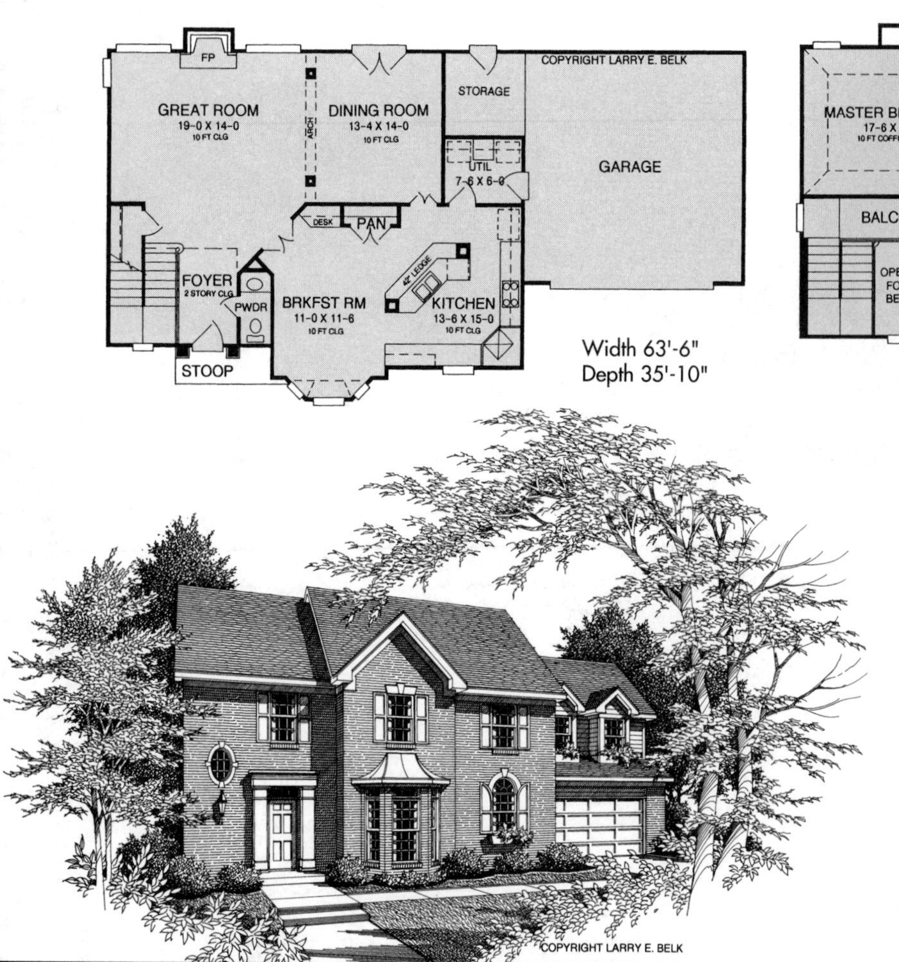
COPYRIGHT LARRY E. BELK
FP
GREAT ROOM
19-0 X 14-0
10 FT CLG
DINING ROOM
13-4 X 14-0
10 FT CLG
ARCH
STORAGE
UTIL
7-6 X 6-0
GARAGE
DESK
PAN
42" LEDGE
FOYER
2 STORY CLG
PWDR
BRKFST RM
11-0 X 11-6
10 FT CLG
KITCHEN
13-6 X 15-0
10 FT CLG
STOOP
Width 63'-6"
Depth 35'-10"
COPYRIGHT LARRY E. BELK

K.S.
MASTER BATH
MASTER BEDROOM
17-6 X 14-0
10 FT COFFERED CLG
SEAT
BEDROOM 2
13-0 X 14-0
GAME ROOM/
BEDROOM 4
13-8 X 18-0
BALCONY
OPEN TO
FOYER
BELOW
BEDROOM 3
14-6 X 11-6
LIN
K.S.
BATH 2

Design by
Larry E. Belk Designs

Design 8122

First Floor: 1,206 square feet
Second Floor: 1,541 square feet
Total: 2,747 square feet

■ A perfect design for the busy family, this traditional home includes amenities that focus on family living. The oversized kitchen has a large island with a serving bar and a bay breakfast area. The great room is set apart from the dining room with an elegant arch. The second level features the handsome master suite that's complete with a lush, compartmented bath and a walk-in closet. Finishing this story are two family bedrooms, a game room and a large hall bath with twin vanities and a compartmented toilet and bath area. Please specify crawlspace or slab foundation when ordering.

Design 9109

First Floor: 2,114 square feet
Second Floor: 1,116 square feet
Total: 3,230 square feet

Design by
Larry W. Garnett & Associates, Inc.

■ Elaborate brick detailing, a steeply pitched roof and the repetitive arch theme throughout the windows and porch accent this impressive home. The raised foyer overlooks a formal dining room with built-in display niche. The spacious living room features a fireplace, French doors leading to the porch and full-length windows. The master suite has twin walk-in closets, a through-fireplace to the bath and an adjacent study. The unique kitchen has a cathedral ceiling. Three bedrooms, a game room and two baths finish the second level.

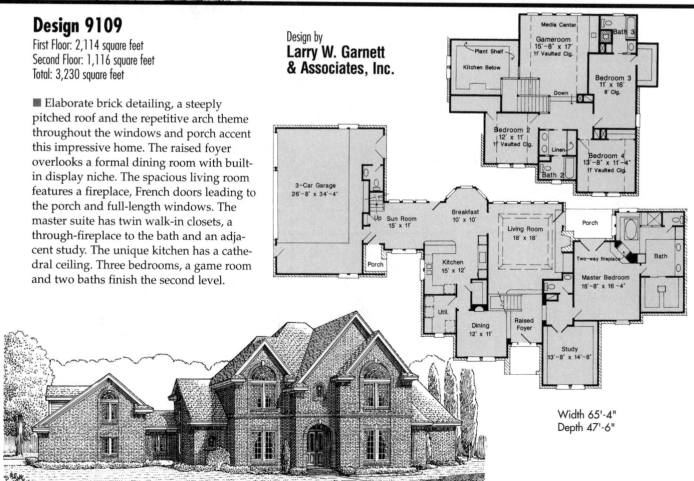

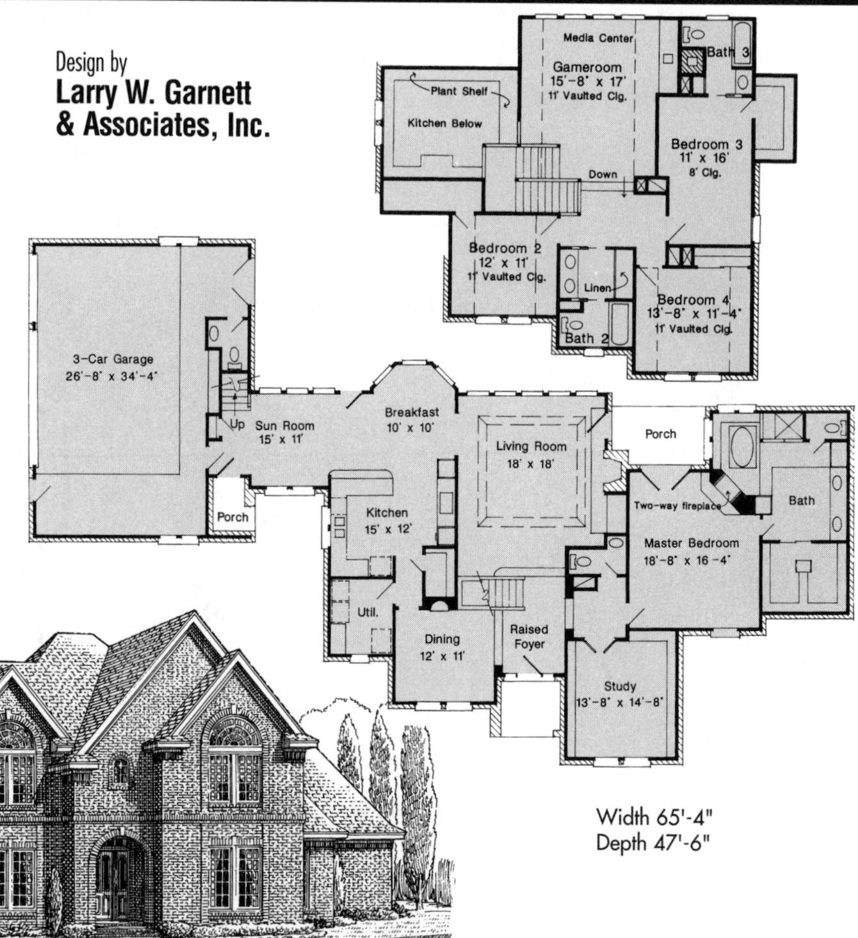
Media Center
Gameroom
15'-8" x 17'
11' Vaulted Clg.
Bath 3
Plant Shelf
Kitchen Below
Bedroom 3
11' x 16'
8' Clg.
Down
Bedroom 2
12' x 11'
11' Vaulted Clg.
Linen
Bedroom 4
13'-8" x 11'-4"
11' Vaulted Clg.
Bath 2
3-Car Garage
26'-8" x 34'-4"
Up
Sun Room
15' x 11'
Breakfast
10' x 10'
Living Room
18' x 18'
Porch
Two-way fireplace
Bath
Kitchen
15' x 12'
Master Bedroom
18'-8" x 16-4"
Util.
Dining
12' x 11'
Raised
Foyer
Study
13'-8" x 14'-8"
Width 65'-4"
Depth 47'-6"

Design 9351

First Floor: 2,839 square feet
Second Floor: 1,111 square feet
Total: 3,950 square feet

Design by
Design Basics, Inc.

■ A two-story foyer introduces the formal living zones of this plan: a den with a ten-foot ceiling, a dining room with a butler's pantry, a living room with a fireplace and a high ceiling. For more casual living, the gathering room shares space with the octagonal breakfast area and the kitchen. Sleeping arrangements include a first-floor master bedroom. It offers a sitting area with a fireplace, a bath with a corner whirlpool and compartmented toilet, and an extensive closet. The second floor holds three bedrooms—all feature walk-in closets and private baths.

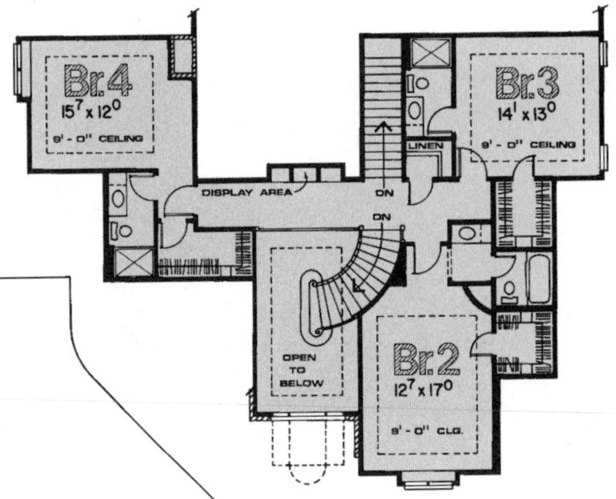

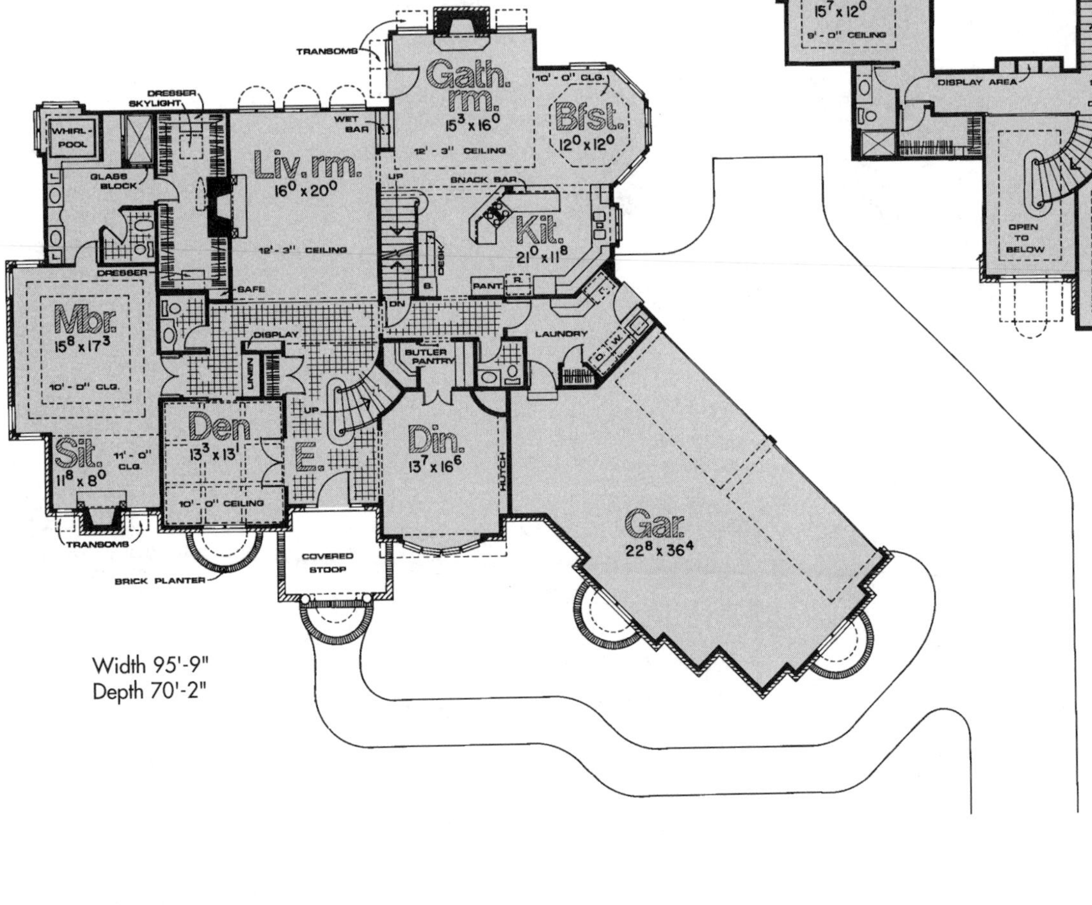

Width 95'-9"
Depth 70'-2"

Design 9886

First Floor: 1,165 square feet
Second Floor: 1,050 square feet
Total: 2,215 square feet

Design by
Design Traditions

■ Classic design knows no boundaries in this gracious two-story home. From the formal living and dining areas to the more casual family room, it handles any occasion with ease. Of special note on the first floor are the L-shaped kitchen with attached breakfast area and the guest-pampering half bath. Upstairs are three bedrooms including a master suite with a fine bath and a walk-in closet. A fourth bedroom can be developed in bonus space as needed. This home is designed with a basement foundation.

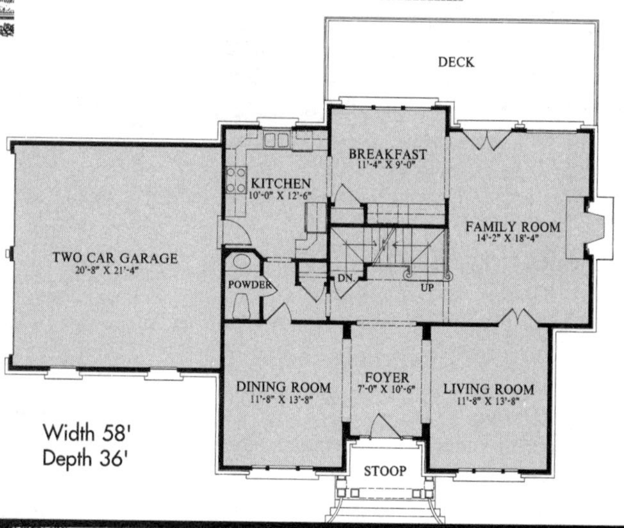
DECK
BREAKFAST
11'-4" X 9'-0"
KITCHEN
10'-0" X 12'-6"
FAMILY ROOM
14'-2" X 18'-4"
TWO CAR GARAGE
20'-8" X 21'-4"
POWDER
DN.
UP
DINING ROOM
11'-8" X 13'-8"
FOYER
7'-0" X 10'-6"
LIVING ROOM
11'-8" X 13'-8"
STOOP
Width 58'
Depth 36'

Design 9842

First Floor: 1,053 square feet
Second Floor: 1,053 square feet
Total: 2,106 square feet
Bonus Room: 237 square feet

■ Brick takes a bold stand in grand traditional style in this treasured design. The front study has a near-by full bath, making it a handy guest bedroom. The family room with fireplace opens to a cozy breakfast area. For more formal entertaining there's a dining room just off the entry. The kitchen features a prep island and huge pantry. Upstairs, the master bedroom has its own sitting room and a giant-sized closet. Two family bedrooms share a full bath. This home is designed with a basement foundation.

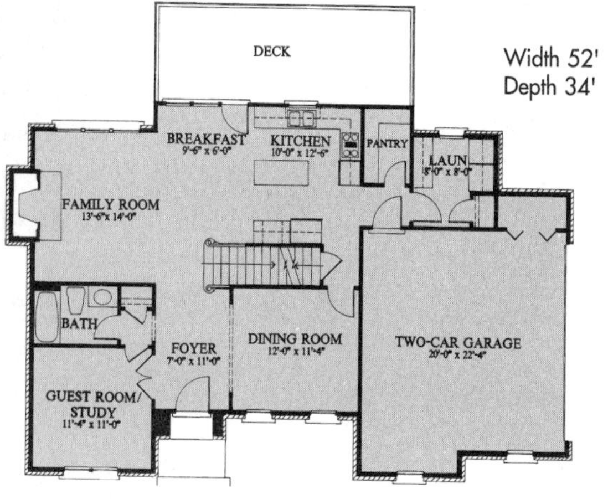
DECK
Width 52'
Depth 34'
BREAKFAST
9'-6" x 6'-0"
KITCHEN
10'-0" x 12'-6"
PANTRY
LAUN
8'-0" x 8'-0"
FAMILY ROOM
13'-6" x 14'-0"
BATH
FOYER
7'-0" x 11'-0"
DINING ROOM
12'-0" x 11'-4"
TWO-CAR GARAGE
20'-0" x 22'-4"
GUEST ROOM/
STUDY
11'-4" x 11'-0"

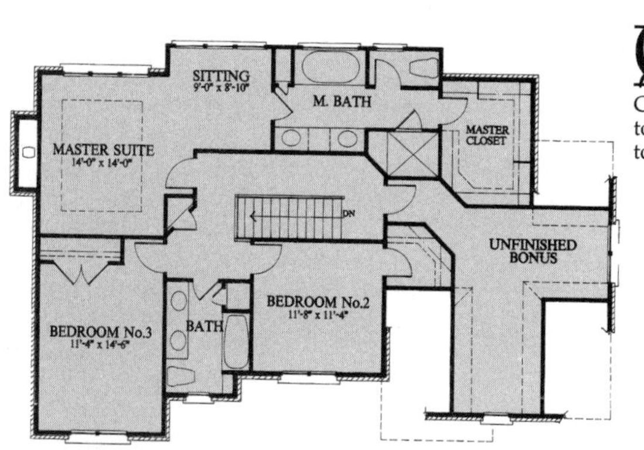
SITTING
9'-0" x 8'-10"
M. BATH
MASTER CLOSET
MASTER SUITE
14'-0" x 14'-0"
DN
UNFINISHED BONUS
BEDROOM No.2
11'-8" x 11'-4"
BATH
BEDROOM No.3
11'-4" x 14'-6"

QUOTE ONE®
Cost to build? See page 342 to order complete cost estimate to build this house in your area!

Design by
Design Traditions

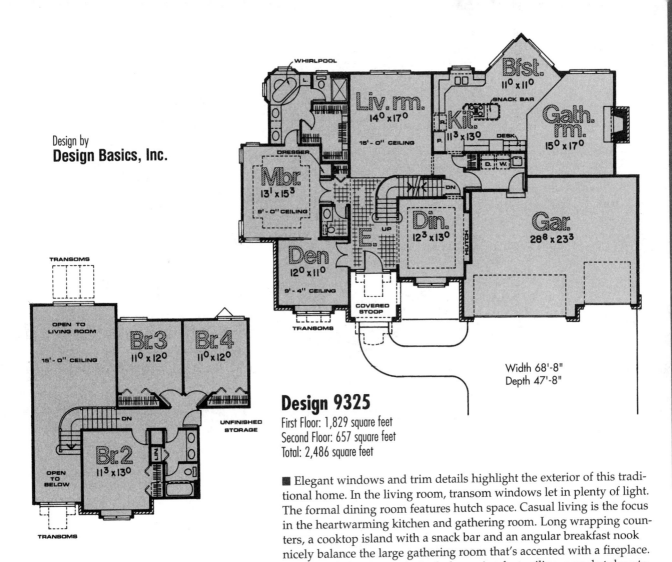

Design by
Design Basics, Inc.

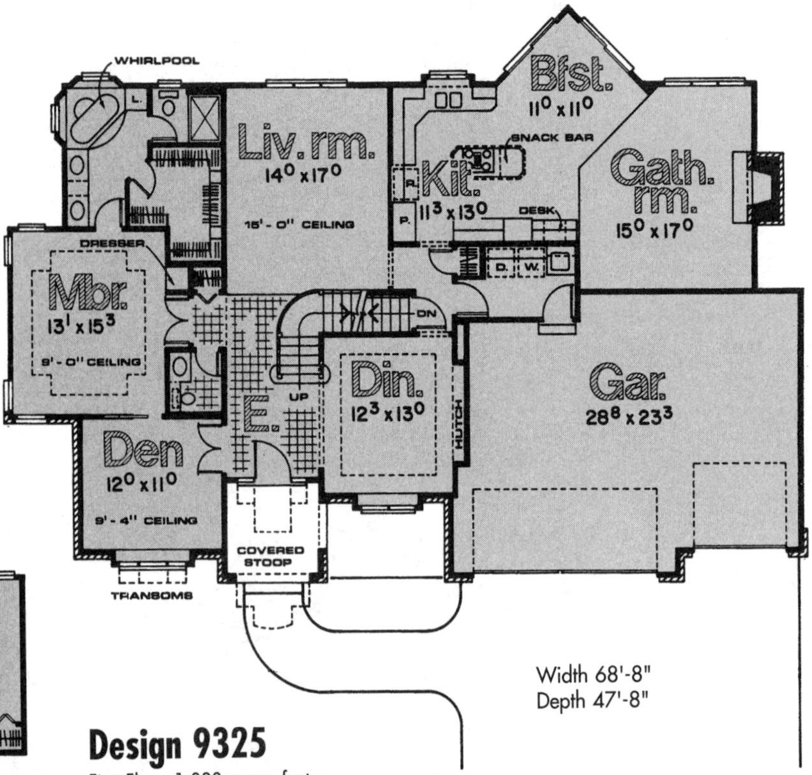

Mbr. 13¹ x 15³ 9'-0" CEILING
WHIRLPOOL
DRESSER
Liv. rm. 14⁰ x 17⁰ 15'-0" CEILING
Bfst. 11⁰ x 11⁰
SNACK BAR
Kit. 11³ x 13⁰
DESK
Gath. rm. 15⁰ x 17⁰
Den 12⁰ x 11⁰ 9'-4" CEILING
E.
Din. 12³ x 13⁰
HUTCH
Gar. 28⁸ x 23³
COVERED STOOP
TRANSOMS

TRANSOMS
OPEN TO LIVING ROOM 15'-0" CEILING
Br. 3 11⁰ x 12⁰
Br. 4 11⁰ x 12⁰
UNFINISHED STORAGE
Br. 2 11³ x 13⁰
OPEN TO BELOW
TRANSOMS

Width 68'-8"
Depth 47'-8"

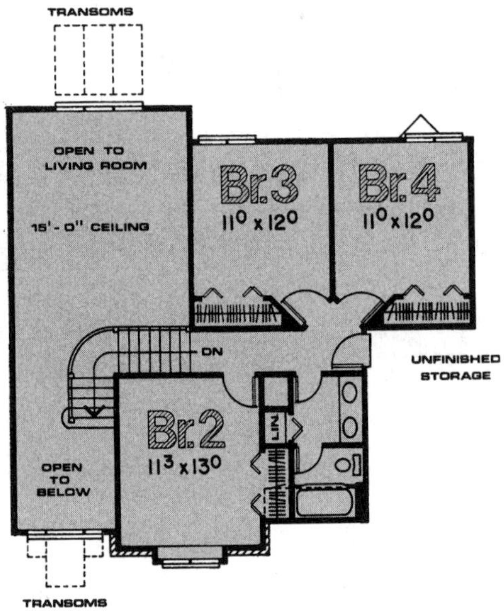

Design 9325

First Floor: 1,829 square feet
Second Floor: 657 square feet
Total: 2,486 square feet

■ Elegant windows and trim details highlight the exterior of this traditional home. In the living room, transom windows let in plenty of light. The formal dining room features hutch space. Casual living is the focus in the heartwarming kitchen and gathering room. Long wrapping counters, a cooktop island with a snack bar and an angular breakfast nook nicely balance the large gathering room that's accented with a fireplace. The secluded master suite includes a nine-foot ceiling, a pocket door to the den, a corner whirlpool and a huge walk-in closet. Three family bedrooms are on the second level.

G. MacDonald

Design 9849

First Floor: 780 square feet
Second Floor: 915 square feet
Total: 1,695 square feet

■ Columns, brickwork and uniquely shaped windows and shutters are reminiscent of the best homes in turn-of-the-century America. Inside, contemporary amenities are abundant. To the left of the foyer is the powder room. Opposite is a formal dining room with passage to the kitchen, which is open to the breakfast area and great room. This area is particularly well-suited to entertaining both formally and informally, with an open, airy design to the kitchen. The large fireplace is well placed and framed by glass and light. Opening from the great room are a two-car garage and a staircase to the second level. The master suite's double-door entrance, tray ceiling and fireplace are of special interest. The adjoining master bath and walk-in closet complement this area well. The laundry room is found on this level, convenient to any of the bedrooms. Two family bedrooms that share a full bath complete this level. This home is designed with a basement foundation.

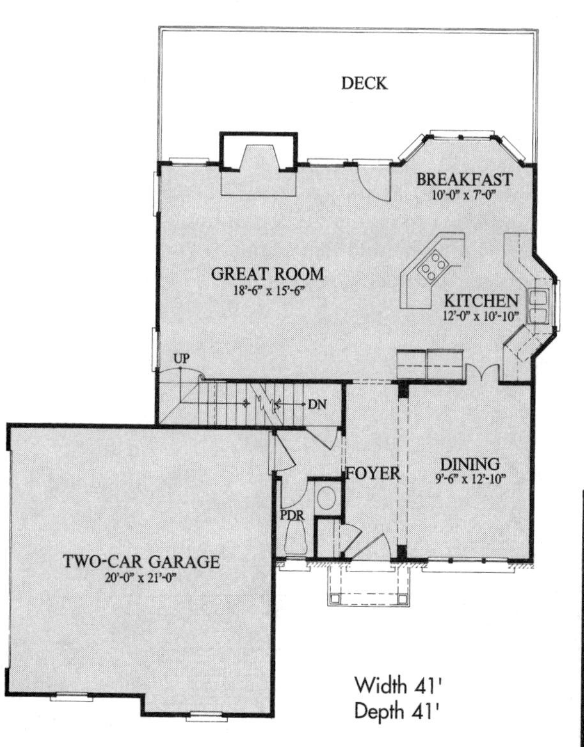
DECK
BREAKFAST
10'-0" x 7'-0"
GREAT ROOM
18'-6" x 15'-6"
KITCHEN
12'-0" x 10'-10"
UP
DN
FOYER
DINING
9'-6" x 12'-10"
PDR
TWO-CAR GARAGE
20'-0" x 21'-0"
Width 41'
Depth 41'

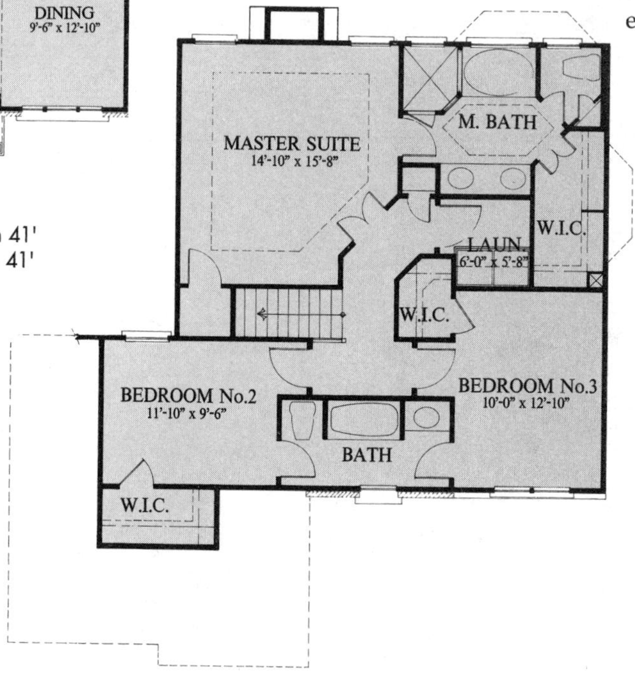

MASTER SUITE
14'-10" x 15'-8"
M. BATH
W.I.C.
LAUN.
6'-0" x 5'-8"
W.I.C.
BEDROOM No.2
11'-10" x 9'-6"
BEDROOM No.3
10'-0" x 12'-10"
BATH
W.I.C.

Design by
Design Traditions

Design 9807

Square footage: 2,785

■ The balance and symmetry of this European home have an inviting quality. An entry foyer allowing a grand view out of the back of the house leads directly to the great room. Just off the great room are a convenient and functional gourmet kitchen and a bright adjoining bay-windowed breakfast room. The master suite enjoys privacy in its position at the rear of the home. Three other bedrooms, one which might serve as a guest room or children's den and one that might work well as a study, round out the sleeping accommodations. This home is designed with a basement foundation.

2-CAR GARAGE 21'-3" x 26'-0"
LAUN.
BREAKFAST 11'-6" x 12'-0"
KITCHEN 14'-0" x 16'-6"
PAN.
DN
GREAT ROOM 16'-0" x 20'-6"
SITTING
M. BATH
MASTER SUITE 15'-6" x 23'-3"
MASTER CLOSET
BEDROOM No.3 12'-0" x 13'-6"
DINING ROOM 13'-0" x 13'-6"
FOYER
STUDY/ BEDROOM No.2 13'-0" x 13'-6"
GUEST ROOM/ CHILDRENS DEN 13'-6" x 16'-9"

Width 72'
Depth 73'

Design by
Design Traditions

QUOTE ONE®

Cost to build? See page 342 to order complete cost estimate to build this house in your area!

PORCH
BREAKFAST
10'-0" X 10'-0"
GREAT ROOM
16'-0" X 18'-0"
MASTER BEDROOM
15'-0" X 14'-0"
W.I.C.
MASTER BATH
POWDER
KITCHEN
14'-0" X 11'-4"
FOYER
5'-0" X 9'-0"
BEDROOM NO. 2
11'-2" X 11'-0"
DINING ROOM
10'-6" X 13'-0"
BEDROOM NO. 3
10'-6" X 10'-0"
BATH
LAUND
5'-2" X 10'-6"
DN.
TWO CAR GARAGE
20'-4" X 19'-4"

Width 60'
Depth 58'-6"

Design 9872

Square Footage: 1,815

Design by
Design Traditions

■ Inside, the foyer of this lovely European home opens into the great room with a vaulted ceiling and a dining room defined by columns. Kitchen tasks are made easy with this home's step-saving kitchen and breakfast bar. Nestled away at the opposite end of the home, the master suite combines perfect solitude with elegant luxury. Features include a double-door entry, tray ceiling, and niche details. Two family bedrooms share a private bath. This home is designed with a basement foundation.

QUOTE ONE®

Cost to build? See page 342 to order complete cost estimate to build this house in your area!

Copyright 1992 Stephen S. Fuller, Inc.

Copyright 1992 Stephen S. Fuller, Inc.

Design by
Design Traditions

QUOTE ONE®

Cost to build? See page 342 to order complete cost estimate to build this house in your area!

Design 9904

Square Footage: 2,090

■ This home's European styling will work well in a variety of environments. As for livability, this plan has it all. Begin with the front door which opens into the dining and great rooms—the latter complete with fireplace and doors that open onto the back porch. The kitchen combines with the breakfast nook to create ample space for meals. This plan incorporates four bedrooms; you may want to use one bedroom as an office and another as a study. The master bedroom houses a fabulous bath with twin walk-in closets and a spa tub. This home is designed with a basement foundation.

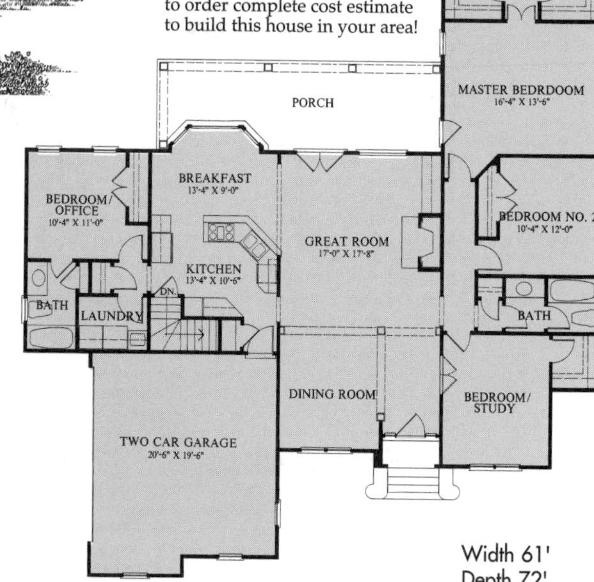
MASTER BATH
PORCH
MASTER BEDRDOOM
16'-4" X 13'-6"
BEDROOM/ OFFICE
10'-4" X 11'-0"
BREAKFAST
13'-4" X 9'-0"
GREAT ROOM
17'-0" X 17'-8"
BEDROOM NO. 2
10'-4" X 12'-0"
KITCHEN
13'-4" X 10'-6"
DN.
BATH
LAUNDRY
BATH
DINING ROOM
BEDROOM/ STUDY
TWO CAR GARAGE
20'-6" X 19'-6"

Width 61'
Depth 72'

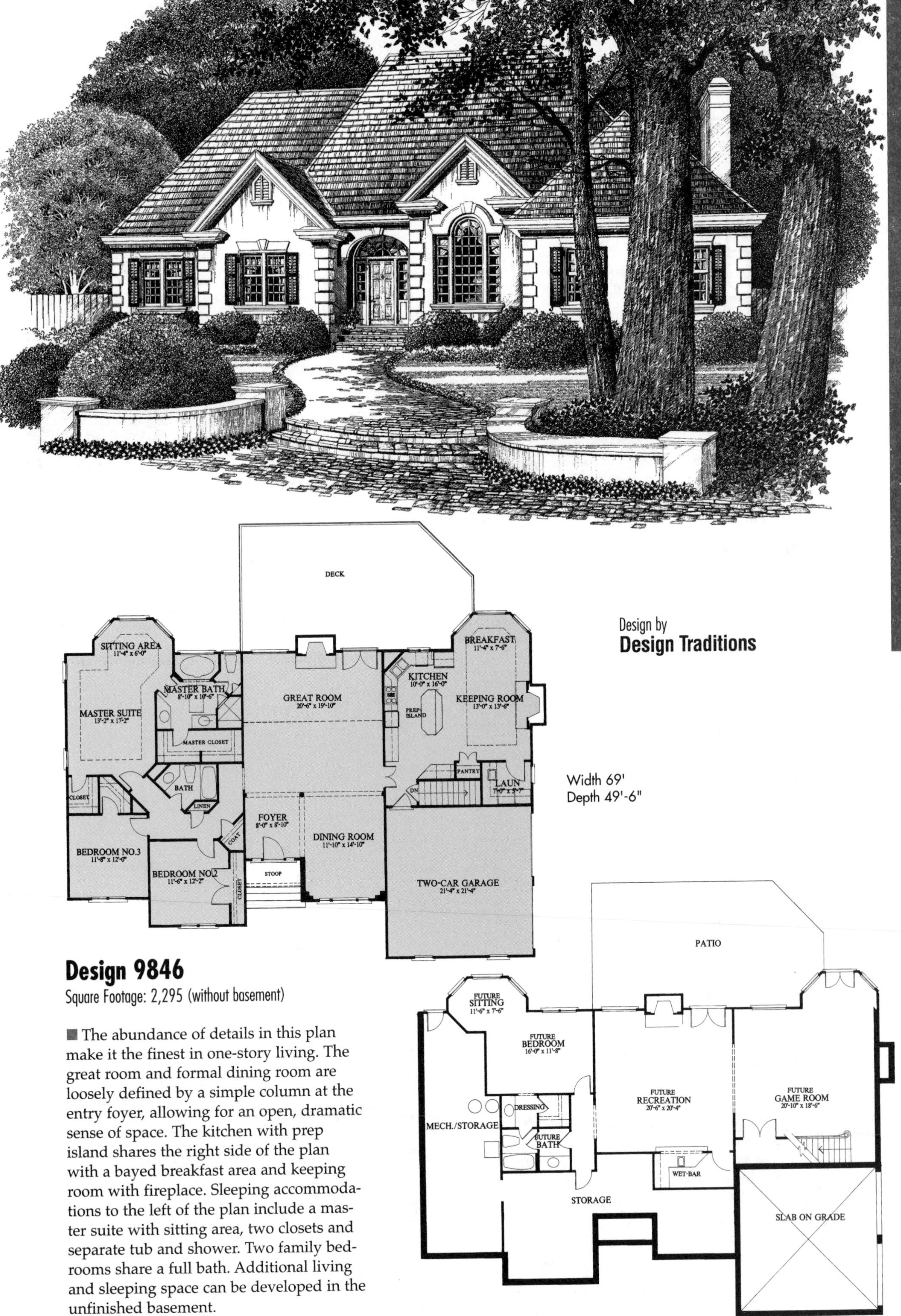
DECK
SITTING AREA
11'-4" x 6'-0"
MASTER BATH
8'-10" x 10'-6"
MASTER SUITE
13'-2" x 17'-2"
MASTER CLOSET
GREAT ROOM
20'-6" x 19'-10"
BREAKFAST
11'-4" x 7'-6"
KITCHEN
10'-0" x 16'-0"
PREP ISLAND
KEEPING ROOM
13'-0" x 13'-6"
PANTRY
LAUN
7'-0" x 5'-7"
DN
CLOSET
BATH
LINEN
COAT
FOYER
8'-0" x 8'-10"
DINING ROOM
11'-10" x 14'-10"
BEDROOM NO.3
11'-8" x 12'-0"
BEDROOM NO.2
11'-6" x 12'-2"
CLOSET
STOOP
TWO-CAR GARAGE
21'-4" x 21'-4"
PATIO
FUTURE SITTING
11'-6" x 7'-6"
FUTURE BEDROOM
16'-0" x 11'-8"
DRESSING
MECH./STORAGE
FUTURE BATH
FUTURE RECREATION
20'-6" x 20'-4"
WET-BAR
FUTURE GAME ROOM
20'-10" x 18'-6"
STORAGE
SLAB ON GRADE

Design by
Design Traditions

Width 69'
Depth 49'-6"

Design 9846

Square Footage: 2,295 (without basement)

■ The abundance of details in this plan make it the finest in one-story living. The great room and formal dining room are loosely defined by a simple column at the entry foyer, allowing for an open, dramatic sense of space. The kitchen with prep island shares the right side of the plan with a bayed breakfast area and keeping room with fireplace. Sleeping accommodations to the left of the plan include a master suite with sitting area, two closets and separate tub and shower. Two family bedrooms share a full bath. Additional living and sleeping space can be developed in the unfinished basement.

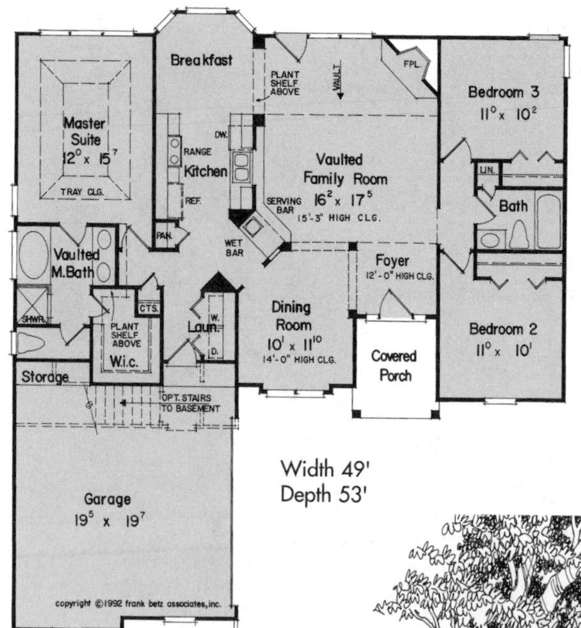

Breakfast
PLANT SHELF ABOVE
VAULT
FPL.
Bedroom 3
11⁰ x 10²
Master Suite
12⁰ x 15⁷
TRAY CLG.
DW.
RANGE
Kitchen
REF.
Vaulted Family Room
16² x 17⁵
15'-3" HIGH CLG.
SERVING BAR
LIN.
Bath
PAN.
WET BAR
Foyer
12'-0" HIGH CLG.
Vaulted M.Bath
CTS.
SHWR.
PLANT SHELF ABOVE
W.i.c.
Laun.
W.
D.
Dining Room
10¹ x 11¹⁰
14'-0" HIGH CLG.
Covered Porch
Bedroom 2
11⁰ x 10¹
Storage
OPT. STAIRS TO BASEMENT
Garage
19⁵ x 19⁷
copyright ©1992 frank betz associates, inc.
Width 49'
Depth 53'

Design P110

Square Footage: 1,429

■ This home's gracious exterior is indicative of the elegant, yet extremely livable, floor plan inside. Volume ceilings that crown the family living areas combine with an open floor plan to give the modest square footage a more spacious feel. The formal dining room is set off from the foyer and vaulted family room with stately columns. The spacious family room has a corner fireplace, rear-yard door and serving bar from the open galley kitchen. A bay-window breakfast nook flanks the kitchen on one end while a laundry center and wet-bar/serving pantry lead to the dining room on the other. The split-bedroom plan allows the amenity-rich master suite maximum privacy. A pocket door off the family room leads to the hall housing the two family bedrooms and a full bath. Please specify basement, crawlspace or slab foundation when ordering.

Design by
Frank Betz Associates, Inc.

Design P232

Square Footage: 1,544
Bonus: 284 square feet

■ A steep front gable and a delightful arch framing the entry porch give this stately European home a distinctive look. Open design describes the spacious family room and formal dining room—tall ceilings and decorative touches like a column and fireplace set them apart. The efficient kitchen has wraparound counters and a cozy breakfast nook. Two family bedrooms and a full bath are split from the master suite for privacy. The master suite has a vaulted master bath, tray ceiling and a large walk-in closet. Please specify basement or crawlspace foundation when ordering.

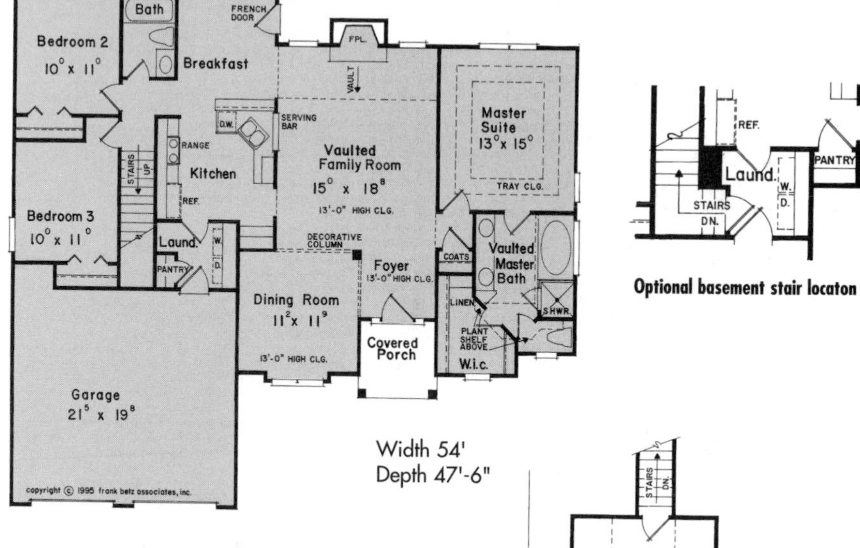

Bath
FRENCH DOOR
Bedroom 2
10⁰ x 11⁰
Breakfast
FPL.
VAULT
D.W.
SERVING BAR
RANGE
Kitchen
STAIRS UP
REF.
Master Suite
13⁰ x 15⁰
TRAY CLG.
Vaulted Family Room
15⁰ x 18⁸
13'-0" HIGH CLG.
Bedroom 3
10⁰ x 11⁰
Laund.
W.
D.
PANTRY
DECORATIVE COLUMN
Foyer
13'-0" HIGH CLG.
COATS
Vaulted Master Bath
LINEN
SHWR.
Dining Room
11² x 11⁹
13'-0" HIGH CLG.
Covered Porch
PLANT SHELF ABOVE
W.i.c.
Garage
21⁵ x 19⁸
copyright © 1995 frank betz associates, inc.
Width 54'
Depth 47'-6"
REF.
Laund.
PANTRY
STAIRS DN.
W.
D.
STAIRS DN.
Opt. Bonus Room
13⁵ x 19⁸

Optional basement stair locaton

Optional bonus room plan

Design by
Frank Betz Associates, Inc.

KEEPING ROOM
PORCH
MASTER BEDROOM
W.I.C.
BREAKFAST
DINING ROOM
GREAT ROOM
MASTER BATH
PANTRY
KITCHEN
LAUNDRY
PWDR.
FOYER
BEDROOM NO. 3
BEDROOM NO. 2/ STUDY
BATH
STOOP
TWO CAR GARAGE

Design 9831

Square Footage: 2,150

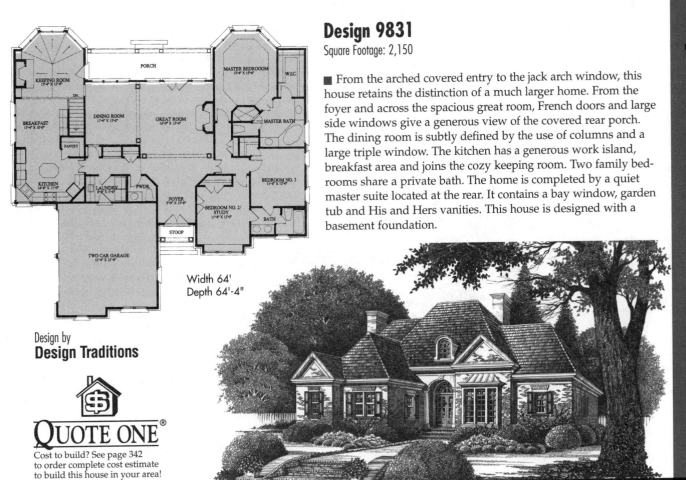

■ From the arched covered entry to the jack arch window, this house retains the distinction of a much larger home. From the foyer and across the spacious great room, French doors and large side windows give a generous view of the covered rear porch. The dining room is subtly defined by the use of columns and a large triple window. The kitchen has a generous work island, breakfast area and joins the cozy keeping room. Two family bedrooms share a private bath. The home is completed by a quiet master suite located at the rear. It contains a bay window, garden tub and His and Hers vanities. This house is designed with a basement foundation.

Width 64'
Depth 64'-4"

Design by
Design Traditions

QUOTE ONE®

Cost to build? See page 342 to order complete cost estimate to build this house in your area!

Design 9862

Square Footage: 2,170

■ This classic cottage features a stone and wooden exterior with an arch-detailed porch and box bay window. The family room is centrally located, just beyond the foyer. From the master suite hallway, double doors open to the den with a fireplace. The master suite features a lush bath and opens onto the rear porch. A short hallway from the sunroom and kitchen area leads to two bedrooms with large closets and shared full bath featuring double vanities. This home is designed with a basement foundation.

Design by
Design Traditions

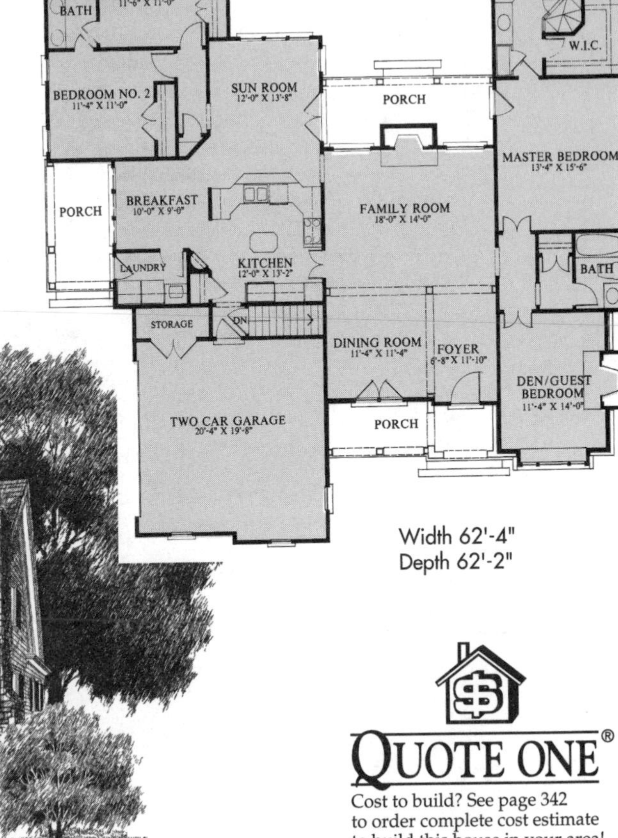

BATH
BEDROOM NO. 3
11'-6" X 11'-0"
BEDROOM NO. 2
11'-4" X 11'-0"
SUN ROOM
12'-0" X 13'-8"
PORCH
MASTER BATH
W.I.C.
MASTER BEDROOM
13'-4" X 15'-6"
PORCH
BREAKFAST
10'-0" X 9'-0"
FAMILY ROOM
18'-0" X 14'-0"
LAUNDRY
KITCHEN
12'-0" X 13'-2"
BATH
STORAGE
DN
DINING ROOM
11'-4" X 11'-4"
FOYER
6'-8" X 11'-10"
DEN/GUEST BEDROOM
11'-4" X 14'-0"
TWO CAR GARAGE
20'-4" X 19'-8"
PORCH

Width 62'-4"
Depth 62'-2"

QUOTE ONE®

Cost to build? See page 342 to order complete cost estimate to build this house in your area!

MASTER BATH
SITTING RM.
11'-6" X 10'-0"
DECK
KEEPING ROOM
15'-3" X 15'-3"
VLT. CLG.
MASTER SUITE
18'-0" X 16'-0"
W.I.C.
GREAT ROOM
15'-6" X 17'-3"
KITCHEN
14'-0" X 13'-3"
BREAKFAST
14'-0" X 13'-0"
DN.
BEDROOM NO. 3
12'-0" X 12'-0"
W.I.C.
W.I.C.
POWDER
LAUNDRY
FOYER
BATH
BEDROOM NO. 2
13'-3" X 11'-6"
DINING ROOM
13'-3" X 18'-6"
2-CAR GARAGE
21'-6" X 21'-6"
STOOP
VLT. CLG.

Width 71'
Depth 66'

Design 9855

Square Footage: 2,935

■ This spacious one-story easily accommodates a large family, providing all the luxuries and necessities for gracious living. For formal occasions, there is a grand dining room just off the entry foyer. It features a vaulted ceiling and is just across the hall from the gourmet kitchen. The great room offers a beautiful ceiling treatment and access to the rear deck. For more casual times, the breakfast nook and adjoining keeping room with a fireplace fill the bill. The master suite is spacious and filled with amenities that include sitting room, a walk-in closet and access to the rear deck. Two family bedrooms share a full bath. Each of these bedrooms has its own lavatory. This home is designed with a basement foundation.

Design by
Design Traditions

Design by
Larry E. Belk Designs

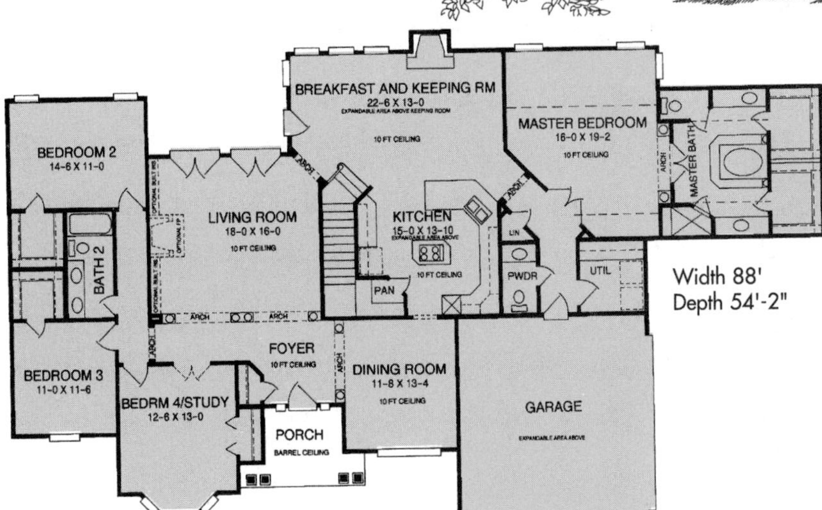
BREAKFAST AND KEEPING RM
22-6 X 13-0
10 FT CEILING
MASTER BEDROOM
16-0 X 19-2
10 FT CEILING
MASTER BATH
BEDROOM 2
14-6 X 11-0
LIVING ROOM
18-0 X 16-0
10 FT CEILING
KITCHEN
15-0 X 13-10
10 FT CEILING
PAN
LIN
PWDR
UTIL
BATH 2
FOYER
10 FT CEILING
DINING ROOM
11-8 X 13-4
10 FT CEILING
BEDROOM 3
11-0 X 11-6
BEDRM 4/STUDY
12-6 X 13-0
PORCH
BARREL CEILING
GARAGE

Width 88'
Depth 54'-2"

Design 8076

Square Footage: 2,733

■ The heart of this beautiful home is its breakfast and keeping room which are complemented by the full kitchen. They are flanked by a large living room with double French doors and the master bedroom with French doors into the elegant master bath. Three other bedrooms, or two bedrooms and a study, are positioned at the opposite end of the house for privacy. Bedrooms 2 and 3 have their own walk-in closets. Please specify slab or crawlspace foundation when ordering.

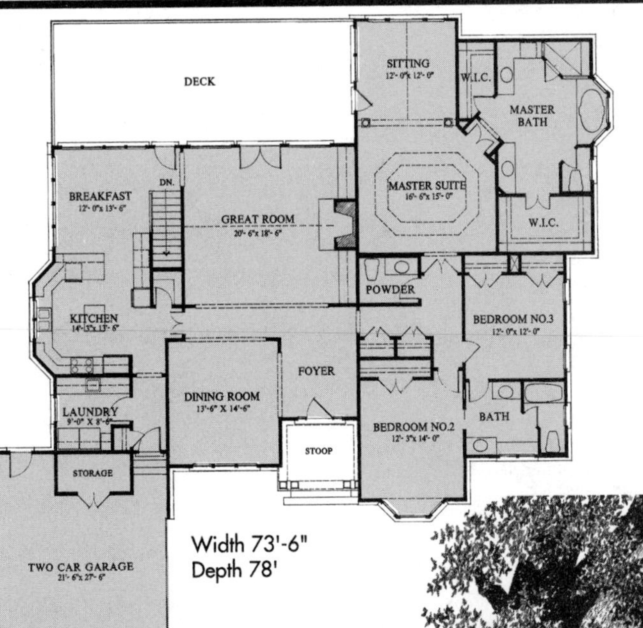
DECK
SITTING
W.I.C.
MASTER BATH
BREAKFAST
GREAT ROOM
MASTER SUITE
W.I.C.
POWDER
KITCHEN
BEDROOM NO.3
FOYER
DINING ROOM
LAUNDRY
BATH
STOOP
BEDROOM NO.2
STORAGE
TWO CAR GARAGE

Width 73'-6"
Depth 78'

Design 9854

Square Footage: 2,770

■ This foyer of this English cottage opens to both the dining room with vaulted ceiling and great room with fireplace and built-in cabinetry. Surrounded by windows, the breakfast room opens to a gourmet kitchen. Two bedrooms with large closets are joined by a full bath with individual vanities and a window seat. Through double doors at the end of a short hall, the master suite awaits with tray ceiling and adjoining sunlit sitting room. The master bath has His and Hers closets, separate vanities, an individual shower, a water closet and a garden tub with bay window.

Design by
Design Traditions

Design 9840

Square Footage: 1,684
(without basement)

■ Charmingly compact, this one-story home is as beautiful as it is practical. The impressive arch over the double front door is repeated with an arched window in the formal dining room. This room opens to a spacious great room with fireplace and is nearby the kitchen and bayed breakfast area. Split sleeping arrangements put the master suite with His and Hers walk-in closets at the right of the plan and two family bedrooms at the left. Additional space in the basement can later be developed as the family grows. This plan is designed with a basement foundation.

QUOTE ONE®
Cost to build? See page 342
to order complete cost estimate
to build this house in your area!
WORKSHOP/
STORAGE
FUTURE
FAMILY ROOM
14'-0" X 17'-6"
FUTURE
GAME ROOM
11'-4" X 18'-6"
FUTURE
GUEST BEDROOM
11'-10" X 14'-6"
MECHANICAL
STOOP
ABOVE
UP
FUTURE
BATH
STORAGE
SLAB ON GRADE
DECK
BREAKFAST
11'-4" X 8'-6"
BEDROOM NO. 3
11'-6" X 11'-0"
GREAT ROOM
14'-0" X 17'-6"
KITCHEN
11'-4" X 10'-0"
MASTER
BEDROOM
12'-4" X 15'-6"
BATH
HIS
FOYER
6'-6" X 5'-0"
DN
PWDR.
MASTER
BATH
BEDROOM NO. 2
11'-0" X 12'-2"
DINING ROOM
11'-4" X 10'-6"
STOOP
LAUNDRY
HERS
TWO-CAR GARAGE
20'-4" X 19'-4"

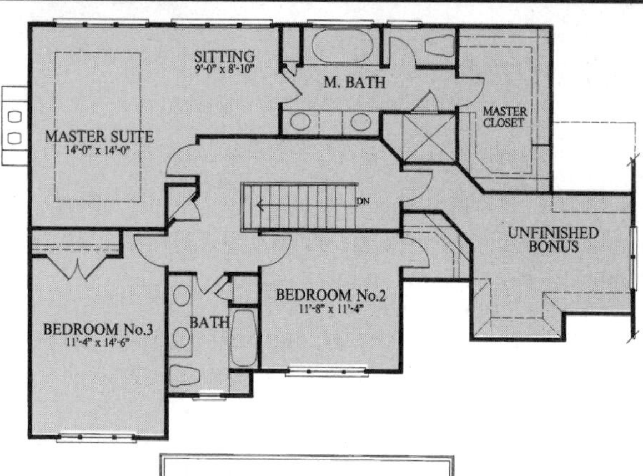

Width 55'-6"
Depth 57'-6"

Design by
Design Traditions

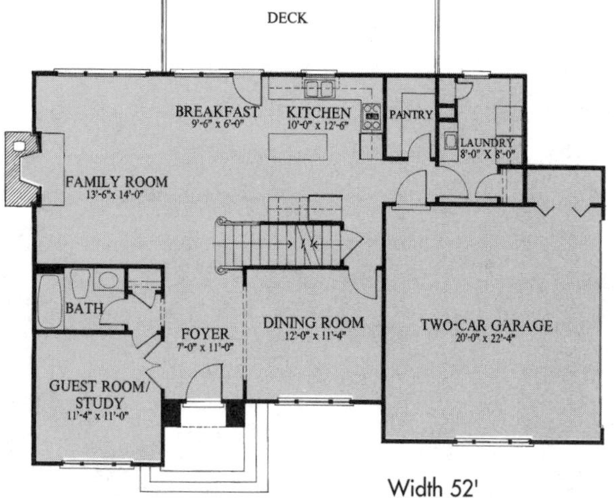
SITTING
9'-0" x 8'-10"
M. BATH
MASTER
CLOSET
MASTER SUITE
14'-0" x 14'-0"
DN
UNFINISHED
BONUS
BEDROOM No.3
11'-4" x 14'-6"
BATH
BEDROOM No.2
11'-8" x 11'-4"
DECK
BREAKFAST
9'-6" x 6'-0"
KITCHEN
10'-0" x 12'-6"
PANTRY
LAUNDRY
8'-0" X 8'-0"
FAMILY ROOM
13'-6"x 14'-0"
BATH
FOYER
7'-0" x 11'-0"
DINING ROOM
12'-0" x 11'-4"
TWO-CAR GARAGE
20'-0" x 22'-4"
GUEST ROOM/
STUDY
11'-4" x 11'-0"

Width 52'
Depth 34'

Design 9900

First Floor: 1,103 square feet
Second Floor: 1,103 square feet
Total: 2,206 square feet
Bonus Room: 212 square feet

Design by
Design Traditions

■ A stucco exterior gives European appeal to this family home. An expansive family room provides space for entertaining. The formal dining room is just off the foyer. Upstairs, the master suite includes a sitting area and enormous bath with dual vanity, whirlpool tub, separate shower and a walk-in closet. Two family bedrooms share a full bath with dual vanity. The bonus room makes a great home office. This home is designed with a basement foundation.

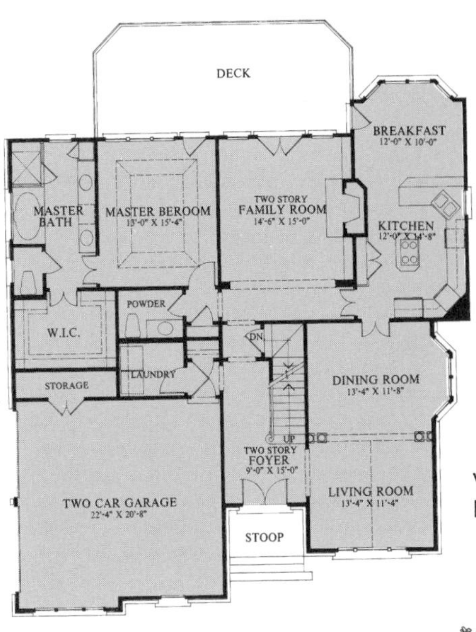
DECK
BREAKFAST
12'-0" X 10'-0"
MASTER BATH
MASTER BEDROOM
13'-0" X 15'-4"
TWO STORY FAMILY ROOM
14'-6" X 15'-0"
KITCHEN
POWDER
W.I.C.
LAUNDRY
DN.
STORAGE
DINING ROOM
13'-4" X 11'-8"
UP
TWO STORY FOYER
9'-0" X 15'-0"
LIVING ROOM
13'-4" X 11'-4"
TWO CAR GARAGE
22'-4" X 20'-8"
STOOP

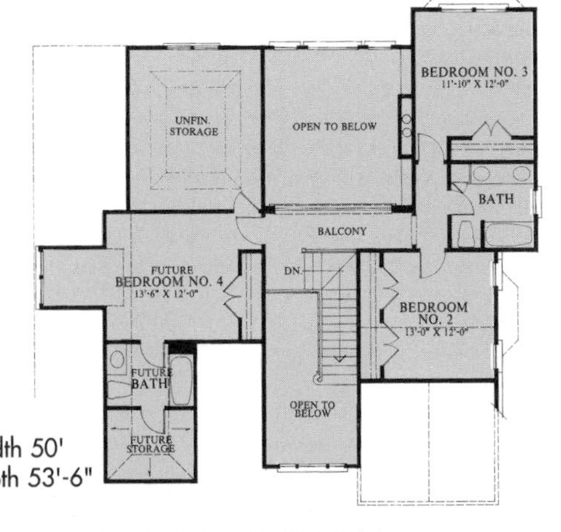
UNFIN. STORAGE
OPEN TO BELOW
BEDROOM NO. 3
11'-10" X 12'-0"
BATH
BALCONY
FUTURE BEDROOM NO. 4
13'-6" X 12'-0"
DN.
BEDROOM NO. 2
13'-0" X 12'-0"
FUTURE BATH
OPEN TO BELOW
FUTURE STORAGE

Width 50'
Depth 53'-6"

Design 9907

First Floor: 1,720 square feet
Second Floor: 545 square feet
Total: 2,265 square feet

Design by
Design Traditions

■ This French Country Cottage is a charming example of European architecture. A two-story foyer opens to a two-story family room with fireplace. To the right, the formal living and dining rooms are separated by columns. The island kitchen is adjoined by a breakfast room with a bay window. A large master bedroom is located on the first floor, while the second floor provides two bedrooms and a full bath, as well as an optional fourth bedroom with an attached bath. This home is designed with a basement foundation.

Design 9916

First Floor: 1,165 square feet
Second Floor: 1,050 square feet
Total: 2,215 square feet

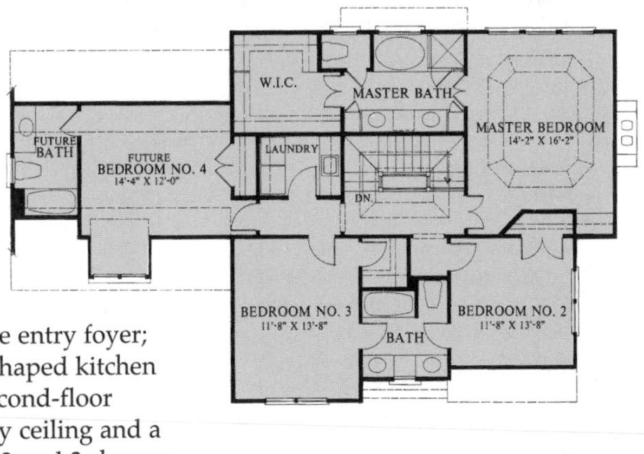
W.I.C.
MASTER BATH
MASTER BEDROOM
14'-2" X 16'-2"
FUTURE BATH
FUTURE BEDROOM NO. 4
14'-4" X 12'-0"
LAUNDRY
DN.
BEDROOM NO. 3
11'-8" X 13'-8"
BATH
BEDROOM NO. 2
11'-8" X 13'-8"

Design by
Design Traditions

■ This beautiful European-styled stucco home puts luxury features into only 2,215 square feet. The main living areas are found on the first floor: formal living and dining rooms flanking the entry foyer; family room with a fireplace; and an L-shaped kitchen with an attached breakfast room. The second-floor master bedroom is a real treat with a tray ceiling and a thoughtfully appointed bath. Bedrooms 2 and 3 share a full bath with a double-bowl vanity. This home is designed with a basement foundation.

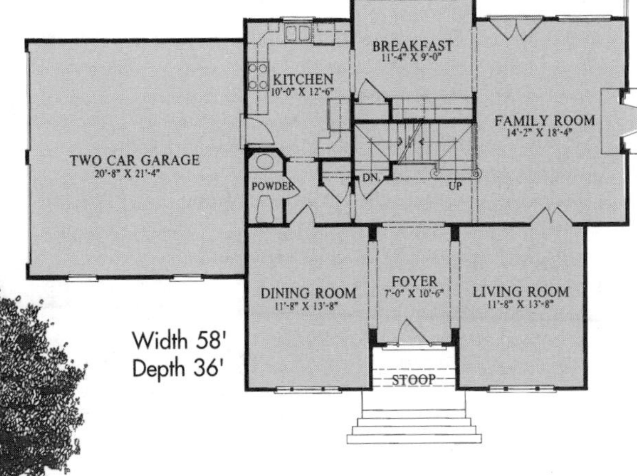
DECK
BREAKFAST
11'-4" X 9'-0"
KITCHEN
10'-0" X 12'-6"
FAMILY ROOM
14'-2" X 18'-4"
TWO CAR GARAGE
20'-8" X 21'-4"
POWDER
DN.
UP
DINING ROOM
11'-8" X 13'-8"
FOYER
7'-0" X 10'-6"
LIVING ROOM
11'-8" X 13'-8"
STOOP

Width 58'
Depth 36'

Design 9893

First Floor: 1,660 square feet
Second Floor: 665 square feet
Total: 2,325 square feet

■ This European design is filled with space for formal and informal occasions. Informal areas include an open kitchen, breakfast room and family room with fireplace. Formal rooms surround the foyer, with the living room on the left and dining room on the right. The master suite is conveniently placed on the first floor, with a gorgeous master bath and a walk-in closet. Each of the family bedrooms upstairs also features a sizable walk-in closet and access to a full bath. Additional storage space is found in the hallway. A fourth bedroom, not included in the square footage, is optional. This home is designed with a basement foundation.

Design by
Design Traditions

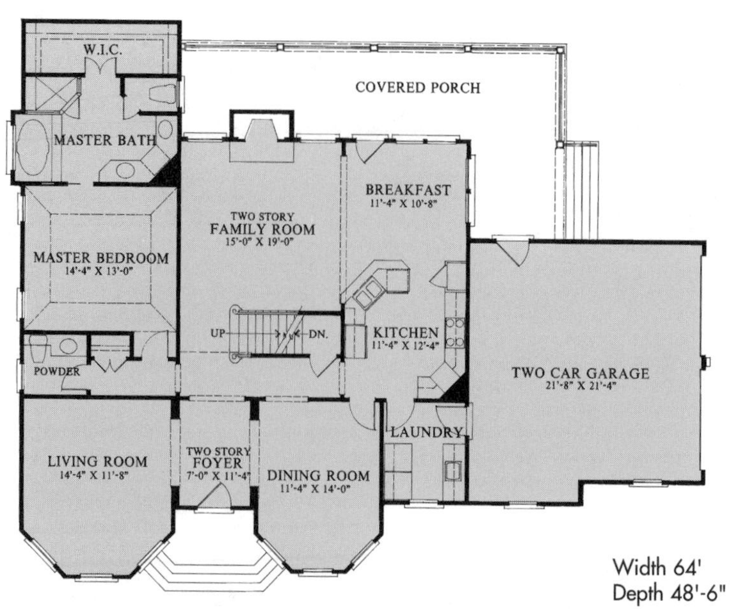
W.I.C.
COVERED PORCH
MASTER BATH
BREAKFAST
11'-4" X 10'-8"
TWO STORY
FAMILY ROOM
15'-0" X 19'-0"
MASTER BEDROOM
14'-4" X 13'-0"
UP
DN.
KITCHEN
11'-4" X 12'-4"
TWO CAR GARAGE
21'-8" X 21'-4"
POWDER
LAUNDRY
LIVING ROOM
14'-4" X 11'-8"
TWO STORY
FOYER
7'-0" X 11'-4"
DINING ROOM
11'-4" X 14'-0"

Width 64'
Depth 48'-6"

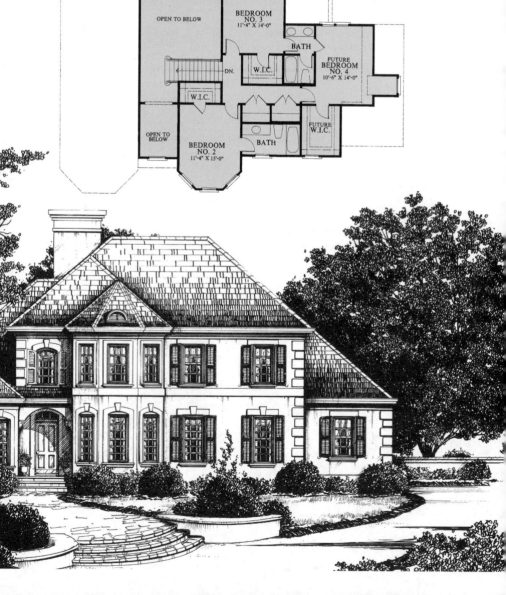

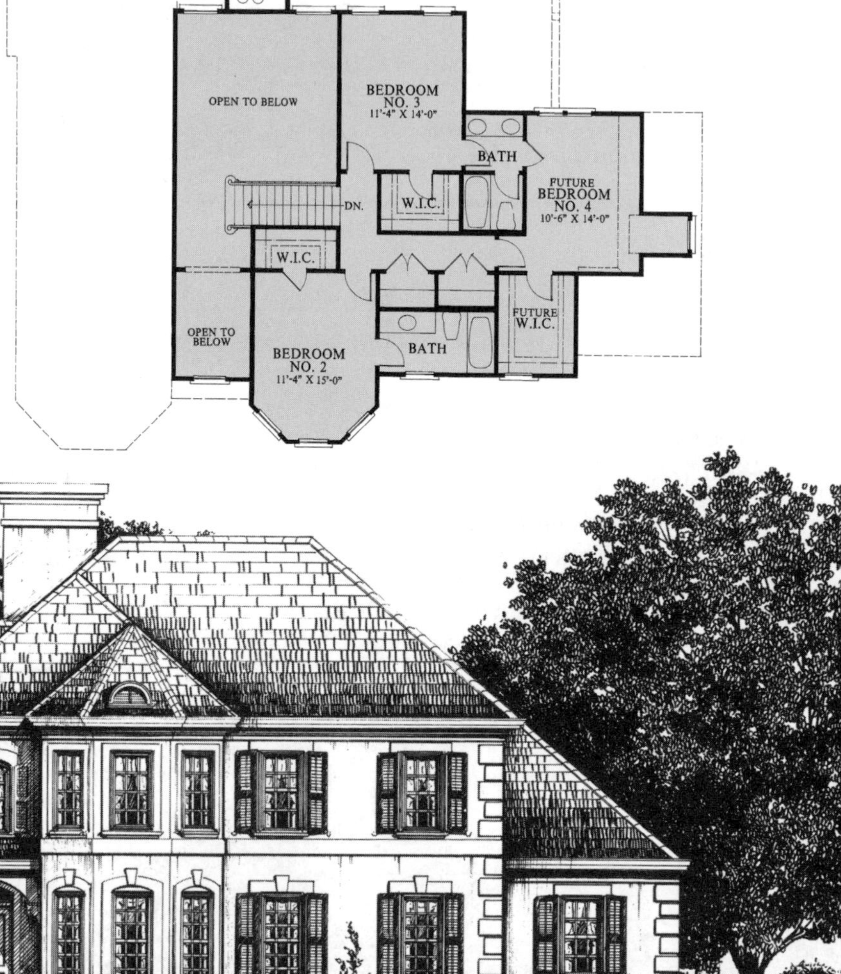
OPEN TO BELOW
BEDROOM
NO. 3
11'-4" X 14'-0"
BATH
FUTURE
BEDROOM
NO. 4
10'-6" X 14'-0"
DN.
W.I.C.
W.I.C.
FUTURE
W.I.C.
OPEN TO
BELOW
BEDROOM
NO. 2
11'-4" X 15'-0"
BATH

DECK
TWO STORY GREAT ROOM 14'-0" X 18'-0"
BREAKFAST 10'-0" X 10'-0"
KITCHEN 12'-6" X 11'-6"
MEDIA ROOM 12'-0" X 15'-6"
UP
DN
LAUNDRY
POWDER
DINING ROOM 12'-0" X 11'-6"
UP
TWO STORY FOYER 10'-6" X 10'-8"
LIVING ROOM 13'-4" X 10'-6"
TWO CAR GARAGE 21'-10" X 22'-0"
STOOP

Design 9864

First Floor: 1,395 square feet
Second Floor: 1,210 square feet
Total: 2,605 square feet

■ The well-balanced use of stucco and stone combined with box-bay window treatments and a covered entry make this English country home especially inviting. The two-story foyer opens on the right to the attractive living and dining rooms with large windows. The step-saving kitchen and breakfast areas flow easily into the two-story great room and a media room with a see-through fireplace. The second floor offers a pleasing combination of open design and privacy. The master bedroom has a modified tray ceiling and is complete with a sitting area. The compartmented master bath has a double vanity, separate shower and a large walk-in closet. Double vanities are also found in the full bath off the hall. Bedrooms 2 and 3 are ample in size and feature walk-in closets. This home is designed with a basement foundation.

Design by
Design Traditions

QUOTE ONE®
Cost to build? See page 342 to order complete cost estimate to build this house in your area!

Width 47'
Depth 49'-6"

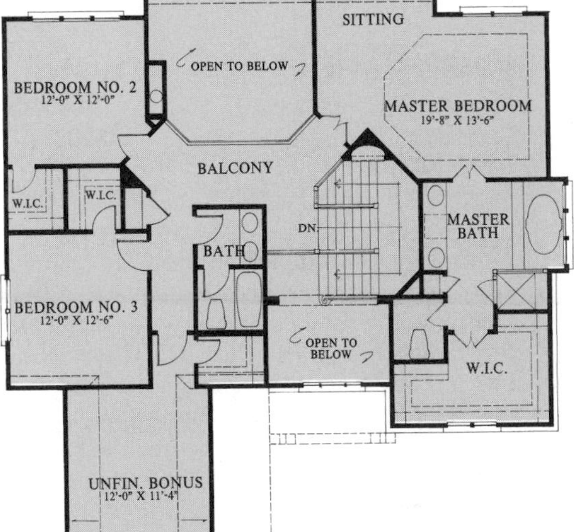
SITTING
OPEN TO BELOW
BEDROOM NO. 2 12'-0" X 12'-0"
MASTER BEDROOM 19'-8" X 13'-6"
BALCONY
W.I.C.
W.I.C.
DN
MASTER BATH
BATH
BEDROOM NO. 3 12'-0" X 12'-6"
OPEN TO BELOW
W.I.C.
UNFIN. BONUS 12'-0" X 11'-4"

BEDRM 2
13-4 X 11-0
OPEN TO LIVING ROOM BELOW
BEDRM 5
13-6 X 15-0
ATTIC STORAGE
BATH 2
BALCONY
BATH 3
BEDRM 3
13-6 X 11-8
OPEN TO FOYER BELOW
BEDRM 4
11-4 X 12-8
EXPANDABLE AREA

Design 8045

First Floor: 1,844 square feet
Second Floor: 1,103 square feet
Total: 2,947 square feet

Design by
Larry E. Belk Designs

■ A stucco finish and front porch sporting a metal roof dress up this home designed for the growing family. The spacious, efficient kitchen paired with the breakfast room and the family room provide a perfect place for family gatherings. A two-story living room and a dining room with a ten-foot ceiling are perfect for more formal entertaining. The master bedroom is located downstairs with a luxuriously appointed master bath. The second floor has three bedrooms (Design 8044) or four bedrooms (Design 8045) and full bath. Please specify crawlspace or slab foundation when ordering.

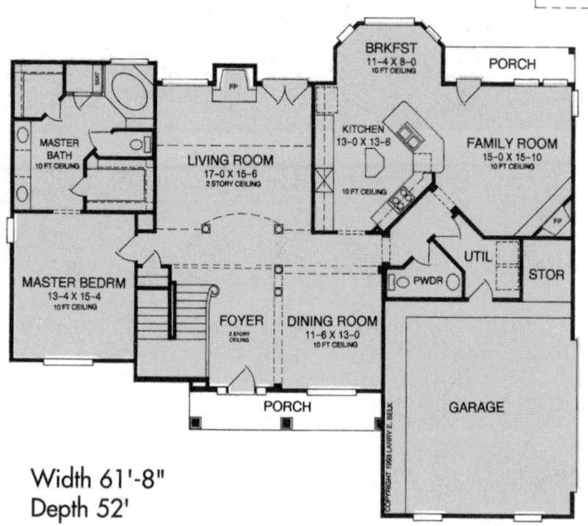

BRKFST
11-4 X 8-0
10 FT CEILING
PORCH
MASTER BATH
10 FT CEILING
LIVING ROOM
17-0 X 15-6
2 STORY CEILING
KITCHEN
13-0 X 13-6
10 FT CEILING
FAMILY ROOM
15-0 X 15-10
10 FT CEILING
UTIL
STOR
PWDR
MASTER BEDRM
13-4 X 15-4
10 FT CEILING
FOYER
2 STORY CEILING
DINING ROOM
11-6 X 13-0
10 FT CEILING
PORCH
GARAGE

Width 61'-8"
Depth 52'

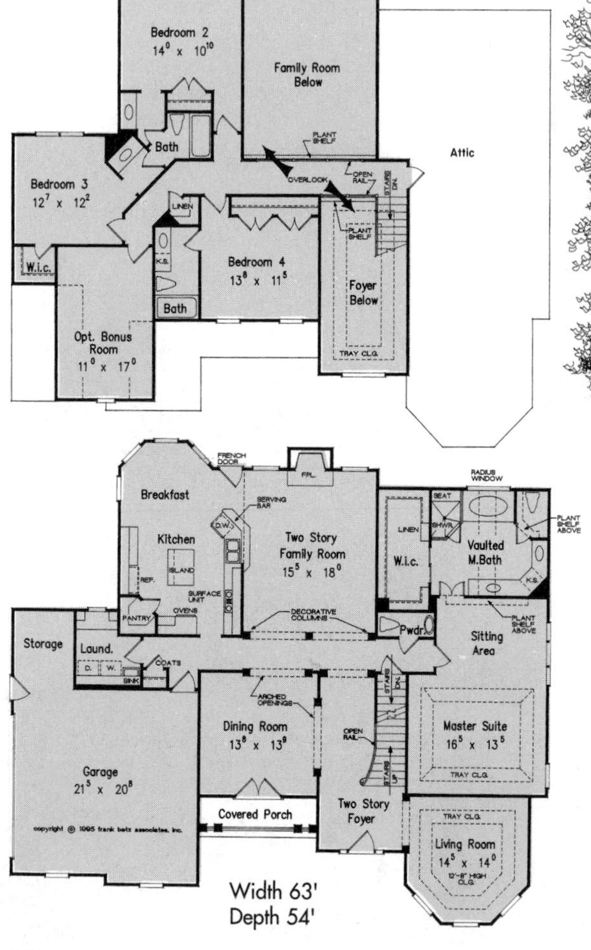

RADIUS WDW.
Bedroom 2
14^{0} x 10^{10}
Family Room Below
PLANT SHELF
Attic
Bath
Bedroom 3
12^{7} x 12^{2}
OVERLOOK
OPEN RAIL
STAIRS DN
LINEN
W.i.c.
Bedroom 4
13^{8} x 11^{5}
Foyer Below
Bath
Opt. Bonus Room
11^{0} x 17^{0}
TRAY CLG.
FRENCH DOOR
FPL.
RADIUS WINDOW
Breakfast
SERVING BAR
Kitchen
Two Story Family Room
15^{5} x 18^{0}
LINEN
SEAT
SHWR.
W.i.c.
Vaulted M.Bath
PLANT SHELF ABOVE
PANTRY
OVENS
DECORATIVE COLUMNS
Pwdr.
Storage
Laund.
COATS
Sitting Area
ARCHED OPENINGS
Dining Room
13^{8} x 13^{8}
OPEN RAIL
Master Suite
16^{5} x 13^{5}
TRAY CLG.
Garage
21^{3} x 20^{8}
Covered Porch
Two Story Foyer
TRAY CLG.
Living Room
14^{5} x 14^{0}
12'-8" HIGH CLG.

Width 63'
Depth 54'

Design P118

First Floor: 2,044 square feet
Second Floor: 896 square feet
Total: 2,940 square feet
Bonus Room: 197 square feet

Design by
Frank Betz Associates, Inc.

■ A gracious front porch off the formal dining room and a two-story entry set the tone for this elegant home. A front living room is set to the front of the plan, thoughtfully separated from casual family areas that radiate from the kitchen. The two-story family room is framed by a balcony hall and accented with a fireplace and serving bar. The first-floor master suite features a sitting area, lush bath and a walk-in closet. Upstairs, two family bedrooms share a private bath while a third enjoys a private bath. Please specify basement or crawlspace foundation when ordering.

Design 7803

First Floor: 1,475 square feet
Second Floor: 1,460 square feet
Total: 2,935 square feet

■ French entry doors open to a formal dining room on the left with excellent frontal views, and a formal living room on the right that leads to a quiet corner media room. The great room is a full two stories and has excellent views to the rear yard, thanks to an expanse of windows. A large island kitchen with a bayed breakfast nook completes the first floor of this plan. Upstairs, two family bedrooms share a full bath, while a third bedroom enjoys a private bath. The master suite features a bayed sitting area and an exquisite master bath with a wonderful vanity area, walk-in closet and a spa-style tub. This home is designed with a basement foundation.

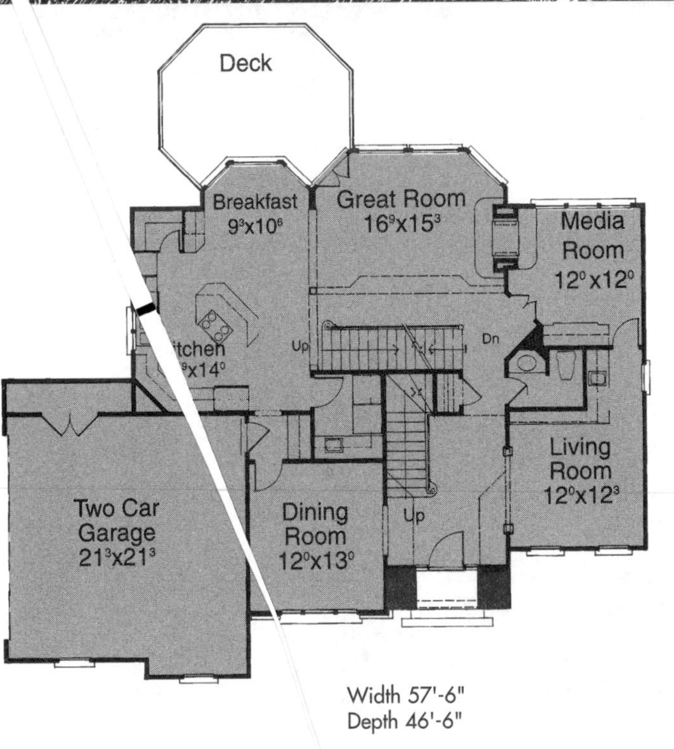
Deck
Breakfast
$9^{3}x10^{6}$
Great Room
$16^{9}x15^{3}$
Media Room
$12^{0}x12^{0}$
itchen
$x14^{0}$
Up
Dn
Living Room
$12^{0}x12^{3}$
Two Car Garage
$21^{3}x21^{3}$
Dining Room
$12^{0}x13^{0}$
Up
Width 57'-6"
Depth 46'-6"

Design by
Design Traditions

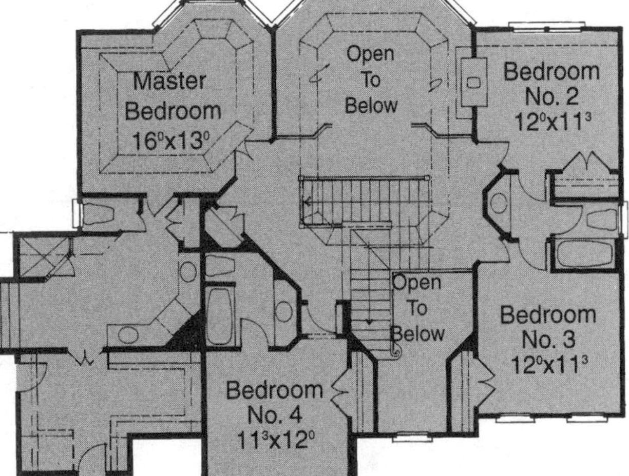
Master Bedroom
$16^{0}x13^{0}$
Open To Below
Bedroom No. 2
$12^{0}x11^{3}$
Open To Below
Bedroom No. 3
$12^{0}x11^{3}$
Bedroom No. 4
$11^{3}x12^{0}$

Design 8023

First Floor: 2,109 square feet
Second Floor: 1,060 square feet
Total: 3,169 square feet

■ Old-world charm blends a warm, inviting exterior with a traditional, efficient floor plan. From the foyer, note the curved wall that rises with the staircase. The kitchen is a delight with its large cooktop island, walk-in pantry and a sunlit sink with a corner grouping of windows. The pampering master suite offers access through French doors to a covered patio and includes a relaxing master bath with His and Hers walk-in closets, a corner whirlpool tub surrounded by windows and dual vanities. Bedroom 4 may be used as a study or would be ideal used as an office. Upstairs, a curved balcony overlooks the two-story living room. Bedroom 2 features a full bath, a walk-in closet and access to an upper deck. Bedroom 3 has access to its own full bath. A game room with french doors opening to an upper deck completes the second floor.

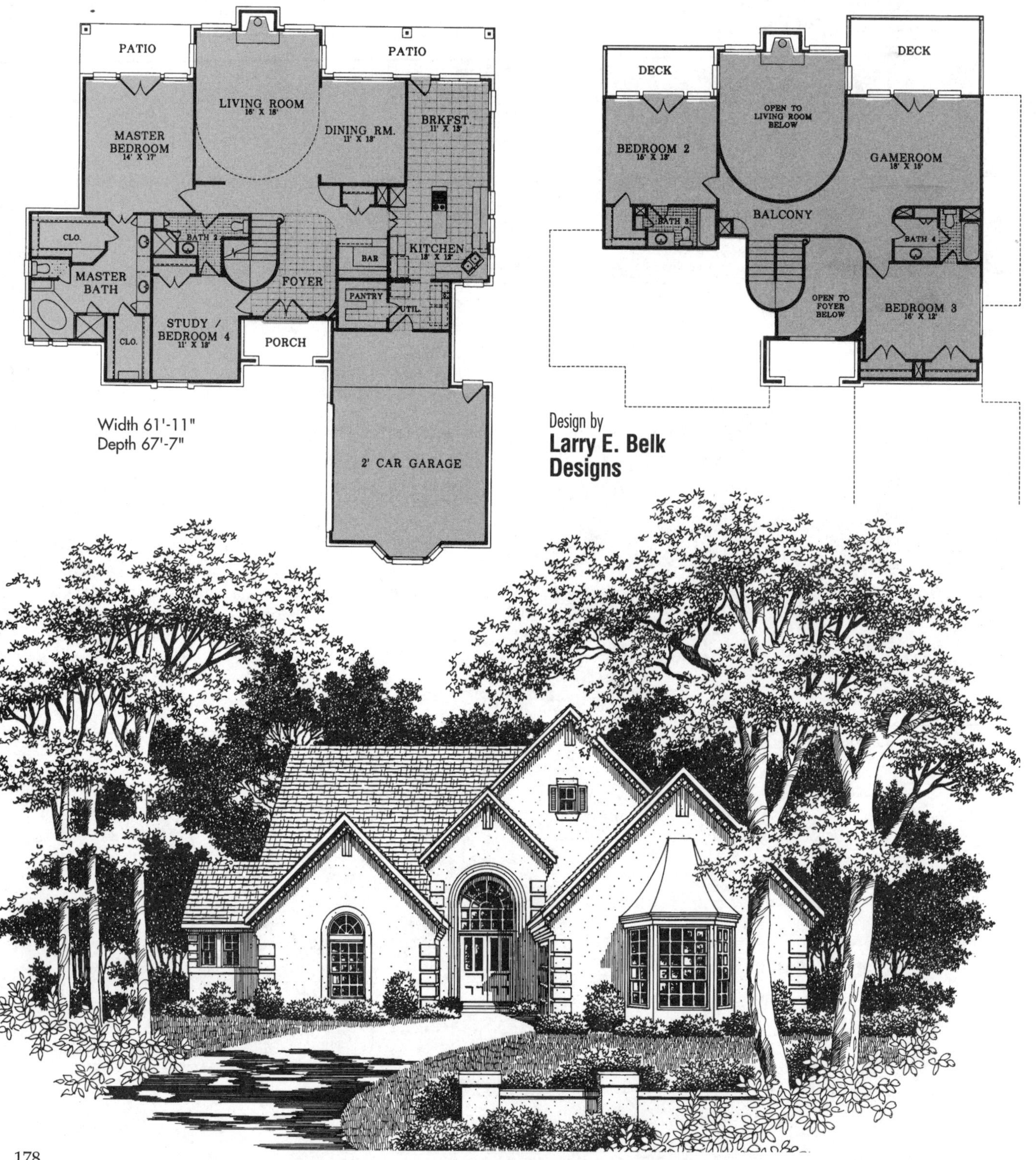
PATIO
PATIO
LIVING ROOM
MASTER BEDROOM
DINING RM.
BRKFST.
CLO.
BATH 2
KITCHEN
BAR
MASTER BATH
FOYER
PANTRY
UTIL.
STUDY / BEDROOM 4
CLO.
PORCH
2' CAR GARAGE
DECK
DECK
OPEN TO LIVING ROOM BELOW
BEDROOM 2
GAMEROOM
BATH 3
BALCONY
BATH 4
OPEN TO FOYER BELOW
BEDROOM 3

Width 61'-11"
Depth 67'-7"

Design by
Larry E. Belk Designs

Width 73'-6"
Depth 49'
DECK
LAUNDRY
BREAKFAST
KITCHEN
GREAT ROOM
TWO CAR GARAGE
PORTE'-COCHERE
FOYER
DINING ROOM
LIVING ROOM
MASTER BATH
MASTER BEDROOM
W.I.C.
BATH
GUEST BEDROOM
DEN
OPEN TO BELOW
BEDROOM NO. 2
BEDROOM NO. 3
BATH

QUOTE ONE®

Cost to build? See page 342 to order complete cost estimate to build this house in your area!

Design 9814

First Floor: 1,370 square feet
Second Floor: 1,673 square feet
Total: 3,043 square feet

Design by
Design Traditions

■ This English Georgian home features a dramatic brick exterior. The series of windows and jack-arch detailing are second only to the drama created by the porte cochere. Enter into the two-story foyer where the unusually shaped staircase and balcony overlook create a tremendous first impression. Separated only by a classical colonnade detail, the living and dining rooms are perfect for entertaining. Upstairs is a guest room, a children's den area, two family bedrooms and a master suite. This home is designed with a basement foundation.

Design 9825

First Floor: 2,129 square feet
Second Floor: 895 square feet
Total: 3,024 square feet

Design by
Design Traditions

■ Reminiscent of the country estates in Europe, this stucco home makes a grand statement. The foyer offers an impressive view of the dining room, family room and through to the back of the house. The kitchen enjoys the vaulted breakfast/sunroom area. The master suite promises privacy and comfort with its lovely sitting room and doors leading to the back deck. All guests will enjoy maximum comfort with the downstairs guest room. Upstairs are two more bedrooms, plus storage space, and a large, sunny playroom overlooking the breakfast area below. This home is designed with a basement foundation.

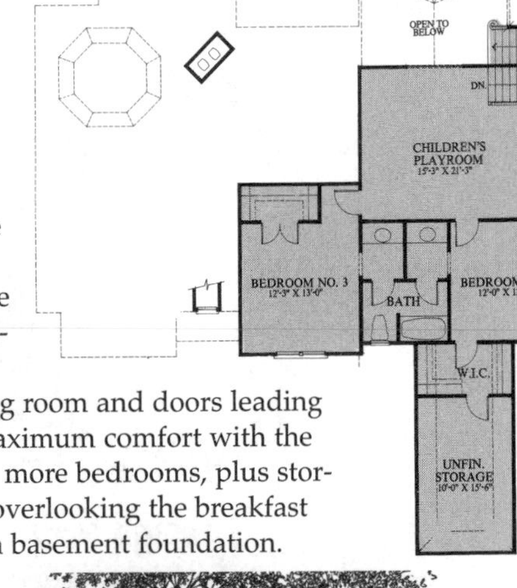

OPEN TO BELOW
DN
CHILDREN'S PLAYROOM
BEDROOM NO. 3
BATH
BEDROOM NO. 2
W.I.C.
UNFIN. STORAGE

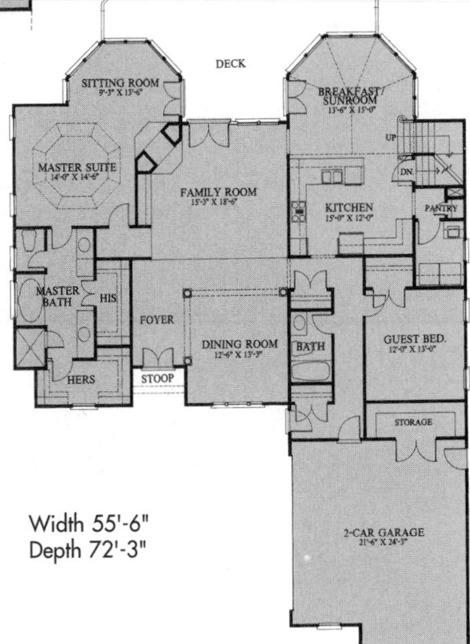

DECK
SITTING ROOM
BREAKFAST/ SUNROOM
MASTER SUITE
FAMILY ROOM
KITCHEN
PANTRY
MASTER BATH
HIS
HERS
FOYER
DINING ROOM
BATH
GUEST BED.
STOOP
STORAGE
2-CAR GARAGE
Width 55'-6"
Depth 72'-3"

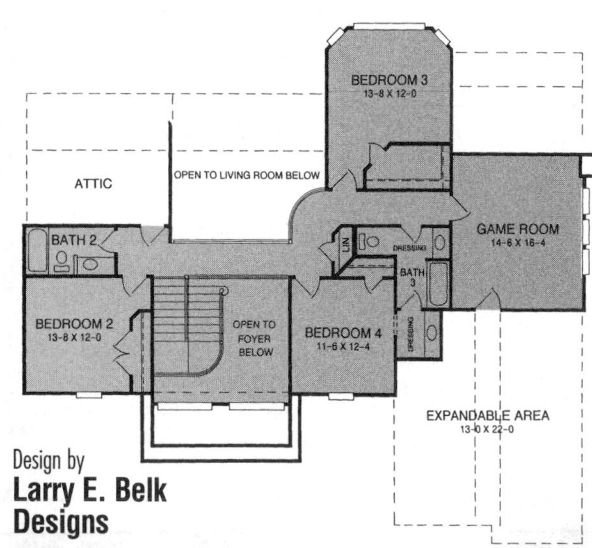
BEDROOM 3
13-8 X 12-0
ATTIC
OPEN TO LIVING ROOM BELOW
GAME ROOM
14-6 X 16-4
BATH 2
LIN
DRESSING
BATH 3
BEDROOM 2
13-8 X 12-0
OPEN TO FOYER BELOW
BEDROOM 4
11-6 X 12-4
EXPANDABLE AREA
13-0 X 22-0

Design by
Larry E. Belk Designs

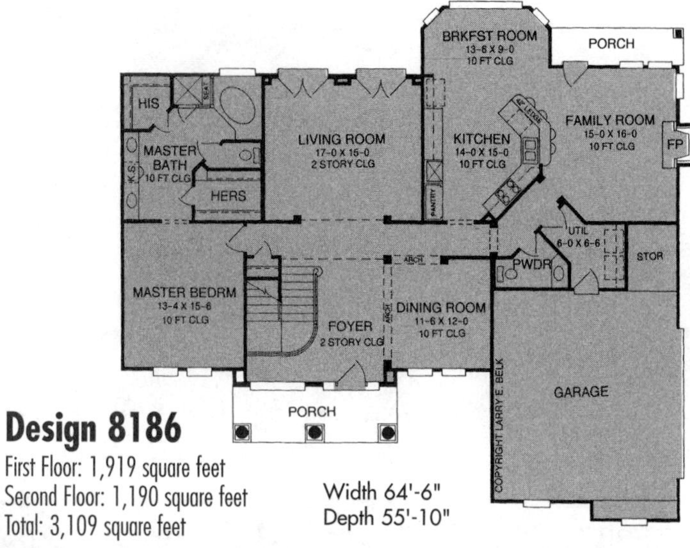
BRKFST ROOM
13-6 X 9-0
10 FT CLG
PORCH
HIS
MASTER BATH
10 FT CLG
HERS
LIVING ROOM
17-0 X 15-0
2 STORY CLG
KITCHEN
14-0 X 15-0
10 FT CLG
PANTRY
FAMILY ROOM
15-0 X 16-0
10 FT CLG
FP
UTIL
6-0 X 6-6
STOR
PWDR
MASTER BEDRM
13-4 X 15-6
10 FT CLG
FOYER
2 STORY CLG
DINING ROOM
11-6 X 12-0
10 FT CLG
PORCH
GARAGE
COPYRIGHT LARRY E. BELK

Design 8186

First Floor: 1,919 square feet
Second Floor: 1,190 square feet
Total: 3,109 square feet

Width 64'-6"
Depth 55'-10"

■ Flower boxes, arches and multi-paned windows all combine to create the elegant facade of this four-bedroom home. Inside, the two-story foyer has a formal dining room to its right and leads to a two-story living room that is filled with light. An efficient kitchen has a bayed breakfast room and shares a snack bar with a cozy family room. Located on the first floor for privacy, the master suite is graced with a luxurious bath. Upstairs, three secondary bedrooms share two full baths and have access to a large game room. For future growth there is an expandable area accessed through the game room. Please specify crawlspace or slab foundation when ordering.

HIS
HERS
M. BATH
MASTER SUITE
17'-3" x 18'-6"
SEE THRU F.P.
BEDROOM No.3
13'-3" x 12'-0"
DN
OPEN TO BELOW
BEDROOM No.2
15'-0" x 13'-3"
VLT.CLG.
UNFINISHED STORAGE
11'-0" x 21'-9"
DECK
BREAKFAST/ KEEPING ROOM
21'-3" x 13'-0"
DINING ROOM
13'-6" x 15'-0"
LIVING ROOM
17'-3" x 18'-6"
SEE THRU F.P.
KITCHEN
18'-3" x 11'-9"
DN
BALCONY ABOVE
FOYER
UP
OPTION ROOM
GUEST ROOM
/MUSIC ROOM
15'-0" x 13'-0"
LAUN.
2-CAR GARAGE
21'-9" x 21'-6"

Width 53'-6"
Depth 60'-6"

Design 9802

Design by
Design Traditions

First Floor: 1,811 square feet
Second Floor: 1,437 square feet
Total: 3,248 square feet

■ Topping the arched entry is a lovely transom window, which admits sunlight to enhance the magnificence of the two-story foyer. The formal atmosphere of the living and dining rooms is brought together by a through-fireplace. Generously sized windows in these rooms allow views of outside living areas or children's play areas. An additional fireplace can be found in the corner of the keeping room, adjacent to the enormous kitchen and the breakfast area, which is set off by a bay window. The master suite features an expansive master bath with a large walk-in closet. This home is designed with a basement foundation.

Photo by Frank Grillo

Design 8026

First Floor: 2,188 square feet
Second Floor: 1,110 square feet
Total: 3,298 square feet

■ This brick and stucco home with European style showcases an arched entry and presents a commanding presence from the curb. Inside, the living room, the dining room and the family room are located at the rear of the home to provide wide open views of the rear grounds beyond. A colonnade with connecting arches defines the space for a living room with a fireplace and the dining room. The spacious master suite features a relaxing sitting area, His and Hers closets and an extravagant master bath. Take special note of the private His and Hers bathrooms. On the second floor, three bedrooms, two baths and a game room complete the home.

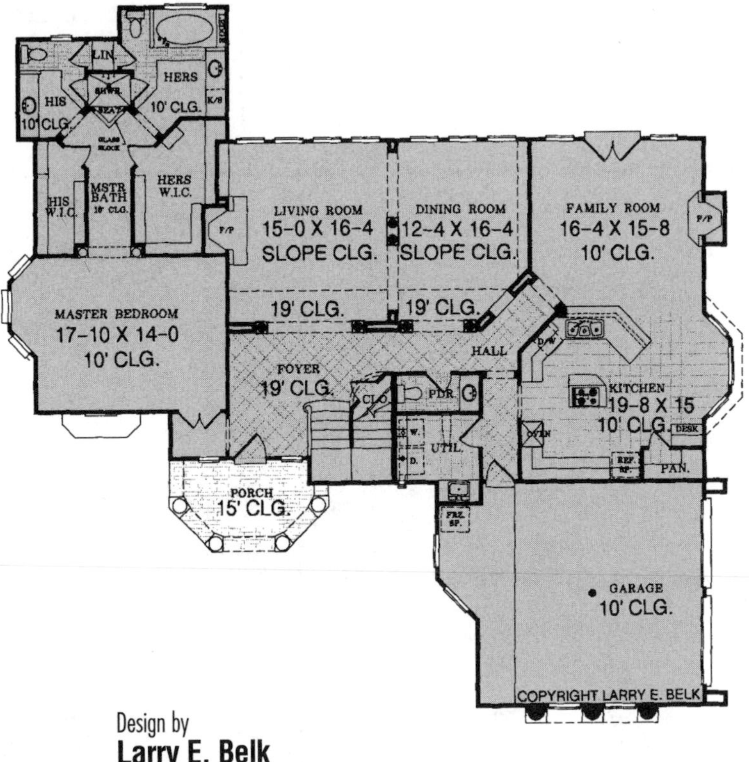
LIN.
HERS
HIS
10' CLG.
HERS
10' CLG.
HIS W.I.C.
MSTR BATH
HERS W.I.C.
LIVING ROOM
15-0 X 16-4
SLOPE CLG.
DINING ROOM
12-4 X 16-4
SLOPE CLG.
FAMILY ROOM
16-4 X 15-8
10' CLG.
MASTER BEDROOM
17-10 X 14-0
10' CLG.
19' CLG.
19' CLG.
HALL
FOYER
19' CLG.
CLO.
PDR
UTIL.
KITCHEN
19-8 X 15
10' CLG.
DESK
PAN.
PORCH
15' CLG.
GARAGE
10' CLG.
COPYRIGHT LARRY E. BELK

Design by
Larry E. Belk Designs

Width 69'
Depth 64'-8"

QUOTE ONE®

Cost to build? See page 342 to order complete cost estimate to build this house in your area!

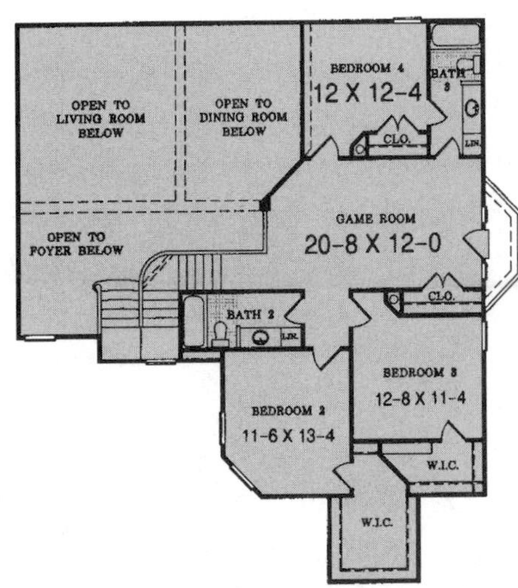
OPEN TO
LIVING ROOM
BELOW
OPEN TO
DINING ROOM
BELOW
BEDROOM 4
12 X 12-4
BATH 3
CLO.
LIN.
GAME ROOM
20-8 X 12-0
OPEN TO
FOYER BELOW
CLO.
BATH 2
LIN.
BEDROOM 3
12-8 X 11-4
BEDROOM 2
11-6 X 13-4
W.I.C.
W.I.C.

Width 60'
Depth 48'-6"

Design 9833

First Floor: 1,683 square feet
Second Floor: 1,544 square feet
Total: 3,227 square feet
Bonus Room: 176 square feet

Design by
Design Traditions

■ This country cottage's stucco exterior, mixed with stone and shingles, creates a warmth that is accented with a fanlight transom and fancy door frame. The two-story foyer opens onto the staircase and then flows easily into the dining room, living room and family room. The great room features a fireplace and bookcases and opens to a well-lit breakfast and kitchen area. Upstairs are three additional bedrooms and space for a bonus or play room. The master suite features a tray ceiling, sitting area and a lush master bath. This home is designed with a basement foundation.

Design 9970

First Floor: 1,980 square feet
Second Floor: 1,317 square feet
Total: 3,297 square feet

Design by
Design Traditions

■ The contemporary floor plan of this French country cottage begins with a soaring foyer that opens onto the formal living and dining rooms. Casual living is enjoyed at the rear of the plan in the L-shaped kitchen, the family room and the light-filled breakfast/sunroom. A guest bedroom is tucked behind the family room for privacy. Upstairs, an exquisite master suite features a lavish bath and a huge walk-in closet. Two family bedrooms, a full bath and unfinished bonus space complete the second floor. This home is designed with a basement foundation.

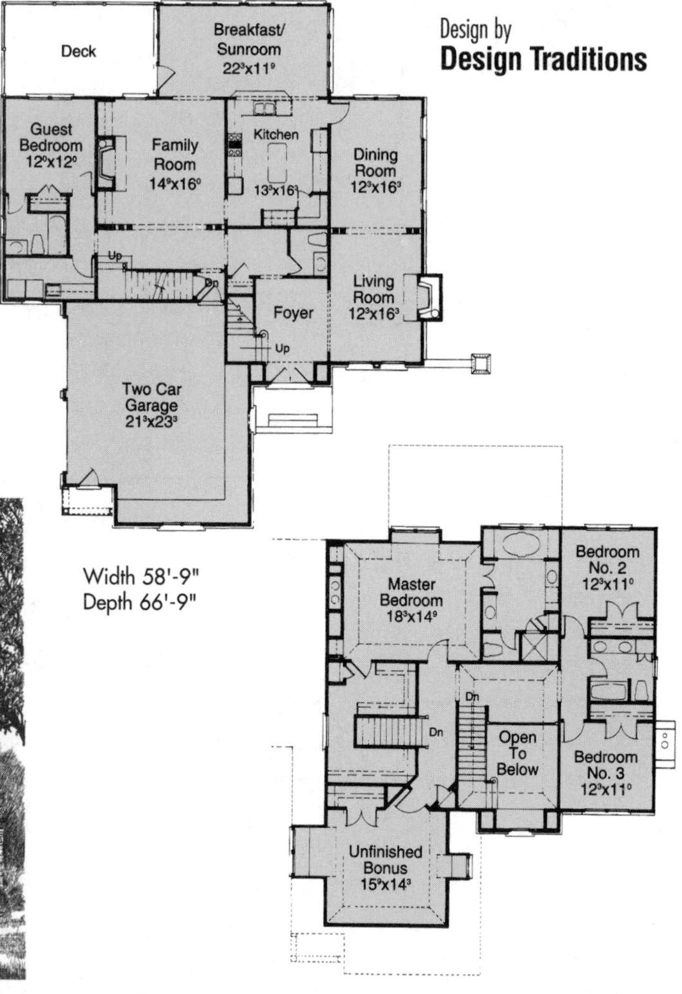
Deck
Breakfast/ Sunroom 22³x11⁹
Guest Bedroom 12⁰x12⁰
Family Room 14⁹x16⁰
Kitchen 13⁵x16¹
Dining Room 12³x16³
Living Room 12³x16³
Foyer
Up
Dn
Two Car Garage 21³x23³
Width 58'-9"
Depth 66'-9"
Master Bedroom 18³x14⁹
Bedroom No. 2 12³x11⁰
Open To Below
Bedroom No. 3 12³x11⁰
Unfinished Bonus 15⁶x14³

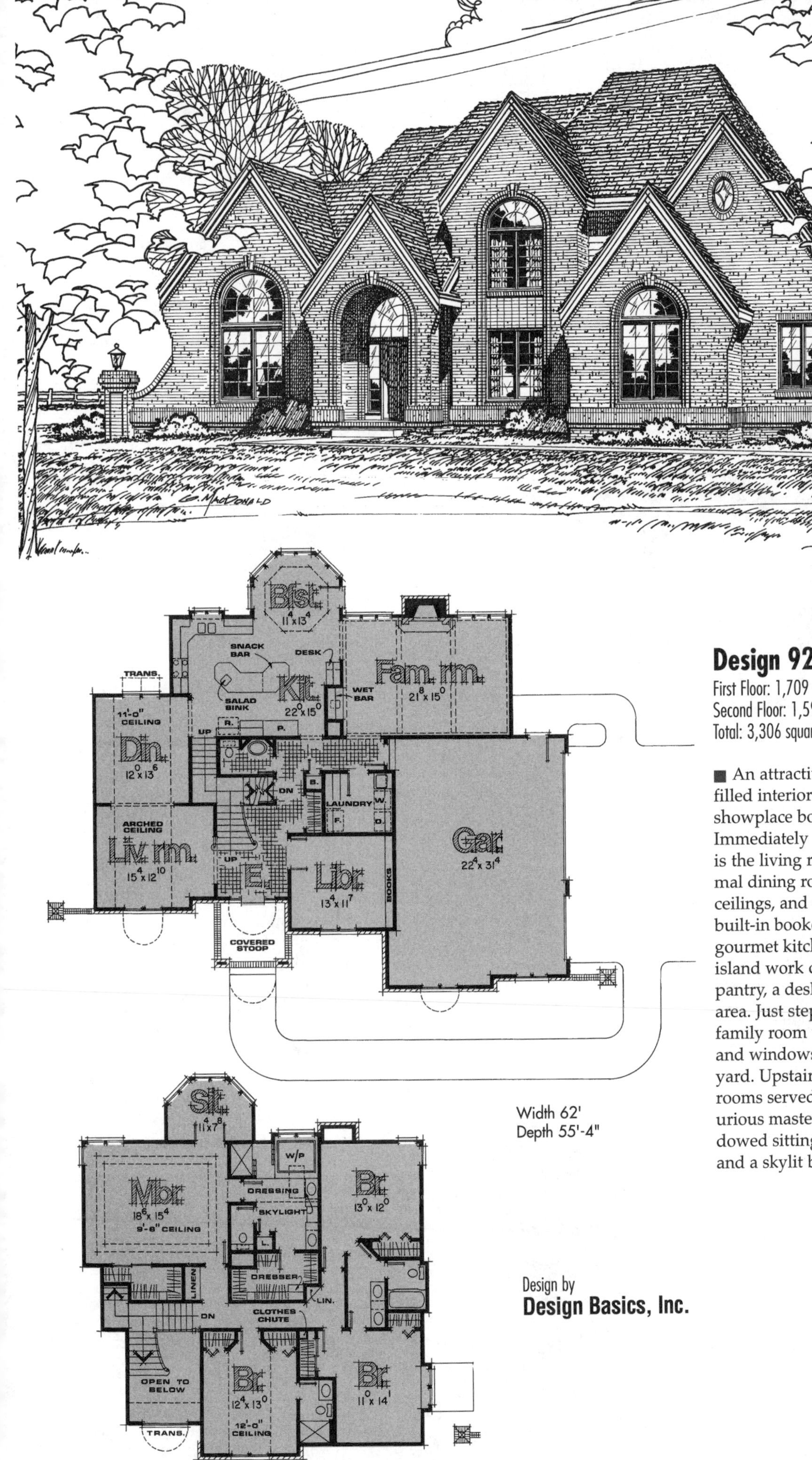
Bfst.
11^4x13^4
SNACK BAR
DESK
Kit.
22^0x15^0
SALAD SINK
WET BAR
Fam. rm.
21^8x15^0
TRANS.
11'-0" CEILING
Din.
12^0x13^6
R.
P.
UP
DN
B.
LAUNDRY
W.
F.
D.
ARCHED CEILING
Liv. rm.
15^4x12^{10}
UP
E.
Libr.
13^4x11^7
BOOKS
Gar.
22^4x31^4
COVERED STOOP
Sit.
11^4x7^8
W/P
Mbr.
18^6x15^4
9'-8" CEILING
DRESSING
SKYLIGHT
L.
Br.
13^0x12^0
DRESSER
LINEN
LIN.
DN
CLOTHES CHUTE
OPEN TO BELOW
Br.
12^4x13^0
12'-0" CEILING
Br.
11^0x14^1
TRANS.

Width 62'
Depth 55'-4"

Design by
Design Basics, Inc.

Design 9229

First Floor: 1,709 square feet
Second Floor: 1,597 square feet
Total: 3,306 square feet

■ An attractive facade and amenity-filled interior make this home a showplace both outside and in. Immediately off the two-story foyer is the living room and connecting formal dining room, both with arched ceilings, and the quiet library with built-in bookcases. The enormous gourmet kitchen features a large island work counter/snack bar, a pantry, a desk and a gazebo breakfast area. Just steps away is the spacious family room with a grand fireplace and windows overlooking the back yard. Upstairs are three family bedrooms served by two baths and a luxurious master suite with a bay-windowed sitting room, detailed ceiling and a skylit bath with a whirlpool.

Design 8048

First Floor: 2,469 square feet
Second Floor: 1,025 square feet
Total: 3,494 square feet

QUOTE ONE®

Cost to build? See page 342 to order complete cost estimate to build this house in your area!

■ A lovely double arch gives this European-style home a commanding presence. Once inside, a two-story foyer provides an open view directly through the formal living room to the rear grounds beyond. A spacious kitchen with work island and the bayed breakfast area share space with the family room. The private master suite features dual sinks, twin walk-in closets, a corner garden tub and a separate shower. A second bedroom, which doubles as a nursery or a study, and a full bath are located nearby. Two bedrooms and a bath are located on the second floor. A large game room completes this wonderful family home. Please specify crawlspace or slab foundation when ordering.

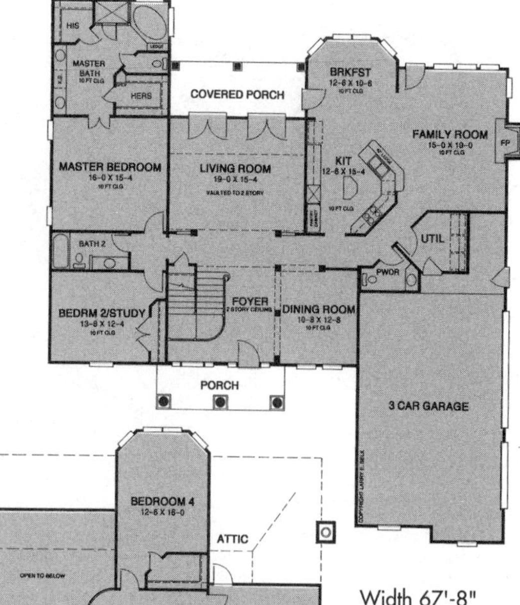
MASTER BATH
HERS
COVERED PORCH
BRKFST
12-6 X 10-6
FAMILY ROOM
15-0 X 19-0
MASTER BEDROOM
16-0 X 15-4
LIVING ROOM
19-0 X 15-4
KIT
12-6 X 15-4
UTIL
BATH 2
PWDR
BEDRM 2/STUDY
13-8 X 12-4
FOYER
DINING ROOM
10-8 X 12-8
PORCH
3 CAR GARAGE

COPYRIGHT 1993 LARRY E. BELK

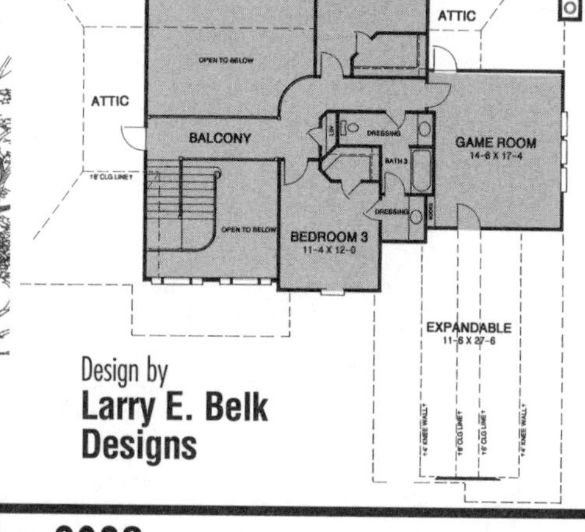
BEDROOM 4
12-6 X 16-0
ATTIC
ATTIC
BALCONY
GAME ROOM
14-6 X 17-4
BEDROOM 3
11-4 X 12-0
EXPANDABLE
11-8 X 27-6

Width 67'-8"
Depth 74'-2"

Design by
Larry E. Belk Designs

Design 8032

First Floor: 2,520 square feet
Second Floor: 1,305 square feet
Total: 3,825 square feet

Design by
Larry E. Belk Designs

■ Distinctive touches to this elegant European-style home make an inviting first impression. The two-story foyer is graced by a lovely staircase and a balcony overlook from the upstairs. To the right is the formal dining room; to the left, a study. The great room directly leads to the two-story double bay windows that introduce the kitchen and keeping room. A huge walk-in pantry and adjacent butlers pantry connect the dining room to the kitchen. A marvelous master suite features a sitting room and pampering bath. Upstairs, three bedrooms and two full baths complete the plan.

SITTING
KEEPING RM
11-6 X 16-0
BRKFST
MASTER BEDROOM
19-4 X 16-6
GREAT ROOM
18-0 X 19-6
KIT
14-0 X 17-6
UTIL
MASTER BATH
PWDR
PAN
DOUBLE GARAGE
FOYER
STUDY
13-4 X 11-6
DINING ROOM
13-0 X 14-2
PORCH

Width 73'-8"
Depth 58'-6"

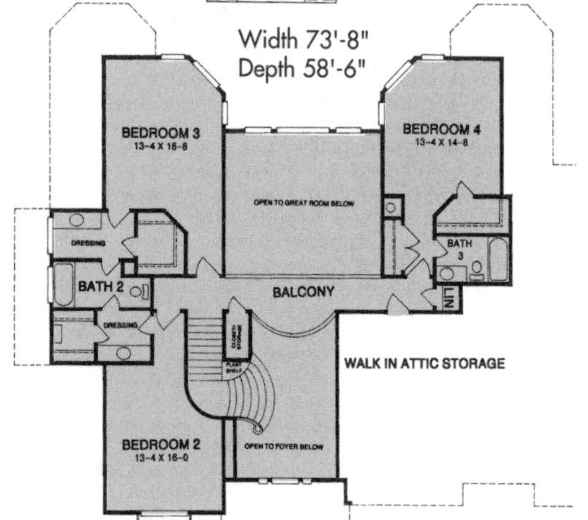
BEDROOM 3
13-4 X 16-8
BEDROOM 4
13-4 X 14-8
BATH 3
BATH 2
BALCONY
LIN
WALK IN ATTIC STORAGE
BEDROOM 2
13-4 X 16-0

COPYRIGHT 1993 LARRY E. BELK

COPYRIGHT 1993 LARRY E. BELK

Design 8086

First Floor: 2,733 square feet
Second Floor: 1,003 square feet
Total: 3,736 square feet

■ This Mediterranean-style villa is distinguished by a stunning octagonal front porch. The second-story dormer above the porch draws the eye and accents the entry to this lovely home. The home is designed to capture views to the rear grounds and is perfect for a golf course or lake. Through arched openings flanked by columns, the adjoining living room and dining room open off the two-story foyer. A see-through fireplace separates the two rooms. The gourmet kitchen, family room and breakfast room flow together. The master suite is at the rear of the home and provides access to a private screened porch. A curved staircase leads to a balcony hall and two bedrooms, each with a private bath. Please specify crawlspace or slab foundation when ordering.

SCREENED PORCH
LIVING ROOM
16-0 X 19-0
TWO STORY CEILING
DINING ROOM
12-0 X 13-0
10 FT CEILING
FAMILY ROOM
18-0 X 18-6
10 FT CEILING
MASTER BEDROOM
14-0 X 18-0
10 FT CEILING
EXERCISE
10-4 X 8-6
10 FT CEILING
MASTER BATH
BEDRM 2/STUDY
12-0 X 13-0
9 FT CEILING
BATH 2
FOYER
TWO STORY CEILING
PWDR
PAN
KITCHEN
12-6 X 15-0
BRKFST
12-10 X 13-4
10 FT CEILING
PORCH
UTIL
STOR
GARAGE
Width 74'-8"
Depth 76'-3"
BEDROOM 3
14-0 X 20-0
OPEN TO LIVING ROOM BELOW
BEDROOM 4
12-6 X 20-0
BALCONY
ATTIC STORAGE
BATH 3
LIN
CEDAR CLOSET
BATH 4
OPEN TO FOYER BELOW
DISPLAY LEDGE
ATTIC STORAGE

Design by
Larry E. Belk Designs

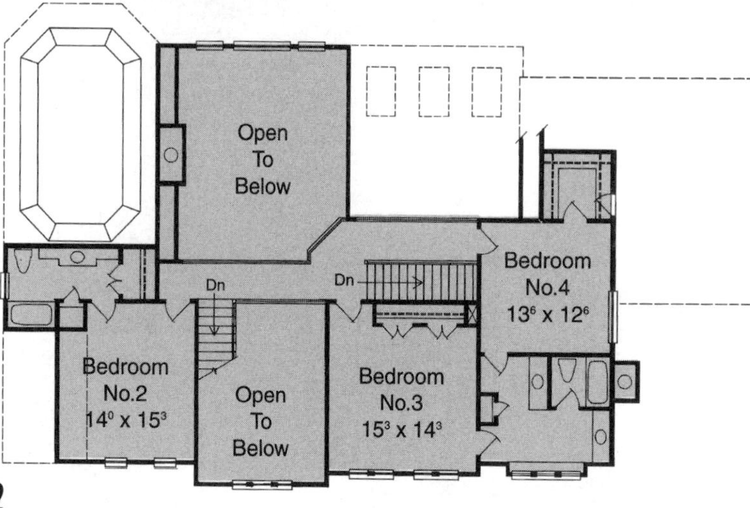
Open
To
Below
Dn
Dn
Bedroom
No.4
13^{6} x 12^{6}
Bedroom
No.2
14^{0} x 15^{3}
Open
To
Below
Bedroom
No.3
15^{3} x 14^{3}

Design by
Design Traditions

Design 9932

First Floor: 2,420 square feet
Second Floor: 1,146 square feet
Total: 3,566 square feet

■ Multi-pane glass windows, double French doors and ornamental stucco detailing are complementary elements on the facade of this home. An impressive two-story foyer opens to the formal living and dining rooms. Natural light is available through the attractive windows in each room. The kitchen features a pass-through to the two-story family room and an adjoining sky-lit breakfast room. The first-floor master suite offers an elegant vaulted bedroom ceiling, a bath with twin vanities, a separate shower and tub, and two spacious walk-in closets. Upstairs, Bedroom 2 has its own bath and can be used as a guest suite. Two other bedrooms share a large bath with twin vanities. This home is designed with a basement foundation.

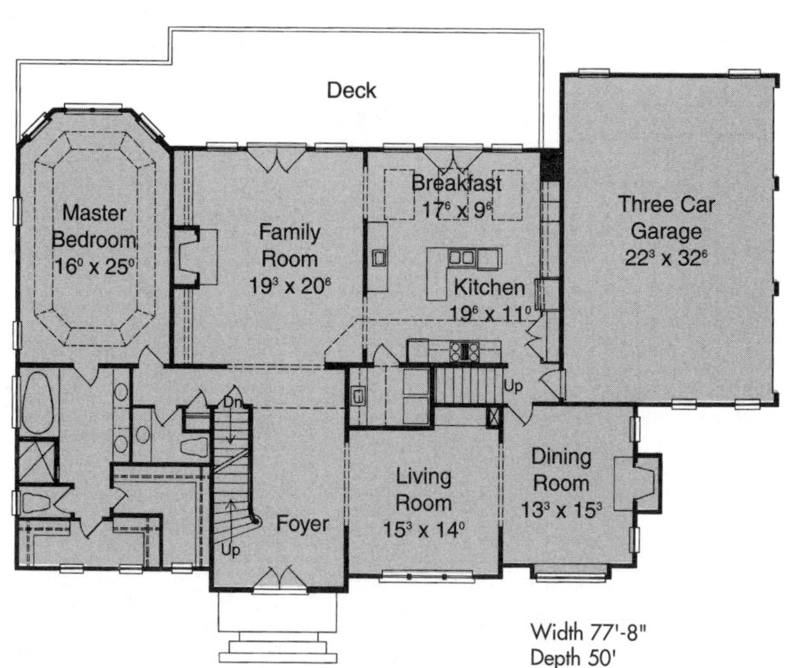
Deck
Master
Bedroom
16^{0} x 25^{0}
Family
Room
19^{3} x 20^{6}
Breakfast
17^{6} x 9^{6}
Kitchen
19^{6} x 11^{0}
Three Car
Garage
22^{3} x 32^{6}
Dn
Up
Up
Foyer
Living
Room
15^{3} x 14^{0}
Dining
Room
13^{3} x 15^{3}
Width 77'-8"
Depth 50'

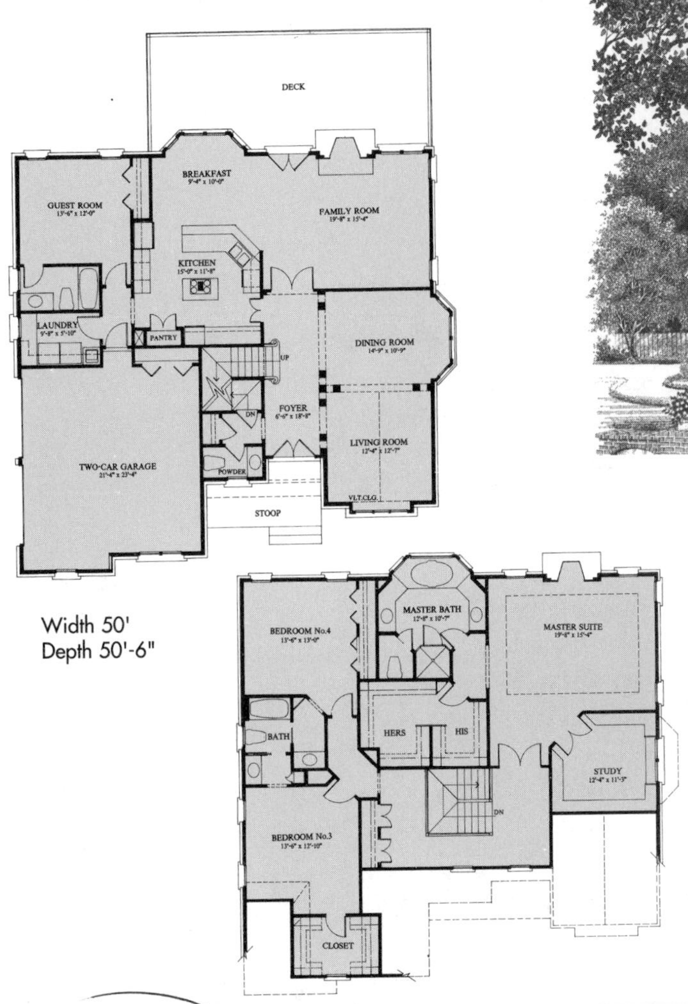
DECK
BREAKFAST
GUEST ROOM
FAMILY ROOM
KITCHEN
LAUNDRY
PANTRY
DINING ROOM
FOYER
LIVING ROOM
TWO-CAR GARAGE
POWDER
STOOP
BEDROOM No.4
MASTER BATH
MASTER SUITE
BATH
HERS
HIS
STUDY
BEDROOM No.3
CLOSET

Width 50'
Depth 50'-6"

Design 9819

First Floor: 1,678 square feet
Second Floor: 1,677 square feet
Total: 3,355 square feet

Design by
Design Traditions

■ This English Manor home features a dramatic brick and stucco exterior accented by a gabled roofline and artful half-timbering. Inside, the foyer opens to the formal living room and dining room. Through the double doors lies the center of family activity: a spacious family room, kitchen and breakfast room. For your guests, a bedroom and bath are located on the main level. The second floor provides two additional bedrooms and a private bath. The master suite has a tray ceiling, fireplace and private study. The master bath has separate vanities, a garden tub and separate shower along with oversized closets. This home is designed with a basement foundation.

Design 9930

First Floor: 2,346 square feet
Second Floor: 1,260 square feet
Total: 3,606 square feet

Design by
Design Traditions

■ The European character of this home is enhanced through the use of stucco and stone on the elevation, giving this Country French estate home its charm and beauty. The foyer has access to the dining room and study/living room. The two-story family room is positioned for convenient access to the back staircase, the kitchen, the wet bar and the deck area. The master bedroom suite is privately located on the right side of the home with an optional entry to the study and a large garden bath. Upstairs are three more large bedrooms; two have a shared bath and private vanities and one has a full private bath. All bedrooms have convenient access to the back staircase and open-rail views to the family room below. This home is designed with a basement foundation.

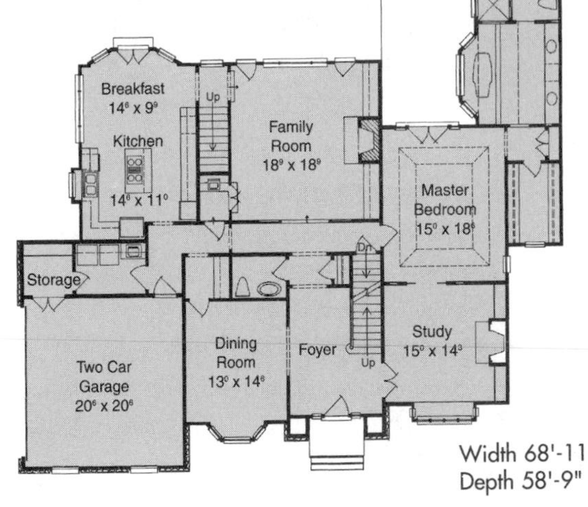
Breakfast
14^6 x 9^9
Kitchen
14^6 x 11^0
Family Room
18^9 x 18^9
Master Bedroom
15^0 x 18^6
Storage
Dining Room
13^0 x 14^6
Foyer
Study
15^0 x 14^0
Two Car Garage
20^6 x 20^6

Width 68'-11"
Depth 58'-9"

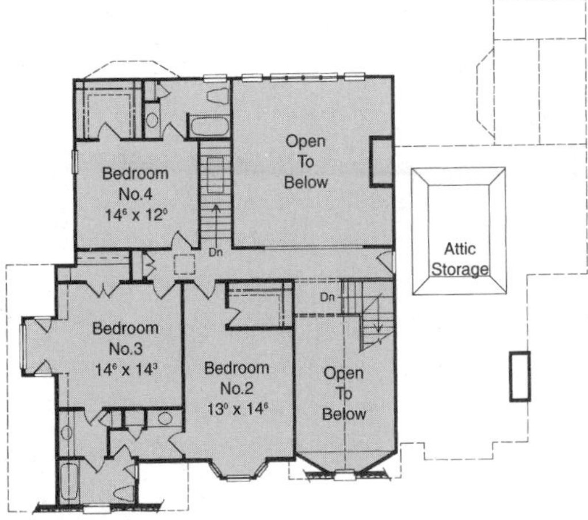
Open To Below
Bedroom No.4
14^6 x 12^0
Attic Storage
Bedroom No.3
14^6 x 14^3
Bedroom No.2
13^0 x 14^6
Open To Below

Design 8034

First Floor: 2,639 square feet
Second Floor: 1,625 square feet
Total: 4,264 square feet

■ European traditional style is the hallmark of this bestselling plan. The two-story foyer is graced by a lovely staircase and a balcony overlook from upstairs. Two columns flank the entry to the great room notable for its beautiful window wall facing the rear grounds. Two-story double bays on the rear of the home form the keeping room and the breakfast room on one side and the master bedroom and its sitting area on the other. A huge walk-in pantry and an adjacent butler's pantry connect the dining room to the kitchen. Rear stairs from the kitchen join the family gathering area with the three bedrooms and game room upstairs. With a large study downstairs and walk-in attic storage available for expansion upstairs, this home provides all the amenities needed for today's busy family.

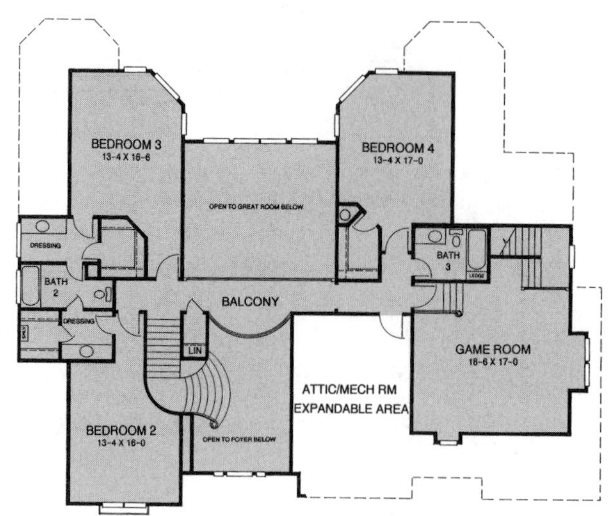
BEDROOM 3
13-4 X 16-6
OPEN TO GREAT ROOM BELOW
BEDROOM 4
13-4 X 17-0
DRESSING
BATH
2
DRESSING
BATH
3
BALCONY
LIN
GAME ROOM
18-6 X 17-0
ATTIC/MECH RM
EXPANDABLE AREA
BEDROOM 2
13-4 X 16-0
OPEN TO FOYER BELOW

Design by
Larry E. Belk Designs

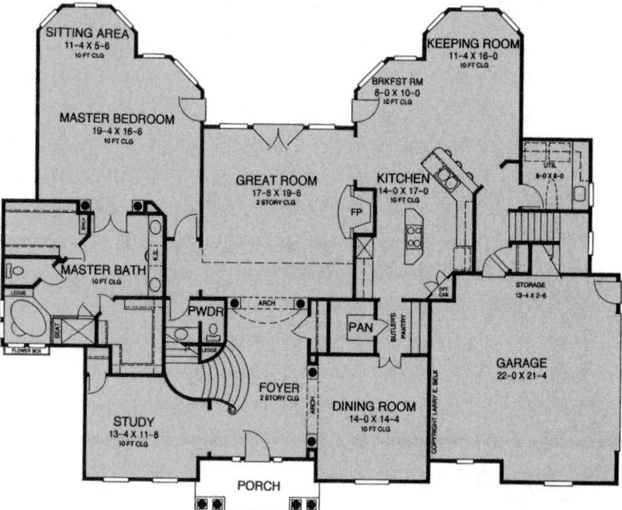
SITTING AREA
11-4 X 5-6
KEEPING ROOM
11-4 X 16-0
BRKFST RM
8-0 X 10-0
MASTER BEDROOM
19-4 X 16-6
GREAT ROOM
17-6 X 19-6
2 STORY CLG
KITCHEN
14-0 X 17-0
FP
MASTER BATH
STORAGE
13-4 X 2-6
PWDR
ARCH
PAN
BUTLER'S PANTRY
GARAGE
22-0 X 21-4
FOYER
2 STORY CLG
STUDY
13-4 X 11-8
DINING ROOM
14-0 X 14-4
PORCH
COPYRIGHT LARRY E. BELK

Width 73'-8"
Depth 58'-6"

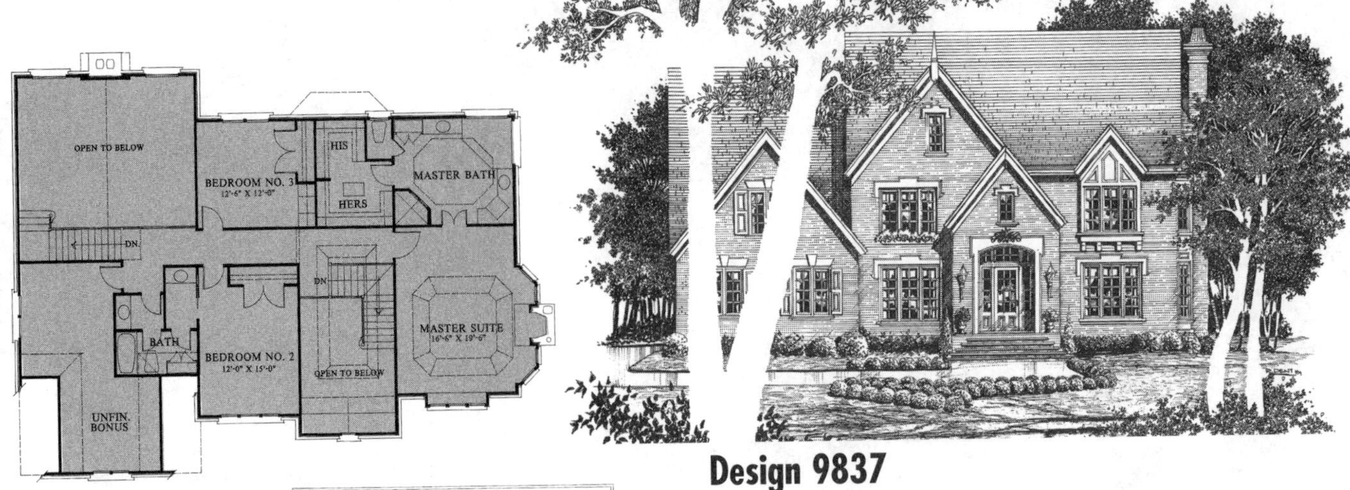
OPEN TO BELOW
BEDROOM NO. 3
12'-6" X 12'-0"
HIS
HERS
MASTER BATH
DN.
BATH
BEDROOM NO. 2
12'-0" X 15'-0"
DN
MASTER SUITE
16'-6" X 19'-6"
OPEN TO BELOW
UNFIN. BONUS

DECK
FAMILY ROOM
21'-3" X 17'-6"
BREAKFAST
14'-6" X 11'-0"
KITCHEN
12'-9" X 12'-0"
DINING ROOM
14'-3" X 16'-3"
UP
VLT. CLG.
LAUNDRY
DN
STOR.
BATH
LIVING ROOM
16'-0" X 16'-6"
UP
STUDY/
GUEST BED
12'-0" X 12'-0"
FOYER
2-CAR GARAGE
21'-6" X 22'-0"
STOOP

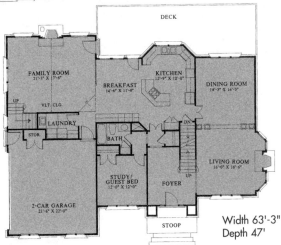

Width 63'-3"
Depth 47'

Design 9837

First Floor: 1,847 square feet
Second Floor: 1,453 square feet
Total: 3,330 square feet

Design by
Design Traditions

■ To suit those who favor Classic European styling, this English Manor home features a dramatic brick exterior which is further emphasized by the varied roofline and the finial atop the uppermost gable. The main level opens with a two-story foyer and formal rooms on the right. The living room contains a fireplace set in a bay window. The dining room is separated from the living room by a symmetrical column arrangement. The more casual family room is to the rear. For guests, a bedroom and bath are located on the main level. The second floor provides additional bedrooms and bath for family as well as a magnificent master suite. This home is designed with a basement foundation.

Design 9919

First Floor: 2,461 square feet
Second Floor: 1,114 square feet
Total: 3,575 square feet

■ This unique stair-stepped facade provides each room at the front of the home with a corner view. To the right of the striking foyer is the formal dining room. An efficient L-shaped kitchen and bayed breakfast nook are conveniently located to the dining area. The living room has a welcoming fireplace and opens to the rear terrace. The private master suite provides access to the rear terrace and adjacent study. The master bath is sure to please with its relaxing garden tub, separate shower, grand His and Hers walk-in closets and a compartmented toilet. The second floor contains three large bedrooms, one with a private bath, while the others share a bath. This home is designed with a basement foundation.

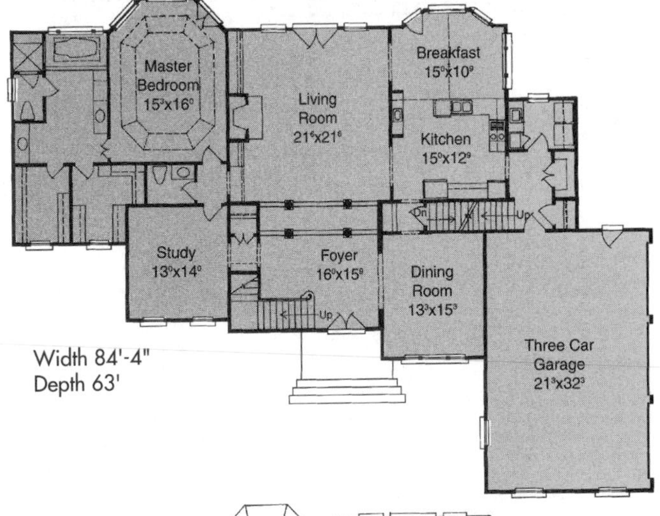
Master
Bedroom
15⁰x16⁰
Living
Room
21⁶x21⁶
Breakfast
15⁰x10⁹
Kitchen
15⁰x12⁹
Dn
Up
Study
13⁰x14⁰
Foyer
16⁰x15⁹
Up
Dining
Room
13⁹x15³
Three Car
Garage
21⁹x32³

Width 84'-4"
Depth 63'

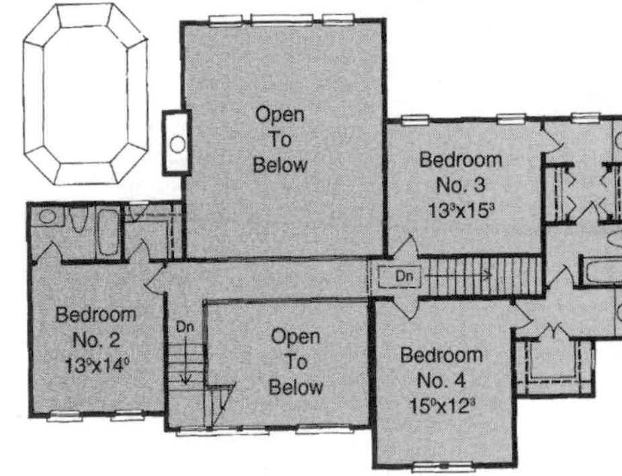
Open
To
Below
Bedroom
No. 3
13⁹x15³
Dn
Bedroom
No. 2
13⁹x14⁰
Dn
Open
To
Below
Bedroom
No. 4
15⁰x12⁸

Design by
Design Traditions

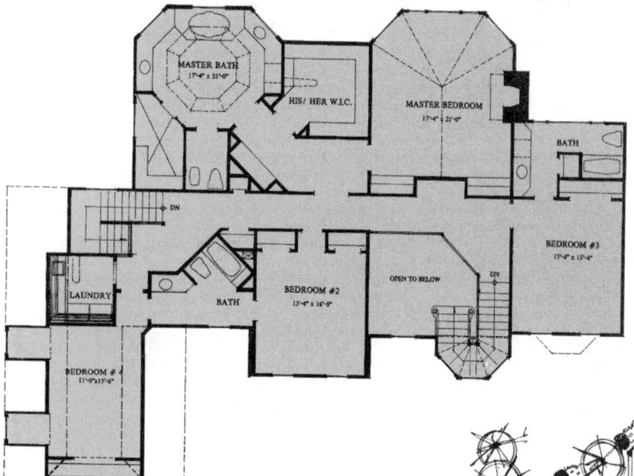

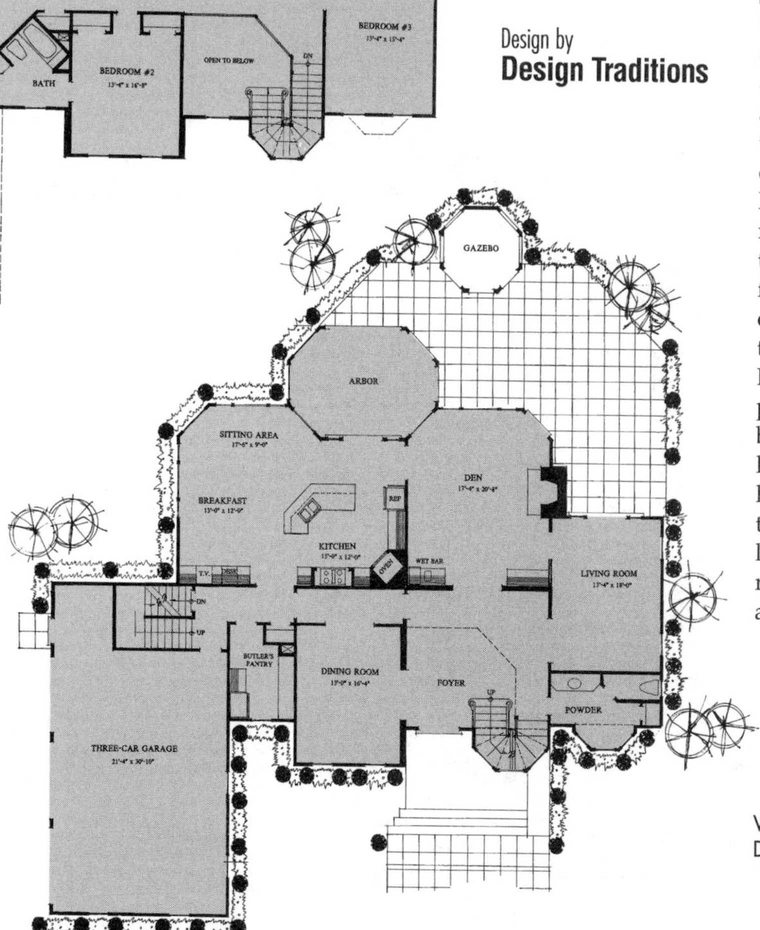
GAZEBO
ARBOR
SITTING AREA
BREAKFAST
DEN
KITCHEN
WET BAR
LIVING ROOM
THREE-CAR GARAGE
BUTLER'S PANTRY
DINING ROOM
FOYER
POWDER

Design 9889

First Floor: 2,161 square feet
Second Floor: 2,110 square feet
Total: 4,271 square feet

■ A blend of stucco and stone create the charm in this country French estate home. The asymmetrical design and arched glass windows add to the European character. Inside, the plan offers a unique arrangement of rooms conducive to today's lifestyles. A living room and a dining room flank the foyer, creating a functional formal area. The large den or family room is positioned at the rear of the home with convenient access to the kitchen, patio and covered arbor. Equally accessible to the arbor and patio are the kitchen and breakfast/sitting area. A large butler's pantry is located near the kitchen and dining room. Upstairs, the vaulted master suite and three large bedrooms provide private retreats. This home is designed with a basement foundation.

Design by
Design Traditions

Width 76'-2"
Depth 60'-11"

Design 8148

First Floor: 2,693 square feet
Second Floor: 2,027 square feet
Total: 4,720 square feet

■ This fantastic home is both a romantic castle retreat and a luxurious custom home. The grand foyer opens to a round study on the left and a formal dining room on the right. The expansive great room has a towering fireplace and is framed by a tiered staircase that opens to a balcony on the second floor. The oversized kitchen has a work island, a wraparound snack bar and a sunny breakfast nook. A thoughtful guest suite with a private bath is tucked behind the great room. Upstairs, the luxurious master suite is accented with a separate sitting room, a fireplace, tiered ceiling and a spa-style bath with two large walk-in closets. One additional family bedroom has a private bath and a walk-in closet. A delightful game room completes this fantasy home. Please specify crawlspace or slab foundation when ordering.

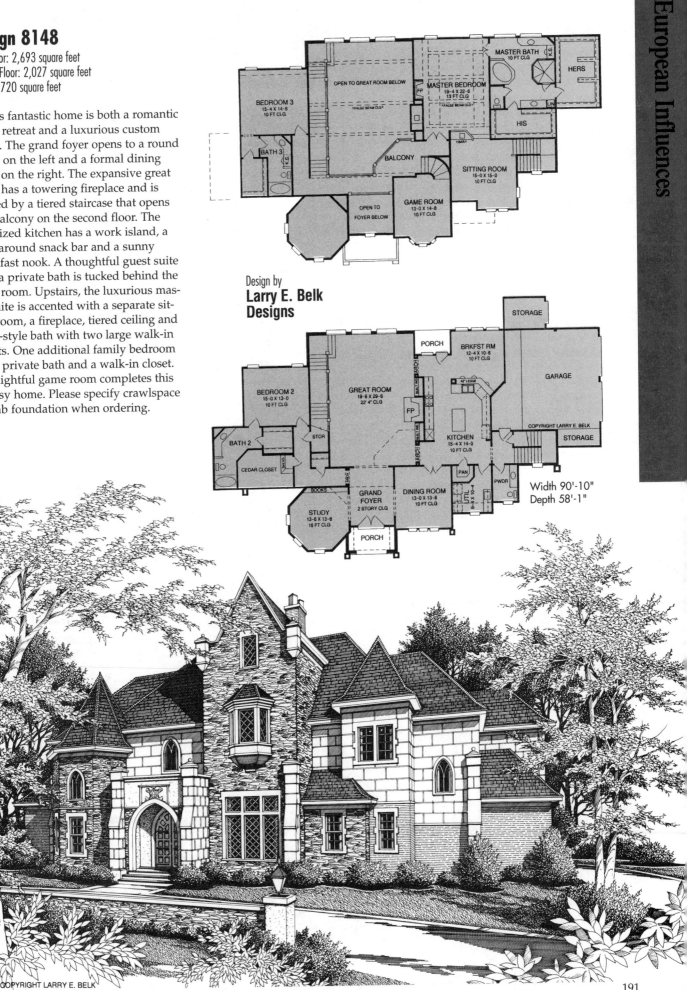

Design by
Larry E. Belk Designs

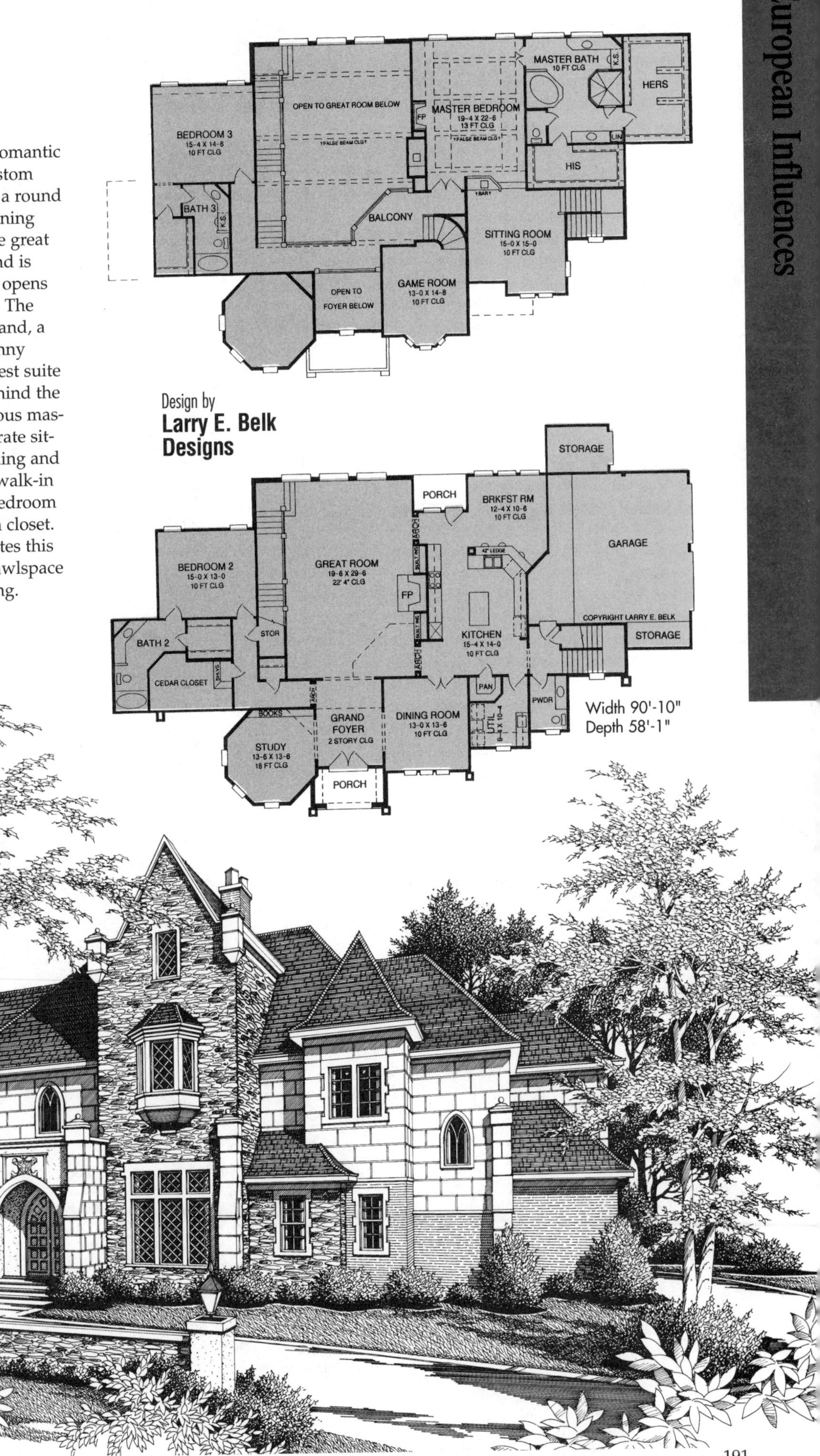
MASTER BATH
10 FT CLG
HERS
HIS
OPEN TO GREAT ROOM BELOW
MASTER BEDROOM
19-4 X 22-6
13 FT CLG
BEDROOM 3
15-4 X 14-6
10 FT CLG
BATH 3
BALCONY
SITTING ROOM
15-0 X 15-0
10 FT CLG
OPEN TO FOYER BELOW
GAME ROOM
13-0 X 14-8
10 FT CLG
STORAGE
PORCH
BRKFST RM
12-4 X 10-6
10 FT CLG
GARAGE
BEDROOM 2
15-0 X 13-0
10 FT CLG
GREAT ROOM
19-6 X 29-6
22' 4" CLG
FP
KITCHEN
15-4 X 14-0
10 FT CLG
COPYRIGHT LARRY E. BELK
STORAGE
BATH 2
STOR
CEDAR CLOSET
PAN
PWDR
BOOKS
GRAND FOYER
2 STORY CLG
DINING ROOM
13-0 X 13-6
10 FT CLG
STUDY
13-6 X 13-6
18 FT CLG
PORCH
COPYRIGHT LARRY E. BELK

Width 90'-10"
Depth 58'-1"

Design 9989

First Floor: 2,058 square feet
Second Floor: 712 square feet
Total: 2,770 square feet

■ If you've always dreamed of owning a villa, we invite you to experience this European lifestyle—on a perfectly manageable scale. This home offers the best of traditional formality and casual elegance. The foyer leads to the great room with a bold but stylish fireplace and three French doors to the rear terrace—sure to be left open during fair weather. The large kitchen opens gracefully to a private dining room that has access to a covered outdoor patio. The master suite combines great views and a sumptuous bath to complete this winning design. Upstairs, a balcony hall overlooking the great room leads to two family bedrooms that share a full hall bath. This home is designed with a basement foundation.

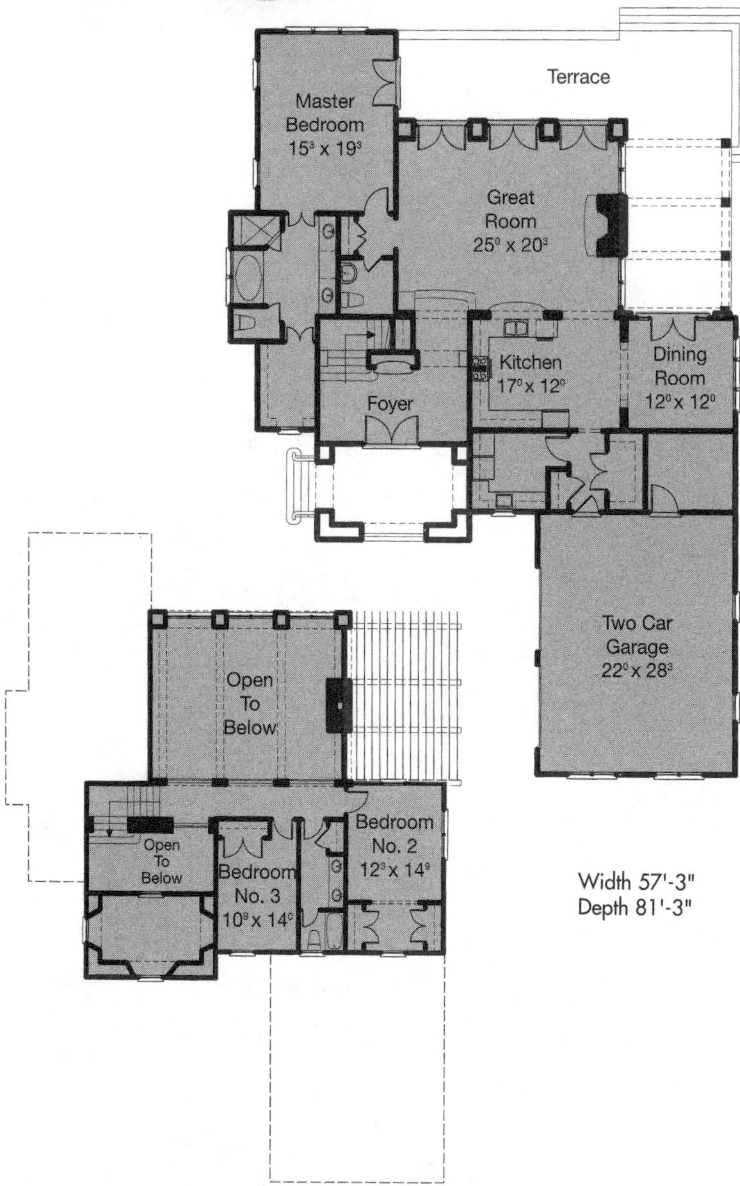

Terrace
Master Bedroom
15³ x 19³
Great Room
25⁰ x 20³
Kitchen
17⁰x 12⁰
Dining Room
12⁰x 12⁰
Foyer
Two Car Garage
22⁰x 28³
Open To Below
Open To Below
Bedroom No. 2
12³x 14⁹
Bedroom No. 3
10⁹x 14⁰
Width 57'-3"
Depth 81'-3"

Design by
Design Traditions

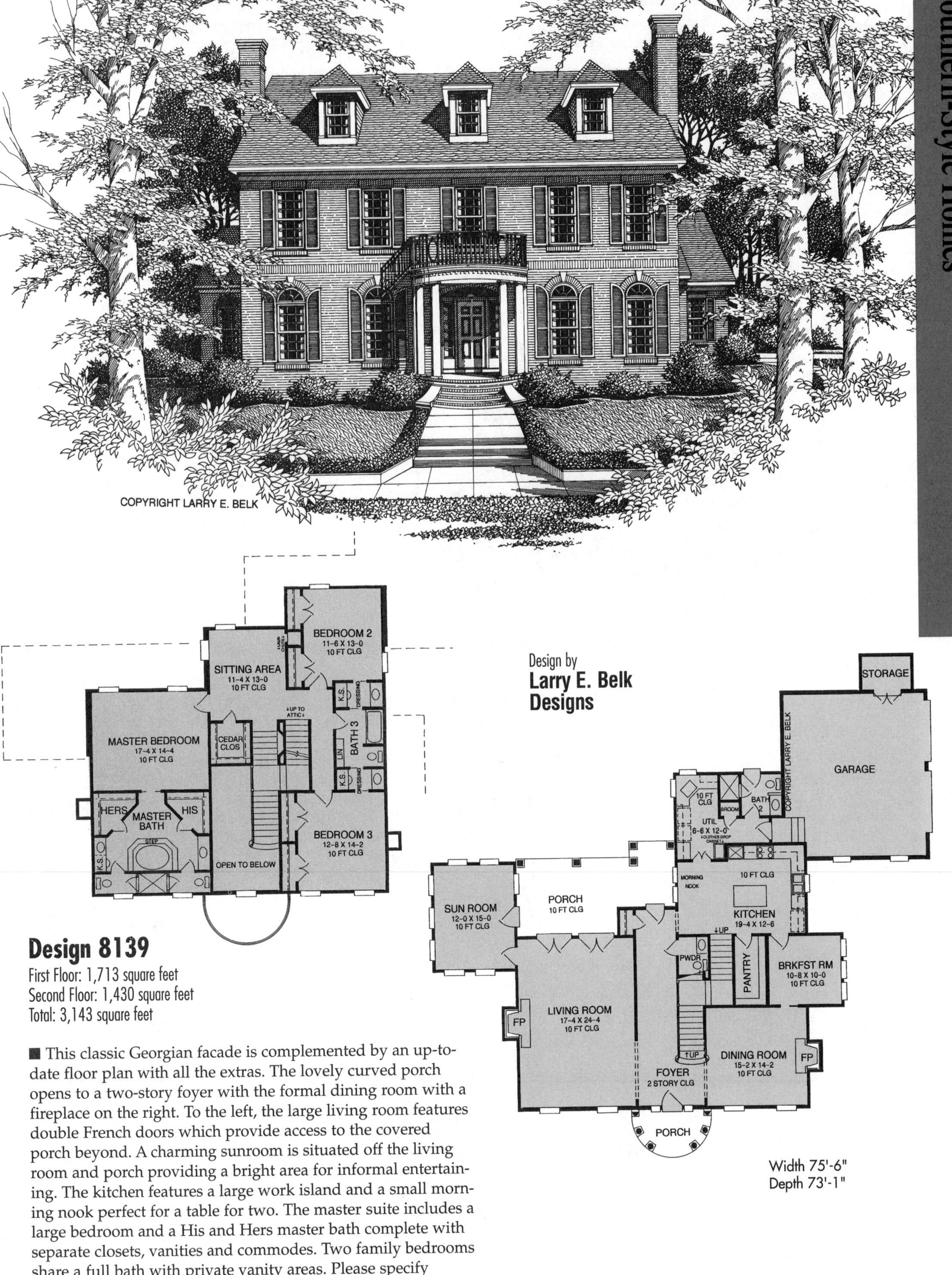
COPYRIGHT LARRY E. BELK
BEDROOM 2
11-6 X 13-0
10 FT CLG
SITTING AREA
11-4 X 13-0
10 FT CLG
MASTER BEDROOM
17-4 X 14-4
10 FT CLG
CEDAR CLOS
UP TO ATTIC
K.S.
DRESSING
BATH 3
LIN
HERS
MASTER BATH
HIS
STEP
OPEN TO BELOW
BEDROOM 3
12-8 X 14-2
10 FT CLG
STORAGE
GARAGE
COPYRIGHT LARRY E. BELK
10 FT CLG
BROOM
BATH 2
UTIL
6-6 X 12-0
MORNING NOOK
10 FT CLG
KITCHEN
19-4 X 12-6
UP
SUN ROOM
12-0 X 15-0
10 FT CLG
PORCH
10 FT CLG
PWDR
PANTRY
BRKFST RM
10-8 X 10-0
10 FT CLG
FP
LIVING ROOM
17-4 X 24-4
10 FT CLG
UP
DINING ROOM
15-2 X 14-2
10 FT CLG
FP
FOYER
2 STORY CLG
PORCH

Design by
Larry E. Belk Designs

Design 8139

First Floor: 1,713 square feet
Second Floor: 1,430 square feet
Total: 3,143 square feet

■ This classic Georgian facade is complemented by an up-to-date floor plan with all the extras. The lovely curved porch opens to a two-story foyer with the formal dining room with a fireplace on the right. To the left, the large living room features double French doors which provide access to the covered porch beyond. A charming sunroom is situated off the living room and porch providing a bright area for informal entertaining. The kitchen features a large work island and a small morning nook perfect for a table for two. The master suite includes a large bedroom and a His and Hers master bath complete with separate closets, vanities and commodes. Two family bedrooms share a full bath with private vanity areas. Please specify crawlspace or slab foundation when ordering.

Width 75'-6"
Depth 73'-1"

Design P102

First Floor: 1,135 square feet
Second Floor: 917 square feet
Total: 2,052 square feet
Bonus Room: 216 square feet

Design by
Frank Betz Associates, Inc.

■ This grand two-story home proves that tried and true traditional style is still the best! Thoughtful planning brings formal living areas to the forefront and places an open, casual living areas to the rear of the plan. Bedroom 4 serves as a multi-purpose room, providing the flexibility desired by today's homeowner. The second floor is devoted to the relaxing master suite, two secondary bedrooms, a full hall bath and a balcony overlook. Please specify basement or crawlspace foundation when ordering.

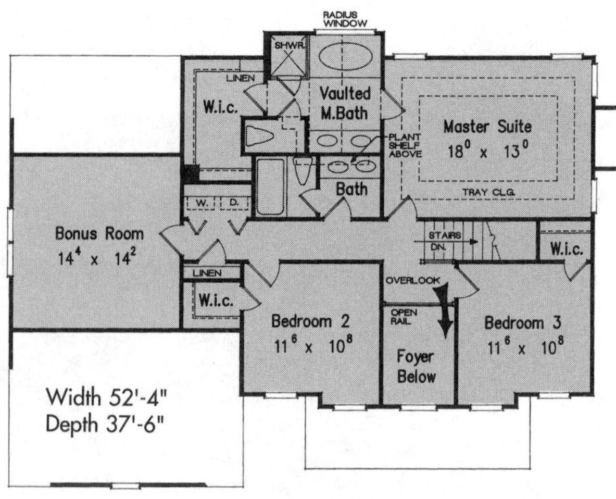
RADIUS WINDOW
SHWR.
LINEN
W.i.c.
Vaulted M.Bath
PLANT SHELF ABOVE
Master Suite 18⁰ x 13⁰
W. D.
Bath
TRAY CLG.
Bonus Room 14⁴ x 14²
STAIRS DN.
W.i.c.
LINEN
W.i.c.
OVERLOOK
OPEN RAIL
Bedroom 2 11⁶ x 10⁸
Bedroom 3 11⁶ x 10⁸
Foyer Below
Width 52'-4"
Depth 37'-6"

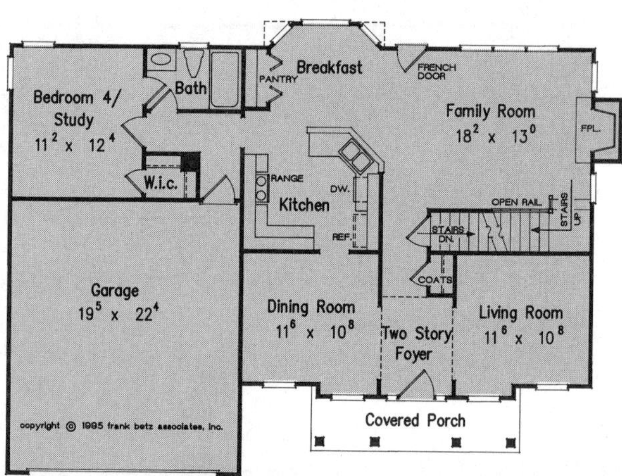
Breakfast
PANTRY
FRENCH DOOR
Bath
Bedroom 4/ Study 11² x 12⁴
Family Room 18² x 13⁰
FPL.
W.i.c.
RANGE
DW.
Kitchen
OPEN RAIL
STAIRS DN.
STAIRS UP
REF.
COATS
Garage 19⁵ x 22⁴
Dining Room 11⁶ x 10⁸
Two Story Foyer
Living Room 11⁶ x 10⁸
Covered Porch
copyright © 1995 frank betz associates, inc.

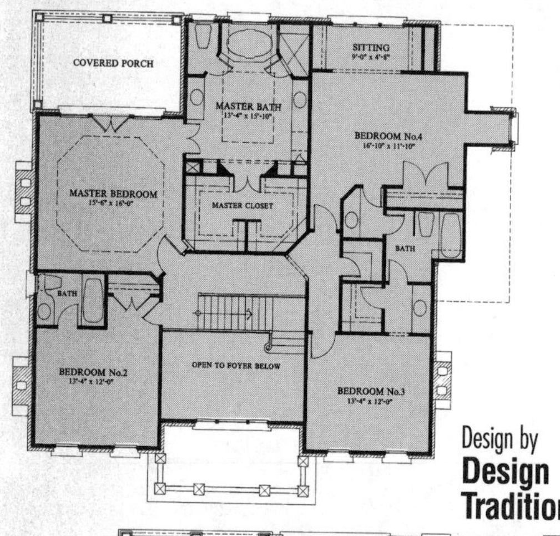
COVERED PORCH
SITTING
MASTER BATH
BEDROOM No.4
MASTER BEDROOM
MASTER CLOSET
BATH
BATH
BEDROOM No.2
OPEN TO FOYER BELOW
BEDROOM No.3

Design by
Design Traditions

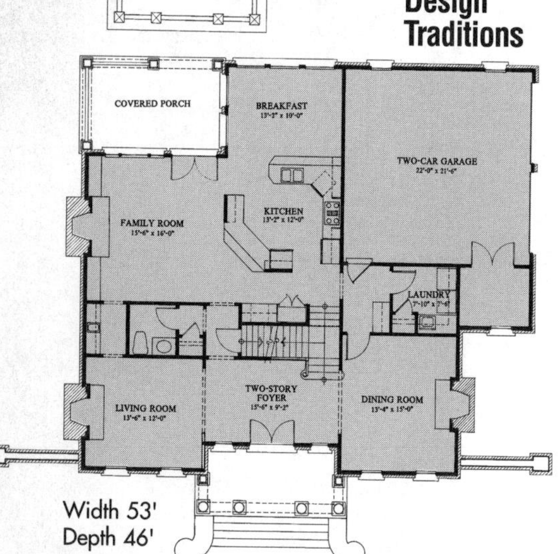
COVERED PORCH
BREAKFAST
TWO-CAR GARAGE
FAMILY ROOM
KITCHEN
LAUNDRY
LIVING ROOM
TWO-STORY FOYER
DINING ROOM
Width 53'
Depth 46'

Design 9828

First Floor: 1,455 square feet
Second Floor: 1,649 square feet
Total: 3,104 square feet

QUOTE ONE®

Cost to build? See page 342 to order complete cost estimate to build this house in your area!

■ The double wings, twin chimneys and center portico of this home work in concert to create a classic architectural statement. The two-story foyer is flanked by the spacious dining room and formal living room, each containing its own fireplace. A large family room with a full wall of glass beckons the outside in while it opens conveniently onto the sunlit kitchen and breakfast room. The master suite features a tray ceiling and French doors that open onto a covered porch. A grand master bath with all the amenities, including a garden tub and huge closet, completes the master suite. Two other bedrooms share a bath while another has its own private bath. The fourth bedroom also features a sunny nook for sitting or reading. This home is designed with a basement foundation.

OPEN TO BELOW
BEDROOM NO. 4
BALCONY
BEDROOM NO. 2
OPEN TO BELOW
W.I.C.
BATH
W.I.C.
BATH
W.I.C.
PLAY ROOM
BEDROOM NO. 3
PORCH
LAUNDRY
TWO CAR GARAGE
MASTER BEDROOM
GREAT ROOM
BREAKFAST
MASTER BATH
STAIR HALL
POWDER
PORCH
HERS
KITCHEN
HIS
PANTRY
LIVING ROOM
FOYER
DINING ROOM
PORCH
Width 77'-4"
Depth 58'-4"

QUOTE ONE®

Cost to build? See page 342 to order complete cost estimate to build this house in your area!

Design by
Design Traditions

Design 9830

First Floor: 2,380 square feet
Second Floor: 1,295 square feet
Total: 3,675 square feet

■ Finely crafted porches—front, side and rear—make this home a classic in traditional Southern living. Past the large French doors, the impressive foyer is flanked by both the formal living and dining rooms. Beyond the stair is a vaulted family room with an expanse of windows, a fireplace and built-in bookcases. From here the breakfast room and kitchen are easily accessible and open onto a private side porch. The master suite provides a large bath, two spacious closets, a fireplace and a private entry that opens to the covered rear porch. The second floor contains three bedrooms with private bath access and a children's playroom. This home is designed with a basement foundation.

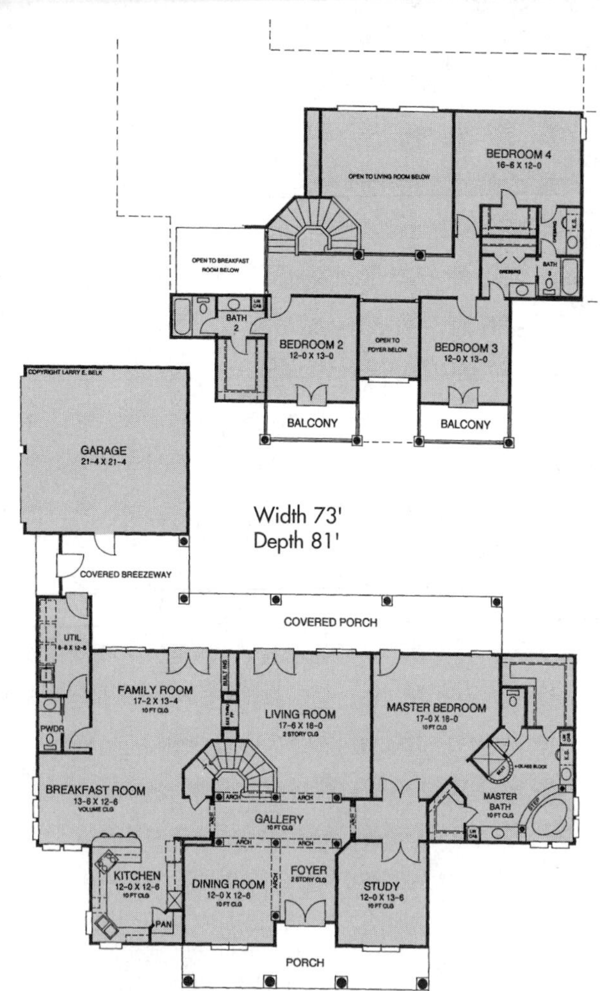
COPYRIGHT LARRY E. BELK
BEDROOM 4
16-6 X 12-0
OPEN TO LIVING ROOM BELOW
OPEN TO BREAKFAST ROOM BELOW
BATH 2
BEDROOM 2
12-0 X 13-0
OPEN TO FOYER BELOW
BEDROOM 3
12-0 X 13-0
BATH 3
DRESSING
BALCONY
BALCONY
GARAGE
21-4 X 21-4
Width 73'
Depth 81'
COVERED BREEZEWAY
COVERED PORCH
UTIL
FAMILY ROOM
17-2 X 13-4
LIVING ROOM
17-6 X 18-0
MASTER BEDROOM
17-0 X 18-0
PWDR
BREAKFAST ROOM
13-6 X 12-6
ARCH
GALLERY
MASTER BATH
KITCHEN
12-0 X 12-6
DINING ROOM
12-0 X 12-6
FOYER
STUDY
12-0 X 13-6
PAN
PORCH

Design 8077

First Floor: 2,553 square feet
Second Floor: 1,085 square feet
Total: 3,638 square feet

Design by
Larry E. Belk Designs

■ Traditional Southern ambience distinguishes this stately antebellum home. The dining and living rooms open off the foyer and are defined by a gallery of columns with graceful connecting arches. A see-through fireplace serves both the living and family rooms. The kitchen is designed for efficiency with a corner walk-in pantry, a breakfast bar and a sunny corner window above the sink. The master suite includes a luxury bath with a corner tub accented by columns, as well as a large shower, a vanity area with knee space, two linen cabinets and twin walk-in closets. Upstairs, the two front bedrooms have private balconies; all three bedrooms have private bath access. Please specify crawlspace or slab foundation when ordering.

Design 9364

First Floor: 1,717 square feet
Second Floor: 1,518 square feet
Total: 3,235 square feet

Design by
Design Basics, Inc.

■ Stately columns highlight the facade of this beautiful Southern Colonial. The open entry allows for views into formal areas and up the tapering staircase. The dining room joins the kitchen through double doors. The living room can be divided from the sunken family room by pocket doors. Step down into the huge family room to find large windows, a fireplace, a built-in entertainment center, and bookcases. The kitchen features a gazebo breakfast area, serving bar and cooktop island. Upstairs, three family bedrooms share two full baths. The private master suite features a tiered ceiling, two walk-in closets, and a roomy, bayed sitting area.

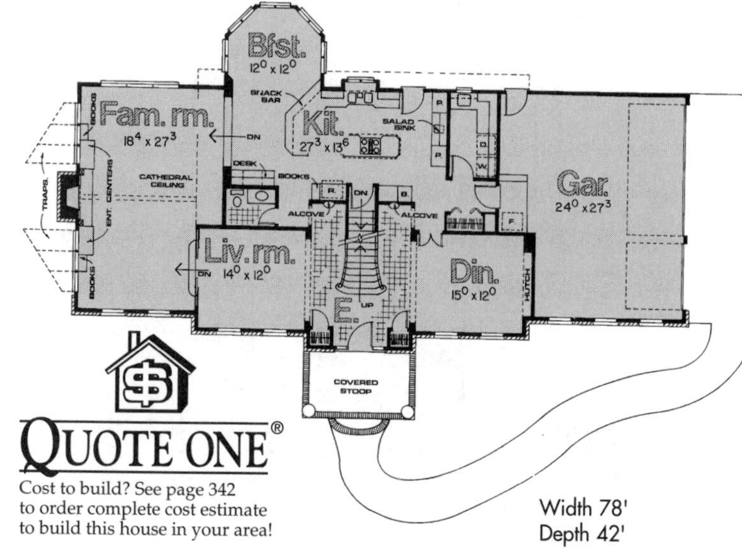
Bfst.
12⁰ x 12⁰
SNACK BAR
Fam. rm.
18⁴ x 27³
CATHEDRAL CEILING
Kit.
27³ x 13⁶
SALAD SINK
DESK
BOOKS
ALCOVE
ALCOVE
Gar.
24⁰ x 27³
Liv. rm.
14⁰ x 12⁰
Din.
15⁰ x 12⁰
HUTCH
E
UP
COVERED STOOP
Width 78'
Depth 42'

QUOTE ONE®
Cost to build? See page 342 to order complete cost estimate to build this house in your area!

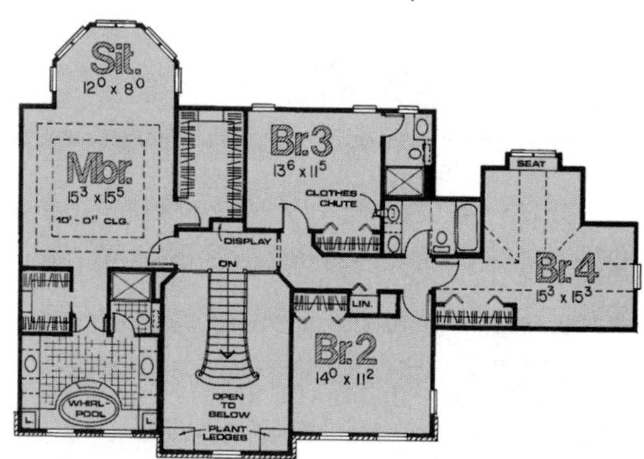
Sit.
12⁰ x 8⁰
Mbr.
15³ x 15⁵
10'-0" CLG.
Br.3
13⁶ x 11⁵
CLOTHES CHUTE
SEAT
DISPLAY
DN
LIN.
Br.4
15³ x 15³
Br.2
14⁰ x 11²
WHIRLPOOL
OPEN TO BELOW
PLANT LEDGES

PORCH
50'-0" X 8'-0"
MASTER BEDROOM
13'-0" X 14'-0"
GREAT ROOM
18'-4" X 14'-0"
UP
KEEPING ROOM
13'-4" X 12'-0"
DN.
MASTER BATH
POWDER
BREAKFAST
14'-0" X 10'-0"
FOYER
4'-8" X 11'-6"
DINING ROOM
13'-8" X 11'-6"
KITCHEN
13'-4" X 9'-6"
W.I.C.
STOOP
PORCH
LAUNDRY
9'-6" X 6'-0"
TWO CAR GARAGE
20'-4" X 20'-4"

Width 53'
Depth 59'

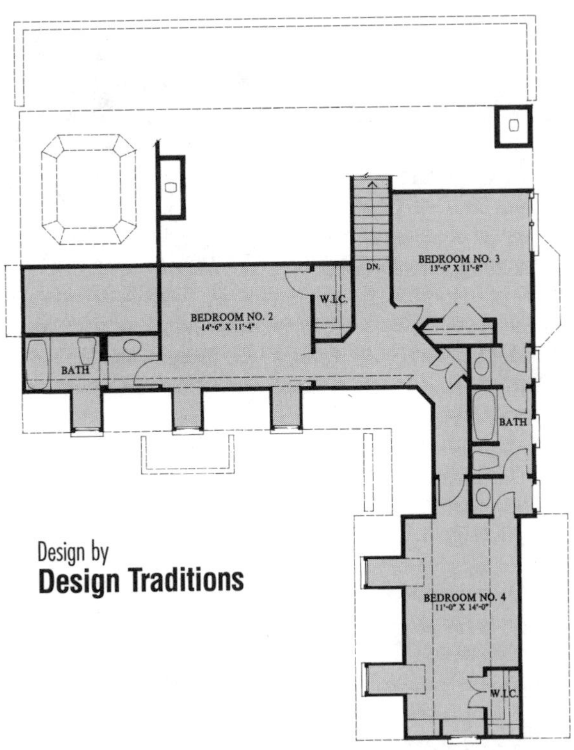
DN.
BEDROOM NO. 3
13'-6" X 11'-8"
W.I.C.
BEDROOM NO. 2
14'-6" X 11'-4"
BATH
BATH
BEDROOM NO. 4
11'-0" X 14'-0"
W.I.C.

Design by
Design Traditions

Design 9818

First Floor: 1,640 square feet;
Second Floor: 1,030 square feet;
Total: 2,670 square feet

■ This home with its classic Georgian detailing features brick jack arches that frame the arched front door and windows. Dormers above and a motorcourt entry garage add to the charm and elegance of this classically detailed home. Inside, the foyer leads directly to the large great room with a fireplace and French doors that lead outside. Just off the foyer, the dining room is separated by an open colonnade and receives brilliant light from the arched window. The kitchen and breakfast room with bay window offer every convenience including a handy cooking island. Adjacent to the breakfast room is the keeping room which incudes a corner fireplace and French doors that lead to the large rear porch. Comfort and privacy describe the master suite, complete with elegant tray ceilings, an accommodating bath and spacious walk-in closet. Upstairs, two additional bedrooms share convenient access to a bath while, down the hall, a fourth bedroom flaunts its own private bath. This home is designed with a basement foundation.

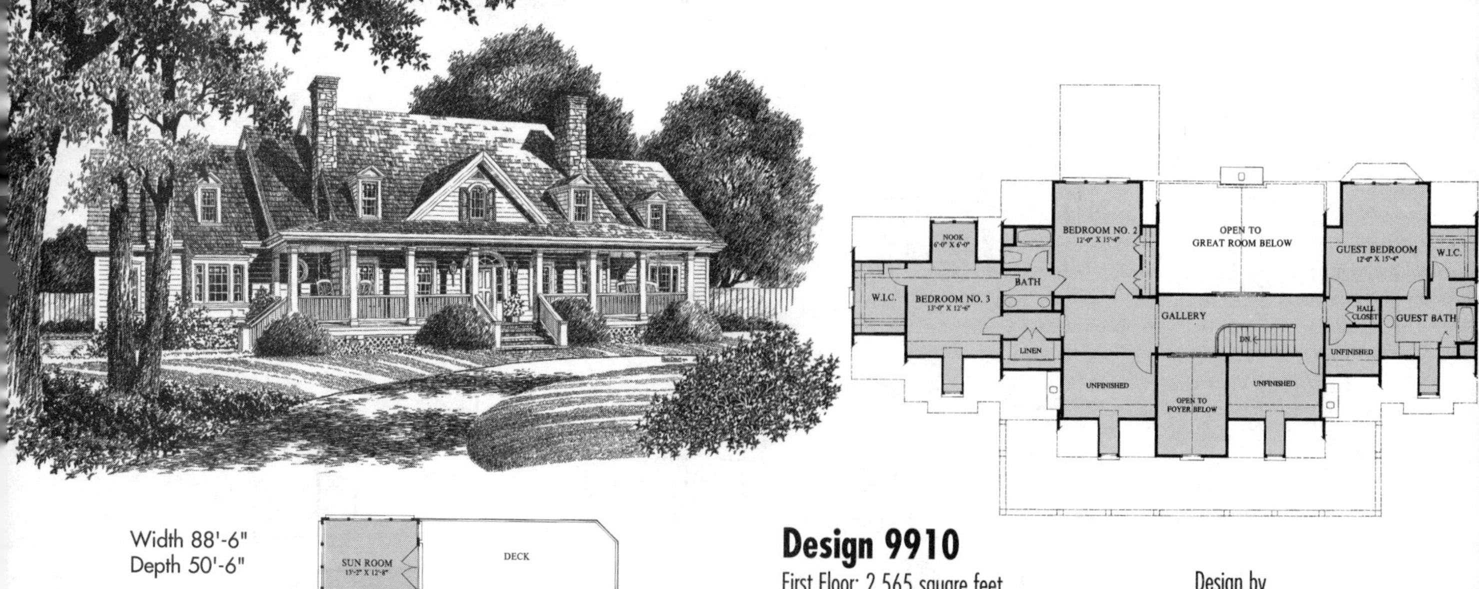
NOOK
BEDROOM NO. 2
OPEN TO GREAT ROOM BELOW
GUEST BEDROOM
W.I.C.
BATH
BEDROOM NO. 3
GALLERY
HALL CLOSET
GUEST BATH
LINEN
UNFINISHED
OPEN TO FOYER BELOW
UNFINISHED
UNFINISHED

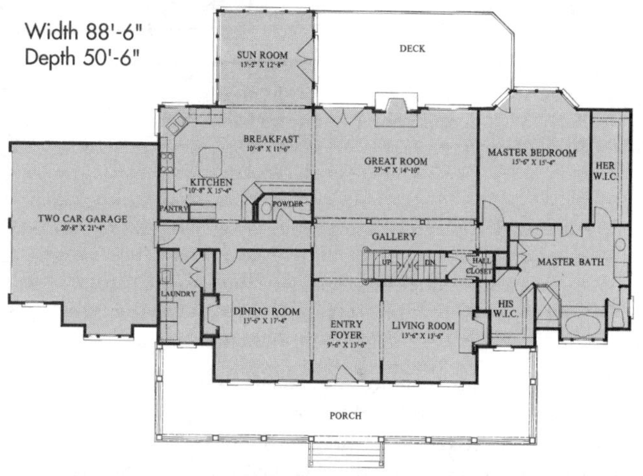
Width 88'-6"
Depth 50'-6"
SUN ROOM
DECK
BREAKFAST
KITCHEN
GREAT ROOM
MASTER BEDROOM
HER W.I.C.
TWO CAR GARAGE
PANTRY
POWDER
GALLERY
HALL CLOSET
MASTER BATH
LAUNDRY
DINING ROOM
ENTRY FOYER
LIVING ROOM
HIS W.I.C.
PORCH

Design 9910

First Floor: 2,565 square feet
Second Floor: 1,375 square feet
Total: 3,940 square feet

Design by
Design Traditions

■ A symmetrical facade with twin chimneys makes a grand statement. A covered porch welcomes visitors and provides a pleasant place to spend cool evenings. The entry foyer is flanked by formal living areas: a dining room and a living room, each with a fireplace. A third fireplace is the highlight of the expansive great room to the rear. The large eat-in kitchen openly joins the sunroom and the great room. The master bedroom has a bay window, spa-style bath and twin walk-in closets. The second floor offers three bedrooms, two full baths and plenty of storage space. This home is designed with a basement foundation.

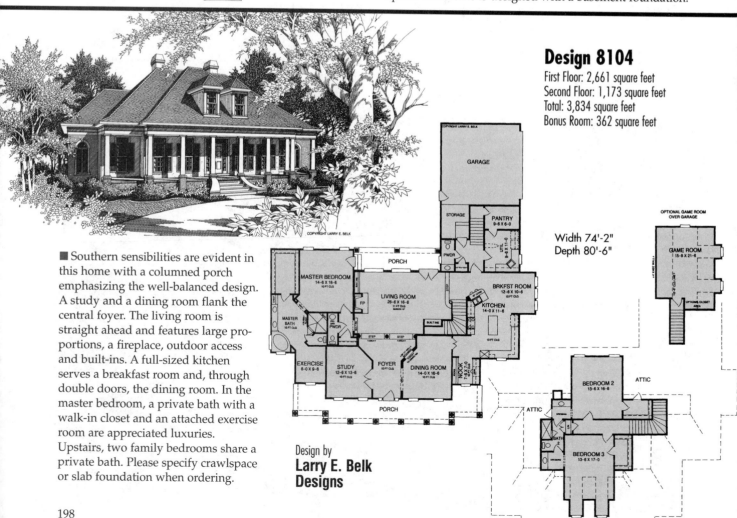

Design 8104

First Floor: 2,661 square feet
Second Floor: 1,173 square feet
Total: 3,834 square feet
Bonus Room: 362 square feet

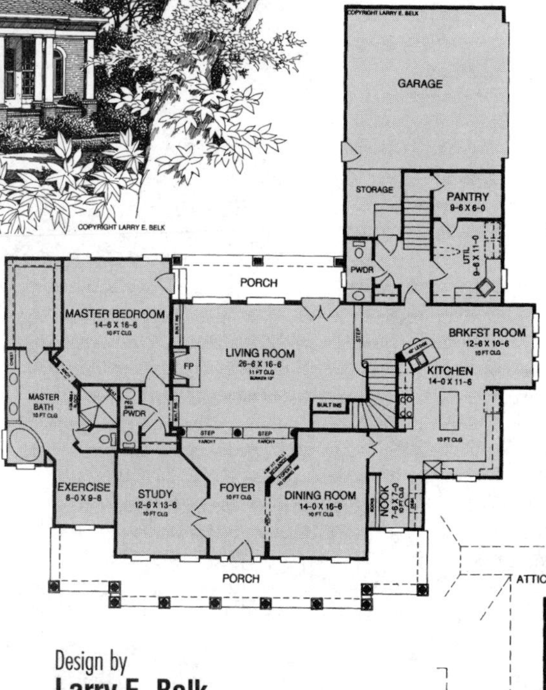

Width 74'-2"
Depth 80'-6"

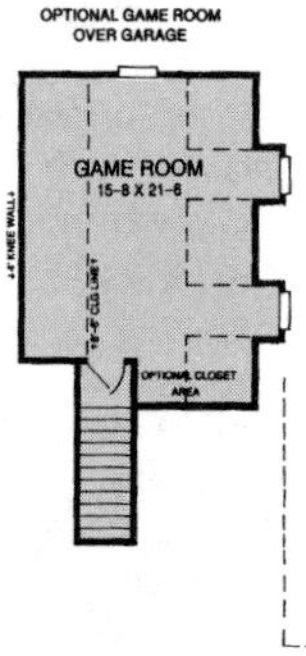

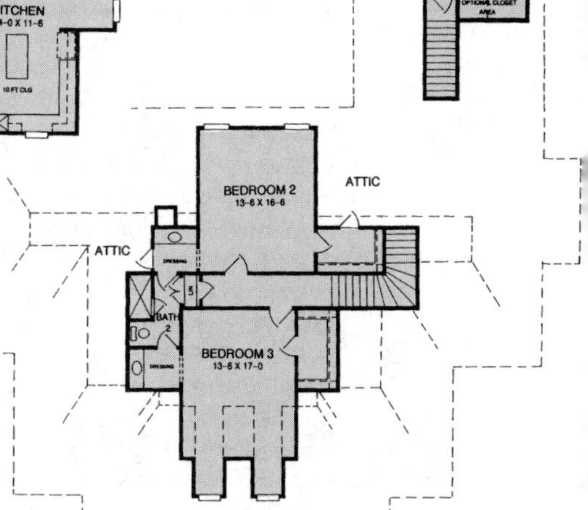

■ Southern sensibilities are evident in this home with a columned porch emphasizing the well-balanced design. A study and a dining room flank the central foyer. The living room is straight ahead and features large proportions, a fireplace, outdoor access and built-ins. A full-sized kitchen serves a breakfast room and, through double doors, the dining room. In the master bedroom, a private bath with a walk-in closet and an attached exercise room are appreciated luxuries. Upstairs, two family bedrooms share a private bath. Please specify crawlspace or slab foundation when ordering.

Design by
Larry E. Belk Designs

B. NATHAN

Design 7616

Square Footage: 2,450
Bonus Room: 647 square feet

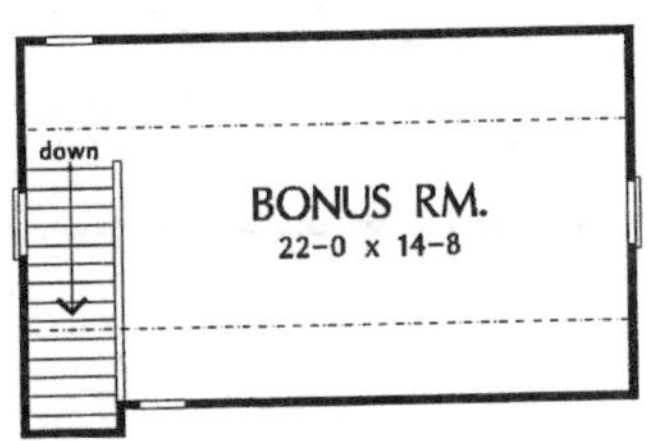
down
BONUS RM.
22-0 x 14-8

■ A handsome display of columns frames the porch of this gracious Southern home. The foyer opens to the dining room and to a study, which could also be an additional bedroom. The open living room and family room are joined under a dramatic cathedral ceiling, divided with a showpiece fireplace that opens to both rooms. The efficient corner kitchen has a handy breakfast nook that opens to a morning porch and a work island with a cooktop and curved snack bar. The master suite has a stylish tray ceiling, twin walk-in closets and a compartmented bath with an elegant bumped-out tub.

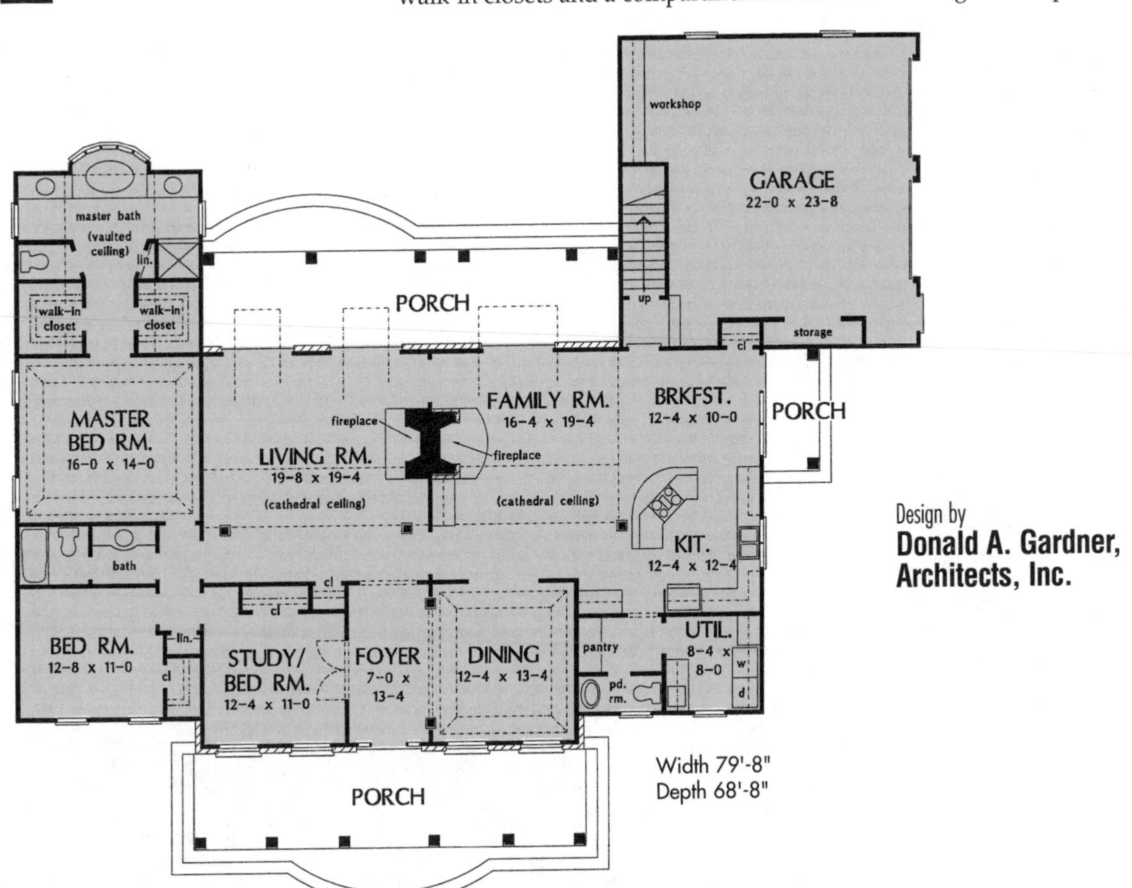
workshop
GARAGE
22-0 x 23-8
up
storage
cl
master bath
(vaulted ceiling)
lin.
walk-in closet
walk-in closet
PORCH
MASTER BED RM.
16-0 x 14-0
fireplace
fireplace
FAMILY RM.
16-4 x 19-4
BRKFST.
12-4 x 10-0
PORCH
LIVING RM.
19-8 x 19-4
(cathedral ceiling)
(cathedral ceiling)
KIT.
12-4 x 12-4
bath
cl
cl
UTIL.
8-4 x 8-0
BED RM.
12-8 x 11-0
lin.
cl
STUDY/ BED RM.
12-4 x 11-0
FOYER
7-0 x 13-4
DINING
12-4 x 13-4
pantry
pd. rm.
w
d
PORCH
Width 79'-8"
Depth 68'-8"

Design by
Donald A. Gardner, Architects, Inc.

Design 8143

Square Footage: 2,648

■ This vintage elevation has all the extras desired by today's homeowner. Twelve-foot ceilings give a spacious feel in the study, dining room and the great room. The kitchen has a cooktop work island, a pantry and a snack bar. The master suite includes His and Hers closets and an amenity-filled master bath. Two family bedrooms have roomy closets and share a private, compartmented bath. Please specify crawlspace or slab foundation when ordering.

Design by
Larry E. Belk Designs

COPYRIGHT LARRY E. BELK

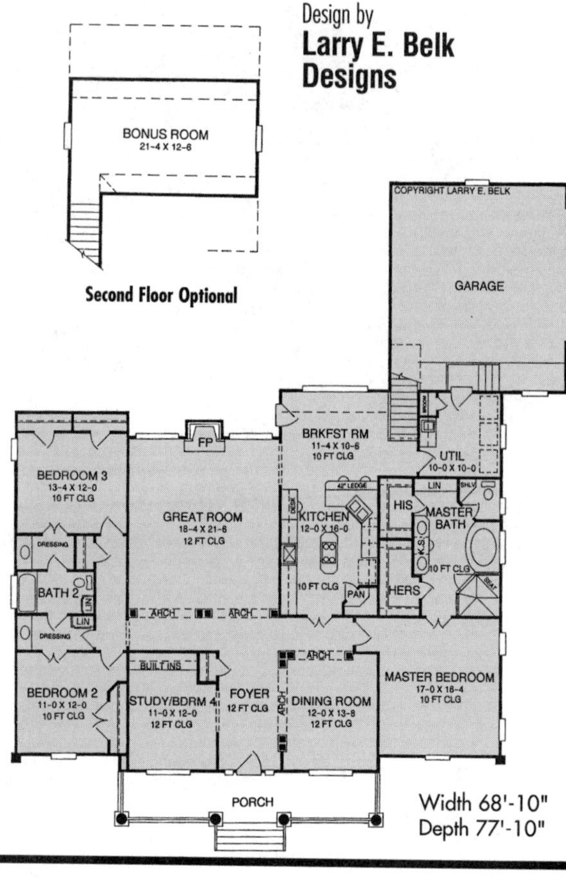
BONUS ROOM
21-4 X 12-6
Second Floor Optional
COPYRIGHT LARRY E. BELK
GARAGE
BRKFST RM
11-4 X 10-6
10 FT CLG
UTIL
10-0 X 10-0
BEDROOM 3
13-4 X 12-0
10 FT CLG
GREAT ROOM
18-4 X 21-8
12 FT CLG
KITCHEN
12-0 X 16-0
HIS
MASTER BATH
BATH 2
HERS
MASTER BEDROOM
17-0 X 18-4
10 FT CLG
BEDROOM 2
11-0 X 12-0
10 FT CLG
STUDY/BDRM 4
11-0 X 12-0
12 FT CLG
FOYER
12 FT CLG
DINING ROOM
12-0 X 13-8
12 FT CLG
PORCH

Width 68'-10"
Depth 77'-10"

Design P115

Square Footage: 1,856

■ A delightful covered porch with a recessed entry is crowned with the smart addition of a front gable. A symmetrical plan of living areas places the living and dining rooms to either side of the foyer, with the large family room directly ahead. A graceful arched opening and a fireplace flanked by windows are complemented by extra-high ceilings in the foyer and family room. An efficiently designed kitchen features an abundance of counter and cabinet space along with a serving bar to the breakfast nook. The master suite is split from the two family bedrooms for privacy—a perfect owner's retreat. A tray ceiling in the bedroom, a vaulted ceiling in the amenity-filled bath and a walk-in closet are a few of the luxurious details. Please specify basement, crawlspace or slab foundation when ordering.

Design by
Frank Betz Associates, Inc.

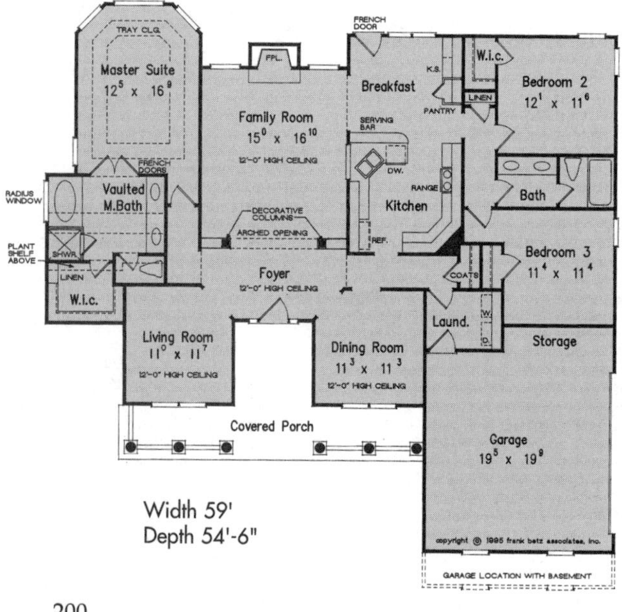
Bedroom 3
Laund.
Garage
Optional Basement Stair Location
Master Suite
Family Room
Breakfast
Bedroom 2
Kitchen
Vaulted M.Bath
Bath
Foyer
Bedroom 3
W.I.c.
Laund.
Storage
Living Room
Dining Room
Covered Porch
Garage
copyright © 1995 frank betz associates, inc.
GARAGE LOCATION WITH BASEMENT

Width 59'
Depth 54'-6"

QUOTE ONE®
Cost to build? See page 342 to order complete cost estimate to build this house in your area!

Width 65'-3"
Depth 67'-3"
2-CAR GARAGE
LAUNDRY
STORAGE
VERANDA
MASTER BATH
MASTER SUITE
W.I.C.
BREAKFAST
GREAT ROOM
KITCHEN
BEDROOM NO. 3
POWDER
BATH
PANTRY
DINING ROOM
FOYER
BEDROOM NO. 2
PORTICO

Design 9806

Square Footage: 2,697

■ Dual chimneys—one a false chimney created to enhance the aesthetic effect—and a double stairway to the covered entry of this home create a balanced architectural statement. The sunlit foyer leads straight into the spacious great room, where French doors and large side windows provide a generous view of the covered veranda. The great room features a tray ceiling and a fireplace bordered by twin bookcases. Another great view is offered from the spacious kitchen with breakfast bar and a roomy work island. The master suite provides a large bath, a spacious closet, and a glassed sitting area with access to the veranda. This home is designed with a basement foundation.

Design by
Design Traditions

Design 8013

Square Footage: 2,409
Optional Second Floor: 490 square feet

■ The stately elegance of this lovely home is evident from first glance. Upon entering the great room through two square columns, the focus is on a large masonry fireplace. The kitchen is equipped with a snack bar, walk-in pantry and planning desk. The master suite is located at the rear of the house with a luxury master bath that includes large walk-in His and Hers closets. Two family bedrooms share a full hall bath. A staircase from the kitchen area rises to an expandable second floor. With a future bedroom, game room and bath upstairs, this home will fit the needs of a growing family. Please specify crawlspace or slab foundation when ordering.

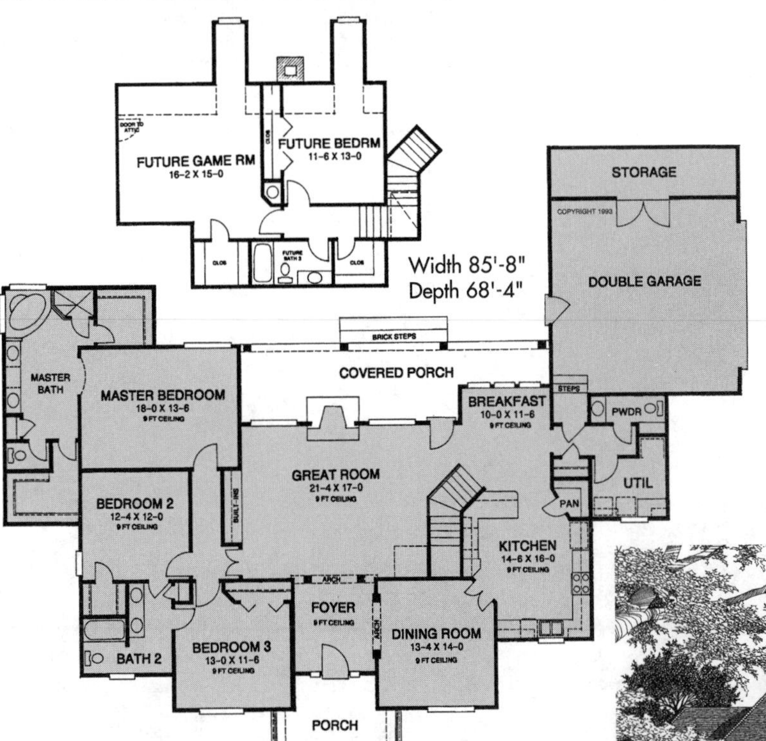

FUTURE GAME RM
16-2 X 15-0
FUTURE BEDRM
11-6 X 13-0
Width 85'-8"
Depth 68'-4"
STORAGE
DOUBLE GARAGE
BRICK STEPS
COVERED PORCH
MASTER BATH
MASTER BEDROOM
18-0 X 13-6
BREAKFAST
10-0 X 11-6
STEPS
PWDR
GREAT ROOM
21-4 X 17-0
UTIL
PAN
BEDROOM 2
12-4 X 12-0
KITCHEN
14-6 X 16-0
FOYER
DINING ROOM
13-4 X 14-0
BATH 2
BEDROOM 3
13-0 X 11-6
PORCH

QUOTE ONE®
Cost to build? See page 342 to order complete cost estimate to build this house in your area!

Design by
Larry E. Belk Designs

COPYRIGHT 1993 LARRY E. BELK

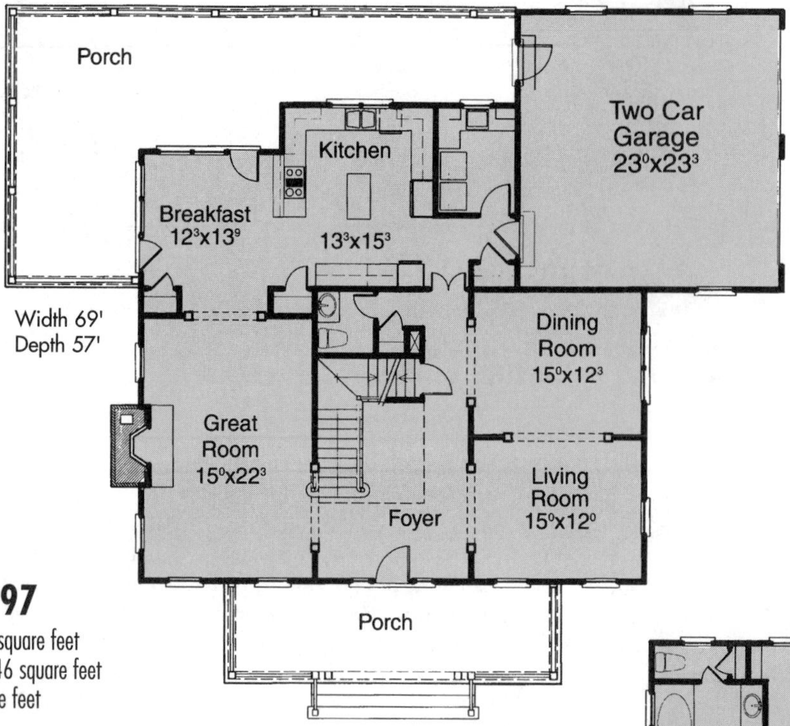

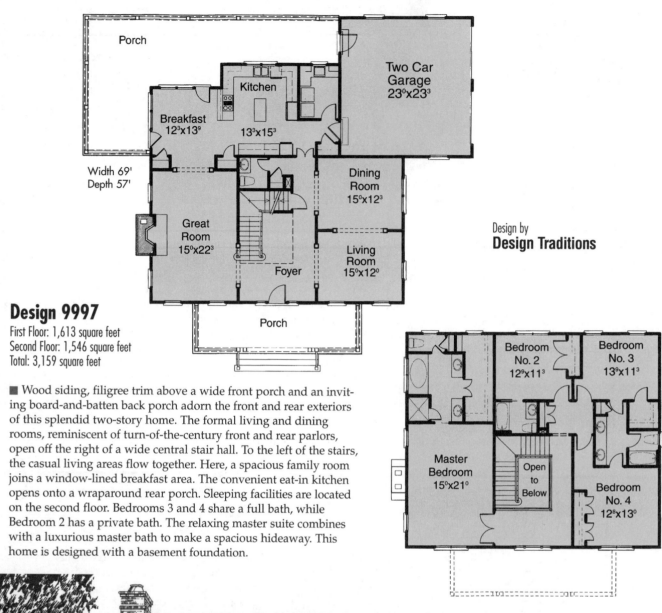

Width 69'
Depth 57'

Design by
Design Traditions

Design 9997

First Floor: 1,613 square feet
Second Floor: 1,546 square feet
Total: 3,159 square feet

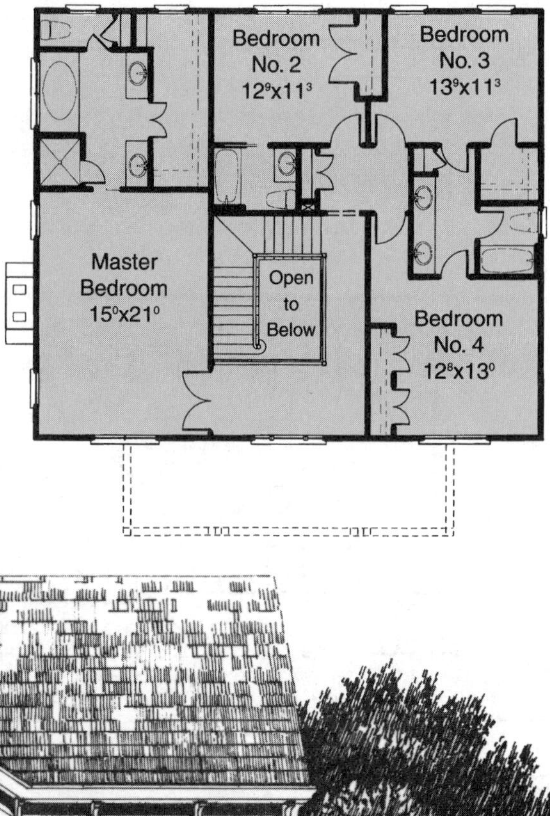

■ Wood siding, filigree trim above a wide front porch and an inviting board-and-batten back porch adorn the front and rear exteriors of this splendid two-story home. The formal living and dining rooms, reminiscent of turn-of-the-century front and rear parlors, open off the right of a wide central stair hall. To the left of the stairs, the casual living areas flow together. Here, a spacious family room joins a window-lined breakfast area. The convenient eat-in kitchen opens onto a wraparound rear porch. Sleeping facilities are located on the second floor. Bedrooms 3 and 4 share a full bath, while Bedroom 2 has a private bath. The relaxing master suite combines with a luxurious master bath to make a spacious hideaway. This home is designed with a basement foundation.

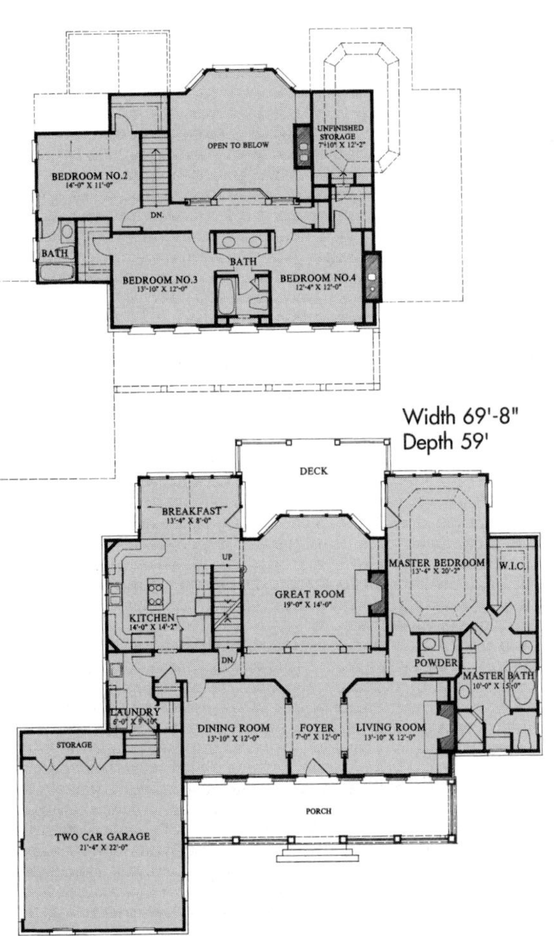
BEDROOM NO.2
14'-0" X 11'-0"
OPEN TO BELOW
UNFINISHED STORAGE
7'10" X 12'-2"
DN.
BATH
BATH
BEDROOM NO.3
13'-10" X 12'-0"
BEDROOM NO.4
12'-4" X 12'-0"
Width 69'-8"
Depth 59'
DECK
BREAKFAST
13'-4" X 8'-0"
UP
GREAT ROOM
19'-0" X 14'-0"
MASTER BEDROOM
13'-4" X 20'-2"
W.I.C.
KITCHEN
14'-0" X 14'-2"
DN.
POWDER
MASTER BATH
10'-0" X 15'-0"
LAUNDRY
6'-0" X 9'-10"
DINING ROOM
13'-10" X 12'-0"
FOYER
7'-0" X 12'-0"
LIVING ROOM
13'-10" X 12'-0"
STORAGE
PORCH
TWO CAR GARAGE
21'-4" X 22'-0"

Design by
Design Traditions

Design 9850

First Floor: 1,960 square feet
Second Floor: 905 square feet
Total: 2,865 square feet

QUOTE ONE®
Cost to build? See page 342 to order complete cost estimate to build this house in your area!

■ Georgian symmetry balances the living room and dining room to the right and left of the foyer. The main level continues into the two-story great room with built-in cabinetry, a fireplace and a large bay window. A dramatic tray ceiling, a wall of glass and access to the rear deck complete the master bedroom. The master bath features separate vanities and a large walk-in closet. Left of the great room, the main level includes a large kitchen that opens to the breakfast area. Upstairs, each bedroom features ample closet space and direct access to a bathroom. This home is designed with a basement foundation.

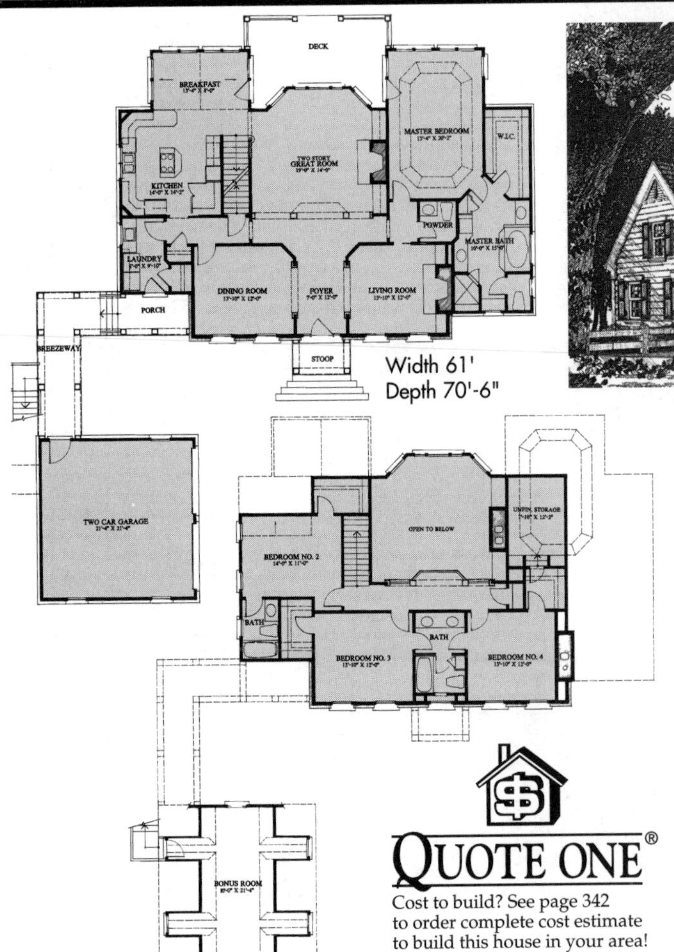
DECK
BREAKFAST
KITCHEN
TWO STORY GREAT ROOM
MASTER BEDROOM
W.I.C.
POWDER
MASTER BATH
LAUNDRY
DINING ROOM
FOYER
LIVING ROOM
PORCH
BREEZEWAY
STOOP
Width 61'
Depth 70'-6"
TWO CAR GARAGE
BEDROOM NO. 2
OPEN TO BELOW
UNFIN. STORAGE
BATH
BATH
BEDROOM NO. 3
BEDROOM NO. 4
BONUS ROOM

Design 9823

First Floor: 1,960 square feet
Second Floor: 905 square feet
Total: 2,865 square feet
Bonus Room: 297 square feet

Design by
Design Traditions

■ Traditionalists will appreciate the classical styling of this Colonial home. The foyer opens to both a banquet-sized dining room and formal living room with fireplace. Just beyond, is the two-story great room. The entire right side of the main level is occupied by the master suite. The other side of the main level includes a large kitchen and breakfast room just steps away from the detached garage. Upstairs, each bedroom features ample closet space and direct access to bathrooms. The detached garage features an unfinished office or studio on its second level. This home is designed with a basement foundation.

QUOTE ONE®
Cost to build? See page 342 to order complete cost estimate to build this house in your area!

Design by
Design Traditions

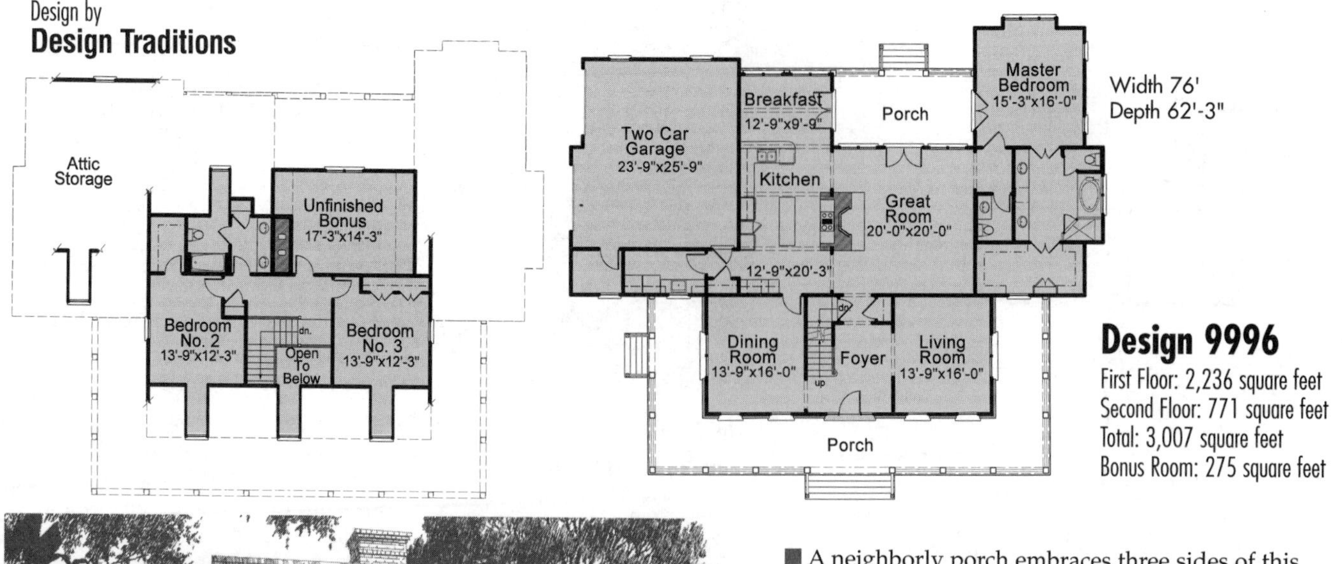

Attic
Storage
Unfinished
Bonus
17'-3"x14'-3"
Bedroom
No. 2
13'-9"x12'-3"
dn.
Open
To
Below
Bedroom
No. 3
13'-9"x12'-3"
Two Car
Garage
23'-9"x25'-9"
Breakfast
12'-9"x9'-9"
Porch
Master
Bedroom
15'-3"x16'-0"
Kitchen
Great
Room
20'-0"x20'-0"
12'-9"x20'-3"
Dining
Room
13'-9"x16'-0"
up
dn.
Foyer
Living
Room
13'-9"x16'-0"
Porch

Width 76'
Depth 62'-3"

Design 9996

First Floor: 2,236 square feet
Second Floor: 771 square feet
Total: 3,007 square feet
Bonus Room: 275 square feet

■ A neighborly porch embraces three sides of this comfortable home, extending a hearty welcome. Inside, rooms open directly onto one another, preserving an old-fashioned farmhouse atmosphere. Openings on both sides of a warming fireplace in the family room lead to a country kitchen. A sun-drenched breakfast area and an expansive master suite that features a bay window and a sumptuous bath frame the rear porch. Upstairs, dormers accent two family bedrooms and a shared bath, while bonus space can easily be a fourth bedroom. This home is designed with a basement foundation.

Design 8997

Square Footage: 2,077

■ Don't be misled by the traditional, Southern charm of this home—the floor plan is simply contemporary while fostering a down-home, country spirit. The open foyer leads past the formal dining room and into the large living room, with both rooms defined by half-walls. The casual living room features built-in cabinets, bookshelves and a media center. From the living room, a large counter borders the country kitchen that's equipped with an island work-top and breakfast nook. The master suite is accessed through a solarium/office and features dual walk-in closets and a grand bath. Two additional bedrooms, one of which can be a study, share a full hall bath.

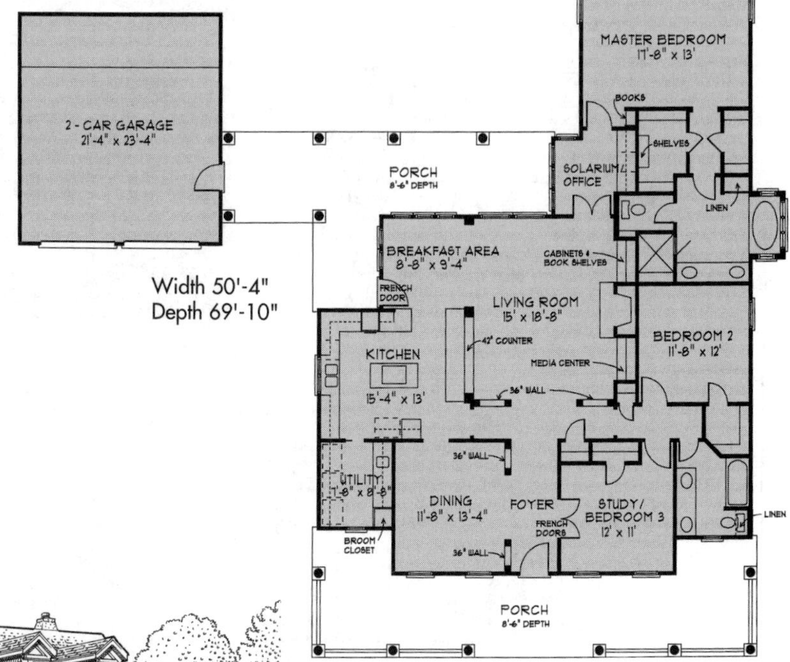

2-CAR GARAGE
21'-4" x 23'-4"
PORCH
8'-6" DEPTH
MASTER BEDROOM
17'-8" x 13'
BOOKS
SHELVES
SOLARIUM/
OFFICE
LINEN
BREAKFAST AREA
8'-8" x 9'-4"
CABINETS & BOOK SHELVES
FRENCH DOOR
LIVING ROOM
15' x 18'-8"
42" COUNTER
MEDIA CENTER
BEDROOM 2
11'-8" x 12'
KITCHEN
15'-4" x 13'
36" WALL
UTILITY
7'-8" x 8'-8"
DINING
11'-8" x 13'-4"
FOYER
FRENCH DOORS
STUDY/
BEDROOM 3
12' x 11'
LINEN
BROOM CLOSET
PORCH
8'-6" DEPTH

Width 50'-4"
Depth 69'-10"

Design by
Larry W. Garnett & Associates, Inc.

Design by
Donald A. Gardner, Architects, Inc.

Design 7622

First Floor: 2,920 square feet
Second Floor: 853 square feet
Total: 3,773 square feet

■ This home has a traditional symmetry in design that is a hallmark of Southern homes. The welcome feel of the front porch is translated throughout the plan with an open arrangement of the formal living and dining rooms with the expansive great room. The kitchen is designed for efficiency with a nearby laundry room and a large breakfast nook. The master bedroom has an elegant tray ceiling and a posh bath. Upstairs, a balcony hall leads to two family bedrooms that share a compartmented bath.

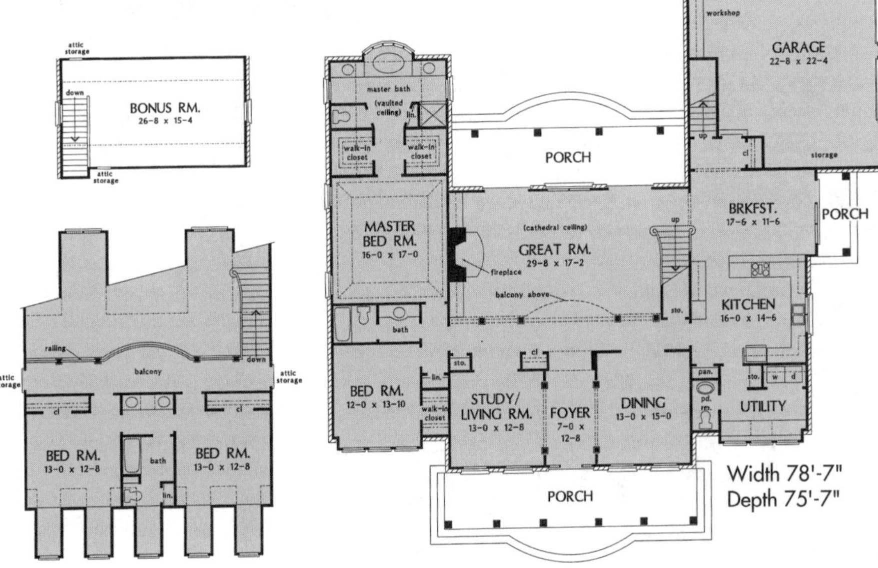
workshop
GARAGE
22-8 x 22-4
storage
master bath
(vaulted ceiling)
walk-in closet
walk-in closet
PORCH
MASTER
BED RM.
16-0 x 17-0
(cathedral ceiling)
GREAT RM.
29-8 x 17-2
fireplace
balcony above
BRKFST.
17-6 x 11-6
PORCH
KITCHEN
16-0 x 14-6
bath
BED RM.
12-0 x 13-10
STUDY/
LIVING RM.
13-0 x 12-8
FOYER
7-0 x
12-8
DINING
13-0 x 15-0
UTILITY
PORCH

Width 78'-7"
Depth 75'-7"

Design 9977

Square Footage: 3,066

■ Inspired by America's Tidewater country, this updated adaptation retains the charm of a Southern cottage at the same time it offers an elegance that is appropriate in any climate. Central to the social flow in the house, the great room opens to the kitchen, the breakfast room and the rear porch that runs across the back. The private master suite includes twin walk-in closets that lead to a lavish master bath. Two additional bedrooms share a bath, while a fourth bedroom (located on the other side of the house) enjoys a high level of privacy that makes it an ideal guest room. This home is designed with a basement foundation.

Width 73'
Depth 70'-6"

Design by
Design Traditions

Design by
Design Traditions

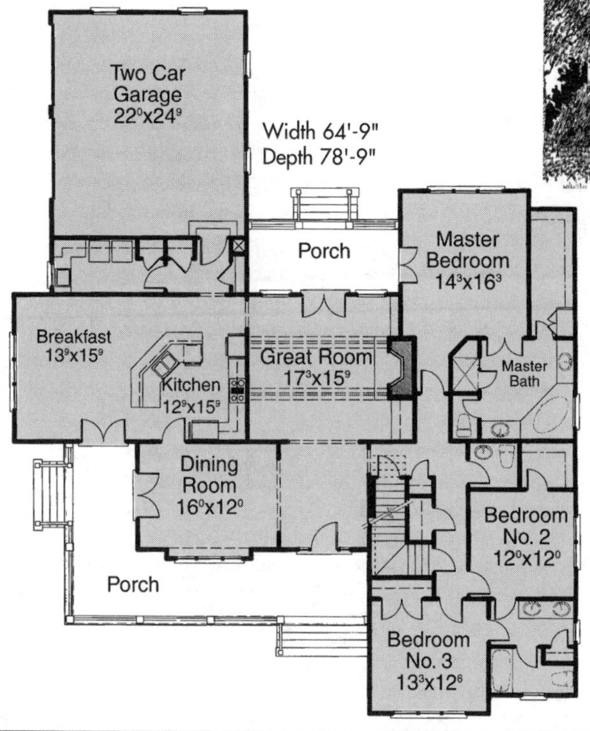

Two Car Garage 22°x24⁹
Width 64'-9"
Depth 78'-9"
Porch
Master Bedroom 14³x16³
Breakfast 13⁹x15⁹
Kitchen 12⁹x15⁹
Great Room 17³x15⁹
Master Bath
Dining Room 16°x12°
Bedroom No. 2 12°x12°
Porch
Bedroom No. 3 13³x12⁶

Design 7807

Square Footage: 2,485

■ Wood siding and a wraparound porch give this early American adaptation a warm, inviting quality. The foyer opens to the formal dining room and the great room, where a fireplace and French doors to the rear porch are highlights. The kitchen has a fantastic, angled island and a spacious breakfast room with French doors to the porch. Two family bedrooms that share a private bath balance the large master suite. This home is designed with a basement foundation.

Design by
Design Traditions

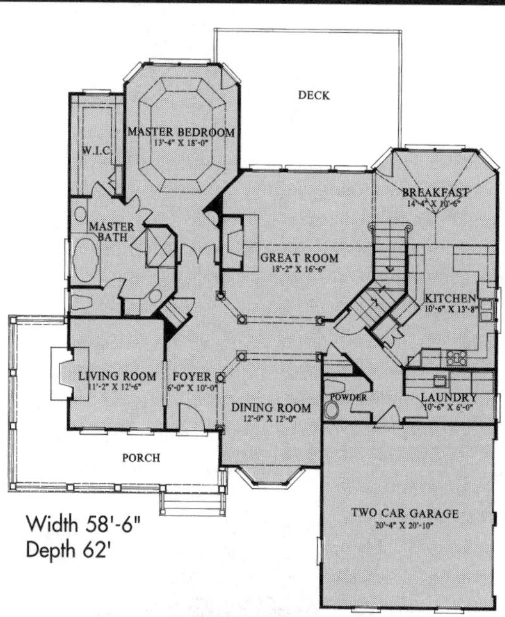

DECK
MASTER BEDROOM
W.I.C.
BREAKFAST
MASTER BATH
GREAT ROOM
KITCHEN
LIVING ROOM
FOYER
DINING ROOM
POWDER
LAUNDRY
PORCH
TWO CAR GARAGE
Width 58'-6"
Depth 62'

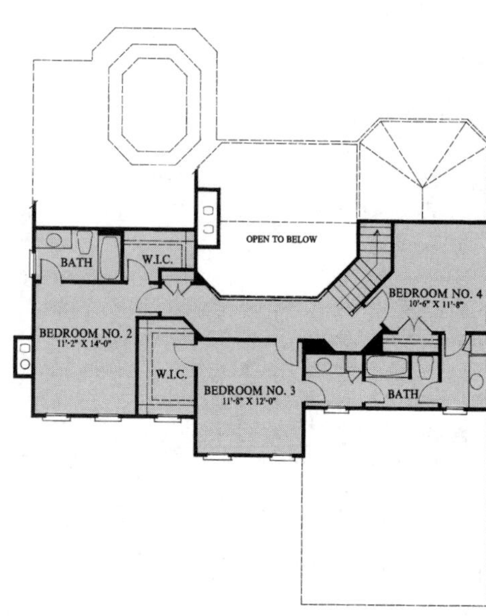

OPEN TO BELOW
BATH
W.I.C.
BEDROOM NO. 4
BEDROOM NO. 2
W.I.C.
BEDROOM NO. 3
BATH

Design 9852

First Floor: 1,840 square feet
Second Floor: 950 square feet
Total: 2,790 square feet

■ The appearance of this early American home brings the past to mind with its wraparound porch, wood siding and flower-box detailing. Inside, columns frame the great room and dining room. Left of the foyer lies the living room with a warming fireplace. The angular kitchen joins a sunny breakfast nook. The master suite has a spacious master bath and walk-in closet. Stairs to the second level lead from the breakfast area to an open landing overlooking the great room. Three family bedrooms with large walk-in closets and a private bath access complete this level. This home is designed with a basement foundation.

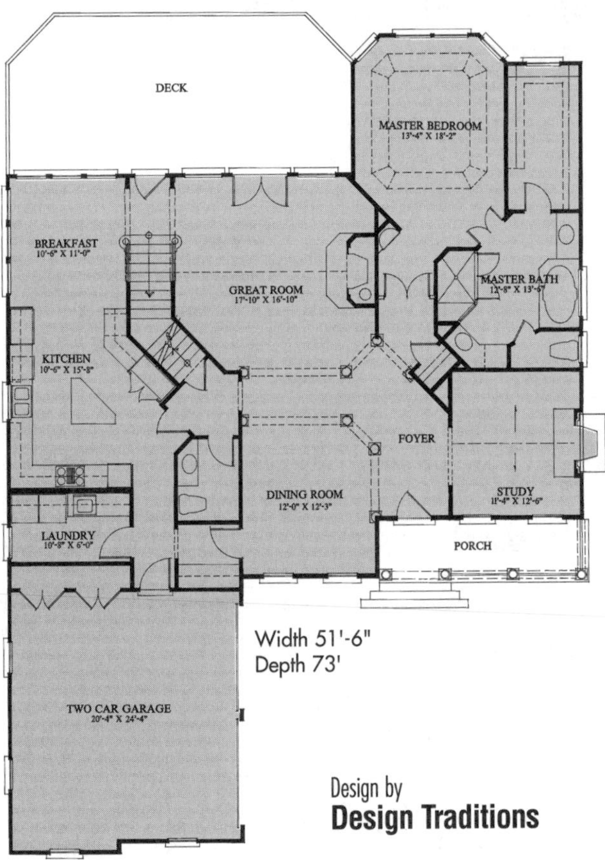
DECK
MASTER BEDROOM
BREAKFAST
GREAT ROOM
MASTER BATH
KITCHEN
FOYER
STUDY
DINING ROOM
LAUNDRY
PORCH
TWO CAR GARAGE

Width 51'-6"
Depth 73'

■ This gracious home combines warm informal materials with a modern, livable floor plan to create a true Southern classic. The dining room, study and great room work together to create one large, exciting space. Just beyond the open rail, the breakfast room is lined with windows. Plenty of counter space and storage make the kitchen truly usable. The master suite, with its tray ceiling and decorative wall niche, is a welcome owners' retreat. Upstairs, two additional bedrooms each have their own vanity within a shared bath while the third bedroom or guest room has its own bath and walk-in closet. This home is designed with a basement foundation.

Design 9822

First Floor: 1,944 square feet
Second Floor: 954 square feet
Total: 2,898 square feet

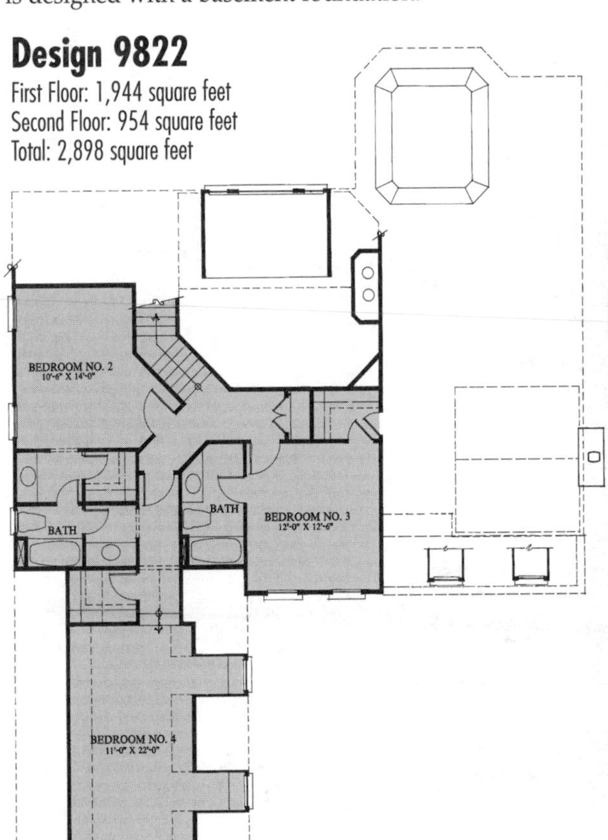
BEDROOM NO. 2
BATH
BATH
BEDROOM NO. 3
BEDROOM NO. 4

Design by
Design Traditions

QUOTE ONE®

Cost to build? See page 342 to order complete cost estimate to build this house in your area!

Design 8018

Square Footage: 2,846

■ This Southern Colonial home is distinguished by its columned porch and double dormer. Inside, the angled foyer is defined by columns and connecting arches. The master suite is located away from the other bedrooms for privacy and includes a large master bath and a walk-in closet. Three additional bedrooms are located adjacent to the family room. The kitchen, breakfast area and family room are open—perfect for informal entertaining and family gatherings. The foyer, living room and dining room have twelve-foot ceilings. Ten-foot ceilings are used in the family room, kitchen, breakfast area and master suite to give this home an open, spacious feeling. Please specify crawlspace or slab foundation when ordering.

Design by
Larry E. Belk Designs

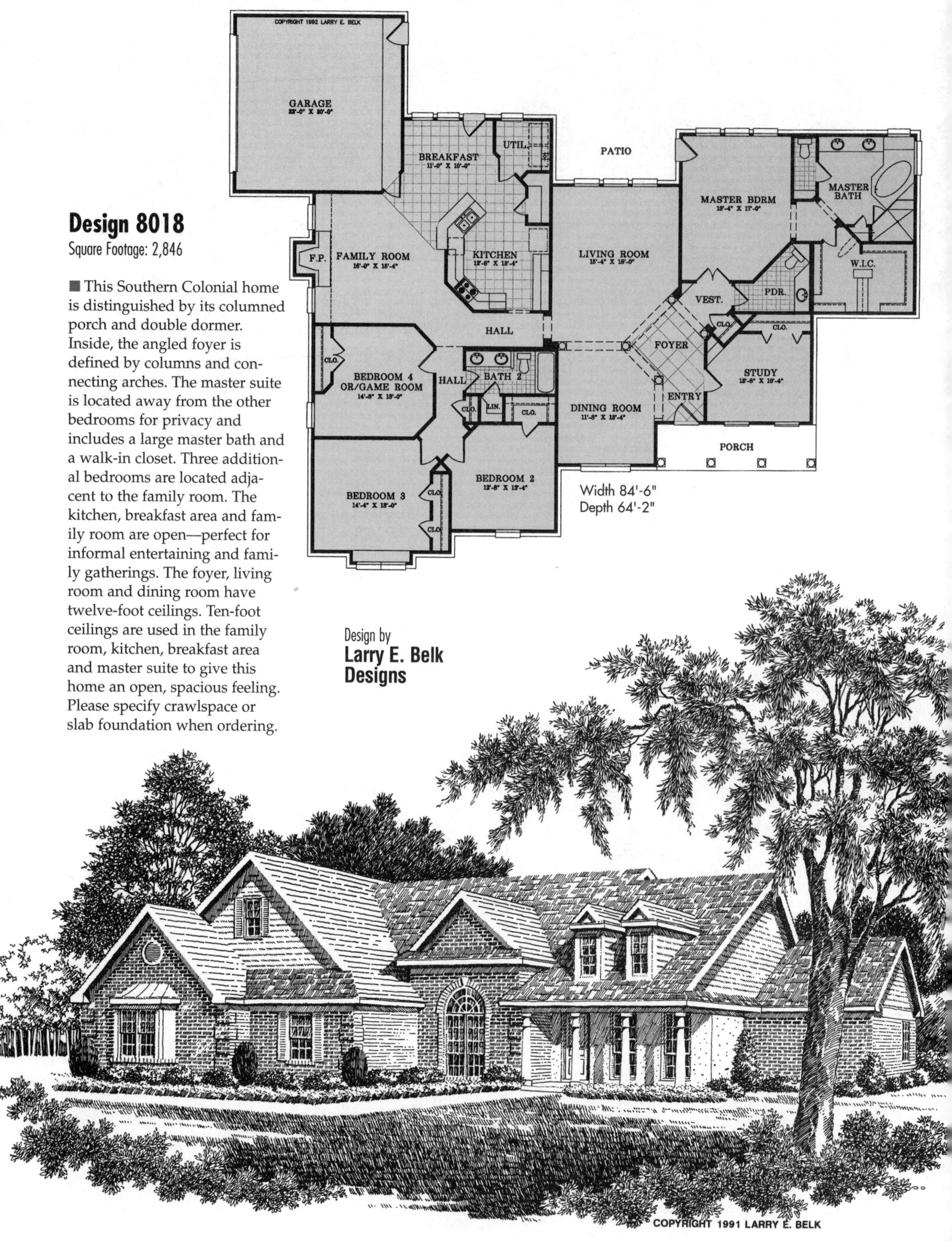
COPYRIGHT 1992 LARRY E. BELK
GARAGE
BREAKFAST
UTIL.
PATIO
MASTER BDRM
MASTER BATH
F.P.
FAMILY ROOM
KITCHEN
LIVING ROOM
W.I.C.
VEST.
PDR.
CLO.
HALL
FOYER
BEDROOM 4 OR/GAME ROOM
HALL
BATH 2
STUDY
LIN.
DINING ROOM
ENTRY
PORCH
BEDROOM 2
BEDROOM 3
Width 84'-6"
Depth 64'-2"
COPYRIGHT 1991 LARRY E. BELK

Design 9632

First Floor: 1,756 square feet
Second Floor: 565 square feet
Total: 2,321 square feet

QUOTE ONE®

Cost to build? See page 342 to order complete cost estimate to build this house in your area!

■ A wraparound covered porch at the front and sides of this house and an open deck at the back provide plenty of outside living area. The spacious great room features a fireplace, cathedral ceiling and clerestory with an arched window. The island kitchen has an attached, skylit breakfast room complete with a bay window. The first-floor master bedroom contains a generous closet and a master bath with garden tub, double-bowl vanity and shower. The second floor sports two bedrooms and a full bath with double-bowl vanity. An elegant balcony overlooks the great room. Please specify basement or crawlspace foundation when ordering.

Design by
Donald A. Gardner, Architects, Inc.

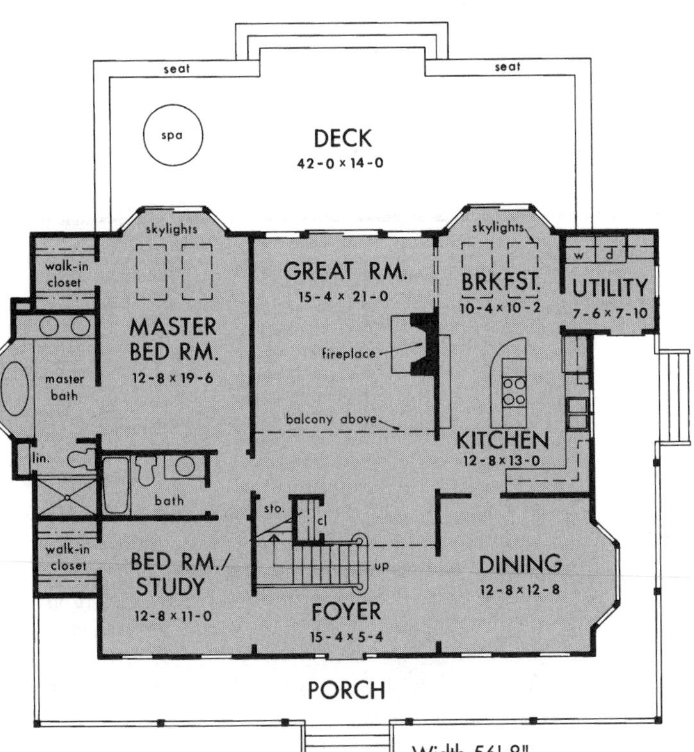
seat
seat
spa
DECK
42-0 x 14-0
skylights
skylights
walk-in closet
GREAT RM.
15-4 x 21-0
BRKFST.
10-4 x 10-2
w
d
UTILITY
7-6 x 7-10
MASTER BED RM.
12-8 x 19-6
fireplace
master bath
balcony above
KITCHEN
12-8 x 13-0
lin.
bath
sto.
cl
walk-in closet
BED RM./ STUDY
12-8 x 11-0
up
DINING
12-8 x 12-8
FOYER
15-4 x 5-4
PORCH

Width 56'-8"
Depth 54'-4"

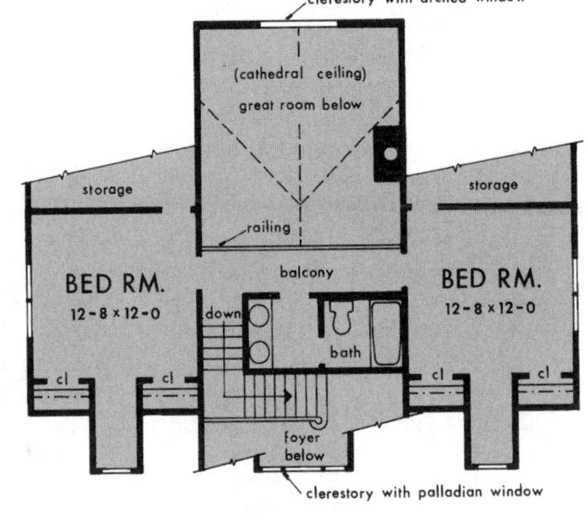
clerestory with arched window
(cathedral ceiling)
great room below
storage
storage
railing
balcony
BED RM.
12-8 x 12-0
BED RM.
12-8 x 12-0
down
bath
cl
cl
cl
cl
foyer below
clerestory with palladian window

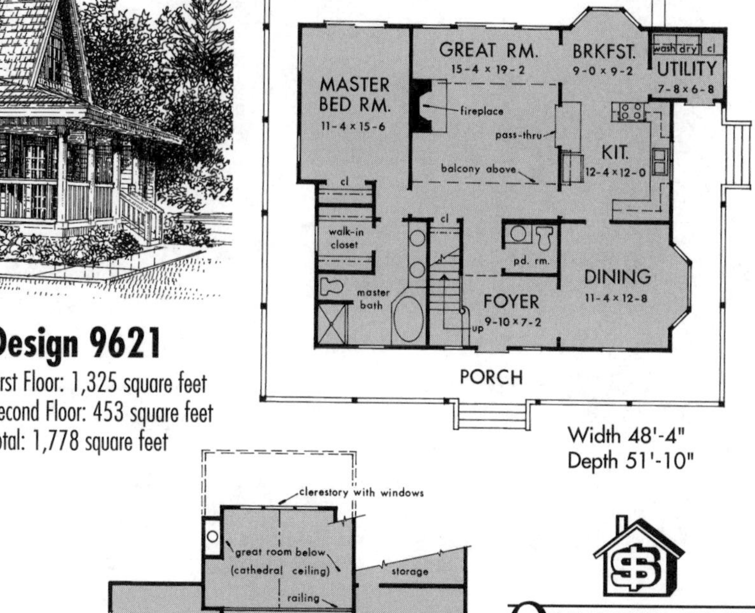
seat
seat
DECK
41-10 x 13-4
spa
GREAT RM.
15-4 x 19-2
BRKFST.
9-0 x 9-2
wash dry cl
UTILITY
7-8 x 6-8
MASTER
BED RM.
11-4 x 15-6
fireplace
pass-thru
KIT.
12-4 x 12-0
balcony above
cl
walk-in closet
master bath
cl
pd. rm.
DINING
11-4 x 12-8
FOYER
9-10 x 7-2
up
PORCH
Width 48'-4"
Depth 51'-10"
clerestory with windows
great room below
(cathedral ceiling)
railing
storage
BED RM.
11-4 x 10-2
down
BED RM.
11-4 x 10-2
bath
cl
cl
cl
cl
foyer below
clerestory with palladian window

■ This compact design has all the amenities available in larger plans with little wasted space. The spacious great room has a fireplace, a cathedral ceiling and clerestory windows. A second-level balcony overlooks this gathering area. The kitchen is centrally located for maximum flexibility and features a pass-through to the great room. Besides the generous master suite with a full bath, there are two family bedrooms located on the second level sharing a full bath with a double vanity. Please specify basement or crawlspace foundation when ordering.

Design 9621

First Floor: 1,325 square feet
Second Floor: 453 square feet
Total: 1,778 square feet

Design by
Donald A. Gardner, Architects, Inc.

QUOTE ONE®
Cost to build? See page 342 to order complete cost estimate to build this house in your area!

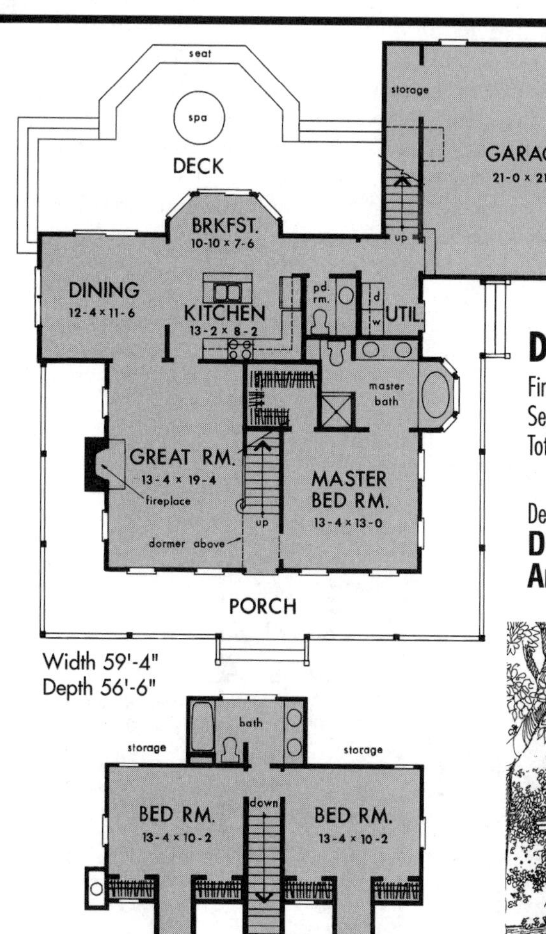
seat
spa
DECK
storage
GARAGE
21-0 x 21-8
BRKFST.
10-10 x 7-6
up
DINING
12-4 x 11-6
KITCHEN
13-2 x 8-2
pd. rm.
d
w
UTIL
master bath
GREAT RM.
13-4 x 19-4
fireplace
MASTER
BED RM.
13-4 x 13-0
up
dormer above
PORCH
Width 59'-4"
Depth 56'-6"
bath
storage
storage
BED RM.
13-4 x 10-2
down
BED RM.
13-4 x 10-2

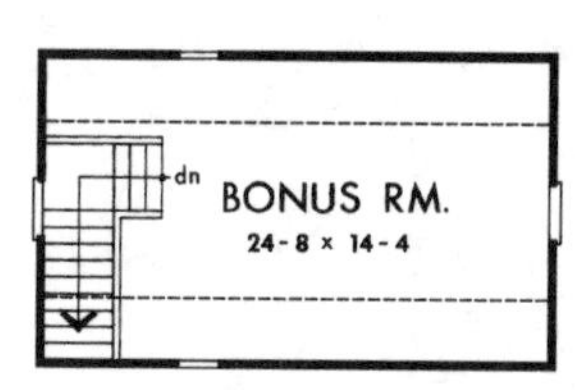
dn
BONUS RM.
24-8 x 14-4

QUOTE ONE®
Cost to build? See page 342 to order complete cost estimate to build this house in your area!

Design 9690

First Floor: 1,145 square feet
Second Floor: 518 square feet
Total: 1,663 square fee

Design by
Donald A. Gardner, Architects, Inc.

■ Look this plan over and you'll be amazed at how much livability can be found in less than 2,000 square feet. A wraparound porch welcomes visitors to the home. Inside lies an enormous great room with a fireplace. To the rear of the home, the breakfast and dining rooms have sliding glass doors to a large deck with room for a spa. The master bedroom contains a walk-in closet and an airy bath with a whirlpool tub. Two bedrooms are found on the second floor, as well as a bonus room over the garage.

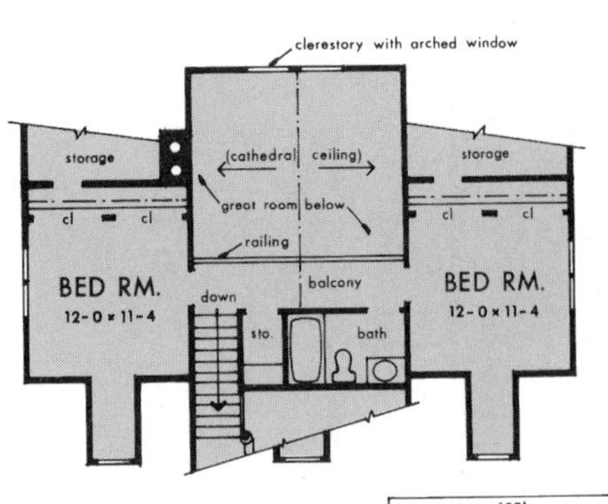
clerestory with arched window
storage
(cathedral ceiling)
storage
cl
cl
great room below
cl
cl
railing
BED RM.
12-0 × 11-4
down
balcony
BED RM.
12-0 × 11-4
sto.
bath

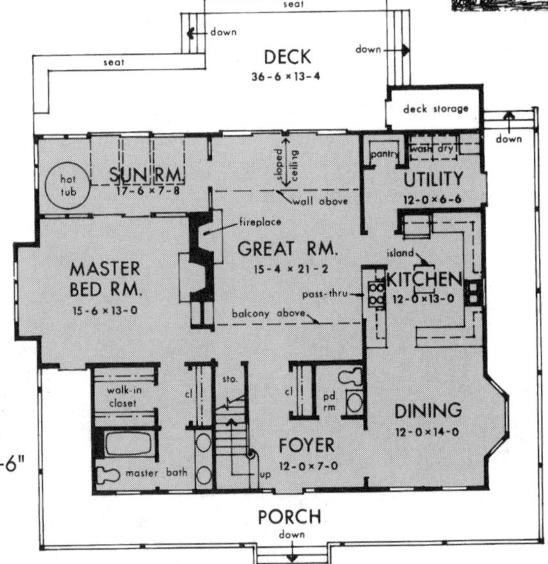
seat
down
seat
DECK
36-6 × 13-4
down
deck storage
down
pantry
wash dry
hot tub
SUN RM.
17-6 × 7-8
sloped ceiling
UTILITY
12-0 × 6-6
wall above
fireplace
GREAT RM.
15-4 × 21-2
island
MASTER
BED RM.
15-6 × 13-0
KITCHEN
12-0 × 13-0
pass-thru
balcony above
walk-in closet
cl
sto.
cl
pd rm
DINING
12-0 × 14-0
FOYER
12-0 × 7-0
master bath
up
PORCH
down

Width 54'
Depth 44'-6"

Design 9605

First Floor: 1,562 square feet
Second Floor: 537 square feet
Total: 2,099 square feet

Design by
Donald A. Gardner, Architects, Inc.

■ Outdoor living is encouraged in a wraparound covered porch at the front and sides of this house, as well as the open deck with storage to the rear. The country feel is updated with arched rear windows and a sunroom. The spacious great room has a fireplace, cathedral ceiling and clerestory windows. The kitchen occupies a central location between the dining room and the great room for equally convenient formal and informal occasions. A generous master suite has a fireplace and access to the sunroom and covered porch. The second level features two family bedrooms, a full bath and storage space.

■ The welcoming charm of this country farmhouse is expressed by its many windows and its covered, wraparound porch. A two-story entrance foyer is enhanced by a Palladian window in a clerestory dormer above to allow natural lighting. A first-floor master suite allows privacy and accessibility. The master bath includes a whirlpool tub, a shower and double-bowl vanity along with a walk-in closet. The second floor provides two additional bedrooms, a full bath, and plenty of storage space. A bonus room provides room to grow. Please specify basement or crawlspace foundation when ordering.

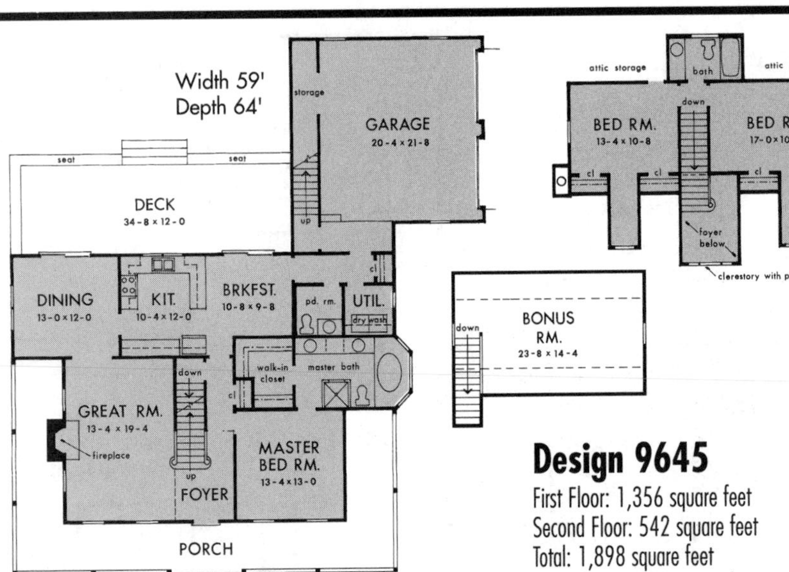
Width 59'
Depth 64'
storage
GARAGE
20-4 × 21-8
seat
seat
DECK
34-8 × 12-0
up
cl
DINING
13-0 × 12-0
KIT.
10-4 × 12-0
BRKFST.
10-8 × 9-8
pd. rm.
UTIL.
dry wash
down
walk-in closet
master bath
cl
GREAT RM.
13-4 × 19-4
fireplace
MASTER
BED RM.
13-4 × 13-0
up
FOYER
PORCH
attic storage
bath
attic storage
down
BED RM.
13-4 × 10-8
BED RM.
17-0 × 10-8
cl
cl
cl
cl
foyer below
clerestory with palladian window
down
BONUS
RM.
23-8 × 14-4

Design 9645

First Floor: 1,356 square feet
Second Floor: 542 square feet
Total: 1,898 square feet
Bonus Room: 393 square feet

Design by
Donald A. Gardner, Architects, Inc.

QUOTE ONE®

Cost to build? See page 342 to order complete cost estimate to build this house in your area!

Design by
Donald A. Gardner, Architects, Inc.

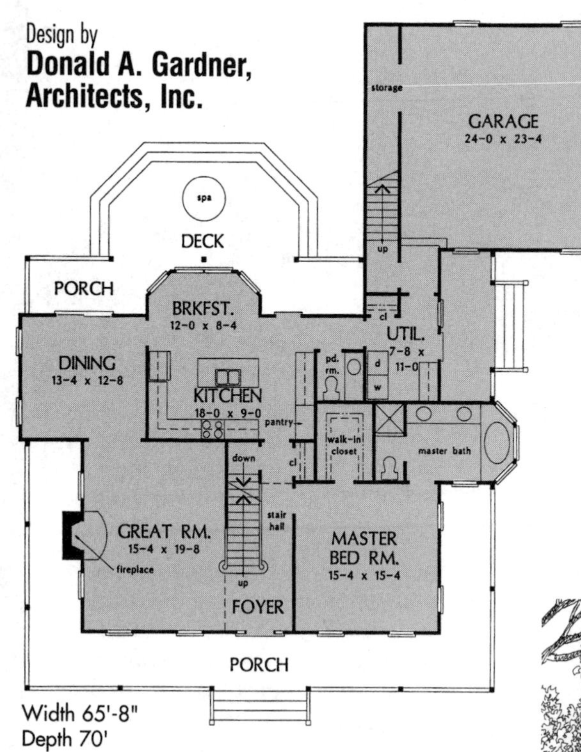

GARAGE
24-0 x 23-4
storage
DECK
spa
PORCH
BRKFST.
12-0 x 8-4
DINING
13-4 x 12-8
KITCHEN
18-0 x 9-0
pantry
UTIL.
7-8 x 11-0
pd. rm.
walk-in closet
master bath
GREAT RM.
15-4 x 19-8
fireplace
stair hall
MASTER BED RM.
15-4 x 15-4
FOYER
PORCH

Width 65'-8"
Depth 70'

Design 9694

First Floor: 1,537 square feet
Second Floor: 641 square feet
Total: 2,178 square feet

■ This charming farmhouse has a two-story entrance foyer with a Palladian window in a clerestory dormer above for natural light. The master suite, with its large walk-in closet, is on the first level for privacy and accessibility. The master bath includes a whirlpool tub, a shower and a double-bowl vanity. The second level has two bedrooms, a full bath and plenty of storage. Please specify crawlspace or basement foundation when ordering.

Width 76'-4"
Depth 74'-2"

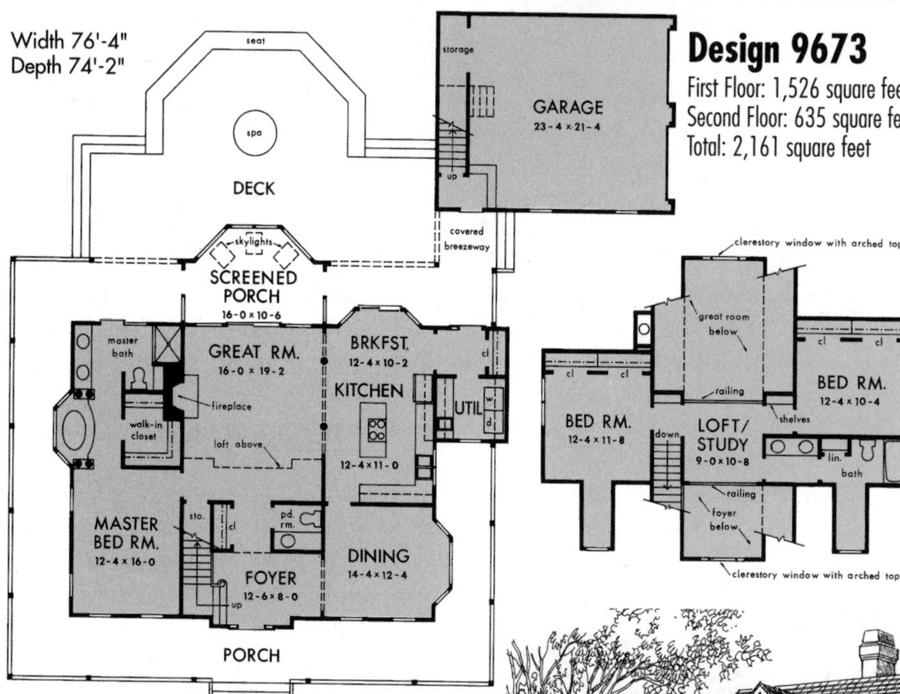

seat
spa
DECK
storage
GARAGE
23-4 x 21-4
covered breezeway
skylights
SCREENED PORCH
16-0 x 10-6
master bath
GREAT RM.
16-0 x 19-2
fireplace
walk-in closet
loft above
BRKFST.
12-4 x 10-2
KITCHEN
12-4 x 11-0
UTIL.
MASTER BED RM.
12-4 x 16-0
pd. rm.
FOYER
12-6 x 8-0
DINING
14-4 x 12-4
PORCH
clerestory window with arched top
great room below
railing
BED RM.
12-4 x 10-4
BED RM.
12-4 x 11-8
LOFT/ STUDY
9-0 x 10-8
shelves
lin.
bath
foyer below
clerestory window with arched top

Design 9673

First Floor: 1,526 square feet
Second Floor: 635 square feet
Total: 2,161 square feet

■ This beautiful farmhouse boasts all the extras a three-bedroom design could offer. Clerestory windows with arched tops enhance the exterior both front and back as well as allowing natural light to penetrate into the foyer and the great room. A kitchen with an island counter and a breakfast area is open to the spacious great room through a cased opening with a colonnade. The exquisite master suite has a generous bedroom, a large walk-in closet and a lush master bath. The second level has two bedrooms sharing a full bath and a loft/study area overlooking the great room.

Design by
Donald A. Gardner, Architects, Inc.

QUOTE ONE®

Cost to build? See page 342 to order complete cost estimate to build this house in your area!

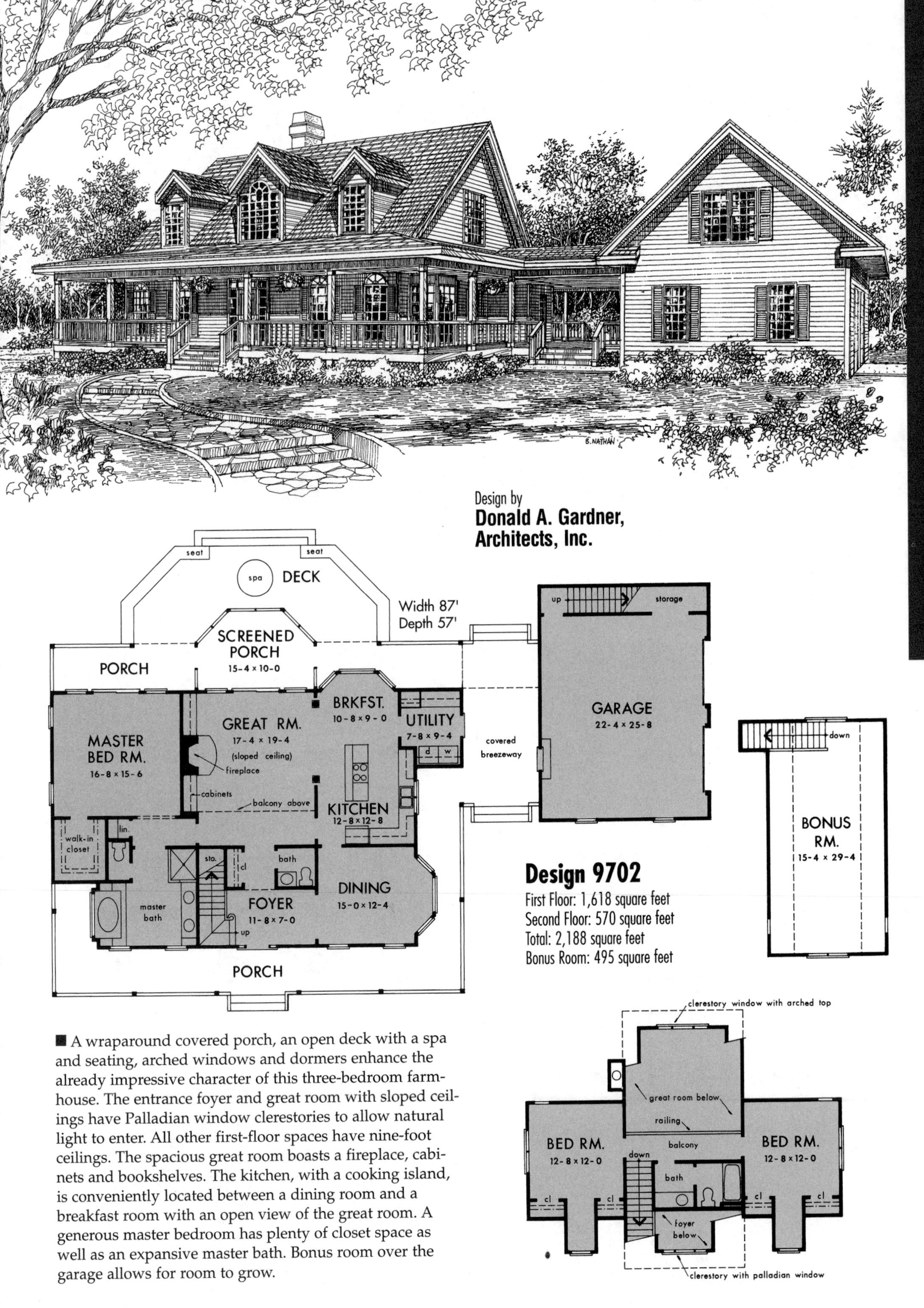
E. NATHAN
seat
seat
spa
DECK
Width 87'
Depth 57'
SCREENED PORCH 15-4 x 10-0
PORCH
MASTER BED RM. 16-8 x 15-6
GREAT RM. 17-4 x 19-4 (sloped ceiling)
fireplace
cabinets
balcony above
BRKFST. 10-8 x 9-0
UTILITY 7-8 x 9-4
d
w
KITCHEN 12-8 x 12-8
walk-in closet
lin.
sto.
cl
bath
master bath
FOYER 11-8 x 7-0
up
DINING 15-0 x 12-4
PORCH
covered breezeway
up
storage
GARAGE 22-4 x 25-8
down
BONUS RM. 15-4 x 29-4
clerestory window with arched top
great room below
railing
balcony
BED RM. 12-8 x 12-0
down
bath
BED RM. 12-8 x 12-0
cl
cl
cl
cl
foyer below
clerestory with palladian window

Design by
Donald A. Gardner, Architects, Inc.

Design 9702

First Floor: 1,618 square feet
Second Floor: 570 square feet
Total: 2,188 square feet
Bonus Room: 495 square feet

■ A wraparound covered porch, an open deck with a spa and seating, arched windows and dormers enhance the already impressive character of this three-bedroom farmhouse. The entrance foyer and great room with sloped ceilings have Palladian window clerestories to allow natural light to enter. All other first-floor spaces have nine-foot ceilings. The spacious great room boasts a fireplace, cabinets and bookshelves. The kitchen, with a cooking island, is conveniently located between a dining room and a breakfast room with an open view of the great room. A generous master bedroom has plenty of closet space as well as an expansive master bath. Bonus room over the garage allows for room to grow.

Design 9623

First Floor: 1,651 square feet
Second Floor: 567 square feet
Total: 2,218 square feet

■ A wonderful wraparound covered porch at the front and sides of this house and the open deck with spa at the back provide plenty of outside living area. Inside, the spacious great room is appointed with a fireplace, cathedral ceiling and clerestory with arched window. The kitchen is centrally located for maximum flexibility in layout and features a food preparation island for convenience. Besides the master bedroom with access to the sun room, there are two second-level bedrooms that share a full bath. Please specify basement or crawlspace foundation when ordering.

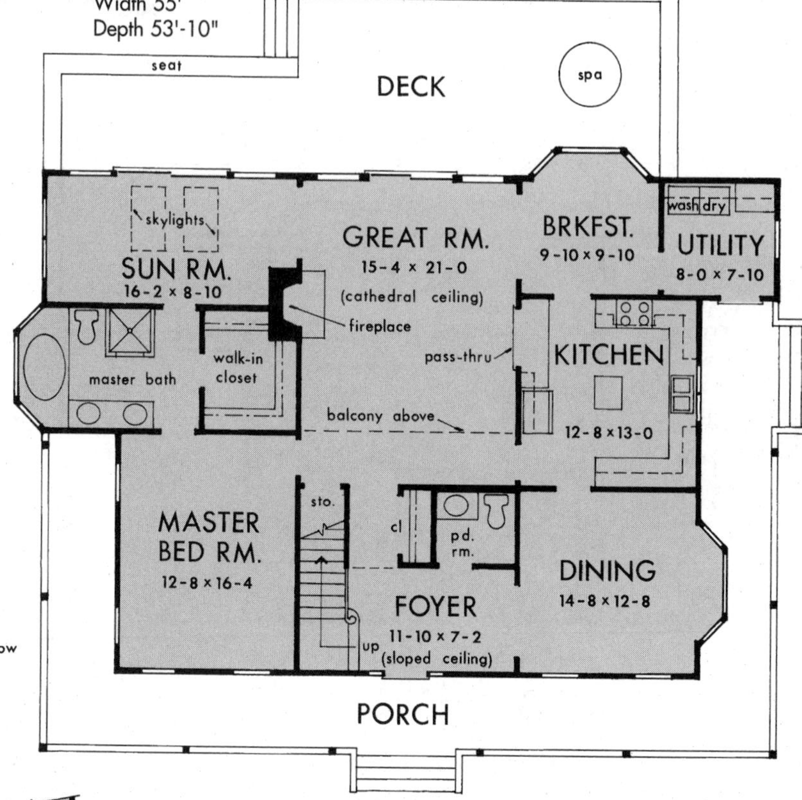
Width 55'
Depth 53'-10"
seat
seat
DECK
spa
skylights
SUN RM.
16-2 x 8-10
GREAT RM.
15-4 x 21-0
(cathedral ceiling)
fireplace
BRKFST.
9-10 x 9-10
wash dry
UTILITY
8-0 x 7-10
master bath
walk-in closet
pass-thru
KITCHEN
12-8 x 13-0
balcony above
sto.
cl
pd. rm.
MASTER BED RM.
12-8 x 16-4
DINING
14-8 x 12-8
FOYER
11-10 x 7-2
up
(sloped ceiling)
PORCH

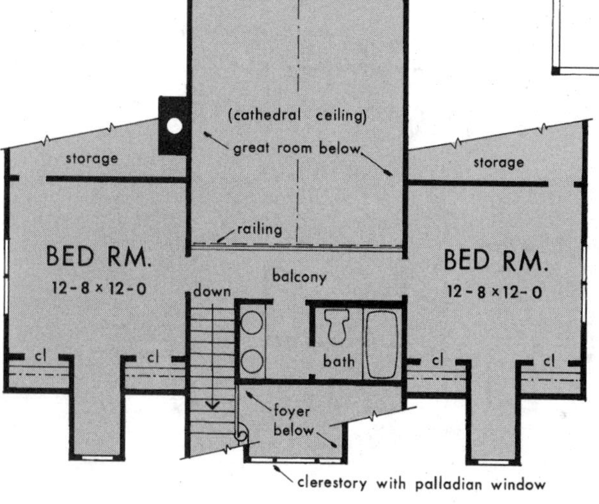
clerestory with arched window
(cathedral ceiling)
great room below
storage
storage
railing
BED RM.
12-8 x 12-0
balcony
BED RM.
12-8 x 12-0
down
bath
cl
cl
cl
cl
foyer below
clerestory with palladian window

Design by
Donald A. Gardner, Architects, Inc.

QUOTE ONE®

Cost to build? See page 342 to order complete cost estimate to build this house in your area!

■ This grand four-bedroom farmhouse with wraparound porch has eye-catching features: a double-gabled roof, Palladian window at the upper level, arched window on the lower level and intricately detailed brick chimney. The exceptionally large family room allows for more casual living. Look for a fireplace, wet bar and direct access to a porch and deck here. The lavish kitchen boasts a cooking island and serves the dining room, breakfast and deck areas. The master suite on the second level has a large walk-in closet and a master bath with a whirlpool tub, shower and double-bowl vanity. Three additional bedrooms share a full bath.

Design 9667

First Floor: 1,357 square feet
Second Floor: 1,204 square feet
Total: 2,561 square feet

Design by
Donald A. Gardner, Architects, Inc.

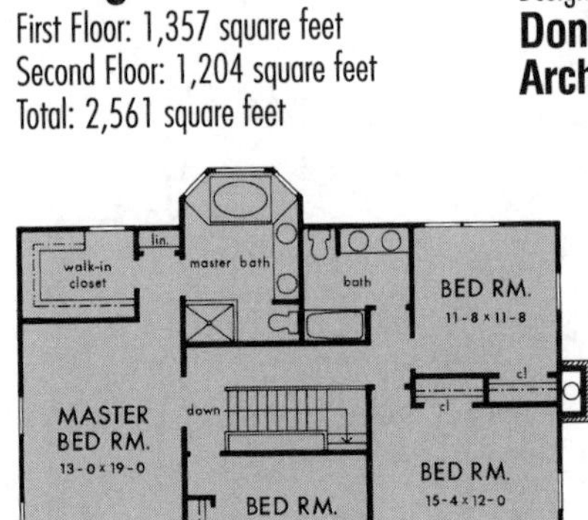

walk-in closet
lin.
master bath
bath
BED RM.
11-8 x 11-8
MASTER BED RM.
13-0 x 19-0
down
BED RM.
12-4 x 10-0
BED RM.
15-4 x 12-0
cl

QUOTE ONE®

Cost to build? See page 342 to order complete cost estimate to build this house in your area!

Width 80'
Depth 57'

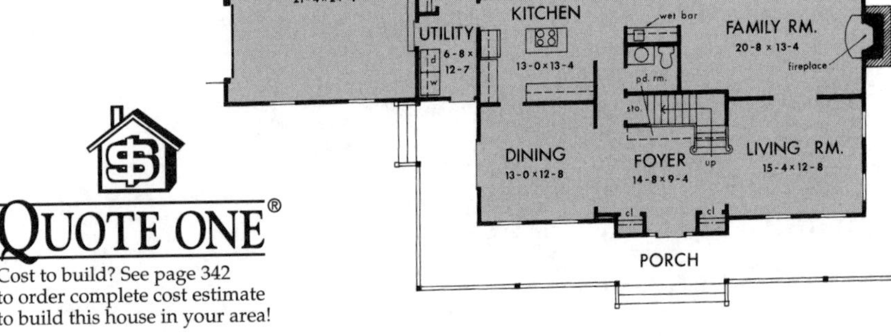

seat
DECK
spa
PORCH
GARAGE
21-4 x 24-4
BRKFST.
9-4 x 9-10
KITCHEN
13-0 x 13-4
UTILITY
6-8 x 12-7
wet bar
FAMILY RM.
20-8 x 13-4
fireplace
pd. rm.
sto.
DINING
13-0 x 12-8
FOYER
14-8 x 9-4
up
LIVING RM.
15-4 x 12-8
cl
PORCH

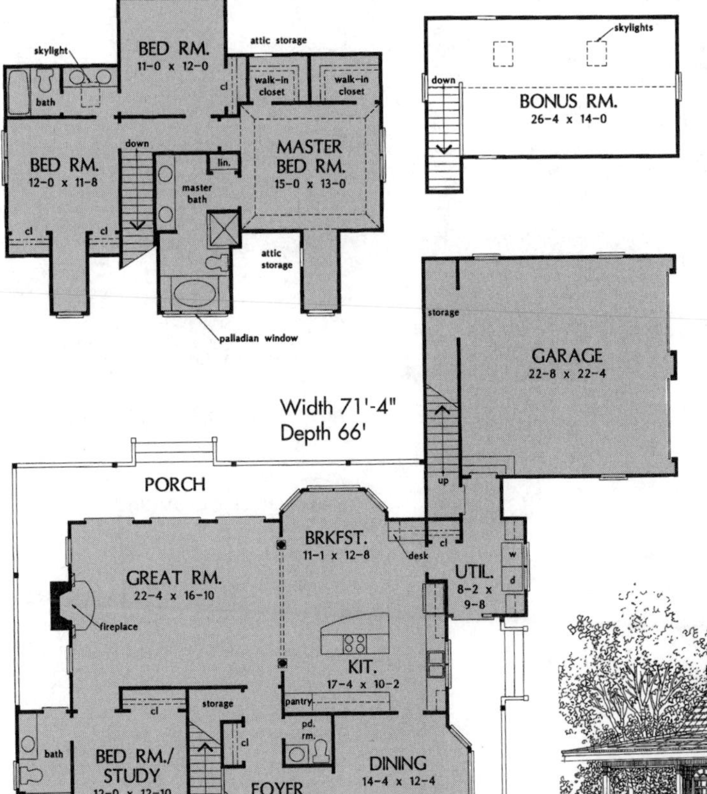

skylight
BED RM.
11-0 x 12-0
attic storage
walk-in closet
bath
BED RM.
12-0 x 11-8
down
lin.
master bath
MASTER BED RM.
15-0 x 13-0
cl
attic storage
palladian window
skylights
down
BONUS RM.
26-4 x 14-0
storage
GARAGE
22-8 x 22-4
Width 71'-4"
Depth 66'
PORCH
up
BRKFST.
11-1 x 12-8
desk
UTIL.
8-2 x 9-8
GREAT RM.
22-4 x 16-10
fireplace
KIT.
17-4 x 10-2
storage
pantry
pd. rm.
bath
BED RM./ STUDY
12-0 x 12-10
FOYER
11-8 x 7-0
DINING
14-4 x 12-4
PORCH

Design 9745

First Floor: 1,576 square feet
Second Floor: 947 square feet
Total: 2,523 square feet
Bonus Room: 405 square feet

Design by
Donald A. Gardner, Architects, Inc.

■ Enjoy balmy breezes as you relax on the wraparound porch of this delightful county farmhouse. The foyer introduces a dining room to the right and a bedroom or study to the left. The expansive great room—with its cozy fireplace—has direct access to the rear porch. Columns define the kitchen, with its large island cooktop, and a sunny breakfast area. A built-in pantry and a desk are popular features here. A powder room and a utility room are located nearby. The master bedroom features a tray ceiling and a luxurious bath. Two additional bedrooms share a skylit bath.

Design 9708

First Floor: 2,238 square feet
Second Floor: 768 square feet
Total: 3,006 square feet

■ This grand country farmhouse with wraparound porch offers comfortable living at its finest. The open floor plan is accented by a vaulted great room and entrance foyer with clerestory windows. The large kitchen has lots of counter space, a sunny breakfast nook and a cooktop island with a bumped-out snack bar. The master suite has beautiful bay windows, a well-designed master bath and a spacious walk-in closet. The second level has two large bedrooms, a full bath and plenty of attic storage.

Design by
Donald A. Gardner, Architects, Inc.

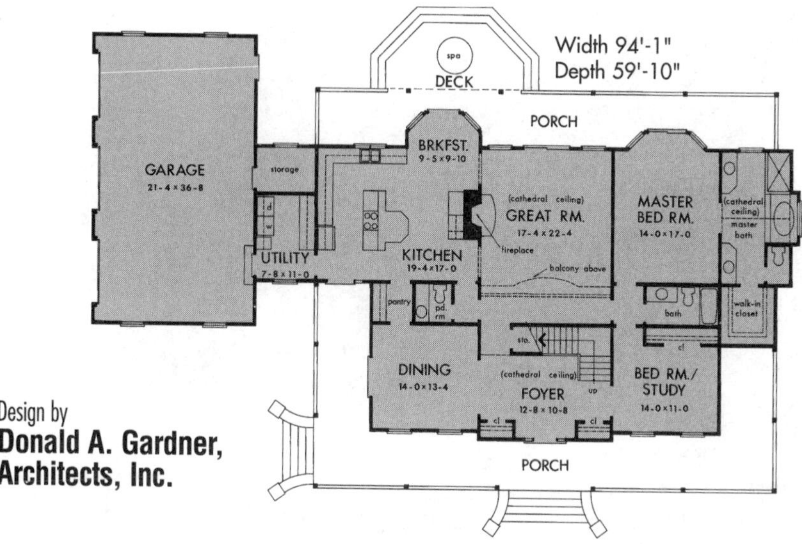

Width 94'-1"
Depth 59'-10"
spa
DECK
PORCH
GARAGE
21-4 x 36-8
storage
BRKFST.
9-5 x 9-10
(cathedral ceiling)
GREAT RM.
17-4 x 22-4
fireplace
balcony above
MASTER
BED RM.
14-0 x 17-0
(cathedral ceiling)
master bath
KITCHEN
19-4 x 17-0
UTILITY
7-8 x 11-0
pantry
pd. rm.
bath
walk-in closet
DINING
14-0 x 13-4
(cathedral ceiling)
FOYER
12-8 x 10-8
BED RM./
STUDY
14-0 x 11-0
PORCH

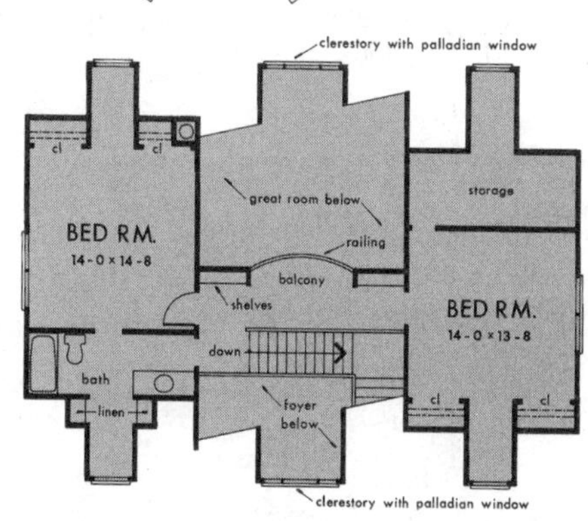

clerestory with palladian window
storage
great room below
railing
BED RM.
14-0 x 14-8
balcony
shelves
BED RM.
14-0 x 13-8
down
bath
linen
foyer below
clerestory with palladian window

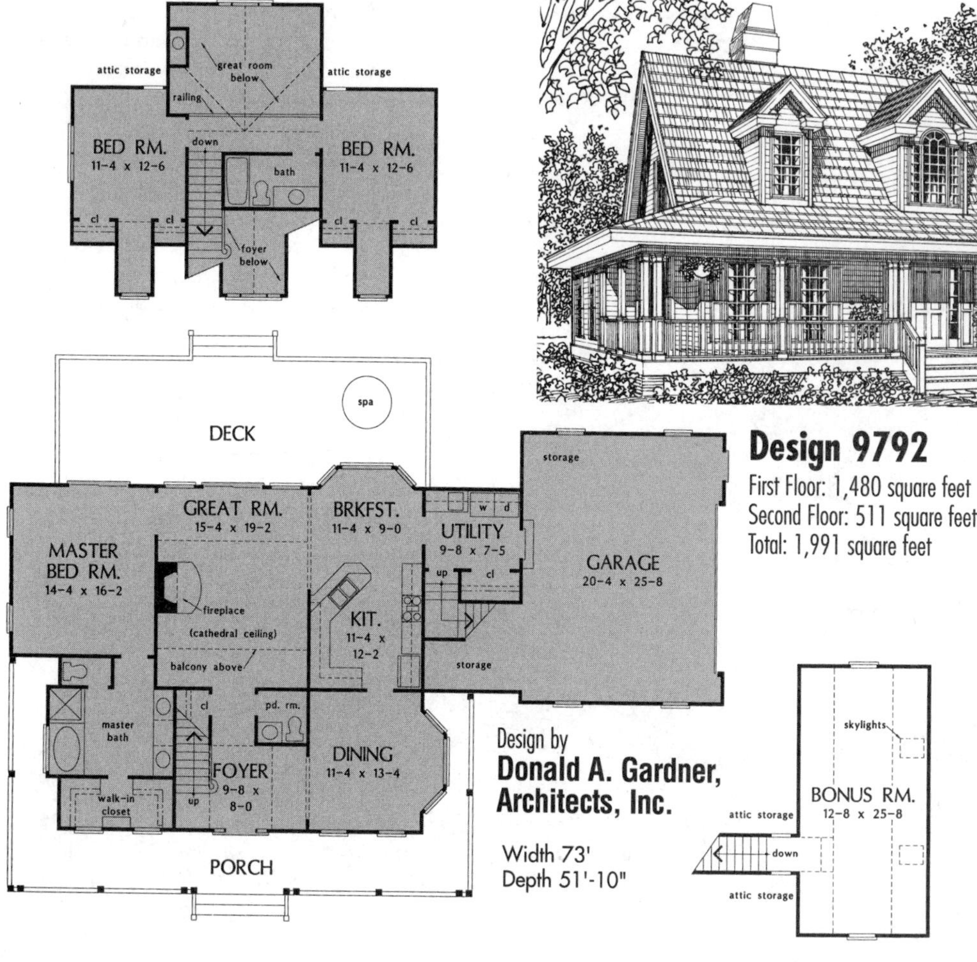

attic storage
great room below
attic storage
railing
BED RM.
11-4 x 12-6
down
bath
BED RM.
11-4 x 12-6
foyer below
spa
DECK
storage
GREAT RM.
15-4 x 19-2
BRKFST.
11-4 x 9-0
UTILITY
9-8 x 7-5
MASTER
BED RM.
14-4 x 16-2
GARAGE
20-4 x 25-8
fireplace
(cathedral ceiling)
KIT.
11-4 x 12-2
balcony above
storage
master bath
pd. rm.
FOYER
9-8 x 8-0
DINING
11-4 x 13-4
walk-in closet
PORCH
skylights
BONUS RM.
12-8 x 25-8
attic storage
down
attic storage

Design 9792

First Floor: 1,480 square feet
Second Floor: 511 square feet
Total: 1,991 square feet

■ This farmhouse has plenty to offer, from its covered front porch to its rear deck with a spa. Inside, the amenities continue, including a bayed formal dining room, a great room with fireplace and a bayed breakfast nook. A deluxe master bedroom pampers you with a luxurious bath made up of a whirlpool tub, a separate shower, twin vanities and a walk-in closet. Upstairs, away from the master bedroom for privacy, two family bedrooms share a full hall bath and a balcony overlooking the great room.

Design by
Donald A. Gardner, Architects, Inc.

Width 73'
Depth 51'-10"

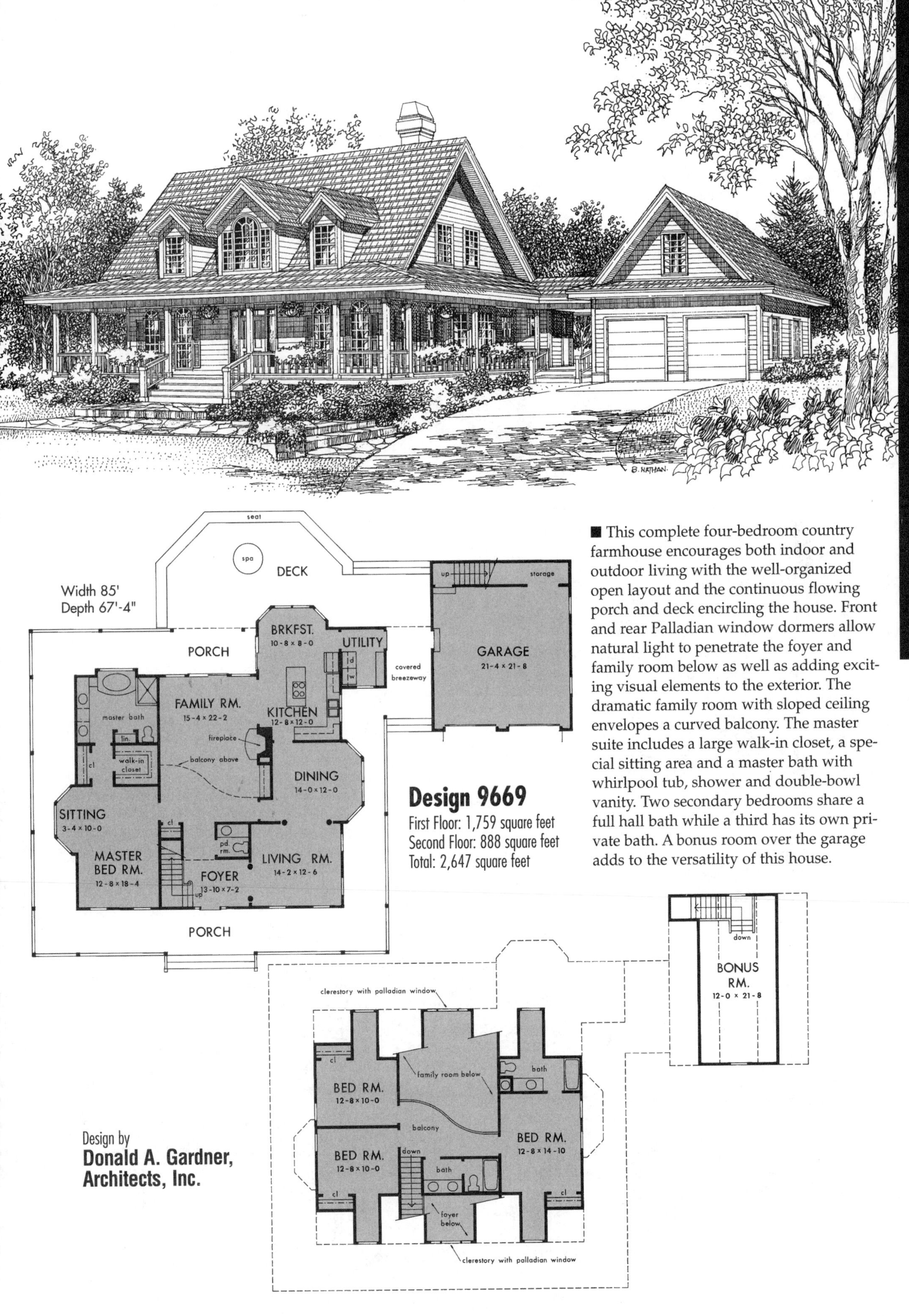
B. NATHAN
seat
spa
DECK
Width 85'
Depth 67'-4"
up
storage
BRKFST.
10-8 x 8-0
UTILITY
PORCH
GARAGE
21-4 x 21-8
covered breezeway
master bath
FAMILY RM.
15-4 x 22-2
KITCHEN
12-8 x 12-0
lin.
fireplace
cl
walk-in closet
balcony above
DINING
14-0 x 12-0
SITTING
3-4 x 10-0
cl
pd. rm.
MASTER BED RM.
12-8 x 18-4
LIVING RM.
14-2 x 12-6
FOYER
13-10 x 7-2
up
PORCH
down
BONUS RM.
12-0 x 21-8
clerestory with palladian window
cl
family room below
bath
BED RM.
12-8 x 10-0
balcony
BED RM.
12-8 x 14-10
BED RM.
12-8 x 10-0
down
bath
cl
cl
foyer below
clerestory with palladian window

■ This complete four-bedroom country farmhouse encourages both indoor and outdoor living with the well-organized open layout and the continuous flowing porch and deck encircling the house. Front and rear Palladian window dormers allow natural light to penetrate the foyer and family room below as well as adding exciting visual elements to the exterior. The dramatic family room with sloped ceiling envelopes a curved balcony. The master suite includes a large walk-in closet, a special sitting area and a master bath with whirlpool tub, shower and double-bowl vanity. Two secondary bedrooms share a full hall bath while a third has its own private bath. A bonus room over the garage adds to the versatility of this house.

Design 9669

First Floor: 1,759 square feet
Second Floor: 888 square feet
Total: 2,647 square feet

Design by
Donald A. Gardner, Architects, Inc.

Design 9773

First Floor: 1,499 square feet
Second Floor: 665 square feet
Total: 2,164 square feet

■ The warm, down-home appeal of this country house is as apparent inside as it is out. A wraparound front porch and a rear deck with a spa provide plenty of space to enjoy the surrounding scenery. Inside, a two-story foyer and a great room give the home an open feel. The great room leads to a breakfast area and an efficient kitchen with an island work area and a large pantry. The master bedroom is situated on the left side of the house for privacy. It features deck access, a large walk-in closet and a bath that includes dual vanities, a whirlpool tub and a separate shower. Three bedrooms, a full bath and bonus space are located upstairs.

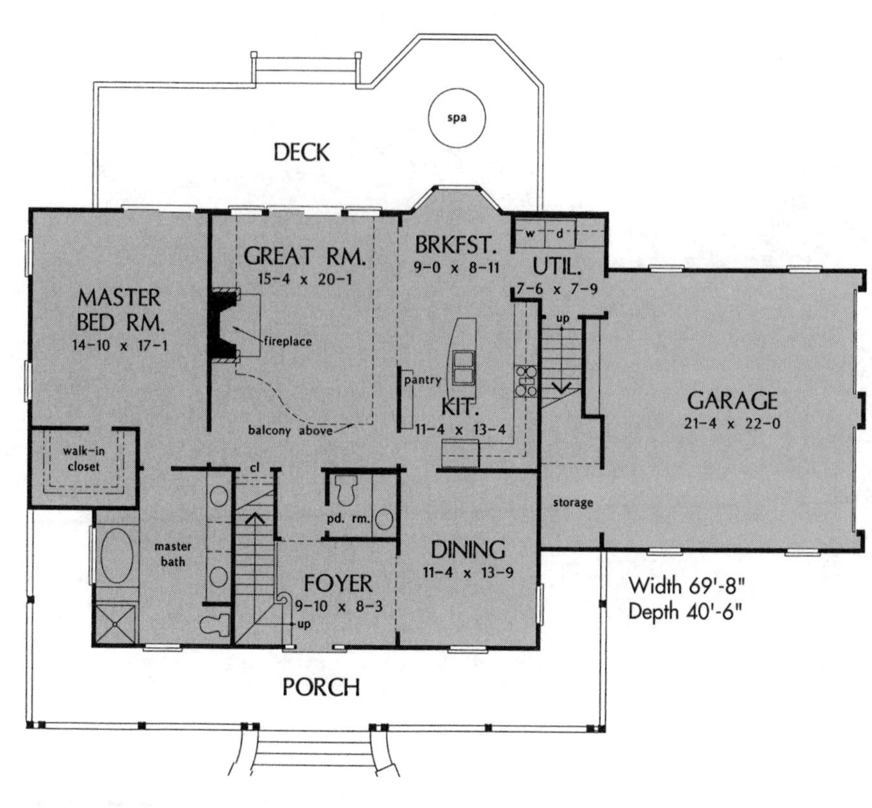

spa
DECK
MASTER BED RM. 14-10 x 17-1
GREAT RM. 15-4 x 20-1
fireplace
BRKFST. 9-0 x 8-11
w d
UTIL. 7-6 x 7-9
up
pantry
KIT. 11-4 x 13-4
balcony above
GARAGE 21-4 x 22-0
walk-in closet
cl
pd. rm.
storage
master bath
DINING 11-4 x 13-9
FOYER 9-10 x 8-3
up
Width 69'-8"
Depth 40'-6"
PORCH

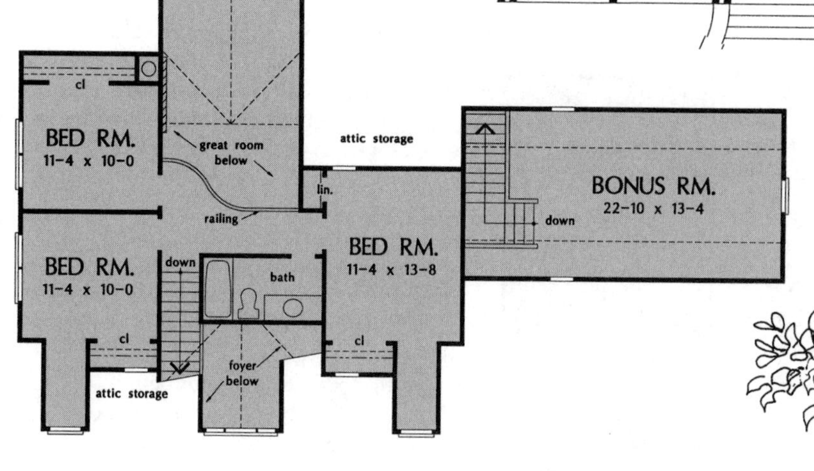

cl
BED RM. 11-4 x 10-0
great room below
attic storage
railing
lin.
BONUS RM. 22-10 x 13-4
down
BED RM. 11-4 x 10-0
down
bath
BED RM. 11-4 x 13-8
cl
cl
foyer below
attic storage

Design by
Donald A. Gardner, Architects, Inc.

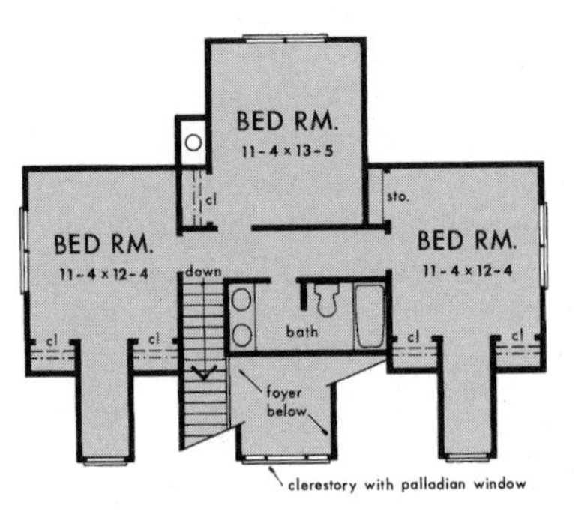
BED RM.
11-4 x 13-5
BED RM.
11-4 x 12-4
BED RM.
11-4 x 12-4
bath
foyer below
clerestory with palladian window

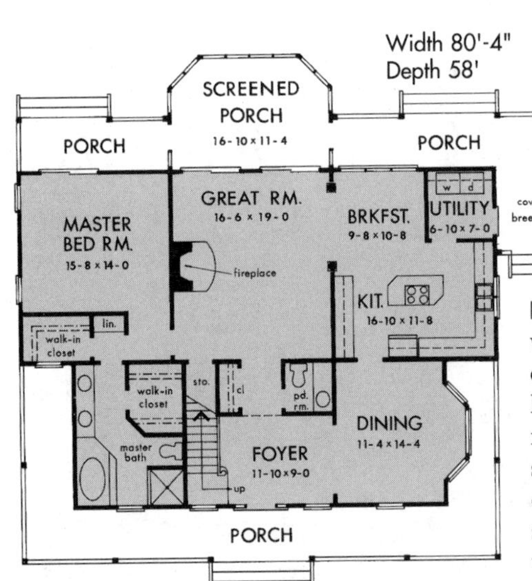
Width 80'-4"
Depth 58'
SCREENED PORCH
16-10 x 11-4
PORCH
PORCH
MASTER BED RM.
15-8 x 14-0
GREAT RM.
16-6 x 19-0
BRKFST.
9-8 x 10-8
UTILITY
6-10 x 7-0
KIT.
16-10 x 11-8
DINING
11-4 x 14-4
FOYER
11-10 x 9-0
PORCH
GARAGE
21-4 x 24-4
covered breezeway
BONUS RM.
12-0 x 24-4

Design by
Donald A. Gardner, Architects, Inc.

Design 9706

First Floor: 1,585 square feet
Second Floor: 731 square feet
Total: 2,316 square feet

■ This complete farmhouse projects an exciting and comfortable feeling with its wraparound porch, arched windows and dormers. A Palladian window in the clerestory above the entrance foyer allows an abundance of natural light. The large kitchen with cooking island easily services the breakfast area and dining room. The generous great room with fireplace offers access to the spacious screened porch for carefree outdoor living. The master bedroom suite, located on the first level for privacy and convenience, has a luxurious master bath. The second level allows for three bedrooms and a full bath. Don't miss the garage with bonus room—both meet the main house via a covered breezeway.

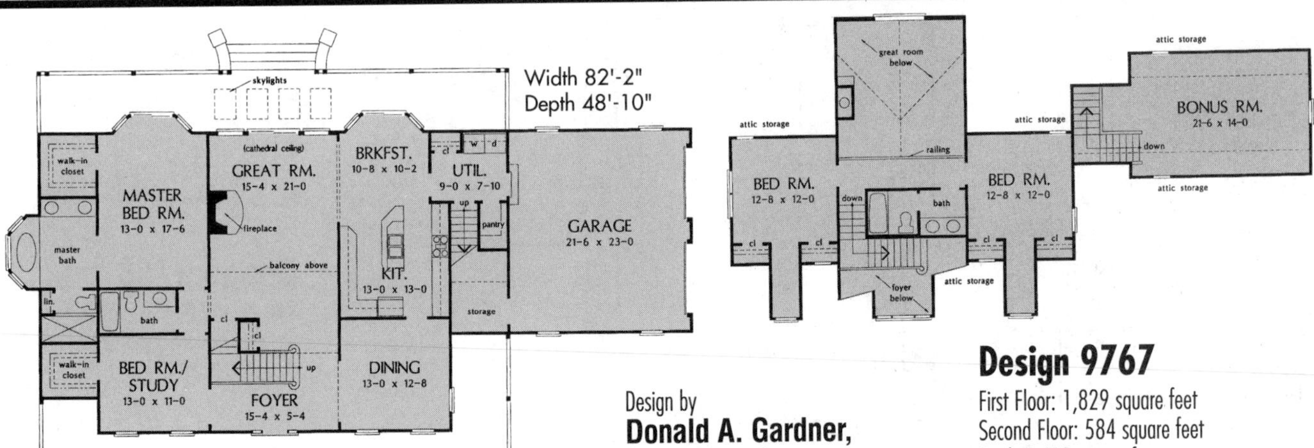
Width 82'-2"
Depth 48'-10"
MASTER BED RM.
13-0 x 17-6
GREAT RM.
15-4 x 21-0
BRKFST.
10-8 x 10-2
UTIL.
9-0 x 7-10
KIT.
13-0 x 13-0
GARAGE
21-6 x 23-0
BED RM./ STUDY
13-0 x 11-0
FOYER
15-4 x 5-4
DINING
13-0 x 12-8
PORCH
BED RM.
12-8 x 12-0
BED RM.
12-8 x 12-0
BONUS RM.
21-6 x 14-0

Design 9767

First Floor: 1,829 square feet
Second Floor: 584 square feet
Total: 2,413 square feet

Design by
Donald A. Gardner, Architects, Inc.

■ Spaciousness and lots of amenities earmark this design as a family favorite. The front wraparound porch leads to the foyer where a bedroom/study and dining room open. The central great room presents a warming fireplace, a cathedral ceiling and access to the rear porch. In the master bedroom suite, a private bath with a bumped-out tub and a walk-in closet are extra enhancements. Upstairs, two bedrooms flank a full bath. A bonus room over the garage allows for future expansion.

Design 9723

First Floor: 2,064 square feet
Second Floor: 594 square feet
Total: 2,658 square feet
Bonus Room: 464 square feet

■ You'll find country living at its best when meandering through this spacious four-bedroom farmhouse with wraparound porch. A front Palladian window dormer and rear clerestory windows at the great room add exciting visual elements to the exterior while providing natural light to the interior. The large great room boasts a fireplace, bookshelves and a raised cathedral ceiling, allowing a curved balcony overlook above. The great room, master bedroom and breakfast room are accessible to the rear porch for greater circulation and flexibility. Special features such as the large cooktop island in the kitchen, the wet bar, the bedroom/study, the generous bonus room over the garage and ample storage set this plan apart.

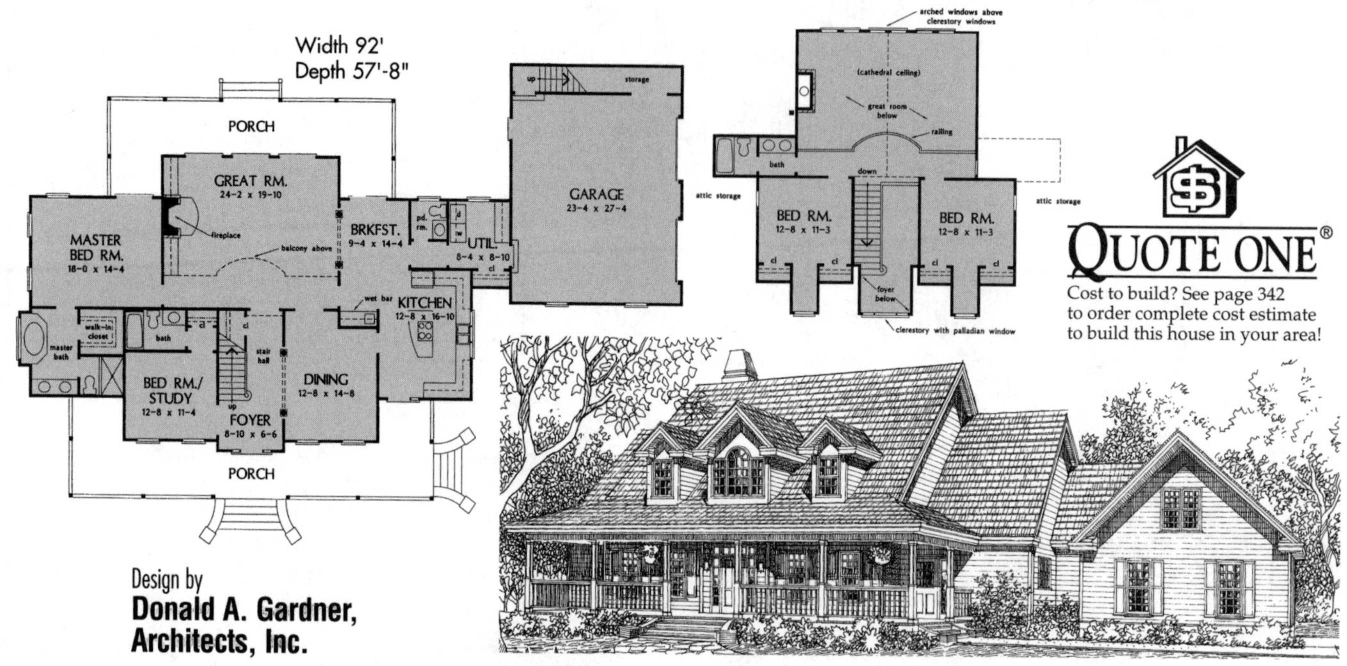
Width 92'
Depth 57'-8"
PORCH
GREAT RM.
24-2 x 19-10
fireplace
balcony above
MASTER
BED RM.
18-0 x 14-4
BRKFST.
9-4 x 14-4
UTIL.
8-4 x 8-10
GARAGE
23-4 x 27-4
storage
KITCHEN
12-8 x 16-10
wet bar
walk-in closet
master bath
bath
stair hall
BED RM./
STUDY
12-8 x 11-4
DINING
12-8 x 14-8
FOYER
8-10 x 6-6
PORCH
arched windows above clerestory windows
(cathedral ceiling)
great room below
railing
bath
down
attic storage
BED RM.
12-8 x 11-3
BED RM.
12-8 x 11-3
foyer below
clerestory with palladian window
Design by
Donald A. Gardner,
Architects, Inc.

QUOTE ONE®

Cost to build? See page 342 to order complete cost estimate to build this house in your area!

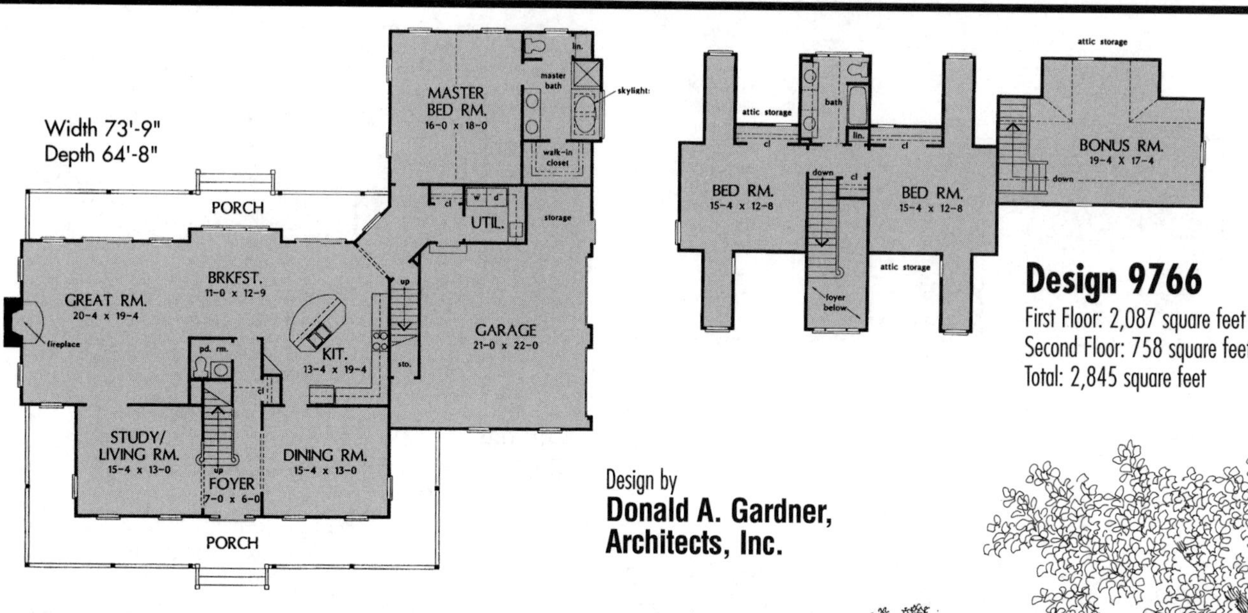
Width 73'-9"
Depth 64'-8"
MASTER
BED RM.
16-0 x 18-0
master bath
skylight
walk-in closet
PORCH
UTIL.
storage
GREAT RM.
20-4 x 19-4
fireplace
BRKFST.
11-0 x 12-9
KIT.
13-4 x 19-4
GARAGE
21-0 x 22-0
STUDY/
LIVING RM.
15-4 x 13-0
DINING RM.
15-4 x 13-0
FOYER
7-0 x 6-0
PORCH
attic storage
bath
BED RM.
15-4 x 12-8
BED RM.
15-4 x 12-8
BONUS RM.
19-4 X 17-4
foyer below

Design 9766

First Floor: 2,087 square feet
Second Floor: 758 square feet
Total: 2,845 square feet

Design by
Donald A. Gardner, Architects, Inc.

■ This handsome country exterior will be a pleasure to come home to—the front and rear porches, invite relaxation. Inside, the great room has an expanse of windows and a fireplace for added warmth. The breakfast area takes advantage of views out the back while the kitchen serves this area with the help of a large island cooktop. A formal dining room and front living room make entertaining a joy. The master bedroom suite is privately located at the rear of the plan. Two secondary bedrooms upstairs and a bonus room over the garage finish the plan.

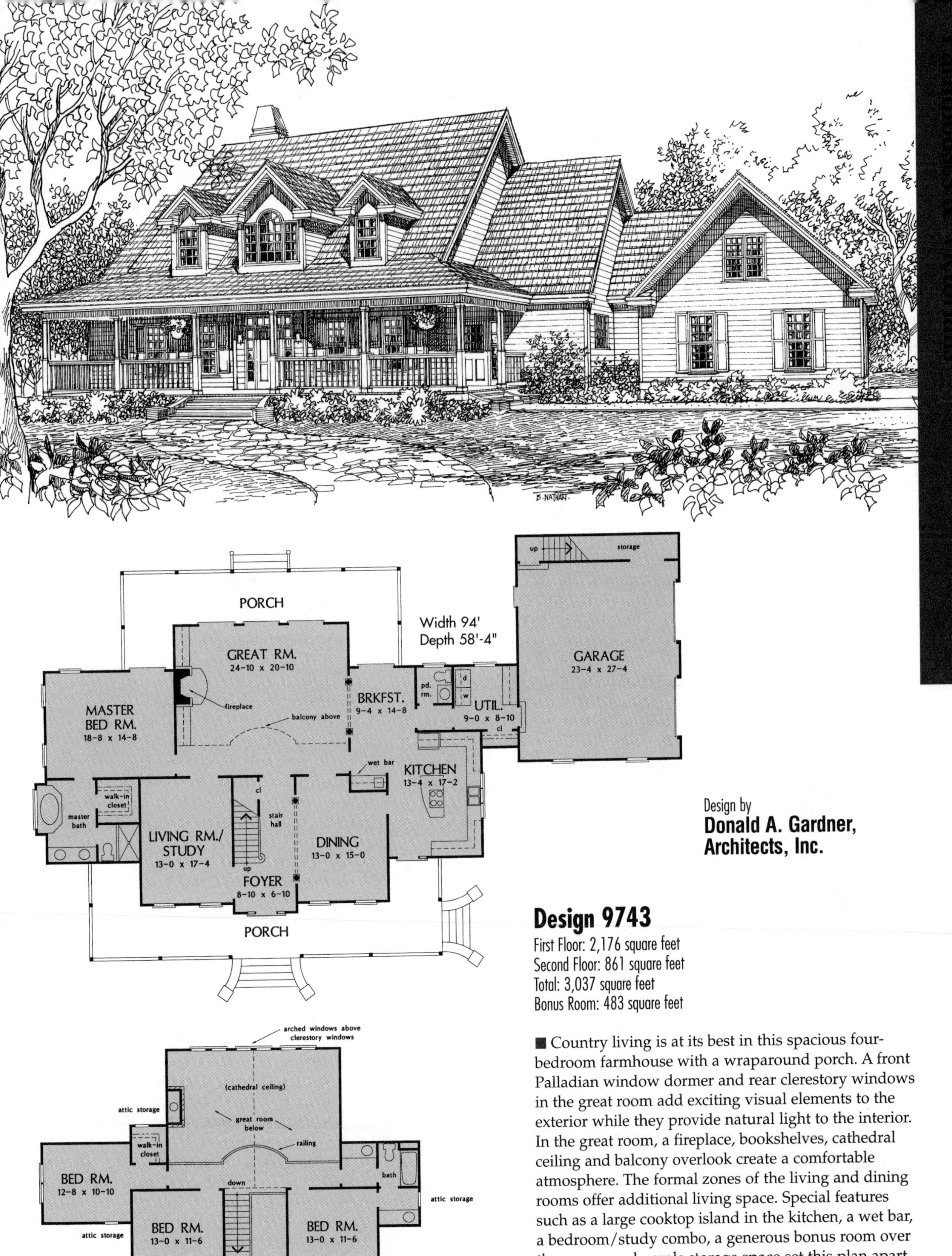
B. NATHAN
PORCH
Width 94'
Depth 58'-4"
GREAT RM.
24-10 x 20-10
fireplace
balcony above
BRKFST.
9-4 x 14-8
pd. rm.
UTIL.
9-0 x 8-10
cl
GARAGE
23-4 x 27-4
up
storage
MASTER BED RM.
18-8 x 14-8
walk-in closet
master bath
LIVING RM./ STUDY
13-0 x 17-4
stair hall
up
FOYER
8-10 x 6-10
DINING
13-0 x 15-0
wet bar
KITCHEN
13-4 x 17-2
PORCH
arched windows above clerestory windows
(cathedral ceiling)
attic storage
great room below
railing
walk-in closet
BED RM.
12-8 x 10-10
down
bath
attic storage
BED RM.
13-0 x 11-6
BED RM.
13-0 x 11-6
attic storage
cl
cl
cl
cl
foyer below
clerestory with palladian window

Design by
Donald A. Gardner, Architects, Inc.

Design 9743

First Floor: 2,176 square feet
Second Floor: 861 square feet
Total: 3,037 square feet
Bonus Room: 483 square feet

■ Country living is at its best in this spacious four-bedroom farmhouse with a wraparound porch. A front Palladian window dormer and rear clerestory windows in the great room add exciting visual elements to the exterior while they provide natural light to the interior. In the great room, a fireplace, bookshelves, cathedral ceiling and balcony overlook create a comfortable atmosphere. The formal zones of the living and dining rooms offer additional living space. Special features such as a large cooktop island in the kitchen, a wet bar, a bedroom/study combo, a generous bonus room over the garage and ample storage space set this plan apart from others. You'll also love the fact that the master bedroom suite, the great room and the breakfast room all directly access the rear porch.

Design 9721

First Floor: 2,316 square feet
Second Floor: 721 square feet
Total: 3,037 square feet
Bonus Room: 545 square feet

■ This gracious farmhouse with its wraparound porch offers a touch of symmetry in a well-defined, open plan. The entrance foyer has a Palladian clerestory window that gives an abundance of natural light to the interior. The vaulted great room furthers this feeling of airiness with a second-floor balcony above and two sets of sliding glass doors leading to the porch out back. The country kitchen with an island countertop, the bayed breakfast nook and the dining room all enjoy nine-foot ceilings. Upstairs, each family bedroom has two closets. A full bath with a double-bowl vanity rests to one side of the hall. For privacy, the master suite occupies the right side of the first floor. With a sitting room and all the amenities of a spa-style bath, this room won't fail to please.

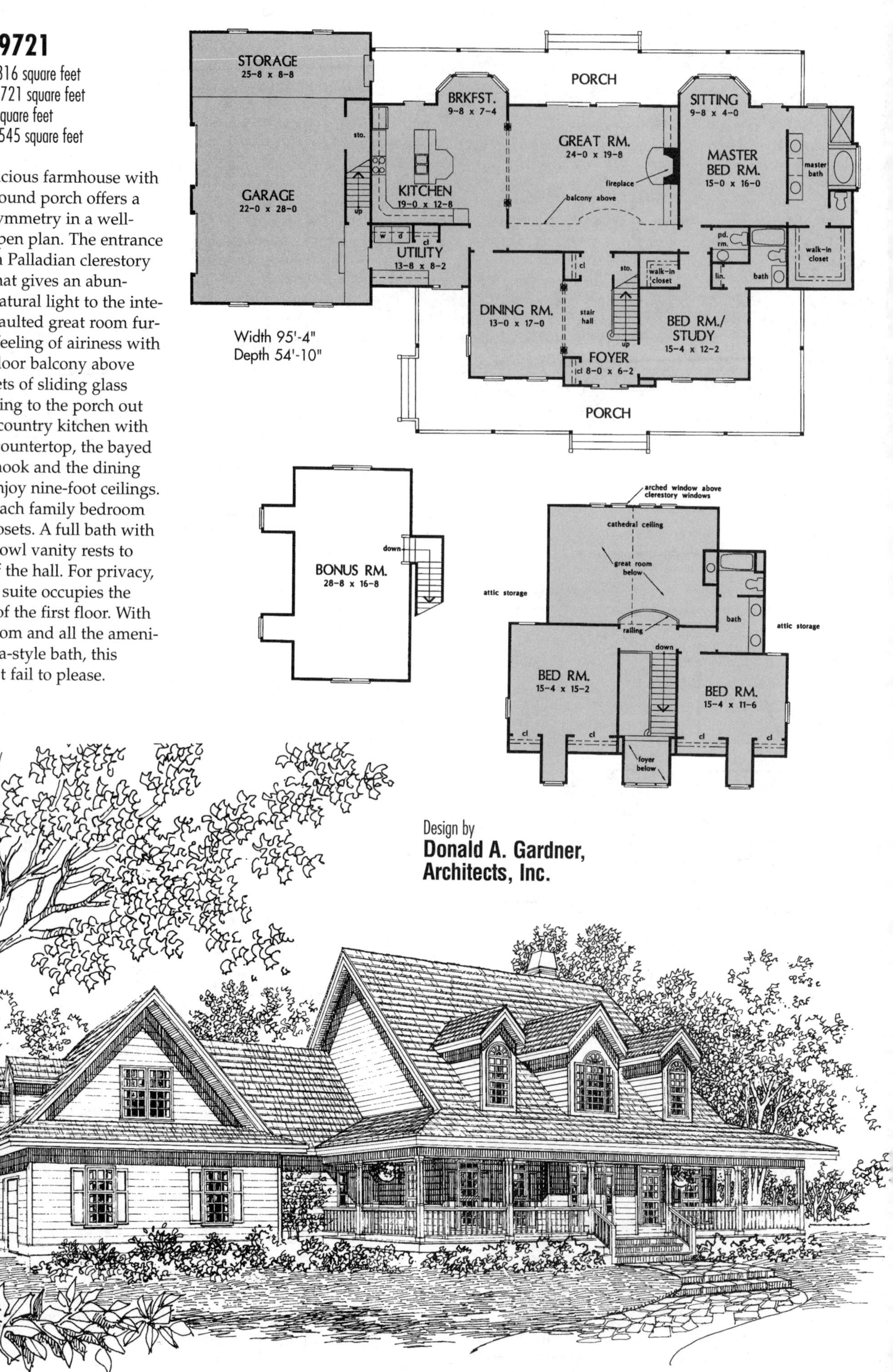
STORAGE
25-8 x 8-8
GARAGE
22-0 x 28-0
sto.
up
KITCHEN
19-0 x 12-8
BRKFST.
9-8 x 7-4
PORCH
GREAT RM.
24-0 x 19-8
fireplace
balcony above
SITTING
9-8 x 4-0
MASTER
BED RM.
15-0 x 16-0
master bath
pd. rm.
lin.
bath
walk-in closet
w
d
cl
UTILITY
13-8 x 8-2
cl
DINING RM.
13-0 x 17-0
stair hall
sto.
walk-in closet
BED RM./
STUDY
15-4 x 12-2
up
FOYER
cl 8-0 x 6-2
PORCH
Width 95'-4"
Depth 54'-10"
BONUS RM.
28-8 x 16-8
down
arched window above
clerestory windows
cathedral ceiling
great room below
attic storage
bath
attic storage
railing
down
BED RM.
15-4 x 15-2
BED RM.
15-4 x 11-6
cl
cl
cl
cl
foyer below

Design by
Donald A. Gardner, Architects, Inc.

■ This stylish country farmhouse offers style and the flexibility to choose the total number of bedrooms while maximizing use of space. Choose between a living room with a half bath (Design 9730) or a bedroom/study with a full bath (Design 9731) depending on your family needs. A loft/study on the second floor overlooks the elegant foyer and great room below. The master bedroom and breakfast area admit natural light through bay windows and skylights. Private covered porches are accessible from the master bedroom and the living room/study. Three bedrooms and two full baths occupy the second floor.

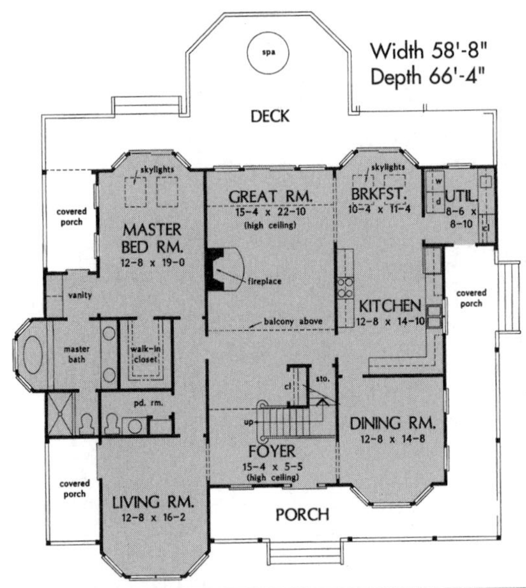
Width 58'-8"
Depth 66'-4"
spa
DECK
covered porch
skylights
MASTER BED RM.
12-8 x 19-0
GREAT RM.
15-4 x 22-10
(high ceiling)
fireplace
balcony above
BRKFST.
10-4 x 11-4
UTIL.
8-6 x 8-10
KITCHEN
12-8 x 14-10
covered porch
vanity
master bath
walk-in closet
pd. rm.
sto.
up
FOYER
15-4 x 5-5
(high ceiling)
DINING RM.
12-8 x 14-8
covered porch
LIVING RM.
12-8 x 16-2
PORCH

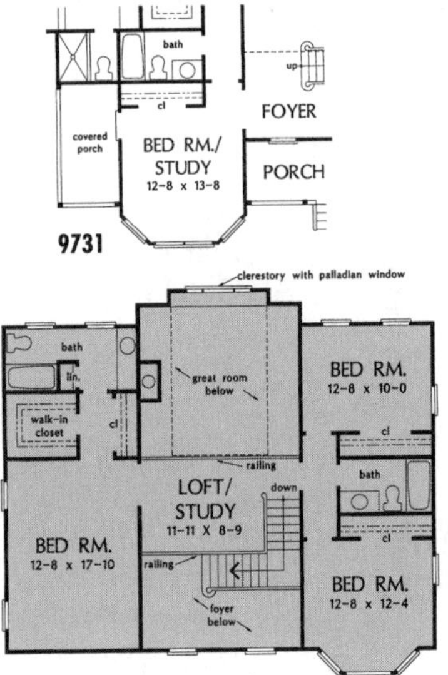
bath
cl
FOYER
covered porch
BED RM./ STUDY
12-8 x 13-8
PORCH
9731
clerestory with palladian window
bath
walk-in closet
great room below
BED RM.
12-8 x 10-0
railing
LOFT/ STUDY
11-11 X 8-9
down
bath
BED RM.
12-8 x 17-10
railing
foyer below
BED RM.
12-8 x 12-4

Design 9730/9731

First Floor: 1,976 square feet
Second Floor: 970 square feet
Total: 2,946 square feet

Design by
Donald A. Gardner, Architects, Inc.

Design 9729

First Floor: 2,176 square feet
Second Floor: 861 square feet
Total: 3,037 square feet

■ Country living is at its best in this spacious, five-bedroom farmhouse with a wraparound porch. A front Palladian window dormer and rear clerestory windows add exciting visual elements to the exterior and provide natural light to the interior. The large great room boasts a fireplace, bookshelves and a raised cathedral ceiling allowing the curved balcony to overlook from above. Special features such as a large cooktop island in the kitchen, a wet bar, a bedroom/study combo and generous bonus room over the garage set this plan apart from the rest.

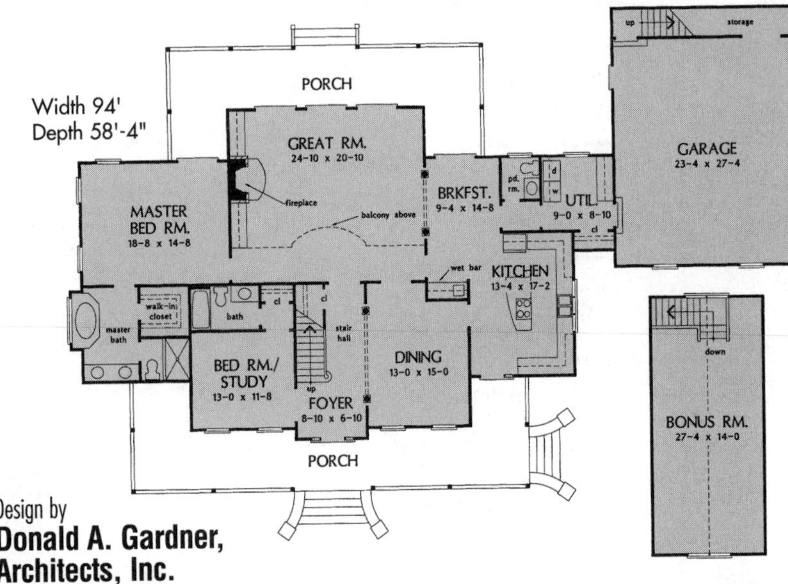
Width 94'
Depth 58'-4"
PORCH
GREAT RM.
24-10 x 20-10
fireplace
balcony above
MASTER BED RM.
18-8 x 14-8
BRKFST.
9-4 x 14-8
pd. rm.
UTIL.
9-0 x 8-10
GARAGE
23-4 x 27-4
storage
wet bar
KITCHEN
13-4 x 17-2
walk-in closet
bath
master bath
stair hall
BED RM./ STUDY
13-0 x 11-8
DINING
13-0 x 15-0
FOYER
8-10 x 6-10
PORCH
down
BONUS RM.
27-4 x 14-0

Design by
Donald A. Gardner, Architects, Inc.

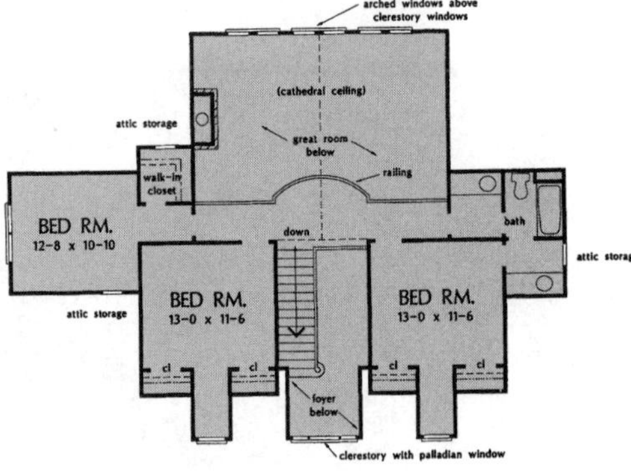
arched windows above clerestory windows
(cathedral ceiling)
attic storage
great room below
walk-in closet
railing
BED RM.
12-8 x 10-10
down
bath
attic storage
attic storage
BED RM.
13-0 x 11-6
BED RM.
13-0 x 11-6
foyer below
clerestory with palladian window

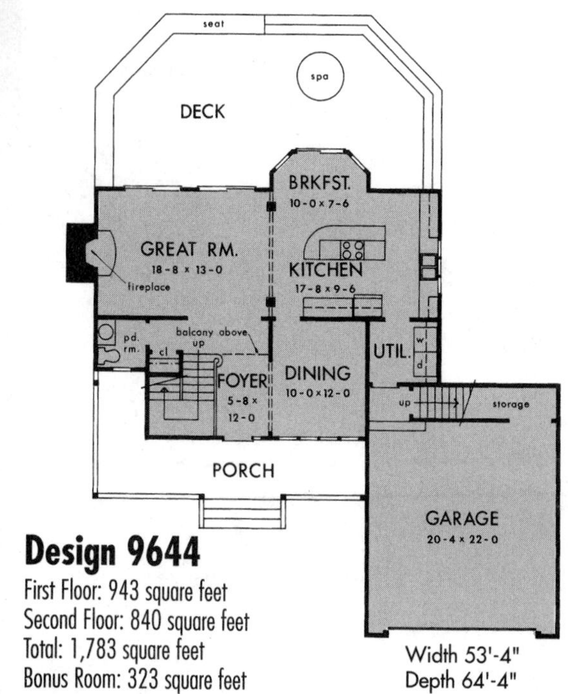
seat
spa
DECK
BRKFST.
10-0 x 7-6
GREAT RM.
18-8 x 13-0
fireplace
KITCHEN
17-8 x 9-6
pd. rm.
cl
balcony above
up
FOYER
5-8 x 12-0
DINING
10-0 x 12-0
UTIL.
w
d
up
storage
PORCH
GARAGE
20-4 x 22-0

Design 9644

First Floor: 943 square feet
Second Floor: 840 square feet
Total: 1,783 square feet
Bonus Room: 323 square feet

Width 53'-4"
Depth 64'-4"

Design by
Donald A. Gardner, Architects, Inc.

■ Roundtop windows and an inviting covered porch offer an irresistible appeal for this three-bedroom plan. A two-story foyer provides a spacious feeling to this well-organized open layout. Round columns between the great room and kitchen add to the impressive quality of the plan. An expansive deck promotes casual outdoor living to its fullest. The master suite with walk-in closet and complete master bath is on the second floor along with two additional bedrooms and a full bath. The bonus room over the garage offers room for expansion.

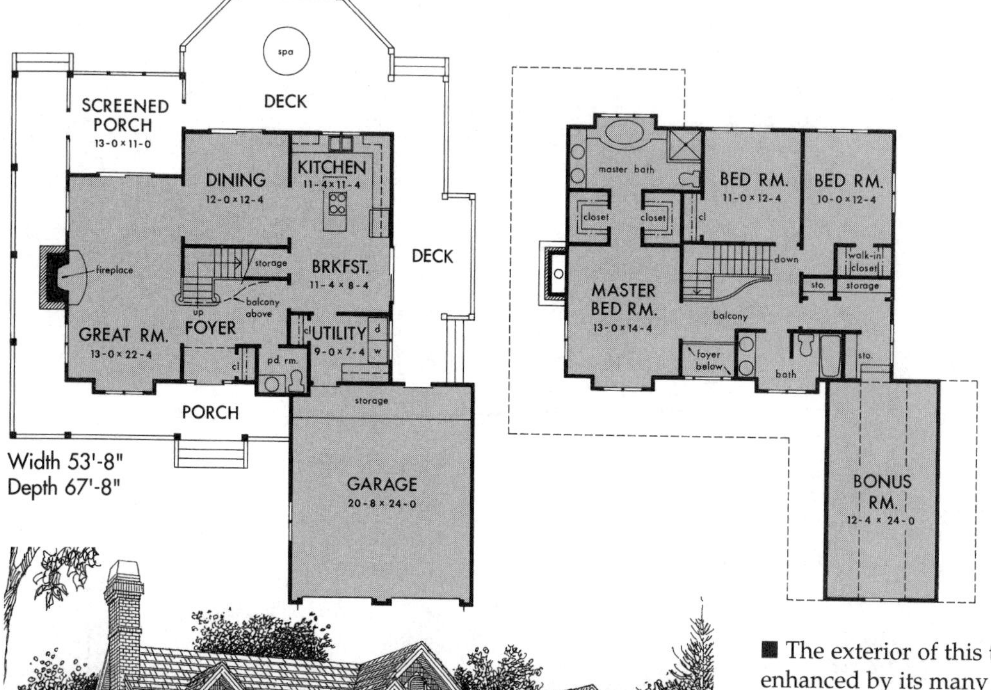
spa
SCREENED PORCH
13-0 x 11-0
DECK
DINING
12-0 x 12-4
KITCHEN
11-4 x 11-4
fireplace
storage
BRKFST.
11-4 x 8-4
DECK
balcony above
up
GREAT RM.
13-0 x 22-4
FOYER
UTILITY
9-0 x 7-4
cl
pd. rm.
storage
PORCH
GARAGE
20-8 x 24-0
master bath
BED RM.
11-0 x 12-4
BED RM.
10-0 x 12-4
closet
closet
cl
down
walk-in closet
sto.
storage
MASTER BED RM.
13-0 x 14-4
balcony
foyer below
bath
sto.
BONUS RM.
12-4 x 24-0

Width 53'-8"
Depth 67'-8"

Design by
Donald A. Gardner, Architects, Inc.

Design 9662

First Floor: 1,025 square feet
Second Floor: 911 square feet
Total: 1,936 square feet

QUOTE ONE®

Cost to build? See page 342 to order complete cost estimate to build this house in your area!

■ The exterior of this three-bedroom home is enhanced by its many gables, arched windows and wraparound porch. A large great room with impressive fireplace leads to both the dining room and screened porch with access to the deck. An open kitchen offers a country-kitchen atmosphere. The second-level master suite has two walk-in closets and an impressive bath. Two family bedrooms share a full bath and plenty of storage. There is also bonus space over the garage.

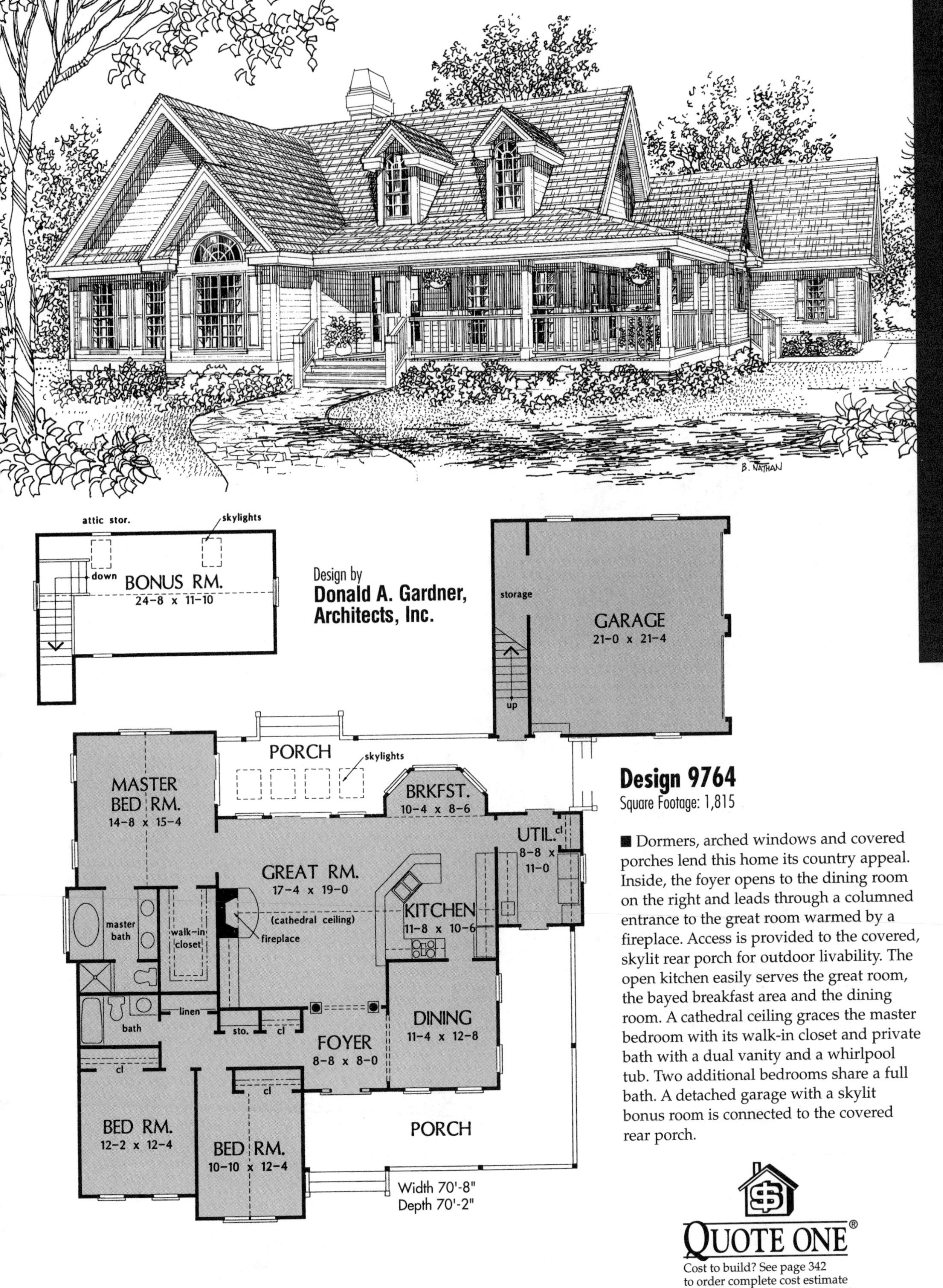
B. NATHAN
attic stor.
skylights
down
BONUS RM.
24-8 x 11-10
storage
GARAGE
21-0 x 21-4
up
PORCH
skylights
MASTER
BED RM.
14-8 x 15-4
BRKFST.
10-4 x 8-6
UTIL.
8-8 x 11-0
cl
GREAT RM.
17-4 x 19-0
(cathedral ceiling)
fireplace
KITCHEN
11-8 x 10-6
master bath
walk-in closet
linen
bath
sto.
cl
FOYER
8-8 x 8-0
DINING
11-4 x 12-8
cl
cl
BED RM.
12-2 x 12-4
BED RM.
10-10 x 12-4
PORCH
Width 70'-8"
Depth 70'-2"

Design by
Donald A. Gardner, Architects, Inc.

Design 9764

Square Footage: 1,815

■ Dormers, arched windows and covered porches lend this home its country appeal. Inside, the foyer opens to the dining room on the right and leads through a columned entrance to the great room warmed by a fireplace. Access is provided to the covered, skylit rear porch for outdoor livability. The open kitchen easily serves the great room, the bayed breakfast area and the dining room. A cathedral ceiling graces the master bedroom with its walk-in closet and private bath with a dual vanity and a whirlpool tub. Two additional bedrooms share a full bath. A detached garage with a skylit bonus room is connected to the covered rear porch.

QUOTE ONE®

Cost to build? See page 342 to order complete cost estimate to build this house in your area!

Design 9779

Square Footage: 1,632

Design by
Donald A. Gardner, Architects, Inc.

■ This country home has a big heart in a cozy package. Special touches—interior columns, a bay window and dormers—add elegance. The central great room features a cathedral ceiling and a fireplace. A clerestory window splashes the room with natural light. The open kitchen easily services the breakfast area and the nearby dining room. The private master suite, with a tray ceiling and a walk-in closet, boasts amenities found in much larger homes. The bath features skylights over the whirlpool tub. Two additional bedrooms share a bath. The front bedroom features a walk-in closet and would make a nice study with an optional foyer entrance.

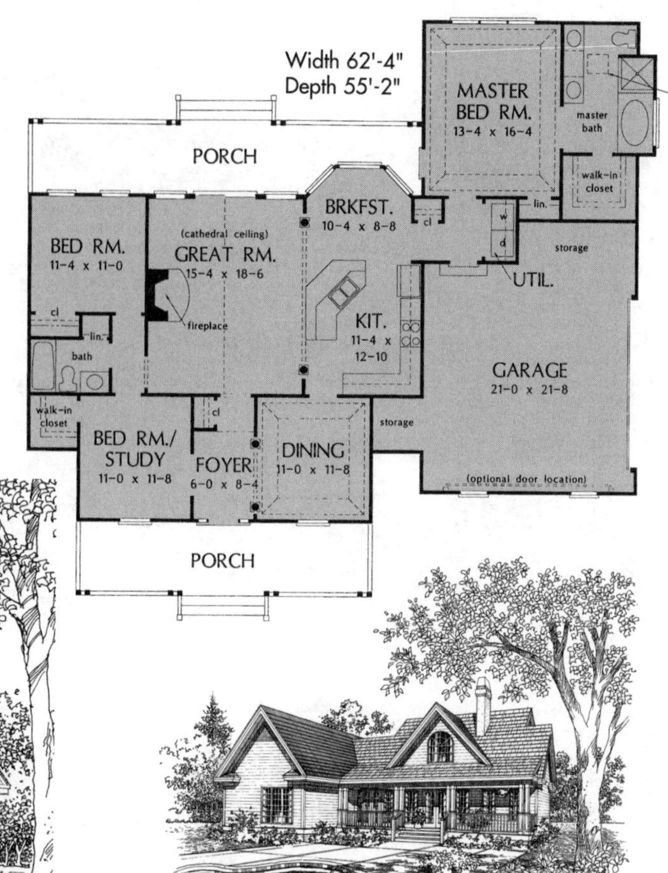

Width 62'-4"
Depth 55'-2"
MASTER BED RM. 13-4 x 16-4
master bath
walk-in closet
lin.
PORCH
BRKFST. 10-4 x 8-8
cl
w
d
storage
UTIL.
BED RM. 11-4 x 11-0
(cathedral ceiling)
GREAT RM. 15-4 x 18-6
fireplace
KIT. 11-4 x 12-10
GARAGE 21-0 x 21-8
cl
lin.
bath
walk-in closet
BED RM./ STUDY 11-0 x 11-8
cl
FOYER 6-0 x 8-4
DINING 11-0 x 11-8
storage
(optional door location)
PORCH

Design 7603

Square Footage: 1,864

Design by
Donald A. Gardner, Architects, Inc.

■ Two covered porches, sunny dormers and multi-pane windows combine to give this three-bedroom home plenty of curb appeal. Directly from the foyer, the spacious great room offers a cathedral ceiling, fireplace and doors to the rear porch. The spacious kitchen is thoughtfully set between the sunny breakfast nook and the formal dining room. The sleeping zone is split, with two family bedrooms and a full bath set to the rear of the plan. The master suite has a tray ceiling, walk-in closet and a compartmented bath.

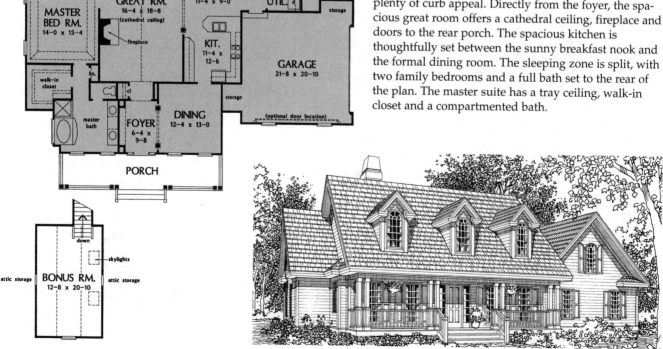

Width 65'
Depth 59'-8"

BED RM. 10-8 x 11-0
BED RM. 10-8 x 11-0
PORCH
MASTER BED RM. 14-0 x 15-4
GREAT RM. 16-4 x 18-8 (cathedral ceiling)
BRKFST. 11-4 x 9-0
UTIL.
KIT. 11-4 x 12-6
GARAGE 21-8 x 20-10
FOYER 6-4 x 9-8
DINING 12-4 x 13-0
PORCH
BONUS RM. 12-8 x 20-10

Design 9783

Square Footage: 1,832

■ This plan rises with a cathedral ceiling in the great room and dormer windows shedding light on the foyer, front bedroom and the formal dining room. The kitchen is completely open to the great room and features a stylish snack-bar island and a bay window at the breakfast nook. The master suite has a tray ceiling and a skylit bath. Two secondary bedrooms are split for privacy and share a full hall bath. Bonus space may be developed over the garage.

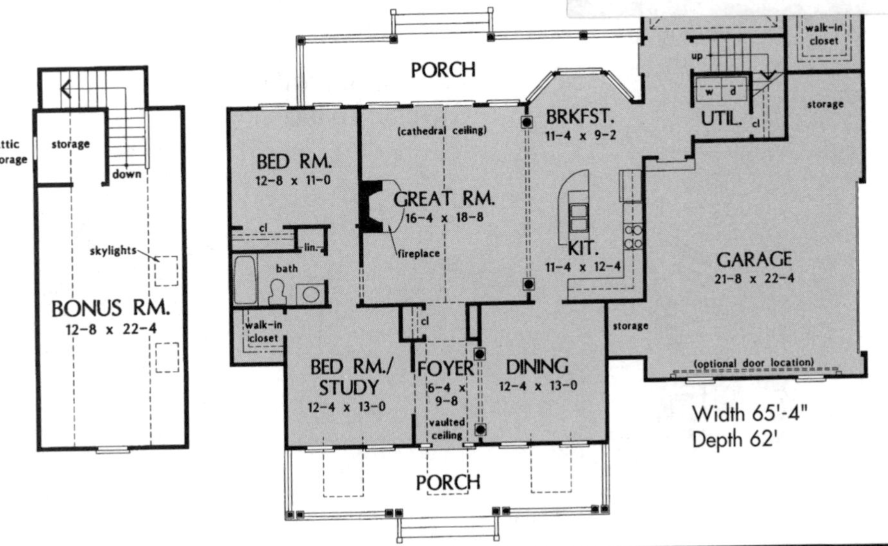

attic storage
storage
down
skylights
BONUS RM.
12-8 x 22-4
PORCH
BRKFST.
11-4 x 9-2
(cathedral ceiling)
BED RM.
12-8 x 11-0
GREAT RM.
16-4 x 18-8
fireplace
cl
lin.
bath
walk-in closet
KIT.
11-4 x 12-4
UTIL.
up
storage
walk-in closet
GARAGE
21-8 x 22-4
storage
(optional door location)
BED RM./ STUDY
12-4 x 13-0
FOYER
6-4 x 9-8
vaulted ceiling
DINING
12-4 x 13-0
PORCH
Width 65'-4"
Depth 62'

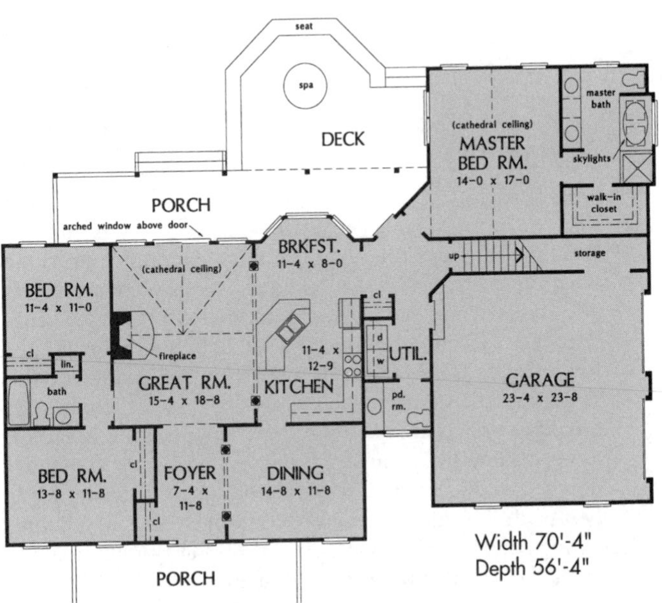

seat
spa
DECK
(cathedral ceiling)
MASTER BED RM.
14-0 x 17-0
master bath
skylights
walk-in closet
PORCH
arched window above door
BRKFST.
11-4 x 8-0
up
storage
(cathedral ceiling)
BED RM.
11-4 x 11-0
cl
lin.
bath
fireplace
GREAT RM.
15-4 x 18-8
11-4 x 12-9
KITCHEN
UTIL.
pd. rm.
GARAGE
23-4 x 23-8
BED RM.
13-8 x 11-8
FOYER
7-4 x 11-8
cl
DINING
14-8 x 11-8
PORCH
Width 70'-4"
Depth 56'-4"

down
skylights
BONUS RM.
14-4 x 23-8

Design 9749

Square Footage: 1,864
Bonus Room: 420 square feet

Design by
Donald A. Gardner, Architects, Inc.

■ Quaint and cozy on the outside with porches front and back, this three-bedroom country home surprises with an open floor plan featuring a large great room with a cathedral ceiling. Nine-foot ceilings add volume throughout the home. A central kitchen with an angled counter opens to the breakfast and great rooms for easy entertaining. The privately located master bedroom has a cathedral ceiling and adjacent access to the deck. Operable skylights over the tub accent the luxurious master bath. Two secondary bedrooms share a full hall bath. A bonus room makes expanding easy. Please specify crawlspace or basement foundation when ordering.

eet
re feet
e feet

...loor planning gives this effi- ...hree-bedroom home a much ...ger feeling. The two-story foyer leads to the great room and dining area which sports a vaulted ceiling accented with skylights. The eat-in kitchen has a stylish angled snack bar that opens to the great room. Privacy is assured in the first-floor master suite which features a walk-in closet and a pampering bath. Upstairs, a balcony hall that overlooks the great room leads to two family bedrooms with a full bath shared in between.

Design by
Donald A. Gardner, Architects, Inc.

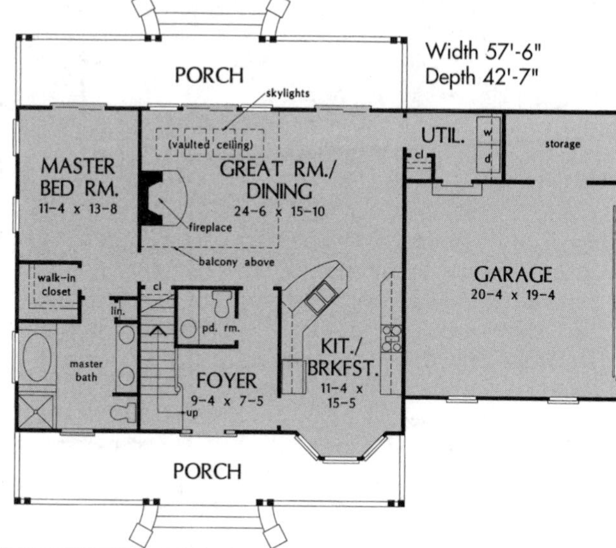
Width 57'-6"
Depth 42'-7"
PORCH
skylights
(vaulted ceiling)
MASTER BED RM.
11-4 x 13-8
GREAT RM./ DINING
24-6 x 15-10
fireplace
balcony above
UTIL.
storage
GARAGE
20-4 x 19-4
walk-in closet
lin.
pd. rm.
master bath
FOYER
9-4 x 7-5
up
KIT./ BRKFST.
11-4 x 15-5
PORCH

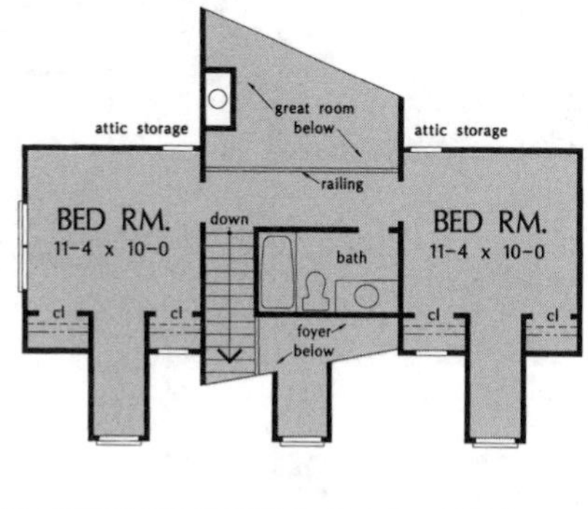
great room below
attic storage
attic storage
railing
BED RM.
11-4 x 10-0
down
bath
BED RM.
11-4 x 10-0
foyer below

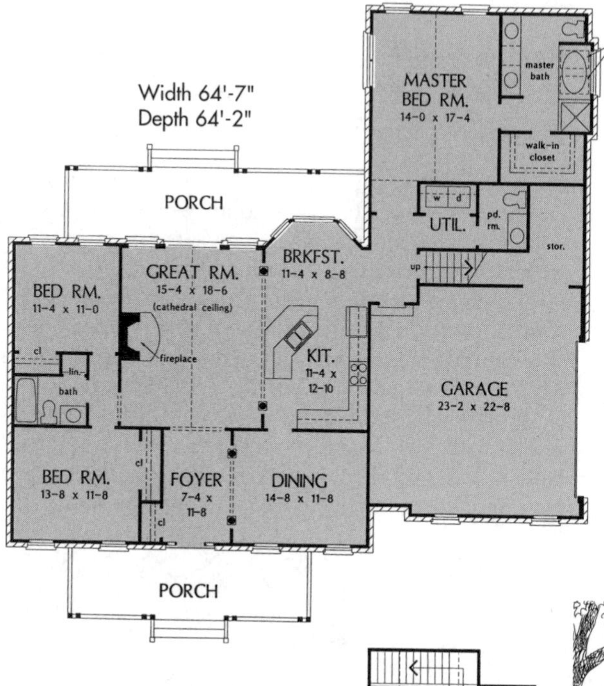
Width 64'-7"
Depth 64'-2"
skylights
MASTER BED RM.
14-0 x 17-4
master bath
walk-in closet
PORCH
UTIL.
pd. rm.
stor.
BED RM.
11-4 x 11-0
GREAT RM.
15-4 x 18-6
(cathedral ceiling)
BRKFST.
11-4 x 8-8
up
fireplace
bath
KIT.
11-4 x 12-10
GARAGE
23-2 x 22-8
BED RM.
13-8 x 11-8
FOYER
7-4 x 11-8
DINING
14-8 x 11-8
PORCH

Design 9771

Square Footage: 1,927

■ Sunlight takes center stage in this delightful country home. Each room, including the garage, has at least two windows to add warmth and radiance, and a clerestory window brightens the foyer. Two bedrooms and a full bath are to the left of the foyer. To the right is the dining room which leads into the L-shaped kitchen with its peninsula cooktop and connecting breakfast area with a bay window. The central great room offers a cathedral ceiling, a fireplace and access to the rear porch. The master suite is separated for privacy and features two walls of windows, a large walk-in closet and a luxurious whirlpool bath with skylights. Additional storage space is available in the garage and in the attic.

down
attic storage
BONUS RM.
23-2 x 19-0

Design by
Donald A. Gardner, Architects, Inc.

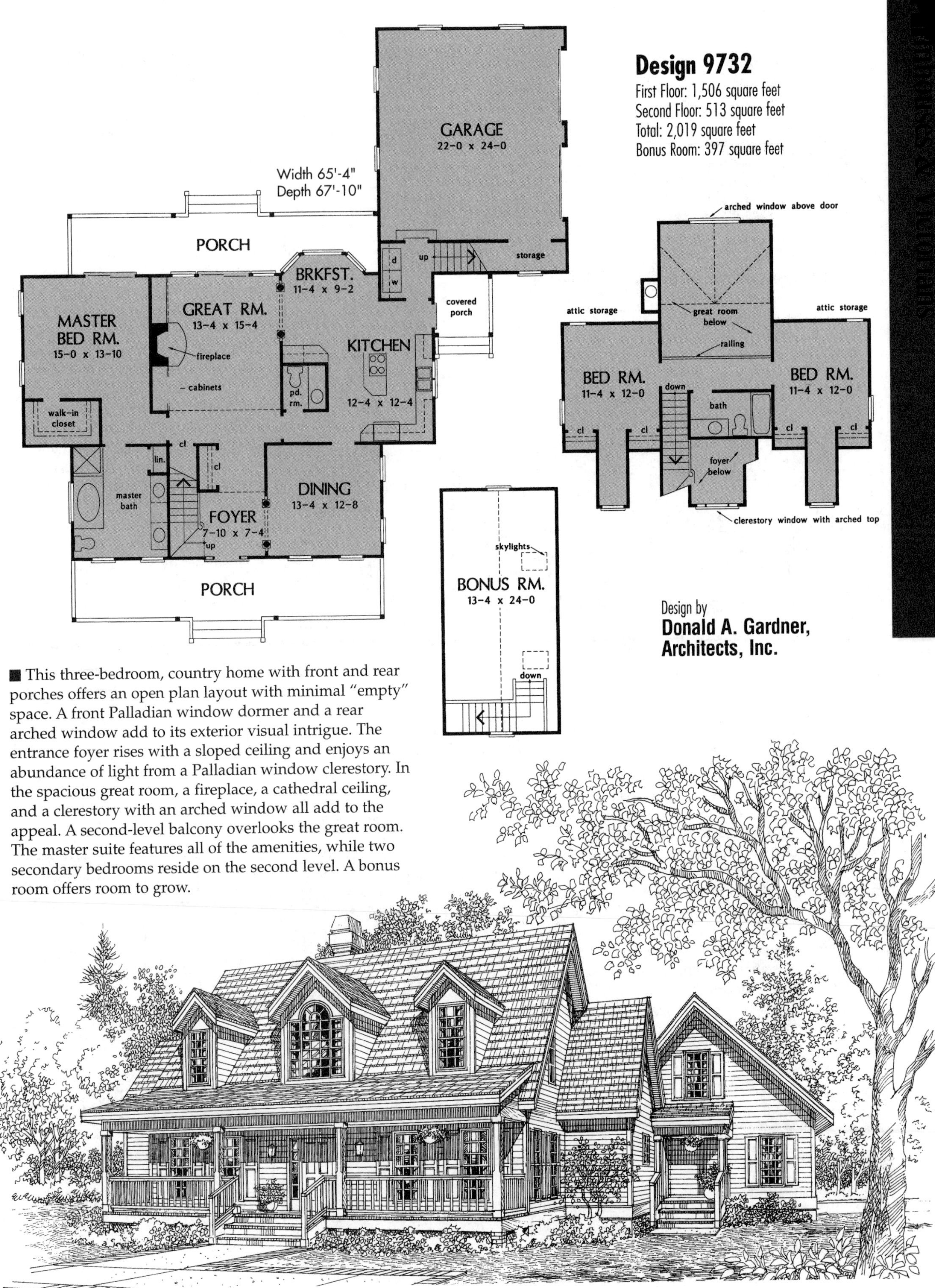
GARAGE
22-0 x 24-0
Width 65'-4"
Depth 67'-10"
PORCH
BRKFST.
11-4 x 9-2
storage
up
covered porch
MASTER
BED RM.
15-0 x 13-10
GREAT RM.
13-4 x 15-4
fireplace
cabinets
KITCHEN
12-4 x 12-4
pd. rm.
walk-in closet
master bath
lin.
cl
FOYER
7-10 x 7-4
DINING
13-4 x 12-8
PORCH
arched window above door
attic storage
great room below
railing
attic storage
BED RM.
11-4 x 12-0
down
bath
BED RM.
11-4 x 12-0
foyer below
clerestory window with arched top
skylights
BONUS RM.
13-4 x 24-0
down

Design 9732

First Floor: 1,506 square feet
Second Floor: 513 square feet
Total: 2,019 square feet
Bonus Room: 397 square feet

Design by
Donald A. Gardner, Architects, Inc.

■ This three-bedroom, country home with front and rear porches offers an open plan layout with minimal "empty" space. A front Palladian window dormer and a rear arched window add to its exterior visual intrigue. The entrance foyer rises with a sloped ceiling and enjoys an abundance of light from a Palladian window clerestory. In the spacious great room, a fireplace, a cathedral ceiling, and a clerestory with an arched window all add to the appeal. A second-level balcony overlooks the great room. The master suite features all of the amenities, while two secondary bedrooms reside on the second level. A bonus room offers room to grow.

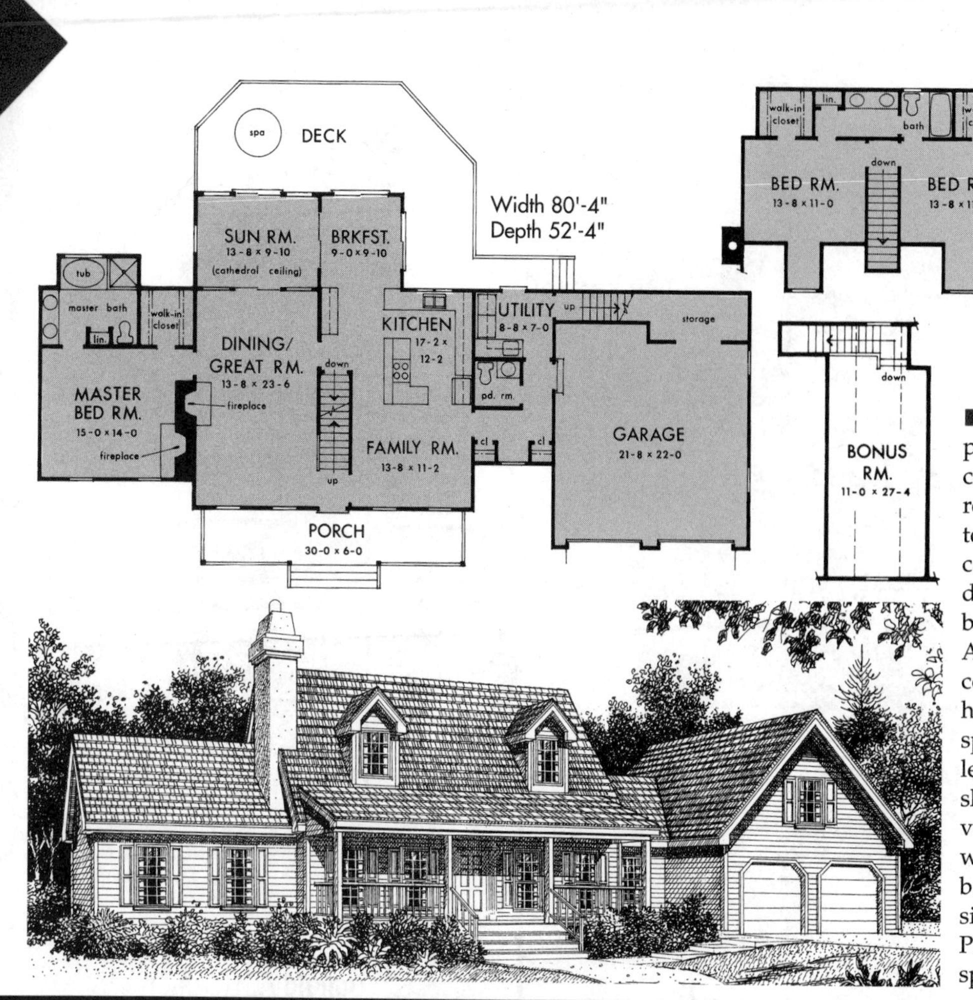
DECK
spa
SUN RM.
13-8 x 9-10
(cathedral ceiling)
BRKFST.
9-0 x 9-10
Width 80'-4"
Depth 52'-4"
tub
master bath
walk-in closet
lin.
DINING/
GREAT RM.
13-8 x 23-6
KITCHEN
17-2 x 12-2
UTILITY
8-8 x 7-0
up
storage
MASTER
BED RM.
15-0 x 14-0
fireplace
fireplace
down
pd. rm.
FAMILY RM.
13-8 x 11-2
cl
cl
GARAGE
21-8 x 22-0
up
PORCH
30-0 x 6-0
walk-in closet
lin.
bath
walk-in closet
down
BED RM.
13-8 x 11-0
BED RM.
13-8 x 11-0
down
BONUS
RM.
11-0 x 27-4

Design by
Donald A. Gardner, Architects, Inc.

Design 9625

First Floor: 1,581 square feet
Second Floor: 549 square feet
Total: 2,130 square feet
Bonus Room: 334 square feet

■ Great flexibility is available in this plan—the great room/dining room can be reworked into one large great room with the dining room relocated to the family room. A sunroom with cathedral ceiling and sliding glass door to the deck is accessible from both the breakfast and dining rooms. A large kitchen boasts a convenient cooking island. The master bedroom has a fireplace, walk-in closet and spacious master bath. Two second-level bedrooms are equal in size and share a full bath with double-bowl vanity. Both bedrooms have a dormer window and a walk-in closet. A large bonus room over the garage is accessible from the utility room below. Please specify basement or crawlspace foundation when ordering.

Design 9654

First Floor: 1,578 square feet
Second Floor: 554 square feet
Total: 2132 square feet

■ Enjoy outdoor living with a covered porch at the front of this home and an expansive deck to the rear. The floor plan allows for great livability and privacy with the master suite on the first floor. The kitchen and family room give a relaxing space for casual living while the dining area and great room can take on more formal entertaining. Upstairs, two family bedrooms each enjoy a walk-in closet and share a full bath. There is also bonus space above the garage for a studio, study or play room. Please specify basement or crawlspace foundation when ordering.

Design by
Donald A. Gardner, Architects, Inc.

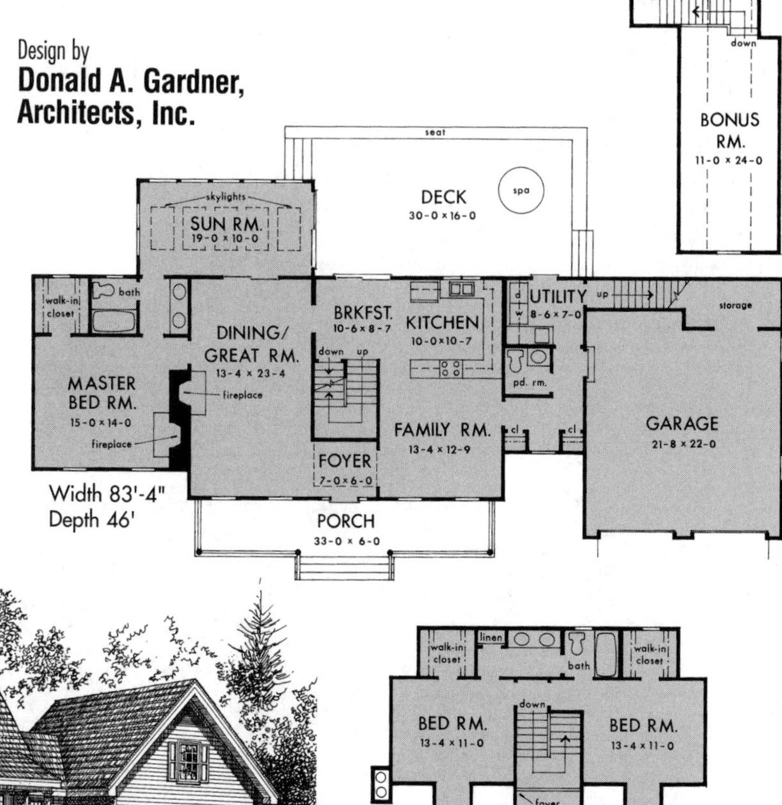
down
BONUS
RM.
11-0 x 24-0
seat
DECK
30-0 x 16-0
spa
skylights
SUN RM.
19-0 x 10-0
walk-in closet
bath
DINING/
GREAT RM.
13-4 x 23-4
BRKFST.
10-6 x 8-7
KITCHEN
10-0 x 10-7
UTILITY
8-6 x 7-0
up
storage
down up
fireplace
MASTER
BED RM.
15-0 x 14-0
fireplace
pd. rm.
FAMILY RM.
13-4 x 12-9
cl
cl
GARAGE
21-8 x 22-0
FOYER
7-0 x 6-0
Width 83'-4"
Depth 46'
PORCH
33-0 x 6-0
linen
walk-in closet
bath
walk-in closet
down
BED RM.
13-4 x 11-0
BED RM.
13-4 x 11-0
foyer below
clerestory with palladian window

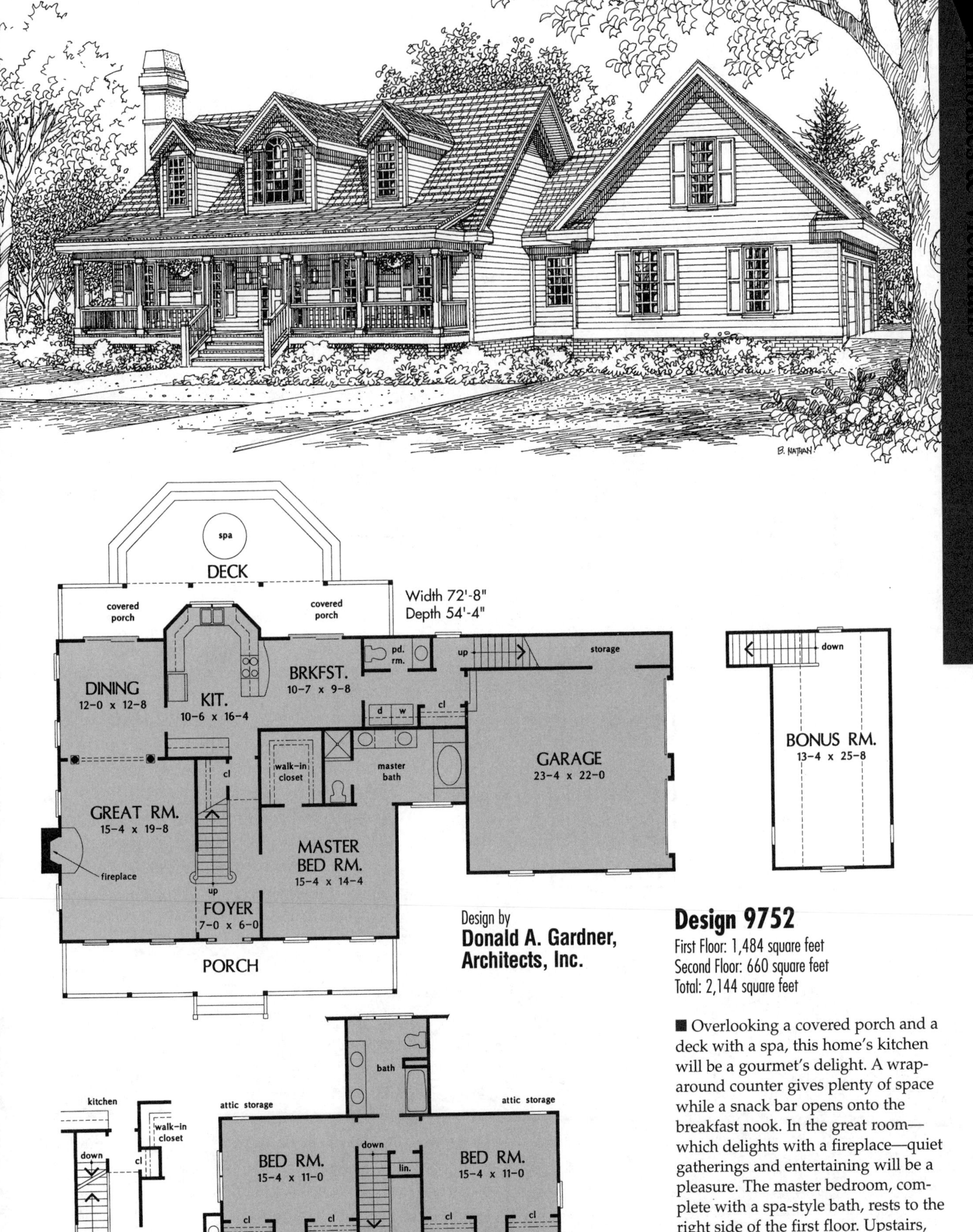
B. NATHAN
spa
DECK
covered porch
covered porch
Width 72'-8"
Depth 54'-4"
pd. rm.
up
storage
down
DINING
12-0 x 12-8
KIT.
10-6 x 16-4
BRKFST.
10-7 x 9-8
d w
cl
BONUS RM.
13-4 x 25-8
walk-in closet
master bath
GARAGE
23-4 x 22-0
cl
GREAT RM.
15-4 x 19-8
fireplace
MASTER
BED RM.
15-4 x 14-4
up
FOYER
7-0 x 6-0
PORCH
bath
kitchen
walk-in closet
attic storage
attic storage
down
cl
down
lin.
BED RM.
15-4 x 11-0
BED RM.
15-4 x 11-0
cl
cl
cl
cl
up
foyer
foyer below
Optional Basement Stair

Design by
Donald A. Gardner, Architects, Inc.

Design 9752

First Floor: 1,484 square feet
Second Floor: 660 square feet
Total: 2,144 square feet

■ Overlooking a covered porch and a deck with a spa, this home's kitchen will be a gourmet's delight. A wrap-around counter gives plenty of space while a snack bar opens onto the breakfast nook. In the great room—which delights with a fireplace—quiet gatherings and entertaining will be a pleasure. The master bedroom, complete with a spa-style bath, rests to the right side of the first floor. Upstairs, two bedrooms and a full hall bath comfortably house family and guests. Please specify basement or crawlspace foundation when ordering.

Design 9756

Square Footage: 2,207
Bonus Room: 435 square feet

■ This quaint four-bedroom home with front and rear porches reinforces its beauty with arched windows and dormers. The pillared dining room opens on your right while a study that could double as a guest room is available on your left. Straight ahead lies the massive great room with its cathedral ceiling, enchanting fireplace and access to the private rear porch and the deck with a spa and seat. Within steps of the dining room is the efficient kitchen and the sunny breakfast nook. The master suite enjoys a cathedral ceiling, rear deck access and a master bath with a skylit whirlpool tub, a walk-in closet and a double vanity. Two additional bedrooms are located at the opposite end of the house and share a full bath with dual vanities.

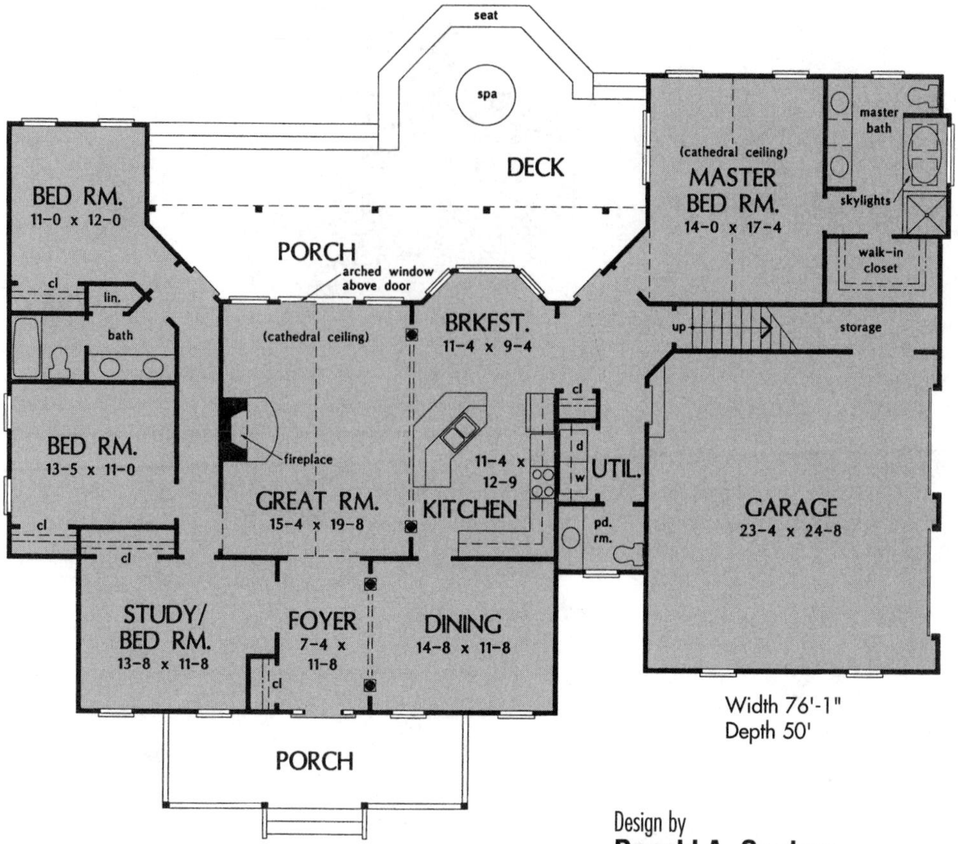

Width 76'-1"
Depth 50'

Design by
Donald A. Gardner, Architects, Inc.

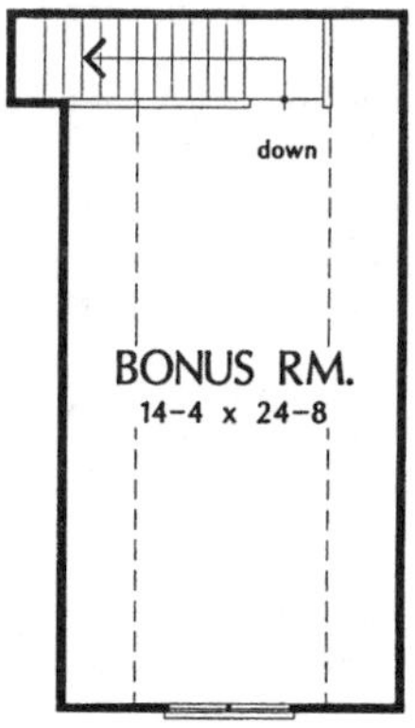

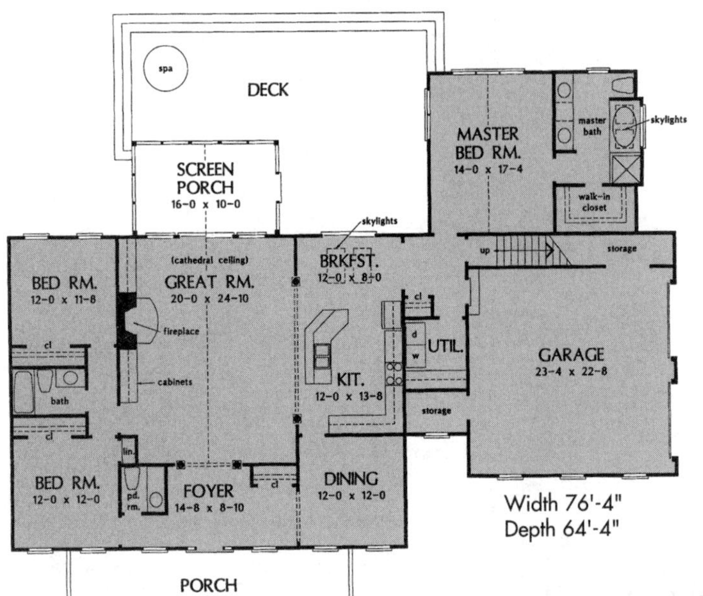

spa
DECK
SCREEN PORCH 16-0 x 10-0
MASTER BED RM. 14-0 x 17-4
master bath
skylights
walk-in closet
BED RM. 12-0 x 11-8
(cathedral ceiling)
GREAT RM. 20-0 x 24-10
fireplace
cabinets
BRKFST. 12-0 x 8-0
KIT. 12-0 x 13-8
UTIL.
GARAGE 23-4 x 22-8
storage
bath
BED RM. 12-0 x 12-0
lin.
pd. rm.
FOYER 14-8 x 8-10
DINING 12-0 x 12-0
PORCH

Design 9738

Square Footage: 2,136

Design by
Donald A. Gardner, Architects, Inc.

■ This exciting three-bedroom country home overflows with amenities. Traditional details such as columns, cathedral ceilings, and open living areas combine to create the ideal floor plan for today's active family lifestyle. The spacious great room features built-in cabinets, a fireplace and a cathedral ceiling which continues into the adjoining screen porch. An efficient kitchen with a preparation island is conveniently grouped with the great room, the dining room and the skylit breakfast area. A private master bedroom features a cathedral ceiling, a large walk-in closet and a relaxing master bath with a skylit whirlpool tub and a separate shower. Two secondary bedrooms share a full bath. A bonus room above the garage provides flexibility for growth.

Width 76'-4"
Depth 64'-4"

BONUS RM. 14-4 x 26-4

QUOTE ONE®

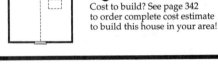

Cost to build? See page 342 to order complete cost estimate to build this house in your area!

Design 9782

Square Footage: 2,192

Design by
Donald A. Gardner, Architects, Inc.

■ Exciting volumes and nine-foot ceilings add elegance to a comfortable, open plan while secluded bedrooms are pleasant retreats in this home, designed for today's family. Sunlight fills the airy foyer from a vaulted dormer and streams into the great room. A formal dining room, delineated from the foyer by columns, features a tray ceiling. Hosts whose guests always end up in the kitchen will enjoy entertaining here, with only columns to separate them from the great room. Family bedrooms share a full bath complete with a linen closet. The front bedroom doubles as a study for extra flexibility and is accented by a tray ceiling. The master suite is highlighted by a tray ceiling and a lush bath.

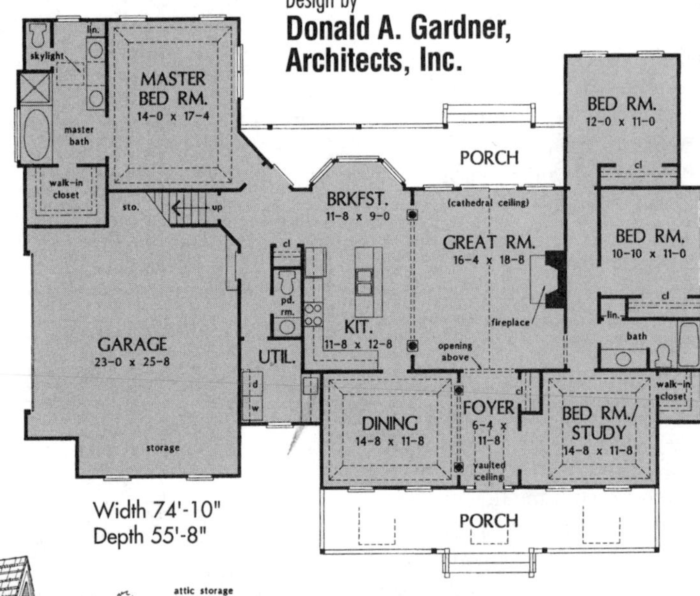

MASTER BED RM. 14-0 x 17-4
master bath
skylight
walk-in closet
PORCH
BED RM. 12-0 x 11-0
BRKFST. 11-8 x 9-0
(cathedral ceiling)
GREAT RM. 16-4 x 18-8
BED RM. 10-10 x 11-0
fireplace
KIT. 11-8 x 12-8
GARAGE 23-0 x 25-8
UTIL.
opening above
bath
DINING 14-8 x 11-8
FOYER 6-4 x 11-8
vaulted ceiling
BED RM./ STUDY 14-8 x 11-8
storage
PORCH

Width 74'-10"
Depth 55'-8"

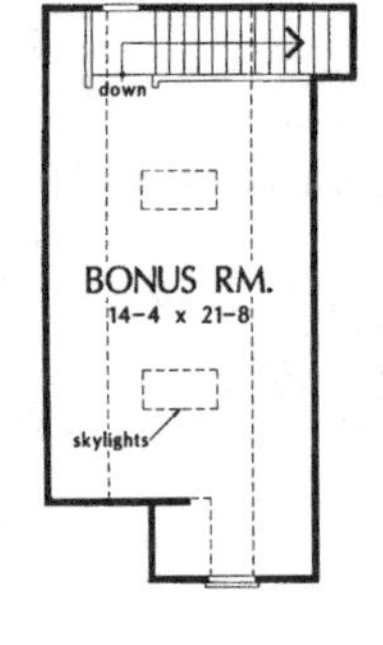

attic storage
down
BONUS RM. 14-4 x 21-8
skylights

Design by
Donald A. Gardner, Architects, Inc.

Design 9707

First Floor: 1,632 square feet
Second Floor: 669 square feet
Total: 2,301 square feet
Bonus Room: 528 square feet

■ This open country plan boasts front and rear covered porches and a bonus room for future expansion. The entrance foyer with a sloped ceiling has a Palladian window clerestory to allow natural light in. The spacious great room has a fireplace, cathedral ceiling and a clerestory with arched windows. The second-floor balcony overlooks the great room. A U-shaped kitchen provides the ideal layout for food preparation. For flexibility, access is provided to the bonus room from both the first and second floors. This plan is available with a crawlspace foundation.

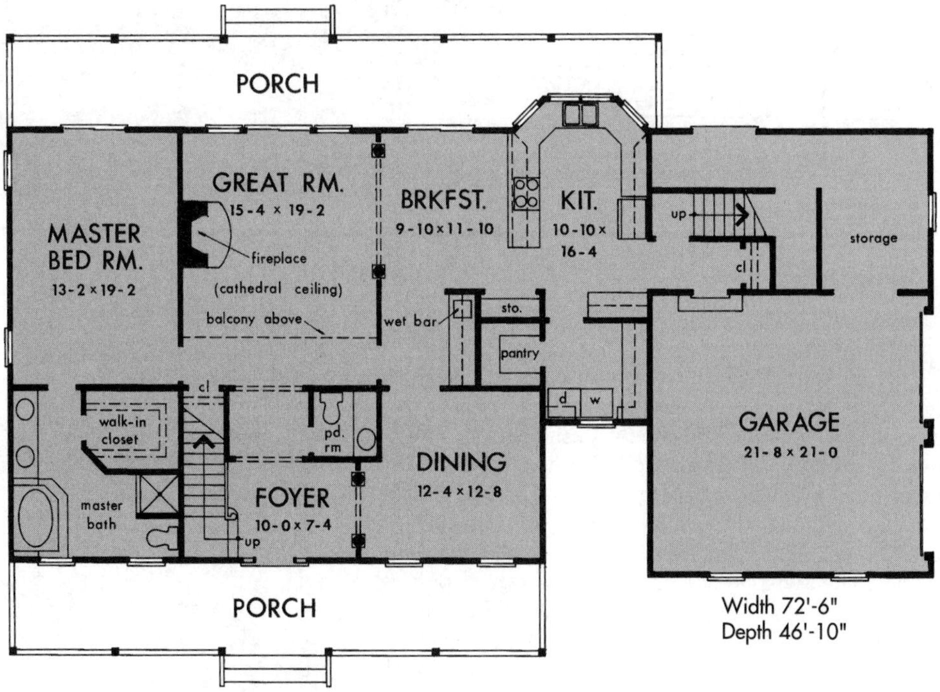

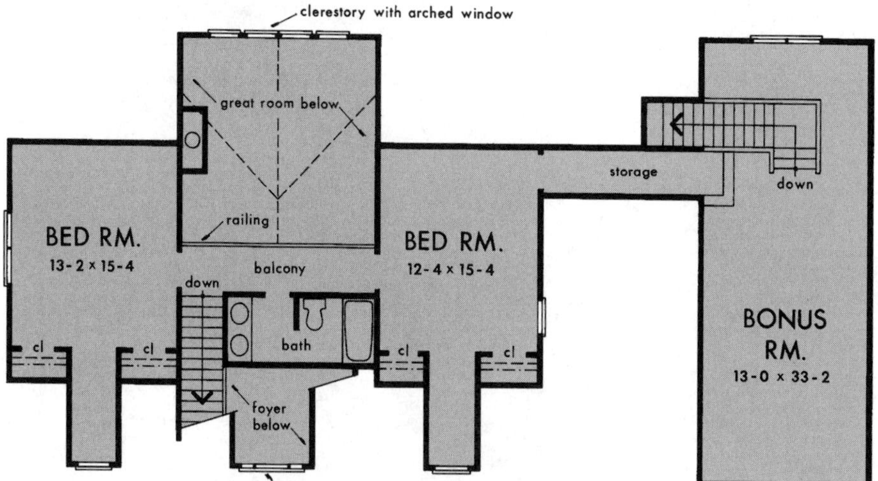

Width 72'-6"
Depth 46'-10"

QUOTE ONE®

Cost to build? See page 342 to order complete cost estimate to build this house in your area!

GARAGE
22-4 × 21-4
spa
DECK
covered breezeway
clerestory with arched window
(cathedral ceiling)
GREAT RM.
19-8 × 19-2
fireplace
walk in closet
skylight
master bath
cab.
railing
BRKFST.
9-8 × 10-6
UTIL.
8-0 × 9-4
wet bar
KITCHEN
13-0 × 16-4
MASTER BED RM.
13-0 × 15-4
bath
up
BED RM./ STUDY
12-0 × 11-0
FOYER
5-0 × 13-6
DINING
12-0 × 13-2
PORCH
30-4 × 8-0
Width 70'
Depth 79'-2"

Design by
Donald A. Gardner, Architects, Inc.

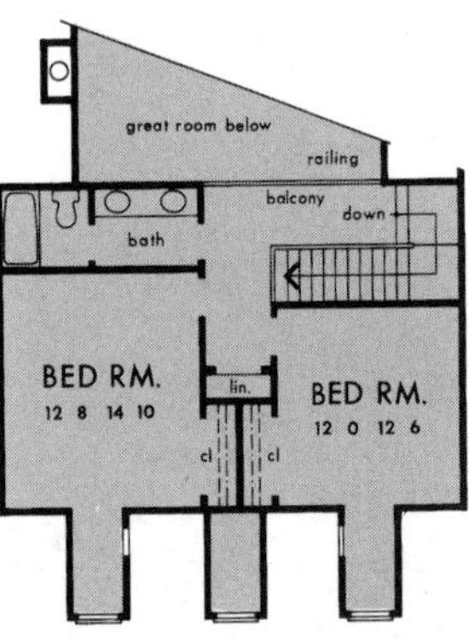
great room below
railing
balcony
down
bath
BED RM.
12 8 14 10
lin.
BED RM.
12 0 12 6
cl
cl

Design 9703

First Floor: 1,783 square feet
Second Floor: 611 square feet
Total: 2,394 square feet

■ Onlookers will delight in the symmetry of this facade's arched windows and dormers. The interior offers a great room with cathedral ceiling. This open plan is also packed with the latest design features, including a kitchen with large island, wet bar, bedroom/study combo on the first floor and a gorgeous master suite with a spa-style bath. Upstairs, two family bedrooms share a compartmented hall bath. An expansive rear deck and generous covered front porch offer maximum outdoor livability.

Design 9712

First Floor: 1,766 square feet
Second Floor: 670 square feet
Total: 2,436 square feet

Design by
Donald A. Gardner, Architects, Inc.

■ This four-bedroom farmhouse celebrates sunlight with a Palladian window dormer, a skylit screened porch and a rear arched window. The clerestory window in the two-story foyer throws natural light across the loft to a great room with a fireplace and a cathedral ceiling. The central island kitchen and the breakfast area open to the great room through an elegant colonnade. The first-floor master suite is a calm retreat and opens to the screened porch through a bay area. A garden tub, dual lavatories and a separate shower are touches of luxury in the master bath. The second floor provides two bedrooms with private baths and a loft area.

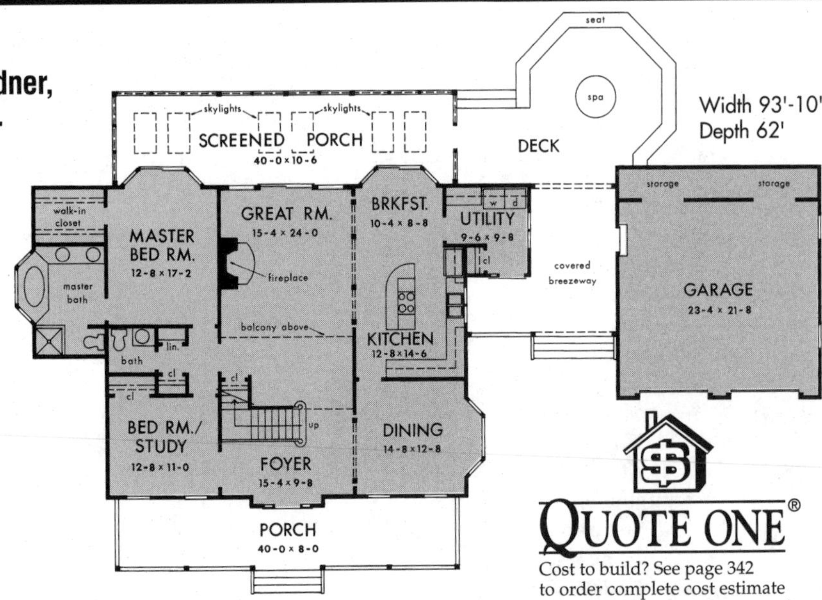
seat
spa
skylights
skylights
SCREENED PORCH
40-0 × 10-6
DECK
Width 93'-10"
Depth 62'
walk-in closet
master bath
MASTER BED RM.
12-8 × 17-2
GREAT RM.
15-4 × 24-0
fireplace
BRKFST.
10-4 × 8-8
UTILITY
9-6 × 9-8
storage
storage
covered breezeway
GARAGE
23-4 × 21-8
balcony above
KITCHEN
12-8 × 14-6
bath
lin.
cl
BED RM./ STUDY
12-8 × 11-0
up
FOYER
15-4 × 9-8
DINING
14-8 × 12-8
PORCH
40-0 × 8-0

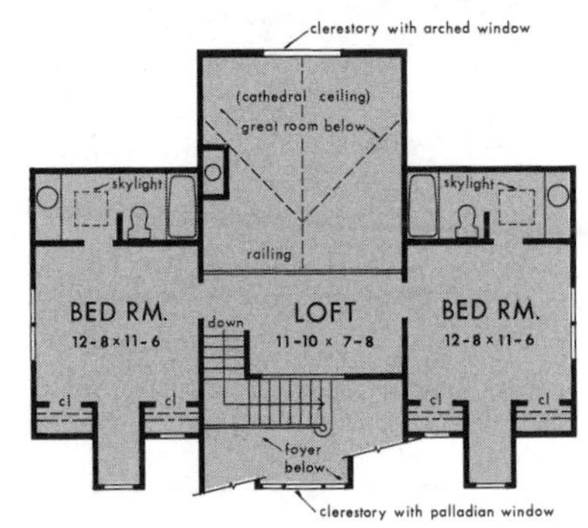
clerestory with arched window
(cathedral ceiling)
great room below
skylight
skylight
railing
BED RM.
12-8 × 11-6
down
LOFT
11-10 × 7-8
BED RM.
12-8 × 11-6
cl
cl
cl
cl
foyer below
clerestory with palladian window

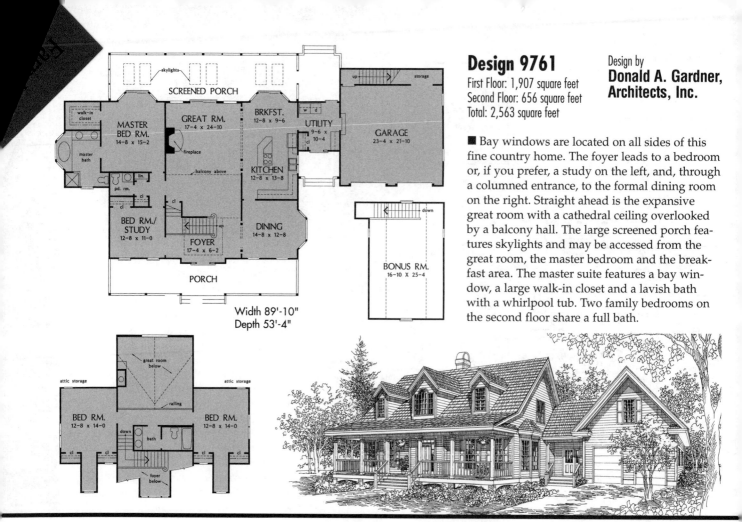

Design 9761

Design by
Donald A. Gardner, Architects, Inc.

First Floor: 1,907 square feet
Second Floor: 656 square feet
Total: 2,563 square feet

■ Bay windows are located on all sides of this fine country home. The foyer leads to a bedroom or, if you prefer, a study on the left, and, through a columned entrance, to the formal dining room on the right. Straight ahead is the expansive great room with a cathedral ceiling overlooked by a balcony hall. The large screened porch features skylights and may be accessed from the great room, the master bedroom and the breakfast area. The master suite features a bay window, a large walk-in closet and a lavish bath with a whirlpool tub. Two family bedrooms on the second floor share a full bath.

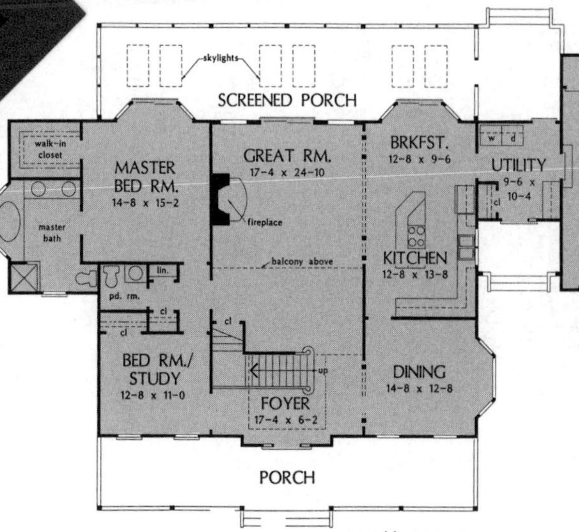

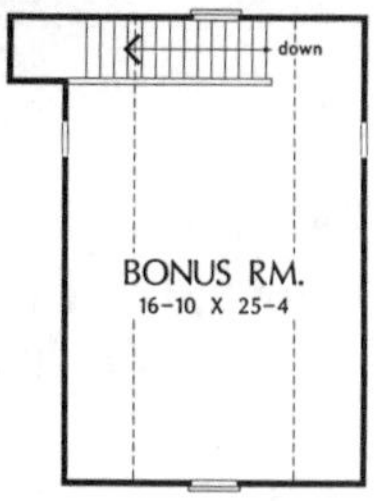

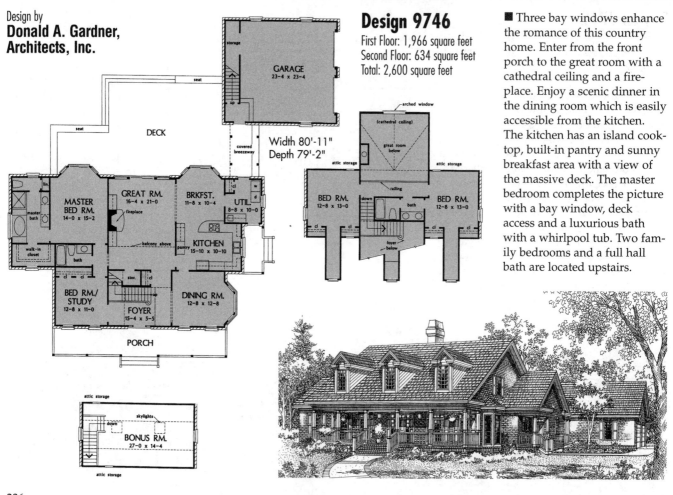

Width 89'-10"
Depth 53'-4"

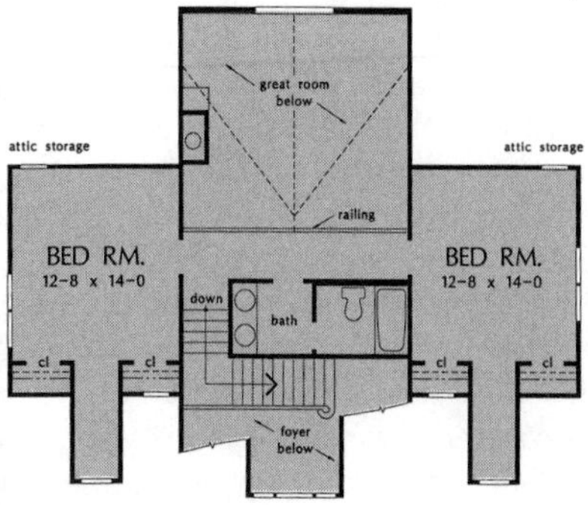

Design 9746

Design by
Donald A. Gardner, Architects, Inc.

First Floor: 1,966 square feet
Second Floor: 634 square feet
Total: 2,600 square feet

■ Three bay windows enhance the romance of this country home. Enter from the front porch to the great room with a cathedral ceiling and a fireplace. Enjoy a scenic dinner in the dining room which is easily accessible from the kitchen. The kitchen has an island cooktop, built-in pantry and sunny breakfast area with a view of the massive deck. The master bedroom completes the picture with a bay window, deck access and a luxurious bath with a whirlpool tub. Two family bedrooms and a full hall bath are located upstairs.

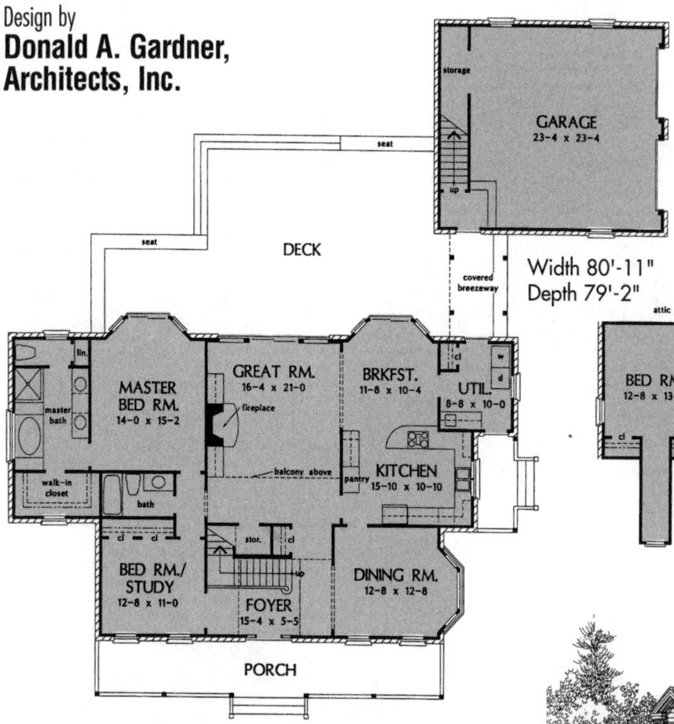

Width 80'-11"
Depth 79'-2"

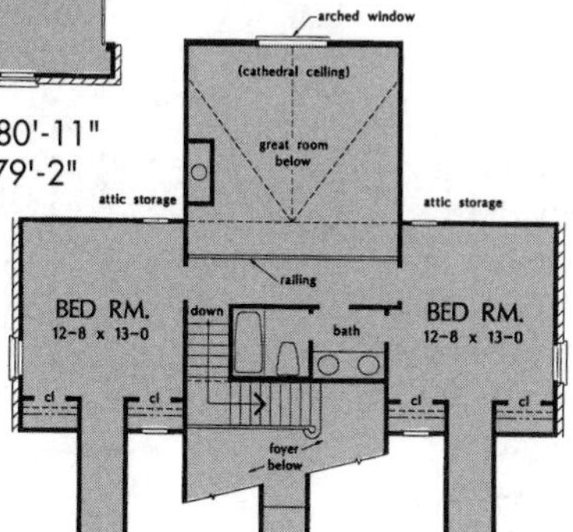

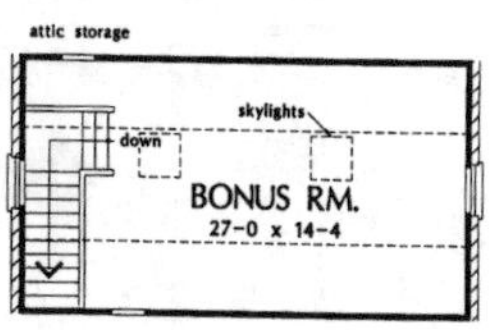

■ The two-story great room will soon become the focal point of this exquisite farmhouse. It is easily accessible from all areas of the house and features a cathedral ceiling, interior columns, an inviting fireplace and an overhead balcony. It is readily served by the kitchen with an island cooktop, a large pantry and a nearby utility room. The private master bedroom has direct access to the covered porch and includes a master bath with a double-bowl vanity, a whirlpool tub, a separate shower and a large walk-in closet. The front bedroom, with its separate full bath, can also convert to a study. Two additional bedrooms are located on the second floor and share a full bath. Attic storage areas are easily accessible.

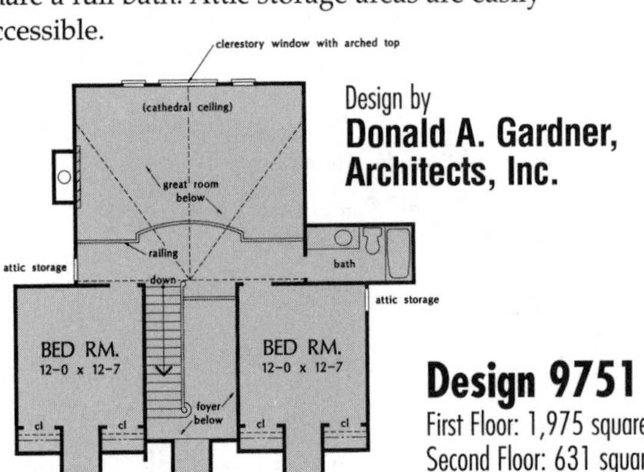
clerestory window with arched top
(cathedral ceiling)
great room below
railing
attic storage
bath
attic storage
down
BED RM.
12-0 x 12-7
BED RM.
12-0 x 12-7
foyer below
cl
cl
cl
cl

Design by
Donald A. Gardner, Architects, Inc.

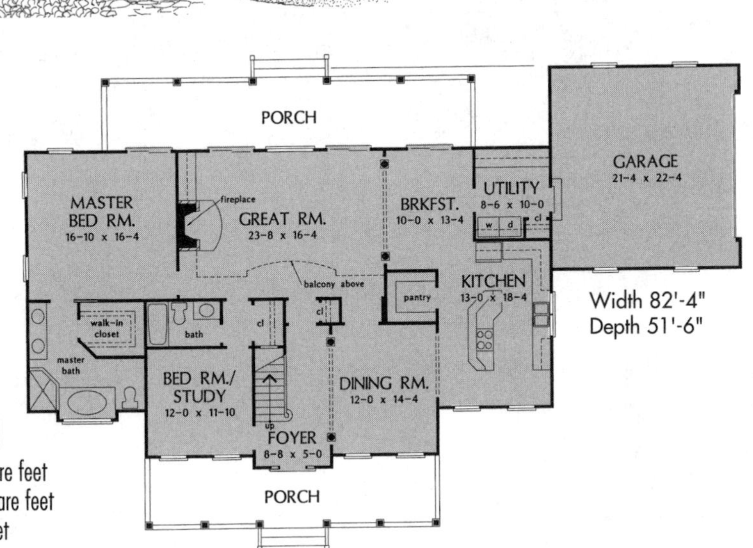
PORCH
MASTER BED RM.
16-10 x 16-4
fireplace
GREAT RM.
23-8 x 16-4
balcony above
BRKFST.
10-0 x 13-4
UTILITY
8-6 x 10-0
GARAGE
21-4 x 22-4
KITCHEN
13-0 x 18-4
pantry
walk-in closet
bath
master bath
cl
cl
BED RM./ STUDY
12-0 x 11-10
DINING RM.
12-0 x 14-4
up
FOYER
8-8 x 5-0
PORCH
Width 82'-4"
Depth 51'-6"

Design 9751

First Floor: 1,975 square feet
Second Floor: 631 square feet
Total: 2,606 square feet

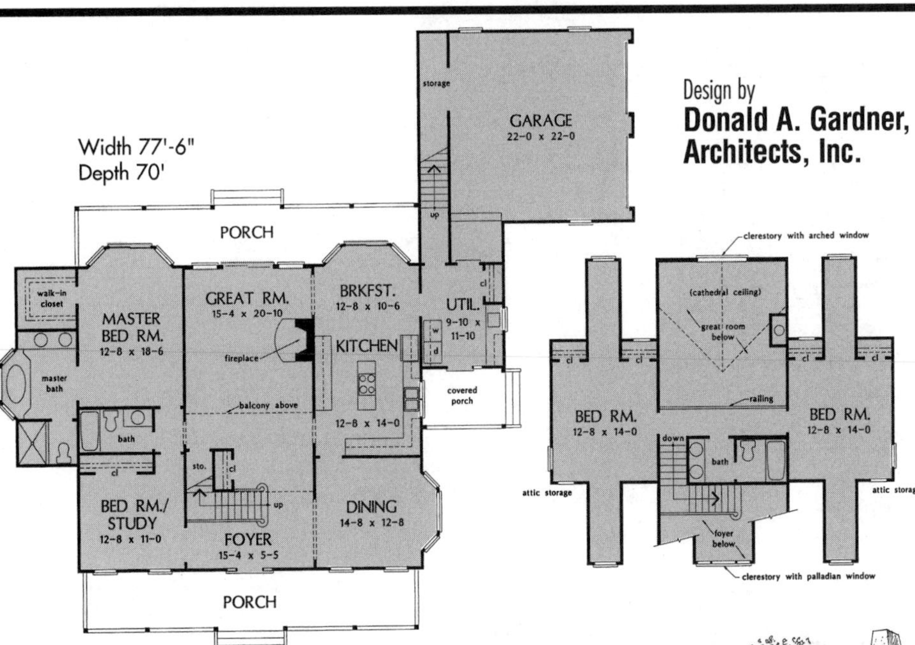
storage
GARAGE
22-0 x 22-0
Width 77'-6"
Depth 70'
up
PORCH
walk-in closet
MASTER BED RM.
12-8 x 18-6
master bath
GREAT RM.
15-4 x 20-10
fireplace
balcony above
BRKFST.
12-8 x 10-6
KITCHEN
12-8 x 14-0
UTIL.
9-10 x 11-10
covered porch
bath
cl
BED RM./ STUDY
12-8 x 11-0
sto.
cl
up
FOYER
15-4 x 5-5
DINING
14-8 x 12-8
PORCH

Design by
Donald A. Gardner, Architects, Inc.

clerestory with arched window
(cathedral ceiling)
great room below
railing
BED RM.
12-8 x 14-0
BED RM.
12-8 x 14-0
down
bath
attic storage
attic storage
foyer below
clerestory with palladian window

■ This fetching four-bedroom country home has porches and dormers at both front and rear to offer a welcoming touch. The spacious great room enjoys a large fireplace, cathedral ceiling and an arched clerestory window. An efficient kitchen is centrally located to the dining room and bayed breakfast area and includes a cooktop island. The expansive master suite is located on the first floor with a generous walk-in closet and a luxurious master bath. A front bedroom would make a lovely study or guest room. The second level is highlighted by a balcony hall that leads to two family bedrooms that share a full bath.

Design 9733

First Floor: 1,871 square feet
Second Floor: 731 square feet
Total: 2,602 square feet
Bonus Room: 402 square feet

Design by
Larry W. Garnett & Associates, Inc.

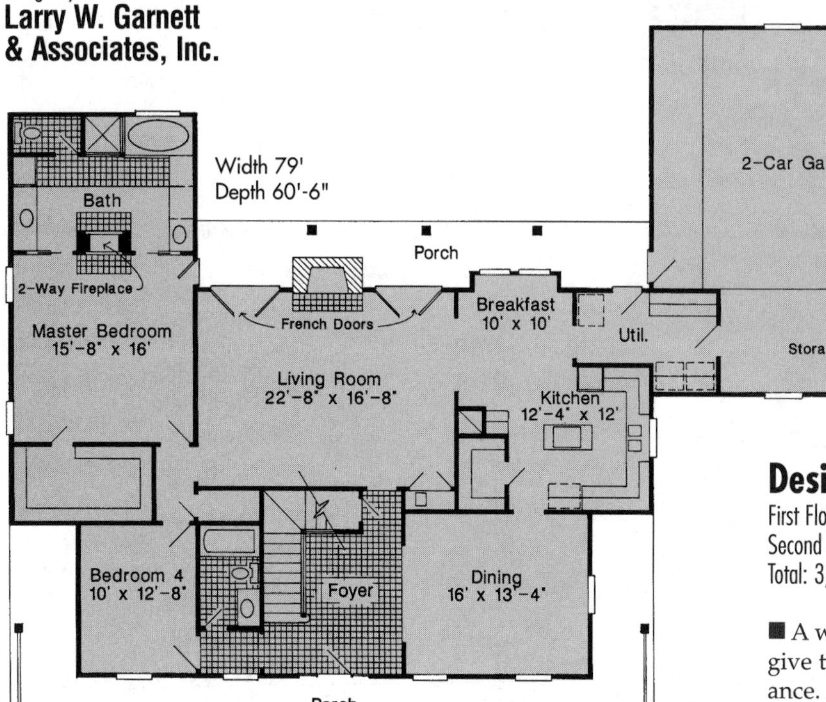

Width 79'
Depth 60'-6"
2-Car Garage
Bath
Porch
2-Way Fireplace
French Doors
Breakfast
10' x 10'
Util.
Storage
Master Bedroom
15'-8" x 16'
Living Room
22'-8" x 16'-8"
Kitchen
12'-4" x 12'
Bedroom 4
10' x 12'-8"
Foyer
Dining
16' x 13'-4"
Porch

QUOTE ONE®
Cost to build? See page 342
to order complete cost estimate
to build this house in your area!

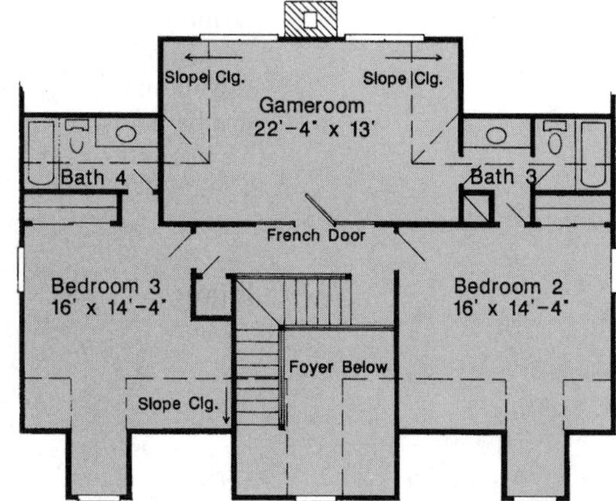

Slope Clg.
Slope Clg.
Gameroom
22'-4" x 13'
Bath 4
Bath 3
French Door
Bedroom 3
16' x 14'-4"
Bedroom 2
16' x 14'-4"
Foyer Below
Slope Clg.

Design 9005

First Floor: 1,995 square feet
Second Floor: 1,077 square feet
Total: 3,072 square feet

■ A wraparound front porch and dormer windows give this home a casual and comfortable appearance. A leaded-glass transom above the front door, along with the dormer window in the sloped ceiling, fill the foyer with natural light. The large living room features French doors on each side of an elegant fireplace, and a built-in wet bar. An island cooktop, along with a walk-in pantry are part of the well-planned kitchen. The utility room, with extra work space, leads to an attached two-car garage and storage area. The master bedroom has generous closet space and a two-way fireplace opening into the master bath. His and Hers lavatories, an oversized tub and a glass-enclosed shower complete this elegant master bath. The second-floor balcony has French doors opening into a large game room. Bedroom 3 has a private bath, while Bedroom 2 shares access to a bath with the game room. Each bedroom has a sloped ceiling and a cozy alcove created by the dormer window.

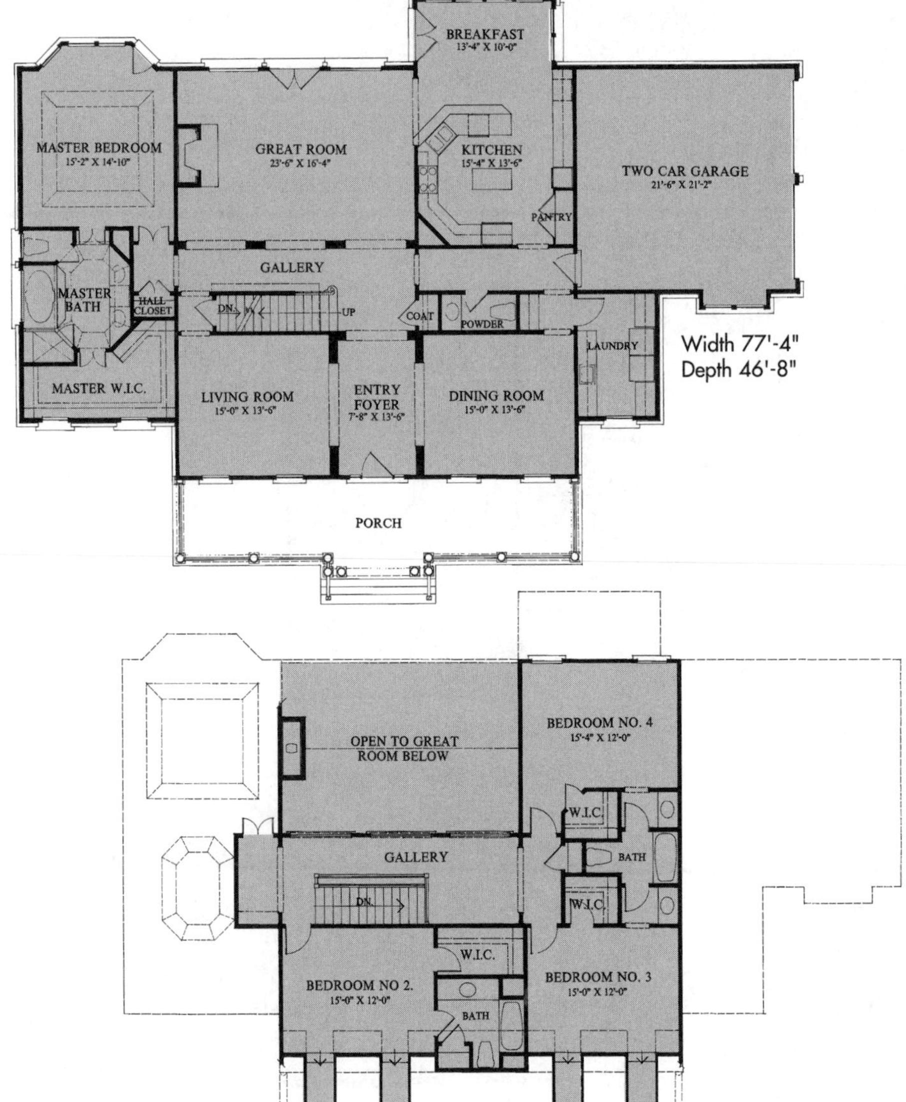

BREAKFAST
13'-4" X 10'-0"
MASTER BEDROOM
15'-2" X 14'-10"
GREAT ROOM
23'-6" X 16'-4"
KITCHEN
15'-4" X 13'-6"
TWO CAR GARAGE
21'-6" X 21'-2"
PANTRY
GALLERY
MASTER BATH
HALL CLOSET
DN
UP
COAT
POWDER
LAUNDRY
MASTER W.I.C.
LIVING ROOM
15'-0" X 13'-6"
ENTRY FOYER
7'-8" X 13'-6"
DINING ROOM
15'-0" X 13'-6"
Width 77'-4"
Depth 46'-8"
PORCH
OPEN TO GREAT ROOM BELOW
BEDROOM NO. 4
15'-4" X 12'-0"
W.I.C.
BATH
GALLERY
DN
W.I.C.
W.I.C.
BEDROOM NO 2.
15'-0" X 12'-0"
BATH
BEDROOM NO. 3
15'-0" X 12'-0"

Design 9912

First Floor: 2,315 square feet
Second Floor: 1,200 square feet
Total: 3,515 square feet

■ This grand home displays the finest in farmhouse design. Dormer windows and a traditional brick and siding exterior create a welcoming facade. Inside, the entry foyer opens to a formal zone consisting of a living room to the left and a dining room to the right. The kitchen enjoys a pass-through to the breakfast area—the great room is just a step away. Here, a fireplace graces the far end of the room while a wall of glass allows light to penetrate the interior of the room. Double doors grant passage to the back yard. Beyond the first-floor gallery, the master bedroom boasts a tray ceiling, a window bay and a lavish bath. Upstairs, three family bedrooms all have walk-in closets and direct access to a bath. This home is designed with a basement foundation.

Design by
Design Traditions

…91

…4 square feet
…r: 1,061 square feet
…,545 square feet

Design by
Donald A. Gardner, Architects, Inc.

■ With two covered porches that invite outdoor living and an open layout, this farmhouse has plenty to offer. Columns define the living room which can option to be a study. The great room is graced by a fireplace and has access to the rear porch. The sunny, bayed breakfast room is convenient to the U-shaped island kitchen. A formal dining room is located to the front of the plan and is enhanced by a boxed-bay window. Three bedrooms upstairs include a deluxe master suite complete with sitting area framed by a bay window, a lavish bath and walk-in closet. Two family bedrooms share a full hall bath. A large bonus room would make a great guest suite or a studio.

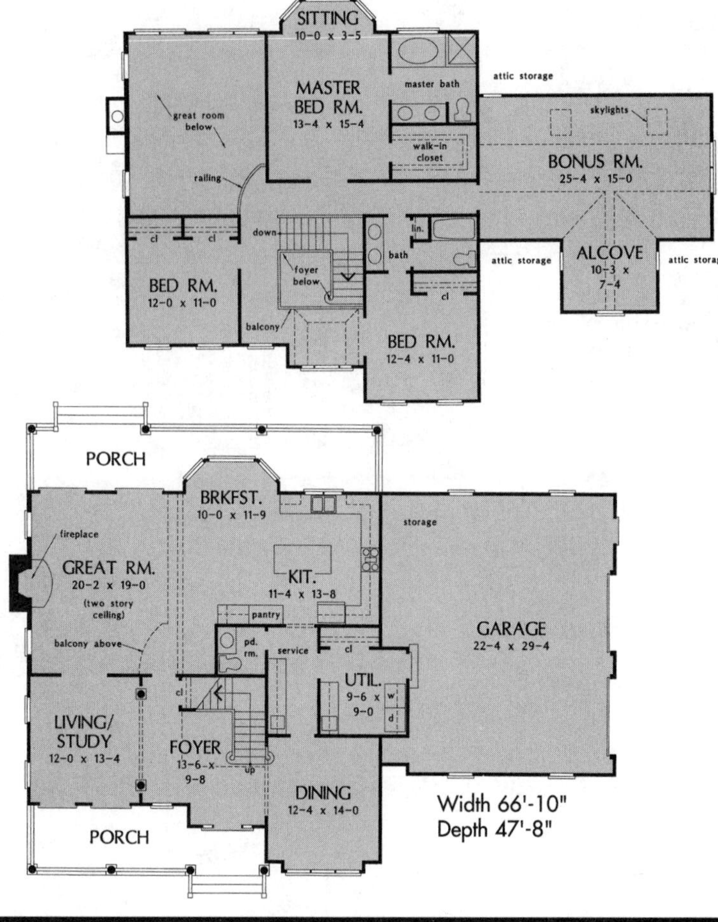
SITTING
10-0 x 3-5
MASTER
BED RM.
13-4 x 15-4
master bath
walk-in closet
great room below
railing
attic storage
skylights
BONUS RM.
25-4 x 15-0
ALCOVE
10-3 x 7-4
attic storage
attic storage
down
foyer below
bath
lin.
cl
BED RM.
12-0 x 11-0
balcony
BED RM.
12-4 x 11-0
PORCH
BRKFST.
10-0 x 11-9
storage
fireplace
GREAT RM.
20-2 x 19-0
(two story ceiling)
KIT.
11-4 x 13-8
pantry
balcony above
pd. rm.
service
GARAGE
22-4 x 29-4
UTIL.
9-6 x 9-0
w
d
LIVING/
STUDY
12-0 x 13-4
FOYER
13-6 x 9-8
up
DINING
12-4 x 14-0
PORCH
Width 66'-10"
Depth 47'-8"

Design 7319

First Floor: 1,086 square feet
Second Floor: 1,033 square feet
Total: 2,119 square feet

Design by
Design Basics, Inc.

■ Down-home charm is exuded from this hospitable, wood-sided home. A front gable gives definition to the covered porch as it leads to this traditional plan. A parlor and formal dining room flank the entry foyer where an open staircase leads to the second floor. The large family room has a grand fireplace and open views of the sunny breakfast nook and the efficient kitchen. The master suite is joined on the second floor by three family bedrooms and a compartmented hall bath.

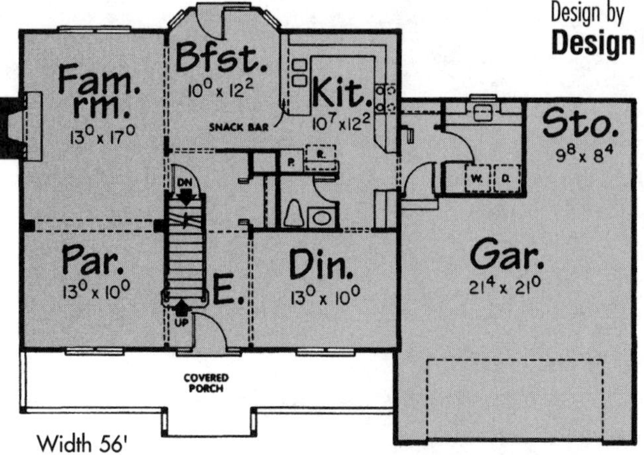
Fam. rm.
13^0 x 17^0
Bfst.
10^0 x 12^2
SNACK BAR
Kit.
10^7 x 12^2
Sto.
9^8 x 8^4
W.
D.
DN
Par.
13^0 x 10^0
E.
UP
Din.
13^0 x 10^0
Gar.
21^4 x 21^0
COVERED PORCH
Width 56'
Depth 38'

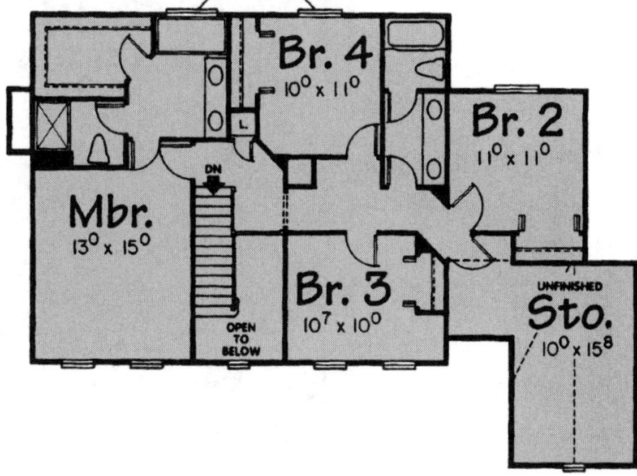
Br. 4
10^0 x 11^0
Br. 2
11^0 x 11^0
DN
Mbr.
13^0 x 15^0
Br. 3
10^7 x 10^0
OPEN TO BELOW
UNFINISHED
Sto.
10^0 x 15^8

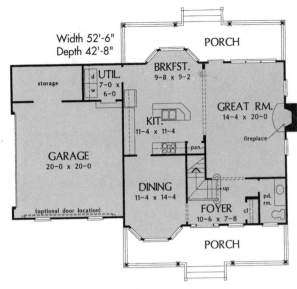

Width 52'-6"
Depth 42'-8"

PORCH
storage
UTIL. 7-0 x 6-0
BRKFST. 9-8 x 9-2
GREAT RM. 14-4 x 20-0
fireplace
KIT. 11-4 x 11-4
pan.
GARAGE 20-0 x 20-0
DINING 11-4 x 14-4
up
FOYER 10-6 x 7-8
pd. rm.
(optional door location)
PORCH

Design 7600

First Floor: 959 square feet
Second Floor: 833 square feet
Total: 1,792 square feet

Design by
Donald A. Gardner, Architects, Inc.

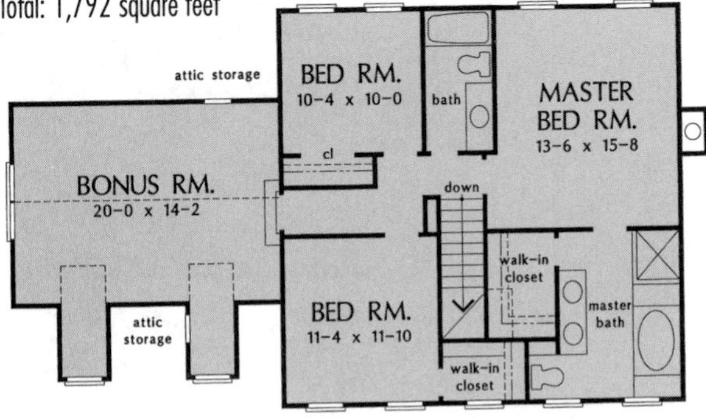

attic storage
BED RM. 10-4 x 10-0
bath
MASTER BED RM. 13-6 x 15-8
cl
BONUS RM. 20-0 x 14-2
down
walk-in closet
BED RM. 11-4 x 11-10
master bath
attic storage
walk-in closet

■ From its covered front porch to its covered rear porch, this farmhouse is a real charmer. The formal dining room is filled with light from a bay window and has direct access to the efficient kitchen. A matching bay is found in the cozy breakfast room. The large great room is graced with a warming fireplace and even more windows. An L-shaped staircase leads up to the sleeping zone containing two family bedrooms, a full bath and a master suite full of luxuries. A bonus room extending over the garage can be developed into a game room, a fourth bedroom or a study at a later date.

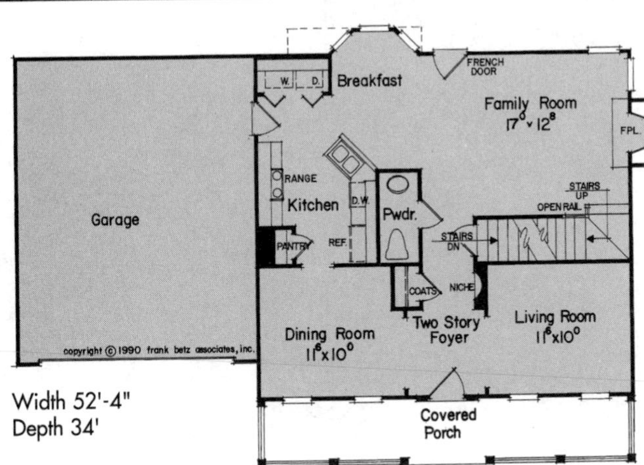

Breakfast
FRENCH DOOR
Family Room $17^0 \times 12^8$
FPL.
RANGE
Kitchen
D.W.
Pwdr.
STAIRS UP
OPEN RAIL
Garage
PANTRY
REF.
STAIRS DN
COATS
NICHE
Two Story Foyer
Living Room $11^6 \times 10^0$
Dining Room $11^6 \times 10^0$
copyright © 1990 frank betz associates, inc.
Covered Porch
Width 52'-4"
Depth 34'

Design P103

First Floor: 828 square feet
Second Floor: 772 square feet
Total: 1,600 square feet

Design by
Frank Betz Associates, Inc.

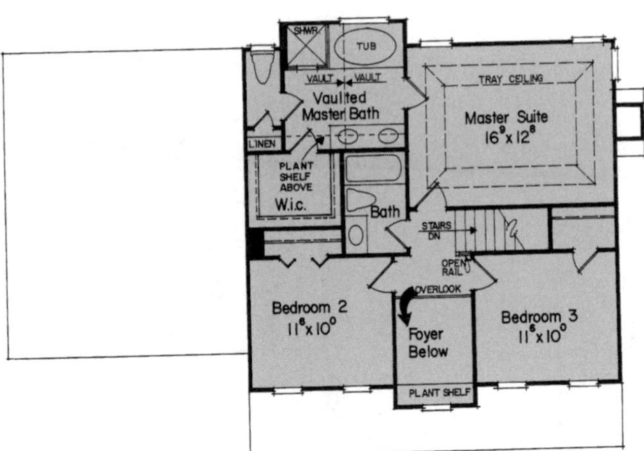

SHWR.
TUB
VAULT
Vaulted Master Bath
TRAY CEILING
Master Suite $16^0 \times 12^8$
LINEN
PLANT SHELF ABOVE
W.i.c.
Bath
STAIRS DN
OPEN RAIL
OVERLOOK
Bedroom 2 $11^6 \times 10^0$
Foyer Below
Bedroom 3 $11^6 \times 10^0$
PLANT SHELF

■ Traditional farmhouse symmetry is apparent throughout this family plan. The wide front porch invites relaxation besides offering a nice introduction to the two-story foyer. The formal dining and living rooms are split off of the foyer with each having two multi-pane windows facing forward. The comfortable family room has a fireplace at the far end and a French door to the rear yard. Most notable is the spacious feeling that comes from the family room being open to the breakfast room and the kitchen. Upstairs, the master suite is detailed with a tray ceiling and a vaulted master bath with a garden tub, compartmented toilet and walk-in closet. Two family bedrooms and a hall bath complete this plan. Please specify basement, slab or crawlspace foundation when ordering.

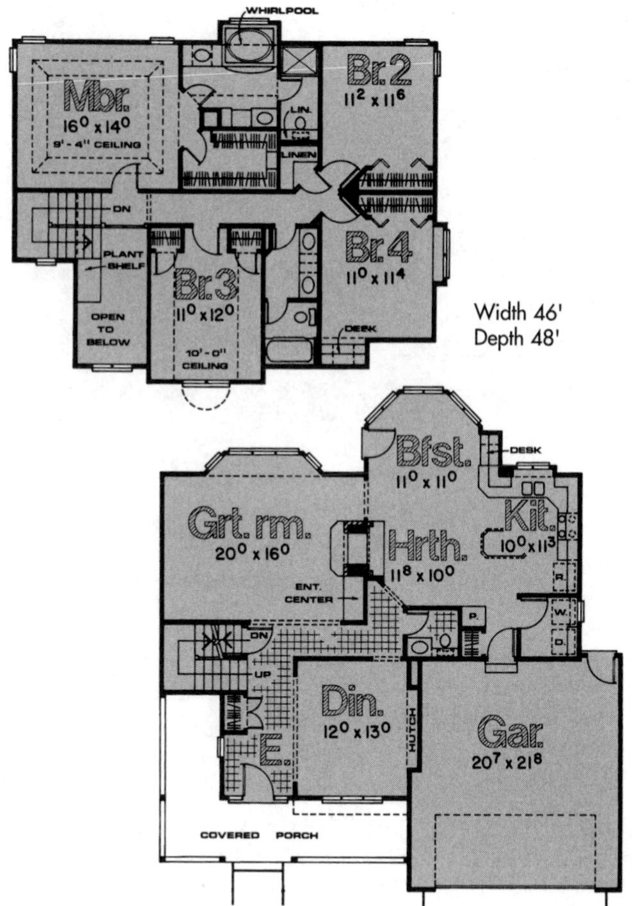

WHIRLPOOL
Mbr.
16⁰ x 14⁰
9'-4" CEILING
LIN.
LINEN
Br. 2
11² x 11⁶
DN
PLANT SHELF
OPEN TO BELOW
Br. 3
11⁰ x 12⁰
10'-0" CEILING
Br. 4
11⁰ x 11⁴
DESK
Width 46'
Depth 48'
Bfst.
11⁰ x 11⁰
DESK
Grt. rm.
20⁰ x 16⁰
Hrth.
11⁸ x 10⁰
Kit.
10⁰ x 11³
ENT. CENTER
DN
UP
P.
W.
D.
Din.
12⁰ x 13⁰
HUTCH
E
Gar.
20⁷ x 21⁸
COVERED PORCH

Design 9312

First Floor: 1,150 square feet
Second Floor: 1,120 square feet
Total: 2,270 square feet

Design by
Design Basics, Inc.

■ A covered porch enhances the elevation of this popular farmhouse. An entertainment center, through-fireplace and bayed windows add appeal to the great room. Families will love the spacious kitchen, breakfast and hearth room. Enhancements include a gazebo dinette, wrapping counters, prep island and a planning desk. Upstairs, comfortable secondary bedrooms and a sumptuous master suite feature privacy by design. Bedroom 3 is highlighted by a half round window, volume ceiling and double closets while Bedroom 4 features a built-in desk. The master suite has a vaulted ceiling, large walk-in closet, compartmented toilet/shower area and an oval whirlpool tub.

Design 9688

First Floor: 1,569 square feet
Second Floor: 929 square feet
Total: 2,498 square feet

Design by
Donald A. Gardner, Architects, Inc.

■ This home's striking exterior is reinforced by its gables and arched glass window. The central foyer leads to all spaces in the home's open layout. Both the living room and great room boast fireplaces and round columns. The efficient U-shaped kitchen offers a cooking island for added luxury to serve both the dining room and breakfast area. The master bedroom holds a large walk-in closet and generous bath with whirlpool, shower and double-bowl vanity. Two additional bedrooms share a full bath. A bedroom on the first level can easily double as a study.

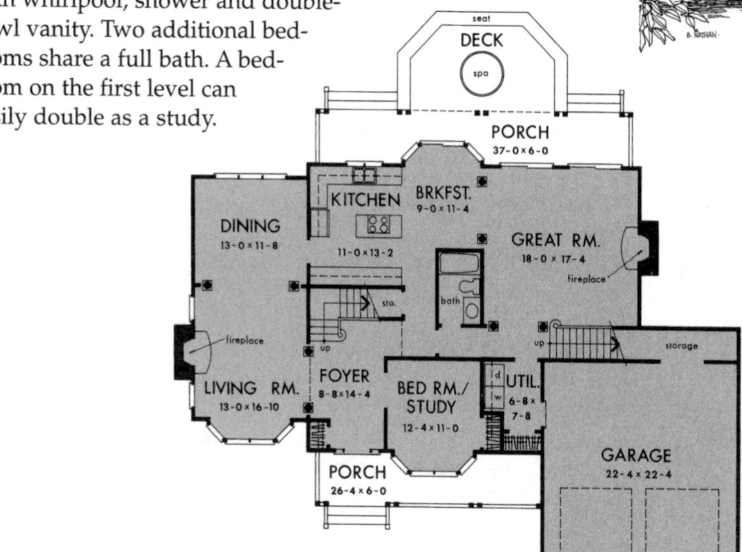

seat
DECK
spa
PORCH
37-0 x 6-0
KITCHEN
BRKFST.
9-0 x 11-4
DINING
13-0 x 11-8
11-0 x 13-2
GREAT RM.
18-0 x 17-4
fireplace
bath
sto.
up
fireplace
storage
LIVING RM.
13-0 x 16-10
FOYER
8-8 x 14-4
BED RM./
STUDY
12-4 x 11-0
UTIL.
6-8 x 7-8
GARAGE
22-4 x 22-4
PORCH
26-4 x 6-0

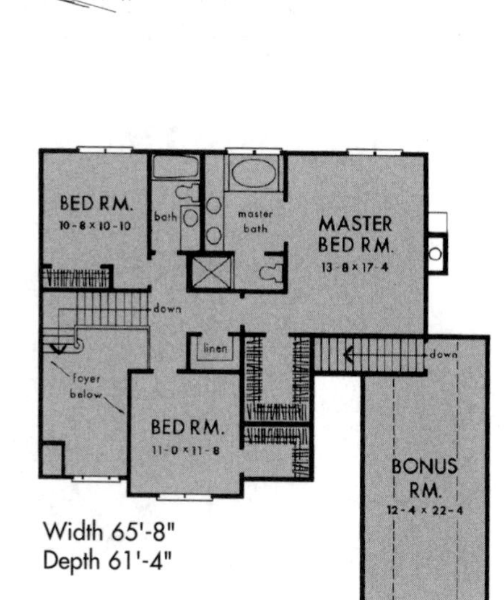

BED RM.
10-8 x 10-10
bath
master bath
MASTER
BED RM.
13-8 x 17-4
down
linen
foyer below
BED RM.
11-0 x 11-8
down
BONUS
RM.
12-4 x 22-4
Width 65'-8"
Depth 61'-4"

B. NATHAN

Design 9725

First Floor: 1,346 square feet
Second Floor: 836 square feet
Total: 2,182 square feet

Design by
Donald A. Gardner, Architects, Inc.

■ This classy, two-story home with wraparound covered porch offers a dynamic open floor plan. The entrance foyer and the spacious great room both rise to two stories—a Palladian window at the second level floods these areas with natural light. The kitchen is centrally located for maximum flexibility in layout and, as an added feature, also has a breakfast bar. The large dining room delights with a bay window. The generous master suite has plenty of closet space as well as a bath with a whirlpool tub, a shower and a double-bowl vanity. On the second level, three bedrooms branch off the balcony that overlooks the great room. One large bedroom has a private bath and a walk-in closet while the other bedrooms share a full bath.

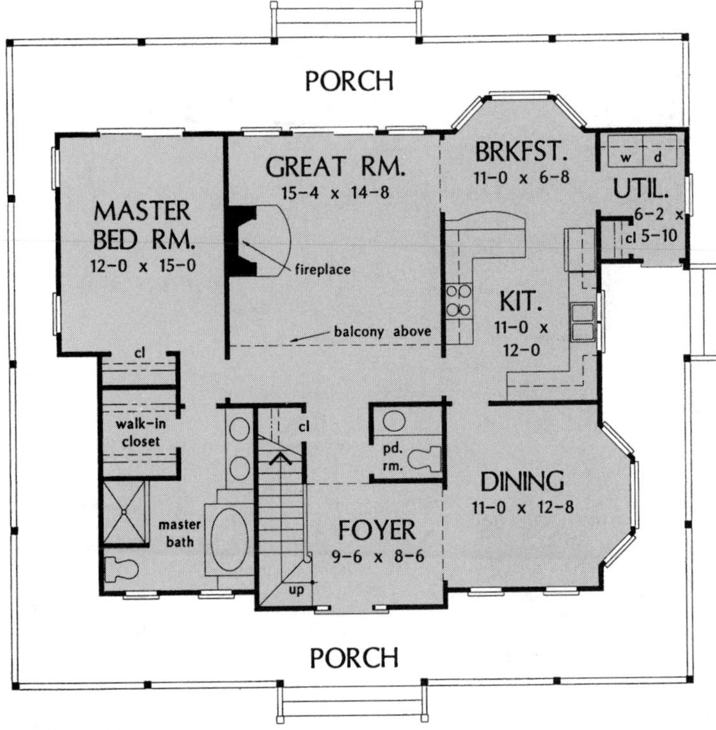
PORCH
GREAT RM.
15-4 x 14-8
BRKFST.
11-0 x 6-8
w d
UTIL.
6-2 x 5-10
cl
MASTER
BED RM.
12-0 x 15-0
fireplace
KIT.
11-0 x 12-0
balcony above
cl
walk-in closet
cl
pd. rm.
DINING
11-0 x 12-8
master bath
FOYER
9-6 x 8-6
up
PORCH

Width 49'-5"
Depth 45'-4"

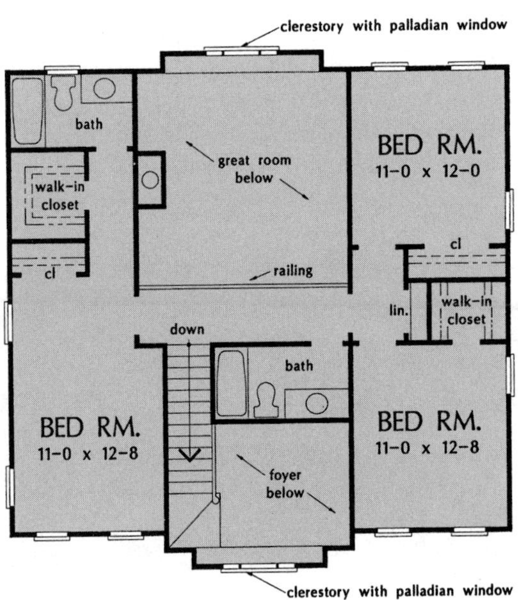
clerestory with palladian window
bath
great room below
BED RM.
11-0 x 12-0
walk-in closet
cl
railing
cl
lin.
walk-in closet
down
bath
BED RM.
11-0 x 12-8
foyer below
BED RM.
11-0 x 12-8
clerestory with palladian window

Design 7294

First Floor: 1,365 square feet
Second Floor: 1,185 square feet
Total: 2,550 square feet

Design by
Design Basics, Inc.

■ With its brick and wood siding facade, this farmhouse presents a strong and solid image, while its cool covered porch invites the gentle pleasure of relaxation. Inside, the formal living and dining room flank the traditional foyer. The family room at the rear of the plan has a warming fireplace and is thoughtfully open to the oversized country kitchen. An expanse of wrapping counters, a prep island and a bay breakfast nook make the kitchen the true heart of the house. Upstairs, three family bedrooms and a hall bath balance out the comfortable master suite.

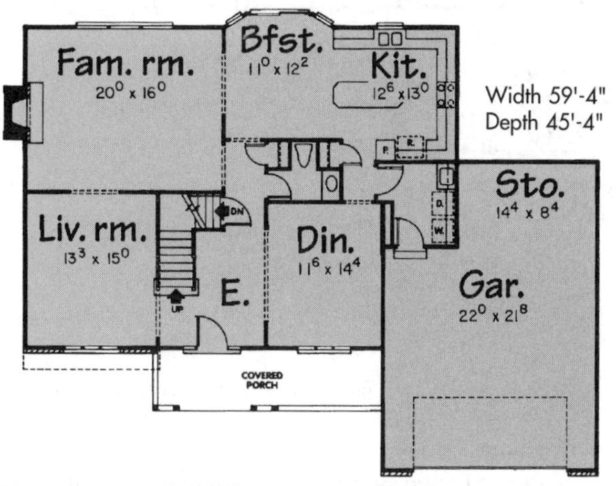
Fam. rm.
20^0 x 16^0
Bfst.
11^0 x 12^2
Kit.
12^6 x 13^0
Liv. rm.
13^3 x 15^0
Din.
11^6 x 14^4
E.
Sto.
14^4 x 8^4
Gar.
22^0 x 21^8
COVERED PORCH

Width 59'-4"
Depth 45'-4"

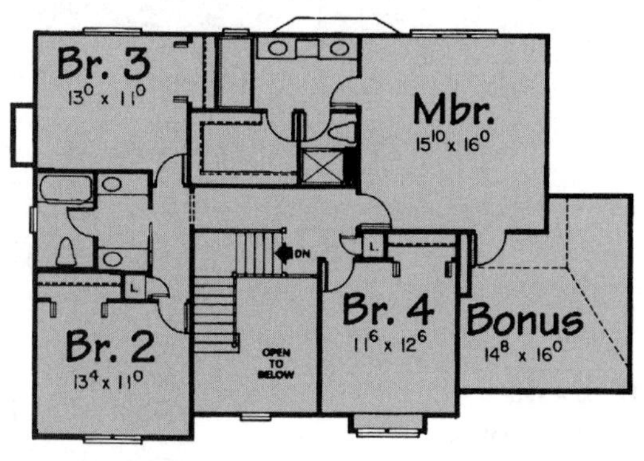
Br. 3
13^0 x 11^0
Mbr.
15^10 x 16^0
Br. 2
13^4 x 11^0
OPEN TO BELOW
Br. 4
11^6 x 12^6
Bonus
14^8 x 16^0

Design 9298

First Floor: 1,881 square feet
Second Floor: 814 square feet
Total: 2,695 square feet

Design by
Design Basics, Inc.

■ Oval windows and an appealing covered porch lend character to this country home. Inside, a volume entry views the formal living and dining rooms. Three large windows and a raised-hearth fireplace flanked by bookcases highlight a volume great room. An island kitchen with huge pantry and wrapping counters serves a captivating gazebo dinette. In the master suite, a cathedral ceiling, corner whirlpool and roomy dressing area deserve careful study. A gallery wall for displaying family mementos and prized heirlooms graces the upstairs corridor that leads to three family bedrooms.

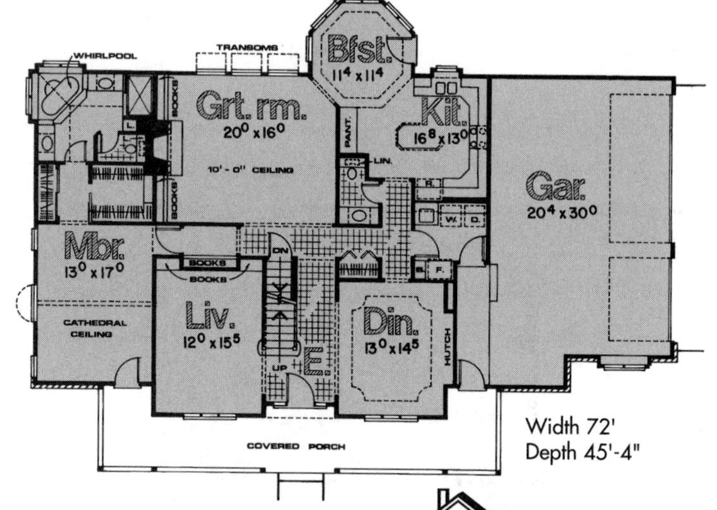
WHIRLPOOL
TRANSOMS
Bfst.
11^4 x 11^4
Grt. rm.
20^0 x 16^0
10'-0" CEILING
Kit.
16^8 x 13^0
Gar.
20^4 x 30^0
Mbr.
13^0 x 17^0
CATHEDRAL CEILING
Liv.
12^0 x 15^5
Din.
13^0 x 14^5
E.
COVERED PORCH

Width 72'
Depth 45'-4"

QUOTE ONE®
Cost to build? See page 342 to order complete cost estimate to build this house in your area!

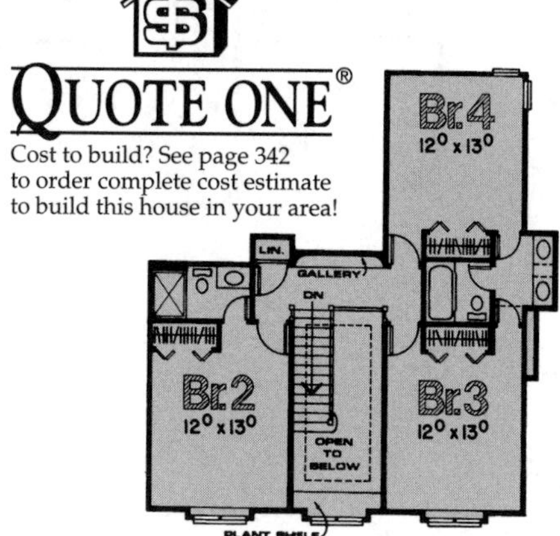
Br.4
12^0 x 13^0
GALLERY
Br.2
12^0 x 13^0
OPEN TO BELOW
Br.3
12^0 x 13^0
PLANT SHELF

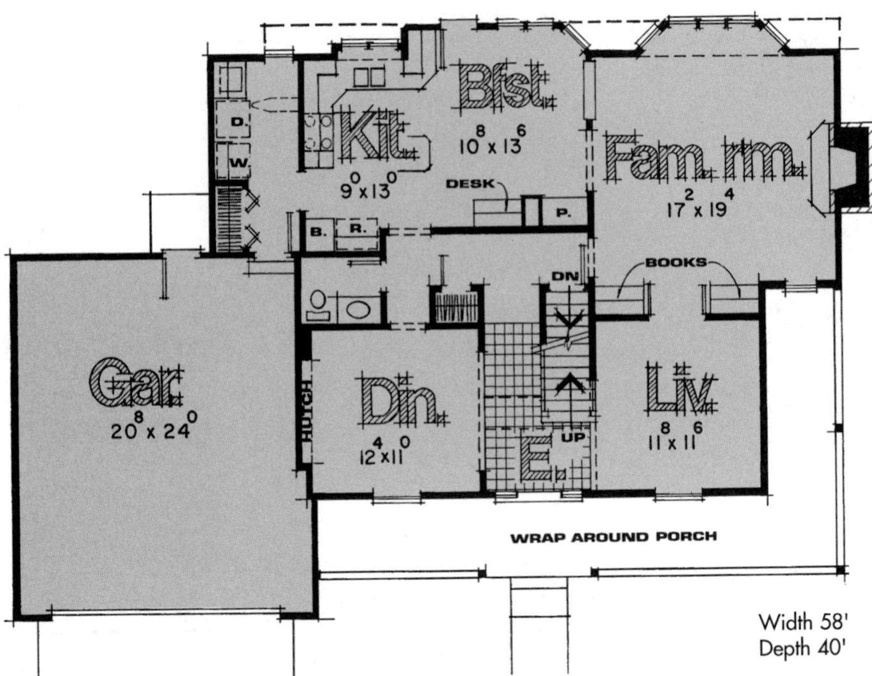
Bfst. 10⁸ x 13⁶
Kit. 9⁰ x 13⁰
Fam. rm. 17² x 19⁴
DESK
P.
B.
R.
D.
W.
BOOKS
DN
UP
Gar. 20⁸ x 24⁰
HUTCH
Din. 12⁴ x 11⁰
E.
Liv. 11⁸ x 11⁶
WRAP AROUND PORCH

Width 58'
Depth 40'

Design 9214

First Floor: 1,188 square feet
Second Floor: 1,172 square feet
Total: 2,360 square feet

■ Beginning with the interest of a wraparound porch, there's a feeling of country charm in this two-story plan. Formal dining and living rooms, visible from the entry, offer ample space for gracious entertaining. The large family room is truly a place of warmth and welcome with its gorgeous bay window, fireplace and French doors to the living room. The kitchen, with island counter, pantry and desk, makes cooking a delight. Upstairs, the secondary bedrooms share an efficient compartmented bath. The expansive master suite has its own luxury bath with double vanity, whirlpool, walk-in closet and dressing area.

Design by
Design Basics, Inc.

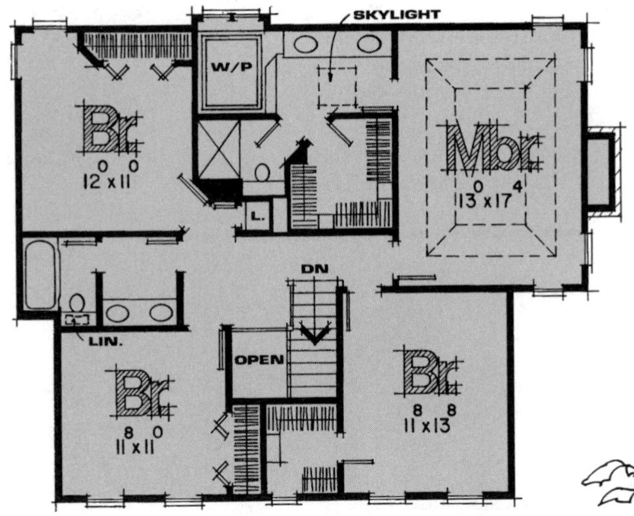

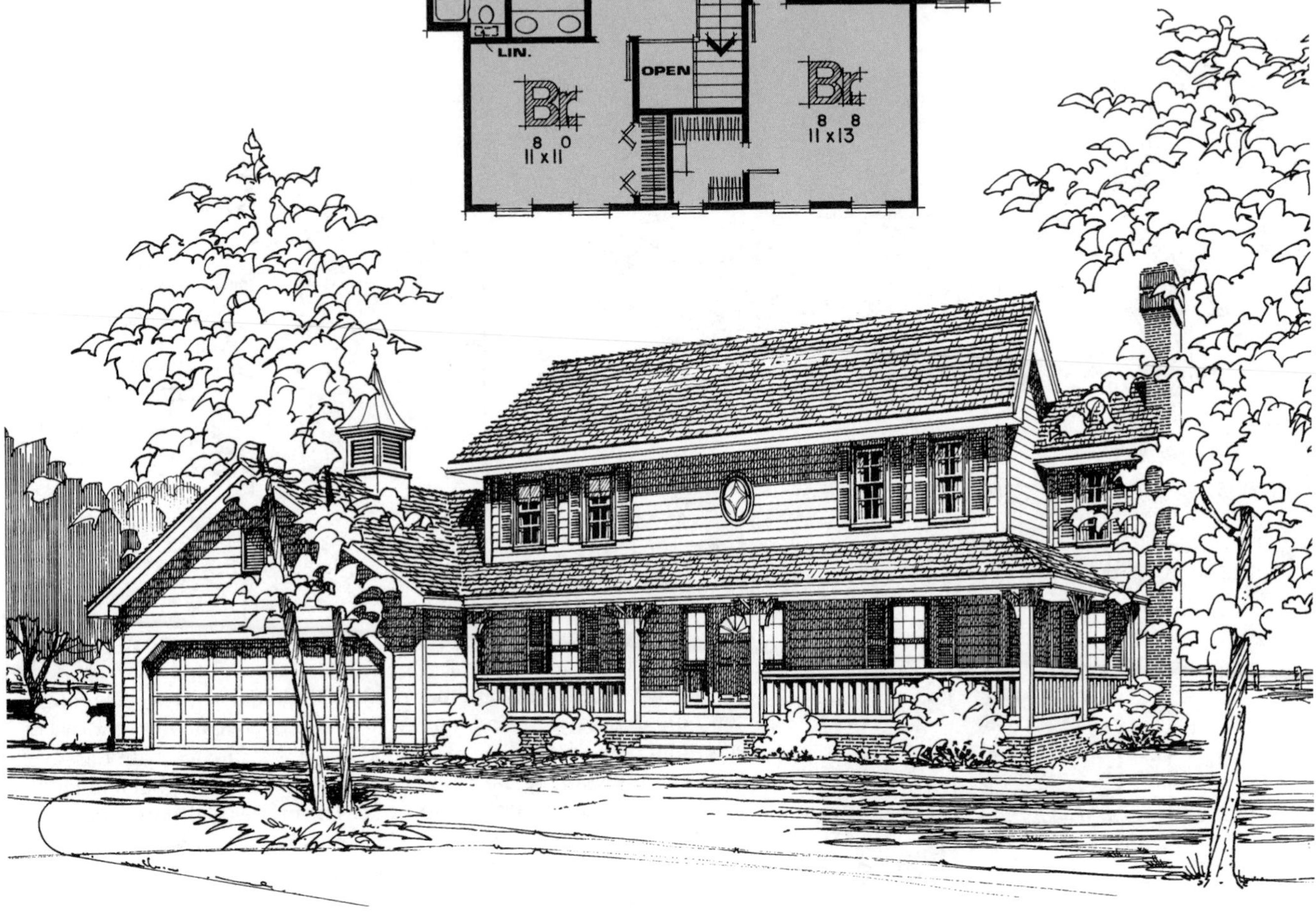

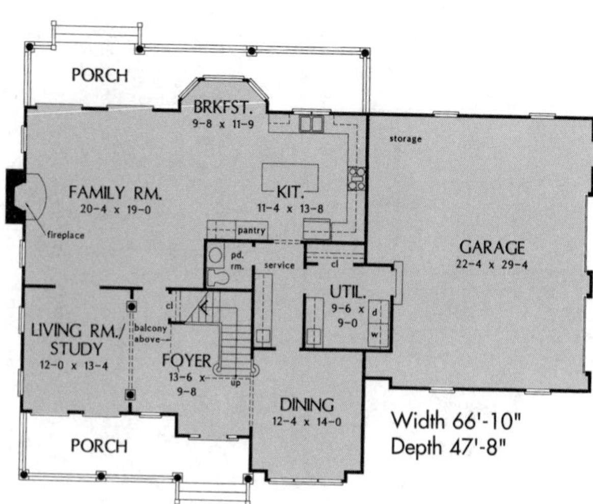

PORCH
BRKFST.
9-8 x 11-9
storage
FAMILY RM.
20-4 x 19-0
KIT.
11-4 x 13-8
fireplace
pantry
pd. rm.
service
cl
GARAGE
22-4 x 29-4
UTIL.
9-6 x 9-0
LIVING RM./ STUDY
12-0 x 13-4
balcony above
FOYER
13-6 x 9-8
up
DINING
12-4 x 14-0
PORCH
Width 66'-10"
Depth 47'-8"

Design 9798

First Floor: 1,483 square feet
Second Floor: 1,349 square feet
Total: 2,832 square feet

Design by
Donald A. Gardner, Architects, Inc.

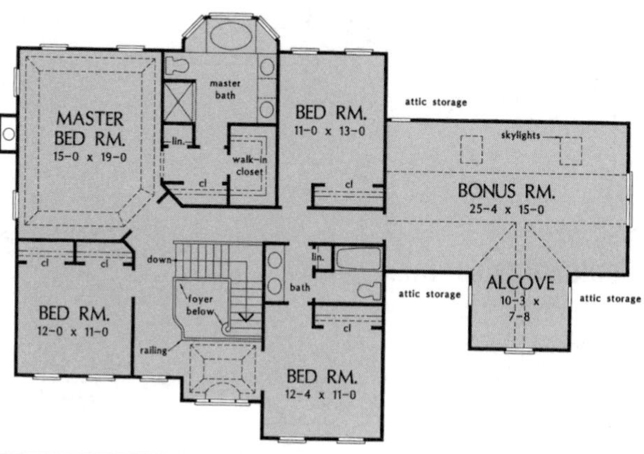

MASTER BED RM.
15-0 x 19-0
master bath
lin.
walk-in closet
cl
BED RM.
11-0 x 13-0
attic storage
skylights
BONUS RM.
25-4 x 15-0
cl
down
foyer below
bath
lin.
BED RM.
12-0 x 11-0
railing
attic storage
ALCOVE
10-3 x 7-8
attic storage
BED RM.
12-4 x 11-0

■ With two covered porches to encourage outdoor living, multi-pane windows and an open layout, this farmhouse has plenty to offer. Columns define the living room/study area. The family room is accented by a fireplace and has access to the rear porch. An adjacent sunny, bayed breakfast room is convenient to the oversized island kitchen. Four bedrooms upstairs include a deluxe master suite with a lush bath and walk-in closet. Three family bedrooms have plenty of storage space and share a full hall bath.

Design by
Larry E. Belk Designs

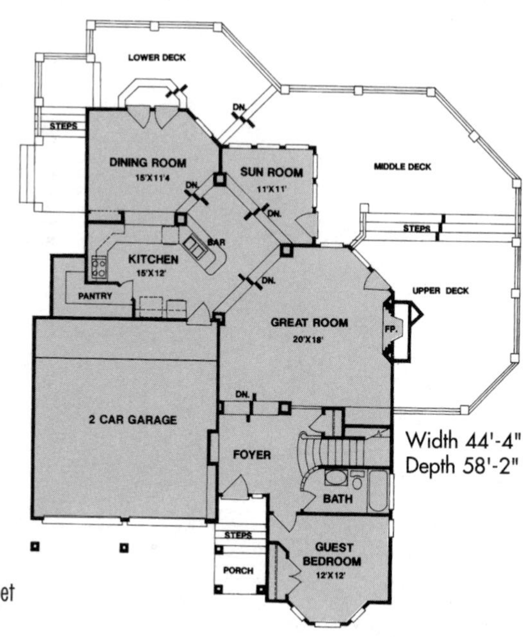

LOWER DECK
STEPS
DN.
DINING ROOM
15'X11'4
SUN ROOM
11'X11'
MIDDLE DECK
DN.
BAR
STEPS
KITCHEN
15'X12'
PANTRY
DN.
UPPER DECK
GREAT ROOM
20'X18'
FP.
2 CAR GARAGE
DN.
FOYER
BATH
STEPS
PORCH
GUEST BEDROOM
12'X12'
Width 44'-4"
Depth 58'-2"

Design 8001

First Floor: 1,309 square feet
Second Floor: 1,343 square feet
Total: 2,652 square feet

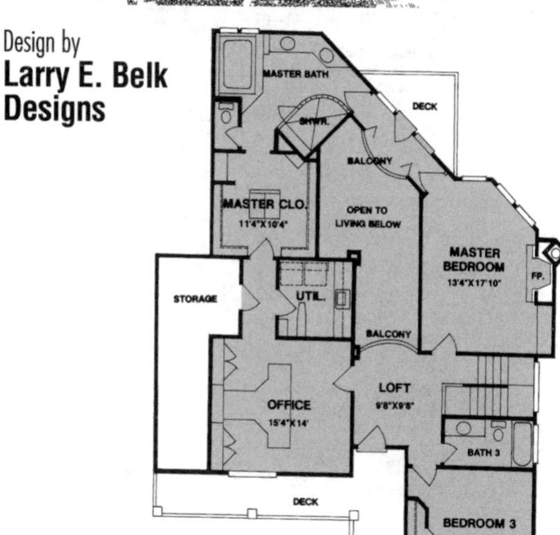

MASTER BATH
SHWR.
DECK
BALCONY
MASTER CLO.
11'4"X10'4"
OPEN TO LIVING BELOW
MASTER BEDROOM
13'4"X17'10"
FP.
STORAGE
UTIL.
BALCONY
OFFICE
15'4"X14'
LOFT
9'8"X9'8"
BATH 3
DECK
BEDROOM 3
11'8"X12'4"

■ Clean, contemporary lines, a unique floor plan and a metal roof with a cupola set this farmhouse apart. Remote-control transoms in the cupola open to create an airy and decidedly unique foyer. The great room, sunroom, dining room and kitchen flow from one to another for casual entertaining with flair. The rear of the home is fashioned with plenty of windows overlooking the multi-level deck. A front bedroom and bath would make a comfortable guest suite. The master bedroom and bath upstairs are bridged by a pipe rail balcony that also gives access to a rear deck. An additional bedroom, home office and bath complete this very special plan.

Design 9909

First Floor: 1,700 square feet
Second Floor: 1,585 square feet
Total: 3,285 square feet
Bonus Room: 176 square feet

Design by
Design Traditions

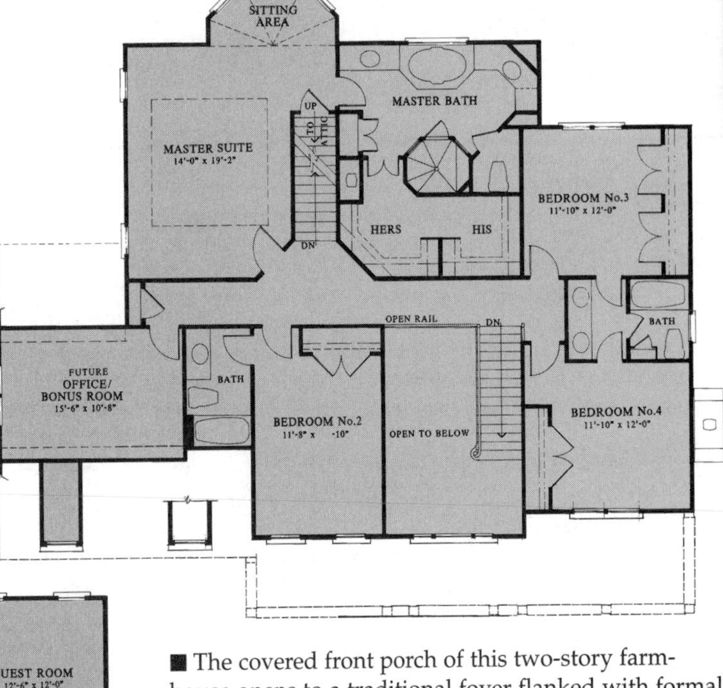
SITTING AREA
MASTER BATH
MASTER SUITE 14'-0" x 19'-2"
UP
TO ATTIC
DN
HERS
HIS
BEDROOM No.3 11'-10" x 12'-0"
OPEN RAIL
DN
BATH
FUTURE OFFICE/ BONUS ROOM 15'-6" x 10'-8"
BATH
BEDROOM No.2 11'-8" x -10"
OPEN TO BELOW
BEDROOM No.4 11'-10" x 12'-0"

Width 60'
Depth 47'-6"

DECK
BREAKFAST 10'-10" x 7'-0"
KITCHEN 14'-0" x 13'-4"
UP
GREAT ROOM 17'-2" x 19'-2"
GUEST ROOM 12'-6" x 12'-0"
LAUNDRY 10'-2" x 5'-8"
DN
STORAGE
TWO-CAR GARAGE 21'-4" x 21'-4"
DINING ROOM 11'-0" x
FOYER 11'-10" x 17'-0"
LIVING ROOM 14'-0" x 13'-6"
UP
STOOP

■ The covered front porch of this two-story farmhouse opens to a traditional foyer flanked with formal areas. A cozy living room with a fireplace sits on the right and an elongated dining room—perfect for an elegant table—is on the left. For casual family living, a great room—also with a fireplace—and a kitchen with a breakfast area will surely serve the family's needs. A lovely deck just off the breakfast room invites outdoor dining. A comfortable guest room has a nearby full bath. Upstairs, the master suite has a bayed sitting area and a private bath with an oversized closet. Two family bedrooms share a private, compartmented bath while a third has a private bath. A bonus room would make a great office or additional bedroom. This home is designed with a basement foundation.

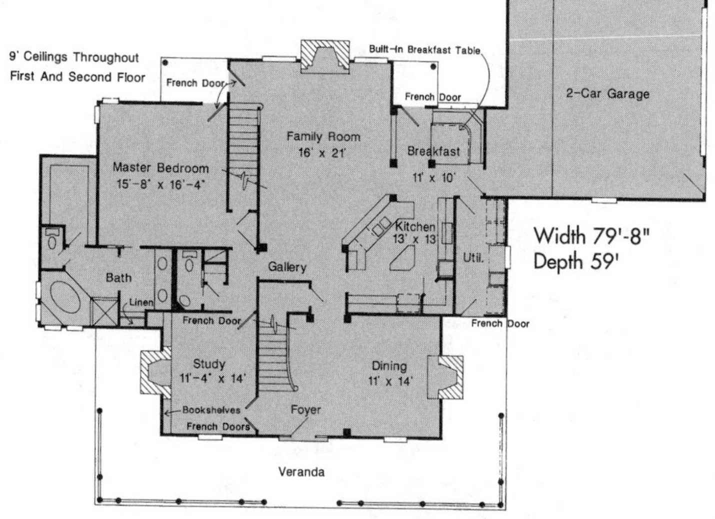
9' Ceilings Throughout
First And Second Floor
French Door
Built-In Breakfast Table
French Door
2-Car Garage
Family Room
16' x 21'
Breakfast
11' x 10'
Master Bedroom
15'-8" x 16'-4"
Kitchen
13' x 13'
Util.
Gallery
Bath
Linen
French Door
French Door
Study
11'-4" x 14'
Dining
11' x 14'
Bookshelves
French Doors
Foyer
Veranda
Width 79'-8"
Depth 59'

Design 9067

First Floor: 1,999 square feet
Second Floor: 933 square feet
Total: 2,932 square feet

Design by
Larry W. Garnett & Associates, Inc.

■ Opening directly to the formal dining room, the two-story foyer offers extra space for large dinner parties. Double French doors lead to the study with raised paneling and a cozy fireplace. A spacious gourmet kitchen features plenty of counter space, a work island and a pass-through snack bar that opens onto the family room. The private master suite features a corner garden tub, glass-enclosed shower and a walk-in closet. A rear staircase provides convenient access to the second floor from the family room. Three family bedrooms include two that share a bath and one with a private bath.

QUOTE ONE®

Cost to build? See page 342 to order complete cost estimate to build this house in your area!

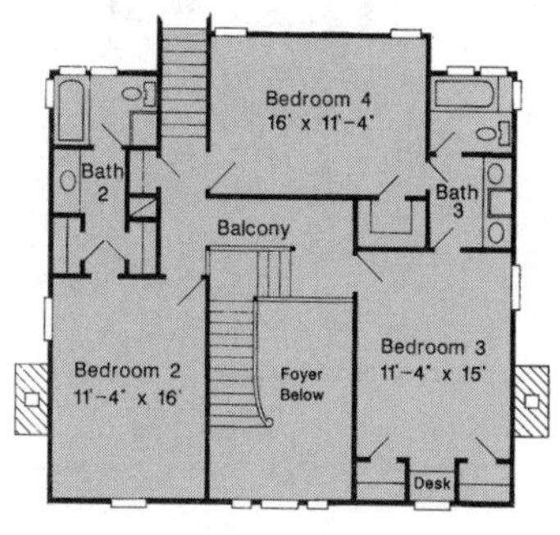
Bedroom 4
16' x 11'-4"
Bath 2
Bath 3
Balcony
Bedroom 2
11'-4" x 16'
Foyer Below
Bedroom 3
11'-4" x 15'
Desk

Design 9288

First Floor: 1,421 square feet
Second Floor: 578 square feet
Total: 1,999 square feet

Design by
Design Basics, Inc.

■ Victorian details and a covered veranda lend a peaceful flavor to the elevation of this popular home. A volume entry hall views the formal dining room and luxurious great room. Imagine the comfort of relaxing in the great room which features a 12'-10" ceiling and abundant windows. The kitchen and breakfast area includes a through-fireplace, snack bar, walk-in pantry and wrapping counters. The secluded master suite features a vaulted ceiling, luxurious dressing/bath area and corner whirlpool tub. Upstairs, the family sleeping quarters feature special amenities unique to each.

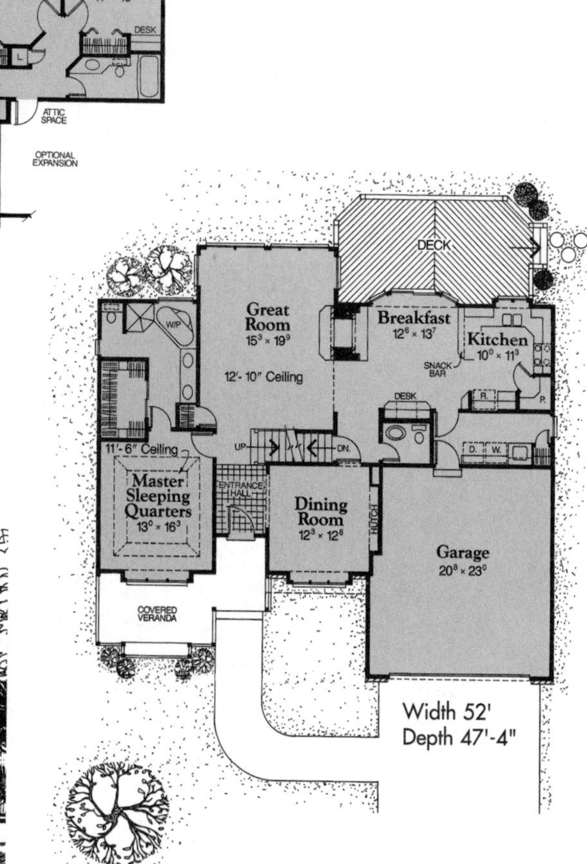
Sleeping Quarters
11⁰ × 11⁴
Sleeping Quarters
11⁰ × 10⁰
DESK
OPEN TO BELOW
DN.
ATTIC SPACE
Sleeping Quarters
11³ × 11³
10'-0" Ceiling
OPTIONAL EXPANSION
DECK
Great Room
15³ × 19⁹
12'-10" Ceiling
Breakfast
12⁶ × 13⁷
Kitchen
10⁰ × 11³
SNACK BAR
DESK
W/P
UP
DN.
11'-6" Ceiling
Master Sleeping Quarters
13⁰ × 16³
ENTRANCE HALL
Dining Room
12³ × 12⁶
HUTCH
Garage
20⁹ × 23⁰
COVERED VERANDA
Width 52'
Depth 47'-4"

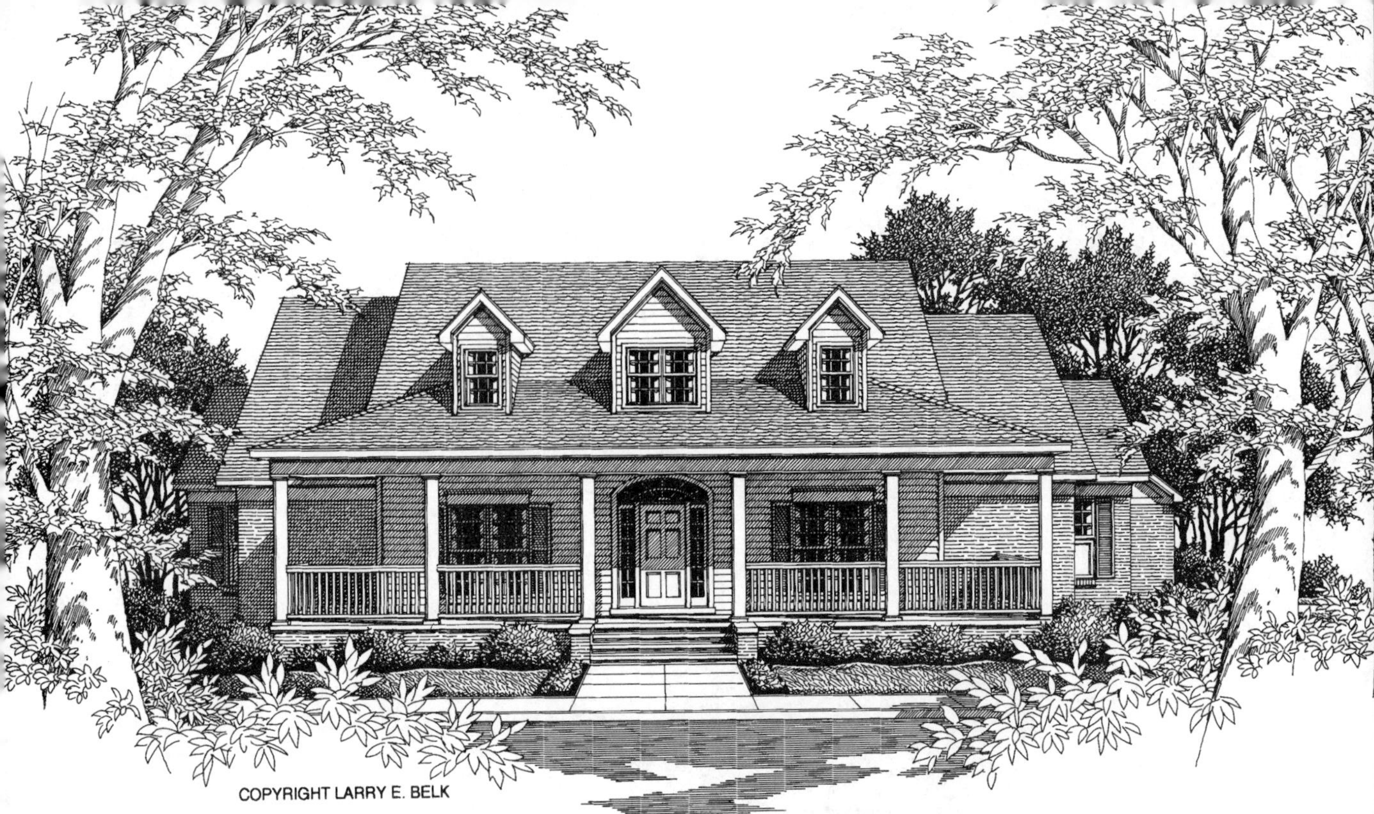

Design by
Larry E. Belk Designs

Design 8157

First Floor: 2,465 square feet
Second Floor: 788 square feet
Total: 3,253 square feet

■ Designed to meet the needs of today's lifestyles, this historical elevation is a familiar one. Inside, the large great room is designed with entertaining in mind. The nearby kitchen boasts all the latest features, including a snack bar and breakfast room. The bedroom wing features a luxurious master suite with a lush bath and twin walk-in closets. Two additional bedrooms are comfortably sized and share a private bath. The upper level can be finished later and is designed to add a bedroom, a bath and a large game room. Please specify crawlspace or slab foundation when ordering.

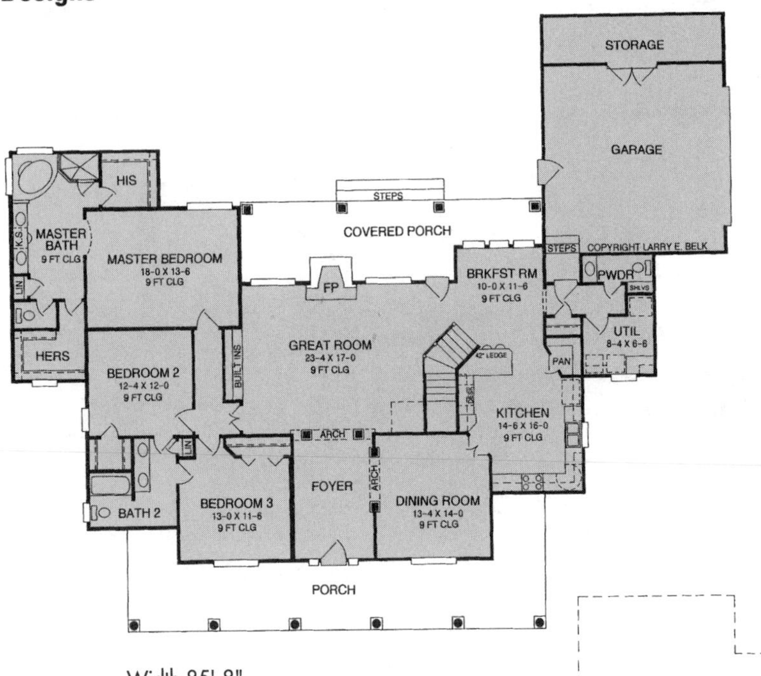
STORAGE
GARAGE
HIS
MASTER BATH
9 FT CLG
MASTER BEDROOM
18-0 X 13-6
9 FT CLG
STEPS
COVERED PORCH
COPYRIGHT LARRY E. BELK
FP
BRKFST RM
10-0 X 11-6
9 FT CLG
PWDR
UTIL
8-4 X 6-6
HERS
BEDROOM 2
12-4 X 12-0
9 FT CLG
GREAT ROOM
23-4 X 17-0
9 FT CLG
BUILT INS
PAN
KITCHEN
14-6 X 16-0
9 FT CLG
ARCH
BEDROOM 3
13-0 X 11-6
9 FT CLG
FOYER
DINING ROOM
13-4 X 14-0
9 FT CLG
BATH 2
PORCH

Width 85'-8"
Depth 70'-7"

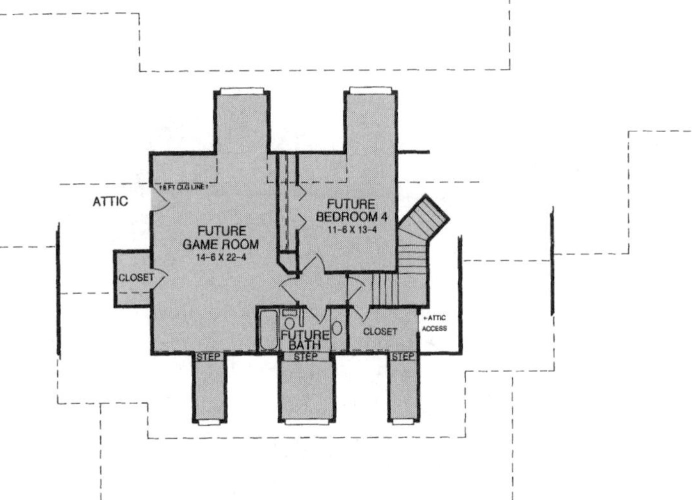
ATTIC
FUTURE GAME ROOM
14-6 X 22-4
FUTURE BEDROOM 4
11-6 X 13-4
CLOSET
FUTURE BATH
CLOSET
STEP
STEP
STEP

DECK
Breakfast
9⁸ × 12⁰
Kitchen
10⁰ × 10⁰
DESK
Gathering Room
17³ × 15⁰
8'-8" Ceiling
STORAGE
Dining Room
12⁰ × 12⁰
DN.
ENTRANCE HALL
UP
Garage
19⁴ × 22⁰
Parlor
12⁰ × 16⁴
12'-0" Ceiling
COVERED VERANDA
W.
D.
SKYLIGHT
SKYLIGHT
W/P
Sleeping Quarters
11⁰ × 10⁰
9'-0" Ceiling
Master Sleeping Quarters
12⁰ × 17⁰
DN.
L
Sleeping Quarters
10⁰ × 11⁰
Sleeping Quarters
11⁰ × 12⁸
11'-6" Ceiling
QUOTE ONE®

QUOTE ONE®

Cost to build? See page 342 to order complete cost estimate to build this house in your area!

Width 46'
Depth 41'-5"

Design 9252

First Floor: 1,113 square feet
Second Floor: 965 square feet
Total: 2,078 square feet

Design by
Design Basics, Inc.

■ Elegant detail, a charming veranda and a tall brick chimney make a pleasing facade on this Victorian home. From the large, bayed parlor with a sloped ceiling to the sunken gathering room with a fireplace, there's plenty to appreciate about the floor plan. The formal dining room opens to the parlor for convenient entertaining. An L-shaped kitchen with attached breakfast room is nearby. Upstairs quarters include a master suite with a private dressing area and whirlpool, and three family bedrooms.

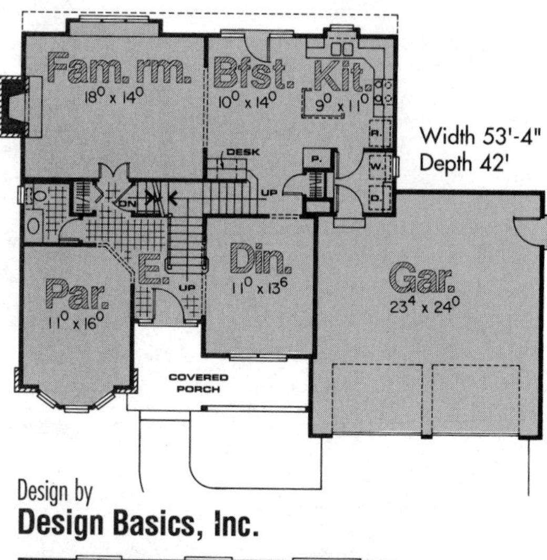
Fam. rm.
18⁰ x 14⁰
Bfst.
10⁰ x 14⁰
Kit.
9⁰ x 11⁰
DESK
P.
W.
D.
DN
UP
E.
UP
Din.
11⁰ x 13⁶
Par.
11⁰ x 16⁰
Gar.
23⁴ x 24⁰
COVERED PORCH

Width 53'-4"
Depth 42'

Design by
Design Basics, Inc.

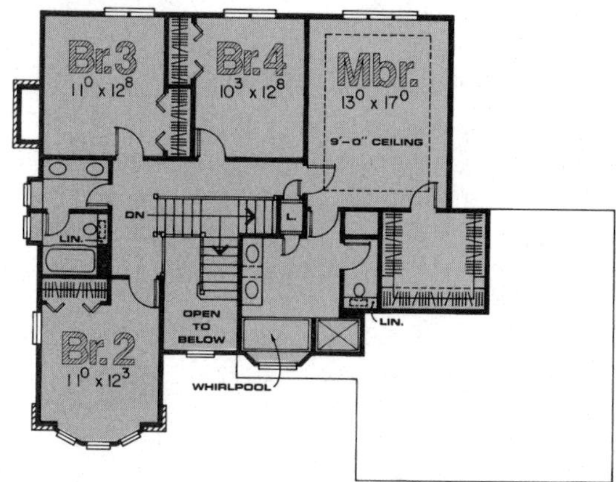
Br.3
11⁰ x 12⁸
Br.4
10³ x 12⁸
Mbr.
13⁰ x 17⁰
9'-0" CEILING
DN
L
LIN.
OPEN TO BELOW
LIN.
Br.2
11⁰ x 12³
WHIRLPOOL

Design 7312

First Floor: 1,134 square feet
Second Floor: 1,149 square feet
Total: 2,283 square feet

■ Victorian embellishments give a time-honored elegance to this classic family plan. Left of the entry, the front parlor opens to reveal a dramatic bay window. The formal dining room is large enough for a grand party and has easy access to the kitchen. Casual living is sure to center around the corner kitchen with a prep island and the joining breakfast room as they flow into the spacious family room. A split stair leads to the second level, where an oversized master suite is accompanied by three family bedrooms and a full hall bath.

Design 9251

First Floor: 1,653 square feet
Second Floor: 700 square feet
Total: 2,353 square feet

■ Beautiful arches and elaborate detail give the elevation of this four-bedroom, 1½-story home an unmistakable elegance. Inside the floor plan is equally appealing. Note the formal dining room with bay window, visible from the entrance hall. The large great room has a fireplace and a wall of windows out the back. A hearth room, with bookcase, adjoins the kitchen area with a walk-in pantry. The private, first-floor master suite features a pampering bath that contains a large whirlpool and double lavatories. Upstairs quarters share a full bath with compartmented sinks.

Design by
Design Basics, Inc.

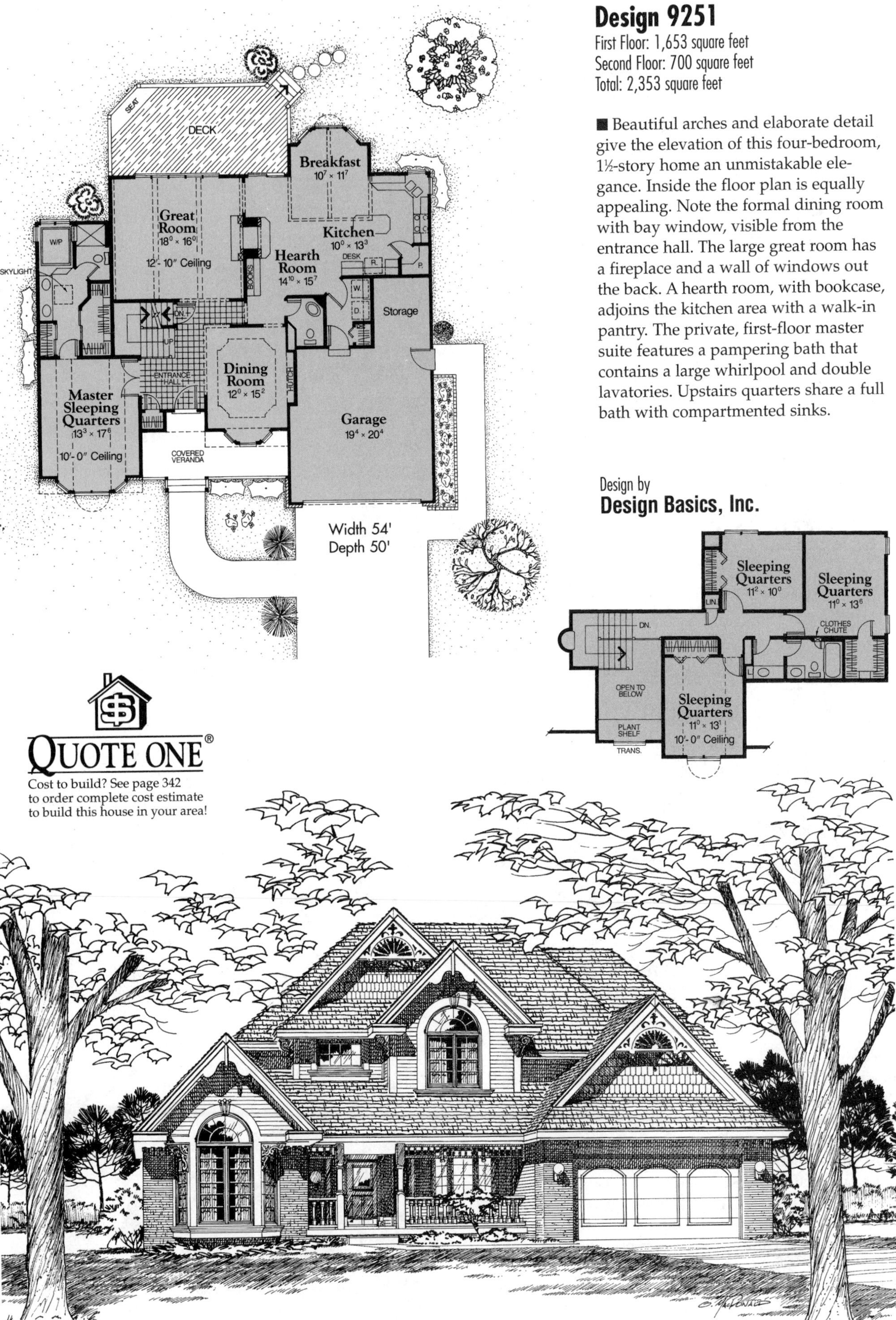

DECK
SEAT
Breakfast
10⁷ × 11⁷
Great Room
18⁰ × 16⁰
12'-10" Ceiling
Kitchen
10⁰ × 13³
Hearth Room
14¹⁰ × 15⁷
BOOKS
DESK
W/P
SKYLIGHT
Storage
ENTRANCE HALL
Dining Room
12⁰ × 15²
Master Sleeping Quarters
13³ × 17⁶
10'-0" Ceiling
Garage
19⁴ × 20⁴
COVERED VERANDA
Width 54'
Depth 50'
Sleeping Quarters
11² × 10⁰
Sleeping Quarters
11⁰ × 13⁶
CLOTHES CHUTE
DN.
LIN.
OPEN TO BELOW
PLANT SHELF
TRANS.
Sleeping Quarters
11⁰ × 13¹
10'-0" Ceiling

QUOTE ONE®
Cost to build? See page 342 to order complete cost estimate to build this house in your area!

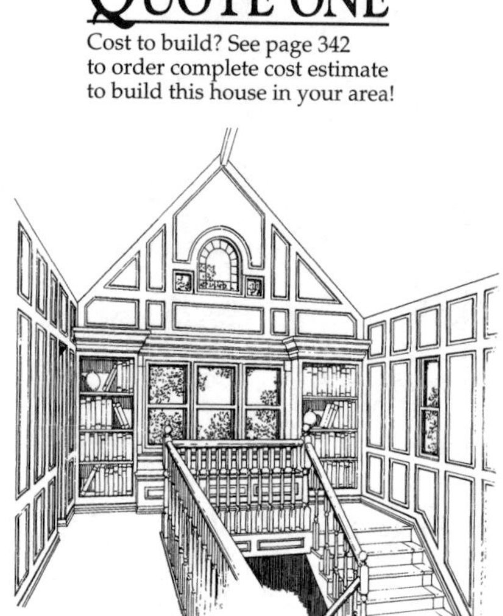

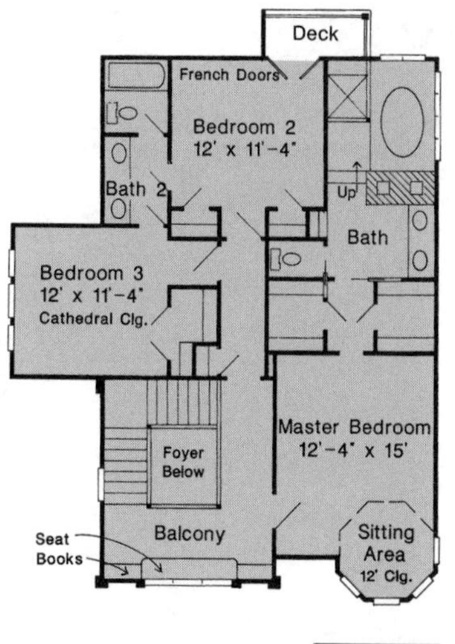

Deck
French Doors
Bedroom 2
12' x 11'-4"
Bath 2
Up
Bath
Bedroom 3
12' x 11'-4"
Cathedral Clg.
Foyer
Below
Master Bedroom
12'-4" x 15'
Seat
Books
Balcony
Sitting
Area
12' Clg.
Incline Ladder
Bath
Below
Exercise Loft
15 x 13

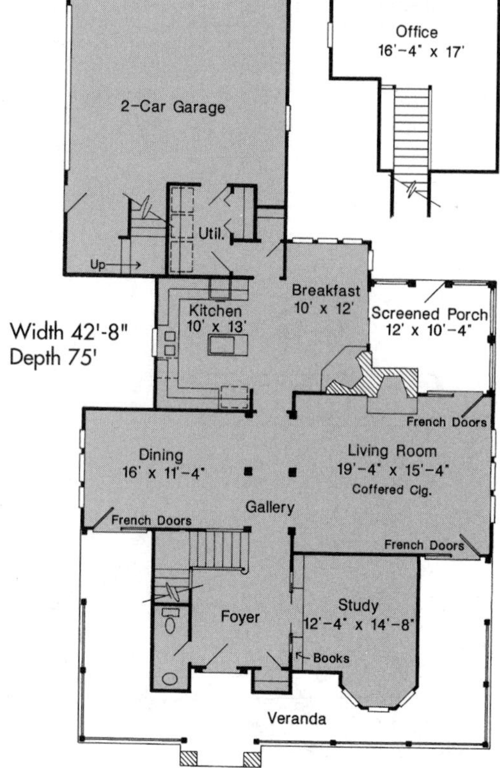

Width 42'-8"
Depth 75'
2-Car Garage
Office
16'-4" x 17'
Up
Util.
Breakfast
10' x 12'
Kitchen
10' x 13'
Screened Porch
12' x 10'-4"
French Doors
Dining
16' x 11'-4"
Living Room
19'-4" x 15'-4"
Coffered Clg.
Gallery
French Doors
French Doors
Foyer
Study
12'-4" x 14'-8"
Books
Veranda

Design 9012

First Floor: 1,357 square feet
Second Floor: 1,079 square feet
Total: 2,436 square feet

Design by
Larry W. Garnett & Associates, Inc.

■ A wraparound veranda with delicate spindlework and a raised turret with leaded-glass windows recall the Queen Anne-style Victorians of the late 1880s. Double doors open from the two-story foyer to a study with built-in bookcases and a bay window. A fireplace adds warmth to the breakfast area and the island kitchen. Above the two-car garage is an optional area that is perfect for a home office or guest quarters. Upstairs, the balcony overlooks the foyer below. An octagon-shaped ceiling and leaded-glass windows define a cozy sitting area in the master suite. A raised alcove in the master bath contains a garden tub and glass-enclosed shower. An optional exercise loft and plant shelves complete this elegant master bath. Two additional bedrooms, one with a private deck, and the other with a cathedral ceiling share a dressing area and bath.

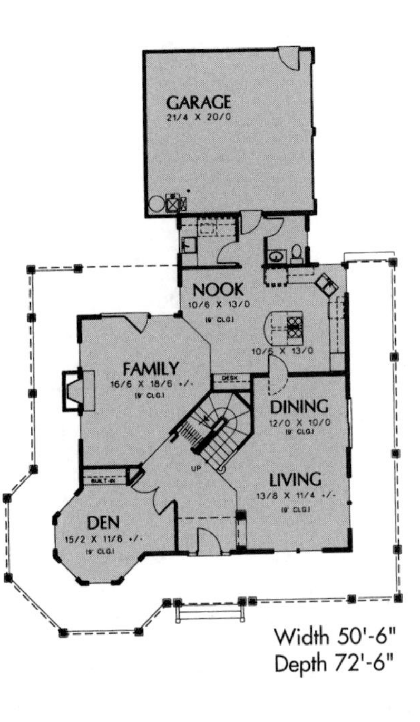
GARAGE
21/4 X 20/0
NOOK
10/6 X 13/0
10/6 X 13/0
FAMILY
16/6 X 18/6 +/-
DINING
12/0 X 10/0
LIVING
13/8 X 11/4 +/-
DEN
15/2 X 11/6 +/-

Width 50'-6"
Depth 72'-6"

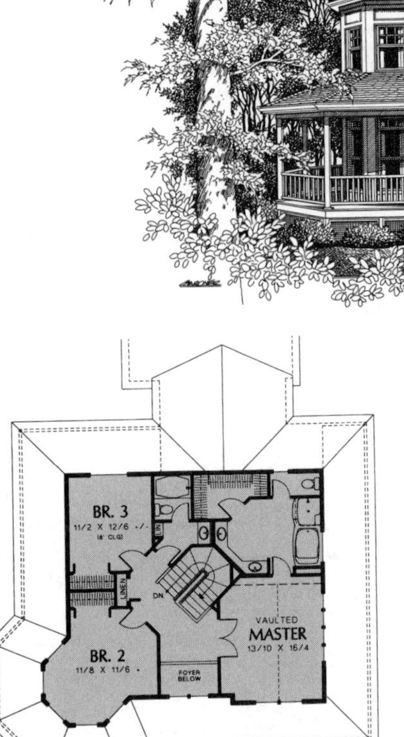
BR. 3
11/2 X 12/6 +/-
LINEN
DN
VAULTED
MASTER
13/10 X 16/4
BR. 2
11/8 X 11/6
FOYER BELOW

Design by
Alan Mascord Design Associates, Inc.

Design 9585

First Floor: 1,337 square feet
Second Floor: 1,025 square feet
Total: 2,362 square feet

■ An octagonal tower, a wraparound porch and rich amenities combine to give this house tons of appeal. The tower is occupied by a sunny den on the first floor and a delightful bedroom on the second floor. A large efficient kitchen easily serves both the formal dining room and the cheerful nook. Upstairs, two bedrooms share a full hall bath while the master bedroom revels in its luxurious private bath.

Design 9063

First Floor: 1,236 square feet
Second Floor: 835 square feet
Total: 2,071 square feet

Design by
Larry W. Garnett & Associates, Inc.

■ The living room of this spectacular Queen Anne style home features a fireplace and a bay-windowed alcove. The centrally located kitchen overlooks a dining area that has full-length windows and a French door. The master bedroom features a large walk-in closet and French doors opening to the rear veranda. Upstairs, double doors open into a game room. Bedroom 2 offers a walk-in closet and a ten-foot sloped ceiling. Bedroom 3 also provides a walk-in closet and a raised octagon-shaped ceiling. Plans are included for a detached two-car garage and an optional screened porch.

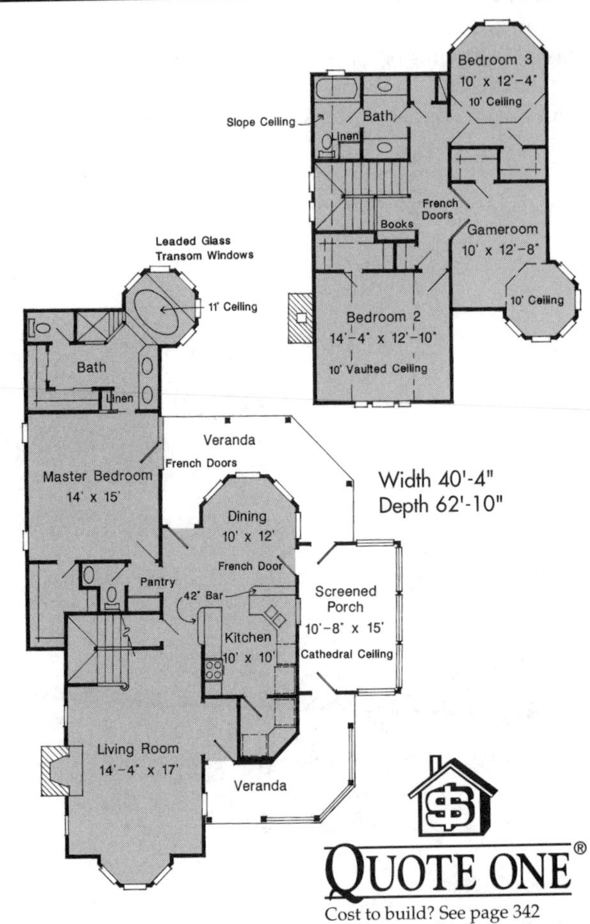
Bedroom 3
10' x 12'-4"
10' Ceiling
Slope Ceiling
Bath
Linen
French Doors
Books
Gameroom
10' x 12'-8"
10' Ceiling
Bedroom 2
14'-4" x 12'-10"
10' Vaulted Ceiling
Leaded Glass
Transom Windows
11' Ceiling
Bath
Linen
Veranda
French Doors
Master Bedroom
14' x 15'
Width 40'-4"
Depth 62'-10"
Dining
10' x 12'
French Door
Pantry
42" Bar
Kitchen
10' x 10'
Screened
Porch
10'-8" x 15'
Cathedral Ceiling
Living Room
14'-4" x 17'
Veranda

Cost to build? See page 342 to order complete cost estimate to build this house in your area!

Design 9017

First Floor: 1,617 square feet
Second Floor: 1,818 square feet
Total: 3,435 square feet
Optional Loft: 136 square feet

■ With its cantilevered gable sloping with a gentle curve to the first floor and a raised turret, this design is representative of late 19th-Century style. The raised foyer overlooks the living and dining rooms, both with expansive windows and coffered ceilings. Two steps up from the foyer is a mezzanine-level study with curved walls. An open serving bar provides the kitchen with a full view of the family area, with its built-in window seats and massive fireplace. The second floor master suite offers an alcove with high windows that is perfect for a king-size bed and a raised sitting area with an 11' ceiling. A curved, glass-block shower and a whirlpool tub beneath expansive casement windows are part of the exquisite bath. Three additional bedrooms boast private baths and walk-ins, along with special features.

Design by
Larry W. Garnett & Associates, Inc.

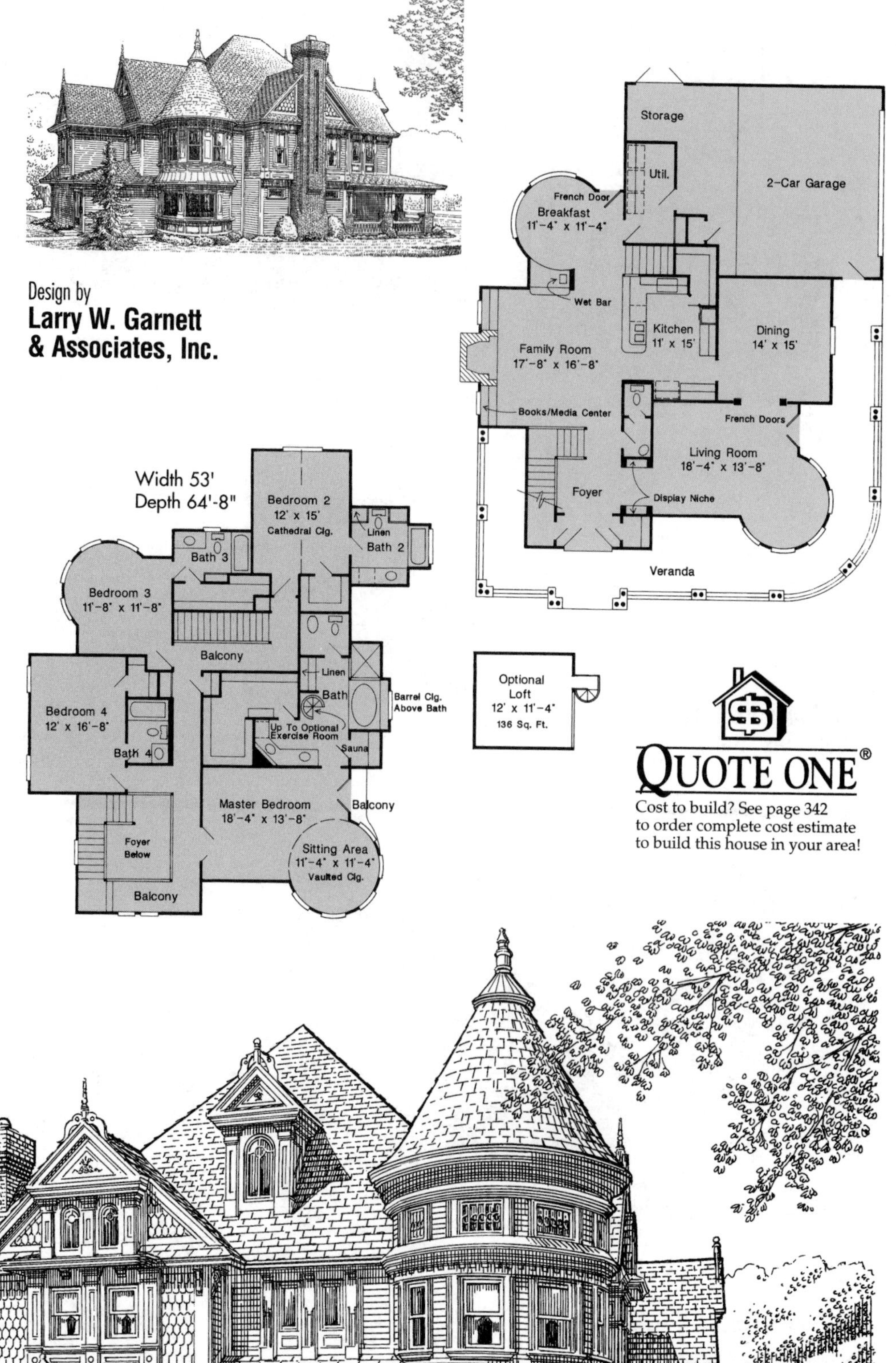
Storage
Util.
2-Car Garage
French Door
Breakfast
11'-4" x 11'-4"
Wet Bar
Kitchen
11' x 15'
Dining
14' x 15'
Family Room
17'-8" x 16'-8"
Books/Media Center
French Doors
Living Room
18'-4" x 13'-8"
Foyer
Display Niche
Veranda
Width 53'
Depth 64'-8"
Bedroom 2
12' x 15'
Cathedral Clg.
Linen
Bath 2
Bath 3
Bedroom 3
11'-8" x 11'-8"
Balcony
Linen
Bath
Barrel Clg.
Above Bath
Bedroom 4
12' x 16'-8"
Bath 4
Up To Optional
Exercise Room
Sauna
Master Bedroom
18'-4" x 13'-8"
Balcony
Foyer
Below
Sitting Area
11'-4" x 11'-4"
Vaulted Clg.
Balcony
Optional
Loft
12' x 11'-4"
136 Sq. Ft.

QUOTE ONE®

Cost to build? See page 342 to order complete cost estimate to build this house in your area!

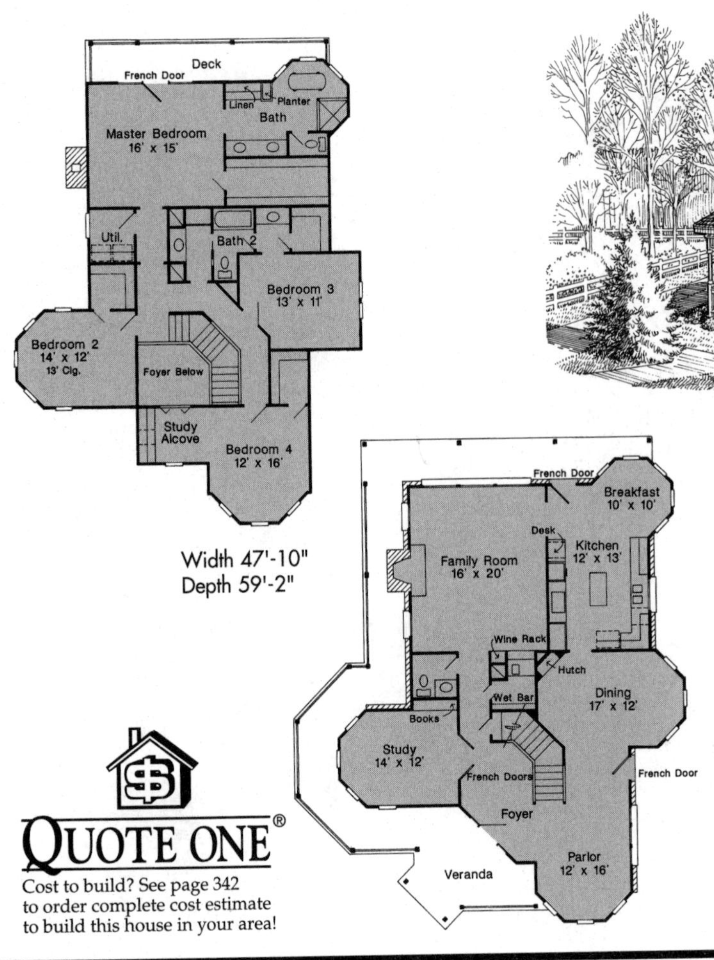
Deck
French Door
Planter
Linen
Bath
Master Bedroom
16' x 15'
Util.
Bath 2
Bedroom 3
13' x 11'
Bedroom 2
14' x 12'
13' Clg.
Foyer Below
Study
Alcove
Bedroom 4
12' x 16'
French Door
Breakfast
10' x 10'
Desk
Kitchen
12' x 13'
Family Room
16' x 20'
Wine Rack
Hutch
Wet Bar
Dining
17' x 12'
Books
Study
14' x 12'
French Doors
French Door
Foyer
Parlor
12' x 16'
Veranda

Width 47'-10"
Depth 59'-2"

QUOTE ONE®

Cost to build? See page 342 to order complete cost estimate to build this house in your area!

Design 9014

First Floor: 1,565 square feet
Second Floor: 1,598 square feet
Total: 3,163 square feet

Design by
Larry W. Garnett & Associates, Inc.

■ This Queen Anne Victorian has an angled entry that opens to a grand foyer and a formal parlor with expansive windows and a French door leading to the side yard. French doors open from the foyer to the large study with bookcases and full-length windows. The spacious family room has a fireplace and a wet bar. The kitchen is fashioned with a work island, abundant cabinet space and a sunny breakfast room. Upstairs, the master bedroom has a private deck and a lush bath with a claw-foot tub. Three additional bedrooms each have walk-in closets and distinctly special features. Plans for a two-car detached garage are included.

Design 9056

First Floor: 1,354 square feet
Second Floor: 1,418 square feet
Total: 2,772 square feet

Design by
Larry W. Garnett & Associates, Inc.

■ Inside this charming turn-of-the-century design, classical columns separate the foyer and dining room. A French door opens from the living room to a lattice-covered side arbor. Double doors in both the living and family rooms provide access to a bay-windowed study with built-in bookcases and a desk. Upstairs, the master suite features an elegant bath with a garden tub inset in a bay window, and a walk-in closet. Bedrooms 3 and 4 share a bath, while Bedroom 2 has a private bath and a bay-windowed alcove.

QUOTE ONE®

Cost to build? See page 342 to order complete cost estimate to build this house in your area!

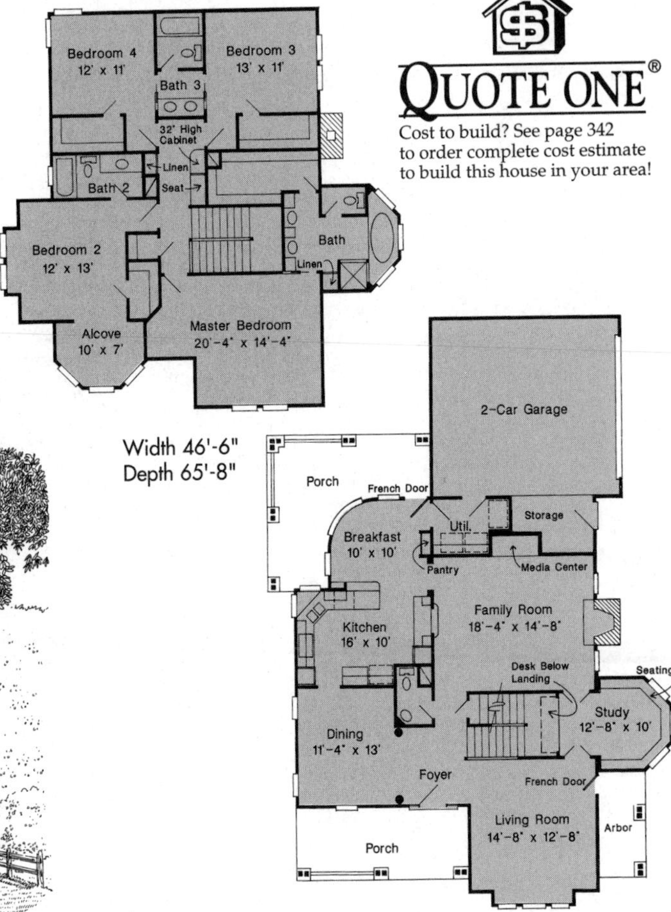
Bedroom 4
12' x 11'
Bedroom 3
13' x 11'
Bath 3
32" High Cabinet
Linen
Seat
Bath 2
Bedroom 2
12' x 13'
Bath
Linen
Alcove
10' x 7'
Master Bedroom
20'-4" x 14'-4"
2-Car Garage
Porch
French Door
Storage
Util.
Breakfast
10' x 10'
Pantry
Media Center
Family Room
18'-4" x 14'-8"
Kitchen
16' x 10'
Desk Below Landing
Seating
Study
12'-8" x 10'
Dining
11'-4" x 13'
Foyer
French Door
Living Room
14'-8" x 12'-8"
Arbor
Porch

Width 46'-6"
Depth 65'-8"

Design 9638

Square Footage: 1,865

■ This distinctive Victorian exterior conceals an open, contemporary floor plan. The entrance foyer with round columns offers visual excitement. The octagonal great room has a high tray ceiling and a fireplace. A generous kitchen with an angular island counter is centrally located, providing efficient service to the dining room, breakfast room and deck. The luxurious master bedroom suite has a large walk-in closet and a compartmented bath. Two additional bedrooms—one that would make a lovely study by including an entrance off the foyer—and a full hall bath round out this favorite plan.

Design by
Donald A. Gardner, Architects, Inc.

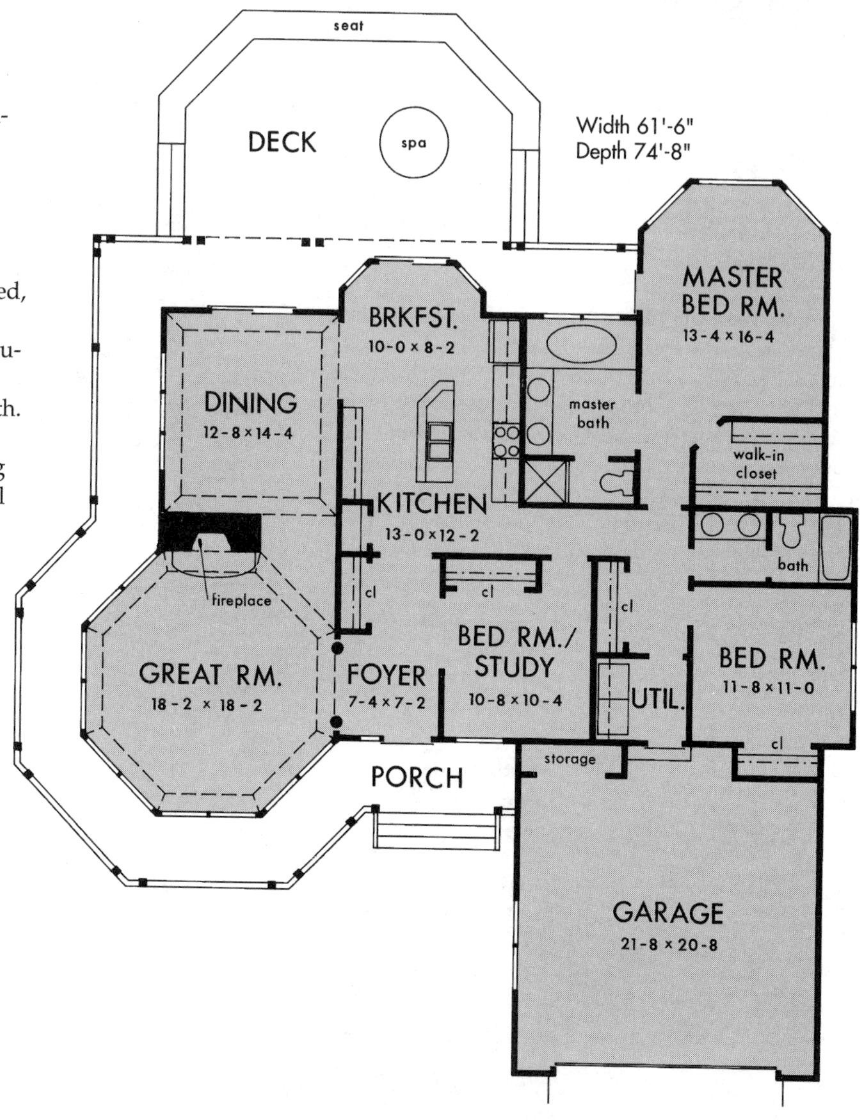

seat
DECK
spa
Width 61'-6"
Depth 74'-8"
MASTER BED RM.
13-4 × 16-4
BRKFST.
10-0 × 8-2
DINING
12-8 × 14-4
master bath
walk-in closet
KITCHEN
13-0 × 12-2
bath
cl
cl
cl
fireplace
GREAT RM.
18-2 × 18-2
FOYER
7-4 × 7-2
BED RM./ STUDY
10-8 × 10-4
UTIL.
BED RM.
11-8 × 11-0
cl
storage
PORCH
GARAGE
21-8 × 20-8

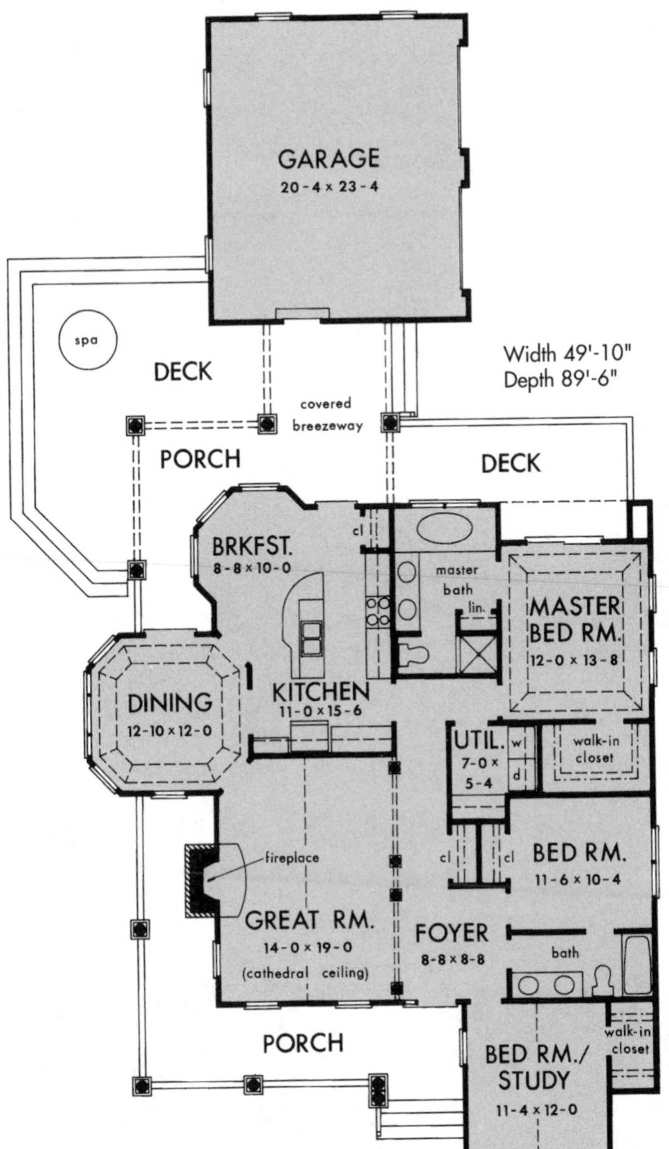
GARAGE
20-4 x 23-4
spa
DECK
covered
breezeway
Width 49'-10"
Depth 89'-6"
PORCH
DECK
BRKFST.
8-8 x 10-0
cl
master
bath
lin.
MASTER
BED RM.
12-0 x 13-8
DINING
12-10 x 12-0
KITCHEN
11-0 x 15-6
UTIL.
7-0 x
5-4
w
d
walk-in
closet
fireplace
cl
cl
BED RM.
11-6 x 10-4
GREAT RM.
14-0 x 19-0
(cathedral ceiling)
FOYER
8-8 x 8-8
bath
PORCH
BED RM./
STUDY
11-4 x 12-0
walk-in
closet

Design 9693

Square Footage: 1,677

■ This cozy, three-bedroom plan with arched windows and a wraparound porch displays a sense of elegance uncommon to a plan this size. Cathedral ceilings grace both the great room and the bedroom/study, while tray ceilings appear in the dining room and master bedroom. The open kitchen design allows for a serving island which is convenient to the breakfast area, dining room and rear porch. The master suite has direct access to the deck and also features a large walk-in closet and master bath with double-bowl vanity, shower and whirlpool tub. A covered breezeway connects the garage to the house.

Design by
Donald A. Gardner, Architects, Inc.

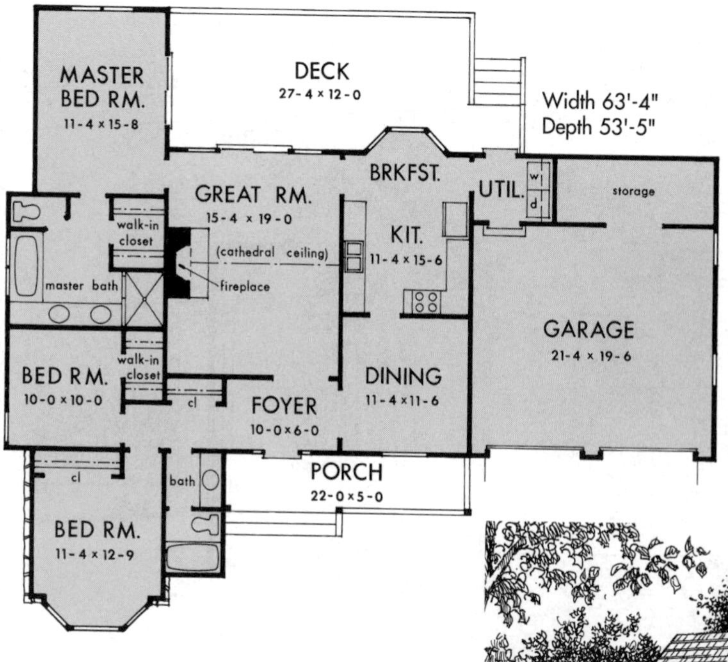

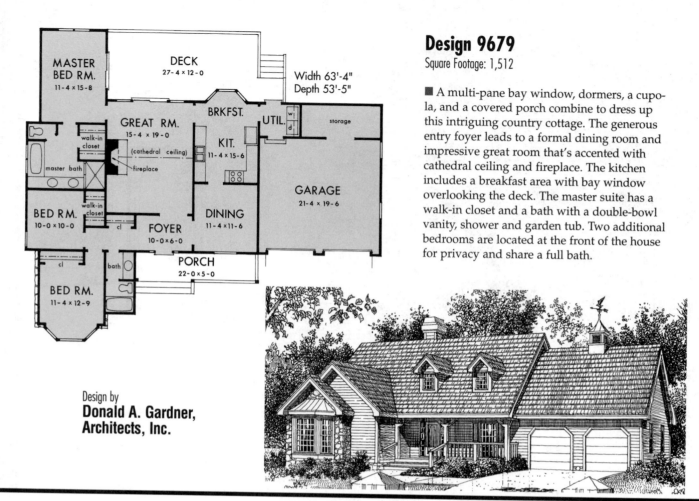

MASTER BED RM. 11-4 x 15-8
DECK 27-4 x 12-0
GREAT RM. 15-4 x 19-0 (cathedral ceiling)
BRKFST.
KIT. 11-4 x 15-6
UTIL.
storage
GARAGE 21-4 x 19-6
walk-in closet
master bath
fireplace
BED RM. 10-0 x 10-0
walk-in closet
cl
FOYER 10-0 x 6-0
DINING 11-4 x 11-6
bath
PORCH 22-0 x 5-0
BED RM. 11-4 x 12-9

Width 63'-4"
Depth 53'-5"

Design 9679

Square Footage: 1,512

■ A multi-pane bay window, dormers, a cupola, and a covered porch combine to dress up this intriguing country cottage. The generous entry foyer leads to a formal dining room and impressive great room that's accented with cathedral ceiling and fireplace. The kitchen includes a breakfast area with bay window overlooking the deck. The master suite has a walk-in closet and a bath with a double-bowl vanity, shower and garden tub. Two additional bedrooms are located at the front of the house for privacy and share a full bath.

Design by
Donald A. Gardner, Architects, Inc.

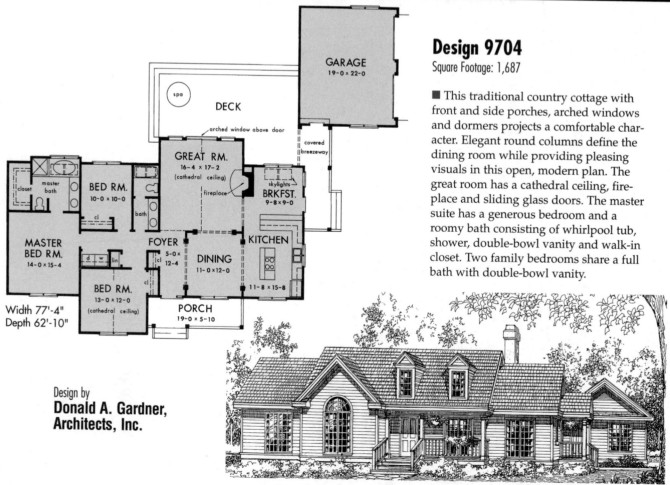

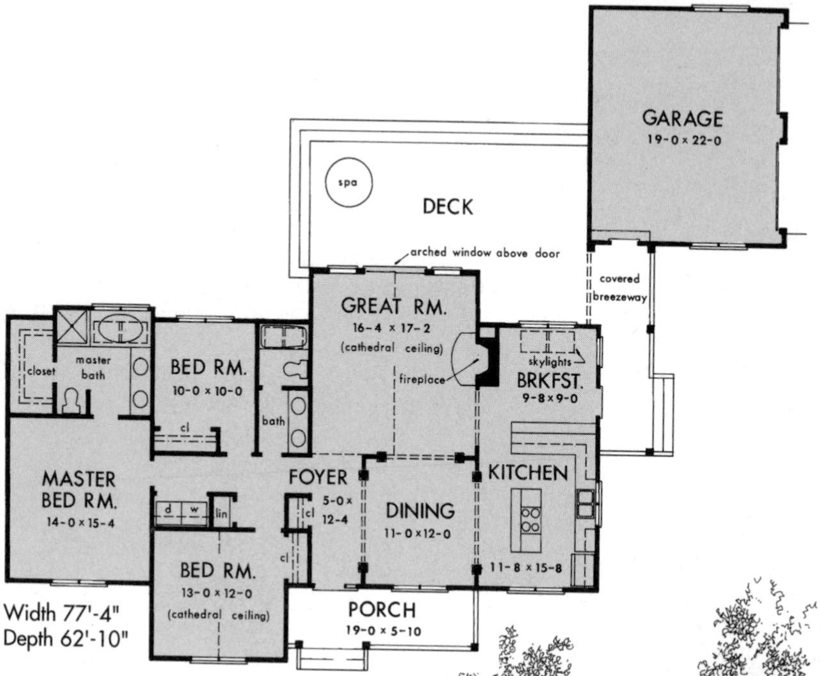

GARAGE 19-0 x 22-0
spa
DECK
arched window above door
covered breezeway
GREAT RM. 16-4 x 17-2 (cathedral ceiling)
skylights
fireplace
BRKFST. 9-8 x 9-0
closet
master bath
BED RM. 10-0 x 10-0
cl
bath
MASTER BED RM. 14-0 x 15-4
FOYER 5-0 x 12-4
cl
d w lin
DINING 11-0 x 12-0
KITCHEN 11-8 x 15-8
cl
BED RM. 13-0 x 12-0 (cathedral ceiling)
PORCH 19-0 x 5-10

Width 77'-4"
Depth 62'-10"

Design 9704

Square Footage: 1,687

■ This traditional country cottage with front and side porches, arched windows and dormers projects a comfortable character. Elegant round columns define the dining room while providing pleasing visuals in this open, modern plan. The great room has a cathedral ceiling, fireplace and sliding glass doors. The master suite has a generous bedroom and a roomy bath consisting of whirlpool tub, shower, double-bowl vanity and walk-in closet. Two family bedrooms share a full bath with double-bowl vanity.

Design by
Donald A. Gardner, Architects, Inc.

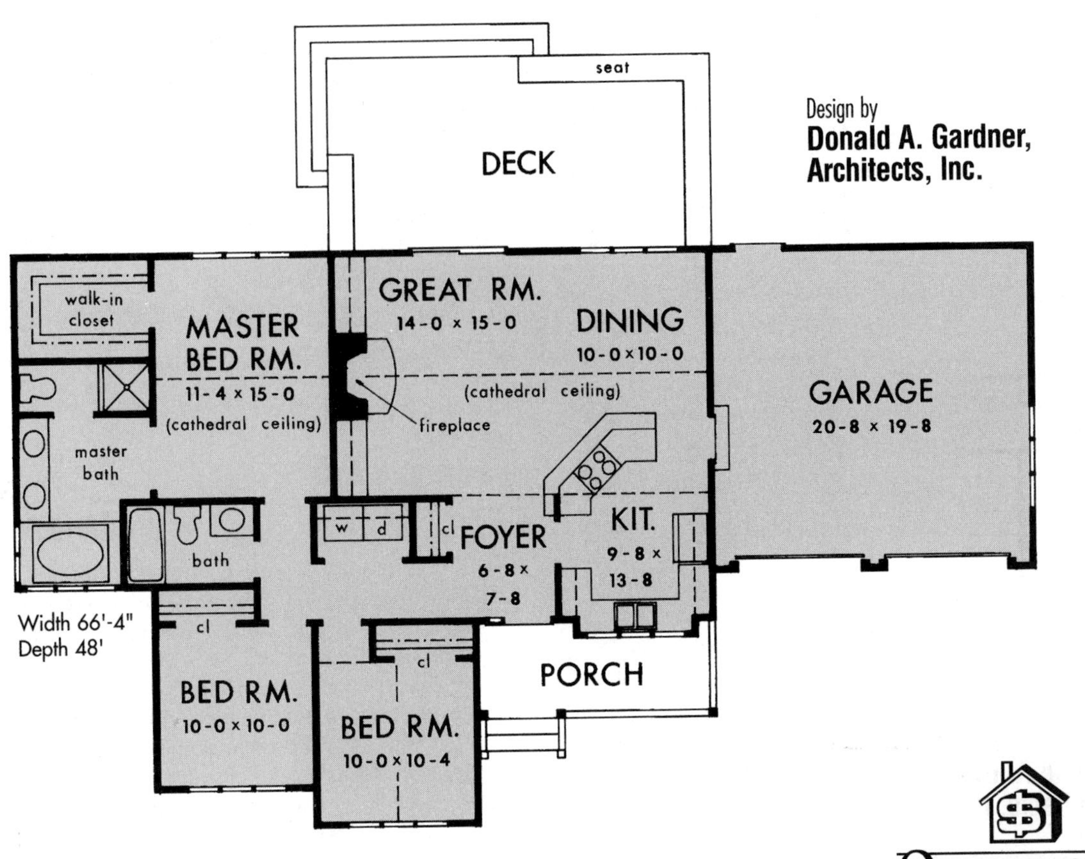
seat
DECK
walk-in closet
MASTER BED RM.
11-4 x 15-0
(cathedral ceiling)
GREAT RM.
14-0 x 15-0
DINING
10-0 x 10-0
(cathedral ceiling)
fireplace
GARAGE
20-8 x 19-8
master bath
bath
w d
cl
FOYER
6-8 x 7-8
KIT.
9-8 x 13-8
cl
cl
PORCH
BED RM.
10-0 x 10-0
BED RM.
10-0 x 10-4
Width 66'-4"
Depth 48'

Design by
Donald A. Gardner, Architects, Inc.

QUOTE ONE®

Cost to build? See page 342 to order complete cost estimate to build this house in your area!

Design 9664

Square Footage: 1,287
Optional Basement Square Footage: 1,319

■ This economical plan offers an impressive visual statement with its comfortable and well-proportioned appearance. The entrance foyer leads to all areas of the house. The great room, dining area and kitchen are all open to one another allowing, visual interaction. The great room and dining area are joined under a dramatic cathedral ceiling that is punctuated with a grand fireplace flanked by bookshelves and cabinets. The master suite has a cathedral ceiling, walk-in closet and master bath with double-bowl vanity, whirlpool tub and shower. Two family bedrooms and a full hall bath complete this cozy home. Please specify basement or crawlspace foundation when ordering.

B. NATHAN

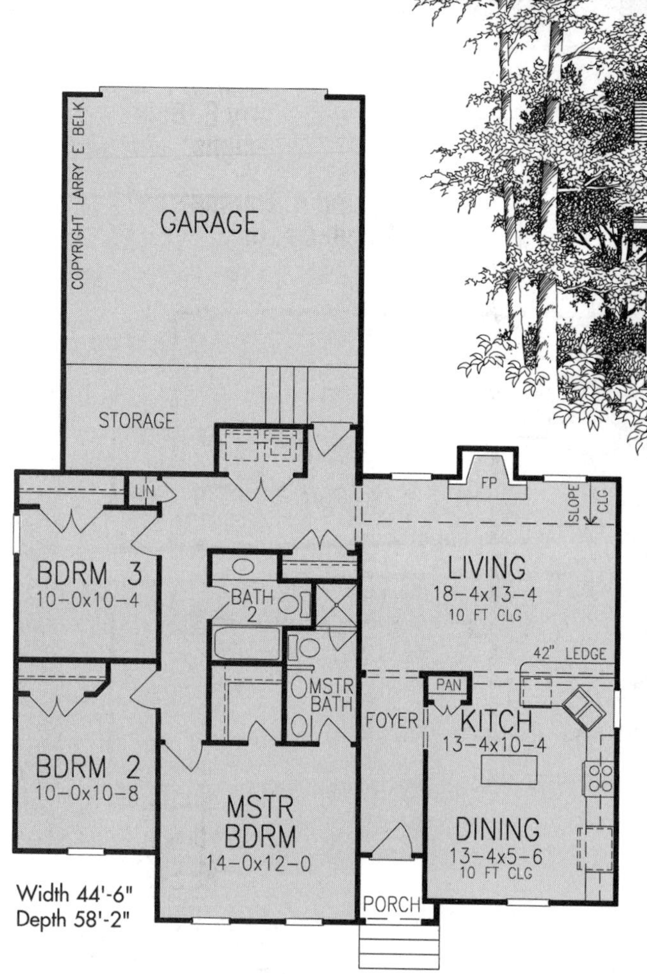
COPYRIGHT LARRY E. BELK
GARAGE
STORAGE
LIN
BDRM 3
10-0x10-4
BATH 2
MSTR BATH
BDRM 2
10-0x10-8
MSTR BDRM
14-0x12-0
FP
SLOPE CLG
LIVING
18-4x13-4
10 FT CLG
42" LEDGE
PAN
FOYER
KITCH
13-4x10-4
DINING
13-4x5-6
10 FT CLG
PORCH
Width 44'-6"
Depth 58'-2"

Design 8250

Square Footage: 1,322

Design by
Larry E. Belk Designs

■ A fine first impression is offered with the delightful chalet roofline on the entry of this efficient country design. A traditional foyer opens to the large living room. Accents include a sloped ten-foot ceiling, a snack bar from the kitchen and windows that frame the fireplace. The kitchen has a corner sink, island prep area and a dining nook. The front-facing master bedroom has a walk-in closet and a twin-sink vanity in the bath. Two family bedrooms share a hall bath. A hallway laundry center and a two-car garage, discreetly set at the rear of the house, complete this plan.

Design by
Larry E. Belk Designs

Design 8165

Square Footage: 1,772

■ A Victorian flair gives this home its curb appeal. Inside, a large living room boasts a centerpiece fireplace and coffered ceiling. The kitchen has a 42"-high breakfast bar and a pantry. The master suite includes a ten-foot coffered ceiling and a luxury bath complete with a corner whirlpool tub, a separate shower, His and Hers vanities and a roomy walk-in closet. Two additional bedrooms and a bath are nearby. A two-car garage plan is included with this design and can be connected to the home with a breezeway. Please specify crawlspace or slab foundation when ordering.

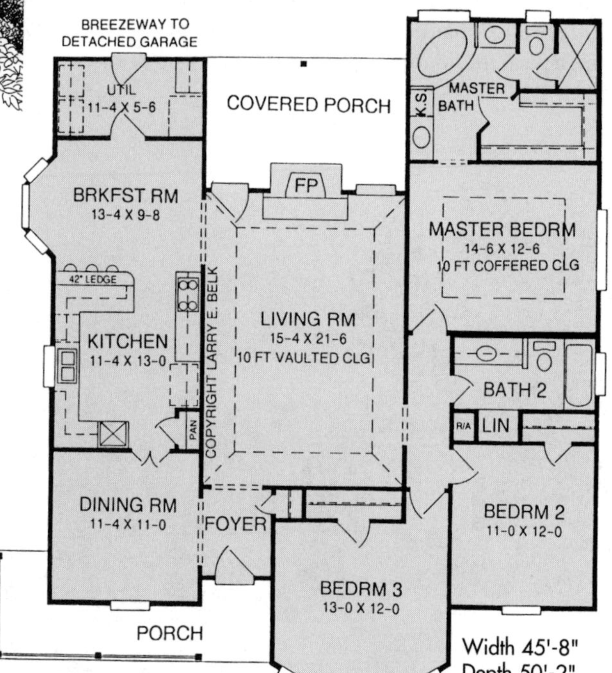
BREEZEWAY TO DETACHED GARAGE
UTIL
11-4 X 5-6
COVERED PORCH
K.S.
MASTER BATH
BRKFST RM
13-4 X 9-8
FP
MASTER BEDRM
14-6 X 12-6
10 FT COFFERED CLG
42" LEDGE
KITCHEN
11-4 X 13-0
COPYRIGHT LARRY E. BELK
LIVING RM
15-4 X 21-6
10 FT VAULTED CLG
BATH 2
PAN
R/A
LIN
DINING RM
11-4 X 11-0
FOYER
BEDRM 2
11-0 X 12-0
BEDRM 3
13-0 X 12-0
PORCH
Width 45'-8"
Depth 50'-2"

COPYRIGHT LARRY E BELK
GARAGE
STORAGE
UTILITY
B/C
FP
GREAT ROOM
17-8x16-0
11 FT CLG
BRKFST
11-0x10-6
9 FT CLG
BDRM 2
10-8x13-8
9 FT CLG
BDRM 3
11-0x10-0
9 FT CLG
42" LEDGE
KITCH
12-6x
13-8
9 FT CLG
HALL
9 FT CLG
BATH 2
FOYER
11 FT
CLG
DINING
12-4x13-8
11 FT CLG
LIN
PANTRY
MSTR
BATH
9 FT CLG
MSTR BDRM
12-4x16-8
10 FT CLG
PORCH
SEAT
Width 54'-10"
Depth 69'-10"

Design by
Larry E. Belk Designs

Design 8239

Square Footage: 1,654

■ The modest size of this quaint cottage doesn't hinder the great design working inside. The foyer opens to a formal dining room that is set apart from the great room with columns. A fireplace with built-in bookcases and plenty of windows give the great room charm. The stylish kitchen takes on new angles to maximize space and efficiency. A large master bedroom enjoys a walk-in closet and an oversized, spa-style bath. Two additional bedrooms share a full hall bath. Please specify crawlspace or slab foundation when ordering.

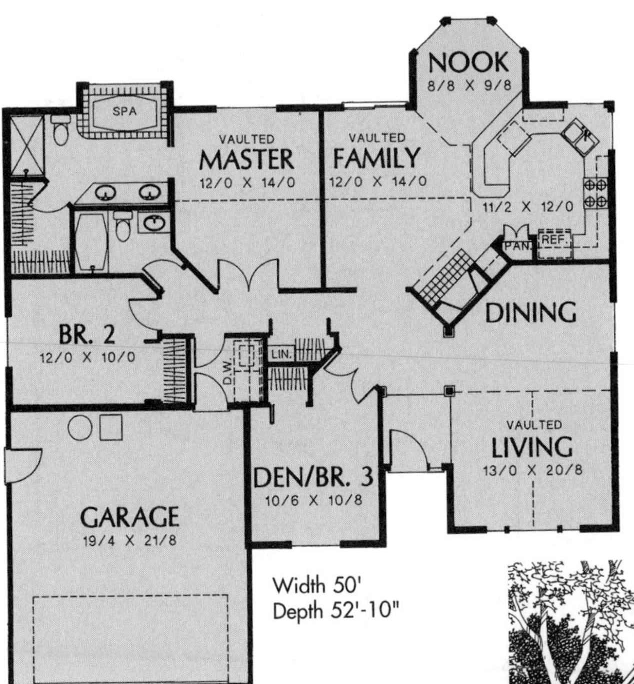
NOOK
8/8 X 9/8
SPA
VAULTED
MASTER
12/0 X 14/0
VAULTED
FAMILY
12/0 X 14/0
11/2 X 12/0
PAN.
REF.
DINING
BR. 2
12/0 X 10/0
D.W.
LIN.
VAULTED
LIVING
13/0 X 20/8
DEN/BR. 3
10/6 X 10/8
GARAGE
19/4 X 21/8
Width 50'
Depth 52'-10"

Design 9403

Square Footage: 1,565

■ If you're looking for a traditional-styled ranch, this one with front-facing gables and a combination of cedar shingles and vertical cedar siding fits in with many locales. The vaulted living room faces the street and is set off with a gorgeous Palladian window. The family room, accented with an angled fireplace, and the master bedroom also contain vaulted ceilings. The master bath has a delightful spa tub, a large shower and walk-in closet. Through French doors in the entry is a den that could be used as a third bedroom, while another bedroom shares a full hall bath.

Design by
Alan Mascord Design Associates, Inc.

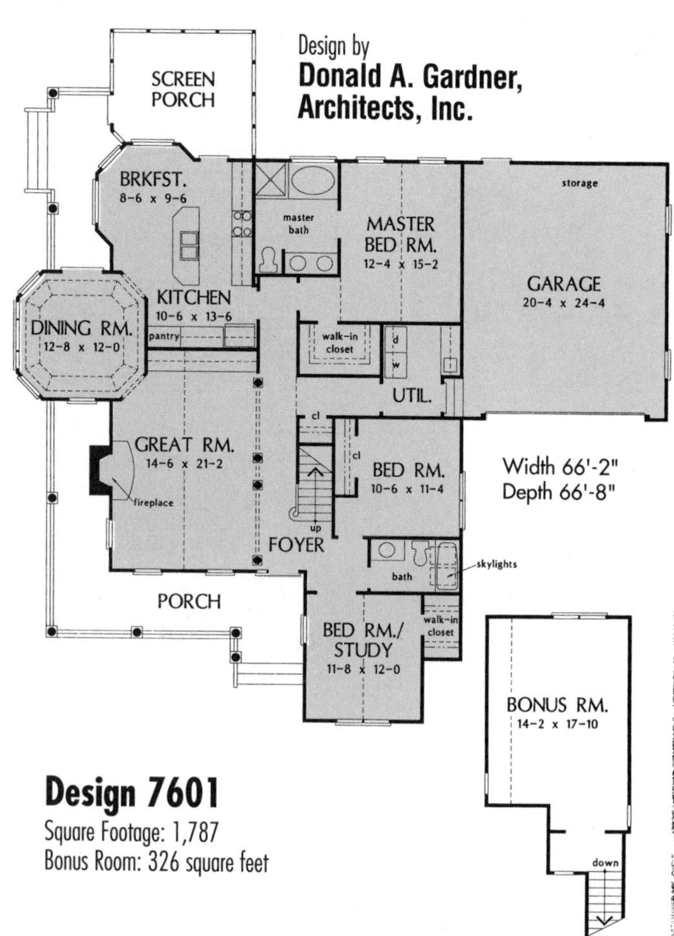
SCREEN PORCH
BRKFST.
8-6 x 9-6
master bath
MASTER BED RM.
12-4 x 15-2
storage
GARAGE
20-4 x 24-4
KITCHEN
10-6 x 13-6
DINING RM.
12-8 x 12-0
pantry
walk-in closet
d
w
UTIL.
cl
GREAT RM.
14-6 x 21-2
fireplace
cl
BED RM.
10-6 x 11-4
up
FOYER
bath
skylights
PORCH
BED RM./ STUDY
11-8 x 12-0
walk-in closet
BONUS RM.
14-2 x 17-10
down

Design by
Donald A. Gardner, Architects, Inc.

Width 66'-2"
Depth 66'-8"

Design 7601

Square Footage: 1,787
Bonus Room: 326 square feet

■ Cathedral ceilings bring a feeling of spaciousness to this charming cottage. The great room features a fireplace, cathedral ceiling and built-in bookshelves. The kitchen is designed for efficient use with a food prep island and a large pantry. A premiere dining room is fashioned between the kitchen and great room and features an elegant tray ceiling and an expanse of windows. The master suite provides a welcome retreat with a cathedral ceiling, a walk-in closet and a luxurious bath. Two additional bedrooms, one with a walk-in closet, share a hall bath that's accented with skylights. A second-floor bonus room is perfect for a study or a play area. Please specify basement or crawlspace foundation when ordering.

Design 9430

First Floor: 1,150 square feet
Second Floor: 543 square feet
Total: 1,693 square feet

■ While fitting on the smallest of lots, this great plan still encompasses some dynamic features. A dramatic, two-story hearth room serves as the main living area in the home. Tall windows flank the fireplace and a glass door leads to the outdoor area. The master bedroom is conveniently located on the main floor overlooking the back yard, with direct access to the full bath serving the lower floor. A balcony hall overlooking the hearth room leads to two family bedrooms and a full hall bath.

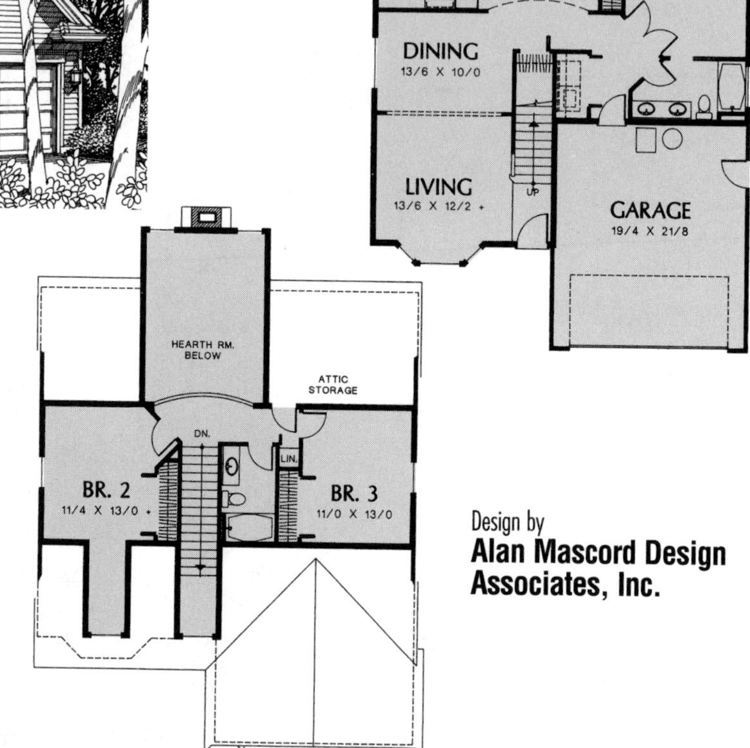
VAULTED
HEARTH ROOM
12/0 X 16/6
10/0 X 10/6
REF.
P.
MASTER
12/4 X 14/10
DINING
13/6 X 10/0
LIVING
13/6 X 12/2 +
UP
GARAGE
19/4 X 21/8
HEARTH RM. BELOW
ATTIC STORAGE
DN.
LIN.
BR. 2
11/4 X 13/0 +
BR. 3
11/0 X 13/0

Width 38'
Depth 50'

Design by
Alan Mascord Design Associates, Inc.

Design 7613

First Floor: 1,116 square feet
Second Floor: 442 square feet
Total: 1,558 square feet

Design by
Donald A. Gardner, Architects, Inc.

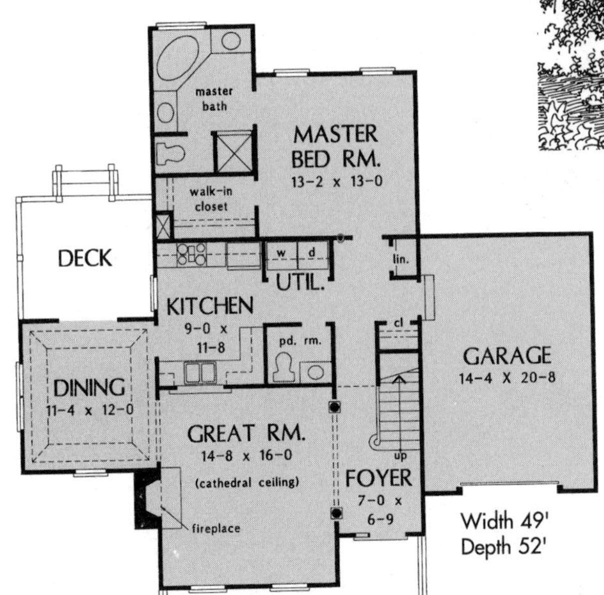

master bath
MASTER BED RM.
13-2 x 13-0
walk-in closet
DECK
w d
UTIL.
lin.
KITCHEN
9-0 x 11-8
pd. rm.
cl
GARAGE
14-4 X 20-8
DINING
11-4 x 12-0
GREAT RM.
14-8 x 16-0
(cathedral ceiling)
fireplace
up
FOYER
7-0 x 6-9
Width 49'
Depth 52'
PORCH

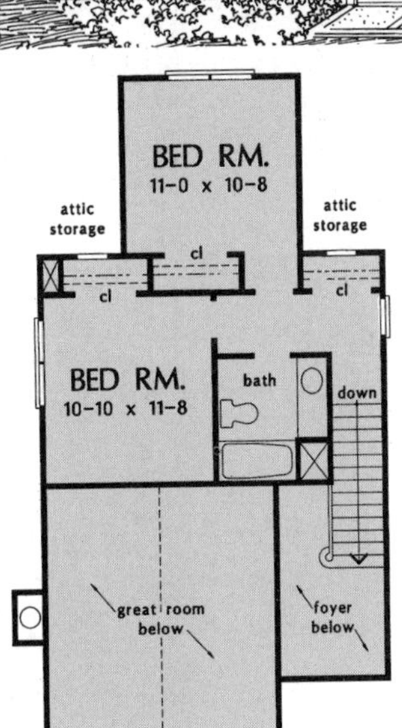

BED RM.
11-0 x 10-8
attic storage
attic storage
cl
cl
cl
BED RM.
10-10 x 11-8
bath
down
great room below
foyer below

■ The front porch and the foyer open through a columned entrance to the large great room with a cathedral ceiling and a fireplace. A dining room with a tray ceiling is centered between the great room, kitchen and the deck. The master bedroom is located at the rear of the home for privacy and features a walk-in closet and a corner whirlpool tub. Upstairs, two family bedrooms share a full hall bath.

Design by
Donald A. Gardner, Architects, Inc.

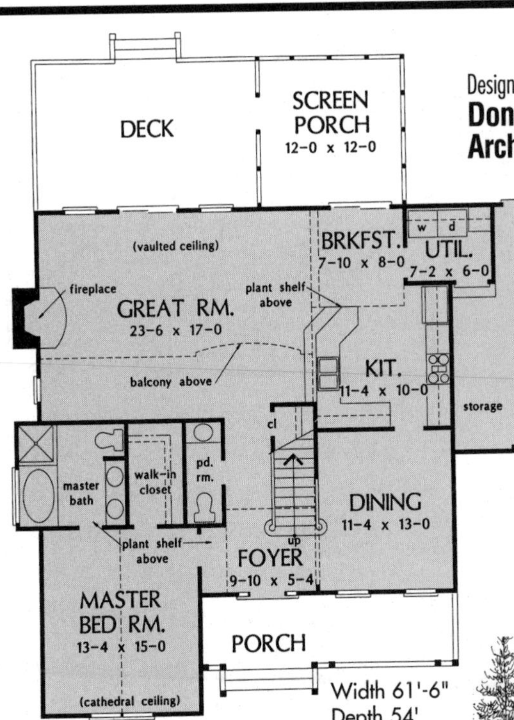

DECK
SCREEN PORCH
12-0 x 12-0
(vaulted ceiling)
BRKFST.
7-10 x 8-0
w d
UTIL.
7-2 x 6-0
fireplace
plant shelf above
GREAT RM.
23-6 x 17-0
GARAGE
19-8 x 20-0
KIT.
11-4 x 10-0
balcony above
storage
cl
master bath
walk-in closet
pd. rm.
DINING
11-4 x 13-0
plant shelf above
up
FOYER
9-10 x 5-4
MASTER BED RM.
13-4 x 15-0
PORCH
(cathedral ceiling)
Width 61'-6"
Depth 54'

great room below
skylight
attic storage
railing
down
BED RM.
12-2 x 12-0
bath
BED RM.
11-4 x 12-0
cl
cl
cl
foyer below

■ This farmhouse exudes welcoming charm. Inside, the large great room with cathedral ceiling, fireplace and rear deck access is convenient to the efficient kitchen. The breakfast room has sliding glass doors to a screened-in porch for carefree outdoor dining. The location of the master bedroom downstairs and two other bedrooms upstairs maintains privacy.

Design 9747

First Floor: 1,335 square feet
Second Floor: 488 square feet
Total: 1,823 square feet

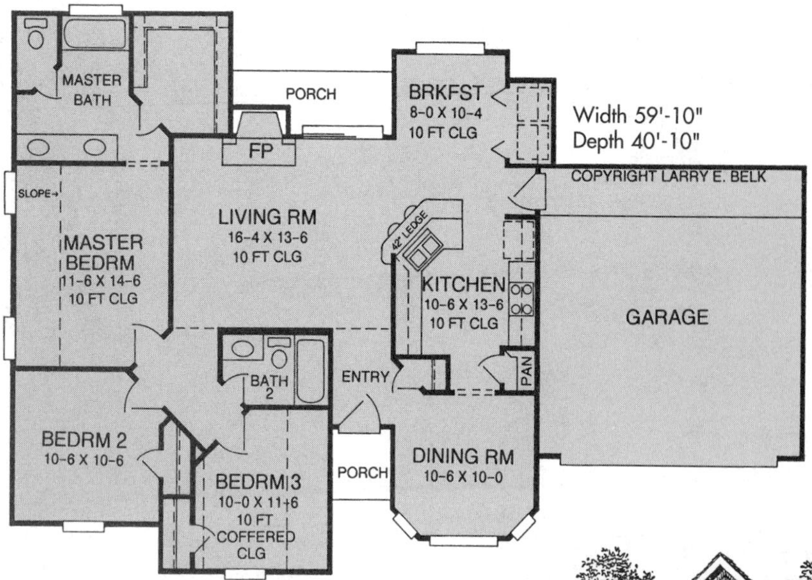

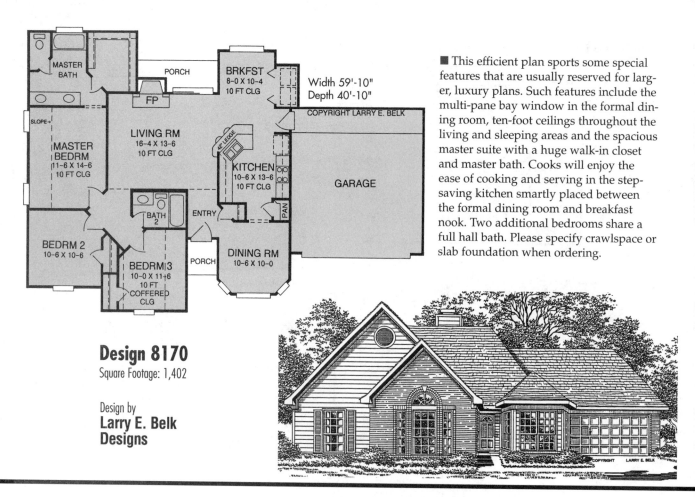

Width 59'-10"
Depth 40'-10"

■ This efficient plan sports some special features that are usually reserved for larger, luxury plans. Such features include the multi-pane bay window in the formal dining room, ten-foot ceilings throughout the living and sleeping areas and the spacious master suite with a huge walk-in closet and master bath. Cooks will enjoy the ease of cooking and serving in the step-saving kitchen smartly placed between the formal dining room and breakfast nook. Two additional bedrooms share a full hall bath. Please specify crawlspace or slab foundation when ordering.

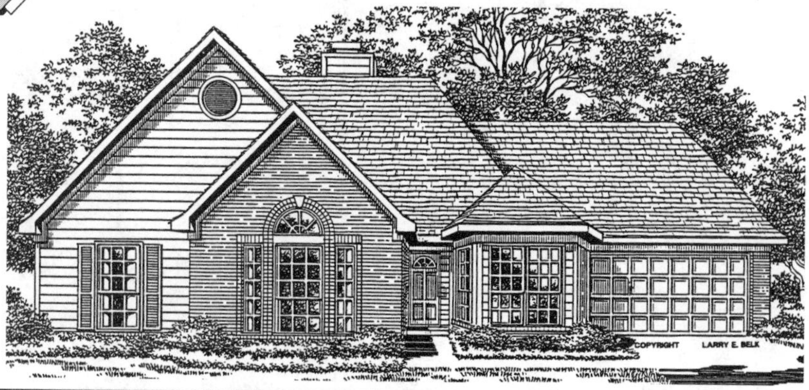

Design 8170

Square Footage: 1,402

Design by
Larry E. Belk Designs

Design 8169

Square Footage: 1,310

■ This charming plan is perfect for families just starting out or for the empty-nester looking to pare down. Every room is designed for maximum livability, from the living room with a corner fireplace to the efficient kitchen with a snack bar and hidden washer and dryer. The master bedroom is fashioned with a dual-vanity bath and a walk-in closet equipped with shelves. Two additional bedrooms each have a walk-in closet and share a hall bath. Please specify crawlspace or slab foundation when ordering.

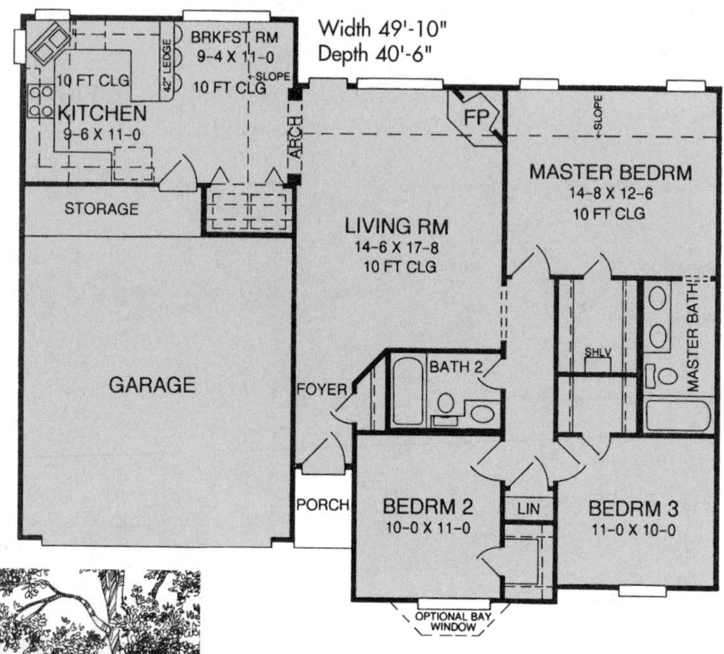
Width 49'-10"
Depth 40'-6"
BRKFST RM
9-4 X 11-0
10 FT CLG
SLOPE
42" LEDGE
10 FT CLG
KITCHEN
9-6 X 11-0
ARCH
FP
STORAGE
MASTER BEDRM
14-8 X 12-6
10 FT CLG
LIVING RM
14-6 X 17-8
10 FT CLG
GARAGE
BATH 2
SHLV
MASTER BATH
FOYER
PORCH
BEDRM 2
10-0 X 11-0
LIN
BEDRM 3
11-0 X 10-0
OPTIONAL BAY WINDOW

Design by
Larry E. Belk Designs

Design 8171

Square Footage: 1,087

■ This quaint brick home has definite curb appeal. From the multi-pane windows to the corner quoins, the home's facade is enchanting. Inside, attractive arches flank the entryway; one arch leads to a cheerful breakfast room and an efficient kitchen, the other to the deluxe master suite. Directly ahead of the foyer is the large great room that offers access to the rear yard and the two family bedrooms. In the master suite, a sumptuous bath offers a double-bowl vanity and a large walk-in closet. Two family bedrooms are located on the opposite end of the home and share a full hall bath. Please specify crawlspace or slab foundation when ordering.

Design by
Larry E. Belk Designs

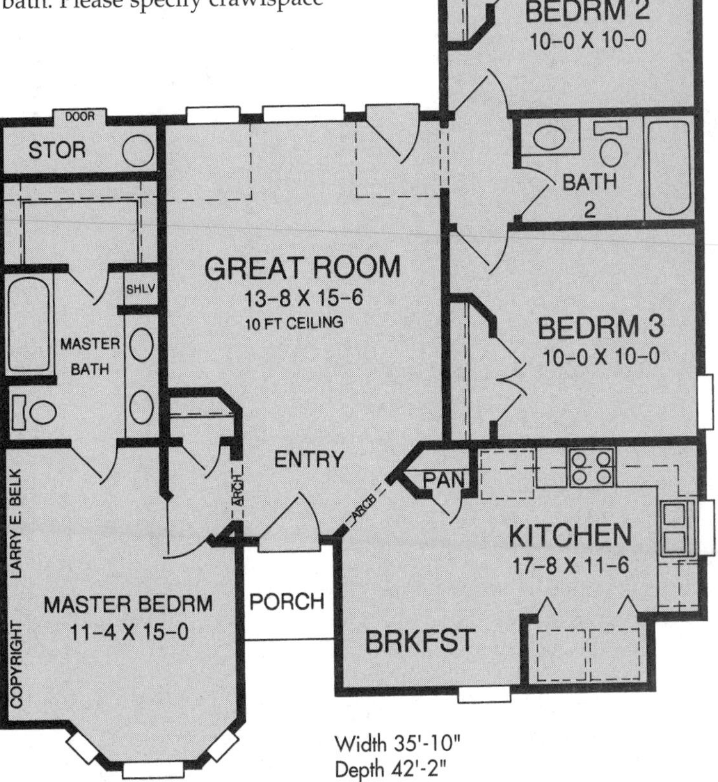
BEDRM 2
10-0 X 10-0
DOOR
STOR
BATH
2
GREAT ROOM
13-8 X 15-6
10 FT CEILING
SHLV
MASTER
BATH
BEDRM 3
10-0 X 10-0
ENTRY
PAN
ARCH
ARCH
KITCHEN
17-8 X 11-6
LARRY E. BELK
COPYRIGHT
MASTER BEDRM
11-4 X 15-0
PORCH
BRKFST

Width 35'-10"
Depth 42'-2"

■ This economical, rustic three-bedroom plan sports a relaxing country image with both front and back covered porches. The openness of the great room to the kitchen/dining areas and the loft/study area is reinforced with a shared cathedral ceiling. The first level allows for two bedrooms, a full bath and a utility area. The master suite on the second level has a walk-in closet and a master bath with whirlpool tub, shower and double-bowl vanity.

Design 9666

First Floor: 1,027 square feet
Second Floor: 580 square feet
Total: 1,607 square feet

Design by
Donald A. Gardner, Architects, Inc.

QUOTE ONE®
Cost to build? See page 342 to order complete cost estimate to build this house in your area!

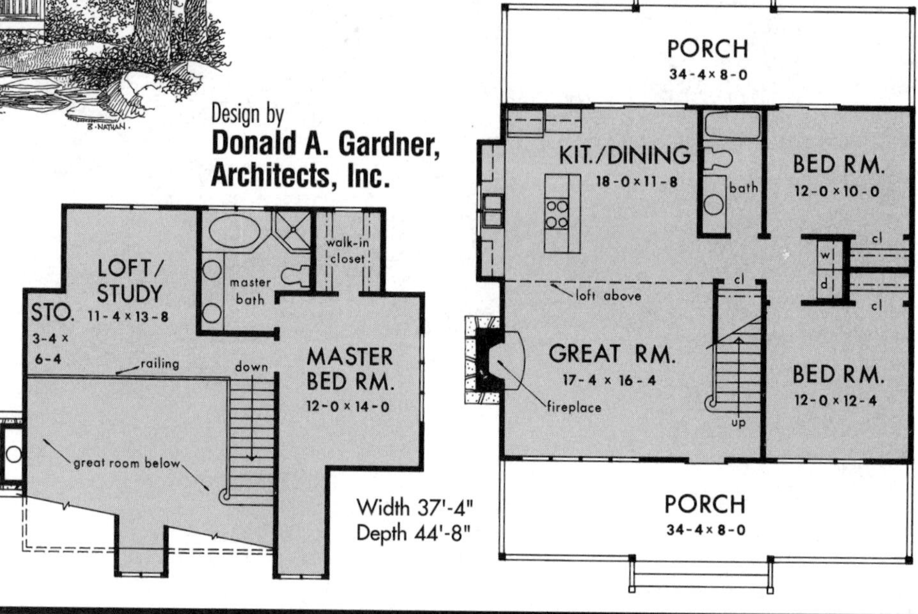
PORCH
34-4 × 8-0
KIT./DINING
18-0 × 11-8
bath
BED RM.
12-0 × 10-0
cl
w
d
cl
loft above
cl
GREAT RM.
17-4 × 16-4
fireplace
up
BED RM.
12-0 × 12-4
PORCH
34-4 × 8-0
LOFT/
STUDY
11-4 × 13-8
master
bath
walk-in
closet
STO.
3-4 × 6-4
railing
down
MASTER
BED RM.
12-0 × 14-0
great room below

Width 37'-4"
Depth 44'-8"

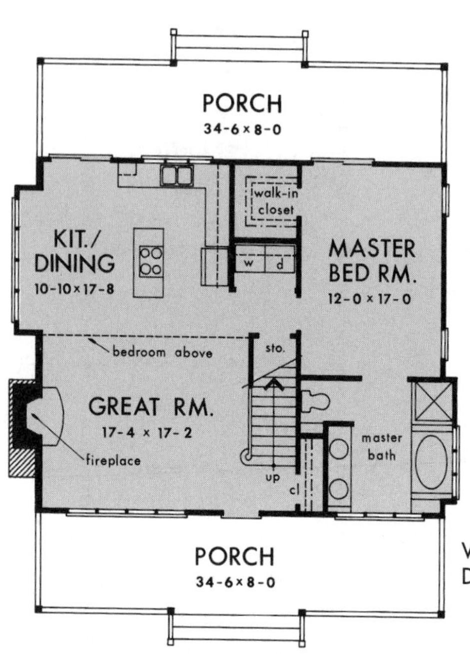
PORCH
34-6 × 8-0
KIT./
DINING
10-10 × 17-8
walk-in
closet
w
d
MASTER
BED RM.
12-0 × 17-0
bedroom above
sto.
GREAT RM.
17-4 × 17-2
fireplace
up
cl
master
bath
PORCH
34-6 × 8-0

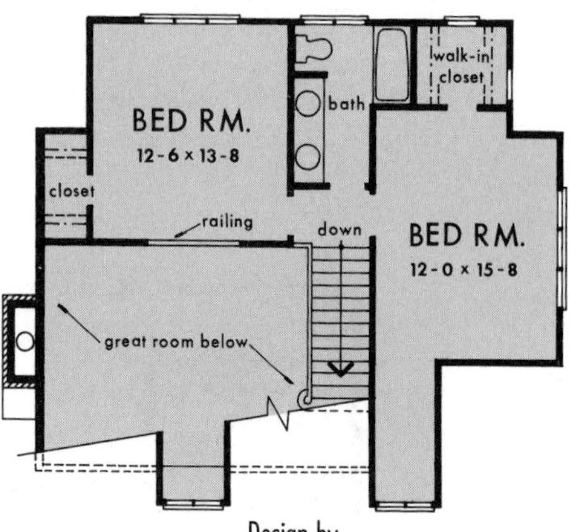
BED RM.
12-6 × 13-8
bath
walk-in
closet
closet
railing
down
BED RM.
12-0 × 15-8
great room below

Design 9697

First Floor: 1,039 square feet
Second Floor: 583 square feet
Total: 1,622 square feet

Width 37'-9"
Depth 44'-8"

Design by
Donald A. Gardner, Architects, Inc.

■ Charming and compact, this delightful two-story cabin is perfect for the small family or empty-nester. Designed with casual living in mind, the two-story great room is completely open to the dining area and the spacious island kitchen. The master suite is on the first floor for privacy and convenience. It features a roomy bath and a walk-in closet. Upstairs, two comfortable bedrooms—one has a dormer window, the other has a balcony overlooking the great room—share a full hall bath.

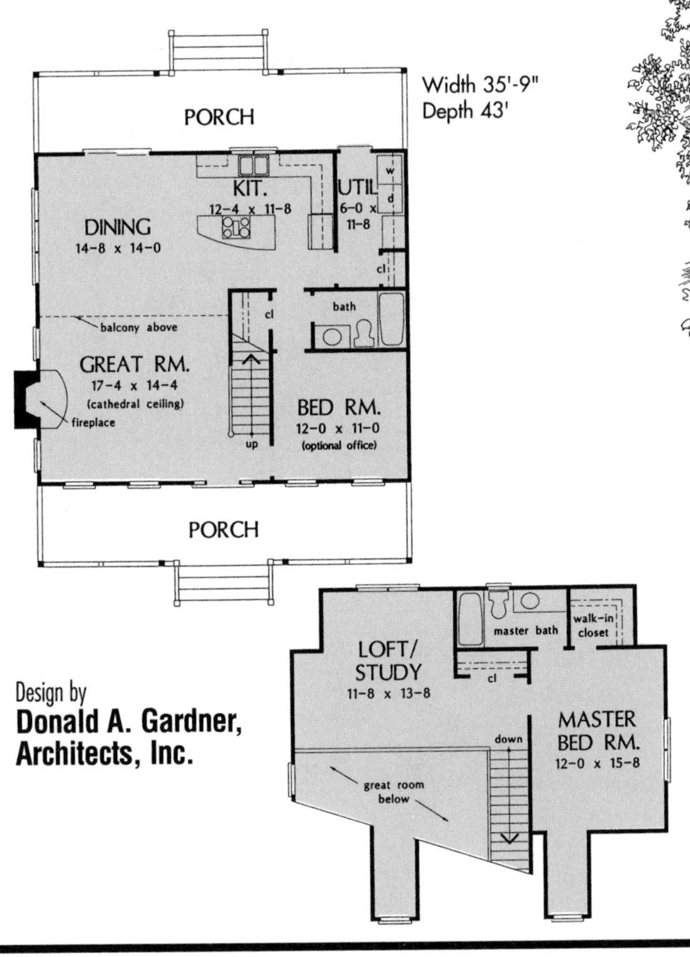
PORCH
KIT.
12-4 x 11-8
UTIL
6-0 x 11-8
DINING
14-8 x 14-0
balcony above
bath
GREAT RM.
17-4 x 14-4
(cathedral ceiling)
fireplace
BED RM.
12-0 x 11-0
(optional office)
up
PORCH
LOFT/
STUDY
11-8 x 13-8
master bath
walk-in closet
MASTER
BED RM.
12-0 x 15-8
down
great room
below

Width 35'-9"
Depth 43'

Design by
Donald A. Gardner, Architects, Inc.

Design 9769

First Floor: 966 square feet
Second Floor: 584 square feet
Total: 1,550 square feet

■ A country farmhouse exterior combined with an open floor plan creates a comfortable home or vacation getaway. The great room, warmed by a fireplace and opened by a cathedral ceiling, combines well with the dining room and the kitchen. Adjacent to the kitchen is a convenient utility room. Flexibility is offered with a front bedroom and full bath that easily double as a home office. The second floor contains the master bedroom with a walk-in closet and a private bath. Overlooking the great room below is the loft/study. Front and rear porches provide plenty of room for outdoor enjoyment.

■ A relaxing country image projects from the front and rear covered porches of this rustic three-bedroom home. Open planning extends to the great room, the dining room and the efficient kitchen. A shared cathedral ceiling creates an impressive space. Completing the first floor are two family bedrooms, a full bath and a handy utility area. The second floor contains the master suite featuring a spacious walk-in closet and a master bath with a whirlpool tub and a separate corner shower. A generous loft/study overlooks the great room below.

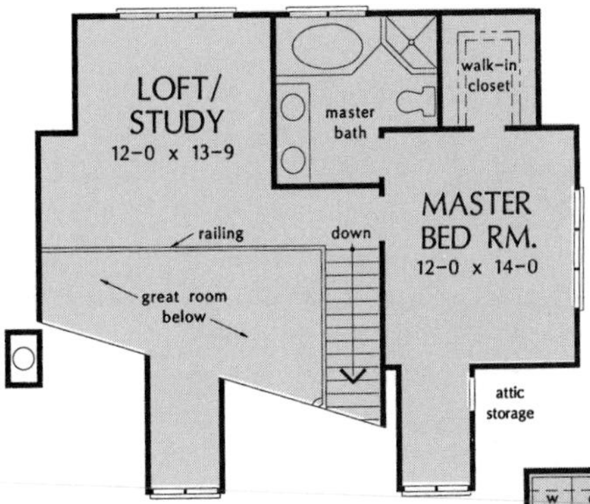

LOFT/
STUDY
12-0 x 13-9
master bath
walk-in closet
MASTER
BED RM.
12-0 x 14-0
railing
down
great room
below
attic storage

Design 9759

First Floor: 1,100 square feet
Second Floor: 584 square feet
Total: 1,684 square feet

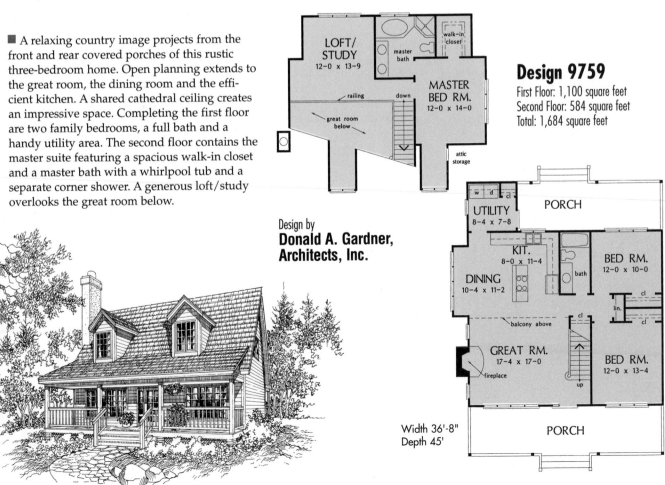

Design by
Donald A. Gardner, Architects, Inc.

UTILITY
8-4 x 7-8
PORCH
KIT.
8-0 x 11-4
DINING
10-4 x 11-2
bath
BED RM.
12-0 x 10-0
lin.
balcony above
GREAT RM.
17-4 x 17-0
fireplace
up
BED RM.
12-0 x 13-4
PORCH

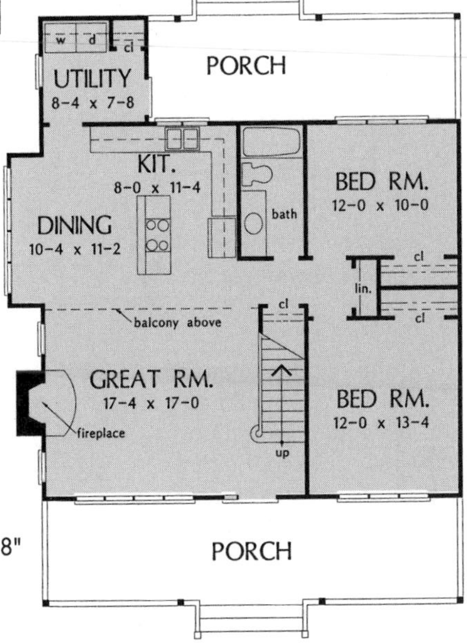

Width 36'-8"
Depth 45'

Design 9663

First Floor: 1,002 square feet
Second Floor: 336 square feet
Total: 1,338 square feet

■ A mountain retreat, this rustic home features covered porches front and rear. Open living is enjoyed in a great room and kitchen/dining room combination. Here, a fireplace provides the focal point and a warm welcome that continues into the L-shaped island kitchen. The cathedral ceiling that graces the great room gives an open, inviting sense of space. Two bedrooms—one with a walk-in closet—and a full bath on the first level are complemented by a master suite on the second level which includes a walk-in closet and deluxe bath. There is also attic storage on the second level. Please specify basement or crawlspace foundation when ordering.

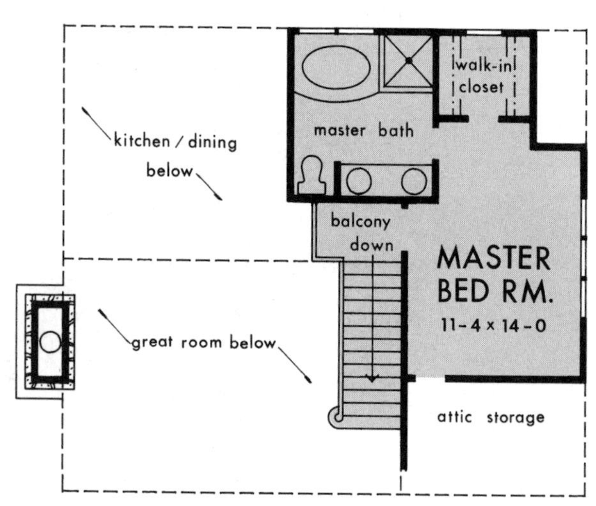
walk-in closet
master bath
kitchen / dining below
balcony down
MASTER BED RM.
11-4 × 14-0
great room below
attic storage

Width 36'-8"
Depth 44'-8"

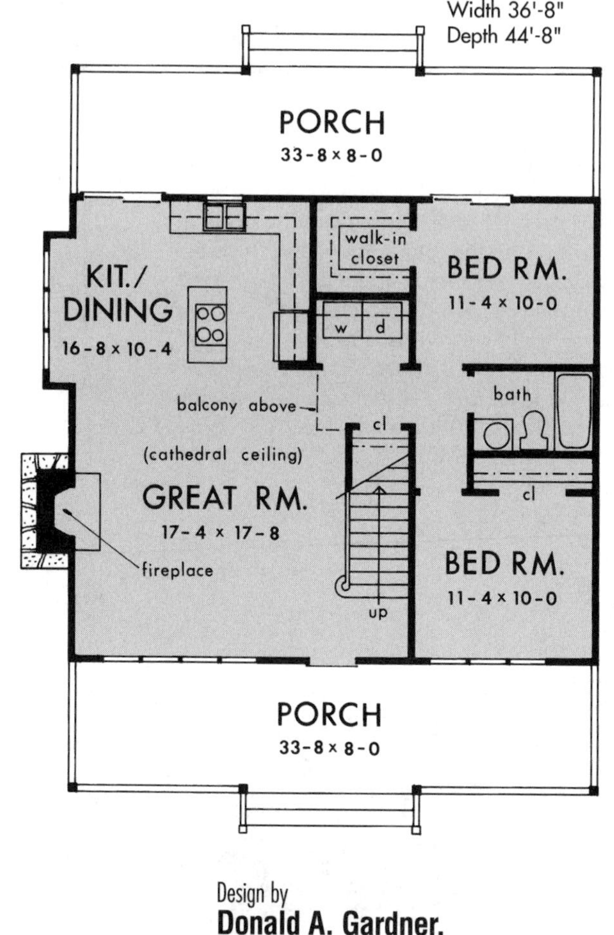
PORCH
33-8 × 8-0
walk-in closet
KIT./ DINING
16-8 × 10-4
BED RM.
11-4 × 10-0
w
d
balcony above
bath
cl
(cathedral ceiling)
GREAT RM.
17-4 × 17-8
fireplace
up
cl
BED RM.
11-4 × 10-0
PORCH
33-8 × 8-0

Design by
Donald A. Gardner, Architects, Inc.

Porch
Master
Bedroom
15⁶x14⁰
Great
Room
16⁹x24³
Bedroom
No. 2
11⁹x12⁰
Bedroom
No. 3
10⁹x14⁰
Kitchen
12⁶x9⁰
Dining
Room
9⁰x16³
Stoop
Width 56'
Depth 56'-3"
Unfinished
Loft
16⁰x24⁰
Open to
Below
W.I.C.

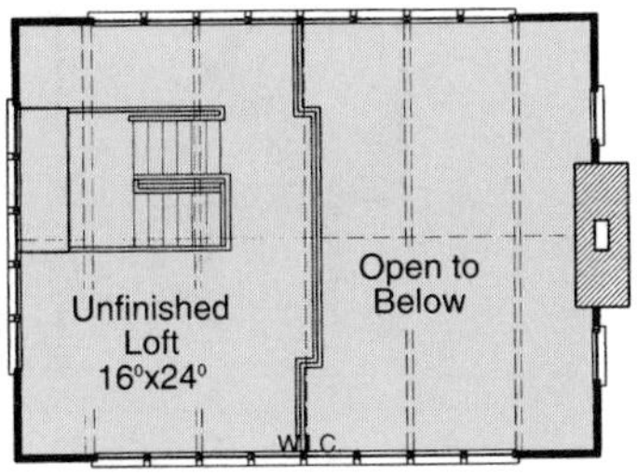

Design 9995

Square Footage: 2,019
Loft: 363 square feet

Design by
Design Traditions

■ This design takes inspiration from the casual fishing cabins of the Pacific Northwest and interprets it for modern livability. It offers three options for a main entrance. One door opens onto a mud porch, where a small hall leads to a galley kitchen and the vaulted great room. Two French doors on the side porch open into a dining room with bay-window seating. Another porch entrance opens directly into the great room. The great room is centered around a massive stone fireplace and is accented with a beautiful wall of windows. The secluded master bedroom features a master bath with a claw-foot tub and twin pedestal sinks, as well as a separate shower and walk-in closet. Two more bedrooms share a spacious bath. Ideal for a lounge or extra sleeping space, an unfinished loft looks over the great room.

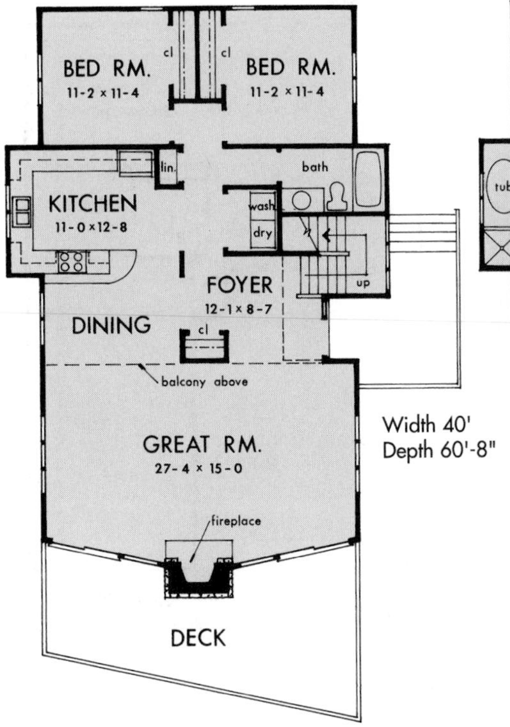

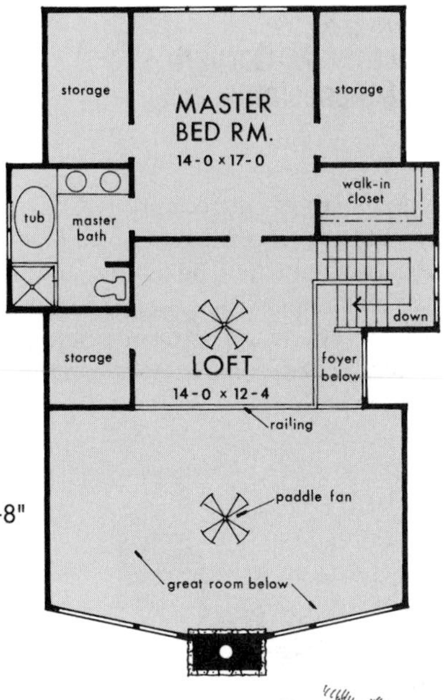

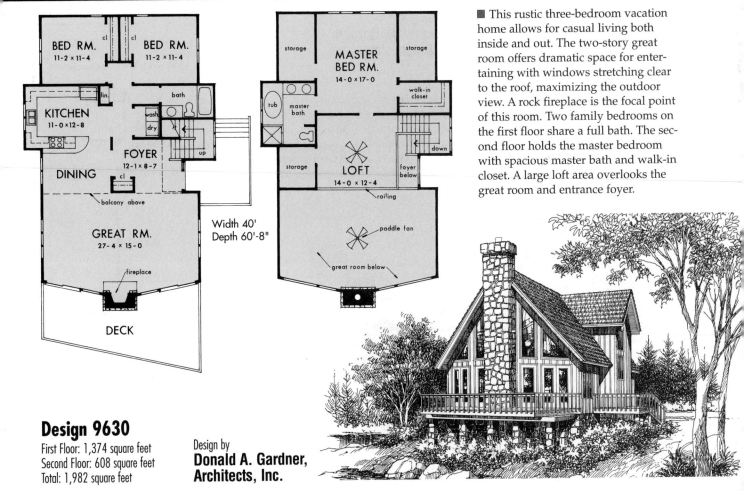

■ This rustic three-bedroom vacation home allows for casual living both inside and out. The two-story great room offers dramatic space for entertaining with windows stretching clear to the roof, maximizing the outdoor view. A rock fireplace is the focal point of this room. Two family bedrooms on the first floor share a full bath. The second floor holds the master bedroom with spacious master bath and walk-in closet. A large loft area overlooks the great room and entrance foyer.

BED RM. 11-2 x 11-4
BED RM. 11-2 x 11-4
KITCHEN 11-0 x 12-8
FOYER 12-1 x 8-7
DINING
GREAT RM. 27-4 x 15-0
DECK
MASTER BED RM. 14-0 x 17-0
LOFT 14-0 x 12-4

Width 40'
Depth 60'-8"

Design 9630

First Floor: 1,374 square feet
Second Floor: 608 square feet
Total: 1,982 square feet

Design by
Donald A. Gardner, Architects, Inc.

Design 9590

First Floor: 1,205 square feet
Second Floor: 1,123 square feet
Total: 2,328 square feet

■ A covered porch, multi-pane windows and shingle with stone siding combine to give this bungalow plenty of curb appeal. Inside, the foyer is flanked by the formal living room and an angled staircase. The formal dining room joins the living room and the kitchen is accessible through double doors. A large family room is graced by a fireplace and opens off a cozy eating nook. The second level presents many attractive angles. The master suite has a spacious walk-in closet and a sumptuous bath complete with a garden tub and separate shower. Three family bedrooms share a full hall bath.

Design by
Alan Mascord Design Associates, Inc.

Width 57'-2"
Depth 58'-7"

NOOK
8/0 X 15/0
10/0 X 13/4
FAMILY
15/0 X 13/4
DINING
13/0 X 10/0
LIVING
13/0 X 12/4
GARAGE
23/0 X 21/4
MASTER
12/6 X 16/0
BR. 2
10/0 X 12/0
BR. 3
13/0 X 11/0
BR. 4
10/8 X 10/0
PLANT SHELF

Design 8956

First Floor: 845 square feet
Second Floor: 845 square feet
Total: 1,690 square feet

Design by
Larry W. Garnett & Associates, Inc.

■ An angled foyer and staircase lends diversity to this three-bedroom plan. The large living room, with a front-facing sitting area, affords amenities such as a fireplace and lots of wall space for various furniture arrangements. The dining room is bright and sunny and offers access outside via a French door. The U-shaped kitchen enjoys a built-in pantry, plenty of counter and cabinet space and convenience to the nearby utility room. The second floor offers two family bedrooms that share a full bath, and a master bedroom that boasts a fine angled bath.

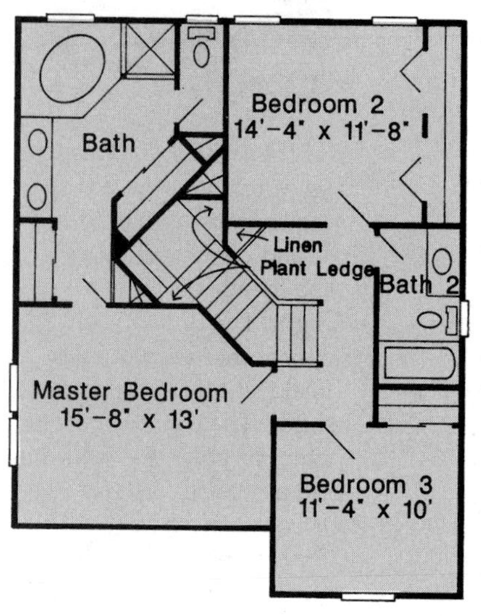
Bath
Bedroom 2
14'-4" x 11'-8"
Linen
Plant Ledge
Bath 2
Master Bedroom
15'-8" x 13'
Bedroom 3
11'-4" x 10'

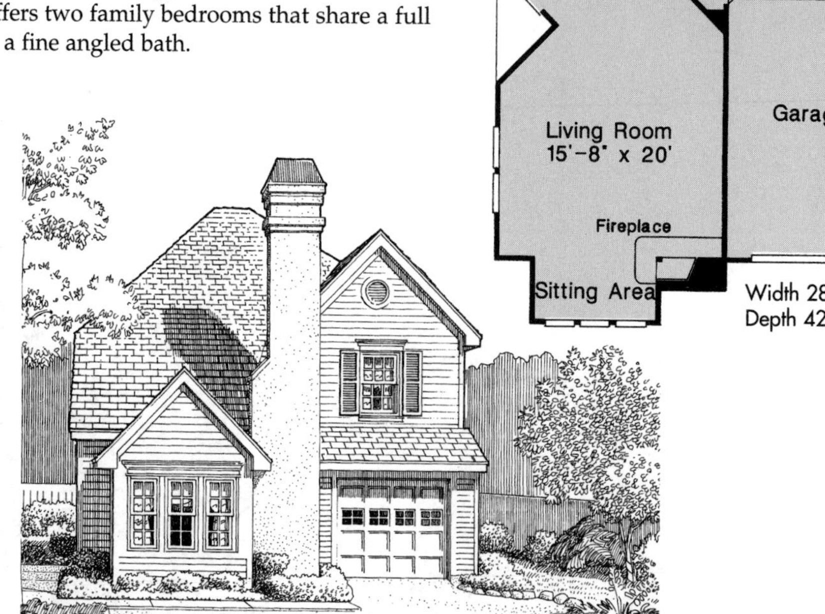
French Door
Dining
12' x 11'
Kitchen
15' x 10'
Pantry
Stor.
1/2 Bath
Util.
Foyer
Garage
Living Room
15'-8" x 20'
Fireplace
Sitting Area

Width 28'
Depth 42'-4"

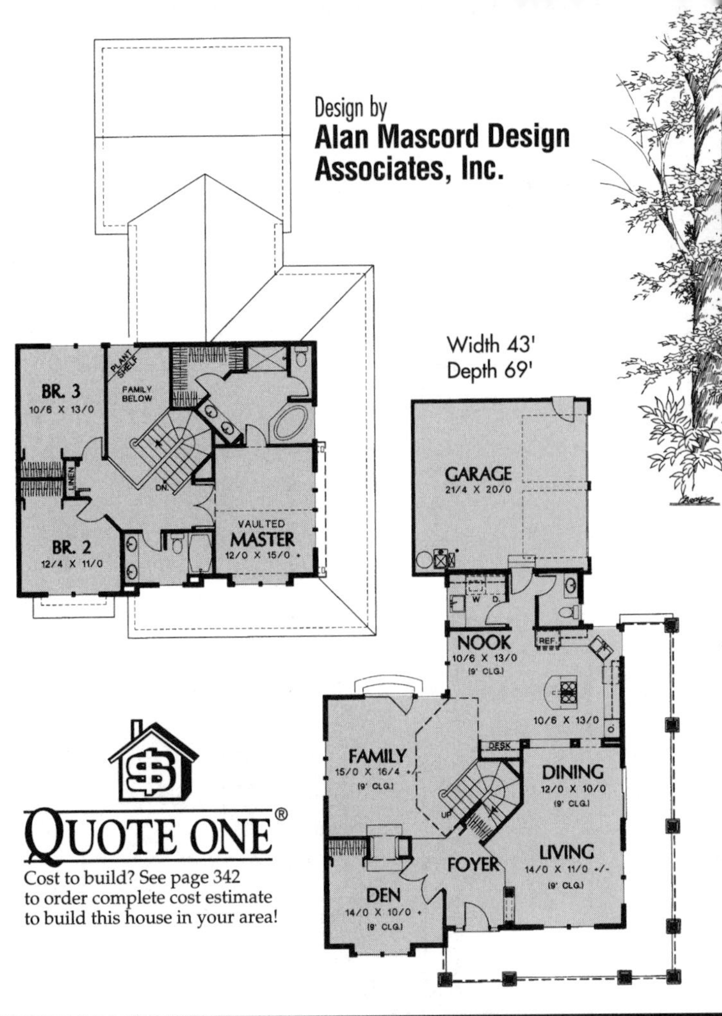
BR. 3
10/6 X 13/0
FAMILY BELOW
PLANT SHELF
LINEN
DN.
BR. 2
12/4 X 11/0
VAULTED
MASTER
12/0 X 15/0 +
GARAGE
21/4 X 20/0
W
D
NOOK
10/6 X 13/0
(9' CLG.)
REF.
10/6 X 13/0
DESK
FAMILY
15/0 X 16/4 +/-
(9' CLG.)
DINING
12/0 X 10/0
(9' CLG.)
UP
FOYER
LIVING
14/0 X 11/0 +/-
(9' CLG.)
DEN
14/0 X 10/0 +
(9' CLG.)

Design by
Alan Mascord Design Associates, Inc.

Width 43'
Depth 69'

QUOTE ONE®
Cost to build? See page 342 to order complete cost estimate to build this house in your area!

Design 9557

First Floor: 1,371 square feet
Second Floor: 916 square feet
Total: 2,287 square feet

■ The decorative pillars and the wraparound porch give a perfect introduction to this charming bungalow. Inside, from the foyer where an angled stairway leads to the second level, French doors lead to the den that shares a see-through fireplace with the two-story family room. The large island kitchen includes a writing desk, corner sink, breakfast nook and an efficient utility room. Upstairs, the master suite is a real treat with its French-door access, vaulted ceiling and luxurious bath. Two secondary bedrooms and a full bath complete the second floor.

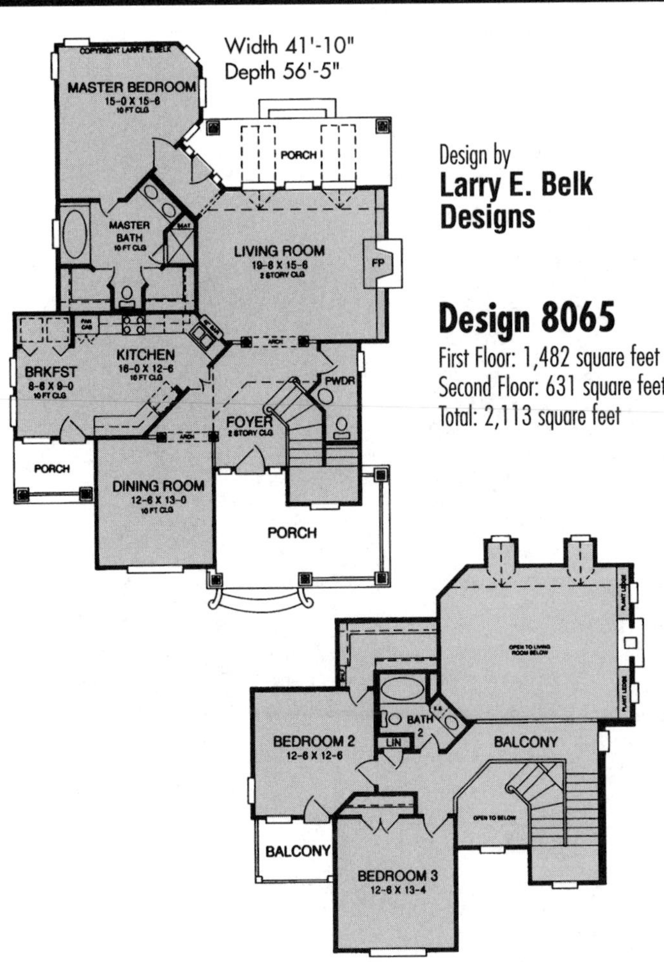
MASTER BEDROOM
15-0 X 15-6
PORCH
MASTER BATH
LIVING ROOM
19-8 X 15-6
2 STORY CLG
FP
BRKFST
8-6 X 9-0
KITCHEN
16-0 X 12-6
PWDR
FOYER
2 STORY CLG
PORCH
DINING ROOM
12-6 X 13-0
PORCH
BEDROOM 2
12-6 X 12-6
BATH 2
LIN
BALCONY
BALCONY
BEDROOM 3
12-6 X 13-4

Width 41'-10"
Depth 56'-5"

Design by
Larry E. Belk Designs

Design 8065

First Floor: 1,482 square feet
Second Floor: 631 square feet
Total: 2,113 square feet

■ Four-square design reminiscent of the 1940s gives this home its landmark look. An inviting porch opens to a two-story foyer. Straight ahead, the living room is visible through two columns mounted on pedestals and connected by a graceful arch. Dormers located in the living room's vaulted ceiling flood the area with natural light. The dining room is situated nearby and entered through another arched opening. A large kitchen and a sunny breakfast room invite casual conversations and lingering over coffee. The master bedroom includes a luxurious master bath with His and Hers walk-in closets, a soothing whirlpool tub and a separate shower. Two additional bedrooms (one with a balcony) and a full bath share the second floor. Please specify crawlspace or slab foundation when ordering.

Design 9525

First Floor: 1,396 square feet
Second Floor: 523 square feet
Total: 1,919 square feet

Design by
Alan Mascord Design Associates, Inc.

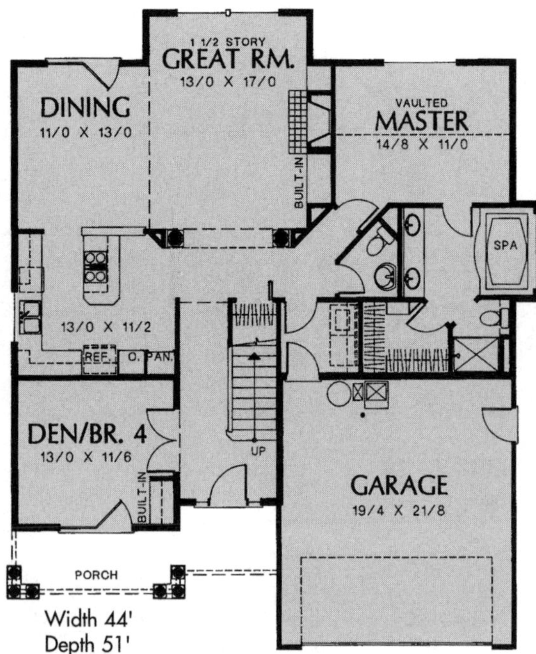

1 1/2 STORY
GREAT RM.
13/0 X 17/0
DINING
11/0 X 13/0
VAULTED
MASTER
14/8 X 11/0
BUILT-IN
SPA
13/0 X 11/2
REF.
O. PAN.
DEN/BR. 4
13/0 X 11/6
BUILT-IN
UP
GARAGE
19/4 X 21/8
PORCH
Width 44'
Depth 51'

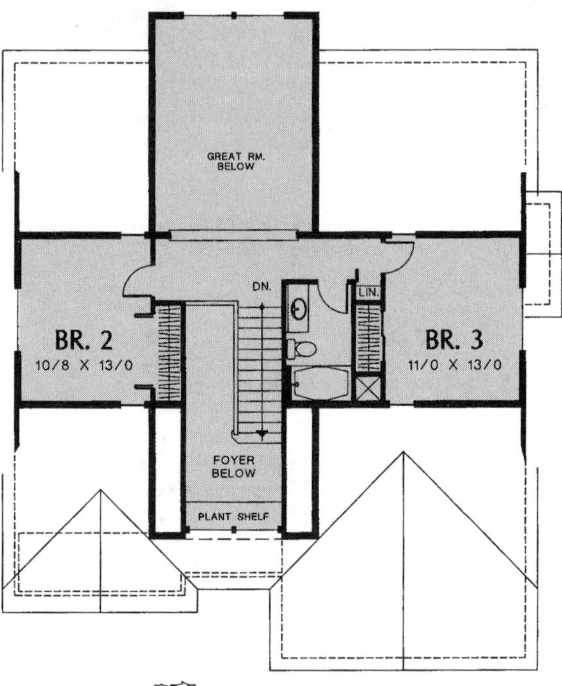

GREAT RM.
BELOW
DN.
LIN.
BR. 2
10/8 X 13/0
BR. 3
11/0 X 13/0
FOYER
BELOW
PLANT SHELF

■ Double pillars reminiscent of the Craftsman style set a comfortable tone in this charming bungalow. A two-story foyer leads to a modern floor plan starting with the front den (or make it a fourth bedroom). Living areas center on the casual life and include a great room with fireplace that opens directly to the dining room. The kitchen is L-shaped for convenience and features an island cooktop. The master suite is on the first floor and sports a vaulted ceiling and bath with spa tub and separate shower. The upper floor holds two secondary bedrooms and a full bath. The open staircase is decorated with a plant shelf that receives light from double windows over the foyer.

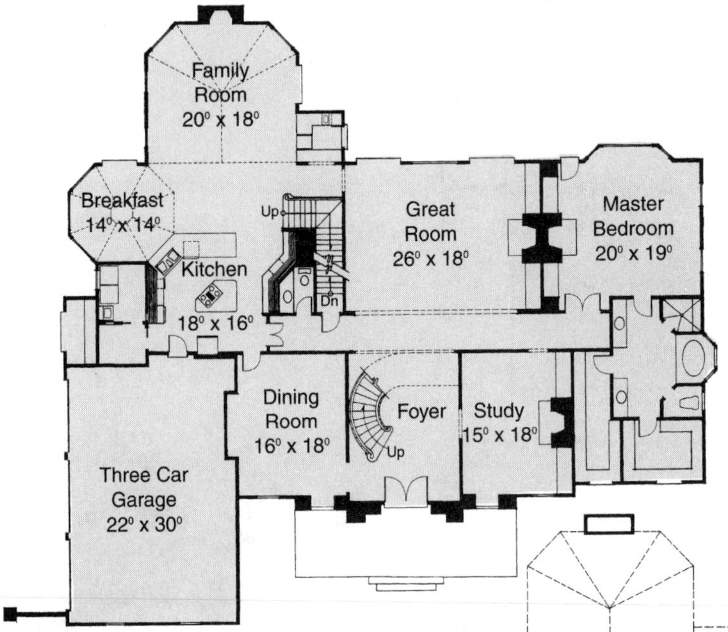

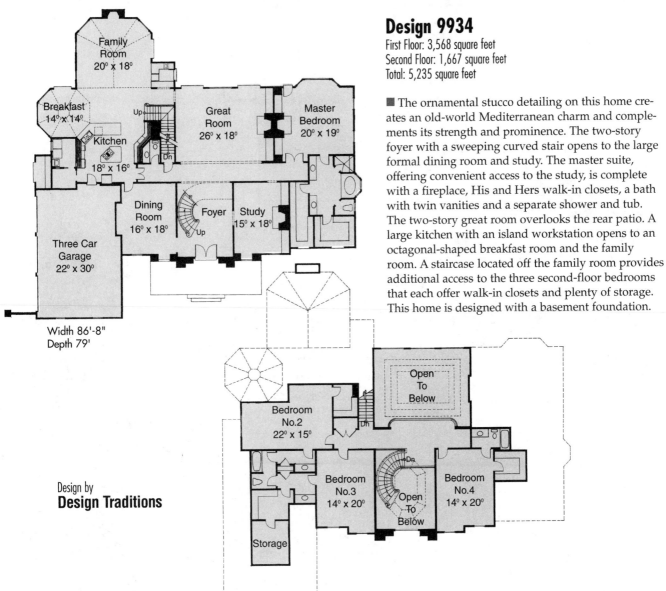

Design 9934

First Floor: 3,568 square feet
Second Floor: 1,667 square feet
Total: 5,235 square feet

■ The ornamental stucco detailing on this home creates an old-world Mediterranean charm and complements its strength and prominence. The two-story foyer with a sweeping curved stair opens to the large formal dining room and study. The master suite, offering convenient access to the study, is complete with a fireplace, His and Hers walk-in closets, a bath with twin vanities and a separate shower and tub. The two-story great room overlooks the rear patio. A large kitchen with an island workstation opens to an octagonal-shaped breakfast room and the family room. A staircase located off the family room provides additional access to the three second-floor bedrooms that each offer walk-in closets and plenty of storage. This home is designed with a basement foundation.

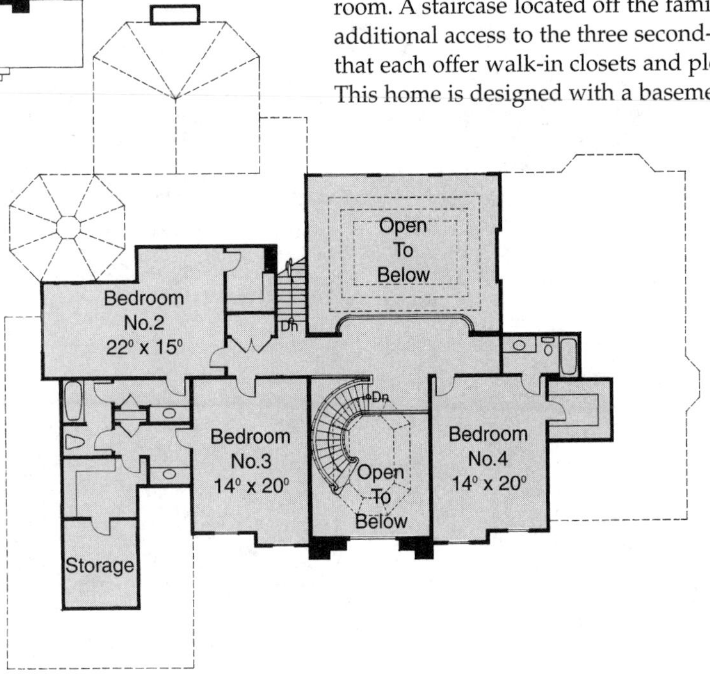

Width 86'-8"
Depth 79'

Design by
Design Traditions

Design 9936

First Floor: 3,902 square feet
Second Floor: 2,159 square feet
Total: 6,061 square feet

■ The entry to this classic home is framed with a sweeping double staircase and four large columns topped with a pediment. The two-story foyer is flanked by spacious living and dining rooms. Beyond the foyer, the home is designed with rooms that offer maximum livability. The two-story family room, which has a central fireplace, opens to the study and a solarium. A spacious U-shaped kitchen features a central island cooktop. An additional staircase off the breakfast room offers convenient access to the second floor. Of the five bedrooms, the master suite is the most impressive. It features deck access and a bath fit for a king. A walk-in closet with an ironing board will provide room for everything. Four bedrooms upstairs enjoy large proportions. This home is designed with a basement foundation.

Design by
Design Traditions

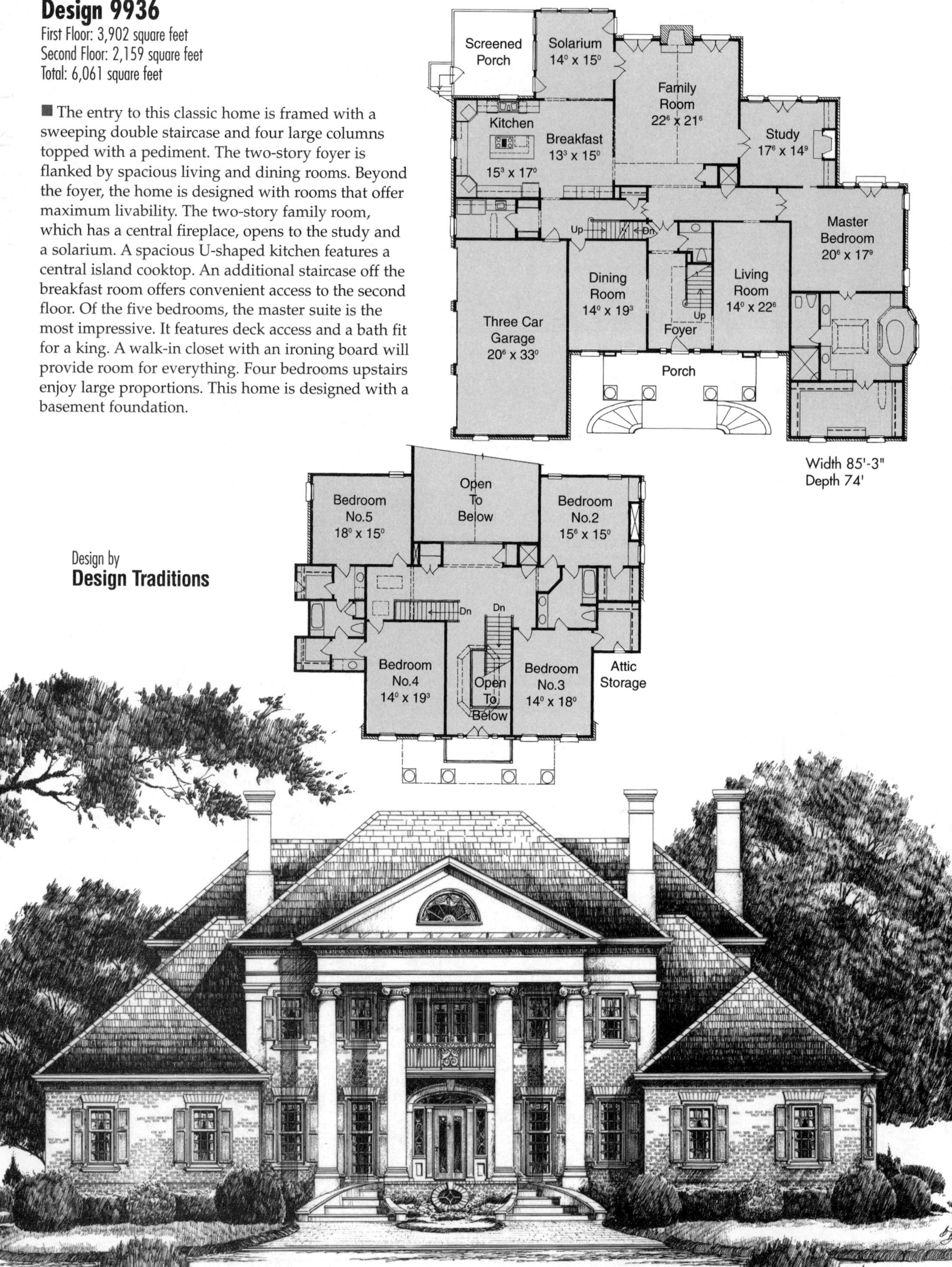

Screened Porch
Solarium 14^{0} x 15^{0}
Family Room 22^{6} x 21^{6}
Kitchen 15^{3} x 17^{0}
Breakfast 13^{3} x 15^{0}
Study 17^{6} x 14^{9}
Master Bedroom 20^{6} x 17^{9}
Up
Dn
Three Car Garage 20^{6} x 33^{0}
Dining Room 14^{0} x 19^{3}
Foyer
Up
Living Room 14^{0} x 22^{6}
Porch
Width 85'-3"
Depth 74'
Bedroom No.5 18^{0} x 15^{0}
Open To Below
Bedroom No.2 15^{6} x 15^{0}
Dn
Dn
Bedroom No.4 14^{0} x 19^{3}
Open To Below
Bedroom No.3 14^{0} x 18^{0}
Attic Storage

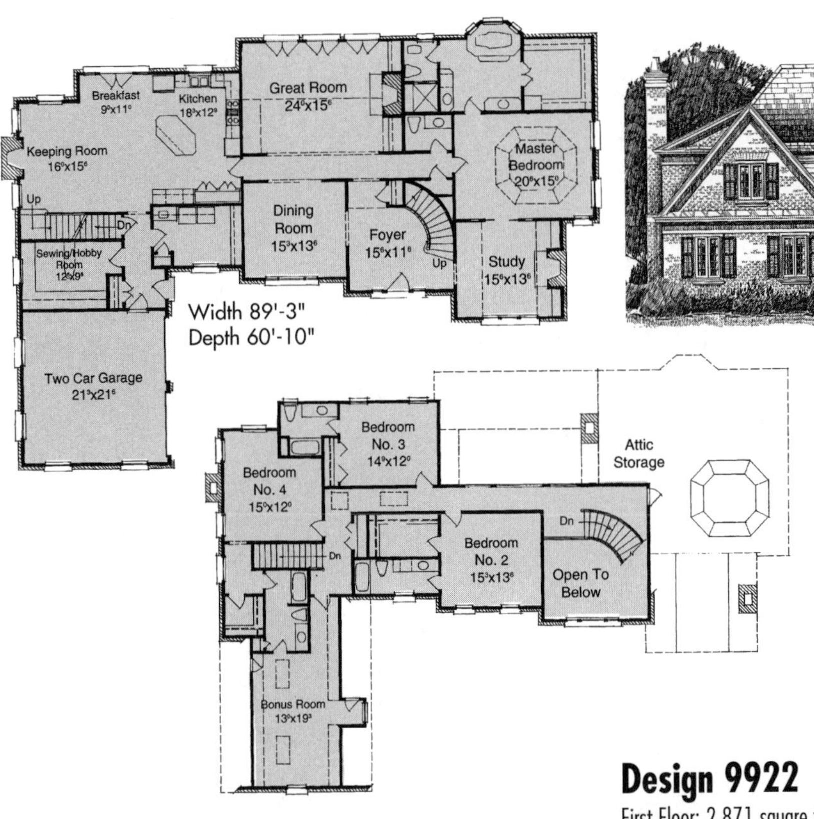
Breakfast
9⁹x11⁰
Kitchen
18⁹x12⁹
Great Room
24⁰x15⁶
Keeping Room
16⁰x15⁶
Master
Bedroom
20⁰x15⁹
Up
Dn
Dining
Room
15³x13⁶
Foyer
15⁶x11⁶
Sewing/Hobby
Room
12⁶x9⁶
Up
Study
15⁰x13⁶
Width 89'-3"
Depth 60'-10"
Two Car Garage
21⁵x21⁶
Bedroom
No. 3
14⁶x12⁰
Attic
Storage
Bedroom
No. 4
15⁶x12⁰
Dn
Dn
Bedroom
No. 2
15³x13⁶
Open To
Below
Bonus Room
13⁹x19³

Design 9922

First Floor: 2,871 square feet
Second Floor: 1,407 square feet
Total: 4,278 square feet
Bonus Room: 324 square feet

Design by
Design Traditions

■ Brick details, casement windows and large expanses of glass add an Old World touch of glamour to this gracious two-story home. Sunlight streams in the two-story foyer which is highlighted by the sweeping curves of the balustrade. For formal occasions, look to the spacious dining room, the inviting study and the vaulted great room. The kitchen, breakfast room and keeping room are designed for casual family living. The master suite provides a quiet retreat with access to the study through pocket doors. Luxury abounds in the spacious master bedroom and the sumptuous bath. Upstairs, three secondary bedrooms each have private baths. This home is designed with a basement foundation.

Design 8079

First Floor: 3,722 square feet
Second Floor: 1,859 square feet
Total: 5,581 square feet

■ A richly detailed entrance sets the elegant tone of this luxurious design. Rising gracefully from the two-story foyer, the staircase is a fine prelude to the great room beyond, where a fantastic span of windows on the back wall overlooks the rear grounds. The dining room is located off the entry and has a lovely coffered ceiling. The kitchen, breakfast room and sunroom are conveniently grouped for casual entertaining. The elaborate master suite has a coffered ceiling, private sitting room and a spa-style bath. The second level consists of four bedrooms with private baths and a large game room featuring a rear stair.

Design by
Larry E. Belk Designs

SUN ROOM
ADDITIONAL GARAGE
PORCH
BRKFST AREA
MASTER BEDROOM
PORCH
SIDE PORCH
SITTING
DRESSING AREA
KITCHEN
GREAT ROOM
DOUBLE GARAGE
HIS CLOSET
MASTER BATH
HER CLOSET
PANTRY
STUDY
ENTRY
DINING ROOM
STORAGE
SINGLE GARAGE
PORCH
Width 127'-10"
Depth 83'-9"
BALCONY
BEDROOM 5
BEDROOM 4
GAME ROOM
ATTIC
BALCONY
BEDROOM 2
BEDROOM 3

Design 8908

First Floor: 3,985 square feet
Second Floor: 2,278 square feet
Total: 6,263 square feet

Design by
Larry W. Garnett & Associates, Inc.

■ First- and second-story bay windows with copper roofs and detailed brick arches at the front entry and veranda recall classic estate homes of the 1920s. The magnificent foyer features an impressive staircase and balcony. The gallery offers a view into the formal living room, which has a fireplace and doors to the terrace. The master suite has a fancy sitting room, a corner fireplace and a lavish bath. The formal dining room shares a two-way fireplace with the pub. Charming French doors close the kitchen and breakfast area to the sun-drenched solarium and family room. Upstairs, four bedrooms with private baths are joined with a game room and library.

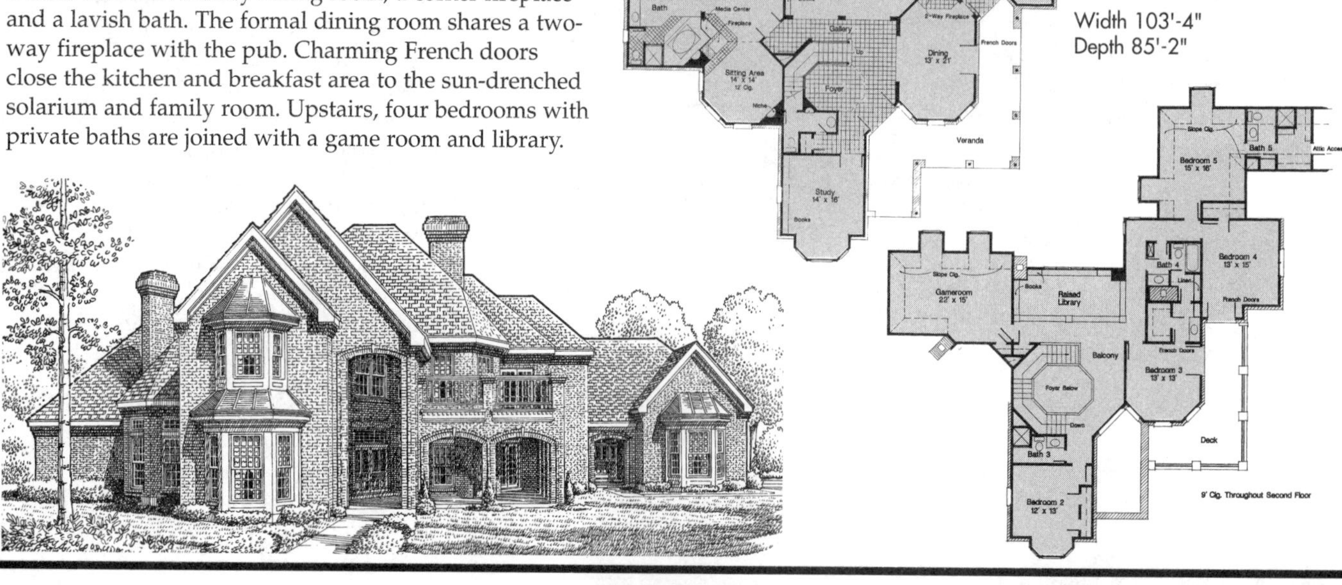
Width 103'-4"
Depth 85'-2"

■ Elegance and luxury define this stately brick-and-stucco home. Creative design continues inside with a dramatic foyer that leads to the formal living and dining rooms and the casual two-story family room. A butler's pantry links the dining room to the grand kitchen. Casual gatherings will be enjoyed in the family room that joins with the breakfast room and kitchen. Here, a solarium and porch invite outdoor living. The exquisite master suite features a lush bath and sunny sitting area. Upstairs, two family bedrooms with private baths, a home office and a hobby room round out the plan. This home is designed with a basement foundation.

Design 9990

First Floor: 3,065 square feet
Second Floor: 1,969 square feet
Total: 5,034 square feet

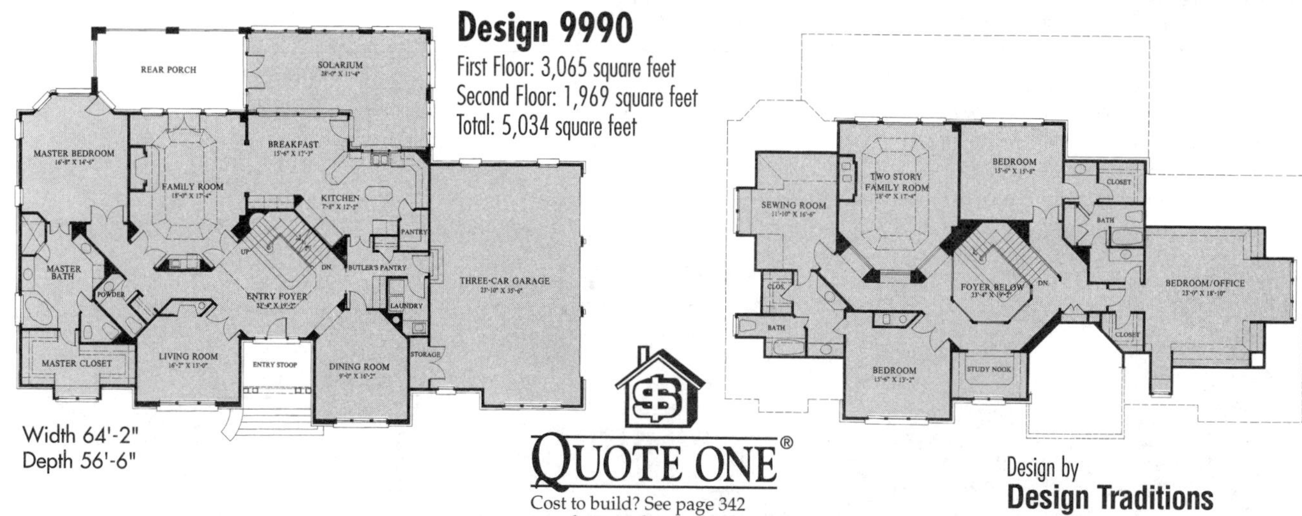
REAR PORCH
SOLARIUM
MASTER BEDROOM
FAMILY ROOM
BREAKFAST
KITCHEN
PANTRY
MASTER BATH
POWDER
ENTRY FOYER
BUTLER'S PANTRY
THREE-CAR GARAGE
LAUNDRY
MASTER CLOSET
LIVING ROOM
ENTRY STOOP
DINING ROOM
STORAGE
SEWING ROOM
TWO STORY FAMILY ROOM
BEDROOM
CLOSET
BATH
FOYER BELOW
BEDROOM/OFFICE
BEDROOM
STUDY NOOK
Width 64'-2"
Depth 56'-6"

QUOTE ONE®

Cost to build? See page 342 to order complete cost estimate to build this house in your area!

Design by
Design Traditions

Design by
Larry W. Garnett & Associates, Inc.

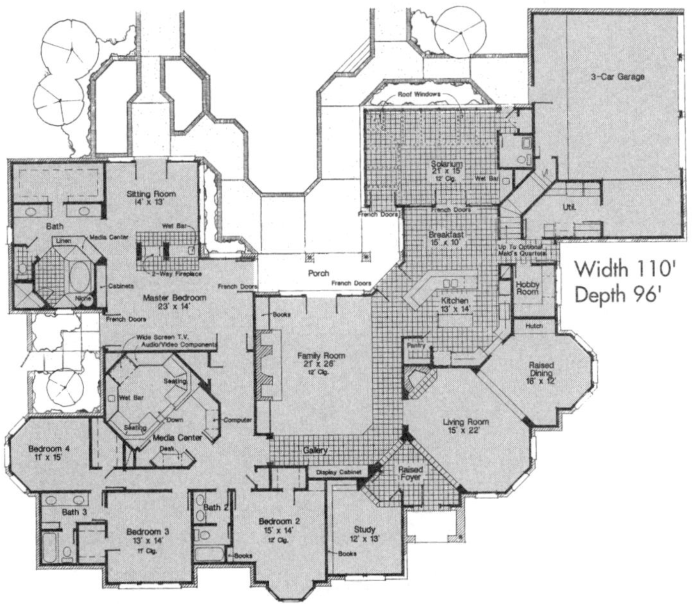
3-Car Garage
Solarium
Breakfast
Kitchen
Util.
Hobby Room
Porch
Sitting Room
Bath
Master Bedroom
Family Room
Raised Dining
Living Room
Media Center
Bedroom 4
Gallery
Raised Foyer
Bath 3
Bedroom 3
Bath 2
Bedroom 2
Study
Width 110'
Depth 96'

Design 8905

Square Footage: 4,958

■ The stately facade of this traditional estate belies the remarkably contemporary floor plan within. Surely a highlight in this open, elegant plan is the media center, just off the main gallery. Fireplaces warm the spacious family and living rooms. A study to the left of the foyer provides built-in bookshelves. The kitchen, with a work island and a large pantry, serves the family room, breakfast room and raised dining room with ease. French doors open to a commodious solarium. Three family bedrooms, one with a bay window, are accompanied by two full baths. The master suite, to the rear of the home, includes a two-way fireplace to the bedroom and the sitting room, easy access to three separate outdoor areas, a built-in media center, and a bath with a separate shower and tub.

Design 8030

First Floor: 2,528 square feet
Second Floor: 1,067 square feet
Total: 3,595 square feet

Design by
Larry E. Belk Designs

■ The massive entry to this beautiful home insures that all who pass will take note of this stately elevation. Upon entering, one steps into a two-story foyer with a gallery effect created by oversized columns and connecting arches. A graceful curved staircase rises from the foyer to the second floor. The dining room is showcased off the foyer. Situated with views to the side and rear of the home, the great room is designed with an offset perfect for a grand piano or a game table. The kitchen and breakfast room are centrally located for access to the rear yard. The master suite features a sitting area and a luxury bath with a two-way fireplace. The second floor completes the home with three bedrooms, two baths and a game room.

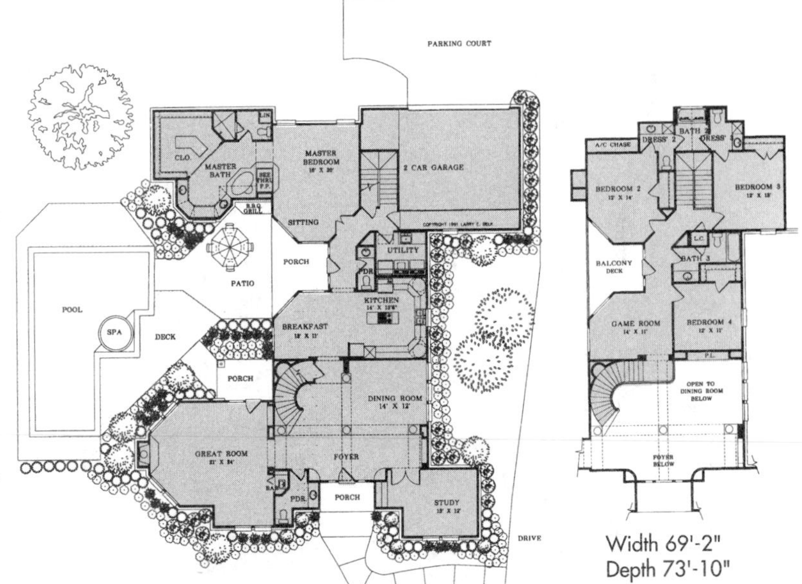
PARKING COURT
MASTER BEDROOM
2 CAR GARAGE
SITTING
PORCH
PATIO
UTILITY
KITCHEN
BREAKFAST
POOL
SPA
DECK
PORCH
DINING ROOM
GREAT ROOM
FOYER
PORCH
STUDY
DRIVE
BEDROOM 2
BEDROOM 3
BALCONY
GAME ROOM
BEDROOM 4
Width 69'-2"
Depth 73'-10"

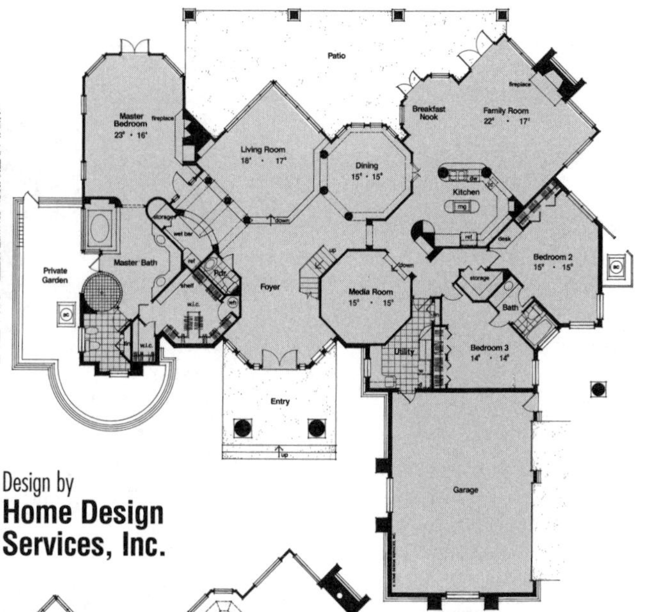

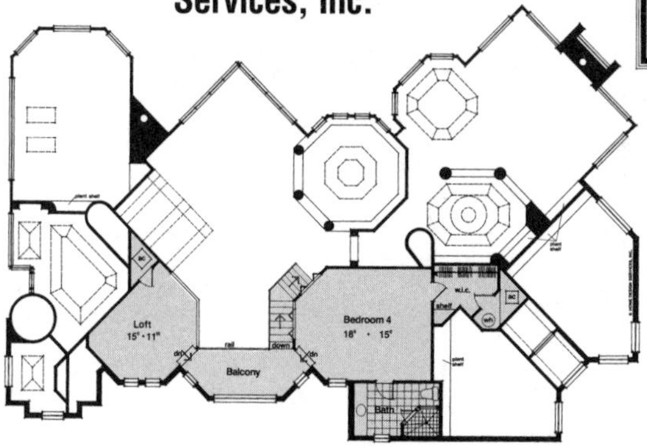

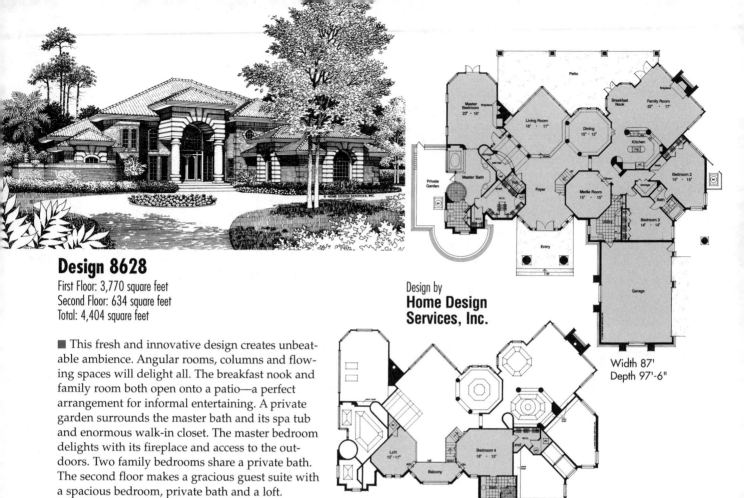

Design 8628

First Floor: 3,770 square feet
Second Floor: 634 square feet
Total: 4,404 square feet

Design by
Home Design Services, Inc.

Width 87'
Depth 97'-6"

■ This fresh and innovative design creates unbeatable ambience. Angular rooms, columns and flowing spaces will delight all. The breakfast nook and family room both open onto a patio—a perfect arrangement for informal entertaining. A private garden surrounds the master bath and its spa tub and enormous walk-in closet. The master bedroom delights with its fireplace and access to the outdoors. Two family bedrooms share a private bath. The second floor makes a gracious guest suite with a spacious bedroom, private bath and a loft.

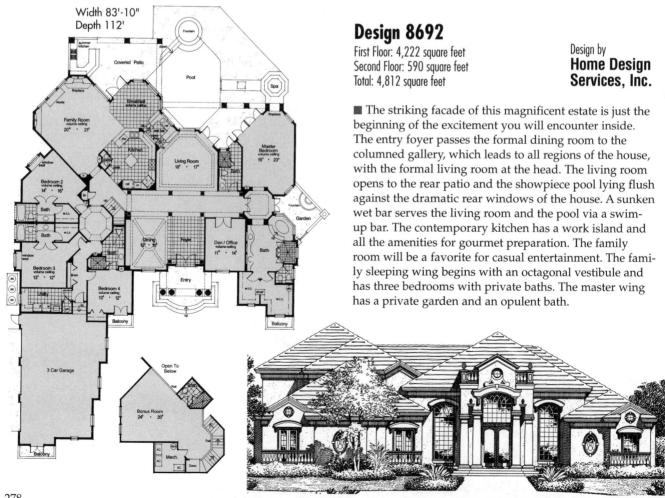

Width 83'-10"
Depth 112'

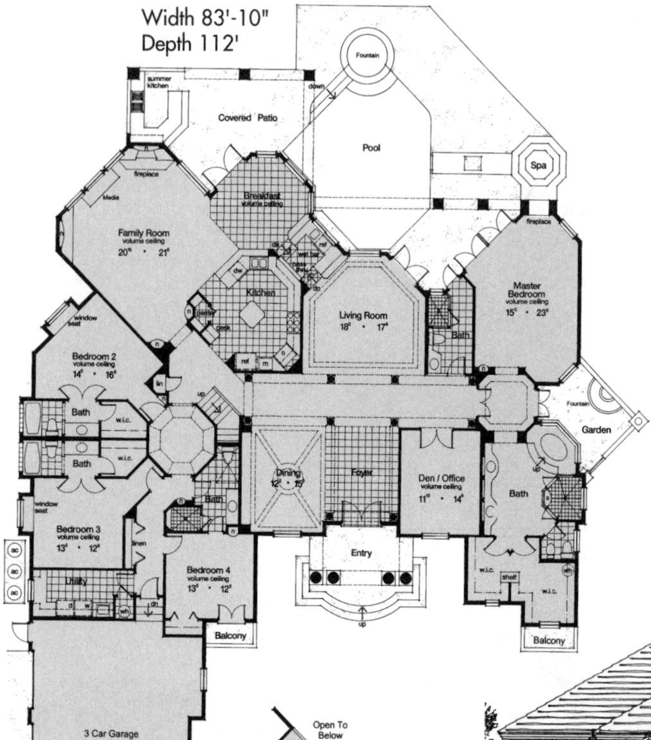

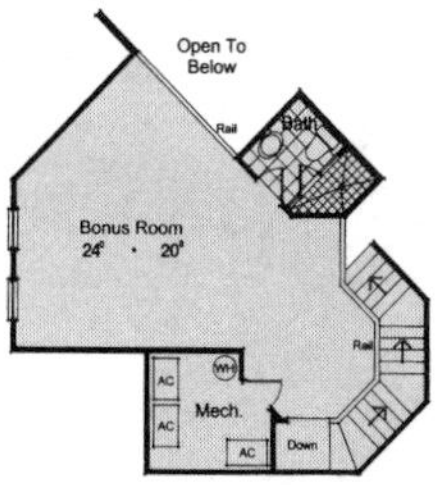

Design 8692

First Floor: 4,222 square feet
Second Floor: 590 square feet
Total: 4,812 square feet

Design by
Home Design Services, Inc.

■ The striking facade of this magnificent estate is just the beginning of the excitement you will encounter inside. The entry foyer passes the formal dining room to the columned gallery, which leads to all regions of the house, with the formal living room at the head. The living room opens to the rear patio and the showpiece pool lying flush against the dramatic rear windows of the house. A sunken wet bar serves the living room and the pool via a swim-up bar. The contemporary kitchen has a work island and all the amenities for gourmet preparation. The family room will be a favorite for casual entertainment. The family sleeping wing begins with an octagonal vestibule and has three bedrooms with private baths. The master wing has a private garden and an opulent bath.

Design 8626

First Floor: 3,236 square feet
Second Floor: 494 square feet
Total: 3,730 square feet

■ If you want to build a home that is light years ahead of most other designs, non-traditional, yet addresses every need for your family, this showcase home is for you. From the moment you walk into this home you are confronted with wonderful interior architecture that reflects contemporary, yet refined taste. The exterior says European Villa; the interior creates special excitement. Note the special rounded corners found throughout the home and the many amenities. The master suite is especially appealing with fireplace and grand bath. Upstairs are a library/sitting room and a very private den or guest bedroom.

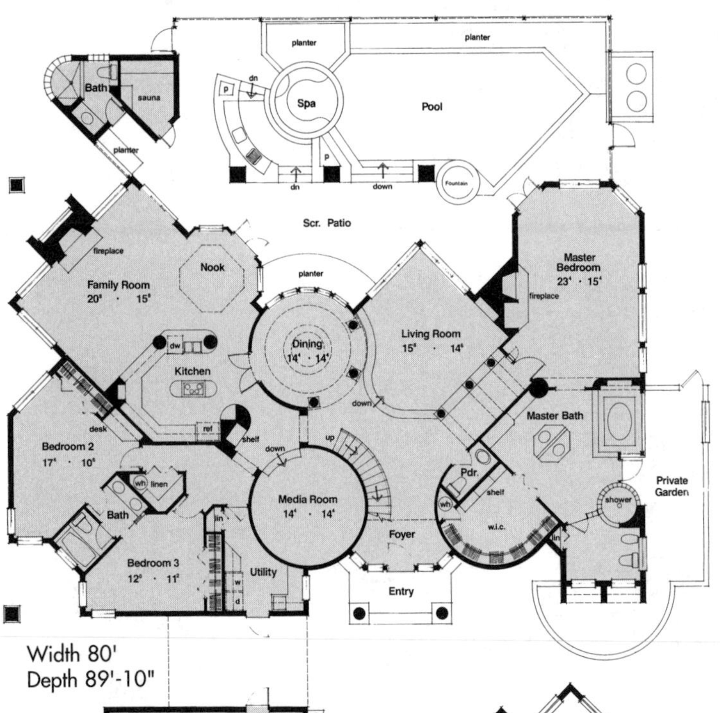
planter
planter
Bath
sauna
Spa
Pool
Fountain
Scr. Patio
fireplace
Family Room
20' · 15'
Nook
planter
Dining
14' · 14'
Living Room
15' · 14'
Master Bedroom
23' · 15'
fireplace
Kitchen
Bedroom 2
17' · 10'
desk
Media Room
14' · 14'
Master Bath
Private Garden
shower
Pdr.
shelf
w.i.c.
Bath
linen
Bedroom 3
12' · 11'
Utility
Foyer
Entry
Width 80'
Depth 89'-10"
Double Garage

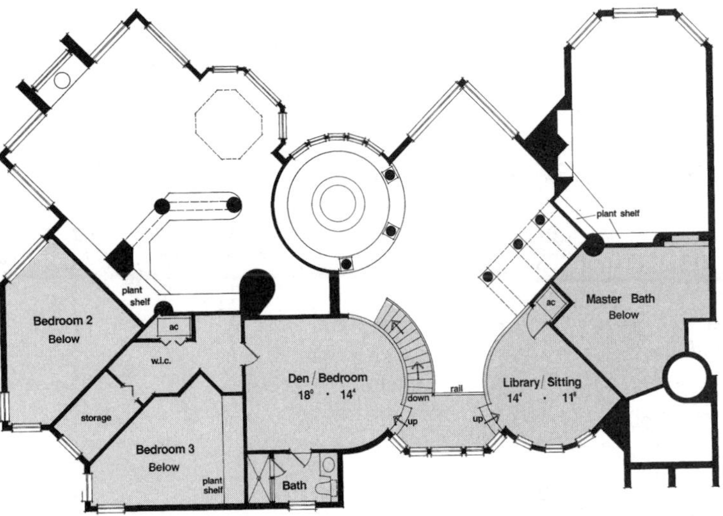
plant shelf
Bedroom 2
Below
w.i.c.
storage
Bedroom 3
Below
plant shelf
Den / Bedroom
18' · 14'
rail
down
up
Library / Sitting
14' · 11'
Master Bath
Below
plant shelf
Bath

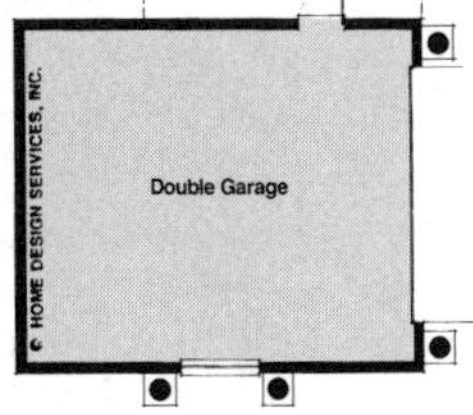

Design by
Home Design Services, Inc.

Design 6635

First Floor: 4,760 square feet
Second Floor: 1,552 square feet
Total: 6,312 square feet

QUOTE ONE®

Cost to build? See page 342 to order complete cost estimate to build this house in your area!

Design by
The Sater Design Collection

■ As beautiful from the rear as from the front, this home features a spectacular blend of arch-top windows, French doors and balusters. An impressive, informal leisure room has a sixteen-foot-high tray ceiling, an entertainment center and a grand ale bar. The large, gourmet kitchen is well appointed and easily serves the nook and formal dining room. The master suite has a large bedroom and a bayed sitting area. Walk-in closets and a curved, glass-block shower are highlights in the bath. The staircase leads to the secondary guest suites, two of which have observation decks to the rear.

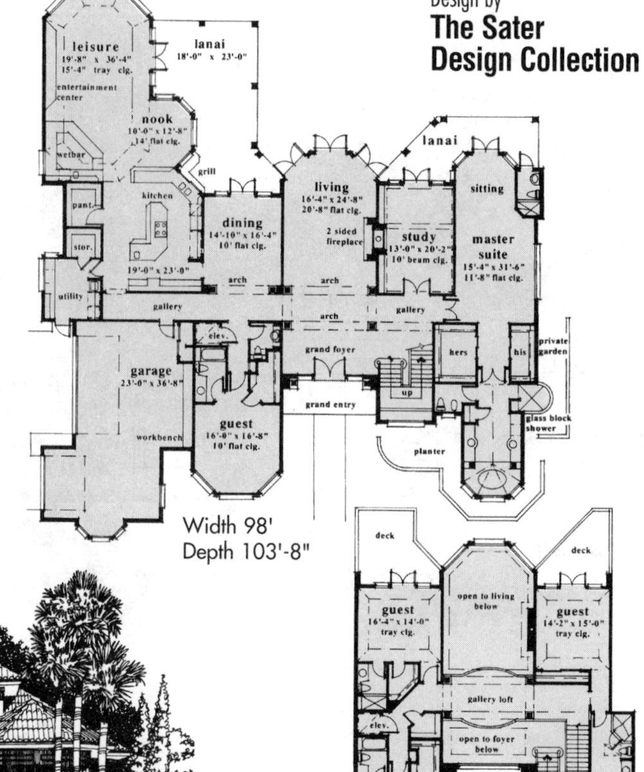
leisure
lanai
entertainment center
nook
wetbar
grill
kitchen
pantry
stor.
utility
dining
living
2 sided fireplace
study
lanai
sitting
master suite
arch
gallery
grand foyer
elev.
hers
his
private garden
glass block shower
garage
workbench
guest
grand entry
up
planter
Width 98'
Depth 103'-8"
deck
deck
guest
open to living below
guest
gallery loft
elev.
open to foyer below
down
guest

Design by
Home Design Services, Inc.

Design 8690

Square Footage: 3,556

■ A beautiful curved portico provides a majestic entrance to this one-story estate. Curved volume ceilings in the formal living and dining rooms continue the extraordinary style. The family wing is geared for casual living with a modified galley kitchen with a cooktop island and breakfast nook, a comfortable family room and a private hall leading to two family bedrooms that share a compartmented bath. The master suite has a two-way fireplace, a sitting room, an exercise area with a wet bar and a luxurious twin bath.

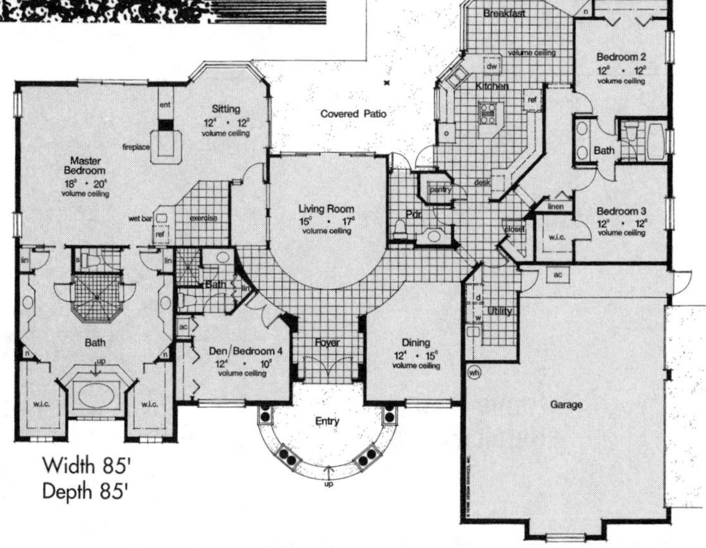
summer kitchen
fireplace
Family Room
vaulted ceiling
Breakfast
Bedroom 2
volume ceiling
Kitchen
Covered Patio
Sitting
volume ceiling
Master Bedroom
volume ceiling
fireplace
exercise
wet bar
Living Room
volume ceiling
pantry
Pdr.
Bath
linen
Bedroom 3
volume ceiling
w.i.c.
Bath
Den/Bedroom 4
volume ceiling
Foyer
Dining
volume ceiling
Utility
Garage
w.i.c.
w.i.c.
Entry
up

Width 85'
Depth 85'

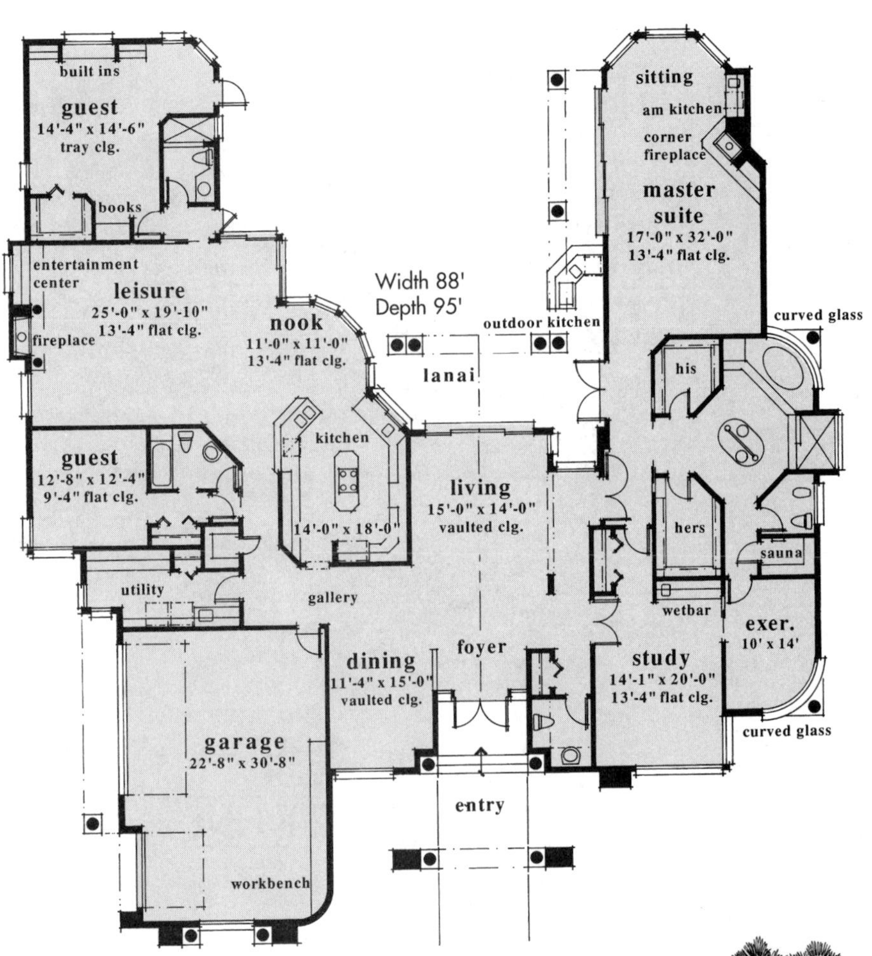
built ins
guest
14'-4" x 14'-6"
tray clg.
books
entertainment center
leisure
25'-0" x 19'-10"
13'-4" flat clg.
fireplace
nook
11'-0" x 11'-0"
13'-4" flat clg.
Width 88'
Depth 95'
outdoor kitchen
lanai
kitchen
14'-0" x 18'-0"
guest
12'-8" x 12'-4"
9'-4" flat clg.
living
15'-0" x 14'-0"
vaulted clg.
utility
gallery
dining
11'-4" x 15'-0"
vaulted clg.
foyer
garage
22'-8" x 30'-8"
workbench
entry
sitting
am kitchen
corner fireplace
master suite
17'-0" x 32'-0"
13'-4" flat clg.
curved glass
his
hers
sauna
wetbar
exer.
10' x 14'
study
14'-1" x 20'-0"
13'-4" flat clg.
curved glass

Design 6636

Square Footage: 4,565

■ A free-standing entryway is the focal point of this luxurious residence. It has an arch motif that is carried through to the rear using a gable roof and a vaulted ceiling from the foyer out to the lanai. High ceilings are found throughout the home, creating a spacious atmosphere. The kitchen that features a cooktop island and plenty of counter space, opens to the leisure area with a handy snack bar. Two guest suites with private baths are just off this casual living area. The master wing is truly pampering, stretching the entire length of the home. The suite has a large sitting area, a corner fireplace and a morning kitchen. The bath features an island vanity, a raised tub with a curved glass wall overlooking a private garden, a sauna and separate closets. An exercise room has a curved glass wall and a pocket door to the study, where a wet bar is ready to serve up refreshment. Outdoor living will be welcome, thanks to a lovely rear lanai and an outdoor kitchen.

Design by
The Sater Design Collection

Design 6619

First Floor: 2,725 square feet
Second Floor: 1,418 square feet
Total: 4,143 square feet

Design by
The Sater Design Collection

QUOTE ONE®
Cost to build? See page 342 to order complete cost estimate to build this house in your area!

■ Florida living takes off in this grand design. A grand room gains attention as a superb entertaining area. A through-fireplace here connects this room to the dining room. Sets of sliding glass doors offer passage to an expansive rear deck. In the bayed study, quiet time is assured—or slip out onto the deck for a breather. A full bath connects the study and Bedroom 2. Bedroom 3 sits on the opposite side of the house and enjoys its own bath. The kitchen is fully functional with a large work island and a sunny connecting breakfast nook. Upstairs, the master bedroom suite is something to behold. His and Hers baths, a through-fireplace and access to an upper deck all characterize this room. A guest bedroom suite with a bay window is located on the other side of the upper floor and will make visits a real pleasure.

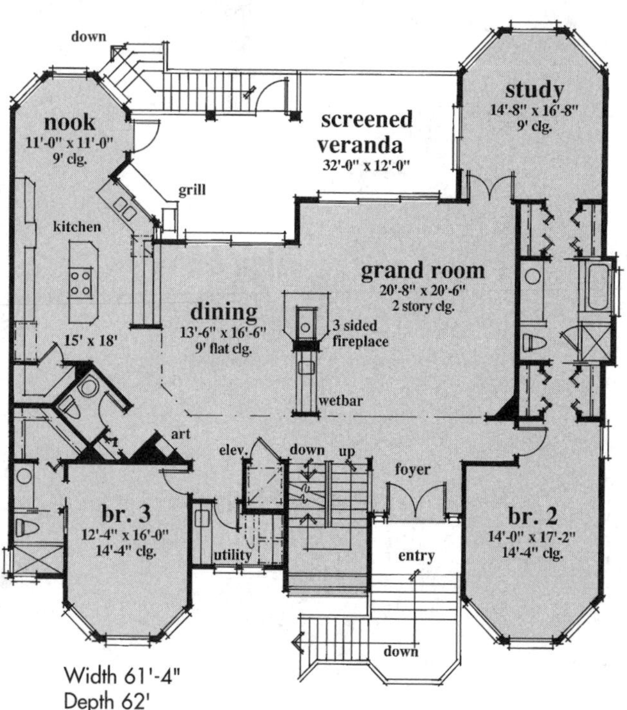
down
nook
11'-0" x 11'-0"
9' clg.
screened
veranda
32'-0" x 12'-0"
study
14'-8" x 16'-8"
9' clg.
grill
kitchen
grand room
20'-8" x 20'-6"
2 story clg.
dining
13'-6" x 16'-6"
9' flat clg.
3 sided
fireplace
15' x 18'
wetbar
art
elev.
down
up
foyer
br. 3
12'-4" x 16'-0"
14'-4" clg.
utility
entry
br. 2
14'-0" x 17'-2"
14'-4" clg.
down

Width 61'-4"
Depth 62'

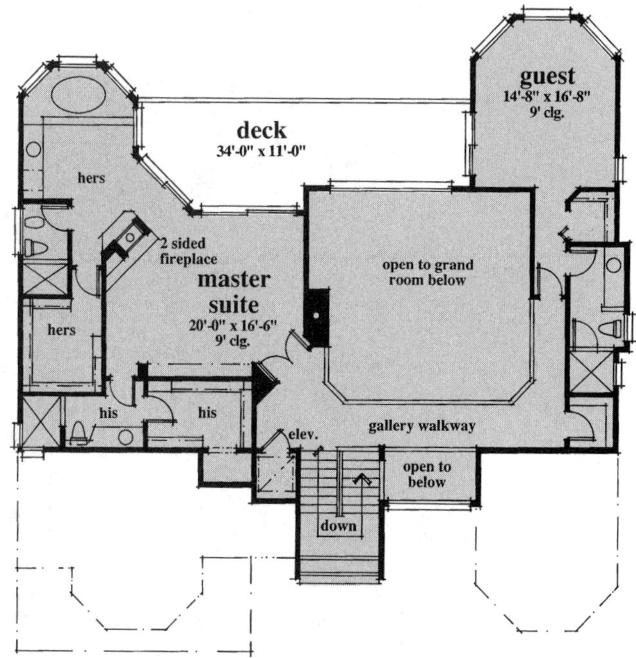
guest
14'-8" x 16'-8"
9' clg.
deck
34'-0" x 11'-0"
hers
2 sided
fireplace
master
suite
20'-0" x 16'-6"
9' clg.
open to grand
room below
hers
his
his
elev.
gallery walkway
open to
below
down

© The Sater Group, Inc.
HOLZHAUER INC. 95

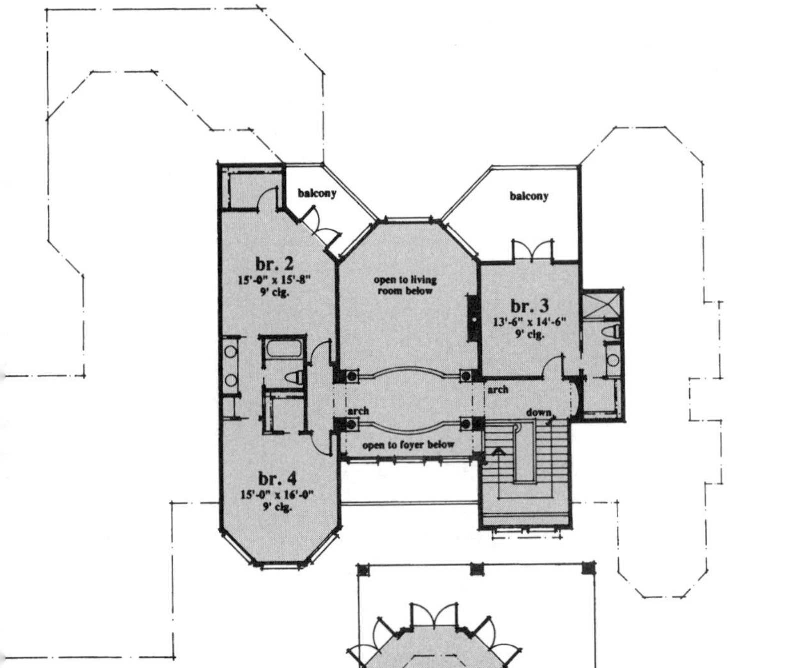

■ A marvelously arched entry welcomes you to call this beautiful mansion home. Inside, the two-story foyer leads under the second floor balcony into the lavish living room which is graced by a through-fireplace to the study and three sets of double French doors to the rear terrace. A huge octagonal leisure room at the back of the plan offers a built-in entertainment center and mirrors the living room's three sets of double French doors. A large kitchen with a cooktop island easily serves both the formal dining room and the sunny breakfast nook. The master suite, located at the far right of the plan, is lit from the bay window and has access to a rear veranda. Large His and Hers walk-in closets will fulfill all your storage needs and a sumptuous master bath is designed to pamper. Upstairs, three family bedrooms each have walk-in closets. Two share a full bath with twin vanities while the third has a private bath. A three-car garage will easily handle the family fleet. Please specify basement or slab foundation when ordering.

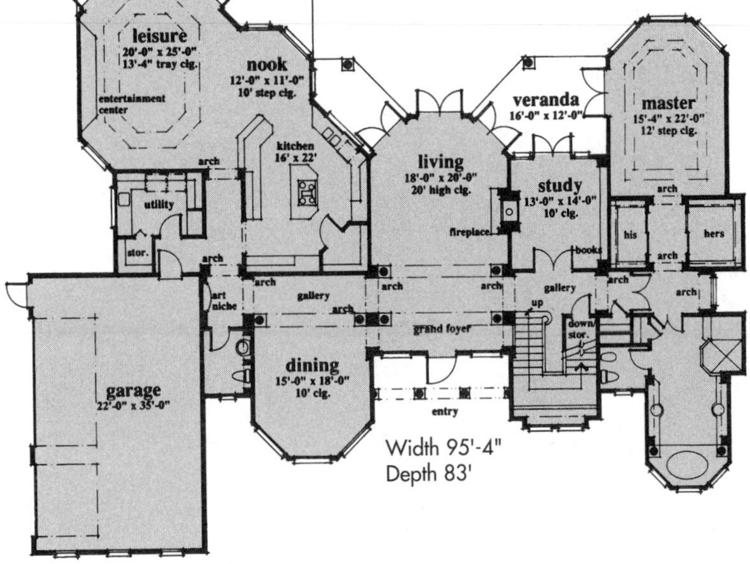

Design 6651

First Floor: 3,546 square feet
Second Floor: 1,213 square feet
Total: 4,759 square feet

Design by
The Sater Design Collection

Width 95'-4"
Depth 83'

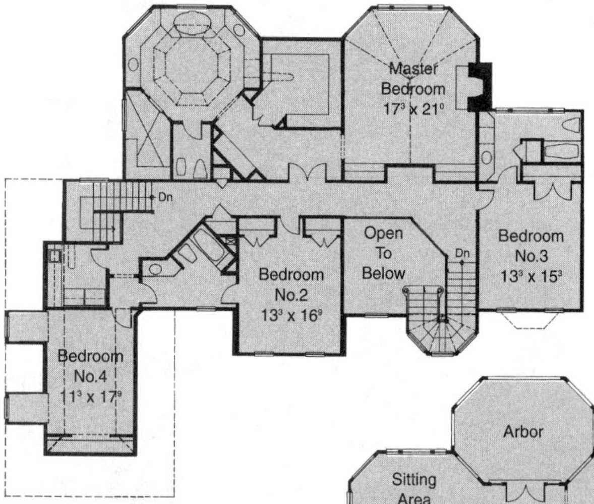

Design 9931

First Floor: 2,161 square feet
Second Floor: 2,110 square feet
Total: 4,271 square feet

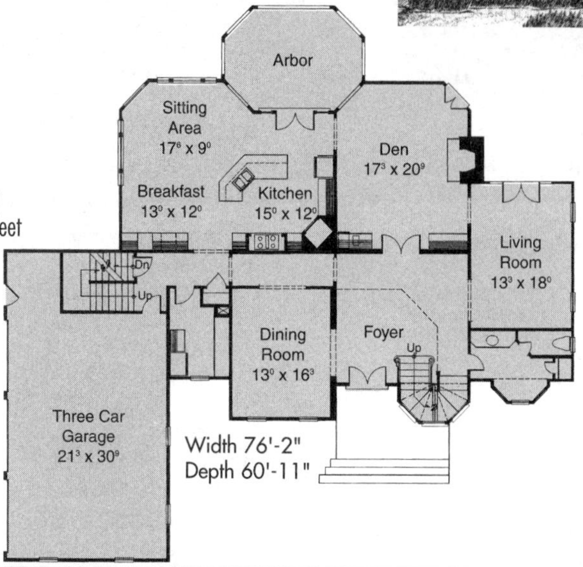

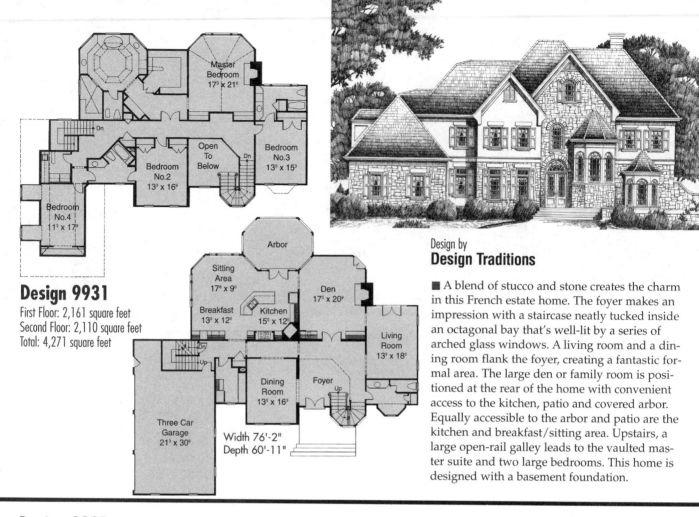

Width 76'-2"
Depth 60'-11"

Design by
Design Traditions

■ A blend of stucco and stone creates the charm in this French estate home. The foyer makes an impression with a staircase neatly tucked inside an octagonal bay that's well-lit by a series of arched glass windows. A living room and a dining room flank the foyer, creating a fantastic formal area. The large den or family room is positioned at the rear of the home with convenient access to the kitchen, patio and covered arbor. Equally accessible to the arbor and patio are the kitchen and breakfast/sitting area. Upstairs, a large open-rail galley leads to the vaulted master suite and two large bedrooms. This home is designed with a basement foundation.

Design 9921

First Floor: 2,832 square feet
Second Floor: 1,664 square feet
Total: 4,496 square feet
Bonus: 425 square feet

Design by
Design Traditions

■ Inside this exquisite country estate, the arrangement of rooms is well-suited for a variety of lifestyles. The large dining room and great room provide the opportunity for formal receiving and entertaining. For casual living, look to the spacious kitchen, the multi-windowed breakfast room or the cozy keeping room with its welcoming fireplace. Conveniently, yet privately located, the master suite is designed to take full advantage of the adjacent study and family area. The second floor contains three bedrooms, three full baths and a bonus room that also functions as Bedroom 5. This home is designed with a basement foundation.

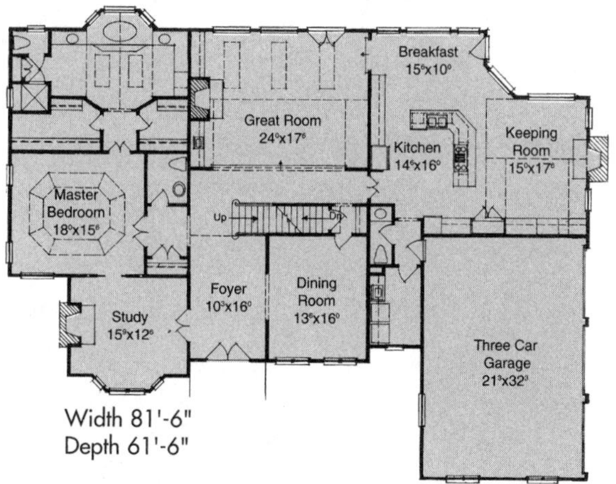
Breakfast 15⁶x10⁰
Great Room 24⁰x17⁶
Kitchen 14⁰x16⁰
Keeping Room 15⁰x17⁶
Master Bedroom 18⁰x15⁶
Up
Dn
Foyer 10⁶x16⁰
Dining Room 13⁶x16⁰
Study 15⁶x12⁶
Three Car Garage 21⁵x32³
Width 81'-6"
Depth 61'-6"

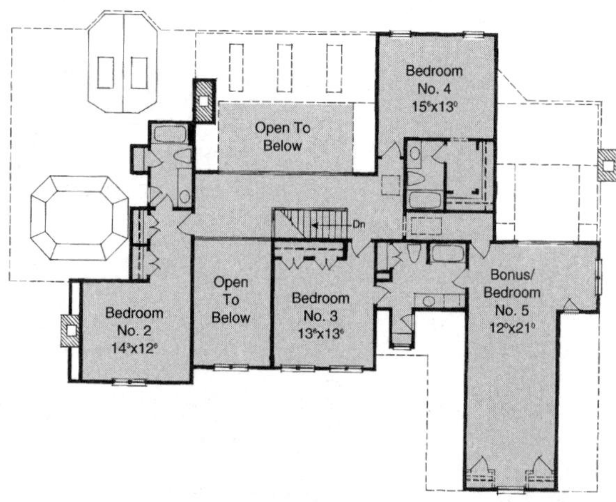
Bedroom No. 4 15⁶x13⁰
Open To Below
Dn
Bedroom No. 2 14⁰x12⁰
Open To Below
Bedroom No. 3 13⁶x13⁶
Bonus/ Bedroom No. 5 12⁰x21⁰

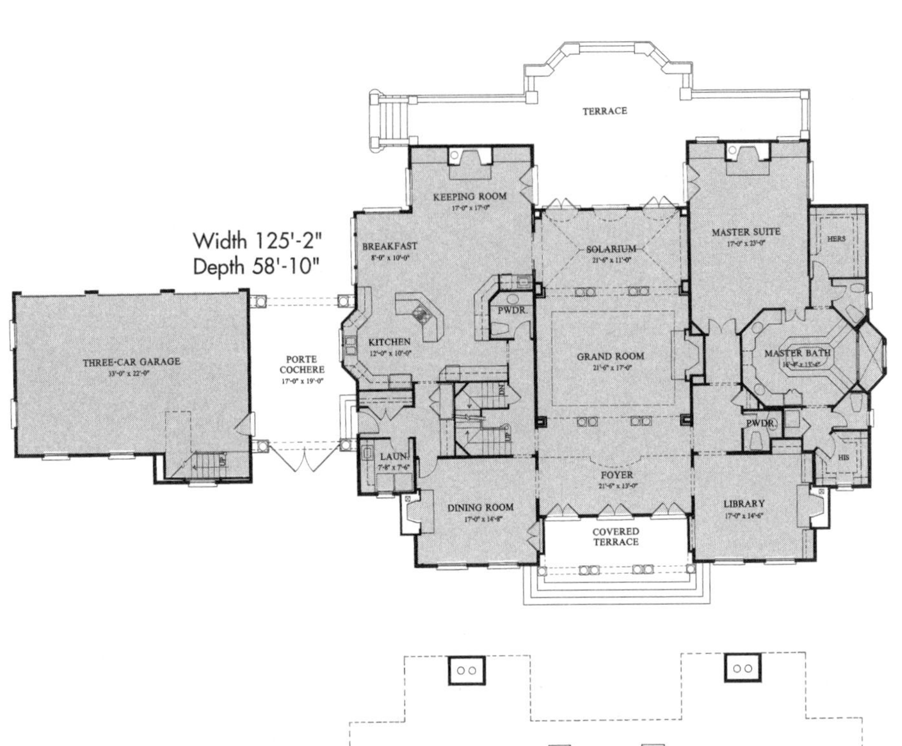
Width 125'-2"
Depth 58'-10"
TERRACE
KEEPING ROOM
BREAKFAST
SOLARIUM
MASTER SUITE
HERS
KITCHEN
PWDR
GRAND ROOM
MASTER BATH
THREE-CAR GARAGE
PORTE COCHERE
PWDR
LAUN
HIS
FOYER
DINING ROOM
LIBRARY
COVERED TERRACE
FUTURE KID'S DEN/ PLAYROOM
BEDROOM
BATH
FUTURE MAID'S SUITE
HALLWAY
FUTURE STUDIO
BATH
BATH
BEDROOM
OPEN TO FOYER BELOW
BEDROOM

Design 9937

First Floor: 3,703 square feet
Second Floor: 1,427 square feet
Total: 5,130 square feet

■ This magnificent estate is detailed with exterior charm: a porte cochere connecting the detached garage to the house, a covered terrace and oval windows. The first floor consists of a lavish master suite, a cozy library with a fireplace, an absolutely stupendous grand room/solarium combination, an elegantly formal dining room with another fireplace and a kitchen/breakfast room/keeping room that will delight everyone in the family. The second floor is equally impressive. Three large bedrooms dominate this level, each with a walk-in closet. For the kids there is a play room/ kid's den and up another flight of stairs is a room for future expansion into a deluxe studio with a fireplace. Over the three-car garage and attached to the second floor via the roof of the porte cochere, there is a room for a future mother-in-law suite or maid's suite. This home is designed with a basement foundation.

Design by
Design Traditions

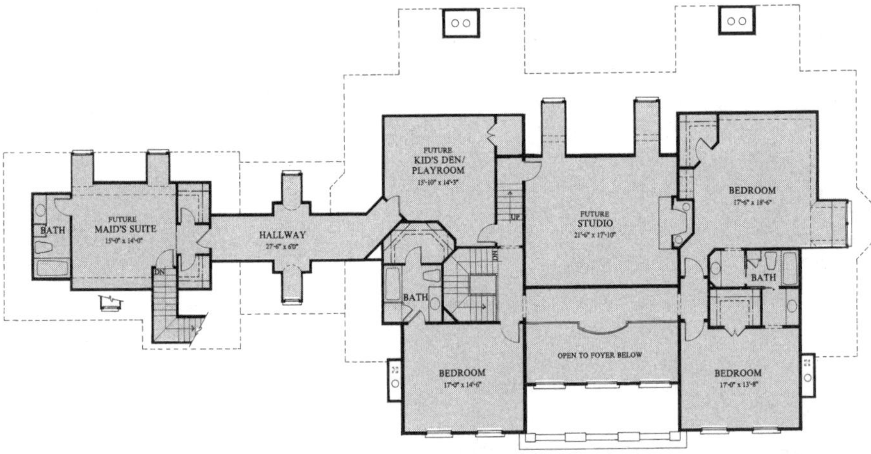

Design 8084

First Floor: 3,328 square feet
Second Floor: 868 square feet
Total: 4,196 square feet

■ The combination of stucco, stacked stone and brick adds texture and character to this country French home. The foyer offers views to the study, dining room and living room. Double French doors open to the study with built-in bookcases and a window seat overlooking the rear deck. The breakfast room, family room and the spacious kitchen make a nice backdrop for family living. The master suite is enhanced by a raised, corner fireplace and a bath with an exercise room. Upstairs, two family bedrooms and a full bath are balanced by a large game room.

Width 108'-2"
Depth 61'-6"
GARAGE
SCREENED PORCH
14-6 X 10-6
PATIO WITH TRELLIS
DECK
HOT TUB
EXERCISE RM
MASTER BATH
PORCH
BATH 3
COVERED PORCH
FAMILY ROOM
15-6 X 16-0
BREAKFAST
11-6 X 12-0
LIVING ROOM
15-0 X 17-6
STUDY/BEDROOM 3
14-6 X 13-6
MASTER BEDROOM
15-4 X 16-6
BEDROOM 4
11-6 X 13-0
PAN
UTIL
KITCHEN
21-0 X 13-6
DINING ROOM
15-4 X 15-4
FOYER
BATH 2
BEDROOM 2
12-0 X 14-0
PORCH

Design by
Larry E. Belk Designs

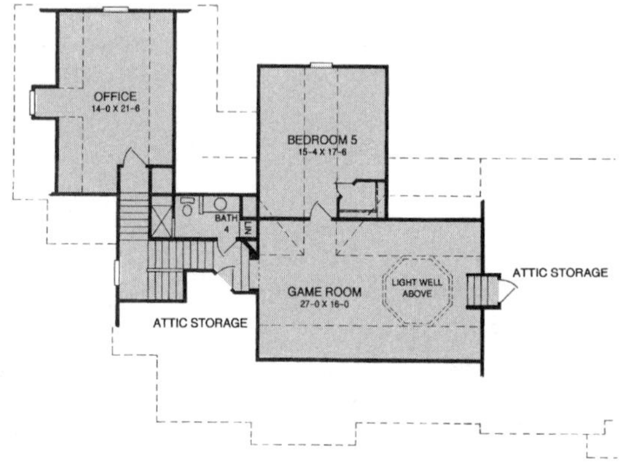

OFFICE
14-0 X 21-6
BEDROOM 5
15-4 X 17-6
BATH 4
GAME ROOM
27-0 X 16-0
LIGHT WELL ABOVE
ATTIC STORAGE
ATTIC STORAGE

Design 8083

First Floor: 4,383 square feet
Second Floor: 1,544 square feet
Total: 5,927 square feet

Design by
Larry E. Belk Designs

■ Two Palladian windows focus attention on the double-gable entry of this fine European style home. Through double doors, a lovely music room opens off the foyer while the open dining room remains the focal point upon entering. The large great room is crowned with a two-story ceiling and a grand fireplace. Family living takes off in the comfortable kitchen with a cooktop island, snack bar and breakfast nook—all convenient to the cozy family room. The master suite is fashioned with a pampering bath and a private exercise studio. Two first-level family bedrooms complement the upstairs accommodations that consist of two bedrooms with private baths, a sporty loft and a game room.

Width 114'-2"
Depth 85'-5"

SCREENED PORCH
FAMILY ROOM
BREAKFAST
EXERCISE ROOM
MASTER BATH
SITTING AREA
MASTER SUITE
STORAGE
GREAT ROOM
CEDAR CLOSET
DOUBLE GARAGE
KITCHEN
BEDROOM 2
BATH 2
PANTRY
FOYER
UTIL
SINGLE GARAGE
DINING ROOM
GRAND FOYER
MUSIC ROOM
BEDROOM 3
PORCH

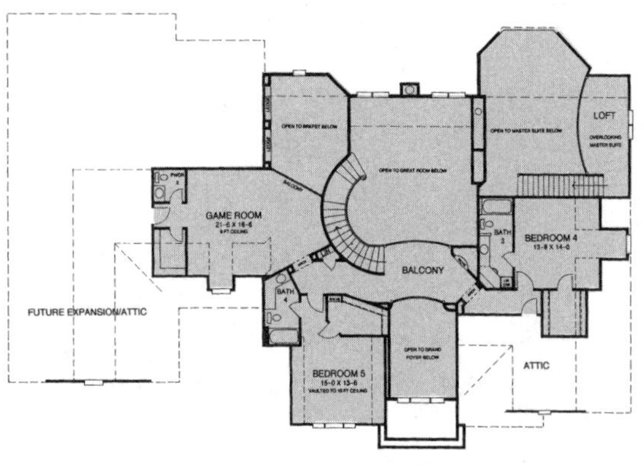

LOFT
GAME ROOM
BEDROOM 4
BALCONY
BATH 4
FUTURE EXPANSION/ATTIC
ATTIC
BEDROOM 5

COPYRIGHT 1993 LARRY E. BELK

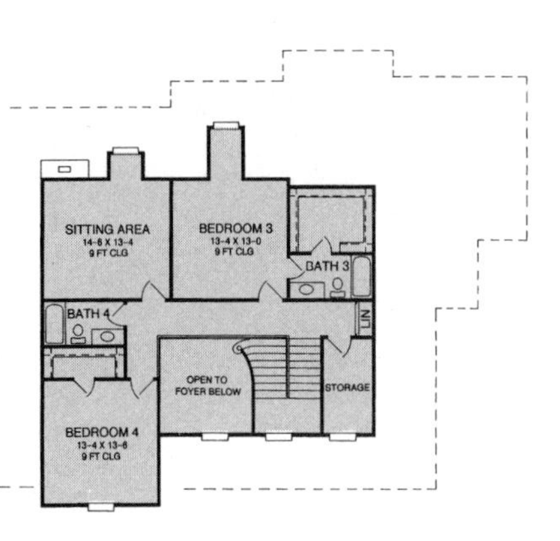
SITTING AREA
14-6 X 13-4
9 FT CLG
BEDROOM 3
13-4 X 13-0
9 FT CLG
BATH 3
BATH 4
LIN
OPEN TO
FOYER BELOW
STORAGE
BEDROOM 4
13-4 X 13-6
9 FT CLG

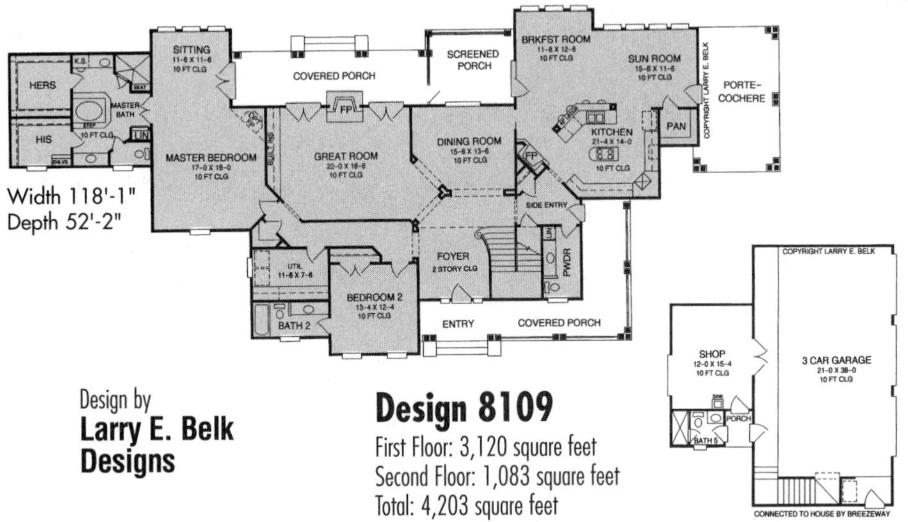
HERS
HIS
MASTER BATH
SITTING
11-6 X 11-6
10 FT CLG
COVERED PORCH
SCREENED PORCH
BRKFST ROOM
11-6 X 12-6
10 FT CLG
SUN ROOM
15-6 X 11-6
10 FT CLG
PORTE-COCHERE
PAN
KITCHEN
21-4 X 14-0
MASTER BEDROOM
17-0 X 18-0
10 FT CLG
GREAT ROOM
22-0 X 18-6
10 FT CLG
DINING ROOM
15-6 X 13-6
10 FT CLG
SIDE ENTRY
UTIL
11-6 X 7-6
FOYER
2 STORY CLG
PWDR
BEDROOM 2
13-4 X 12-4
10 FT CLG
BATH 2
ENTRY
COVERED PORCH
COPYRIGHT LARRY E. BELK

Width 118'-1"
Depth 52'-2"

COPYRIGHT LARRY E. BELK

SHOP
12-0 X 15-4
10 FT CLG

3 CAR GARAGE
21-0 X 38-0
10 FT CLG

PORCH

BATH 5

CONNECTED TO HOUSE BY BREEZEWAY

Design by
Larry E. Belk Designs

Design 8109

First Floor: 3,120 square feet
Second Floor: 1,083 square feet
Total: 4,203 square feet

■ The blending of natural materials and a nostalgic farmhouse look gives this home its unique character. Inside, a sophisticated floor plan includes all the amenities demanded by today's upscale family. Three large covered porches, one on the front and two on the rear, provide outdoor entertaining areas. The kitchen features a built-in stone fireplace visible from the breakfast and sunrooms. The master suite includes a large sitting area and a luxurious bath. Upstairs, two additional bedrooms and a large game room will please family and guests. Please specify crawlspace or slab foundation when ordering.

Design 8057

First Floor: 3,359 square feet
Second Floor: 2,174 square feet
Total: 5,533 square feet

■ A truly unique luxury home, this farmhouse has all the amenities. The fantastic covered porch surrounds three sides of the home and provides a wonderful area for outdoor living. A two-story foyer angles to draw the eye through double arches to the elegant living room with a fireplace flanked by built-ins and an area for the grand piano. The kitchen, breakfast room and family room join for casual living. Also on the first level: a home office, a game room and a cozy study. Upstairs, the master bedroom is luxuriously appointed and opens to a private sun deck. Three family bedrooms each have walk-in closets and private bath access.

Width 96'-5"
Depth 85'-6"

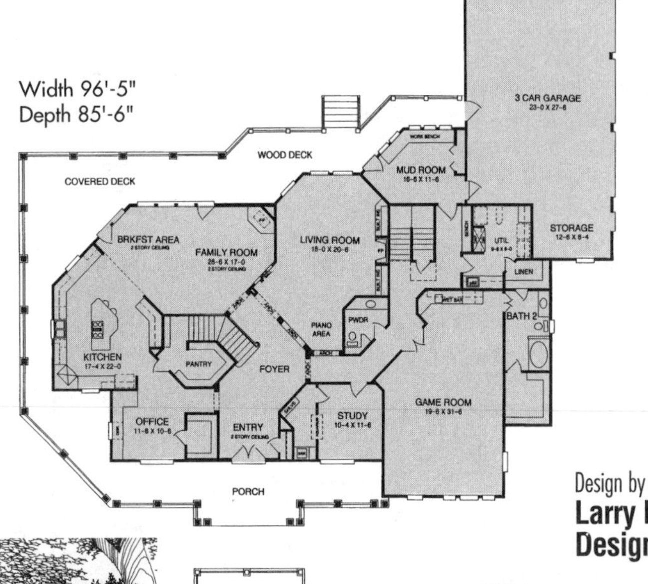
3 CAR GARAGE
WOOD DECK
COVERED DECK
MUD ROOM
STORAGE
BRKFST AREA
FAMILY ROOM
LIVING ROOM
UTIL
LINEN
BATH 2
PIANO AREA
PWDR
KITCHEN
PANTRY
FOYER
GAME ROOM
OFFICE
ENTRY
STUDY
PORCH

Design by
Larry E. Belk Designs

SUN DECK
OPEN TO BELOW
BEDROOM 4
ATTIC
BEDROOM 2
14-4 X 15-0
MASTER BEDROOM
17-0 X 22-0
BATH 4
LIN
BALCONY
BATH 3
MASTER BATH
ATTIC
BEDROOM 3

Design 9928

First Floor: 2,959 square feet
Second Floor: 1,326 square feet
Total: 4,285 square feet

■ The impressive two-story facade with a raised front pediment gives this home a stately image. Inside, the two-story foyer opens to an adjacent study and dining room. An open rail from the gallery above looks down on the foyer and living room below to give a very open appeal to the formal area of the home. The master suite—with rich appointments and access to the study—provides the perfect retreat. The kitchen is situated in a casual arrangement with the breakfast area and keeping room. Upstairs, three large bedrooms and an optional guest suite, maid's quarters or bonus room meet the needs of a growing family. This home is designed with a basement foundation.

Design by
Design Traditions

Keeping Room
18^{6}x12^{9}
Master Bedroom
17^{6}x16^{9}
Living Room
17^{9}x22^{9}
Breakfast
11^{9}x11^{0}
Width 90'
Depth 58'-8"
Kitchen
18^{0}x15^{9}
Up
Storage
Storage
Up
Dn
Three Car Garage
21^{3}x32^{6}
Study
16^{3}x14^{9}
Foyer
10^{0}x14^{6}
Dining Room
16^{0}x14^{9}
Attic Storage
Open To Below
Bedroom No. 4
14^{6}x14^{6}
Dn
Future Guest Bedroom
17^{0}x12^{3}
Dn
Bedroom No. 2
16^{3}x14^{9}
Open To Below
Bedroom No. 3
16^{3}x14^{9}

© 1991 HOME DESIGN SERVICES, INC.
BRADSHAW

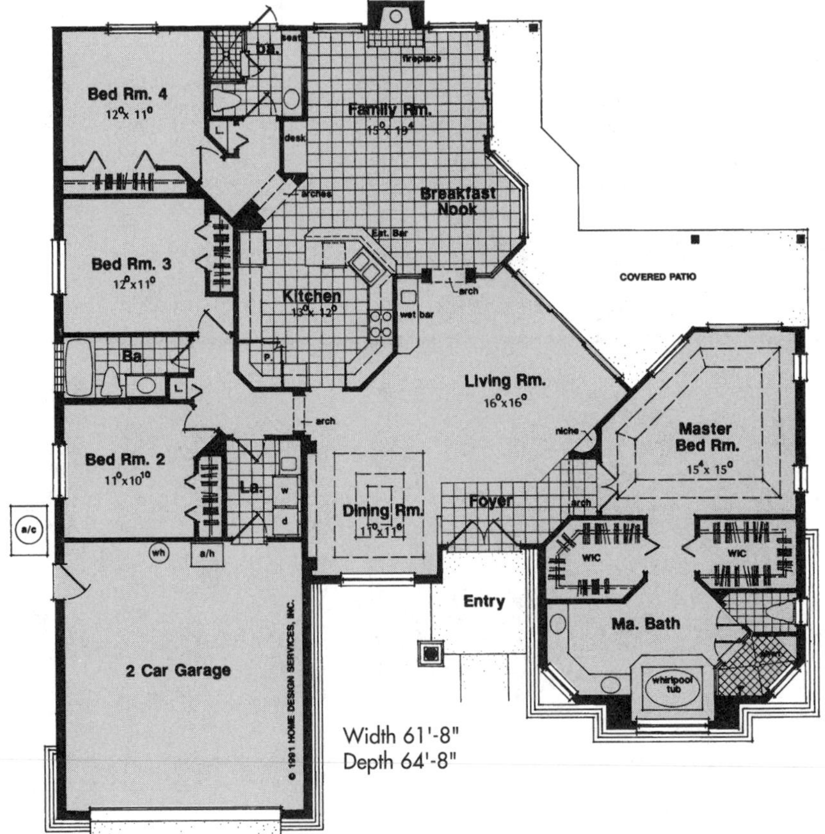
Bed Rm. 4
Ba.
seat
fireplace
Family Rm.
desk
arches
Breakfast Nook
Eat. Bar
Bed Rm. 3
Kitchen
wet bar
arch
COVERED PATIO
Ba.
Living Rm.
niche
Master Bed Rm.
Bed Rm. 2
La.
arch
Dining Rm.
Foyer
arch
WIC
WIC
a/c
wh
a/h
Entry
Ma. Bath
whirlpool tub
2 Car Garage
© 1991 HOME DESIGN SERVICES, INC.

Width 61'-8"
Depth 64'-8"

Design 8646

Square Footage: 2,352

■ An array of varied, arched windows sets off this striking Italianate home. Double doors reveal the foyer, which announces the living room accented by a wet bar, niche and patio access. The coffered dining room combines with the living room to create a perfect space for formal entertaining. An arched entry to the informal living area presents a bayed breakfast nook and adjoining family room warmed by a fireplace. A pass-through kitchen comes with a deep pantry and informal eating bar. Double doors open to the coffered master bedroom. Its sumptuous bath has two walk-in closets, a dual vanity and spa tub. Arched entries lead to three additional bedrooms: two share a full bath and the third boasts a private bath with yard access. Blueprints include an alternate elevation at no extra charge.

Design by
Home Design Services, Inc.

© 1991 HOME DESIGN SERVICES, INC.
BRADSHAW

Design 8687

Square Footage: 2,278

■ The grand entrance of this one-story home offers a fine introduction to an open, spacious interior. A delightful formal living and dining room sized for large get-togethers, extends from the foyer. To the left, a short hall accented with a decorator's niche, precedes the master suite, which includes a sitting area, two walk-in closets and a spa-style bath. Family living centers in the kitchen where wrapping counters, a walk-in pantry and an angular snack bar balance out the spacious family room and breakfast nook. Two family bedrooms are split from the master suite and share a full hall bath.

Design by
Home Design Services, Inc.

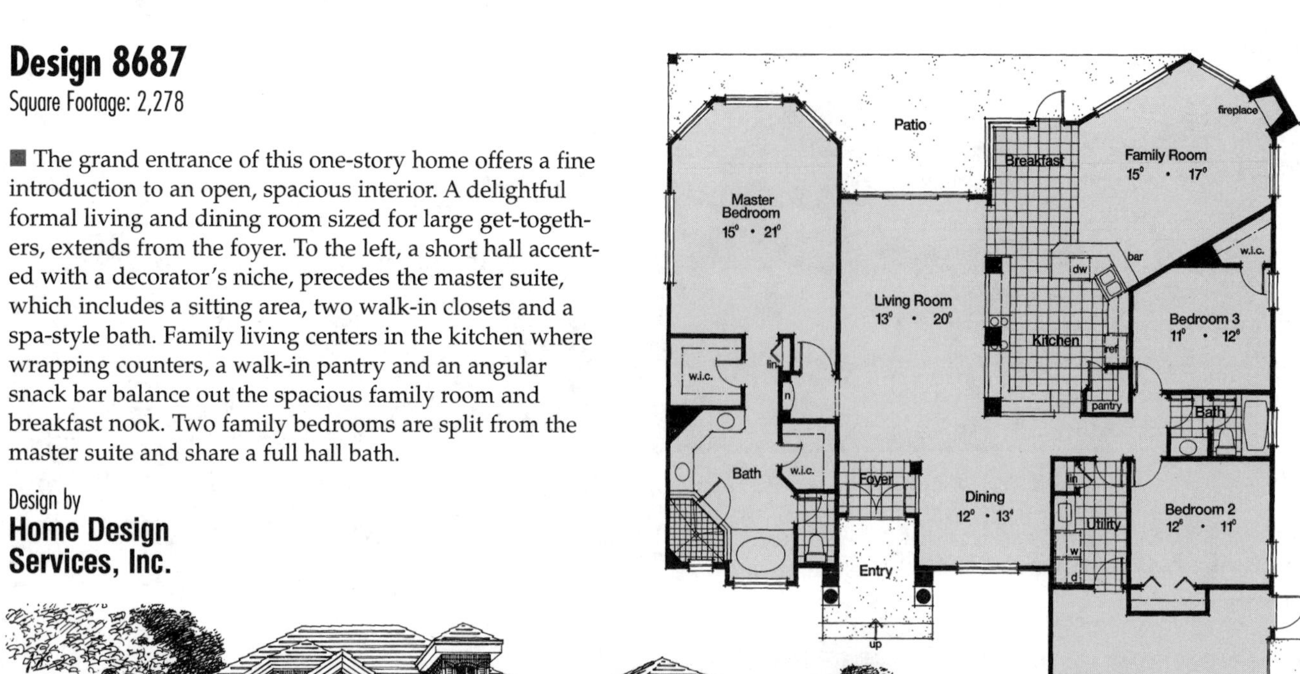

Patio
Breakfast
Family Room
fireplace
Master Bedroom
Living Room
bar
w.i.c.
Bedroom 3
Kitchen
pantry
Bath
Foyer
Dining
Utility
Bedroom 2
Entry
Double Garage

Width 57'-9"
Depth 71'-8"

Design by
Home Design Services, Inc.

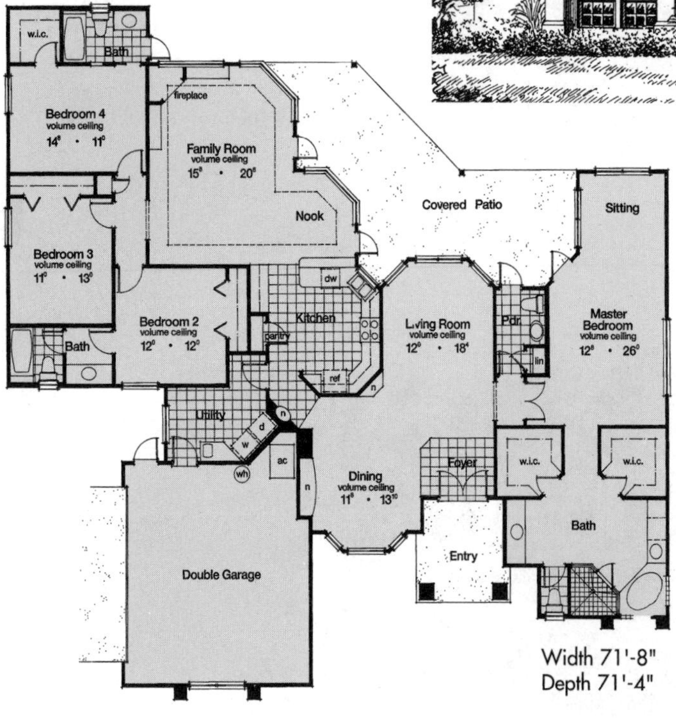

Width 71'-8"
Depth 71'-4"

Design 8688

Square Footage: 2,636

■ A towering entry welcomes all into the foyer of this soaring contemporary design with a multitude of elegant volume ceilings. The open dining room and living room each have sunny bay windows and built-in features. The spacious family room has a charming corner fireplace, plenty of windows and a breakfast nook easily in reach of the roomy kitchen. Three family bedrooms are just off the family room. The master suite has a sitting area, twin closets and an oversized bath designed for relaxing.

Master Bedroom
18⁰ • 16⁰
tray ceiling
see-thru fireplace
Master Bath
linen
w.i.c.
ac
Utility
w
d
Covered Patio
summer kitchen
Breakfast Nook
vaulted ceiling
dw
Kitchen
rng
ref
desk
pantry
Family Room
vaulted ceiling
16⁰ • 23⁸
fireplace
shelves
Bedroom 2
14⁰ • 11⁰
Bath 2
lin
Bedroom 3
11⁸ • 12⁰
linen
Bath 3
Bedroom 4
12⁰ • 11⁰
wh
shelves
Dining
vaulted ceiling
11⁰ • 12⁰
Foyer
Entry
Living Room
vaulted ceiling
12⁰ • 13⁰
planter
3 Car Garage
Width 70'
Depth 76'
© HOME DESIGN SERVICES, INC.
J.N. HANSEN P.T.L.

Design 8653

Square Footage: 2,962

■ Enter the formal foyer of this home and you are greeted with a traditional split living and dining room layout. The family room is where the real living takes place—whether gathered around the fireplace or expanding the space with the help of sliding glass, to include the outside patio and summer kitchen. The ultimate master suite contains coffered ceilings, a "boomerang" vanity and angular mirrors that reflect the bayed soaking tub and shower. Efficient use of space creates a huge closet with little dead center space. Two family bedrooms are situated to share a hall bath. Another bedroom has a semi-private bath, offering guests luxurious comfort.

Design by
Home Design Services, Inc.

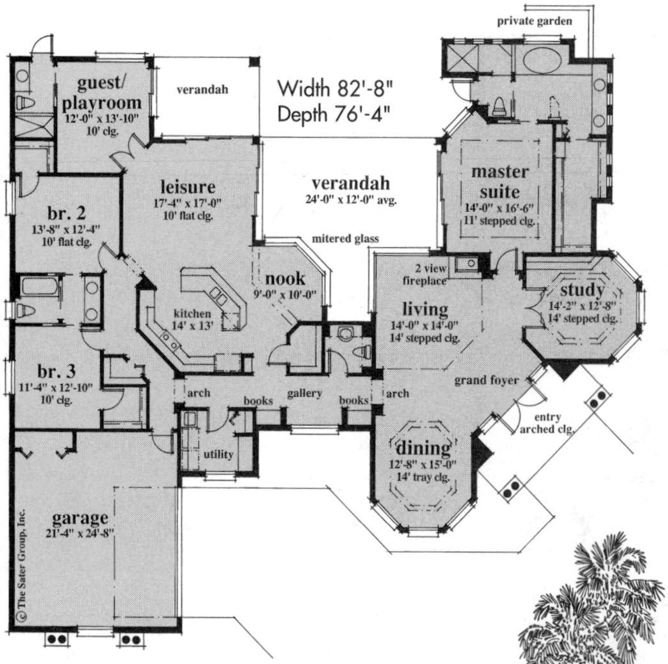

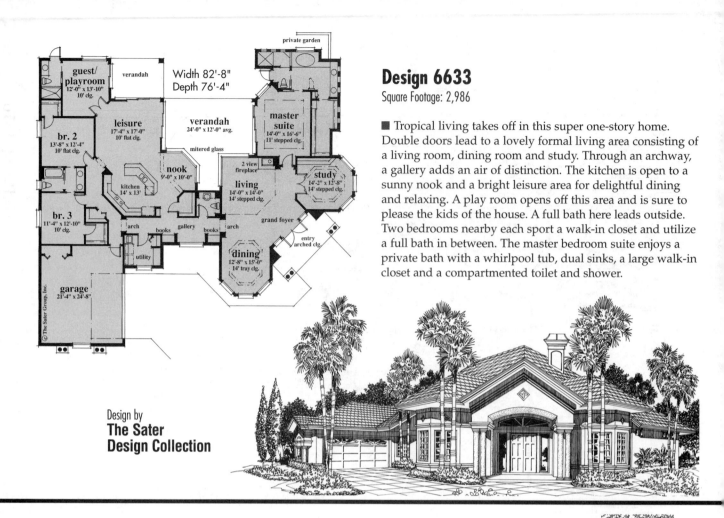

Design 6633

Square Footage: 2,986

■ Tropical living takes off in this super one-story home. Double doors lead to a lovely formal living area consisting of a living room, dining room and study. Through an archway, a gallery adds an air of distinction. The kitchen is open to a sunny nook and a bright leisure area for delightful dining and relaxing. A play room opens off this area and is sure to please the kids of the house. A full bath here leads outside. Two bedrooms nearby each sport a walk-in closet and utilize a full bath in between. The master bedroom suite enjoys a private bath with a whirlpool tub, dual sinks, a large walk-in closet and a compartmented toilet and shower.

Width 82'-8"
Depth 76'-4"

Design by
The Sater Design Collection

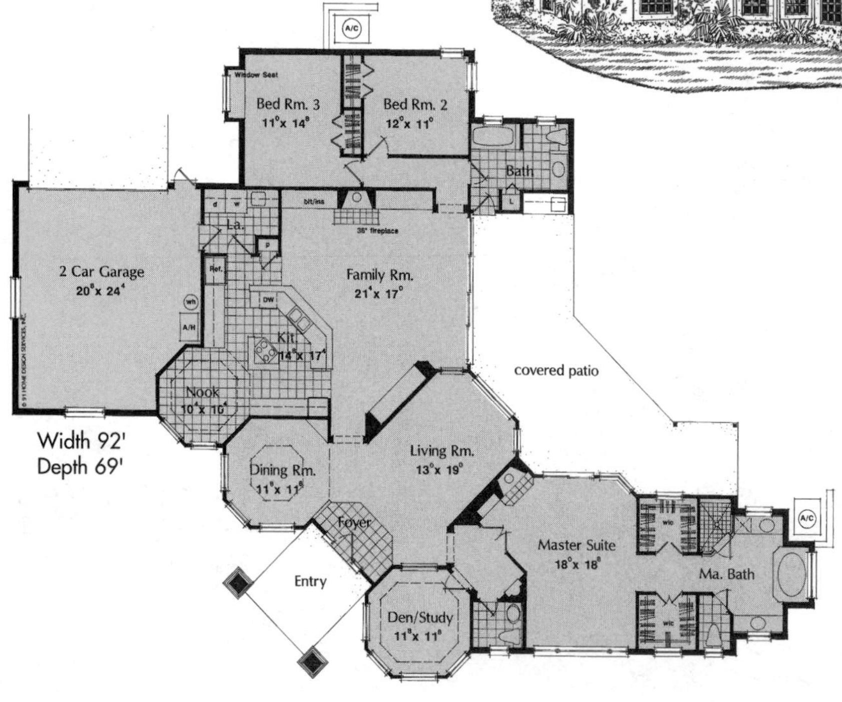

Design 8603

Square Footage: 2,656

■ A graceful design sets this charming home apart from the ordinary and transcends the commonplace. From the foyer, the dining room branches off the sunny living room, setting a lovely backdrop for entertaining. Casual living is the focus in the oversized family room, where sliding doors open to the patio and the eat-in, gourmet kitchen is open for easy conversation. Two family bedrooms and a cabana bath are just off the family room. The master suite has a cozy fireplace in the sitting area, twin closets and a compartmented bath. A large covered patio adds to the living area.

Width 92'
Depth 69'

Design by
Home Design Services, Inc.

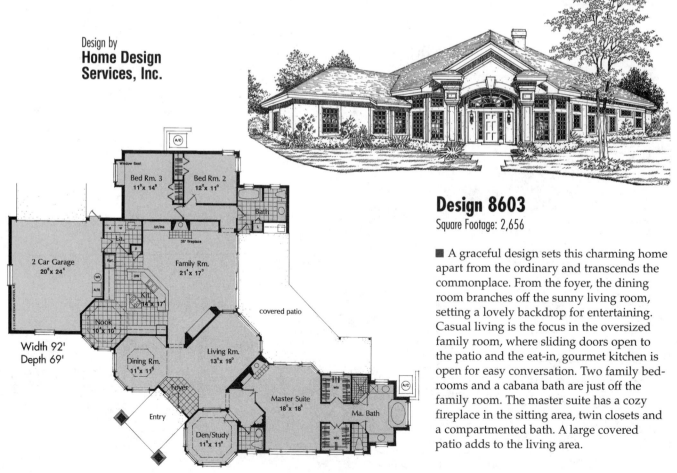

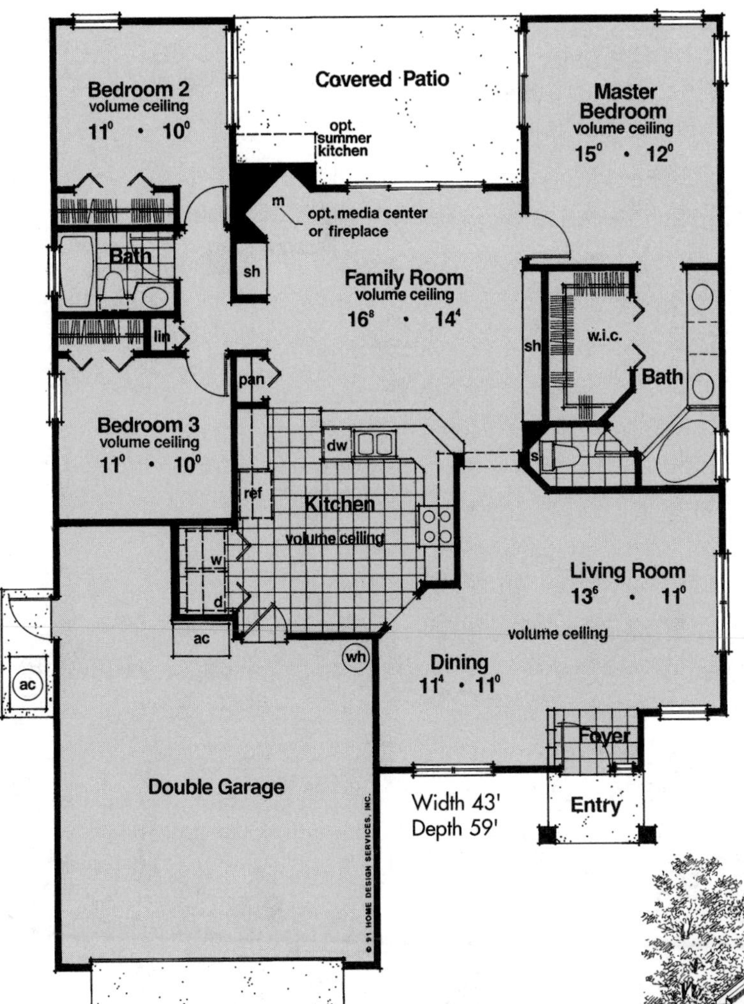
Bedroom 2
volume ceiling
11⁰ · 10⁰
Covered Patio
opt. summer kitchen
Master Bedroom
volume ceiling
15⁰ · 12⁰
m
opt. media center or fireplace
Bath
sh
Family Room
volume ceiling
16⁸ · 14⁴
lin
sh
w.i.c.
Bath
pan
Bedroom 3
volume ceiling
11⁰ · 10⁰
dw
ref
Kitchen
volume ceiling
s
w
d
Living Room
13⁶ · 11⁰
volume ceiling
ac
wh
Dining
11⁴ · 11⁰
ac
Foyer
Double Garage
Entry
Width 43'
Depth 59'
© 91 HOME DESIGN SERVICES, INC.

Design 8630

Square Footage: 1,550

■ Enjoy resort-style living in this striking sun-country home. Guests will always feel welcome when entertained in the formal living and dining areas, but the eat-in country kitchen overlooking the family room will be the center of attention. Casual living will be enjoyed in the large family room and out on the patio with the help of an optional summer kitchen and view of the fairway. Built-in shelves and an optional media center give you decorating options. The master suite features a volume ceiling and oversized master bath. Two secondary bedrooms accommodate guests or family and share a full hall bath. Plans for this home include a choice of two exterior elevations.

Design by
Home Design Services, Inc

Design 6612

Square Footage: 1,487

■ Here's an offer too good to pass up! Two elevations and a wealth of modern livability is presented in this compact one-story home. Inside, a great room with a vaulted ceiling opens to the lanai, offering wonderful options for either formal or informal entertaining. Or step out onto the lanai from the delightful kitchen with its bay-windowed breakfast nook. Two secondary bedrooms—each with its own walk-in closet—share a full bath. Finally, enjoy the lanai from the calming master suite and pampering bath featuring a corner tub, a separate shower and a large walk-in closet.

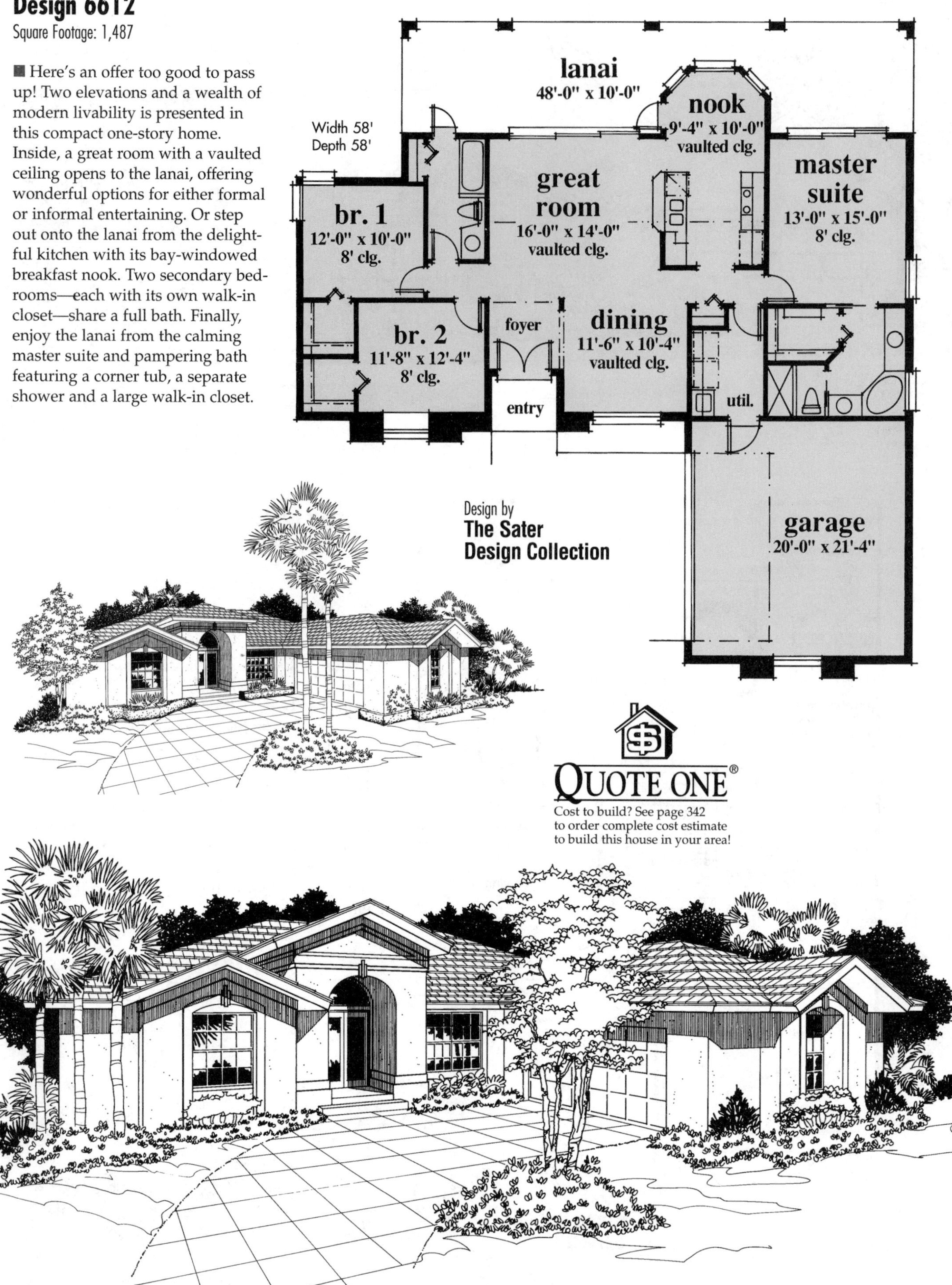

Width 58'
Depth 58'
lanai
48'-0" x 10'-0"
nook
9'-4" x 10'-0"
vaulted clg.
master suite
13'-0" x 15'-0"
8' clg.
great room
16'-0" x 14'-0"
vaulted clg.
br. 1
12'-0" x 10'-0"
8' clg.
br. 2
11'-8" x 12'-4"
8' clg.
foyer
dining
11'-6" x 10'-4"
vaulted clg.
entry
util.
garage
20'-0" x 21'-4"
Design by
The Sater Design Collection
QUOTE ONE®
Cost to build? See page 342 to order complete cost estimate to build this house in your area!

Design by
Donald A. Gardner, Architects, Inc.

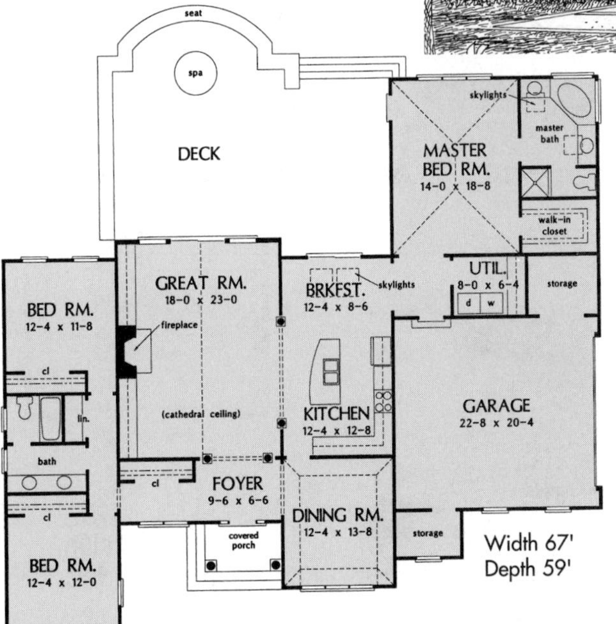

seat
spa
DECK
skylights
master bath
MASTER BED RM. 14-0 x 18-8
walk-in closet
UTIL. 8-0 x 6-4
d w
storage
GREAT RM. 18-0 x 23-0
fireplace
(cathedral ceiling)
BED RM. 12-4 x 11-8
cl
lin.
bath
cl
BED RM. 12-4 x 12-0
BRKFST. 12-4 x 8-6
skylights
KITCHEN 12-4 x 12-8
GARAGE 22-8 x 20-4
cl
FOYER 9-6 x 6-6
covered porch
DINING RM. 12-4 x 13-8
storage
Width 67'
Depth 59'

Design 9744

Square Footage: 2,090

■ This exciting Southwestern design is enhanced by the use of arched windows and an inviting arched entrance. The large foyer opens to a massive great room with a fireplace and built-in cabinets. The kitchen features an island cooktop and a skylit breakfast area. The master suite has an impressive cathedral ceiling and a walk-in closet as well as a luxurious bath that boasts separate vanities, a corner whirlpool tub and a separate shower. Two additional bedrooms are located at the opposite end of the home for privacy and share a full bath. Please specify crawlspace or slab foundation when ordering.

Design by
Donald A. Gardner, Architects, Inc.

Design 9755

Square Footage: 1,315

■ Southwestern influences are evident in this design, from the tiled roof to the warm stucco exterior. A covered porch leads indoors where the great room gains attention. A cathedral ceiling, a fireplace and built-ins enhance this area. The dining room remains open to this room. In the kitchen, a pass-through cooktop counter allows the cook to converse with family and friends. Three bedrooms include two family bedrooms that share a hall bath and a master suite with skylights, a walk-in closet and a private bath. Please specify crawlspace or slab foundation when ordering.

covered porch
skylights
skylights
walk-in closet
MASTER BED-RM. 11-4 x 15-0
(cathedral ceiling)
master bath
skylight
bath
GREAT RM. 14-4 x 15-0
DINING 9-8 x 12-0
(cathedral ceiling)
fireplace
w d
cl
KIT. 9-8 x 13-8
foyer
GARAGE 20-8 x 21-8
cl
BED RM. 10-0 x 10-0
cl
BED RM. 10-0 x 10-0
(cathedral ceiling)
covered porch
Width 66'-4"
Depth 44'-4"

Design 8662

Square Footage: 2,005

■ A super floor plan makes this volume home that much more attractive. Inside you'll find a formal dining room—defined by columns—to the right and a living room—with an optional fireplace—to the left. Beyond this area is an expansive great room with a vaulted ceiling and openness to the kitchen and breakfast room. Two secondary bedrooms complete the right side of the plan. Each features a volume ceiling, ample closet space and the use of a full hall bath. The master bedroom enjoys its own bath with a whirlpool tub, separate shower, dual vanity and compartmented toilet.

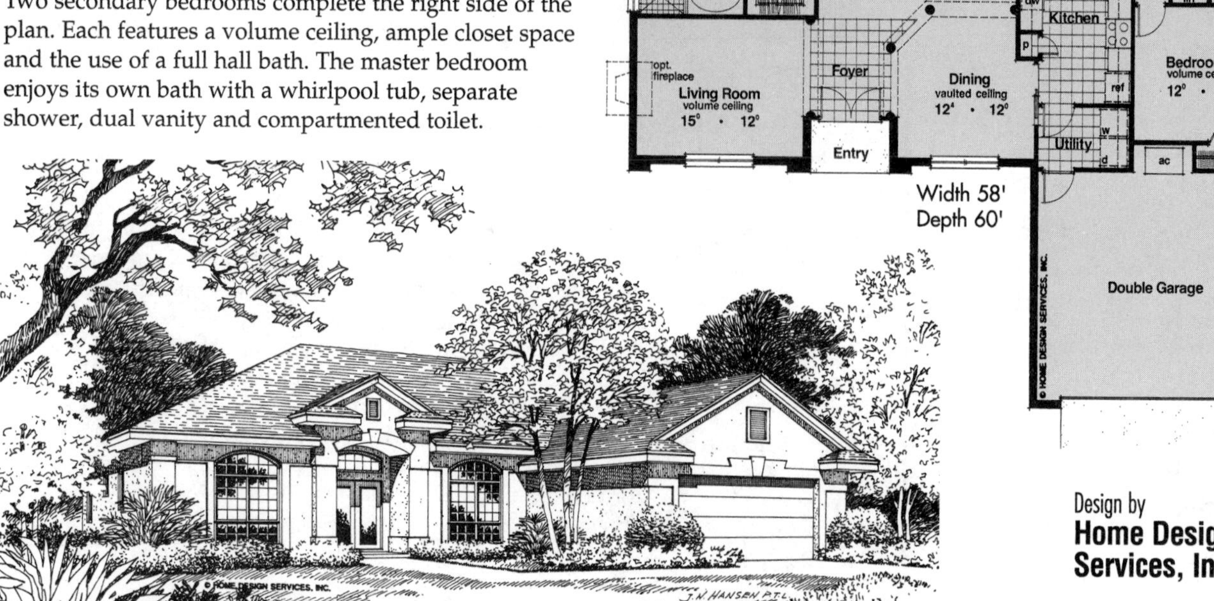
Master Bedroom
volume ceiling
16⁰ · 12⁰
Covered Patio
Bedroom 2
volume ceiling
13¹⁰ · 12⁰
Breakfast
Great Room
vaulted ceiling
20⁰ · 18⁰
Bath
w.i.c.
lin
Kitchen
Bedroom 3
volume ceiling
12⁰ · 11⁸
opt. fireplace
Living Room
volume ceiling
15⁰ · 12⁰
Foyer
Dining
vaulted ceiling
12⁴ · 12⁰
Entry
Utility
Double Garage
© HOME DESIGN SERVICES, INC.
J.N. HANSEN P.T.L.

Width 58'
Depth 60'

Design by
Home Design Services, Inc.

Design 6658

Square Footage: 1,647

■ This glorious sun-country cottage gives you the option of two elevations: choose from a hipped or gabled roof at the front entrance. Either way, this plan gives a new look to comfortable resort living. Designed for casual living, the foyer opens to the dining and grand rooms while providing great views of the rear lanai and beyond. The grand room has a built-in entertainment center and a snack bar served from the kitchen. The galley kitchen has a gazebo dining nook with a door to the lanai. The master suite is split from the family sleeping wing and features a walk-in closet and a compartmented bath. Two secondary bedrooms, a study and full cabana bath complete this luxurious vacation home.

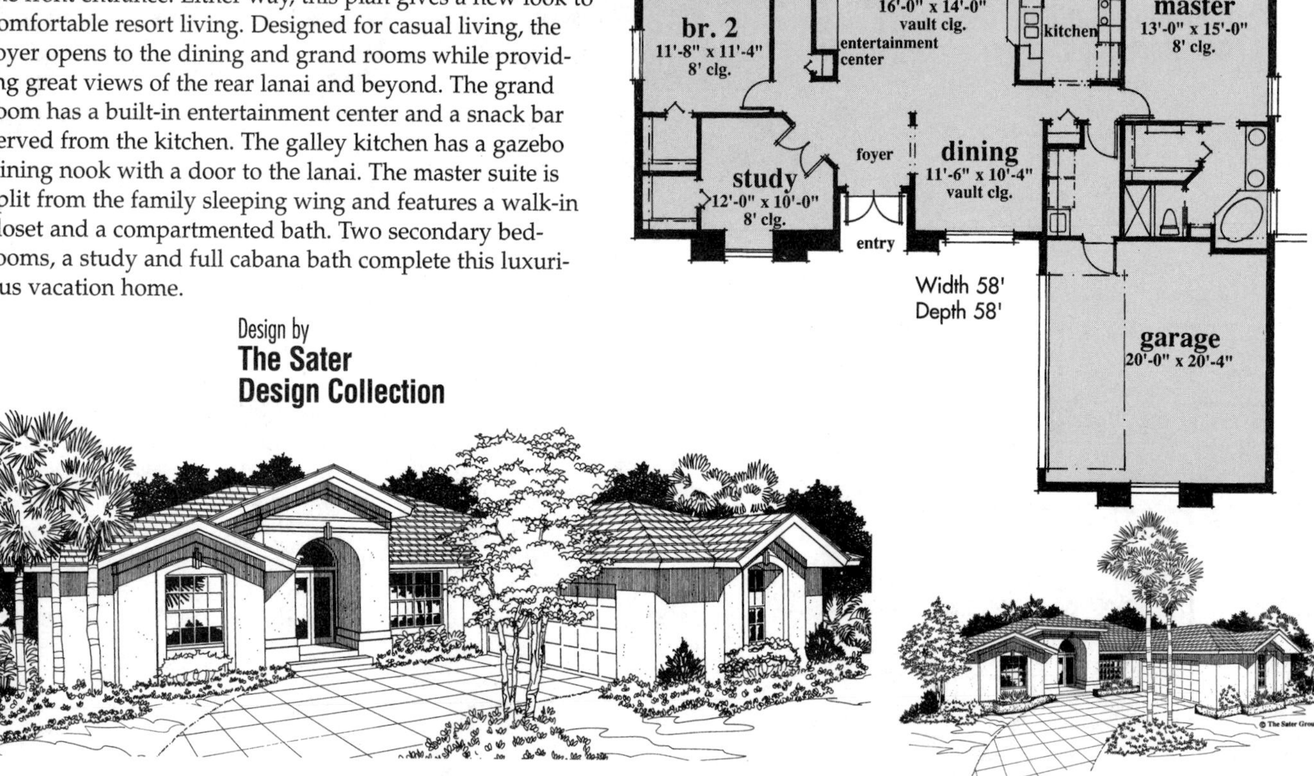
br. 1
11'-8" x 10'-4"
8' clg.
lanai
13'-6" x 10'-0"
lanai
nook
9'-0" x 9'-0"
grand room
16'-0" x 14'-0"
vault clg.
entertainment center
kitchen
master
13'-0" x 15'-0"
8' clg.
br. 2
11'-8" x 11'-4"
8' clg.
study
12'-0" x 10'-0"
8' clg.
foyer
dining
11'-6" x 10'-4"
vault clg.
entry
garage
20'-0" x 20'-4"
© The Sater Group, Inc.

Width 58'
Depth 58'

Design by
The Sater Design Collection

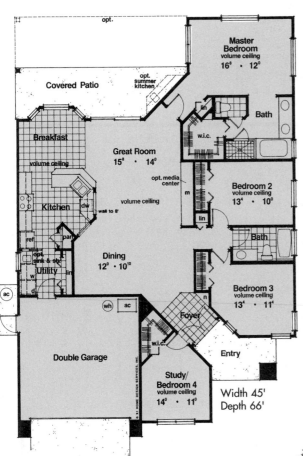

© 91 HOME DESIGN SERVICES, INC.

opt.
Master Bedroom volume ceiling 16⁸ · 12⁰
Covered Patio
opt. summer kitchen
lin
Bath
w.i.c.
Breakfast
Great Room 15⁸ · 14⁰
volume ceiling
opt. media center
m
Bedroom 2 volume ceiling 13⁴ · 10⁰
volume ceiling
Kitchen
dw
wall to 8'
lin
ref
pan
Bath
opt. sink & sh.
Utility
lin
w
d
Dining 12⁰ · 10¹⁰
Bedroom 3 volume ceiling 13⁴ · 11⁴
n
ac
wh
ac
Foyer
w.i.c.
Double Garage
Entry
Study/ Bedroom 4 volume ceiling 14⁰ · 11⁰
Width 45'
Depth 66'

Design 8633

Square Footage: 1,865

■ This innovative plan takes advantage of an angled entry into the home, maximizing visual impact and making it possible to include four bedrooms. The joining of the family and dining space makes creative interior decorating possible. The master suite also takes advantage of angles. The master bath is designed with all the amenities usually found in much larger homes. The kitchen and breakfast nook overlook the outdoor living space where you can even have an outdoor kitchen area—a great design for entertaining. The traditional feel of the exterior and the up-to-date interior make this house the perfect design for the 90s.

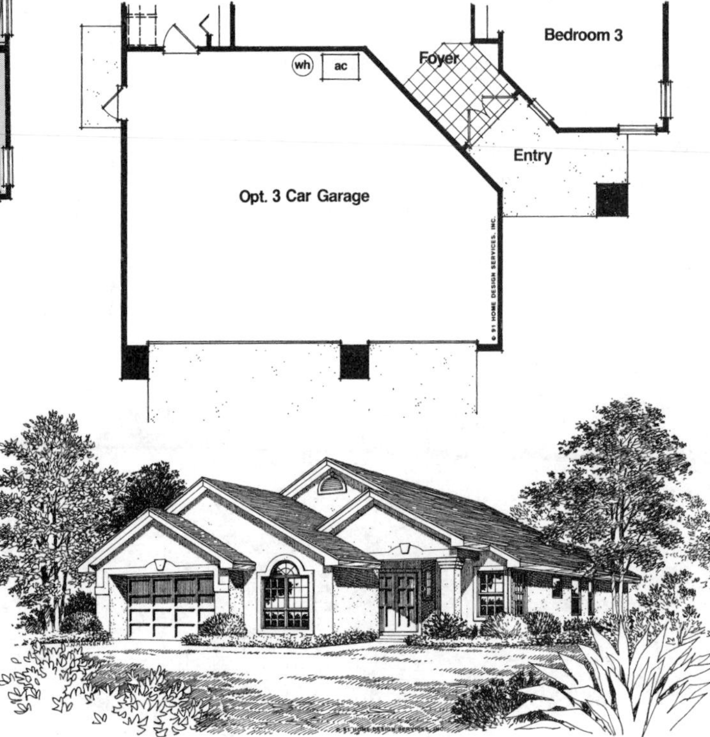
wh
ac
Foyer
Bedroom 3
Entry
Opt. 3 Car Garage

Design by
Home Design Services, Inc.

Design 6626

Square Footage: 2,589

■ This plan has a contemporary Mediterranean look that gives an Old World feel. The formal living areas are off the foyer. The large living and dining room are easily accessible to the wet bar. An archway leads to the family areas. An ample kitchen has a walk-in pantry and desk message center. The nook and leisure room face the rear. The owners' wing features a bayed study with bookshelves, a large sleeping quarter and a bayed sitting area. The bath has His and Hers walk-in closets, a glass shower and a garden tub.

Design by
The Sater Design Collection

Width 64'
Depth 81'

opt. fireplace
leisure 20'-6" x 16'-0"
lanai 28'-0" x 14'-6"
nook 10'-0" x 9'-0"
sitting
kitchen
br. 2 12'-0" x 11'-0"
master suite 13'-0" x 21'-0"
living 17'-0" x 13'-6" avg.
desk
dining 14'-0" x 12'-0"
grand foyer
opt. wetbar
his
hers
br. 3 12'-0" x 11'-0"
opt. built ins
study 10'-8" x 14'-0"
entry
garage 20'-8" x 27'-0"
© 1994 The Sater Group, Inc.

Design 6629

Square Footage: 2,214

■ Make yourself at home in this delightful one-story home. The dramatic entry—with an arched opening—leads to a comfortable interior. Volume ceilings highlight the main living areas which include a formal dining room and a great room with access to one of the verandas. In the turreted study, quiet time is assured with double doors closing off the rest of the house. The master bedroom suite features a luxury bath with a double-bowl vanity, a bumped-out whirlpool tub and a compartmented toilet and shower. The secondary bedrooms reside on the other side of the house and utilize a full bath that also accommodates outdoor living areas.

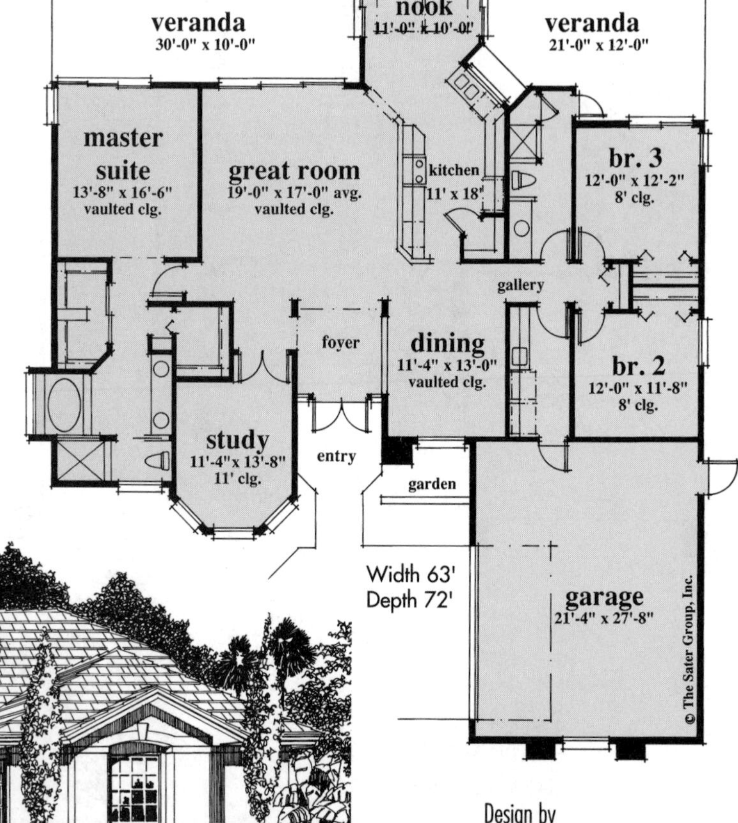
skylights above
veranda 30'-0" x 10'-0"
nook 11'-0" x 10'-0"
veranda 21'-0" x 12'-0"
master suite 13'-8" x 16'-6" vaulted clg.
great room 19'-0" x 17'-0" avg. vaulted clg.
kitchen 11' x 18'
br. 3 12'-0" x 12'-2" 8' clg.
gallery
foyer
dining 11'-4" x 13'-0" vaulted clg.
br. 2 12'-0" x 11'-8" 8' clg.
study 11'-4" x 13'-8" 11' clg.
entry
garden
Width 63'
Depth 72'
garage 21'-4" x 27'-8"
© The Sater Group, Inc.

Design by
The Sater Design Collection

Design 6661

Square Footage: 3,265

■ This dazzling Floridian home offers the best in formal and elegant living. A striking living room opens through sliding glass doors to the rear veranda and has built-in cabinetry, a fireplace and a wet bar for easy entertaining. The oversized kitchen is rich with amenities such as an angular snack bar, a cooktop island and walk-in pantry. Sunny windows frame the eating nook as it introduces the cozy leisure room that's complete with a built-in entertainment center. A smart guest room with a full cabana bath is just off the leisure room. Two family bedrooms are set against a gallery hall and are designed to share a compartmented bath. The master suite is stylishly set off with arches and a private garden visible from a lovely window seat and the luxurious bath. A multitude of windows makes the bedroom an elegant retreat.

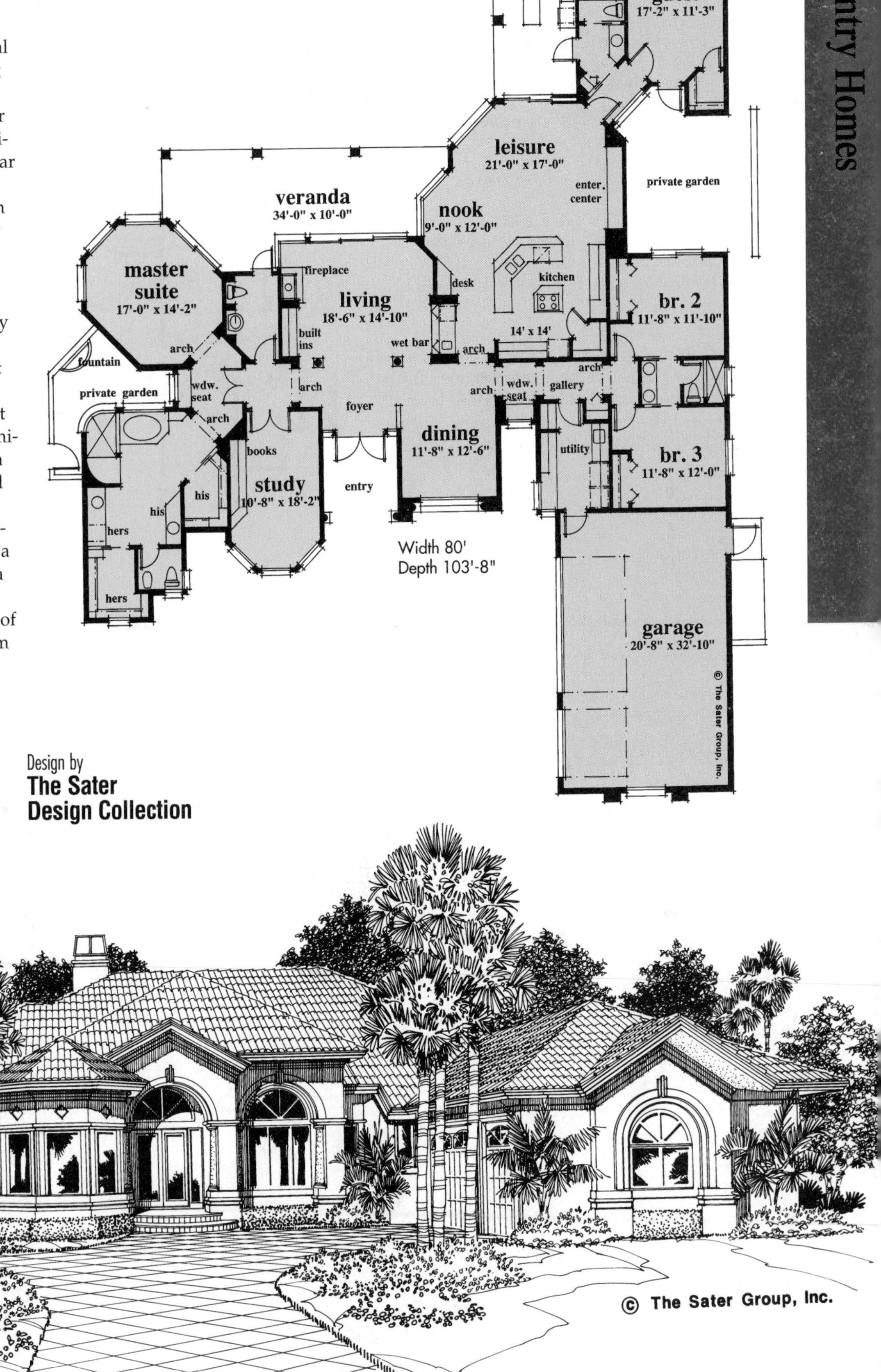
grill
guest
17'-2" x 11'-3"
leisure
21'-0" x 17'-0"
private garden
enter. center
veranda
34'-0" x 10'-0"
nook
9'-0" x 12'-0"
master suite
17'-0" x 14'-2"
fireplace
living
18'-6" x 14'-10"
desk
kitchen
br. 2
11'-8" x 11'-10"
built ins
wet bar
14' x 14'
arch
fountain
private garden
wdw. seat
arch
foyer
wdw. seat
gallery
arch
dining
11'-8" x 12'-6"
utility
br. 3
11'-8" x 12'-0"
books
study
10'-8" x 18'-2"
his
his
hers
hers
entry
Width 80'
Depth 103'-8"
garage
20'-8" x 32'-10"
© The Sater Group, Inc.
© The Sater Group, Inc.

Design by
The Sater Design Collection

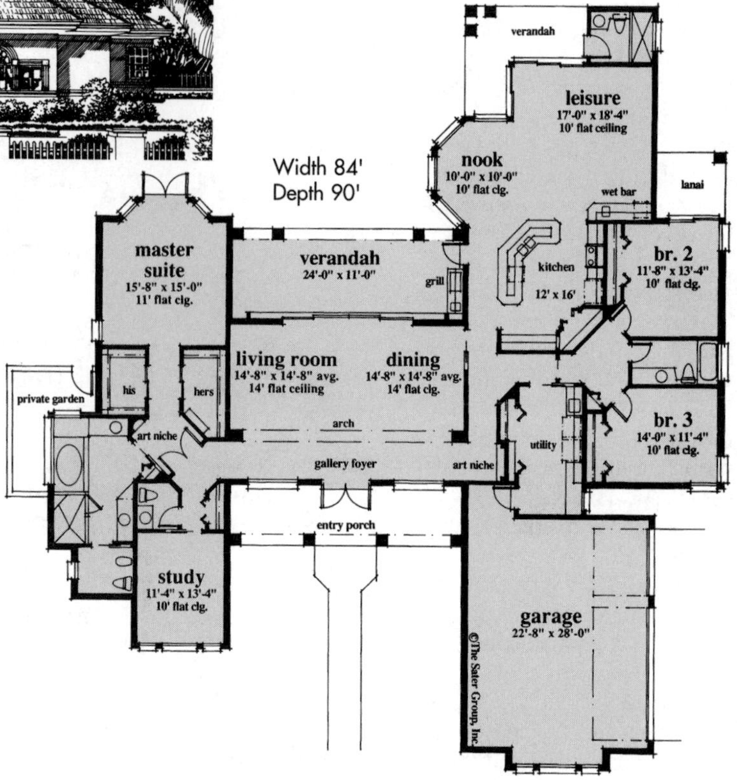

Width 84'
Depth 90'

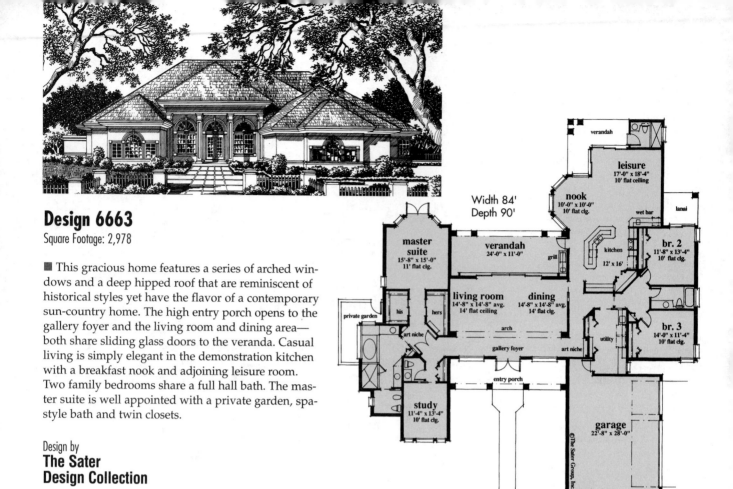

Design 6663

Square Footage: 2,978

■ This gracious home features a series of arched windows and a deep hipped roof that are reminiscent of historical styles yet have the flavor of a contemporary sun-country home. The high entry porch opens to the gallery foyer and the living room and dining area—both share sliding glass doors to the veranda. Casual living is simply elegant in the demonstration kitchen with a breakfast nook and adjoining leisure room. Two family bedrooms share a full hall bath. The master suite is well appointed with a private garden, spa-style bath and twin closets.

Design by
The Sater Design Collection

Width 95'
Depth 88'-8"

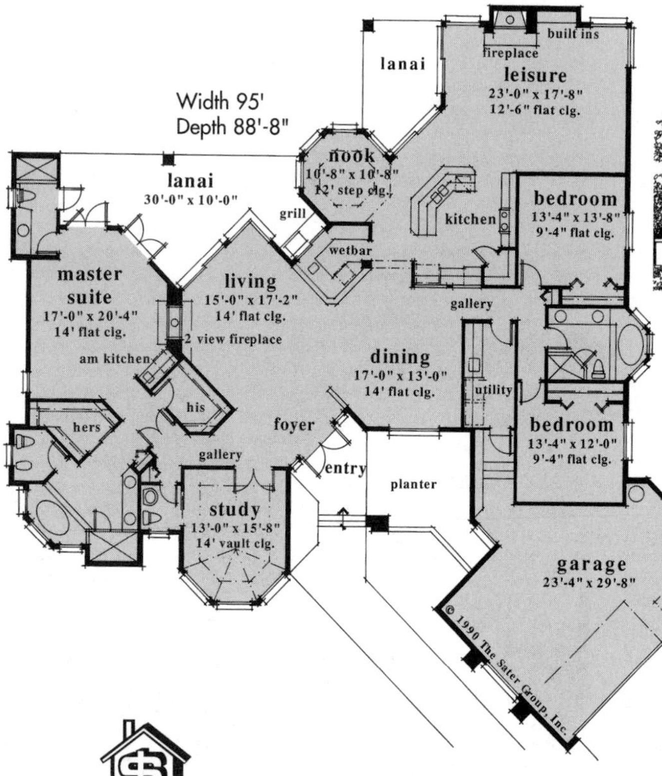

Design 6634

Square Footage: 3,477

■ Make dreams come true with this fine sunny design. An octagonal study provides a nice focal point both inside and outside. The living areas remain open to each other and access outdoor areas. A wet bar makes entertaining a breeze, especially with a window pass-through to a grill area on the lanai. The kitchen enjoys shared space with a lovely breakfast nook and a bright leisure room. Two bedrooms are located near the family living center. In the master bedroom suite, luxury abounds with a two-way fireplace, a morning kitchen, two walk-in closets and a compartmented bath. Another full bath accommodates a pool area.

QUOTE ONE®
Cost to build? See page 342 to order complete cost estimate to build this house in your area!

Design by
The Sater Design Collection

■ An arched, covered porch presents fine double doors leading to a spacious foyer in this decidedly European home. A two-story bay-windowed tower contains an elegant formal dining room on the first floor and a spacious bedroom on the second floor. The grand room is aptly named, with three sets of doors opening onto a roofed veranda, a fireplace and a built-in entertainment center. A large kitchen is ready to please the gourmet of the family with a big walk-in pantry for storage. A sunny, bay-windowed eating nook is nearby and has access to a second covered veranda. The secluded master suite is luxury in itself. A bay-windowed sitting area, access to the rear veranda, His and Hers walk-in closets and a lavish bath are all set to pamper you. Upstairs, two bedrooms, both with walk-in closets, share a full hall bath with twin vanities. Bedroom 2 has its own private deck. Please specify basement or slab foundation when ordering.

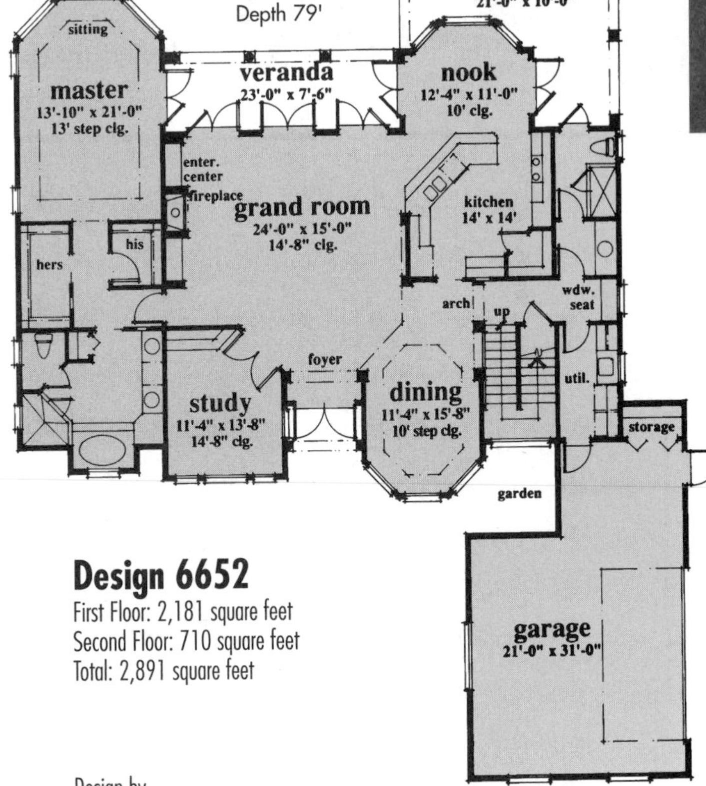
Width 66'-4"
Depth 79'
veranda
21'-0" x 10'-0"
sitting
master
13'-10" x 21'-0"
13' step clg.
veranda
23'-0" x 7'-6"
nook
12'-4" x 11'-0"
10' clg.
enter. center
fireplace
grand room
24'-0" x 15'-0"
14'-8" clg.
kitchen
14' x 14'
his
hers
arch
up
wdw. seat
foyer
util.
study
11'-4" x 13'-8"
14'-8" clg.
dining
11'-4" x 15'-8"
10' step clg.
storage
garden
garage
21'-0" x 31'-0"

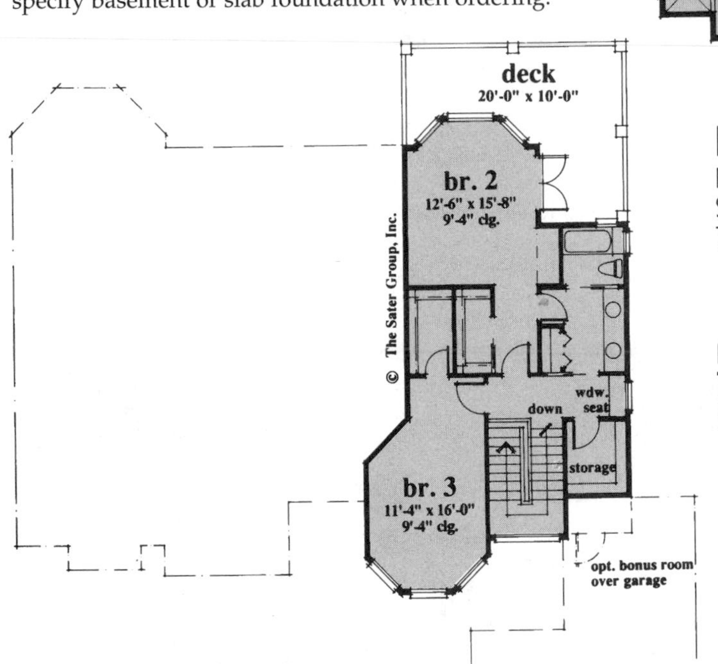
deck
20'-0" x 10'-0"
br. 2
12'-6" x 15'-8"
9'-4" clg.
© The Sater Group, Inc.
wdw. seat
down
storage
br. 3
11'-4" x 16'-0"
9'-4" clg.
opt. bonus room over garage

Design 6652

First Floor: 2,181 square feet
Second Floor: 710 square feet
Total: 2,891 square feet

Design by
The Sater Design Collection

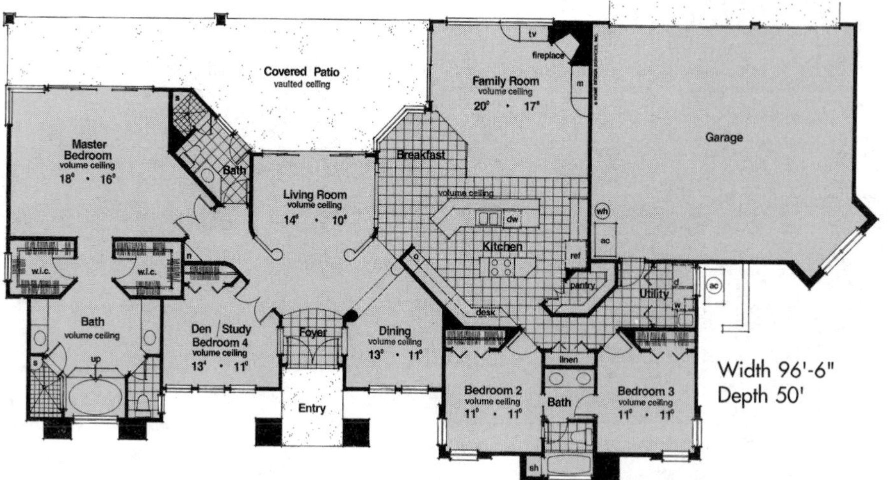
Covered Patio
vaulted ceiling
Family Room
volume ceiling
20° · 17°
tv
fireplace
Garage
Master
Bedroom
volume ceiling
18° · 16°
Bath
Living Room
volume ceiling
14° · 10°
Breakfast
volume ceiling
Kitchen
dw
ref
pantry
Utility
w.i.c.
w.i.c.
Bath
volume ceiling
up
Den / Study
Bedroom 4
volume ceiling
13° · 11°
Foyer
Dining
volume ceiling
13° · 11°
desk
Bedroom 2
volume ceiling
11° · 11°
linen
Bath
Bedroom 3
volume ceiling
11° · 11°
Entry
sh
ac

Width 96'-6"
Depth 50'

© HOME DESIGN SERVICES, INC.

Design 8663

Square Footage: 2,597

■ The angles in this home create unlimited views and spaces that appear larger. Majestic columns of brick add warmth to a striking elevation. Inside, the foyer commands special perspective on living areas including the living room, dining room and the den. The island kitchen serves the breakfast nook and the family room. A large pantry provides ample space for food storage. In the master bedroom suite, mitered glass and a private bath set the tone for simple luxury. Two secondary bedrooms share privacy and quiet at the front of the house. The den may also convert to a fourth bedroom, if desired.

Design by
Home Design Services, Inc.

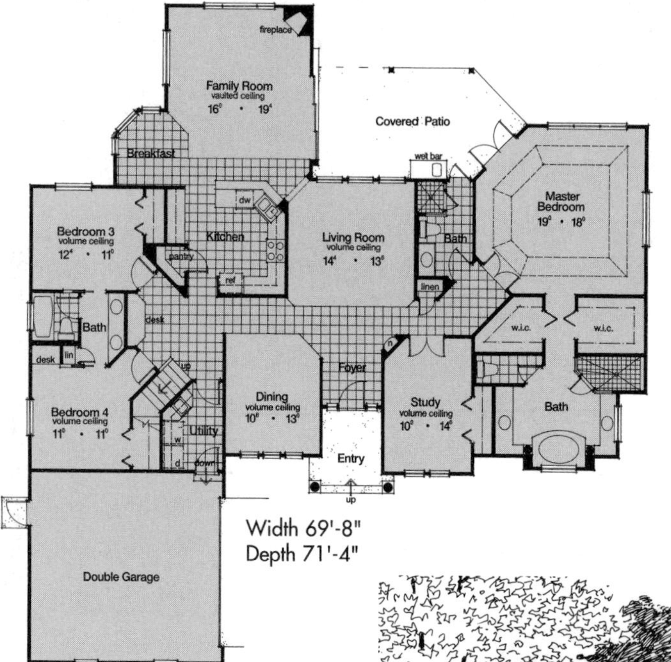
fireplace
Family Room
vaulted ceiling
16° · 19°
Covered Patio
Breakfast
wet bar
Master
Bedroom
19° · 18°
Bedroom 3
volume ceiling
12° · 11°
dw
Kitchen
pantry
ref
Living Room
volume ceiling
14° · 13°
Bath
linen
Bath
desk
desk
lin
w.i.c.
w.i.c.
up
Foyer
Bedroom 4
volume ceiling
11° · 11°
Utility
Dining
volume ceiling
10° · 13°
Study
volume ceiling
10° · 14°
Bath
Entry
down
up
Double Garage

Width 69'-8"
Depth 71'-4"

Design 8682

Square Footage: 2,551
Bonus Room: 287 square feet

■ Shutters and multi-pane windows dress up the exterior of this lovely stucco home. Formal and informal areas flow easily, beginning with the dining room sized to accommodate large parties and function with the adjacent living room. A gourmet kitchen is complete with a walk-in pantry and a cozy breakfast nook. Double doors lead to the spacious master suite. The lavish master bath features His and Hers walk-in closets, a tub framed by a columned archway and an oversized shower. Off the angular hallway are two bedrooms that share a pullman-style bath and a study desk. A bonus room over the garage provides additional space.

Bonus
11° · 20°

Design by
Home Design Services, Inc.

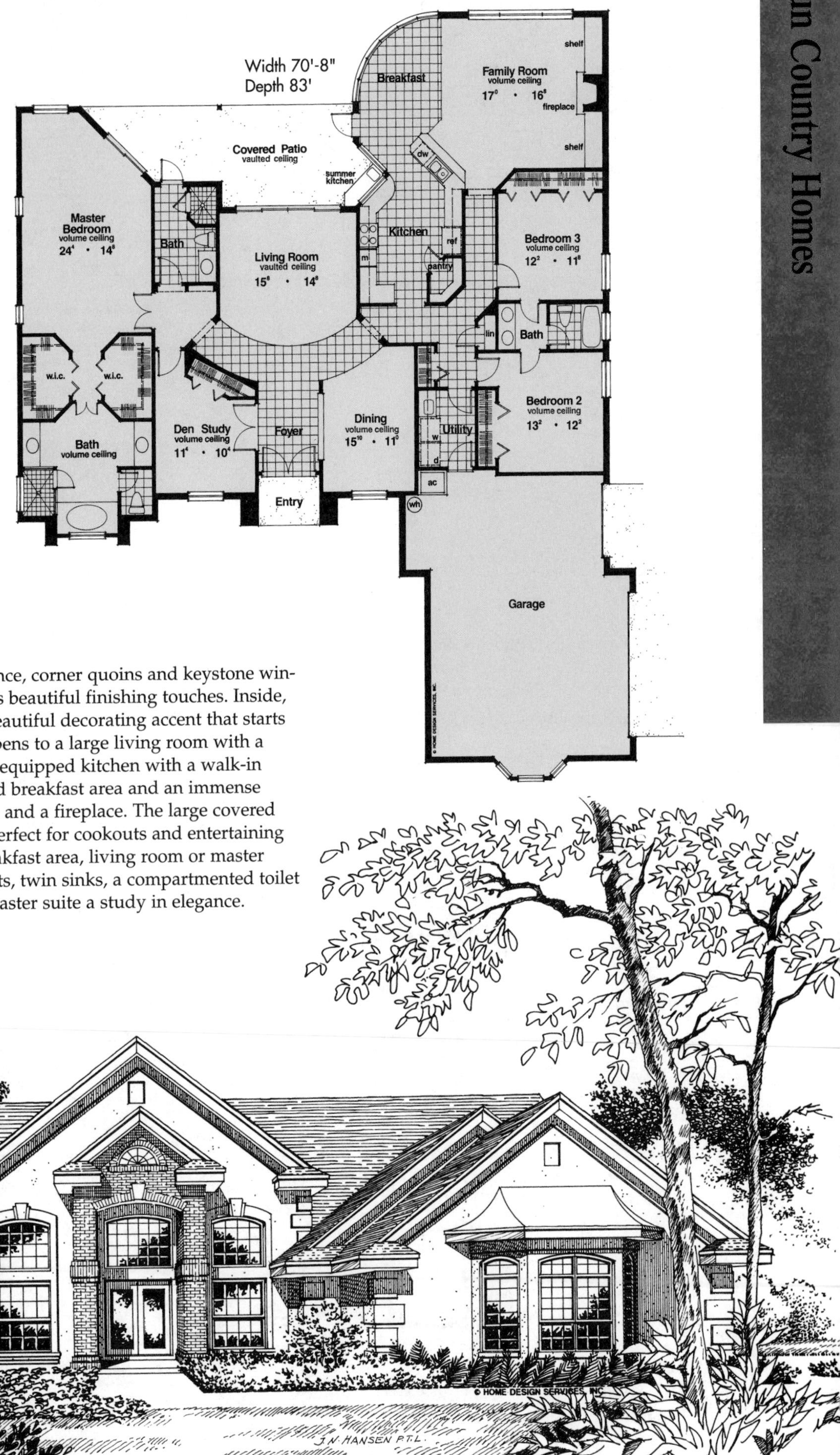

Width 70'-8"
Depth 83'
Breakfast
Family Room
volume ceiling
17^0 · 16^8
shelf
fireplace
shelf
Covered Patio
vaulted ceiling
summer kitchen
dw
Master Bedroom
volume ceiling
24^4 · 14^8
Bath
Living Room
vaulted ceiling
15^8 · 14^8
Kitchen
ref
pantry
Bedroom 3
volume ceiling
12^2 · 11^8
lin
Bath
w.i.c.
w.i.c.
Bath
volume ceiling
Den Study
volume ceiling
11^4 · 10^4
Foyer
Dining
volume ceiling
15^{10} · 11^0
Utility
Bedroom 2
volume ceiling
13^2 · 12^2
ac
wh
Entry
Garage
© HOME DESIGN SERVICES, INC.
J.N. HANSEN P.T.L.

Design by
Home Design Services, Inc.

Design 8666

Square Footage: 2,931

■ The bricked French-door entrance, corner quoins and keystone windows are just a few of this home's beautiful finishing touches. Inside, rich tile flows throughout for a beautiful decorating accent that starts from the ground up. The foyer opens to a large living room with a vaulted ceiling. The wonderfully equipped kitchen with a walk-in pantry opens up to the windowed breakfast area and an immense family room with built-in shelves and a fireplace. The large covered patio with a summer kitchen is perfect for cookouts and entertaining and is accessible through the breakfast area, living room or master suite. His and Hers walk-in closets, twin sinks, a compartmented toilet and a windowed tub make the master suite a study in elegance.

Design 6639

Square Footage: 3,944

■ Innovative design and attention to detail create true luxury living. This clean contemporary style features a raised, columned entry with an interesting stucco relief archway. The foyer opens into the formal living room which overlooks the lanai and waterfall through walls of glass. The formal dining room has a curved wall of windows and a built-in buffet table. Two guest suites each have a walk-in closet and private bath. The owners' wing features a foyer with views of a fountain and a sunny sitting area which opens to the lanai. The bath has a soaking tub, a round shower and a large wardrobe area.

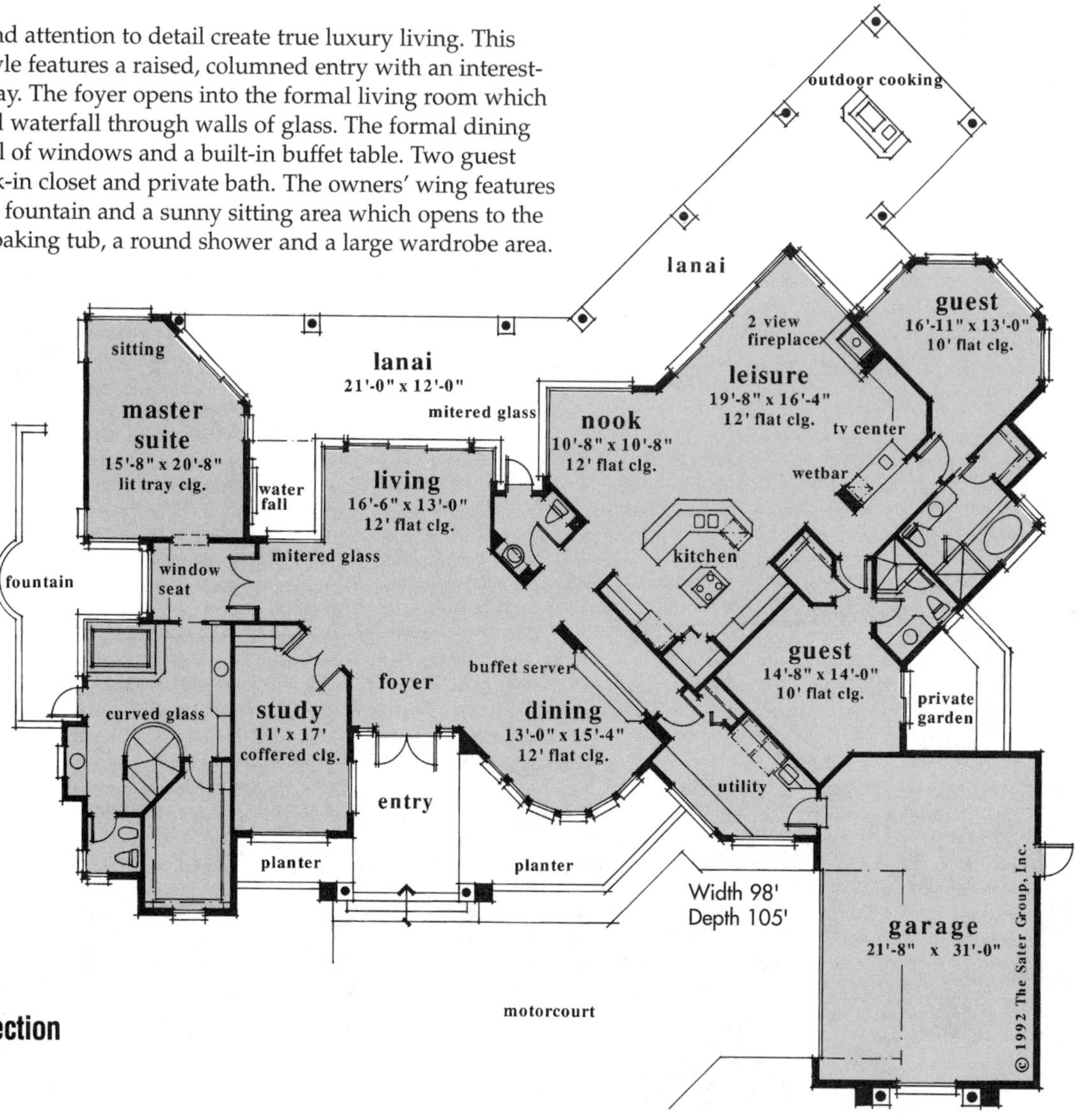

Width 98'
Depth 105'

Design by
The Sater Design Collection

Design 6640

Square Footage: 3,866

■ This modern home adds a contemporary twist to the sunny family living. The turret study and bayed dining room add a sensational look from the streetscape. The main living areas open up to the lanai and offer broad views to the rear through large expanses of glass and doors. The family kitchen nook and leisure room focus on casual living with amenities like an entertainment center and ale bar. The guest suite has a private bath and morning kitchen. An additional bedroom has use of a full cabana bath. The master suite features a lovely sitting area and a lush spa-style bath.

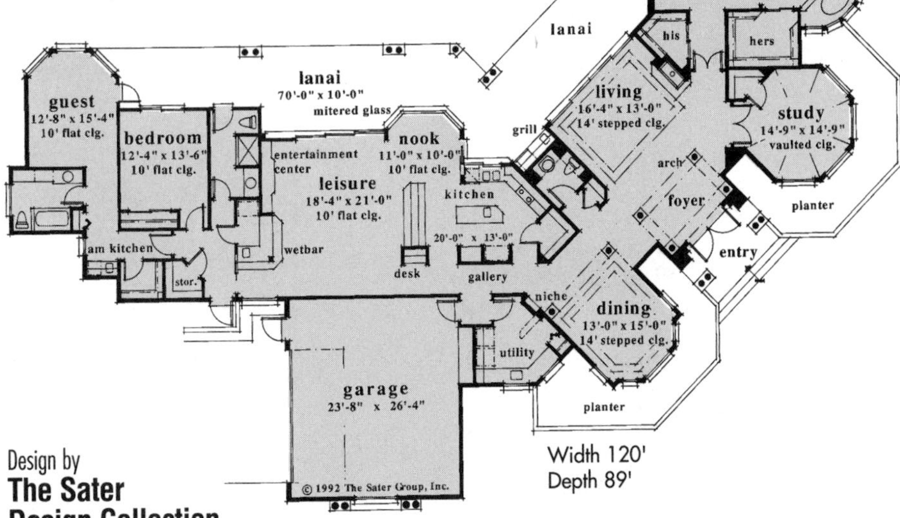
sitting
master suite
14'-10" x 23'-6"
12'-8" flat clg.
lanai
his
hers
lanai
70'-0" x 10'-0"
mitered glass
guest
12'-8" x 15'-4"
10' flat clg.
bedroom
12'-4" x 13'-6"
10' flat clg.
entertainment center
nook
11'-0" x 10'-0"
10' flat clg.
leisure
18'-4" x 21'-0"
10' flat clg.
grill
living
16'-4" x 13'-0"
14' stepped clg.
study
14'-9" x 14'-9"
vaulted clg.
arch
kitchen
foyer
planter
am kitchen
wetbar
20'-0" x 13'-0"
stor.
desk
gallery
entry
niche
dining
13'-0" x 15'-0"
14' stepped clg.
utility
garage
23'-8" x 26'-4"
planter
© 1992 The Sater Group, Inc.

Width 120'
Depth 89'

Design by
The Sater Design Collection

Design 8601

Square Footage: 2,125

■ A luxurious master suite is just one of the highlights offered with this stunning plan—an alternate plan for this suite features a sitting room, wet bar and fireplace. Two family bedrooms to the right of the plan share a full bath with a dual vanity, and a gallery hall that leads directly to the covered patio. Tile adds interest to the living area and surrounds the spacious great room, which offers a fireplace and access to the rear patio. A formal dining room and a secluded den or study flank the foyer.

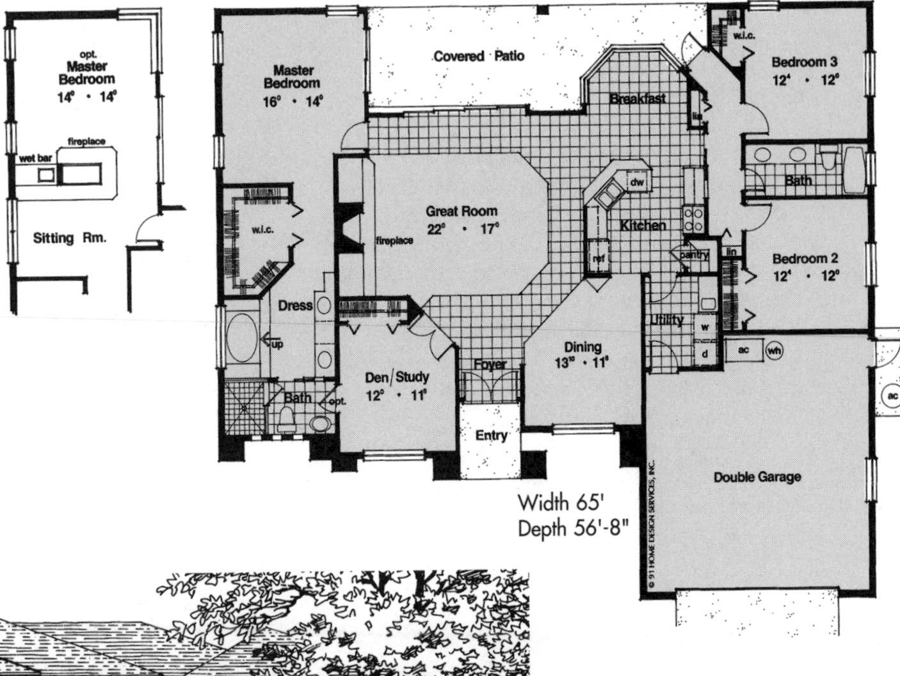
opt. Master Bedroom
14° • 14°
fireplace
wet bar
Sitting Rm.
Master Bedroom
16° • 14°
Covered Patio
Bedroom 3
12⁴ • 12°
w.i.c.
Breakfast
Great Room
22° • 17°
Bath
w.i.c.
fireplace
Kitchen
dw
ref
pantry
Bedroom 2
12⁴ • 12°
Dress
Utility
up
Dining
13¹⁰ • 11⁸
Den/Study
12° • 11°
Foyer
Bath
opt.
Entry
ac
wh
Double Garage
© 91 HOME DESIGN SERVICES, INC.

Width 65'
Depth 56'-8"

© 91 HOME DESIGN SERVICES, INC.

Design by
Home Design Services, Inc.

Design by
Home Design Services, Inc.

Design 8649

Square Footage: 2,691

■ Italianate lines add finesse to the formal facade of this home. Strong symmetry, a soaring portico and gentle rooflines are the prized hallmarks of this relaxed, yet formal design. To the right of the foyer, columns and a stepped ceiling offset the dining room. A plant shelf heralds the living room which also has a twelve-foot ceiling. An angled cooktop counter adds flair to the kitchen, which also has a desk and walk-in pantry and serves the breakfast nook. A corner fireplace, high ceiling and patio enhance the family room. An arch opens the entry to the lavish master suite. Two additional bedrooms come with separate entries to a full bath.

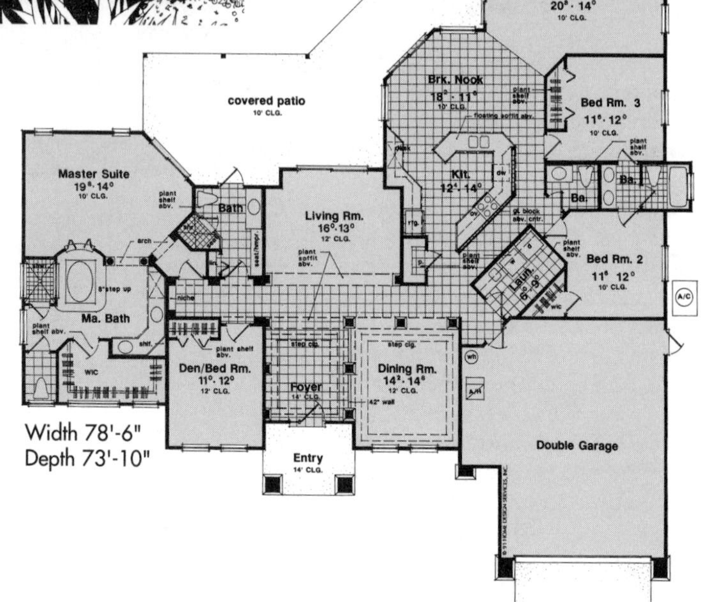

Family Rm.
Brk. Nook
Bed Rm. 3
covered patio
Master Suite
Bath
Living Rm.
Kit.
Ba.
Bed Rm. 2
Ma. Bath
Den/Bed Rm.
Foyer
Dining Rm.
Entry
Double Garage
Width 78'-6"
Depth 73'-10"

Design 8683

First Floor: 2,254 square feet
Second Floor: 608 square feet
Total: 2,862 square feet

■ Indoor and outdoor living are enhanced by the beautiful courtyard that decorates the center of this home. A gallery provides views of the courtyard and leads to a kitchen featuring a center work island and adjacent breakfast room. Combined with the family room, this space will be a favorite for informal gatherings. To the left, the gallery leads to the formal living room and master suite. The secluded master bedroom features a tray ceiling and double doors that lead to a covered patio. Retreat to the master bath, where a relaxing tub awaits to pamper and enjoy. The second floor contains a full bath shared by two family bedrooms and a loft that provides flexible space for an additional bedroom.

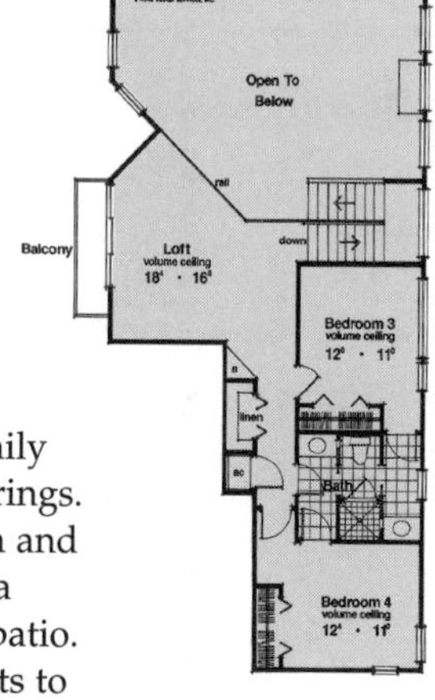

Open To Below
Balcony
Loft
Bedroom 3
Bath
Bedroom 4

Design by
Home Design Services, Inc.

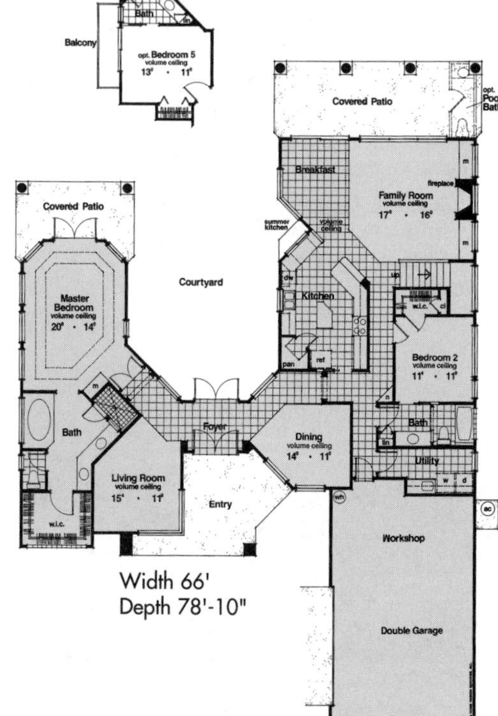

Bath
Balcony
opt. Bedroom 5
Covered Patio
opt. Pool Bath
Breakfast
Family Room
Covered Patio
Courtyard
Master Bedroom
Kitchen
Bedroom 2
Bath
Foyer
Dining
Bath
Utility
Living Room
Entry
Workshop
Double Garage
Width 66'
Depth 78'-10"

© 1989 The Sater Group, Inc.

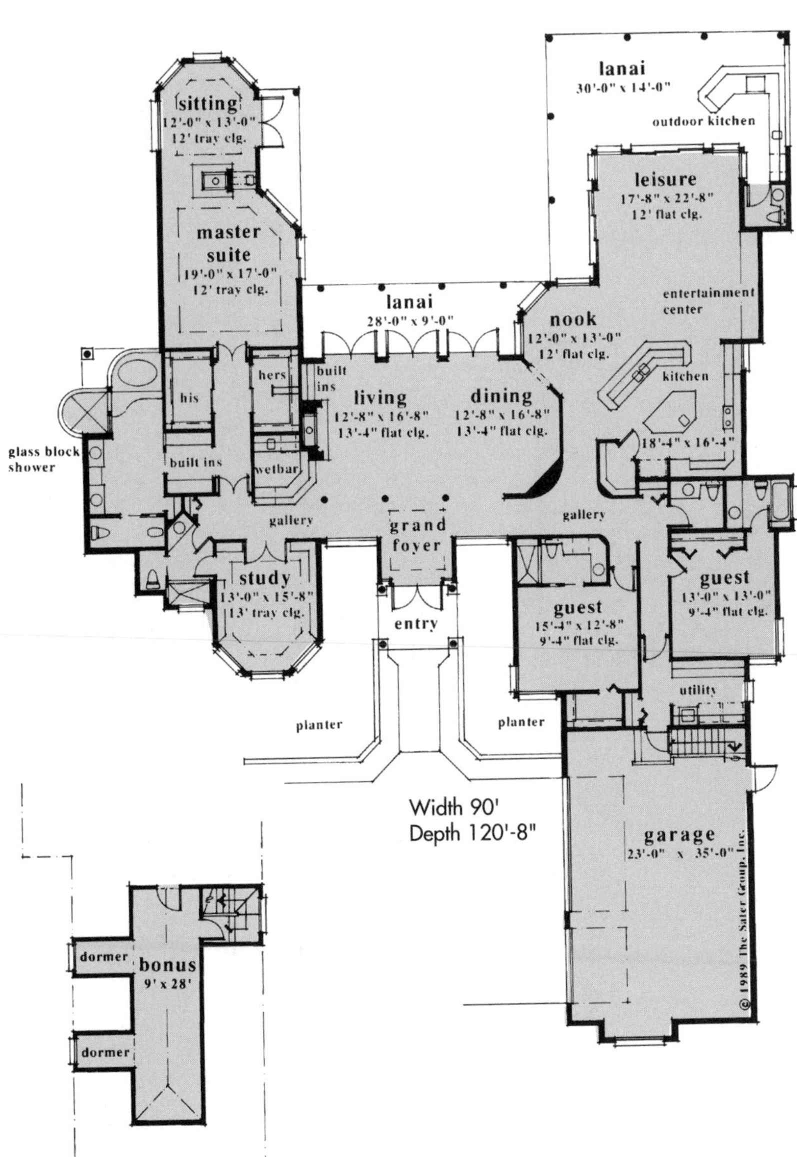
lanai
30'-0" x 14'-0"
outdoor kitchen
sitting
12'-0" x 13'-0"
12' tray clg.
master
suite
19'-0" x 17'-0"
12' tray clg.
leisure
17'-8" x 22'-8"
12' flat clg.
entertainment
center
lanai
28'-0" x 9'-0"
nook
12'-0" x 13'-0"
12' flat clg.
hers
his
built
ins
living
12'-8" x 16'-8"
13'-4" flat clg.
dining
12'-8" x 16'-8"
13'-4" flat clg.
kitchen
18'-4" x 16'-4"
glass block
shower
built ins
wetbar
gallery
grand
foyer
gallery
study
13'-0" x 15'-8"
13' tray clg.
entry
guest
15'-4" x 12'-8"
9'-4" flat clg.
guest
13'-0" x 13'-0"
9'-4" flat clg.
utility
planter
planter
Width 90'
Depth 120'-8"
garage
23'-0" x 35'-0"
© 1989 The Sater Group, Inc.
dormer
bonus
9' x 28'
dormer

Design 6641

Square Footage: 3,896

■ This elegant exterior blends a classical look with a contemporary feel. Corner quoins and round columns highlight the front elevation. The formal living room, complete with a fireplace and a wet bar, and the formal dining room access the lanai through three pairs of French doors. The well-appointed kitchen features an island prep sink, walk-in pantry and a desk. The secondary bedrooms are full guest suites, located away from the private owner's wing. The master suite has enormous His and Hers closets, built-ins, a wet bar and three-sided fireplace that separates the sitting room and the bedroom. The luxurious bath features a stunning, rounded glass-block shower and a whirlpool tub.

Design by
The Sater Design Collection

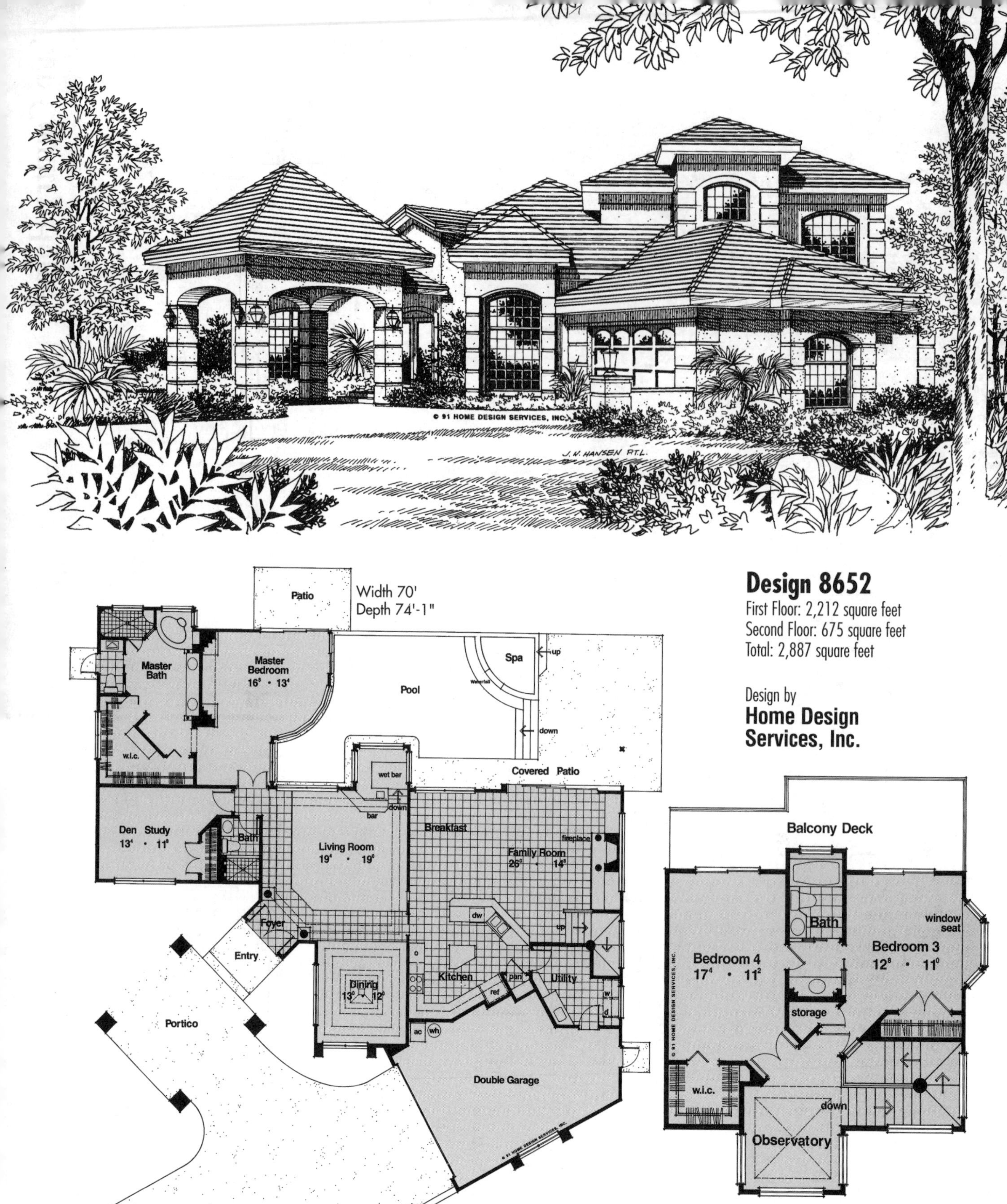
© 91 HOME DESIGN SERVICES, INC.
J.V. HANSEN RTL.
Patio
Width 70'
Depth 74'-1"
Master Bath
Master Bedroom
$16^{8} \cdot 13^{4}$
Spa
up
Pool
Waterfall
down
w.i.c.
Covered Patio
wet bar
bar
down
Den Study
$13^{4} \cdot 11^{8}$
Bath
Living Room
$19^{4} \cdot 19^{0}$
Breakfast
fireplace
Family Room
$26^{0} \cdot 14^{8}$
dw
up
Foyer
Entry
Dining
$13^{0} \cdot 12^{0}$
Kitchen
pan
ref
Utility
w
d
ac
wh
Portico
Double Garage
Balcony Deck
Bath
window seat
Bedroom 4
$17^{4} \cdot 11^{2}$
Bedroom 3
$12^{8} \cdot 11^{0}$
storage
w.i.c.
down
Observatory

Design 8652

First Floor: 2,212 square feet
Second Floor: 675 square feet
Total: 2,887 square feet

Design by
Home Design Services, Inc.

■ As you drive up to the porte cochere entry of this home, the visual movement of the elevation is breathtaking. The multi-roofed spaces bring excitement the moment you walk through the double-doored entry. The foyer leads into the wide glass-walled living room. To the right, the formal dining room features a tiered pedestal ceiling. To the left is the guest and master suite wing of the home. The master suite with its sweeping, curved glass wall has access to the patio area and overlooks the pool. The master bath, with its huge walk-in closet comes complete with a columned vanity area, a soaking tub and a shower for two. Two large bedrooms on the second floor—one with a bay window and one with a walk-in closet—share a sun deck, a full bath and an activity area.

Design by
Home Design Services, Inc.

Design 8645

Square Footage: 2,224

■ Arches crowned by gentle, hipped rooflines provide an Italianate charm in this bright and spacious, family-oriented plan. A covered entry leads to the foyer that presents the angular, vaulted living and dining rooms. A kitchen with a V-shaped counter includes a walk-in pantry and looks out over the breakfast nook and family room with a fireplace. The master suite features a sitting room, two walk-in closets and a full bath with garden tub. Two additional bedrooms share a full bath located between them. A fourth bedroom, with its own bath, opens off the family room and works perfectly as a guest room.

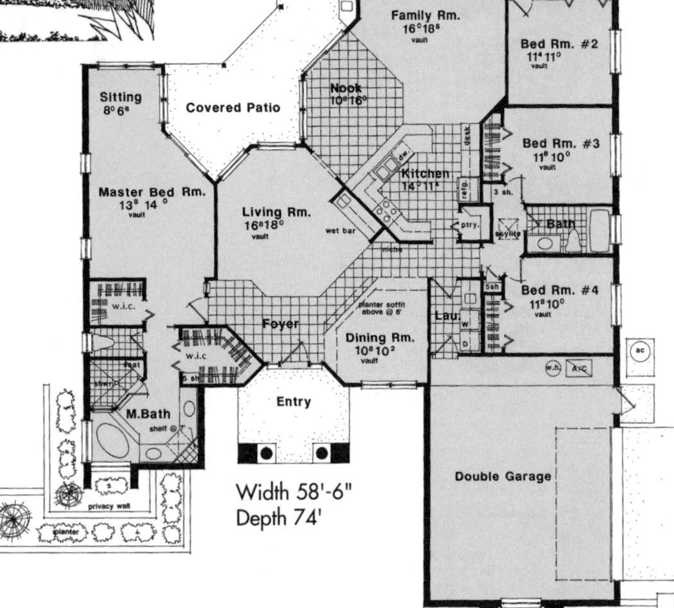
window above
opt. summer kitchen
fireplace
Family Rm.
Bath
Bed Rm. #2
Nook
Sitting
Covered Patio
Kitchen
Bed Rm. #3
Master Bed Rm.
Living Rm.
wet bar
Bath
Bed Rm. #4
w.i.c.
Foyer
Lau.
Dining Rm.
Entry
M.Bath
Double Garage
privacy wall
planter

Width 58'-6"
Depth 74'

Design 8637

Square Footage: 2,089

■ This four-bedroom, three-bath home offers the finest in modern amenities. The formal living spaces have a classic split design, perfect for quiet time and conversation. The huge family room, which opens up to the patio with twelve-foot, pocket sliding doors, has space for a fireplace and media equipment. Two family bedrooms share their own bath while one bedroom has a private bath with patio access, making it the perfect guest room. The master suite, located just off the kitchen and nook, is private yet easily accessible. It has a double-door entry and a bed wall with glass above. The angled entry to the bath makes for a luxurious view of the corner tub. The step-down shower and private toilet room, walk-in linen closet, lavish vanity and closet make this a super bath!

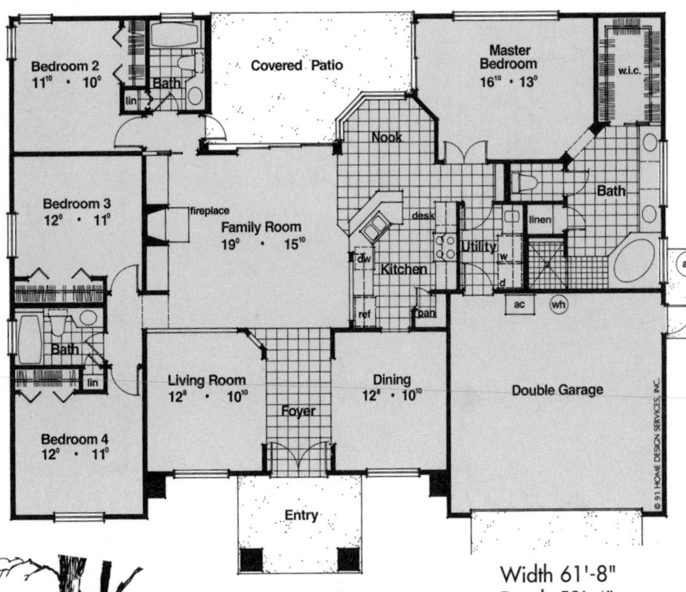
Bedroom 2
Bath
Covered Patio
Master Bedroom
w.i.c.
Nook
Bedroom 3
fireplace
Family Room
Bath
Kitchen
Utility
Bath
Living Room
Dining
Double Garage
Foyer
Bedroom 4
Entry

Width 61'-8"
Depth 50'-4"

Design by
Home Design Services, Inc.

■ This exquisite plan features two tower structures that enhance its dramatic facade. Inside, the living areas radiate around the central hallway which also contains the stairway to the second floor. The areas are large, open and convenient for both casual and formal occasions. Three bedrooms upstairs include two family bedrooms and a grand master suite with a bath fit for a king. An oversized walk-in closet and vaulted ceiling are found here. Bonus space over the garage can be developed at a later time to suit changing needs.

Design by
Alan Mascord Design Associates, Inc.

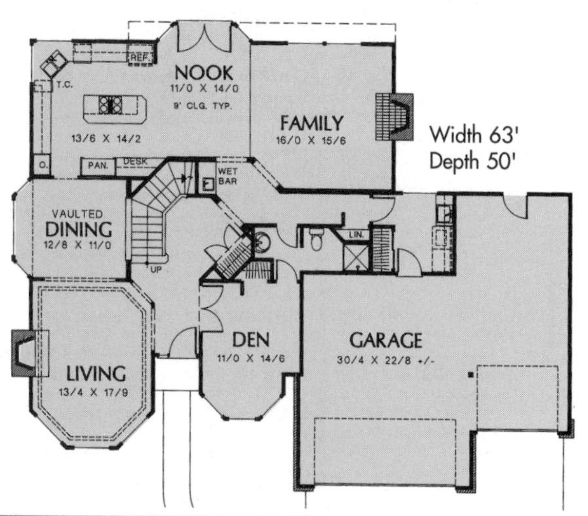

REF.
NOOK
11/0 X 14/0
9' CLG. TYP.
T.C.
13/6 X 14/2
PAN.
DESK
FAMILY
16/0 X 15/6
WET BAR
VAULTED
DINING
12/8 X 11/0
UP
LIN.
DEN
11/0 X 14/6
GARAGE
30/4 X 22/8 +/-
LIVING
13/4 X 17/9
Width 63'
Depth 50'

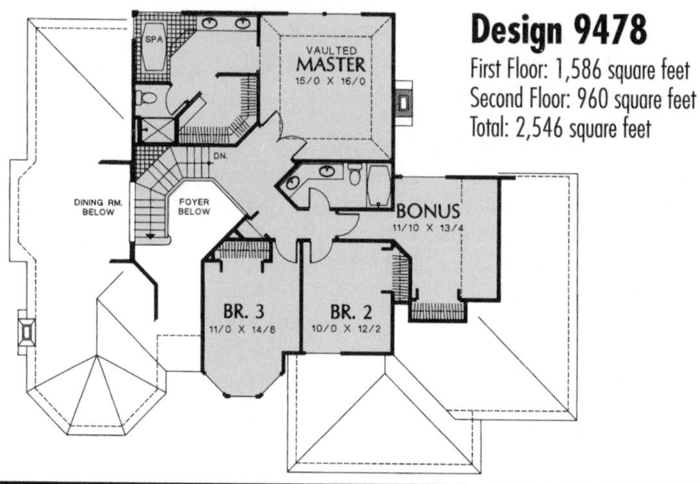

SPA
VAULTED
MASTER
15/0 X 16/0
DN.
DINING RM. BELOW
FOYER BELOW
BONUS
11/10 X 13/4
BR. 3
11/0 X 14/8
BR. 2
10/0 X 12/2

Design 9478

First Floor: 1,586 square feet
Second Floor: 960 square feet
Total: 2,546 square feet

Design 8684

Square Footage: 1,898

■ Family living is at the core of this brick one-story home. To the left of the foyer, double doors open to the den/study. The master suite features a pampering bath with a large walk-in closet, a separate shower and a relaxing tub. The family room combines well with the kitchen and the bay-windowed breakfast nook. The sleeping wing to the right contains two secondary bedrooms that share a full bath and patio access.

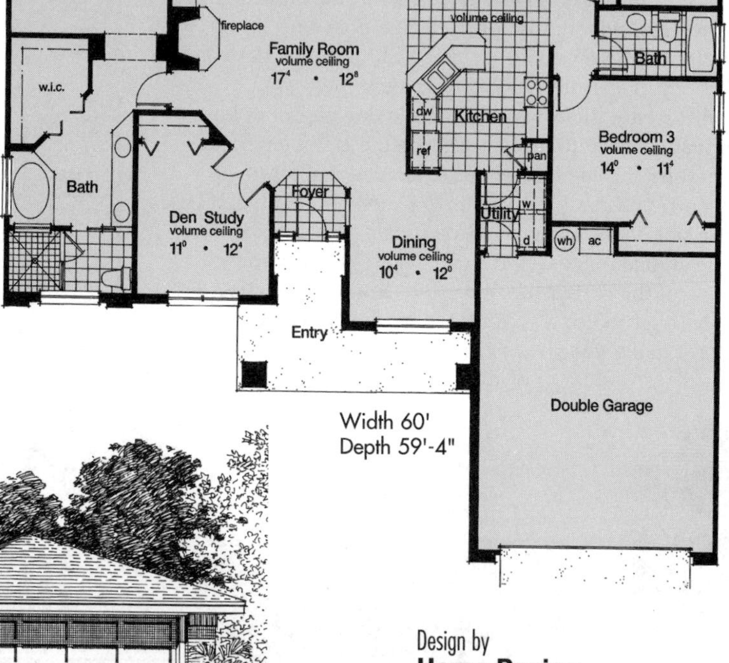

Covered Patio
Master Bedroom
volume ceiling
$13^{0} \cdot 16^{0}$
Bedroom 2
volume ceiling
$11^{4} \cdot 11^{0}$
Breakfast
med
fireplace
volume ceiling
Family Room
volume ceiling
$17^{4} \cdot 12^{8}$
lin
Bath
w.i.c.
dw
Kitchen
ref
pan
Bedroom 3
volume ceiling
$14^{0} \cdot 11^{4}$
Bath
Foyer
Den Study
volume ceiling
$11^{0} \cdot 12^{4}$
Utility
w
d
wh
ac
Dining
volume ceiling
$10^{4} \cdot 12^{0}$
Entry
Double Garage
Width 60'
Depth 59'-4"

Design by
Home Design Services, Inc.

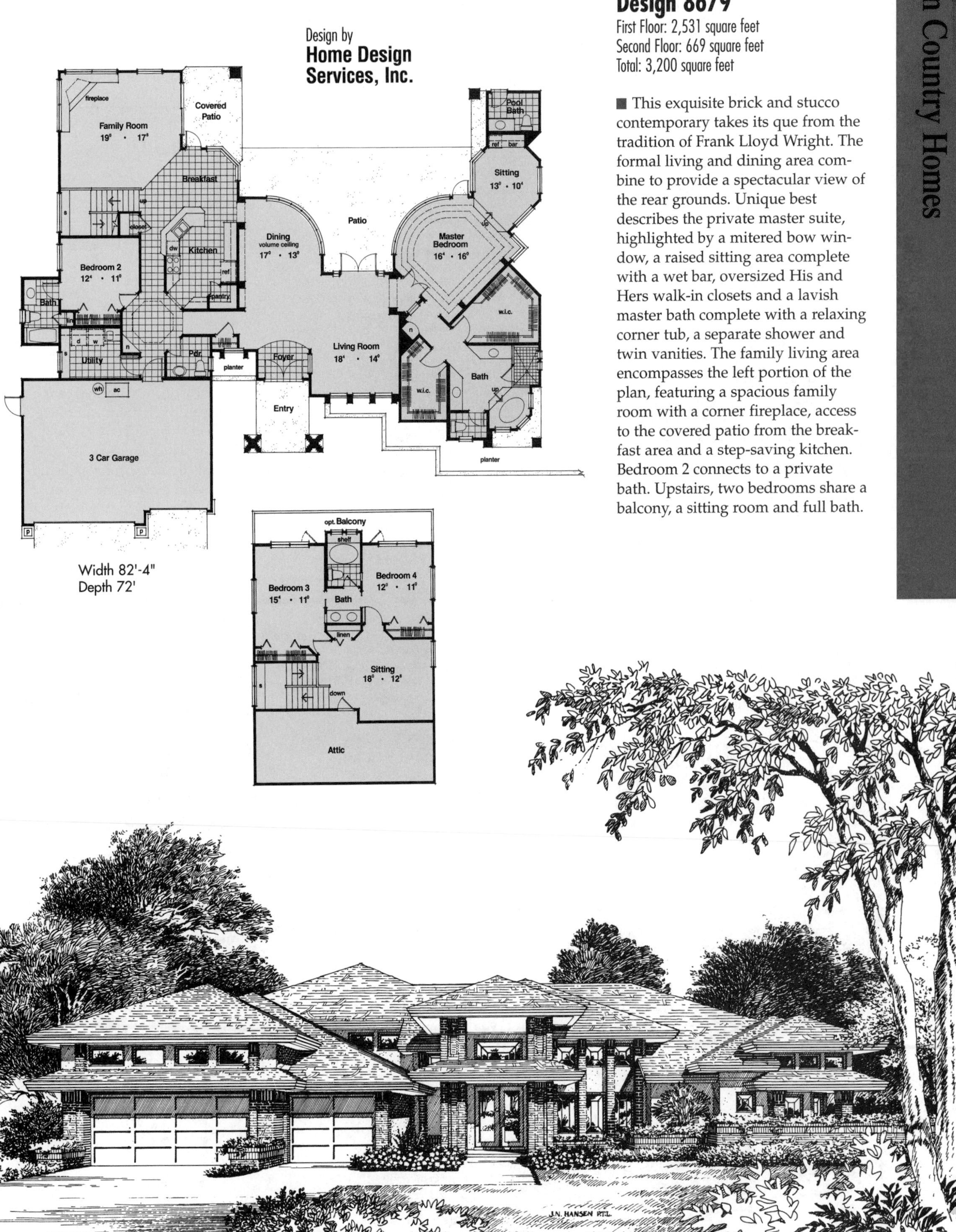
Design by
Home Design Services, Inc.
fireplace
Family Room
19⁰ · 17⁸
Covered Patio
Breakfast
Pool Bath
ref bar
Sitting
13⁰ · 10⁴
Patio
Dining
volume ceiling
17⁰ · 13⁰
Master Bedroom
16⁴ · 16⁰
Kitchen
Bedroom 2
12⁴ · 11⁰
Bath
pantry
w.i.c.
Utility
Pdr
planter
Foyer
Living Room
18⁴ · 14⁰
w.i.c.
Bath
Entry
3 Car Garage
planter
Width 82'-4"
Depth 72'
opt. Balcony
shelf
Bedroom 4
12⁰ · 11⁰
Bedroom 3
15⁴ · 11⁰
Bath
linen
Sitting
18⁰ · 12⁸
down
Attic
J.N. HANSEN P.T.L.

Design 8679

First Floor: 2,531 square feet
Second Floor: 669 square feet
Total: 3,200 square feet

■ This exquisite brick and stucco contemporary takes its que from the tradition of Frank Lloyd Wright. The formal living and dining area combine to provide a spectacular view of the rear grounds. Unique best describes the private master suite, highlighted by a mitered bow window, a raised sitting area complete with a wet bar, oversized His and Hers walk-in closets and a lavish master bath complete with a relaxing corner tub, a separate shower and twin vanities. The family living area encompasses the left portion of the plan, featuring a spacious family room with a corner fireplace, access to the covered patio from the breakfast area and a step-saving kitchen. Bedroom 2 connects to a private bath. Upstairs, two bedrooms share a balcony, a sitting room and full bath.

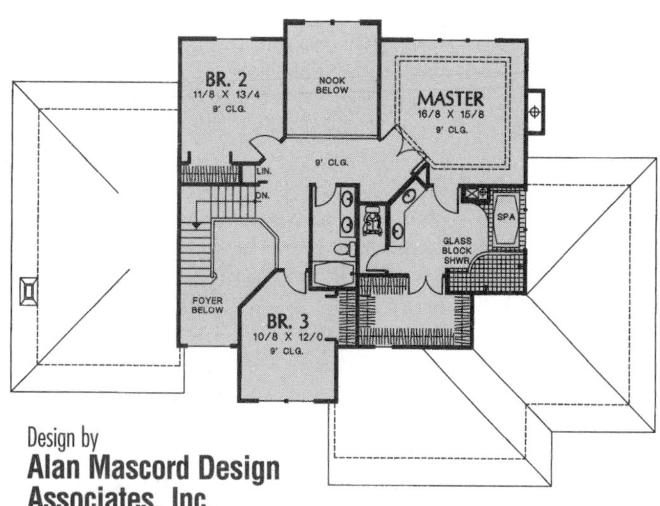
BR. 2
11/8 X 13/4
9' CLG.
NOOK BELOW
MASTER
16/8 X 15/8
9' CLG.
LIN.
DN.
9' CLG.
SPA
GLASS BLOCK SHWR.
FOYER BELOW
BR. 3
10/8 X 12/0
9' CLG.

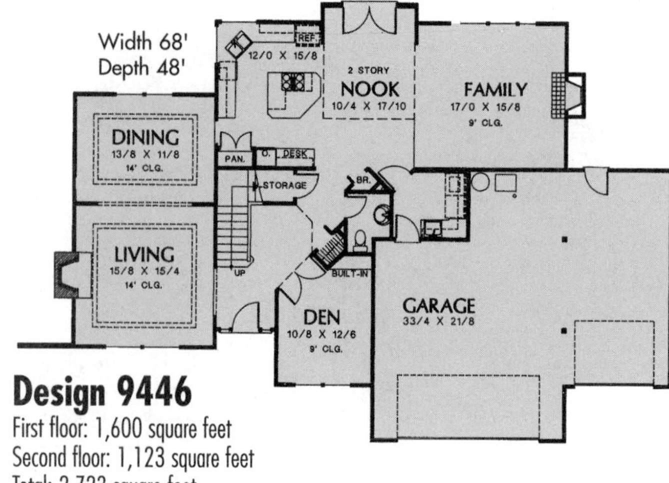
Width 68'
Depth 48'
12/0 X 15/8
REF.
2 STORY
NOOK
10/4 X 17/10
FAMILY
17/0 X 15/8
9' CLG.
DINING
13/8 X 11/8
14' CLG.
PAN.
DESK
STORAGE
BR.
LIVING
15/8 X 15/4
14' CLG.
UP
BUILT-IN
DEN
10/8 X 12/6
9' CLG.
GARAGE
33/4 X 21/8

Design by
Alan Mascord Design Associates, Inc.

Design 9446

First floor: 1,600 square feet
Second floor: 1,123 square feet
Total: 2,723 square feet

■ Beyond the contemporary facade of this home lies a highly functional floor plan. First-floor living areas include formal living and dining rooms, a private den, and a large family room that connects directly to the breakfast nook and island kitchen. The upper level contains three bedrooms, including a master suite with a nine-foot tray ceiling and a sumptuous master bath which encompasses a huge walk-in closet, a whirlpool spa and a double vanity in the bath. A fine hall bath completes this floor.

Design by
Alan Mascord Design Associates, Inc.

Design 9581

First Floor: 1,896 square feet
Second Floor: 568 square feet
Total: 2,464 square feet

MASTER 13/0 X 16/0 (10' CLG.)
SPA
Width 45'
Depth 64'
DEN 11/0 X 10/0 (9' CLG.)
TWO STORY FAMILY 17/4 X 16/8 +/-
(9' CLG.)
NOOK 11/4 x 10/0 (9' CLG.)
11/0 X 11/4 +/-
MEDIA CENTER
LINEN
BUILT-IN
REF.
UP
DINING 12/0 x 10/10 (10' CLG.)
GARAGE 20/4 X 21/8
LIVING 13/0 x 14/6 (10' CLG.)

■ Inside the grand entrance of this contemporary home a large foyer offers a gracious introduction to the formal living and dining rooms. Nearby, the L-shaped island kitchen serves formal and informal areas with equal ease. A two-story family room with a built-in media center and a corner fireplace shares space with a sunny nook. The private master suite features a walk-in closet and a luxurious master bath. The second floor contains two bedrooms and a full bath.

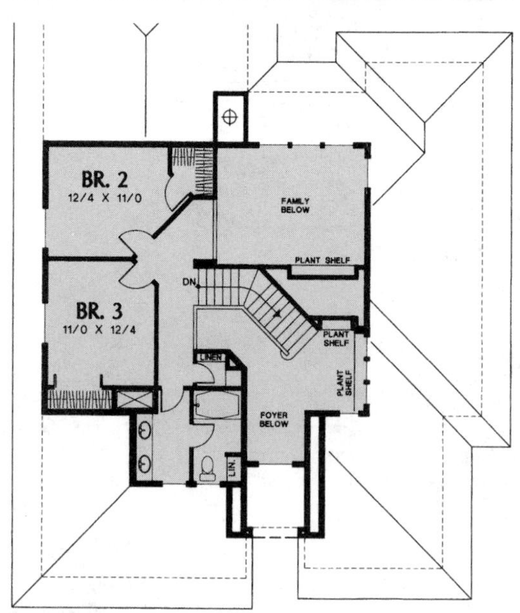
BR. 2
12/4 X 11/0
FAMILY BELOW
PLANT SHELF
DN
BR. 3
11/0 X 12/4
PLANT SHELF
LINEN
FOYER BELOW
LIN.

■ Luxury abounds in this magnificent contemporary plan. The entry foyer gives way to a den on the left and formal living and dining rooms on the right. A curving staircase leads upstairs to the master suite, and two family bedrooms sharing a full bath. The rear of the plan holds a family room separated from the kitchen/nook area by built-in shelves. A back staircase here makes the upstairs even more accessible. Note special features such as the three-car garage, island prep in the kitchen and bonus room.

Design 9485

First Floor: 2,148 square feet
Second Floor: 1,300 square feet
Total: 3,448 square feet
Bonus Room: 444 square feet

NOOK
11/0 X 11/0
FAMILY
20/0 X 15/8
20/0 X 15/6 +/-
DINING
12/2 X 15/0
DEN
11/6 X 14/0
LIVING
16/6 X 19/10
GARAGE
33/8 X 25/4 +
Width 86'
Depth 73'
BR. 2
11/0 X 13/4
MASTER
17/4 X 15/8 +/-
BONUS
27/0 X 12/4 +
BR. 3
11/6 X 12/0 +
FOYER BELOW

Design by
Alan Mascord Design Associates, Inc.

Design 9434

First Floor: 2,226 square feet
Second Floor: 1,444 square feet
Total: 3,670 square feet

■ European styling takes center stage in this beautiful two-story. The interior allows for a variety of lifestyle options. For example, the den on the main floor can be used as a convenient guest bedroom thanks to an adjacent full bath. Formal living and dining rooms flank the entry and both feature their share of treasured amenities. The oversized family room provides a fireplace and is adjacent to the breakfast nook and island kitchen. Upstairs are four bedrooms, including a spectacular master suite overlooking the front courtyard. A three-car garage easily accommodates the family fleet.

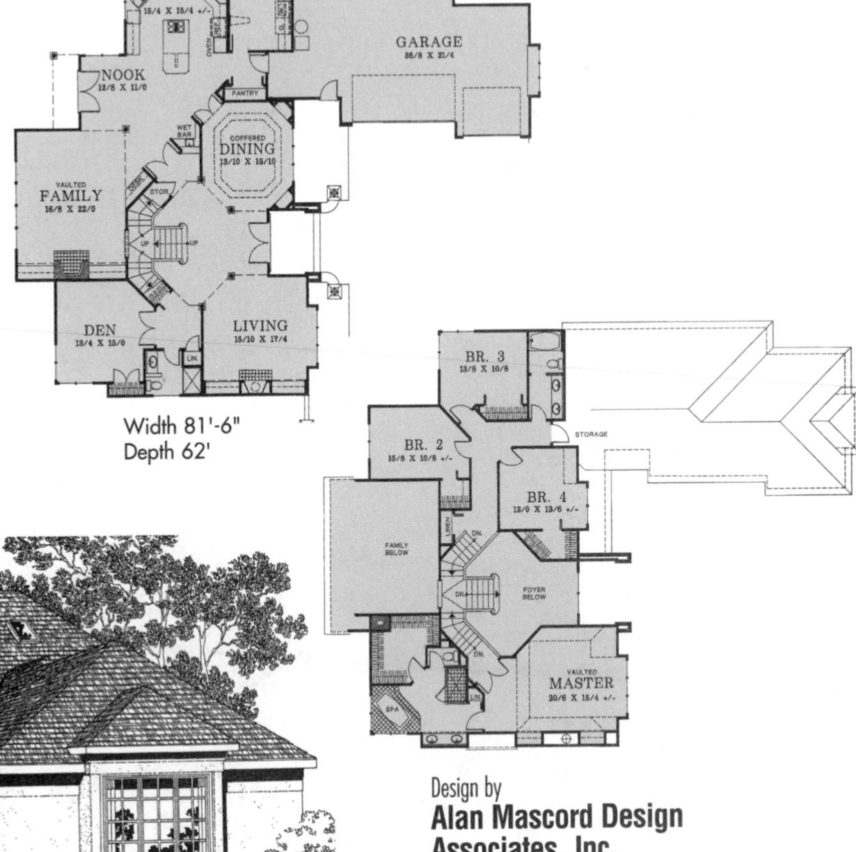
GARAGE
36/8 X 21/4
NOOK
12/8 X 11/0
COFFERED
DINING
13/10 X 15/10
VAULTED
FAMILY
16/8 X 22/0
DEN
13/4 X 15/0
LIVING
15/10 X 17/4
Width 81'-6"
Depth 62'
BR. 3
13/8 X 10/8
BR. 2
15/8 X 10/8 +/-
BR. 4
12/0 X 13/6 +/-
FAMILY BELOW
FOYER BELOW
VAULTED
MASTER
20/6 X 15/4 +/-

Design by
Alan Mascord Design Associates, Inc.

Design 9558

First Floor: 1,322 square feet
Second Floor: 1,000 square feet
Total: 2,322 square feet

Design by
Alan Mascord Design Associates, Inc.

■ A multi-windowed breakfast nook will brighten your mornings. Columns dress up the beam-ceilinged family room and the kitchen. An island cooktop is placed in an efficient work triangle also defined by an angled double sink and a refrigerator. A den with built-ins, a dining room and a rear living room with a fireplace provide ample space for various pursuits. A three-bedroom upstairs includes two secondary bedrooms of ample proportions and a master bedroom suite that opens through double doors.

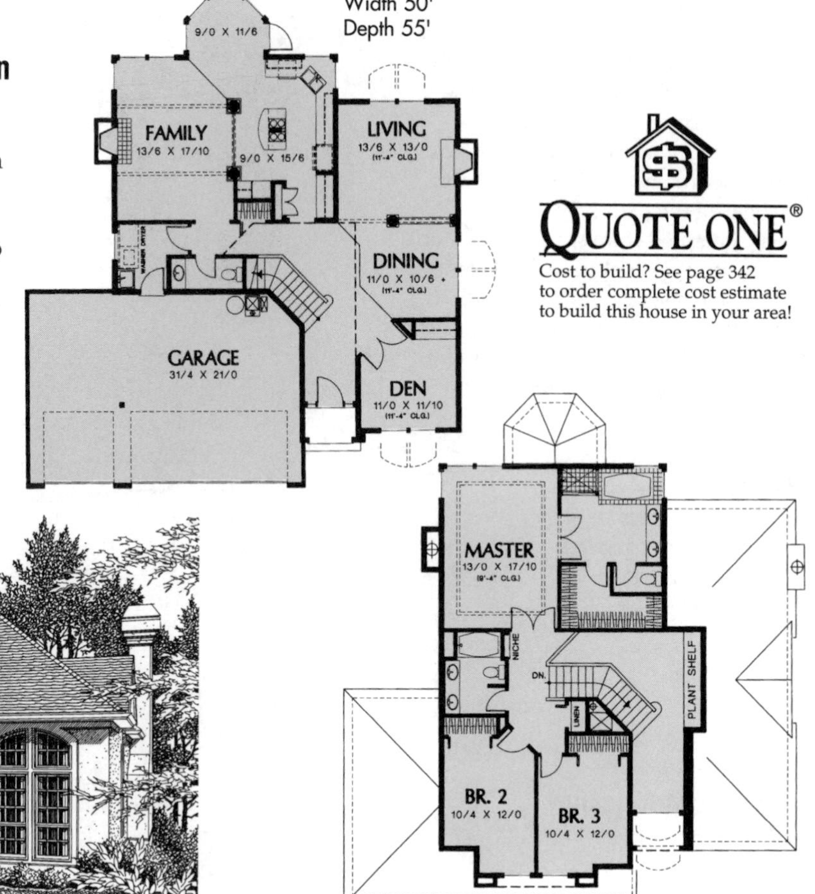

Width 50'
Depth 55'
9/0 X 11/6
FAMILY
13/6 X 17/10
9/0 X 15/6
LIVING
13/6 X 13/0
DINING
11/0 X 10/6
GARAGE
31/4 X 21/0
DEN
11/0 X 11/10
MASTER
13/0 X 17/10
NICHE
DN.
LINEN
PLANT SHELF
BR. 2
10/4 X 12/0
BR. 3
10/4 X 12/0

QUOTE ONE®
Cost to build? See page 342 to order complete cost estimate to build this house in your area!

Design 8659

First Floor: 1,230 square feet
Second Floor: 649 square feet
Total: 1,879 square feet

■ The tiled foyer of this two-story home opens to a living/dining space with a soaring ceiling, a fireplace in the living room and access to a covered patio that invites outdoor livability. The kitchen has an oversized, sunny breakfast area with a volume ceiling. The first-floor master bedroom offers privacy with its sumptuous bath; a corner soaking tub, dual lavatories and a compartmented toilet lend character to the room. Upstairs, a loft overlooking the living spaces could become a third bedroom. One of the family bedrooms features a walk-in closet. Both bedrooms share a generous hall bath.

Width 38'
Depth 53'-6"

Design by
Home Design Services, Inc.

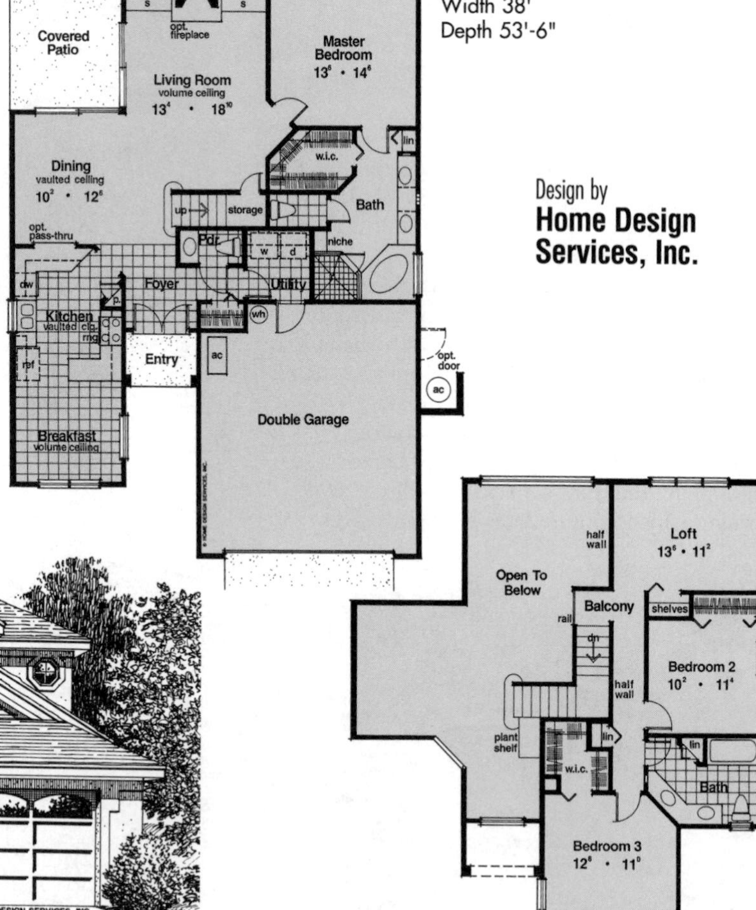

Covered Patio
opt. fireplace
Living Room
volume ceiling
13⁴ • 18¹⁰
Master Bedroom
13⁶ • 14⁶
Dining
vaulted ceiling
10² • 12⁶
w.i.c.
storage
Bath
Pdr
niche
opt. pass-thru
Foyer
Utility
Kitchen
vaulted clg.
Entry
opt. door
Double Garage
Breakfast
volume ceiling
Open To Below
half wall
Loft
13⁶ • 11²
Balcony
shelves
Bedroom 2
10² • 11⁴
plant shelf
w.i.c.
Bath
Bedroom 3
12⁶ • 11⁰

© HOME DESIGN SERVICES, INC.

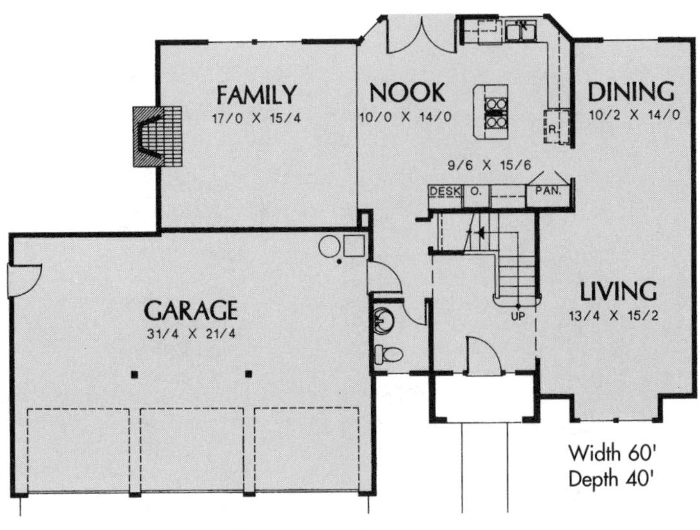
FAMILY
17/0 X 15/4
NOOK
10/0 X 14/0
DINING
10/2 X 14/0
9/6 X 15/6
DESK
PAN.
GARAGE
31/4 X 21/4
LIVING
13/4 X 15/2
UP

Width 60'
Depth 40'

Design 9442

First Floor: 1,172 square feet
Second Floor: 1,214 square feet
Total: 2,386 square feet

Design by
Alan Mascord Design Associates, Inc.

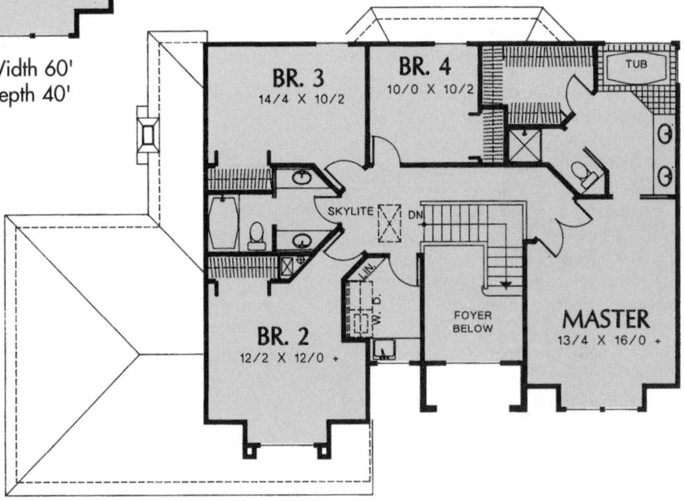

■ This home's entry opens to a most convenient floor plan. Formal living and dining rooms are to the right and provide a gracious backdrop for entertaining. The family room and kitchen/nook area combine into a large casual space that's perfect for everyday activities. The family room has a cozy fireplace and outdoor access. A three-car garage connects to the main house near a handy powder room. Upstairs there are four bedrooms. One is the master suite with a double-bowl vanity and a separate tub and shower. Three family bedrooms share a full bath with separate vanity and bathing areas. A laundry room is also placed on the second floor for convenience.

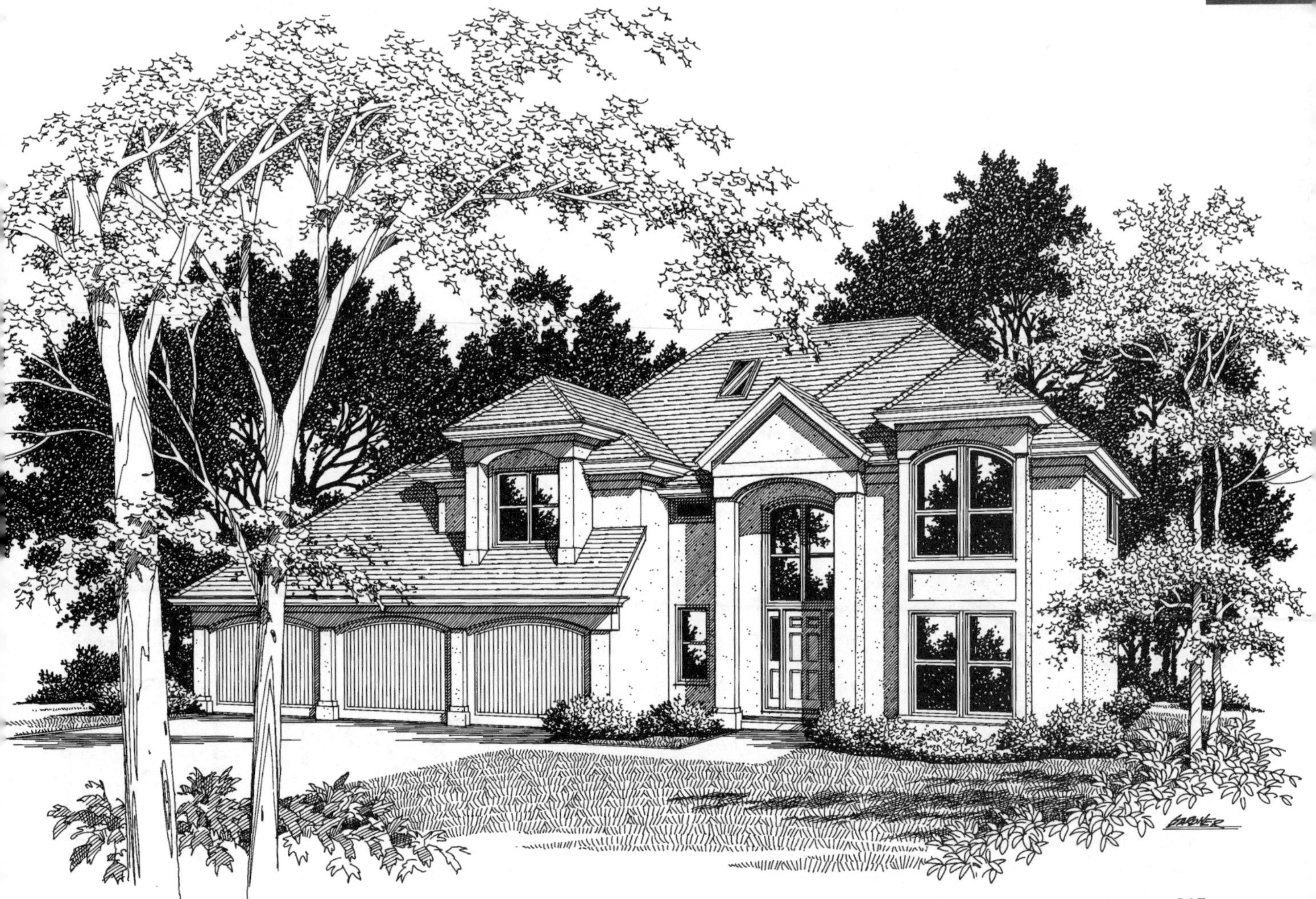

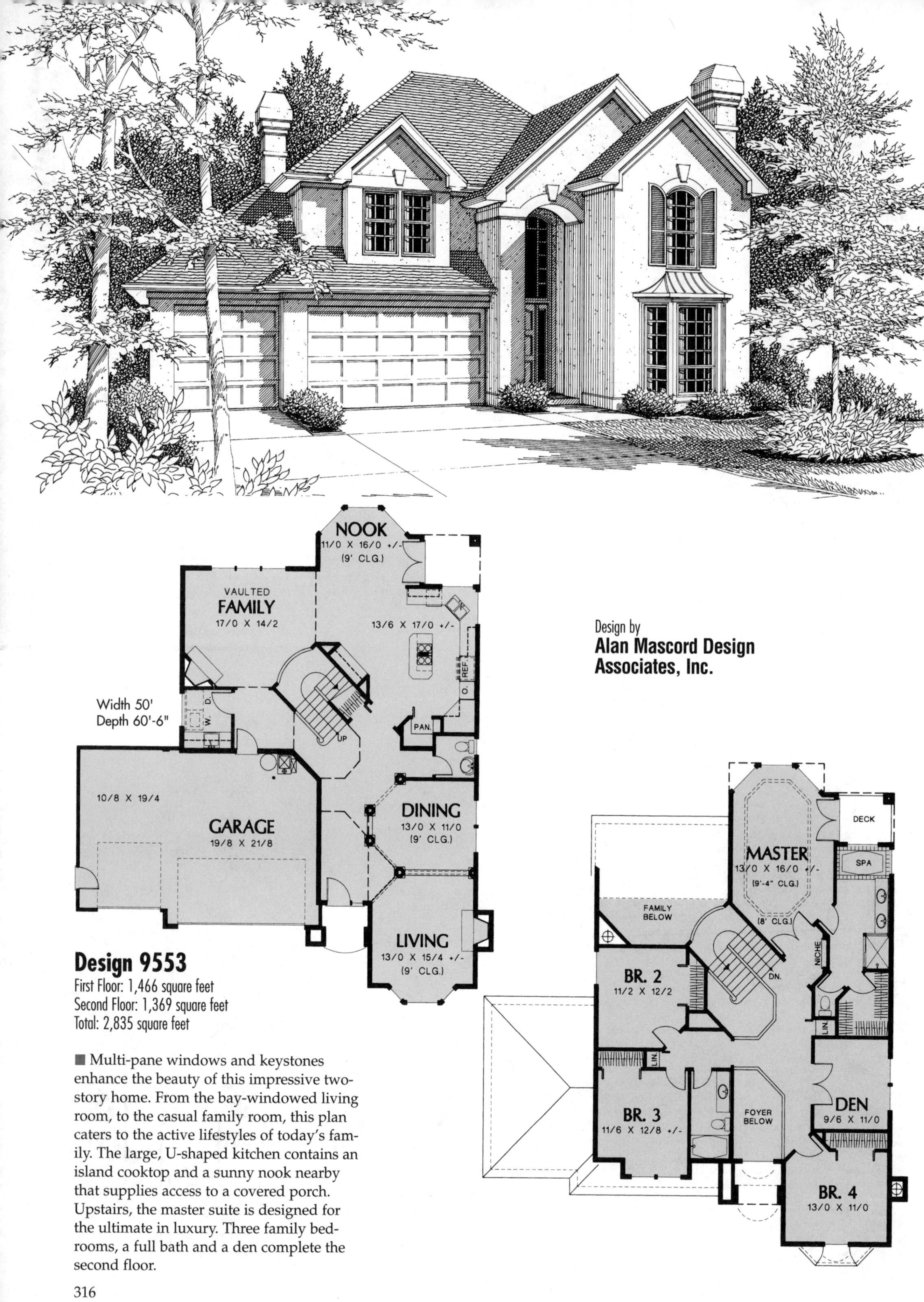
NOOK
11/0 X 16/0 +/-
(9' CLG.)
VAULTED
FAMILY
17/0 X 14/2
13/6 X 17/0 +/-
REF.
PAN.
UP
GARAGE
10/8 X 19/4
19/8 X 21/8
DINING
13/0 X 11/0
(9' CLG.)
LIVING
13/0 X 15/4 +/-
(9' CLG.)
DECK
MASTER
13/0 X 16/0 +/-
(9'-4" CLG.)
(8' CLG.)
SPA
FAMILY
BELOW
NICHE
BR. 2
11/2 X 12/2
DN.
LIN.
BR. 3
11/6 X 12/8 +/-
FOYER
BELOW
DEN
9/6 X 11/0
BR. 4
13/0 X 11/0

Width 50'
Depth 60'-6"

Design by
Alan Mascord Design Associates, Inc.

Design 9553

First Floor: 1,466 square feet
Second Floor: 1,369 square feet
Total: 2,835 square feet

■ Multi-pane windows and keystones enhance the beauty of this impressive two-story home. From the bay-windowed living room, to the casual family room, this plan caters to the active lifestyles of today's family. The large, U-shaped kitchen contains an island cooktop and a sunny nook nearby that supplies access to a covered porch. Upstairs, the master suite is designed for the ultimate in luxury. Three family bedrooms, a full bath and a den complete the second floor.

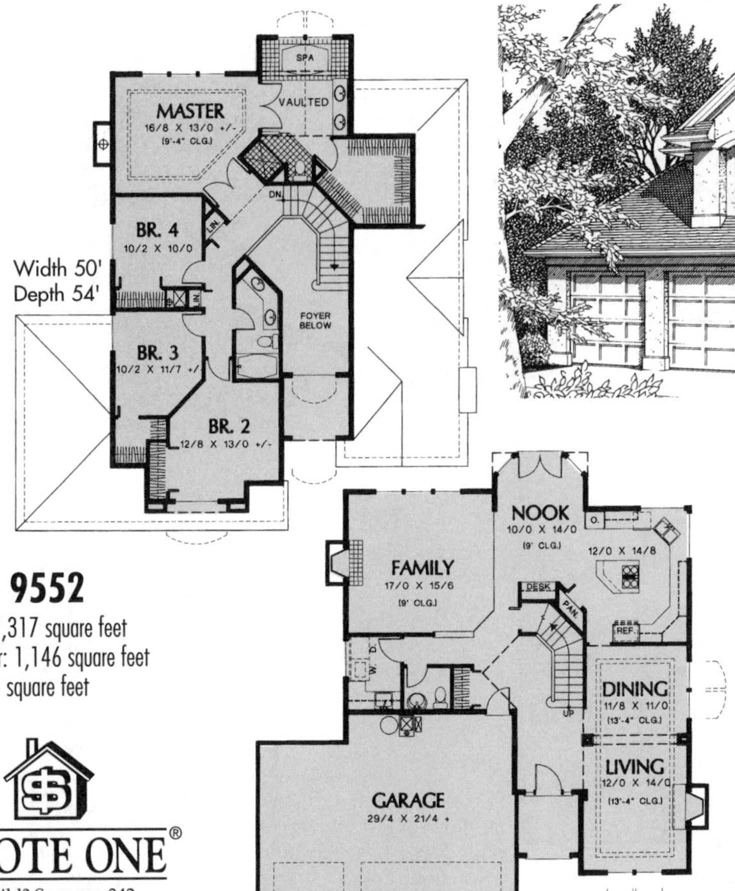
SPA
MASTER
16/8 X 13/0 +/-
(9'-4" CLG.)
VAULTED
DN.
BR. 4
10/2 X 10/0
LIN.
Width 50'
Depth 54'
FOYER BELOW
BR. 3
10/2 X 11/7 +/-
BR. 2
12/8 X 13/0 +/-
NOOK
10/0 X 14/0
(9' CLG.)
12/0 X 14/8
FAMILY
17/0 X 15/6
(9' CLG.)
DESK
PAN.
REF.
DINING
11/8 X 11/0
(13'-4" CLG.)
UP
LIVING
12/0 X 14/0
(13'-4" CLG.)
GARAGE
29/4 X 21/4 +

Design by
Alan Mascord Design Associates, Inc.

Design 9552

First Floor: 1,317 square feet
Second Floor: 1,146 square feet
Total: 2,463 square feet

QUOTE ONE®
Cost to build? See page 342 to order complete cost estimate to build this house in your area!

■ This striking home incorporates fine design elements throughout the plan, including a columned formal living and dining area with a boxed ceiling and a fireplace. A gourmet kitchen accommodates the most elaborate—as well as the simplest—meals. The large family room is just off the kitchen for easy, casual living. A lovely curved stair leads to a balcony overlooking the foyer. The master bedroom suite contains many fine design features, including a luxury bath with a vaulted ceiling and a spa-style bath. Two comfortable family bedrooms share a full hall bath.

Design 9560

First Floor: 1,178 square feet
Second Floor: 1,592 square feet
Total: 2,770 square feet

■ The angular placement of this home's three-car garage creates an expansive and very stylish facade. The foyer is punctuated with a dramatic stair and opens on the right to formal living areas before continuing back into the inviting family room. A fireplace and plenty of windows in the family room are a nice balance to the country kitchen. Amenities include a breakfast nook, cooktop island and rear access to the formal dining room. Three family bedrooms and a full hall bath join the luxurious master suite on the second floor.

NOOK
9/0 X 12/0 +/-
FAMILY
15/0 X 15/2
DINING
12/6 x 13/0
LIVING
15/6 x 14/0
GARAGE
34/0 X 21/4 +
DEN
11/0 X 12/0 +
Width 78'
Depth 65'

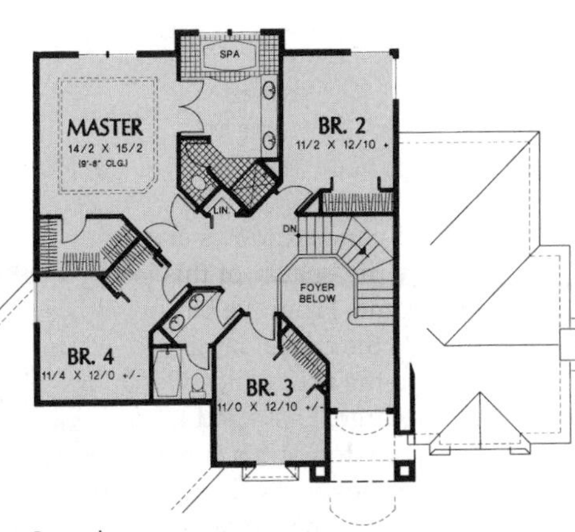
SPA
MASTER
14/2 X 15/2
(9'-8" CLG.)
BR. 2
11/2 X 12/10 +
LIN.
DN.
FOYER BELOW
BR. 4
11/4 X 12/0 +/-
BR. 3
11/0 X 12/10 +/-

Design by
Alan Mascord Design Associates, Inc.

Design 6616

First Floor: 1,136 square feet
Second Floor: 636 square feet
Total: 1,772 square feet

QUOTE ONE®

Cost to build? See page 342 to order complete cost estimate to build this house in your area!

■ The covered entry of this coastal design with its dramatic transom window leads to a spacious living room highlighted by a warming fireplace. To the left, the dining room and kitchen both provide access to a side deck through double doors. Two bedrooms and a full bath complete the first floor. The luxurious master suite is located on the second floor for privacy and features an oversized walk-in closet and a pampering master bath that enjoys a relaxing whirlpool tub, a double-bowl vanity and a compartmented toilet.

down
screened verandah
20'-0" x 7'-8"
kitchen
great room
21'-0" x 14'-0"
vault. clg.
fireplace
dining
12'-6" x 9'-0"
8' clg.
sundeck
up
down
foyer
study
10'-0" x 13'-0"
8' clg.
br. 2
11'-8" x 11'-6"
8' clg.
entry porch
down
Width 41'-9"
Depth 45'
open to below
master suite
12'-3" x 20'0"
8' clg.
down
loft
w.i.c.

Design by
The Sater Design Collection

Design 6654

First Floor: 1,342 square feet
Second Floor: 511 square feet
Total: 1,853 square feet

■ Amenities abound in this delightful two-story Floridian. The foyer opens directly onto the fantastic grand room, which offers a warming fireplace and two sets of double doors to the rear deck. The dining room also has access to this deck, and to a second deck shared with Bedroom 2. A convenient kitchen and another bedroom also reside on this level. Upstairs the master bedroom reigns supreme. Entered through double doors, it pampers with a luxurious bath, a walk-in closet, a morning kitchen and a private balcony.

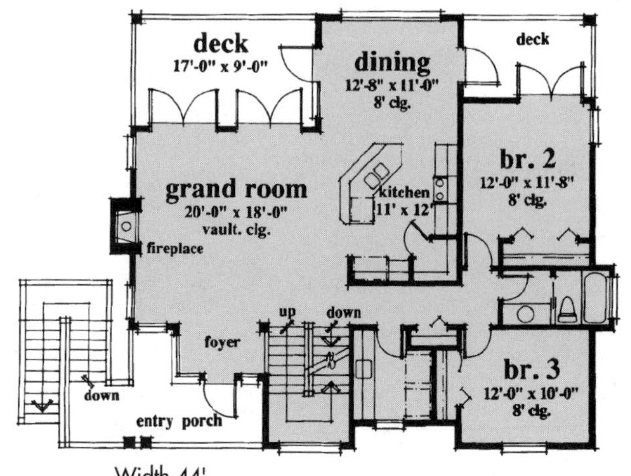
deck
17'-0" x 9'-0"
dining
12'-8" x 11'-0"
8' clg.
deck
grand room
20'-0" x 18'-0"
vault. clg.
kitchen
11' x 12'
br. 2
12'-0" x 11'-8"
8' clg.
fireplace
up
down
foyer
br. 3
12'-0" x 10'-0"
8' clg.
down
entry porch

Width 44'
Depth 40'

Design by
The Sater Design Collection

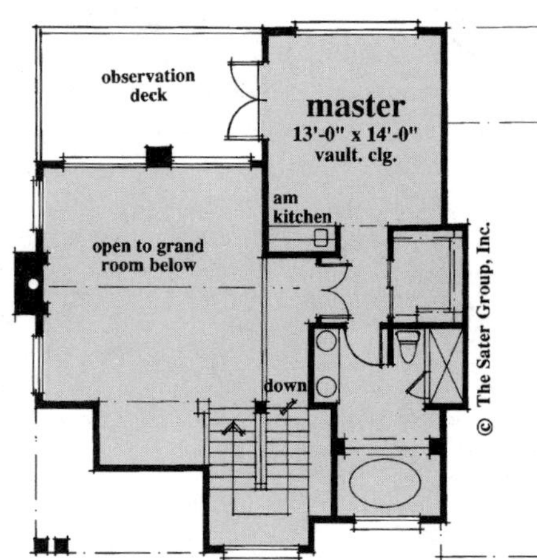
observation deck
master
13'-0" x 14'-0"
vault. clg.
am kitchen
open to grand room below
down

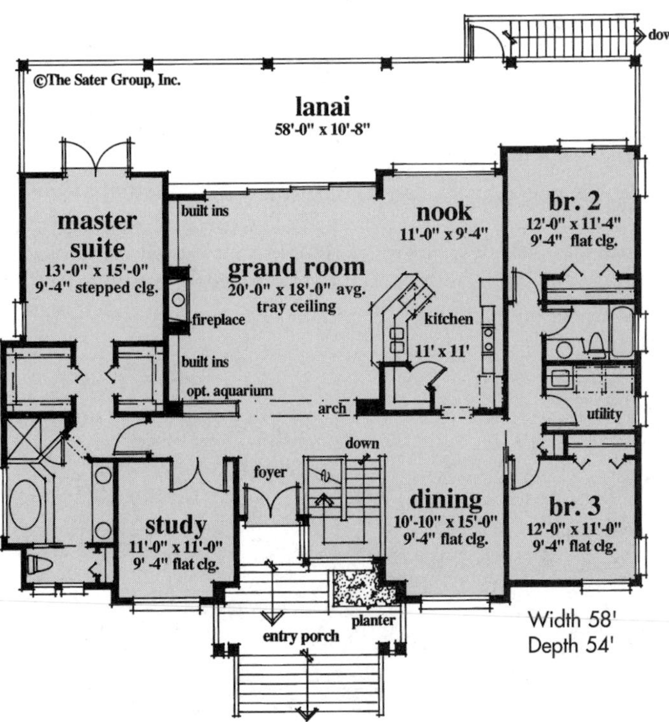

down
©The Sater Group, Inc.
lanai
58'-0" x 10'-8"
master suite
13'-0" x 15'-0"
9'-4" stepped clg.
built ins
grand room
20'-0" x 18'-0" avg.
tray ceiling
fireplace
built ins
opt. aquarium
arch
nook
11'-0" x 9'-4"
kitchen
11' x 11'
br. 2
12'-0" x 11'-4"
9'-4" flat clg.
utility
foyer
down
study
11'-0" x 11'-0"
9'-4" flat clg.
dining
10'-10" x 15'-0"
9'-4" flat clg.
br. 3
12'-0" x 11'-0"
9'-4" flat clg.
planter
entry porch

Width 58'
Depth 54'

QUOTE ONE®

Cost to build? See page 342 to order complete cost estimate to build this house in your area!

Design by
The Sater Design Collection

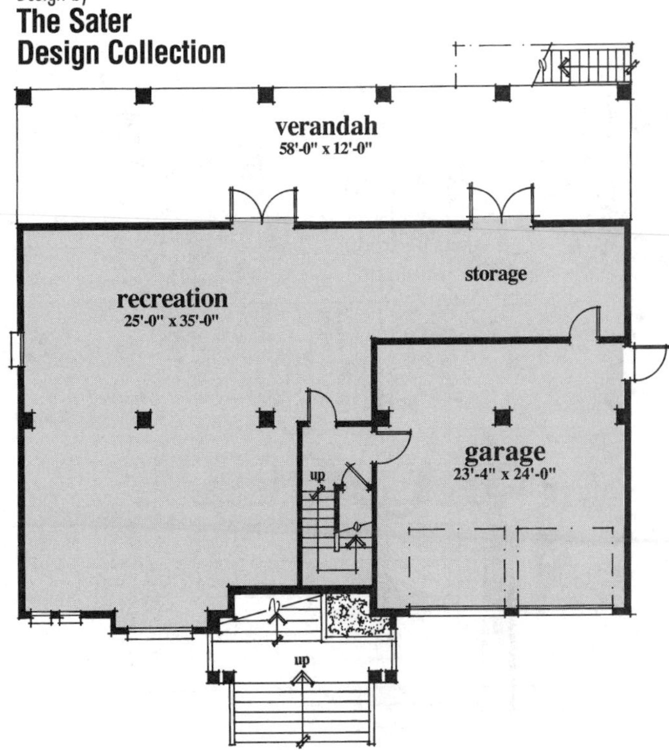

verandah
58'-0" x 12'-0"
recreation
25'-0" x 35'-0"
storage
up
garage
23'-4" x 24'-0"
up

Design 6622

Square Footage: 2,190

■ A dramatic set of stairs leads to the entry of this home. The foyer leads to an expansive living room with a fireplace and built-in bookshelves. A lanai opens off this area and will assure outdoor enjoyments. For formal meals, a front-facing dining room offers a bumped-out bay. The kitchen serves this area easily as well as the breakfast room. A study and three bedrooms make up the rest of the floor plan. Two secondary bedrooms share a full hall bath. A utility area is also nearby. In the master suite, two walk-in closets and a full bath are apppreciated features. In the bedroom, a set of French doors offer passage to the lanai.

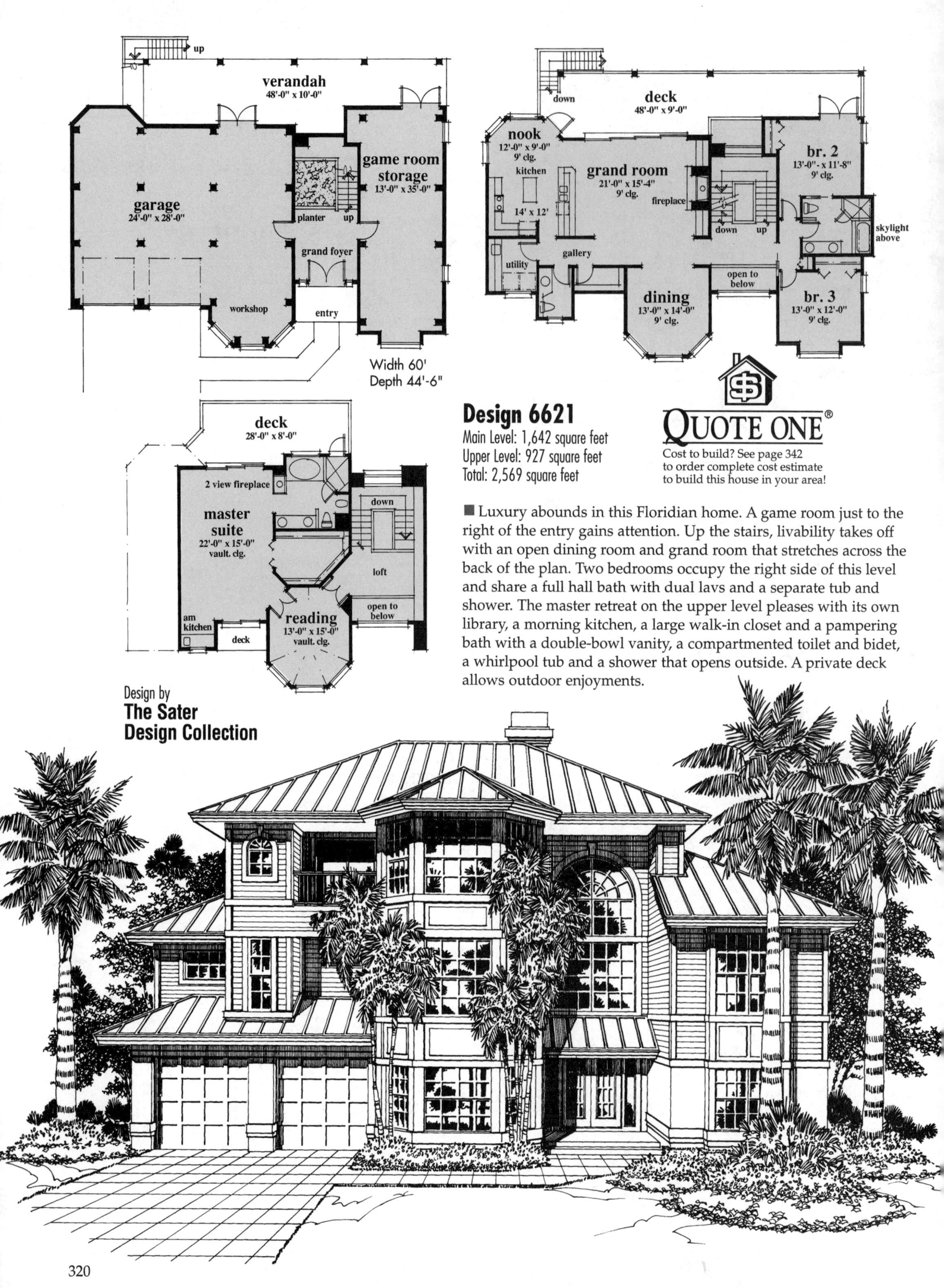
up
verandah
48'-0" x 10'-0"
garage
24'-0" x 28'-0"
planter
up
game room
storage
13'-0" x 35'-0"
grand foyer
workshop
entry
Width 60'
Depth 44'-6"
down
deck
48'-0" x 9'-0"
nook
12'-0" x 9'-0"
9' clg.
kitchen
14' x 12'
grand room
21'-0" x 15'-4"
9' clg.
fireplace
down
up
br. 2
13'-0" x 11'-8"
9' clg.
skylight
above
utility
gallery
open to
below
dining
13'-0" x 14'-0"
9' clg.
br. 3
13'-0" x 12'-0"
9' clg.
deck
28'-0" x 8'-0"
2 view fireplace
master
suite
22'-0" x 15'-0"
vault. clg.
down
loft
open to
below
am
kitchen
deck
reading
13'-0" x 15'-0"
vault. clg.
QUOTE ONE®

Design 6621

Main Level: 1,642 square feet
Upper Level: 927 square feet
Total: 2,569 square feet

Cost to build? See page 342 to order complete cost estimate to build this house in your area!

■ Luxury abounds in this Floridian home. A game room just to the right of the entry gains attention. Up the stairs, livability takes off with an open dining room and grand room that stretches across the back of the plan. Two bedrooms occupy the right side of this level and share a full hall bath with dual lavs and a separate tub and shower. The master retreat on the upper level pleases with its own library, a morning kitchen, a large walk-in closet and a pampering bath with a double-bowl vanity, a compartmented toilet and bidet, a whirlpool tub and a shower that opens outside. A private deck allows outdoor enjoyments.

Design by
The Sater Design Collection

Photo by Bob Greenspan

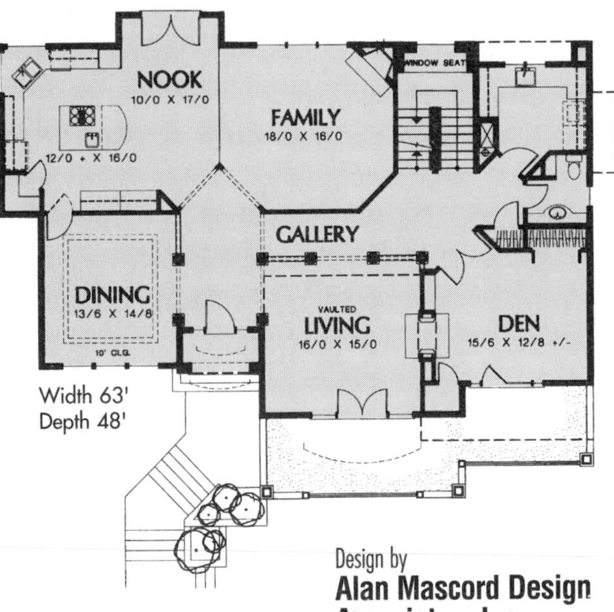
NOOK
10/0 X 17/0
12/0 + X 16/0
FAMILY
18/0 X 16/0
WINDOW SEAT
GALLERY
DINING
13/6 X 14/8
10' CLG.
VAULTED
LIVING
16/0 X 15/0
DEN
15/6 X 12/8 +/-
Width 63'
Depth 48'

Design 9554

Main Level: 1,989 square feet
Upper Level: 1,349 square feet
Total: 3,3383 square feet
Lower Level: 592 square feet

QUOTE ONE®

Cost to build? See page 342 to order complete cost estimate to build this house in your area!

■ Dramatic balconies and spectacular window treatment enhance this stunning luxury home. Inside, a through-fireplace warms the formal living room and a restful den. Both living spaces open onto a balcony that invites quiet reflection on starry nights. The banquet-sized dining room is easily served from the adjacent kitchen. Here, space is shared with an eating nook that provides access to the rear grounds and a family room with a corner fireplace perfect for casual gatherings. The upper level contains two family bedrooms and a luxurious master suite that enjoys its own private balcony. The lower level accommodates a shop and a bonus room for future development.

Design by
Alan Mascord Design Associates, Inc.

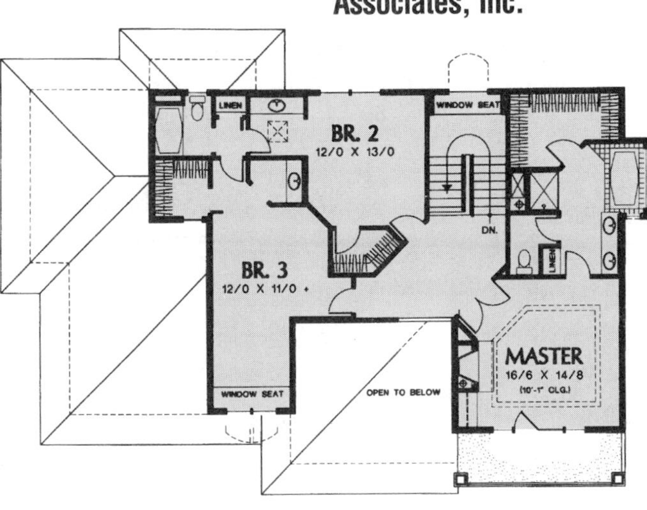
LINEN
BR. 2
12/0 X 13/0
WINDOW SEAT
BR. 3
12/0 X 11/0 +
DN.
LINEN
MASTER
16/6 X 14/8
(10'-1" CLG.)
WINDOW SEAT
OPEN TO BELOW

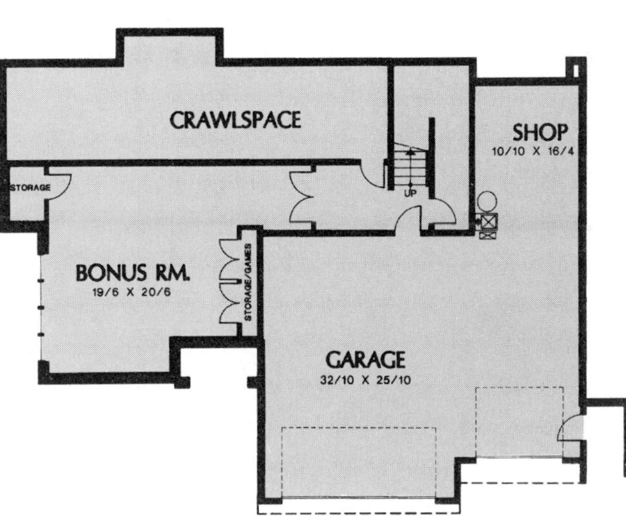
CRAWLSPACE
SHOP
10/10 X 16/4
STORAGE
UP
BONUS RM.
19/6 X 20/6
STORAGE/GAMES
GARAGE
32/10 X 25/10

Design 9576

First Floor: 1,894 square feet
Second Floor: 1,544 square feet
Total: 3,438 square feet

■ Sleek, contemporary lines define the exterior of this home. Steps lead up a front-sloping lot to the bright entry. A front-facing den is brightly lit by a curving wall of windows. Built-ins enhance the utility of this room. A two-story living room offers a fireplace and lots of windows. The nearby dining room is capped by an elegant ceiling. The kitchen serves a sunny breakfast nook and an oversized family room. The family will find plenty of sleeping space with four bedrooms on the second level. The master bedroom suite is a real attention-getter. Its roomy bath includes a spa tub and a separate shower.

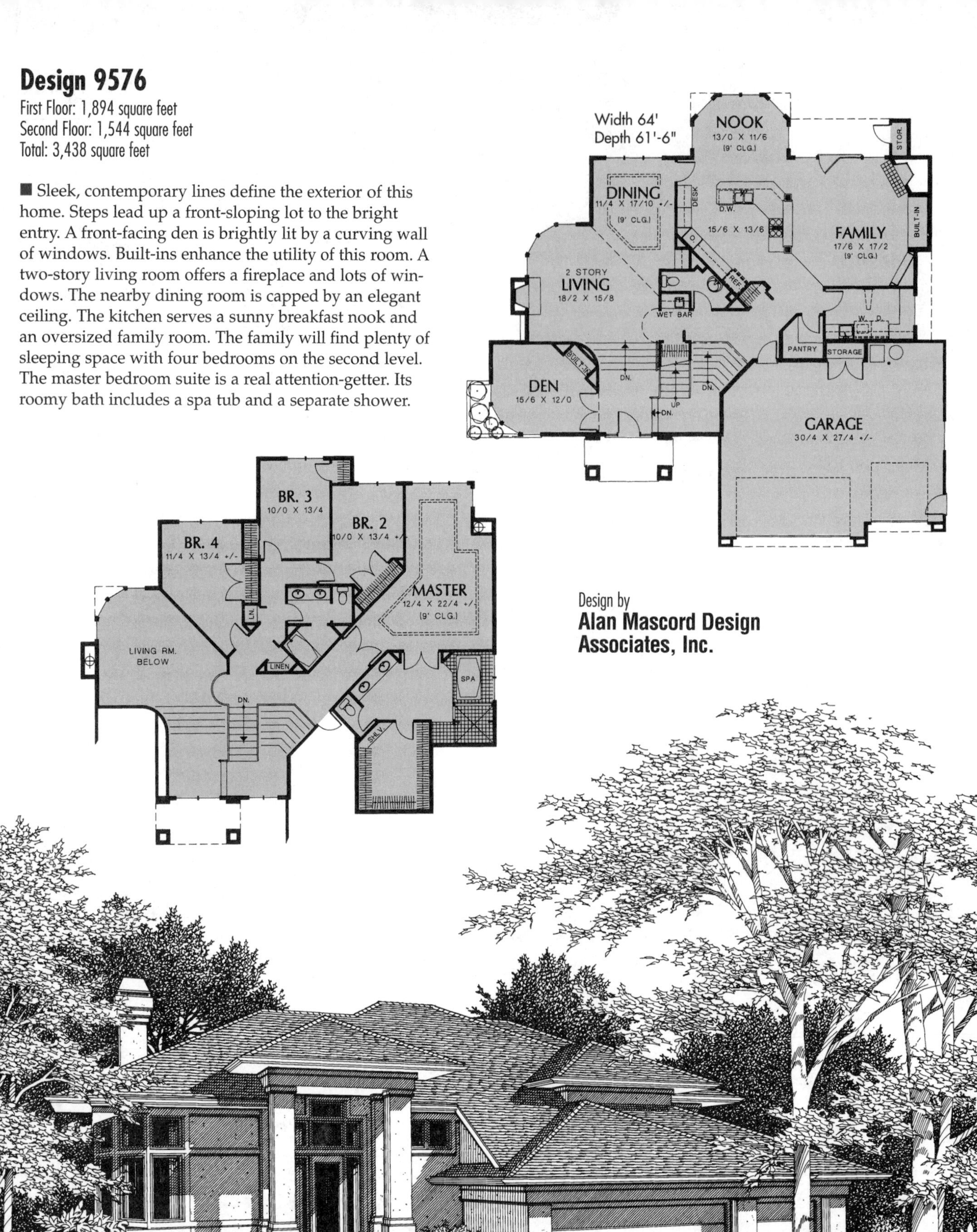

Width 64'
Depth 61'-6"
NOOK
13/0 X 11/6
(9' CLG.)
STOR.
DINING
11/4 X 17/10 +/-
(9' CLG.)
DESK
D.W.
15/6 X 13/6
FAMILY
17/6 X 17/2
(9' CLG.)
BUILT-IN
2 STORY
LIVING
18/2 X 15/8
REF.
WET BAR
W.
D.
PANTRY
STORAGE
BUILT-IN
DEN
15/6 X 12/0
DN.
UP
DN.
GARAGE
30/4 X 27/4 +/-
BR. 3
10/0 X 13/4
BR. 2
10/0 X 13/4 +/-
BR. 4
11/4 X 13/4 +/-
MASTER
12/4 X 22/4 +/-
(9' CLG.)
LN
LINEN
LIVING RM.
BELOW
DN.
SPA
SHLV.

Design by
Alan Mascord Design Associates, Inc.

■ Sleek lines define the contemporary feel of this home. Double entry doors lead to a columned gallery and an expansive great room. It showcases a fireplace, built-ins and a curving wall of windows. The nearby kitchen utilizes efficient zoning. A nook here opens to a wraparound deck. A dining room and a den finish the first-floor living areas. In the master bedroom suite, large proportions and an elegant bath with a see-through fireplace aim to please. The two bedrooms on the lower level have in-room vanities; one has direct access to the compartmented bath. A game room with a fireplace and built-ins leads to outdoor livability.

Design 9539

Main Level: 2,219 square feet
Lower Level: 1,324 square feet
Total: 3,543 square feet

Design by
Alan Mascord Design Associates, Inc.

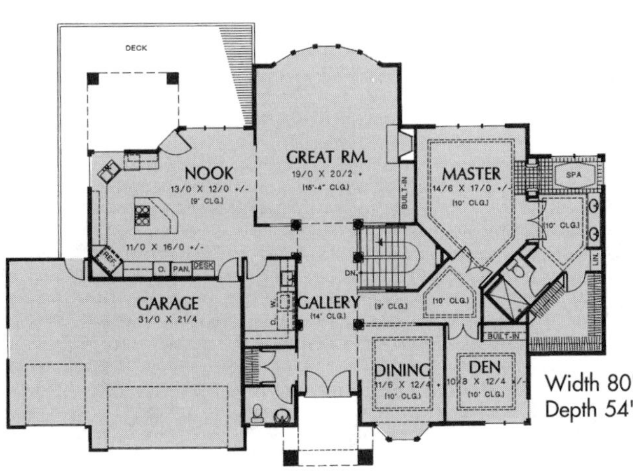
DECK
NOOK
13/0 X 12/0 +/-
[9' CLG.]
GREAT RM.
19/0 X 20/2 +
[15'-4" CLG.]
MASTER
14/6 X 17/0 +/-
[10' CLG.]
SPA
GARAGE
31/0 X 21/4
GALLERY
[14' CLG.]
DINING
11/6 X 12/4
[10' CLG.]
DEN
10/8 X 12/4
[10' CLG.]
Width 80'
Depth 54'-6"

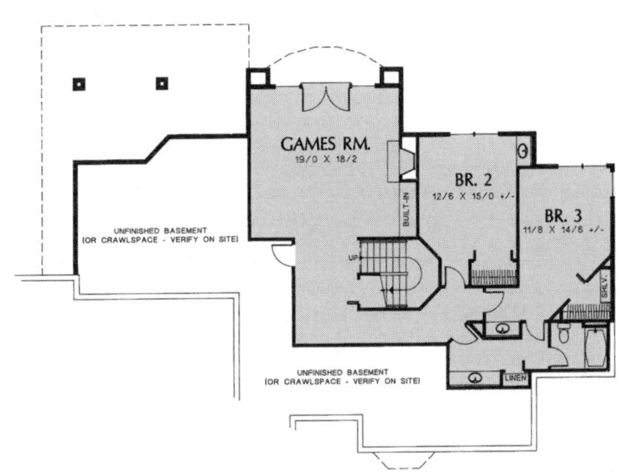
GAMES RM.
19/0 X 18/2
BR. 2
12/6 X 15/0 +/-
BR. 3
11/8 X 14/6 +/-
UNFINISHED BASEMENT
(OR CRAWLSPACE - VERIFY ON SITE)

■ This refined hillside home is designed for lots that fall off toward the rear and works especially well with a view out the back. The kitchen and eating nook wrap around the vaulted family room where arched transom windows flank the fireplace. Formal living is graciously centered in the living room that's directly off the foyer and the adjoining dining room. A grand master suite is located on the main level for convenience and privacy. Downstairs, three family bedrooms share a compartmented hall bath.

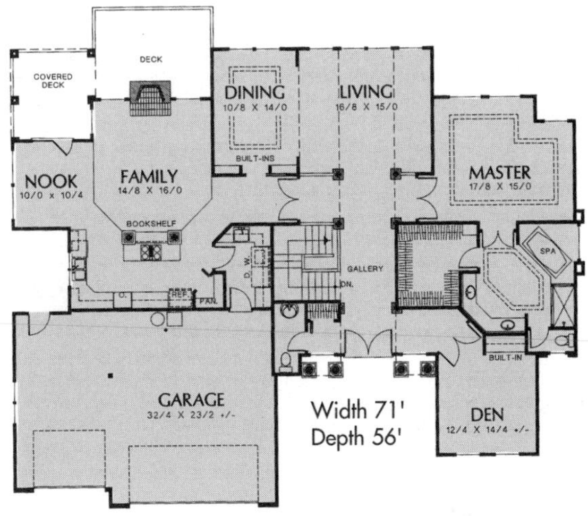
COVERED DECK
DECK
DINING
10/8 X 14/0
LIVING
16/8 X 15/0
NOOK
10/0 x 10/4
FAMILY
14/8 X 16/0
BOOKSHELF
MASTER
17/8 X 15/0
SPA
GALLERY
GARAGE
32/4 X 23/2 +/-
DEN
12/4 X 14/4 +/-
Width 71'
Depth 56'

Design 9417

Main Level: 2,196 square feet
Lower Level: 1,542 square feet
Total: 3,738 square feet

Design by
Alan Mascord Design Associates, Inc.

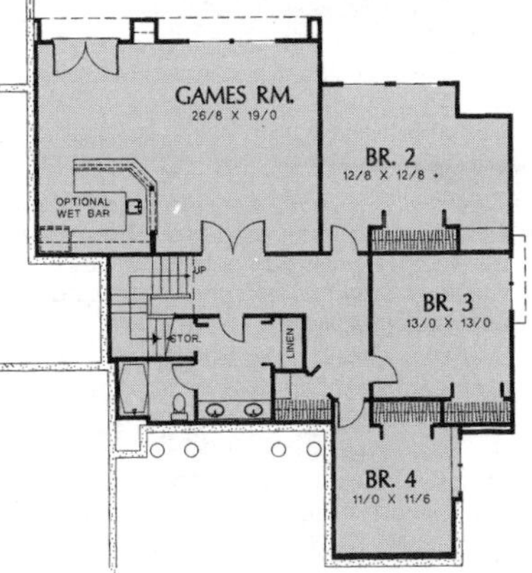

GAMES RM.
26/8 X 19/0
OPTIONAL WET BAR
BR. 2
12/8 X 12/8 +
BR. 3
13/0 X 13/0
BR. 4
11/0 X 11/6

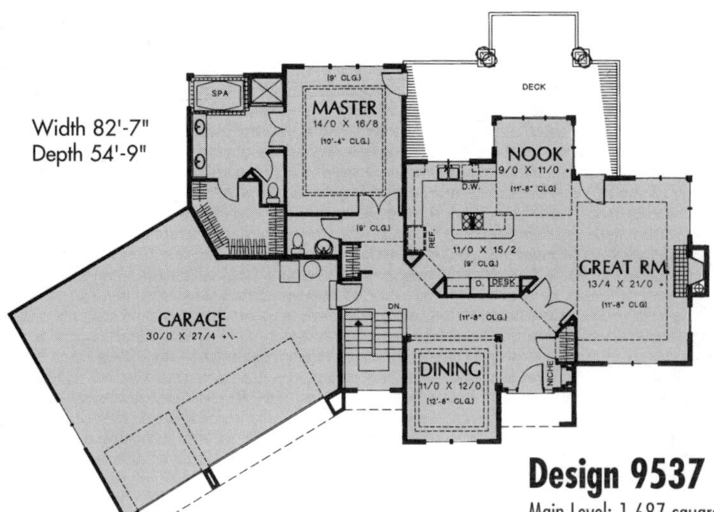

Width 82'-7"
Depth 54'-9"
DECK
SPA
MASTER
14/0 X 16/8
NOOK
9/0 X 11/0
GREAT RM.
13/4 X 21/0
GARAGE
30/0 X 27/4 +\-
DINING
11/0 X 12/0

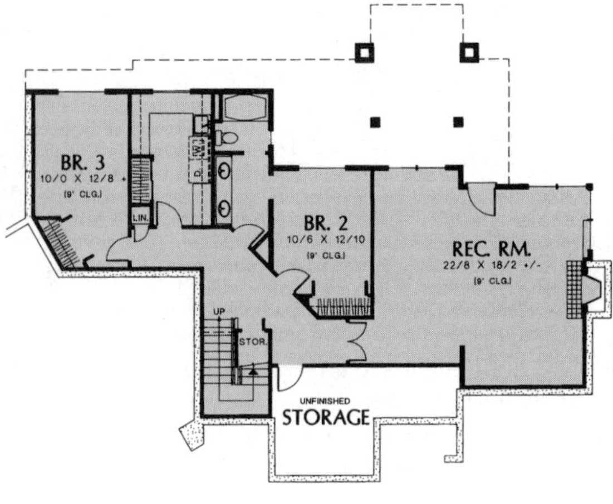

BR. 3
10/0 X 12/8
BR. 2
10/6 X 12/10
REC. RM.
22/8 X 18/2 +/-
UNFINISHED
STORAGE

Design 9537

Main Level: 1,687 square feet
Lower Level: 1,251 square feet
Total: 2,938 square feet

Design by
Alan Mascord Design Associates, Inc.

■ This striking home is perfect for daylight basement lots. An elegant dining room fronts the plan. It is near an expansive kitchen that features plenty of cabinet and counter space. A nook surrounded by a deck adds character. The comfortable great room, with a raised ceiling and a fireplace, shares space with these areas. The master bedroom suite includes private deck access and a superb bath with a spa tub and dual lavatories. Downstairs, two bedrooms, a laundry room with lots of counter space and a rec room with a fireplace cap off the plan.

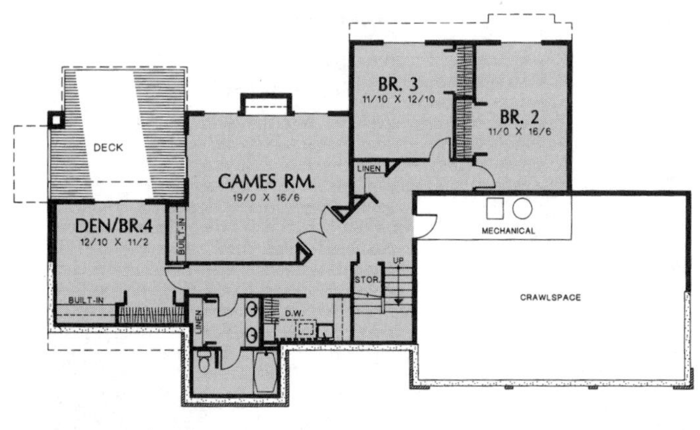

DECK
GAMES RM.
19/0 X 16/6
BR. 3
11/10 X 12/10
BR. 2
11/0 X 16/6
DEN/BR.4
12/10 X 11/2
MECHANICAL
CRAWLSPACE

DECK
MASTER
14/0 X 15/8
SPA
VAULTED
GREAT RM.
19/0 X 16/6
NOOK/KIT.
15/6 X 18/0
DINING
11/0 X 12/0
GARAGE
32/2 X 21/4 +/-
Width 76'
Depth 43'

Design 9484

Main Level: 1,573 square feet
Lower Level: 1,404 square feet
Total: 2,977 square feet

Design by
Alan Mascord Design Associates, Inc.

■ There's something for every member of the family in this captivating hillside plan. The first floor holds a huge great room for family and formal gatherings, a dining room distinguished by columns, an island kitchen with attached nook and an outdoor deck area. The master suite has a lavish bath. The game room downstairs is joined by three bedrooms, or two bedrooms and a den. Look for another deck at this level. Please specify basement or crawlspace foundation when ordering.

Design 9568

Main Level: 1,972 square feet
Lower Level: 837 square feet
Total: 2,809 square feet

■ A gracious facade welcomes all into this delightful family plan. A formal zone, consisting of living and dining rooms, greets you at the foyer. To the right, a double-doored den provides a peaceful place to work or relax. The spacious kitchen has a cooktop island, a pantry and a window-laden breakfast nook. The family room offers passage to the rear deck. The master suite does the same. You'll also find a private bath and a walk-in closet here. Bedroom 2 is nestled in front by a full hall bath. Downstairs, two bedrooms flank a games room. A two-car garage opens to a laundry room.

DECK
NOOK
10/0 X 11/0 +/-
(9'-1" CLG.)
FAMILY RM.
15/8 X 15/4 +/-
(12'-5" CLG.)
MASTER
15/0 X 15/4 +/-
(12'-5" CLG.)
SPA
DESK
PAN
REF.
DINING RM.
13/0 X 10/4
(9'-1" CLG.)
(12'-5" CLG.)
DN.
GARAGE
19/8 X 21/8 +
DEN
10/8 X 10/10
(9'-1" CLG.)
LIVING RM.
13/0 X 13/0 +
(9'-1" CLG.)
BR. 2
10/0 X 12/0
(9'-1" CLG.)
Width 62'
Depth 45'

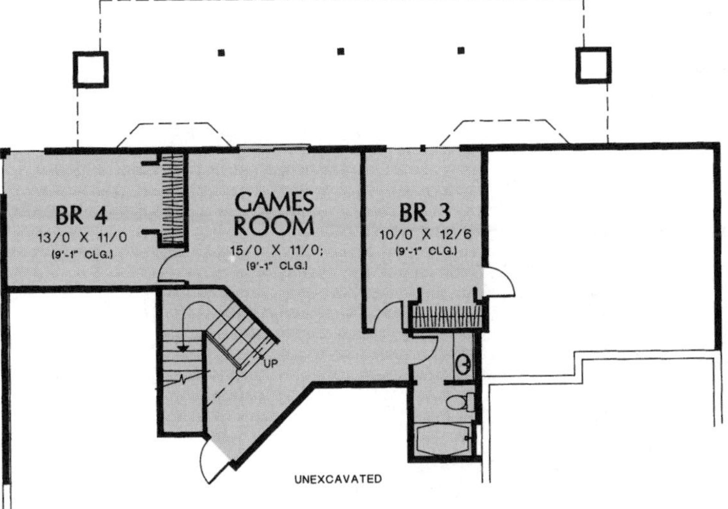
BR 4
13/0 X 11/0
(9'-1" CLG.)
GAMES ROOM
15/0 X 11/0;
(9'-1" CLG.)
BR 3
10/0 X 12/6
(9'-1" CLG.)
UP
UNEXCAVATED

Design by
Alan Mascord Design Associates, Inc.

Design 9914

Square Footage: 1,770

■ Perfect for sloping lots, this European one-story includes living areas on one level and bedrooms on another. The great room contains a fireplace and access to the rear deck. Close by are the U-shaped kitchen and breakfast room with a boxed window. The formal dining room completes the living area and is open to the entry foyer. Bedrooms are a few steps up from the living areas and include a master suite with two walk-in closets and a sumptuous bath with a compartmented toilet. Secondary bedrooms share a full bath with double-bowl vanity. On the lower level is garage space and bonus space that may be used later for additional bedrooms or casual gathering areas. This home is designed with a basement foundation.

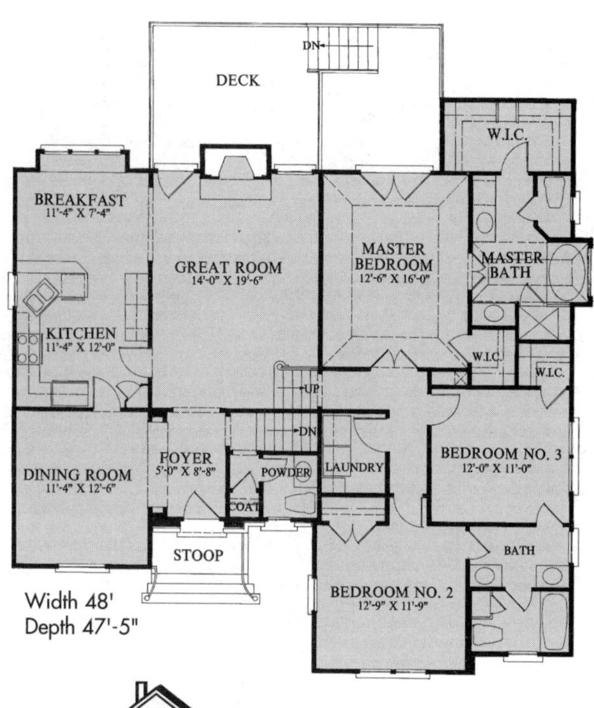

DECK
DN
W.I.C.
BREAKFAST
11'-4" X 7'-4"
GREAT ROOM
14'-0" X 19'-6"
MASTER BEDROOM
12'-6" X 16'-0"
MASTER BATH
KITCHEN
11'-4" X 12'-0"
W.I.C.
W.I.C.
UP
DN
DINING ROOM
11'-4" X 12'-6"
FOYER
5'-0" X 8'-8"
POWDER
LAUNDRY
BEDROOM NO. 3
12'-0" X 11'-0"
COAT
STOOP
BATH
BEDROOM NO. 2
12'-9" X 11'-9"
Width 48'
Depth 47'-5"

QUOTE ONE®

Cost to build? See page 342 to order complete cost estimate to build this house in your area!

Design by
Design Traditions

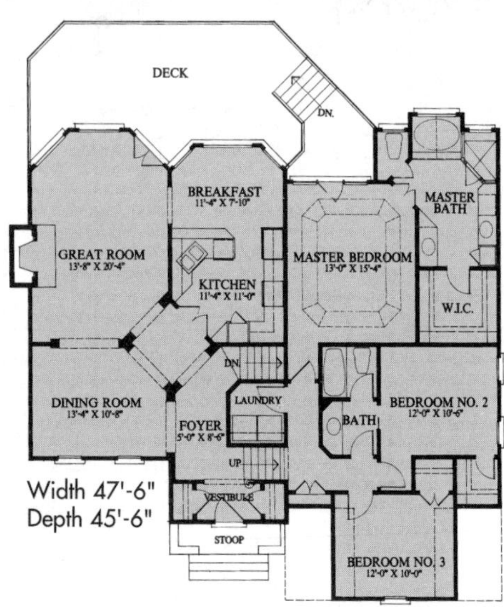

DECK
DN.
BREAKFAST
11'-4" X 7'-10"
MASTER BATH
GREAT ROOM
13'-8" X 20'-4"
MASTER BEDROOM
13'-0" X 15'-4"
KITCHEN
11'-4" X 11'-0"
W.I.C.
DN
DINING ROOM
13'-4" X 10'-8"
LAUNDRY
BEDROOM NO. 2
12'-0" X 10'-6"
FOYER
5'-0" X 8'-6"
BATH
UP
VESTIBULE
STOOP
BEDROOM NO. 3
12'-0" X 10'-0"
Width 47'-6"
Depth 45'-6"

■ European style takes beautifully to a sloped lot. This design tames a slight grade by making use of a hillside garage. The main floor is split into two levels accessed from the foyer. From the entry, the spacious great room and dining room open. Columns and windows give an open, inviting look. The eat-in kitchen has a glorious window in the nook out to the deck. The upper level of the main floor holds the ultra-comfortable master suite and two family bedrooms that share a full bath. The basement has a two-car garage and a storage area.

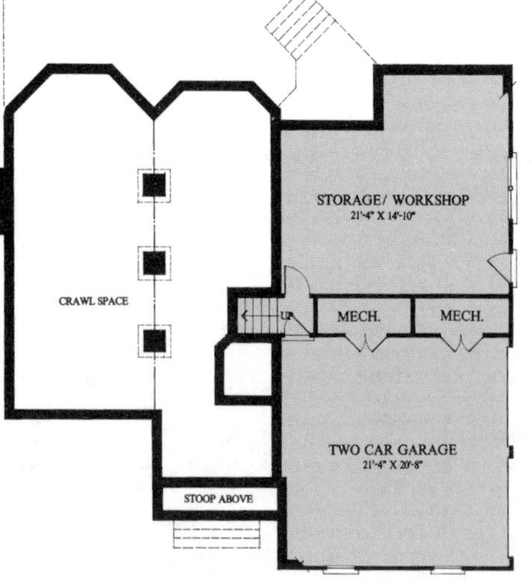

STORAGE/ WORKSHOP
21'-4" X 14'-10"
CRAWL SPACE
UP
MECH.
MECH.
TWO CAR GARAGE
21'-4" X 20'-8"
STOOP ABOVE

Design 9841

Square Footage: 1,725

Design by
Design Traditions

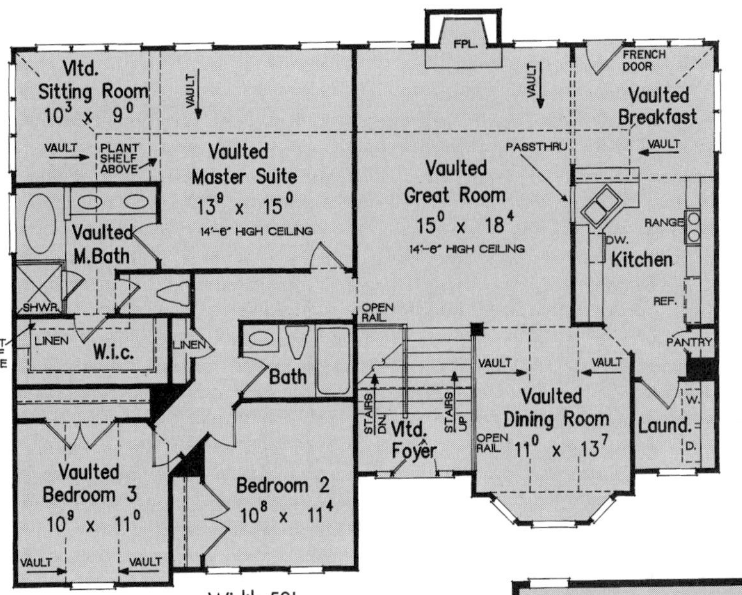
FPL.
FRENCH DOOR
Vltd. Sitting Room 10³ x 9⁰
VAULT
PLANT SHELF ABOVE
Vaulted Master Suite 13⁹ x 15⁰
14'-6" HIGH CEILING
Vaulted Great Room 15⁰ x 18⁴
14'-6" HIGH CEILING
Vaulted Breakfast
PASSTHRU
RANGE
DW.
Kitchen
REF.
PANTRY
Vaulted M.Bath
SHWR.
LINEN
W.i.c.
Bath
OPEN RAIL
STAIRS DN
STAIRS UP
Vltd. Foyer
Vaulted Dining Room 11⁰ x 13⁷
Laund.
W.
D.
Vaulted Bedroom 3 10⁹ x 11⁰
Bedroom 2 10⁸ x 11⁴

Width 50'
Depth 39'-4"

Design P190

Main Level: 1,677 square feet
Lower Level: 40 square feet
Total: 1,717 square feet

■ This elegant home makes the most of the hillside lot by using the lower level for a two-car garage and expandable basement space. A striking stair leads to the entry where another half flight continues up inside. The vaulted dining room has an open rail that overlooks the entry. A vaulted ceiling in the great room accents the fireplace. A modified galley kitchen has a snack bar and a breakfast nook. The master suite features a sitting room, compartmented bath and a walk-in closet. Two family bedrooms share a full hall bath.

Design by
Frank Betz Associates, Inc.

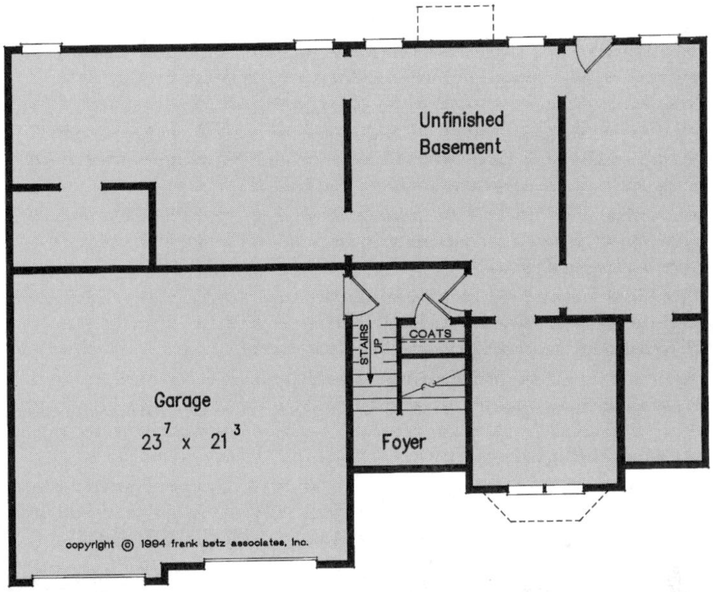

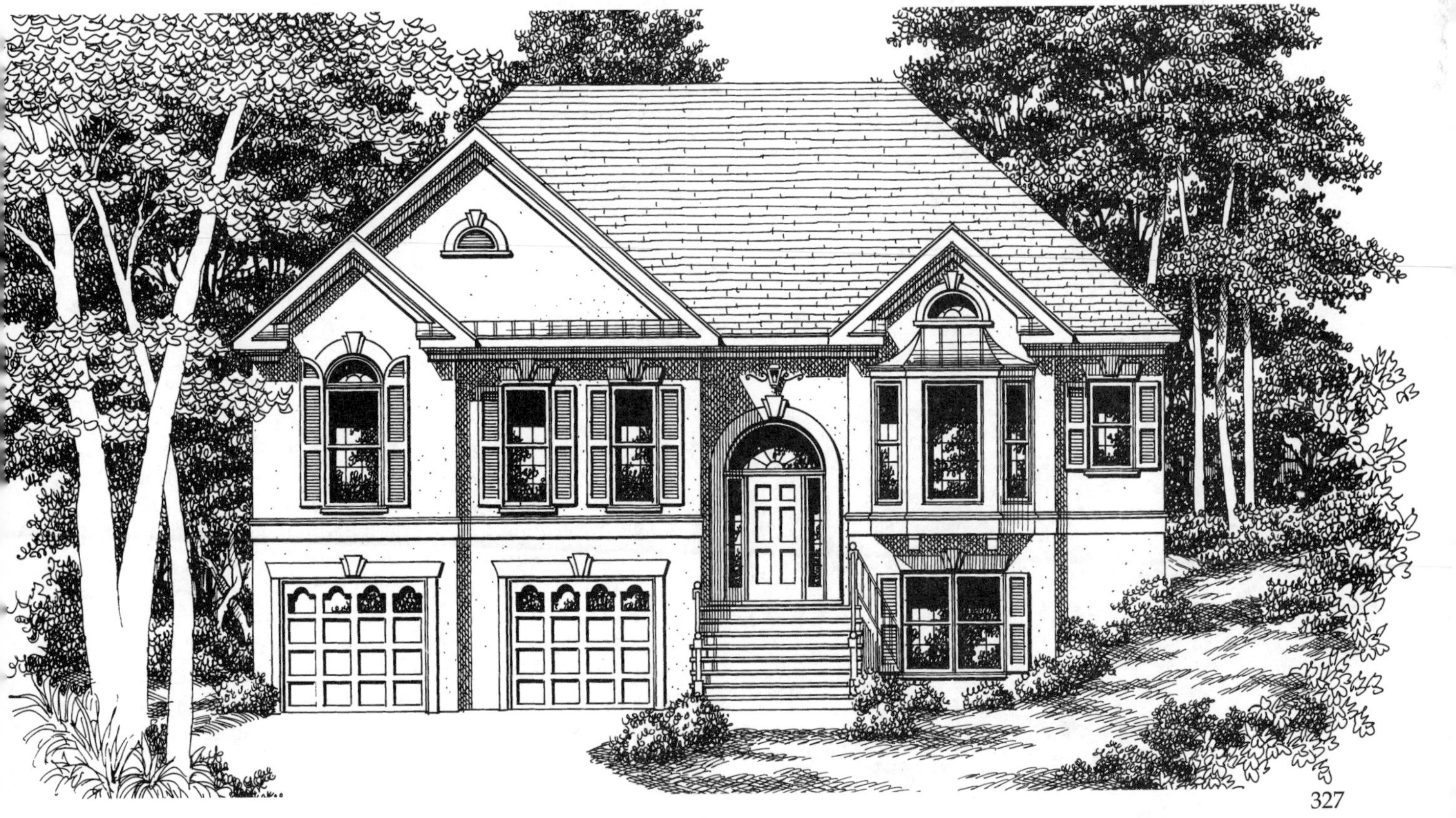

Design 9917

Square Footage: 1,770

■ With European charm and functional floor planning, this fine family home will delight for years to come. A recessed front door opens to a columned dining room that shares space with the family room. A fireplace, tiered ceiling and French doors are just a few of the features that lend elegance to the plan. A bayed breakfast nook enjoys expansive rear views and direct service from the kitchen. Up a half flight of stairs, three bedrooms include two family bedrooms and a master suite. In the master suite, French doors lead to a private deck. An expansive, secluded bath offers dual lavatories, a corner garden tub and a walk-in closet. This home is designed with a basement foundation.

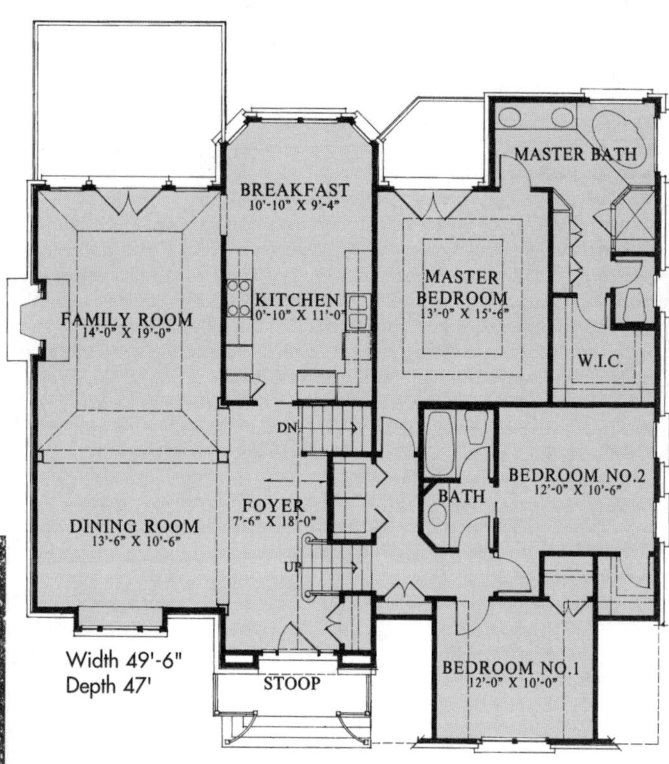
BREAKFAST
10'-10" X 9'-4"
MASTER BATH
FAMILY ROOM
14'-0" X 19'-0"
KITCHEN
10'-10" X 11'-0"
MASTER BEDROOM
13'-0" X 15'-6"
W.I.C.
DN
BATH
BEDROOM NO.2
12'-0" X 10'-6"
FOYER
7'-6" X 18'-0"
DINING ROOM
13'-6" X 10'-6"
UP
BEDROOM NO.1
12'-0" X 10'-0"
STOOP
Width 49'-6"
Depth 47'

Design by
Design Traditions

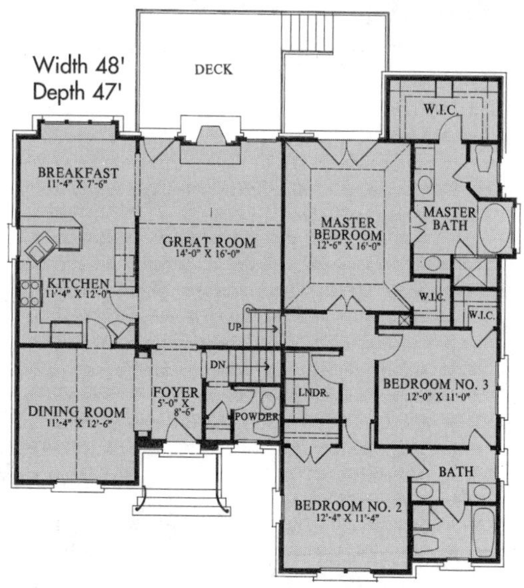
Width 48'
Depth 47'
DECK
W.I.C.
BREAKFAST
11'-4" X 7'-6"
GREAT ROOM
14'-0" X 16'-0"
MASTER BEDROOM
12'-6" X 16'-0"
MASTER BATH
KITCHEN
11'-4" X 12'-0"
W.I.C.
W.I.C.
UP
DN
DINING ROOM
11'-4" X 12'-6"
FOYER
5'-0" X 8'-6"
POWDER
LNDR.
BEDROOM NO. 3
12'-0" X 11'-0"
BATH
BEDROOM NO. 2
12'-4" X 11'-4"

Design by
Design Traditions

QUOTE ONE®

Cost to build? See page 342
to order complete cost estimate
to build this house in your area!

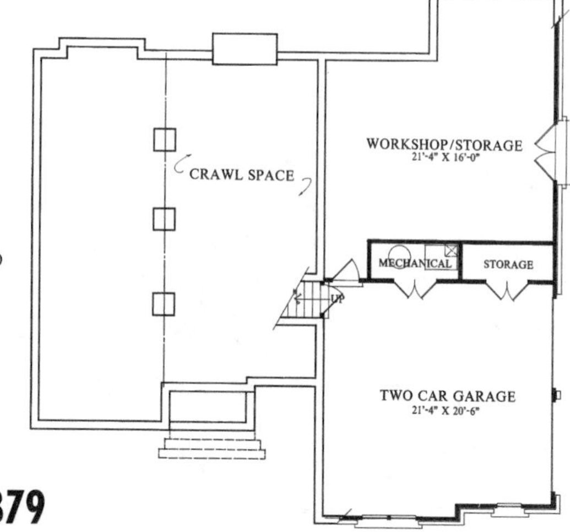
CRAWL SPACE
WORKSHOP/STORAGE
21'-4" X 16'-0"
MECHANICAL
STORAGE
UP
TWO CAR GARAGE
21'-4" X 20'-6"

Design 9879

Square Footage: 1,770

■ The country cottage styling of this stately brick home includes brick detailing framing the front entry and windows. Gables and a multi-level roof help create the soft charm of this design. The foyer provides views into both the large great room with warming hearth and the dining room with vaulted ceiling. From the great room, one enters the kitchen with a spacious work area and adjacent breakfast room. The second level, up a half flight of stairs, offers two bedrooms that share a bath. The master bedroom is entered through large double doors and features a tray ceiling and French doors leading to a private deck. The master bath is generous, and complete with His and Hers vanities, garden tub and large walk-in closet. This home is designed with a basement foundation.

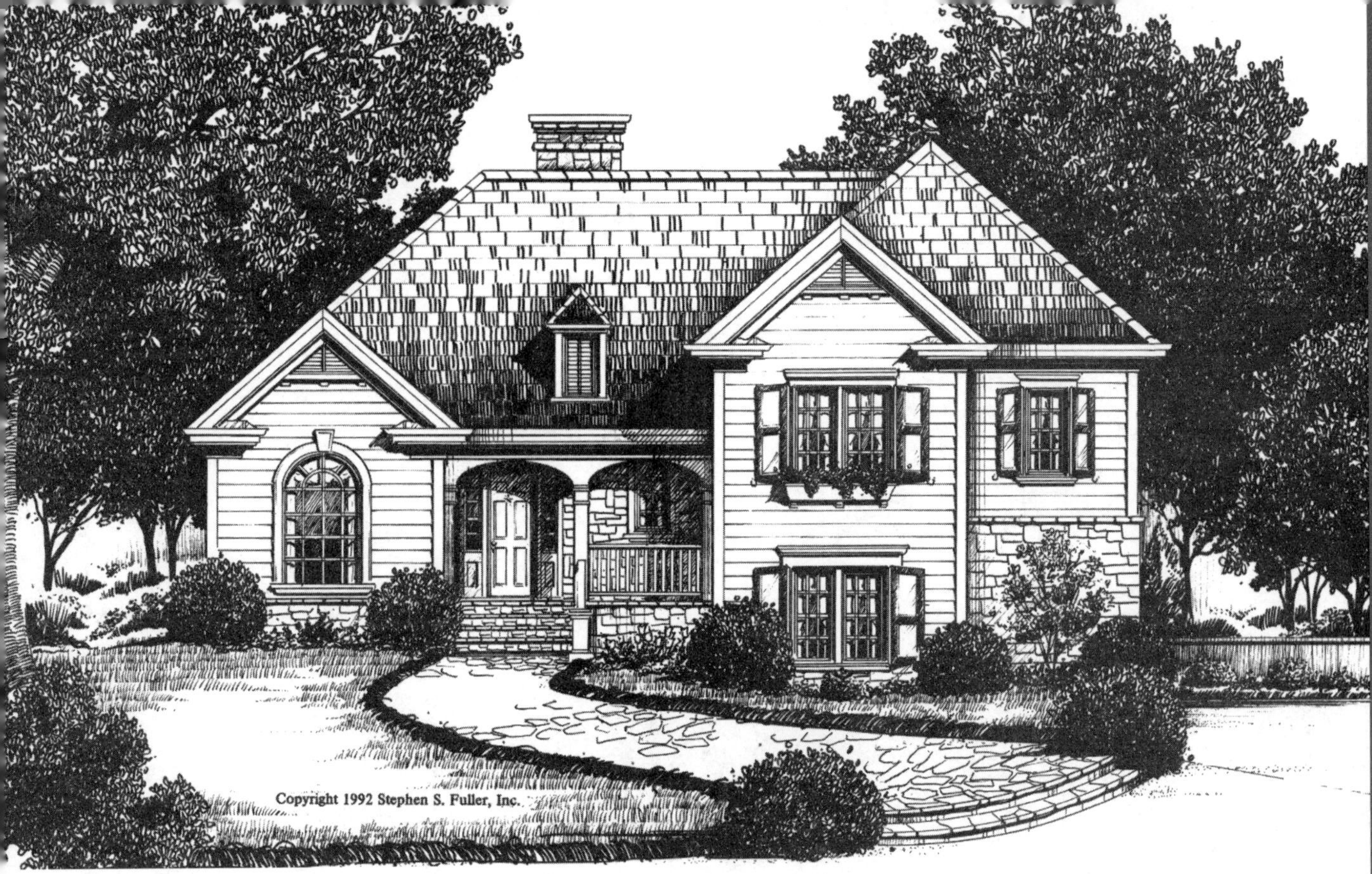

Design by
Design Traditions

Design 9949

Square Footage: 1,770

■ Wood frame, weatherboard siding and stacked stone give this home its country cottage appeal. The concept is reinforced by the double elliptical arched front porch, the Colonial balustrade and the roof-vent dormer. Inside, the foyer leads to the great room and the dining room. The well-planned kitchen easily serves the breakfast room. A rear deck makes outdoor living extra-enjoyable. Three bedrooms include a master suite with a tray ceiling and a luxurious bath. The two secondary bedrooms share a compartmented bath. This home is designed with a basement foundation.

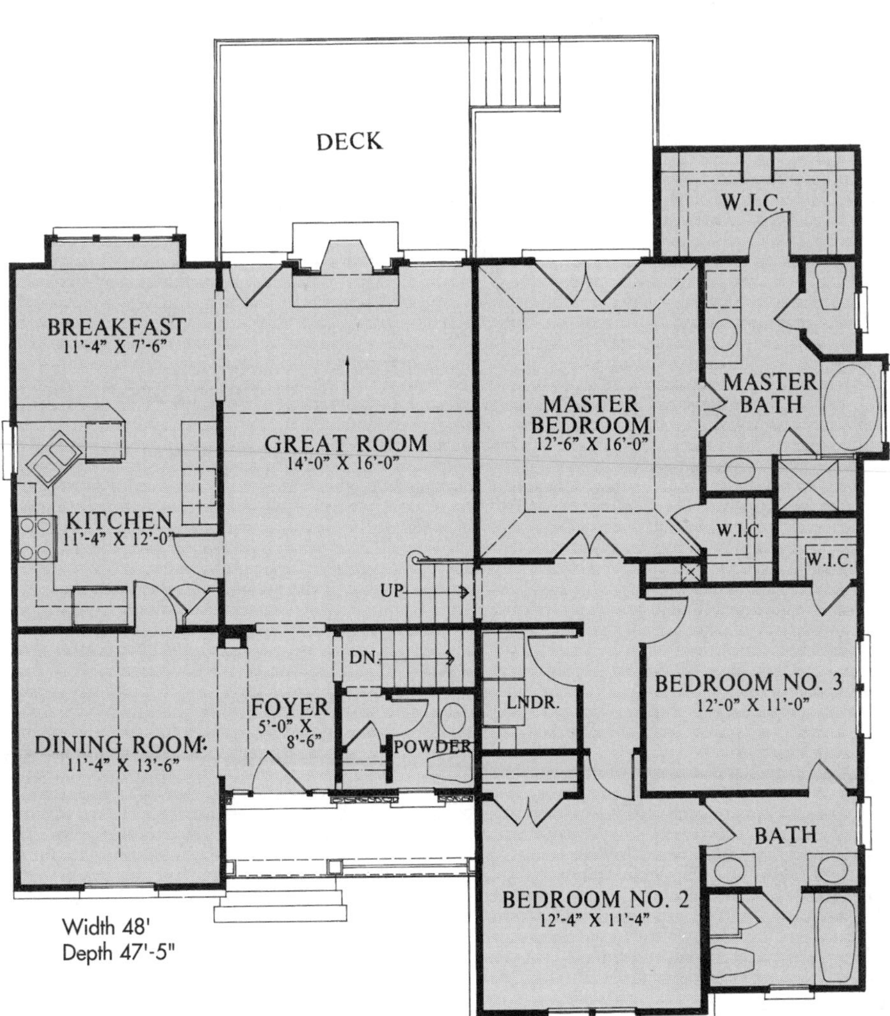
DECK
W.I.C.
BREAKFAST
11'-4" X 7'-6"
MASTER BEDROOM
12'-6" X 16'-0"
MASTER BATH
GREAT ROOM
14'-0" X 16'-0"
KITCHEN
11'-4" X 12'-0"
W.I.C.
W.I.C.
UP
DN.
BEDROOM NO. 3
12'-0" X 11'-0"
FOYER
5'-0" X 8'-6"
LNDR.
DINING ROOM
11'-4" X 13'-6"
POWDER
BATH
BEDROOM NO. 2
12'-4" X 11'-4"
Width 48'
Depth 47'-5"

Design 7277

Main Level: 962 square feet
Lower Level: 668 square feet
Total: 1,630 square feet

■ Efficient site utilization is the focus of this smart home. In the expansive great room, a sloped ceiling and a warming hearth combine for the best in both formal and informal living. The kitchen includes a snack bar for impromptu dining. The master bedroom views the rear grounds through two windows. A secondary bedroom also overlooks this area. Downstairs, a family room provides extra room to grow. Two family bedrooms share a full bath. A laundry room and a one-car garage with built-in shelves finish the plan.

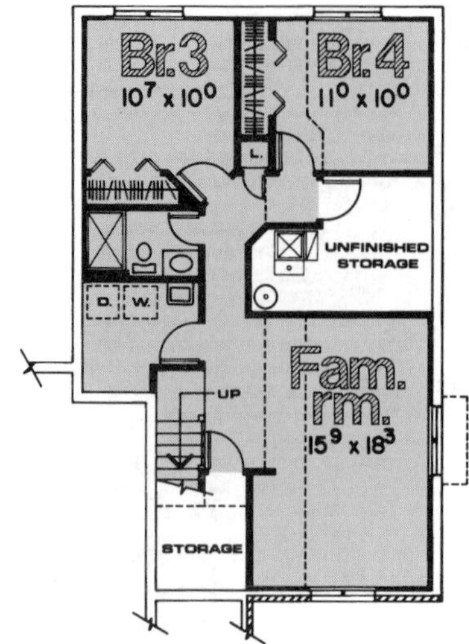
Br. 3
$10^{7} \times 10^{0}$
Br. 4
$11^{0} \times 10^{0}$
L.
UNFINISHED STORAGE
D.
W.
UP
Fam. rm.
$15^{9} \times 18^{3}$
STORAGE

Design by
Design Basics, Inc.

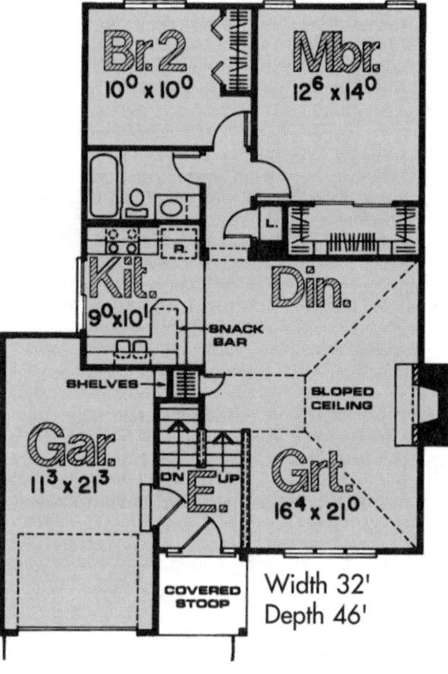
Br. 2
$10^{0} \times 10^{0}$
Mbr.
$12^{6} \times 14^{0}$
L.
R.
Kit.
$9^{0} \times 10^{1}$
Din.
SNACK BAR
SHELVES
SLOPED CEILING
Gar.
$11^{3} \times 21^{3}$
DN
E.
UP
Grt.
$16^{4} \times 21^{0}$
COVERED STOOP

Width 32'
Depth 46'

Design 7229

Square Footage: 1,696

■ This convenient split-entry traditional home features a great room with a fireplace flanked by bookcases and a floor-to-ceiling view of the back yard. The efficient kitchen includes a sunny bay window in the breakfast area. Box ceilings grace both the breakfast nook and the formal dining room. The laundry room is strategically located near the sleeping wing. Two secondary bedrooms offer abundant closet space and a shared full bath. The deluxe master bedroom has a vaulted ceiling, a large walk-in closet and a bath with a whirlpool tub.

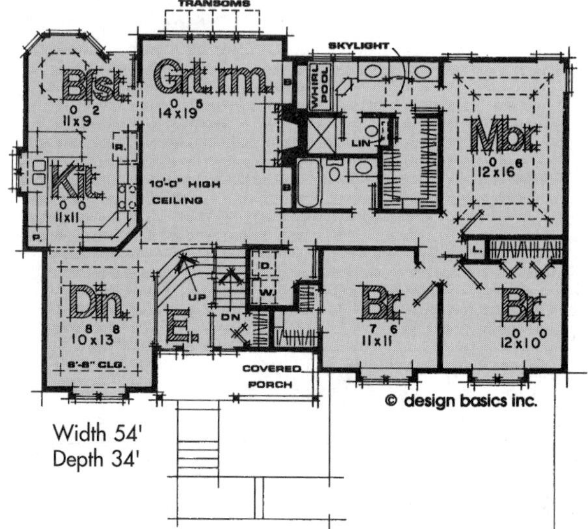
TRANSOMS
SKYLIGHT
Bfst.
$11^{0} \times 9^{2}$
Grt. rm.
$14^{0} \times 19^{5}$
WHIRL POOL
LIN
Mbr.
$12^{0} \times 16^{6}$
Kit.
$11^{0} \times 11^{0}$
R.
P.
10'-0" HIGH CEILING
D.
W.
L.
Din.
$10^{8} \times 13^{8}$
9'-8" CLG.
E.
UP
DN
Br.
$11^{7} \times 11^{6}$
Br.
$12^{0} \times 10^{0}$
COVERED PORCH
© design basics inc.

Width 54'
Depth 34'

Design by
Design Basics, Inc.

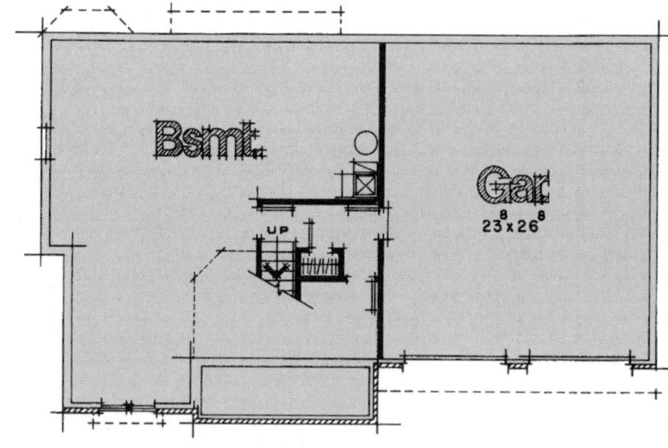
Bsmt.
Gar.
$23^{8} \times 26^{8}$
UP

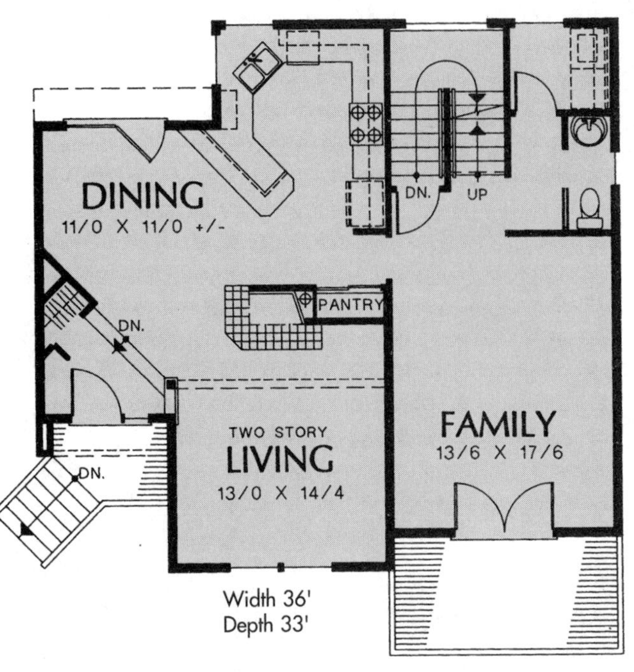
DINING
11/0 X 11/0 +/-
DN.
UP
PANTRY
DN.
TWO STORY
LIVING
13/0 X 14/4
FAMILY
13/6 X 17/6
DN.
Width 36'
Depth 33'

■ This house not only accommodates a narrow lot, but it also fits a sloping site. Notice how the two-car garage is tucked away under the first level of the house. The angled corner entry gives way to a two-story living room with a tiled hearth. The dining room shares an interesting angled space with this area and enjoys easy service from the efficient kitchen. A large pantry and an angled corner sink add character to this area. The family room offers double doors to a refreshing balcony. A powder room and a laundry room complete the main level. Upstairs, three bedrooms include a vaulted master suite with a private bath. Bedrooms 2 and 3 each take advantage of direct access to a full bath.

Design 9509

Main Level: 1,022 square feet
Upper Level: 813 square feet
Total: 1,835 square feet

Design by
Alan Mascord Design Associates, Inc.

BR. 2
10/2 X 13/0
TUB
DN.
BR. 3
10/8 X 11/8
LIN.
LIVING RM.
BELOW
VAULTED
MASTER
13/6 X 12/6

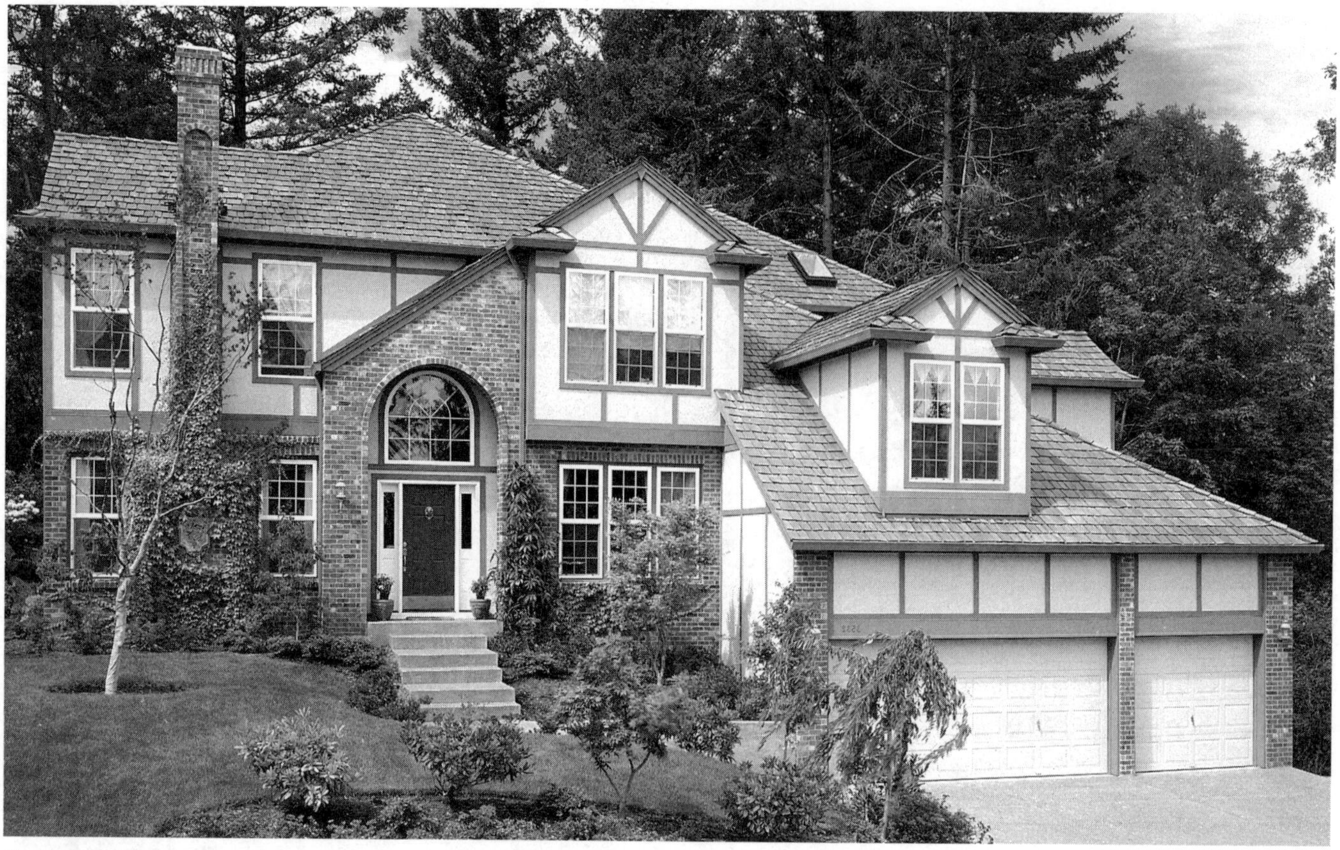

Photo by Bob Greenspan

■ This impressive Tudor is designed for lots that slope up slightly from the street—the garage is five feet below the main floor. Just to the right of the entry, the den is arranged to work well as an office. Formal living areas include a living room with fireplace and an elegant dining room. The family room also has a fireplace and is close to the bumped-out nook—a great casual dining area. All the bedrooms are generously sized, especially the master with plenty of amenities and a huge walk-in closet. A large vaulted bonus room features convenient access from both the family room and the upper hallway.

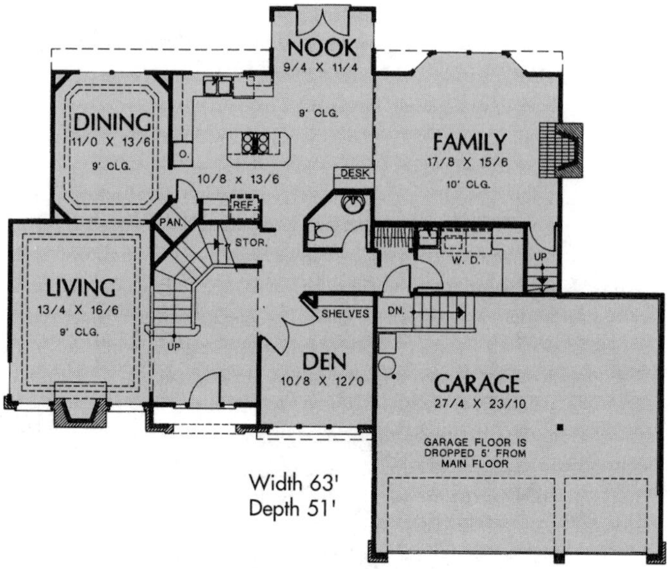

Width 63'
Depth 51'

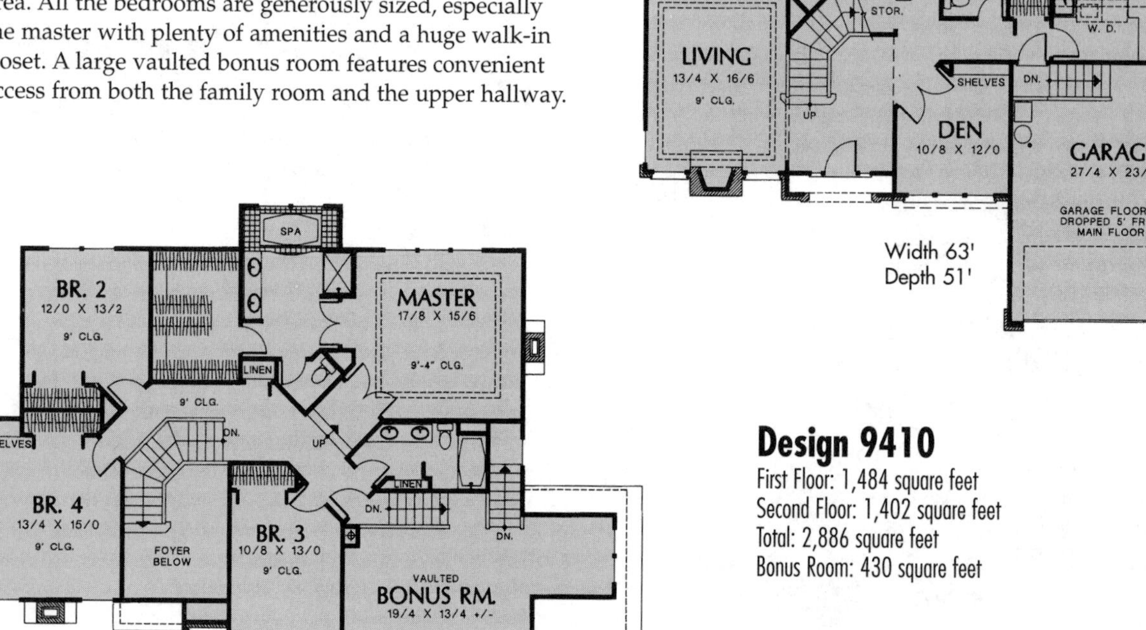
SPA
BR. 2
12/0 X 13/2
9' CLG.
MASTER
17/8 X 15/6
9'-4" CLG.
LINEN
9' CLG.
DN.
UP
SHELVES
BR. 4
13/4 X 15/0
9' CLG.
FOYER
BELOW
BR. 3
10/8 X 13/0
9' CLG.
LINEN
DN.
DN.
VAULTED
BONUS RM.
19/4 X 13/4 +/-

Design 9410

First Floor: 1,484 square feet
Second Floor: 1,402 square feet
Total: 2,886 square feet
Bonus Room: 430 square feet

Design by
Alan Mascord Design Associates, Inc.

■ Designed for sloping lots, this home has much to offer in addition to its visual appeal. It is especially suited to homes that orient with a view to the front (note the decks off the master bedroom and den). The two-story family room, with through-fireplace to the den, is complemented by the more formal parlor with a high ceiling. The parlor is separated from the dining room by a step with columned accents. The kitchen has an island range and a large nook. Three bedrooms upstairs include a master with lavish bath and a tray ceiling. Two family bedrooms share a full bath.

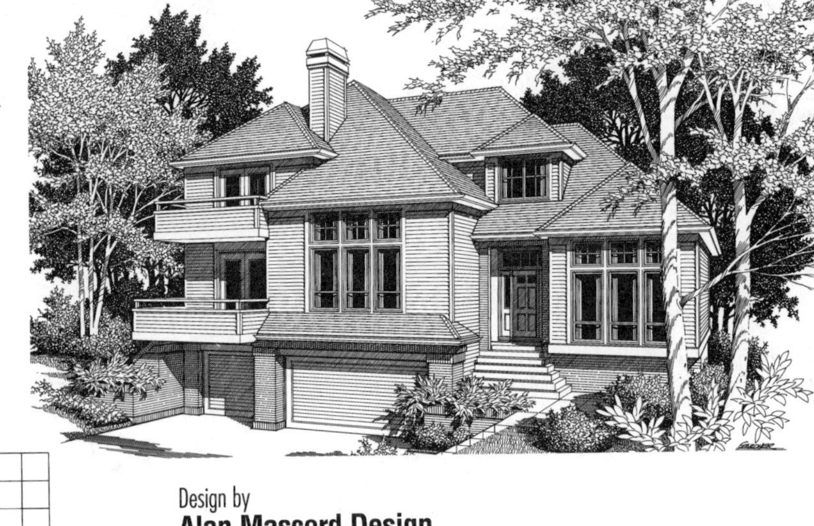

Design 9488

Main Level: 1,713 square feet
Upper Level: 998 square feet
Lower Level: 102 square feet
Total: 2,813 square feet

Design by
Alan Mascord Design Associates, Inc.

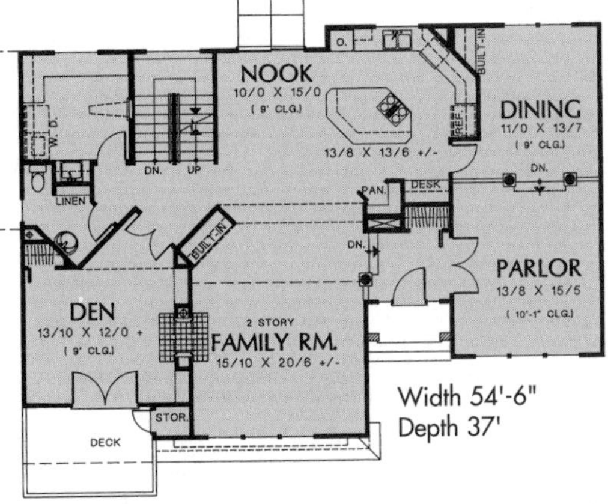
NOOK
10/0 X 15/0
(9' CLG.)
13/8 X 13/6 +/-
DINING
11/0 X 13/7
(9' CLG.)
PARLOR
13/8 X 15/5
(10'-1" CLG.)
DEN
13/10 X 12/0 +
(9' CLG.)
2 STORY
FAMILY RM.
15/10 X 20/6 +/-
LINEN
DESK
PAN.
BUILT-IN
REF.
W. D.
DN.
UP
STOR.
DECK
Width 54'-6"
Depth 37'

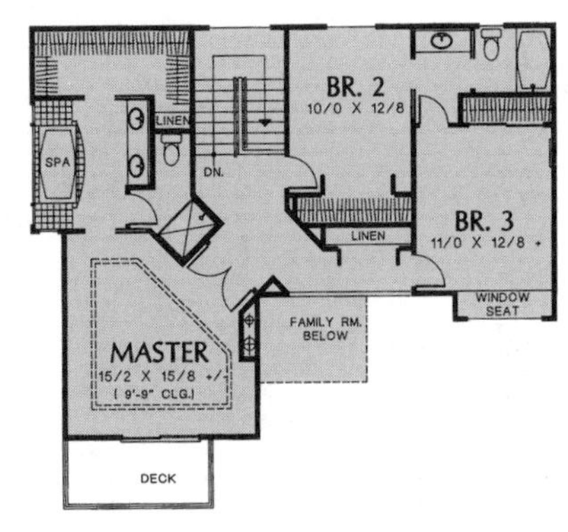
BR. 2
10/0 X 12/8
BR. 3
11/0 X 12/8 +
MASTER
15/2 X 15/8 +/-
(9'-9" CLG.)
SPA
LINEN
FAMILY RM. BELOW
WINDOW SEAT
DN.
DECK

Design 9467

First Floor: 899 square feet
Second Floor: 871 square feet
Total: 1,770 square feet

■ Try packing more features into a plan of less than 1,800 square feet! This plan includes four bedrooms, a separate family room, living room and eating nook, all in a compact plan that works well on even the smallest lots. The family room shares a breakfast bar with an efficiently designed kitchen that overlooks the charming nook with its bay windows projecting into the rear yard. The master bedroom upstairs is spacious. It contains a window seat, bath with walk-in closet and double sinks, and a vaulted ceiling. Three family bedrooms round out the second floor.

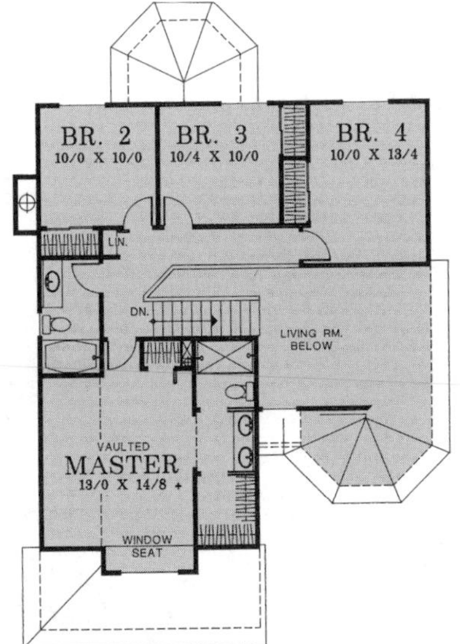
BR. 2
10/0 X 10/0
BR. 3
10/4 X 10/0
BR. 4
10/0 X 13/4
LIN.
DN.
LIVING RM. BELOW
VAULTED
MASTER
13/0 X 14/8 +
WINDOW SEAT

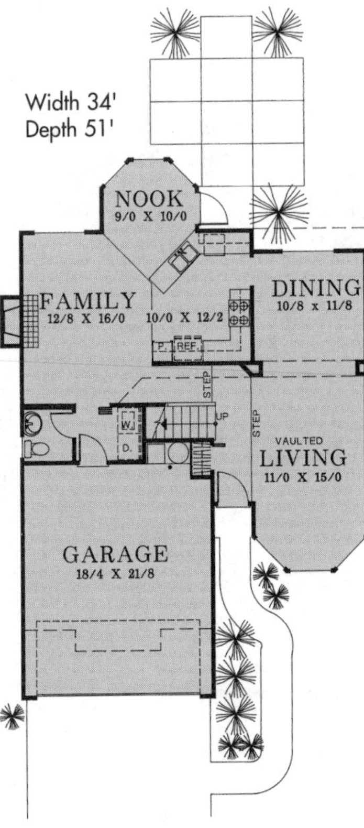
Width 34'
Depth 51'
NOOK
9/0 X 10/0
FAMILY
12/8 X 16/0
10/0 X 12/2
DINING
10/8 x 11/8
REF.
STEP
UP
W.
D.
VAULTED
LIVING
11/0 X 15/0
GARAGE
18/4 X 21/8

Design by
Alan Mascord Design Associates, Inc.

■ Front and back porches, and a dash of Southern charm give this home its warm appeal. The foyer is flanked by a dining room and a living room (or a study). You'll also find a great room with a fireplace for family livability. The kitchen and breakfast room are not far away from here. The first-floor master suite contains porch access, a luxurious private bath and a large walk-in closet. Upstairs, secondary bedrooms accommodate family or guests. This home is designed with a basement foundation.

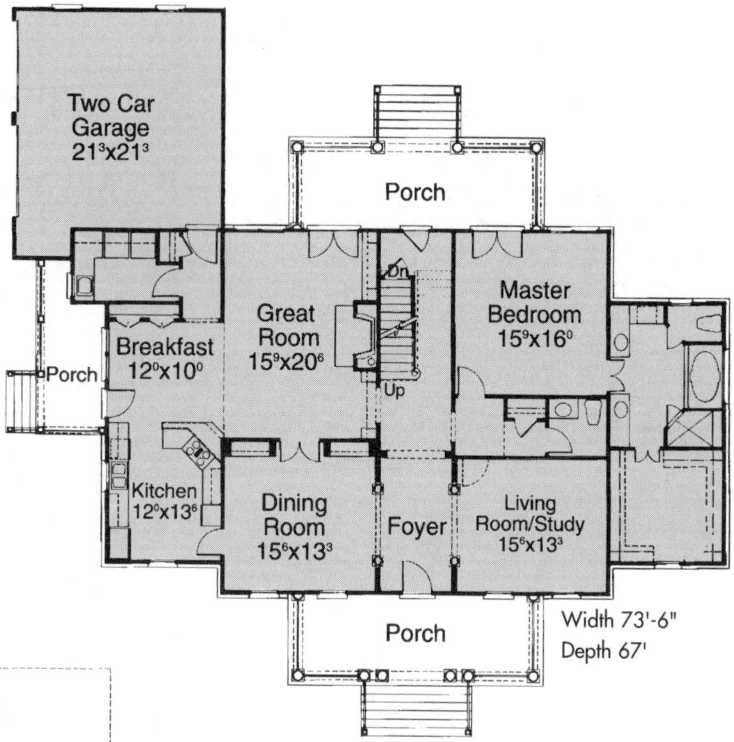

Design by
Design Traditions

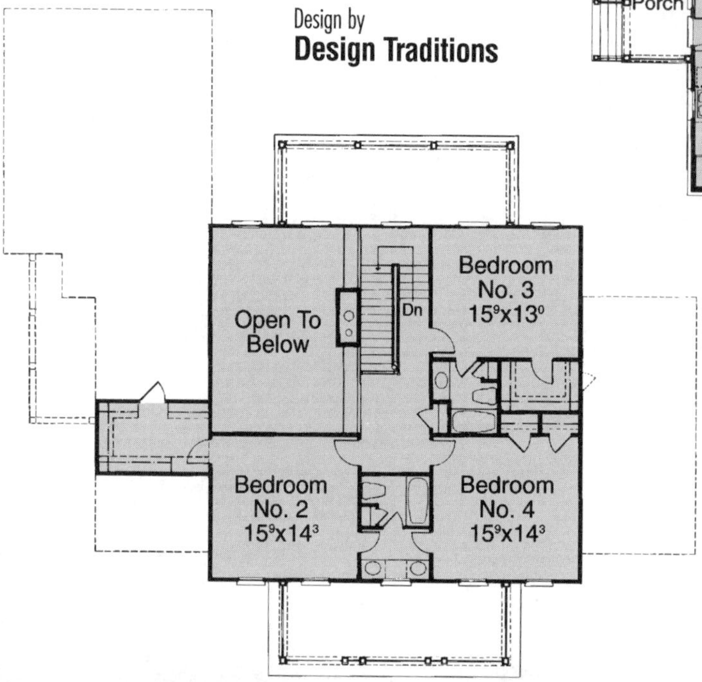

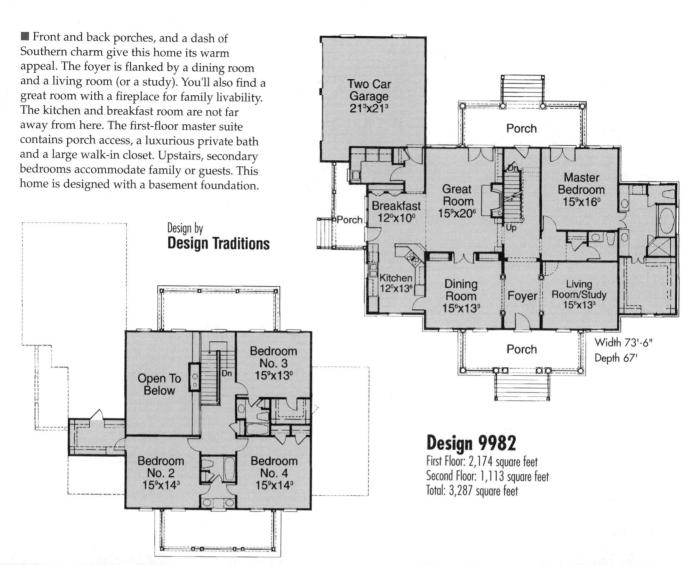

Two Car Garage 21^3x21^3
Porch
Breakfast 12^0x10^0
Great Room 15^9x20^6
Master Bedroom 15^9x16^0
Kitchen 12^0x13^6
Dining Room 15^6x13^3
Foyer
Living Room/Study 15^6x13^3
Porch
Dn
Up
Width 73'-6"
Depth 67'

Open To Below
Dn
Bedroom No. 3 15^9x13^0
Bedroom No. 2 15^9x14^3
Bedroom No. 4 15^9x14^3

Design 9982

First Floor: 2,174 square feet
Second Floor: 1,113 square feet
Total: 3,287 square feet

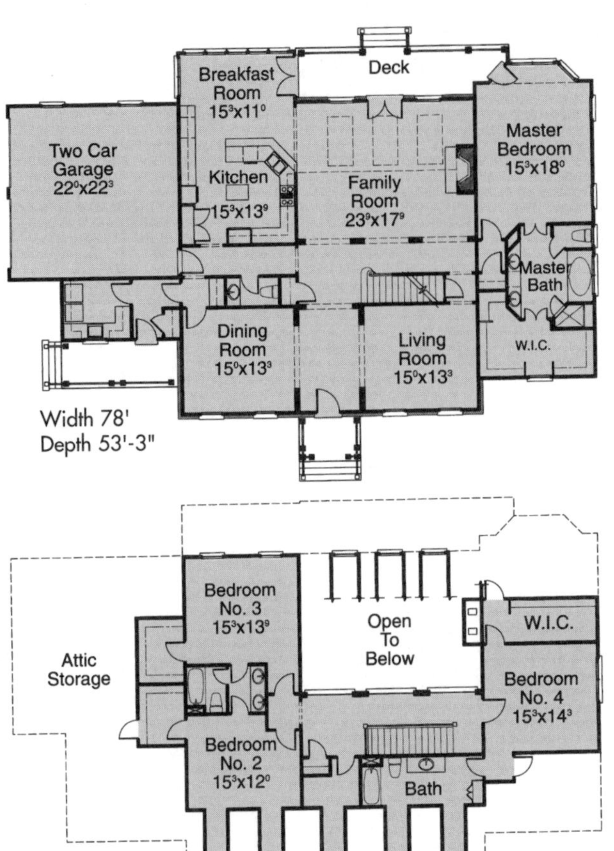

Deck
Breakfast Room 15^{3}x11^{0}
Kitchen 15^{3}x13^{9}
Two Car Garage 22^{0}x22^{3}
Family Room 23^{9}x17^{9}
Master Bedroom 15^{3}x18^{0}
Master Bath
W.I.C.
Dining Room 15^{0}x13^{3}
Living Room 15^{0}x13^{3}
Width 78'
Depth 53'-3"
Bedroom No. 3 15^{3}x13^{9}
Open To Below
W.I.C.
Attic Storage
Bedroom No. 4 15^{3}x14^{3}
Bedroom No. 2 15^{3}x12^{0}
Bath

Design 9991

First Floor: 2,496 square feet
Second Floor: 1,373 square feet
Total: 3,869 square feet
Finished Basement: 1,620 square feet

■ Classical symmetry prevails inside in comparable living and dining rooms that open off either side of the entrance foyer. The less formal living spaces beyond flow easily into one another from a central stair hall. Dormers bathe interior spaces in natural light. A dramatic vaulted great room with three dormers, a window-wrapped breakfast area and a master suite in the right wing all open onto a private rear porch. Five dormers on the front elevation distinguish a second story that includes three bedrooms, two baths and an optional linen closet or a cozy seating area. This home is designed with a basement foundation that can be developed with a bedroom with bath, a family room with a fireplace, a recreation room and plenty of storage.

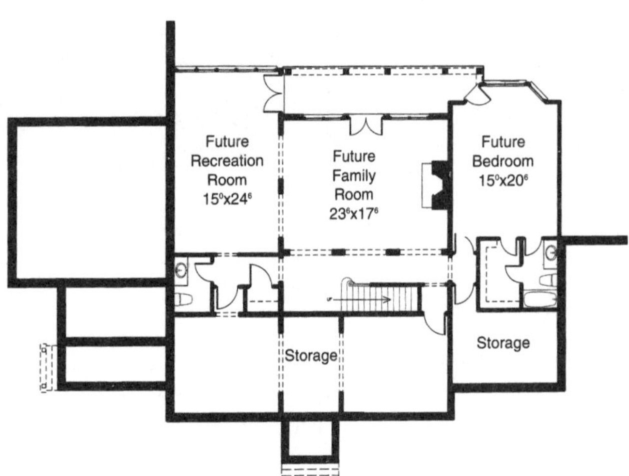

Future Recreation Room 15^{0}x24^{6}
Future Family Room 23^{6}x17^{6}
Future Bedroom 15^{0}x20^{6}
Storage
Storage

Design by
Design Traditions

■ This home's fine proportions contain formal living areas, including a dining room and a living room. At the back of the first floor you'll find a fine kitchen that serves a breakfast nook. A great room with a fireplace and a bumped-out window make everyday living very comfortable. A rear porch allows for outdoor dining and relaxation. Upstairs, four bedrooms include a master suite with lots of notable features. A boxed ceiling, a lavish bath, a large walk-in closet and a secluded sitting room (which will also make a nice study or exercise room) assure great livability. One of the secondary bedrooms contains a full bath. This home is designed with a basement foundation.

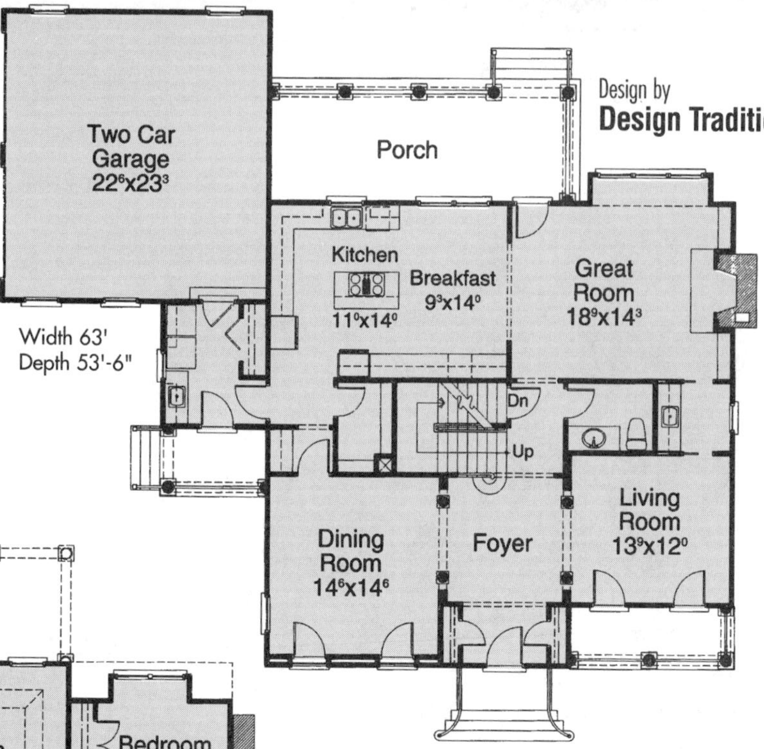

Design by
Design Traditions

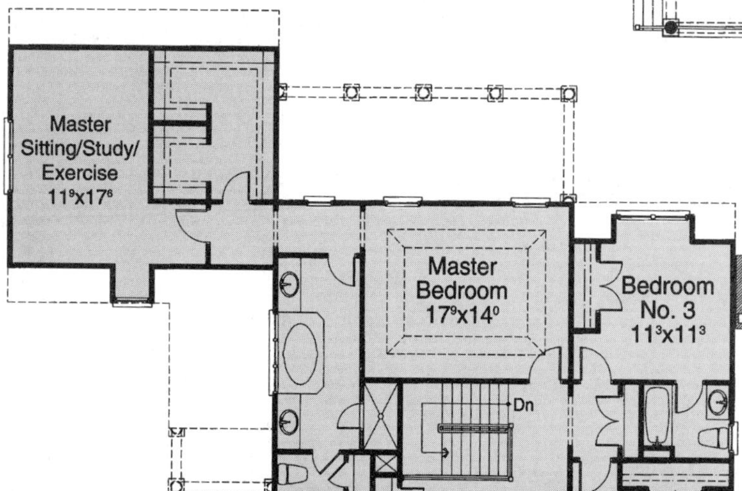

Two Car Garage 22^6x23^3
Porch
Kitchen 11^0x14^0
Breakfast 9^3x14^0
Great Room 18^9x14^3
Dining Room 14^6x14^6
Foyer
Living Room 13^9x12^0
Dn
Up

Width 63'
Depth 53'-6"

Master Sitting/Study/Exercise 11^9x17^6
Master Bedroom 17^9x14^0
Bedroom No. 3 11^3x11^3
Bedroom No. 2 14^6x11^0
Bedroom No. 4 13^9x11^0
Dn

Design 9967

First Floor: 1,567 square feet
Second Floor: 1,895 square feet
Total: 3,462 square feet

Design 9992

First Floor: 1,704 square feet
Second Floor: 1,449 square feet
Total: 3,153 square feet
Bonus Room: 455 square feet

■ The fieldstone exterior and cupola evoke rural Southern appeal. The distinctive railed balcony, bay windows and porch arches recall Colonial detail. Inside, formal and informal spaces are separated by a graceful central stair hall that opens off the front foyer. French doors lead from the front porch into a formal dining room that links both the stair hall and the foyer. The living room, which also opens off the entrance foyer, leads to a cheerful great room that features a fireplace and built-in bookcases. An adjoining breakfast area opens onto a columned rear porch. Upstairs, a spacious master suite overlooks the rear yard. Two additional bedrooms share a convenient hall bath. A generous bonus space above the garage is also available. This home is designed with a basement foundation.

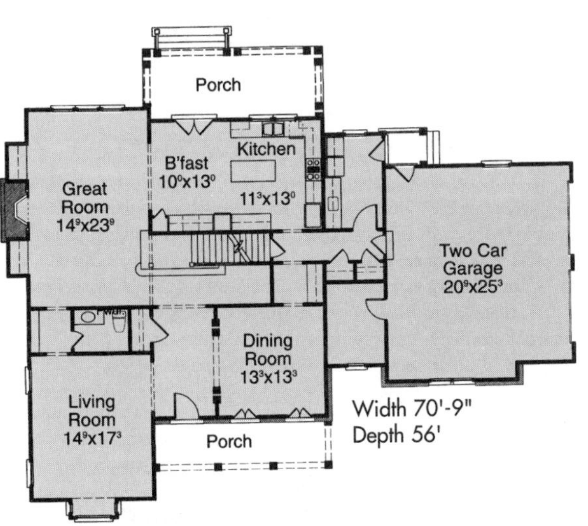
Porch
Great Room 14^{9}x23^9
B'fast 10^{0}x13^0
Kitchen 11^{3}x13^0
Two Car Garage 20^{9}x25^3
Pwdr.
Dining Room 13^{3}x13^3
Living Room 14^{9}x17^3
Porch
Width 70'-9"
Depth 56'

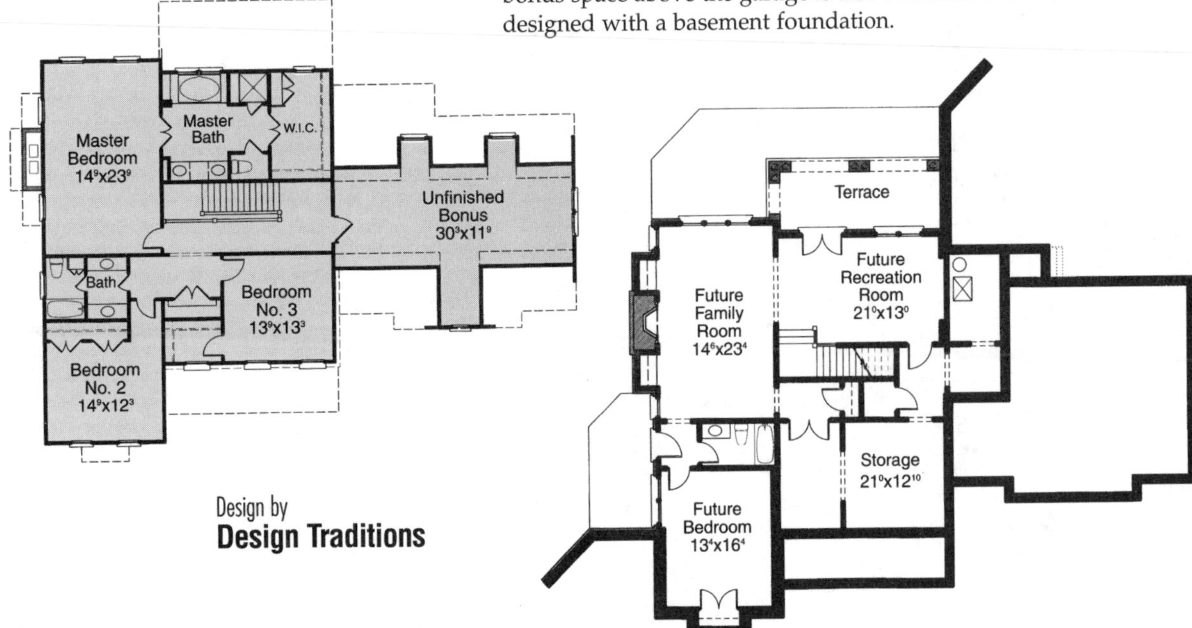
Master Bedroom 14^{9}x23^9
Master Bath
W.I.C.
Unfinished Bonus 30^{3}x11^9
Bath
Bedroom No. 3 13^{9}x13^3
Bedroom No. 2 14^{9}x12^3
Terrace
Future Recreation Room 21^{0}x13^0
Future Family Room 14^{6}x23^4
Storage 21^{0}x12^{10}
Future Bedroom 13^{4}x16^4

Design by
Design Traditions

Design 9993

First Floor: 1,634 square feet
Second Floor: 1,598 square feet
Total: 3,232 square feet
Bonus Room: 273 square feet

■ Only a sloping pediment above double front windows adorns this simple, country-style house, where a side-entry garage looks like a rambling addition. The wide porch signals a welcome that continues throughout the house. A front study doubles as a guest room with an adjacent full bath. A large dining room is ideal for entertaining and a sun-filled breakfast room off a spacious kitchen provides comfortable space for casual family meals. The open, contemporary interior plan flows from a stair hall at the heart of the house. On the private second floor, the master bedroom includes a luxurious bath; two other bedrooms share a bath with dual vanities. An extra room over the kitchen makes a perfect children's play area. This home is designed with a basement foundation.

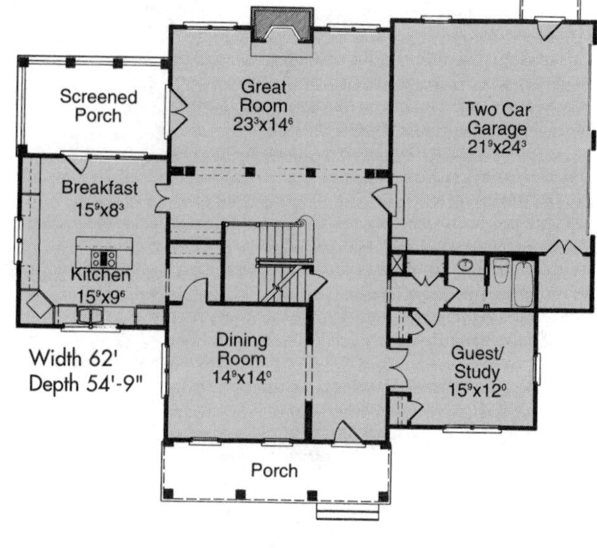
Screened Porch
Great Room 23^{3}x14^{6}
Two Car Garage 21^{9}x24^{3}
Breakfast 15^{9}x8^{3}
Kitchen 15^{9}x9^{6}
Dining Room 14^{9}x14^{0}
Guest/ Study 15^{9}x12^{0}
Porch
Width 62'
Depth 54'-9"

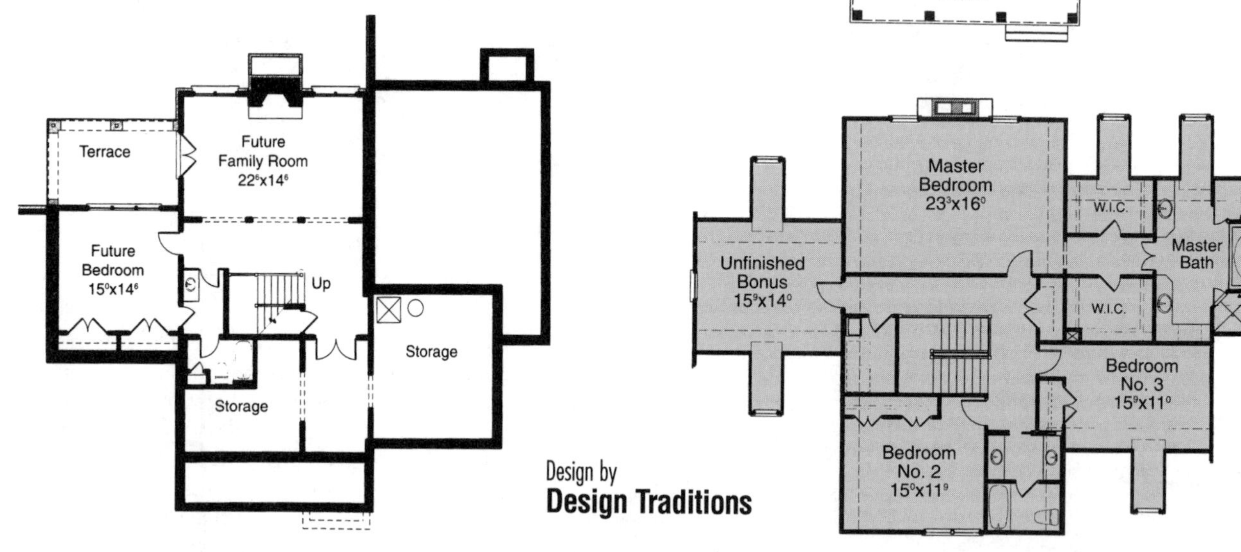
Terrace
Future Family Room 22^{6}x14^{6}
Future Bedroom 15^{0}x14^{6}
Up
Storage
Storage
Master Bedroom 23^{3}x16^{0}
Unfinished Bonus 15^{9}x14^{0}
W.I.C.
Master Bath
W.I.C.
Bedroom No. 3 15^{9}x11^{0}
Bedroom No. 2 15^{0}x11^{9}

Design by
Design Traditions

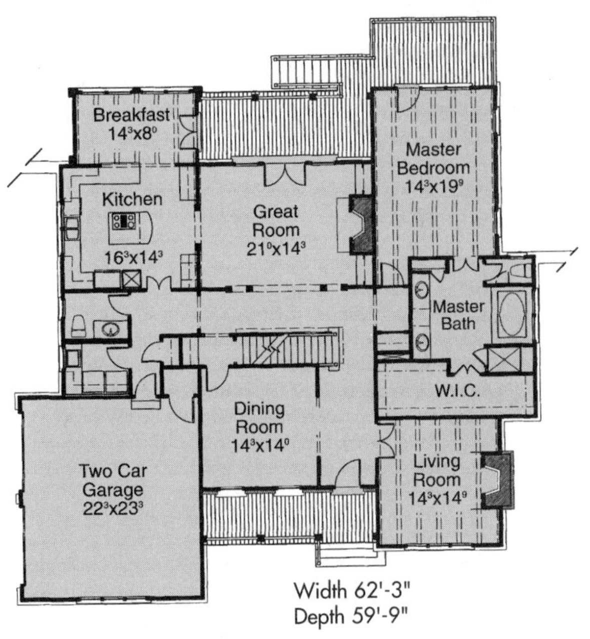
Breakfast
14³x8⁰
Kitchen
16³x14³
Great Room
21⁰x14³
Master Bedroom
14³x19⁹
Master Bath
W.I.C.
Dining Room
14³x14⁰
Living Room
14³x14⁹
Two Car Garage
22³x23³

Width 62'-3"
Depth 59'-9"

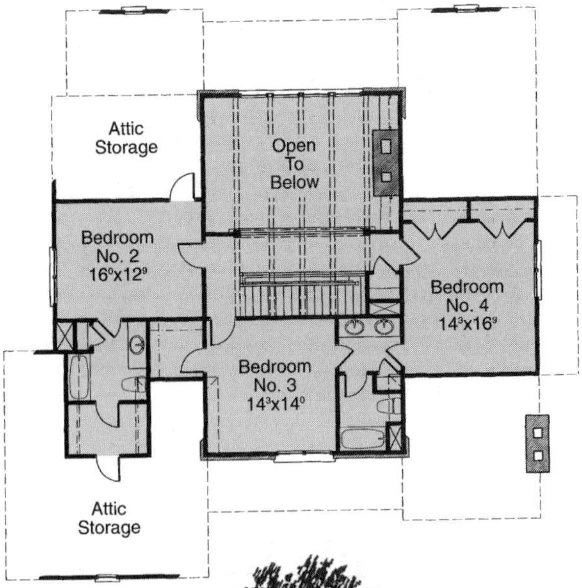

Design 9994

First Floor: 2,270 square feet
Second Floor: 1,128 square feet
Total: 3,398 square feet
Finished Basement: 1,271 square feet

■ Designed for lovers of the outdoors and natural rhythms, this 1½-story home crafts native creek stone and rugged lap siding into a design that blends with the landscape. Massive stone fireplaces set the tone in the formal living room and in the great room. The large kitchen has a sunny breakfast room and a multi-purpose island with a range top and snack bar. A separate vestibule leads to the elegant master bedroom with a luxurious master bath and oversized walk-in closet. Upstairs, three family bedrooms share two full baths. This home is designed with a basement foundation that can be developed with a large bedroom suite, a sunny family room and sitting area with a fireplace and plenty of storage.

Design by
Design Traditions

Attic Storage
Open To Below
Bedroom No. 2
16⁰x12⁹
Bedroom No. 4
14³x16⁹
Bedroom No. 3
14³x14⁰
Attic Storage

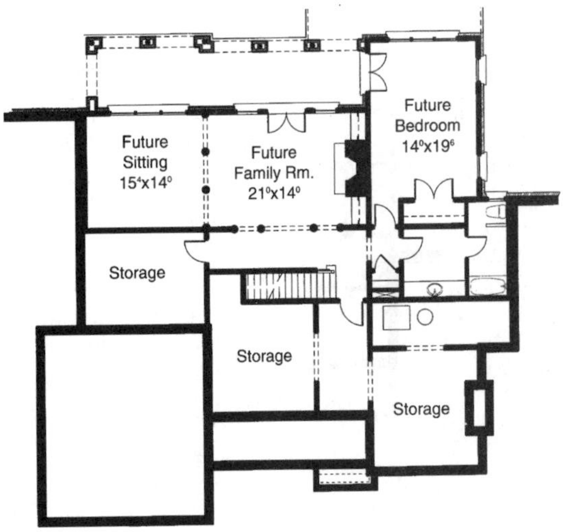

Future Sitting
15⁴x14⁰
Future Family Rm.
21⁰x14⁰
Future Bedroom
14⁰x19⁶
Storage
Storage
Storage

When You're Ready To Order . . .

Let Us Show You Our Home Blueprint Package.

Building a home? Planning a home? Our Blueprint Package has nearly everything you need to get the job done right, whether you're working on your own or with help from an architect, designer, builder or subcontractors. Each Blueprint Package is the result of many hours of work by licensed architects or professional designers.

QUALITY

Hundreds of hours of painstaking effort have gone into the development of your blueprint set. Each home has been quality-checked by professionals to insure accuracy and buildability.

VALUE

Because we sell in volume, you can buy professional-quality blueprints at a fraction of their development cost. With our plans, your dream home design costs only a few hundred dollars, not the thousands of dollars that custom architects charge.

SERVICE

Once you've chosen your favorite home plan, you'll receive fast, efficient service whether you choose to mail or fax your order to us or call us toll free at 1-800-521-6797. For customer service, call toll free 1-888-690-1116.

SATISFACTION

Over 50 years of service to satisfied home plan buyers provide us unparalleled experience and knowledge in producing quality blueprints. What this means to you is satisfaction with our product and performance.

ORDER TOLL FREE 1-800-521-6797

After you've looked over our Blueprint Package and Important Extras on the following pages, simply mail the order form on page 349 or call toll free on our Blueprint Hotline: 1-800-521-6797. We're ready and eager to serve you. For customer service, call toll free 1-888-690-1116.

Each set of blueprints is an interrelated collection of detail sheets which includes components such as floor plans, interior and exterior elevations, dimensions, cross-sections, diagrams and notations. These sheets show exactly how your house is to be built.

Among the sheets included may be:

Frontal Sheet
This artist's sketch of the exterior of the house gives you an idea of how the house will look when built and landscaped. Large ink-line floor plans show all levels of the house and provide an overview of your new home's livability, as well as a handy reference for deciding on furniture placement.

Foundation Plan
This sheet shows the foundation layout includ-

Sample Package

ing support walls, excavated and unexcavated areas, if any, and foundation notes. If slab construction rather than basement, the plan shows footings and details for a monolithic slab. This page, or another in the set, may include a sample plot plan for locating your house on a building site.

Detailed Floor Plans

These plans show the layout of each floor of the house. Rooms and interior spaces are carefully dimensioned and keys are given for cross-section details provided later in the plans. The positions of electrical outlets and switches are shown.

House Cross-Sections

Large-scale views show sections or cut-aways of the foundation, interior walls, exterior walls, floors, stairways and roof details. Additional cross-sections may show important changes in floor, ceiling or roof heights or the relationship of one level to another. Extremely valuable for construction, these sections show exactly how the various parts of the house fit together.

Interior Elevations

Many of our drawings show the design and placement of kitchen and bathroom cabinets, laundry areas, fireplaces, bookcases and other built-ins. Little "extras," such as mantelpiece and wainscoting drawings, plus moulding sections, provide details that give your home that custom touch.

Exterior Elevations

These drawings show the front, rear and sides of your house and give necessary notes on exterior materials and finishes. Particular attention is given to cornice detail, brick and stone accents or other finish items that make your home unique.

Frontal Sheet
Foundation Plans
Detailed Floor Plans
Exterior Elevations
Interior Elevations
House Cross-Sections
RIGHT SIDE
CROSS SECTION B-B
CROSS SECTION C-C
CROSS SECTION D-D
TYPICAL 2ND FLOOR WALL SECTION
ATTIC
HOME PLANNERS, INC.

Important Extras To Do The Job Right!

Introducing eight important planning and construction aids developed by our professionals to help you succeed in your home-building project.

MATERIALS LIST

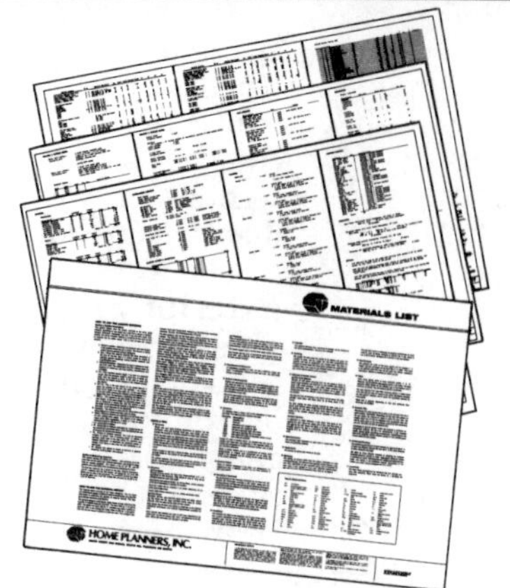

(Note: Because of the diversity of local building codes, our Materials List does not include mechanical materials.)

For many of the designs in our portfolio, we offer a customized materials take-off that is invaluable in planning and estimating the cost of your new home. This Materials List outlines the quantity, type and size of materials needed to build your house (with the exception of mechanical system items). Included are framing lumber, windows and doors, kitchen and bath cabinetry, rough and finish hardware, and much more. This handy list helps you or your builder cost out materials and serves as a reference sheet when you're compiling bids.

SPECIFICATION OUTLINE

SPECIFICATION OUTLINE
SPECIFICATION OUTLINE

This valuable 16-page document is critical to building your house correctly. Designed to be filled in by you or your builder, this book lists 166 stages or items crucial to the building process. It provides a comprehensive review of the construction process and helps in making choices of materials. When combined with the blueprints, a signed contract, and a schedule, it becomes a legal document and record for the building of your home.

QUOTE ONE®

Summary Cost Report / Materials Cost Report

A new service for estimating the cost of building select designs, the Quote One® system is available in two separate stages: The Summary Cost Report and the Materials Cost Report.

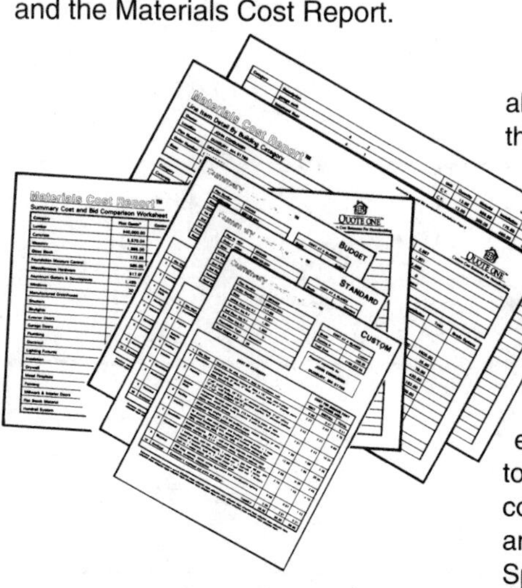

The Summary Cost Report is the first stage in the package and shows the total cost per square foot for your chosen home in your zip-code area and then breaks that cost down into ten categories showing the costs for building materials, labor and installation. The total cost for the report (which includes three grades: Budget, Standard and Custom) is just $19.95 for one home, and additionals are only $14.95. These reports allow you to evaluate your building budget and compare the costs of building a variety of homes in your area.

Make even more informed decisions about your home-building project with the second phase of our package, our Materials Cost Report. This tool is invaluable in planning and estimating the cost of your new home. The material and installation (labor and equipment) cost is shown for each of over 1,000 line items provided in the Materials List (Standard grade) which is included when you purchase this estimating tool. It allows you to determine building costs for your specific zip-code area and for your chosen home design. Space is allowed for additional estimates from contractors and subcontractors, such as for mechanical materials, which are not included in our packages. This invaluable tool is available for a price of $110 ($120 for a Schedule E plan) which includes a Materials List.

The Quote One® program is continually updated with new plans. If you are interested in a plan that is not indicated as Quote One®, please call and ask our sales reps, they will be happy to verify the status for you. To order these invaluable reports, use the order form on page 349 or call 1-800-521-6797.

CONSTRUCTION INFORMATION

If you want to know more about techniques—and deal more confidently with subcontractors we offer these useful sheets. Each set is an excellent tool that will add to your understanding of these technical subjects.

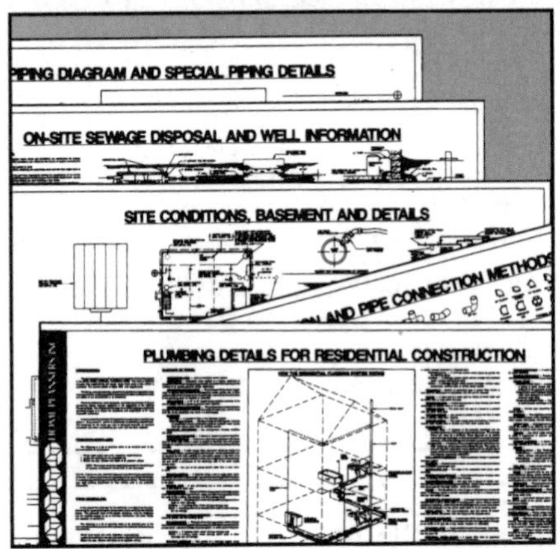
PIPING DIAGRAM AND SPECIAL PIPING DETAILS
ON-SITE SEWAGE DISPOSAL AND WELL INFORMATION
SITE CONDITIONS, BASEMENT AND DETAILS
PLUMBING DETAILS FOR RESIDENTIAL CONSTRUCTION

PLUMBING

The Blueprint Package includes locations for all the plumbing fixtures in your new house, including sinks, lavatories, tubs, showers, toilets, laundry trays and water heaters. However, if you want to know more about the complete plumbing system, these 24x36-inch detail sheets will prove very useful. Prepared to meet requirements of the National Plumbing Code, these six fact-filled sheets give general information on pipe schedules, fittings, sump-pump details, water-softener hookups, septic system details and much more. Color-coded sheets include a glossary of terms.

FLOOR PLAN WIRING DIAGRAM & SPECIAL DETAILS
TYPICAL SWITCH & OUTLET WIRING INSTALLATION DETAILS
SERVICE LOAD REQUIREMENTS & DISTRIBUTION PANEL WIRING
GENERAL INFORMATION & SERVICE ENTRANCE DETAILS
ELECTRICAL WIRING DETAILS FOR RESIDENTIAL CONSTRUCTION

ELECTRICAL

The locations for every electrical switch, plug and outlet are shown in your Blueprint Package. However, these Electrical Details go further to take the mystery out of household electrical systems. Prepared to meet requirements of the National Electrical Code, these comprehensive 24x36-inch drawings come packed with helpful information, including wire sizing, switch-installation schematics, cable-routing details, appliance wattage, door-bell hookups, typical service panel circuitry and much more. Six sheets are bound together and color-coded for easy reference. A glossary of terms is also included.

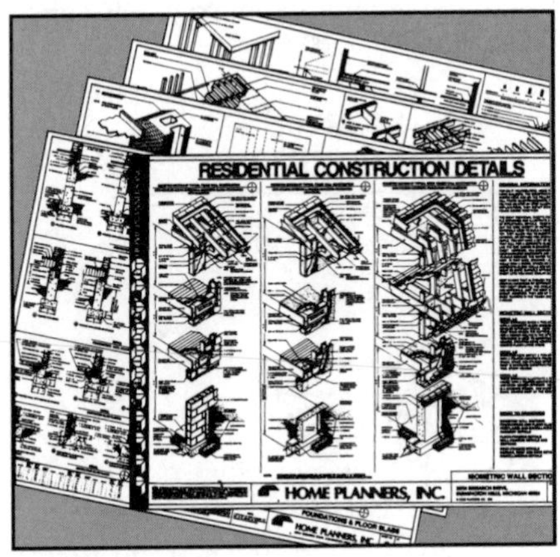
RESIDENTIAL CONSTRUCTION DETAILS
HOME PLANNERS, INC.

CONSTRUCTION

The Blueprint Package contains everything an experienced builder needs to construct a particular house. However, it doesn't show all the ways that houses can be built, nor does it explain alternate construction methods. To help you understand how your house will be built—and offer additional techniques—this set of drawings depicts the materials and methods used to build foundations, fireplaces, walls, floors and roofs. Where appropriate, the drawings show acceptable alternatives. These six sheets will answer questions for the advanced do-it-yourselfer or home planner.

MECHANICAL DETAILS
HOME PLANNERS, INC.

MECHANICAL

This package contains fundamental principles and useful data that will help you make informed decisions and communicate with subcontractors about heating and cooling systems. The 24x36-inch drawings contain instructions and samples that allow you to make simple load calculations and preliminary sizing and costing analysis. Covered are today's most commonly used systems from heat pumps to solar fuel systems. The package is packed full of illustrations and diagrams to help you visualize components and how they relate to one another.

Plan-A-Home®

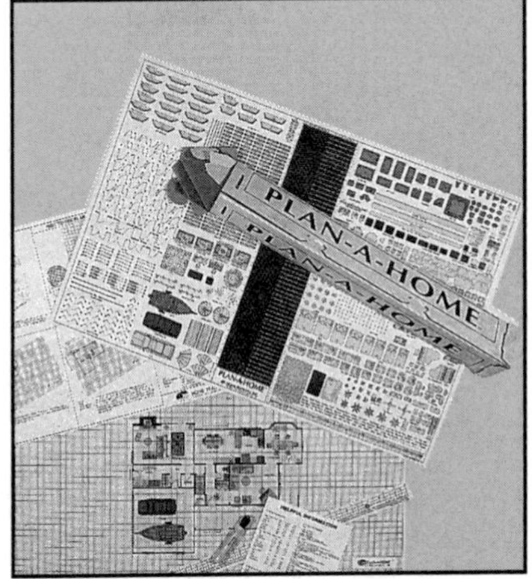
PLAN-A-HOME

Plan-A-Home® is an easy-to-use tool that helps you design a new home, arrange furniture in a new or existing home, or plan a remodeling project. Each package contains:

- **More than 700 reusable peel-off planning symbols** on a self-stick vinyl sheet, including walls, windows, doors, all types of furniture, kitchen components, bath fixtures and many more.
- **A reusable, transparent, 1/4-inch scale planning grid** that matches the scale of actual working drawings (1/4-inch equals 1 foot). This grid provides the basis for house layouts of up to 140x92 feet.
- **Tracing paper** and a protective sheet for copying or transferring your completed plan.
- **A felt-tip pen,** with water-soluble ink that wipes away quickly.

Plan-A-Home® lets you lay out areas as large as a 7,500 square foot, six-bedroom, seven-bath house.

To Order, Call Toll Free 1-800-521-6797

To add these important extras to your Blueprint Package, simply indicate your choices on the order form on page 349 or call us Toll Free 1-800-521-6797 and we'll tell you more about these exciting products. For customer service, call toll free 1-888-690-1116.

Price Schedule & Plans Index

House Blueprint Price Schedule

(Prices guaranteed through December 31, 1999)

Tier	1-set Study Package	4-set Building Package	8-set Building Package	1-set Reproducible Sepias	Home Customizer® Package
A	$390	$435	$495	$595	$645
B	$430	$475	$535	$655	$705
C	$470	$515	$575	$715	$765
D	$510	$555	$615	$775	$825
E	$630	$675	$735	$835	$885

Prices for 4- or 8-set Building Packages honored only at time of original order.

Additional Identical Blueprints in same order..........................$50 per set
Reverse Blueprints (mirror image)..$50 per set
Specification Outlines..$10 each

Materials Lists (available only from those designers listed below):
† Design Basics Designs $75
✸ Alan Mascord Designs...$50
◆ Donald Gardner Designs $50
■ Design Traditions Designs...$50
• The Sater Design Collection...$50
✲ Larry Garnett Designs $50
≠ Larry Belk Designs..$50

Materials Lists for "E" price plans are an additional $10.

Deck Plans Price Schedule

CUSTOM DECK PLANS

Price Group	Q	R	S
1 Set Custom Plans	$25	$30	$35

Additional identical sets $10 each
Reverse sets (mirror image) $10 each

STANDARD DECK DETAILS

1 Set Generic Construction Details ....$14.95 each

COMPLETE DECK BUILDING PACKAGE

Price Group	Q	R	S
1 Set Custom Plans, plus 1 Set Standard Deck Details	$35	$40	$45

Landscape Plans Price Schedule

Price Group	X	Y	Z
1 set	$35	$45	$55
3 sets	$50	$60	$70
6 sets	$65	$75	$85

Additional Identical Sets....................................$10 each
Reverse Sets (mirror image)...............................$10 each

Index

To use the Index below, refer to the design number listed in numerical order (a helpful page reference is also given). Note the price index letter and refer to the House Blueprint Price Schedule above for the cost of one, four or eight sets of blueprints or the cost of a reproducible sepia. Additional prices are shown for identical and reverse blueprint sets, as well as a very useful Materials List for some of the plans. Some plans are also part of our Quote One® estimating service and are indicated by this symbol 🏠. See page 342 for more information.

To Order: Fill in and send the order form on page 349—or call toll free 1-800-521-6797 or 520-297-8200.

DESIGN	PRICE	PAGE	QUOTE ONE®
† 9312	D	242	
† 9323	D	44	
† 9325	D	159	
† 9326	D	94	
† 9328	C	21	
† 9337	E	127	
† 9343	C	151	🏠
† 9344	D	147	
† 9346	E	97	
† 9347	C	44	
† 9351	E	157	
† 9362	C	43	🏠
† 9364	E	196	🏠
† 9366	E	110	🏠
† 9369	D	123	
† 9370	E	95	
† 9375	E	73	🏠
† 9389	E	148	
† 9390	E	155	
† 9395	E	94	
✸ 9403	B	261	
✸ 9410	D	332	
✸ 9417	E	323	
✸ 9427	B	24	
✸ 9430	B	262	
✸ 9434	E	313	
✸ 9440	D	116	
✸ 9442	B	315	
✸ 9446	C	312	
✸ 9453	D	2	
✸ 9459	B	101	
✸ 9462	B	115	
✸ 9465	C	154	
✸ 9467	B	333	
✸ 9468	B	120	
✸ 9477	C	115	
✸ 9478	D	310	
✸ 9484	D	324	
✸ 9485	E	313	
✸ 9486	C	116	
✸ 9487	C	117	
✸ 9488	D	333	
✸ 9509	B	331	
✸ 9511	C	129	
✸ 9521	E	11	
✸ 9525	B	272	
✸ 9537	D	324	
✸ 9539	D	323	
✸ 9541	C	114	
✸ 9542	D	124	
✸ 9552	C	317	🏠
✸ 9553	D	316	
✸ 9554	E	321	🏠
✸ 9557	C	271	🏠
✸ 9558	C	314	🏠
✸ 9560	D	317	
✸ 9568	D	325	
✸ 9576	E	322	
✸ 9578	C	49	🏠
✸ 9581	C	312	
✸ 9584	D	114	
✸ 9585	C	253	
✸ 9590	C	270	
◆ 9601	C	27	
◆ 9605	D	211	
◆ 9606	C	84	🏠
◆ 9616	D	13	
◆ 9619	D	26	
◆ 9620	B	55	
◆ 9621	C	210	🏠
◆ 9622	C	26	
◆ 9623	D	214	🏠
◆ 9625	D	230	
◆ 9626	C	84	🏠
◆ 9630	C	269	
◆ 9632	D	209	🏠
◆ 9634	D	34	
◆ 9638	C	256	
◆ 9639	C	56	
◆ 9644	C	224	
◆ 9645	C	211	🏠
◆ 9646	D	144	
◆ 9654	D	230	
◆ 9660	D	30	
◆ 9661	C	98	🏠
◆ 9662	C	224	🏠
◆ 9663	B	268	
◆ 9664	B	259	🏠
◆ 9666	C	266	🏠
◆ 9667	D	215	🏠
◆ 9669	D	217	
◆ 9671	D	83	
◆ 9673	D	212	🏠
◆ 9679	C	258	
◆ 9688	D	242	
◆ 9690	C	210	🏠
◆ 9692	C	98	
◆ 9693	C	257	
◆ 9694	D	212	
◆ 9695	D	67	
◆ 9696	C	59	
◆ 9697	B	266	
◆ 9702	D	213	🏠
◆ 9703	D	235	
◆ 9704	C	258	
◆ 9705	D	88	
◆ 9706	D	219	
◆ 9707	D	234	🏠
◆ 9708	E	216	
◆ 9709	D	65	
◆ 9712	D	235	🏠
◆ 9713	C	61	
◆ 9721	E	222	
◆ 9723	D	220	🏠
◆ 9725	D	243	
◆ 9726	B	57	
◆ 9727	B	55	
◆ 9728	C	35	
◆ 9729	E	223	
◆ 9730	D	223	
◆ 9731	D	223	
◆ 9732	D	229	
◆ 9733	D	237	
◆ 9734	C	29	🏠
◆ 9736	D	99	
◆ 9738	D	233	🏠
◆ 9739	D	41	
◆ 9742	C	64	
◆ 9743	E	221	
◆ 9744	D	295	
◆ 9745	D	215	
◆ 9746	D	236	
◆ 9747	C	263	
◆ 9748	C	28	
◆ 9749	C	227	
◆ 9750	C	61	
◆ 9751	D	237	
◆ 9752	D	231	
◆ 9753	B	57	
◆ 9755	B	295	
◆ 9756	D	232	
◆ 9757	D	106	
◆ 9759	C	267	
◆ 9760	B	19	
◆ 9761	D	236	
◆ 9763	C	62	
◆ 9764	C	225	🏠
◆ 9766	D	220	
◆ 9767	D	219	
◆ 9769	C	267	
◆ 9771	C	228	
◆ 9773	D	218	
◆ 9774	C	228	
◆ 9775	C	82	
◆ 9778	C	63	
◆ 9779	C	226	
◆ 9780	C	60	
◆ 9782	D	233	
◆ 9783	C	227	

DESIGN	PRICE	PAGE	QUOTE ONE®
◆ 9791	D	240	
◆ 9792	C	216	
◆ 9794	C	63	
◆ 9797	B	54	
◆ 9798	D	246	
9802	D	180	
■ 9805	D	132	
■ 9806	C	201	⌂
■ 9807	C	161	⌂
■ 9808	C	78	⌂
■ 9810	C	78	
■ 9812	C	87	⌂
■ 9813	C	173	⌂
■ 9814	D	179	⌂
■ 9816	C	174	⌂
9818	C	197	
■ 9819	D	187	
■ 9821	C	87	⌂
■ 9822	D	207	⌂
■ 9823	C	203	⌂
9825	D	179	
■ 9828	D	194	⌂
9829	D	141	
■ 9830	D	195	⌂
■ 9831	C	167	⌂
9833	D	182	
■ 9837	D	189	
9838	D	14	⌂
■ 9840	B	170	⌂
9841	B	326	
■ 9842	C	158	⌂
9846	C	163	
9847	B	130	
9849	B	160	
■ 9850	D	203	⌂
9852	C	206	
■ 9853	B	51	⌂
9854	C	169	
9855	D	168	
9857	C	137	
■ 9858	D	135	⌂
■ 9862	C	167	⌂
■ 9864	C	175	⌂
■ 9869	D	140	⌂
■ 9871	D	15	⌂
■ 9872	B	162	⌂
9873	B	28	
■ 9874	B	50	⌂
9876	C	105	
■ 9879	B	328	⌂
■ 9884	C	52	⌂
■ 9885	C	52	⌂
9886	C	158	
9889	E	190	
■ 9892	C	6	⌂
9893	C	172	
■ 9894	B	25	⌂
9895	B	38	
■ 9896	B	104	⌂
9898	D	174	
■ 9899	D	146	⌂
9990	C	170	
9902	B	153	
■ 9904	B	162	⌂
9907	C	171	
9909	D	247	
■ 9910	E	198	
9912	D	239	
■ 9914	B	326	⌂
9916	C	171	
9917	B	328	
9918	D	131	
9919	D	189	
9921	E	284	
9922	E	275	
■ 9928	E	288	
9930	E	187	
9931	E	284	
9932	D	186	
9934	E	273	
9936	E	274	
■ 9937	E	285	
9949	B	329	
9950	C	166	
9967	E	336	
9970	D	182	
9977	D	205	
9979	D	149	
9981	D	149	
9982	D	334	
9984	D	152	
9989	C	192	
■ 9990	E	276	⌂
9991	D	335	
9992	D	337	
9993	D	338	
9994	D	339	
9995	C	269	
9996	C	204	
9997	D	202	
9999	C	80	
P100	B	16	
P101	B	153	
P102	C	194	
P103	B	241	
P104	B	90	
P105	C	154	
P106	B	136	
P107	A	18	
P108	A	150	
P109	B	165	
P110	A	164	
P111	B	23	
P112	C	106	
P113	B	104	
P114	B	136	
P115	B	200	
P116	D	173	
P117	E	126	
P118	D	176	
P119	D	125	
P120	E	108	
P122	B	48	
P123	B	47	
P124	C	130	
P125	B	46	
P127	C	165	
P128	B	47	
P129	B	49	
P132	C	129	
P146	C	53	
P148	C	30	
P152	E	132	
P189	B	20	
P190	B	327	
P230	E	133	
P231	D	128	
P232	B	164	
P233	B	22	
P234	D	3	
P235	A	18	

Before You Order . . .

Before filling out the coupon at right or calling us on our Toll-Free Blueprint Hotline, you may want to learn more about our services and products. Here's some information you will find helpful.

Quick Turnaround
We process and ship every blueprint order from our office within 48 hours. Because of this quick turnaround, we won't send a formal notice acknowledging receipt of your order.

Our Exchange Policy
Since blueprints are printed in response to your order, we cannot honor requests for refunds. However, we will exchange your entire first order for an equal number of blueprints at a price of $50 for the first set and $10 for each additional set; $70 total exchange fee for 4 sets; $100 total exchange fee for 8 sets . . . *plus* the difference in cost if exchanging for a design in a higher price bracket or *less* the difference in cost if exchanging for a design in lower price bracket. One exchange is allowed within a year of purchase date. **(Sepias are not exchangeable.)** All sets from the first order must be returned before the exchange can take place. Please add $18 for postage and handling via ground service; $30 via Second Day Air; $40 via Next Day Air.

About Reverse Blueprints
If you want to build in reverse of the plan as shown, we will include an extra set of reverse blueprints (mirror image) for an additional fee of $50. Although lettering and dimensions will appear backward, reverses will be a useful aid if you decide to flop the plan.

Revising, Modifying and Customizing Plans
The wide variety of designs available in this publication allows you to select ideas and concepts for a home to fit your building site and match your family's needs, wants and budget. Like many homeowners who buy these plans, you and your builder, architect or engineer may want to make changes to them. Some minor changes may be made by your builder, but we recommend that most changes be made by a licensed architect or engineer. If you need to make alterations to a design that is customizable, you need only order our Home Customizer® Package to get you started. As set forth below, we cannot assume any responsibility for blueprints which have been changed, whether by you, your builder or by professionals selected by you or referred to you by us, because such individuals are outside our supervision and control.

Architectural and Engineering Seals
Some cities and states are now requiring that a licensed architect or engineer review and "seal" a blueprint, or officially approve it, prior to construction due to concerns over energy costs, safety and other factors. Prior to application for a building permit or the start of actual construction, we strongly advise that you consult your local building official who can tell you if such a review is required.

About the Designers
The architects and designers whose work appears in this publication are among America's leading residential designers. Each plan was designed to meet the requirements of a nationally recognized model building code in effect at the time and place the plan was drawn. Because national building codes change from time to time, plans may not comply with any such code at the time they are sold to a customer. In addition, building officials may not accept these plans as final construction documents of record as the plans may need to be modified and additional drawings and details added to suit local conditions and requirements. We strongly advise that purchasers consult a licensed architect or engineer, and their local building official, before starting any construction related to these plans.

BLUEPRINTS ARE NOT RETURNABLE

Local Building Codes and Zoning Requirements
At the time of creation, our plans are drawn to specifications published by the Building Officials and Code Administrators (BOCA) International, Inc.; the Southern Building Code Congress (SBCCI) International, Inc.; the International Conference of Building Officials; or the Council of American Building Officials (CABO). Our plans are designed to meet or exceed national building standards. Because of the great differences in geography and climate throughout the United States and Canada, each state, county and municipality has its own building codes, zone requirements, ordinances and building regulations. Your plan may need to be modified to comply with local requirements regarding snow loads, energy codes, soil and seismic conditions and a wide range of other matters. In addition, you may need to obtain permits or inspections from local governments before and in the course of construction. Prior to using blueprints ordered from us, we strongly advise that you consult a licensed architect or engineer—and speak with your local building official—before applying for any permit or beginning construction. We authorize the use of our blueprints on the express condition that you strictly comply with all local building codes, zoning requirements and other applicable laws, regulations, ordinances and requirements. **Notice:** Plans for homes to be built in Nevada must be re-drawn by a Nevada-registered professional. Consult your building official for more information on this subject.

Foundation and Exterior Wall Changes
Most of our plans are drawn with either a full or partial basement foundation. Depending on your specific climate or regional building practices, you may wish to change this basement to a slab or crawlspace. Most professional contractors and builders can easily adapt your plans to alternate foundation types. Likewise, most can easily change 2x4 wall construction to 2x6, or vice versa.

Disclaimer
We and the designers we work with have put substantial care and effort into the creation of our blueprints. However, because we cannot provide on-site consultation, supervision and control over actual construction, and because of the great variance in local building requirements, building practices and soil, seismic, weather and other conditions, WE CANNOT MAKE ANY WARRANTY, EXPRESS OR IMPLIED, WITH RESPECT TO THE CONTENT OR USE OF OUR BLUEPRINTS, INCLUDING BUT NOT LIMITED TO ANY WARRANTY OF MERCHANTABILITY OR OF FITNESS FOR A PARTICULAR PURPOSE.

Terms and Conditions
These designs are protected under the terms of United States copyright Law and may not be copied or reproduced in any way, by any means, unless you have purchased Sepias or Reproducibles which clearly indicate your right to copy or reproduce. We authorize the use of your chosen design as an aid in the construction of one single-family home only. You man not use this design to build a second or multiple dwellings without purchasing another blueprint or blueprints or paying additional design fees.

How Many Blueprints Do You Need?
A single set of blueprints is sufficient to study a home in greater detail. However, if you are planning to obtain cost estimates from a contractor or subcontractors—or if you are planning to build immediately—you will need more sets. Because additional sets are cheaper when ordered in quantity with the original order, make sure you order enough blueprints to satisfy all requirements. The following checklist will help you determine how many you need:

___ Owner

___ Builder (generally requires at least three sets; one as a legal document, one to use during inspections, and at least one to give to subcontractors)

___ Local Building Department (often requires two sets)

___ Mortgage Lender (usually one set for a conventional loan; three sets for FHA or VA loans)

___ TOTAL NUMBER OF SETS

Toll Free 1-800-521-6797

Regular Office Hours:
8:00 a.m. to 8:00 p.m. Eastern Time, Monday through Friday
Our staff will gladly answer any questions during regular office hours. Our answering service can place orders after hours or on weekends.

If we receive your order by 4:00 p.m. Eastern Time, Monday through Friday, we'll process it and ship within 48 hours. When ordering by phone, please have your charge card ready. We'll also ask you for the Order Form Key Number at the bottom of the coupon.

By FAX: Copy the Order Form on the next page and send it on our FAX line: 1-800-224-6699 or 1-520-544-3086.

Canadian Customers
Order Toll-Free 1-800-561-4169

For faster service and plans that are modified for building in Canada, customers may now call in orders directly to our Canadian supplier of plans and charge the purchase to a charge card. Or, you may complete the order form at right, adding 40% to all prices and mail in Canadian funds to:

The Plan Centre 60 Baffin Place
Unit 5
Waterloo, Ontario N2V 1Z7

OR: Copy the Order Form and send it via our Canadian FAX line: 1-800-719-3291.

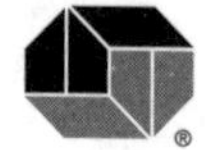

HOME PLANNERS, LLC
Wholly owned by Hanley-Wood, Inc.
3275 WEST INA ROAD, SUITE 110
TUCSON, ARIZONA 85741

ORDER FORM

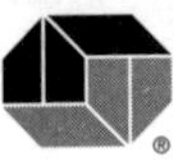

HOME PLANNERS, LLC, Wholly owned by Hanley-Wood, Inc.
3275 WEST INA ROAD, SUITE 110
TUCSON, ARIZONA 85741

THE BASIC BLUEPRINT PACKAGE

Rush me the following (please refer to the Plans Index and Price Schedule in this section):

_____ Set(s) of blueprints for plan number(s) ____________. $________
_____ Set(s) of sepias for plan number(s) ____________. $________
_____ Home Customizer® Package for plan(s)____________. $________
_____ Additional identical blueprints in same order @ $50 per set. $________
_____ Reverse blueprints @ $50 per set. $________

IMPORTANT EXTRAS

Rush me the following:

_____ Materials List: $50
$75 Design Basics. Add $10 for a Schedule E plan Materials List. $________
_____ **Quote One**® Summary Cost Report @ $19.95 for 1, $14.95 for each additional, for plans ____________ $________
Building location: City ____________ Zip Code ____________
_____ **Quote One**® Materials Cost Report @ $110 Schedule A-D; $120 Schedule E for plan____________ $________
(Must be purchased with Blueprints set.)
Building location: City ____________ Zip Code ____________
_____ Specification Outlines @ $10 each. $________
_____ Detail Sets @ $14.95 each; any two for $22.95; any three for $29.95; all four for $39.95 (save $19.85). $________
❑ Plumbing ❑ Electrical ❑ Construction ❑ Mechanical
(These helpful details provide general construction advice and are not specific to any single plan.)
_____ Plan-A-Home® @ $29.95 each. $________

POSTAGE AND HANDLING	1-3 sets	4+ sets
DELIVERY (Requires street address - No P.O. Boxes)		
•Regular Service (Allow 7-10 days delivery)	❑ $15.00	❑ $18.00
•Priority (Allow 4-5 days delivery)	❑ $20.00	❑ $30.00
•Express (Allow 3 days delivery)	❑ $30.00	❑ $40.00
CERTIFIED MAIL (Requires signature) If no street address available. (Allow 7-10 days delivery)	❑ $20.00	❑ $30.00
OVERSEAS DELIVERY Note: All delivery times are from date Blueprint Package is shipped.	fax, phone or mail for quote	

POSTAGE (From box above) $______
SUB-TOTAL $______
SALES TAX (AZ, CA, DC, IL, MI, MN, NY & WA residents, please add appropriate state and local sales tax.) $______
TOTAL (Sub-total and tax) $______

YOUR ADDRESS (please print)

Name ____________________
Street ____________________
City ____________ State ____________ Zip ____________
Daytime telephone number (______) ____________

FOR CREDIT CARD ORDERS ONLY

Please fill in the information below:
Credit card number ____________________
Exp. Date: Month/Year ____________________
Check one ❑ Visa ❑ MasterCard ❑ Discover Card

Signature ____________________
Please check appropriate box: ❑ Licensed Builder-Contractor
❑ Homeowner

ORDER TOLL FREE!
1-800-521-6797 or 520-297-8200

Order Form Key
TB49

ORDER FORM

HOME PLANNERS, LLC, Wholly owned by Hanley-Wood, Inc.
3275 WEST INA ROAD, SUITE 110
TUCSON, ARIZONA 85741

THE BASIC BLUEPRINT PACKAGE
Rush me the following (please refer to the Plans Index and Price Schedule in this section):
_____ Set(s) of blueprints for plan number(s) ____________. $________
_____ Set(s) of sepias for plan number(s) ____________. $________
_____ Home Customizer® Package for plan(s)____________. $________
_____ Additional identical blueprints in same order @ $50 per set. $________
_____ Reverse blueprints @ $50 per set. $________

IMPORTANT EXTRAS
Rush me the following:
_____ Materials List: $50
$75 Design Basics. Add $10 for a Schedule E plan Materials List. $________
_____ Quote One® Summary Cost Report @ $19.95 for 1, $14.95 for each additional, for plans ____________ $________
Building location: City ____________ Zip Code ____________
_____ Quote One® Materials Cost Report @ $110 Schedule A-D; $120 Schedule E for plan____________ $________
(Must be purchased with Blueprints set.)
Building location: City ____________ Zip Code ____________
_____ Specification Outlines @ $10 each. $________
_____ Detail Sets @ $14.95 each; any two for $22.95; any three for $29.95; all four for $39.95 (save $19.85). $________
❑ Plumbing ❑ Electrical ❑ Construction ❑ Mechanical
(These helpful details provide general construction advice and are not specific to any single plan.)
_____ Plan-A-Home® @ $29.95 each. $________

POSTAGE AND HANDLING	1-3 sets	4+ sets
DELIVERY (Requires street address - No P.O. Boxes)		
•Regular Service (Allow 7-10 days delivery)	❑ $15.00	❑ $18.00
•Priority (Allow 4-5 days delivery)	❑ $20.00	❑ $30.00
•Express (Allow 3 days delivery)	❑ $30.00	❑ $40.00
CERTIFIED MAIL (Requires signature) If no street address available. (Allow 7-10 days delivery)	❑ $20.00	❑ $30.00
OVERSEAS DELIVERY Note: All delivery times are from date Blueprint Package is shipped.	fax, phone or mail for quote	

POSTAGE (From box above) $______
SUB-TOTAL $______
SALES TAX (AZ, CA, DC, IL, MI, MN, NY & WA residents, please add appropriate state and local sales tax.) $______
TOTAL (Sub-total and tax) $______

YOUR ADDRESS (please print)
Name ____________________
Street ____________________
City ____________ State ____________ Zip ____________
Daytime telephone number (______) ____________

FOR CREDIT CARD ORDERS ONLY
Please fill in the information below:
Credit card number ____________________
Exp. Date: Month/Year ____________________
Check one ❑ Visa ❑ MasterCard ❑ Discover Card

Signature ____________________
Please check appropriate box: ❑ Licensed Builder-Contractor
❑ Homeowner

ORDER TOLL FREE!
1-800-521-6797 or 520-297-8200

Order Form Key
TB49

Helpful Books & Software

Home Planners wants your building experience to be as pleasant and trouble-free as possible. That's why we've expanded our library of Do-It-Yourself titles to help you along. In addition to our beautiful plans books, we've added books to guide you through specific projects as well as the construction process. In fact, these are titles that will be as useful after your dream home is built as they are right now.

ONE-STORY

ONE-STORY HOMES

1 448 designs for all lifestyles. 860 to 5,400 square feet.
384 pages $9.95

TWO-STORY

TWO-STORY HOMES

2 460 designs for one-and-a-half and two stories. 1,245 to 7,275 square feet.
384 pages $9.95

VACATION

VACATION & SECOND HOMES

3 345 designs for recreation, retirement and leisure.
312 pages $8.95

MULTI-LEVEL

HILLSIDE HOMES
214 Sloping-Lot & Multi-Level Designs

4 214 designs for split-levels, bi-levels, multi-levels and walkouts.
224 pages $8.95

COUNTRY

200 FARMHOUSE & COUNTRY HOME PLANS

5 200 country designs from classic to contemporary by 7 winning designers.
224 pages $8.95

MOVE-UP

200 MOVE-UP

6 200 stylish designs for today's growing families from 9 hot designers.
224 pages $8.95

NARROW-LOT

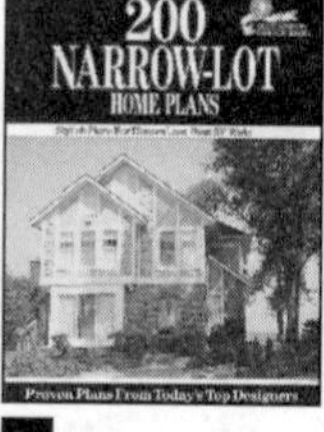
200 NARROW-LOT HOME PLANS

7 200 unique homes less than 60' wide from 7 designers. Up to 3,000 square feet.
224 pages $8.95

SMALL HOUSE

SMALL HOUSE PLANS

8 200 beautiful designs chosen for versatility and affordability.
224 pages $8.95

BUDGET-SMART

200 BUDGET-SMART HOME PLANS

9 200 efficient plans from 7 top designers, that you can really afford to build!
224 pages $8.95

EXPANDABLES

200 EXPANDABLE HOME PLANS

10 200 flexible plans that expand with your needs from 7 top designers.
240 pages $8.95

ENCYCLOPEDIA

ENCYCLOPEDIA OF HOME DESIGNS
500 House Plans
New Revised Edition!

11 500 exceptional plans for all styles and budgets—the best book of its kind!
352 pages $9.95

AFFORDABLE

AFFORDABLE HOME PLANS
300 HOME DESIGNS FOR MODEST & MEDIUM BUDGETS

12 Completely revised and updated, featuring 300 designs for modest budgets.
256 pages $9.95

ENCYCLOPEDIA 2

ENCYCLOPEDIA OF HOME DESIGNS
VOLUME II
500 House Plans

13 500 Completely new plans. Spacious and stylish designs for every budget and taste.
352 pages $9.95

VICTORIAN

Victorian DREAM HOMES

14 160 striking Victorian and Farmhouse designs from three leading designers.
192 pages $12.95

ESTATE

Estate DREAM HOMES
Luxury DREAM HOMES

15 Dream big! Twenty-one designers showcase their biggest and best plans.
208 pages. $15.95

LUXURY

16 154 fine luxury plans-loaded with luscious amenities!
192 pages $14.95

COTTAGES

Cottages

17 25 fresh new designs that are as warm as a tropical breeze. A blend of the best aspects of many coastal styles.
64 pages. $19.95

BEST SELLERS

HOME PLANNERS Gold

18 Our 50th Anniversary book with 200 of our very best designs in full color!
224 pages $12.95

SPECIAL COLLECTION

THE DESIGNS OF WILLIAM E. POOLE
70 Classical House Plans

19 70 Romantic house plans that capture the classic tradition of home design.
160 pages $17.95

COUNTRY HOUSES

Country Houses

20 208 Unique home plans that combine traditional style and modern livability.
224 pages $9.95

CLASSIC

CLASSIC HOME PLANS

21 Timeless, elegant designs that always feel like home. Gorgeous plans that are as flexible and up-to-date as their occupants.
240 pages. $9.95

CONTEMPORARY

CONTEMPORARY Home Plans

22 The most complete and imaginative collection of contemporary designs available anywhere.
240 pages. $9.95

EASY-LIVING

EASY-LIVING HOMES
200

23 200 Efficient and sophisticated plans that are small in size, but big on livability.
224 pages $8.95

SOUTHERN

SOUTHERN Home Plans

24 207 homes rich in Southern styling and comfort.
240 pages $8.95

SUNBELT

SOUTHWEST HOME PLANS

25 215 Designs that capture the spirit of the Southwest.
208 pages $10.95

WESTERN

WESTERN HOME PLANS

26 215 designs that capture the spirit and diversity of the Western lifestyle.
208 pages $9.95

ENERGY GUIDE

RESIDENTIAL ENERGY

27 The most comprehensive energy efficiency and conservation guide available.
280 pages $35.00

Design Software

BOOK & CD ROM

HOME PLANNERS Gold

28 Both the Home Planners Gold book and matching Windows™ CD ROM with 3D floorplans.
$24.95

3D DESIGN SUITE

PLANIX HOME Design Suite 3D

29 Home design made easy! View designs in 3D, take a virtual reality tour, add decorating details and more. $59.95

Outdoor Projects

OUTDOOR

YARD & GARDEN STRUCTURES

30 42 unique outdoor projects. Gazebos, strombellas, bridges, sheds, playsets and more!
96 pages $7.95

GARAGES & MORE

GREAT GARAGES
Sheds & Outdoor Buildings

31 101 Multi-use garages and outdoor structures to enhance any home.
96 pages $7.95

DECKS

DECK PLANNER

32 25 outstanding single-, double- and multi-level decks you can build.
112 pages $7.95

Landscape Designs

EASY CARE

EASY-CARE LANDSCAPE PLANS

33 41 special landscapes designed for beauty and low maintenance. 160 pages $14.95

FRONT & BACK

HOME LANDSCAPER

34 The first book of do-it-yourself landscapes. 40 front, 15 backyards. 208 pages $14.95

BACKYARDS

THE BACKYARD LANDSCAPER

35 40 designs focused solely on creating your own specially themed backyard oasis. 160 pages $14.95

BEDS & BORDERS

Beds & Borders
40 PROFESSIONAL DESIGNS FOR DO-IT-YOURSELFERS

36 Practical advice and maintenance techniques for a wide variety of yard projects. 160 pages. $14.95

BATHROOMS

DESIGNING AND PLANNING BATHROOMS

37 An innovative guide to organizing, remodeling and decorating your bathroom. 96 pages $9.95

KITCHENS

KITCHENS
Design • Remodel • Build

38 An imaginative guide to designing the perfect kitchen. Chock full of bright ideas to make your job easier. 176 pages $14 .95

HOUSE CONTRACTING

Be Your Own HOUSE CONTRACTOR
Save 25% without Lifting a Hammer
CARL HEILDMANN

39 Everything you need to know to act as your own general contractor...and save up to 25% off building costs. 134 pages $14.95

WINDOWS & DOORS

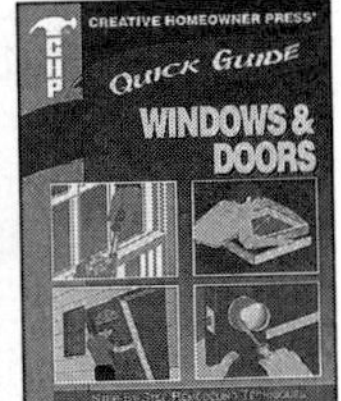
Quick Guide
WINDOWS & DOORS

40 Installation techniques and tips that make your project easier and more professional looking. 80 pages $7.95

ROOFING

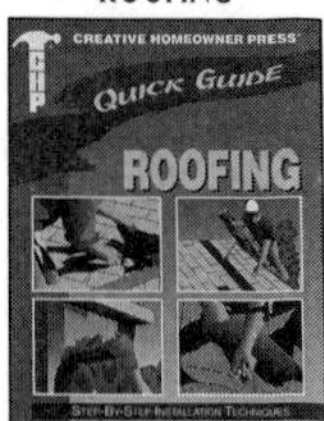
Quick Guide
ROOFING

41 Information on the latest tools, materials and techniques for roof installation or repair. 80 pages $7.95

FRAMING

RESIDENTIAL FRAMING
William P. Spence

42 For those who want to take a more-hands on approach to their dream. 319 pages $19.95

VISUAL HANDBOOK

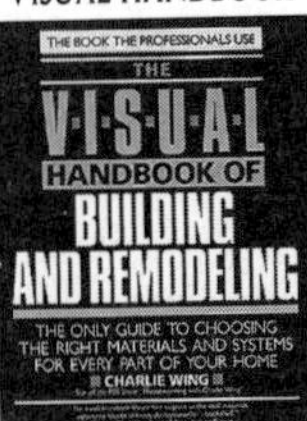
V-I-S-U-A-L HANDBOOK OF BUILDING AND REMODELING

43 A plain-talk guide to the construction process; financing to final walk-through, this book covers it all. 498 pages $19.95

BASIC WIRING

BASIC WIRING

44 A straight forward guide to one of the most misunderstood systems in the home. 160 pages $12.95

PATIOS & WALKS

Quick Guide
PATIOS & WALKS

45 Clear step-by-step instructions take you from the basic design stages to the finished project. 80 pages $7.95

TILE

Working with TILE

46 Every kind of tile for every kind of application. Includes tips on use installation and repair. 176 pages $12.95

PLUMBING

Modern HOME PLUMBING

47 Tackle any plumbing installation or repair as quickly and efficiently as a professional. 160 pages $12.95

TRIM & MOLDING

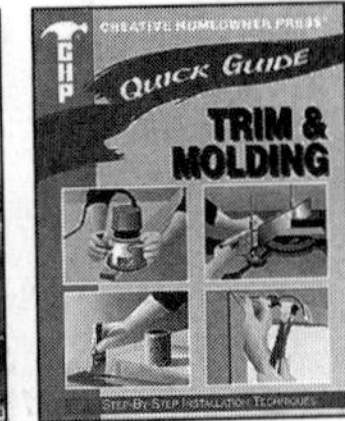
Quick Guide
TRIM & MOLDING

48 Step-by-step instructions for installing baseboards, window and door casings and more. 80 pages $7.95

Additional Books Order Form

To order your books, just check the box of the book numbered below and complete the coupon. We will process your order and ship it from our office within 48 hours. Send coupon and check (in U.S. funds).

YES! Please send me the books I've indicated:

- ☐ 1:VO $9.95
- ☐ 2:VT $9.95
- ☐ 3:VH $8.95
- ☐ 4:VS $8.95
- ☐ 5:FH $8.95
- ☐ 6:MU $8.95
- ☐ 7:NL $8.95
- ☐ 8:SM $8.95
- ☐ 9:BS $8.95
- ☐ 10:EX $8.95
- ☐ 11:EN $9.95
- ☐ 12:AF $9.95
- ☐ 13:E2 .... $9.95
- ☐ 14:VDH $12.95
- ☐ 15:EDH $15.95
- ☐ 16:LD2 .... $14.95
- ☐ 17:CTG $19.95
- ☐ 18:HPG $12.95
- ☐ 19:WEP $17.95
- ☐ 20:CN $9.95
- ☐ 21:CS $9.95
- ☐ 22:CM $9.95
- ☐ 23:EL $8.95
- ☐ 24:SH $8.95
- ☐ 25:SW $10.95
- ☐ 26:WH $9.95
- ☐ 27:RES......... $35.00
- ☐ 28:HPGC $24.95
- ☐ 29:PLANSUITE .. $59.95
- ☐ 30:YG $7.95
- ☐ 31:GG $7.95
- ☐ 32:DP $7.95
- ☐ 33:ECL $14.95
- ☐ 34:HL $14.95
- ☐ 35:BYL $14.95
- ☐ 36:BB $14.95
- ☐ 37:CDB $9.95
- ☐ 38:CKI $14.95
- ☐ 39:SBC $14.95
- ☐ 40:CGD $7.95
- ☐ 41:CGR $7.95
- ☐ 42:SRF $19.95
- ☐ 43:RVH $19.95
- ☐ 44:CBW $12.95
- ☐ 45:CGW $7.95
- ☐ 46:CWT $12.95
- ☐ 47:CMP $12.95
- ☐ 48:CGT $7.95

Canadian Customers
Order Toll-Free 1-800-561-4169

Additional Books Sub-Total $______
ADD Postage and Handling $ 3.00
Sales Tax: (AZ, CA, DC, IL, MI, MN, NY & WA residents, please add appropriate state and local sales tax.) $______
YOUR TOTAL (Sub-Total, Postage/Handling, Tax) $______

YOUR ADDRESS (Please print)

Name ____________________

Street ____________________

City __________ State ______ Zip ______

Phone (_____) _______ — _______

YOUR PAYMENT
Check one: ☐Check ☐Visa ☐MasterCard ☐Discover Card
Required credit card information:

Credit Card Number ____________________

Expiration Date (Month/Year) ________/________

Signature Required ____________________

Home Planners, LLC
Wholly owned by Hanley-Wood, Inc.
3275 W Ina Road, Suite 110, Dept. BK, Tucson, AZ 85741

TB49

ABOUT THE DESIGNERS

The Blue Ribbon Designer Series™ is a collection of books featuring the home plans of a diverse group of outstanding home designers and architects known as the Blue Ribbon Network of Designers. This group of companies is dedicated to creating and marketing the finest possible plans for home construction on a regional and national basis. Each of the companies exhibits superior work and integrity in all phases of the stock-plan business including modern, trendsetting floor planning, a professionally executed blueprint package and a strong sense of service and commitment to the consumer.

Design Basics, Inc.

For nearly a decade, Design Basics, a nationally recognized home design service located in Omaha, has been developing plans for custom home builders. Since 1987, the firm has consistently appeared in *Builder* magazine, the official magazine of the National Association of Home Builders, as the top-selling designer. The company's plans also regularly appear in numerous other shelter magazines such as *Better Homes and Gardens, House Beautiful* and *Home Planner.*

Stephen Fuller/Design Traditions

Design Traditions was established by Stephen S. Fuller with the tenets of innovation, quality, originality and uncompromising architectural techniques in traditional and European homes. Especially popular throughout the Southeast, Design Traditions' plans are known for their extensive detail and thoughtful design. They are widely published in such shelter magazines as *Southern Living* magazine and *Better Homes and Gardens.*

Alan Mascord Design Associates, Inc.

Founded in 1983 as a local supplier to the building community, Mascord Design Associates of Portland, Oregon began to successfully publish plans nationally in 1985. With plans now drawn exclusively on computer, Mascord Design Associates quickly received a reputation for homes that are easy to build yet meet the rigorous demands of the buyers' market, winning local and national awards. The company's trademark is creating floor plans that work well and exhibit excellent traffic patterns. Their motto is: "Drawn to build, designed to sell."

Larry E. Belk Designs

Through the years, Larry E. Belk has worked with individuals and builders alike to provide a quality product. After listening to over 4,000 dreams and watching them become reality all across America, Larry's design philosophy today combines traditional exteriors with upscale interiors designed for contemporary lifestyles. Flowing, open spaces and interesting angles define his interiors. Great emphasis is placed on providing views that showcase the natural environment. Dynamic exteriors reflect Larry's extensive home construction experience, painstaking research and talent as a fine artist.

Larry W. Garnett & Associates, Inc.

Starting as a designer of homes for Houston-area residents, Garnett & Associates has been marketing designs nationally for the past ten years. A well-respected design firm, the company's plans are regularly featured in *House Beautiful, Country Living, Home* and *Professional Builder.* Numerous accolades, including several from the Texas Institute of Building Design and the American Institute of Building Design, have been awarded to the company for excellence in architecture.

Frank Betz Associates, Inc.

Frank Betz Associates, Inc. located in Smyrna, Georgia, is one of the nation's leaders in the design of stock plans. FBA, Inc. has provided builders and developers with home plans since 1977. With their vast knowledge of the speculative home builders business, they specialize in products for a wide variety of locations, price ranges, and markets. Frank Betz Associates, Inc. prides itself in its bi-annual plan magazine, *HOMEPLANS, Designed for Today's Market,* released every February and August featuring the firm's newest and most innovative plans.

Donald A. Gardner, Architects, Inc.

The South Carolina firm of Donald A. Gardner was established in response to a growing demand for residential designs that reflect constantly changing lifestyles. The company's specialty is providing homes with refined, custom-style details and unique features such as passive-solar designs and open floor plans. Computer-aided design and drafting technology resulting in trouble-free construction documents places the firm at the leading edge of the home plan industry.

The Sater Design Collection

The Sater Design Collection has a long established tradition of providing South Florida's most diverse and extraordinary custom designed homes. Their goal is to fulfill each client's particular need for an exciting approach to design by merging creative vision with elements that satisfy a desire for a distinctive lifestyle. This philosophy is proven, as exemplified by over 50 national design awards, numerous magazine features and, most important, satisfied clients. The result is an elegant statement of lasting beauty and value.

Home Design Services, Inc.

For the past fifteen years, Home Design Services of Longwood, Florida, has been formulating plans for the sun-country lifestyle. At the forefront of design innovation and imagination, the company has developed award-winning designs that are consistently praised for their highly detailed, free-flowing floor plans, imaginative and exciting interior architecture and elevations which have gained international appeal.